D1074886

HANDBOOK OF
EARLY CHRISTIANITY

HANDBOOK OF EARLY CHRISTIANITY

Social Science Approaches

Edited by
ANTHONY J. BLASI
JEAN DUHAIME
PAUL-ANDRÉ TURCOTTE

ALTAMIRA PRESS
A Division of Rowman & Littlefield Publishers, Inc.
Walnut Creek • Lanham • New York • Oxford

AltaMira Press
A Division of Rowman & Littlefield Publishers, Inc.
1630 North Main Street, #367
Walnut Creek, CA 94596
www.altamirapress.com

Rowman & Littlefield Publishers, Inc.
4720 Boston Way
Lanham, MD 20706

12 Hid's Copse Road
Cumnor Hill, Oxford OX2 9JJ, England

British Library Cataloguing in Publication Information Available

Library of Congress Cataloging-in-Publication Data

Handbook of early Christianity : social science approaches / edited by Anthony J. Blasi, Paul-André Turcotte, and Jean Duhaime.
    p. cm.
    Includes bibliographical references and index.
    ISBN 0-7591-0015-2 (alk. paper)
    1. Sociology, Christian—History—Early church, ca. 30–600. 2. Church history—Primitive and early church, ca. 30–600. 3. Religion and sociology—Rome. I. Blasi, Anthony J. II. Turcotte, Paul-André, 1943– III. Duhaime, Jean.

BR166 .H36 2002
270.1—dc21   2001053587

Printed in the United States of America

♾ ™ The paper used in this publication meets the minimum requirements of American National Standard for Information Sciences—Permanence of Paper for Printed Library Materials, ANSI/NISO Z39.48-1992.

CONTENTS

Part II: Special Methods

Part III: Contexts and Emergence of the Jesus Movement and Early Christianity

Preface

THIS VOLUME PROVIDES A general orientation and background information for people interested in the social scientific study of early Christianity. The first three chapters provide a general introduction that should help the reader select techniques and use concepts with a genuinely scientific problematic in view. It is the application of theory and method to a research question, not the concepts and techniques themselves, that makes an endeavor a scientific one. Chapters 4 through 9 have more discipline-specific foci—archaeology, history, etc. Some of these chapters will be more informative to social scientists lacking familiarity with literary source criticism or rhetorical analysis, while other chapters present approaches that may be new to New Testament scholars. Chapters 10 through 16 highlight social processes in the sociocultural world in which Christianity emerged, or those within Christian groups themselves. Chapters 17 through 21 deal with the status group and power dimensions of inequality in the world of the early Christians. If room permitted, a treatment of gender would be included among these chapters; as it is, that topic is treated only by way of illustration in Chapter. 13. Chapters 22 through 24 treat the economic dimension of inequality. The final three chapters focus on the individual person, that is, the psychological. The reader will discover that these sections necessarily blend into one another.

We distinguish between works cited by the authors of the individual chapters and a systematic bibliography for the field. The list of references acknowledges works the authors used for specific points or recommend for more extensive treatments of a topic. The bibliography is intended as a reference tool for facilitating research for those working in the field.

Acknowledgments

THE EDITORS WISH TO express their gratitude to Thomas Best, Willi Braun, William R. Garrett, John Kloppenborg, and Amy-Jill Levine for their suggestions in the early stages of planning this volume. The project also depended greatly on the willingness of the members of the Board of Editors to offer advice and to read the draft chapters; they represent a variety of disciplines that complement ours: Lynn Dwyer (anthropology); David G. Horrell, Margaret Y. MacDonald, and Peter Richardson (New Testament); and Luigi Tomasi (sociology). Erik Hanson of AltaMira Press was instrumental in getting the project under way.

T. & T. Clark of Edinburgh graciously permitted us to publish a revision and expansion of David G. Horrell's essay, "Social-Scientific Approaches to New Testament Interpretation: Retrospect and Prospect," an introductory essay that appeared in David G. Horrell (ed.), *Social-Scientific Approaches to New Testament Interpretation* (Edinburgh: T. & T. Clark, 1999), 3–27.

Board of Editors

Lynn Dwyer is an associate professor emerita at Tennessee State University in Nashville. She holds a B.A. and an M.S. from the University of Tennessee and a Ph.D. from American University, in Washington, D.C. Her anthropological research, conducted under federal grants, focused on rural folk in Tennessee, as they faced displacement by hydroelectric projects.

David G. Horrell earned an M.A. and a Ph.D. in New Testament from the University of Cambridge. He is a senior lecturer in New Testament studies in the Department of Theology at University of Exeter in the United Kingdom. His books include *The Social Ethos of the Corinthian Correspondence* (1996), *The Epistles of Peter and Jude* (1998), *Social-Scientific Approaches to New Testament Interpretation* (ed., 1999), *An Introduction to the Study of Paul* (2000), and *Christology, Controversy, and Community* (coeditor, 2000). His articles appear in the *Journal of Biblical Literature, Journal for the Study of the New Testament*, and *Sociology of Religion*.

Margaret Y. MacDonald teaches at St. Francis Xavier University in Antigonish, Nova Scotia. She earned a B.A. from St. Mary's University and a doctorate from the University of Oxford. Her major writings include *The Pauline Churches: A Socio-Historical Study of Institutionalization in the Pauline and Deutero-Paline Writings* (1988) and *Early Christian Women and Pagan Opinion* (1996). She is working on commentaries on Colossians and Ephesians in the Sacra Pagina series.

Peter Richardson earned a B.Arch. from the University of Toronto, a B.D. from Knox College in Toronto, and a Ph.D. from Cambridge University. He is a professor emeritus of Christian origins in the Department for the Study of Religion at the University of Toronto. His books include *Israel in the Apostolic Church* (1969), *Paul's Ethic of Freedom* (1979), *From Jesus to Paul* (coeditor, 1984), *Anti-Judaism in Early Christianity* (ed., vol. I, 1986), *Law in Religious Communities in the Roman Period* (coauthor, 1990), *Gospel in Paul* (coeditor, 1994), *Herod, King of the Jews and Friend of the Romans* (1996), *Common Life in the Early Church* (1998), and *Judaism and Christianity in First-Century Rome* (coeditor, 1998).

Luigi Tomasi teaches at the Università degli Studi di Trento in Italy. He holds advanced degrees in theology (Rome), philosophy (Milan), and sociology (Trento), and a specialization in urban and rural sociology (Urbino). Among his many writings are *Suicidio e società* (1989), *Teoria sociologica e sviluppo* (1991), *Teoria sociologica ed investigazione empirica* (1995), *La scuola sociologico di Chicago* (1997), and *The Tradition of the Chicago School of Sociology* (ed., 1998). He is the Italian representative to the Council of Europe for youth studies and president of the European Centre for Traditional and Regional Cultures.

About the Contributors

Frederick Bird earned a B.A. in history from Harvard College, a B.D. from Harvard Divinity School, and a Ph.D. in religion and society from the Graduate Theological Union in Berkeley. He is a professor of religion at Concordia University in Montréal, Quebec, Canada. His publications appear in the *Journal of Religious Ethics, Studies in Religion, Sociological Analysis, Social Compass,* and *Journal for the Scientific Study of Religion.*

Anthony J. Blasi holds a B.A. in history from St. Edward's University in Texas, an M.A. and Ph.D. in sociology from the University of Notre Dame, an M.A. in biblical studies from the University of St. Michael's College in Toronto, an S.T.L. from Regis College in Toronto, and a conjoint Th.D. from Regis College and the University of Toronto. He is a professor of sociology at Tennessee State University in Nashville. His books include *A Phenomenological Transformation of the Social Scientific Study of Religion* (1985), *Moral Conflict and Christian Religion* (1988), *Early Christianity as a Social Movement* (1989), *Making Charisma: The Social Construction of Paul's Public Image* (1991), *A Sociology of Johannine Christianity* (1996), and *Organized Religion and Seniors' Mental Health* (1999). He is past president of the Association for the Sociology of Religion.

Steven L. Bridge earned a B.A. jointly in psychology, sociology, and religion from Hope College in Holland, Michigan, and an M.A. and Ph.D. in religious studies and biblical theology from Marquette University. He is an assistant professor at St. Joseph's College in Standish, Maine. He has published in the *Journal of Early Christian Studies.*

Warren Carter holds a B.A. from the Victoria University of Wellington in New Zealand, a B.D. and Th.M. in pastoral care from the Melbourne College of Divinity in Australia, and a Ph.D. in New Testament from the Princeton Theological Seminary. He is the Lindsey P. Pherigo Professor of New Testament at Saint Paul School of Theology in Kansas City, Missouri. He has written *Households and Discipleship: A Study of Matthew 19–20* (1994) and *Matthew and the Margins* (2000). His articles appear in the *Catholic Biblical Quarterly, Journal for the Study of the New Testament,* and *Journal of Biblical Literature.*

Nicola Denzey holds a B.A. from the University of Toronto and an M.A. and Ph.D. from Princeton University. She is an assistant professor of religion at Skidmore College in Saratoga Springs, New York.

Jean Duhaime earned a B.A. from the Séminaire de Chicoutimi; a Bachelor's in Secondary-level Religious Education from the Université du Québec à Chicoutimi; a Licentiate in religious studies, an M.A. in theology–biblical studies, and an M.Sc. in sociology from the Université de Montréal; and a Diplôme from the École Biblique et Archéologique Française de Jérusalem. He is professeur titulaire [full professor] d'interprétation de la Bible at the Faculté de Théologie at the Université de Montréal. His books include *Entendre la voix du Dieu vivant* (coeditor, 1994), *Loi et autonomie dans la Bible et la tradition chrétienne* (coeditor, 1994), *L'adhésion à la conscience de Krishna aux États-Unis vers 1970* (1996). His works have also appeared in the *Encyclopedia of the Dead Sea Scrolls, Revue de Qumrân, Revue Scriptura, Religiologiques,* and *Église et Théologie.*

Douglas Edwards earned a B.S. from the University of Nebraska and a Ph.D. from Boston University. He is professor of religion at the University of Puget Sound, Tacoma, Washington. His books include *Religion and Power: Pagans, Jews, and Christians in the Greek East* (1996) and *Archaeology and the Galilee* (coeditor, 1997).

Richard K. Fenn earned a B.A. from Yale University, a B.D. from the Episcopal Theological School, a Th.M. from Princeton Theological Seminary, and a Ph.D. from Bryn Mawr Graduate School. He is Maxwell Upson Professor of Christianity and Society at the Princeton Theological Seminary. His books include *Toward a Theory of Secularization* (1978), *Liturgies & Trials: The Secularization of Religious Language* (1982), *The Spirit of Revolt* (1986), *The Dream of the Perfect Act* (1987), *The Death of Herod* (1992), and *Blackwell Companion to Sociology of Religion* (ed., 2001).

David A. Fiensy holds an A.B. in Christian ministries from the Cincinnati Bible Seminary, an M.A. in classical Greek and Latin from Xavier University in Cincinnati, and a Ph.D. in New Testament from Duke University. He is professor of New Testament at Kentucky Christian College, Grayson, Kentucky. His books include *Prayers Alleged to Be Jewish* (1985), *The Social History of Palestine in the Herodian Period* (1991), *New Testament Introduction* (1994), and *The Message and Ministry of Jesus* (1996). His articles appear in the *Journal for the Study of the New Testament, Journal for the Study of the Pseudepigrapha,* and *Harvard Theological Review.*

Philip A. Harland holds a B.A. in history from the University of Waterloo and an M.A. and Ph.D. in Christian origins from the Centre for the Study of Religion at the University of Toronto. He is an assistant professor of religion (history of Christianity) at Concordia University in Montréal. His articles appear in *Studies in Religion* and the *Journal for the Study of the New Testament.*

David G. Horrell earned an M.A. and a Ph.D. in New Testament from the University of Cambridge. He is a senior lecturer in New Testament studies in the Department of Theology at University of Exeter in the United Kingdom. His books include *The Social Ethos of the Corinthian Correspondence* (1996), *The Epistles of Peter and Jude* (1998), *Social-Scientific Approaches to New Testament Interpretation* (ed., 1999), *An Introduction to the Study of Paul* (2000), and *Christology, Controversy, and Community* (co-editor, 2000). His articles appear in the *Journal of Biblical Literature, Journal for the Study of the New Testament,* and *Sociology of Religion.*

Howard Clark Kee holds a Th.M. from the Dallas Theological Seminary and a Ph.D. from Yale University. He is William Goodwin Aurelio Professor of Biblical Studies, Emeritus, at Boston University. Among his many books are *Jesus in History* (1977), *Community of the New Age: Studies in Mark's Gospel* (1977), *Christian Origins in Sociological Perspective: Methods and Resources* (1980), *Miracle in the Early Christian World: A Study in Socio-Historical Method* (1983), *Knowing the Truth: A Sociological Approach to New Testament Interpretation* (1989), *The Theology of Acts* (1990), *Christianity: A Social and Cultural History* (co-author, 1991), and *Who Are the People of God? Early Christian Models of Community* (1995).

Dimitris J. Kyrtatas earned a First Degree in economics from the University of Thessaloniki and a Ph.D. in sociology from Brunel University, London. He is a fellow at the Research Centre of Greek Society at the Academy of Athens and a professor of ancient history at the University of Crete at Rethymno, Greece. He is the author of *The Social Structure of the Early Christian Communities* (1987) and has published in *International Sociology* and other scholarly publications.

John W. Marshall holds a B.A. from the University of Waterloo, an M.A. from Wilfrid Laurier University, and a Ph.D. from Princeton University. He is an assistant professor in the Department for the Study of Religion at the University of Toronto. He is the author of *Parables of the War: Reading John's Jewish Apocalypse* (2001).

Russell Martin is a doctoral candidate in the Department for the Study of Religion at the University of Toronto.

Donald A. Nielsen holds a B.A. from the State University of New York at Stony Brook, an M.A. in sociology from the University of Illinois, and a Ph.D. in sociology from the New School for Social Research in New York. He is a professor of sociology at the University of Wisconsin at Eau Claire. He has written *Three Faces of God: Society, Religion, and the Categories of Totality in the Philosophy of Émile Durkheim* (1999) and articles in *Sociological Analysis, Sociologia internationalis, Religioni e società,* and *Sociology of Religion.*

Carolyn Osiek earned a B.A. from Fontbonne College, an M.A.T. from Manhattanville College, and a Th.D. from Harvard University. She is professor of New Testament at the Catholic Theological Union in Chicago, Illinois. Her books include *Rich and Poor in the Shepherd of Hermas* (1983), *What Are They Saying about the Social Setting of the New Testament?* (1984), and *Families in the New Testament World: Households and House Churches* (coauthor, 1997). Her articles appear in *Theological Studies, Catholic Biblical Quarterly,* and *Biblical Theology Bulletin.*

Harold Remus earned a B.A. from the University of Minnesota, an M.Div. from Concordia Seminary in St. Louis, and a Ph.D. from the University of Pennsylvania. He is professor emeritus of religion and culture at Wilfrid Laurier University in Ontario. He is the author of *Pagan-Christian Conflict over Miracle in the Second Century* (1983) and *Jesus as Healer* (1997). His articles appear in *Studies in Religion, Journal of Biblical Literature,* and *Second Century.*

Peter Richardson earned a B.Arch. from the University of Toronto, a B.D. from Knox College in Toronto, and a Ph.D. from Cambridge University. He is a professor emeritus of Christian origins in the Department for the Study of Religion at the University of Toronto. His books include *Israel in the Apostolic Church* (1969), *Paul's Ethic of Freedom* (1979), *From Jesus to Paul* (coeditor, 1984), *Anti-Judaism in Early Christianity* (ed., vol. 1, 1986), *Law in Religious Communities in the Roman Period* (coauthor, 1990), *Gospel in Paul* (coeditor, 1994), *Herod, King of the Jews and Friend of the Romans* (1996), *Common Life in the Early Church* (1998), and *Judaism and Christianity in First-Century Rome* (coeditor, 1998).

Jack T. Sanders holds a B.A. from Texas Wesleyan College, an M.Div. from Emory University, and a Ph.D. from Claremont Graduate School. He is professor emeritus of religious studies at the University of Oregon. His books include *The Jews in Luke-Acts* (1987), *Schismatics, Sectarians, Dissidents, Deviants: The First One Hundred Years of Jewish–Christian Relations* (1993), and *Charisma, Converts, Competitors: Societal and Sociological Factors in the Success of Early Christianity* (2000). His articles appear in *New Testament Studies, Social Compass,* and other journals.

Peter Staples earned a Ph.D. from the University of Nottingham in the United Kingdom. He is a professor emeritus of church history and ecumenics at the State University of Utrecht in the Netherlands. His articles appear in *Forum, Religioni e società,* and *Social Compass.*

Nicholas H. Taylor holds a Ph.D. from Durham University. He is a senior lecturer in New Testament studies in the Faculty of Theology at the University of Pretoria, South Africa. He is the author of *Paul, Antioch, and Jerusalem: A Study in Relationships and Authority in Earliest Christianity* (1992) and articles in *Religioni e società,* and *Listening, Religion and Theology.*

Paul-André Turcotte holds a B.A., M.A., and Lic. from the Université de Montréal; a B. Péd. from the Université Laval; a Ph.D. in social sciences from the École des Hautes Études in Sciences Sociales in Paris; and a Ph.D. in theology from the Institut Catholique de Paris. He is professor of social science at the Institut Catholique de Paris (Institut d'Études Économiques et Sociales), Paris, France. His books include *Les chemins de la différence: Pluralisme et aggiornamento dans l'après-concile* (1985), *L'enseignement secondaire public des frères éducateurs* (1988), *Intransigeance ou compromis: Sociologie et histoire du catholicisme actuel* (1994), *Sociologie du christianisme* (1996), and *La religion dans la modernité* (1997). He has edited special issues of *Social Compass* dealing with the sociology of early Christianity.

Ernst R. Wendland holds a B.A. in classics and biblical languages from Northwestern College, an M.A. in linguistics, and a Ph.D. in African languages and literature from the University of Wisconsin; and an S.T.M. in exegetical theology from the Wisconsin Lutheran Seminary. He is an instructor at the Lutheran Seminary in Lusaka, Zambia; a visiting professor (Dept. of Ancient Studies) at the University of Stellenbosch in South Africa; and a translation consultant for United Bible Societies. He is the author of *Preaching That Grabs the Heart: A Rhetorical-Stylistic Study of the Chichewa Revival Sermons of Shadrack Wame* (2000). His articles appear in *Notes on Translation, Neotestamentica, Trinity Journal,* and the *Journal of Translation and Textlinguistics.*

Ritva H. Williams earned a B.A. and an M.A. from Carlton University in Ottawa and a Ph.D. from the University of Ottawa. She is an assistant professor of New Testament at Augustana College in Rock Island, Illinois.

Robert A. Wortham holds a B.A. from Elon College; a M.T.S. from the Candler School of Theology, Emory University; and a Ph.D. from Emory University. He is professor of sociology at North Carolina Central University in Durham, North Carolina. He is the author of *Spatial Development and Religious Orientation in Kenya* (1991) and *Social-Scientific Approaches in Biblical Literature* (1999). His articles appear in *Perspectives in Religious Studies, Social Science Journal, Population Research and Policy Review, Biblical Theology Bulletin,* and *International Sociology.*

Abbreviations

Abbreviations of Non-Canonical Ancient Works

Act. Cypriani—*Acta S. Cypriani proconsularis*
Act. Paul. Thec.—*Acts of Paul and Thecla*
Act. Thom.—*Acts of Thomas*
Acts Scill.—*Acts of the Scillitan Martyrs*
Aeschylus, *Pers.*—*Persians*
Ambrose, *Ep.*—*Letters*
Apoc. Paul.—*Apocalypse of Paul*
Apoc. Pet.—*Apocalypse of Peter*
Appian, *Bell. Civ.*—*Civil Wars*
Apuleius, *Metam.*—*Golden Ass*
Aristides, *Apol.*—*Apology*
Aristotle, *Pol.*—*Politics*
　　　　Rhet.—*Rhetoric*
Arnobius, *Adv. Nationes*—*Against the Gentiles*
Athenagoras, *Leg.*—*Legation for Christians*
Augustine, *Civ. Dei*—*City of God*
Basil of Caesarea, *Ad Adolesc.*—*Address to Young Men*
b.B.Bat.—*Babylonian Talmud, Bava Batra*
b.Ber.—*Babylonian Talmud, Berakhot*
b.Shabb.—*Babylonian Talmud, Shabbat*
Cato, *Agr.*—*Agriculture*
Cicero, *Off.*—*Offices*
　　　　Prov. cons.—*Consular Provinces*
　　　　Verr.—*Verres*

Clement of Alexandria, *Paed.*—*Christ the Educator*
      Quis div.—*Salvation of the Rich*
      Strom.—*Miscellanies*
Cod. Theod.—*Theodosian Code*
Columella, *Rust.*—*Agriculture*
Cyprian, *Ep.*—*Letters*
      Lapsi—*The Lapsed*
      Test.—*To Quirinius: Testimonies against the Jews*
Did.—*Didache*
Dio—Dio Cassius, *History of Rome*
Dio Chrysostom, *Lib.*—*Freedom*
      4 Regn.—*Kingship 4 (Or. 4)*
      Nest.—*Homer's Portrayal of Nestor (Or. 57)*
      Rhod.—*To the People of Rhodes (Or. 31)*
      3 Fort.—*Fortune 3 (Or. 65)*
      Ven.—*The Hunter (Or. 7, Euboean Discourse)*
Diogn.—*Letter to Diognetus*
Ep. Barn.—*Epistle of Barnabas*
Epiphanius, *Pan.*—*Refutation of All Heresies*
Eusebius, *Hist. eccl.*—*Ecclesiastical History*
      Vit. Const.—*Life of Constantine*
Fronto—M. Cornelius Fronto, *Letters*
Gen. Rab.—*Genesis Rabbah*
Gos. Thom.—*Gospel of Thomas*
Gregory of Nazianzus, *Or. Bas.*—*Oration in Praise of Basil*
Herm., *Man.*—*Shepherd of Hermas, Mandates*
      Sim.—*Shepherd of Hermas, Similitudes*
Herodianus—Herodian, *History*
Hippolytus, *Comm. Dan.*—*Commentary on Daniel*
      Haer.—*Refutation of All Heresies*
      Trad. ap.—*Apostolic Traditions*
Ign., *Eph.*—Ignatius, *Letter to the Ephesians*
    Magn.—Ignatius, *Letter to the Magnesians*
    Pol.—Ignatius, *Letter to Polycarp*
    Rom.—Ignatius, *Letter to the Romans*
    Smyrn.—Ignatius, *Letter to the Smyrnaeans*
    Trall.—Ignatius, *Letter to the Trallians*
Irenaeus, *Haer.*—*Against Heresies*
Jerome, *Ep.*—*Letters*

Josephus, *Ant.*—*Jewish Antiquities*
        B.J.—*Jewish War*
        C. Ap.—*Against Apian*
        Vita—*The Life*
Julian (Emperor), *Ep.*—*Letters*
Justin, *1 Apol.*—*First Apology*
        2 Apol.—*Second Apology*
        Dial.—*Dialogue with Trypho*
Juvenal, *Sat.*—*Satires*
Lactantius, *De Mort. Persec.*—*The Deaths of the Persecutors*
        Inst.—*The Divine Institutes*
Let. Aris.—*Letter of Aristeas* (OT Pseudepigripha)
Livy—*From the Founding of the City* (Rome)
Lucian of Samosata, *Fug.*—*The Runaways*
        Peregr.—*Passing of Peregrinus*
Mart. Agape—*Martyrdom of Agape*
Mart. Carp.—*Martyrdom of Saints Carpus, Papylus, and Agathonic*
Mart. Justin—*Martyrdom of Justin*
Mart. Perpet.—*Martyrdom of Perpetua*
Mart. Pionii—*Martyrdom of Pionius*
Mart. Pol.—*Martyrdom of Polycarp*
Martial, *Epig.*—*Epigrams*
        Spect.—*On the Spectacles*
m.Berakoth—*Mishnah, Berakhot*
Minucius Felix, *Oct.*—*Octavius*
m.Peah—*Mishnah, Pe'ah*
m.Pesahim—*Mishnah, Pesahim*
m.Shabb.—*Mishnah, Shabbat*
Novatian, *Spect.*—*The Spectacles*
Origen, *Cels.*—*Against Celsus*
        Hom. Exod.—*Homily on Exodus*
        Hom. Gen.—*Homily on Genesis*
        Princ.—*First Principles*
P. Oxy.—*Oxyrinchos Papyri*
Philo, *Abr.*—*On the Life of Abraham*
        Cher.—*On the Cherubim*
        Contem.—*On the Contemplative Life*
        Decal.—*On the Decalogue*
        Deus.—*On God*

Flaccus—*Against Flaccus*
Fug.—*Flight*
Her.—*Who is the Heir*
Leg.—*Allegorical Interpretation*
Legat.—*On the Embassy to Gaius*
Mos.—*On the Life of Moses*
Mutat.—*On the Change of Names*
Opif.—*On the Creation of the World*
Plant.—*On Planting*
Post.—*On the Posterity of Cain*
Prob.—*That Every Good Person Is Free*
Prov.—*On Providence*
QE—*Questions and Answers on Exodus*
QG—*Questions and Answers on Genesis*
Sacr.—*On the Sacrifices of Cain and Abel*
Somn.—*On Dreams*
Spec.—*On the Special Laws*
Virt.—*On the Virtues*

Plato, *Tim.*—*Timaeus*
Pliny the Elder, *Nat.*—*Natural History*
Pliny the Younger, *Ep.*—*Letters*
    Pan.—*Panegyricus*
Plotinus, *Enn.*—*Enneads*
Plutarch, *Mor.*—*Moralia*
    Pomp.—*Pompey*
    Quaest. Conv.—*Quaestionum convivialum libri IX*
    Sept. Sap. Conv.—*Septem sapientium convivium*
Polycarp, *Phil.*—*To the Philippians*
Pss. Sol.—*Psalms of Solomon*
Qumran, 1QpHab—Qumran Pesher Habakkuk
    4QpNah—Qumran Pesher Nahum Fragments
Seneca, *Ben.*—*On Kindnesses*
    Clem.—*On Mercy*
Sophocles, *Ant.*—*Antigone*
    Phil.—*Philotectes*
Sozomen, *H.E.*—*Ecclesiastical History*
Strabo, *Geogr.*—*Geography*
Suetonius, *Aug.*—*Augustus*
    Dom.—*Domitian*
    Galb.—*Galba*

Nero—*Nero*
Tib.—*Tiberius*
Vesp.—*Vespasian*
Symmachus, *Relatio.*—Quintus Aurelius Symmachus, *Relations*
Tacitus, *Agr.*—*Agricola*
    Ann.—*Annals*
    Germ.—*Germania*
    Hist.—*Histories*
T. Benj.—*Testament of Benjamin*
T. Dan—*Testament of Dan*
Tertullian, *Apol.*—*Apology*
    Cor.—*The Crown*
    Fug.—*Flight in Persecution*
    Idol.—*Idolatry*
    Mart.—*To the Martyrs*
    Paen.—*Repentance*
    Pud.—*Modesty*
    Scap.—*To Scapula*
    Spec.—*The Shows*
Theophilus, *Auto.*—*To Autolycus*
t.Hul.—*Toshefta Hullin*
T. Jud.—*Testament of Judah*
T. Reu.—*Testament of Reuben*
T. Sim.—*Testament of Simeon*
T. Zeb.—*Testament of Zebulon*
Varro, *Rust.*—*On Farming*
Virgil, *Aen.*—*Aeneid*
Vit. Pachom.—*Life of Pachomius*
2 Bar.—*2 Baruch*
1 Clem.—Clement of Rome, *First Letter*
2 Clem.—*Second Clement*
1 En.—*1 Enoch*
2 En.—*2 Enoch*
4 Ezra—*4 Ezra*

Abbreviations of Compilations of Ancient Sources

ANF—*Ante-Nicene Fathers*, 10 vols. Ed. Alexander Roberts and James Donaldson. Buffalo, N.Y.: Christian Literature Publishing, 1885–96; Peabody, Mass.: Hendrickson, 1994.

CII—*Corpus inscriptionum iudaicarum* (Sussidi allo studio delle anichità cristiane, 3.). Ed. Jean-Baptiste Frey. Rome: Pontificio Istituto di Archeologia Cristiana, 1936–52.

CIL—*Corpus Inscriptionum Latinarum*. Berlin: G. Rimerus, 1862– .

CPJ—*Corpus papyrorum judaicarum*. Ed. Victor Tcherikover and Alexander Fuks. Cambridge, Mass.: Harvard University Press, 1957–64.

DFSJ—*Donateurs et fondateurs dans les synagogues juives, répertoire des dédicaces grecques relatives à la construction et à la réfection des synagogues*. Ed. Baruch Lifshitz. Paris: J. Gabalda, 1967.

Dig.—*Corpus juris civilis. Digesta.*

IBithDörner—Dörner, Friedrich Karl. *Bericht über eine Reise in Bithynien* (Denkschriften der österreichische Akademie der Wissenschaften, philosophische-historische Klasse, 75). Wien (Vienna): Rudolf M. Rohrer, 1952.

ICor—*Corinth: Results of Excavations Conducted by the American School of Classical Studies at Athens Volume VIII, Part III, The Inscriptions 1926–1950*. Ed. John Harvey Kent. Princeton, N.J.: American School of Classical Studies at Athens, 1966.

ICURn—*Inscriptiones christianae urbis Romae. Nova Series*. Ed. A. Silvagni, A. Ferrua, and D. Mazzoleni. Rome: Pontificio Istituto di Archeologia Cristiana, 1922–85.

IEph—Engelmann, H., H. Wankel, and R. Merkelbach. *Die Inschriften von Ephesos* (Inschriften griechischer Städte aus Kleinasien, 11–17). Bonn: Rudolf Habelt, 1979–84.

IG—*Inscriptiones graecae*. Editio minor. Berlin, 1924– .

IGR—*Inscriptiones graecae ad res romanas pertinentes*. Ed. René Cagnat et al. Paris: E. Leroux, 1906–27.

IGUR—*Inscriptiones graecae urbis romae* (Studi pubblicati dall'Istituto Italiano per la Storia Antica, 17), comp. Luigi Moretti. Rome: Istituto Italiano per la Storia Antica, 1968–91.

IHierap—Judeich, Walther. "Inschriften." In *Altertümer von Hierapolis* (Jahrbuch des kaiserlich deutschen Archäologischen Instituts, Ergänzungsheft, 4). Ed. Carl Humann, et al., 67–181. Berlin: Georg Reimer, 1898.

ILCV—*Inscriptiones Latinae Christianae Veteres*. Ed. Ernestus Diehl. Dublin: Weidmann, 1970.

ILS—*Inscriptiones Latinae Selectae*. Ed. H. Dessau. Dublin: Apud Weidmannos, 1972 [1892].

IPergamon—*Inschriften von Pergamon* (Altertümer von Pergamon, 8.). Ed. Max Fränkel. Berlin: W. Spemann, 1890–95.

Iside—*Side im Altertum*. I GSK.43. Johannes Nollé. Bonn: Rudolf Habelt, 1993.

ISmyrna—Inschriften von Smyrna (Inschriften griechischer Städte aus Kleinasien, 23). Ed. Georg Petzl. Bonn: Rudolf Habelt, 1982–90.

ITral—Inschriften von Tralleis und Nysa (Inschriften griechischer Städte aus Kleinasien, 23). Ed. Fjodor B. Poljakov. Bonn: Rudolf Habelt, 1989.

LSAM—Lois sacrées de l'Asie Mineure (École française d'Athènes, Travaux et mémoires des anciens membre étrangers de l'école et de divers savants, 9). Ed. Franciszek Sokolowski. Paris: Ed. de Boccard, 1955.

MAMA—Monumenta asiae minoris antiqua (Publications of the American Society for Archaeological Research in Asia Minor). Ed. Josef Keil, et al. Manchester: Manchester University Press, 1928.

NewDocs—New Documents Illustrating Early Christianity. 5 vols. Ed. G. H. R. Horsley. North Ryde, Australia: Ancient History Documentary Research Centre, Macquarie University, 1981–89.

NHL—Nag Hammadi Library. Ed. James M. Robinson. New York: Harper & Row, 1981.

OGIS—Orientis graeci inscriptiones selectae. 2 vols. Ed. W. Dittenberger. Leipzig, 1903–5.

OTP—Old Testament Pseudepigrapha. 2 vols. Ed. James H. Charlesworth. Garden City, N.Y.: Doubleday, 1985.

PIR²—Prosopographia imperii romani. E. Groag, A. Stein, and L. Petersen. Berlin: Walter de Gruyter, 1933.

SEG—Supplementum epigraphicum graecum. Ed. Pierre Roussel, Antonin Salav, Marcus N. Tod, et. al. Lugduni Batavorum (Lyons): A. W. Sijthoff, 1923.

TAM—Tituli Asiae Minoris collecti et editi auspiciis academiae litterarum austriacae. Ed. Ernest Kalinka, Rudolf Heberdey, Frederick Carol Dörner, Josef Keil, and Peter Herrmann. Vindobonae (Vienna): Academiam Scientiarum Austriacam, 1920.

GENERAL PERSPECTIVE I

Social Sciences Studying Formative Christian Phenomena: A Creative Movement

I

DAVID G. HORRELL

T HE LAST THIRTY YEARS or so have seen the introduction of new methods in studies of the New Testament and early Christianity. Alongside the established methods of historical criticism, new approaches have been using theoretical traditions from other disciplines, such as literary criticism and the social sciences.[1] Social scientific interpretation of early Christian phenomena, then, is part of a wider trend, reflecting greater diversity within the discipline of biblical studies and greater interdisciplinarity within the humanities and social sciences. Unlike some forms of literary criticism, the wide variety of social scientific approaches to early Christian texts retain a close link with the aims of historical criticism (Barton 1995); the intention is that the use of the resources that the social sciences offer, along with the other methods of textual and historical criticism, may enable a fuller and better appreciation of the biblical texts and communities within their historical, social, and cultural setting (cf. Elliott 1993: 7–8). John Elliott's recent definition of contemporary social scientific criticism offers a clear summary of the approach as applied to biblical texts.

> Social scientific criticism of the Bible is that phase of the exegetical task which analyzes the social and cultural dimensions of the text and of its environmental context through the utilization of the perspectives, theory, models, and research of the social sciences. As a component of the historical-critical method of exegesis, social scientific criticism investigates biblical texts as meaningful configurations of language intended to communicate between composers and audiences. (1993: 7)

In this chapter, I shall set the modern development of social scientific criticism in its historical context, summarize the different approaches currently represented in

New Testament and early Christian studies, and explore the areas of contemporary debate and the prospects for future development.

The Origins and Revival of Interest in the Social World of Early Christianity

Interest in social aspects of early Christianity is certainly nothing new.[2] In a recent
study of the history of research in this area, Ralph Hochschild (1999) traces the
beginnings of "sociohistorical exegesis" (*sozialgeschichtliche Exegese*) to around the
middle of the nineteenth century, with the contrasting work of Wilhelm Weitling
and Friedrich Lückes.[3] Weitling's 1846 book presented a radical, human Jesus calling people to live in a community of equality and freedom and depicted the early
church as a form of communism, practicing the community of goods. Lückes, on
the other hand, presented the early church as a kind of free association (*freier
Verein*). In each case, the social location and commitments of the author shaped his
view of early Christianity, Weitling reacting against the "bourgeois society" (*bürg-
erliche Gesellschaft*) that Lückes regarded so positively. Although these early works
have had virtually no impact on the subsequent literature, it is interesting to see
the extent to which their different perspectives are paradigmatic for sociohistorical analyses of the character of the earliest churches (Hochschild 1999: 45–63).

Hochschild goes on to trace the process by which sociohistorical questions
about early Christianity became established in scholarly discourse. There are a
number of significant approaches and directions, both within and outside the theologians' guild. From among the theologians, Hochschild examines the works
published around the 1880s by C. F. Georg Heinrici, Gerhard Uhlhorn, and
Heinrich Holtzmann (Hochschild 1999: 64–78). Also important are the works
on early Christianity produced at approximately the same time by members of the
socialist movement, notably Friedrich Engels and Karl Kautsky.[4] Around the turn
of the century important contributions to our understanding of the social history
of early Christianity were made by scholars such as Adolf Deissmann
(1866–1937) and Ernst Troeltsch (1865–1923). Deissmann paid particular attention to the recently discovered papyri and their implications for understanding
the social world of the New Testament, especially of Paul (see Deissmann 1911,
1927). Troeltsch's monumental work on the social teaching of the Christian
churches, published in 1912 (Troeltsch 1931), underpins Gerd Theissen's much
more recent arguments about the "love-patriarchalism" that developed, especially
in the Pauline tradition.[5] Troeltsch's analysis of the distinction between "church"
and "sect" has also been widely influential.[6]

Other important developments include the rise of form criticism, pioneered
by the German Old Testament scholar Hermann Gunkel (1862–1932), and its

application to the New Testament, especially by Martin Dibelius (1883–1947) and Rudolf Bultmann (1884–1976). Form criticism connected different types of textual material to their particular *Sitz im Leben*, or setting in life; it aimed to recover the earliest form of a tradition by relating the development of textual traditions to their use in specific social settings. Hence in 1925 Oscar Cullmann insisted that form criticism would require the development of a "special branch of sociology devoted to the study of the laws which govern the growth of popular traditions."[7]

In America interest in the sociology of early Christianity was especially pursued in the work of the so-called Chicago School, whose members included Shirley Jackson Case and Shailer Mathews.[8] Case's book, *The Social Origins of Christianity* (1923), is among the best-known examples of the school's work. Case argues for a "social-historical" approach to the New Testament, contrasting what he sees as the traditional concern for the "recovery of the distinctive teachings" or dogmas of early Christianity with his own focus on "the more comprehensive and fundamental matter of social experience as a key to the understanding of the genesis and early history of the Christian movement" (1923: v–vi). His focus is less on the meaning of the New Testament texts than on the movement that the texts represent, understood within its social context. Case proceeds to sketch the development of the early Christian movement from its Jewish origins through its transition to a gentile environment to its success in meeting the religious needs of the time and its consolidation and confrontation with rivals in the fourth century. At the close of the book something of Case's own theological agenda emerges: the recovery of New Testament doctrine, as was the aim of the Reformers, is hardly appropriate for an age in which historic doctrines are no longer accepted as authoritative. "Modern Christianity is becoming less and less doctrinally motivated and is directing its energies more and more toward the realization of effective action on the part of Christian individuals and groups as functioning factors in society" (1923: 251). For proponents of such a social gospel, inspiration comes not from the repetition of early Christian doctrines but from the dynamism with which early Christianity arose, grew, and adapted successfully to its environment.

Also among the members of the Chicago School, though less well known now than Case and Mathews, was Donald Riddle, who, indebted to Case for the development of his approach, published a series of works in the 1920s and 1930s.[9] In *The Martyrs* (1931), Riddle begins from an interest in the role of religion in social control and proceeds to study how the early Christian movement exercised control over its members such that they were willing to pay the price of martyrdom rather than conform to the demands of the Roman state. He considers such factors as the importance of group loyalty and belonging, the Christian view of rewards for faithful confession and punishments for apostasy, the support offered by Christians to those of their number imprisoned and tried, and especially the role of martyrologies and their precursors in the New Testament as a type of "control literature." The Markan passion narrative, in particular, is seen as "a primitive martyrology" (1931: 196).

But despite such energetic pursuit of social-historical understanding of the early Christian movement, from around the 1920s until the 1970s interest in the social dimensions of early Christianity declined.[10] There were a number of reasons for this. One was the failure of form criticism, particularly in the hands of its most prominent exponent, Rudolf Bultmann, to explore the social context in which the traditions were preserved and developed. It is often remarked that Cullmann's call for a sociological dimension to form criticism went virtually unheeded. In practice form criticism focused not on the wider social context, as might be implied in the term *Sitz im Leben*, but on the *Sitz im Glauben*, the setting in faith, or the setting in the life of the church (Theissen 1993: 9–10; also note 7 above). Also significant was the fact that Bultmann became concerned to promote a hermeneutic of demythologization and the formulation of the word of the gospel in existentialist terms, as a challenge to the "I" for a radically new self-understanding (see Bultmann 1960, 1985). Thus in Bultmann's work the New Testament kerygma becomes essentially detached from its sociohistorical context, just as does its contemporary reformulation (cf. Kee 1989: 4–5). Another important reason was the influence, indeed an influence on Bultmann, of Karl Barth's (1886–1968) dialectical theology, a break with the then established theological liberalism first announced in his Tambach lecture of 1919 and in the successive editions of his famous commentary on Romans (1st ed. 1918; 2nd ed. 1922; see further Scholder 1987: 40–45).[11] For Barth the revealed Word of God is radically "other" than all humanly and socially constructed patterns of religiosity. The gospel stands as a radical challenge to all forms of human society and can never be identified with any particular social organization. As Gerd Theissen points out, this aversion to a connection between theology and society was profoundly related to the specific social context in which Barth was located and the struggles of the Confessing Church against National Socialism and the German Christians (Theissen 1993: 8–15; Scholder 1987). Hochschild also suggests broader reasons for the turn away from sociohistorical research, at least in West Germany: there was neither the experience of massive social inequality nor problems concerning the societal position of the church of the previous decades, so that central motivations for previous socially orientated historical studies were no longer of social relevance (1999: 209).

The tide began to turn in the 1960s, and a revival of interest in the social aspects of early Christianity began. One landmark was the 1960 publication of Edwin Judge's *The Social Pattern of the Christian Groups in the First Century*, which, in the following decade or two, played a significant role in encouraging this renewed interest.[12] Other notable works of social history were published (e.g., Martin Hengel 1969, 1973; cf. Scroggs 1980: 168–71). However, in contrast to much of the work undertaken earlier in the century, what was new in the early 1970s was the creative and varied use of methods, models, and theories from the social sciences in studies of early Christianity.

Why, then, the revival of interest in social aspects of early Christianity, and why the experimentation with new methods? Undoubtedly one major factor was dissatisfaction with the established methods of New Testament study. This dissatisfaction is perhaps best summarized in the oft-quoted words of Robin Scroggs:

> To some it has seemed that too often the discipline of the theology of the New Testament (the history of *ideas*) operates out of a methodological docetism, as if believers had minds and spirits unconnected with their individual and corporate bodies. Interest in the sociology of early Christianity is no attempt to limit reductionistically the reality of Christianity to social dynamic; rather it should be seen as an effort to guard against a reductionism from the other extreme, a limitation of the reality of Christianity to an inner-spiritual, or objective-cognitive system. In short, sociology of early Christianity wants to put body and soul together again. (1980: 165–66)

The new interest in the sociology of early Christianity must also be understood in the light of wider developments in society at the time. The dissatisfaction of which Scroggs speaks, for example, may perhaps be linked with the widespread protests of the "radical" 1960s (cf. Theissen 1993: 16). At least partly as a product of the communitarian and radical concerns of this period, there was something of a shift in the methods of doing history, away from a focus on the "great" figures and toward a concern with communities, social relations, popular movements, and popular culture: in short, history not "from above" but "from below" (cf. Barton 1997: 278). The 1960s also witnessed an expansion in the disciplines of the social sciences and an increase in their influence and prominence in universities and in society (cf. Barton 1992: 401). All that happened in the 1970s, Theissen suggests, was that "exegesis caught up with what had already developed elsewhere" (1993: 18). The interest in the use of social scientific methods in biblical studies thus stems from the social context that also gave rise to feminist and political/liberationist hermeneutics, for example, and more generally to widespread and creative experimentation with a whole range of "new methods" in biblical studies.[13] Social scientific approaches retain a much closer connection with the concerns of historical criticism than many of these other new methods, particularly some of the forms of literary criticism (Barton 1995).

Innovative Studies of the 1970s

Two "events" of the early 1970s, one in the United States, the other in Germany, deserve particular notice. One is the formation in 1973 of a SBL (Society of Biblical Literature)[14] group devoted to the study of the social world of early Christianity (see J. Z. Smith 1975). One of the group's founding members was Wayne Meeks, who had already (in 1972) published a groundbreaking essay on John's Gospel, using perspectives from the sociology of knowledge to argue that the Christology of the Fourth Gospel reflects and legitimates the social situation of a sectarian community that is alienated and isolated from the world.[15] Another founding member was Jonathan Smith, who offered an outline of what he saw as the major tasks and opportunities in the field (J. Z. Smith 1975). The group devoted a number of years to the study of early Christianity in a particular location, Antioch, seeking to give concrete and specific focus to their studies of the social context in which the early Christians lived (see Meeks and Wilken 1978).[16]

The second notable event (not strictly a single "event") was the publication of a series of articles between 1973 and 1975 by Gerd Theissen, then of the University of Bonn, now at Heidelberg. These articles, which encompass both the Palestinian Jesus movement and the Pauline church at Corinth, remain among the most influential and groundbreaking contributions to the sociology of early Christianity.[17] They combine a detailed and careful use of historical evidence with a creative and eclectic use of sociological theory. Notably, the essays on the synoptic material demonstrate a close connection with the methods and concerns of form criticism, while exploring the sociological questions about *Sitz im Leben* that form criticism evidently failed to address (Theissen 1993: 10 n.11, 33–37). The detailed methodological and exegetical reflections in these essays (see Theissen 1979: 3–76) underpin the more popular presentation in Theissen's much discussed *Soziologie der Jesusbewegung*, translated into English as *Sociology of Early Palestinian Christianity* (in the United States) or *The First Followers of Jesus* (in the United Kingdom; see Theissen 1978).[18]

Other notable groundbreaking publications in this period include Robin Scroggs's essay of 1975, the first systematic attempt to apply the sociological model of the religious "sect" to early Christianity, and John Gager's book *Kingdom and Community* (1975). Gager sketched the ways in which a number of different social scientific theories might be applied to early Christianity. These include the models resulting from studies of millenarian movements and Melanesian cargo cults, undertaken by anthropologists in the 1950s and 1960s; Max Weber's concept of charisma and its routinization; the process of institutionalization; and cognitive dissonance theory, developed by Leon Festinger and others in the 1950s through the study of groups that predicted the end of the world but did not disappear when their prediction failed to come true. Although the brevity of Gager's studies left him open to criticism, notably by Smith (1978),[19] many of his suggested avenues have been explored in more detail in subsequent work. Bengt Holmberg (1978/1980), for example, has applied Weber's notions of charisma and its routinization to the structures of authority in the primitive church, and Margaret MacDonald (1988), influenced in part by Holmberg, has undertaken a detailed study of institutionalization in the Pauline churches. Robert Jewett (1986) has applied the "millenarian model" to the Thessalonian churches. The theory of cognitive dissonance has also proved fruitful in further studies (see, e.g., Gager 1981; Segal 1990a; and Taylor 1992, 1997a, 1997b).

In the late 1970s and early 1980s interest in the field continued to grow, and an increasing number of widely varied publications appeared.[20] Book-length introductions to the area were written by Derek Tidball (1983) and Carolyn Osiek (1984), both of which remain useful entrées into the subject.[21] More recently, as well as biblical scholars developing an interest in the social sciences, some sociologists have turned their attention to early Christianity. Notable examples include Anthony Blasi's *Early Christianity as a Social Movement* (1988) and Rodney Stark's *The Rise of Christianity* (1996), the latter a book that has generated considerable discussion.[22]

A number of attempts have been made to classify this varied and ongoing work according to the method employed and the scope of the investigation. John Elliott distinguishes the following five categories: (1) "investigations of *social realia* . . . generally to illustrate some feature or features of ancient society but with no concern for analyzing, synthesizing, and explaining these social facts in social scientific fashion"; (2) studies that seek "to construct a *social history* of a particular period or movement or group" but with a predominantly historical conceptual framework and "an eschewing of social theory and models"; (3) studies of "the social organisation of early Christianity," and of "the social forces leading to its emergence and its social institutions," which include "*the deliberate use of social theory and models*"; (4) studies that focus on "*the social and cultural scripts* influencing and constraining social interaction" in the "cultural environment of the New Testament"; and (5) studies that use "the research, theory, and models of the social sciences . . . in the *analysis of biblical texts*" (1993: 18–20).[23] Hochschild offers a fourfold model, categorizing approaches on two axes according to their methodological and hermeneutical stance. His four categories are (1) "social-descriptive" (*sozialdescriptiv*), (2) "social-proclamatory" (*sozialkerygmatisch*), (3) "social-scientific" (*sozialwissenschaftlich*), and (4) "materialist" (*materialistich*) (1999: 26, 243).[24] Categories 1 and 2 are described as methodologically conservative, eschewing the use of social scientific models, whereas categories 3 and 4 are methodologically innovative, taking up various approaches from the social sciences. However, on the other axis, the hermeneutical stance, categories 2 and 4 stand close together in giving prominence to the significance of the texts for the contemporary world, whereas categories I and 3 tend to distance themselves from such explicit hermeneutical concerns.

Any categorization can of course be questioned, since the boundaries between types of work are never neat or clear. In Hochschild's case, rather a lot is encompassed within category 3, despite some significant disagreements and differences of approach among scholars classified as belonging to that group (see further Horrell forthcoming-a). There are also relevant theoretical debates concerning the adequacy of any methodological distinction between history and social science (see Horrell 1996a: 26–31). However, in terms of the assessment of published work, there clearly is a significant distinction to be drawn between works of social history that explicitly eschew the use of social scientific theories or models (e.g., Clarke 1993 and Gooch 1993)[25] and those that employ them as tools in the task of historical investigation (e.g., Meeks 1983). Also significant is the distinction that has emerged between those who may be termed "social historians" (yet who use social scientific methods) and the "social scientists" who have developed a rigorous and model-based approach (Martin 1993: 107).[26] What may be questioned, though, is the legitimacy of a claim to eschew the discussion of theory. Any approach to history is guided by the methods, presuppositions, and convictions of the researcher, and the adoption of a merely empirical interest in the data must be seen as a concealment of (implicit) theory, which theoretically conscious works aim to render conspicuous and therefore open to critical scrutiny (cf. Horrell 1996a: 27–28, in criticism of Clarke 1993). Indeed, the desire to be open and explicit about methods and models has been a motivation in much social scientific exegesis (cf. Esler 1987: 15 and Elliott 1993: 36–59).

In the following sections I shall focus on three types of approach that emerged as significant in the 1980s and 1990s and between which there are important differences. This will prepare the ground for a brief overview of areas of criticism, current debate, and prospects for future development.

Cultural Anthropology and the Context Group

In 1981 Bruce Malina published his groundbreaking book *The New Testament World: Insights from Cultural Anthropology*, in which he outlined a series of models derived from the work of various anthropologists for understanding the pivotal values of Mediterranean culture—the social world inhabited by the first Christians. Malina's concern was to enable his readers to appreciate the strangeness and difference of that cultural context when viewed from the perspective of twentieth-century America. In order to displace the implicit ethnocentric and anachronistic assumption that people then were pretty much like modern Americans, Malina sought to provide models of a culture that operated in very different ways. The central features and values of that culture, he proposed, were honor and shame, dyadic rather than individual personality,[27] the perception of limited good,[28] distinctive norms of kinship and marriage, and a set of purity rules to distinguish clean and unclean (Malina 1981).

In 1986 Malina published another book of models, drawn from the work of various anthropologists, notably Mary Douglas, and intended to provide further resources for study of the social and cultural world of the New Testament (Malina 1986a). Also in 1986 the "Context Group" was formed, with Bruce Malina as a prominent and founding member. This group, formally organized in 1989, comprises an international (though largely American) group of scholars who meet "annually to plan, mutually discuss, and evaluate their individual and collaborative work in social-scientific exegesis" (Elliott 1993: 29). In the words of the announcement for their 1997 conference, "the Context Group is dedicated to understanding and interpreting the Biblical text within the context of the social and cultural world of traditional Mediterranean society." The pivotal values of Mediterranean society as outlined in Malina's 1981 book have remained foundational to the Context Group's work (see, e.g., Neyrey 1991; Esler 1994: 19–36; and Rohrbaugh 1996), and a basic motivation for their work remains the avoidance of ethnocentric and anachronistic readings of biblical texts (see, e.g., Elliott 1993: 11). Drawing on studies of the Mediterranean, both ancient and modern, and using models developed by anthropologists, they have consistently developed and applied a range of reading strategies to illuminate the foreign world of the early Christians. Contrasts between Mediterranean and American society are often explicitly detailed or tabulated (e.g., Malina and Neyrey 1988: 145–51; Malina 1993: 56–58, 82–86; and Malina and Neyrey 1996: 227–31).

Another early and influential member of the group is Jerome Neyrey, whose many publications since the mid-1980s have also pursued this approach to the New Testament, often in collaboration with Malina and other members of the Context Group.[29] Others whose interest in social scientific methods began independently but who have since become closely involved with the group's work include John Elliott, who in 1981 published a pioneering study of I Peter using what he then termed "sociological exegesis,"[30] and Philip Esler.[31] Recent products of the group's collaborative efforts include the collection of essays on Luke-Acts, edited by Neyrey (1991); Malina and Richard Rohrbaugh's *Social-Science Commentary on the Synoptic Gospels* (1992); *Social Scientific Models for Interpreting the Bible*, the *Festschrift* for Bruce Malina, edited by John Pilch (2001); and an accessible presentation of the Context Group's models edited by Rohrbaugh (1996), which provides perhaps the best place to begin an encounter with their approach. Their individual and collaborative output has been impressive and extensive and can hardly be summarized here.[32]

The main achievements of their approach encompass both method and re-sults. First, by elucidating a clear and explicit set of models they have set out openly the basis for their studies, enabling readers both to appraise the results and employ the models experimentally for themselves, should they so wish (cf. Elliott 1993: 48). Second, the results of their studies have served to illuminate the strik-ingly different social dynamics at work in the biblical texts and thus to guard against any hermeneutic that elides the distinction between ancient and modern contexts. Yet there are also critical questions to be raised, some of which will be considered below.

Historical Sociology/Social History

All proponents of the use of the social sciences in studies of early Christianity ac-knowledge that such work stands in close connection with historical-critical study. The social sciences provide a further (and, many would argue, essential) compo-nent of historical study, enabling the social context, dynamics, and impact of the texts to be better understood (e.g., Elliott 1993: 7–16 and Esler 1994: 2–3). However, in contrast to the Context Group, whose members have developed a par-ticular set of social scientific models and applied them consistently, others have adopted social scientific methods in a more eclectic and piecemeal way, regarding themselves primarily as social historians, or have used social theory to develop a theoretical or research framework, but have rejected a specifically model-based ap-proach.[33] The work of Gerd Theissen, for example, already mentioned above, may appropriately be described in this way. Certainly Theissen is acutely theoretically conscious (see 1979: 3–76 and 1993: 231–87), yet his use of sociological (and psychological—see 1987) theory is eclectic and experimental, and often linked closely with other historical studies. Particular mention should also be made of the magisterial study by Wayne Meeks, *The First Urban Christians* (1983). In this wide-ranging examination of the Pauline churches, Meeks explicitly declares his identity as "social historian" and states that he adopts his social scientific the-ory—both sociological and anthropological—"piecemeal, as needed, where it fits" (1983: 6). Meeks seeks to appreciate the particularities of the early Christ-ian communities, something he sees as essentially a historian's concern, which he contrasts with the social scientist's search for law-like generalizations (1982: 266; cf. 1983: 1–7). However, in my view, the contrasts between a search for what is distinctive and for what is typical, between open-ended theoretical frameworks and cross-cultural models, may be related to two sides of a debate *within* the so-cial sciences about the nature of social science, rather than to a supposed contrast between history and social science (see Garrett 1992 and Horrell 1996a: 9–32). Furthermore, it is not surprising that this debate is played out also in New Testament studies (see below) and corresponds with a significant division among scholars who use the social sciences in their studies of early Christianity: Elliott (1985) and Malina (1985b), for example, have criticized Meeks's book for its lack of consistent theoretical foundation, while Theissen declared himself "deeply impressed" (1985: 113).

Other studies that use social scientific theory yet remain closely connected with historical scholarship and concerns include those of Howard Kee (1980); Francis Watson (1986); Philip Esler (1987); Margaret MacDonald (1988); and, more recently, John Barclay (1992, 1995a, 1995b, 1996). Barclay has employed the social sciences to provide fruitful and heuristic lines of questioning and enquiry, new ways of seeing and conceptualizing old issues, yet is concerned primarily to be a historian, and so to wrestle with the scanty and often ambiguous evidence from the period and to appreciate the distinctiveness and variety in patterns of social interaction and practice.

Historical studies of early Christianity after the New Testament period have also turned to the social sciences for theoretical and conceptual tools. For example, James Jeffers (1991) draws on Max Weber's types of legitimate authority and the sociology of sects (especially following Bryan Wilson) in his analysis of the contrasts in Roman Christianity exemplified by *1 Clement* and the *Shepherd of Hermas*. Harry Maier (1991) employs the coauthored theoretical work of Peter Berger and Thomas Luckmann (1966) in his study of the development of patterns of ministry in the *Shepherd of Hermas, 1 Clement,* and the letters of Ignatius. While there clearly is a difference between such approaches and the work of those social historians who reject the use of contemporary social theory, and while there clearly have been differences in approach between historians, sociologists, and anthropologists, I follow those who argue that there is no sustainable methodological distinction between history and social science and therefore maintain that the distinction between historical sociology and social history is, or should become, meaningless.[34] Historical studies that avoid any discussion of theory or any use of social scientific insights, as I suggested above, merely impoverish their analyses, or conceal the implicit theoretical presuppositions of their approach.

Nonetheless, despite a common acceptance of the value of using the social sciences, there remain significant differences of approach between those who follow the method pioneered by Malina and those who follow the kind adopted by Theissen and Meeks. Members of the Context Group adopt a model-based approach that draws primarily upon anthropology and stresses the cultural gap between the early Christian world and the present one, whereas those sometimes labeled "social historians" have tended to draw their theoretical resources more from sociology (e.g., the sociology of sects, the sociology of knowledge, etc.) and to use their social scientific resources more as a way of constructing a framework for understanding and of sensitizing the researcher to previously ignored questions and issues.

Radical Social History and Emancipatory Theologies

Just as Marxist scholars in the late nineteenth and early twentieth centuries were among those who demonstrated an interest in the social dimensions of early Christianity, so in recent years a number of scholars have developed a variety of what may be termed "radical" sociopolitical perspectives on early Christianity, often allied to the concerns of some form of emancipatory or liberation theology.[35] In these types of work, as Hochschild points out, the hermeneutical interests are more explicit (1999: 242–43): the exploration of the social history of earliest Christianity is undertaken with an interest in the significance of the texts for the contemporary world. Not all radical approaches to the New Testament are in any sense social scientific, but a good number are. Some derive theoretical resources from Marxist traditions of sociology, and thus develop a "materialist" reading of the New Testament (e.g., Bélo 1974). Also indebted at least indirectly to Marxism, as well as to other versions of critical social theory, are approaches that employ a critical conception of "ideology" and thus attempt to unmask the ways in which language/texts are used to legitimate and sustain relations of power and domination.

One prominent achievement is the development of feminist social-historical perspectives on the New Testament. Feminist studies represent one form of ideology-critique, in that they seek to expose patriarchal structures of domination in both past and present and to call them into question. A landmark publication in this regard is Elisabeth Schüssler Fiorenza's *In Memory of Her: A Feminist Theological Reconstruction of Christian Origins* (1983/1995). Although she does not explicitly adopt social scientific methods,[36] her work does represent a creative attempt to recover the social history of the early Christian movement, especially of women within that movement, from behind the veil of androcentric texts and the tradition of androcentric interpretation. She argues that an early "discipleship of equals" was gradually marginalized by a process of patriarchalization within the first-century churches. Among the many and varied contributions that might also be mentioned, the writings of Luise Schottroff represent notable studies in feminist social history (see Schottroff 1993, 1995). Schottroff's feminist commitment is closely allied to a commitment to the cause of liberation theology, the emancipation of the poor from structures of oppression (see e.g., Schottroff 1985/1999).

While these varied radical approaches make clear their sociopolitical commitments, it is perhaps misleading to refer to them as "committed" readings, at least if that is taken as an implicit contrast with supposedly "uncommitted" readings. As Schottroff (1999: 285) briefly notes, the claim to objectivity in much New Testament scholarship is a claim that conceals the interests and commitments that actually underpin the perspective that is adopted. One may perhaps feel that some of the radical readings present a "history" that is an idealized reflection of contemporary commitments more than of historical reality—such as the utopian ideal of the discipleship of equals, or the egalitarian church of the poor in which the rich abandoned their social privileges. Nevertheless, they represent an important challenge to "bourgeois" interpreters to consider the possibility of other perspectives on the history of early Christianity, perspectives that may perhaps sit less comfortably with the presuppositions of their socioeconomic location and commitments. Moreover, they press interpreters to confront the unacknowledged commitments that inevitably mean that evidence is seen from a particular perspective—or sometimes overlooked altogether—because of the interpreter's own context.

Significant Areas of Current Debate and Prospects for Future Development

In such a rich and diverse field of scholarship there are numerous differences and disagreements that could be highlighted. In what follows I focus on certain important points of contemporary debate and on what seem to me the main areas for future development in social scientific study of early Christianity.

Critical Questions

Those who advocate the use of the social sciences in studies of early Christianity maintain that the fruit of a variety of social scientific research offers new ways of framing questions, new perspectives, and critical theoretical resources and alerts the researcher to previously unexplored aspects of social behavior. The question then, as posed by Philip Esler, is "not 'Do we need the social sciences?' but rather 'How can we get along without them?'" (1994: 18). Nevertheless, objections to the enterprise have been raised.[37] Cyril Rodd (1981) has questioned whether the ancient sources yield adequate data of a kind suitable for sociological analysis (compared with the contemporary opportunities for interviews, observation, etc.). He highlights the danger that a theory or model may be used to fill in the gaps and assume things for which evidence is lacking. Edwin Judge similarly expresses the concern that sociological models or theories may be imposed upon the ancient evidence, without the painstaking study of that evidence necessary to ascertain the "social facts of life characteristic of the world to which the New Testament belongs"

(1980: 210). Philip Esler rightly questions Judge's apparently empiricist presuppositions; namely the idea that one can simply search for social facts, for uninterpreted data, innocent of the need for theoretical discussion or reflection on the presuppositions of particular approaches to history (1987: 13–16; see also MacDonald 1988: 25–27). For Esler, social scientific models should not predetermine the results of an inquiry, but serve as heuristic tools, suggesting new perspectives and illuminating comparisons. Nevertheless, there is a significant debate—a debate within the social sciences and within New Testament studies—about the appropriate methods for social scientific research and about the philosophical and epistemological assumptions that underpin different types of approach. While an untheoretical empiricism of the kind Judge seems to advocate is to be rejected, there are still important questions to be asked about how particular methods and approaches shape the way in which the evidence is interpreted.

A second criticism often mentioned is that of reductionism, that is, the idea that social scientific theories will "explain" religious phenomena purely in terms of social or economic forces.[38] Certainly some traditions of social theory—that is, some forms of Durkheimian or Marxist sociology—are more crudely reductionist and deterministic than others. Yet even if such traditions are avoided, the reductionist criticism cannot be dismissed quite as easily as some suppose.[39] The social sciences prioritize certain aspects of human experience and interaction—the "social"—and regard human knowledge and culture as essentially "socially constructed" (see Berger 1967). Hence their stance is one of what Peter Berger calls "methodological atheism" (1967: 180).[40] A more profound and extended version of this critique has been articulated by John Milbank (1990), who argues that the creation of a secular polity—a novel modern achievement—was based on certain "theological" decisions and that this in turn facilitated the rise of "secular" disciplines such as economics, sociology, and anthropology, which have antitheological assumptions at their heart. The social sciences serve theoretically to marginalize and privatize religion, naming the public sphere as a secular space to be comprehended by secular reason. Milbank rejects the practice whereby theologians draw on the social sciences to understand and explain as far as they can, or borrow from the social sciences their fundamental account of reality, and then see whether there are any theologically significant "bits" left (1990: 380). He argues that social science and theology offer fundamentally different and competing narratives about human society and that it is the business of theologians to articulate the Christian narrative, rather than to cede priority to the narrative of social science. Milbank's aim, bluntly expressed, is "to 'end' the dialogue between theology and sociology" (1990: 4).

I am not convinced that the theoretical narratives of theology and social science are so fundamentally incommensurable, nor as monolithic, as Milbank seems to suggest. Nevertheless, there are important theoretical presuppositions underpinning various forms of social theory that should be carefully and critically appraised. While there is more variety within the traditions and contemporary formulations of social theory than Milbank acknowledges, there is, it seems to me, an important truth in Milbank's argument that sociology and theology offer "narratives" about human society with fundamentally different priorities and assumptions at their heart and that *some* forms of social science offer explanations of early Christianity that stand in tension with "theological" perspectives. Of course, whether that tension or opposition is an attraction or a problem for the scholar of early Christianity will depend upon personal commitments and beliefs, but what should certainly be avoided is the naïve belief that any form of social science can be used to study the early church without any serious theoretical conflict between that perspective and more theological understandings.[41]

These various criticisms should not therefore be too lightly dismissed, but neither do they require the abandonment of the enterprise. Those who practice social scientific criticism, in whatever form, themselves often stress the need for ongoing methodological reflection and critical discussion. Important theoretical issues need to be debated and clarified, but in the context of ongoing and creative attempts to use social scientific resources in studies of early Christianity. The social sciences offer tools for exploring the social context within which the "theology" of early Christianity was forged and resources for investigating the ways in which early Christian writings formed and shaped patterns of interaction within the congregations. They bring new and different questions onto the agenda for the study of early Christianity, without in any way implying or requiring the abandonment of more traditional, theological modes of inquiry. For example, a social scientist may ask about the ways in which particular aspects of early Christian belief and practice constructed a distinct sense of group identity and formed boundaries around the membership of the early Christian communities. This enables comparison with the ways in which other groups, then and now, construct and maintain their identity and boundaries, but it does not negate or undermine attempts to understand and articulate the particular ideas and practices that constitute that specifically Christian identity. In some cases, of course, a social scientific explanation of some aspect of the rise of Christianity will conflict with a Christian theological understanding of that process: in such cases Milbank's notion of competing narratives seeking to "out-narrate" one another may well be apposite. But the academy is surely the place where even such deeply opposed forms of description and explanation can and should be articulated, considered, and tested by critical scrutiny.

Theory, Methods, and Models

Many of those who have written about this use of social scientific methods have stressed the importance of ongoing methodological reflection (e.g., Stowers 1985 and Elliott 1986). Susan Garrett, for example, insists, "It is . . . increasingly urgent that scholars of Christian origins engage in sustained reflection on the philosophical implications of the perspectives and models they choose to employ" (1992: 93). She draws a contrast between "a rigorous model-testing approach"—characteristic, as we have seen, of the work of the Context Group—and the more "interpretive" approach adopted by "ethnographic" anthropologists (i.e., those who seek to immerse themselves in the culture of the people they are studying and then to offer a "thick description"; see Garrett 1992: 92). Garrett sees Meeks's book (1983) as a fine example of the latter approach, which she favors (Garrett 1992: 95–96).

This, then, is an important point of contemporary debate and disagreement (cf. Martin 1993: 107–10). On the one hand there are those who insist that a social scientific approach should involve the employment and testing of models that have been formulated on the basis of cross-cultural research. Malina, a prominent practitioner of this approach, defines a model as "an abstract, simplified representation of some real world object, event or interaction" (1982: 231). Equipped with an appropriate set of social scientific models the researcher can approach the evidence and test whether the data fit. Those who advocate a model-based approach insist that their use of models is heuristic and not prescriptive, and that only if the data fit the model will its use be justified (Esler 1994: 12–13; 1995a: 4). But any particular model *shapes* the way in which evidence is selected and interpreted; theoretical questions about the nature of a model or research framework are therefore as crucial as the pragmatic question as to how well the data fit.

Others have doubts about this "scientific" approach to the study of human societies and consider that a model-based approach can result in the evidence being fitted into a particular mold that insufficiently allows for variations across space and change over time. They argue instead for an approach that, while theoretically informed, uses theory as a "sensitizing" tool and seeks to explore the particularities of each specific sociocultural context (cf. Garrett 1992; Horrell 1996a: 9–18, 2000d; and Barclay 1995a: 118).

A comparable division among classicists influenced by anthropology is noted by Paul Cartledge:

> On the one hand, there are those who believe it is possible and fruitful to generalize across all modern Greece (and sometimes, more broadly still, to "the Mediterranean world," for example) and to use such generalized comparative data to supplement as well as interpret the lacunose primary data of antiquity. . . . On the other hand, there are those who . . . believe . . . that such comparison should be used chiefly to highlight fundamental cultural difference rather than homogenize heterogeneous cultures, or fill gaps in the extant primary sources. (1994: 5)

This debate reflects a similar one within the social sciences themselves, where some (e.g., Turner 1987: 156–94) advocate an approach that seeks to generalize and explain human behavior in laws and precise models, while others argue for a more interpretive, or hermeneutically informed, version of social science, which emphasizes the uniqueness of particular contexts and seeks explanations in those particularities rather than in generalizations (e.g., Giddens 1984: xiii–xxxvii, 1–40; see also Horrell 1996a: 9–32). In the current "postmodern" climate there has certainly been a move away from grand theory and model building. Some contemporary anthropologists, for example, have specifically criticized "generalizations" about supposed cultural zones, such as "the Mediterranean," calling instead for "ethnographic particularism" (Herzfeld 1980: 349; cf. Peristiany and Pitt-Rivers 1992: 5–6 and note 44 below).

Such philosophical and theoretical issues are an important area of current debate, with implications for the way in which a historical approach informed by the social sciences should develop. It is hardly to be expected, nor necessarily to be desired, that the current diversity of method and practice will disappear. But it is important to explore and debate the theoretical issues that underpin the variety of approaches, in order to clarify what is basically in dispute and to refine and reformulate new directions for research.[42]

Anthropology and the Understanding of the Ancient Mediterranean Context

As noted above, members of the Context Group have developed and applied a consistent set of models based on the work of various anthropologists, which, they propose, enable the interpreter to avoid the perils of anachronism and ethnocentrism and to appreciate the cultural dynamics of the ancient Mediterranean. The group's work has done much to draw attention to the social and cultural dynamics of the early Christian world and to highlight the differences between that world and the twentieth-century West. However, critical questions may also be raised. First, there seems to be an overdependence on the basic set of models outlined in Malina's work of 1981, which in any case lack the reference to extrabiblical ancient sources necessary to demonstrate the models' validity as a representation of ancient Mediterranean culture (cf. Gager 1983: 195–96).[43] Some of these models, notably that of honor and shame, and the idea that contests for honor are played out in public encounters of challenge–riposte, have been repeatedly cited and applied (e.g., Malina and Rohrbaugh 1992; Malina and Neyrey 1991a; and Neyrey 1994). Certainly these studies have helped to show the extent to which such social values are visible in the biblical texts, but the illumination is not necessarily increased with frequent repetition. It may also be suggested that the models have sometimes become somewhat inflexible tools, which lead to a rather "homogenized" view of "Mediterranean culture" and give scant opportunity for the subtleties and variations of local contexts to emerge (cf. Garrett 1988, 1992; Chance 1994: 146–49; and Meggitt 1998a). This is especially to be noted since recent anthropological studies stress the variety of ways in which honor or shame (and not necessarily both) may be instantiated in particular contexts and encourage the researcher to be open to the rich diversity of local cultures, rather than adopt or assume a single model.[44] Moreover, a number of the anthropological studies employed by Malina et al. are of the modern Mediterranean, and the implicit assumption that modern and ancient Mediterranean cultures are broadly continuous and similar may be sharply questioned (Meggitt 1998a). To some extent the underlying issue and point of debate is a methodological one: Should a social scientific approach involve the testing of generalized cross-cultural models or a more inductive, interpretive, particularist approach?[45]

A fundamental achievement of the work of Malina and others has been to bring the insights, methods, and models of the discipline of anthropology into fruitful engagement with the study of early Christianity. Whatever the precise method used to employ these resources, there is surely much to be gained from continued critical engagement with recent anthropological work on societies that bear closer comparison with the early Christian communities than do the industrialized market economies of the contemporary developed world. Indeed, Dale Martin suggests that "most scholars engaged in social approaches to the New Testament claim to find sociology less and less helpful and anthropology and ethnography more and more interesting" (Martin 1993: 115). Martin's recent book (1995) represents an interesting and important study, not using a model-based approach, but employing cross-cultural studies and drawing briefly on theories of ideology, which illustrates how ancient sources may be used to reconstruct the diverse and contrasting ancient views of the social and individual body, and of disease in the body, thereby also stressing the gap between that social world and our own.[46] In other work too, the anthropologically informed appreciation of cultural dynamics that Malina et al. have done so much to promote is drawn in alongside other kinds of historical and social scientific evidence, thus indicating ways in which distinctions in contemporary approaches to research, outlined above, might be broken down (see, e.g., Witherington 1998b; Osiek and Balch 1997). Other directions in anthropological research might also prove fruitful for studies of early Christian texts: the use of literary texts as sources for ethnography, for example, has more obvious parallels to the kind of study that is possible with early Christian sources than the more traditional anthropological method of participant observation.[47]

Radical or Conservative? Early Christianity, Its Interpreters, and the Critique of Ideology

The work of feminists, liberation theologians, and other radical scholars (see above) has helped to focus attention on particular sociopolitical questions about the history of early Christianity and the character of the New Testament texts: To what extent and in what sense was the early church egalitarian? To what extent, if at all, did the early Christian communities reject or subvert the dominant social and patriarchal hierarchy of their society? Does the teaching of Jesus, or Paul, or other early Christian voices, challenge that patriarchal hierarchy and promote equality and liberation, or does it reinforce established patterns of domination and subordination? Although the presuppositions and commitments of each interpreter undoubtedly affect the ways in which these questions are posed and the style of the answer, a particular perspective by no means necessarily follows from a specific interpretative commitment. Feminist scholars, for example, disagree as to whether the New Testament offers some evidence of, and resources to support, the liberation and equality of women (e.g., Schüssler Fiorenza 1983; Schottroff 1993) or whether the whole Jewish-Christian tradition is so irredeemably patriarchal that it must be abandoned altogether (e.g., Daly 1986; Hampson 1996). Radical and Marxist scholars of the New Testament and of ancient history disagree as to whether early Christianity's message challenged the social order of the day, or whether it merely helped sustain it.[48] What is important is that these critical sociological questions have been placed prominently onto the agenda of early Christian studies, and it is to be hoped that further debate will seek to clarify not only the range of possible answers to such questions, but also the ways in which theoretical resources from the traditions of Marxism and critical social theory might be used to develop historically plausible radical perspectives on the early church.[49] The question of historical plausibility is important, since some attempts to "rediscover" a radical, liberating Jesus, Paul, or whomever seem to end up pressing the more awkward texts into an implausible mold in order to construct the kind of ideal figure who is a reflection of the author's own commitments.[50]

Among the wide variety of recent and postmodern approaches to biblical criticism are developments in ideological criticism, where interpreters inquire into the interests that underpin particular textual formulations and how those texts function in a discourse of power, to sustain hierarchies, to marginalize and exclude, and to conceal or naturalize relations of domination.[51] These critical questions clearly connect with the concerns of feminist and liberation theologies, which seek to unmask the strategies by which men legitimate or conceal their domination of women, or by which the rich maintain and conceal their oppression of the poor. But these questions about (concealed) interests are now being addressed not only to ancient texts but also to their contemporary interpreters, whose interests and commitments are equally bound up with the perspectives they adopt and promote. Thus a whole series of critical (and sometimes disturbing) questions are beginning to be raised, and there is the potential for further development of an interesting coalescence of concerns: from ideology-critique, critical social theory, emancipatory theologies, and radical or materialist approaches to history.

Links with Literary and Rhetorical Approaches

Another major new direction in biblical studies of the last quarter-century or so is the development of a wide variety of literary approaches, ranging from narrative and rhetorical studies to reader-response, poststructuralism, and deconstruction. Some of these methods have virtually nothing in common with social scientific approaches, as they consciously eschew any interest in the social world in which the text was originally produced. However, since the study of early Christian texts, whatever else it may be, is certainly the study of literature, tools for literary analysis and criticism can hardly but be important to sociohistorical investigations. Any responsible historical or social scientific study must take account of the literary character of the texts that comprise the primary evidence and must consider carefully how historical evidence can be drawn from texts that are written to exhort and persuade, often with a polemical and argumentative thrust. In recent years some scholars have sought to develop methods that incorporate both literary and social scientific approaches to interpretation. Norman Petersen's (1985) study of Paul's letter to Philemon is a good example. Vernon Robbins has given considerable attention to the task of developing an integrated approach to New Testament interpretation that encompasses both literary-rhetorical and social scientific methods, and has coined the term "socio-rhetorical criticism" (see Robbins 1996a, 1996b). In three recent "socio-rhetorical" commentaries on the Corinthian letters (1995a), Acts (1998a), and the Gospel of Mark (2001), Ben Witherington has independently[52] also sought to combine the insights of social scientific and rhetorical approaches in a historical analysis. Such attempts to integrate social scientific and literary methods are important and timely and point the way to an important direction for continuing research.

The Continued Revitalization of the Study of Early Christian History, Ethics, and Theology

Since the 1970s "sociological" perspectives have become increasingly widely infused into New Testament and early Christian studies. It is now commonplace, for example, to hear about the sectarian character of the Johannine community, or the social function of the Jewish law in debates about understanding Paul. Such perspectives have undoubtedly helped to root the discussion of early Christian texts much more concretely in the social situations of human communities and within a theoretical framework that fosters an appreciation of the social dynamics of human interaction and conflict. In terms of Scroggs's critique of much New Testament study up to the 1970s (cited above) it seems that the introduction of social scientific perspectives has indeed helped "to put body and soul together again" and has led to the "revitalising of historical criticism" (Barton 1997: 286; cf. 1995). The continued creative and careful use of a variety of social scientific approaches—some no doubt yet to be discovered by biblical or patristic scholars or applied to early Christianity by social scientists—should enable this revitalization to progress further.

At the close of a recent essay introducing social scientific criticism Stephen Barton suggests that the introduction of social scientific perspectives may perhaps also bear fruit in revitalizing the study of New Testament theology and ethics (Barton 1997: 286: "it remains to be seen"). Barton mentions the work of William Countryman (1989) and Wayne Meeks (1993) as "promising beginnings." There is an obvious overlap of concern between the study of ethics—if ethics is conceived of as reflection on the ways in which human beings should behave in relation to one another and their environment—and the social scientific study of patterns of social interaction in communities and of the ways in which texts both arise from and shape their social context. If the social sciences do influence the study of early Christian ethics then they will surely direct the focus away from individuals and their decisions of right and wrong on specific moral questions and toward the ways in which the early Christian texts shape social relationships in particular community contexts (cf. Barton 1992). Hence Meeks prefers to speak of the New Testament texts as instruments of "moral formation" (1996: 317). The questions raised by social scientists also have a direct bearing on the critical study of Christian ethics: Who is urging what particular course or pattern of behavior, and whose interests does that exhortation reflect? How is power used to manipulate or coerce? There would seem then to be the scope for the fruitful enrichment of the study of early Christian ethics with perspectives and questions from the social sciences.

If "theology" is seen not as the elucidation of abstract and unchanging truths but as "a contingent historical construct emerging from, and reacting back upon, particular social practices conjoined with particular semiotic and figural codings" (Milbank 1990: 2), then, *pace* Milbank, the study of theology is surely closely linked with the concerns of social science. In terms of the study of early Christian theology (or theologies) the social sciences offer tools to enrich the historical study of the social context within which such theology was formed, and provide theoretical tools to analyze the ways in which the theology (expressed in texts) acted back upon—shaped—social interaction in the early Christian communities. In this field of study too, then, the social sciences have an important role to play.

Conclusion

The use of the social sciences in studies of early Christianity is now widespread and firmly established. Whether in the study of the social context in which a text was written, the ideology and impact of a text itself, the character and expansion of the early Christian communities, or indeed of the social location and interests of contemporary interpreters, the social sciences have shown that they offer rich resources to complement both the already established and the newly developing methods of biblical criticism. In the last thirty years or so, the development of social scientific approaches has indeed been a creative movement in the study of early Christian phenomena. The sheer diversity of approach, and the increasingly widespread impact of social scientific study, make the field ever more difficult to survey and assess. With links established to both historical criticism and literary methods, the social sciences have made their presence and their value very widely felt. Yet even though social scientific methods and findings are now widely institutionalized into the mainstream of early Christian studies, new and creative approaches will in all likelihood continue to be developed. All the signs indicate that in a wide variety of directions, some perhaps new and unexpected, the social sciences will continue to enrich and inform the study of early Christianity.[53]

Notes

This chapter is based on David G. Horrell, "Social-Scientific Interpretation of the New Testament: Retrospect and Prospect," in *Social-Scientific Approaches to New Testament Interpretation*, ed. David G. Horrell (Edinburgh: T. & T. Clark, 1999), pp. 3–27. It has been substantially revised by the author for use here with the kind permission of T. & T. Clark Publishers. I am very grateful to Harriet Harris, Todd Still, and especially John Barclay for comments on a draft of the original essay. Any errors or indiscretions naturally remain my own responsibility.

1. On the diversity of methods now practiced in New Testament studies see Anderson and Moore (1992); Haynes and McKenzie (1993); Green (1995); and Porter (1997b). On the use of the social sciences in studies of the Hebrew Bible/Old Testament, see Mayes (1989); Osiek (1989); and Chalcraft (1997).

2. This point is often made; see e.g., Scroggs (1980: 164) and Theissen (1979: 3–6).

3. For an outline of Hochschild's book, and some critical reflections, see Horrell (2001b).

4. See Marx and Engels (1957) for essays by Engels published in the 1880s and Kautsky (1910). See also Schottroff (1985/1999) and Hochschild (1999: 79–96).

5. See Troeltsch (1931: 69–89) and Theissen (1982: 107–10, 138–40, 163–64). For a critical discussion of Theissen's thesis see Horrell (1996a, esp. 126–98, 233–37), and Schottroff (1999).

6. See Troeltsch (1931: 331–43); MacDonald (1988); and Gill (1996: 4, 56–68).

7. Cullmann (1925), quoted in MacDonald (1988: 19). See also Maier (1991: 5) and Esler (1987: 3).

8. On the Chicago School, see Keck (1974); Funk (1976); Scroggs (1980: 164–65); and Hochschild (1999: 197–206).

9. For example, Riddle does not appear in the bibliography of works published before 1960 in Hochschild (1999: 246–51). For more of Riddle's publications see the bibliography to this volume.

10. Theissen (1993: 1–29) divides his survey of the interest in the sociological interpretation of the New Testament into three phases: 1870–1920, 1920–70, 1970s onward. His analysis, which focuses on German scholarship, perceptively relates the various approaches adopted by scholars to their social and political contexts. Hochschild's work (1999), originally a thesis supervised by Theissen, now offers a more detailed study of the history of research.

11. Hochschild is cautious about explaining the decline of sociohistorical investigation directly by the rise of dialectical theology, though he does note that the directions in theological discussion prominent in dialectical theology were unfavorable for the pursuit of sociohistorical research into early Christianity (1999: 208).

12. Compare Theissen (1993: 19, note 23): "This little book deserves a place of honor in the history of modern sociological exegesis." Judge was a professor of ancient history at Macquarie University in Sydney, Australia, where since the 1960s interest in the social history of early Christianity has been energetically pursued.

13. See Barton for a more extensive list of the influences on the renewed interest in the "communal dimension of earliest Christianity" (1992: 399–406).

14. The SBL is the major U.S.-based organization for biblical studies. On the various SBL groups that have since been formed see Osiek (1989: 268–69).

15. See especially Meeks (1972: 70); Scroggs (1980: 176–77); Holmberg (1990: 125–28); and Barton (1993: 145–52).

16. Given the group's focus on a specific location, it is notable that one of Jonathan Smith's (1978) criticisms of Gager (1975) was that the latter did not relate his analyses to particular places or communities.

17. Note the comments of Scroggs (1980: 174–75); Holmberg (1990: 44–54, 119–25); and Elliott (1993: 21–23). Theissen's work was collected in book-form as *Studien zur Soziologie des Urchristentums* (1979/1988). The essays on Corinth are available in English in *The Social Setting of Pauline Christianity* (1982); the essays on the Jesus movement and other more recent articles in *Social Reality and the Early Churches* (1992/1993).

18. Among the important critiques of this book are Stegemann (1984); Elliott (1986); and Horsley (1989).

19. See also Bartlett (1978); Tracy (1978) (all three review essays in the same issue of *Zygon*).

20. Useful surveys and assessments of this early period are provided by Scroggs (1980); Harrington (1980); Judge (1980); Best (1983); Edwards (1983); and Richter (1984). Richter in particular offers extensive and classified bibliographical information. Elliott also offers a comprehensive survey (1993: 17–35).

21. Tidball's book was reissued in 1997; a second edition of Osiek's was published in 1992.

22. See, e.g., Klutz (1998), Hopkins (1998), Castelli (1998), and a response from Stark (1998a) (all articles in an issue of the *Journal of Early Christian Studies*). See also Malina (1997).

23. Similar classifications are offered, e.g., by J. Z. Smith (1975) and Richter (1984).

24. For category 1 Hochschild refers to work such as that by Martin Hengel; for category 3 Wayne Meeks, Gerd Theissen, Bruce Malina, and Jerome Neyrey et al. are key exemplars. For category 2 Hochschild's key example is the work of Luise Schottroff and Wolfgang Stegemann (1978/1986) and for 4 Fernando Bélo (1974). On these latter two categories see below on "Radical Social History and Emancipatory Theologies."

25. Note also the comments of Garrett (1992: 94) on Malherbe (1977).

26. Both of these categories are encompassed within Hochschild's "social-scientific" category.

27. That is, where persons form their notion of self-identity in terms of what others perceive and relate to them: "A dyadic personality is one who simply needs another continually in order to know who he or she really is" (Malina 1981: 55). For Malina, this stands in contrast with modern (U.S.) individualism.

28. That is, where all goods are deemed to be finite and thus where "an individual, alone or with his family, can improve his social position only at the expense of others" (Malina 1981: 75).

29. See, e.g., Neyrey 1990, 1994, 1998. See also the following collaborations with Malina: Malina and Neyrey 1988, 1991a, 1991b, 1996, etc.

30. See Elliott (1981: 7–11; 1986: 1). For more recent reflections and approach see Elliott's later work (1986, 1993, 1995a, 1995b).

31. Esler (1987); compare more recent work by Esler (1994, especially 19–36; 1995a and b). In his most recent work, Esler has combined the basic approach to Mediterranean culture derived from Malina with the tools of Social Identity Theory, as developed especially by social psychologist Henri Tajfel (see Esler 1996, 1998b, 2000b).

32. See Elliott (1993: 29–30) and bibliographical data at http://www.serv.net/~oakmande/bibliog/context.htm. See also Malina's more recent books (1996a, 2000).

33. Cf. Osiek (1989: 268–74) and Martin (1993: 107–10), both of whom refer to the different groups now constituted under the auspices of the SBL and representing the differences of approach between the "social historians" and the "social scientists."

34. E.g., Anthony Giddens, Philip Abrams, Peter Burke, etc.; see Horrell (1996a: 29–30).

35. A concern with human emancipation, or liberation, is shared by a range of perspectives, including those of feminism and liberation theology. For examples in New Testament studies see Schottroff and Stegemann (1978), Schottroff and Stegemann (1984), Gottwald and Horsley (1993), Myers (1988), Rowland and Corner (1990), Elliott (1994), Schottroff (1985/1999).

36. For this reason there is little justification for Schüssler Fiorenza's claim, based on the omission of mention of her book in recent overviews of social scientific approaches

by Kee (1985) and Martin (1993), that: "According to such 'scientific' historical records of the discipline, feminist historical and social-scientific work still does not exist" (Schüssler Fiorenza 1983/1995: xxxv, note 2).

37. Cf. the summary in Osiek (1989: 275–77).

38. See, e.g., Scroggs (1980: 166–67); Malina (1982: 237–38); Meeks (1983: 2–4); Esler (1987: 12–13); Holmberg (1990: 149–50); Theissen (1979: 58–60; 1993: 187–88); and Horrell (1996a: 18–22).

39. E.g., Malina (1982: 237–38); see also Esler: "There is little to be said for the reductionist criticism" (1987: 12).

40. Berger has offered his own theological response to the issue of this atheistic stance (1969).

41. See further the range of critical reactions to Milbank's book presented in Gill (1996: 429–70), especially that by sociologist Kieran Flanagan. Gill's articles are extracts from fuller presentations in *New Blackfriars* 73 (June 1992).

42. Cf. Osiek (1989: 269–74, 277) and Martin (1993: 107–10). For the two sides of the ongoing debate see Garrett (1992) and response in Esler (1995a: 4–8). See also Horrell (1996a: 9–32), with critique and response in Esler (1998a), taken up again most recently in Horrell (2000d) and Esler (2000a). For a model-based approach see e.g., Malina (1981, 1986); Elliott (1986); Neyrey (1991); and Rohrbaugh (1996).

43. Note, however, the detailed use of ancient sources in, e.g., Neyrey (1994); Elliott (1995b); and Malina and Neyrey (1996).

44. See especially Herzfeld (1980); Chance (1994); Gilmore (1987); and Peristiany and Pitt-Rivers (1992). Peristiany and Pitt-Rivers for example, referring to the use of the term "Mediterranean Society" in the subtitle of their earlier work (Peristiany 1965) state that this "led sometimes to the misunderstanding that we were proposing to establish the Mediterranean as a 'culture area.' This was not the case. . . . In fact we were as much interested in the differences of culture as in the similarities among the peoples surrounding the Mediterranean" (1992: 6). I am also indebted here to Louise Lawrence's research on honor and shame in anthropology and biblical studies. See also the debate between Horrell (2000d) and Esler (2000a).

45. Cf. the critical comments of Sanders (1993: 100–14), relating particularly to the use of Mary Douglas's theory by Malina and Neyrey (1988).

46. See further the review in Horrell (1996b). For another recent book using cultural anthropology see Gordon (1997).

47. For examples of such work among anthropologists see Schapera (1977); Hill (1995); and Whitehead (1995). I am indebted here to my research student Louise Lawrence, who is using such resources to write a "literary ethnography" of Matthew's gospel.

48. See the positive view of a "liberating" Paul in Elliott (1994) (review in Horrell 1997); the "love–hate" relationship with the New Testament—essentially positive about Jesus, negative about Paul—expressed by Mayer (1983); and the negative comments on the impact of early Christianity in de Ste. Croix (1975; 1981: 103–11, 416–41).

49. See the careful discussion of method in Meggitt (1998b), concerning the approach to doing history "from below" and the use of élite sources to reconstruct popular culture.

50. See the comments of Mitchell on Elliott (1994):

E. blithely and swiftly dismisses all the evidence for Paul as a social conservative. . . . The constructive argument depends upon a pileup of questionable assumptions. . . . One should not . . . accept unquestioningly the rigid dichotomy which controls E.'s work (that Paul was either oppressor or liberator) but should press for more complex, mixed, and nuanced portraits of one who offers no simple social legacy. (Mitchell 1996: 547)

For similar comments, see Horrell (1997). The famous comments of Albert Schweitzer on those whose reconstructions of the historical Jesus in fact bear the image of their own reflection remain apposite (Schweitzer 2000: 6). Now, of course, we are more aware of the extent to which every historical reconstruction reflects the context and interests of the interpreter. Yet, unless we abandon the idea that history can be written at all, then it remains the case that historical reconstructions can be more or less plausible in their treatment of the available evidence.

51. For a brief introduction to ideological criticism see Pippin (1997); also, linked with the wider concerns of postmodern biblical criticism, see Adam (1995) and the Bible and Culture Collective (1995). I have sought to apply a critical conception of ideology in the context of a social scientific approach (in Horrell 1993, 1995, 1996a, 1999b).

52. Witherington does acknowledge, "It appears that the term 'socio-rhetorical' was first used by Vernon K. Robbins" (1995a: xii note 8).

53. Extensive bibliographical information can be found in the classified bibliography in this volume. For other bibliographical sources see Harrington (1988); Theissen (1988, 331–70); May (1991); Barton (1992); Elliott (1993); and Hochschild (1999). Useful book-length introductions to the social sciences and New Testament interpretation are Tidball (1983); Osiek (1984; 2nd edition 1992); Holmberg (1990); and Elliott (1993). Shorter introductions and assessments of the field may be found in the dictionary articles by Kee (1985); Garrett (1992); and articles by Osiek (1989); Barton (1992, 1995, 1997); and Martin (1993).

Major Social Scientific Theories: Origins, Development, and Contributions 2

PAUL-ANDRÉ TURCOTTE

Introduction

THE DEVELOPMENT OF SOCIOLOGICAL THOUGHT and, more generally, of social scientific theory has taken on such a literary magnitude over the last century that it is impossible to give a complete account here. Commentators (inter alia Ritzer 1988, 1992, 1996; Morrow and Brown 1994; Kivisto 2000; McDonald 1993) have traced the histories of the various theoretical traditions and how the traditions have been interwoven. In the social scientific study of Christian origins we find a parallel diversity of approach.

We need to orient ourselves amidst the many theories and assess their cognitive validity. Doing so requires a surgical selection. In the case of social science, the enterprise requires referring to the classics and retrieving the ideas that have proven fruitful for the continuation and nourishment of research and discussion. We know Aristotle's famous remark in his *Politics*, "The best knowledge of things requires considering them in their origin" (I.2.1252a). That holds true for both Christian origins and social scientific theory.

Origin of the Sciences of Society and the Conditions of Their Development

The term "sociology," in the sense of a science of society, appeared for the first time in 1839, in a digression in the forty-seventh lesson of the *Cours de philosophie positive* of Auguste Comte (1798–1857). The expression stuck, even though its inventor had preferred "social physics." The French thinker was not the first to construct a systematic and critical reflection on society, but he had the merit of incorporating the social thought of authors as diverse as Vico, Montesquieu, Hume, Condorcet, and Saint-Simon in an original systematization.

One should add to this list, among others, Aristotle (384–322 B.C.E.), with his writings on politics and morals (*Politics, Nicomachean Ethics*); Augustine of Hippo (354–430 C.E.), with his *City of God*; and Ibn Khaldun (1332–1406), with his Muqaddamah, the introductory volume to his *Universal History*. Khaldun, an Arabic language writer, was born in Tunis and educated in Koranic studies, mathematics, and history. He developed a number of ideas that anticipated modern sociology, such as the importance of rational disinterested inquiry, the necessity of empirical investigation, a preoccupation with a search for the causes of social phenomena, and cross-cultural comparison. He devotes special attention in his works to economic and political institutions. His studies led him to be annoyed with the established powers; he spent two years in prison in Morocco for having stated that the rulers of the state were not leaders by divine right. The originality of Khaldun's ideas is widely recognized, but this precursor has had no real influence on the classics of modern sociology.

The first modern sociologists were philosophers by education, such as Auguste Comte, Émile Durkheim (1858–1917), Karl Marx (1818–1883), and Ernst Troeltsch (1865–1922). They tried to understand their times and sought solutions for the social problems that emerged in the wake of political revolutions, untamed industrialization, and massive urbanization. They pursued the philosophical goal of explaining reality in its totality; to that end they valued inductive over deductive methods, embracing the factual aspects of social reality rather than the normative aspects.

From 1880 to 1920, the period of classical sociological thought, the discussion concerned the nature and problems of modern society, as well as the distinction between the natural and cultural sciences. The shadows of Kant (1724–1806) and Hegel (1770–1831) hovered over the highly articulated program statements of Wilhelm Dilthey (1833–1911) and Max Weber (1864–1920). Rather than the explanatory method and external perspective of the natural sciences, both favored a comprehensive method for the human sciences that would not be determinist and would be able to grasp the meaning of lived experience. At the same time it was all-important to break with the vain abstractions of metaphysics and incorporate history and comparisons into the science of society on the basis of observation and experience.

A displacement took place in Europe with the emergence of science and the advance of formal education, and the decline of the public influence of institutional religions. These latter no longer guaranteed the basis of life in society, on account of their being devalued in the name of liberty and reason. However, religion would not be neglected by the founders; it was treated in several of their books. Christian origins were approached, notably by Friedrich Engels (1820–1892), Max Weber, Ernst Troeltsch, and their followers. Each of these pursued an analysis of Western culture from its origins, the history of which is marked by the spirit of Christianity and the emergence of capitalism and the Enlightenment.

Two tendencies become evident in the analysis of religion and society. The first tendency highlights the invariant content and supposed permanent essence of every religion in the society. Émile Durkheim and Karl Marx are the figures known for doing this. The second observes the different historical forms of religious reality and seeks to extricate them from the interactions that develop within a specific social context, in terms of constants, recurrences, and changes in religion or society. Friedrich Engels, Max Weber, and Ernst Troeltsch exemplify this tendency, which can sometimes overlap with the preceding one. The examination of biblical texts is associated with the sociohistorical and comparative tendency.

All the classical thinkers attributed a rational character to religious action in society. Positivism had seen in the religious interpretation of the world a relatively primitive stage in the evolution of human thought. The attack had been directed more against theology than religion since religion would not be an object of study in a perspective that was not specifically religious or in a perspective shared with inquiries into other historical phenomena. Ironically, social science would appear as the heir of religion insofar as it seeks to unveil and name the hidden, the invisible beyond appearances.

The classics also positioned themselves in relation to socialism, which many people continued to espouse. Moreover, their thought developed in combination with teaching, research, publications in periodicals, and advocacy in public discussions. This combination was foremost in the development of the sciences of society. In brief, these sciences were born of conditions propitious to their creation and asserted themselves amidst the teeming ideas of the era.

Factors in the Postclassical Development of the Social Sciences

In the period between the two world wars, interest shifted toward problems of method, including techniques of inquiry, the application of ideas from the theoretical classics, and action for social change. Some of the linkages to the earlier theoretical classics help in sketching the contours of the great theoretical currents and their methods. Thus functionalism draws from Herbert Spencer (1820–1903) and Émile Durkheim; the critical theories look back to G. W. F. Hegel, Karl Marx, and Sigmund Freud (1856–1939); action theorists appeal to Max Weber or Vilfredo Pareto (1848–1923); conflict theorists look to Karl Marx and Georg Simmel (1858–1918); and symbolic interactionism, the theory and method that Herbert Blumer (1900–1987) would formulate in the 1930s, was inspired by George H. Mead (1863–1931). The interwar theorists would extend and rearticulate the ideas of the classic writers. The theoretical and methodological lineages and references, once begun, continue up to the present.

The development of mathematics, especially statistics, of transportation and technology; the demand for inquiries into various social phenomena; and the institutionalization of universities for research and instruction benefited social scientific thought in the 1950s and after. Great nationwide surveys were conducted at governmental request, especially after 1960. From 1950 to 1970 specialization and the diversification of objects of research and theory contributed to thematic and theoretical fragmentation. At the same time, thinkers such as Robert K. Merton (1910–), Alfred Schutz (1899–1959), and Norbert Elias (1897–1990) took up anew the ideas advanced in the classics and the theoreticians of the interwar period. Networks were created on a continental and international scale. The growth of electronic communication after 1980 consolidated a movement already well under way. Over the last twenty years the volume of social scientific work has reached impressive proportions, even concerning relatively new areas such as the sociology of biblical societies.

Overspecialization did not cease to increase after the 1960s, often in concert with professionalization in education and the branching out of programs of study under technobureaucratic guidance. The rationalization and complexification of social scientific work reflects that of the society as a whole. Grand syntheses are born, which hearken back to successive earlier harvests of copious, often disparate crops. At the international level the development differs from society to society, particularly according to the available economic means, the freedom of public expression or the cultivation of the critical spirit, and the institutional support provided by universities, public and private. Studies of religious phenomena and, more so, texts of founders of given denominations were affected by these conditions. A perspective that would not be directly religious was especially promoted. Thus more generally, the focus in places of scholarship went beyond the local circuit or that of even more parochial circles.

In the course of the growth of the sciences of society, the relationship between perspectives or disciplines oscillated between compartmentalization and interaction. Sociology, psychology, anthropology, and history, for example, engage in borrowing, observing combinations, only to insist on the peculiarity of their own cognitive procedures. The test of what pertains to sociology, whether considered as a discipline with its own cognitive framework or as a distinct perspective of knowledge, can be used by history and anthropology as well. To the combination of means and places of production are added methods, perspectives, or objects of theory. The borders among the social sciences have become movable, if not clashing. In this context, it is important to retrace the lineages that serve as alternative reference points.

Function, System, and Structure

If there is a particularly tentacle-like current, it is that of theories about function, system, and structure.[1] It is spread out through the length of the historical course of social science, and it is found in philosophy as well. This current has furnished a fecund conceptual and analytical apparatus for explaining or comprehending relationships, behaviors, and organizations in society. The concepts utilized in analyses are put forth in a diverse and prolific scholarly production reporting ties among the psychosocial individual, the society, and the culture.

One of the beneficial results of functionalism, which is an essentially analytical current, is that it raised and maintained discussions of basic questions for the social sciences about the cognitive presuppositions and the conditions of validity of knowledge. The underlying or explicit conception of society turns on certain features: the interdependence of the social relations at the heart of a totality, the organism-like arrangement of the social whole and its constitutive parts, the reproduction of the society in its invariants. These features merge and separate, whether they are expressed in a dynamic or a static fashion. They continue to stimulate discussion about the implications and limitations of their use and conceptualization.

According to the functionalists, society is formed from an ensemble of relations that turn on a social response to emergent needs, on the cooperation of forces, and on the coincidence among divergent interests, or at least by the delimitation of the areas proper to each. Correlatively, the components of society are not simply juxtaposed to one another; rather they are coordinated in socially patterned relationships, thus giving them the form of a system, that is, an arrangement of components. The social arrangement brings us back to structures, so that we understand that some configurations are determining the development of relations and, thereby, the distribution of roles and positions, functions, and powers. The relations between the interdependent elements and the resultant whole follow rules that are set forth by the scientists in logical terms of which the groups and individuals under study are to some degree unaware. It is an organic vision of social relations, in which such relations have purposes and rules.

The spirit of system arises from the Durkheimian theme of the shared consciousness and constraint of society on its members. Max Weber's observations about bureaucratization constitute another stimulating reference point. So too are the remarks of Herbert Spencer (1820–1903) on the similarities and differences between the organization and evolution of living organisms and of societies. One notes, in this regard, that in both cases evolution occurs through an increasing differentiation and specialization of organs or components, and therefore through a multiplication of structures and functions. The political organ has no equivalent in a living organism, and this fact highlights how the comparison allows for sketching simple analogies that lead to thinking of social reality as an ensemble of relations among interdependent parts that constitute an integrated totality. Like Spencer, A. R. Radcliffe-Brown (1891–1955) repeats the organicist analysis and clarifies the concepts of structure and social function (1952).

From the point of view of method, Vilfredo Pareto (1848–1923), an economist by training, tried to create conceptual tools for the study of society and give it a scientific methodological rigor. He maintained that it is important to consider the social system, to examine its nature and properties in dynamic terms, not static. Hence the social reality is represented in a simplified manner, stylized in some way. Economists tend to presuppose logical and rational conduct, albeit conduct influenced by sentiment and nonlogical behavior. Sociology seeks to explain rationally the relations among sentiments, rationalization, and nonlogical activity on the one hand and on the other the interdependent relations between nonlogical and logical action. Contemporary rational choice theory resembles the economic approach.

In the wake of Pareto, as well as Talcott Parsons (1902–1979), Bronislaw Malinowski (1884–1942), and Robert Merton (1910–), the notions of system, structure, and function constituted as many intellectual tools for analyzing social reality from the angle of the interdependence of the social bonds contained in a totality. Parsons's structural functionalism analyzes society as much as possible with abstract and global terms, in lieu of pursuing, as Malinowski did, the analysis of cultural and social elements. Parsons addresses every problem in terms of the state of the system as an ensemble; he made structure a characteristic element of systems. Merton too promoted a system conception of the social, with the slight difference of not beginning with the concept of system in his analysis. Rather, he centered his attention on the empirically delimited elements of the social reality and so was led to attribute a function to them. In this case, the concept of system emerged from the analysis without being thereby an object of formal theory, as it was with Parsons. For Parsons, structure constituted the rule according to which the elements of the system were arranged; that narrowed the theoretical possibilities that were left for the workings of functions. For Merton, the limitation of possibilities of variation at the heart of the system is expressed by the notion of structural constraint, which comes to limit the number of imaginable functional substitutes.[2]

Dysfunction, Equilibrium, and Social Conflict

Robert K. Merton found fault with the absolute functionalism of Malinowski, especially the postulate that holds that every cultural or social element fills a function and that therefore it should be functionally indispensable. Instead, each element can have several functions, just as a single function can be performed by interchangeable elements. Moreover, he recognized dysfunction as a factual social process that hampers the adaptation or adjustment of the system. And while there are manifest or intended functions, there are also latent functions, that is, ones not sought for or implicated in the point of view of the persons in the situation. More generally, analyzing functions and systems allows one to specify a problem or situation with great rigor, but it can become a conservative, static, if not utilitarian conception of social relations. This assessment would be shared by a number of critics from the ranks of neo-functionalists and conflict theorists.[3]

For Norbert Elias (1970), it is explicitly a matter of the too frequent association of social function with social norm. Indeed are not social relations changeable, and are not unregulated relations structures in their own way? In life, in society as in a game, rules are not identified in concrete practice, and what we catalog as social disorder has a coherence and underlying logic, a structure proper to it in some way. Otherwise, the notion of function is a relational notion, at the same time a notion of interdependence and reciprocity, and the reciprocal functions between interdependent social agents coincide with the equilibrium of social forces.

I propose, in dwelling on the critique by Elias, that social function can be understood as a relation of reciprocity under control, by reason notably of power relations among the social actors implicated in them. Social actors create disturbances that upset any social equilibrium, thereby dynamically restructuring society. In particular, the relations between a church, as the Catholic Church, and the modern European state can be expressed in terms of dependence in a conflictual reciprocity between two instances of domination over monopolistic claims, and this in return for some level of recognition of the distinction between the two domains of control and the areas of symbolic reference. The legitimation of domination and social equilibrium is intended directly; it requires a body of criteria that would be acceptable by the definers and the receivers, thus justifying at one and the same time the positions of reciprocity in an unequal power relationship. These concepts derive from a sociology of conflict, such as that found in Max Weber or Georg Simmel. Conflict, according to them, is a form of social relation; it is the product of an activity, deliberate or not, neither self-generated nor the product of causal conditioning.

The conflict theorists dwell more on the production of society than on its reproduction. They focus their analysis on the social actor and make it clear that social structures entail constraint and alienation. They go as far as deciphering the discourse that camouflages the self-serving interests that profit from the social system. They analyze dysfunctions in society, even unveiling how interests benefit from protest, that is, from questioning the established order in the name of divergent interests, indeed in the name of some utopia in the sense of a protest that simultaneously attests in some way to an idealized reality. It is a matter of a radical protest, if the critique attacks the *raison d'être* of the basis of life in society and imagines it entirely and decisively changed (transformation) rather than partially and temporarily altered. In short, conceptualizations about conflict range from highlighting social functions, as with the *Functions of Social Conflict* (1956) by Lewis Coser (1913–   ), to radical sociology as represented by C. Wright Mills (1916–1962), especially his *Power Elite* and *Sociological Imagination*.

Reading the same social facts alternatively in functional and conflict terms continues today and often provokes intense discussion. This is the case with the First Letter of Peter. Its exegesis goes in opposite directions: either the integration of Christians into Anatolian society was elevated so much that dissent was relegated to the religious domain, or the Christians maintained an active distance from public practices and representations. Larry Miller has shown that the doctrine of the letter, from a sociological point of view, opposed the attempt on the part of Anatolian society to functionally transform the fundamental character of the Christian movement, and that it advocates a Christianity that is voluntary, utopian, relatively radical, and essentially pacific (1999: 521–43). The critical social exegete would maintain, consistent with Jean Séguy, that as long as a voluntary group supports a utopia, a protest and conflict with the environing society persists (1999: 233–75). It is only its form and intensity that change. Similarly, implicit or indirect protest can prove to be as critical and utopian as direct or explicit protest.

An issue of strategy is often in question, which one must most of all not confound with the intent of the movement. This is as true for early Christianity as for other historical cases (Turcotte 1990). Conflictual relations within a sociopolitical or a socioreligious system span the origin and institutionalization of Christianity. From the utopian mystical experience of Jesus, one comes to a church that, while based on that foundational experience, establishes a doctrinal, moral, and ritual apparatus in a permanent and more compact system. The formation of the institution issues forth from a socioreligious movement, not without being torn and systematized.

Émile Durkheim and the French School: Explaining the Social with the Social

One of the most notable contributions of Durkheim is the principle that an explanation of a social fact ought to be sought always in another social fact. This basic idea was elaborated in *Le suicide* in a critique of Italian positivism (Durkheim 1979: 83–106). The latter maintained that suicide was more frequent in the summer than in the winter because heat excites the senses. Durkheim countered that rather than physical causation operating in suicide, it was the intensity of social life; the suicide rate is higher in summer because the social life is more intense. The rhythm of the seasons is involved, but, most importantly, so is the ensemble of rhythms that modify social life.

Further, social phenomena ought to be conceived as external to individuals, i.e., as "things" that are not immediately intelligible. Moreover, their analysis should be inductive, as in all science, even if the intuition of them plays a very important role. Comparison, observation, and experimentation lead to transparency in the comprehension of a social fact that would not otherwise be explained causally. It is the rules of sociological method that help achieve an accounting of a social "thing" by means of the social (Durkheim 1982).

Religion occupies an important place in Durkheim's works. For him, the desacralization of the society signifies the expulsion of the gods from social life and, more specifically, the suppression of references to a sacred order or religious values. Then the problem of the basis of the social tie arises: How can individuals live in society, bereft of the sacrality that comes from religion when they face competing interests, values, and worldviews? Durkheim believed that it is important to believe in a secular sacred, a sacred in and of the world, and not from beyond it, to establish a modern synthesis of meaning and social ethics.

In the final analysis, religion represents a complex of symbols and practices synthesizing the constraints of a society. The individual is inscribed in a common consciousness by the constraining synthesis, thus assuring cohesion in the social bond and meaning for individual and collective existence. Far from being a simple residue, religion is essential to every society. It is produced in moments of "social effervescence" evocative of a transcending of everyday life, moments that are far from individual routine. Such times are laden with communal feeling. The basis of social life resides in the shared consciousness that, inasmuch as the transfiguration and symbolic thought of society, is imposed on individuals and also demands obedience and respect from them, it thus constitutes a social force that ties individuals together into a moral person with an anonymous character that transcends individual singularities. Indeed, every society involves a moral authority for the collectivity over the individual; this authority is exercised through the respect that is the source of the sacred and consequently explains the phenomenon of religion as a shared consciousness (*conscience collective*). In brief, the only real force that transcends individuals and takes the form of an anonymous and diffuse force is society itself (Durkheim 1968, the "long conclusions").

These are the usual conclusions from research on the elemental forms of religious life: the separation of the sacred from the profane, the prohibited from the permitted, and so forth. The position was not unrelated to the diminishment of the importance of churches in society, in favor of the state and the public sector, with the intent of separating church and state. At the end of his life, Durkheim would affirm that the divinity as well as the collectivity could play the role of a richer moral reality than the sum of individuals. The arguments provided by choosing one or the other of the two left him indifferent. The essential remained thus: morality, the system of duties and obligations, made society "a moral person qualitatively distinct" from the individuals who compose it (Durkheim 1963: 72–73).

The first condition of solidarity, be it mechanical or organic, resides there. Mechanical solidarity is proper to archaic societies where the individuals are similar to one another, sharing the same sentiments, respecting the same beliefs, and obeying the same rules. In that case sameness creates solidarity, which comes to reinforce a legal system of an especially punitive nature; the shared consciousness (*conscience collective*) is strong and expansive, and the sanction of a forbidden act takes the form of punishment. Organic solidarity characterizes modern societies and results from the differential organization of individuals; these are bound to one another because they exercise different roles and functions in the interior of the social system. Consciousness of individuality is linked to the enlargement of demographic growth, itself at the origin of the division of labor for purposes of increasing economic productivity. However, an indicator of the diversification and demographic growth of society is that punitive laws diminish. Acts that impede the functioning of organic solidarity can be sanctioned with restitutive law— commercial or civil law (Durkheim 1984).

The fecundity of Durkheim's thought is also noted by anthropologists and ethnologists. Some of them, beginning with Marcel Mauss (1873–1950), have investigated the opposition of the sacred and the profane. Does not everything appear religious in tribal societies: the orientation of the house, various ceremonies of the lifeways, the cycle of activities? In fact all societies are religious to a greater or lesser degree; nevertheless, principal social phenomena have a religious dimension, as they have political, cultural, and economic dimensions. Consequently, religion is, in the famous formula of Mauss, a multidimensional "total social phenomenon."

In a related vein, societies are shaped by economic imperatives and the division of labor, but equally by symbols, traditions, and beliefs. Indeed, religions are a source of the intelligibility of collective life, just as they explore through introspection the interior realm of the experience of belief. An analogy is even proposed with science as general explanation of the human, except science rejects the distortion in religion and denounces it as its adversary (Dumont 1980: 348–52). The discussion poses the problem of mediations, the relationships of reciprocity between distinct, indeed opposite, elements, without fusion or confusion.

In the wake of Durkheim and Mauss, the French school of sociology affirmed the primacy of the whole over the parts in a system, the importance of the study of correlations among the elements of a structure. Among the studies produced by this school, one work treats Christian origins directly, *La topographie légendaire des évangiles en Terre Sainte*, by Maurice Halbwachs (1971). Following a reading from a pilgrim from Bordeaux, the author takes his exploration to Bethlehem, to the Cenacle and the tomb of David, Pilate's praetorium, the Via Dolorosa, the Mount of Olives, Nazareth, and Lake Tiberias. His fine and nuanced reflections identify the foundation of collective memories, a foundation made from their projection onto concrete space. Halbwachs then fleshes out his preoccupation by finding the presence of the social in the sources of consciousness, and he looks further back in the task of identifying the primitive historical data beneath the traditions that had been projected onto the land.[4]

Economy, Religion, and History: Karl Marx and Friedrich Engels

These two German thinkers—at once philosophers, historians, and sociologists—are popularly known through later interpreters who hardened their positions. Consequently, there is a reason for taking up the original texts of Marx and Engels themselves. The two are monuments of characteristically nineteenth-century thought, in relation to which Max Weber and Ernst Troeltsch, among others, would situate themselves. Marx and Engels were the creators of the sociology of knowledge, the specialty that is given over to the dialectical examination of human representations and the conditions and modes of their construction.

Put simply, the Marxian concept of society[5] distinguishes between those who own the means of production, planning them and extracting benefits from them, and those who are deprived of the means of production but nevertheless produce the surplus value and receive a remuneration guaranteeing them survival as a workforce and consumer market. This results in a bipolar social categorization—domination by the business class (bourgeoisie) and alienation of the working class (proletariat). Consequently, the return to a condition of nonalienation constitutes an ethical task of the highest order.

The analysis typical of the Marxian conception of history contributes to a raising of consciousness leading to disalienation. According to this conception, the determining factor in history in the final analysis is the production and reproduction of real life. In a letter to Ernst Bloch Engels emphasizes that the factor in question does not reduce to economics (Marx/Engels 1964: 274–75). The economic situation is the foundation, but elements of the "superstructure" (various theories, religious conceptions, etc.) enter into the course of historical struggles. There is an interaction of different factors in a movement where the economic element ends up entering in as a necessity.

In the course of history, "ideology" consists of the nonmaterial production—ideas, representations, conscience, and religion. This production of a spiritual kind is conditioned by the material production and the corresponding social relations. In the situation of human distress, religion is the sigh of the oppressed, the opium for the occasion, in lieu of a correction of the real human conditions. Religion is the horizon of a totally other world; by virtue of that it can detract from the raising of consciousness about misery and from the action of reversing the conditions of distress, just as it can contribute to the understanding of liberation and the class struggle against oppression. Religion thus has a double function.

The double function is found in Christian history. Among the writings on this subject, Engels's essay on early Christianity (Marx/Engels 1964: 316–47) remains the most significant. As sociological historian, Engels shows how the integration of antagonistic elements undermines their capacity for social revolution. The work appears to be more of a sketch than a careful and well-documented study. It consists essentially in placing in opposition the revolutionary character of the first Christian movement and its alienating diversion into an institutional church in the pay of oppressive classes. Engels never turns thoughtlessly toward a Manichean dichotomy; for example, he indicates the existence of the class struggle at the very heart of the church, which presupposes a difference of positions inside the institution. The historical description is centered on the relationship between the forces of production and representations of reality. The representations either generate or detract from actions for social change.

Engels's position, as sharp as it may be, raises a host of questions. For example, what and how can religion be at the same time a product of society and an agent for its transformation, especially if this society is alienated? Does not the capacity for disalienation require some autonomy of religion relative to sociohistorical conditions? Would it not be an irreducibility of a religion that would give it the capacity of constituting a force for change in the social relations, of being an agent of active protest and not only a reproducer of factors that undermine consciousness?

In a similar vein, what of a religion such as Christianity whose original message is addressed to the most deprived, in coming to reach various sectors and levels of the global society? This religion has every chance of counting adherents among every social class, and by that very fact it will reproduce the conflicts among these classes in the very being of its institutions. In that case, organized religion is presented as the site for the struggles between social reproduction and the confrontation of social classes, in short, a site susceptible of feeding the class struggle and, in the case of Christianity, furnishing it with a symbolic reference. In a flourish, Engels claims that religion, particularly Christianity, cultivates transactions with society that are as much on a material or institutional order as a symbolic one.

In phenomenological terms, religion maintains a relationship with the sa-cred—the representation of perfect harmony between contraries, and thus the re-verse of worldly conditions. It also sustains a relationship with the profane, which is opposed to the sacred. The dialectical character of religion, as with any human product, allows us to avoid a mechanical perception or simplistic reduction. En-gels did not entirely escape this, because of an assumption on his part by which he assimilated religion with the reversal of worldly conditions. He identifies reli-gion as much with the sacred as he does revolutionary change with a reversal of the conditions of production. These very conditions, however, contaminate the whole of Christian religion, making it an alienating reproduction, turning it away from its original goals. On the other hand, and indirectly, Engels recognized the symbolic potential for radical transformation that the original Christian message offered.

From the perspective of the sociology of knowledge, the sacred and the utopian together express the reversal of existing human conditions, in the form of an otherness. The sacred adds an element of delocalization and autonomy, losing any tie with the world. It is religion that comes back to establish and cultivate bonds between the sacred and the human conditions. With its mediations, the sacral representations become capable, if necessary, of engendering the utopian imagery that eventually goes so far as to sacralize and, in a way, legitimate radical historical change, that is, legitimate the intent to restructure society in globally dif-ferent terms. Utopian imagery joins delocalization and relocalization in a project whose alterity would reverse specific conditions of existence.

The relations of production between the representations of things of life and the different levels of social existence can be expressed without any utopian im-agery. Thus, the ideas, models, or positions involved in religion refer to an alterity constructing the very experience of the transcendent. In knowing the representa-tions and models that help elucidate the links between means and ends as well as produce, maintain, or eradicate meaning, the symbolic also participates in the in-stitution of the concrete social relations as the conditions in which those symbolic representations have taken form. At the heart of the dialectic social actors—who develop inside the structures—take their places. They take the form of subjects in social interaction who react against constraints and prescriptions, which they might otherwise internalize or simply receive as exterior to the self (Turcotte 1999b: 86–89).

The followers of Marx and Engels appeared in unexpected places. Inside the churches, critics of Christianity have been inspired by Marxian theory to conduct a sociohistorical analysis, even taking up Christian origins again and focusing on a New Testament book. Fernando Bélo undertakes this exercise in his exegesis of the Gospel of Mark (1974). He based it on a lengthy development of the modes

of production, including those of the symbolic order, and with a structural textual analysis he cleared the way for an attempt at a materialist ecclesiology. The
shadow of Feuerbach[6] hovers over this effort, which also draws from post-1960
French Marxian production. At the beginning of the twentieth century, Walter
Rauschenbusch (1991) began a sociohistorical analysis of Christianity from its
roots in the prophets of the Old Testament. He devoted one chapter to Jesus and
another to early Christianity; then he showed the distortions of and breaks from
the founding project in the era of the church. His analysis leads to a call for action to eradicate miserable conditions of life in American cities. The United States
had just industrialized and undergone massive urbanization, especially in the
poorer sections of New York. Rauschenbusch was preoccupied with restoring
utopian Christianity to the strength of its mint condition and thereby with revitalizing ecclesiology, Baptist ecclesiology in his case. The aim meshes with Bélo's,
with the difference that the American study ends not only with reflections of a
theoretical order but also with an exposition of concrete undertakings.

Historical Mediations, Implications, and Social Complexity: Weber and Troeltsch

Engels shows how the utopian sacred in human history was sidetracked, especially
in what concerned Christianity after the dominant classes took control of the life
of the church. His reasoning was far from being endorsed unconditionally by
Weber and Troeltsch.[7] For them, the sacred, as social imagery of an alterity, constitutes a reference on the symbolic plane in social life traversed by historical mediations, one of which is organized religion. The reference to an alterity is expressed
through practices, ethics, ministry, memberships, rites, and identities. More specifically, the extraordinary, be it political or religious, emerges to change behavior and
affect the course of history, provided that it is integrated into the ordinary in life,
and notably that it takes on flesh in the institutions of the society.

Max Weber remains in essence a sociologist of modernity, the latter understood as an opposition to the exceptional: modernity entails the rationalization
and demagicalization of life in society. Moderns live in a world of value pluralism, which entails a divergence of interests and tension among the cultures and
levels of human existence (economy, religion, and so forth). Weber declined to
center the understanding of the complexity on invariants or to reduce it to some
single principle of knowledge. The understanding that he promoted and practiced
was not monocausal; it included the meaning that social actors give to their actions, be those activities in harmony or competition with those of others. Such action can be rational in purpose, rational in value, affective if under the influence
of emotion or passion, or traditional through a conformity to custom.

These features overlap the kinds of legitimation of domination ("authority," as we term it) that require an ensemble of criteria acceptable to those who impose and those who receive authoritative decisions. The acceptance of such criteria serves to justify asymmetrical social relationships. Always, according to Weber, this legitimation is traditional ("That's the way it is"), rational-legal by conformity to rationally established rules, or charismatic in a confidence in a chief bearer of charisma. These concepts, among others, help to trace the ruptures leading to modernity and show how religion, specifically in a Protestant Puritan form, participates in modern rationalization, by means of a radicalization of the transcendence of God and, its corollary, the uselessness of magical manipulation. There is a demand for signs of belonging among those chosen by God in his inscrutable designs; these signs of divine election are manifest in faith, and above all in its efficacy within everyday life, which success in tasks in the world signifies (Weber 1958).

Troeltsch left a varied literary legacy in philosophy, theology, exegesis, and politics. Like his friend Weber, he sought to understand and explain the genesis of the modern world. He was also preoccupied with reconciling the absolute nature of Christian faith as far as divine revelation is concerned, and such historical relativism as that which occurs with cultures. His research was centered on European Christianity. In his lengthy sociohistorical analysis of the social teachings of the churches and Christian groups (1911), he pays great attention to early Christianity. He devoted highly suggestive and well-documented studies to this significant period of Christian history. Troeltsch relied on Weberian concepts in his analyses, but his research also influenced Weber. Both were immensely productive, and their influence lasts even to the present.

Despite sharing the purpose of Weber's inquiry, Troeltsch's intellectual project was not confounded entirely with that of Weber. Weber, we know, centered his study on domination as a social relation. The Weberian understanding of life in society focused more on action and the patterns of organization produced by social actors. He focused especially on rules of conduct issuing from commands, obedience to which legitimation supports. Thus systems of reference, of the religious or political kind, come and go over the course of history. Their production and reproduction are tied to social change. There indeed is the formulation of a theory that points to the thought of Marx and Engels, but the latter two thinkers were much more interested in the forces of social production of an economic order than was Weber.

Troeltsch sought to show that Christianity overtook the world as much as the world transformed Christianity. Christian representations, without being determined in the final analysis by the relations of production, knew a historical development marked by general social conditions. The Christian impact on the world would be indirect—hence the eminently historical character of Christianity. Moreover, as a prophetic religion it affords the greatest importance to ethics in matters of social relationships and to the historical mediations of God's will. These mediations encompass, beyond ritual, principally great personages and organizational models. The great personages are subject to influences of every kind, but the religious ideation that they affirm or confirm would not be reduced to an ideological reflection of external factors, especially economic. Similarly, the social organization of religious groupings mediates the influence of the global society on Christian ideation and the influence that the latter can socially exercise. This line of thought goes back to Weber's point of view; to repeat, representations of the world borne in societies engender ethics of conduct and attitude that leave effects in the social world.

A key concept for understanding Weber and Troeltsch is *compromis* (tense union, uneasy alliance, dilemma, risky influence, oppositional implication).[8] This simple expression denotes oppositional transactions between different sectors of life, such as religion and the world. Thus social representations cannot avoid the cluster of historical mediations in the workings of variants and invariants. We confront these complex workings after the period of Christian origins. Troeltsch would make *compromis* one of the motifs of his analysis of Christianity. Just as in Weber, the operative concept was not made the object of a particular theorization; it is an analytical concept whose general features we can trace.

In Troeltsch's perspective, *compromis* is not confounded with compromise (*compromission*) and concerns all the religious groupings in their relationship with the world. In particular, spiritual people willingly practicing "Nicodemism" (see Jn 3.1–12) have fixed ideas about the organization of the world, while criticizing it as it is. Relationships with the world pose the most problems for the sect. In the name of evangelical radicalism, the sect undertakes negative relations with the world, ranging from daily annoyance to dissent from the state. In this case, *compromis*, if there is room for it, occurs case by case, is undergone more than it is explicitly recognized. In contrast, in the case of church one can investigate efforts to extend the Kingdom, evangelize humanity, and penetrate the culture in order to manifest the gospel tradition. Nevertheless, ecclesial *compromis* has limits (e.g., the problem of collective sin), and a combination of the church with the sect is possible, as in the case of the free church or the religious order (Séguy 1998: 26–42; Turcotte 1999).

The concept of *compromis* in Max Weber (Ouedraogo 1997: 611–25) represents a tool refracting only some aspects of reality, and this ideal type, when sketched out, aims at an understanding of processes of social genesis. This intent is particularly evident in Weber's treatment of the transformation of the religion of virtuosos into that of the masses. In the form of radical religion, religious virtuosity offers an intellectual production that responds to the quest for meaning and salvation—for a solution to the problem of evil through redemption while disqualifying magic as a means of access to salvation. The situation is completely different for those who do not have a musical ear for religion but show interest in salvation. On the one hand, monks, charismatic communities, sectarian groups, and reformers search for salvation based on a necessity or an interior distress, based on meaning in a way of life that obtains unity with oneself, with other humans, and with the cosmos. On the other hand, with a laity foreign to intellectualism, religiosity is no longer animated by necessities of an interior order but bears the mark of external problems and is consequently remote from theological considerations about the meaning of the world and close to the cultural needs of the masses and the organizational constraints bound to the question of salvation.

In the process of transformation *compromis* appears around the interpretation of the world, the method of salvation, and the relationship with the world. For example, charging interest eventually came to be accepted in Christianity, political arrangements intrude upon universal religions, and magic periodically emerges in religion. Consequently, *compromis* assures the perpetuation of only some virtuoso religiosity. It goes without saying that such is the symptom of a mass reception of Christian ideas and their influence on everyday life. One should always take care lest *compromis* come after mass religiosity spreads or after the reduction of Christianity to syncretism. Generally, it is a departure from the quest for meaning, as the religious production is covered over and the organizational apparatus guarantees a liaison with institutions and entities of the world.

To the extent that it consists of a relation of reciprocity between actors in a situation of opposition in the symbolic or institutional order, *compromis* indicates a terrain where divergent interests can be expressed and arrive at an *entente*. This is so for both the sect and the religiosity of virtuosos in their relationships with the world or the masses. Some externalization is necessary, some expression that would be the public manifestation of a collectivity, no matter its size. From this point of view, mystical spirituality tends toward individual *compromis*, notably by the reception of sacraments otherwise considered not essential for salvation, but does not indulge in *compromis* of a collective character on account of a spirit of relativizing the exteriority of a church and membership in it, reconceptualizing the church as a spiritual communion. The exteriority of the church type includes ritual, beliefs, dogmatic formulae, and a certain constraint. Moreover, the church presents minimal conditions for gaining salvation, such as baptismal membership in the ecclesiastical institution, the practice of its other sacraments, obedience to its precepts (be they commandments of God or of the church), and conformity to the virtues attached to one's state in life or earthly vocation (Remy and Turcotte 1997: 627–40; Turcotte 1999a, 1999b). The administration of the symbolic does not limit itself to the maintenance of a system that otherwise houses some elements of charisma or utopia, should the occasion arise.

Prophetic Charisma and Its Institutionalization

From the point of view of Max Weber, charisma has nothing ethereal about it (1978: 246–54, 1121–23; Séguy 1982 and 1998; Turcotte 1999: 102–9). Charismatic personages are humans who act in history; they are produced by it to some extent, and in turn they produce it in their way. An individual claiming legitimacy for actions or sayings on the basis of a personal experience rises above the ordinary; in all probability charisma could be accounted for by changes in appearance and the acceptance of some outstanding characteristic. Perhaps more important than the level of personal inspiration is its being paired with an open rejection of institutional mediations. In the case in which disciples survive the charismatic personage and establish socioreligious forms that are more or less rapidly institutionalized, personal charisma changes into office charisma.

Office charisma is a deviation from personal charisma in that the latter is borne by flesh and blood humans, and hence by relational beings; office charisma is also different because its legitimation rests essentially on the ritual mediation of an institution that is said to be the proprietor of the founding charisma and its exclusive interpreter. On the other hand, this institution, as a social organization, can only lay claim to office charisma to the extent that it unites believers in its specific grace. Moreover, the religious institution has to face the problem of reformulating its charismatic legitimation amidst historical events and changes of all kinds. Thus it does not constitute a purely objective reality. Doesn't the concentration of social and symbolic interactions perpetuate an ensemble of structures that are only relatively autonomous from adherents and from the course of history? Or else, what credibility would there be in the adherence of the believer and in the demand for obedience to authority?

The social dynamic of charisma turns on the acceptance of a claim to extraordinariness by reference to some reality other than what is commonly accepted and the humdrum events of everyday life. To reduce the distortions that compromise the credibility of office charisma, notably if orthodoxy is in question, wily camouflage and shortcuts represent an eventual tactical measure. Whether the strategy aims at the unconditional acceptance of a coercive measure or of a message made equivalent to truth, it is highly likely that a monopolistic use of the symbolic or structural order will ensue. There is, for example, the limitation of access to the means of salvation, and the civil authority can always be used to enforce ecclesiastical rules. The institutional channel of grace authoritatively prevails over grace acquired by the subjective experience of belief. Nevertheless, personal charisma is susceptible to emerging at any moment, especially in times of flux and shifting systems of existential reference.

From the point of view of the actors affected by the administration of institutional symbolic goods, and also perhaps more so in subordinate roles, office charisma sets out in search, when needed, of an added personalization of charisma to make up for a lack of credibility and social legitimacy on the part of the institution. The quest eventually comes to a private personal charisma, which projects an inventive mentality, even while manifestly preserving the institutional character and resisting innovation. In short, charisma consists in the acceptance of the extraordinary, mediated either through personal experience or institutional ritual.

Transactions constitute the texture of the institutionalization of personal prophetic charisma. In this case the relationship between the extraordinary and the ordinary can be known from the perspective of the quotidianization[9] of what was originally exceptional. In prophetic religion, these relationships are understood more as a tension in the unfolding history between the reference to a personage-mediated transcendence on the one hand (i.e., mediated by uncommon activity, notably apart from ritual) and, on the other hand, the constraints of ordinary life coming to terms with the representations or models of existence as well as with the requirements of the calculation and clarification of means and ends.

The insertion of the original extraordinariness into daily life is supposed to guarantee the historical continuation of an experience that, packed with a new host of references, is constituted as an autonomous (at least relatively so) historical social force. It is a matter of a process, the indicators of which are notably diachronic. For Christianity, what is important is the passage from a community of the faithful, those who place their confidence in a recognized charismatic leader, to the institutional community that governs adherence to disciplines, rituals, and doctrines officially harmonized with the intent of the founder and presented as the way of salvation. This transformation operates through "quotidianization," in the sense of a confrontation and merging with the necessities and ordinary hazards of life. This brings about a banalization of the exceptional. "Quotidianization" does not proceed without a "routinization," which denotes at the same time both repetition and the insertion of the inspiration into individual and collective living processes. "Routinization" promotes institutionalization, the transformation of what was established, what was raised up from the movement, the creation of something system-like in institutional form.

Decisive changes are interspersed through a more or less extended period of time, varying with, among other factors, the historical conditions, the force of the original inspiration, and the interplay of the actors directly or indirectly involved. Even so the institutionalization process proceeds, paired with a spirit of invention on the fringes of the institutional boundaries and "wanderings in the wilderness" outside of the institutional framework altogether.

The passage from the instituted to the institution includes an intersection of processes that are no more frequently serial than simultaneous, while the institutionalization occurs slowly or rapidly, decisively or reversibly, wholly or partially, etc. Principally, the processes can elaborate a permanent specialization of tasks and formalize the group's internal life and regulations, the hierarchization of members, and administrative rationalization, as well as functional integration with the environing society. This list is not exhaustive, and related developments connect with the controlling transformation processes. For example, by virtue of the specialization of tasks, a division of labor commensurate with competence increases in the group itself; the performance of permanent duties of office replaces provisional missions, the training of "ministers" (as socialization elsewhere) is arranged along the lines of an institutional program, and the selection of candidates takes into account criteria that have little antiquity behind them. The codification of the Christian life itself signifies a progressive adoption of charters, statutes, and written impersonal rules, which tend to be substituted for the personal and often changeable decisions of the charismatic leader. With legal formalization a bureaucratic kind of governmental apparatus develops, which practices an administration of goods marked by calculation and very elaborate economic planning. Functional integration completes the picture: it aims at social or religious utility, a rapprochement with dominant authorities, and the reduction of socioreligious distinctiveness by the adoption of practices found in the environment. In that way, the institution, insofar as it results from a process of systemic coordination, breaks away from the extraordinariness that characterized its origin. The relationship between the two poles reveals itself as more than a simple inversion in time, in the passage from movement to system.

From Jesus the Christ to the Church
around the Episcopal See

Troeltsch's socio-critical reading of the Gospels led him to insist on the importance of the social, cultural, and political context, but at the same time he did not understand the Jesus movement only in terms of the conditions of its time. Most importantly, the preaching of the good news is also presented as a religious message and not as a social program; it is a matter essentially of an ethical discourse inspired by an extraordinary spiritual experience. Moreover, its universalist message accentuates the individuality of the conversion process and not a collective project. As for the New Testament, its redaction was influenced by Stoicism, one of the currents in vogue in a society fending off revolutionary movements.

In this regard, Troeltsch noted that Christianity has indeed inspired revolutionaries, but the question of the function of dissent and protest on the basis of Christian ideas remains open. For example, the Middle Ages were a period in which Catholicism appeared as a chief work of *compromis*. It produced and reproduced a society prone to entirely open dissent, but a deeper analysis of even the extreme cases of this dissent uncovers mere faults or interstices of the system of reproduction and purportedly subversive contestations. In brief, in one way or another one's perspective and method greatly predetermine findings concerning production and reproduction, dissent and protest.

Troeltsch proceeded with a typological historical reading of Christianity. Each historical moment represents a synthesis that cannot be repeated, and these moments are theoretically framed by three types—mysticism, sect, and church. In neutral terms, the church is opposed to the sect, as extension and *compromis* are opposed to intensity and radicalism, and both church and sect are opposed to mysticism in the way that exteriority is opposed to interiority. However, these different types of organizational mediation appear throughout Christian history. Differences between periods or among types of communion are woven with the thread of displacement, conflict, and rupture in the dialectical relations between religious ideals and society.

Thus it is necessary to find, after the disappearance of the master, another principle of unity that should maintain a link with him. This was the belief in the resurrection of Jesus and his exaltation at the right hand of the Father; at the same time Christian rituals were constituted, giving pattern to the mission of Jesus. At the beginning of the second century faith in the resurrected and exalted Jesus and in a community marking presence from the absent and confirming conversion with baptism and the Eucharist, slides toward a belief in the church, a church ruled by an episcopate and attached to tradition. This is a passage from the mystical or the sect type to the church type, in a search for an organization conformed to Christian ideals, both autonomous and comfortable with the environing world at the same time. Some tensions arose that endure even to our day, for example in relation to ties between sacrament and gospel, the distinction between clergy and laity, and the double ethic of commandments for the masses and evangelical counsels for the religious virtuosos. In the transition, the practice of charity is juxtaposed to ritual formalization, provided that the church defines its selected oppositions to the world and its integration into the ruling classes (Troeltsch 1911: 39–199; Wackenheim 1992: 197–202).

Max Weber died before completing his sociology of early Christianity. We are left with his notes and sketchy observations. They deal with relationships between Judaism and Christianity, relations of borrowing and preparation, and also relations with the world—at times relations of tension, accommodation, and indifference—and finally continuities and discontinuities among Jesus, Paul, and the church. The details Weber recorded and his summary headings suggest that the elites (Jewish rabbis and Christian missionaries) have greatly contributed to the cultural distinction between the religion that issued from the Jesus movement and Talmudic Judaism. Some borrowings were decisive, such as the Jewish spirituality of exile that inspired the Pauline mission. Indeed, redemptive suffering, especially in the suffering servant of God passages in Isaiah 40–55, offered a reference that made the Christian doctrine of sacrificial death of the divine savior thinkable. Otherwise, the originality of Christianity lies in the opposition of Jesus to the social and cultural environment and in his intent of developing a religiosity of faith and not law. He subordinated everything to an attitude of unlimited confidence in God. At its origin, Christianity was set up against the biblical and juridical erudition of the Jews, against the aristocratic soteriology of the Gnostics, and even against ancient philosophy. Given this opposition, Christianity had to break with Judaism and organize its own communities according to its specific spirit.

Paul became the great organizer of communities after his conversion on the road to Damascus. He clarified the role of the intellect in a religiosity of faith. Thus the emergence of an ethic of verifying prophecies replaced the emotional content of the original charisma of Jesus, in the milieu of tensions between a true religiosity of faith in God and specific ethical exigencies. Jesus attracted principally the poor, the oppressed, the publicans, and fishers, while Paul and his traveling companions addressed the middle levels of the urban societies, people who displayed a cultural level characteristic of the petite bourgeoisie. After it had been established, the Pauline community continued to merit the identity of the charismatic and prophetic Jesus movement; it showed an emotional character more than traits of rational socialization, and it was ruled in principle by the effective presence of members. These traits also made the Pauline Christian community autonomous from the synagogue.

The apostle also devoted himself to lessening the tension between religious equality and social distinction. The equality was threatened by charisms, the use of which was to be subordinated to the edification of the community. He was equally attentive to assuring a guiding coordination among the local communities raised up under his authority. A network was woven together among the communities that came close to the sect rather than the church type.

The postapostolic age features a decline in eschatological expectation and, consequently, an increasing immersion into everyday affairs. With the passage to the quotidian, personal charisma gave way more and more to office charisma and the bureaucratization of power in the hands of bishops and presbyters. This occurred while indifference on the part of Christians over socioeconomic and political affairs lessened. The church came into being, an institution that was formally charismatic, born from the reification of the charisma of its origins, from an essentially pneumatic charisma. This church encompassed various elements simultaneously—a sacerdotal caste properly under control and separated from the world, an intent to expand universally that entailed a religious leveling of is members, a rationalization and systematic instruction in dogma and cult, and the institutionalization of charisma and transformation of it into office charisma. Indeed, the church was the first rational bureaucracy in history, thanks notably to the administrative and legal genius of the Romans. However, the church is not only a bureaucratic organization; it is what institutionalizes the grace that it communicates in the rite of ordination. The rite determines the efficacy of the gift of grace rather than charismatic personages doing so.

Some other matters drew Weber's attention. For example, the numerical growth of the faithful stratified the social fabric, creating new inequalities. The authorities wanted to harmonize the religious stratification with the social; thus bishops formed a caste at the beginning of the fourth century. Originally they came from the ranks of artisans, merchants, even slaves. Moreover, the Christian world was marked by pluralism from the first, on account of the diversity of ways that the baptized followed. Whether these ways were that of individual perfection of religious virtuosos such as martyrs, ascetics, and hermits, that of the quest for salvation in light of a charismatic transmission of grace as in ancient monasticism, that of the complete dissociation between the gift of grace and the merit of those who receive it, the option for an ecclesiastical institution was made. At the same time solicitations and oppositions from outside accentuated pluralism: The debate between early Christianity and Greek philosophy gave birth to Christian theology, and the Gnostics presented a direct threat, with their religious alternative to Christian soteriology. In both cases the exigencies of the religious ethic typical of prophetic religion engendered distinctive identities that combined with the economic, political, and scientific elements of the sociocultural environment (Ouedraogo 1999; Wackenheim 1992: 190–97).

The Chicago School, Symbolic Interactionism, and Their Transformations

The department of sociology at the University of Chicago opened its doors in 1892, under the direction of Albion Small (1854–1926).[10] Researchers joined and succeeded him in the 1930s; their methodological and theoretical contribution still inspires thought and research in the social sciences. Among the figures leaving their mark on the "first Chicago School" (1892–1934) were William I. Thomas (1863–1947), Florian Znaniecki (1882–1958), Robert Ezra Park (1864–1944), and George H. Mead (1863–1931). Jane Addams (1860–1935) and her work with immigrants exerted a major influence as well, though she was not a member of the department. Each of the university scholars was interested in questions of method and theoretical conceptualization. Symbolic interactionism is the most impressive social scientific tradition to emerge from their work. This current of thought, considered typically American, is still elaborating and enriching its methods and conceptualizations.

At its founding, the department of sociology concentrated its research effort on the solution of social problems, with a view toward ameliorating living conditions in the urban context. The researchers did not hesitate to place their confidence in scientific inquiry. The early Chicago sociologists were always refining their methods and applying them to the study of a growing number of subjects. By the end of the 1920s, Chicago had become an internationally recognized center for the use of social scientific methods, especially quantitative methods. The reflection that was focused on the cognitive presuppositions and operationality of methods was applied to the human geography of cities and to theory construction. The city was a privileged object for research, manifesting elements of typical social relations: racial and ethnic boundaries, neighbor relations in the ghetto, immigration and social integration, urban mobility, social ecology, and interethnic conflicts. The success of the research endeavors owed greatly to the fact that they were carried out and staffed in cooperation with theology schools and institutes of social intervention.

The Chicago sociologists openly challenged positivism and its tendency to accept only directly observable and measurable observations, similar to the natural sciences. They also maintained that the nature of social scientific work was to take into consideration how social actors defined the social facts in which they were involved. What is more, the analysis of a social situation required that both objective and subjective factors be taken into account at the same time, the observable objective facts and the shared representation of those facts. Thus the Chicago sociologists went well beyond positivism.

Today we benefit from insights drawn from the famous study by Thomas and Znaniecki (1956), *The Polish Peasant in Europe and America*. Among the theoretical contributions of the work, the concept of the "definition of the situation" led to extensive developments. According to this concept, social actors respond to a situation not only in step with its objective character but also with the meaning that it has for them, in step with the representation that they make of it, with the manner in which they define it. In short, as the "Thomas theorem" puts it, "Situations defined as real are real in their consequences" (Thomas and Thomas 1970 [1928]; further developed by Merton 1948). In this case, the researcher gains every advantage from cultivating intuition, an attentiveness on the alert for the unexpected, a shrewd mind.

The Thomas theorem contains symbolic interactionism in a nutshell. Symbolic interactionism is chiefly interested in the social actor, all that pertains to human action in society, and influences that change society, not only the objective conditions of social life. Attention is focused on social interaction, even more on imagery in the minds of the interactants to the extent that it takes symbolic form (language, values, norms, definitions of reality) in step with the sociohistorical circumstances of the social exchanges. The symbolic expression of social imagery is grasped by means of acts and speech, the gestures and words of individuals and groups. Thus symbolic interaction, which refers to the signification of things in life and their purposes, reflects and reveals the social relationships in their cultural and structural aspects. Moreover, as Znaniecki keenly defends it, culture is not enslaved, condemned to reproduce and justify the economic and social world; it is principally the occasion in which social actors exercise their judgment, express their values, and recognize one another.

According to Herbert Blumer (1969), human beings are not content to simply react to the acts of another; indeed they interpret or define such acts for themselves, and the meanings that acts have will serve as the basis for a response that becomes an interaction. Consequently, interaction is mediated by the use of symbols, interpretation, the significance accorded to the action of another. In this conceptualization of social relations, the functioning of society is understood through the representations of the actors involved and not through structures or some functionality or dysfunctionality in a system. Firm in this position, the analyst clarifies the conditioning and fashioning of individual representations of social life, discovers how a worldview is socially constructed and how that worldview constitutes a subjective reality characteristic of a social actor situated in a given history, society, and culture. At the same time the investigation takes up the social production of individual and shared imagery, and such imagery as a product of a society. Thus are relations between culture and structure, social imagery and social functioning analyzed (Berger and Luckmann 1966).

Interactionism is directly linked to philosophical pragmatism, since communication determines the whole of social regulation: economic, political, culture. The idea is found throughout Park's studies of the city and interethnic relations. He advocated a method having several facets—recourse to history, entries in diaries, participant observation, utilization of suitable statistics, and definitions of basic concepts. He made his own Simmel's (1968) conceptualization of social life. For Simmel, the individual and society were inseparable. Clearly people simultaneously make and are subject to society, are its product and producer. Society is fundamentally interaction, the reciprocal action of individuals who give it its existence. Individuals are mutually swayed and bound by reciprocally experienced influences. Social relationships take on an objective character gradually. Thus supraindividual structures are only crystallizations of reciprocal interactions, means of consolidating them. Even when they become permanent and take on a life of their own and come to be experienced as outside consciousness, they are not at first objective and binding realities but reciprocal actions of association or antagonism, collaboration or opposition among humans. By a kind of precipitation from interindividual exchanges social entities are fashioned for the long term maintaining the group in one or another definite form. The form passes gradually from a processual state to that of being a substantial reality. In short, interactions determine social life, the locus of exchanges that are reciprocal and exchanges that are crystallized, detached, external to the consciousness of individuals and groups.

From a methodological perspective and in Dilthey's terms, the understanding of symbolic productions presupposes an inside access to the systems of meaning that underlie them (1990). Intuition plays an important role in this access, and it would arrive at an understanding, not a causal explanation. The conditions necessary for such access are attainable because the people who interpret are symbolic beings, participants in the very humanity who produce it. If natural phenomena are diverse, changeable, and external to us, the data proper to the mental sciences (Dilthey's *Geisteswissenchaften*) must immediately deal with an already constituted totality. The world of mental phenomena is presented as an "interactive complex," as opposed to the causal world of nature. The knowledge of the social world depends on empathy and distance, on entering into a system and deconstructing it by making a critique in the sense of a detached theorization.

Dilthey and Simmel, as well as Weber, created the intellectual background that inspired symbolic interactionism through their impact on George H. Mead (see Joas 1985) and John Dewey. Mead and Dewey, with others, founded the pragmatist school of philosophy at Chicago, a school marked by a confidence in the scientific method and trusting acceptance of the objective of solving the social, moral, economic, and political problems of the time. The accent was on science and action, the union of thought and deliberate human action, the application of critical thought and experience. The researcher, equipped with these, seeks to learn from experience. Knowledge was a complex of provisional hypotheses, at best probable and never certain.

Mead had written articles but not books in his life, but his most important ideas were brought together in the posthumous volume *Mind, Self, and Society* (1934). Herbert Blumer set about extricating from Mead's thought theoretical and methodological points that he would call "symbolic interactionism." In Mead's symbolic interactionist perspective, society is composed of acting elements. It is a complex of individuals ever confronting varied situations. To contend with situations, the individuals construct cooperative actions in which they adjust their acts to those of others. These actions constitute life in society. Mead distinguished between nonsymbolic interaction and symbolic; the first arises from direct and involuntary responses, almost reflexes, on the part of individuals to acts of some kind or another. The second, symbolic interaction, consists in establishing the meaning of another's action, whatever its form (comment, facial expression, hand signal, intonation, etc.), and acting on the basis of this interpretation in arriving at ways to make indications to the other about how to act. The result is that the participants in a symbolic interaction adjust their actions to the actions of the others. A process is set in motion by which collective action is constructed.

Moreover, human beings are described as organisms endowed with "selves," as beings who can be objects to themselves, acting toward themselves as they would toward others—perceiving themselves, having ideas of themselves, communicating with themselves, reproaching themselves, encouraging themselves, being angry with themselves, appraising themselves. The subject perceives its own nature as object because the indication gives it a meaning. The meaning is based on ongoing activity and, beginning with it, the person is oriented toward the indicated object. In the processes of interaction with themselves, individuals also make indications of other objects, determine the meanings of those objects, and organize their actions toward those objects. The self is introduced in the process through which humans interpret what confronts them and act on the basis of the interpretation. By way of illustration, there is an important and subtle difference between simply feeling hungry and being cognizant of the fact that one is hungry. The self is constituted by a reflexive process that permits one to face the world and control one's conduct. We should not confound the self, as Mead described it, with a psychological structure as, for example, the ego. The latter is not reflective and cannot thus act toward itself; one is left simply to express an ego.

The actions of an individual are not simple expressions of psychological structures under the effect of external stimuli. They are constructed in a process of interaction with the self; human beings determine what they want to do, the goals they will pursue, taking into account the situations in which they find themselves, and, indicating to themselves specific objects, they draw up plans for action. Actions are not elaborated at a glance; they are constructed step-by-step. Individuals are ever reevaluating the situations in which they find themselves, the objects they will take into account, and their own actions—all this in an unending interaction with themselves. Because of the reflectivity of the self, the actor is not simply taken up in an action or submerged in an environment. The actor is situated at a remove and acts toward a situation according to the way it is defined and interpreted. An action is always situated. In this respect, the actor is not at the mercy of structural pressures, organic needs, or role requirements. Psychological and social structures are constraints that enter into the construction of an action only because the human being takes them into account and interprets them; the constraints do not simply determine action. One can thus find in the actor's effort at interpretation the link between specific conditions in which the individual is found and the individual's activity. However, saying of human beings that they construct their actions does not mean that they act for the better. Individuals are not implacably rational. Actions are constructed through interpretations that actors make of the situations in which they find themselves.

Mead's theoretical statements plunge us into the realm of symbolic interactionism. That realm encompasses the above-mentioned theory of the social construction of reality, which is largely indebted to the phenomenological sociology of Alfred Schutz (1899–1959). The sociology of everyday life was also created along the lines of symbolic interactionism, which decisively influenced the dramaturgical sociology of Erving Goffman (1922–1982). Ethnomethodology can be associated in some respects with these two theoreticians.

The expression "ethnomethodology" was coined by Harold Garfinkel in 1954, on the occasion of his research on juries. He discovered that they conducted themselves in the course of a hearing as they would if engaging in scientific research; they were in a kind of inquiry as though they were experts on the social world and on the veracity or sociological pertinence of the arguments advanced. By extension, the scientific project of ethnomethodology is the analysis of methods or procedures used by individuals for finding their way through the various activities that they perform in their everyday life. In other words, the object is the analysis of the ordinary ways of doing things that social actors rely upon to perform their ordinary actions. In Garfinkel's words, it is "practical sociological reasoning" exercised by the members of a society or social group in order to objectify the world. Correlatively, ethnomethodology considers social facts not as things but as practical accomplishments that are the product of the continuous activity of people who put to work their know-how, methods, rules of conduct, and modes of organization. We thus live in a describable, intelligible, and analyzable world. The task of the sociologist is to account for this by means of close participant observation.

Rational choice theory takes its inspiration from economics, where it is used as a tool for theorizing market behavior and decision making. The theory rests on the postulates that the social actor is egoistic and acts for personal gain, that he knows from acquired information the utility of all possible options, that he establishes an order of preference among alternative actions in accordance with a cost/benefit calculus, and that he is rational, selecting among alternatives to maximize "utility." Thus, the actor always seeks a maximum gain and chooses among all possible options the one that will yield the most and cost the least.

Critical discussion has given birth to a "theory of limited rationality." It introduces new elements: the actor decides on the basis of information that is possessed, and can consider a lack of information when making the decision. The actor's motivations are not necessarily limited to personal interest. In making a decision, there is the notion of preexisting principles of action, obviating the task of reanalyzing the entire situation anew each time. The actor is not an isolated being but makes decisions in relation to the environing milieu and is influenced by the interactions in which she participates. Above all, the actor, when faced by a difficulty in making the best possible choice, stops at the threshold of a utility satisfying for him rather than maximizing utility. The revised theory has the advantage of enabling one to objectify the study of behavior. It conceals limitations that block its ascendance from the status of a tool of objectivation to that of a full sociological paradigm. In particular, if it allows for a comprehension of the process of making decisions that leads to adopting a strategy, thus to making choice, with a view to attaining a given good; it does not allow for clarifying motivations that have led to the choice of that end. By virtue of this limitation, rational choice theory remains essentially a tool of objectivation usable on a case by case basis.

The Blending of Theories and Perspectives

The theories generally sketched above are found in the different sciences of society. They have sources shared by more than one science, as do anthropology and sociology in the case of functionalism. They advance conceptualizations that overlap and interpenetrate, for example in the relations between symbolic interactionism and social psychology. Their use is often eclectic in addressing a question in different ways. We know that the understanding of reality lends itself to distinct or diametrically opposed methodological positions. Setting out deductively from a principle of knowledge with logic leads to a different product from that which is elicited inductively from a situation in its irrational aspects as well as rational, subjective as well as objective, and implicit as well as explicit. There we have major points of difference among the perspectives used by the major social scientific theories.

Works on biblical materials from the period of early Christianity are affected by such issues. In addition, archaeology and similar disciplines that deal with antiquity are relevant. The social sciences and their interconnected theoretical traditions are more than supplementary elements for sketching the context of that kind of social fact. They are necessary where it is difficult gain an adequate focus even while intending to be scientific. For this reason, the social sciences would risk losing their cognitive validity and capacity for widening the horizons of knowledge if they were to advance an unvarying theory that is closed in on itself or trapped within a compartmentalized perspective. This calls for vigilance, particularly when the object of study is the time of the founding of a world religion.

There are many questions that remain open. By way of example, the relationship between psychoanalysis and sociology poses basic problems. In the case of an analysis that rejects a sharp separation between the psychological and the social, like the separation made by Durkheim, or especially an analysis that integrates actors and their psychology in its fields of study, it is a matter of seeing from which psychology one will expect complementary interpretations and if it will retain the hypothesis of the unconscious that is fundamental to the psychoanalytical approach. In this regard, Sigmund Freud (1856–1939) inquired into the ties between the individual unconsciousness and culture. Freud did not consider the individual in isolation from the social environment. It is understood in the interlacing of its ties with its milieu, the culture in which it acts and to which it submits. The many ties, modified over time and circumstance, form a close texture that the subjects enter. The ideas advanced by Freud in the wake of this position continue to stimulate discussion, and we know of disagreements among the founders of psychoanalysis.

Between history and sociology, the stumbling block appears in methodology and in turf wars. Nevertheless, historical sociology claims a heritage going back to Max Weber and Ernst Troeltsch. The discussion is open concerning the differences and ties between the various approaches to social reality. I have only indicated what is proper to the various social scientific theories and dwelt on those that have contributed or may contribute in a major way to our knowledge of Christian origins.

Notes

1. On functionalism, see Coenen-Huther (1984), Eastby (1985), Emmet (1972), Isajiw (1969), and Jarvie (1973).

2. See Malinowski (1954), Parsons (1954), and Merton (1968).

3. On conflict theory, see Coser (1967) and Freund (1983).

4. Another text merits attention, Saint Besse, *Étude d'un culte alpestre* (in Hertz 1970: 110–60). Hertz's whole anthropological analysis turns on the birth of a cult as an occasion for affirming an identity; its author reaches the theoretical level without ever losing contact with the data. Another work on Christian origins is Czarnowski (1919) on the cult of Saint Patrick in Ireland. The author shows how the saints are particular cases of the social type "hero," from the point of view of their genesis and function, after having sought to determine how the legend of Saint Patrick had formed and what the conditions of the production of legends about national heroes in Ireland were. These studies follow in the theoretical footsteps of Durkheim without taking on the inflexibility of some of his positions.

5. On Marxian thought and religion, see Desroche (1962).

6. Ludwig Feuerbach (1804–1872) was a critic of religion who influenced Marx's thought. Feuerbach thought of religion as a projection into God of things missing in earthly life. Thus an unjust society would have a God of justice.

7. On Weber, see Bendix (1977), Käsler (1988), Lash and Whimster (1987), and Sica (1988); on Troeltsch, see Drescher (1991), Dumais (1995), Séguy (1980), and Yasukata (1986).

8. There is no simple equivalent to the French term, used in the same way as O'Dea (1966: 90–97) used "dilemma" in his essay on the dilemmas of institutionalization, and as Gurvitch (1962) used "implication dialectique mutuelle." The relevant French defini-

tion among several for *compromis* would be "that which one willingly constitutes from very different elements, as in an architecture of *compromis*."

9. Weber's English language translators use the expression "routinization" for this; I make distinctions below between making something part of everyday experience (quotidianization) and making it banal or routine.

10. On the Chicago School, see Bulmer (1984), Matthews (1977), Prus (1996), and the essays in Tomasi (1998).

General Methodological Perspective   3

ANTHONY J. BLASI

Introduction

PROFESSORS OF NEW TESTAMENT commonly ask their students to take up one of the Gospels and read it from beginning to end. They want their students to see it as a whole rather than know of it only in the way that it is presented in worship services—one small passage at a time. It is not that a focused reading of a small passage is not useful; indeed exegetes cultivate the art of "reading slowly" and drawing out implications from details. However, a whole gospel provides the literary context for each detail; one cannot understand the full significance of a detail without considering the context. One of the contextual characteristics of which a reader of an entire gospel will become aware is the dramatic tension that the gospel communicates to the reader. Jesus, portrayed as moved by religious inspiration, presents an appealing and even idealistic spiritual message, but in doing so he encounters a current of mistrust and opposition. People ask him what gives him the right to teach. They criticize his disciples for breaking customs. They ask him trick questions. Eventually they plot against his life.

One cannot imagine how the portrayed undercurrent against Jesus could be retained in the traditional narratives and recorded as a salient fact in the written Gospels if some experience of mistrust and opposition were not familiar to the authors and their intended audience. The very suggestion that Jesus failed to persuade so many of his hearers would not be a convenient fact for the early Christians unless they themselves evidently experienced tension with unpersuaded neighbors of their own. The fact that Jesus faced that same problem made the gospel narrative meaningful for them. This is certainly not the only important characteristic of the four Gospels and the other major works of early Christian literature, but it is instructive. Most of the evidence we have on the early Christian movement is literary in character. The literature often purports to relate information about John the Baptizer, Jesus of Nazareth, Paul of Tarsus, and other early personages, but inadvertently it is also informative about the authors and audiences of the literary works, as well as their typical experiences. We therefore have more than one kind of information available to us from early Christian literature, and whenever we have information about people, we have the possibility of using it in a social scientific study of them and their worlds. In the case of the New Testament and related literature, we have information about two religious movements—the Jesus movement in its social environment and early Christian churches in their worlds. We may refer to all these collectively as the "early Christian movement."

The Jesus movement consisted of the following that Jesus of Nazareth enjoyed in his travels about rural Palestine, as well as in Jerusalem, in the third and fourth decades of the first century C.E. We have no writings from the Jesus movement, but the Gospels—both canonical and non-canonical—purport to tell the reader narratives about it. Early Christian churches were the organized aspects of the movement that developed after the death of Jesus, having as their unifying theme the cult of Jesus as the Messiah. The writings that we have from the early church Christians mean by "Messiah" inter alia the judge coming in a universal final judgment or the presence of the creator God to the human world in the person of Jesus and in the Spirit that lives among the unified Christians themselves. Some modern commentators object to the expression "Christian," claiming that the movement cannot be distinguished from Jewish religiosity until a later point in history, when both Christian ecclesiastical structures and Jewish rabbinical traditions emerged. There is validity to that claim, insofar as the first Christians were religiously oriented to the Hebrew Scriptures and the Temple[1] in Jerusalem, but the movement whose literature identified Jesus of Nazareth as the Christ or Messiah and meant by "Messiah" the final judge or the presence of God in the human world is clearly distinct and identifiable; there is no reason not to use the word "Christian" for it.[2] I am concerned in this chapter with scientific inquiry into this identifiable movement of people, as well as the Jesus movement.[3]

"Science"

"Science" is not a neutral term in contemporary discourse. The successes in engineering and medicine that have resulted from the practical applications of the natural sciences have led people to accord a great deal of legitimacy to scientific research. Consequently there is a temptation to use the term as a form of secular legitimation and to take on the appearances of science whether or not one is engaged in genuinely scientific inquiry. That temptation need not lead to a deliberate deception on the part of some dishonest propagandist; someone with a genuine personal conviction might liken the impression of truth associated with the conviction to the impression created by scientific procedure and evidence. Scientific mannerisms may thereby accompany the demonstration of a belief to which one had come by a nonscientific procedure. Thus we have the expression "Christian Science" and the claim of scientific status for creationism.

For this reason it is fundamentally important in science to set aside "truth" (in the sense of "conviction"). Science is inquiry, and inquiry is not authentic if the "truth" is already known. Inquiry needs to be autonomous; its course cannot be channeled by convention, prior belief, or habits of thought without a denaturing of the inquiry itself. When an inquiry is fully free from such influences, it should not matter who is conducting it. A fervent believer and a convinced atheist should be able to study early Christianity scientifically and arrive at similar conclusions. In order to guarantee that kind of autonomy in inquiry, it is necessary to clarify concepts, describe procedures, and delimit the matter of examination; in short, it is necessary to be explicit about theory, method, and the matter of observation. Most important of all, it is the problematic with which one proceeds that needs to be scientific. I will spend the greater part of this chapter describing various dimensions of that problematic. Taken together, these various dimensions involve the human mind learning from evidence. If one were to seize upon the concepts, instrumentation, and even findings of any particular science without using these to learn from evidence, the scientific problematic would be absent and the endeavor would be a case of misplaced erudition.

As a preliminary step toward characterizing the use of genuine social science in the study of early Christianity, it is useful to distinguish scientific from particulate knowledge. Particulate knowledge is the product of aimless fact gathering. Like so many thousands of grains of sand, thousands of aimlessly gathered facts take on no enduring shape. The same grains might one day form one shape and another day a different one, depending on the changing winds. Isolated facts might one day suggest one conclusion, and on another day suggest a different one, depending on the slightest alterations in the predispositions of the observer. A kind of education that rewards students for committing facts to memory and repeating them in examinations is responsible for a great deal of particulate knowledge in the world. Fundamentalists are appropriately criticized for memorizing biblical passages in particulate form, without developing a critical capacity that would lead them to think about what biblical works say rather than find proof texts for defending received opinions and conventional stances. The problem is not limited to fundamentalists, however; free spirits, ready to break with tradition and convention, may similarly acquire facts in an unsystematic way and use them to support a preselected argument. Any inquiry may begin with some initial fact gathering, but it is necessary to go beyond that activity. Because the social scientific vision understands literary texts as products of ongoing social interaction—interaction that is typical, recurrent, and general—it presupposes a necessity to both base itself on and go beyond particularity (MacDonald 1988: 23).

Science stands in contrast to philosophy as well as to particulate knowledge. While particulate knowledge represents a failure to draw out the contours and general geography underneath a desert of granular fact, philosophy begins with a map and never looks to actual terrain. Philosophy proceeds in the manner of Descartes (*cogito ergo* . . .). The development of thinking skills in philosophical activity is undoubtedly important as a preliminary step toward scientific inquiry, but it is necessary to put aside thought as an end in itself. One cannot fixate on ideas and then succeed in science; the use of any given idea needs to be warranted by evidence. It is especially important that potentially circular courses of reasoning be avoided, lest evidence be prevented from breaking in and inspiring the drawing out of unanticipated implications. One kind of circularity to be avoided is the self-confirming idea. Concepts that are overly generalizable do not lend themselves to the disconfirmation of a thesis in which they play a part; they therefore lead to self-confirmation. The proposition that biblical societies were pervaded by an "honor/shame" principle, for example, cannot be disconfirmed, irrespective of what any given biblical passage may say, because "honor/shame" is too vague. If the prodigal son comes to his senses and returns to his father, his motive can be that of avoiding embarrassment in the foreign land even though he returns to his father's household diminished in status. If someone turns the other cheek or offers a second garment to one who has already taken a first, it is a scheme to embarrass an aggressor by rising above embarrassment. It does not matter whether a biblical figure improves in honorific standing or worsens; the motive is said to be the same. Using such passages to "confirm" the relevance of honor/shame themes would be circular. That circularity arises from a concept that does not enable one to distinguish definitively between honor/shame behavior and non-honor/shame behavior. A genuinely scientific inquiry cannot be tantamount to a philosophy built around a concept of that kind.

Early Christian Materials and Scientific Procedures

The Literary Materials

Most of the evidence for the early Christian movement is literary in nature, though archaeology has provided important nonliterary information (Charlesworth 1988: 103–30). Literature involves a spectrum of materials, ranging from the physical to the symbolic. The physical objects include the writing materials with which ancient authors and copyists worked and the extant manuscripts we have from the early Christian communities. Writing materials and manuscripts were more valuable in ancient times than they are today; there were no printing presses for the mass production of works and no pulp paper. Consequently, a book, treatise, or other work was not normally a fixed text that remained constant through a series of reproductions but a unique physical object that was prepared for a specific setting. "Luke" would have written the canonical two-part book (Gospel of Luke and Acts) for the library of "Theophilos" (Lk I.1–4; Acts I.I), perhaps for use in worship by a church that met in the latter's house. Neither the real name of the author nor that of the owner of the manuscript would appear in the text of the work because of the controversial and illegal nature of the Christian sect; such a document could be used in a legal proceeding against both the author and the owner. If someone else wanted the two-part book by "Luke," a scribe would write revisions into the copy that might be needed to fit the education and cultural background of the intended owner of that "copy," as well as the church that might be using it. It was the paper and the labor of editing and copying that was valuable, not a copyrightable fixed text. Only after a work had been designated "scared scripture" in a canon would the exact text become fixed. Until that happened for a given work, the text reflected the needs of the people for whom it was first written and the people for whom it was later "copied" or adapted.

It is a working rule of literary analysis that textual criticism must precede source criticism and redaction criticism. That is to say, we establish how a given text read before deciding whether someone copied it (as Matthew and Luke copied Mark's gospel and copied the "Q" sayings, making revisions in both in the process) and why that person placed the text in its new literary context. Usually the scholars who are responsible for critical editions of the Greek New Testament and other ancient works have done the text criticism for us. It is generally bad procedure to base an interpretive argument about a text on the grounds that one can find a variant reading of the passage somewhere in a museum (unless one is studying the community for whom the variant was intended). When one is interested in a text that is no longer extant but was copied into another work, it is necessary to reconstruct how it must have read before setting out to propose interpretations of it. A topic of interest, for example, might be the sociology of the users and hearers of the source text from which both Matthew and Luke took most of their non-Markan material,[4] or the social context proper to the earlier layers of the Gospel of John independently of the social contexts proper to the later layers and vice versa.[5]

While modern Christians generally prefer to use the whole canonical New Testament in their worship (and sometimes insist upon a particular translation of it), a scientific analysis must take each work in the New Testament as a separate entity and consider as well extracanonical works. Since the circumstances of authorship are important, it becomes necessary to dissociate the Deutero-Pauline literature, for example, from the Pauline. As noted above, the intent of the original author of a work was not as central an issue in the ancient world as it is today; authorship was simply not important. Many works were anonymous or written under pseudonyms. Indeed, it was an act of politeness and humility not to put one's own name on a work, and authors often honored a predecessor by putting the latter's name on their works. In using works that underwent multiple revisions, such as the Coptic Gospel of Thomas, it is necessary to ascertain whether its sources were independent of the canonical gospels or not, and if they were it is necessary to reconstruct how those sources read.[6]

Measures and Indicators

In order for inquiries to succeed, it is necessary first to guarantee that the elementary research acts by which observations are received, categorized, and manipulated neither impose arbitrary characteristics on what is observed nor obscure the features that reside in the observed objects. Concerning these elementary research acts, methodologists distinguish among three kinds of observation: nominal indication, ordinal measurement, and interval measurement. Nominal indications involve classifying observable objects by means of a typology. For example, distinguishing references to Christ that represent a high Christology from those that represent a low Christology is using a typology of Christologies for categorizing the references. Most observables in literary materials in fact lend themselves to analyses with nominal indications. In some cases, we are able to use statistical procedures that are based on frequencies with nominal data; thus one may ascertain whether one New Testament book has a higher percentage of high christological references in its texts that refer to Christ than another book. Similarly, if one has apportioned the passages of a New Testament book among two or more layers of tradition, one may ascertain whether one layer has a higher percentage of high christological references than another layer does. One may use similar comparisons with friendly versus hostile references to governing powers, Jewish customs, and the like. It is also possible to ascertain whether two such nominal variations are related to each other; for example, are the books of the New Testament that appear to be oriented to gentile Christians rather than Jewish Christians the same books that have high rather than low Christologies?

When using nominal indicators, it is important that the two (or more) counterposed types be mutually exclusive of one another. A book must be oriented to Gentile Christians or Jewish Christians, but not both, if only two types are employed. If it is thought that one or more New Testament authors directed their works to mixed Jewish and Gentile congregations, it is necessary to provide a third type. Again, if one or more authors appear to have directed their works to both

Jewish and Gentile congregations but not mixed ones, it is necessary to provide a fourth type. Any given observable (in this case, any given book of the New Testament) must fall into one and only one type. The discovery of what types are needed for accommodating the observables is an important part of the research process; it leads to conceptualizations that are "grounded" (Glaser and Strauss 1967).

It is best that the *units* of observation derive from the literary material itself. References in the Greek texts, for example, were made by the authors who were responsible for the texts. Similarly, most of the books of the New Testament were units established by the original authors. However, verses as numbered in modern Bibles are not optimal units of observation because the numbering was established not by the ancient authors but rather by early modern printers. Similarly, one should use Greek texts rather than translations in research. Moreover, if one uses the books of the New Testament as units of observation, the Resurrection narratives added to the Gospel of Mark may need to be counted as a separate book, as may the original wording of a source such as Q in the Gospels of Matthew and Luke. Second Corinthians may need to be considered as three rather than one observable, if one believes three letters were edited together to create it. One can readily see that literary source-critical issues often need to be confronted to a researcher's satisfaction before typologies can be applied to New Testament material.

Ordinal measures follow the logical progression of ordinal numbers in most languages—first, second, third, etc. As in an auto race, there is no suggestion that the distance between the first and second places is equal to that between the second and third places. Strictly speaking, it is not correct to perform arithmetical operations on ordinal data. Similarly, it is something of a mistake in arithmetic to calculate grade point averages from educational transcripts, as educators often do, after converting "A" grades to 4, "B" to 3, and so forth. It is also a mistake to convert Likert-type response categories ("strongly agree," "agree," "not sure," "disagree," "strongly disagree") to numerical scores and then perform arithmetical calculations on those scores. There is no reason to believe that the quantitative difference between an "A" and a "B" on a transcript is the same as that between a "C" and a "D," or that the quantitative difference between "strongly agree" and "agree" responses on a Likert-type questionnaire is the same as that between "not sure" and "disagree" responses. Thus one should avoid if possible treating such categories as "very high," "high," "moderate," "low," and "very low" Christologies with any mathematical procedure other than frequency counts and percentages, or to see "Jewish and Gentile" congregations and "mixed" congregations as somehow representing a quantity lying between "Jewish" and "Gentile" that lends itself to any kind of arithmetical operation.[7]

An interval measure is one in which there is a metric that lends itself to arithmetical operations. Chronological indications using years, for example, lend themselves to calculations because the passage of time between the years 30 C.E. and 40 C.E. is the same as that between the years 110 C.E. and 120 C.E. We are often able to put dates on texts by ascertaining whether they reflect knowledge of events that historians have dated (e.g., the destruction by fire of the Temple in Jerusalem in 70 C.E. and the reigns of rulers), whether the texts cite other works to which we are able to affix dates, and whether the texts are cited *by* other works to which we are able to affix dates. The fact that an author knows about an event is stronger evidence than an absence of any mention of it, since the author can simply choose not to mention something known (Neusner 1988: 133). Normal travel time between ancient cities and the population sizes of those cities similarly lend themselves to arithmetical operations (see Stark 1991, 1996: 129–45). It makes sense to create time lines and other graphs with interval measures, while it does not make sense to create graphs with nominal indictors and ordinal measures.

Whenever using such measures or indicators, it is necessary to address the issues of reliability and validity. Reliability is the consistency with which a particular observational procedure yields the same indication. For example, if a particular personality test found an individual to be domineering by nature when the test was administered once but found that the same individual was compliant by nature and willing to yield to others when the test was administered again, one might conclude that the test itself is not reliable. By analogy, a particular linguistic usage—that is, the combination of paratactic clause linkages (and . . . and . . . and) and the use of the Greek expression *euthus*—may either reliably or unreliably indicate Markan versus non-Markan authorship. Validity is a matter of whether an indicator really shows what one might be using it to indicate or whether it may alternatively indicate something else. Does a personality test really indicate an enduring trait of a personality, or alternatively might it indicate a fleeting mood brought on by an immediate situation in which the individual happens to be taken up? Can an adage such as "The first shall be last and the last shall be first" be used as an indicator of an honor-obsessed culture, or might it simply be an expression that was traditionally used to instruct the young in manners?

Induction

Induction is the process of reasoning toward a conclusion from particular facts or individual cases. It involves an inherent dilemma insofar as the particular facts or individual cases from which it sets out have not warranted in any direct way the categories with which the researcher is initially prepared to reason. In the natural sciences, the facts and cases are not thinking subjects at all, but mindless objects. The stars, planets, satellites, and other objects that constitute the universe do not know that they are more or less "obeying" the laws of gravity. We cannot make inquiries *of* such natural objects about the logics they follow. Consequently, we need to make an assumption, in the manner of Galileo, that they conform to mathematical logic. We assume that, since in mathematics two plus three yields five, two quarts of a liquid plus three quarts of it will yield five quarts. There is no absolute reason why the natural universe and its elements should conform to our logical operations, but the everyday materials before us in our worlds appear to do so for the most part. When physicists explore the world of subatomic particles, however, the correspondence between the natural and the mathematical worlds cannot be taken for granted.

In the social sciences, the relationship between the logics of the matters of inquiry and of the inquiring minds is quite tenuous. If the people whom we study think as we do, there would be little problem in our understanding their activities. However, people's activities often follow personal habits, social customs, and patterns that they have tacitly and haphazardly negotiated with the people they live with, while social scientists seek to proceed with a careful and openly deliberated logic. There is a chasm between the scientists' reasoning procedures and the emergent reasons that underlie the social activities that they would want to understand. Unlike the natural scientists, however, who cannot communicate with their matter of inquiry, the social scientists can make inquiries *of* the people whose activity they study. The relationship between different logics need not resort to assumptions that resemble those that were presupposed by Galileo's mathematicalization of physics; rather, the relationship becomes a hermeneutic question for research.

In hermeneutics, the matter of inquiry is meaningful; what is studied is a tendency on the part of a subject to respond to a sign or symbol in a particular way. The social scientific study of early Christianity, having for the most part ancient texts of religious literature to work with, has the hermeneutic problem of establishing valid understandings as one of its objectives.[8] It is possible to know about the origin of a passage, its subsequent usage in a book of the New Testament or other ancient collection, its reception in the early history of the Christian churches, and how we ourselves respond to it. Our understanding of the passage will not be identical to the originary understanding or even identical to that of the redactor of the larger work in which it appears, *but it is our understanding that is the key to our comprehension of the originary and redactive understandings.* We rely upon the analogy between our understandings and the ancient ones.

For example, consider this brief passage: "When reviled, we bless; when prosecuted, we endure," λοιδορούμενοι εὐλογοῦμεν, διωκόμενοι ἀνεχόμεθα (I Cor 4.12b). It appears to be an allusion to a traditional saying of Jesus; Paul cites it again elsewhere (Rom 12.14), and it appears in the Q source of Jesus sayings used by both Luke (6.28, 32, 27b) and Matthew (5.44b, 46), as well as the *Didache*

(1.3b). Paul uses the allusion to argue against Christians seeking status in the church: "Already you are filled! Already you have become rich! Without us you have become kings! And would that you did reign, so that we might share the rule with you!" (I Cor 4.8 RSV). The meaning in Luke seems related to a countercultural stance; he introduces it with "Woe to you, when all people speak well of you" (Lk 6.26a RSV). Matthew uses the saying similarly to recommend a higher ethic than that recommended by most people: "You have heard . . . but I say to you" (Mt 5.43–44 RSV). In the *Didache* it is used to characterize one of two ways to live. In the context of secular Hellenistic beliefs about the good life, the saying, which may go back to Jesus himself, was clearly countercultural, perhaps reminiscent of the Cynics (Vaage 1994: 57, 165 at note 13).[9] Let us propose that Jesus used the saying, shocking his listeners (as he frequently did with his parables) in the superficially Hellenized context of Galilee by recommending a countercultural stance toward the world, but from the perspective of Jewish Messianism; that would succeed in offending "Jew" (Pharisee) and "Greek" (Herodian) alike. Paul uses the statement ironically, suggesting that the Christian movement itself deserved a countercultural critique from within its own ranks. Q, Matthew, Luke, and the *Didache* go back to the countercultural impact of the saying, but they are all rather removed from the potential shock of using a Hellenistic form of social critique in a Jewish perspective. So what is the valid "meaning" of the saying? The lexically correct meaning is "valid" enough, just as it was for the readers of Paul, Matthew, Luke, and the *Didache*. The *relevances* attached to that meaning vary, however, and the social sciences have the discovery of those relevances as one of their tasks.

One could well use a musical metaphor. The natural or acoustical contents of a particular performance of a work do not comprise its meaning. Instrumentation, performance pitch, and conventional "readings" of scores, which establish the acoustical contents, change. It is the experience of going through time with the musical retentions and protentions that is the "meaning" of the music (see Schutz 1964), the response shared among composer, performers, and audience. Similarly, it is what a passage accomplishes in a reader that is its meaning. A gospel may make the reader aware of a dialectic between a pleasant spiritual inspiration and an undercurrent of human unwillingness. A parable may shock the reader, forcing a reconsideration of everyday events. A letter may relativize denomination-like norms and encourage an acceptance of an authentic spirituality on the part of other groups of people on their own cultural terms. What *happens* between author and audience, redactor and reader, is the primary datum. This performative meaning, reasonably expected by author and redactor to follow upon a recital or other kind of execution of the text, is the particular fact or individual case out of which induction proceeds. It has the same importance in research that employs literary materials that the back-and-forth among social actors has for the ethnographer; it is the "symbolic interaction" that warrants any types that would be applied by a researcher.[10]

The warranting of any given type by a meaning that has been occasioned by a text is unique to that text alone. Just as ethnographers cannot legitimately generalize to other settings the meaningful life worlds they portray in their separate reports, the social scientist who analyzes the Jesus movement or early Christianity on the basis of a text can only associate an interpretation or conclusion to the particular originators and early hearers of that text, not to the whole of early Christianity or the whole of the ancient Mediterranean region. Induction is a modest enterprise. It leads to understandings and interpretations. Understandings are those responses that are analogous to responses by the ancients who used a particular passage in their social interactions. Interpretations place the understood text in the context of other observables that one has reason to associate with the text. Interpretation is a nongeneralizable moment that follows upon understanding.[11]

One needs to be wary of the pitfalls hidden within the concept "culture." Culture is not an object, preserved in some pickled form. It is not similar to word definitions printed on the pages of a dictionary. It is processual. Culture consists of lived experiences; it *happens* among people. It only exists, for social scientific research purposes, in the present tense. Thus even past people, people from antiquity, experienced their culture in the present tense. Their "now" is more analogous to our "now" than to our "then." It is therefore scientifically illegitimate to subsume ancient meaning systems into a broad pattern that obtains within a "then" perspective for us; we cannot, for example, legitimately associate aspects of "ancient Mediterranean culture" with every text that comes from one or more individuals who happened to inhabit the Mediterranean geographical region in antiquity, disregarding evidence of whether those individuals acted in a "Mediterranean-like" manner at all. We need to warrant for a given author, redactor, or member of an ancient readership or audience *every* meaning that we want to associate with those individuals. It is perfectly possible for them to be a unique circle of people, for them to inhabit a closely circumscribed subcommunity, or to be engaging in a countercultural expression. In no instance should a researcher substitute some general cultural pattern for missing evidence; that is deduction, not induction. American politicians have an adage—all politics is local. In a parallel way, all real culture is local. Even in societies that have mass media, how particular programming is received and interpreted varies from locality to locality, even from one subgroup within a locality to another. How much more is this so in the case of ancient societies, which did not even have the printing press!

Moreover, collecting a number of observations from a cultural setting (be it a community or large geographical region) and finding a theme common among them does not warrant the inference that the theme is particularly characteristic of the culture in question. For example, finding references to meals, food, and banquets in ancient Hellenistic, Roman, Jewish, and Christian literature does not make the activity of eating peculiarly "Mediterranean," somehow in contrast to "Western" culture. It is necessary to examine references in comparable texts from a number of cultural systems and find what is present in the one(s) of interest that is not present elsewhere in order to find anything particularly characteristic of the former. That is to say, we need to examine comparison cases as much as the case(s) of principal concern. Social scientists refer to the comparison cases as the "control group."[12]

Theorizing

Comparison is the simplest kind of theoretical work. It is not possible to compare two acts of understanding both as present experiences; either one will contaminate the other so that neither is experienced separately, or one will reside in memory under the guise of a type while the other is occurring. Memory does not allow for a duplication of an ongoing experience of a past act but rather records a past act as having been a particular kind or type of event.[13] The ability to make an object out of an experience and thereby make note of it as one or another type of event is what enables us both to remember events in any meaningful way and to make comparisons. When we make a comparison, we identify two events as either two instances of the same type or instances of different types. If the two instances are more dissimilar than similar, we are establishing a contrast rather than a comparison. With inquiry into early Christianity, we principally compare the performative meaning of texts for one combination of originators (authors or redactors) and audience (or readers) with the performative meaning of other texts for another combination of originators and audience. Our interest is in establishing in a comparison whether both sets of performative meaning fit under one type, or alternatively in a contrast whether they belong in different types (see, e.g., Elliott 1995a).

The methodological question that needs be addressed for the procedure to be scientific is whether the type or types used in the comparative (or contrasting) enterprise are "adequate" with respect to the performative meanings of the texts for their originators and early audience. We have established the adequacy of an analytical type if we can say that the actors whose performative meaning is in question acted under a subjective meaning state that corresponds to the type that we are using (Schutz 1972: 235, in a critique of Weber 1978). This amounts to finding a similar type or types in both the ancient actors' and our own stocks of knowledge (see Schutz and Luckmann 1973: 99ff.). That is to say, we rely on the fact that the ancient actors were in a situation similar to ours insofar as they had to employ types in order to categorize and commit to memory their own meaningful acts. Consequently, we need to find traces in their texts of their own efforts to define ("typ-ify") their situations. Our ability to categorize and to make comparisons depends on our exploration of their definitional proceedings ("typifications").

Consider the following passage: "For I delivered to you as of first importance what I also received, that Christ died for our sins in accordance with the Scriptures, that he was buried, that he was raised on the third day in accordance with the Scriptures, and that he appeared to Cephas, then to the twelve (I Cor 15.3–5 RSV). Then consider this one: "For I received from the Lord what I also delivered to you, that the Lord Jesus on the night when he was betrayed took bread, and when he had given thanks, he broke it, and said, 'This is my body which is for you. Do this in remembrance of me'" (I Cor 11.23–24 RSV). These and similar passages suggest that a *reception and delivery* of such statements (as distinct from the contents of the statements) is a part of the stock of knowledge of Paul and his Corinthian readers. Invoking the type (we might call it tradition) occurs in order to reinforce doctrine in the case of I Corinthians 15 and to give focus to ritual in I Corinthians 11. The two occurrences are of a type, "invocations of tradition," but they are aimed at different matters (doctrine versus practice).

If we can establish a relationship among a number of types the adequacy of which has been demonstrated for a given set of originators and audience of related texts, we can speak of generating a "model."[14] For example, the cited Pauline texts, buttressed by other ones on morality, may lead us to propose a model of a legitimatory enterprise, wherein not all spiritual quests are accepted as inspired by the deity but only those that proceed in accord with a specific doctrinal tradition, ritual focus, and moral order. Each element in the model needs to be developed as a meaningful type and found in the stock of knowledge of the appropriate circle of people. It would not be scientific to assume that some type that helps comprise the model and that is found among some other circle of ancient people, or even among some other early Christians, "must" exist for the circle of people under consideration. Typical elements of a model cannot be used to substitute for evidence; that would be deduction of a philosophical kind, not deduction in scientific theory.

Theorizing involves three dialectical processes; the one that is logically last (hence third) is an unpredictable dialectic between two provinces of meaning within which each of two other dialectics occur (Gurvitch 1962: 233ff.). First of the logically prior two is a meaning type that emerges within the social actors' life world; it is not a static psychological construct because its significance changes with the historical context that envelops it. For example, the significance of a wandering Christian charismatic before the Jewish Wars could almost suggest an appeal to the Hellenistic countercultural Cynic movement, but after the wars could instead suggest a displaced Judaic authenticity. The crucial datum is not some permanent relevance of the Wandering Christian Charismatic type it-self but the relevance it takes on in the changing historical contexts. This kind of evolving relevance constitutes a dialectic of meaning within the life worlds of the social actors. Second, types change their theoretical significance in the discourse of the scientists. At one point in the history of the social sciences, the Wander-ing Christian Charismatic type may be associated with Max Weber's model of so-cial change, wherein charisma legitimates a break from tradition and may lead to a routinization of charisma in a rational organization (Weber 1978: 241–51). At a later point in social scientific history, the same type may be seen as an instance of social marginality, wherein a desire to engage society in the form of critique motivates people to maintain non-normative religious subcultures, often at great cost. With both the social actors' meaning systems and the social scientists' the-oretical apparatus in flux, the dialectic between these two life worlds and the types shared by them makes the matter of establishing the adequacy of the types unpredictable. Indeed, it becomes a challenging task.

Interpretive Theorizing

Social scientific interpretive theories elaborate a different dialectic, that between a text and its life world context. This kind of theory develops in the course of model building. Generally, the researcher develops an account of a micro-level phenomenon and places it in a broad macro-level context. By "micro" we simply mean what pertains to a small setting.[15] An individual's everyday social persona, status, or role is a micro phenomenon, as is a small group. A setting under the study of an ethnographer is micro. Typically, a literary work from the early Chris-tian movement reflects a micro setting most directly because the early Christian movement was small and intimate. A macro phenomenon is a structure that is characteristic of a whole society. The Roman Empire, for example, was held to-gether by power—power founded on military success and maintained on the ba-sis of law. Were one to elaborate the full set of implications of the macro context of the Roman Empire for a given Christian micro-level setting, one would be pur-suing a problematic of describing the "total societal phenomenon" relevant to that setting. Alternatively, one may interpret a text that reflects directly a micro-level setting by placing it in the context of an organizational-level or a community-level context, intermediate levels between the micro and the macro.

There are such interpretations other than the sociological. Some operate in the manner of the sociological, placing a small textually evidenced setting into a larger context. One may, for example, portray the economic environment of Palestine (see Freyne 1995), and place Jesus' Temple demonstration within that context. In a rather different procedure, one may apply modern psychological theories to ancient attitudinal structures; for example, one may apply the cognitive dissonance school of social psychology to the stances that Paul of Tarsus takes in his letters (see Taylor 1996b and 1997b). The types that appear in the thinking of Paul differ from the types employed by cognitive dissonance theorists, but the theorist may argue persuasively that the stance taken by Paul is a "case" of a particular type that appears in the disciplinary stock of knowledge of the psychologist. What is optimal in that kind of analysis is that a phenomenon from early Christianity is placed into a modern scientific disciplinary context and interpreted, without misunderstanding the original stance.

Deduction

Pure deduction, of course, is a philosophical enterprise. One begins with premises and by means of logic proceeds to conclusions. The premise is often an observation rather than a concept. In the famous case of the Cartesian *cogito*, the philosopher observed that he was thinking. In the natural scientific procedure followed by Galileo, the operative processes occurring in the physical world were assumed to parallel the logical processes of mathematics. In the social sciences, the issue emerges of whether cogitated logical relationships among social scientific types have any parallels in the life experiences of the social actors under study.

One approach to this issue takes the form of applying "laws" to social conduct. The laws in question would not be customary or legal norms of a society but analogs to Newton's "law" of gravity. In an absolute sense, a law would be an invariant statement. For example, one may formulate the proposition that *all societies have family systems, that is, institutional arrangements of marriage and infant care*. Such invariant propositions, however, are rarely interesting. More often, social scientists identify "tendential regularities," propositions that seem for the most part to be consistent with evidence and therefore serve as approximate summaries of the evidence. The scientific task then becomes one of ascertaining the utility of the propositions as summary statements by "testing" them with evidence.[16] The relationship among types that appear in such propositions becomes at most a linkage that gives form to a heuristic device. The "force" of the propositions comes to be found not in the logics by which their major terms are linked but in their conformance to evidence.

The major terms in theoretical propositions are of necessity quite general. The statement *all societies have family systems, that is, institutional arrangements of marriage and infant care*, for example, would embrace all kinds of human groupings under the term "societies" and a wide variety of contracts and ceremonies under the term "marriage." Was the Roman Empire a society or a collection of societies? Was the early Christian grouping a society? Were the slaves and lower-ranked affiliates of the ancient household members of families? Did marriages have any bearing on the status of these people in the households? Was infant care an aspect of the family or of the household? Left in the abstract, the proposition can neither be affirmed nor disconfirmed by the evidence because the major terms of the proposition are less specific than the types that can be derived from the evidence. Consequently, it becomes necessary to specify the major terms of the proposition. The investigator does this by deriving a more focused statement from the theoretical proposition; for example, one might derive the statement *Self-sufficient human populations all have family arrangements that are marked by marriage rituals or contracts and such arrangements legitimate the conduct of or delegation of infant care.* The Roman Empire was a self-sufficient human population, but early Christianity was not. A family system was therefore not necessary for early Christianity, but useful for its continuance through time in the empire. Many of the dilemmas within early Christianity occurred with respect to questions of family because the latter was tied in to the workings of the extra-Christian dimensions of life in the empire. Notice that the theoretical proposition does not tell us more about early Christianity directly, but to the extent that it usefully summarizes relevant information it helps us pose questions about early Christianity and its environment. This is what is meant by a "heuristic" function.

As noted, the research problematic becomes one of affirming or disconfirming a derived proposition. Affirmation is not confirmation; any inquiry that does not entail all possible cases (including future ones) cannot be shown to be true. Rather, correspondences between the proposition and evidence strengthen the confidence one might have in the utility of applying the proposition. Disconfirmation does not refute the proposition so much as limit its applicability. Consequently the propositions are not statements of truth but working hypotheses. Whenever one entertains a hypothesis, one must simultaneously entertain its opposite—usually termed a "null hypothesis." If no evidence that one may possibly collect can support the null hypothesis, one does not really learn anything from "findings" that support the hypothesis; the research project would not really be *testing* the hypothesis. Thus as one is not really asking a question if the answer cannot be either "Yes" or "No" or some other alternative responses ("When did you stop beating your wife?"), one is not really engaging in research if the findings cannot either affirm or disconfirm the main hypothesis. Hypotheses must be falsifiable. While this may appear to be an elementary point, it is deceptively easy to make claims in the social and behavioral sciences that are not falsifiable.

Human worlds tend to be complex. Each individual person takes many situational factors into account in performing each act, and no two individuals are in a position to account for each factor from the same perspective. Indeed, the same individual may act differently in similar situations at different points in life. Individuals find themselves caught up in complex situations; they find it necessary to do things that ordinarily they would not want to do. "Father, if thou art willing, remove this cup from me; nevertheless not my will, but thine, be done" (Lk 22.42 RSV). Consequently it is not easy to apply simple propositions to human activity. It becomes necessary to revise and elaborate the propositions until they begin to become complex and cumbersome statements. In order to apply them at all, one must use them before they become entirely too unwieldy. Many of the cases to which one would apply them will therefore not support the best of hypotheses, even if the hypotheses are for the most part true. In making judgments about hypotheses, the researcher needs to be prepared to deal with "error." There are generally two kinds of error. In Type 1 error, one rejects a true null hypothesis and accepts a false main hypothesis. In Type 2 error, one accepts a false null hypothesis and rejects a true main hypothesis. When social scientists use statistics in their studies, they systematically consider a large enough representative sample of cases so that they can prepare probability models for Type 1 errors occurring; they tend to pay less systematic attention to Type 2 errors. Apart from studies of word usage in ancient texts, the evidence on early Christianity is insufficiently extensive to use statistical procedures; we cannot survey a random sample of 1,500 early Christians. Consequently, it becomes necessary to follow up every tested hypothesis with supplementary considerations that address in some other manner the possibility of both Type 1 and Type 2 errors, but especially Type 1. This necessity derives from the fact that the hypothesis testing procedure is concerned with the utility of a heuristic device, not with grounded types.

Conclusion

The deceptively simple concept of science as inquiry brings with it a series of dilemmas. One dilemma is that of the relationship between relevant types in the realm of the observable and meaningful types in the thinking of the observer. A second dilemma is that of the relationship between operative processes in the former realm and logical procedures in the latter realm. The dilemmas become compounded in the social sciences by the fact that the people whose conduct is under consideration, in the present instance members of the Jesus movement or of the early Christian communities, were thinking agents themselves. They lived through dilemmas themselves—that of the relationship between types relevant to the events they experienced and the types that emerged as meaningful in their thinking, and that of the relationship between the processes relevant to the events they experienced and the logics they themselves entertained. The scientific problematic for those who would conduct inquiry into the conduct of the ancient Christians needs to organize itself around the relationship between modern and ancient conceptualizations and logics, among other things.

In light of these dilemmas, one should be cautious about overly simple and formulaic approaches to the use of the modern social sciences in inquiry into ancient Christianity. Contemporary social scientific concepts and models are not "cookie cutters" that can stamp out preestablished shapes in an otherwise formless dough of ancient information. The social scientific concepts and models are not "answers" to be substituted for missing evidence but questions. Science in general is not a shortcut; it is an art that requires practice. I have elsewhere argued that a good preparation for using the social sciences with ancient material is the study of its use with contemporary phenomena (Blasi 1993); the dilemmas inherent in social scientific research require sufficiently sophisticated responses on the part of the researcher and thus they are best addressed by those responses becoming "second nature" aspects of the inquirer's mind rather than by their codification as research rules. Codification has its purpose—specifically, communication about methodological questions—but can be too cumbersome in research activity. One does not memorize rules in driving an automobile or playing a game, though the codification of the relevant rules has its purposes; one "learns by doing." Research is at least as sophisticated an enterprise as automobile driving or game playing; it calls for craftsmanship. This should not discourage anyone from beginning, but invite one to begin with full cognizance of the length and trials of the journey.

Notes

1. Taylor (1999) notes that the earliest Christians made a point of locating themselves in Jerusalem because of the role of the Temple in their eschatological expectations.

2. Some also argue against using the term "Jewish," claiming that the proper translation from ancient texts should read "Judaean." Many ancient *Ioudaioi*, however, did not live in Judaea and were religiously oriented to the Hebrew Scriptures (sometimes in Greek translation) and to the Temple in Jerusalem. Especially in the decades after the Jewish Wars, culminating in the destruction of the Temple and expulsion of the inhabitants from Jerusalem, most *Ioudaioi* were Jews, not Judaeans.

3. For earlier discussions of methodology in this area of study, see Blasi (1988: 199–218, and 1993).

4. On this source, Q, see Kloppenborg (1988).

5. This was the problematic in Blasi (1996).

6. On anonymous and pseudonymous authorship, see Meade (1986). Charlesworth (1988) provides a review of literary materials that have come to the attention of archaeologists in the past century. Other relevant extracanonical Christian literature is found in the "apostolic fathers" volumes of patristic collections (e.g., Lightfoot and Harmer 1992); see also Milavec (1989) on the *Didache*; Kloppenborg, Meyer, Patterson, and Steinhauser (1990) on Q and Coptic Thomas; and Hock (1995) on the Gospel of James and the Infancy Gospel of Thomas.

7. While some purists might insist that arithmetic operations, including advanced linear statistical modeling, should never be applied to nominal and ordinal data, it is common practice to include indications of gender (e.g., 1 for male, 2 for female) and religious identity (e.g., 1 for Episcopal, 2 for Methodist, etc.) in complex linear regression models. It is at the point of making decisions about such matters that what would be an exact science becomes an art. It is my own preference that no more than one such variable in any given statistical model violate assumptions of levels of measurement in that manner. Analogously, in treating literary evidence in a social scientific analysis, no more than one instance of violating the assumptions of the levels of measurement should be allowed in arriving at any one conclusion.

8. On understanding, see Weber (1978: 4ff.), criticized by Schutz (1972: 20ff.). Abel (1948) gives a brief account of the history of understanding as a research operation, as well as a general description of it. Social scientists often use the German expression *Verstehen* for the operation.

9. The suggestion that Jesus could use cultural references does not mean that he identified with or imitated the historical Cynics. It does mean that people did demonstrate deliberate distance from established cultures in antiquity—the Cynics did it and the Jesus movement did it.

10. On the primacy of the "back and forth" between people, see Mead (1934) and Blumer (1969). In explicating the approach of John Dominic Crossan, Robbins (1995) speaks of the story in a parable "doing things to us as readers"; he counterposes this approach to what is inaccurately presented by some as *the* social scientific approach.

11. Weber speaks of "interpretive understanding" (1978: 4); he gives a conceptual account of understanding but approaches the interpretive moment more by illustration from the literature of his day.

12. The rationale for always having a control group comes from the logic of the experiment. In examining "natural situations" rather than ones that we might contrive for purposes of an experiment, we look for "natural experiments" that observable history provides.

13. See Schutz for an account of differences between knowledge about predecessors and about contemporaries (1972: 207ff.).

14. This approach to models differs from but is by no means inconsistent with that provided by Elliott (1986). I wish simply to highlight the empirical warranting of models by constituting them out of "grounded" types.

15. The distinction between micro and macro is as old as scientific sociology itself; it was intrinsic to the thought of Émile Durkheim (1982), for example, who emphasized the macro. By introducing attitudes (*Ethik* and *Geist*) into sociology, Weber (1958) emphasized the micro, without ignoring the macro. The terms "micro" and "macro" appeared as mainstays in the methodological treatises of Georges Gurvitch (see 1947: 49 and 1958b).

16. For a treatise on testing as a general method of social science, see Zetterberg (1965).

SPECIAL METHODS

II

Archaeological and Architectural Issues and the Question of Demographic and Urban Forms

4

CAROLYN OSIEK

W E WOULD LIKE TO BE ABLE to go to some designated archaeological area in an ancient city like Ephesus or Rome and point to the ruins of a Christian house church. Although this is not possible, it *is* possible to walk into first-century houses elsewhere that must have been very similar to those in which the earliest generations of Christians worshipped. But care must be exercised not to do it too selectively, wearing Christian blinders. First, the whole of the housing evidence must be studied, and then conclusions drawn for the life of early Christianity.

Like most archaeological evidence, that for domestic and assembly space is preserved randomly. In some cases, Christian/Jewish interest spurred excavations, as at Capernaum in lower Galilee. In other cases, preservation occurred sporadically or haphazardly as the result of natural causes or human actions. An outstanding example of destruction by natural causes is the burial of cities by the eruption of Vesuvius in August of 79 C.E., especially Pompeii and Herculaneum, to be rediscovered by accident in the sixteenth and seventeenth centuries. An outstanding example of deliberate human destruction is the filled-in siege wall, prepared for the Persian invasion of 256 C.E. at Dura Europa on the Euphrates River. An entire line of buildings constructed along one wall of the city, including a mithraeum, a house synagogue, and a house church, were preserved nearly perfectly. Thus we have a rare example where we can say for sure that Christians worshipped in that space, recognized by its reconstruction and iconography.

The Material Evidence

The forerunner of housing patterns for the early Christian period in Palestinian archaeology is the so-called "four-room house" of the Israelite period in which three long rooms form a U-shape around a courtyard with one open end that is closed not by a building but by a wall and gate. These buildings may have had second stories in which the family sleeping quarters were located. They establish a basic pattern that with considerable variations continued for hundreds if not thousands of years in the region: rooms surrounding a common courtyard that can be closed off at will from the outside world. All rooms have direct access to the courtyard. By its very design, such a structure aids its occupants in coping with the climate and the social situation. The climate includes rainfall for only a few months, a warm, dry climate for up to eight months of the year, searing heat by day and cooling by night. Shade can be sought during the heat of the day, and life can return to the open when the sun is not immediately overhead. The roofless central space allows cool night air to descend and enter all the rooms. Most of daily life can be lived outdoors, yet privacy from outsiders is readily available if desired. The courtyard door can lie open for easy access or closed for privacy and protection.

The excavated domestic buildings at Capernaum on the north shore of the Lake of Galilee give an idea of the basic housing unit that was probably used throughout the region at that time and perhaps in villages in many areas of the Mediterranean world (see sketch in Snyder 1985: 72). Here, modest separate buildings of one or more rooms are built around a common courtyard, the whole complex surrounded by a common outer wall. While most of the housing evidence, the earlier "four-room" house described above and much later material, suggests somewhat small family units living together rather than large extended families, the housing arrangement seen at Capernaum allows for the possibility of larger family units living together in one compound. While the typical house seems large enough only for a nuclear family and its dependents, we do not know whether and to what extent those living in units near, next to, or across the courtyard were members of the same extended family.

Another variant of the same basic pattern from roughly the same period can be seen at the recently excavated Bethsaida in the northeast corner of the lake's floodplain. Several large houses have been excavated and restored. The room design varies, but each house can be accessed through an open courtyard. Just a few miles up the hill and away from the lake is Chorazim, where a development from later times can be seen. Characteristic of the Byzantine period, discrete houses are built around a common courtyard. All open onto the courtyard, but each contains complexes of rooms, many of which do not have immediate access to the outside.

Several wealthy houses from the upper city of Roman Jerusalem were discovered and excavated in 1969, before the structures of today's Jewish Quarter were built over them. Most of these houses were destroyed in the conflagration of the city's destruction in 70 C.E. One of them, now known and accessible as the "Herodian Mansion" or Wohl Museum, was a very large complex built around a central courtyard, containing an elaborate reception hall, guest rooms, and at least one upper story. Some of the first-floor walls of this house contained painted floral frescoes that were then plastered over and painted again in a style that closely resembles that of Pompeii. Another room was decorated in white plaster incised to resemble ashlars, large building stones (Avigad 1980: 83–120).

The Greek peristyle house follows the same general design of rooms grouped around a common courtyard, but the open space consists of a covered ambulatory around the outside, with a roof supported by rows of columns. Because the space in the center is open to the sky, rainwater flows in. This water is usually channeled and caught into some kind of container, a pool, basin, or sometimes an underground cistern. Many variations and differences of design are known. In some cases the peristyle is so small that there is room in the middle only for a small paved area, perhaps with a well. In other cases the open space of the peristyle is extensive and can be planted with charming gardens. Greek peristyle and courtyard houses from the classical period (fourth century B.C.E.) are preserved at Olynthus in Macedonia (one floor plan is given in Wallace-Hadrill 1994: 8). Simple peristyle houses from the Roman period can be seen in a number of places, including Pergamon and Ephesus at the center of Roman civilization in Asia, Delos in the Aegean Sea region, Sepphoris in lower Galilee, and Palmyra and Zeugma on the eastern edges of the empire.

The peristyles of the luxurious "terrace houses" of Roman Ephesus, located on the north slope of Mount Koressos to the south of the main east–west street of the city, are paved but provide a pleasant place to work or enjoy the open air. The houses are built higher on the hill to catch the better air; much more modest houses lie below them at a lower level. The latter are essentially smaller rooms behind and above shops that open onto the main street. The more affluent houses had at least a second, and perhaps a third, story, so that sleeping quarters were above the ground floor where most of the daytime activity occurred. There are at least five houses of this type built on the same hill, all with running water and with heating pipes built into the walls. At least one house had its own bath and another its own kitchen. While most affluent houses had some means for preparing food, these installations were luxury features in a Roman city, since the public baths were there for everyone and food and drink was readily available in the street shops below.

The peristyle first appeared in Greek houses in the Hellenistic period and soon spread to the West. The characteristic difference in the traditional Italian house, however, is the presence of a different kind of open space just inside the front door, the atrium, with its opening in the middle of the roof, usually smaller than that of a peristyle and not supported by a colonnade. The open space in the roof was originally meant to allow smoke to escape, since in the older Italian house, the hearth was placed there. When the hearth was moved or abandoned, the small opening in the roof took on the function of the *compluvium*, allowing rain-water to enter into a pool or basin below, the *impluvium*. This was originally the source of the house's water supply, since in central and northern Italy, there is sufficient rainfall to collect water in this manner. When later in the imperial period a city water supply supplanted this need, the atrium–*impluvium* combination remained a standard feature in many houses, even though the rainwater was no longer used and had to be channeled out into the street. These channels can still be seen in some Pompeian houses today.

In the Julio–Claudian period (30 B.C.E.–62 C.E.), the flourishing period of Pompeii and Herculaneum, two architectural tendencies have been observed. One is the disappearance of an office area (the *tablinum*) for the business of the *paterfamilias*, or the penchant for making it into an open sitting room (Richardson 1988: 240–41). Thus this architectural and decorative feature was no longer the central focus of the house, which implies a similar shift in the social function of the room. This need not mean that the conducting of business in the house declined but that it became less formal. The business of the *paterfamilias* could be conducted anywhere in the house that he chose. The other tendency is increased interest in gardens and peristyles, with the peristyle replacing the atrium. Those who did not have space for an actual garden decorated their walls with scenes of flowers and birds.

Roman houses used less furniture than modern houses, and most of it was lightweight and movable, which made it possible for the same space to be used for different functions at different times of the day. This made use of space very flexible and made it possible for whole rooms to be completely decorated (Zanker 1998: 11–12). Houses of this period were decorated elaborately, the walls in many cases literally covered with paintings, some with bold red or black backgrounds: mythological scenes, pastoral scenes, gardens, views of houses, scenes from everyday life, architectural fantasies with optical illusions of depth and breadth, even simple depictions of fruits and vegetables. Ceilings were often decorated and the floors covered with mosaics or patterned marble. The chaste white marble statues that we admire today in museums were painted to look lifelike, and many a wealthy householder was an art collector. What greeted the eyes of a visitor to a well-to-do house was a barrage of visualizations, on walls and corridors, in rooms and peristyles, in bedrooms, everywhere, often with very large figures in a relatively small room. A good example of such a room, in which everything but the ceiling is preserved, is that containing the Dionysiac frescoes in the Villa of the Mysteries at Pompeii. Important paintings were sometimes used for instruction and illustration, and some of these domestic paintings may have served that function. The rhetorical art of *ekphrasis* verbally recreated the image so vividly that the listener was drawn into the depiction just as surely through words as through im-

age. Many of these household paintings must have been used this way, to entertain and to instruct.

These descriptions should not lead to the conclusion that every Greek house
had a neatly constructed peristyle and every Roman house both an atrium and
peristyle. Quite the opposite is the case. As usual, the classic description by a theorist does not match what we see in reality. In Pompeii and Herculaneum, only 41
percent of houses have an atrium; not all have peristyles; and in a sampling of
three city blocks, only 10 percent of the peristyles have the classic design of
colonnade on all four sides (Wallace-Hadrill 1994: 84, 86). Thus the distribution
of features of the classic description in actual houses is quite irregular or, to put
it another way, variation in architectural pattern is considerable.

Before going on to the social interpretation of the use of space in the Roman
house, we need to consider several other kinds of housing and entertainment facilities that are relevant to the interpretation of early Christian life. The majority
of urban dwellers lived not in the kinds of houses just described but in apartment
houses (*insulae*), multiple-unit dwellings, some of which were spacious and comfortable, others squalid and dangerous.[1] The evidence for such apartment buildings is not extensive in the earlier pre-Vespasianic remains of the cities of Vesuvius, but it is there: at Pompeii, large dwellings like the House of Fabius Rufus
and the Sarno Bath complex with its more than one hundred rooms and luxury
facilities. It also seems that the famous Villa of the Mysteries, while built all on
ground level, was used as multi-rental property in the last phase of its existence,
as was the House of Pansa (Osiek and Balch 1997: 17–18). At Herculaneum, the
House of the Bicentenary and the House "a Graticcio" are examples of rather
simple multiple-resident and multiple-story dwellings, while the Insula Orientalis
is the only one to be found in the Vesuvian cities of the type later to become popular at Ostia, the port city of Rome (Wallace-Hadrill 1994: 104). Augustus limited their height to seventy feet; Trajan later to sixty. Such buildings could therefore go as high as four and five poorly built stories often in danger of collapsing
or burning (Strabo, *Geogr.* 5.3.7; Juvenal, *Sat.* 3.190-208). Such buildings were increasingly present in Rome and, it can be assumed, in most cities of the empire.

Greater evidence for multi-unit housing comes from Ostia in the second to
fourth centuries. This style of living seems to have become more popular then,
even for those who could afford their own separate houses. The well-known
House of Diana is lined with shops on its ground floor, facing the principal street.
It must have been fairly pleasant to live in, especially at the lower levels above the
ground, with large windows and balconies to the outside and an inner light well
to provide light and air to the rooms. Other buildings like it line the same street.
Some writers refer to apartment houses of this sort as "luxury apartments." Other
examples of multiple-unit housing include the so-called "Garden Houses" and

Casette tipo, which depart from the traditional central open space in their ground plans. Here, short connecting passageways link four or five rooms with each other within a rectangular space. The same floor plan is repeated four times on the ground level, side by side, with stairs going up to further levels and sometimes pedestrian passageways between the buildings. These are modest individual apartments built next to and on top of each other.

Another aspect of social life that is preserved in the material evidence is the rental dining room for banquets and entertainment. While facilities for regular bathing were provided by the city, dining was, except on rare special occasions of commemoration or celebration, a private affair. The poor and those of more moderate means probably ate mostly from the *thermopolia*, *tavernae*, and *cauponae* that were available everywhere, providing drinks, food, and even rental lodging. One example of these dining rooms in a sacral context is the Asclepion of Corinth, where a series of small dining rooms were located at ground level, each with eleven individual couches around the walls of the room and place for a table to hold food in front of each. This is an important setting for I Corinthians 8.10, where one of the settings of the problem of eating meat offered to idols is the listener "reclining in the temple of an idol." A less religiously associated rented dining room can be found in the House of Julia Felix at Pompeii. It is the largest residential unit so far excavated. Here a freeborn successful businesswoman offered five-year leases on baths, shops, taverns, and upper-floor apartments, while she kept a series of entertainment rooms looking out onto a large and beautiful peristyle. At least one of them had a fountain of running water that flowed down marble tile between the two couches, each of which could hold several people for elegant dining.

Social Interpretation

Ancient terminology for "house" and "family" is fluid and different from modern usage. Both English words can be used to mean the Greek οἶκος or οἰκία (*oikos* or *oikia*) and the Latin *domus* and to some extent *familia*. *Oikos* and *domus* more frequently connote the material structure of the house than the other terms do, yet both can mean quite different things. The house can mean the structure itself or all of its belongings as well. Both Greek words and the Latin *familia* more often mean all the persons belonging to the household, especially the slaves. It may include, but never means exclusively, wife and children. Married children and their own *familia* may also be included in the *familia* of the *paterfamilias*, as may be his ancestors. The one thing that none of these terms means is the first thing that the English words connote: the nuclear family, for which ancient Greeks and Romans had no distinct word even though both archaeological and literary evidence indicates living groups based on it rather than extended blood kinship. Where a community or group has no term for something social, there is in all likelihood no reality to correspond to that term.

The early Augustan Roman architect Vitruvius describes the Greek house as one in which entry is obtained through a narrow passageway from the street into a colonnaded peristyle, around which are located dining rooms, guest rooms, and spaces for the entertaining of male guests and conducting of business. Beyond this, through another passageway to the back of the house, lie the family area, slave quarters, and the area where women spend their days (called together the *gynaikonitis* (γυναικονῖτις, or women's quarters), where the domestic life of the household is lived separately from what goes on with the business of the male head of the household (*De architectura* 6.7.1–5). In other words, the social use of space in the Greek house is determined by gender. It is with regard to this architectural arrangement that Philo's famous words on the seclusion of women can be understood. He opines that the public forum is male territory, while women should remain indoors, unmarried girls going only as far as the middle doors that separate the women's from the men's quarters, while mature women can go as far as the outer door (Philo, *Spec.* 3.171).

An interpretive problem arises when very few Greek houses that survive, even from the pre-Roman period, exhibit a floor arrangement that would correlate with this idea of segregation by sex, while some of the later larger houses of Roman Pompeii do, in spite of lack of literary evidence that the social arrangement was the same. Wallace-Hadrill suggests a pattern of segregation by sex in a house of Olynthus (1994: 8), but the house is relatively small and the pattern of segregation is not obvious from the floor plan. There is of course always the possibility or even the likelihood of a second story accessible by ladder or a staircase that has not survived, in which case the women's quarters could be located on the upper floor. Many of the larger houses at Pompeii exhibit a front area around the atrium and a narrow passageway leading to an interior part of the house around a rear peristyle, but nearly any house large enough will have separate sections to it.

The atrium of the Roman house usually has rooms that open immediately onto it. The *tablinum*, in which the head of the household received clients, conducted business, kept records, and read, was usually placed directly at the back of the atrium. Beyond the atrium of the Roman house is often the familiar peristyle, also with rooms opening onto it as onto a central courtyard. If we had only Vitruvius's account of the Greek house, we might read into the design of these houses men's quarters in the front around the atrium and women's quarters in the back around the peristyle. However, we would also observe that in many houses of Pompeii and Herculaneum that have both atrium and peristyle, the most elegantly decorated rooms are not off the atrium but off the peristyle.

Some of these are dining rooms, usually arranged as a *triclinium* with three straight couches in a U-shaped design with the open end facing the outside. Each couch accommodated three persons, thus the ideal dinner party consisted of nine persons. The *triclinium* had a hierarchical seating arrangement with the most honored positions at the back left where the view was best. An alternative form of dining couch, the *stibadium*, formed a single half circle. Originating in Greek outdoor dining on leaves or stuffed cushions thrown on the ground, the *stibadium* was associated with more of a picnic atmosphere than formal dining and did not have the strict hierarchical seating pattern associated with the *triclinium*. By the late fourth century, this was the preferred dining arrangement because there was more free space and a better view for more participants. However, its original informality of seating had usually given way by that time to the same formality of the *triclinium* (Dunbabin 1991). Nearly all banquet scenes in Christian funerary art depict the participants on *stibadia*.

Formal rooms of the house could also be general reception rooms, called singularly an *oecus* by Vitruvius, where women do their spinning during the morning and men entertain later in the day. Moreover, the higher the status of the owner, the more elaborate these entertainment facilities would be (*De architectura* 6.7.2, 5; 5.1–2). The *oecus* in some important houses became larger and more significant, even sometimes adding an apsed end in imitation of the public basilica, a Roman building that was used for law courts and public offices. Thus elegant dining and reception areas are a sign of the social importance of the owners.

While space in the Greek house is divided by gender, in the Roman house, it is divided by time of day (Wallace-Hadrill 1994: 47; Laurence 1994: 127, 131–32), and there is a more flexible arrangement of the use of space in general. Some of the small rooms that surround the atrium are not for entertaining at all, but sleeping quarters for anyone, including members of the family. In the atrium women do their spinning, which means they gather socially (Livy 1.5.7); children play (Virgil, *Aen.* 7.379–80); and men conduct business, but at different times of the day. In the early morning the front space of the house belongs to the *paterfamilias*, who receives clients and conducts business there; later in the day, women and children frequent it until midafternoon, when it becomes the first-order reception area.

According to Wallace-Hadrill (1988: 52) some houses were constructed under Roman influence with social rank distinctions in mind. In larger houses the distinction between family and entertaining area and service area is pronounced, the latter accessible only down long narrow corridors as in the House of the Faun or of the Menander at Pompeii. Where decoration is preserved, the difference in style, quality, or just existence of artistic expression clearly distinguishes the public areas of the house. At the extensive villa of Oplontis at Torre Annunciata near Pompeii, public areas of the house bear elegant painted decoration while service areas are painted with crude stripes (illustration Osiek and Balch 1997: 29; Wallace-Hadrill 1994: 42). In the service areas are spaces for cooking and washing and for slaves' sleeping quarters.

The most surprising notion from a modern point of view is the way in which certain areas of the homes of important people were considered open to the public. Every house that could afford one had an *ostiarius* or doorkeeper (sometimes a female *ostiaria*: cf. Jn 18.17; Acts 12.13), a slave whose responsibility it was to supervise who entered and to deny access when appropriate. Yet Vitruvius remarks that everyone has a right to enter the atrium and peristyle of the houses of important people, leaving only bedrooms, dining rooms, and baths as the private area of the family (*De architectura* 6.5.1). The construction of reception halls within homes also indicates the degree to which public architecture and therefore public business was actualized within the "private" house.

Moreover, the *tablinum*, usually immediately visible from the front door across the atrium, more often had a backing of movable curtain or wood panels; when the room was not in use, the backing could be swung aside, allowing an axial view from the front door through the atrium and across the peristyle to an imposing dining room or reception hall. Thus when entertaining was going on, everyone who walked by, even without entering the house, could look in and see what important people were inside and what important things were happening. The modern notion of the home as a private place away from business and the public sphere of politics is not applicable here. The head of the household daily received clients at home and conducted as much business as possible in the comfort and security of the house. Much "public" business happened in the "private" sphere of the house. The concepts of public and private worked very differently than in modern thinking or even in older Greek society. "The Greek house is concerned with creating a world of privacy, of excluding the inquisitive passerby; the Roman house invites him in and puts its occupants on conspicuous show. Vitruvius's contrast is not between space for visitors and space for family but between space for uninvited and for invited visitors" (Wallace-Hadrill 1994: 45).

In Roman religion, the household gods were represented and worshipped daily at the domestic shrine. The *lararium* or shrine of the household gods is still to be seen in many Pompeiian houses. Good examples are in the House of the Vettii and of the Menander. The *lares familiares*, usually depicted as dancing figures, were joined by molded heads or busts of male ancestors and the painted image of the *genius*, or personal protective spirit of the *paterfamilias*, usually depicted as a snake. Each morning the whole household gathered there for sacrifice, led by the *paterfamilias* as priest and the *materfamilias* as priestess of the family cult.

In view of all these considerations, it is clear that there was little personal privacy, whether in sleeping, eating, dressing, bathing, or defecating. All of these activities were done in common, at home or at the baths. Public bathing was done in common, apparently at some times and places with both sexes together, though on other occasions there is literary evidence of separation of the sexes by time of day: women in the morning, males slaves in early afternoon, and free men after that—at the time of day when the water was hottest. Some baths, like the Stabian baths at Pompeii, have separate smaller and poorer facilities with a back entrance that could have been either for women or for slaves. The public latrines that have been preserved, as at Philippi, Corinth, or Ephesus, usually use the runoff from the baths to provide running water under the stone seats, but there are no signs of separations between seats for privacy.

Even in those areas of the house that were off-limits to strangers, the continual mingling of free persons and slave attendants made impossible anything that would approach the modern concept of privacy (Clarke 1991: 1–2, regarding Roman Italy). Those who could afford them had personal attendants who ministered to the most intimate bodily needs. Those who could not lived in constantly crowded conditions. Clement of Alexandria (c. 150–220 C.E.) remarks that modest Christian women who would not think of revealing themselves in front of male relatives will not hesitate to strip in front of male slaves at the baths (*Paed.* 3.5).

Another social implication of the material evidence is that there was little segregation by wealth or status. Though there were wealthier and poorer areas of any city, different social levels rubbed elbows with each other constantly in daily interactions. *Domus* and *insula* were built in the same areas. Beggars were everywhere. In larger houses, those slaves who were not personal attendants slept in separate and poorer quarters, but during the day, their lives were intertwined with proprietor members of the household. In smaller houses, slaves and owners lived in constant interaction. Brothels were located throughout the city, as amply shown by the twenty-eight establishments in Pompeii. Other prostitutes plied their trade in one-room units in the best of neighborhoods, as in a room adorned with mosaics across the street from the luxurious House of Neptune and Amphitrite at Herculaneum.

Clients of different social levels frequented the houses of their patrons, and passersby of any social level gaped at the door or wandered into the atrium or peristyle, into the same space where in the late evening the household prepared for sleep in cubicles immediately attached. There may thus have been more social mixing in the *domus* than in the *insula*. Certain slaves could exercise great authority as porters (Schneider 1916), pedagogues (Osiek and Balch 1997: 68ff.), chief cooks, managers of hospitality, and administrators of households (Martin 1990: 9–10), with power to discipline children, forbid access to the house or its head, or seat guests by rank at dining couches even though the guests might not like where they were placed. The Roman house was designed to display status not be-

cause its inhabitants were isolated from those of different status, but precisely because those of so many different statuses were constantly coming and going in it
and would be duly impressed.

The considerable theoretical social differences between the Greek and Roman
house raise the question whether we are dealing with cultural, geographic, or
chronological differences, or all of the above. In the early Christian period, are we
to assume that Greek-speaking households lived like the Greek household with its
segregation by sex while Latin speakers lived like Romans in their mixture of public and private within the house, or that East and West lived differently, or that
Roman influence had become so extensive by this time that the Greek model of
the household had disappeared?

Stones and walls do not always give an answer. The Roman houses of Ephesus
do not seem by their design to have a separate place for women's quarters, but as
we have seen, many of the large houses of Pompeii could be interpreted as having
them, if we did not know better from literary texts about Roman customs. By the
first century C.E. a pervasive adaptation to Roman culture was happening. The Pax
Romana, the Augustan myth of stability, was contagious. The imperial cult was creating a uniform civic–religious system that instilled loyalty to the conquerors in exchange for stability and peace. In places like Pompeii, Ephesus, or Caesarea, we see
the increasing uniformity of Romanization in decorative style, monumental architecture, and dedicatory inscriptions. Moreover, Roman colonies of legionary veterans and commercial freedmen were established in refounded Greek cities such as
Philippi and Corinth. Roman influence was everywhere among the educated social
levels, probably less so among the lower classes. Yet the tastes and practices of the
elites filtered down and were imitated whenever possible by nonelites, creating a
dominant culture that was voluntarily accepted by those who did not belong to the
elite Roman hegemony. We can consequently assume something of a cultural continuity among most urbanites, based on Roman values and practices.

If there are any differences to be hypothesized between eastern and western
Mediterranean culture at this time, they can perhaps be detected in what is one
of the major social tension points in most cultures: gender. We have already
noted Vitruvius's comments about how the social structure of the Greek house
secludes women from the public male world, while in the Roman house women
mingle more freely with men. This is a general tendency of which people at the
time were probably aware: the greater integration of the sexes in daily life in the
West than in the East. Vitruvius is not the only one to comment on this difference. Cornelius Nepos, writing in Rome in the year 35 B.C.E., remarks that Roman men do not hesitate to take their wives to dinner parties and matrons do not
hesitate to be participants in celebrations in their own houses. "It is very different in Greece: neither is she allowed at dinner parties except with relatives, nor

does she appear anywhere in the house except in the interior part called the women's quarters, where no one enters except close relatives" (*On Illustrious Men*, preface 6–7). A little later, in the early first century C.E., Valerius Maximus (*Factorum et dictorum memorabilim* 2.1.2) comments that the traditional way for men and women to dine together, men reclining and women sitting alongside, is now less frequently observed. This change is corroborated by Petronius's mid–first-century *Satyricon* (67), where Scintilla reclines at dinner with the men.

Yet the custom of separating men and women at dinner did not die out completely. At the marriage of Octavian and Livia, the couple reclined together. However, for official public events such as military triumphs, when a more traditional image was preferred, Livia gave a separate banquet for the women while Octavian presided at the men's banquet (Dio 48.44.3; 55.2.4, 8.2; 57.12.5). Later depictions of funerary meals from all over the empire continue to show men reclining and women sitting next to them, even some of the Christian catacomb paintings of the fourth century C.E.. But whether it is a case of reclining alongside men or sitting next to their couch, women were present and integrated into the meal. When Plutarch, writing a century after Valerius Maximus, still maintains that women do not belong at a formal meal, he echoes the traditional Greek way; yet even he depicts a dinner scene in which two respectable women are present, one apparently reclining and the other sitting (*Quaest. Conv.* 612F–613A, 8–9; *Sept. Sap. Conv.* 150B–155E).

In contrast is the famous story of Verres's misuse of his governorship as reported by Cicero (*Verr.* 2.1.26.65–68), in which Verres creates a public outrage while he was a guest in the house of a noble Greek family by insisting on seeing the unmarried daughter of the host, whose household resorts to violence rather than let this happen. But the fact that the story is intelligible in Rome a generation before Cornelius Nepos shows that the Roman audience is close enough to the social reality of the seclusion of women to understand and object to Verres's actions.

In view of this literary evidence, it is difficult to agree with Richardson's interpretation that each time we see evidence of more than one dining or reception room in Pompeiian houses, one of them is a "ladies' dining room" (1988: 156–58, 164–70, 174–75), even when two apparent dining rooms are side by side, as in the House of the Vettii at Pompeii, or in parallel position on either side of an *oecus*, as in the House of the Labyrinth. They could instead be alternate dining or reception areas. For example, Vitruvius gives advice about having several rooms that face different directions, to catch the benefits of the different seasons: south in the winter and north in the summer. In the absence of evidence for a separate dining room, as in the House of Meleagro, Richardson concedes that the new custom could be invoked: "We must conclude that here ladies sometimes reclined in company with the men, as Valerius Maximus (2.1.2) said was becoming customary in Rome in his day, toward the end of the reign of Tiberius" (1988: 322).

There is evidence from many places in the empire of women running busi-nesses and acting as patrons to persons and professional societies. For example, at Pompeii Julia Felix leased real estate. Lydia of Thyatira was a merchant of luxury cloth with her own *oikos* at Philippi (Acts 16). Eumachia was patron of the fullers' guild at Pompeii with a statue erected to her in gratitude. Plancia Magna of early second-century Perge in Pamphylia was a public patron of the city. The freed-woman Manlia Gnome of Rome boasts on her epitaph of her many clients (*CIL* 6.21975). The Christian deacon Phoebe of Cenchrae near Corinth was an ac-knowledged patron of Paul (Rom 16.2). While some differences between East and West are to be expected in the question of women's social functions, the real factor was likely to have been the degree of Romanization affecting the particular place and status level concerned.

Architectural Adaptations by Religious Groups

The first gatherings of religious groups were often in private homes, and they per-haps continued that way for some time. We are accustomed to thinking of the first generations of Christians meeting in houses for their ritual meal. We are less ac-customed to thinking of them meeting in a rented space or small private apart-ment of an *insula*. There is no direct archaeological evidence of this, but there is indirect evidence: in Ostia in the *insula* of Diana one of the ground rooms was adapted decoratively and fitted out as a *mithraeum*, an indication that specified rooms or areas of these buildings could be dedicated to religious purposes. The titular churches of Rome are thought to have been built over an original place where Christian gatherings took place at an earlier date. The later church of Saints John and Paul on the Caelian hill was built over what seems to have been an apartment house (illustrations in White 1997: 2.214–15). Similarly, the church of San Clemente was built partially over a house with a series of rooms that had been made into a *mithraeum* (probably in the first century) and partly over an ad-joining large building, either a public building of some kind, perhaps a warehouse or an apartment building.

One big question is whether a Christian group meeting in an apartment building (sometimes nicknamed a "tenement church": see Jewett 1993) would have the same hierarchical status structure that could be expected of one hosted in a *domus*. We know very little about social life in an *insula* except from the Ro-man satirists. "Those who belong to Chloe" (1 Cor 1.11) may be such a group, though there are other possible explanations for that reference (they could be be-lieving members of the household of a nonbeliever, for example); what is certain from the language is that they are not a house church. This is a topic that needs further investigation.

Christians were not the only ones who began their gatherings in private houses and eventually adapted them architecturally for religious use. Synagogues too seem to have begun this way, as well as *mithraea* and other religious groups. In late second or early third century B.C.E. Philadelphia in Lydia, for example, a man named Dionysius set up a cult center devoted to a number of traditional Greek gods in his *oikos*. While the term can mean sanctuary or shrine in religious usage, there is reason to think that the meeting place was actually in his house. The inscription is interesting for comparative purposes because it sets delimitations of moral conduct for membership (Barton and Horsley 1981: 15–16, 31–33).

The case of Dura Europa is instructive. There, down one line of city buildings, two originally private houses had been adapted for religious use: one as a synagogue, and one as a Christian church. The social implications of their proximity are intriguing. Everyone in the neighborhood must have known of the uses being made of these dwellings, which are literally "down the street" from each other. Not too far away, in the military barracks along the same street, was another area set aside for religious use, here as a *mithraeum*. Both synagogue and church showed evidence of stages of remodeling. Both had begun as peristyle houses. The synagogue eventually acquired adjoining property and expanded to become large assembly space, adorned with the remarkable biblical scenes that can now be seen in the Archaeological Museum in Damascus.

The church did not expand in total size, but took down one wall between two rooms to make a larger assembly space, now rectangular in shape. On the other side of the courtyard, a baptistery was installed in one corner of a smaller room. Fragments of fresco indicate that the whole room was adorned with paintings (floor plans in Snyder 1985: 68–71 and White 1997: 125–27). This architectural adaptation of an already existing domestic structure represents the second stage of Christian assembly space and organization, usually called the *domus ecclesiae*. The architectural adaptation from private house to remodeled house, preserved with archaeological certainty at Dura Europa by the felicitous tragedy of invasion, can be presumed to have been in widespread practice.

Reading Christian Texts in Context

Both the archaeological evidence and our knowledge of social structures must be brought to bear on the interpretation of Christian texts. The problem that has overshadowed biblical and classical archaeology for more than a century to some degree also applies here: Does the text illustrate history or does history illustrate the text? Does one use the biblical account of the fall of Jericho to interpret the material remains or vice versa? Does reading Homer help in excavating Troy, or does an excavation of Troy illuminate readings of Homer? There are also such minimalist and maximalist positions in the interpretation of early Christianity.

With the exception of the *domus ecclesiae* at Dura Europa, there is no single structure before the fourth century that can be said with certainty to have been a center of Christian assembly. A maximalist can walk into one of the spacious houses of Pompeii or Herculaneum and imagine the meeting of a house church, while the minimalists will say that Christians never met in houses like these. Though there has been good work done in recent years on the social levels of Christians, we still know next to nothing about how social rankings in the systems of power, property, and prestige translated into specifics about housing. The square footage of Pompeiian houses has been catalogued and analyzed, but very little is known in most cases about the kinds of person who lived there, much less any correlation of those findings with what we know of Christians.[2]

Though the Gospels are set not in the Greco-Roman but in the rural Palestinian context, even here some of our knowledge of the material and social environment is helpful for interpretation. There has been intensive study in recent years of the archaeology, material culture, and social environment of Roman Galilee. The continuing excavations at Sepphoris have demonstrated the extension of Greco-Roman material culture into the cities. Discussion continues about dating and interpretation of important finds there such as the beautiful *triclinium* mosaic floor of the "villa" with its Dionysiac themes or the large residential quarter in which each house has what could either be interpreted as a bathhouse or a *mikveh*, the clarification of which would help determine how Jewish the city was at the time.

Details of gospel narratives are illumined by archaeological and social data. An example is the woman who enters where Jesus is at table to wash his feet with her tears and dry them with her hair (Lk 7.36–50). It can be presumed from everything we know about the desire to imitate elite customs that Galilean notables would live in as Romanized a manner as possible, or at least that Luke thinks they would. He envisions the Greco-Roman custom of reclining at table, whereby Jesus' feet would be easily accessible. The less clear element in the story is the question of how she got into the house uninvited. Here, awareness of the structure of houses with axial view to the dining room and the practice of keeping the front door open during important dinners tells us that she simply walked in. In view of the evidence that at least in important houses the front doors stood open during dinner, the question must be asked whether the meal was not eaten in potential public view (note the "outsider" who comes in during prayer and cannot make sense of it, I Cor 14.16).

The configuration of house church meetings is a topic about which a great deal is known, yet much is still unknown, and perhaps always will be. The frequent Pauline expression "the church (assembly, ἐκκλησία, *ekklesia*) that is in (someone's) house (*oikos*)" can be understood to mean inside the physical location of the building, within and among the persons who live there, or both simultaneously. We know the names of some of the people who hosted house churches in the Pauline years: the couple Prisca and Aquila (I Cor 16.19; Rom 16.3–5); Philemon, Apphia, and Archippos (Phlm 1); and Lydia (Acts 16.14–15, 40). The house of Mary mother of John Mark was a gathering place for the first believers in Jerusalem (Acts 12.12). To this list could be added Nympha (Col 4.15), and Tavia of Smyrna about fifty years later (Ign. *Smyrn.*13.2).

The patronage system upon which nonkinship relations were built is operative here. Those who hosted meetings of the Christian assembly regularly in their house became the patrons of the community. Clients were normally understood to be of lesser status than their patrons. Consequently, all members, at least free male members, were below their house church patron, who was the natural and expected leader of the congregation because of his or her status, both for celebration of the ritual meal and for other functions of the community, as in Paul's exhortation to submission to authority in I Thessalonians 5.12–13. A more explicit connection is I Corinthians 16.15–16, where Stephanas, head of the first *oikia* to convert in the area of Corinth, is the example of the leader who deserves submission from others.

The case of women who are leaders of house churches, Lydia, Nympha, and Mary mother of John Mark, deserves special consideration, as does that of Phoebe the deacon in Romans 16.1–2, whom Paul calls his patron (προστάτις or *prostatis*). There is as yet no thorough study on women and patronage, but there is ample evidence of the economic initiative and independence of women, from nonelites like Julia Felix to elites like Eumachia and Plancia Magna. Nor is it well understood how patronage functioned in the case of a founding figure like Paul. There are other examples of women heading households known from ancient literature, for example, the elites Ummidia Quadratilla (Pliny the Younger *Ep.* 7.24) and Matidia, great-aunt of Marcus Aurelius (Fronto 1.301; 2.94–97), but little is known of how they conducted the social life of their houses. Since Quadratilla planned her own dinner entertainment, she must have presided at table, something that would have been thought quite unusual. There are ample discussions of patriarchal household management in the Greco-Roman world. The relative silence about how women managed their own households, though there must have been many, may have occurred precisely because such activity was not the norm, so writers did not know how to deal with it.

When Christian groups met in peristyle houses of whatever modest dimensions, the host leaders and most distinguished guests or community members reclined in the *triclinium* while everyone else either reclined or sat on movable couches or tables and chairs, within hearing of those in the *triclinium*. Whether women reclined with men, sat next to them, or reclined or sat separately depended on local custom.

Other issues of cultural accommodation among Christian groups arise in different social contexts all having to do with dining customs. The dilemma of the believer and food offered to idols in I Corinthians 8 and 10 has three aspects. The first is accepting a dinner invitation at a rented dining room in a temple, where the meat no doubt comes from sacrifice and there will be a further sacrificial offering during the course of the meal (I Cor 8.10). The second is the general question of purchasing meat sold in the market, since much if not most of it was left over from temple sacrifices and wholesaled to the markets (I Cor 10.25). The third is accepting dinner invitations at the homes of unbelievers (I Cor 10.27). All three situations have to do with issues of purity and pollution, or understood another way, cultural accommodation, but in different social contexts all having to do with dining customs.

The problem of celebration of the Lord's Supper in I Cor 11.17–34 has to do with various social strata not respecting the needs and concerns of each other. Here the meal seems not to be supplied by the patron in whose house they meet, but by different people bringing food, after the model of a *thiasos* (θίασος or religious association meeting—I Cor 11.21–22, 33–34). However, the seating arrangement probably remains the same as that of the patronage model of hospitality, whereby the host leaders and most distinguished guests or community members reclined in the triclinium while everyone else either reclined or sat on movable couches or tables and chairs within hearing of those in the *triclinium*. It is likely that the seance of prayer, prophecy, and tongues described in I Corinthians 14 is the second part of the supper, following the model of the symposium with eating first and discussion or entertainment afterward, rather than a distinct meeting. I Corinthians 14.30 implies that most in attendance are sitting rather than reclining and that this is a rather freely structured session in which anyone can rise and speak. This arrangement necessitates that all present can hear what anyone in the group says, which may mean that many early Christian groups were quite small.

The early pattern of church organization was probably to keep each unit small enough to be able to meet together in one house or apartment house room. Some house churches must have consisted solely of the members of the household in which it met, especially if the entire household had been baptized, as were the households of Stephanas (I Cor 1.16; 16.15), Cornelius at Caesarea (Acts 10.2, 44–48), Lydia (Acts 16.14–15, 40), and the unnamed jailer at Philippi (Acts 16.31–33). Others had to be made up of members of various households, since there is ample evidence that individuals were accepted for baptism distinct from their family structure and independently from a *paterfamilias* (I Cor 7.13–16; I Pt 3.1). Thus a given house church assembly could be composed of the host household plus other women and men, married and unmarried, free and slave, probably with children from outside the household accompanying their parents. The total group was probably kept small enough that each assembly could attend to the needs of all its members. When it grew too large, another unit was formed in another house.

Sometime in the second century, the numbers began to outgrow this structure. Interior remodeling of houses began to take place to accommodate larger numbers in the *domus ecclesiae*, and it was probably at this time that the ritual became detached from an actual meal. The position of worshippers was now standing or sitting in a rectangular space facing a table behind which the presider and other leaders stood. There were precedents for both this architectural and social arrangement. Architecturally, the *oecus* or reception room in some houses had grown to be a major social space, sometimes even with an apse in imitation of the public basilica building. Though nothing of this is preserved in a surely Christian place of worship, some of these architecturally adapted worship spaces may also have contained apses. Thus it was no great leap a century and a half later when Christians began building public spaces in the shape of the basilica.

Some descriptions of early church worship of the second and third centuries are therefore to be located in the *domus ecclesiae*. Justin Martyr, writing from Rome in the middle of the second century, describes the baptism of new converts. They are first brought to a place where there is water, which could be a baptistery built into one of the rooms as at Dura Europa, and baptized in a ritual washing (*1 Apol.* I.61). Then they are led to the waiting assembly, across the peristyle into the assembly room, where prayers are raised for the newly baptized and other concerns. The prayers are followed by the ritual exchange of peace. Then the president of the assembly receives bread and a cup of wine mixed with water that are brought to him. When he has completed the thanksgiving prayer and all have answered "Amen," deacons distribute the bread and wine mixed with water to everyone present before taking a portion also to those who are absent (1.65). On the first day of the week (the day called "of the sun"), all who live either in the city or in the country come together for readings and instruction by the president. When the instruction is completed, all rise together for the prayers, after which bread, wine, and water are brought in for the Eucharist; a distribution is made by the deacons as previously described; and at the end a collection is taken up for the needy (1.67). All of this description of movement is more comprehensible in a *domus ecclesiae* than in the confines of a private house.

A more concrete description of Christian worship in a *domus ecclesiae* is that of the *Didascalia Apostolorum* from third-century Syria. The bishop (a term not used by Justin) is instructed how to arrange the assembly in good order, which is firmly patriarchal. The bishop is to be seated in the eastern part of the house and the presbyters seated with him (the Dura house church assembly hall is oriented southwest to northeast). After them are to be seated the men, and then the women of the congregation. When they rise to pray all must face east; the motive given is

Psalm 67(68): 34: God rides on the heavens to the east. One deacon stands by the table of offerings to assist, while another supervises those who enter by the door. Seating is strictly according to status and age: senior men and women sit apart from each other, while girls and women with children either sit apart or stand behind the women if there is no place to sit. The usher-deacon must see that everyone sits in the proper place. When there are visitors, the deacon inquires as to their status and seats them accordingly, considering along the way if perchance they belong to some heresy (but nothing is said about whether such a person is to be treated differently). Visiting presbyters are to be welcomed by the local presbyters, a visiting bishop seated with the bishop and invited to speak. If someone of social significance, man or woman, enters during the service, the bishop must continue speaking, and people in the congregation will receive him or her for seating. If they do not, the deacon must oust the youngest person in the suitable category to provide a free seat. But if a poor man or woman enters, the bishop must be sure that this person is honorably received, even—in rhetorical flourish—if the bishop has to sit on the ground (*Didascalia* 29–30; cf. Jas 2.1–4).

Here specific seating arrangements have been institutionalized, with clergy in front, followed by laymen and then women. The impression is given that some might be arriving from a distance and at various times during the service rather than all gathered at the beginning. Visitors from other churches may also apparently drop in without being known to the local leaders. The congregation and the space are large enough that separate seating arrangements are possible, yet small enough that one deacon can supervise. The seats are presumably movable and can be rearranged according to need. People sit during part of the service but rise for the offering of prayers, including the eucharistic prayer. Because seating is segregated, the exchange of peace is given within the various groups, especially men with men and women with women, as specified in some other texts.

The case of Paul of Samosata (from the late third century) is also illuminating. As bishop of Antioch in the 260s C.E., Paul headed one of the most powerful churches in the world. But he came under fire not only from the Antiochene intelligentsia but from bishops in many parts of the eastern Mediterranean, not only for his questionable Christology but also for his eccentric behavior. A formal written charge was made against him by the Christian presbyter Malchion, head of one of the rhetorical schools of Antioch. Based on his report, a group of bishops who had come to inspect the situation drafted a statement to the bishops of Rome and Alexandria, the other two leading churches. Among the charges against Paul was his love of worldly honor, so that he behaved not as a bishop should, but as a civil magistrate would. He received people at a *bema* or raised platform that he had constructed and in a private audience room as if he were a magistrate. He also, according to the charge, deflected liturgical singing from Christ to himself and was too free with the *subintroductae*, women living chastely with clerics, a practice that nearly always produced trouble. The synod of bishops declared Paul excommunicated and deposed from his bishopric. He, however, refused to relinquish the *oikos tês ekklesias* (οἰκος τῆς ἐκκλησίας or *domus ecclesiae*); the bishops appealed to the emperor Aurelian, who decided in favor of those in communion with the bishop of Rome and sent in imperial forces to oust him (Eusebius, *Hist. eccl.* 7.29.1–30.19).

Several elements of the story deserve comment in view of the question of Christian social and archaeological history. Bearing in mind that accounts of leaders made by their enemies are usually biased, still Paul seems to have thought of himself as some kind of mini-magistrate. In spite of the growing monarchical tendencies of bishops, his detractors found this to be too much to bear. The text does not say where Paul erected his *bema*. It could have been in the assembly hall itself. Wherever it was, clearly such a structure was an innovation at the time, considered inappropriate by other bishops. The property seems to have been entirely in Paul's hands, to do with as he pleased. Paul had a popular following among his assembly, and both his theology and his behavior were causing rifts in the community. The building he refused to move out of was literally the "house of the church," no doubt a domestic structure adapted for use as a church assembly, as at Dura Europa. His refusal to leave it means that he acted as proprietor of the property. This is the first recorded use of imperial power by one Christian group against another. Many would follow.

The move from house to building used exclusively for worship had social consequences, especially when that building came to be acquired by the church community in the person of its bishop, as seems to be the case by the time of Paul of Samosata. A significant aspect of personal patronage was eliminated as the meeting place of the assembly was no longer in the hands of individual members but of the church in the person of the bishop. Gradually all patronal authority became concentrated in the hands of the bishop, who controlled all assets, both the real property and money collected for distribution to the needy. With his deacon assistants as his direct representatives, he exercised primary patronage toward the whole community.

Yet one kind of personal patronage seems to have endured for a while: the hosting of a *cena dominica*, a "Lord's Supper" that was probably not a Eucharist in spite of Paul's designation of the eucharistic gathering by that term (1 Cor 11.20). Chapter 28 of Hippolytus's *Apostolic Tradition*, believed to date to the early third century and to represent traditions from Rome and perhaps from Egypt, depicts an invitation to dinner from a wealthy Christian patron, complete with *apoforeton* (ἀποφόρετον), a Greek term for a gift given at a banquet by a patron to his or her clients. If a bishop is present, he directs the conversation, or likewise a presbyter or deacon in the absence of a bishop. All receive the "blessed bread" from the presbyter or deacon. Catechumens may be present, and their bread is first exorcised—a sure sign that it is not the Eucharist. Another way to exercise patronage is by inviting widows to dinner; they must be of mature age and sent away before evening. If they cannot attend a meal at one's house, they are to be given food and wine and sent home (*Apostolic Tradition*, chapter 30).

We are still in the realm of private houses and invitations given by patrons to exercise clientage toward those of lesser social status and lesser economic means. Yet in the first instance, the presence of a bishop, presbyter, or deacon upstages the role of the patron to preside and therefore directs the conversation and sets the style for the dinner. The bishop becomes patron wherever he is. The social tension thus engendered eventually find its resolution in persons of higher status assuming the role of bishop (Bobertz 1993: 182) but also in the automatic elevation of the person selected as bishop to high status regardless of whether he originally possessed it or not.

Conclusion

Through careful examination of the material remains of Mediterranean antiquity, we can construct some ideas and impressions about the daily lives of early Christians. By careful comparison with texts, some of the empty spaces in our knowledge can be filled in. We are now in a position to see some of the patterns of the development of Christian forms and structures in the first few hundred years. Many questions still remain. Perhaps future new discoveries will help to answer them.

Notes

1. The ancient use of the word *insula* to refer to one of these apartment buildings should not be confused with the modern archaeological use of the word to mean a city block.

2. Attempts to demonstrate an actual Christian presence in Pompeii and Herculaneum through ambiguous inscriptions and one very questionable wall plaque have not been convincing and are not under consideration here, even though such presence is historically plausible.

An Illustration of Historical Inquiry: 5
Histories of Jesus and Matthew 1.1–25

RITVA H. WILLIAMS

Introduction

"TO WRITE HISTORY is to be engaged in endless argument" (Marius 1999: 5). Nowhere is this truer than in the contemporary study of Jesus. Was Jesus an eschatological prophet (Sanders 1993), a cynic-like teacher of wisdom (Crossan 1991), a shaman-like healer and exorcist (Davies 1995), or a radical politician seeking to win support for a new vision of the king-dom of God on earth (Wright 1999)? Was he born in Bethlehem, or perhaps in Nazareth? Are the stories of Jesus' birth recounted in the New Testament Gospels history remembered, history metaphorized, or prophecy historicized?[1] Are they a cover-up for a scandalous, illegitimate birth (see Schaberg 1990; Lüdemann 1998)? Perhaps they are simply fictions patterned after the birth narratives of Greco-Roman heroes, rulers, and philosophers.

For some, the seemingly endless arguments of historical Jesus scholars are a cause for embarrassment or for discrediting the entire historical enterprise. Some condemn historical scholarship as destructive of traditional understandings of Jesus and Christian origins. This response seems to grow out of a sense that there is only one "right" way to view these matters that must be accepted without ques-tion. Others deride historians for their inability to reach consensus and/or for producing hopelessly biased and subjective analyses. On occasion both of these objections are used in tandem to justify rejecting or ignoring the work of his-torical scholars. Here we see a legacy of ways of thinking rooted in the Enlight-enment that valorize value-free, neutral, and objective scientific approaches to knowledge and truth.[2]

The current state of affairs in historical studies of Jesus is not a cause for despair but a sign of such work's relevance and importance for our times. We investigate and analyze our pasts in order to understand who we are in the present. We want to know why we are who and what we have become. Through this process we become aware of alternative possibilities for the future. We research and study the life and teachings of Jesus because they are theologically and ethically important to us. For me as for many Christians, Jesus of Nazareth was and is the Word/Wisdom of God made flesh. Historical study is one way (among others) to gain a deeper understanding of the character and expectations of the God whom Jesus reveals. It can be a way to do theology. From an ethical standpoint, a perspective that sees Jesus as an oppressed Jew living in a Roman-dominated Jewish homeland stands as a corrective to Christianity's anti-Semitic tendencies. As a first-century Jewish person, the historical Jesus is not one of us and so calls us to account for trying to co-opt him to our own ends. Historical Jesus studies can, additionally, serve as a case study within or a microcosm of a larger historical enterprise that encourages not only critical reasoning, but also empathy for and tolerance of diversity and plurality, virtues much needed in religious and public life. I teach historical Jesus studies in a church-related liberal arts college for these reasons.

The Historical Enterprise

"The *reality* of the past is the written report rather than the *past as it actually was*" (Munslow 1997: 2). What this means is that in common everyday usage "history" refers to events that occurred in the past, but what we actually know about the past is limited to history, to stories that are told about those events. History as an account of the past does not correspond exactly to the circumstances that it describes. The main reasons for this have to do with the nature of the evidence and the interpretative process. Such bits and pieces of the past—archaeological remains, artwork, official documents, personal writings, and so forth—as survive into the present make up the primary sources that are the basis of all historical research. Even for the most recent happenings the extant evidence is always incomplete, fragmentary, and representative of the personal interests and concerns of the individuals who produced and preserved it. These primary sources do not "speak for themselves"; they must be evaluated, interpreted, and explained by the researcher.

The interpretive narratives produced by historians constitute secondary sources for the study of the past. Each one of these histories "is as much the product of the historian who wrote it as of the people who actually lived the events it attempts to describe" (Furay and Salevouris 1988: 4). This element of subjectivity can lead to unwarranted skepticism about, and even disdain for, the results of historical scholarship. History, like all other academic disciplines including science, indeed all discourse and analysis, is conditioned by cultural and personal frames of reference. A historian's subjectivity is exercised in her interactive relationship with the evidence,[3] in which each modifies and challenges the other. The resulting history is not merely one scholar's private, personal opinion but part of the public discourse of the academic community.[4] The historian's conclusions are subject to testing by his colleagues, and to a lesser extent by the educated general public. Histories are judged by their appeals to the extant evidence and their coherence, plausibility, and persuasiveness.

Our ability to develop coherent, plausible explanations and interpretations of primary sources from the past, as well as to evaluate effectively the secondary sources produced by scholars, depends on our ability to develop a critical "historical-mindedness" (Furay and Salevouris 1988: 16). Most importantly, this means developing sensitivity to how the past differs from the present. Researching the past is often compared to spending time in a foreign country where one cannot function comfortably without learning the local language, customs, values, and laws. The historian must learn to empathize, that is, to think with and think like the subjects that he or she is studying.[5] This requires the ability to set aside personal beliefs and sociocultural circumstances temporarily, including on occasion our knowledge of how things turned out (see Frederiksen 1999: 34–41). Failure to do so can lead to anachronistic and ethnocentric misinterpretations of primary source data.

Other aspects of critical historical-mindedness include an awareness of continuity and change in human institutions and affairs, of the existence and validity of multiple perspectives in any given situation along with the alternative interpretations that can arise from these, and of all written history as imprecise and tentative. Histories need to be rewritten. Evidence can be overlooked or misinterpreted, or new evidence comes to light, necessitating a reassessment of previous histories. A particular set of data can be viewed from different perspectives, yielding alternative explanations that often are not mutually exclusive. A historical interpretation may lose its relevance as the interests and preoccupations of society change. New circumstances need to be explained in terms of continuity or discontinuity with the past. This is why writing history involves engaging in dialogue and argument without end.

The following discussion of Matthew 1.1–25 is an illustration of how I, as a historian, read this text. My goal is to understand Matthew's narrative in its originating social, cultural, and historical context while at the same time assessing its content for historical information about Jesus and his origins. Before turning to that task it is necessary to say something about the challenges that Matthew's Gospel presents when treated as a source for historical information.

Matthew as Historical Source

Historical Jesus studies are particularly challenging due to the scarcity of primary sources and the nature of the evidence that we do have. An investigation into the circumstances surrounding the birth of Jesus, for instance, immediately runs into the fact that we have no documentary data from the lifetime of Jesus himself concerning this or any other aspect of his life. Our primary sources for the birth of Jesus are the Gospels of Matthew and Luke. I like to work with Matthew's account because it is less familiar to students whose knowledge of Jesus' origins generally derives from the conflated version celebrated at Christmas. Most are unaware that the "Christmas story" contains elements drawn from two different narratives.

The Gospel According to Matthew is generally believed to be the work of an anonymous Greek-speaking Jewish Christian scribe writing about the year 85 C.E. for a Greek-speaking Jewish Christian audience located in northern Galilee or Syria. Analysis of its form, content, and function indicates that it (along with the other New Testament Gospels) is "a distinctive type of ancient biography combining . . . Hellenistic form and function with Jewish content" (Aune 1987: 22). In keeping with Greco-Roman literary and cultural conventions, the evangelist focused almost exclusively on the public life of Jesus, who he presented as a stylized "type" acting out recognized, and stereotypical, social roles such as prophet, teacher, healer, and so forth (Aune 1987: 28, 56–57). Matthew's story of Jesus is "Christian literary propaganda" intended to reinforce the faith of believers and/or to awaken faith in unbelieving members of Christian households. Jesus personifies and legitimates the Christian beliefs and values of the author (Aune 1987: 59–63; Ehrman 2000: 55–59). This does not deny a priori the historicity of events recorded in the gospel, but it does call for a critical assessment of each one and an awareness of its rhetorical function in the gospel as a whole.

Like other ancient biographers, Matthew relied on previous sources, incorporating both written and oral—what we would call hearsay—information into his portrait of Jesus. Only one of Matthew's sources has survived into the present, the Gospel According to Mark (70 C.E.), 90 percent of which was incorporated into "Matthew's" composition. Matthew seems to have had access to a collection of sayings of Jesus (the reconstructed Q document or something like it) that probably predated Mark, as well as an assortment of materials of unknown origin and date, designated as M. Finally, Matthew drew on themes found in the Jewish Scriptures to shape his sources into a coherent narrative reflecting his personal perspectives and concerns.

What all this means from a historical perspective is that we are dealing here with a source that is highly complex. Matthew's Gospel is much more like a secondary source, a narrative about Jesus written many years after the fact and based largely on primary sources that have not survived into the present. Without access to that truly primary data it is almost impossible to corroborate the information that is contained in Matthew's Gospel. Cultural values and perspectives quite different from those of most modern historical Jesus scholars have shaped his composition. The Gospel of Matthew is deeply biased in favor of Jesus and the Christian beliefs and values that Jesus epitomizes in them. This text is likely to tell us as much about the gospel writer and his concerns as about Jesus.

We are faced, then, with the problem of retrieving historical data from Matthew's narrative. How to go about such a task? Most scholars work under the assumption that earlier sources are likely to be more historically reliable than later ones. Hence, primary consideration is given to determining the date of a text and its origin in a particular source. Matthew 1.1–25 is part of the M materials that we are unable to locate in terms of date or derivation. Some scholars regard it as a late tradition dating from the time of the writing of the gospel (85 C.E.) and therefore by definition historically suspect.[6] Others argue that the common material in Matthew and Luke's birth narratives points to an earlier common tradition that predates both the M and uniquely Lukan (L) sources on which they are based (Brown 1993: 34; Meier 1991: 214). While issues of date and source are useful beginning points, they are not conclusive.

The content of a gospel text can also be assessed on the basis of certain other criteria. Information that is attested in multiple independent sources is usually accepted as historically accurate, particularly if one of the sources is considered to be early. Material that is likely to have caused embarrassment or discomfort to the early Christian movement may be judged historically reliable, since early Christians would seem to have little motive to make up such things. A similar assumption applies to material that is dissimilar to the gospel writer's theological agenda. The criterion of dissimilarity should not be used to exclude material just because it is similar to the developing Christian tradition. Some continuity between Palestinian Judaism, Jesus' teachings and practices, and the practices of his followers is to be expected. Information about Jesus should be contextually credible and free of anachronisms. Material presented in terms that are memorable is deemed more likely to accurately reflect the oral culture in which Jesus lived. Historically accurate information is likely to help explain developments in the Jesus traditions. The criterion of coherence allows scholars to include as authentic poorly attested material if it shares a common content or form with well-attested texts. Scholars use these criteria in order to ascertain what might be reasonably considered factual about Jesus (Powell 1998: 46–50).

Like other scholars I use these criteria, in particular the criteria of contextual credibility, multiple attestation, and embarrassment, to illustrate how scholars assess the historicity of information contained in Matthew's birth narrative, although my own particular interest goes beyond simply gathering facts about Jesus. I am especially concerned with exploring and developing contextually credible readings of gospel stories. Given Matthew's context—late first-century

Hellenized Jewish Christian—was he really arguing for a virginal conception, as is commonly assumed? Or to put it another way, would an assertion of a virginal conception have been contextually credible in a Greek-speaking Jewish Christian community in 85 C.E.? How likely is it that such a story might have originated among the members of Jesus' Jewish family or his first followers (i.e., the possible originators of the M source)? What were M and/or Matthew trying to tell their audiences about Jesus? Were M and Matthew saying the same thing? Why? What circumstances in the life of Jesus and/or the early church would account for the way M and later Matthew tells the story of Jesus' birth?

The Genealogy—Matthew 1.1–17

Matthew's genealogy presents Jesus' family tree in three sets of fourteen ancestors, Abraham to David; David to Jechoniah, who was deported to Babylon; and finally Jechoniah to Joseph, the husband of Jesus' mother Mary. All of the names in the first two divisions may be found in existing biblical genealogies (e.g., Ruth 4.18–22; I Chr 1–3). Nine names in the third set are completely unknown and uncorroborated.[7] The organizational pattern is Matthew's and indicates that this genealogy is "artificial rather than strictly historical" (Brown 1993: 74). Genealogies in the ancient world were rarely constructed primarily to record biological descent; rather their main purpose was to establish claims to social status, rank, or a particular office, such as priest or king (Malina and Rohrbaugh 1992; Brown 1993: 65). This was important in the ancient world where a person's social worth and identity (honor) were rooted in ethnic affiliation, clan/tribe, ancestors, and family (Neyrey 1998: 91). Matthew's genealogy connected Jesus with the founding fathers of Israel (Abraham, Isaac, and Jacob), its most noble tribe (Judah), and its most prominent family (the house of David—Neyrey 1998: 98).

The purpose of the genealogy, then, was to assert that Jesus was born into and deserved a most exalted and honorable status. Is there any evidence that such a claim was historically warranted, or was it simply prompted by Matthew's desire to glorify Jesus? Luke also linked Jesus to the house of David through Joseph (1.27, 32; 2.4; 3.23–38). This information comes from Luke's special source L, which like M is of unknown date and derivation. There are assertions of a Davidic connection in early Christian texts that predate both Matthew and Luke. Mark, writing about 70 C.E., reports that during his lifetime Jesus was hailed as the "son of David" by those seeking his help (10.46–52//Mt 9.27–31, 20.29–34//Lk 18.35–43).[8] Paul, writing about 58 C.E. to the church at Rome, refers to Jesus as having been "descended from David according to the flesh" (1.3). At first glance, we seem to have four independent sources here, two early (Paul and Mark) and two of unknown date (M, L). It is possible that Matthew and Luke picked up the Davidic connection from Mark and inserted it into their special sources, in which case we would have only double attestation.

At any rate, our two earliest sources do affirm a Davidic link of some sort. Paul, reciting received tradition, asserts that Jesus was a descendant of David. In Mark "son of David" may be a messianic title. We are left wondering about the relationship of these two ideas. Did those who hailed Jesus as the Messiah assume a Davidic lineage? Or was Jesus' connection to the house of David one of the reasons for his ascribed messianic status? Due to the paucity of our sources we may never know. What we can conclude is that Jesus was linked in some way to the house of David perhaps during his lifetime, and certainly was regarded as a descendant of David in some early Christian circles.[9] Matthew probably constructed his genealogy in order to support that tradition as one of the bases of Jesus' claim to honor and status.

The most curious feature of Matthew's genealogy is the inclusion of four women, who represent an intrusion into an otherwise entirely patrilineal genealogy.[10] Their stories seem to call into question Jesus' honorable origins. Tamar was a childless young widow, who, disguised as a prostitute, had intercourse with her father-in-law Judah (Mt 1.3; Gn 38). Rahab was a prostitute in Jericho who negotiated with Israelite spies to save her family (Mt 1.5; Jos 2.1–21). Ruth, another childless young widow, sexually compromised Boaz, the head of her deceased husband's clan (Mt 1.5; Ruth 2–4). The wife of Uriah (Bathsheba) was an adulteress whose unexpected pregnancy led to her husband's murder by her lover, King David (Mt 1.6; 2 Sm 11–12).

Each of these women lacked sexual exclusivity, the basis of a woman's honorable status in the ancient world. Each woman's reputation was restored when a man acknowledged his guilt in his relationship with her (Judah, David) or accepted responsibility for her (Joshua, Boaz). Each became a wife and the mother of a son (or sons), thus assuring her a place of honor within society. By naming these four women, Matthew inserted (and/or acknowledged) into the family tree of Jesus a history of closely averted scandal arising from women's socially risky sexual behavior. How could such women enrich the illustrious status Matthew seems to claim for Jesus?

Neyrey has recently shown that according to the rules of Greco-Roman rhetoric these four women could contribute to Jesus' honor in one of two ways. An ancient storyteller, hearer, or reader might have compared them to the dishonorable kings named in the genealogy (Abijah, Joram, Uzziah, Ahaz, and Manasseh). Both groups could be ennobled by Jesus' excellence, a possibility "encoded in Jesus' very name as the one who would 'save his people from their sins,' past as well as present" (Neyrey 1998: 99). An alternative understanding for Matthew and his audience might have arisen from Jewish midrashic and postbiblical traditions about these women in which they were depicted as being rescued from shame by divine intervention. From an early Christian perspective, the four women attest to the divine favor and patronage enjoyed by Jesus' ancestors, and hence by Jesus himself (Neyrey 1998: 98–99).[11] This second option seems preferable, since such a reading would prepare the reader for the story that follows of Joseph's dilemma in the face of his betrothed's premarital pregnancy.

Matthew concludes the genealogy with "Jacob the father of Joseph the husband of Mary, of whom Jesus was born" (1.16). Malina and Rohrbaugh indicate that "For purposes of historical reconstruction, only the last three generations in genealogies from oral societies are likely to be accurate" (1992: 25). If this is correct, we might expect that here we have some fairly solid historical data. Jesus' mother's name is given as Mary in both Matthew's and Luke's birth narratives (M, L sources), in Mark (6.3//Mt 13.55), and in Acts (1.14). The last is not an independent witness since it is a sequel to the Gospel of Luke, written by the same author. We therefore have one or three witnesses to the name of Jesus' mother, depending on how one construes the relationship between Mark, Matthew, and Luke at this point, and how faithfully one thinks their authors replicated their sources.

Joseph is named as Mary's husband in both New Testament birth narratives (Mt 1.16, 18–25; Lk 1.27, 2.5). This would give us M and L as independent sources. Jesus is called the "son of Joseph" (with a disclaimer) in Luke 3.23, again part of the L source. The same title is bestowed on Jesus by one of his disciples, this time without a disclaimer in John 1.45, perhaps pointing to the Jewish Christian belief that he was Joseph's son. "Son of Joseph" also occurs in Luke 4.22 and in John 6.42. These may be independent revisions of the statement in Mark 6.3 claiming that Jesus is the "son of Mary." Joseph is not mentioned at all in Mark, although we could argue that his existence is presupposed by the early and well-attested tradition of Jesus' siblings.[12] Although we lack an early witness to the name of Joseph, it does occur independently in M, L, and John.

Matthew's designation of Jacob as the father of Joseph is problematic. Luke's version of Jesus' family tree identifies Heli as the father of Joseph (Lk 3.23). The issue is further complicated by Matthew's characterization of Mary's husband, Joseph son of Jacob, as a man who regularly received revelations in dreams and went to Egypt to save a special child from an evil king. The story line parallels the biblical story of Joseph son of Jacob (Gn 37, 39–50), who interpreted dreams and went down to Egypt (Gn 37, 39–50). There he and his descendants settled until a king "who did not know Joseph" plotted to kill all the Hebrew baby boys, and so set in motion the story of Moses (Ex 1.8ff). Given the widely attested, albeit relatively late, traditions connecting Jesus and/or his mother to a man named Joseph, I do not think that Matthew made up the name based on the earlier biblical story. As Brown has argued, "the parallelism between the two Josephs depends on the similarity of name and is made possible by the lack of historical knowledge about the career of the NT Joseph" (Brown 1993: 112). At any rate, the designation of Joseph's father as Jacob seems unlikely.

Matthew's genealogy is not a historically accurate record of Jesus' ancestors. That Jesus was the son of Mary, who was married to a man named Joseph, is undisputed. Jesus' connection with the house of David may also date to his own lifetime. Unfortunately, the scarcity of evidence makes it impossible to determine the basis for that link. Matthew's genealogy is his attempt to support that tradition, and so demonstrate Jesus' noble status within Jewish society.

Jesus' Birth—Matthew 1.18–25

The story of Jesus' birth as told in Matthew 1:18–25 is often dismissed as a literary creation containing little or no historically factual information. Matthew's narrative contains parallels with popular first-century Jewish expansions of the birth of Moses. In the version recounted by Josephus, for example, Moses' father receives divine assurance in a dream that his soon-to-be-born son will escape the murderous intentions of Pharaoh and will grow up to deliver his people from their bondage in Egypt (*Ant.* 2.9, 212, 215–6).[13] The obvious parallels are that the fathers have dreams and the unborn children will grow up to be liberators of their people, but the situations are markedly different. In Matthew 1.18–25, no evil king threatens Jesus' existence; rather Mary's untimely pregnancy threatens Joseph's righteousness and honor. It is the differences, rather than the similarities, that carry the weight of Matthew's message.

Matthew writes that Mary was betrothed but not yet living together with her husband when it was discovered that she was pregnant (1.18). Luke similarly indicates that not only the conception but the actual birth of Jesus occurred while Mary and Joseph were still betrothed (Lk 1.27, 2.5). Although this situation does not seem to constitute a problem for Luke, in Matthew's account Joseph planned to "dismiss her" (i.e., divorce her) because of the pregnancy. This response is the clearest indication that Joseph was not responsible for his fiancée's condition. Luke also indicates that Joseph was not the biological father of Jesus (1.26–38). The tradition that Mary's pregnancy was untimely and that her betrothed was not responsible may also be supported by the early tradition found in Mark 6.3 that people in Nazareth called him "son of Mary," and the independent tradition alleging illegitimacy in John 8.41 (more about these texts below).

Matthew's narrative reflects first-century Jewish marriage customs and values. Jewish families arranged marriages for their daughters in two stages. The father betrothed his daughter, at puberty, to her future husband. This involved an agreement, usually a written contract, legally transferring guardianship from the father to the future husband. For this reason, a formal divorce was required to break the betrothal. The actual marriage, or home-taking, followed at least a year later at which time the bride took up residence in the groom's home (Safrai 1976). Sexual relations during the interim period were fiercely discouraged in some regions, perhaps tolerated if not approved in others (Schaberg 1990: 43–44). Loss of virginity prior to the wedding was not only a source of shame, but could have serious repercussions for the woman (cf. Dt 22.13–21). Sexual intercourse with a betrothed woman was treated like adultery; both parties were to be stoned to death (Dt 22.23–24). An exception was made if it could be determined that the betrothed woman had been raped. If she cried out for help when accosted in town, or if the incident occurred in the open country where there was no one to help her, the woman was not to be punished (Dt 22.23–27). Some postbiblical Jewish texts advocate that such a woman be divorced by her fiancé (Schaberg 1990: 48).

Let us think through the logic of Matthew's narrative with the above first-century assumptions in mind. Joseph wished to spare Mary from public disgrace by divorcing her quietly. The divorce would certainly indicate to observers that he found something objectionable about his betrothed. Mary's pregnancy would make it clear to people what the problem was. In the absence of a charge of adultery, the community would probably come to the conclusion that Mary had been raped. Joseph's planned action therefore suggests that he thought Mary had been raped, and/or was willing to let people think that was the case. As a rape victim she might be the subject of "pity and fellow-feeling" (Philo, *Spec.* 3.76), rather than an object of public disgrace. Of course in Matthew's story, Mary is saved from such a shameful situation by divine intervention. Yet, we cannot help wonder why the story of Jesus begins with this socially precarious situation that is only resolved by an angelic vision. Is this simply dramatic storytelling designed to highlight the virginal conception of Jesus, or can we detect a historical remembrance here?

Mark records an incident in which citizens of Nazareth offended by Jesus' teaching in the synagogue identify him as "the son of Mary" (6.3).[14] In the context of that incident, the epitaph was clearly intended to put Jesus in his place, but what precisely did it signify? One suggestion is that the Nazarene crowd was simply highlighting Jesus' ordinariness; Mary is named because she was present in the synagogue at the time of the controversy. It meant nothing more ominous than "Why, he's only Mary's son!" (Meier 1991: 227). Others argue that the villagers called Jesus "son of Mary" because Joseph was long dead (Brown 1993: 519, 540). The difficulty with these readings is that their proponents would have us believe that the residents of Nazareth were offended by Jesus' prophetic pretensions because he was just an ordinary fellow like them, or because his mother was a widow. But why then did Matthew change Mark's "Is this not the carpenter, the son of Mary" to "Is this not the carpenter's son? Is not his mother's name Mary?" Luke (4.22) and John (6.42) appear to have gone one step further and have Jesus' critics name him as "the son of Joseph." These revisions to the Markan text suggest that the "son of Mary" was not only a putdown, but a potentially embarrassing or scandalous way of naming Jesus.

In the first century people were normally identified by their father's name.[15] The epitaph "son of Mary" probably does not point to an absent, because dead, father, but could indicate an *unknown* father. Understood within the social and cultural norms of a patrilineal society, the epitaph was a slur on Jesus' paternity (Schaberg 1990: 160). This reading of the text is supported by the Jewish legal principle that "a man is illegitimate when he is called by his mother's name" (Schaberg 1990: 161). It has been argued that since this principle was not articulated in this way until much later, we cannot be sure that it applied to Jesus' first-century context (Brown 1993: 540). This would be a valid objection if it could be shown that this legal principle indicated a change, rather than a codification of custom, in the way individuals were named in Jewish society. It appears to have been the norm throughout Jewish history, as evident in the Hebrew Bible, to identify individuals as the offspring of their fathers.[16] Samaritan and Mandaean texts also support the reading of "son of Mary" as pointing to illegitimacy. These texts are admittedly considerably later than the Gospels, but do show that the ancient peoples could and did interpret "son of Mary" this way. The thesis of Jesus' illegitimacy is not simply a peculiar modern reading of the evidence.

Mark 6.3 could therefore provide evidence that in his hometown during his lifetime suspicions were raised about Jesus' legitimacy. The villagers may have been offended by Jesus' prophetic claims because they regarded him as Mary's premaritally conceived, and therefore illegitimate, child. Alternatively, Mark 6.3 could indicate that the evangelist was aware of such allegations circulating among Jews who disparaged early Christian claims about Jesus' status. Independent support for charges of illegitimacy among first-century opponents of Jesus and his followers may be found in John 8.41. Here Jesus is portrayed as being engaged in an increasingly hostile debate with "the Jews." When Jesus asserts that their intention to kill him calls into question their status as Abraham's children, they reply, "We are not illegitimate children" (Jn 8.39–41). The emphatic "we" could imply that Jesus is. Even if the incident as reported does not go back to the lifetime of Jesus, it does suggest that the evangelist was aware of such charges and innuendoes circulating in the Jewish community.

Both early (Mark) and later (John) sources support the contention that suspicions and/or allegations of Jesus' illegitimacy circulated in the first century and may even go back to the lifetime of Jesus. The later revisions of Mark 6.3 are clear indications that the gospel writers sought to suppress or correct this potentially scandalous information. These charges may been particularly nasty examples of first-century ad hominem polemics. Yet they seem to have had some basis in the memory of a premarital pregnancy that is doubly attested (M, L) and that the gospel writers seek to legitimate. This is precisely the sort of historical data that would be embarrassing to the early church and that from the second century onward gave rise to the widespread tradition of Jesus' illegitimacy, which was spread by opponents of emerging Christian movements. The most (in)famous of these is the "ben Panthera" tradition recorded by Celsus (Origen, *Cels.* 1.28–39) and in several rabbinic passages (e.g., *b.Shabb.* 104; *t.Hul.* 2.22).

It is the historical memory of a premarital pregnancy and its possible meaning that Matthew acknowledges and seeks to explain in his birth narrative. In Matthew's narrative, Joseph's dilemma is resolved when an angel appears to him in a dream. At this point a modern reader might decide that what follows cannot be historical. Such a judgment would be premature. Dreams and visions are common human experiences. Ordinary people in the first century, many persons today, and countless individuals in the centuries in between have believed (and continue to believe) that God communicates with humanity through such occurrences. What is at stake here are two distinct, though related issues: an event and the interpretation of that event. There are many whose lives have been changed dramatically as a consequence of visionary episodes. Historians need not, indeed they should not, deny the fact that people have dreams and visions. What is problematic for historical study is the impossibility of objectively verifying the content of such experience. What the historian can do, however, is ask, given an event interpreted as a vision, what that experience might have meant to the recipient.

In Matthew's birth narrative, the angel told Joseph that the child Mary was carrying was "from a spirit that is holy" (Mt 1.20). What would a first-century Jewish person conclude upon hearing that the child conceived in a woman's womb was "from a spirit that is holy?" Bow's assessment of birth stories in the Hebrew Bible and in extrabiblical Jewish texts indicates that the possibility of divine–human sexual unions in Jewish stories was generally denied. Although God was thought to exercise power over human reproduction, that power was not a substitute for normal sexual relations between a man and a woman. In a few instances spiritual or demonic beings were said to have mated with human women, but such activity was viewed quite negatively, even with horror. The offspring of such unions were regarded as unnatural, turning out to be models of depravity (the giants in *1 En.* 6–11), criminality (Cain in rabbinic literature), or bizarre oddities (Melchizedek in *2 En.*; see Bow 1995: 310–26, 434).

If Mary's Jewish fiancé had received a message such as that delivered by the angel, it is highly unlikely that he would have understood it to mean that Mary conceived without having sexual intercourse with a human male. Such a child would have been "unholy" from a Jewish perspective. For Joseph, the angel's message would probably have meant that *regardless of the circumstances* surrounding the conception of this child, he "represents the will of God" (Horton 1987: 186). It would not negate suspicions that a seduction or rape had occurred. In fact, the angel's message did not address Mary's situation at all. The child she was carrying, and his future role as savior of his people, was the main focus of that message. What is being proposed is that God's plan of salvation was worked out in and through the actions of human beings, even seemingly shameful and scandalous actions.[17] Joseph responded to the angel's command to take Mary as his wife not because he had been assured of her chastity, but to promote the interests of his people, whose salvation depended upon this child (Horton 1987: 188). Joseph completed his marriage to Mary, but refrained from having sexual relations with her until the child was born, and he named him Jesus. In naming the child, Joseph accepted Mary's son into his household and assumed the role of father to him. If this story formed part of a pre-Matthean tradition about Jesus' birth[18] and if it originated among Jesus' family or first followers, these people would also have interpreted it as conveying that Jesus was holy regardless of the circumstances surrounding his conception and birth. But would it have meant the same thing to our gospel writer? Our answer will depend on how Jewish and/or how Hellenized we think Matthew was.

People from a Greco-Roman background were raised on narratives (mythological and biographical) in which gods or divine spirits caused women to conceive either directly through sexual contact or indirectly in a nonsexual manner.[19] Claims of divine parentage were put forward on the behalf of heroes (e.g., Herakles), rulers (e.g., Alexander the Great, Augustus), and philosophers (e.g., Plato). Whether Greco-Roman audiences understood such assertions literally is unclear. Plutarch denied that gods literally mated with human women but does seem to allow for the possibility of nonsexual divine generation.[20] Another possibility is that stories of divine conceptions were understood as indicating dual paternity. In other words, divine fathering need not negate the possibility of a normal human conception (see Gordon 1977).

Had Matthew been a Greco-Roman writer confronted by a narrative tradition in which an angel claimed that an unborn child came from a spirit that is holy, he likely would have read it one of two ways. One possibility would be that the child had no human father but was divinely generated, in this case without sexual contact between the spirit and the human mother. This is in fact how many early gentile Christians read and understood Matthew's birth narrative. It remains the dominant reading to this day. Alternatively, a Greco-Roman might have thought the angel's message implied that the child was conceived in the normal fashion, but some divine power was at work in the child's conception and life. This view is somewhat similar to the Jewish understanding explicated above, except for the attribution of dual paternity. That some gentile Christians thought this way about Jesus might be suggested by a passage in the *Gospel of Philip*. In his argument against Jesus' conception by the Holy Spirit the author asserted that "the Lord would not have said, 'My Father who is in Heaven,' unless he had had another father."[21] Here were Christians who interpreted the words of the Lord's Prayer to mean that Jesus had both an earthly and a heavenly father, and who denied conception by the Holy Spirit.

The question remains, would Matthew have understood the angel's message to imply either dual paternity or divine generation? If Matthew was indeed a Jewish-Christian scribe, our answer would have to be "probably not." But the situation is more complicated than that; Matthew, we have presupposed, was a Greek-speaking Jewish Christian. How much and in what ways would his Hellenistic education have influenced his understanding of his pre-gospel sources and/or his creative editing of those materials? Paul and Philo of Alexandria, two other first-century Greek-educated Jewish writers, might provide useful analogies. Paul does refer to Isaac as the "child who was born according to the Spirit" in contrast with Ishmael, the "child who was born according to the flesh" (Gal 4.29). This is within the context of an allegorical interpretation of Genesis that in no way negates the human paternity of Isaac or any of the other patriarchs (Rom 9.8–10). In his allegorical interpretation of the stories of the patriarchs Philo seems to assert that their mothers were virgins impregnated by God. Philo's point, however, is not that Isaac, Reuben, Jacob, Esau, and Gershom were the results of virgin conceptions, but that the virtues, the most "divine" aspect of humanity, are generated by God within the human soul.[22]

What we see in the writing of Paul and of Philo is that these Hellenistic Jewish writers used the language of divine generation allegorically, not literally. Their example suggests that Matthew likewise would probably not have understood the angel's message in a Greco-Roman fashion as implying a literal conception by a spirit, or even dual paternity. Matthew's Jewish Christian reading of the angelic message is more likely to have been symbolic, not literal. That an angel declared Mary's unborn child to be from a spirit that is holy would be a sign of God's favor. Jesus was chosen by the deity to save God's people; the circumstances surrounding his premarital conception were irrelevant in light of divine election. What counted for Matthew was that Joseph accepted Mary's son into his household and into the royal line of David. The purpose of Matthew's birth narrative is to explain how Jesus came to be a member of the house of David, the point made in the genealogy.

At this point the reader might object that something important has been left out. Where does the prophecy from Isaiah that a virgin would conceive fit into all this? Some have argued that this passage actually gave rise to the birth narratives in the Gospels. The idea seems to be that some early Christian, having decided that Jesus was the Son of God, searched the Scriptures until he found a text that could be interpreted as prophesying a miraculous birth and proceeded to create a narrative by elaborating on that text (Crossan 1995: 18). An alternative hypothesis arises when one notes that the recitation of Isaiah 7.14 is intrusive and awkward. The story is quite coherent without it, and as Brown has noted "even flows more smoothly" (1993: 100). This is true of four of the five citations of scripture in Matthew's birth narrative,[23] and suggests that these citations may have been added to an already existing pre-Matthean narrative. We might ask, for what purpose?

Neyrey has shown that the scriptural citations associated with place-names function to legitimate reversals of status. Bethlehem was a satellite village dependent upon Jerusalem.[24] It was a small and insignificant place that had no claim to fame aside from the memory that long ago King David had been born and raised there (1 Sm 17.12, 15) and an ancient prophecy that it would be the birthplace of a future king (Mi 5.2). Similarly, Nazareth, where Jesus' grew up, was a satellite village of Sepphoris in Galilee. Its first-century honor rating may be discerned in Nathanael's query, "Can anything good come out of Nazareth?" (Jn 1.46), yet Matthew tried to redeem this lowly place with a bit of midrashic exegesis. He connected the place-name, Nazareth, with the concept of the *nazir*, a holy one dedicated to God (Is 4.3; Jgs 3.5–7), or to the notion of the *netzer* or branch of David's line (Is 11.1; Zec 3.8, 6.12). Neyrey argues that the point Matthew was trying to make with these citations was that Jesus deserved respect and honor because he overcame the disadvantages of being born in an lowly village and raised in a cultural backwater (Neyrey 1998: 96–97). The citations are arguments from higher authority intended to counter the first-century evaluation of places associated with Jesus' life.

A similar status reversal may be effected by the citation of Isaiah 7.14. Jesus was the product of a premarital pregnancy for which Joseph, his mother's fiancé, was not responsible. A more ignominious origin for the savior of Israel could hardly be imagined. The angel's message assured Joseph that despite these circumstances Mary's unborn child was holy. Not content to rely on this personal revelation, Matthew added the biblical citation to legitimate this unlikely situation. Holy Scripture, the evangelist asserts, actually predicted that a "virgin" would give birth to a child who would be a sign of the divine presence with God's people.

There was nothing about this text in its Isaianic context that suggested a miraculous or virginal conception. The oracle about the impending birth of a child called "Immanuel" was originally the second of three addressed to King Ahaz during the Syro-Ephraimite War (735–732 B.C.E.). The birth of this child was intended to be a sign of divine protection for the city of Jerusalem. The Hebrew text referred to an *almah*, a young woman of marriageable age, giving birth. Although the Septuagint (Matthew's source) used the Greek word *parthenos* (virgin), it was probably understood in the same sense (Meier 1991: 222). Nothing in the Jewish tradition would have prepared a Jewish Christian writer or audience to see in this text the miraculous divine generation of their Messiah. In Matthew's context, Isaiah 7.14 functioned as an argument from higher authority to legitimate the overturning of normal status requirements.[25]

Mary's premarital pregnancy is a matter of historical remembrance and not dramatic storytelling. It may have given rise to suspicions and allegations of illegitimacy during Jesus' lifetime and to similar charges from the opponents of the early church (Mk 6.3, 8.41). Mary's socially risky pregnancy also gave rise to two very different legitimating narratives. Luke's gentile Christian gospel claimed a virginal conception and divine paternity for Jesus. Matthew's Jewish Christian narrative claimed for Jesus a Davidic lineage and explained how that came about. Joseph, a member of the house of David, accepted Jesus as his son. In doing so Matthew argued that Mary's shameful pregnancy and the child's unknown biological origins were not definitive factors for determining Jesus' status. Matthew supported his case by appealing to historical precedent (Tamar, Rahab, Ruth, and Bathsheba), the angel's message, and the prophecy of Isaiah. For Matthew and his Jewish Christian audience, this birth narrative affirmed Jesus' Davidic rather than divine status.

Conclusions

What then are the results of this historical analysis of Matthew 1.1–25? By using the criterion of multiple independent attestation we find that Jesus' mother's name was Mary, her husband's name was Joseph, Jesus was linked to the house of David, and Jesus was born as the result of a premarital pregnancy. That Joseph changed his mind about divorcing Mary because of a dream is plausible but unverifiable. We are unable to affirm a genealogical connection between Jesus (through Joseph) and David. Our evidence is too meager to allow us to determine whether messianic claims for Jesus led to attributions of a Davidic lineage or if Jesus' Davidic lineage gave rise to messianic claims. A decision on this issue might be inferred by comparison with other early Jewish messianic claimants (e.g., Simon bar Giora or Simon bar Kochba). In none of the cases of which I am aware was any connection with the house of David implied. That being the case, it seems more likely that the developing Jesus tradition attributed Davidic lineage to Jesus after his death on the basis of an assumed messianic status.

Mary's premarital pregnancy was found to be explicitly attested by Matthew (M) and Luke (L), and implied in Mark 6.3 and John 8.41. A premarital pregnancy has the value of offering an explanation for the allegations of illegitimacy recorded by Mark and John, and for the widespread second-century charges made by opponents of early Christian groups. Given the potentially embarrassing nature of a premarital pregnancy, it does not seem likely that early Christians would have made up this information. Indeed, the revision of "son of Mary" (Mk 6.3) by Matthew, Luke, and John points to early Christian efforts to suppress, or at the very least correct, such an understanding of Jesus' origins. Matthew's birth narrative does not deny the premarital pregnancy nor its shameful implications but argues on the basis of historical precedent, divine revelation, and scriptural authority that these factors do not invalidate Jesus' claim to honor and status within Israel.

Historical-mindedness required us to try to read Matthew empathetically, with Jewish eyes. Having done this, we saw that Matthew was probably not asserting a virginal conception for Jesus (i.e., that Jesus was divinely generated in Mary's womb without sexual contact with any human or divine being). Neither were Matthew's sources doing so; neither was any member of Jesus' family or circle of first followers. Presupposing that all of these persons were of Jewish origin, the notion that any of them would have created or told a story about a virginal conception fails to meet the criterion of contextual credibility. Jewish texts prior to Matthew either denied the possibility of such conceptions or regarded them negatively. Hellenistic Jews occasionally allegorically used language about being born of the spirit or of divine generation, but not literally about real human persons. Jewish Christians after Matthew insisted that Jesus was the son of Joseph.

This way of contextual reading also shows that the meaning of Matthew's birth narrative is not in the words of the text itself, but is to a certain extent the product of the audience's social location. In a Jewish context, without prior knowledge of a virginal conception, Matthew's story might assert no more than that Jesus was holy in spite of the uncomfortable circumstances surrounding his conception and birth. However, Matthew's narrative did not remain the property of his Jewish Christian community but became the favored gospel of the early church. Gentile Christians approaching the birth narrative with different presuppositions may have concluded that it was a tale of dual (human and divine) paternity or of divine generation. The dominant Christian reading is one possibility only, arising out of a gentile interpretation of that originally Jewish story. This should serve as a caution against asserting that "mine" or "ours" is the "right" or "true" understanding of the text to the exclusion of other readings and of those who propose them. We do not need to make heretics, as the early church did, of those who cannot for whatever reasons affirm "our" interpretations of the text.

The most disturbing part of this study will probably be my assertion that the logic of Matthew's story points to the possibility that Jesus was a child of rape, perhaps even seduction. I am not the first to come to such a conclusion. My method of getting there is once again an attempt to read empathetically. In this instance I asked myself, if I were a first-century observer, a neighbor watching the drama unfold, what would I conclude? Admittedly my ability to think like a first-century resident of Nazareth is limited; I will never get it completely right. But I do know beyond any shadow of a doubt that a first-century Jewish observer could not hold twenty-first-century Western Christian ideas about what was going on. Historical study demands that we attempt to see through another's eyes as a way of disciplining our tendency for personal, cultural, and temporal distortion. This holds true even if, or perhaps especially if, we find the resulting view unpleasant.

It should also be noted that I am not saying that Matthew ascribed to or wished to promote the view that Jesus may have been a child of rape. Matthew was silent about the circumstances leading up to Mary's premarital pregnancy. His argument was that Mary's child was a holy sign of God's presence in spite of that unspoken but clearly troubling situation.

My motives for doing historical Jesus studies are theological and ethical; I have already made my pitch for the tolerance of diversity and pluralism in biblical interpretation. If Jesus is the Word/Wisdom of God made flesh, then according to my reading of Matthew's birth narrative, he/she became incarnate in an illegitimate child who grew up in a cultural backwater. It seems to me that there is some good news here for those who find themselves in similar circumstances and an open plea for tolerance toward those so disadvantaged.

Notes

1. For the meanings of these terms see Crossan (1991) and Borg (1999a).
2. For an excellent discussion of this issue see Appleby, Hunt, and Jacob (1994), chapter 7.
3. Appleby, Hunt, and Jacob define historical objectivity as an interactive relationship between an inquiring subject and an external object (1994: 261).
4. Crossan defines history in a similar way (1999: 3).
5. This notion is the basis of the work of the Context Group; see, for example, Malina (1993) and Neyrey (1991).
6. Funk and the Jesus Seminar suggest a late first- or early second-century date (1998: 498). See also Borg (1999b).
7. Luke's genealogy (3.23–38) has a completely different organization, and a completely different set of names from Jesus to Zerubbabel.
8. Matthew makes this a standard form of address for those seeking Jesus' help; see Mt 12.23; 15.22; 21.9; 15. Mark (12.35–37; Mt 22.42–45; /Lk 20.41–44) also records a saying of Jesus in which he contests the notion that the messiah will be or is the "son of David."

9. Funk and the Jesus Seminar dismiss this tradition as "popular piety" (1998: 501). I wonder if such a thing could emerge at so early a date.

10. The biblical model in Ruth 4.18–22 is entirely patrilineal, while genealogies in Chronicles do contain the name of the occasional woman. Tamar is named in 1 Chr 2.4, and Bathshua the mother of Solomon in 1 Chr 3.5.

11. Schaberg argues that the stories of these four women show a significant lack of intervention on God's part (1990: 20–34).

12. See 1 Cor 9.5; Gal 1.19; Mk 3.21; Mk 3.31–35//Mt 12.46–50//Lk 8.19–31; Mk 6.3//Mt 13.55//Jn 6.42; Jn 2.12; 7.3, 5, 10; Acts 1.14.

13. Crossan curiously finds the closest parallels with the version contained in the medieval *Book of Remembrance* (1995: 12–15). Brown argues for a pre-Matthean birth narrative patterned on the infancy of Moses (1993: 104–19).

14. This wording represents the dominant reading of Mark's text. The variant reading "the son of the carpenter and Mary" attested in a few ancient manuscripts is regarded as later scribal emendation to bring the Markan text into agreement with Matthew and Luke (see Brown 1993: 537–41; Meier 1991: 225).

15. Ilan includes a few examples from Josephus where the metronyme is a nickname (either derogatory or complimentary) or where the mother is a person of high status (1992: 23–45). These examples do not seem to provide useful parallels to Mark.

16. The only exception seems to be the "sons of Zeruiah" in 1 Sm 26.6, 2 Sm 2.13, and so on. See the discussion in Meier (1991: 226).

17. Schaberg's discussion of the Targums that deal with Tamar and Judah is especially illustrative on this point (1990: 24). In those texts, following Judah's admission that Tamar is pregnant by him, a voice from heaven declares, "It is from me that this thing comes."

18. Brown argues for a pre-Matthean birth narrative built around angelic dream appearances to Joseph (1993: 108–9). He regards the reference to a "spirit that is holy" as a Matthean insertion. This isn't necessary for the pre-Matthean story to have had Jewish roots.

19. For a detailed treatment of this literature see Hyland (1998: 117–54).

20. See Plutarch, *Quaest. Conv.* 8.1.717–8 and *Numa* 4.4.

21. Reproduced in Barnstone (1984: 89).

22. Philo, *Cher.* 45, 47; see discussion in Crouch (1991: 34–38), Brown (1993: 524), and Hyland (1998: 174–67).

23. The exception is the combined recitation of Mi 5.2 and 2 Sm 5.2 in Mt 2.5b–6.

24. Bruce Chilton (2000: 7–9) argues on the basis of Jos 19.15, Talmudic references, and undisclosed archaeological evidence that Jesus was born not in Bethlehem of Judaea, but in Bethlehem of Galilee, the site of a flour mill seven miles from Nazareth. Although such a location would strengthen Neyrey's reading of Matthew, Chilton's claim has yet to be assessed.

25. Carter also concludes that the citation of Is 7.14 destabilizes the status quo and represents Jesus as a sign of resistance to imperial power (2000c: 503–20).

Literary Source and Redaction Criticism 6

STEVEN L. BRIDGE

SOCIAL RESEARCHERS LOOKING FOR INFORMATION in early Christian documents have a myriad of critical methodologies at their disposal. Among them,
source criticism and redaction criticism are invaluable tools for exploring the
often complex compositional histories of the extant literature. Source criticism
seeks to determine the presence of earlier literary materials in an extant text, while
redaction criticism seeks to determine what a writer or editor tends to do in the
course of using and reformulating such earlier material. Both identifying source
materials and distinguishing them from later passages are essential for sorting out
what periods in Christian history the given texts reflect. Since redaction criticism
has evolved (both historically and methodologically) from source criticism, the majority of this chapter will be devoted to source analysis. At the conclusion of our
source study, I shall briefly outline the purpose and method of redaction criticism,
and then consider two examples to demonstrate its application.

Literary Source Criticism

Before examining the purpose and methodology of literary source criticism, it is
necessary to offer some preliminary remarks in order to clarify some prevailing
misconceptions. To begin with, the title, "literary source criticism," is something
of a misnomer. Traditionally, the study of the diachronic structure of a text—
including its sources—was one of the hallmarks of literary criticism (see, e.g.,
Streeter 1925; Beardslee 1971). Gradually, however, "literary criticism" has come
to refer to a more synchronic reading of the text, involving narrative criticism,
rhetorical criticism, and the study of narrative rhetoric (Neirynk 1993: 12–13;
Peterson 1978). In fact, some of the most recent works on literary criticism and
the New Testament contain no source critical analysis whatsoever (e.g., Ryken

1984; Moore 1989). The alternative, of course, is to understand "literary" to indicate the *types* of sources involved in an author's composition. But even this recourse is problematic, since scholars today tend to speak of "cycles of oral tradition" rather than, or in addition to, written documents (Kselman and Witherup 1990: 1134–35).

The use of the term "source" can be equally misleading. Raymond Brown defines sources as "the antecedents from which the NT writers drew their information" (1997: 21). Brown's definition is general enough, but in practice, source critics have tended to restrict such antecedents to those traditions that originated with or appeared after the historical Jesus. They have tended *not* to label those traditions that circulated *prior* to Jesus (e.g., those found in the Old Testament and in the intertestamental literature) as "sources." For the sake of convention, we will also maintain this distinction, yet acknowledge that these earlier traditions can have as much influence upon the content and structure of an author's work as his contemporary "sources."

The *Mercer Dictionary of the Bible* offers this explanation of source criticism:

> The basic purpose of source criticism is to determine whether a given textual unit—be it a short passage or an entire book—is from a single hand or is a composite based on one or more written sources. If there are indications that a previous source existed, then the exegete seeks to determine as much as possible about the author(s) of the source, the time and place in which it was written, its character and purpose, and the extent of its incorporation into the present text. (Knight 1990: 853)

Given this purpose, why would one want to identify an author's source(s)? At least four reasons can be adduced. First, literary relationships provide valuable information regarding compositional history. In particular, they can offer clues as to the dating, authorship, origin, or circulation of the text in question. A second reason concerns historicity. While earlier sources/texts are not necessarily more historically reliable than later sources/texts, they do have the advantage of being chronologically nearer to the events described. Thus, a text that relies on earlier sources could prove to be more valuable in reconstructing history than one that relies on later sources. A third reason involves hermeneutics. In some instances, a text cannot be adequately comprehended without some knowledge of its source. This is often the case when intertextual quotations, allusions, or typologies are involved, but it also pertains to traditional source-critical examples as well. Finally, source criticism lays the groundwork for redaction criticism. Once source dependency is established, one can begin the work of investigating an author's editorial activity, which would reflect the time and social situation of that author rather than the time and place reflected in a source.

Source-critical methods can be grouped into two categories, depending on whether the documents involved are paralleled or non-paralleled. "Paralleled" documents can be defined as material that demonstrates "conspicuous agreements" with an extant literary predecessor or contemporary (Conzelmann and Lindemann 1988: 87). "Non-paralleled" refers to those lacking "conspicuous agreements." The guidelines proposed by Hays (1989: 27–33) can be useful in alleviating some of the subjectivity surrounding the term "conspicuous."

Discerning Sources in Non-Paralleled Texts

Modern source criticism evolved gradually from the insights of Richard Simon (1638–1712), Jean Astruc (1684–1766), and Julius Wellhausen (1844–1918). Working with the Torah, or Pentateuch, these pioneers recognized that certain peculiar literary features—duplicate stories, alternating names of God, chronological discrepancies, etc.—could best be explained if originally diverse sources were collected and synthesized at a later point in time. This discipline, therefore, emerged from documents whose sources, for the most part, had long since disappeared. To facilitate the recognition of source dependency in these types of text, it became necessary to establish a certain number of "objective" criteria.

There are at least eight different criteria used to discern sources in non-paralleled literature. (These criteria can also be applied to paralleled texts, but since they involve additional considerations, they shall be treated separately.) The criteria include (a) changes in literary style, (b) shifts in vocabulary, (c) breaks in continuity of thought or presentation, (d) the presence of secondary linking and connecting statements, (e) changes in theological and other viewpoints, (f) duplications or repetition of material, (g) clearly defined and isolatable sub-units, and (h) chronological, factual, or other inconsistencies (Hayes 1987: 76–77).

We can clarify these criteria and demonstrate how they are applied by considering a variety of examples from early Christian literature. First, three qualifications should be noted: the representatives below are not intended to be exhaustive; some passages may actually qualify for more than one criterion, and any given assignment is subject to alternative interpretations.

Changes in literary style. Various factors contribute to an author's "style." These include the type of Greek employed (e.g., Semitized or Hellenized), habits of sentence and paragraph construction, vocabulary, and rhetorical proclivities. Because most individuals write consistently, an abrupt change in literary style can signal source dependency.

Some commentators, for example, have detected stylistic differences in the main narrative sections of John 1–12. Specifically, they cite stronger Semitic affinities (verb before subject, absence of connective particles, etc.) here than elsewhere, evidence that may indicate an underlying "Sign Source" (Brown 1966–70: I.xxix). Similarly, others have observed a strong Aramaic presence in Acts I.I–5.16, 9.31–II.I8, and parts of chapters 12 and 15. Because these sections describe the first days of the Jerusalem church and the early ministry of Peter, they have been ascribed to a Palestinian-based source (Bruce 1954: 22–23; Fitzmyer 1998: 80–89).

This criterion is one of the primary tools used to evaluate the authenticity of the Pauline Epistles. Stylistic analysis of Romans, for example, suggests that Paul had a good Hellenistic education and was familiar with the popular rhetoricians of his day (Fitzmyer 1993: 90–92). He employs specific literary forms (e.g., the diatribe, *testimonia* lists, chiasmus), repeats particular phrases (e.g., "Certainly not!" "What then?"), and follows certain grammatical customs (e.g., using the passive to express something done by God). Based on these types of stylistic traits, biblical scholars have judged seven of the "Pauline" letters genuine (I Thes, Gal, Phil, I & 2 Cor, Rom, and Phlm), three dubious (2 Thes, Col, and Eph), and three pseudonymous (I & 2 Tm and Ti).

Outside of the Pauline corpus, stylistic analysis favors a single author for the seven letters of Ignatius (bishop of Antioch, early second century), but different authors for John/I John, I & 2 Peter, and *1 & 2 Clement* (bishop of Rome, late first century).

Shifts in vocabulary. Changes in literary style are often accompanied by changes in vocabulary. Occasionally, these "internal" indicators coincide with "external" textual evidence. This is the case with the ending of Mark's Gospel. Although the earliest manuscripts suggest that Mark 16 ends at v. 8, some of the ancient witnesses add vv. 9–20, the so-called "longer ending" of Mark. An appeal to vocabulary indicates that vv. 9–20 are decidedly non-Markan. At least nine of the words or phrases contained in this section ("proceed," vv. 9, 15; "after this," v. 12; "afterwords," v. 14; "unbelief," v. 14; "saw," v. 14; "harm," v. 18; "confirm," v. 20; "work," v. 20; "accompany," v. 20) are found nowhere else in Mark. Furthermore, at least one of the phrases used to designate the disciples ("those who had been with him," v. 10) is completely foreign to the rest of the New Testament (Metzger 1971: 125).

An analogous example involves the pericope of the woman caught in adultery (Jn 7.53–8.11). Like the ending to Mark's Gospel, its textual support is weak. It is missing altogether from many early and diverse manuscripts, and those that do include it place it at different locations, after 7.52, 7.36, 7.44, and even after Luke 21.38! For this reason, it is suspected to be non-Johannine. A vocabulary analysis confirms this suspicion. There are several words or phrases (e.g., "Mount of Olives," v. I; "at daybreak," v. 2; "the scribes," v. 3) that are otherwise absent from John. Furthermore, at least two of the literary constructions are strongly reminiscent of Luke/Acts (e.g., "stand there in front of everybody," v. 3, cf. Acts 4.7; "so that they could have something to accuse him of," v. 6, cf. Lk 6.7). It is possible, therefore, that this pericope originally belonged to the Lukan tradition.

Shifts in vocabulary alone do not necessarily indicate source dependency. For instance, the "epilogue" to John's Gospel (Jn 21) contains twenty-eight words that do not appear elsewhere in this gospel. However, since this is the only fishing scene in John, one should expect a certain percentage of distinctive terminology (Brown 1966–70: 2.1079). This material should probably be attributed to another source, but this conclusion is based less on vocabulary, and more on the next criterion.

Breaks in continuity of thought or presentation. It is not so much the vocabulary of John 21 that suggests source dependency, but the closing statement found immediately before it:

> Now Jesus did many other signs in the presence of [his] disciples that are not written in this book. But these are written that you may [come to] believe that Jesus is the Messiah, the Son of God, and that through this belief you may have life in his name. (Jn 20.30–31)

The continuity of this gospel appears to be broken by material appended to its original conclusion. This practice is not uncommon in early Christian literature, as the "epilogues" in I John 5.13–21 (cf. 5.1–12), and I Peter 4.12–5.11 (cf. 4.7–11) demonstrate. Breaks in continuity of thought or presentation can also take place within the body of a text. Once such example occurs in John 14.31b. Following an extended discourse (Jn 14.1–31a), Jesus says to his disciples, "Get up, let us go." Inexplicably, another series of long discourses follows this statement (Jn 15–17). These discourses delay the departure of Jesus and his company until 18.1.

Well-known cases of literary disruption also appear in the Pauline literature. For instance, 2 Corinthians 2.14–7.4 intrudes rather awkwardly upon Paul's otherwise cogent description of his travel to Macedonia (cf. 2.12–13 with 7.5–13). Within this intrusion, 6.14–7.1 interferes with Paul's attempt to cultivate more receptive attitudes among the Corinthians (cf. 6.11–13 with 7.2–4). Similarly, the defensive exhortation in Philippians 3.2-21 is clearly disjunctive with the hopeful outlook expressed by Paul toward the Philippians (cf. 2.25–3.1 with 4.1–23). While a few commentators speculate that such dramatic shifts in thought or content may serve some sort of intentional rhetorical strategy, most agree that they represent a displacement of originally unrelated material.

The presence of secondary linking and connecting statements. An author drawing information from one or more sources may find it necessary to "fill in the gaps" between literary units. These so-called "bridge passages" are designed to smooth the transition from one originally independent section to another.

There are at least two reasons why this criterion does not always denote source dependency. First, even texts that are composed without sources require transitional statements for the sake of narrative progression. Second, the more successful an author is at blending bridge passages into the document, the more difficult it will be to determine whether sources are involved. Functionally, this criterion is almost the opposite of breaks in continuity.

The emphasis, therefore, should be on the word "secondary." In other words, the connecting statements should show evidence that they are not essentially related to the material that they bridge. For example, Paul writes:

> Now you are Christ's body, and individually parts of it. Some people God has designated in the church to be, first, apostles; second, prophets; third, teachers; then, mighty deeds; then gifts of healing, assistance, administration, and varieties of tongues. Are all apostles? Are all prophets? Are all teachers? Do all work mighty deeds? Do all have the gifts of healing? Do all speak in tongues? Do all interpret? Strive eagerly for the greatest spiritual gifts. (1 Cor 12.27–31a)

Then, in v. 31b, he offers this transitional statement: "But I shall show you a still more excellent way." This is followed by 13.1–13, a poetic eulogy that extols love above all other endowments. Paul's transition at its conclusion ("Pursue love, but strive eagerly for the spiritual gifts, above all that you may prophesy," 14.1) completely glosses over the eulogy, and returns to the topic of 12.27–31a. Therefore, both 12.31b and 14.1 can be considered good examples of bridge passages.

The *Epistle of Barnabas* (a pseudonymous letter dating to the mid-second century) contains a transition similar to Paul's. Following a concluding summary in chapter 17, the text abruptly announces, "Now let us pass on to another lesson and teaching" (*Ep. Barn.* 18.1). This notation introduces the "Two Ways" material (18.1–20.1)—a Jewish/Christian "doctrine" that is thought to have circulated independently prior to the composition of *Barnabas*.

Secondary statements are not confined to the beginnings or endings of source units. They may also include explanatory remarks located within an inherited tradition. Tenney (1960) has identified fifty-nine such "footnotes" in John's Gospel. These comments serve to translate foreign terms (e.g., Jn 1.38, 41, 42; 9.7), identify characters (e.g., 11.2; 18.13–14), clarify misconceptions (e.g., 2.21, 12.33), provide psychological insight (e.g., 6.6), explain cultural norms (e.g., 4.9), or draw attention to the fulfillment of Old Testament prophecies (e.g., 18.9).

Changes in theological and other viewpoints. Detecting change in theological viewpoints can be more subjective than, say, detecting change in narrative viewpoints. What one scholar may regard as "inconsistency," another may regard as "nuance." Generally, the more blatant the contradiction, the more likely a source is involved.

One such contradiction is exemplified in Mark's narrative of the Gerasene demoniac (Mk 5.1–20). Following the expulsion of the legion of demons that inhabited him (vv. 1–17), the Gerasene begs to remain with Jesus (v. 18). Jesus denies his request, and directs the man to return to his people and "to announce to them all that the Lord had done for him" (v. 19). Jesus' injunction counters his tendency in Mark to keep his identity concealed. The discrepancy is readily apparent in a survey of Mark's seventeen other healings and exorcisms. Of these, seven (41 percent) include some sort of censure of a demon speaking out or injunction of the cured person not to spread the news of the miracle (1.21–28, 32–34, 40–45; 3.7–12; 5.21–24, 35–43; 7.31–37; 8.22–26). Of the remainder, nine (53 percent) have no command—positive or negative—regarding the spread of information (1.29–31, 35–39; 2.1–12; 3.1–6; 5.25–34; 6.53–56; 7.24–30; 9.14–29; 10.46–52). Mark 5.1–20 is the only healing/exorcism in which Jesus explicitly charges an individual to broadcast his experience. Therefore, this pericope opposes Mark's otherwise consistent portrayal of Jesus' "Messianic Secret" (Wrede 1971).

As mentioned earlier, changes in narrative viewpoints are often easier to recognize. One of the most dramatic examples occurs in Acts. While much of this document is written from a third-person perspective, there are five lengthy sections written in the first-person plural (Acts 16.10–17; 20.5–8, 13–15; 21.1–18; 27.1–28.16). There is no scholarly consensus as to whether these so-called "we passages" constitute a stylistic device or an eyewitness warranty. In either case, they probably originated from the same source—a source that should be distinguished from the third-person accounts.

Duplications or repetition of material. Several factors can explain literary duplications or repetition. It is possible that an author relied upon multiple sources that attest to the same event. Rather than omit one, the author may have chosen to include them both. Alternatively, an author may have known of only one instance of an event, but duplicated it for stylistic or rhetorical purposes. Of course, it is also possible that the event(s) described occurred more than once, so that the literary repetition is merely a matter of coincidence. One cannot always be certain which is the case.

Mark's Gospel contains two stories in which Jesus miraculously feeds a crowd of thousands (Mk 6.34–44, 8.1–10) and two instances of Jesus healing a blind man (8.22–26, 10.46–52). Many exegetes consider these pairs to be variations of the same event. On the other hand, within the first five chapters of Acts, Luke records two sermons by Peter (Acts 2.14–36, 3.12–26), two arrests of the apostles (4.3, 5.18), two defenses before the Sanhedrin (4.8–12; 5.29–32), two estimates of the number of converts (2.41, 4.4), and two references to communal goods (2.44–45, 4.32–35). Many scholars judge these doublets to be the result of a coincidental cycle of historical circumstance (e.g., Bruce 1954: 23).

Source dependency is more certain when duplications betray an author's attempt to harmonize incongruous material. This situation is evidenced in the

Shepherd of Hermas (a Christian "apocalypse" dating to the mid-second century). The Fifth Similitude in *Hermas* is about a servant who faithfully tends his master's vineyard while he is away. Upon returning home, the master rewards his servant by making him joint-heir with his son (Herm., *Sim.* 5.2). The extended "explanation" of this parable contains not one, but three (!) varying interpretations. In the first (5.1, 3) the servant epitomizes the "perfect fast." In the second (5.5.2–5.6.3) the servant symbolizes the Son of God. In the third (5.6.4–5.7.4) the servant personifies the flesh, which bore the Holy Spirit on earth. The fact that these explanations contradict each other suggests that they are the products of three different authors.

Clearly defined and isolatable sub-units. It is here that source criticism meets form criticism (the division, classification, and study of textual units according to their literary genre). This is not to say that every distinct form has independent origins. Rather, the challenge for source critics is to determine whether the author of a given literary block has merely adopted a conventional style of expression, or is relying on a source for his content as well. The criteria discussed so far can be of great assistance in making this determination.

It has been observed that certain literary forms are more likely than others to signal the incorporation of inherited material. For instance, the hymns, poetry, and prayers found inserted into narratives or epistles often show signs of prior circulation. Luke's so-called "Magnificat of Mary" (Lk 1.46–55) and "Canticle of Zechariah" (1.68–79) fit this category. So, too, do the poetic renderings found in the Gospel of John (Jn 1.1–18), Colossians (Col 1.15–20), Philippians (Phil 2.6–11), and First Corinthians (1 Cor 13.1–13). To these examples, the invocation near the conclusion of *1 Clement* (59.3–61.3) can also be added.

Chronological, factual, or other inconsistencies. Chronological discrepancies can be classed into two types. The first affects the sequencing of narrative events. For instance, in John's account of the raising of Lazarus, Mary is introduced as "the one who had anointed the Lord with perfumed oil and dried his feet with her hair" (Jn 11.2). According to John's story line, however, Mary's anointing of Jesus has not happened yet—it takes place some fifty-seven verses later (12.3–8)!

A similar example concerns Silas's travel itinerary in Acts. A delegation consisting of Paul, Barnabas, Judas, and Silas travels together from Jerusalem to Antioch (Acts 15.22–31). After they arrive, Judas and Silas return back to Jerusalem (vv. 32–33), while Paul and Barnabas remain in Antioch (v. 35). Paul and Barnabas then have a disagreement over whether to allow John Mark to accompany them on their next missionary journey (vv. 36–38). Unable to resolve their differences, Barnabas takes John Mark to Cyprus (v. 39), and Paul takes Silas (who is presumably still in Jerusalem) to Syria and Cilicia (v. 40). These examples are likely the result of inattentive editing—editing that suggests source dependency.

A second type of chronological problem pertains specifically to historical time frames. Most experts judge that the same individual wrote Luke and Acts (e.g., Fitzmyer 1998: 49–51). However, the timetables surrounding Jesus' post-Resurrection activities in these texts do not agree. In Luke, Jesus rises, appears to his disciples, and ascends, all on Easter Sunday (Lk 24). In Acts, these same events span a period of forty days (Acts 1.1–12). The chronological differences, which somewhat jeopardize "the facts," indicate that Luke gathered his information about Jesus' last days from two separate traditions.

Not all matters of chronology bear upon "the facts," nor are all factual inconsistencies related to chronology. An example of this latter point is evidenced in John's record of Jesus' baptismal ministry. In one place, John writes that "Jesus and his disciples went into the land of Judea; there he remained with them and baptized" (3.22). Elsewhere, John claims "Jesus himself did not baptize, but only his disciples" (4.2). It is likely that John transcribed 3.22 from his source and then added his own editorial gloss (see the section on changes in theological and other viewpoints, above) in 4.2.

The preceding survey has intentionally overlooked those texts, or portions thereof, that are paralleled by their literary predecessors or contemporaries. This situation, which is not uncommon among early Christian writings, poses a unique problem for those reconstructing compositional histories. Therefore, certain criteria have been established to help determine source relationships among paralleled literature.

Determining Literary-Source Relationships among Paralleled Literature
One of the goals of source criticism is to explain the interrelationship between paralleled texts. When only two texts are involved (e.g., 2 Pt 2//Jude 4–16; Gal 3//Rom 4; Eph 5–6//Col 3; Jas 4//1 Pt 5; Ep *Barn.* 18–20//*Did.* 1–6, etc.) at least five possibilities exist. Either (a) both works were written by the same author, (b) the first work is dependent upon the second, (c) the second work is dependent upon the first, (d) both works draw independently upon a third, common source, or (e) the similarities are coincidental, based upon shared experiences or cultural milieus. Of these five, the first is an option normally reserved for works attributed to the same individual, and the last is unlikely to explain detailed verbal agreement.

Literary relationships become exponentially more complicated when three or more paralleled texts are involved. This is the case with the Gospels of Matthew, Mark, and Luke—collectively referred to as the "synoptics" since their portrayals of Jesus share such a similar perspective. This similar perspective can be translated statistically: over 80 percent of the material in Mark appears in Matthew, and about 65 percent of it appears in Luke (Brown, 1997: 263). Furthermore, Matthew and Luke share additional material (mainly sayings of Jesus) that is not found in Mark. Determining the precise literary association between these gospels constitutes the "synoptic problem."

Biblical scholarship has traditionally not approached the synoptic problem from a completely objective starting point (assigning equal probability to every possible literary combination). Indeed, some of the earliest internal and external evidence militates against this. Luke, for example, makes reference to the many who have "undertaken to compile a narrative of the events that have been fulfilled among us," and to those "ministers of the word [who] handed them down to us" (Lk 1.1–2). Moreover, the testimony of Papias (the bishop of Hierapolis in the early second century) recorded by Eusebius (fourth-century Christian historian) claims that "Matthew compiled the sayings of our Lord in Aramaic, and everyone translated them as well as he could" (*Hist. eccl.* 3.39.16). Because of these (and other) traditions, it was assumed that Matthew, Mark, and Luke wrote their gospels consecutively, each with the knowledge of the previous one(s). This assumption, which explains the order found in the New Testament, prevailed until the rise of historical criticism in the eighteenth century.

The Greisbach Hypothesis (1783) represents the first serious challenge to the above order. This theory maintains Matthean priority, but judges Mark to be a conflation of Matthew and Luke. This arrangement is also referred to as the "Two-Gospel Hypothesis" because it holds that Mark depended upon the two other Gospels.

Five decades after the Greisbach Hypothesis was formulated, C. H. Weisse (1838) proposed a theory of Markan priority. According to Weisse, both Matthew and Luke used Mark independently. To explain the material common to Matthew and Luke, but absent from Mark, Weisse hypothesized another "source" (or *Quelle* in German; the letter "Q" has since been used to designate this source). Since Weisse maintained that Matthew and Luke each composed their gospels using two primary sources (Mark and Q), his theory is also referred to as the "Two Source Hypothesis."

In recent years, some commentators have attempted to challenge the Two Source Hypothesis. Most notably, Farrer (1985) champions a consecutive Mark, Matthew, Luke arrangement; Farmer (1964) revives the Griesbach Hypothesis; and Gundry (1993) argues that Luke depended on Mark, Q, and Matthew (the "Three Source Hypothesis"). Despite these (and other) proposals, the majority of scholars still judge the Two Source Hypothesis to be the best solution to the synoptic problem (Tuckett 1983).

Ultimately, all theories of synoptic relationship are accountable to the same set of source-critical criteria. Specifically, these criteria compare texts on the basis of (a) difficulty, (b) length, (c) style, and (d) order. Underlying each of these criteria is the quest to detect redactional activity. We can clarify these principles and demonstrate how they are applied by considering various examples from paralleled Christian literature. Since they were largely excluded from the first part of the chapter, the synoptics will now constitute the primary—though not exclusive—focus of our attention. Again, the following examples are not intended to be exhaustive, some may fit more than one criterion, and any given assignment may be subject to different interpretations.

Difficulty. Enigmatic passages can take many forms. Authors working with inherited material are often inclined to omit or change that which they judge to be (a) erroneous, (b) cryptic, (c) theologically unsound, or (d) defamatory. Therefore, documents that contain comparatively more instances of these types of readings are presumed to be earlier. For the sake of clarity, these subdivisions can be considered separately.

(a) Factual errors that occur in Mark's Gospel tend to be corrected by Matthew and Luke. For instance, Mark cites "Isaiah the prophet: 'Behold I am sending my messenger ahead of you; he will prepare your way. A voice of one crying out in the desert: Prepare the way of the Lord, make straight his paths.'" (1.2–3). The trouble is that the first part of this quotation actually comes from Malachi 3.1. Both Matthew (Mt 3.3) and Luke (Lk 3.4–6) delete it. (Scriptural misattributions also occur in Matthew [e.g., 13.35, 27.9], but these texts lack synoptic parallels.)

A similar mistake appears where Mark (2:26) refers to "Abiathar" as the high priest who supplied David with the showbread from the Temple. According to 1 Samuel 21.2–7, it was not Abiathar, but Ahimelech, the father of Abiathar, who did this. Matthew (12.4) and Luke (6.4) simply avoid naming the high priest at all.

Two other Markan "errors" are found in the passion account. First, Mark's Jesus predicts that Peter will deny him three times before the cock crows twice (14.30). After Peter's third denial, the cock does indeed crow a second time (14.72). The problem is that Mark never records its first crowing. Both Matthew (26.34, 74) and Luke (22.34, 60) remedy the problem by reducing this double sign to a single one.

Second, Mark (15.25) reports that Jesus is crucified at the "third hour," 9 A.M.; darkness spreads over the land at the "sixth hour," 12 P.M. (15.33); and Jesus breathes his last at the "ninth hour," 3 P.M. (15.34–37). Mark's Jesus is thus on the cross for six hours (9 A.M. to 3 P.M.). Both Matthew (27.33–50) and Luke (23.33–46) shorten this to three hours by omitting Mark's first reference. Jesus' crucifixion now begins at noon—a detail corroborated by John's account (Jn 19.14).

There are narrative errors in Matthew and Luke that appear more correctly in Mark (e.g., Mt 26.67–68//Mk 14.65; Lk 22.65–66//Mk 14.72–15.1). In these cases, however, the mistakes are almost certainly the result of Matthew and Luke's reorganization of Mark's text. Therefore, we will examine these pericopes more closely under (b) and (d) below.

(b) Many references in the synoptic Gospels can be considered "cryptic." Although it is true that some rather obtuse Markan passages appear nowhere else (e.g., the seed growing secretly in Mk 4.26–29, or the fleeing of the naked man in 14.51–52), similar examples can be culled from Matthew (e.g., Mt 7.6, 13.51–52, 17.24–27) and Luke (e.g., Lk 10.18–19, 16.1–9, 20.18). Therefore, the mere presence of "cryptic" passages does not necessarily indicate chronological priority.

More telling for source analysis are instances where attempted clarifications are introduced. For example, in one of his teachings on parables, Mark's Jesus tells his disciples, "To you has been given the mystery of the kingdom of God, but for those outside everything is in parables" (Mk 4.11). Taken literally, this statement doesn't seem to place the disciples at much of an advantage. Both Matthew and Luke illuminate Jesus' meaning by adding, "to you it has been given *to understand* the mysteries of the kingdom" (Mt 13.11; Lk 8.9).

A similar example is found in Mark 10.49–50: "Everyone will be salted with fire. Salt is good, but if salt becomes insipid, with what will you restore its flavor? Keep salt in yourselves and you will have peace with one another." Both Matthew and Luke remove the puzzling fire element and shift the emphasis from retaining salt to becoming more like it (Mt 5.13; Lk 14.34–35). In Mark's case, salt appears to be some sort of spiritual quality; in Matthew and Luke's, it becomes a paradigm for discipleship.

(c) Theologically problematic passages can be as difficult to define as those that are cryptic. Many commentators claim that Matthew or Luke (or both) deliberately excised a number of Markan passages (e.g., Mk 7.31–37, 8.22–26, 10.18, 13.32, 15.44) for doctrinal reasons. But again, similar lists can be made from material unique to Matthew (e.g., Mt 5.17–30, 6.15, 18.23–25, 18.17, 28.17) or to Luke (e.g., Lk 2.41–50, 6.24–26, 12.47–48).

Editorial revisions can demonstrate this criterion more convincingly. As noted above, two of Jesus' arduous healings in Mark (7.31–37, 8.22–26) are missing from Matthew and Luke. By itself, this could indicate that Mark had access to material unknown to his synoptic counterparts. However, two other instances of troublesome healings in Mark have evidently been improved. In the first, Mark's Jesus goes to Nazareth, where he could do "*no* mighty work there" because of the people's unbelief (Mk 6.1–6). Although Luke does not retain this pericope, Matthew clarifies it slightly by stating that Jesus "did not do *many* mighty works there" (Mt 13.58).

In the second case, Mark's Jesus charges a dumb and deaf spirit to depart from a young boy (Mk 9.25). Once the demon is exorcised, the child appears so lifeless that the crowd takes him to be dead (9.26). Only after Jesus takes him by the hand does the boy revive (9.27). Matthew and Luke both remove the embarrassing result and the second attempt. Luke states, "Jesus rebuked the unclean spirit and healed the boy" (Lk 9.42). Matthew is more emphatic: "Jesus rebuked him, and the demon came out of him, and the boy was cured *instantly*" (Mt 17.18). This evidence, coupled with the omissions above, suggests that Matthew and Luke found aspects of Mark's miracle accounts to be incompatible with their christological sensibilities.

Analogous synoptic patterns only reinforce Matthew and Luke's theological concerns. For instance, Jesus' emotional reactions in Mark (e.g., 1.43, 10.14, 11.12–16, 14.34) tend to be raw and unflattering compared to the parallel versions in Matthew and Luke. Furthermore, Mark's Jesus is addressed only once as "Lord" (7.28)—his more usual title is "rabbi," "teacher." In Matthew and Luke, "Lord" occurs nineteen and sixteen times, respectively (Streeter 1925: 162).

(d) Subsequent authors may improve "difficult" personal profiles as well. In this regard, Matthew and Luke appear to have omitted and/or changed some of the material in Mark that casts Jesus' family in a negative light (e.g., Mk 3.19–21, 31–35; 6.1–6). A similar tendency can be discerned regarding Jesus' disciples, who often appear confrontational and ignorant in Mark (e.g., Mk 8.32–33, 9.33–36, 16.8). Luke goes to greater lengths than Matthew to salvage apostolic reputations; nevertheless, even he allows some material that could be considered defamatory (e.g., Lk 11.27–28). Curiously, this type of character rehabilitation is not limited to those closest to Jesus. For instance, none of the three synoptics hold Pilate responsible for Jesus' death. However, both Matthew and Luke underscore his blamelessness. In Matthew 27.24, Pilate literally washes his hands of Jesus' blood. In Luke 23.4, 14–15, 22, Pilate explicitly declares Jesus innocent three times.

The first criterion of "difficulty"—with each of its four sub-divisions—seems to favor the chronological priority of Mark's Gospel. As we shall see, the remaining three criteria generally confirm this assessment.

Length. Source analysis has demonstrated that as textual units are passed on, they tend to expand rather than contract. This is because authors working with a source often find it necessary to explain confusing information, add supplemental details, or fill in narrative gaps.

Of the synoptics, Mark's Gospel is by far the shortest (661 verses, compared to 1,068 in Matthew and 1,149 in Luke). This appears to be due, in part, to Matthew and Luke's reliance on a source (Q) unknown to Mark. However, even when this material is accounted for (about 220 verses), Matthew and Luke still remain 200 to 300 verses longer than Mark. Therefore, the sheer brevity of Mark's Gospel suggests its chronological priority. Similar conclusions have been drawn for other paralleled literature from early Christianity: Galatians (149 verses) is considered to be earlier than Romans (433 verses), Colossians (95 verses) earlier than Ephesians (155 verses), and the "Two Ways" material in *Barnabas* (22 verses) earlier than the *Didache* (42 verses).

Many of the Matthean and Lukan expansions are readily identifiable. Mark's Gospel begins with Jesus' baptism and ends with Jesus' death. Both Matthew and Luke extend this account with stories of Jesus' childhood (Mt 1–2; Lk 1–2) and his resurrection (Mt 28; Lk 24). They also incorporate large blocks into Mark's story line, including material about John the Baptist (Mt 3.1–17; Lk 3.1–22), Jesus' temptation (Mt 4.1–11; Lk 4.1–13), and Jesus's sermon (Mt 5–7; Lk 6.20–49).

Despite these augmentations, exegetes have noted that several individual episodes in Mark are significantly longer than those parallels in Matthew (e.g., Mk 2.1–12//Mt 9.1–8; Mk 5.1–20//Mt 8.28–34; Mk 5.21–43//Mt 9.18–26). This phenomenon, which has been used to support Matthean priority, under-scores some important exceptions to this criterion. While most textual units grow over time, later authors may shorten or omit passages judged to be difficult (as discussed above), loquacious, or superfluous. Truncations can also arise uninten-tionally, as from parablepsis (shifting one's eyes from one's source). Mark and Matthew offer a good test case for this criterion in their versions of Jesus' experi-ence following the Sanhedrin's condemnation.

> Some began to spit on him, and to cover his face, and to strike him, saying to him, "Prophesy!" And the guards received him with blows. (Mk 14.65–66)

> Then they spat in his face, and struck him; and some slapped him, saying, "Prophesy to us, you Christ! Who is it that struck you?" (Mt 26.67–68)

A simple word-count of these two texts favors the priority of Matthew (twenty-one Greek words) over Mark (twenty-three Greek words), but several peculiarities recommend closer inspection. Matthew actually has an *expanded* form of the taunt-ing of the aggressors. Their taunt clarifies their intentions—they do not want Jesus merely to prophesy; they want him to indicate which one of them hit him. In light of this elaboration, why is Matthew's version shorter? The answer(s) re-late to the exceptions noted above. First, Matthew eliminates superfluous infor-mation by subsuming the blows delivered by the guards (Mk 14.66) into the litany of abuses that Jesus initially suffers: "they spat . . . struck . . . *and some slapped him*" [emphasis added] (Mt 26.67). This makes for smoother reading.

Matthew's version is also shorter because he commits a parablepsis. In his ap-parent effort to improve Mark, Matthew specifies where the people spat on Jesus (his "face"). But because Matthew returns to the word "face" in Mark's text, he inadvertently omits the description of Jesus' blindfolding. (Interpreting this evi-dence the other way makes little sense. If Mark added the blindfold to clarify Matthew's version, then why would he render the tormentor's words more am-biguous?) Without this obstruction, the "prophesy challenge" in Matthew 26.68 becomes meaningless. With it, Matthew's version would gain another five words (raising his total to twenty-six). Therefore, the criterion of length—with all its exceptions—favors Markan priority.

Style. As noted above, style can refer to the type of language employed, habits of sentence and paragraph construction, vocabulary, and rhetorical proclivities. When paralleled texts are compared, the one with the more refined style is generally judged to be the later.

Most biblical experts agree that Mark writes Greek with less polish than Matthew or Luke. Many factors support this conclusion. Mark uses a number of rather primitive Aramaisms (e.g., Mk 3.17; 5.41; 7.11, 34; 8.10; 14.36; 15.22, 34). Matthew retains only one ("Golgatha," Mt 27.33), and renders another into Hebrew ("Eli, Eli, lema sabachthani?" Mt 27.46). Luke removes them altogether.

Grammatically speaking, Mark frequently strings his pericopes together with the phrase "(and) immediately" (Mk 1.12, 21, 29, etc.), resulting in a narrative of almost breathless pace.[1] The parallels in Matthew and Luke demonstrate more varied and creative transitions. Mark is also fond of double expressions, such as "that evening, when the sun had set" (Mk 1.32; see also 1.35, 42; 2.20; 4.35; 10.30; 13.24; 14.12, 43; 15.42; 16.2). Matthew and Luke typically eliminate one member of the pair.[2]

With respect to vocabulary, Matthew and Luke often replace Mark's rare or unusual words with more common ones. For example, Mark writes that after Jesus' baptism, the heavens were "ripped apart" (Mk 1.10). Matthew and Luke change this to "opened" (Mt 3.16, Lk 3.21). Mark has Jesus "cast out" into the desert by the Spirit (Mk 1.12). In Matthew and Luke he is "led" (Mt 4.1, Lk 4.1). Mark describes Peter as "cast upon himself" following his denial of Jesus (Mk 14.72). In Matthew and Luke, he "weeps bitterly" (Mt 26.75, Lk 22.62).

Theoretically, Mark would employ his characteristic inferior style if he were rewriting Matthew and Luke freely. But most Greisbach defenders contend that Mark had Matthew and Luke before him, and frequently copied them word for word. Under these circumstances, this type of literary deterioration is difficult to justify (so Marcus 1999: 44). So the criterion of style suggests that Mark's Gospel was the first to be written.

d) *Order.* Authors with inherited material tend to arrange it so that their finished document is structurally cogent, with thematic groupings and smooth transitions. When two paralleled texts are compared, the earlier one will generally evince a more disjunctive arrangement of material. Two non-synoptic examples may help to clarify this principle.

The Epistles of Jude and 2 Peter both condemn false teachers within the early Christian community. In this context, they rely on a similar set of examples from the past to demonstrate God's judgment of the unrighteous (Jude), and his salvation of the elect (2 Pt). Jude includes the experiences of the Egyptians, the primordial angels, Sodom and Gomorrah, the devil (at Moses' death), Cain, Balaam, and Korah (Jude 5–13). The list in 2 Peter is slightly different: primordial angels, Noah and his generation, Sodom and Gomorrah (and Lot), and Balaam (2 Pt 2). A close inspection of these two lists reveals that Jude presents his examples in random order; the Egyptians, the devil (at Moses' death), Cain, and Korah are all out of chronological sequence. Coincidentally (or not), none of these examples appears in 2 Peter. Instead, 2 Peter's list is arranged according to correct historical appearance. Therefore, based on the criterion of order, 2 Peter is probably later than Jude.

A second comparison involves the *Epistle of Barnabas* and the *Didache* (an early Christian "handbook" dating to the mid-second century). Both documents contain the "Two Ways" material, but they arrange it differently. *Barnabas* lists unrelated injunctions rather haphazardly:

> Thou shall share. . . . thou shall not be forward to speak. . . . be not one who stretches out the hand to take, but shuts to give. . . . thou shall love all who speak the word of the Lord. . . . thou shall remember the day of judgment. . . . thou shall seek the society of the saints. . . . thou shall not hesitate to give. (*Barn.* 19.8–11)

The *Didache* organizes this same material thematically: "be not one who stretches out the hand to take, but shuts to give. . . . thou shall not hesitate to give. . . . thou shall not turn away the needy" (Did. 4.5–8). The ordering of the "Two Ways" material suggests that the version in *Didache* is later than the version in *Barnabas.*

Much has been written regarding order in the synoptics (see Neville 1994). To date, however, the most persuasive evidence seems to favor Markan priority. Matthew and Luke both follow Mark's order closely, but when one departs, the other usually adheres. Furthermore, Matthew and Luke both contain instances of literary displacement (narrative incongruities that can best be explained by appeal to an original Markan sequence). An example from Luke can clarify this point: Matthew and Mark's versions of Jesus before the Sanhedrin were compared above. Luke contains a similar episode, but it occurs at a different place in the narrative (Lk 22.63–65). Evidently, Luke sought to clarify the identity of Mark's "some" (Mk 14.65). In its context, this reference implies that certain members of the Jewish council beat Jesus. Luke remedies this problem by moving this scene to the period of Jesus' detention the night before his Sanhedrin appearance. According to Luke, Jesus suffers under his captors, not at the hands of the Jewish elders. This also improves the transition at the end of the assembly. Once the council announces its decision (Lk 22.71), Jesus is immediately taken to Pilate (23.1).

While Luke's order does improve the narrative sequence, it also creates a literary problem. His preceding pericope ends as Peter, following his denial of Jesus, "went out and began to weep bitterly" (Lk 22.62). However, the realigned text uses only pronouns in reference to Jesus: "The men who held *him* in custody were ridiculing and beating *him*" (Lk 22.63). In other words, Luke's transposition makes it appear as though the soldiers were beating Peter! This problem, of course, is readily apprehended in light of Mark's original order.

Before concluding this section on paralleled texts and turning to the subject of redaction criticism, the outcomes of these criteria should be clarified. If a certain degree of consistency emerges when the above criteria are applied to paralleled texts, then chronological priority can usually be established. Furthermore, if sufficient verbal correspondence exists, then it can be argued that the earlier text is a source for the later. This is the situation between Mark and Matthew, and Mark and Luke. However, paralleled texts sometimes produce conflicting results with respect to these criteria. In these cases, there is an increased likelihood that a third, independent source is involved. Variations in the *Didache* and the *Shepherd of Hermas* help to demonstrate this point. For the sake of comparison, the conspicuous agreements between these two documents have been italicized.

Did. 1.5–6

"Give to everyone that asks you," and do not refuse, for the Father's will is that we give to all from the gifts we have received. Blessed is he that gives according to the command, for he is innocent. Woe to him who receives, for if any man receives alms under pressure of need, he is innocent. But he who received it without need shall be tried as to why he took and for what, and being in prison he shall be examined as to his deeds, and "he shall not come out until he pays the last penny." Concerning this it was also said, "Let your alms bring sweat into your hands, until you know to whom you are giving."

Herm., Man. 2.4–6

Do good, and of all your toil which God gives you, give in simplicity to all who need, not doubting to whom you shall give and to whom not: *give to all, for to all God wishes gifts to be made of his own bounties. Those then who receive shall render an account to God why they received it and for what. Those who accepted through distress shall not be punished, but those who accepted in hypocrisy shall pay the penalty.* He therefore who gives is innocent; for as he received from the Lord the fulfillment of this ministry, he fulfilled it in simplicity, not doubting to whom he should give or not give.

It can be readily seen that the section in *Hermas* is shorter, initially indicating chronological priority. However, *Hermas*'s length is somewhat a reflection of its grammatical refinement. The *Didache* retains double expressions (e.g., "give to everyone that asks you, and do not refuse") which *Hermas* may have found superfluous. So the *Didache* could be earlier. On the other hand, the *Didache* contains three scriptural quotations that *Hermas* has not included (Lk 6.30, Mt 5.26, and a third of unknown origin; see Bridge 1997). Since *Hermas* frequently employs similar quotations elsewhere, their absence here suggests that *Hermas* did not obtain this material from the *Didache*.

It is likely, therefore, that both *Didache* and *Hermas* independently drew upon a third, common source, and then altered it according to their purposes.

An analogous situation exists between Matthew and Luke. As noted earlier, these two gospels share a considerable amount of material not found in Mark (for the specific contents of this material, see Brown 1997: 117 n. 31, 118–19). While it is possible that one evangelist relied upon the work of the other, an appeal to the above criteria suggests otherwise. Refinements of vocabulary and grammar occasionally appear in Matthew, and other times in Luke (see *Critical Edition of Q*). The ordering of this material similarly suggests a shared source; although Matthew and Luke almost always insert Q into different narrative contexts, their underlying sequencing remains virtually identical. This phenomenon is readily explained if they borrowed from a common tradition, but difficult to justify if one knew the other, given their fidelity to Mark's order.

Redaction Criticism

Having examined the source-critical criteria for both non-paralleled and paralleled texts, we have laid the necessary groundwork for redaction criticism. Redaction criticism evolved, in part, as an effort to balance the "atomizing" tendencies of source and form criticism. Whereas source and form critics begin with completed texts and work their way "backward" to isolate the various strands of inherited tradition, redaction critics do just the opposite. They begin with the literary antecedents and work their way "forward" to determine how and why the final authors used source(s) in the ways that they did.

Redaction criticism takes place on both the micro and macro level. At the micro level, individual passages are examined to assess precisely *how* an author has incorporated, altered, augmented, or omitted his source(s). As shown above, when paralleled texts are involved, this type of redaction is all but "inseparable" from source criticism (Neirynk 1990: 593). On the macro level, exegetes consider the editorial decisions an author has made throughout an entire work. The accumulated data create a profile of an author's literary, rhetorical, and theological interests, and often help to explain *why* an author has shaped the source(s) in a particular way. Because our preceding source analysis contains numerous examples of redaction criticism at the micro level, we shall confine our remaining investigation to the macro level. Moreover, since the above evidence recommends Markan priority, we shall concentrate on the editorial tendencies in Matthew and Luke (vis-à-vis Mark).

Redaction in the Gospel of Matthew

Of the synoptic writers, Matthew writes from a decidedly Jewish perspective. He conveys it with (1) frequent references to prophecies from the Hebrew Bible, (2) use of typologies from the Hebrew Bible, (3) demonstrated familiarity with Jewish customs, and (4) emphasis on the Jewish law.

(1) Matthew records more explicit instances of prophecy fulfillment than Mark and Luke combined. Five alone appear in his account of Jesus' birth (Mt 1.22–23; 2.5–6, 15, 17, 23). In fact, Matthew's zeal for aligning the details of Jesus' life with "predictions" from the Hebrew Bible may explain several peculiar changes he makes to Mark's record. For example, Mark's Jesus enters Jerusalem riding on a colt (Mk 11.1–10); Matthew positions Jesus awkwardly upon a colt and an ass, evidently in fulfillment of Zechariah 9.9: "See, your king shall come to you; a just savior is he; meek, and riding on an ass, on a colt, the foal of an ass." Similarly, at Golgotha Mark's Jesus is offered "wine mixed with myrrh" (Mk 15.23); Matthew's Jesus is offered "wine mingled with gall" (Mt 27.34). The latter corresponds more closely to Psalm 69.22: "Instead they put gall in my food; for my thirst they gave me vinegar." Matthew's appeal to the Hebrew Bible also explains several unique features in his gospel. The thirty pieces of silver paid to Judas (Mt 26.15) parallels Zechariah 11.12. The crowd's rebuke of Jesus (Mt 27.43) echoes Psalm 22.9. And the circumstances surrounding Judas's death (Mt 27.3–10) recall Zechariah 11.12–13, Jeremiah 19.1–13, and Jeremiah 32.6–9.

(2) In addition to prophetic fulfillment, Matthew also develops a number of typologies from the Hebrew Bible. For instance, the details within Jesus' infancy narrative (Mt 1.18–2.23) evoke the stories of Joseph the patriarch, Moses, the Exodus, and David (for details, see Brown 1993). Matthew's is also the only gospel in which John the Baptist is explicitly associated with Elijah (Mt 11.14). Even the structure of his gospel serves a typological function. Matthew has arranged his material around five major sermons delivered by Jesus (Mt 5–7, 10, 13, 18, 23–25). These discourses, recalling the five books of the Torah, help establish Jesus as the "new Moses." This is reinforced by Matthew's regular placement of Jesus on top of a mountain (e.g., Mt 5.1, 28.16).

(3) Matthew demonstrates his (and his audience's) familiarity with Jewish customs in a variety of ways. One of the most telling is his omission of Mark's description of Jewish purification practices (Mk 7.3-4), a reference he probably found superfluous. He also alters Mark 15.42, which incorrectly presents the day of preparation for the Sabbath as continuing into the night. Matthew consistently changes Mark's "Kingdom of God" to "Kingdom of Heaven," presumably out of respect for the Divine name. And he demonstrates a concern for Sabbath rest, as evidenced by his addition to the Markan apocalypse (cf. Mk 13.18, Mt 24.20).

(4) Matthew's concern for the law is suggested by Jesus' repeated affirmation of it (Mt 5.17-19, see also 23.1-3). Indeed, Matthew changes or omits those occasions on which Mark's Jesus appears to relax the law (e.g., Mk 2.27, 7.19), and counters with even more stringent requirements (e.g., Mt 5.21–48, 15.1–9).

Space does not allow our pursuing other redactional tendencies in this gospel. However, from the evidence above, it is obvious that Matthew perceives Jesus as the Jewish Messiah. Because Jesus is the fulfillment of the promises made to the descendents of Abraham, their salvation constitutes his first and foremost concern (Mt 10.5–6, 15.24).

Redaction in the Gospel of Luke

While Matthew has cast Jesus' ministry in a decidedly Jewish light, Luke places more emphasis on the inclusive character of Jesus' outreach, particularly as this applies to (1) the Gentiles, (2) "sinners," (3) women, and (4) the poor.

(1) In Mark, Jesus has limited contact with Gentiles (so Mk 5.1–20, 7.24–8.9). Jesus responds to them as he does to the Jews, but he interacts with them separately. In Luke, the Jews and Gentiles have more equal opportunities before Jesus. For instance, Jesus' Sermon on the Plain is addressed to "a great crowd of his disciples and a large number of people from all of Judaea and Jerusalem and the coastal regions of Tyre and Sidon" (Lk 6.17). When given such opportunity, Luke's Gentiles often respond more favorably than the Jews. This is the case with the Samaritan leper who returned to thank Jesus (17.11–19). It also holds true for the "Good Samaritan" who stopped to assist the man left for dead (10.29–37).

(2) While each of the synoptics agrees that Jesus "came not to call the righteous, but sinners" (Mk 2.17//Mt 9.13//Lk 5.32), Luke places a special emphasis on this theme. In Luke, Jesus' concern for the sinner is evidenced in the triad of three parables that epitomize the joy experienced in heaven over the repentance of one who is "lost" (the lost sheep, 15.1–7; the lost coin, 15.8–10; the lost son 15.11–32). Luke also records three separate instances of Jesus associating "sinful" tax collectors with his movement (5.27–32, 18.9–14, 19.1–10). Luke even adapts some of Mark's contents in accordance with this motif. For instance, in Mark, the anointing at Bethany serves to prepare Jesus for his approaching suffering and death (Mk 14.3–9); Luke repositions this episode, emphasizes the sinful character of the woman involved, and uses this scene as a lesson on forgiveness (Lk 7.36–50). Similarly, those who are crucified with Mark's Jesus revile him from their crosses (Mk 15.32); in Luke, however, one of the criminals repents (Lk 25.39–42). Jesus assures him, "Today you will be with me in Paradise" (25.43).

(3) Luke has a tendency to lend a gender balance to his narratives. In his nativity stories of John and Jesus, Zechariah's experience matches that of Mary's. Both are approached by Gabriel (1.19, 26–27) and are initially troubled (1.12, 29). Both are informed about the miraculous conceptions (1.13, 31) and the

unique missions of their sons (1.15–16, 32–33). Both question Gabriel (1.18, 34) and are told what to name their offspring (1.13, 31). Analogous pairings appear throughout Luke's writings; both Simeon (2:25–35) and Anna (2:36–38) recognize Jesus at his presentation in the Temple. The twelve disciples are augmented by a number of women followers (8.1–3). Jesus raises a widow's son (7.11–17) and a man's daughter (8.40–56). And Jesus heals both a woman (13.10–17) and a man (14.1–6) on the Sabbath. In several of these examples, Luke has supplemented Mark's male characters with female characters. Luke's interest in the role of women in Jesus' ministry is further evidenced by other episodes that only he records (e.g., Elizabeth and Mary, Lk 1–3; Martha and Mary, 10.38–42; the persistent widow, 18.1–8; the women weeping, 23.27–31).

(4) Throughout the synoptics, Jesus speaks to the issues of wealth and poverty (e.g., Mk 4.18–19, 10.17–31, 12.41–44, and parallels). In Luke, however, his message is made more emphatic. In the Sermon on the Plain, Jesus blesses the poor (Lk 6.20; cf. Mt 5.3, "the poor in spirit") and chastises the rich (Lk 6.24). This is reflected in Mary's "Magnificant," where she declares that God "has filled the hungry with good things, but the rich he has sent away empty" (1.53). Two of Luke's parables—the rich fool (12.16–21), and the rich man and Lazarus (16.19–31)—place importance on sharing with the poor. Indeed, Luke's Jesus advocates disinterested charity (e.g., Lk 6.27–36, 14.7–14).

These examples demonstrate that Luke understood Jesus' ministry as one that encompasses all people, regardless of their prior religious or moral backgrounds, their gender, or their economic standing. In fact, according to Luke, Jesus directs his ministry precisely to those individuals who might otherwise be considered "disadvantaged."

Conclusion

We have explored the unique perspectives, aims, and contributions of literary source and redaction criticism. As with all critical tools, these methods have their own limitations. Nevertheless, they have proven to be invaluable to those interested in examining the compositional histories of the early Christian literature. While source criticism has increased our awareness of the rich deposits of tradition from which the ancient writers drew, redaction criticism has lent us insight into how and why these traditions were employed. Together, these methodologies deepen our understanding of the early Christians and of the profound experiences that they sought to convey. An awareness and use of these methods is necessary for the utilization of early Christian literary materials in developing social scientific accounts of the early Christian movement.

Notes

1. Some see this as a rhetorical ploy, but its purpose remains unclear. More likely it reflects poor style.

2. The occasions on which Matthew retains one half and Luke the other (e.g., Mt 8.16; Lk 4.40) are cited by Greisbach proponents as evidence of Markan conflation.

Statistical Textual Analysis: A Special Technique 7

ROBERT A. WORTHAM

Sᴄʜᴏʟᴀʀꜱ ꜱᴛᴜᴅʏɪɴɢ ᴛᴇxᴛꜱ associated with Christian origins have a broad cross section of interpretive techniques at their disposal that enable them to investigate a text's literary development, structure, and meaning. These techniques include such established hermeneutical methods as form criticism (McKnight 1969), literary criticism (Petersen 1978), and redaction criticism (Perrin 1969) and newer approaches such as structural exegesis (Patte 1976) and social scientific criticism (Elliott 1993). These approaches have enabled researchers to identify distinct structural patterns in the sayings attributed to Jesus as they were transmitted from oral tradition to formal narratives (Bultmann 1963), uncover the literary dynamics of the parables (Via 1967; Crossan 1973), document the historical transmission and corruption of early Christian manuscripts (Metzger 1968), explore the association between Markan narrative structures and the semantic and symbolic universes embedded in the text (Patte 1978), and demonstrate how social stratification and inequality could generate conflict among various power groups in Corinth (Theissen 1982).

Both the established and newer exegetical approaches enable researchers to gain significant insight into the historical, literary, social, and cultural development of the "religious imaginations" (Greeley 1989: 94–95; 1990: 38–44) of the different early Christian communities. With these interpretive tools scholars can raise significant questions concerning (1) multiple authorship and editorship of existing texts, (2) the documenting of layers of tradition, (3) problems of dependence and independence among parallel texts, and (4) a text's social and cultural setting (*Sitz im Leben*) as well as its manifest (surface structure) and latent (deep structure) meaning, its meaning effect (*effet de sens*).

In addressing such issues, several alternative theories are typically offered as plausible solutions to a research problem. For example, rival theories of source dependence among the synoptic Gospels have been offered (Bultmann 1963; Farmer 1976; and Stoldt 1980). Stylistic and literary evidence is cited to support one argument over another, but empirical tests utilizing statistical measures and tests of statistical significance have generally not been employed. Here is where statistical textual analysis represents a promising tool that researchers could add to their exegetical arsenal. By investigating statistical associations among linguistic units, theories of multiple authorship and source dependence could be evaluated within an empirical, hypothesis-testing framework.

This chapter presents a basic introduction to statistical textual analysis. This is accomplished by offering a methodological primer on the hypothesis testing method, introducing the major tenets of statistical linguistics, and providing case studies of statistical textual analysis. The methodological primer on the hypothesis testing method addresses such issues as research design, variables, and tests of significance. Statistical linguistics addresses such issues as word length, word sequencing, and verbal agreement. These linguistic phenomena can be quantified and utilized as data in evaluating claims concerning a text's multiple authorship or the presence of different layers of tradition. Existing biblical studies involving the use of statistical analysis are as diverse as the "Bible Code" and the analysis of letter sequencing patterns (Drosnin 1997; Witztum, Rips, and Rosenberg 1994), computer-assisted structural analysis (Parker 1976), the Computer Bible project (Baird and Freedman 1971), and the testing of theories of source dependence based on the statistical analysis of verbal agreement patterns (Honoré 1968; Wortham 1999). Finally, two case studies illustrating statistical textual analysis are offered. The two case studies address issues concerning the common authorship or editorship of John's prologue (Jn 1.1–18) and the antitheses section of the Sermon on the Mount (Mt 5.21–48).

Methodological Primer

The Research Process

Empirical research is based on the analysis of observable phenomena and is concerned with the description, analysis, and explanation of what is rather than what ought to be. The goal is to generate testable explanations of observable phenomena. Within this context researchers are to remain neutral. Perceptual and methodological biases are to be minimized and hopefully acknowledged (Hoover 1988: 3–41). In reality, it is impossible to eliminate bias from research completely insofar as researchers will favor certain theoretical and methodological approaches in their data analysis and practice selective observation and selective interpretation (Spradley and McCurdy 1988 [1972]: 13–15). Prior experiences and procedural preferences color any research endeavor. However, by formally and explicitly stating theories and derived propositions and by comparing these to evidence, bias can be given less chance to force conclusions.

The hypothesis testing method is an expression of the empirical research process. Wallace (1971) offers a classic statement of the procedure. The key elements of his "cycle of scientific inquiry" are theory, hypotheses, data, and generalizations. A modified version of this model is offered in figure 7.1. The model indicates that the four components are connected and that a two-way association exists between theory and data. These linkages signify that these elements are interdependent. Each is an integral part of the research process. The interaction between theory and data suggests that a scholar may approach a research topic from either an inductive or deductive perspective. If one takes an inductive approach, one may focus more on how empirical observations may lead to the development of new theoretical constructs, which can then be tested within a hypothesis testing framework. Conversely, with the deductive approach, one begins with the theoretical construct and then collects data to see if the theory maintains its explanatory power within a new empirical context. The latter is what will be outlined below. With either approach, theory construction (inductive approach) or theory validation (deductive approach), the research design hinges on the interdependence of theory, hypotheses, data, and conclusions.

The deductive approach begins with theories, which may be described as points of view, and every discipline is characterized by a variety of theoretical

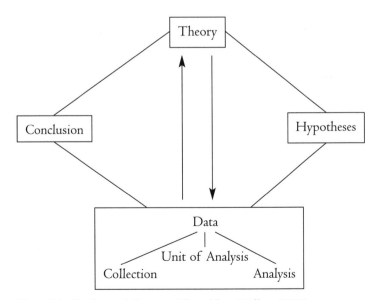

Figure 7.1. The Research Process. *Adapted from Wallace (1971).*

perspectives. A more formal definition of theory suggests that a theory is a set of statements and concepts that attempt to describe observable phenomena or behavior (Schutt 1996: 19–23). An example of a sociological theory is functionalism. According to this theoretical perspective, society is a system of parts. Each part has a specific purpose or intent. The purpose of the family, a social institution, may be to provide identity and child rearing. The different parts of society work together to provide a sense of order and control. Likewise, biblical scholars are familiar with source criticism and the various theories that attempt to specify patterns of source independence and dependence among the Gospels of Matthew, Mark, Luke, John, Thomas, and Q (Bultmann 1963; Farmer 1976; and Funk, Hoover, and the Jesus Seminar 1993).

The second component of the research process involves hypotheses. A hypothesis is often described as an "educated guess" that is based on a theory. This definition obscures the fact that an association between "variables" is being tested. A hypothesis may be defined as a tentative statement about the association between two or more variables that reflect two or more theoretical concepts. Concepts are the basic ideas of a discipline, whereas a variable includes observable characteristics that can be logically related to one another (Hoover 1988: 16–20, 27–31). A hypothesis proposes a claim such as "educational attainment is higher in urban areas" or "there is no difference in educational attainment in rural and urban areas (the null hypothesis).

In a recent statistical analysis of source-dependent associations among the infancy narratives preserved in Matthew, Luke, and the *Protevangelium of James*, Wortham generated three general and twelve specific hypotheses in order to identify specific patterns of source dependence (1999: 105–28). One general hypothesis was the null hypothesis. This hypothesis stated, "no source dependent associations exist among the infancy of Jesus narratives preserved in Matthew, Luke and the Protevangelium of James." One of the specific hypotheses was a restatement of Conrady's thesis that "the *Protevangelium of James* is the common source of Matthew and Luke, but Matthew is earlier than Luke" (Cullmann 1963: 372).

Data collection and analysis is the third component of the research process. Empirical inquiry is based on the assumption that phenomena can be observed and measured. These measurable observations are data. In social research, data may take the form of individual responses in a survey questionnaire or vital statistics, such as birth rates, that can be aggregated at the county or state level. Aggregations of different sizes and individual data represent different "units of analysis." The unit of analysis is the "who" or the "what" that is being studied. Therefore, the unit of analysis may be individual responses, group responses such as males versus females, institutional responses such as private versus public schools, or ecological units such as census tracts or counties (Stark 2001: 8–12).

Data sources that are relevant to the study of early Christianity are available. Standard sources include pottery, coins, and inscriptions, as well as narrative texts and sayings sources.[1] Scholars who choose to employ statistical textual analysis may quickly discover that important statistical data include word length, verse length, total word count, and verbal agreement. The research process does not end with the collection and description of data, however. Within a hypothesis testing framework, data must be analyzed. Various statistical techniques are available to aid researchers with data analysis. These statistical procedures may involve basic frequency counts or percentage differences or more sophisticated approaches like correlation, regression, or discriminant analysis. Statistical techniques provide researchers with ways of identifying patterns or general trends in the data and specify important associations among various measures and indicators. In his study of the synoptic problem, Honoré employed word counts, verbal agreement frequencies, and the ratio of total agreement to total word length to test synoptic problem hypotheses (1968: 96–98).

The fourth component of the research process is the drawing of conclusions. Conclusions represent the general findings of the study as revealed by the data analysis. These findings enable the researcher to test hypotheses and evaluate theoretical claims. The conclusions indicate whether the hypothesis should be accepted or rejected and whether the theory is supported within the present context or perhaps needs to be revised. The success of a research project does not hinge on accepting the hypothesis or reifying the theory. Valuable information is gained from the rejection of a hypothesis that is not supported by an analysis. Problems are encountered when an analysis is misleading—for example, a researcher rejecting a hypothesis when in reality the hypothesis should be accepted or accepting a hypothesis when in reality it should be rejected. The first problem is an example of a Type 1 error or false rejection error, while the second problem is an example of a Type 2 or false acceptance error (Bohrnstedt and Knoke 1994: 100–101).

Hypothesis Testing

Hypothesis testing involves evaluating associations among variables. It assumes that concepts can be "operationalized" as measures that vary, that data are available, that patterns of association may be evaluated statistically, and that statistically significant relationships can be identified. But what does each of the assumptions entail? As noted above, variables represent concepts that are logically related (Levin and Fox 2000: 1–2). Operationalization concerns how a variable is measured (Babbie 1979: 138–46). In many sociological studies, social class is an index operationalized as a composite of years of education, income level, and an occupational prestige ranking. Likewise, in the statistical study of early Christian infancy narratives, Wortham distinguishes exact verbal agreement and partial verbal agreement (1999: 106–7). Exact verbal agreement was operationalized as the employment of grammatically equivalent linguistic expressions in two parallel texts. Exact verbal agreements were subsequently assigned the value 1.0. On the other hand, partial verbal agreement was operationalized as linguistic agreement among parallel words or phrases based on variant grammatical forms. Partial verbal agreements were consequently assigned the value 0.5.

Research studies are only as sound as the data upon which they are based. Confidence in a data source is enhanced if the data are representative, reliable, and valid. Sample data are representative if they reflect the characteristics of the larger population from which they are drawn. Measures are valid if they measure the phenomenon they are intended to measure, and they are reliable if a measurement system yields consistent findings. Replication studies often function to enhance the validity and reliability of the study variables (Schutt 1996: 96–100, 160; Theissen 1982: 178–80; and Babbie 1979: 129–32).

When attempting to analyze biblical texts, the representative nature of a text can be problematic because the available manuscript evidence does not necessarily include all the documents produced by the various religious communities. Researchers are limited to identifying the most plausible reconstruction of extant texts based on the available manuscript evidence. This is essentially what researchers are provided with in the Nestle-Aland critical edition of the Greek New Testament (*Novum Testamentum Graece*) and critical editions of other ancient texts. To the extent that the texts presented in this critical edition are based on the most current manuscript evidence, they are at least *assumed* to be representative. Likewise, biblical researchers employing statistical textual analysis may be working under the assumption that verbal agreement is a valid and reliable measure of linguistic association and source dependence. Repeated tests of source-dependent associations such as those offered by Honoré (1968) and Wortham (1999) increase confidence in the validity and reliability of verbal agreement measures as indicators of linguistic and source dependent associations.

Hypotheses are accepted or rejected based on the meeting of predetermined criteria. A hypothesis is accepted if the measure of association is statistically significant and if the direction of the association indicated by the appropriate statistical measure is consistent with the stated hypothesis. A measure is statistically significant if the probability that the observed association is due to random error does not exceed 5 percent ($p \leq .05$ level) or 1 percent ($p \leq .01$ level). Observed associations significant at the $p \leq .05$ level have a one in twenty chance of being attributed to random error, whereas, associations significant at the $p \leq .01$ level have a one in a hundred chance of being attributed to random error (Stark 1998b: 21–29).

Before turning to a study of a textual issue, a nontextual example can be instructive. A study by Stark is a straightforward example of how the hypothesis testing format can be applied to the statistical study of early Christian phenomena. First, in his study of the diffusion of early Christianity throughout the twenty-two largest urban centers in the Greco-Roman world during the first four centuries C.E., Stark hypothesized that larger urban centers would be more receptive to Christianity than smaller urban centers (1996: 131–35). Population estimates for 100 C.E. for twenty-two Greco-Roman urban centers came from Chandler and Fox (1974). Receptivity to Christianity was measured on the basis of whether a church was located in the urban center by 100 C.E., 200 C.E., or was still lacking by 200 C.E. Stark grounded his receptivity hypothesis on Claude Fischer's studies of urban life. Fischer (1975) maintained that larger urban areas attract more unconventional behavior. Since early Christianity could be treated as a deviant sect within Judaism, Christianity should be present earlier in the larger cities of the Greco-Roman Empire. As population size increases, receptivity to Christianity increases also. One of the statistical techniques Stark employed to test this hypothesis was correlation analysis. Bivariate (two variable) correlations can range from $+1.0$ to -1.0. Positive correlations indicate that both variables move in the same direction, whereas negative correlations indicate that the variables are moving in different directions. Correlations close to zero indicate that no association exists between the two variables, and correlations close to a positive or negative one suggest that a strong association exists between the two variables. Stark observed that the correlation between population size and receptivity to Christianity is 0.32 (1996: 139). The weak, positive correlation is in the direction proposed by the hypothesis, but the correlation is not statistically significant at either the $p \leq .05$ or $p \leq .01$ level. Since the hypothesis is not supported by the data, it is rejected. This finding suggests that larger urban centers were no more receptive to the expansion of early Christianity than were smaller urban centers.

A hypothesis testing illustration dealing with a textual question is provided by Wortham's (1999) study of the infancy narratives of Matthew, Luke, and the *Protevangelium of James*. One theory of source dependence assumed that chronological source-dependent associations exist among these infancy narratives. Since many scholars argue that the *Protevangelium of James* is an apocryphal, second- or third-century C.E. work (Cameron 1982), the infancy traditions preserved in it are assumed to be later. In fact the *Protevangelium of James* infancy narratives have been viewed as a conflation of Matthean and Lukan accounts (Cullmann 1991; Cameron 1982; and Miller 1992). Consequently, one hypothesis states that the chronological sequence of the infancy narratives is Matthew (A), Luke (B), and the *Protevangelium of James* (C). In testing a chronological sequence hypothesis, it is assumed, following earlier analytical models developed by Honoré (1968), that B's use of A (the earliest source) is greater than C's (the latest source) use of B and that C's use of B will be greater than C's use of A. This assumption could also be restated as B's knowledge of A (the earliest source) is greater than C's (the latest source) knowledge of B and that C's knowledge of B will be greater than C's knowledge of A. Latter sources are thus assumed to incorporate lesser amounts of commonly shared linguistic expressions. However, researchers should be cautioned that a text's editor may be aware of an earlier source and not use it if does not conform to the editor's intent and purpose. Honoré's statistical test does not evaluate this possibility. It is simply one test of source dependence based on the assumption that latter sources will incorporate lesser amounts of commonly shared linguistic material.

Since use (knowledge of a text's existence) is measured as degree of shared verbal agreement expressed as a percentage of word (count) length, a pattern of declining percentages would suggest chronological sequence. For the sequence Matthew–Luke–*Protevangelium*, the following use percentages were noted (Wortham 1999: 115). Luke's (B) use of Matthew (A) is 11.10 percent, while the *Protevangelium of James*'s (C) use of Luke (B) is 16.70 percent and the *Protevangelium of James*'s (C) use of Matthew (A) is 24.70 percent. Some researchers argue that when percentage differences are being compared, a percentage difference of less than 10 percentage points is not statistically significant (Riordan and Mazur 1988: 14). Here the percentage difference is 13.6 percent, suggesting that the finding is statistically significant, but the percentage sequence does not confirm the hypothesized pattern. Rather than observing a declining pattern of verbal agreement, the pattern is actually increasing. This finding would lead one to question whether the latest infancy narrative accounts are included in the *Protevangelium of James*. The only statistically significant declining verbal agreement pattern is observed for the Matthew–*Protevangelium of James*–Luke chronological sequence (Wortham 1999: 116–17). This finding suggests that the *Protevangelium of James* does not include the least amount of commonly shared linguistic material and, on the basis of this criterion, may not be the latest infancy narrative source.

Major Tenets of Statistical Linguistics

Statistical textual analysis is an empirically based exegetical method. It provides biblical scholars with an opportunity to test theories of source dependence within a hypothesis testing framework. Source dependence can be measured by such variables as exact and partial verbal agreement, and patterns in the data may be identified using statistical measures like percentage differences. In this regard statistical textual analysis is an important empirical complement to traditional redaction criticism and source criticism. Furthermore, in many respects statistical textual analysis is an extension of statistical linguistics to biblical criticism.

Languages are complex symbol systems. These symbols may be associated with sounds and gestures that can be combined in ways that produce shared meanings (Haviland 1999: 95–100). Language is a shared, cultural phenomenon, and the components of a language can be identified and measured empirically. Linguistics addresses the empirical study of language characteristics, structures, and patterns (Fowler 1974: 19). Words, phrases, sentences, and verses are linguistic expressions that can be measured and analyzed statistically. Statistical linguistics may be employed by researchers as a tool to identify an author's distinctive writing style, test for multiple authorship, and distinguish authentic and inauthentic texts (Hubert 1980). Linguistics, and more specifically statistical linguistics, provides the theoretical and methodological foundation for statistical textual analysis.

If linguistics is primarily concerned with the empirical study of language units and patterns, what are some of the basic linguistic units? Linguistics includes, but is not limited to, the study of phones, phonemes, morphemes, syntax, and semantics (Fowler 1974: 19–42; Haviland 1999: 95–105). A *phone* is a minimal unit of sound in a given language. In English and Greek, this could be the letters of the alphabet (a, b, c, . . . and α, β, γ, . . .). With the *phoneme*, the focus shifts to the smallest unit of sound within a given language that also indicates a change in meaning. A phoneme could be comprised of only one phone such as "I" or two or more phones such as "a" + "t" = "at." In many languages a syllable is a primary example of a phoneme. A *morpheme* is a set of phonemes that are logically related and produce words. These words generate shared meanings that are collectively understood by the language's users. Morphemes may be either *bound* or *free*. Free morphemes stand alone, whereas bound morphemes include prefixes and suffixes. An example of a free morpheme would be the word "American." "Anti-American" and "Americans" are examples of bound morphemes (Haviland 1999: 95–105).

Languages are also characterized by rules of combination. These rules are applied to the combination of phones, phonemes, morphemes (words), phrases, sentences, and verses. The rules of combination are known as *syntax* or *grammar*. Syntax deals with sound combinations and word order and specifies a language's surface structure. Thus, in many English sentences a verb and a possible object follow a subject. On the other hand, the use of "!" at the beginning of a word like "!Kung" is an example of a phone that is not commonly utilized in English.

The final linguistic concept introduced in this overview is *semantics*. How does thought come to expression, and how is meaning derived from word order? Linguistic researchers speak of linguistic phenomena in terms of their surface structure properties or *syntax* and their deep structure properties or *semantics* (Fowler 1974: 32–34; Haviland 1999: 95–105). Often the meaning of a linguistic expression is ambiguous, and meaning must be derived from the expression's context rather than word order. For example, the ending phrase in the Greek text of John

1.1, καὶ θεὸς ἦν ὁ λόγος, is somewhat ambiguous. Traditionally, the phrase is translated "and the Word was God" (RSV, KJV). However, two additional plausible
translations are "and the Word was divine" or "and the word was a god"
(Haenchen 1984: 109). Ambiguity arises because θεός occurs in this phrase without the article ὁ. Earlier in the verse it appears with the article (τὸν θεόν). In translating the latter part of the phrase, translators regard λόγος and θεός as equivalent
expressions and translate the expression θεός without the article as a reference to
the high god of the Judaeo-Christian tradition. But is this the meaning intended
by the author, authors, or editors that produced this text, and is this the meaning
the earliest hearers would have attributed to this text? Did this text arise in a Hellenistic or Palestinian Jewish context or even a possible Gnostic context (Brown
1966; Bultmann 1971; Beasley-Murray 1987)?

Given these possible interpretive contexts, this phrase could have multiple
meanings. Thus, the relationship between syntax and semantics is complex and is
mediated by a text's multiple social and cultural contexts. Questions concerning a
text's social setting (*Sitz im Leben*), the social world and social status of the text's
author or authors and subsequent editors, and the social and cultural worlds of a
text's intended and subsequent hearers are major issues addressed by the sociology
of literature and sociolinguistics (Haviland 1999: 99–101, 110–23; Theissen
1992: 33–37; Theissen 1999: 1–18, 323–31). Thus, insights from linguistics, sociolinguistics, and the sociology of literature could aid in clarifying findings from
statistical textual analysis, which are based more on syntax measures.

The methodological, empirical basis of statistical textual analysis is complemented by measures derived from statistical linguistics. According to Hubert statistical linguistics enables researchers to measure and classify linguistic patterns,
which may answer questions concerning a text's authorship and a language's distinctive features and linguistic complexity (1980: 223). Hubert maintains that a
society's organizational and cultural complexity is reflected in the complexity of
its language. This is a restatement of the Sapir-Whorf hypothesis, whereby language is viewed as a powerful tool that can "shape" one's perception of reality in
addition to "encoding" reality (Haviland 1999: 110–13).

Four major linguistic indicators that can be quantified are (1) word frequency,
(2) vocabulary size, (3) word length, and (4) sentence length (Hubert 1980: 223).
Word frequency analysis deals with documenting word occurrences within a document. Occurrences may be ranked according to frequency of occurrence. Vocabulary size measures may be employed to identify a particular author's writing style.
Here the focus shifts to identifying distinct words utilized by an author and the
author's vocabulary range. Word-length indicators and sentence length can be employed in a similar manner as average number of letters and/or syllables per word
or average sentence length could be utilized as an indicator of an author's style. In

fact, in a classic biblical study addressing the authenticity of the various letters attributed to Paul, A. G. Morton utilized sentence-length measures to test Pauline authenticity (Hubert 1980: 247–48).

Linguistic research testing the validity of these indicators with different languages reveals some important findings. First, an inverse association exists between a word's frequency of occurrence in a document and its rank (Zipf's law).[2] Second, a word's frequency of occurrence decreases as its word length increases. Third, as the length of function words such as prepositions and conjunctions increases, their frequency of occurrence decreases. On the other hand, the frequency of occurrence of context words such as nouns and verbs does not vary by word length. Finally, authors tend to prefer a limited vocabulary, a concept known as the "principle of least effort," but listeners (intended audiences) prefer broader vocabulary ranges because they minimize a particular communicator's possible alternate meanings (Hubert 1980: 234–47). These findings based on cross-cultural research suggest that statistical indicators such as word frequency, vocabulary size, word length, and sentence length are valid and reliable measures and would be appropriate for use in studying linguistic associations embedded in New Testament manuscripts.

Statistical Linguistic Analysis: Case Studies

The Prologue of John (Jn 1:1–18)

Preliminary statistical textual analyses of John 1.1 and 1.1–18 are offered as illustrations of this approach's usefulness in evaluating authorship hypotheses. These passages are appropriate test cases since the Johannine authorship of the prologue and its relationship to the rest of John's Gospel has been questioned (Haenchen 1984: 81; Beasley-Murray 1987: 3). Some theories suggest that only verses 1–3 and 13 were part of the earliest version of the prologue, while others have suggested that verses 1–5, 10–11, 14, and 16–17 were part of an Aramaic hymn that was later incorporated (Bultmann 1971: 16–18; Haenchen 1984: 79, 81; and Beasley-Murray 1987: 3). A word-frequency and word-length analysis of John 1.1 is displayed in table 7.1 for illustration purposes. A more comprehensive verse-length analysis of the prologue is portrayed in table 7.2.[3]

The descriptive statistics provided in table 7.1 could help a researcher specify an author's or editor's style, and data could be provided for each of the prologue's eighteen verses in an attempt to test theories of the prologue's textual homogeneity. The preliminary analysis of the first verse suggests that the writer's style is characterized by the use of small words and a high degree of word repetition. The average word length is three letters, and only three of the seventeen words are used

Table 7.1.   Word-Frequency and Word-Length Analysis of John 1:1

Word Rank	Frequency of Occurrence
1. ὁ, τόν	4
2. λόγος	3
3. ἦν	3
4. καί	2
4. θεόν, θεός	2
6. ἐν	1
6. ἀρχή	1
6. πρός	1

Total verse length: 17 words
Mean word length: 3 letters
SOURCE: *Novum Testamentum Graece.*

once. If one wanted to test whether the authorship style of verses 1–5, 10–11, 14, and 16–17 differs significantly from the style characterizing verses 6–9, 12–13, 15, and 18, mean word-length statistics, word-rank, and word-frequency statistics could be calculated for both clusters and then compared to provide an empirical test of the Aramaic hymn hypothesis.

A second statistical test that could be employed to validate the findings from the word frequency and word length analysis of John's prologue is verse length analysis. It is assumed that verse length functions as an indicator of linguistic style in much the same manner as sentence length. Both measures are syntax-based. However, a word of caution is in order. Verse length and sentence length are not exact equivalents, and extensive punctuation and the verse system are later additions to the Greek text (Metzger 1968: 13, 22–27). The verse is essentially a mechanism that is employed to reference different units of thought. The verse system provides plausible linguistic reconstructions or approximations of expressed ideas.

Given these assumptions verse length is treated as a readily available indicator of authorship style, and one could expect the verse lengths for the Aramaic hymn section of the prologue to differ significantly from the other verses. Even if the author of the prologue has edited the Aramaic hymn section, and earlier material has been woven into the text, traces of the Aramaic hymn author's style would probably survive the translation and redaction process. To test the Aramaic hymn hypothesis, a difference in means test for small samples could be employed. This test would involve calculating the mean verse length $(\overline{X})$ and the estimated sample variance (S^2) for each verse cluster and then employing a t-test to determine whether the difference in means for the Aramaic and non-Aramaic verses is statistically significant (Levin and Fox 2000: 212–17; Mueller, Schuessler, and Costner 1977: 430–36).

If the hypothetical Aramaic and the remaining portions of the prologue were by the same author, then one would expect the difference in mean verse length for these two clusters to be zero or close to zero. This may be stated formally as:

$$H_0: \overline{X} - \overline{Y} = 0$$
$$H_1: \overline{X} - \overline{Y} \neq 0$$

The first hypothesis (H_0) indicates that there is no difference in means. The second hypothesis (H_1) suggests that the mean for the Aramaic hymn verse cluster $(\overline{X})$ could be higher or lower than the mean for the non-Aramaic hymn verse cluster $(\overline{Y})$.

The formulas used in calculating the means (formulas 1 & 2), the estimated sample variance (formulas 3 & 4), the t-test (formula 5), and the degrees of freedom (formula 6) are taken from standard statistical texts (Levin and Fox 2000: 212–16; Mueller, Schuessler, and Costner 1977: 430) and are stated below. The formulas for the means are:

$$\overline{X} = \frac{\sum X_i}{N_x} \qquad \overline{Y} = \frac{\sum Y_i}{N_y} \qquad \text{(formulas 1 \& 2)}$$

X_i and Y_i represent the word length of individual verses, and N_x and N_y represent the total number of verses in each group. The $\sum$ sign indicates that the different verse lengths for each cluster are to be added. The formulas for calculating the sample variance (S^2) estimates are:

$$S_x^2 = \frac{\sum X_i^2}{N_x} - \overline{X} \qquad S_y^2 = \frac{\sum Y_i^2}{N_y} - \overline{Y} \qquad \text{(formulas 3 \& 4)}$$

The formula for the t-test statistic (t) is:

$$t = \frac{\overline{X} - \overline{Y}}{\sqrt{(N_x S_x^2 + N_y S_y^2)/(N_x + N_y - 2) \times (N_x + N_y)/N_x N_y}}$$

(formula 5)

The formula for the degrees of freedom (df) is:

$$df = N_x - N_y - 2 \qquad \text{(formula 6)}$$

The findings of the verse length analysis of the Aramaic hymn and the non-Aramaic hymn verses in John 1.1–18 are summarized in table 7.2. The mean ($\overline{X}$) verse length of the Aramaic hymn verses is 13.7 words, while that of the non-Aramaic verses is 14.375 words. Obviously, the means are not the same, but is the difference in means statistically significant? To determine this a two-tailed t-test is employed.

The hypothesis of no difference in means (H_0: $\overline{X} - \overline{Y} = 0$) will be accepted if $-t_{.005} \leq t \leq t_{.005}$. Using formula 5 to calculate the t statistic, the t value is -0.501 (see table 7.2). It is assumed that the t statistic will be statistically significant if the probability of a chance finding does not exceed $p \leq .05$; however, more confidence is placed with measures significant at the $p \leq .01$ level. This means that the chance that the t value calculated is the result of random error does not exceed 1 percent. Since a two-tailed t-test is used, the chance of an erroneous low value or high value is 0.5 percent. The values for the low end ($-t_{.005}$) and high end ($t_{.005}$) critical t values are derived from "a distribution of t table" (Levin and Fox 2000: 432). This table is included in the appendix of most elementary statistics textbooks. The critical value selected is for a two-tailed test at the $p \leq .01$ significance level for $10 + 8 - 2$

Table 7.2.   Verse-Length Analysis of Aramaic Hymn and Non-Aramaic Hymn Verses in John 1:1–18

Verse (N_x)	A. Aramaic Verses Verse Length in Words (X_i)	X_i^2
1	17	289
2	7	49
3	12	144
4	12	144
5	13	169
10	16	256
11	10	100
14	23	529
16	12	144
17	15	225
	137	2,049

$N_1 = 10$

$$\overline{X} = \frac{\Sigma X_i}{N_1} = \frac{137}{10} = 13.7$$

$$S_x^2 = \frac{\Sigma X_i^2}{N_x} - \overline{X}_2 = \frac{2,049}{10} - (13.7)^2 = 17.21$$

B. Non-Aramaic Verses

Verse (N_y)	Verse Length in Words (Y_i)	Y_i^2
6	8	64
7	14	196
8	11	121
9	13	169
12	16	256
13	16	256
15	22	484
18	15	225
	115	1,771

$N_2 = 8$

$$\overline{Y} = \frac{\Sigma Y_i}{N_y} = \frac{115}{8} = 14.375$$

$$S_y^2 = \frac{\Sigma Y_i^2}{N_y} - \overline{Y}^2 = \frac{1,771}{8} - (14.375)^2 = 14.734$$

$$t = \frac{\overline{X} - \overline{Y}}{\sqrt{(N_x S_x^2 + N_y S_y^2)/(N_x + N_y - 2) \times (N_x + N_y)/N_x N_y}}$$

$$t = \frac{13.7 - 14.375}{\sqrt{\left(\frac{10(17.21) + 8(14.734)}{10 + 8 - 2}\right)\left(\frac{10 + 8}{(10)(8)}\right)}} = -0.501$$

$$\overline{X} = \frac{198}{10} = 19.8$$

= 16 degrees of freedom. This critical t value is ± 2.921. Since −2.921 ≤ − 0.501 ≤ 2.921, the hypothesis of no difference in means (H_0: $\overline{X} - \overline{Y} = 0$) is accepted. This means that the difference in mean verse length for the Aramaic hymn verse cluster ($\overline{X}$) and the non-Aramaic hymn verse cluster ($\overline{Y}$) is not statistically significant. This statistical test indicates that the verses included in the prologue (Jn 1.1–18) display a linguistic style that is similar enough to suggest that they are from the same author or editor. The findings of this empirical test cast doubt on the Aramaic hymn hypothesis.

Testing the Jesus Seminar Authorship Authenticity Designations

Verse length analysis could be employed also in testing for the presence of multiple authors and/or editors of the Jesus tradition preserved in the gospel accounts. In *The Five Gospels* (1993), the members of the Jesus Seminar have attempted to distinguish authentic or probable words of Jesus from those judged to be less

probable or inauthentic. The group has evaluated each of the statements attributed to Jesus preserved in Matthew, Mark, Luke, John, and Thomas and placed
them in one of four groups. These groups are: (1) not a Jesus saying, (2) not a Jesus saying but contains ideas similar to Jesus', (3) probably a Jesus saying, and (4)
a Jesus saying (Funk, Hoover, and the Jesus Seminar 1993: 35–37).

In providing a test of the validity and reliability of the Jesus Seminar's authenticity designations, the "antithesis sayings" from the Sermon on the Mount
(Mt 5:21–48) are subjected to verse length analysis. Since each Jesus saying can
be placed in one of four possible authenticity categories, analysis of variance
(ANOVA) is employed to test the differences in authenticity category means.
Analysis of variance is an appropriate measure to use when the means for three or
more groups are being evaluated. It is assumed that each authenticity category represents a separate sample, and between group (authenticity categories) and within
group (each authenticity category) variation (association) can be assessed (Levin
and Fox 2000: 240–41).

The Greek text of the antithesis section is again based on Nestle-Aland Greek
text (*Novum Testamentum Graece*). The two hypotheses tested are:

- Null Hypothesis
  The antithesis section of the Sermon on the Mount is a collection of sayings
  by a common author.

$$(\overline{H}_0: \overline{X}_1 = \overline{X}_2 = \overline{X}_3 = \overline{X}_4)$$

- Research Hypothesis
  The antithesis section of the Sermon on the Mount is a collection of sayings by multiple authors.

$$(\overline{H}_1: \overline{X}_1 \neq \overline{X}_2 \neq \overline{X}_3 \neq \overline{X}_4)$$

With the research hypothesis, it is assumed also that the antithesis section could
have been created by multiple authors and / or revised by one or more editors. The
Jesus Seminar participants maintain that the antithesis section contains authentic,
probable, similar, and inauthentic Jesus sayings (Funk, Hoover, and the Jesus Seminar 1993: 141–45).

Authorship categories and verse length data for the antithesis section verses are
presented in table 7.3. Included also are mean verse length calculations for each
authenticity category and the square of each verse's length. Verses 22, 42, 44, and
45 have been excluded from the analysis since these verses include phrases that
would cause a verse to be included in more than one authenticity category. Also,
the phrase ἐγὼ δὲ λέγω ὑμῖν has been removed from the word count for verses 34
and 39 so that the verse would conform to only one authenticity category. The
mean verse length for the inauthentic verses $(\overline{X}_1)$ is 13.9 words, whereas the mean

Table 7.3.   Proposed Authorship, Verse, Verse Length, and Mean Length of Verses Included in the Antithesis Section (Mt 5.21–48) of the Sermon on the Mount

A. Sayings Not by Jesus

Verse (N_1)	Verse Length in Words (X_1)	Length Square (X_1^2)
21	15	225
27	5	25
28	20	400
31	11	121
32	23	529
33	15	225
38	10	100
43	12	144
$\Sigma = 111$		$\Sigma = 1{,}769$

$$\bar{X}_1 = \frac{111}{8} = 13.9$$

B. Ideas Similar to Jesus

Verse (N_2)	Verse Length in Words (X_2)	Length Square (X_2^2)
23	19	361
24	22	484
29	33	1089
30	32	1024
34*	12	144
35	19	361
36	15	225
37	17	289
47	17	289
48	12	144
$\Sigma = 198$		$\Sigma = 4{,}410$

$$\bar{X}_2 = \frac{198}{10} = 19.8$$

C. Probably by Jesus

Verse (N_3)	Verse Length in Words (X_3)	Length Square (X_3^2)
25	30	900
26	13	169
46	16	256
$\Sigma = 59$		$\Sigma = 1{,}325$

$$\bar{X}_3 = \frac{59}{3} = 19.7$$

| | *D. Jesus Saying* | |
Verse (N_3)	*Verse Length in Words* (X_3)	*Length Square* (X_3^2)
39*	18	324
40	15	225
41	10	100
	$\Sigma = 43$	$\Sigma = 649$

$$\overline{X}_4 = \frac{43}{3} = 14.3$$

*The phrase ἐγὼ δὲ λέγω ὑμῖν has been omitted and is not included in the verse-length count.
**The Jesus Seminar scholars indicated that verses 22, 42, 44, and 45 contain phrases by multiple authors and/or editors. These verses were excluded from the analysis of variance.

verse length for the similar idea $(\overline{X}_2)$, probable $(\overline{X}_3)$, and authentic $(\overline{X}_4)$ verses is 19.8, 19.7, and 14.3 words respectively.

ANOVA is employed next to evaluate the null and research hypotheses. This procedure involves calculating the individual cluster means, total sum of scores, sum of squared scores, number of subjects, group mean, total sum of squares, within-group and between-group sum of squares, between-group and within-group degrees of freedom, within-group mean square, between-group mean square, the F ratio, and the critical F ratio. The following formulas and analytical steps (1–14) are employed in conducting the analysis of variance of the antithesis material. These formulas and steps are derived from Levin and Fox (2000: 253–56). For larger textual data sets, researchers could utilize either the Statistical Package for the Social Sciences (SPSS) or the Statistical Analysis System (SAS) to import and analyze the relevant, coded textual data. Each statistical package includes various analysis of variance procedures.[4]

1. sample means:

$$\overline{X}_I = \frac{\Sigma X_I}{N_I}$$

$\overline{X}_1 = 13.9$ (See table 7.3)
$\overline{X}_2 = 19.8$
$\overline{X}_3 = 19.7$
$\overline{X}_4 = 14.3$

2. sum of scores:

$$\Sigma\, X_{TOTAL} = \Sigma\, X_1 + \Sigma\, X_2 + \Sigma\, X_3 + \Sigma\, X_4$$
$$\Sigma\, X_{TOTAL} = 111 + 198 + 59 + 43$$
$$= 411$$

3. sum of squared scores:

$$\Sigma\, X^2{}_{TOTAL} = \Sigma\, X_1{}^2 + \Sigma\, X_2{}^2 + \Sigma\, X_3{}^2 + \Sigma\, X_4{}^2$$
$$\Sigma\, X^2{}_{TOTAL} = 1769 + 4410 + 1325 + 649$$
$$= 8153$$

4. number of subjects:

$$N_{TOTAL} = N_1 + N_2 + N_3 + N_4$$
$$N_{TOTAL} = 8 + 10 + 3 + 3$$
$$= 24 \text{ verses}$$

5. group mean:

$$\overline{X} = \frac{\Sigma\, X_{TOTAL}}{N_{TOTAL}}$$
$$= \frac{411}{24} = 17.1 \text{ words}$$

6. total sum of squares:

$$SS_{TOTAL} = \Sigma\, X^2{}_{TOTAL} - N_{TOTAL}\, \overline{X}^2{}_{TOTAL}$$
$$SS_{TOTAL} = 8153 - (23)(17.1)^2$$
$$= 1135.2$$

7. within-group sum of squares:

$$SS_{WITHIN} = \Sigma\, X^2{}_{TOTAL} - \Sigma\, N_{GROUP}\, \overline{X}^2{}_{GROUP}$$
$$SS_{WITHIN} = 8153 - [\, 8(13.9)^2 + 10(19.8)^2 + 3(19.7)^2 + 3(14.3)^2\,]$$
$$= 8153 - 7243.82$$
$$= 909.18 \approx 909$$

8. between-group sum of squares:

$$SS_{BETWEEN} = \Sigma\, \overline{N}_{GROUP}\, \overline{X}^2{}_{GROUP} - \overline{N}_{TOTAL}\, \overline{X}^2{}_{TOTAL}$$
$$SS_{BETWEEN} = [8(13.9)^2 + 10(19.8)^2 + 3(19.7)^2 + 3(14.3)^2] - 24(17.1)^2$$
$$= 7243.82 - 7017.84$$
$$= 225.98$$

9. between-group degrees of freedom:

$$df_{BETWEEN} = k - 1$$
$$df_{BETWEEN} = 4 - 1$$
$$= 3$$

10. within-group degrees of freedom:

$$df_{WITHIN} = N_{TOTAL} - k$$
$$df_{WITHIN} = 24 - 4$$
$$= 20$$

11. within-group mean square:

$$MS_{WITHIN} = \frac{SS_{WITHIN}}{df_{WITHIN}}$$
$$MS_{WITHIN} = \frac{909}{20}$$
$$= 45.45 \approx 45.5$$

12. between-group mean square:

$$MS_{BETWEEN} = \frac{SS_{BETWEEN}}{df_{BETWEEN}}$$
$$MS_{BETWEEN} = \frac{225.98}{3} = 75.327 \approx 75.3$$

13. calculated F ratio:

$$F\ ratio = \frac{MS_{BETWEEN}}{MS_{WITHIN}}$$
$$F\ ratio = \frac{75.3}{45.5} = 1.65$$

14. critical F ratio:
   degrees of freedom (between = 3; within = 20)
   significance level (p ≤ .01)
   critical F ratio = 4.94.[5]

Since the calculated F ratio (1.65) is less than the critical F ratio (4.94) at the p ≤ .01 level of significance, the null hypothesis is accepted. The analysis of variance findings suggest that the antithesis section (Mt 5.21–48) of the Sermon on the Mount in its present form appears to be the work of a common author or a common editor. The material could have come from Jesus, a Matthean redactor, or an unknown source that was inserted by a Matthean redactor. The multiple authorship and/or editorship designations within the antithesis section of the Sermon on the Mount proposed by the Jesus Seminar are not supported by this statistical analysis of verse length data. However, additional linguistic measures other than verse length should be tested, and other passages within the Sermon on the Mount must be analyzed before a common authorship or editorship theory for the Sermon on the Mount material can be accepted. Nevertheless, statistical textual analysis represents an additional tool that biblical researchers can utilize to empirically test authorship theories and authenticity models.

Conclusion

Although biblical researchers have applied statistical analysis to the study of textual variants since the early decades of the twentieth century (Metzger 1968: 163–69), the potential usefulness of this method has not been sufficiently explored. Radday and Shore's (1985, 1977a, and 1977b) application of computer-assisted statistical linguistic analysis to the study of authorship problems associated with the Books of Genesis and Joshua represents a pioneering effort to demonstrate the validity and usefulness of this emerging exegetical approach. The analysis of shared word sequences and shared vocabulary by McIver (1997) represents a more recent attempt by a New Testament scholar to apply statistical textual analysis to the study of synoptic source relationships. The case studies offered in this brief introduction to statistical textual analysis offer additional examples of the approach's potential usefulness. Researchers employing this exegetical approach will need to share an appreciation for statistical analysis and the empirical method. However, statistical textual analysis will provide an additional opportunity to test authorship and textual authenticity claims empirically as well as foster a productive dialogue between researchers in the humanities, the social sciences, computer science, and mathematics. Statistical textual analysis is truly an interdisciplinary exegetical approach.

Notes

1. In addition Stark reminds researchers that such measures as city size, distance from religious (Jerusalem) and political (Rome) centers, and the time period of the known presence of religious groups such as Judaism and Gnosticism are important examples of data that can be utilized in studying the diffusion of early Christianity (1996: 129–45).

2. See table 7.1 for an example of what is meant by *rank* in this context.

3. Again, these analyses are based on *Novum Testamentum Graece*, twenty-seventh edition (Nestle-Aland Greek text).

4. See George and Mallery (2000: 131–63) for SPSS procedures and Cody and Smith (1997: 150–89) for SAS procedures.

5. Taken from a table of critical F values. See Levin and Fox (2000: 435).

Aspects of Rhetorical Analysis Applied to New Testament Texts

8

ERNST R. WENDLAND

OR CENTURIES SCHOLARS, including such notable practitioners as Augustine (himself a teacher of rhetoric), the Venerable Bede, Erasmus, Philip Melanchthon, and John Calvin have applied a rhetorical approach to the study of New Testament (NT) literature. For the past 200 years or so such rhetorical analyses have increased significantly in both quantity and quality, right up to the present day when it has become almost impossible to ignore the results of this text-based research, no matter what one's specialization. Space here does not allow an adequate diachronic or synchronic survey of the field; we will leave that task to others.[1] I will define the discipline in a general way and then give a selective overview of several prominent methodologies that may be useful when working in the social scientific study of early Christianity. I have included a number of shorter NT examples to complement the longer application of a rhetorical model to I Peter.

What Is "Rhetoric" and Why Study It?

A thorough discussion, description, or analysis involving the popular concept of "rhetoric" must necessarily begin with a careful definition of the term itself. But here we encounter a major difficulty. As Martin Kessler observed many years ago, "The basic problem with rhetorical criticism is that English literary critics are by no means agreed as to what that well-worn term 'rhetoric' signifies or ought to signify. In the light of this it can hardly be deemed surprising if biblical critics wonder" (1982: 1). This problem presents itself because, as the word has become more widespread and commonly used in the literary analysis of biblical discourse (cf. Hughes 1989: 23), it has also been employed with an increasingly wide referential scope. Thus its signification may range from a strict application of the basic principles and terminology of ancient Greco-Roman rhetoric (e.g., Watson

1988) to an all-embracing reference to virtually any type of semiotic social inter-action (e.g., Robbins 1984: 6).

In its narrow classical sense "rhetoric" is the *art* and *technique* of persuasion, *ars rhetorica* (Aristotle, *Rhet.*). In practice this entails the use of a definite and clearly definable literary strategy that aims through conventional but skillfully utilized means of argumentation to modify (i.e., to reinforce or change) the cognitive, emotive, and/or volitional stance of the intended audience. The term "art" sug-gests a specific ability or proficiency that one is simply endowed with, while "tech-nique" implies a compositional skill that can be learned and perfected on the ba-sis of some concrete heuristic principles and procedures. The critical evaluation of this rhetorical component or characteristic of literary discourse (i.e., its "rhetori-city") is called "rhetorical criticism."

Although conservative theologians may be reluctant to speak about the use of "argument" or "artistry" in relation to the Holy Scriptures, the obvious facts of the case still need to be confronted. Unless one decides to deny or to downplay the patent literary-stylistic attributes of the biblical text (which have been demon-strated in many published studies), one needs to give such features due consider-ation in any current exposition or application of its intended message. Since a rhetorical method was undoubtedly practiced, whether consciously or intuitively, during the initial event of the oral or written composition of the Scriptures (He-brew or Greek), it is a factor that contemporary analysts and interpreters of the Word must also give particular attention. The aim is to ensure that this vital as-pect of the original text is properly recognized and accounted for in any type of contemporary exposition.

While overlapping in varying degrees with respect to aims, objects, and meth-ods, the study of "rhetoricity" may be distinguished from that of "artistry" in lit-erature by its primary focus. An analysis of artistry tends to stress compositional *form* (impersonal structure or style) within a given text, whereas the examination of rhetoricity emphasizes its communicative *function* or pragmatic (interpersonal) intent. The latter may be viewed as being progressively realized with respect to the twofold aim of *conviction* (cognitive emphasis) plus *persuasion* (emotive + volitional elements). Thus the fact that a person has been cognitively convinced will accord-ingly be manifested by a significant reinforcement or change in thought or behav-ior (actions, words).

There is considerable overlap in the textual realization and the subsequent crit-ical assessment of these two crucial aspects or attributes of literary discourse—artistry and rhetoricity. Many of the same literary-linguistic devices may be in-volved in their operation and evaluation (i.e., the practice of rhetorical criticism versus "stylistics" or "poetics"). Furthermore, both dimensions together con-tribute to the overall *connotative* component of text "meaning" in terms of impact and appeal. For this reason, some analysts lump the two together in their classification of literary technique, e.g., "argumentative" and "compositional" rhetoric (Trible 1994). In any case, there are a number of familiar stylistic devices that feature prominently in the "persuasive" shape of discourse in both secular debate and formal argument and in theological exhortation and admonition. These include rhetorical questions, irony/sarcasm, enigma, paradox, semantic paronomasia, repetition (exact or synonymous), direct speech, and word order variations for differing semantic or pragmatic emphases.

De Waard and Nida make a number of helpful observations from a broader perspective on the subject of rhetoric in their book on "functional equivalence in Bible translating" (1986). Thus the rhetorical aspect of meaning in a text, which is related to its larger discourse structure, is viewed as being realized or manifested by the principal linguistic macro-operations of *selection* and *arrangement*. Rhetoric typically effects such major communicative functions as wholeness, aesthetic appeal, impact, appropriateness, coherence, progression, cohesion, focus, and emphasis (de Waard and Nida 1986: chapter 5). This rhetorical dimension is produced by means of a number of literary techniques, such as repetition, compaction, connection, rhythm, shifts in expectancies, and the exploitation of similarities and contrasts (chapter 6). The main difficulty with such an approach concerns the rather expanded scope of the field of rhetoric, which now encompasses many of the textual features that are commonly investigated within the general framework of "discourse analysis."[2]

Rather than this wider conception of rhetoric, I will restrict the notion more to its classical understanding of *effective communication*. Thus "rhetoricity" pertains to a literary text that accomplishes a particular communicative function (or set of them) that relates to the principal goal of audience *persuasion*. Thus the various devices that contribute to the unity, diversity, structure, or any other literary characteristic simultaneously effect one or more of these functions in and through the text at hand, e.g., expressive, directive, referential, ritual, etc. While such notions may be helpful in a general sense when analyzing a biblical passage, it is probably more helpful for analytical purposes to be more specific. To this end, the various concepts, categories, and procedures associated with "speech act theory," including its extension to "text acts" and "relevance," may be used profitably (Hatim and Mason 1990: 78–79, 95–96).

The perception of and response to biblical rhetoric, just as the religious significance of the text's essential content, will obviously differ for current, as opposed to the initial, consumers of a given book or passage. For many readers or hearers of the Scriptures in today's world, these two so-called "horizons" of hermeneutics, distinguished by terms such as "source-language" and "receptor-language" settings,[3] are complicated by a third. This is the "interposed" horizon of a translation in a language *and culture* that is not their own, e.g., English and French for the majority in Africa or Spanish and Portuguese in Latin America.

While in one sense we are all outsiders "listening in" on a very distant original text, the acuity of some individuals is sharper than that of others. This is due to their ability to access the source text directly and/or their greater knowledge of several of the key situational factors, such as the historical background, sociological setting, political and religious establishment, economic environment, material culture, geography, and climate.[4] A person's textual interpretive competence may also be enhanced by utilizing the analytical techniques supplied by linguistics, literary theory, semiotics, anthropology, biblical studies, communication science, and related disciplines (e.g., multimedia technology). Functionally focused and situation-sensitive studies can furnish some useful insights into the ongoing process of contextualizing, or "framing," one's external ("alien") horizon further along in the direction of that of an internal ("indigenous") original. This includes the use of extratextual tools in modern Bibles such as footnotes, sectional headings, glossary entries, and illustrations to help bridge the ever-present communications gap that exists between the biblical texts' sociocultural contexts and those of today.

Rhetorical Criticism (RC)

There are many different types of "rhetorical criticism" that are being practiced nowadays with respect to the varied literature of the Scriptures. Although these diverse methodologies are related to a greater or lesser extent by their special concern for the *functional*, pragmatic aspect of literary analysis, they are distinct enough to warrant separate consideration. I will not attempt to cover the entire field of study but will focus instead on those approaches that appear to be most helpful in giving the analyst a credible understanding of how the forms of biblical discourse operate to effect various interpersonal functions within their initial as well as current communicative settings.

The practice or application of the ability, skill, craft, and/or technique of "rhetoric" (τέχνη ῥητορική) has been carried out over the years in diverse ways and with a number of important differences with regard to the particular purpose in mind. Consequently, the definition of "rhetorical criticism" has become manifold, even somewhat blurred, as various investigators have tended to focus their attention upon one or another of the basic components involved in the interpersonal communication of biblical literature. Generally speaking, scholarly interest has been shifting from left to right in relation to the three essential constituents shown in figure 8.1 (and their extratextual settings, or *contexts*).

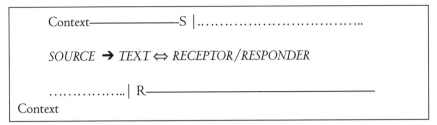

Figure 8.1. Essential Constituents of Rhetorical Studies

The Greco-Roman (GR) Model

Ancient and to a great extent also contemporary practitioners of the discipline of classical rhetoric place a decided emphasis upon the persuasive strategies and compositional techniques of the original *source* of communication, whether oral (an orator) or written (an author). They also place great importance on a text's actual setting, the so-called "rhetorical situation."[5] In its classical sense, the notion of "persuasion" appears to have had a somewhat broader referential domain than its meaning nowadays (Kennedy 1980: 4), including the effects of discourse upon a person's actions or behavior as well as one's thoughts and emotions (i.e., the "imperative" along with the "emotive" and "informative" functions of language; de Waard and Nida 1986: 29–30). Thus an elaborate taxonomy of forms and functions has long been established to both describe and interpret the communicative event from this "premodern" perspective.[6]

A modern eclectic methodology based upon the principles of ancient Greco-Roman, or Hellenistic, rhetoric and applied to biblical discourse is summarized below. This is derived from one of its earliest and best-known practitioners, George Kennedy.[7]

- First, the total scope of the pericope, or "rhetorical unit," to be analyzed is delineated as to its discourse boundaries with respect to "a discernable beginning and ending" (Kennedy 1984: 34), whether a complete work or only a portion of one.
- Next the "rhetorical situation," or contextual setting, of the pericope is described following the model of Lloyd Bitzer (1968: 1–14). This rhetorical situation encompasses all of the relevant factors, personal and impersonal, that together occasion some crisis or stimulus (*exigence*) that calls for an appropriate human response in the form of a verbal discourse.
- The third preliminary matter to deal with is the specific problem, question, or issue (*stasis*) under consideration along with the particular manner (*species*) of rhetoric that has been chosen to present it: *judicial*

(concerning accusation and/or defense of justice or wrong—with a past temporal orientation), *deliberative* (confirmation or refutation according to what is beneficial or expedient—future focus), or *epideictic* (celebration or condemnation of seminal beliefs and values—present time setting).

- The text itself is then analyzed in terms of invention, arrangement, and style. Invention (*inventio*) concerns the choice of various proofs and topics to best support the case being argued, whether according to *ethos* (character), *pathos* (emotions), or *logos* (modes of reasoning). Arrangement (*dispositio*) involves the compositional structure of the discourse in terms of ordered constituents, such as the *exordium* (introduction), *narratio* (initial statement of the case), *probatio* (main body of the argument), and *peroratio* (conclusion) according to the principles of logical deduction or experiential induction. Matters of style (*elocutio*) pertain to the specifics of how a particular speech is put together in a persuasive way through the use of devices such as distinctive diction, repetition, syntax, and figures of speech or thought.[8]

- A proper GR analysis concludes with a careful evaluation of the overall effectiveness of the rhetorical processes utilized in the text. For example, how well do these techniques succeed in meeting the major exigence, and what are the chief implications of the discourse, as delivered, for the audience (or readers)?

Many other formal distinctions and devices could be mentioned, but the preceding five steps provide a basic overview of the main procedures involved in the GR methodology, certainly as capably applied by Kennedy and Watson. The second step deals most directly with the rhetorical dynamics of any situation by calling for persuasive argumentation of one sort or another. It also points stylistic and rhetorical critics alike in the direction of making a more relevant application of their analysis by focusing on human interactive communication in contexts of crisis, celebration, or need.

However, certain problems arise when one attempts to put into practice the other steps of this set of rhetorical procedures. A typical application of the last step, for example, turns out to be rather perfunctory and hence not very helpful. Such an "evaluation of the rhetoric" is generally very short (e.g., less than two pages in Watson 1988: 78–79), highly concentrated in technical terminology, and characteristically positive in nature, as in, "Jude's rhetoric conforms to its [i.e., GR rhetoric's] best principles" (Watson 1988: 78). The third step causes some serious difficulties on account of the imprecision presented by the three so-called "species" of rhetoric, which allow for too much leeway, and hence subjectivity, in one's classification. There is also a great deal of arbitrariness involved in the attempt to categorize any complete text (of the Scriptures at any rate) with reference to a single time frame. The first step corresponds essentially to the first stage of a Muilenburg-type RC analysis (see below), and the fourth amounts to a conventional stylistic "close-reading," clothed (or is it overdressed?) in the jargon of classical rhetoric. The chief divisions proposed do not differ that much from the normal "beginning–middle–ending" of any well-formed discourse.

Much more helpful in this regard is Mack's outline of "the major moves of the rhetorical speech [or 'thesis'] in terms of the major types of proof or argumentation":[9]

> *introduction* (= *exordium*, e.g., a word of praise or commendation)
> *proposition* (the case to be argued, injunction to be supported, or thesis to be defended, often stated in the form of a syllogism, maxim, proverb, anecdote [*chreia*], or traditional commonplace)
> *rationale* (the reason[s] for the proposition—why it is just, true, expedient, appealing, advantageous, etc. according to conventional logical arguments)
> *opposite* (any contrary perspective on the proposition, a demonstration of the truth or validity of its inverse; a dialectic argument of formal refutation)
> *analogy* (general cases or universal principles taken from the world of experience, especially the natural sphere of the environment or that of everyday human activity)
> *example* (well-known stories retold or alluded to from the arena of actual history or facts based upon familiar social institutions and important cultural settings)
> *citation* (quotation from a recognized philosophical or literary authority who has come to a similar conclusion or has adopted the same stance with respect to the main proposition, including appropriate references to the virtues and vices of the gods)
> *conclusion* (a final exhortation that returns the discourse in a memorable way to its initial point of departure)

This sequence and its various transformations (repetition, deletion, perturbation) provide a useful way of summarizing, albeit in very general terms, the mixed "judicial–deliberative–epideictic" type of rhetoric that we find in many of the NT Epistles.

Other difficulties associated with an overly strict application of the GR method of analysis is well summarized by Watson and Hansen.[10]

> There is the question of the degree that rhetorical theory influenced the epistolary genre . . . and if it is rightly used in analyzing Jewish texts, particularly

those from a specifically Palestinian context. . . . Greco-Roman rhetorical analysis may leave peculiar features of early Christian rhetoric unappreciated or
undiscovered. . . . There is the danger of glossing over the changes rhetoric must
undergo in the transition from oral to written form or from one written genre
to another. . . . there is also the danger of a too rigid application of rhetorical
categories to the biblical texts. Black (1989) notes "a disquieting tendency to
press oracles or letters into elaborate rhetorical schemes of organization (from
proem to *epilogos*)." (1994: 111)

The final point noted above is especially problematic when depending upon the
rhetorical theory of the handbooks alone in the analysis of an ancient text, without making a comparative, confirmatory study of actual contemporary speeches
and letters (Mitchell 1992: 9; cf. Stowers 1986: 25). Other criticisms of a general nature could be mentioned: the imprecise (hence often debatable) use of the
elaborate rhetorical categories and foreign terminology; the lack of any alternative
or complementary perspective on the overall organization of a given discourse;
and all too often an undiscriminating application of the GR framework, with the
result that one tends to lose sight of the forest in the thick description of each
and every one of its trees.

"Form Criticism and Beyond"—Muilenburg's Extension into Rhetorical Criticism

James Muilenburg is the recognized pioneer of the modern rhetorical critical movement in American biblical studies, proposing a *text*-based methodology that is simplified and in other ways rather distinct from the classical approach.[11] Dissatisfied
with the discourse-fragmenting procedures of both source and form criticism,
Muilenburg made a revolutionary appeal to respect the integrity and literary
artistry of the biblical text as received (following conservative emendation, if necessary). In his groundbreaking presidential address to the annual meeting of the
Society of Biblical Literature in 1968, [12] Muilenburg argued that "Form and content are inextricably related. They form an integral whole. The two are one. . . . It
is the creative synthesis of the particular formulation of the pericope with the content that makes it the distinctive composition that it is" (Muilenburg in House
1992: 54). Convinced that much of biblical literature was "skillfully wrought . . .
with consummate skill and artistry" under the guiding influence of "conventional
rhetorical practices," Muilenburg went on to propose that "Persistent and painstaking attention to the modes of Hebrew literary composition will reveal that the pericopes exhibit linguistic patterns, word formations ordered or arranged in particular ways, verbal sequences which move in fixed structures from beginning to end"
(Muilenburg in House 1992: 68–69). The strong emphasis of RC upon the text

itself as the principal object of investigation is evident from the preceding citations. This manner of analysis is characteristic also of the secular "New Critical" or "stylistic" school of literary study and is typical of all those who more or less followed Muilenburg's directives. His "concrete" concept of rhetoric is reflected in Eugene Nida's treatment, where the term "includes not merely stylistic flourishes but a highly important level of language structure and significance" (1982: 324). A broader "text-centered approach" also forms the basis for Bruce Johanson's comprehensive rhetorical study of I Thessalonians (1987: 3–6).

In paying tribute to the scholarly insights to be derived from form-critical (FC) studies of the Hebrew Scriptures, Muilenburg noted three things in particular: the broad comparative nature upon which FC analyses were based (including all other literatures of the ancient Near East); their careful attention to matters pertaining to literary genres along with associated formal features (structure and style); and a concern to reveal the social and religious functions that recognizable genres performed in specific cultural settings (Muilenburg in House 1992: 50–51). However, Muilenburg went on to point out several serious deficiencies that he thought needed correcting in the typical FC approach to analysis. Among the most crucial of these was its "tendency to be too exclusive in its application of the method" with the result that it would "lay such stress upon the typical and representative that the individual, personal, and unique features of the individual pericope were all but lost to view" (52–53). In order to counteract such undue emphasis upon the general and the traditional (or expected) in both oral and written texts, Muilenburg proposed a more stylistic and aesthetic critical perspective. However, it is a method that also pays special attention to the larger organization of biblical discourse:

> What I am interested in, above all, is in understanding the nature of Hebrew literary composition, in exhibiting the structural patterns that are employed for the fashioning of a literary unit, whether in poetry or in prose, and in discerning the many and various devices by which the predications are formulated and ordered into a unified whole. (57)

In order to accomplish these objectives, a basic two-step procedure is set forth, one that lays the foundation for any structural analysis through the delimitation of the essential elements of a literary composition. This is coupled with a description of the primary interrelationships of these units, both to one another and to the whole that they comprise. In step one, therefore, the rhetorical critic will seek "To define the limits or scope of the literary unit, to recognize precisely where and how it begins and where and how it ends" (57). Muilenburg carries out this externally oriented aspect of the analysis by noting compositional techniques such as the *inclusio*, colonic or strophic arrangement (in poetry), and the stylistic marking of points of climax leading to a finale. This procedure in fact overlaps with the second, which adopts an internal perspective on the discourse as demarcated, namely:

> To recognize the structure of a composition and to discern the configuration of its component parts, to delineate the warp and the woof out of which the literary fabric is woven, and to note the various rhetorical devices that are employed for marking, on the one hand, the sequence and movement of the pericope, and on the other, the shifts or breaks in the development of the writer's thought. (59)

To this end the analyst should investigate the frequency, distribution, collocation, and function of literary features such as repetition, parallel phrasing, figures of speech, transitional particles, vocatives, and rhetorical questions.

Muilenburg's exercise of what he termed "rhetorical criticism" (in House 1992: 57, 69) is clearly very stylistic or form-centered in nature, albeit in a different sense from the methodology that he desired to move "beyond." For this reason the practitioners of this approach have been criticized as being victims "of that 'rhetoric restrained,' that is, victims of the fateful reduction of rhetoric to stylistics, and of stylistics in turn to the rhetorical tropes or figures" (Wuellner 1987: 451). On the other hand, it may be argued that this method of rhetorical criticism has either initially stimulated or been subsequently broadened into various forms of *literary analysis*, a field of research that has been applied with increasing frequency and success in NT studies of the past few decades, especially with respect to the narrative texts of the Gospels.[13]

Reader-Response (RR) Rhetoric

In recent years RC analysts have become cognizant of the need, first of all, to sensitize themselves to "the oral orientation of ancient literary units," and second, to move "beyond" Muilenburg, as it were, and considerations of literary style in order to "articulate the impact of the literary unit on its audience" (Watson and Hauser 1994: 12, 14). Indeed, some have gone so far as to tailor a definition of their discipline with this focus in mind. For example, rhetoric is "the means by which a text establishes and manages its relationship to its audience in order to achieve a particular effect" (Patrick and Scult 1990: 12). Such an emphasis upon "reader-response," however, may be in danger of moving too far in the direction of the "receptor" side of the communication cycle (see figure 8.1), thus denying Muilenburg's expressed concern (as well as that of GR critics) for probing the rhetorical intentions of the biblical author, or message "source" (Muilenburg in House 1992: 50, 54). RR critics appear to recognize that "The form or shape of a discourse is the key to how it functions for an audience. . . . Through the shape into which speakers cast their message they tell the audience how they mean it to be engaged and therefore to be understood" (Patrick and Scult 1990: 14–15). But most RR interpreters tend to downplay or disregard this principle and perspective by suggesting that such textual "cues or indicators" may not be so important after all. Thus, the "text's meaning is not inherent in its linguistic configuration or its author's intentions, but rather in the transaction or conversation between the text and the spiritual seeker addressed by its rhetoric" (1990: 19). The problem here involves that old hermeneutical conundrum of whether or not to recognize the validity—and ultimately also a priority in terms of original authority—with respect to the two traditional horizons, or contexts, of interpretation: "what a text meant" in its biblical setting and "what it means" for people today. For most current reader-response critics of Scripture, this fundamental distinction does not really apply, and therefore it is up to the present interpreter to "synthesize the meanings a text has had into the meaning it has in order to understand it fully," thus stimulating a "rhetorical re-enactment of the text's meaning" and transforming this amalgam from the past into some current ideal—"the best text it can be" (Patrick and Scult 1990: 20–23). So-called "postmodern" theorists have of course pushed this position a step further in the direction of a contemporary milieu and mind-set, one that favors idiosyncratic interpretation and a localized, here-and-now application of what amounts to a *context-less* biblical text.[14]

Semitic *(Rabbinic)* Rhetoric

This is an important field of RC that has been comparatively neglected in NT studies. The gap here is rather significant since the rhetoric of the Jewish rabbis—appropriated, adapted, and in various respects uniquely developed by Jesus the Christ (as recorded in the Gospels)—represents a sort of midway point between the literature of the Old Testament and that of the New. Jesus' discourses appear to have much in common with the prevailing literary style of the Hebrew prophets as well as that of the contemporary teachers and preachers of his day. The following is a summary description (with illustrative references) of seven of the main artistic and rhetorical features of "Jesus' Speak."[15]

- *Authoritative demeanor/aspect.* Jesus spoke with full divine authority (*ethos*) as the Son of God. This is clearly reflected, for example, in his utterance of categorical blessings or curses and in his many imperative, legislative, judicial, revelatory, and predictive assertions (Mt 5.17, 21; 11.11; 19.4ff.).
- *Prophetic style.* Jesus preached and taught like a Hebrew prophet of old, as evidenced by his calls to sincere repentance in order to avoid future divine judgment (Mt 11.21–24); his reverence for, devotion to, and emphasis upon "the word of the Lord" (Mt 9.12–13); his bluntly honest,

hypocrisy-condemning message, on occasion including irony, hyperbole, and sarcasm (Mt 10.34); and his gracious invitations to enter the "kingdom of God" in both its present (Mt 11.28) and future manifestations (Mt 24.34–36).

- *Wisdom tradition.* In addition to their strong "prophetic" flavor, the speeches of Jesus also reveal significant influence from the "wisdom school" of ancient Hebrew theology and rhetoric. Thus his verbal style also features a simple directness of expression; concrete, picturesque, down-to-earth language—yet dealing with the "deep issues" of life and death, goodness and evil, right and wrong, God and man; the use of questions, both real and rhetorical, and evocative analogies, often expanded into narrative parables; and above all, a predilection for contrast, antithesis, hyperbole, the maxim, and other forms of aphoristic utterance (Mt 5.14–15, 7.2–5, 11.10–13).

- *Dialogic technique.* The rabbinic style favored dialogue, especially interaction with the audience by means of question and answer, or question and counter-question—the method of debating known (today) as "challenge-and-riposte" (Mt 4.1–11).[16] Most of Jesus' controversies with the "scribes and Pharisees" (or with skeptical crowds) are initiated by such an exchange, for example, in Matthew 12 concerning the issues of picking grain on the Sabbath (2–3), healing on the Sabbath (10–11), exorcising a demoniac (22–25), seeking a "sign" (38–39), and Jesus' true "mother and brothers" (46–50).

- *Speaking in specifics.* Jesus' discourses are permeated with specific, life- and people-related imagery and figures of speech (especially simile and metaphor) that are based upon the local environment and everyday experience of his hearers. Such imagery appeals not only to the sense of sight and other sensory impressions (e.g., drowning in the sea or burning in fire—Mt 18.6, 8), it also strikes deeply into one's emotions as well. Often a "focal instance" or "extreme example" (Tannehill 1975: 53) having great shock value is involved (e.g., the series recorded in Mt 5.39–42). Jesus' criticisms are never conveyed in the abstract, but they are normally accompanied by brief, dramatic "case studies" or parables designed to drive home his point along with the underlying spiritual principle (e.g., Mt 6.1–2). In this skillful and insightful manner of speaking, Jesus "contextualized" his teachings inductively in order to illumine both the minds and the hearts of his hearers. The "kingdom of God" as he portrayed it was not something purely conceptual and far away; rather, it became an immediate living experience for all who entered in (Mt 18.2–3, 21.31–32).

- *Audience appeal and involvement.* Several of the features already noted, the dialogic method in particular, indicate how close Jesus was, in communicative terms, to his audience. His many questions were a prominent aspect of this style of instructive engagement—the *rhetorical* type being a standard rabbinical tool (e.g., "What do you think?" Mt 18.12), but also *real* interrogation at times to find out their thinking on particular issues (Lk 10.26–27, 36–37; 14.4). While he favored an economical manner of expression, he would often replace the particular—not with the abstract or general—but with audience-appealing allusion. They could then fill in the blanks or paint the full picture in their own minds, creating a conceptual background for his message (Mt 12.3–4, 25; 13.33, 47, 57). Jesus' enigmatic sayings would certainly tax and test the thinking, opinions, attitudes, and level of commitment of his listeners, even the twelve who were closest to him (Mt 8.22; 9.13, 15, 24). Also attractive to Jesus' audiences undoubtedly were the various touches of either subtle or hyperbolic humor that color his teachings (Mt 7.3–5; 15.14; 23.24, 27).
- *Poetic compositio.* Jesus was a poet with words, first of all with regard to the many minor stylistic features of his discourse—the images, figures, hyperboles, repetitions, questions, wordplays, parallelisms (synonymous or contrastive, Mt 7.7–8, 23.12), and rhythmic cadences. Jesus frequently spoke in the form of balanced, poetically patterned sense and sound units, as we hear in Matthew 6.19–20. Such larger structural arrangements characterize a great many of his didactic passages, particularly those recorded in John's Gospel. It is for this reason no doubt that Luke describes Jesus' words as being exceptionally "pleasing" (with χάρις, Lk 4.22) and having amazing "power/authority" (ἐξουσία, Lk 4.32; cf. Mt 7.29). This would be a good way to characterize the nature and effect of literary rhetoric in Christ's provocative parables in general (e.g., the extended linear parallelism in Mt 7.24–27), and to indicate how his masterful speeches, whether they have come down to us in the original or only in translation, surpassed the prevailing standards of his day. This poetic-rhetorical feature is also especially evident (in Greek!) in his many proverbial sayings.

Clearly such investigation of the diverse rhetoric of Jesus is a potentially rewarding field of study that requires considerably more research, particularly with reference to and in comparison with Jewish rabbinic contemporaries.

"New Rhetoric" (NR)

A relatively recent development in the field of rhetorical criticism, known as "New Rhetoric," zeros in on the various effects that a literary argument has upon the *receptors* (audience/readers) of verbal discourse. This development was popularized in particular by Perelman and Olbrechts-Tyteca's groundbreaking work, *The New Rhetoric: A Treatise on Argumentation* (1969). However, as characterized by Margaret Mitchell, this important text

> Does not claim to be a handbook of ancient rhetoric, but rather a revision and reappropriation of it to modern philosophical problems, particularly that of epistemology. Its intention is at basic points contrary to these [its disciples] New Testament scholars—it aims at expanding the realm of argumentation rather than classifying particular texts according to form or arrangement. (1992: 7)

Mitchell claims that followers of "the audience-based perspective of the New Rhetoric" tend to misconstrue the method's basic orientation and objectives, and hence they have confused the rhetorical analysis of NT literature through the application of terminology that has been subtly "redefined."[17] A more positive way of characterizing this "new" development in rhetorical study is that it adopts a "process approach" in seeking to better "understand the dynamic of persuasion and its function in social contexts" (Guthrie 1994: 30). It therefore focuses on "the inducement or enhancement of an audience's adherence to particular values by means of various strategies of practical reasoning," i.e., quasi-logical arguments and those based upon cause and effect, specific cases to general principles, and distinct "dissociating concepts" (Black 1995: 263, 272).[18]

The basic nature and purpose of NR investigation has, as in the case of RR criticism, been significantly modified, with a decided move from the speaker-orientation of the GR method to the results of rhetorical discourse upon an audience (Watson and Hauser 1994: 113). Primary emphasis is thus placed upon "readers as active, creative, productive," their "status" having been changed from "that of judges and critics to that of validators" (Wuellner 1987: 461). This perspective involves a shift in the primary focus of attention from the initial to the current setting of communication, again at times with a consequent distortion (occasionally a complete obliteration) of the "two-horizons" concept of interpretation (Thistleton 1992: 499–508). The application of NR argumentation strategy procedures to the analysis of New Testament epistolary discourse has thus far been comparatively limited, but this may change if a way can be found to formulate its theoretical principles and practical procedures in a less abstract, dense, and esoteric manner.

The Rhetoric of an Epistolary "Argument"

As a more holistic and potentially more helpful example of the narrower, rhetoric-as-argument approach in biblical studies, we may consider the following method of dealing with the "argument structure" of a New Testament Epistle. This features a multifaceted framework that is designed to highlight the principal elements of content, both explicit as well as implicit, and to link these up with the pragmatic, context-specific relations that generate the discourse of a typical "paraenetic" text.[19] The latter is defined as an oral or written work "consisting of exhortation and admonition, aimed at affecting the attitudes and behavior" of its addressees (Thuren 1995: 18).

The discourse of argument is normally intended to influence the thinking of an audience—to *convince* them of the truth, correctness, validity, expediency, etc. of a certain assertion or position (based on "logical" reasoning, *logos*). In addition, an author may also wish to move people to action, that is, to *persuade* them to change or modify their behavior in some significant way. This desire may be effected through an appeal to the emotions, whether self-oriented (*ethos*) or directed toward their own feelings and attitudes (*pathos*). The relationship between these two aspects of a paraenetic argument, conviction and persuasion, is that the latter normally builds upon the former.

> In order to persuade, the author usually needs to give reasons for the change: to give such reasons, and to justify them so that the recipient's opinions are affected, [sic] is called argumentation. But an argumentation may have its goal and result only that the recipient should see something as valid. . . . It becomes *persuasion* if the goal is also to create in the recipient a volition to act in some way. (Thuren 1995: 51)

Arguments pertaining to both conviction (one's intellect) and persuasion (one's motives, emotions, and volition) are closely interrelated in I Peter, for example, where the author's primary goal is to "exhort" his receptors to "stand" firmly based upon the "testimony" that they had received concerning the truth of the gospel *kerygma* and the ideals of its implicated lifestyle (5.12). In this case, a solid conviction regarding the reliable good news of Jesus Christ (e.g., 1.18–21) was needed first of all in order to persuade his harassed addressees not to return to their former way of living (4.3–4) or to adopt the immoral practices of contemporary pagan society (2.11–12). In short, Peter's aim was—under the guidance of the Holy Spirit (1.12)—to reinforce and enhance their appreciation of the inestimable value of remaining faithful to the theology and ethics that befitted their high spiritual calling as "a chosen and holy people belonging to God" (2.9; cf.1.2, 15). This should be done despite the audience's being separated and estranged from the society at large due to their Christian faith-life (1.1; 2.11).

In order to fully analyze and assess an author's method of epistolary argumentation then, a number of situationally related factors need to be investigated. Nine possible, mutually interactive elements may be described with respect to one another in an approximate manner as shown on in figure 8.2.[20] The essential triad

that underlies every biblical argument involves a particular "problem" (e.g., a the-
ological/spiritual/moral/ethical need, lack, test, trial, or fault), whether known or
previously unknown to the audience, for which the writer (or speaker) desires to
propose a godly solution.[21] He does this by making an appropriate "appeal" or
exhortation that either promotes or prohibits a certain way of thinking or behav-
ing; he encourages them either directly (e.g., imperative) or indirectly (e.g., by way
of a theological/moral assertion) to make a change or to strongly adhere to some
specific thought, attitude, value, action, or situation in life.

   Such an appeal is supported by one or more "motivation(s)," that is, reasoning of various kinds proofs, facts, testimonies, examples, analogies, case studies,
etc.), which relate to content (*logos*), emotion (*pathos*), and/or the author's own
credibility and authority (*ethos*).[22] The problem at issue thus motivates a certain
communicative intention (*"illocution"*) in the mind of the speaker for getting the
audience to deal with the difficulty in a particular way. This is then verbalized in
what he believes to be the most rhetorically effective (convincing/persuasive) manner in terms of linguistic and literary structure and style, specifically, the concrete
"locution" or "text." Particularly important for analysis are the specific rhetorical devices (or "marks"; Murphy 1994: 7) that serve to verbally distinguish or reinforce
what the writer is arguing for and how. This concerns the relative degree of excellence and effectiveness with regard to the manner in which the "appeal" is constructed and supported by its "motivation(s)."

   Invariably associated with this basic rhetorical triad is a set of subsidiary factors that usually do not need to be explicitly asserted but may be mentioned or alluded to, depending on the circumstances, for the sake of emphasis or recollec-
tion. First we have the surrounding *context*, which is comprised of two distinct
components: The "setting" is the *general* social, cultural, religious, historical, and
environmental milieu in which the act of communication takes place. This is coupled with the specific *interpersonal* "situation" that occasioned or provoked the
"problem" in question that calls for a response from the individuals concerned.
The combination of situation and setting (or "rhetorical exigency") with refer-

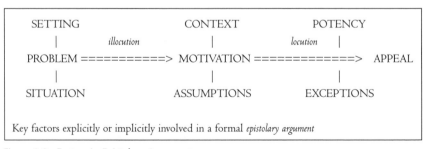

Figure 8.2. Factors in Epistolary Argument

ence to the original context has been the focus of much analysis by the prominent social scientific school of biblical criticism.[23]

Every oral or written text (argument) also occurs within a concrete verbal "cotext," which would encompass portions of the same discourse, whether immediate (the *paratext*) or more remote, especially some preceding passage (an *intratext*). Included here would be all those external texts to which the present pericope is somehow related to or based upon (i.e., an *intertext*, selected for example from a relevant literary corpus such as the New Testament Epistles).

Further allied with every segment of argumentation is a number of underlying "assumptions," or "warrants" (Thuren 1995: 42; Murphy 1994: 13–14). This refers to the various thoughts, attitudes, values, and emotions that the speaker shares with his audience that he presupposes can be readily accessed and understood by them as applying to the present locution, in particular, the relationship that links the problem with the appeal and its motivation. Such background information, which is frequently left unstated (or "implicit"), derives from their prior knowledge and experience and includes their common worldview, way of life, value system, and fundamental social institutions. This conceptual inventory naturally differs from one person to the next, but it may be "averaged out" for any envisioned group. These assumptions will vary in their level of *generality* (e.g., "all," "most," "any," "whenever," "usually," etc.) as well as in their relative *strength* (reliability, validity, viability, relevance, etc.), depending on what they are based upon, that is, their "backing": experience or observation, accepted definition, citation of recognized authority, theoretical principles, and logical consistency (Murphy 1994: 24).

Within the framework of a particular argument, especially a more elaborate one, a possible "exception" or two (a contrast, antithesis, counter-case, opposing evidence, potential rebuttal, etc.) may be optionally incorporated. This is done by way of anticipation, namely, in view of how the speaker surmises at least some in the intended audience will react to the message. Finally, one's formulation of the "appeal" may be deliberately varied through different linguistic-literary devices with regard to its "potency," that is, its relative directness, urgency, or degree of *mitigation* in terms of verbal expression. A recognized gradient is possible depending on the language, literary tradition, author, and type of text that is concerned. This may range from the most to the least "potent" as follows, to cite some common New Testament epistolary possibilities:[24]

An overt imperative (command) form > [> signifies "is more 'potent' than"]
    some closely associated verbal (e.g., an "imperatival" participle) >
        a direct "appeal" (παρακαλέω) by the author to his addressees >
            the performative mention of an order or prohibition followed by indirect speech >
            reference to a specific divine command >

> use of the verbs "ought" (ὀφείλω) or "must" (δει) >
> a 'ινα "final" clause >
> a positive or negative qualitative assertion that implies a related imperative
> (e.g., "in which you exalt . . . you exalt with inexpressible joy" (1.6, 8)
> => therefore, rejoice!)[25]

The strategy of paraenetic argumentation outlined above may be applied at any convenient point in the text at hand or at any given compositional level in the hierarchy of discourse organization. To illustrate its potential utility and value as an analytical tool in New Testament studies, for social scientists in particular, I have utilized this [problem ➔ motivation ➔ appeal] framework to examine one important pericope in the epistle of 1 Peter. This passage sets forth one of the central concepts in the author's overall argument, namely, the believing community as constituting the new "elected" people of God (2.1–10). I will begin with a literary-structural outline and stylistic summary of this particular portion of the letter.[26]

Testify to the "Priesthood" to Which You Belong (2.1–10)

Let's consider the final section of 1 Peter's first principal division. It begins with "therefore" (ὀυν), after a strong *closure* at 1.25. The reference to "newborn" (ἀρτιγέννητα, v. 2) echoes related concepts in 1.3 and 23. This is arguably the central text of the entire letter, with its strong emphasis on the professing "people-priesthood" of God as a fulfillment of Old Testament prophecy. The beginning of this passage syntactically parallels that of the preceding unit, featuring a complex plural participial + ὡς construction (2.1–2//1.13–14), except that the latter is negative while the former is positive in outlook (structural *anaphora*, i.e., section-initial parallels). The end of this section is signaled by another prominent passage of closure (2.10, with a pointed allusion to Hosea 1.6, 9; 2.1, 22). The mention of "mercy" (ἐλεε–) in v. 10 forms an *inclusio* (boundary marker) with the start of this major division in 1.3, while the verb stem –αγγελ– (v. 9) links up *epiphorically* (i.e., parallel section endings) with concluding correspondents in 1.12 and 25. As was the case in the two preceding sections of this division (1.3–12, 13–25), each of the three constituent paragraphs is syntactically encoded in Greek as a single periodic sentence with end stress (climax):

- *Demonstrate your salvation in spiritual growth* (2.1–3)
  This paragraph is dominated by the "milk" imagery of its second half, which is probably a figurative designation for the gospel "word" mentioned at the end of the preceding section (1.25). The present unit concludes with a word of OT confirmation in the unmistakable allusion

to Psalm 34.8, which turns out in Greek to be a christological pun: χρηστός (= χριστός) ὁ κύριος. We note also a dramatic contrast effected by this reference to God's "goodness"—*contra* the actual or potential behavior of those referred to in v. I.

- *Our holy priesthood is built on the foundation of Christ* (2.4–6)
  The leitmotif of λίθον "stone" (3X) lends perceptible cohesion to this central paragraph and also links it to the next (2X). This figurative reference to Christ and his church is again carefully grounded in the Scriptures (Is 8.14), set in prominent position at the close of the unit (v. 6).
- *Proclaim your priesthood in contrast to unbelievers* (2.7–10)
  Anadiplosis (sectional boundary overlapping) with πιστεύω (vv. 6b–7a), coupled with an inferential οὖν, sets up a forceful contrastive pattern that continues throughout the paragraph. This culminates in the crucial "people of God" synonymy (their nature, v. 9a, and purpose, 9b), which is highlighted in turn by the graphic dark–light imagery of 9c, followed by the decisive confirmatory citation from Hosea in verse 10. Verses 9–10 thus form a distinct paragraph of *closure* that foregrounds the principal word of encouragement for Peter's addressees. They have become "God's people" as a result of this salvific divine work, which was previewed by way of summary both at the beginning of the division in 1.3–5 (*inclusio*) and in the letter's salutation (v. 2).

The individual, interrelated components in the structure of argumentation (see figure 8.2) as it applies to I Peter 2.1–10 may now be summarized as follows.

SETTING: This would be the same as that posited for the letter as a whole, but with a special focus (in view of what is said in 2.9–10) upon the addressees' increasing isolation in the wider community due to their uncompromising Christian faith. They were indeed spiritual "strangers" in the world at large, people who could be "scattered" again even further abroad (i.e., from northern Asia Minor) at any time as a result of increasing persecution and prejudicial purges (2.11; cf. 4.12). Also pertinent here, although implicit, is their apparent relatively low social status (like that of their Lord, vv. 4, 7b; note the emphasis on "slaves" [2.18–20], which would obviously resonate with their "not being a people" [v. 10], also in a socioeconomic sense).[27]

SITUATION: In the case of I Peter and many other NT letters, this factor is very difficult to specify with any degree of certainty. Whether the Apostle had ever met any of his readers in person is hard to say, but he does seem to be quite familiar with their interpersonal circumstances and hence the type of Christian encouragement that was most appropriate. In addition to the major threat of surrounding hostility, they also needed to be exhorted about the potential or actual internal tensions among them (2.1; cf. 3.8; 4.8–10) which, if left unchecked, could flare up to tear their community apart from the inside.[28]

PROBLEM: The mutually inflammatory interaction of setting and situation gave rise to a certain difficulty (or a complex of them) within the fellowship of believers. Although the addressees have been chosen by God, sanctified by the Spirit, and redeemed by Christ (1.1–2), their lives did not always measure up to their high calling. On the contrary, it appears that their Christian fellowship was often tested and troubled by such common interpersonal sins as malice, guile, hypocrisy, envy, and slander (2.1). In addition to this overt problem that Peter deals with in the present section, he also implicitly relates his exhortation to the larger difficulty presented by their current hostile life "setting," namely, that of coping with their increasing social alienation and incipient external persecution. Both of these negative factors seem to have diverted the attention of these relatively new believers away from their true source of strength in the Holy Scriptures (including subsequent apostolic testimony; cf. 2 Pt 1.15–16) and this Word's encouraging promises for the people of God.

APPEAL: Peter makes three distinct, but interrelated, appeals in this section, two at the beginning and another in conclusion. He first admonishes his hearers (readers) to rid their Christian lives of all lingering vices, such as those listed by way of illustration in 2.1. Next (2.2) he encourages them to grow in their knowledge of God's life-giving and nourishing Word (the gospel of "salvation"). The third exhortation occurs in an interesting split and separated format. It is introduced in verse 5 as the addressees are figuratively called upon to "offer spiritual sacrifices" which are "pleasing to God," that is, to present their lives in religious devotion to him, according to the leading of his Spirit. This notion is later clarified and augmented in verse 9 through descriptive characterization and the directive that their life-purpose as the people of God must be to "proclaim [his] praises" as a concrete testimony to his mighty acts of (realized) deliverance (v. 10).

POTENCY: The appeal with the strongest linguistic force is the direct aorist active imperative "long for, crave" (ἐπιποθήσατε) in verse 2. The emphasis that is placed upon the authoritative Scriptures in this pericope (and the epistle as a whole) would surely justify such special prominence. This is preceded by a somewhat less obvious (due to its potential ambiguity) but still stressed (due to its initial position) "imperatival participle" in verse 1: Ἀποθέμενοι "put[ting] away from yourselves."[29] Considerably more mitigated and implicit is Peter's charge for his addressees "to offer" (ἀνενέγκαι, infinitive of purpose) themselves as spiritual sacrifices that serve to "laud" God's good deeds (ἐξαγγείλητε, aorist subjunctive in a ὅπως, "so that," purpose clause). This last injunction is foregrounded, never-theless, because of its distinct, compound nature and the inclusion of its second half within the climactic verse 9 near the close of the pericope. It is also previewed by the assertion in verse 3 that "the Lord is good"—hence most worthy of praise in both word and deed (implied).

MOTIVATION: There are three essential motivating thoughts that urge acceptance of and compliance with the interrelated appeals of this segment: (a) the *high status* of the addressees as "chosen priests" and the "holy people" of God (2.5, 9); (b) the *assurance* that is available in the Word of God to strengthen their faith and the certainty of their salvation (2.2b); and (c) the *obligation* to ren-der concrete thanks (i.e., also in their lifestyle) appropriate to the God who has been so "good" to them (2.3) and has shown them so much undeserved "mercy" by bringing them into the light of his saving grace (2.9b–10).

COTEXT: The interpretation of any text-internal pericope will naturally be influenced (*intra*textually) by the material that has preceded it in the discourse. Thus the "motivation" noted above continues the development that was initiated already at the beginning of the epistle in 1.1–2, particularly in the closely related notions of "election" and "sanctification." Accordingly, the opening transitional conjunction "therefore" (οὐ ν) in 2.1 carries on in a negative manner from the positive appeal to loving "obedience" in 1.22 as well as the opening exhortations of 1.13–14. Other concepts with clear intratextual antecedents are "new born" (2.2; cf. "born again" in 1.3); "word-based" (λογικόν, 2.2; cf. "word preached as good news" in 1.25); and "holy" (2.9; cf. the same term in 1.16).[30] This section is also clearly packed with *inter*textual (apostolic as well as prophetic) references and reflections, particularly in the several mutually resonant "stone" passages (2.6–8; cf. Is 8.14, 28.16; Ps 118.22; Acts 4.11, with a possible evocation also of Mt 16.18), but also in the evident allusion to Psalm 34.8 (v. 3); in the vari-ous "praise names" for the people of God in verse 9 (old/Israelite => new/Christian; cf. Is 43.20–21, 61.6, 62.12); and in the announcement of their life-changing spiritual transformation in verse 10 (cf. Hos 1.6, 9; 2.1, 22).[31] The impressive array of biblical testimony and background material that is "re-con-textualized" here is an obvious indication of the thematic centrality of this peri-cope in 1 Peter.

ASSUMPTIONS: There are several basic assumptions that underlie the move-ment from motivation to exhortation in Peter's line of argumentation: (a) God's "holy" people by their very nature and in view of their high status do not willingly practice any behavior akin to that of a pagan lifestyle (vv. 1, 8); (b) further study of God's Word is necessary to enable Christians to grow spiritually and in the power to perform their assigned role in his "spiritual house" adequately, including the offering of God-pleasing "spiritual sacrifices" (vv. 2, 5); (c) the addressees, living in believing fellowship, constitute a fulfillment of biblical prophecy concerning the identity and character of God's holy people (vv. 5, 9); and (d) people naturally ought to thank someone who has been so kind to them (an experience that they have actually "tasted," v. 3) and has mercifully blessed them in so many marvelous ways, especially by bringing them to the gospel "light" which leads to eternal salvation (vv. 4, 9–10).

EXCEPTION: In order to highlight the prevailing positive aspect of his encouraging message, Peter includes an extended and vivid reference to its antithesis, that is, by means of a prophetically based reference to all who oppose the Lord and persecute his followers (cf. 1.6–7). By rejecting Christ and his Word in unbelief, these persons "stumble" upon the divinely selected "rock" and thereby exclude themselves from his holy house (vv. 5, 8), which constitutes a new, multiethnic "chosen people" (vv. 9–10). In effect, this element of dramatic contrast serves as an implicit warning against such a contrary faith-response and hence also a type of negative "motivation" to the first, admonitory aspect of Peter's appeal (2.1). How the chosen inhabitants of this "spiritual" dwelling are to conduct themselves in view of their being surrounded by such an immoral, antagonistic society and culture becomes the topic of focal concern in the entire body of this epistle (2.11–5.11).

The preceding was only a partial "rhetorical exegesis" of the pericope of 1 Peter 2.1–10. My aim was to illustrate how such an "argument-oriented" perspective can help one probe more deeply and systematically into a particular paraenetic passage. The detail required will naturally depend on its purpose and the relative scope of the project concerned. As already noted, this methodology is not meant to be employed on its own, but rather needs to be applied either as a follow-up to or in conjunction with a complete literary-structural overview of the discourse, a specific social scientific study, as well as a thorough semantic-propositional, text-based exposition. It may be further complemented by a so-called "speech-act" analysis whereby the sequence of "locutionary" units is examined on both the micro- and macro-levels of textual organization with a view toward determining their respective "illocutionary" implications: encouragement, warning, instruction, edification, commendation.[32]

Conclusion: The Significance of Rhetorical Criticism for NT Critics

Does it make any difference at all precisely how "rhetoric" is defined and subsequently applied? It would certainly seem so, judging from the diversity in interpretation that results from equally thorough studies of a given biblical text. The reader-response and neo-rhetorical approaches are exegetically less helpful due to their chosen emphasis upon the critical activity of individual *contemporary* receptors in the hermeneutical process. It is not that such interpretation is viewed as being without value, only that it is of a secondary, applicative nature. It must therefore be derived from and based upon the results of a complete examination of the original (primary) setting and event of communication—as nearly as this may be determined using all of the analytical techniques at our disposal, including those of the social sciences.

But from another perspective, given the desirability of mutual correction and supplementation, one might conclude that these different rhetorical methodologies are not so distinct or antithetical at all. Rather, they complement one another (when coupled with other analytical approaches) to give one a fuller, more accurate picture of the manifold rhetorical (logical-argumentative) and artistic (structural-stylistic) complexities of biblical discourse, especially with respect to the New Testament epistolary literature where it has been most widely practiced.[33]

Thus, most effective Bible interpreters recognize the fact that utilizing the manifold resources of rhetoric, both ancient and modern, in relation to the source as well as the target language, is not sufficient in and of itself. A single rhetorical analysis cannot guarantee an adequate understanding or communication of the message of the Scriptures, whether an individual passage or a complete document. It represents a major facet, but certainly not the only one, contributing toward a fuller comprehension of the biblical text from the perspective of the hermeneutical horizon of either the original setting or that of any subsequent translation or time. Rhetoric deals largely with matter of literary form and function, but the more fundamental factor of conceptual, notably theological, content also needs to be considered, as was pointed out earlier.

Content in turn is a function of situational setting, and here is where our major present interpretive problems arise—in terms of the total cognitive environment of the original text (historical, sociocultural, religious, etc.). How serious is this communication gap and how can it be bridged or compensated for in a text? The preparation of contextually conditioned expository notes—"relevant" (i.e., efficient as well as effective) and responsive to both the biblical and the current contextual settings—is one important way of dealing with the critical hermeneutical deficit that cripples many people who interact with the Bible today. Situationally selective commentary of this nature, whether conveyed personally (i.e., by human instructors) or via some mediate pedagogical device—aurally, electronically, in written form, or by audiovisual means—would thus provide a reliable vehicle for transporting today's receptors conceptually back to the life- and thought-world of the Scriptures. In this manifold effort aimed at "contextualizing" a contemporary audience and readership to the complexities of the Word, it is clear that social scientists of every sort have a crucial role to play.

Notes

1. See the extensive studies and bibliographies in Porter (1997a), Porter and Olbricht (1993), Kennedy (1984), Lausberg (1998), Robbins (1996b), and Watson and Hauser (1994). However, some recent anthologies still seem to overlook the importance of rhetoric and rhetorical criticism (e.g., Barton 1998).

2. E.g., Robbins broadly defines rhetoric as referring "to the way language in a text is a means of communication among people" (1996a: 1). His "socio-rhetorical approach" to NT literature "focuses on values, convictions, and beliefs both in the texts we read and in the world in which we live." This methodology features the application of "five different angles to explore multiple textures within texts: (a) inner texture; (b) inter-texture; (c) social and cultural texture; (d) ideological texture; and (e) sacred texture" (1996a: 3). Only the first of these categories deals substantially with the text itself, the traditional domain of rhetorical critics, while the other four analyze the various topics that would be common in most sociological studies. For this reason, Robbins's writings may present the best entry point for scholars in the social scientific community who wish to add rhetorical criticism to their repertory (for an extensive application of this approach in a commentary on Hebrews, see de Silva 2000).

3. E.g., de Waard and Nida (1986: 11–15). The expression "receptor language," which reflects a rather crude conduit theory of "message transmission," is potentially misleading. "Target language" is not much better. Perhaps "consumer language," or even "response language," would be more to the point in that these terms serve to highlight the *active* hermeneutical role that a contemporary audience has in the overall communication process.

4. Recent studies in various fields of the social sciences have contributed greatly to our understanding of the ancient Near Eastern setting that contextualized the different texts of the NT. These results have been so significant that no responsible biblical exegete nowadays can afford to ignore them.

5. The communication-centered "rhetorical situation" (Kennedy 1984: 12, 34) is not to be confused with the more broadly conceived *Sitz im Leben* of Form Criticism (Elliot 1990: 95).

6. For a summary, see Nida, Louw, and Cronje (1983: 172–90); a semio-syntactic reorganization is found in Plett (1985).

7. Kennedy (1984: 33–38); see also Watson (1988: 8–28) and Watson and Hauser (1994: 110–11). Kennedy has more recently extended his productive rhetorical studies by means of an insightful, cross-cultural comparative approach (1998).

8. There are actually two other "rhetorical canons" in classical rhetoric, namely, *memoria*, which deals with the process of effectively committing a speech to memory, and *pronunciatio*, which focuses on the techniques used to dramatically deliver a speech. The latter needs to be given more attention, considering the prominent oral–aural character of many NT texts (Wendland 2000: 26–33). Another important aspect of the "style" of rhetoric not mentioned here concerns the study of various types of *chreiai* (sg. *chreia*), characteristic and memorable sayings (less often actions) that were associated with a given illustrious personage in GR as well as rabbinic oral and written literature. These sayings, which may be cate-

gorized into different types (e.g., wish, maxim, explanation, syllogism), were regarded as being instructive, affective, or beneficial in some notable way. Consequently, they were frequently strung together as either "statements" or "responses" and employed in the composition of the biographies of famous persons (particularly in exposition and argumentation). The analysis of *chreiai* is an important aspect of the form critical and redactional study of the Gospels (cf. Watson 1992: 104–6; Watson and Hauser 1994: 115–20).

9. Mack (1990: 42–46); see further, Bailey and vander Broek (1992: 63). For a more detailed form-functional typology, see Gammie (1990: 47).

10. See also the various essays in Porter and Olbricht (1993).

11. See the testimonies to Muilenburg in Patrick and Scult (1990: 11), Mack (1990: 12), and Kennedy (1984: 4). Personally, I think that Muilenburg's method of biblical text analysis is one of the best in terms of "relevance," both efficiency (being comparatively easy to apply) and effectiveness (providing useful results). Due to its major focus upon the original text of Scripture for its own sake, the Muilenburg approach might be characterized as being "modern," as distinct from both the "premodern" GR interest in the persuasive activity of the author and contemporary "postmodernism," which emphasizes the subjective hermeneutical activity and response of today's text "consumers."

12. Published in 1969, reprinted in House (1992).

13. For three good examples of "narrative criticism" with a rhetorical bent, see Howell (1990), Mack and Robbins (1989), and Witherington (2001).

14. Alter and Kermode observe that a postmodern approach is "one recent sectarian manifestation that radically disavows all unities" in literature and operates according to the "fundamental dogma" that "every text is divided against itself" (1987: 25, 35). This critical characterization is well put.

15. These are largely characteristic of an *inductive* didactic style. However, Jesus also employed *deductive* techniques in his argumentative discourse, e.g., *ad hominem* (Mt 24); *a fortiori* (Mt 6.30, 7.11); and *reductio ad absurdum* (Mk 3.23–26). For a discourse-oriented exploration of Jesus' persuasive manner of teaching, see Wendland (1996); for a classical Greco-Roman perspective on the Gospels and "Jesus' speech," see Kennedy (1984: chapter 5); for a more literary-based overview, especially with reference to John, see Ryken (1992: chapter 17); also Robbins (1984: chapter 1) and Witherington III (1994: chapter 4).

16. Malina and Rohrbaugh (1992: 42, 188). For a structured sequence of such "challenge-and-riposte" episodes, see Mk 2.1–3.6 (Dewey 1980).

17. Mitchell (1992: 7); but see further Hansen (1993: 824) and Black (1995: 271).

18. For an extended application to a NT book, see Hansen, who analyzes Galatians in terms of five methods of NR argument—that by "authority," "definition," "dissociation of ideas," "severance of the group and its members," and "sacrifice" (1989, with a summary in Hansen 1993: 824–25). For several shorter examples, see Vorster (1990: 120–25, 1992: 298–99) and Lategan (1992: 257–58).

19. This is a summary of my adaptation of the "structure of argumentation" model that Lauri Thuren presents in his detailed 1995 study of 1 Peter (which is itself a development of Stephen Toulmin's analytical method, 1958).

20. Compare with Thuren (1995: 42–43). An analysis of this type would normally be carried out in close conjunction with an examination of a text's overall discourse (semantic) structure, i.e., an exposition of its system of interpropositional relations, as described for example in Sherman and Tuggy (1994: 2–4), with reference to 1 John (cf. Johanson 1987: 6, 9). These underlie or constitute the meaningful linkage between the "appeal" and its "motivation," or the "claim" and its "data" (Thuren 1995: 42; termed "grounds" by Murphy 1994: 6), and are normally of the nature of *cause-and-effect*.

21. "Problem," though not an explicit element of the Toulmin/Thuren model, is an essential aspect of all paraenesis, that is, hortatory discourse.

22. As Thuren correctly points out (1995: 27), the key to understanding a paraenetic argument in the Epistles is an accurate elucidation of its distinctive manner of motivation, including its larger inductive and/or deductive technique, as well as the various linguistic devices that are employed in this process.

23. "Social-scientific criticism of the Bible is that phase of the exegetical task which analyzes the social and cultural dimensions of the text and of its environmental context through the utilization of the perspectives, theory, models, and research of the social sciences" (Elliott 1993: 7; for a sample analysis of 1 Peter, see Elliott 1981: 70–86).

24. I apply a similar selective gradient of mitigation with reference to the author's "appeal" in a structural-rhetorical analysis of 1 John (Wendland 1998). The relative "potency" of these various devices in relation to one another in NT discourse may of course be debated; clearly the subject needs further study.

25. Important in the argumentation of some languages like English, but not so much in others like Greek, are certain independent terms of *modality* called "qualifiers," for example (ranging from stronger to weaker): necessarily, certainly, undoubtedly, presumably, probably, apparently, possibly, perhaps, maybe, conceivably, doubtfully, etc. (cf. Murphy 1994: 32).

26. For an overview of this type of text analysis, see Wendland (1992: 30–37). In the discussion that follows, I interact primarily with the views of Achtemeier, as expressed in his excellent commentary on 1 Peter (1996), which includes many insightful comments on the rhetorical development of this letter. I am here assuming Petrine authorship. Another perspective would of course result in significant changes in certain context-related elements of the argument model; however, a practical application of the methodology remains essentially the same.

27. This point is disputed by Achtemeier (1996: 53–54), who feels that the οἰκέται of 2.18 refers "to slaves of a higher and more cultured ranking [i.e., than δοῦλοι]" (1996: 56). While this may be true, their status was certainly not high enough for them to avoid a "beating" (2.20)!

28. Achtemeier feels that "there is no obvious indication in 1 Peter that the communities addressed are threatened by internal disorder or potential schism" (1996: 57). Thus specific admonitions like those found in 3.8–9 may constitute "routine types of advice, representing Christian commonplaces" (1996: 58).

29. In his detailed commentary on 1 Peter, Achtemeier expresses considerable caution with regard to any construal that posits the "imperatival use of participles" since "such us-

age cannot be said to have been normal practice in Hellenistic Greek" (1996: 117). Such usage does, however, seem to be operative in this strongly paraenetic (deliberative) letter. In this connection we may also note once more Achtemeier's overly cautious interpretive approach to these hortatory details: "because such a list of vices was drawn from common Christian tradition, one *may not* draw inferences from them regarding the particular situation of the readers" (1996: 144, emphasis added). So comprehensive a stricture seems too rigorous.

30. Achtemeier presents a varied list of suggestions as to how segment 2.1–3 relates to verses 4–10, most notably on the basis of the "rock" imagery that derives from Psalm 33 (1996: 153).

31. Achtemeier notes this text as being "one of the largest collections of OT images in the NT" (1996: 150).

32. For a short application of speech-act analysis of 1 John, see Wendland (1998). The importance of such S-A studies for NT hermeneutics in general is pointed out by Thiselton (1999) and even more substantially by Vanhoozer (1998: ch. 5–7).

33. Black concisely summarizes the main benefits of rhetorical criticism for NT studies:

> In the academic marketplace of ideas, the study of rhetoric has proven to be a site for lively exchange among biblical interpreters of many allegiances: historical critics and literary analysts, linguists and social scientists, philosophers and theologians. . . . The prime movers of the early church were the *ethos* of Christ and the *pathos* of a Spirit-imbued life. Creatively fusing form and content, the church's *kerygma* [i.e., *logos*] was designed to construe the Christian experience, to express its power and to persuade others of its truth. To the degree that rhetorical criticism helps to clarify these aspects of the NT, it illumines the text to be interpreted and challenges its modern interpreters. (1995: 276)

For detailed studies of the use of rhetorical analysis in various theological disciplines, see Compier (1999) and especially Murphy (1994).

Structuralism and Symbolic Universes: 9
Second Temple Judaism and the Early
Christian Movement

PETER STAPLES

> *Now it is impossible to conceive of social relations outside a common*
> *framework. Space and time are the two frames of reference we use to situate*
> *social relations. . . . These space and time dimensions are not the same as the*
> *analogous ones used by other disciplines but consist of a "social" space and of*
> *a "social time," meaning that they have no properties outside those which derive*
> *from the properties of the social phenomena which "furnish" them.*

—CLAUDE LÉVI-STRAUSS[1]

Introduction

THE PURPOSE OF THIS CHAPTER is to use a "structurist" method to reconstruct the understanding of social space and social time in Second Temple Judaism (STJ) and its associated ritual practices. This endeavor will
help us to explain why the Jews did what they did at that time and to recognize
some of the continuities between Judaism and Early Christianity. Such continuities have recently been overlooked by scholars who emphasized the discontinuity
between Judaism and the original Jesus movement.[2] This study will show that the
transition from Second Temple Judaism to Christianity was a gradual process
rather than a radical break.[3] When we examine the cultural management of space
and time, we can also consider some of the theoretical insights of sociologists
such as Anthony Giddens, who insists that "An ontology of space-time as constitutive of social practices is basic to the conception of structuration" (1984: 3).

We have three preliminary questions: What is a "symbolic universe?" How did
the people of Second Temple Judaism conceptualize time and space in the framework of their own symbolic universe? Which recursive practices (inherited activities

that reiterated time and space concepts) were associated with this particular conceptualization of time and space? If we can answer these questions, we will be able to understand more precisely the puzzling relationship between structure and agency that has recently become a major issue in social-historical explanation (Giddens 1984: chapter I; Lloyd 1986, 1993).

It is important not to compartmentalize structure and agency. If we were to insist on doing that, we would generate descriptions of structures in which nobody ever does anything or descriptions of actions and events in which agents do "that which is right in their own eyes." Agents would no longer seem to be constrained by social contexts, nor would they be capable of acting together with other agents because there would be no medium of communication that would allow them to coordinate their actions. A better understanding of structure will help us to explain the actions of human agents and what we will call their *recursive practices*.

We should be clear about what we mean when we talk about a *structure*, a *symbolic universe*, or a *Gestalt*. There are important differences between *structuralism*, *symbolic realism*, *structuration*, *symbolic interactionism*, and *structurism* (Lloyd 1986), and these approaches do different things with patterns, or structures.[4] One of the advantages of a structurist methodology is that it not only elucidates the structures but also helps explain more convincingly the dialectical relationship between symbolic universes and the actions of the human agents who have internalized them (Lloyd 1993: 93).[5]

A good starting point for understanding structuralism is the account Jean Piaget first published in French in 1968, bearing in mind that this term is difficult to define because "the structures invoked by the . . . 'structuralists' have acquired increasingly diverse significations" (1970: 3). Structures have "certain common and perhaps necessary properties." A structure is also "a system of transformations" rather than "a mere collection of elements." Its transformations "never yield results external to the system." Nor do they involve elements that are "external to it." The notion of structure includes three elements: (i) the idea of wholeness, (ii) the idea of transformation, and (iii) the idea of self-regulation. Piaget also insists that structuralism is an alternative to atomism (1970: 5, 8).[6]

Structuralism not only entails a holistic rather than an atomistic approach to science, but also presupposes that the whole is always more than the sum of its parts. There is a crucial difference between natural science and the human sciences: the latter admits the notion of self-regulation. The human sciences differ from the natural in that transformations in the social world are always the result of human agency. In physics inanimate entities do not have the capacity to change the "rules of the game" (alias the "laws of nature"). In society, however, humans make transformations within their "rules" even in the process of adhering to them. Roger Bastide speaks of individuals, who are influenced by groups, families, religions, and political traditions, not reviving everything that can be had from "collective memory" but only particular images (1971: 79).

Piaget and the anthropologist Claude Lévi-Strauss both also emphasize the importance of Gestalt psychology in structuralistic thinking, because it too is based upon the notion of *wholeness* (Piaget 1970: 55). Lévi-Strauss not only recognizes the affinity between Gestalt psychology and structuralist anthropology, he also sets out to operationalize its insights in the domain of social science (1963: chapter 16).[7] An advantage of Gestalt psychology is that it allows us to recognize the same configuration even if its sequence has been disrupted, if one or two elements have been changed, if one or two elements have been removed, or if something new is added to a Gestalt.

An example is a chain of beads marked with the following symbols: 2, 3, 4, 5, 6, 7, 8, 9, 10, J, Q, K, A. Anybody who has played with a conventional pack of cards will easily recognize this configuration, even if its elements have been shuffled. We can also see that the addition of a Joker not only adds to the configuration, but also changes the rules of the game. Moreover, if I pick up a similar chain that now includes a subset labeled B, V, and H rather than J, Q, and K, I am still confronted by the same configuration because the Dutch use a pack in which the high cards are marked differently. The Jack is now the Boer (= the farmer); the Queen is the Vrouw (= the woman); and the King is the Heer (= the man). Such transformations change neither the Gestalt nor the rules of the game (unless we add Jokers or suchlike), even if three of the symbols in the chain now look different and even if we change their rank ordering. Three of the symbols (the signifiers) have changed, but what they signify still remains the same.

We can operationalize these insights when we reconstruct what I call the Temple Restoration Gestalt in Second Temple Judaism. First, however, we must realize that any structure (such as a pack of playing cards) always consists of a set of symbols. This is part of the *symbolic universe* of games such as bridge. A set of symbols is not the whole, however, because the whole also includes the rules of the game.[8] And we must never forget that, even if we have described the whole of *the* game, we have still not described and explained *a* game—what four human agents do when they have internalized this symbolic universe and begin to play a game of cards. This explains why we must never compartmentalize structure and events; both are ultimately the result of human agency. It also explains why we cannot describe and explain *a* game unless we have first understood *the* game.

Structure and Human Agency

Piaget points to the danger of losing sight of humans as social beings when using some kinds of structural analysis. He acknowledges that "his own constructivist theory of cognitive structure is intimately connected with Lévi-Strauss's doctrine of the primacy of (individual) structure in social life" (1970: chapter 6, note 19). He calls Lévi-Strauss "the very incarnation of the structuralist faith in the permanence of human nature and the unity of reason." But Piaget claims that Lévi-Strauss stood Durkheim on his head. Whereas sociologist Émile Durkheim insisted upon "the primacy of the social over the intellectual," Lévi-Strauss insists that "all social life . . . presupposes an intellectual activity in man of which the formal properties cannot . . . be a reflection of the concrete organization of society" (Piaget 1970: 107). Lévi-Strauss did not stand Durkheim completely on his head, however, because he also insists that "customs are given as external norms before they give rise to internal sentiments, and these norms . . . determine the sentiments of individuals" (Piaget 1970: 108).

Lévi-Strauss still insists that structures "emanate from the intellect" (Piaget 1970: 112). This explains why he conceives of them as prior to rather than derived from the social order. Structurists such as Christopher Lloyd, however, insist that all social structures are ultimately the result of human actions. In other words, social structures do emanate from the human mind, but they do not actually become structures unless actions have taken place. The *prior existence* of symbolic structures not only enables actions to take place, but also constrains them to a certain extent (as Giddens also suggests). Because he focuses primarily upon mental activities, however, Lévi-Strauss seems to lack the more robust understanding of human agency that we find in structurist thinking.

In the light of Lloyd's structurist philosophy of human science, the question of whether to begin with preexisting social structures or with mental operations begins to appear less problematic because we must begin at both ends: especially when we consider the phenomenon of human agency. Agency obviously entails mental operations; but not when we are dealing with undeliberated, involuntary, or reflex actions. For example, actions are always performed by human agents, but they are never performed in a structural vacuum. More precisely, actions are never performed in a structural vacuum once structures are in place. But we can no longer reconstruct the first social structures, nor can we reenact the first mental operations. This means that we cannot answer the question of priority.[9] More precisely: *once symbolic universes are already in place*, we are no longer dealing with a straight line but with a "loop." This is the sociological circle of externalization, objectivation, and internalization (Berger and Luckmann 1966, three moments summarizing the process the sociologist Alfred Schutz focused upon in his phenomenological sociology; see Schutz and Luckmann 1973).

Piaget agrees: "there is no longer any need to choose between the primacy of the social or that of the intellect; the collective intellect is the social equilibrium resulting from the interplay of the operations that enter into all cooperation"

(1970: 114). This is not only consistent with Lloyd's "structurist" methodology but also one of his starting points (1986: 145–47 and chapter 14). He says that Piagetian epistemology is obviously opposed to any form of apriorism or reductionism. It supports the general idea of an emergent realism, or what he called *constructivism* or *structurationism*. There is a central notion of the human subject and objective reality in a dialectical relationship.

> Piaget has also significantly influenced agency theories of structural change. His epistemology rests upon a well-developed agency conception of man as subject: structuring and transforming the world and his mind as he acts in the world. Many sociologists from the dialectical tradition have drawn upon his ideas in developing their theories of action and social history. . . . *There is no structure apart from construction*, either abstract or genetic. (Lloyd 1986: 146–47, 240; original italics)

Lloyd now begins to move from structuralism to constructionism. He backs away from Lévi-Strauss (but not from Piaget) for three reasons. First, because the structural analyses of Lévi-Strauss "were almost exclusively confined to the cultural products of the human mind and he had little to say about the structures or relations of society, or about how they change" (Lloyd 1986: 243). Second, because Lévi-Strauss attempted "to reduce structures of culture to their atomistic [!] elements in order to rearrange them into logico-mathematical patterns" (1986: 247). Third, because social reality and human agency "should always be approached from the point of view of the actor's understandings" (1986: 264). In other words, "What remains sociologically essential is the recognition that all symbolic universes . . . are human products; their existence has its base in the lives of concrete individuals, and has no empirical status apart from those lives" (Berger and Luckmann 1966: 146, which Lloyd [1986: 268] cites). This is also the point at which Lloyd moves closer to symbolic interactionism and the phenomenological sociology of Schutz and of Berger and Luckmann when he explains how human agents *symbolize the world*. We can now pass from structuralism and Gestalt psychology to the social construction of symbolic universes within the explanatory framework that Lloyd calls *symbolic realism* (1986: chapter 13).

What Is a Symbolic Universe?

When we consider symbolic realism, we must also consider Peter Berger's *The Sacred Canopy*.[10] This book was an attempt to apply the insights Berger and Luckmann developed from Schutz's phenomenological sociology to the study of religious phenomena (Berger1967: vi–vii). When Lloyd moves from structuralism toward symbolic realism, he begins to think in terms of "systems of symbols and ideas, forms of consciousness, and the social actions that grow out of actors' symbolic understandings" (Lloyd 1986: 263). More precisely, symbolic realists (such as Berger) treat society as "a symbolically constructed order of meanings, rules, conventions, and so on." Such an *Umwelt* (as he calls it; see Schutz 1973: 126–27, on the constituting of the "world of culture"), or cognitively constructed environment, is not only the structural context of human action but also the *locus* of power, morality, and beliefs. It is continually reproduced by the "agential powers" of human actors (Lloyd 1986: 265). Symbolic realism is not a radically new methodology, however, because its roots can be traced back to symbolic interactionism, phenomenology, and philosophical hermeneutics (Lloyd 1986: 194). The most influential source of Lloyd's symbolic realism is George H. Mead's posthumously published lectures, *Mind, Self, and Society* (1934), which he calls "one of the key texts of twentieth-century social thought." Mead insisted that all human behavior is *social* behavior because "it takes place as a process of symbolically mediated action between an individual self and a social group" (Lloyd 1986: 264).

It is the capacity of *human* agents to construct the "social worlds" in which they live and move and have their being that ultimately distinguishes them from the other members of the animal species. In the process of constructing, reproducing, or transforming these social worlds, they make their own history and construct their cultures (Plummer in Turner 1996: 223). In order to do this, agents always need a medium of communication that enables them to coordinate their actions with those of others. This means that the shared meanings that emerge during the interactions between two or more people depend upon the existence of language (Lloyd 1986: 264). This implies that language is the most important component of every symbolic universe. Without language they would not even exist!

There is a problem here, however, because symbolic interaction begins with interactions between two people even though we can also examine face-to-face groups. This raises the question of whether we are still entitled to think in terms of symbolic interaction when we also take into consideration the symbolic products and the actions of human agents who do not interact with each other face-to-face. So it seems that symbolic interactionists can only cope with micro-level phenomena. Lloyd concedes that explanation always begins at the micro level, but he also insists that "it does not have to stay at that level" (1986: 265). Nevertheless, it is quite obvious that symbol systems such as language are capable of transcending the face-to-face interactions of individuals. For example, English is now spoken throughout the whole of the world. Several religions are "world religions." When these are involved, we are no longer dealing with micro phenomena. So the next important question is, How is this possible?[11]

To answer this question, we can look at Berger's *Sacred Canopy* (1967), where he explains *externalization, objectivation,* and *internalization.* "Only if these three moments are understood together can an empirically adequate view of society be maintained" (1967: 4). With the help of such concepts, we can now begin to understand how the social construction of social reality is possible, even if we move up from the micro level to even higher levels of social construction and reproduction. First of all, "It is through externalization that society is a human product. It is through objectivation that society becomes a reality *sui generis*. It is through internalization that man is a product of society" (1967: 4). More succinctly: "Society is a human product. Society is an objective reality" (Berger and Luckmann 1966: 79). Humans themselves are social products. We have now entered the "sociological circle." The next question is, How did we get there?

Berger, following Schutz, insists that a social world is ultimately constituted by the actions of human agents as they interact with each other in the processes of social construction. This implies that the construction of social reality must inevitably be a collective enterprise. It is only in this way that "the products of those activities persist over time." This means that "The 'stuff' out of which society and all its formations are made" (such as its configurations, *Gestalten* and symbolic universes) consists of meanings that have already been externalized by human agents (Berger 1967: 7–8; see Schutz and Luckmann 1973: 99ff. on the "stock of knowledge").

Having externalized what Berger calls the "stuff" (out of which symbolic structures have already been constructed), the agents who originally produced them begin to assume that those structures must be located *outside themselves*. From the actor's point of view, they now seem to consist of real objects that are capable of resisting their desires, even though they themselves are still in the process of reproducing them. Once a social world has been constructed by human agents, however, "it cannot simply be wished away." This implies that the structures already constructed by human agents now seem to assume "the status of objective reality" (Berger 1967: 8–11). This is the transformation that Berger calls *objectivation*. The sheer objectivity of society includes all of its constituent elements: institutions, social roles, recursive practices, together with both individual and group identities. These explain why the socially constructed world seems to confront its producers as "an external facticity." It is ultimately apprehended by us as such (Berger 1967: 13–15). That not only brings us to the mechanism of internalization but also closes the sociological circle of externalization, objectivation, and internalization. The upshot is that we now begin to comprehend the various elements of an "objectivated world" as if they were *inside our own consciousness* while *simultaneously* apprehending them "as phenomena of *external* reality" (Berger 1967: 15; my italics). This is what Berger means by *internalization*.

Internalization is also related to the mechanism of socialization (becoming a competent member of a society). But Berger also insists that socialization is rather different because it typically involves a learning process. The mechanism of internalization includes another dimension as well because an individual "not only learns the objectivated meanings [of symbolic universes] but [also] identifies with and is shaped by them." So we not only learn about the constituent elements of the social worlds in which we live and move and have our being during the processes of primary and secondary socialization, but also continue to reproduce them throughout the rest of our lives, unless we try to transform them by means of our actions! Berger also insists that total socialization is "theoretically impossible" as well as "empirically non-existent." This implies that we must now think in terms of "different degrees of success" in the processes of socialization. This is what sociologists mean when they talk about *oversocialization* and *undersocialization*. In other words, "The success of socialization depends upon the establishment of symmetry between the objective world of society and the subjective world of the individual" (Berger 1967: 15–16).

Complete symmetry and complete asymmetry, however, are never encountered in the real social world because even deviants need a common language, and historians are well aware that social worlds gradually change through time and there are also episodes of rapid transformation. When we try to explain the relative stability of social worlds that are religious, an additional concept is helpful. This is the notion of *sacralization* (Mol 1976: 1–15). It denotes the process by means of which humanity "has . . . safeguarded and reinforced [the] complex of orderly interpretations of reality, rules, and [their] legitimations." It breaks down into at least four analytically separable mechanisms, the most important of which are (1) objectification, (2) commitment, (3) ritual, and (4) myth (1976: 15). Three points are important here. Processes of sacralization not only tend to stabilize religious systems, but also protect them from the pressures of endogenous and exogenous change. This accounts for their relative stability in the *longue durée*. They also seem to endow religious systems with qualities such as untouchability (which usually means "hands off" in practice!). This implies that they are highly resistant to change once their symbolic universe is already in place. Religious systems are also legitimated by a transcendental point of reference that nonreligious social systems (by definition) do not provide (Mol 1976: 5–11).

But there is a problem here, because Mol seems to prefer group identities with well-defended boundaries that are buttressed by "prejudice" (1976: 80–93). This seems to suggest that he has a normative preference for religious groups that "oversocialize" their members. The problem now is that transformations in religious systems not only seem to be illegitimate when considered from his point of view but also (theoretically speaking) quite impossible, despite the fact that they do occur throughout the course of history. This means that sociologists also have to explain manifestations of religion that are more flexible and tolerant rather than resistant to change. Whenever they overprioritize the hard-shelled social systems in their theoretical "scaffolding" (as Mol calls it), sociologists of religion are no longer capable of predicting historical change because the possibility of radical transformation does not play an equally prominent role in their theoretical models.

The Conceptualization of Time and Space in Second Temple Judaism

Having discussed several attempts to explain what symbolic universes are and how they are socially reproduced, we can consider the symbolic universe of Second Temple Judaism. I cannot deal with it in its entirety but only consider the conceptualization of sacred time and, to a limited extent, sacred space. We can then examine three recursive practices: (1) pilgrimages, (2) holy war, and (3) Temple restoration. Whenever they were conflated, we are confronted by the complex phenomenon that I call the Temple Restoration Gestalt (Staples 1970, 1999). It remained in place until the final destruction of the Temple (Staples 1999: 490).

We are not dealing with clock time because clock time (as we now know it) had not yet been invented. But social life did have its rhythms and seasons that were determined by the movements of the sun and the moon: night and day, phases of the moon, solstice, and equinox. The length of the month was determined by the phases of the moon. Attempts were made to synchronize lunar months with the tropic year to ensure that festivals took place when young lambs were available or the harvests had just been brought in. This was a difficult business because it is virtually impossible to design a lunar/solar calendar in which the phases of the moon and the tropic year are perfectly synchronous. Without going into all the details, Second Temple Judaism adopted a lunar/solar calendar in which the months were determined by the moon while the years were synchronized with the solar cycle. The discrepancies were partially eliminated by adding an extra lunar month. But it was not necessary to do this every year.

There were earlier calendars such as the pentecontad calendar.[12] An alternative calendar was also used at Qumran (Morgenstern 1966; van Goudoever 1959). But because the recursive practices that I propose to examine were endorsed by the official hierarchy, it is not necessary to consider deviant calendars; the guardians of the Temple (where the climax of the festivals took place) did not open the gates to deviants who wanted to celebrate them at the wrong time. The "right times" were not only determined by the official hierarchy but also legitimated by ancient traditions. Because the coordinates of sacred time and space were elements of the symbolic universe, they were highly stable, even if challenged by deviants and even if some officials argued about certain of the details. But we would not expect to find any radical changes as long as the official hierarchy still remained in power and the symbolic universe of Second Temple Judaism still remained in place.

We can now examine the major festivals: Sukkoth (Tabernacles), Pesach-Mazzoth (Passover), Shabuoth (Feast of Weeks), and Hanukkah (midwinter). The first three were pilgrimage festivals, but Sukkoth, Pesach-Mazzoth, and Hanukkah were the "right times" for dedicating or cleansing the Temple. In the time of Judas Maccabaeus (c. 150 B.C.E.), moreover, the pilgrimage to Jerusalem was not only combined with the cleansing and rededication of the Temple, but also preceded by the ritual of the holy war. The best starting point is the dedication of the Temple in 2 Chronicles 7. It is not a historical account of the dedication of the Temple in the time of King Solomon (c. 970–931 B.C.E.), but we can still use it to reconstruct the symbolic universe at the time when it was written. Because it was written *before* the advent of the New Testament period, we can assume that this element was already in place before the time of Jesus (if we can also find collateral evidence in earlier traditions).

In 2 Chronicles 7.9–10 we are told that Solomon "held the feast at that time . . . seven days. . . . And on the eighth day they held a solemn assembly: for they kept the dedication of the altar seven days and the feast seven days. And on the three and twentieth day of the seventh month he sent the people away." This is an early example of what I call the Double Festal Octave. It began on 8 Tishri, and the first week ended when the Sukkoth began on the 15th (see appendix 9.1 for the Jewish calendar). The second octave (the festival proper) began on 15 Tishri and also lasted a week.[13] An extra day was added to give the worshippers time to go home. Tishri 10 is still the Feast of Yom Kippur (Day of Purification), when the high priest used to enter the Holy of Holies (the *Debir*), which was the most sacred part of the Temple. This generates the following scheme:

Tishri 8–10, 10–15; 15–22 (+23)

Three points are important. (1) The Pre-Festal Octave was subdivided into two periods of three and six days. The three-day period runs from 8 to 10 Tishri and the six-day period from Tishri 10 to 15. (2) The pilgrimage festival (15 to 22 Tishri) could not be properly celebrated if the Temple was "unclean"—more specifically, needed its annual cleaning or had recently been defiled. This means that the main purpose of the Pre-Festal Octave is to ensure that the Temple is clean before the pilgrimage festival proper begins on the 15th. In other words, the ritual of the Pre-Festal Octave is a ritual transformation from unclean to clean. (3) On the third day of the Pre-Festal Octave (Yom Kippur), God was expected to appear; the third day is the Day of Theophany. God was expected to appear either in the desert, on the mountain, or in the Temple.

We can find traces of this Pre-Festal Octave as early as the last redaction of Joshua, which demonstrates that it was already in place before the time of

Solomon. We find it this time in the month of Nisan. It immediately precedes the Pesach-Mazzoth Festival. The people prepare themselves for three days before they cross the Jordan (Jos 1.11; 3.2). They pass through the river on 10 Nisan and celebrate Pesach on 14 Nisan, followed by the Mazzoth Festival (15–22 Nisan; see Jos 4.19; 5.10–11). An extra day was added later to give the people time to return home. This generates the following scheme:

$$\text{Nisan } 8\text{–}10, \ 10\text{–}15; \ 15\text{–}22 \ (+23)$$

These two Double Festal Octaves not only derive from ancient traditions, they also mirror each other. In each case, the Pre-Festal Octave is divided into two periods of three days and six days and followed by a pilgrimage festival. They are not only mirror images of each other, they also occur six months after each other. They are celebrated as close as one can get to the autumn and spring equinoxes, given the discrepancies of the lunar/solar calendar, or more precisely the conjunction of full moon and an equinox. There are two important differences: (1) the festival of Pesach, which was celebrated on the night of the 14th (when young lambs were sacrificed and ritually consumed) only takes place in the spring and (2) the high priest entered the *Debir* only on 10 Tishri. But Nisan 10 was a special day on which the Passover lambs were selected for slaughter.

A similar Double Festal Octave can be found in the ninth month of Chislev, when the Jews still remember the liberation, cleansing, and the rededication of the Temple in the time of Judas Maccabaeus. It became a Sukkoth Festival in the ninth month (2 Mc 1.9). It can be found in Ezra 10, which can be dated before the time of Judas Maccabaeus. Again, the people have three days to get to "the right place" (Ezr 10.8–10; cf. Jos 1.11; 3.2), where they were expected on Chislev 20. When we remind ourselves that Hanukkah began on 25 Chislev, we have another Double Octave that now runs from 18 to 20; 20–25 Chislev and is immediately followed by the eight days of Hanukkah. This Pre-Festal Octave is similarly divided into two periods of three and six days and followed by a major octave. The events that took place on 20 Chislev (the third day) are described in terms of the ancient Canaanite storm theophany: the people trembled because of "the great rain" (Ezr 10.9). In this case, the Double Octave is not linked to the conjunction of full moon and equinox. Like Christmas, it is close to the winter solstice. A Double Octave cannot be found close to the summer solstice, however, presumably because Second Temple Judaism was averse to all manifestations of sun worship.[14]

This illustrates two crucial methodological points. (1) Once we have learned to recognize (part of) a Gestalt, we can now recognize it in other texts.[15] (2) We can even use traditions that are not historically reliable in terms of the *events* that the writers were describing, in order to reconstruct the *symbolic structure* that was in place at the time of writing. Another example clinches the point. If we look at Daniel 10.3–4, we see that the prophet fasted for three weeks until 24 Nisan. This looks rather odd because he ought to have been eating the Passover lamb and the Mazzoth. During the major festivals, fasting was completely forbidden. Having reconstructed the Double Festal Octave, we can now see that the prophet must have been rejecting this part of the symbolic universe.[16] But this passage does contain theophanic language. When God spoke to him, Daniel not only fell unconscious but also trembled and became dumb (10.9–19). God also says "Fear not." The rubric *Fear not* often appears in theophany texts and accounts of "recursive practices" such as holy war and Temple dedication.

We can find collateral evidence for the Double Festal Octave in the Gospels as well as polarity between the major festivals of the Jewish year. This confirms that the conceptualization of time is one of the most important continuities between STJ and Christianity. The most important clues can be found in the Fourth Gospel and Luke's Infancy Narrative. There are also traces of it in Mark, such as in his account of the Transfiguration.[17] Such similarities were not recognized by the form critics and the exponents of *Redaktionsgeschichte* because they insisted that the temporal markers must have been added to the units of tradition by those who compiled the Gospels. Even if they were added later, that would not necessarily imply that they must have been invented by the Evangelists. When we compare their conceptualizations of sacred time with the Gestalt that we have already found in the symbolic universe of STJ, we can easily recognize the basic pattern.

The best place to begin is John 2.13: "And the Passover of the Jews was at hand, and Jesus went up to Jerusalem." We can find the same feature in 6.4 and 11.55. When we read the Fourth Gospel, it is important to remember that Jesus regularly went up to Jerusalem to celebrate the pilgrimage festivals. In 12.1, however, we are told for the first time that Jesus arrived in Bethany (just outside Jerusalem) *six days before Passover*. So whenever we read that Jesus went to Jerusalem *when Passover was at hand*, this must mean "six days before the feast." That indicates that the compilers of the Fourth Gospel must have been aware of the Pre-Festal Octave. Josephus also confirms that the Jews assembled on 8 Xanthicus (Nisan) in order to prepare themselves for the feast (*B.J.* 6.290). This is the eighth day before the beginning of the Mazzoth Festival, which began on 15 Nisan. John 11.55 and Josephus also confirm that the purpose of the Pre-Festal Octave was preparation and purification. Again we are dealing with the ritual transformation from unclean to clean that was already in place in Second Temple Judaism.

Before Jesus "went up" to Jerusalem *six days before the Passover*, he also attended a wedding at Cana *on the third day* (Jn 2.1). This indicates that the compilers of the Fourth Gospel also knew that the six days were preceded by a period of three days, thus completing the Pre-Festal Octave. The wedding is also associated with purification because the six water pots were used "for purification" (Jn 2.6). This suggests that the *six* pots signify the six days that began on the third day of the Pre-Festal Octave. This is also suggested by Mark 14.13: When Jesus was looking for the room where he would celebrate Passover, he was met by a man carrying a single pitcher of water. At Passover-tide (the night of Nisan 14–15), only one water pot would be left because there was only one more day to go.

The problem here is that the Fourth Gospel maintains that Jesus was crucified on Nisan 14, when the Passover lambs were slaughtered, and not on Nisan 15. So we would expect to find *five days* instead of *six* in John 12.1. But this was changed from *six* to *five* in Papyrus 66! When the Fourth Gospel timed the Crucifixion one day earlier than the synoptics (presumably to emphasize that Jesus was the Passover lamb), we must now assume that the traditional temporal markers in the Pre-Festal Octave that were used to frame the narrative were not always consistently transformed. But the basic configuration can still be recognized.

We can recognize traces of the same Gestalt in Luke's Infancy Narrative, but there is an important difference. Luke confirms the polarity of the festal year rather than the Double Festal Octave. There is polarity between Sukkoth and Pesach-Mazzoth because both take place near the conjunction of full moon and equinox, because they are six months apart, while Hanukkah begins close to the winter solstice. The best starting point is Luke 1.36: "this is the sixth month with her that was called barren" (cf. Lk 1.26). The annunciation of the future birth of the Baptist could be assigned to Tishri 10 (Yom Kippur), when the high priest entered the *Debir* (concerning Zechariah as a high priest, according to the tradition, see below). The annunciation of the future birth of Jesus could be assigned to Nisan 10, again, six months later. This means that the birth of Jesus (nine months later) can provisionally be assigned to the Double Festal Octave in the ninth month of Chislev. Furthermore, both the Baptist and Jesus were circumcised on the eighth day after their birth (Lk 1.59; 2.21). This suggests that the birth of Jesus was believed to have taken place on 25 Chislev.[18] In that case, the eight days between the birth and the circumcision could coincide with the eight days of Hanukkah.

This assumption is not absolutely certain because Jesus could not have been presented in the Temple (Lk 2.22) until *after* the festal octave was over. That would imply that the parents of Jesus arrived in Jerusalem (Lk 2. 22, 27) *after Hanukkah was over* even though they did turn up on time every year for Passover (Lk 2.41–50). If this eight-day period coincided with the Pre-Festal Octave, however, this would suggest that Jesus was born on 18 Chislev. If this is correct, we must note that the eight days between birth and circumcision are days of *purification* (Lk 2.22). We cannot be completely certain which of the two octaves we are dealing with. But it is already becoming clearer that this pre-Lukan tradition reflects elements that we have already found in the Jewish conceptualization of sacred time even though we cannot put everything into its right place. It is also possible that the transformations are not consistent because the traditional Gestalt was not always consistently applied.

We are on much firmer ground when we reexamine the two annunciation stories. If the birth of the Baptist was announced on 10 Tishri, we would expect this story to be couched in explicitly theophanic language. We should not be surprised if the announcement was made in the Temple by a priest if we are dealing with a 10 Tishri story. This is precisely what we do find when we look again at Luke 1.8–25. The father of the Baptist was a priest, Zechariah. He went into the Temple to burn incense. When he performed this ritual, the Angel Gabriel (who stands in the presence of God) appeared and fear fell upon him. This is a typical human response to a theophany. Then the angel said, "Fear not," the rubric of comfort that regularly appears in theophany texts. Zechariah was also unable to speak because he became dumb, another of the typical responses to a theophany. Because the third day of the Pre-Festal Octave is always the Day of Theophany, this element seems to fall into its right place. That means that Zechariah's actions are described *as if* they were the actions of a high priest because this is what was expected on Yom Kippur.[19] Even though this story is not historical, it should not be ignored since even unhistorical accounts can supply us with historically correct information about the symbolic universe that was in place at the time when they were written.

The annunciation of the birth of Jesus is also couched in theophanic language because the rubric "Fear not" appears in Luke 1.30. The announcement is also made by the Angel Gabriel. The setting is no longer the Temple because we are now in Nazareth. It seems to be a 10 Nisan text because the second annunciation occurs six months later. Nisan 10 is also the third day of a Pre-Festal Octave. The angel also tells Mary that "the power of the Most High shall *overshadow* you" (Lk 1.35). This is an important clue because the verb "to overshadow" (*episkiazein*) rarely turns up in the New Testament outside the accounts of the Transfiguration. So we must now look at Mark 9.2–7.

The following elements of the symbolic universe are important. *After six days* Jesus was transfigured on a high mountain. *A cloud overshadowed them. A voice came out of the cloud.* The crux of the problem here is that the temporal marker seems to hang in the air. This raises the question "Six days after what?" Given that a period of six days is an important element of the Pre-Festal Octave, we can consider whether the temporal marker in this tradition could have been *six days before* (instead of after) as in the Fourth Gospel, remembering that the sixth day before Nisan 15 was also the third day of the three-day period that immediately precedes it.

Several arguments come to mind. The third day of the Pre-Festal Octave is the Day of Theophany. It was also the sixth day *before* the feast. In the Fourth Gospel, the third day, on which the wedding took place, was also *six days before the feast*. It does not include an account of the Transfiguration, but the third-day story in John 2.1–11 is related to it because changing water into wine was the first "sign" *that Jesus was manifesting his glory* (2.11).[20] The phrase *after six days* comes from the story of the Transfiguration of Moses: "And the *glory of the Lord* abode upon Mount Sinai and the cloud covered it *six days*: and the *seventh day* he called unto Moses out of the midst of the cloud" (Ex 24.16). Once we realize that the *cloud* covered Moses on the first of the six days (but the *voice* was heard six days later), we can see that the original temporal marker in the tradition underlying Mark 9.2 could have been *six days before* rather than *after*. This makes better sense and is also consistent with the reconstruction of the Pre-Festal Octave. It is also consistent with what the Fourth Gospel says about the first manifestation of the glory of Jesus and with what Luke is trying to tell us about the precise time of the announcement of the birth of Jesus.

We can put the temporal markers back in their right place when we have reconstructed the symbolic universe and recognized this part of the Gestalt that also appears in the Gospels. The internal polarity of the festal Gestalt is depicted in figure 9.1.[21] Because these festivals are mirror images of each other, the elements associated with any one of them could also be shunted (so to speak) from any one of them to another. For example, the use of Sukkoth rituals at the winter festival (2 Mc 1.9) or the spring festival (as in the Holy Week narratives) shows that the other Pre-Festal Octaves could also be used for Temple purification. It is not necessary to push back the accounts of Holy Week to the autumn or the midwinter festival (Manson 1951) in order to explain the presence in the Gospels of elements associated with Hanukkah or Sukkoth. Elements associated with Sukkoth could also have been shunted over to Hannukah or Passover. Such transformations are part of the rules of the game.

Chislev 18 – 20 – 25 + Hanukkah

Tishri 8 – 10 – 15 + Sukkoth   Nisan 8 – 10 – (14) – 15 + Mazzoth

[Double Festal Octave is missing]

Note the six-month polarity of Tishri and Nisan, the symmetry of the Double Festal Octaves in Tishri, Chislev, and Nisan, and the lack of polarity between the winter festival and the summer season. Shabuoth does not fall into this scheme because it was celebrated fifty days after Pesach-Mazzoth.

Figure 9.1   Festal Octaves

In Luke's infancy narrative, the markers of sacred space are also significant. Space is important in this context not as a place in the world of things but symbolic space, a coherent structure or system of collective images (Bastide 1971: 81). Although the birth of the Baptist was announced in the Temple, he was destined to become a man of the desert (Lk 1.80). Although the birth of Jesus was announced outside the Temple, Jesus was taken to Jerusalem in utero (Lk 1.39). He was also taken there after his circumcision (2.22) and when he was twelve years old (Lk 2.41, 42). Both the synoptics and the Fourth Gospel confirm that Jesus "went up" to Jerusalem to celebrate the annual pilgrimages. His final journey to the Temple coincided with the spring festival. In short, Jesus was destined to be a man of the Temple, not a man of the desert. So there is an interesting crossover pattern in the infancy narratives:

The Baptist: in the Temple → into the desert
Jesus: outside the Temple → toward the Temple

When we turn to the adult Jesus, the pattern becomes more complex; it now looks like this:[22]

Jesus: Desert → Mountain → Temple

The next question is "How do we get there?"

The best place to begin to reconstruct the geographical elements in the symbolic universe of Second Temple Judaism is I Maccabees 1–4. It is an important passage because it is a prime example of the conflation of pilgrimage, holy war, and Temple dedication. It falls to the Double Octave Festival of Hanukkah because the Temple was rededicated on 25 Chislev and the cleansing was done *before* the dedication. Cleansing was necessary because the Temple was polluted by the Syrians (I Mc 1.46) when they placed the Abomination of Desolation on the altar (1.54). It is important to realize that the word "desolation" is not a psychological term, even though the Abomination did provoke profound distress (I Mc 2.7–14; 3.45–46). Whatever this heathen symbol was, its effect is clear enough: it transformed the Holy City into its pristine *desert* state (even though it was still a flourishing Hellenistic city)! We are now confronted by total anomie. The symbolic universe collapsed completely when the Abomination-that-causes-desertification (1.39 and 3.45) was placed in the center of the symbolic cosmos.

Whenever the sacred center is transformed into a desert, the right thing to do is to flee into the empirical desert (I Mc 2.28–29). We frequently find this feature in the Gospels and in Josephus (see Staples 1970: chapter 10 and Staples 1999). This explains why the ministry of Jesus also begins in the desert. The basic transformation now looks like this:

Temple→Desert Temple→Empirical Desert→Mountain→Clean Temple

This is the geographical axis along which the restoration drama is played out. It encompasses the same route that the Israelites traveled when they fled from Egypt after the Exodus. The same route was followed by the sacred ark on its way to the Temple. It is also the traditional pilgrimage route.[23] So when the people go up to Jerusalem to celebrate the pilgrimage festivals, God also goes on pilgrimage with his people.[24] This explains why the ministry of Jesus and the liberation of the Temple city in the time of Judas Maccabaeus were conceived as "reruns" of the Exodus (see I Mc 4.9; Barnett 1980/1981: 688, 699).

Between the starting point (desert) and the final destination (Temple) there is an important station along the way. It is the mountain on which God appears. During the final stage of this ritual, it is also important to note that the mountain is a place from which the Holy City can be seen—the Mount of Olives.[25] Even if it is not stated explicitly, the mountain is always in the vicinity of Jerusalem (I Mc 3.46) because the worshippers proceed from this mountain to the Temple at the climax of the liturgy.

But it is not always certain which mountain it is. In I Maccabees 3.46 it is called Mizpah. In the description of the solemn appearance (*parousia*) of Alexander the Great in Jerusalem Josephus (*Ant.* 11.328–31) tells us that the Temple could be seen from the mountain, but it is not entirely clear which mountain is meant. In the Loeb edition it is called Saphein. This means "a lookout" (*skopon* in Greek). It could also be Mt. Scopus, which is a mile or so north of Jerusalem. In the variant readings we can also find Saphin and Saphan. This suggests that this mountain was also identified with Mount Zaphon in the far north, which was the Mountain of the Gods in ancient Canaanite mythology. That seems less confusing once we recognize that traditions associated with one mountain could be shunted over to another—Horeb↔Sinai, Zaphon↔Zion (the north side), and Zaphon↔Scopus (see Staples 1970: chapter 10 and Clifford 1972). Even though the Alexander episode is blatantly unhistorical, it confirms that the mountain from which the Temple could be seen is an important station along this geographical axis. It provides an important element of the symbolic universe and also confirms that traditions were shunted from one mountain to another. This is another example of a transformation within the system.

More important is the belief that God goes into exile when his people go into exile or whenever the Temple was defiled. The classical text is Ezekiel 9–11. Whenever God forsakes Jerusalem, however, the next question is, "When and how does he come back?" One answer is found in Ezekiel 40–44. The prophet awaits God's return on a very high mountain north of Jerusalem. (The Greek translation says it was "over against" the city.) Ezekiel expected God to return on the tenth of the month "at the beginning of the year." This suggests 10 Tishri because New Year was celebrated in Tishri even though it was the seventh month of the year. The Septuagint calls it the first month, in which case God would have returned from exile on 10 Nisan. Either way, this piece of tradition not only links the return of God to 10 Nisan or 10 Tishri (Yom Kippur) but also locates his arrival on a high mountain overlooking Jerusalem immediately before he is manifest again in the Temple. Either way, God's return was expected on the third day of the Pre-Festal Octave.

There is another problem here. Even though we can put many elements in the gospel traditions back into their "right place" at the "right time" (once we have learned to recognize the basic Gestalt), there are no traces of a theophany in the Temple on the third day of the Pre-Festal Octave either in Mark 11 or anywhere else in the Gospels, suggesting that the Temple restoration ritual could not have been successful! God did manifest himself in the desert (at the time of Jesus' baptism) and on the mountain of Transfiguration.[26] Instead, we now find the third-day resurrection traditions "according to the scriptures."[27] This seems to imply that the resurrection of Jesus on the third day (a Christophany) replaced the theophany in the Temple that was expected on 10 Nisan (if we construe the texts in the light of the symbolic universe). This explains why the Lukan version of the Transfiguration (Lk 9.28–35) says that it happened "about eight days after" (when we would expect to find six days before or after). Luke seems to be treating the Transfiguration as a foretaste of the Christophany on Easter Sunday (the day of Jesus' departure on Nisan 17).

This means that Holy Week (Palm Sunday to Easter Sunday) is a transformation of the traditional Pre-Festal Octave in Nisan (Staples 1970, 1999: 483). It was moved on (as it were) by three days, and the three-day period now follows the six-day period instead of preceding it. Because those transformations are no longer in accordance with the rules, we have now arrived at the first radical breach between STJ and emergent Christianity. Bastide (1971) refers to such transformations as a "bricolage process"—creating structures from events, memories detached from chronology.

Three Recursive Practices

Three recursive practices are related to the Jewish conceptualization of sacred time and sacred space: pilgrimages, the holy war, and Temple dedication. Pilgrimage (*chag*) was mandatory for all adult males who were physically capable of going up to Jerusalem. The three annual pilgrimages (*shaloth regalim*) are required by the legislation in Deuteronomy 16.16, Exodus 23.14–17, and 2 Chronicles 8.3. They are Sukkoth, Pesach-Mazzoth, and Shabuoth. Hanukkah was not a mandatory pilgrimage, but it seems to have assumed the character of the *chag* at a later period, as is shown by the structural parallels between Hanukkah and the spring/autumn *chag* and the use of Sukkoth symbols. Jesus is also said to have gone up to Jerusalem to celebrate the Feast of Dedication (Jn 10). Even though women were not obliged to attend, some did take part, at times taking their children with them (e.g., Lk. 2.41–42).

The holy war (*ha-milchamah*) was also an ancient recursive practice, though it seems to have fallen into disuse immediately after the exile. It was revived during the Maccabean period and continued sporadically until the destruction of the Temple (Staples 1999). This recursive practice was reconstructed by Gerhad von Rad in 1951. War was a sacred institution because God was called the God of Battles (Ex 15.3) and gave his people the power to win victories (1 Sam 17.47). It was also a sacred ritual; so the warriors were also sacred persons. They had to go into battle in a state of purity (Dt 23). Because it was ultimately God who gave the victory, God also manifested himself on the field of battle. This explains the frequent appearance of the rubric "Fear Not" in war texts such as Deuteronomy 31 and 1 Maccabees 4.8. Both warriors and pilgrims were expected to be in a state of purity. More precisely, when the purpose of the war was to retake and dedicate the Temple, the warriors were also pilgrims; the dedication of the Temple also takes place during the *chag*.

When ritual combat was revived, there is another transformation; the ritual could also be performed *without the use of weapons*. In that case, it was believed that God would defeat the enemy because the right rituals had been performed (Staples 1970, 1999). Yonina Talmon suggested in 1962 that millenarian movements can be either "aggressive" or "quietist" in character. There is no evidence in early Christian traditions to demonstrate conclusively that Jesus and his followers were armed when they went in procession to the Temple (give or take one or two swords). But they did operationalize the ritual of combat (Staples 1999). This is demonstrated by the first version of Mark's feeding story (6.40), where we are told that the followers of Jesus sat down in ranks "by hundreds and fifties." This feature also appears in 1 Maccabees 3.55; Judas Maccabeus appointed captains of "hundreds . . . and fifties . . . and tens." This was the traditional deployment of the sacred warriors when they went into battle. Furthermore, if the feeding stories are Nisan 10 stories (as already suggested), this seems to confirm that we have restored them to their right place in the temporal order.[28] And, if this is the right time, then the right place of the feedings in the stories must be somewhere in the vicinity of Jerusalem between the theophany on the Mount of Olives (which seems to lie behind the Transfiguration traditions) and the solemn procession into the Temple.[29]

The narrative of the restoration of the Temple in the time of the Maccabees and what are now called the Holy Week stories in the Gospels describe a Feast of Sukkoth during the Pre-Festal Octave at another turning point of the Jewish year, and both include elements of the traditional ritual of Temple cleansing. This is reflected in the story of the cleansing of the Temple in the Gospels (Mk 11.15–18 and parallels), even though it is impossible to reconstruct precisely what happened on that occasion. In any case, having reconstructed the conceptualization of sacred time and space in STJ, we can now see that most of the basic elements of the traditions do fall into place despite the fact that some transformations have also taken place. But the basic Gestalt can still be recognized. We can also see that we are dealing with a conflation of pilgrimage, war, and Temple restoration.

The only element that is missing in the Gospels is the theophany in the Temple on the third day, which would have confirmed that God had repossessed the Temple. Instead, what we now have in the Gospels is a radically new transformation. It includes a Christophany on the third day after the first day of the Mazzoth Festival. This is the most important difference when we compare the Gospels with the symbolic universe of STJ. Furthermore, when Jesus spoke about the new Temple, he was speaking about the temple of his body (Jn 2.19). This is precisely the point at which early Christianity begins to part company with the various species of Jewish Orthodoxy.

Notes

1. See Lévi-Strauss (1963: 289). The main purpose of this chapter is to operationalize this programmatic statement in the field of biblical studies in a way that is consistent with the methodology of *structuralists* such as Lévi-Strauss and especially Piaget. I shall also consider some of the recent developments in the work of *structurationists* and *structurists* such as Anthony Giddens and especially Christopher Lloyd. None of them operationalized their structural methodologies in the field of biblical studies.

2. The problem of "dissimilarity" in NT studies became acute in the postwar period when exegetes such as Norman Perrin and several disciples of Bultmann insisted that the most historically reliable elements in the Gospels can be identified by applying the principle of "double-dissimilarity" (Staples 1970: 333). In short, the gospel traditions that differ from earlier Judaism and later Christianity are more likely to be historically reliable. This procedure, unless supplemented, failed to capture the continuities between Second Temple Judaism and emergent Christianity.

3. There are some radical changes such as the advent of gentile Christianity and the separation of the Christian movement from Judaism. Chronologically in this chapter, I reach neither of those radical breaks, but I do arrive at some major differences before the cut-off point (the Crucifixion). Jesus transformed the traditional conception of parenthood and kinship (Crossan 1991: 265ff.) to such an extent that the insights of Lévi-Strauss are not directly applicable when we examine radically different *spiritual* relationships demanded by Jesus when he summoned his hearers to enter the Kingdom of God. Such transformations are not possible within the laws of the traditional kinship system. This radical change did not entail a complete breach between the Jesus movement and the social institutions of STJ

at this stage (even though it provoked conflict), because Jesus still continued to worship in the Temple and many of his followers did so until long after his death.

4. The structuralists have already been succeeded by the poststructuralists, some of whom can be classified as postmodernists (e.g., Lemert in Ritzer 1990: chapter 9). This does not imply that postmodernist versions of poststructuralism have completely superseded the earlier manifestations of structuralism; the structuralist methodology still survives, even though it has now been recast in a form that is now called *structurist* (Lloyd 1993: chapters 2, 3) Some exegetes have recently been influenced by the presuppositions and (especially) the aesthetics of postmodernism. I appreciate their holistic approach (when compared with the atomistic approach of some of their predecessors), but I still maintain that the best way to understand the original meaning of biblical texts is to construe them in the light of the symbolic universe that was in place when their authors wrote them. A helpful way to construe texts is to determine what role they play in the processes of constructing, reproducing, and transforming symbolic universes and social institutions. We can call this approach *Symbolgeschichte*.

5. Lloyd seems to have in mind transformations that rearrange elements in preexisting structures (cf. Lévi-Strauss) but also insists that transformations can also add new elements or subtract old ones. One of the problems with structuralism (but not with Piaget's version) is that transformations always seem to take place *within the system*. Lloyd also insists that actors are not always aware of the cumulative effects of their actions. This is what he means by the *unconsciousness* of human agents. Lévi-Strauss construes the unconscious in terms of a lack of direct knowledge of the rules that operate in the human mind whenever transformations within the system are generated. It is never completely clear how this unconscious knowledge ultimately reveals itself (e.g., Jenkins 1979: 12–21). Here, Lloyd insists that a structurist methodology must try to describe and explain what human agents (Giddens's "naive sociologists") do not know about empirical processes of social structuring.

6. Atomism in the humanities entails *methodological individualism*, which is the antithesis of *structuralism* and *structurationism*. "In this ontology, society is not something extra-individual in the sense of relations, rules, shared understandings, and meanings that are not reducible to individuals." It also "denies the legitimacy of the action/society polarity" as well as denying "attempts to conceptualize action and society as being an interpenetrating duality in the sense advocated by Jean Piaget and Anthony Giddens" (Lloyd 1993: 42–43).

7. My first attempt to reconstruct the conceptualization of sacred time and sacred space in STJ was also based upon the insights of Gestalt psychology (Staples 1970: chapters 13 and 14; see also Staples 1999).

8. Harré and Secord (1972) insist that human beings "live according to rule" and it would be absurd to believe otherwise. This is correct as far as it goes but still leaves open the question of whether agents are *totally* constrained by rules. Agents are never totally constrained (or "over-socialized") because we are always confronted by deviance. And, if no human agent is constrained by "the rules of the game" ("under-socialization"), the upshot is a Hobbesian war of all against all or "anomie" (see also Wrong 1995). Berger insists that it is ultimately the "sacred cosmos" that protects religious people from "the terror of anomy" (1969: 27).

9. Attempts by Gilbert (1989) to reconstruct the first human interactions are highly speculative, as we would expect.

10. It was republished in the United Kingdom in 1969 as *The Social Reality of Religion*. Because Lloyd is not a religionist, he does not consider the phenomenon of religion in his theoretical reflections, even though he did consider *The Social Construction of Reality* (Berger and Luckmann 1966).

11. I cannot discuss here the question of whether symbolic interactionists did move up to the meso and macro levels of social interaction. On this see Plummer (in Turner 1996: 238–40). For recent updates on the problem of micro–macro linkage, see Ritzer (in Ritzer 1990: chapter 13) and Turner (1996: part 3, 221–302).

12. The pentecontad calendar consisted of seven periods of fifty days (350 days all told), which were followed by a New Year Festival of two weeks before the next calendar year commenced. Traces of the pentecontad calendar survive in the Shabuoth and Pentecost traditions of STJ.

13. Whether the Double Festal Octave can be traced back to a New Year Festival of two weeks, which was celebrated between two years, each consisting of 7 × 50 days, is a question that cannot be considered here.

14. Attempts were made to abolish the festivals associated with the Maccabees, but Hanukkah was too popular to suppress entirely (Staples 1970: chapter 7).

15. As far as I know, no other scholar has recognized the Double Octave in Chislev. Segal had already realized that the Pre-Festal Octave in Nisan is a ritual transformation from unclean to clean (1963). He also recognized the six-month polarity of Sukkoth and Pesach-Mazzoth (1961).

16. Whether Daniel was a deviant on matters calendrical or performed a prophetic "breaching experiment" (like the prophet who ran naked through the streets) is a question that still cannot be decided.

17. There is also the Feeding Story, which appears twice in Mark (6.35–44 and 8.1–8). The latter contains the three-day temporal marker (8.2). John 8.1–13 contains the phrase "the Passover was at hand," which means "six days before Nisan 15." That confirms that they were originally Nisan 10 stories.

18. The closest day to 25 Chislev in the Roman Calendar is Dec. 25, given the vagaries of a lunar/solar calendar.

19. In some manuscripts of *Protevangelium Jacobi*, Zechariah is explicitly called a high priest.

20. The Feeding in John 6 is also a "sign," suggesting that Jesus performed "signs" not only six days before the feast but also on the Day of Theophany. Jesus' signs are associated with manifestations of the Glory of God (*kabod/doxa*), which is a regular feature of third-day theophany texts (Staples 1970: chapter 11).

21. Laurentin (1957) examined the structure of Luke 1 and 2, and he treated the two parallel cycles as a "diptych" because they are mirror images of each other, but he did not link them directly to the Double Festal Octave.

22. The Desert–Mountain–Temple axis is associated with the three recursive practices of pilgrimage, holy war, and Temple dedication (Staples 1970: chapter 10). It also looms

large in the accounts of ritual combat in Josephus (Staples 1999). The Desert–Mountain–Temple axis was independently reconstructed by Elizabeth Malbon (1991). Her semiotic approach is explicitly Lévi-Straussian (Malbon 1991: xi), but she only deals with the spatial markers and links this geographical axis neither to the temporal ones nor to the events and recursive practices that occurred at the conjunction of sacred time and sacred space. Her explicitly structuralist approach not only lacks a robust account of human agency, it is also focused on movements in the text rather than on the ground.

23. When Jesus went to Jerusalem in utero and as a child, he followed the same route. This is how this pre-Lukan tradition links sacred time and place.

24. The pilgrimage is thus a "split-level" performance. On the "ground level" worshippers perform their actions; on the transcendental level God moves. At important moments in the process, God comes down to ground level, as it were, to reveal himself, to help his people, and to perform actions of his own. God appears first in the desert, then on the mountain, and finally in the Temple, usually on the third day (Staples 1970: chapter 11), demonstrating that this geographical axis is ultimately linked (though not always) in the symbolic universe to the Pre-Festal Octave.

25. The view from Olivet into the Temple was depicted on the Temple coins that were in use at that time.

26. If the Transfiguration was originally a 10 Nisan story (see above), this means that the mountain of Transfiguration must be Olivet. If so, it must have been shunted toward the north at a later point in its transmission history. This is consistent with the rules of transformation.

27. It is almost impossible to identify those scriptures without straining the evidence. This is still a major problem in NT studies.

28. The Gestalt, defeat of the enemy→building a Temple→theophany→victory banquet, is pre-Israelite. It can already be found in the ancient Canaanite myth and ritual pattern (Kapelrud 1963; Habel 1964).

29. Because eating and contact with women were forbidden during the preparation for the manifestation of God on the third day, we can assume that the theophany has already taken place: "And they saw God . . . and they did eat and drink" (Ex 24.10–11); and "Be ready against the third day and come not near a woman" (Ex 19.15—a Shabuoth text that could also be shunted). This is consistent with what Mark says (they were fasting just before they began to eat) and with John 12 (on 10 Nisan Jesus attended a banquet and was anointed by a woman). The fourth Gospel treats the feeding narrative as a Nisan 10 story, but retrojects it to an earlier point in the narrative.

Appendix 9.1

THE JEWISH CALENDAR IS a lunar one having twelve months of twenty-nine or thirty days, with a thirteenth extra month added seven out of every nineteen years to bring its year into a near synchrony with the solar year. Some Jewish groups adhered to a solar calendar, in contrast to the practice of the Temple authorities and the Macedonians. The religious calendar begins in the spring while the civil one begins in the fall.

Month	Religious Number	Civil Number	
Ve-Adar	—	—	Additional month
Nisan	1	7	March/April; Pesach on fourteenth Nisan
Iyyar	2	8	April/May
Sivan	3	9	May/June
Tamuz	4	10	June/July
Ab	5	11	July/August
Elul	6	12	August/September
Tishri	7	1	September/October; Yom Kippur on tenth Tishri
Marheshuvan	8	2	October/November
Chislev	9	3	November/December; Hanukkah on twenty-fifth Chislev
Tebet	10	4	December/January
Shebet	11	5	January/February
Adar	12	6	February/March

CONTEXTS AND EMERGENCE OF THE JESUS MOVEMENT AND EARLY CHRISTIANITY

III

Early Christianity as an Unorganized Ecumenical Religious Movement

10

FREDERICK BIRD

Introduction

T HIS CHAPTER VIEWS with sociological imagination the early history of the
Christian movement until about the year 90 C.E. It views this movement
comparatively and historically much as one might analyze new religious
movements in other periods of time.[1] From the beginning early Christianity was
a missionary religious movement that assumed quite diverse forms.[2] It remained
deeply Jewish in character even as it became a movement distinct from the prevailing forms of Judaism. Through the first several generations this movement
faced a number of crises that threatened its existence and sense of commonality.
Early Christian associations were able to manage this diversity successfully and to
live through these crises for several reasons. These diverse associations shared a
number of highly valued characteristics, they regarded themselves as related to
each other, and they attempted with mixed results to envision their commonality
through several encompassing visions.

I use the term "ecumenical" as a means of capturing with one word several
salient features of this movement. First, it was constituted by varied and dis-
tinctly different kinds of associations, among which existed at times various disputes, disagreements, and rivalries. Still they felt connected with each other as
part of a larger movement. Second, this movement from its early days sought adherents widely, from people shaped by multiple cultural and ethnic traditions.
Third, I use the term "ecumenical" as well to call attention to the several ways
members of these associations sought to affirm their interrelatedness. This ecumenical movement remained unorganized without common authority or decision-making structures.

Historical Setting

Early Christianity emerged as a new religious movement within the Greco-Roman world during the first century C.E. The eastern Mediterranean world in which Christianity developed was politically and militarily dominated by the Romans and culturally deeply influenced by Greek-speaking Hellenistic culture. Christianity initially arose among the Jewish population in Palestine and soon thereafter among diaspora Jews as well, in Syria, Asia Minor, Alexandria, Greece, and elsewhere. Although approximately one million Jews lived in Palestine, nearly four million others lived outside of this area (Stark 1996: 57, citing Johnson 1976 and Meeks 1983). The Christian movement also attracted gentile converts in many of these areas. Jews in Palestine had become increasingly restive. During this period a number of movements arose to protest Roman rule, follow would-be messiahs, question the Jewish religious establishment, protest against various taxes, call for a religious revival, and/or work for social reform. Romans responded brutally to a number of these movements (Horsley and Hanson 1985). Between the years 66 and 70 C.E. a war occurred between the Romans and Jews in Palestine. This war had devastating consequences for Jews. Many villages in Palestine were razed. Many crops were destroyed, and a great number of people died. Ultimately, much of Jerusalem was leveled. The Temple, which served as the center of a wide range of rituals and social practices, was destroyed. Many Jews within Palestine and beyond felt there was a need to find new ways to think about their identity, future, and past. Christianity emerged as a new religion within this larger milieu.

Early Christianity, a Missionary Movement

From its first days the early Christian movement sought to gain additional followers, supporters, and adherents. Christians sought to persuade others to become Christians. They felt compelled to seek out and persuade others to become involved as well. In this broad sense a missionary instinct was characteristic of the movement from its outset.

A social movement may have a missionary character without having to designate specific people as missionaries or establishing organized efforts to proselytize. Missionary movements may assume more ordinary forms. For example, there is considerable evidence that Islam expanded among peoples of Southeast Asia, Indonesia, and the Philippines as commercial traders, who happened to be Muslims, traveled in these areas. The latter incidentally talked of their religious convictions while conducting their business. They were not authorized missionaries. In a similar way Islam spread through large areas of Africa south of the Sahara as a result of travel by individual Muslims visiting other areas in conjunction with trade and by ordinary patterns of migration. Mithraism spread among Roman legionaries almost like a fad rather than the result of organized initiatives. Similarly, during the fourth century Arian Christianity spread among migrating Barbarians in southeastern Europe. Hence, when I describe early Christianity as a missionary movement, I am not assuming that proselytizing efforts were necessarily organized. To be sure, there were a number of specially designated missionaries like Barnabas and Paul, but missionary activity for the most part probably occurred more spontaneously in unplanned ways.

The Acts of the Apostles describes how the early Christian movement spread into a number of areas such as Egypt, Cilicia, Syria, Phoenicia, Cyprus, Cappadocia, Pontus, and Mesopotamia simply as Jews coming to Jerusalem for one of the annual pilgrimages met Christians, were persuaded to join the movement, traveled back home, and gained other supporters there. The Christian movement probably spread into these areas as much by this means as by the efforts of designated emissaries such as described by Eusebius (*Hist. eccl.* I.13; see also Acts 8.14–40, 13.1–14.18; and I Pt I.1, 2).

The quick spread of Christian associations into geographically dispersed areas of the Middle East, Asia Minor, Greece, Alexandria, and Rome indirectly testifies to the missionary character of early Christianity. Not all religious or ideological movements spread so quickly. Many are so closely tied to ethnic or national groups they make no effort to spread. Many religious and ideological movements seek only in modest ways to expand by holding occasional public celebrations or quietly distributing copies of their teachings. From a comparative historical perspective the quick spread of Christianity is noteworthy indeed. Traditional Jews had probably attempted some efforts at proselytizing, often in diaspora areas. It is likely that the large number of diaspora Jews in various parts of the Roman and Hellenistic worlds reflected not only the natural growth of ethnically born Jews but also the expansion of this movement to gain other supporters. Diaspora Jews had begun to welcome those they referred to as God-fearers, that is, people who respected and admired Jewish beliefs, myths, and rites but were not ethnically Jewish. At the beginning of the Common Era Jews were in the unique position of being a very widely dispersed, religiously identified ethnic people. Initially, if nothing else, the early Christian movement represented an altered expression of Judaism that was fervently committed to winning new followers.

This missionary fervor was not accidental or incidental. It was mandated by Jesus. In the collection of sayings found in the Q document, Jesus instructs his followers to take the message he is delivering to others living in dispersed villages. He suggests that many are waiting to hear and will likely respond. Because many are likely to respond favorably, he cautions his followers not to waste their time with those who seem unresponsive. He recognizes that the activity of spreading this message may be risky at times but cautions his followers not to become overly anxious (Lk 10.2–11). He directly tells them that if they speak publicly on his behalf both he and God will somehow find ways to support them (Lk 12.4–6, 8–10). They should not worry about what they wear or what they say: these things will take care of themselves (Lk 12.22–32). He calls for them not only to deliver his message but also to attend those who are ill. It is a mistake to interpret these sayings to mean that all of Jesus' followers were expected to become itinerant preachers. He is not necessarily spelling out a new career that he calls for them all to adopt. Given his interactions with people in quite different circumstances, Jesus seemed to allow for various kinds of responses. No doubt, he called for many followers simply to visit people in neighboring villages. He probably also called for some, especially those already dispossessed (Crossan 1998: 281), to join him at least temporarily as he undertook a preaching campaign in other Galilean towns (Horsley 1989: 117). Additionally, he may have asked a number of followers to join with him for a group pilgrimage to Jerusalem, warning them at the same time that this extended trip might be risky. Without attempting to spell out the precise meaning of Jesus' words more than this kind of retrospective analysis allows, we can observe more generally that Jesus called for and expected his followers to play an active role in spreading the message he was delivering. They were expected to be more than listeners; they were expected to find ways to pass along the message (cf. Lk 11.33–36; 13.18–21; 14.34–35).

This particular kind of missionary impetus may well have been fostered by John the Baptist. Like an ancient Israelite prophet, John had been preaching in wilderness areas and attracting crowds who came out to see and hear him, from Galilee as well as Judaea. He expected that those who came and were baptized as a sign of their commitment to his message would return to their villages and seek more recruits. There is no evidence that these followers were expected to form themselves into commune-like communities. Having heard the word and been baptized, they were expected to act in keeping with John's message. This probably meant among other things speaking with others and encouraging them to go to hear John preach. It appears, moreover, that John was not satisfied simply to wait for contemporary Israelites to come to him. He seems to have commissioned some followers to travel through the countryside to voice his message and baptize those who accepted. Some of Jesus' closest associates, as well as perhaps Jesus himself, had been commissioned in this way (Jn 3.25–4.3). Indirect evidence for the missionary character of the Baptist movement is later found in the Book of Acts on the occasions when early Christians met up with people baptizing the way John did in places as distant as Ephesus (Acts 18.24–28; cf. I Cor 1.12, 3; 3.3, 5).

John was not asking people to become part of a specific new religious movement distinguished from Judaism. Nor was he attempting to establish a distinct denomination within Judaism. Rather, among his fellow Israelites, he initiated a religious revival and reform movement that possessed an unmistakable missionary zeal. John and his followers wanted to win the hearts and minds of their contemporaries to a new or renewed vision of Israel in which membership was not based simply on biological descent but on the willful act of committing themselves to adhere to norms and truths at the heart of their tradition.

The missionary character of the movement begun by Jesus had much the same character. It was a movement spread by the testimonies, conversations, and exemplary actions of individuals as they interacted with neighbors and by the preaching missions of particular individuals (Mk 6.7; Lk 10.1). It was a movement of religious revival and reform among Israelites. It called for a reaffirmation to basic Israelite identity grounded not on biological descent but on a renewed commitment to what the movement regarded as the basic truths of that tradition.

Viewed sociologically, the early Christian movement differed at its outset from the movement begun by John in two important ways. First, it very quickly began to attract adherents among diaspora Jews. In a short period, diaspora Jewish adherents probably outnumbered adherents from Judaea, Samaria, and Galilee (Stegemann and Stegemann 1999: 219). Second, Jesus' followers believed that he had given them some measure of free reign to rearticulate his message in terms that allowed them at once to capture the heart and central character of this message and yet to do so in ways that allowed them to shape it in ways likely to address their quite different audiences. Evidence for this moderate free reign is found both directly in words attributed to Jesus and indirectly in the diverse character of the messages proclaimed by followers in different areas. When Jesus called upon his followers to help spread his message, he told them that they did not need to worry about what to say. In these settings, if they are really dedicated to furthering the movement and its message, they would figure out what to say (Lk 10.1–16, 12.2–12).

Early Christianity, a Movement of Considerable Diversity

From their earliest beginnings Christian associations were diverse in their locale, the character of their writings, many of their ritual practices, the views with which they regarded Jesus, the soteriologies they adopted, the meaning that they attached to membership, and the social forms they assumed. These differences were widespread and the occasion for much conflict. They were as well characteristic of the movement as a whole.

Within twenty years adherents had formed associations in Galilee, Samaria, Judaea, Cyprus, Cilicia, Western Syria, Eastern Syria, Galatea, Macedonia, Rome, and Corinth, as well other locations. These associations included Aramaic and Greek-speaking Jews as well as Gentiles. In the Acts of the Apostles the spread of Christianity is described in a linear fashion as going forth from Jerusalem and then

Antioch. A closer look at the early writings suggests that this spread was much less linear. The Gospels of Mark and Matthew suggest that the movement began and spread as well from Galilee (Mt 26.31–35, 28.16–20; Mk 16.1–8). This view is supported by contemporary scholars who argue that a vibrant movement of followers located in Galilee produced the Q sayings collection (Mack 1988, 1993; Horsley and Silberman 1997). Christian associations probably formed in both Western and Eastern Syria prior to any organized efforts by Christians in Judaea to develop centers there. Additionally, there may well have been Christians in Rome before either Paul or Peter ever reached that city. The Jews who traveled from there to Corinth may well have included some who were already interested in the Christian movement. The willingness of Priscilla and Aquila to house Paul suggests that they may have already been friends of the movement before meeting him (Acts 18.1–4). As noted, the Acts of the Apostles suggests that in an unorganized way diaspora Jewish pilgrims encountered Christians in Jerusalem and then returned to their homes not only as supporters of this new movement but as proponents and potential organizers of local associations (Acts 2.5–13, 11.19).

As a result of these activities, the early Christian movement was able to establish local associations in quite diverse cultural milieus. It is important to emphasize this point even while recognizing that most converts to this movement initially were probably ethnically Jewish. Although ethnically linked, in different locales Jews were likely to be more or less influenced by different local cultures. They also were likely to hold different religious and political views. For example, from the time of Herod to the end of the Jewish wars, at different times large numbers of Palestinian Jews followed several different prophets and would-be messiahs, joined or supported utopian communes such as that at Qumran, participated in popular insurrections, became disciples in reform groups like the Pharisees, allied themselves with the campaigns of Herodians to reestablish an independent Roman-Jewish state, and/or supported the priestly elite associated with the Temple (Horsley and Hanson 1985). To a large degree Galileans regarded themselves as a distinct population different from Judaeans in much the same way, although to a less degree, the Samaritans did (Horsley 1996). They may well have referred to themselves as Galileans or Israelites rather than Jews since the latter term was associated for many with being Judaean (Robinson 1962). The variety of Jews outside of Palestine was no doubt as diverse if not more so. These Jews were not only mostly Greek-speaking but were in varying degrees also influenced by local Syrian, Alexandrian, Cyprian, Achean, Macedonian, and other cultures (Lightstone 1984). As various Palestinian and diaspora Jews joined the emerging early Christian movement, they likely responded to this movement, interpreted it, and articulated its meaning and message in relation to the diverse concerns that moved them and the varied forms of rhetoric to which they had already become accustomed. It seems reasonable to expect diverse receptions to this movement if for no other reason than because of the diversity of the cultural settings of those Jews who responded.

It is not surprising, therefore, to discover that these dispersed early Christian associations used quite different terms to communicate what they regarded as the especially important features of this movement. When we survey the written texts associated with different Christian groups, we find quite different accounts of what was regarded as vital and valued (Koester 1971). Galilean Christians remembered and voiced Jesus' message in terms of a set of prophetic sayings now found in what is referred to as the Q document. Some eastern Syrian Christians viewed the Christian message in term of the *Gospel of Thomas*. These sayings, many parallel to those in Q, were more theosophical, more addressed to individuals interested in personal growth. They were mysterious and not readily comprehensible to ordinary "disciples." In the meantime, other groups, perhaps in both Judaea and Syria, viewed Jesus especially in terms of a cycle of miracle stories, which eventually appeared in similar form and order in the Gospels of John and Mark. There seems to have been a group of Christians in western Syria or upper Galilee who thought of themselves, much as did the Pharisees, as the renewed expression of a Judaism based not only on the accepted written Torah but on a new oral Torah transmitted in the Christian case by and through Jesus, the new Moses. In Matthew's Gospel, not only does Jesus like Moses escape from a murder of the innocents, he also delivers the Law from the Mountain, and sets forth five groups of teaching corresponding to the five books of Torah. In the meantime another group, using imagery and rhetoric similar to that used by the Qumran community, depicted themselves as the true Israelites. This group, whose sentiments are especially expressed in the Gospel of John, set forth their version of the central Christian message in a set of thoughtful and poetic yet discursive stories by and about Jesus. During the same time and earlier, Paul and those who thought of the Christian movement in terms of the images and beliefs he set forth, viewed Christianity largely in terms of the death and rebirth of Jesus as their savior and Lord.

When with a sociological imagination we observe these different expressions by early Christian associations, we are struck by their considerable diversity. Observers are likely not to fully appreciate this diversity if they begin to label some of these expressions as Gnostic, Jewish-Christian, apocalyptic, orthodox, or heterodox. These terms betray a predilection to distinguish central from marginal expressions of this movement. Similarly, observers are likely to overlook or minimize the historicity of this diversity when they begin to see how many of these expressions can be viewed as fitting together when interpreted with what they may regard as appropriate theological spectacles. Other observers are likely to treat this diversity as somehow accidental or uncharacteristic when they seek to discover an original form of this movement either in the Jerusalem church, the Galilean Jesus movement, and/or the Q community.[3] In contrast, what we have observed is that this movement assumed diverse forms from a very early period and that diversity was a characteristic feature during the first several generations.

Christian diversity existed on several levels. The groups differed in terms of many of the rituals they practiced. Some clearly continued to practice circumcision, while others, like the movement in eastern Syria represented by Thomas's Gospel, did not. While Paul criticized formerly gentile Galatian Christians for subsequently deciding to become circumcised, in other communications he seemed to recognize that Christian communities might be constituted by those who chose to be circumcised and those who did not (Romans 2 and 3). Some Christian communities differed in terms of whether and how they practiced prayers, fasting, purifications, and almsgiving (*Gos. Thom.* 5, 14, 89, and 101). They differed on whether women should keep their heads covered when speaking in meetings (I Cor 11.2–16). They split, often quite heatedly, over what foods they were allowed to eat. Some groups of Christians clearly assumed stricter, probably more kosher-like, views than others. We can hear echoes of disputes over this matter in *Thomas* (*Gos. Thom.* 28), Paul's letters (Rom 13 and 14; I Cor 8, 10.14–33; Gal 2), and Acts (Acts 15), as well as in gospel stories of Jesus eating on the Sabbath and with tax collectors and others of low repute.

These groups differed over the regard they held for Jesus. The differences here were probably quite substantial. Some groups, like those associated with Thomas's Gospel, viewed Jesus as a teacher of wisdom. Others, such as the Q community, depicted him as simultaneously a scribe-like teacher and a prophet-like figure, speaking and acting symbolically in ways reminiscent of a long history of Jewish prophets. Many early followers, such as those who collected and recited the cycle of miracle stories in John and Mark, viewed him as a wonder-worker, capable of producing various kinds of cures and healing and finding ample supplies of food and good wine when none seemed to be available. For others, Jesus' most important role seemed to have begun only after he had died. They believed that Jesus had been elevated to the heavens and that he now sent his spirit to intercede in various powerful ways on behalf of his followers. Followers invoked this spirit to account for their capacity to speak in tongues; win numerous converts, especially among diaspora Jews and Gentiles; persuade former critics to become followers; and perform some kinds of healing. Most importantly, a number of followers felt that they had been directly addressed by Jesus' spirit and authorized to spread the movement in his name. The Book of Acts is filled with these kinds of stories. Others, like Paul, viewed Jesus as a savior who through his sacrifice-like dying and subsequent rising occasioned the possibilities of justification and rebirth for followers. There were still other views that variously imagined Jesus as a heavenly high priest, a contemporary Moses, or a heavenly messenger from God. A number of early Christians seemed to have expected Jesus' imminent return. Many observers have already called attention to the quite varied ways in which people within the early Christian movement thought about Jesus. For present purposes it is important not only to note this variety but to recognize as well that these diverse views seem to be held from very early in the history of the movement, within the first two dozen years, and that many of these views were not easily reconciled with each other.

The early Christian associations also held quite different soteriologies. For example, in a number of places Paul, like the Pharisees with whom he had originally been connected, associates this end with a future resurrection of the dead (1 Cor 15; Acts 23.6–10). In other places Paul discusses the end of the Christian life in terms of spiritual rebirth in the present. In still other places he sums up the end of the Christian life as the act of being somehow made righteous in God's eyes. Q associates the end both with the coming realization of the kingless kingdom of God and with an imminent judgment of God. Some early Christians hoped for a new messianic age, while others looked forward to a renewed, more just Israelite society free of Roman rule. Many felt comfortable talking about the end of Christian life as the promise of eternal life. Some simply thought of this end as the blessing or good favor of God that was especially extended to the poor, hungry, grieving, and distressed (Lk 6.20–23). Other observers have called attention to the number and variety of these images. What is especially noteworthy for our present purposes is that these diverse views were likely held within the first two to three decades and that these views imagine the end of the Christian life in ways that are not always easily reconciled.

The early Christian associations used different terms to identify themselves as members. For example, as attested to by the Gospel of Mark, in some settings members of these associations referred to themselves as "disciples." However, this term was scorned (Thomas) or ignored (Q, Paul) by others. In other settings, followers referred to themselves as "brothers" (or "brothers and sisters"), "friends," "believers," "children of God," "saints," and "servants of the word." Many followers probably adopted no special designation but thought of themselves as the true children of Abraham, committed to the renewal of Israel. To be sure, some followers thought of themselves as "Christians," but that title was probably not used by many others. Although Luke's history suggests that the use of this term began in Antioch shortly after Jesus' death, Luke himself seems reluctant to use that term. Instead he refers to followers as disciples or believers or collectively as churches. As we review this information, we can see that Christians had no one term to designate themselves as members of this movement.

Finally, early Christians brought into being associations that took on quite different social forms. For example, the early association of Christians in Jerusalem established a commune-like community in which they shared possessions (Acts 4.32–37). The character of the community presupposed by John's Gospel seems quite similar. Members are presumed to form a close-knit community of the true, and not merely nominal, children of God (Jn 15, 16, 17). In both cases members seems to have lived in close proximity, acted somewhat like an extended family, shared at least some meals, and shared many possessions. The *Gospel of Thomas* seems to be addressed to an association of adherents formed like a theosophical society in which individuals sought to enhance their own personal growth. Members might well have met to hear and recite statements and practice varied forms of meditation. The associations formed by Galilean Christians differed in other ways. Horsley maintains that these associations were constituted by members committed to the reform and renewal of Israelite society (Horsley 1989, 1996; Horsley and Silberman 1997). These associations were constituted by neighbors living in the same villages who were committed to work for these reforms and renewal. Insofar as members traveled, they journeyed among Galilean villages, visiting other like-minded associations and seeking to win supporters for this renewal movement in still other villages. They were dedicated to the renewal of a given, ethnically defined, albeit geographically dispersed, society. These associations may well have held meetings in local synagogues during or after regular synagogue services. In Mack's analysis, other associations in this same area and in Syria may have formed schools much as the Pharisees did or as some of the Greek philosophical movements did (Mack 1993). The Gospel of Matthew presupposes the existence of a Pharisee-like association of Christians, which may have existed as a school but also as a synagogue-like congregation for prayers, readings, initiations, and mutual discipline. The associations established in places like Galatia, Ephesus, Phillipi, Thessalonika, and Corinth were similar in form but were constituted by Gentiles as well as diaspora Jews.

Early Christianity Facing Potentially Divisive Crises

We have noted the several ways in which early Christianity was a very diverse movement. This diversity either occasioned or expressed a number of internal disputes, controversies, and rivalries, all of which may have been potentially divisive. Many of these differences may not ever have been fully settled. It appears in a number of cases that different Christian associations simply agreed to be different and/or that differing Christians within common associations simply lived with their differences. From Paul's letters to Corinthian and Galatian Christians, we can observe that groups within associations in these areas differed quite strongly over a number of issues. These included disagreements and disputes over acceptable practices with regard to what kinds of food were acceptable to eat, over the status and regard assigned to persons able to speak in tongues, over how authority ought to be exercised and by whom, and over whether non-Jewish male converts ought to be circumcised. As is evident from reading 1 Clement, forty years later Christians in Corinth still seemed to be exercised by some of the same kinds of dispute— especially regarding issues associated with authority and spiritual gifts.

In the *Gospel of Thomas* we see evidence for another kind of dispute or rivalry. Here we find followers like Mary, Thomas, and Salome saying things that gain Jesus' approval while Peter, James, and Matthew raise questions and make comments that indicate they do not quite comprehend what Jesus is trying to say. The view of Peter and James expressed here contrasts sharply with the high regard for them both in Acts and Matthew's Gospel. The *Gospel of Thomas* pointedly seems to be arguing that Peter's and James's views of the central Christian message were misguided.

In Jerusalem in the period shortly after Jesus' death, there seems to have been some kind of ongoing dispute or rivalry between diaspora converts and the Galilean leaders of this association. The outcome is fairly clear: a number of diaspora followers left Jerusalem, while the Galilean leaders remained (Acts 6.1–6; 8.2, 3; 11.19–26). Acts overtly describes persecution against the church as the cause. How credible is this account? In an almost undifferentiated way, the author of Acts tends to invoke spontaneous as well as planned persecutions by other Jews as the standard explanation for a wide variety of mishaps (Acts 16.19–24; 17.5–9, 13–15; 18.12; 19.33). For example, Paul's subsequent inability actually to meet with and settle his differences with the Jerusalem church is accounted for as the by-product of a spontaneous attack upon him by other Jews (Acts 21.27–36). Still, even if persecutions were a factor, how do we explain this kind of outcome? Acts does note a dispute between diaspora and Palestinian followers over the distribution of common goods for the benefit of widows. This dispute was seemingly settled by appointing a number of people to address this problem. Still, there seems to be some relation between disputes between these groups, of which the controversies over the common goods was probably only a symptom, and the subsequent division that caused the diaspora followers to exit from this association. They may well have differed because they used different languages— Greek and Aramaic, because they already held different views of Judaism as diaspora and Palestinian Jews, and/or because the diaspora followers were restive with the commune-like character of the association in Jerusalem.

These examples indicate that differences among Christians sometimes led to disagreements, disputes, and rivalries that were often heated and not always resolved. None of these disputes were probably as intense or critical as that which occurred between Paul on one side and Barnabas and Peter on the other. This dispute, which is overtly described in both Acts 15 and in the first two chapters of Paul's letters to the Galatians, has been analyzed by countless observers. It partly concerned the status of Gentiles within Christian associations. The disputants reached a decision that allowed uncircumcised gentile men to become Christians, but they seemed to disagree regarding the status of these converts and about whether they could share in the same common meals. The rupture also seems to have been fueled by different views of the status of the written Torah, the authority of Jesus, and soteriology. It is worth noting that the dispute led to a rupture in the close relationship between two Greek-speaking, diaspora Jews, Paul and Barnabas, who had been colleagues and partners over a period of more than a dozen years. The rupture led Paul to leave for good the Christian association in Antioch with which he had been connected for a long time. There is no evidence that he expected, or they expected him, to return. Paul returned to Jerusalem seven or eight years later with gifts for the Christians in that city from Christian associations in Macedonia, Asia Minor, and Greece. There is no clear evidence that any reconciliation or meeting of minds occurred between Paul and the elders of the church in Jerusalem. Acts describes how diaspora Jews sought to attack Paul, who was eventually protected by Roman officials. There is no account of whether or how the earlier dispute was either raised or resolved. What stands out in the Acts account is the absence of any real meeting or discussion between Paul and the elders in Jerusalem who had previously so strongly disputed his views (Acts 21–26).

Features Common to Early Christian Associations

Although the early Christian movement assumed diverse forms and experienced many rivalries, disagreements, and disputes, it still remained a common, albeit unorganized ecumenical movement. It did not split into a variety of similar but different religious movements. It maintained a sense of commonality, in spite of this diversity and differences, in part because its diverse associations shared a number of common features that they highly regarded. These features were characteristic of Christian associations wherever they were found. I will discuss several of these.

(1) The early Christian movement's associations were characterized by a well-practiced commitment to mutual regard and assistance. This regard and help assumed many forms. Christians were expected to care for and take care of each other. They provided hospitality to each other, especially when receiving travelers. They nursed each other when they were sick. They provided food when others were hungry. They provided charitable assistance when others were economically distressed. Rather than cause animosity between themselves, they forgave each other their debts. They incorporated this principle in their standard common prayer, in which they asked God to forgive them as they forgave each other. They felt that fellow Christians ought to actively seek to make peace with each other before participating in worship services. From the beginning Christians invoked the traditional Jewish com-

mandment to love your neighbor as yourself as their preeminent moral principle. Jesus said the standard summed up the whole of the Torah and the prophets (Mk 12.28–34; Lk 10.25–28). Paul repeatedly invoked the love commandment as a moral principle easily understood by and compelling to both Jews and Gentiles (Rom 13.8–10; I Cor 12, 13, 14). He similarly treated it as a summary of the Ten Commandments. The ethic of mutual assistance powerfully shaped the ethos of this movement. As Stark (1996: 73ff.) has noted, Christians were widely respected for the active, reciprocating way they assisted and cared for each other.

(2) Early Christian associations were marked by a deep, pervasive influence of Jewish cultural traditions. When viewed comparatively with other religious and cultural movements of the ancient Mediterranean and Middle Eastern world, Christian associations appeared similar to Jewish groups in a number of ways. For the most part, they regarded the Jewish Bible as Scripture, usually in its Greek version. Those who authored the early Christian writings that still survive filled their works with images and citations from Jewish texts. This is true not only for works containing many overt references to ancient scriptures, such as Paul's letters, Hebrews, the *Didache, 1 Clement*, and the four extant New Testament Gospels, but also for works such as the sayings collections of Thomas and Q, where the references are more allusive and less textual. Some of the converts to the early Christian movement were Jewish, some of them diaspora Jews, less strongly influenced by Judaean views of Judaism. Some converts were God-fearing, nonethnic individuals whose commitment to and interest in Judaism was based on personal or family choice. To be sure, the early Christian movement also attracted many gentile converts. Furthermore, most local associations, even the most overtly Jewish such as the community associated with John's Gospel, were deeply influenced by Greek cultural values. Stark goes so far as to argue that Christians primarily won support from among disaffected diaspora Jews not only during the first but also during the next two centuries. He notes that their church buildings were typically found in areas of towns where Jews predominantly lived (Stark 1996: 59–69). The fact that most Christian associations treated Jewish texts as their Scriptures indirectly points to the Jewish background of influential adherents.

By different means and to varying degrees, early Christian associations did attempt to distinguish themselves from other Jewish movements. In this way, their stance was much like the Qumran community and the Pharisees, both of whom set themselves apart from the views and practices of the Judaism associated with the priestly establishment. At times the anti-Jewish rhetoric of Christian groups appears to bear witness to intrareligious rivalries. Criticisms of Pharisees in Matthew's Gospel are of this character. The Pharisees are highly praised (Mt 5.17–20, 23.2) at the same time as they are criticized. Similarly, a number of other New Testament references to Jews seem to refer more particularly to rivalries between Galileans and perhaps others as opposed to Judaean Israelites. In places the word "Jews" is used in a series that includes the word "Galileans," Idumeans and Israelites living outside Judaea. In several instances criticisms of Jews seem to have arisen because synagogues in certain areas began to prohibit Christians from participating in their services (Jn 16.2; Rv 2.9; Acts 17.1–9). As the references to Paul's activity and the practices of the Christian community in Jerusalem bear witness, many Christians continued to participate in rituals of the synagogues and Temple. To be excluded aroused their anger. The lengths to which Christians went to criticize particular expressions of Judaism indirectly reflects the extent to which they felt it was necessary to distinguish themselves from the other expressions of Judaism.

The early Christian movement held a fundamentally different view of what it meant to be identified as "children of Israel." In many different ways they said they were not members of a religiously defined ethnic people constituted primarily but not exclusively by descent. They identified themselves as members of voluntary religious associations. The Jews from which they wished to distinguish themselves in various ways all assumed by contrast that they were members of such a religiously defined ethnic people, even though they differed on how to renew, defend, and guide this people.

(3) Early Christian associations used the rite of baptism as a ritual to mark entrance into their associations. No doubt different associations assigned different meanings to this rite. No doubt some viewed the rite in more soteriological terms, like Paul, whereas others viewed it more like John, as the offering of an oath in connection with their entrance into an oath-bound fraternal association dedicated to social and religious renewal. However much they varied in other ways, Christian associations everywhere seemed to practice this rite, and it became an identifying feature.

The conclusion that most if not all Christians underwent this rite is based on several different kinds of observations. The first is the widespread reference to this rite throughout the early Christian writings. The Gospel of Matthew assumes Christians began baptizing in Galilee shortly after Jesus' death (Mt 28.16–20). Acts assumes they began baptizing in Jerusalem after a glossalalic experience by Jesus' closest associates (Acts 2.37–42). John's Gospel assumes Jesus' followers were baptizing even while Jesus was alive (Jn 4.2). Paul presumes that all Christians had been baptized as part of their entrance in and commitment to the Christian movement (1 Cor 1, 2, 3, 4; Rom 6). He does not argue for this act. He takes it for granted. Clearly the Christian associations that he met in Judaea and Syria must have practiced this rite.

The second reason for assuming that most if not all Christian associations practiced this rite comes from considering the close, ambiguous relation between the followers of John the Baptist and the early Christians (Mk 1.14; Mt 4.12). There seems to have been some overlap between the movement of followers associated with John and the movement of followers associated with Jesus. In the Fourth Gospel Jesus and several of his closest associates are described as being followers of John. More precisely, they are described as helping with John's prophetic activities of preaching and baptizing (Jn 3:22–4:3). What happened to the followers of John after he was put into prison for criticizing Herod Antipater and later killed? Did they disappear? Did they become followers of Jesus? Did Jesus continue and at the same time modify what John was doing? We can begin to address these questions by making several observations. There are accounts in the Book of Acts (Acts 8.9–13; 18.24–28; cf. I Cor 1.10–17; 3, 4) that suggest that after Jesus' death followers of John were still proclaiming John's message and baptizing those they convinced. For example, Apollos was described as only knowing the baptism of John although he was ostensibly a follower of Jesus. He is described as baptizing people in Ephesus and Corinth. Others were baptized in Samaria with John's baptism and had to be rebaptized in the spirit by Jesus' followers. In several places John's way of baptizing is distinguished from the baptism administered by Jesus' followers. The latter was described as being connected with a personal experience of the Holy Spirit. From Paul's discussion in his letter to Corinthians and from Acts, we can surmise that those undergoing this baptism often had a glossolalia-like experience (Esler 1994: 37–51). We can also observe a number of passages in Q where efforts are made to show how the movement now following Jesus differs from the earlier movement of John the Baptist (Lk 3.2b, 7–9, 16, 17; 7.1–10, 18–23, 24–27). We can reasonably infer that the need to indicate how the movement following Jesus differed from the movement following John arose because the movements were so closely connected. Because of the close association between these movements, it also seems reasonable to assume that the early Christian movement from the beginning called for those whose comradeship they were seeking to gain to undergo an act of being baptized.

For these several reasons, I think it is reasonable to conclude that all Christians underwent the rite of baptism, whether they were in commune-like groups, theosophical associations, social renewal fraternities, or household congregations. Furthermore, in spite of the diversity of their associations, all were likely to connect this rite with at least two additional features shared in common. The first was the act of committing oneself to a message but also to an association of comrades. The rite helped to bring into being and solidify a new social bond marked, as I have already observed, by an ethic of mutual regard and assistance. The second was an expectation that as a result of this rite a Christian could expect support from God's Spirit. To be sure, this expectation assumed diverse forms. It was connected for many with an expectation of being touched by God's Spirit through a glossolalia-like experience. For others, it was the expectation that God's Spirit would help them say the right thing when confronted by opponents.

(4) Most if not all Christian associations adopted a number of other common ritual practices, including some kind of group ritualized meal. The form of this rite clearly varied, as witnessed by the different accounts in Paul's writing, the *Didache*, the Fourth Gospel, and the synoptic Gospels. As Christians regularly met they partook in some kind of ritualized meal, accompanied with a set recitation of prayers, versicles, readings, and homilies (Crossan 1998: chapter 23). During these services, Christians communicated with each other using primarily what Bernstein refers to as restricted rather than elaborated speech codes (Bernstein 1971). As such, their communications functioned primarily to occasion and reinforce shared sentiments rather than discursively to transmit information, ideas, and/or philosophies.

(5) Early Christian associations were sectarian: they were voluntary associations of people who considered themselves to be religiously and morally qualified.[4] They belonged to their associations not by virtue of birth and normal patterns of socialization but because they had undertaken a personal act of commitment. In this way they were similar to other Jewish reform movements like the Pharisees and the Essenes. Like other sectarian groups, Christians brought into being associations of people who voluntarily committed themselves to live in keeping with standards that called for extra effort, dedication, and virtue. Sect members do not regard themselves as ordinary. They have willingly undertaken activities, identifications, and pursuits that they were not required to assume.

In ways that paralleled beliefs of John's followers, Christians argued that the only way or at least the most fitting way to become true Israelites, authentic children of Abraham or of God, was personally to redevote themselves to God. They assumed that such acts of devotion involved as well acts of repentance. In the process the collectivity that was Israel was reconceived not as a religiously identified ethnic population but as a large voluntary association of persons who had religiously and morally committed themselves to a vision of a renewed society. The Q collection of sayings cites John as advising, "Do not say to yourself, we have Abraham as our ancestor, for I tell you God is able from these stones to raise up children to Abraham" (Lk 3.7–9). In Q Jesus says that the true children of God are not just those who hear God's word—that is, have listened to the recitations of Torah—but rather those who act on God's word (Lk 6.47–49). The Gospel of John begins by asserting that the true children of God are not born of the flesh—that is, by ethnic descent—but by virtue of God's adoption of them by spirit (Jn 1.13, 4.3). With what seems to be an effort to foster conciliation, Paul argues that people may become true Israelites, authentic children of Abraham, either by virtue of descent or by the act of personal commitment and faith. Neither party, he argues, should think of themselves as more virtuous or more authentic (Rom 3.9–11).

Early Christians differed from other Jewish sects in several decisive ways. In composition they included diaspora Jews in much greater numbers, as well as Gentiles. They assumed very diverse social forms as I have already noted. Most importantly, they held different assumptions about the relation of their sectarian movement to Judaism as a whole. In prophetic ways, the Essenes and Pharisees wanted to occasion reforms in Israel. John's movement may have had a similar vocation. In contrast, the Christian movement, and perhaps John's, wanted to remake Israel into a large "sect," that is, a voluntary association of the religious and morally qualified.

(6) All the early Christian associations looked to Jesus as their founder and foundation. Although they thought about Jesus in quite different ways, there were some common elements in their regard for him. Clearly, they all regarded Jesus as the founder of their movement. The movement began with him and not John, for example, or James or Peter or Barnabas. They also all regarded Jesus' words as authoritative and authorizing. They cited what they regarded as his words to legitimate their activities. Whatever they did, they did in Jesus' name. This was true as much for Paul as for the elders in Jerusalem, the social reform movement in Galilee, or the community assumed by Thomas's Gospel. Paul, for example, justifies his activities by claiming that he was personally addressed by Jesus in a vision (Gal 1.11–16; 1 Cor 15.9–11). In other places he refers to Jesus' words either explicitly, as when he discusses rules regarding marriage and divorce (1 Cor 7) and talks about the ritual of the common meal (1 Cor 9.8–14, 11.23–32), or implicitly, as when he invokes the centrality of the love commandment or discusses the flexibility Christians were allowed with respect to kosher rules. Christians felt they were addressed by Jesus through the words and sayings they believed he had spoken. Jesus' words were regarded as authoritative not only because they were viewed as compelling, instructive, wise, and clever but also because they were believed to be true. Whether Christians thought of Jesus as a prophet, seer, teacher, and/or messiah, they regarded his words as expressions that God either inspired, approved, and/or authorized. They treated what they regarded as Jesus' words with great deference and respect.

This point needs to be underlined, I think, precisely because we now know that many if not most of the words attributed to Jesus cannot be considered actual quotations. Many sayings were altered as they were recalled by followers. Many other sayings were probably coined by followers. Nonetheless, I think it does an injustice to the deference and devotion with which followers seem to have regarded Jesus to assume that their phrasings of his words was guided primarily in terms of their own philosophies and agendas. It is credible to think of Jesus as a man who had a remarkable way with words, in much the same way as do great poets and storytellers, and spoke with great authority. Listeners recalled his words as best they could and repeated them to others. However, Jesus not only spoke these words, he also authorized others to take his message and, led by God's spirit, to retell it in ways that were compelling to others who had not directly seen and heard him. Subsequently, believers followed this model as they attempted to restate Jesus' words to other audiences.

Jesus was highly regarded not only as the founder and prophet, but he was also regarded as the source that in the present somehow provided power and inspiration for his followers. Christian associations used a number of different, often very theological, terms to account for what they variously regarded as Jesus' capacity to energize and empower them. They did not seem to agree on these terms. Many, probably most, referred to Jesus as "Lord." Many believed that he had been able to send his or God's spirit into their midst so that they could perform extraordinary things they never expected to do. They connected their capacity to gain supporters; foster strong feelings of community; win converts, especially among those who had formerly opposed them; perform healings; and speak in tongues with presence of God or Jesus' spirit in their midst. They connected the fact of their very existence as associations with Jesus' capacity to send his spirit to inspire, sustain, and comfort them. Thus, they regarded Jesus not only as a man who had once lived and prophesied but as someone able to move his spirit or God's spirit to support, create, and enliven activities and experiences in the present.

For all their real differences and disagreements, early Christians shared a number of very important common traits. They were sectarian associations that practiced baptism and regularly held ritualized common meals. They were largely constituted by Jews and people influenced by Jewish culture. They regularly invoked Jewish traditions and texts. They developed strong emphasis on mutual love and assistance. They regarded Jesus as their founder, inspiration, and ground.

Early Christianity, an Unorganized Ecumenical Movement

I think it is evident that early Christianity was not an organized ecumenical movement in the way that ecumenical movements are today. There was no overarching organization, no regular system of decision making, and no regularly meeting councils. Early Christianity was ecumenical in a much looser, unorganized way— very diverse associations recognized that they were in some important ways part of the same larger movement. Additionally, from time to time people within this movement offered persuasive ways for affirming features all Christians shared in common in spite of these differences. It remained a highly variegated, unorganized ecumenical movement because no one solution for reconciling differences was ever adopted and because no one ecumenical vision ever gained dominance.

Early Christianity quickly emerged as a geographically dispersed movement of quite diverse associations that viewed their aims and identities often in quite different terms. Several potentially divisive disagreements arose among these associations. At the same time these associations shared a number of highly valued family traits. One of the strengths of this movement as whole was the way its associations were able to champion and defend their own particular version of the Christian life while still recognizing shared commonalities. This ecumenical spirit was made both possible and desirable by the mutual coexistence of this diversity and commonality. Several early Christians played major roles in giving life to this ecumenical spirit.

In ways that remained very influential, several first-century authors attempted to weave the diverse elements of early Christianity into what each presented as a common vision that could be held by all. These were Paul, as he wrote what came to be regarded as his Letter to the Romans; Mark, as he wrote his Gospel; and Luke, as he wrote his Gospel and the Acts of the Apostles. I do not have space to analyze these works at length, but I want to show briefly how in each the authors both acknowledged certain forms of diversity existing among the Christian associations and overlooked others, at the same each attempted to offer frameworks in which the at least tacitly acknowledged diversity and the accompanying differences could be reconciled.

Paul argued that there was room in the Christian movement for both uncircumcised Gentiles and circumcised Jews, for those who felt that Jesus' words allowed them to disregard food regulations and those who wanted to comply with respected traditions, for those who regularly had spiritual experiences and those who did not. Paul argued in defense of allowing certain different expressions of the Christian life, especially in his Letter to the Romans. He sharply criticized even while he expressed respect for those in Antioch and Jerusalem who had assumed narrower views (Gal I; 2 Cor II). His was not necessarily a view that would have been adopted by the community associated with John's Gospel, those assumed by Thomas's Gospel, or the Galilean group that collected the sayings of Jesus in Q. There is no evidence it was accepted by the Christian association in Jerusalem. Still, many approved of its particular ecumenical spirit and formed their own view of the Christian movement in relation to it.

Mark's Gospel seems to have offered a different approach. Burton Mack believes that Mark incorporated within one narrative what had previously been two quite different if not antagonistic versions of the Christian message. The gospel at once adopted views of Jesus as an authoritative teacher, a miracle worker, and a dying and rising savior. Mack argues that these views had previous been held by quite different if not antagonistic groups. Galilean Jews largely thought of Jesus as a teacher or miracle worker, while diaspora Jews and Gentiles largely thought of

Jesus as a savior. Mack argues that Mark's genius was in integrating these disparate views into a common narrative. Mark's vision was ecumenical in so far as he acknowledged and attempted to affirm commonality between two different and opposing traditions (Mack 1988). Still, Mark's vision was particular. It did not attempt to deal with views represented by the Fourth Gospel or *Thomas* or the social revitalization visions associated with the sayings in Q.

Luke's Gospel and history constituted a different ecumenical vision. These works overtly acknowledged a number of differences and disputes. Luke's narrative was written in ways that made it seem that most of these disagreements had already been overcome. At times he seemed to distract attention away from conflicts between Christians by noting the influence of external factors, such as, he typically noted, persecutions by hostile Jews. Because of what we learn from other sources, we know that Luke tended to minimize and paper over some of these disputes. Nonetheless, he offered his own ecumenical vision. He attempted to include within his narrative some account of most of the Christian groups he was aware of. He tacitly argued that they all had a place in the unfolding story of early Christianity. He included much of Mark's Gospel as well as most of the sayings in the Q source. He included as well histories of several other early Christian groups; however, he left out references to a number of early Christian movements in Galilee, eastern Syria, and wherever the Johannine community existed. He failed to appreciate and accent the marked difference even among the groups to which he referred.

All three of these expressions were ecumenical. They combined a recognition of diversity with attempts to assert communalities. None of them had become dominant and definitive within the first century. They existed alongside each other. Probably, if any one of these had prevailed, the larger ecumenical character of early Christianity would have been suppressed. While articulating common themes, each was too limited in scope to offer one genuine voice for most groups. As a result the ecumenical spirit was sustained not only because there were diverse associations with common traits but also because early Christians used a variety rather than any single set of images and stories to acknowledge their diversity and affirm their relatedness. In a way the early Christian movement sustained its loose ecumenical character precisely because no single attempt to reconcile their differences was able to become dominant.[5]

Notes

1. This review of early Christianity is based primarily on readings of texts written by members of the movement during this period. I utilize not only first-century NT writings but also works such as *1 Clement*, the *Didache*, and the *Gospel of Thomas*, all written before the

end of the first century C.E. A social movement is a large-scale phenomenon that may include a number of social movement organizations. I use the term "association" here as an economical expression for "social movement organization." I do not mean "formal organization."

2. I am using the phrase "early Christian movement" to refer to all the quite varied groups and movements that arose. Many if not most of the people involved in these groups and associations probably did not think of themselves as part of something called "Christianity" and probably did not think of themselves as "Christians." Some scholars refer to the early followers of Jesus in Galilee and Judaea as members of the "Jesus movement." Would those involved have used this name? I am not sure. I doubt if any in antiquity would have referred to themselves in terms used by other modern scholars, such as members of the "Q community" or "Markan community" or "Matthean community." They variously used terms to describe themselves as "followers," as members of *ekklesia*, as the "new Israel." As I will argue in the main body of this chapter, though they used differing names to refer to their identities within the larger movement, they had a strong sense of being connected together as part of a common movement. I use the phrase "early Christian movement" somewhat anachronistically to describe groups, associations, and congregations that eventually became part of what is recognized as the Christian movement.

3. We can see evidence for this tendency in many who have sought to provide accurate depictions of the historical Jesus as well as in the attempts by several contemporary scholars (Mack 1993; Horsley and Silberman 1997; Schüssler Fiorenza 1983; Crossan 1998) to discover the original and basic form of the Jesus movement. The accounts of these latter scholars, all of whom have established very credible bases for their positions, differ not only because they use somewhat different interpretive spectacles and make somewhat different methodological assumptions but also because they are probably focusing on somewhat different, albeit probably overlapping, expressions of the early Christian movement.

4. This way of viewing sects, which comes from Weber's works, is quite different and, I think, more adequate than the usual views assumed not only by Wilson in his earlier work and Stark, but also by Troeltsch (see Weber 1946: 305). Weber writes,

> A sect in the sociological sense of the word is not a small group . . . is not a group that is split off from another. . . . Rather, the sect . . . aims at being an aristocratic group, an association of persons with full religious qualification. The sect adheres to the ideas of the *ecclesia pura* . . . the visible community of saints. . . . The community functions as a selection apparatus for separating the qualified from the unqualified. (Weber 1978: 1204–10)

Wilson, in his early work, and Stark regard sects as religious groups that have broken away from other religious groups (Wilson 1961; Stark 1996: 33). Troeltsch's view is closer to Weber's but adds what I regard as unwarranted and restrictive assumptions about the characteristics, belief systems, and practices of such groups (Troeltsch 1931/32: chapter 2, section 9; chapter 3, section 4; conclusion). Since his early work, Wilson has assumed a position closer to Weber's (Wilson 1998).

5. The loose, ecumenical character of the early Christian movement gave way in the second century to a more formally organized movement that deliberately attempted to set

limits on how much diversity was permissible. We see the beginnings of this change in the pastoral letters, letters of Ignatius, *1 Clement*, and the writings of Irenaeus. We see evidence for this shift in the efforts to establish the beginnings of a canon, declare certain works as heretical, and craft a common creed. Several factors moved Christians to seek a clearer, more limiting definition of who they were. These developments really lie beyond the scope of this chapter. Still, it is worth mentioning some because of the changes that they represent. (1) As they gained more gentile converts, Christian associations had to deal with those who wanted drastically to limit if not altogether expunge the Jewish character of the movement. For example, some nominal Christians wanted to deny any authority to the Jewish Scriptures. The Christian associations met this challenge by expelling those who denied this authority. (2) Another, earlier, challenge came from the opposite direction: namely, the unwillingness of many if not most ordinary Jews, in and outside of Palestine, to recognize Christians as being in someway Jewish. Christian associations met this challenge by reasserting the movement's Jewish origins and heightening the critique of Jews who rejected their message and movement.

Jesus and Palestinian Social Protest: I I
Archaeological and Literary Perspectives

PETER RICHARDSON AND DOUGLAS EDWARDS

THE QUESTION OF JESUS and Palestinian social protest is, in sociohistorical terms, actually a subordinate question to two more general questions: how closely Palestinian social protest corresponds with other protest movements within the Roman imperial world and whether Jesus' movement corresponds with protest movements before and after his period of activity. To put the question differently, was Jesus' movement related to an extreme form of social protest—social banditry as this arose within a Palestinian setting—and was Palestinian banditry consonant with broader banditry in the region? After sections on theoretical issues and archaeological evidence, we examine the Roman Imperial world, then Syria/Palestine, before assessing the Jesus movement.

Social Protest as a Modern Category and Its Application to Ancient Societies

Social protest takes many forms in ancient and modern societies, social banditry and outright revolt being the most extreme examples. Resistance might occur against an outside power such as the Romans in Palestine or against local elites who are perceived to be associated with that power (e.g., the Herodians) or even other groups who are ethnically different or have different religious or cultural perspectives. Many discussions in New Testament studies of banditry argue that the political-economic environment created social protest and banditry. One of the most ardent proponents of this view, Richard Horsley, acknowledges the role of culture in people's responses but generally interprets culture by situating it in a disproportionate economic system set up by imperialistic powers and their retainers. Banditry in Galilee and elsewhere was caused by acute economic pressure on villagers that resulted in social disintegration (Horsley 1996: 119, 123). This reductionistic approach, while not without merit, misses the complexity of social protest as it existed in first-century Palestine. Current anthropological studies suggest that forms of social protest or resistance have used subtle as well as overt acts to convey their point. Often the protest was intended not so much for those in power, who often are kept out of the loop, but rather for those who feel outside the realm of real power decision making. Patterns found in Palestine are found throughout the Roman Empire during the same period.

Resistance by conquered persons has become central in many modern studies of colonialism (Wells 1999; Scott 1985, 1990; Said 1993), with great variety in forms of protest against foreign control. One common form is the recreation or reclamation of traditional culture, even when moribund for some time ("revitalization movement"). Other forms of common protest include work slowdowns, poor workmanship, arriving late, and creating stories or songs uncomplimentary to those in power (Wells 1999; Scott 1985, 1990; Stoller 1995). But forms of protest can extend even further: insistence on using a language different from those in power, dressing in a manner that stresses allegiance to one's own group, using particular forms of pottery or artifacts or textiles, and emphasizing one's religion and tradition. Such forms of protest are directed against powers that dictate other important aspects of people's lives.

Archaeologically, there is good evidence that the private worlds of Jews offered an outlook different from the public presentation. These private worlds represented means by which they established their identity and at the same time offered a form of protest against Roman power, even if they were the only ones who acknowledged it. Two archaeological examples represent extreme forms of protest or resistance promoting outright revolt. The better known is the siege of Yodefat or Jotapata. Josephus describes at length the struggle between Romans and Jews in the summer of 67 C.E. The town, according to Josephus and now supported by archaeological evidence, was totally destroyed, most of its inhabitants killed or enslaved, and Josephus captured. The destruction represents the commitment of many to outright rebellion against the outside power. In the same war, Gamla, another Jewish village, also revolted against Rome. It met the same end. What is intriguing about both sites (as well as Jerusalem and other areas that revolted) is the evidence for subtler forms of resistance or protest prior to their revolt. We see similar features at other sites that were not destroyed, a point to which we will return.

The second example is Qumran, where an apocalyptically oriented community believed it was participating in the end times. Recent work has shown that many of the references to the *kittim*, the enemy against which the community and God would battle, referred to the Romans. Again we have an example of overt hostility against Roman power, an extreme form of social protest, probably reserved for those in the community or those affiliated with it.

Archaeology has other examples of what appear to be more subtle forms of social protest or resistance. Coins in the Hellenistic and Roman periods typically had images of gods, temples, or political leaders. This tradition was not part of the Hasmonean expression of authority, as they assiduously avoided images of any sort on their coins (except for the occasional palm tree or stalk of wheat). In the first century C.E. Herod Philip, son of Herod the Great, had little problem with placing images on his coins in Gaulanitis. But Herod Antipas of Galilee, whose territory was more extensively Jewish, had no images on his coins. This expression stood in sharp contrast to general practice throughout the Roman Empire. Did this stress Jewish identity? Without question. Understood within the general cultural framework of Roman power, it must be seen as a form of resistance against the pressures of Roman power. Archaeology has also shown that at several sites in Galilee (e.g., Yodefat and Khirbet Cana) and Gaulanitis (Gamla) the vast majority of coins found in first-century contexts are Hasmonean (mostly Alexander Jannaeus). If as some have suggested Hasmonean coins were used as a major part of the local economy, then we have evidence of the reclamation of a tradition—the period when Israel was ruled by its own Jewish kings—and of a form of resistance or social protest. (The coin distribution is different in the more gentile regions just to the north of Lower Galilee.)

Mikvaoth (singular, *mikveh*) are another form of Jewish identity found in archaeological contexts. The usual and probably correct interpretation is that these were for Jewish ritual bathing purposes, although diverse functions cannot be ruled out. What seems certain is that they are found in Judaea and Galilee in Jewish contexts, uniquely associated with Jews. Is this resistance or social protest or simply an architectural feature that only Jews and no one else liked? A minimalist view might argue the latter, but the framework of power in which these features are found needs to be understood. Baths were not normally built this way, while for Jews this was the way one washed ritually. Herod had them. Priests' houses in Jerusalem had them. And they are found at Gamla, Yodefat, Khirbet Cana, Nazareth, and even the city of Sepphoris. City and town had them. They appeared as early as the Hasmonean period (e.g., Jericho) and appear to have the force of tradition behind them. It is not clear whether Herod's and the Qumran community's use of *mikvaoth* were attempts to reemphasize Hasmonean traditions, but it seems likely that both felt they were expressing proper Jewish tradition. Were they forms of social protest? The priests' houses in Jerusalem and the Herodian instances seem perplexing, perhaps, although even Herod did not have images on his palace walls, meaning that he was unwilling to give in completely to prevailing external cultures. The Qumran example was likely based on the community's attitude toward the Romans, as expressed in their literature, and similarly the Galilean examples show a Jewish identity and represent a form of resistance to the general culture.

Stone vessels that appear only in Jewish contexts correspond with this interpretation. Many interpret them as having ritual importance since the *Mishnah* indicates that stoneware does not contract ritual impurity. As noted earlier, one form of protest is to have one's own unique vessels, and the many examples of stoneware fit that general tendency well. No doubt some would use these vessels without a thought to their representing a protest against Rome or the general culture; they might even have appreciated Roman rule for many things. Nevertheless, they were participating in an expression of resistance whether they personally acknowledged it or not. On a similar note, in a provocative study, Andrea Berlin (unpublished paper) has shown that at Gamla, as compared with adjacent towns in more thoroughly gentile territory, there was a marked change in the first-century C.E. use of ceramics. Prior to this period, Jewish inhabitants of Gamla ate off fish-plates and other ceramic vessels, some imported from the gentile coastal cities. Ceramic trade flowed in both directions, and there was no sharp distinction in dining habits. A dramatic change occurred during the reigns of Antipas and Philip. Ceramic trade became one directional. Gentile ceramics were no longer imported, and people now ate out of locally or regionally made (i.e., Jewish) cooking pots. Gentile sites still received ceramics from Jewish manufacturers in the Galilee, while Jews stopped using gentile-made material and adopted eating habits that contrasted with both gentile habits and their own previous practices. Berlin argues that a cultural line-in-the-sand was drawn; when Jews crossed it they entered another world. This is a clear example of subtle social protest, to which we might add the absence of pig bones in Jewish sites. The prohibition against pork was taken seriously, and there is little doubt this was viewed as a symbol of one's identity against the prevailing attitudes.

Circumcision functioned similarly. Together with *mikvaoth*, Hasmonean coins, stone vessels, special ceramic vessels, and lack of pig bones, we find strong indications of efforts to establish a special identity against very powerful outside cultural influences.

One other aspect, important for understanding the environment of the Jesus movement, should be mentioned. The Dead Sea Scrolls are replete with examples of a community that made full use of its traditions to address issues of authority, power, and the community's relationship to the current authorities. Their attitude toward the *kittim* has already been mentioned. Tradition—or better, reclaimed tradition—allowed the community to protest the nature of the powers of this world (especially Roman power but also illegitimate powers in Jerusalem). Their apocalyptic worldview, perhaps the ultimate in social protest (at least literarily), shows where true power lies: not with the Romans or the culture they promote but with God, who works through his righteous community that adheres to strict laws of rightness.

The Romans understood some of these forms of resistance; overt ones were obvious, but they even noted some of the less obvious. They understood the power of religion as a form of protest and as a real problem if not dealt with properly. They walked a fine line. When a soldier exposed his posterior while Jews celebrated Passover, causing a riot, the Romans put the soldier, not the rioters, to death. Roman authorities engaged in a tug-of-war with the priests over control of the high priest's garments; both sides understood their symbolic importance for the identity and traditions of the Jewish people. Both also understood how garments could become the center of (and represent) a form of social protest (Edwards 1994). But the most obvious symbol, which could easily turn to social protest, was the Temple itself. In the first Jewish revolt (66–74 C.E.), as coins attest, various rebel leaders made it the symbol for outright revolt against Roman power (Edwards 1992), upping the ante of the less overt forms of resistance mentioned above. Roman portrayals of its destruction make the Temple's importance absolutely clear. Titus's arch displayed Roman soldiers carrying the Temple's sacred implements in triumph. Even the Romans could not miss which symbol was the focal point of the social revolt, and they emphasized that faith in such symbols was useless. Josephus's account offers a different version, but the final result is much the same: while the Temple served as the central symbol, the leaders of the revolt—bandits as he calls them—had offended God, who withdrew support and gave it to the Romans. Yet Josephus still seeks to preserve a sense of social protest, for it was God who caused the Jews to lose and allowed the Romans to win (though the Romans may not have agreed). The following discussion will summarize what we know of public social protests: banditry, revolts, and riots.

Further Archaeological Evidence of Palestinian Social Unrest

Josephus's Accounts and Archaeological Evidence

Despite the fact that social protest movements generally leave few substantial material remains, the evidence from both the first Jewish revolt (66–74 C.E.) and the second Jewish revolt (Bar Kokhba Revolt, 132–35 C.E.) is reasonably abundant, though largely outside the scope of this chapter. Prior to 70 C.E., however, a few incidents of overt social unrest have left important remains. Those, together with a few general comments on the revolts, are the subjects of this section.

The record of social protest seems to begin with the Hasmonean Revolt (began 168/167 B.C.E.). Its earliest phases, however, have left no marks in the archaeological record, though later developments following this important transformation of society have left clear archaeological remains everywhere in the Holy Land, records both of destruction and of construction, in addition to the smaller finds noted earlier. These evidences of the Hasmonean Revolt, broadly understood, may not be evidence of social protest, for they derive not from the initial protests but from periods of consolidation, wars of conquest, and subsequent settlement (clearly, for example, at Yodefat and Gamla). As a protest movement, the Hasmonean Revolt succeeded and was transformed.

Other protest movements developed in the late Hasmonean period. Records of them come mainly in the context of struggles between the Hasmoneans and the rising power of the Herodian family (Josephus, *B.J.* 1; *Ant.* 13 and 14). No physical evidence of Herod the Great's earliest confrontations with social bandits c. 47 B.C.E. has survived, but two subsequent confrontations have left marks, both about 38 B.C.E. Near Arbel, at a gap in the cliff face where natural caves offered a vantage point, bandits preyed on travelers passing by on the road. The surviving caves provide evidence of an incident in which Herod eradicated many of the bandits from the region by lowering troops on platforms from the top. During the first revolt a wall with towers was built across Mount Nitai to protect these caves from attack from above, as part of Josephus's strengthening of sites in the Galilee (Aviam 1993: 454; Richardson 1996: 68–72, 109–13). Herod returned to the Galilee later in 38 to complete the elimination of bandits; some fled to the Huleh swamp and some to a fortress, no doubt the recently excavated fortress at Keren Naphtali (Aviam 1997). The fortress was first occupied in the late Hellenistic period and marked the eastern boundary of Tyrian territory; evidence of Jewish life suggests the Hasmoneans subsequently took it over, but that occupation ended abruptly at the transition between the Hasmonean and Herodian periods (no Herodian pottery or lamps were found). Aerial photographs from 1945 show a siege camp to the west of the hill with circumvallation. Only Herod the Great's action against the *lêstai* ("bandits") accounts for these siege works, making this the only archaeologically attested evidence of Herod's use of Roman siege techniques.

Another period of social protest followed Herod's death in 4 B.C.E., when several small spontaneous protest movements, some having leaders with messianic pretensions, broke out. Herod had left a will—indeed, a series of different wills (Richardson 1996: 33–38)—but there was still much uncertainty. Popular uprisings destroyed some royal buildings: literarily attested are the Winter Palace at Jericho, the arsenal at Sepphoris, and the palace at Betharamphtha (Josephus, *B.J.* 2. 55–65; *Ant.* 17.269–84). Only the Winter Palace at Jericho has been fully excavated and reported, and its excavations show evidence of fire in the *triclinium*, perhaps from the uprising (Netzer 1993: 690).

Jewish Revolts

The Jewish revolt of 66–74 C.E., which left deep marks on both the Roman and Jewish numismatic records, is included here because of the clarity of its evidence for a successful popular movement. Masada, Herodium, Gamla, and Yodefat are well-known sites, with both defenses and siege activities clearly visible. Josephus refers to the first two as strongholds of "brigands" (*B.J.* 4.555); in both cases they adapted a room in the existing buildings as a synagogue, hinting at religious motivations. By contrast, Yodefat and Gamla were not connected with any specific subgroup; in both cases Josephus himself had reinforced the defenses in 67 C.E. Both sites offer material evidence juxtaposed with literary description; analysis of both kinds of evidence results in a general confirmation of the accuracy of Josephus's description of his work (Aviam and Richardson 2000). One particular small object from Yodefat (the city fell on 20 July 67 C.E.) gives a poignant indication—as interpreted by Mordechai Aviam—of the thoughts of one of the defenders in the waning days of the town's defense. A flat stone was inscribed with crude drawings, on one side a tomb and on the other a crab (representing the month of Tammuz or July), suggesting the meaning "I die in July."

The Bar Kokhba Revolt of 132–35 C.E. has also left physical remains. The primary evidence derives from inaccessible caves high up along the margins of the Dead Sea (the Cave of Horrors, the Cave of Letters, Wadi Muraba`at Caves), others under the main courtyard of Herodium, and some farther away from the center of things in the Shephelah. No conclusive evidence in the Galilee can be associated with the Bar Kokhba Revolt (Aviam 1993: 454). The letters from the Nahal Hever cave are the most important evidence from 132–35 C.E., some of which pertain to the leader and others in the revolt, hinting at the tensions, issues, and relationships. Others pertain to Babatha, an archive of a woman's legal documents, which has provided a rich tapestry of the warp and woof of family life. Babatha carried documents that included the deed to her property, deeds authorized by military and political representatives of the Roman government, the very government Bar Kokhba sought to overthrow (Edwards 1996). Taken together, textual and material remains (clothes, shoes, utensils) have provided a ground-level view of daily life within a revolutionary setting.

Both revolts were triggered by political, religious, cultural, and social aspirations. Their remains are important in providing two of the best collections of materials reflecting widespread social unrest. All were deeply unsettling to Roman authorities. Analysis of social unrest in Judaea and Galilee has been seminal in understanding similar movements in other locations (e.g., Britain, Germany, France, the Danube, North Africa). Having said that, there remains a question about the relevance of the evidence from the revolts for social protest. Both Jewish revolts had a higher degree of organization and deeper religious and political motivations than one might expect to find in a social protest movement, though economic factors certainly played a role as, for example, the oft-cited burning of debt records in the first revolt indicates.

Watchtowers, Guard Posts, and Fortresses
Some have suggested that there was a proliferation of minor fortifications in this period to keep banditry in check. This claim does not stand up well to scrutiny: (1) Where watchtowers were common, especially in western Samaria (second century B.C.E. to second century C.E.; Dar 1993: 1313–16), there is no special evidence of banditry. (2) Both Hasmoneans and Herods had a substantial number of fortresses—the Herodian ones usually renovations of Hasmonean fortresses—but relatively few were in areas troubled by banditry, and there is no record of their use against bandits. (3) The most troublesome areas—hilly borderlands in northern Galilee, southern Lebanon, and southern Syria—had almost no fortresses. The notable exception, Keren Naphtali, was occupied in the Hasmonean but not the Herodian period. Had fortresses been utilized to suppress banditry, one would expect more forts with continuous occupation. Despite the impression conveyed by some of the later Roman sources (below), this particular strategy was not much used in Palestine (contrast Isaac 1990: 107, 428–29). This may also suggest that banditry was not as endemic as some have suggested.

Peasant Life and Urbanization
The common opinion is that the early Roman imperial period was a time of urbanization, with increases in land accumulation, monetization, and increased indebtedness (Fiensy 1991; Horsley 1996). In the Galilee, the cities of Tiberias, Bethsaida, and Caesarea Philippi were founded or refounded; Sepphoris, Caesarea Maritima, and Beth Shean were expanded; and Phasaelis, Archelais, and Julias in Peraea were created. The Augustan peace ushered in a time of open borders and profitable trade, with central development of infrastructure projects such as harbors, warehouses, marketplaces, and roads. The Herods and other entrepreneurs took advantage of these opportunities. These urban elite actions threatened peasant life, it is held: fewer persons held more land, peasants lost their livelihood and were forced off the land, urbanization exploited peasants, and monetization threatened agrarian practices. In support of such views, social anthropology has been used to construct a necessary subordination of peasants whose surplus crops are taken away by the growing urban class (Crossan 2000).

Material remains support this general picture in part, but also offer a subtler picture. For example, the general shift to urbanization from the first century B.C.E. to the first century C.E. has been overstated: the more important movements toward urbanism in the east were earlier, in the late Hellenistic period (roughly the second century B.C.E.), and later, in the middle Roman period (the second century C.E.). The heyday of the great Hellenistic-Roman cities (e.g., Caesarea, Beth Shean, Gerasa) was in the second century C.E., whether in terms of expansion, range of institutional buildings, richness of detailing, imported materials, or patronage and benefaction. Bethsaida, for example (if et-Tell was in fact Bethsaida), which was refounded in the early first century C.E. as one of Philip's capitals, had little first-century building activity; it was busier in the Iron Age than in the first century (contrast Arav and Freund 1995). Both Sepphoris and Tiberias were fairly modest cities in the first century, only a fraction of the later second- and third-century cities.

Complementarily, small rural towns and villages increased both in number and size in this period (Reed 2000: chapter 3). Yodefat, for example, began as a small late Hellenistic fortified farmstead and was taken over by the Hasmoneans as a hilltop town. In the late first century B.C.E. or early first century C.E. it expanded substantially southward. Other small towns such as Cana seem similar. Rural village life expanded and improved at the same time that urbanization was proceeding at Sepphoris and Tiberias (perhaps prompted by the increased opportunities of trade, commerce, and agriculture; Richardson 2000). Decline of village life, abandonment of houses, and reduction of opportunities does not seem apparent. There was no reduction in village numbers or sizes; instead, there seems an increase in numbers of houses, covering a range of types and sizes (Hirschfeld 1995; Guijarro 1997). More critical assessment of these factors is still needed.

The degree of monetization in the period has also been overestimated. Most Galilean excavations have a majority of Hasmonean coins, with relatively few Herodian, procuratorial, and Roman coins, amplified somewhat with Tyrian shekels, sometimes in hoards. This counterintuitive situation might be accounted for on several grounds, but it is incorrect to claim intense monetization with all the pressures that it would bring to bear on a peasant population.

Sources for Understanding Social Protest, First Century B.C.E. to First Century C.E.

The Roman sources for understanding banditry (*lêsteia*) over a two-century period in the empire generally and Syria-Palestine specifically are relatively rich. Only rarely, though, do the sources permit differentiation among organized political revolt, socially or religiously motivated revolt, spontaneous protest with social causes, and robbers singly or in bands without social motivation. The most common word in the Greek sources for most of these activities is *lêstês* and cognates, the focus of the following discussion. It is no coincidence that the *Mishnah* adopts *listîm* as a loanword (applied sometimes even to Roman authorities: see *m.Berakoth.* 1.3; *m.Peah* 2.7; *m.Shabb.* 2.5; *m.Pesahim* 3.7; Jackson 1972: 20–40; Isaac 1984: 183, n. 68).

Sources: The Roman World

Paul's troubles described in 2 Corinthians 11:26 provide an overview of typical dangers; *lêstai* are included alongside natural problems (rivers, wilderness, sea) and social difficulties (Paul's kin, Gentiles, false brothers). This impression is supported by tombstones of persons "killed by bandits" (*interfectus a latronibus*: e.g., Rome, *ILS* 2011, 20307; Dalmatia, *ILS* 5112; Dacia, *CIL* 3.1559; Africa, *ILS* 5795; cf. *CIL* 3.8242). Pliny the Younger names three persons plus slaves that have "disappeared" or "vanished" (*Ep.* 6.25), two of them on the Via Flaminia. Another inscription refers to a fort erected by Commodus (189–192 C.E.) in Numidia "between two highways, for the safety of travelers" (*CIL* 8.2495). Death by bandits was common, according to Roman law (*Dig.* 13.6.5.4; generally, Harland 1993). The evidence spans a broad period, though no doubt the difficulties rose and fell within the period.

Local support of bandits was illegal. A prefect of Egypt says, "it is impossible to root out the bandits apart from those who protect them" (*P. Oxy.* 1408; c. 210 C.E.). Antoninus Pius, when proconsul of Asia, "declared by edict that irenarchs, when they captured brigands, should question them about their associates and about those who sheltered them" (*Dig.* 48.3.6.1). Later formalizations in the *Digest* echo this view: "receivers [supporters] are punished as the bandits themselves. All those persons who could have apprehended the bandits but who let them escape, having received money or part of the loot, are to be treated as in this same category [of bandits]" (*Dig.* 47.16.1). "It is the duty of a good and serious governor to see that the province he governs remains peaceful and quiet. . . . [He] must hunt down . . . bandits (*latrines*) . . . [and] must use force against their collaborators" (*Dig.* 1.18.13).

Strabo (64 B.C.E.–24 C.E.) considers deteriorating social conditions a significant factor in banditry and piracy (which he thinks might still be a valid occupation in Augustus's day, as it had been earlier!). He likens Pamphylians to Cilicians, a rough area where inhabitants "do not wholly abstain from the business of piracy (*tôn lêstrikôn ergôn*)" (*Geogr.* 12.570). Mount Corycus, a similarly rough area, was the haunt of pirates; Lycians also inhabited rough lands but were not pirates (they were *hypo anthrôpôn sôphronôn*; 14.1.32). Rough areas of northern Italy sheltered brigands, a problem solved only by building better roads into the Alps under Augustus (4.204; 4.207, for Pannonia). Strabo is primarily concerned with piracy (*hoi lêstêrioi*; 3.144), which extended west to "the Pillars." In 17.792 he speaks of sea-born activity (*stasis*) of Greeks (for the Black Sea, 7.311), and in 5.232 he describes how even the residents of Antium, near Rome, engaged in acts of "piracy," though they had no harbor. He knows of Egyptian "shepherds who were pirates" (17.802: *hypo boukolôn lêstôn*), and Sicilian horseherds, cowherds, and shepherds who "turned to brigandage in a sporadic way, later they both assembled in great numbers and plundered the settlements." He watched one, Selurus, die in the Forum (6.273). Strabo's descriptions of widespread but similar conditions (mountainous and marginal) are important. Some cases, of course, may not have reflected social protest of the kind discussed here, but some certainly did.

Declamation exercises of the elder Seneca (c. 50 B.C.E.–c. 40 C.E.) often presuppose a person's capture by pirates: a virgin (*Controversiae* 1.2), a man who later married the pirate chief's daughter (1.6), a man who killed two of his brothers (1.7), a good son redeemed by a debauched son (3.3), a youth cast adrift who became a pirate chief and later captured his father (7.1), a son who ransoms his father (7.4). Little light is thrown on the historical situation, but these show that in the late thirties C.E. there was still public concern with piracy and a perception of "humane" piracy. The younger Seneca (4 B.C.E.–65 C.E.) advises readers to have "as little booty as possible on your person . . . if you are empty-handed, the highwayman [*latro*] passes you by; even along an infested road, the poor may travel in peace" (*Ep.* 14.9; cf. Josephus, on Essenes, who "carry nothing whatever with them on their journeys, except arms as a protection against brigands"; *B.J.* 2.125). Seneca's *Epistle* 7 advises avoiding crowds; he parodies the crowd's reaction when a bandit was executed in the amphitheater for killing a traveler.

Plutarch (c. 50–120 C.E.) details Pompey's elimination of piracy (*Pomp.* 24–28), giving a sense of widespread support for it despite the threat it posed. His 500 ships, 120,000 infantry, and 5,000 cavalry meant speedy success, followed by a very liberal settlement of captured pirates in existing and new cities. Pompey thought "that by nature man neither is nor becomes a wild or unsocial creature . . . the habit of vice makes him become something which by nature he is not . . . he can be civilized again by precept and example and by a change of place and of occupation" (*Pomp.* 28). Plutarch, too, thought banditry had social causes and required social solutions.

The *Roman History*[1] of Appian (b. late first century C.E.) emphasizes that piracy was a major problem in the first century B.C.E. (*Bell. Civ.* 1.111) and was resolved only when Pompey was commissioned to eradicate it in 67 B.C.E. (2.23). Rome was even threatened with famine as a result of pirates (*lêsteuomenês*), who are likened to robbers (*Mithridatic Wars* 91–96). They afflicted the Mediterranean as far west as the Pillars of Hercules (93), but they were a more severe problem in the east, especially in Cilicia Tracheia, where piracy began. Piracy extended to Syria, Pamphylia, Cyprus, Pontus—indeed, almost all eastern nations (92). Pompey's eradication of pirates was incomplete, for in 40–38 B.C.E. Octavian accused Pompey's son Sextus of encouraging a "mysterious robbery infesting the sea," so that famine threatened Rome (*Bell. Civ.* 5.77, 80). In fact, Rome itself was "openly infested with bands of robbers" (cf. also *Bell. Civ.* 5.132; Suetonius, *Aug.* 32–33).

Philo of Alexandria (c. 15 B.C.E.–50 C.E.) presupposes *lēsteia*, despite Julius Caesar's clearing the Mediterranean of brigands and pirates (*Legat.* 146: *lēstai, peiratikai*). The ascetic Therapeutae near Alexandria clustered their solitary cells together for fear of robbers (*Contemp.* 24); parents ransomed captured children (*Prob.* 37; cf. 121); the wilds posed general dangers (*Spec.* 1.301). When discussing the commandment not to steal, he refers to oligarchs who perpetrate *lēsteia* (*Decalogue* 136), and he likens Alexandrians to robbers when they attacked Jews (*Legat.* 122), while he praises Flaccus for paying his soldiers well enough so they would not turn into robbers (*Flaccus* 5).

When Dio Cassius (c. 164–229 C.E.) looks back to Pompey, he claims that "large numbers had turned to banditry" (*History of Rome* 36.20.2; also 5.28.1–3, 75.2.4), including some ex-soldiers and slaves (75.2.5–6, 77.10.5). Varus "distributed many of the soldiers to helpless communities . . . for the alleged purpose of guarding various points, arresting brigands, or escorting provision trains" (56.19.1; cf. Suetonius, *Tib.* 37). He mentions especially Bulla Felix—"never really seen when seen, never found when found, never caught when caught" (77.10.2)—who spoke up for slaves and peasants (77.10.5).

Not all brigands were popular. Galen says of a bandit who killed a traveler, "None of the local inhabitants would bury him, but in their hatred of him were glad enough to see his body consumed by the birds which, in a couple of days, ate his flesh, leaving the skeleton as if for medical demonstration" (Galen, *On Anatomical Procedures* 1.2). In sum, from Marius and Sulla through to the second century C.E., brigandage and banditry were severe problems that demanded constant vigilance and strong measures. The problems, however, were not continuous or uniform. And while evidence of popular support for such bandits is not outstandingly strong, there is sufficient evidence, allowing for the upper-class status of the writers on whose comments we must rely, to suggest that much—though certainly not all—banditry had dimensions of social protest and social support. Perhaps occasionally it was even aimed at righting social grievances.

Sources: Syria and Palestine

The sources for Syria and Palestine are both fuller and more limited; there are fewer texts, but those we have offer more circumstantial detail. Strabo is especially helpful as a bridge, since he alludes both to this region and to the broader Roman world. He describes the Lebanon and Anti-Lebanon ranges, saying that the Itureans and Arabians were all robbers (*kakourgoi*), while the plains people were farmers

(*Geogr.* 16.2.18). Pompey destroyed their fortresses, while others later removed threats to Arabian traders (16.2.18, re Trachonitis) by breaking up Zenodorus's band (16.2.20; cf. *OGIS* I.424, reign of Agrippa I or II; Josephus, *B.J.* 1.304–14; Isaac 1990: 78). Strabo includes the Hasmoneans as robbers (*tôn lêstôn lêstêria*; *Geogr.* 16.2.28), interpreting their tyrannies (*ek de tôn tyrannidôn ta lêstêria*) as a result of following Moses' laws, so that "some revolted and harassed the country," subduing much of Syria and Phoenicia (16.2.37). In his view there was little to choose between Zenodorus and the Hasmoneans!

Josephus: Hasmoneans and Herod

The Hasmonean Revolt (167–42 B.C.E.) began as a popular movement that had similarities—to judge from I Maccabees 2.42–48—with social banditry: trouble with authorities, flight to the countryside, and popular support. It is unsurprising that Strabo alluded to its leaders as *lêstai*. Certainly the movement's main characteristics (religion, politics, and tradition or nationalism; Mendels 1992) were similar to those of a social protest, even if it was characterized only for a short time by small bands of dispossessed persons motivated by the struggle for sustenance, of which they had been deprived. For Strabo, *lêsteia* is more abusive epithet than accurate description.

We hear nothing of *lêsteia* in Jewish sources during most of the Hasmonean period. But in the second quarter of the first century B.C.E., when Hasmonean internal conflict prompted Pompey's invasion and led to the triumph of Hyrcanus II and Antipater (64–63 B.C.E.), groups emerged that may have been socially motivated, though their activities do not fit the model well. Some were losers in a power struggle rather than social bandits. The upshot of these conditions (75–40 B.C.E.) was the rise to power of Antipater's second son, Herod, named King of Judaea by the Romans in late 40 B.C.E. (Richardson 1996).

Josephus, on whose accounts of Herod we are so dependent, first uses *lêstês* and cognates (in both *War* and *Antiquities*) when speaking of groups fighting against the young Herod.[2] The hilly location between Galilee and Syria fits well the general conditions described by Strabo. Inhabitants supported themselves and their families by plundering wealthy travelers, a form of violence prompted by revenge for their exploitation or social justice. Herod faced protest of two kinds, *lêstai* who had fled from society but retained support from neighboring towns, and *lêstai* supported by the politically powerful (Harland 1993). The difference between them was that in the second case the exploiters lined their pockets from the activities of the exploited. Initially Herod was a governor in Galilee under Hyrcanus II (Josephus, *B.J.* 1.204–15; *Ant.* 14.158–84; Richardson 1996: 79, 108–13, 250–52). When he executed Hezekiah (an *archilêstês*) for brigandage, Josephus alludes almost

accidentally to popular support for brigands, for some of the Jerusalem elite persuaded Hyrcanus to try Herod for Hezekiah's murder. Support for Hezekiah may
have been simply dislike of Herod; still it shows how Galileans could be linked
with persons in Jerusalem (Crossan 1991: 175–76). Herod's aggressive opposition to social brigandage brought him to Rome's attention, and he was appointed
governor of Coele-Syria and Samaria (47–46 B.C.E.; Josephus, *Ant.* 14.160;
Richardson 1996: 70, 109).

Herod's long campaign to win control of Judaea after being named king
(40–37 B.C.E.) was interrupted to eliminate brigands (*lêstai*) in caves above the road
near Arbel, who were raiding passing traffic (Josephus, *B.J.* 1.304–14; *Ant.*
14.415–30). He subdued them by lowering cages from the cliff tops (Richardson
1996: 155–58). Later, he returned to Galilee and pursued the brigands, partly to
the (Huleh) swamps and partly to a fortress (Keren Naphtali) just west of the
swamps (*B.J.* 1.315–16; *Ant.* 14.431–33; see above).

Not all events using similar language refer to similar situations, so interpretive
caution is necessary. The incidents of 38 B.C.E. may have been primarily a military
campaign by Antigonus's supporters against Herod. Josephus's linking of
Antigonus's strongholds with brigands in caves (*B.J.* 1.303; *Ant.* 14.414–15) need
not refer to social protest; military opposition to Herod is a plausible alternative,
as suggested by the garrison Herod left behind, the pitched battle at Arbel, the use
of an abandoned fortress, and the drowning of Herod's partisans in the Sea of
Galilee (*Ant.* 14.450). The "noble death" motif in the account of the caves (a father kills seven children rather than allow them to go out to Herod) implies a religious rather than a social background; despite Josephus's vocabulary, he may not
be describing the same phenomenon.

Because Herod effectively opposed *lêsteia*, Augustus ceded him Batanea, Au-
ranitis, and Trachonitis (*Ant.* 15.343–49; *B.J.* 1.398–99; Richardson 1996:
139–42, 232), whose two major trade routes—the King's Highway from Aqabah
and the Wadi Sirhan from Arabia—were vulnerable to bandits. Clearing the brigands from Trachonitis was a joint operation of Herod and M. Terrentius Varro
(governor of Syria 24–23 B.C.E.). Josephus and Strabo agree on the complicity of
Zenodorus (tetrarch of the Itureans; see *Ant.* 15.344–48; Strabo, *Geogr.* 16.2.20;
Schürer 1973 I.565–66 for coin evidence: "Zenodorus, tetrarch and high priest").
Lêstai had been constructively resocialized by settling them on land from which
they supported themselves, says Josephus; in 11 B.C.E., however, they returned to
their old ways. This may have been simple banditry. More likely, it was revolt
against Herod's rule (*Ant.* 16.271–75), since Syllaeus of Nabatea and Zenodorus
protected the brigands in exchange for some of the profits. Later, Herod adopted
the Roman policy of allotting land to those who would keep the peace, veterans
in Trachonitis and Babylonian Jews in Batanea (*Ant.* 17.23–28; cf. 16.292).

At Herod's death uncoordinated revolts broke out in various locations (Richardson 1996: chapter 1). Josephus notes the following:

- Herod's demobilized veterans in Idumea armed themselves and fought Archelaus's troops (*B.J.* 2.55; *Ant.* 17.269–70);
- Judas, son of Hezekiah, broke into the Sepphoris armory, equipped his supporters, and attacked Antipas's supporters (*B.J.* 2.56; *Ant.* 17.271–72);
- Simon gathered a group of robbers in Peraea, attacked Jericho, and burned Herod's palace (*B.J.* 2.57–59; *Ant.* 17.273–76);
- Other Peraeans attacked and burned Herod's palace at Betharamphtha across the Jordan from Jericho (*B.J.* 2.59; *Ant.* 17.277); and
- Athrongeus, a shepherd, raised a band in Judaea and attacked Romans and Jews (*B.J.* 2.60–65; *Ant.* 17.278–84).

Josephus uses *lêstrikos* of the group of incidents, and *lêstai* specifically only of Simon in Peraea. The difficulties were put down by Varus (*B.J.* 2.65–79; *Ant.* 17.285–98). He burned two cities, Sepphoris and Emmaus, because they supported the revolutionaries, but in other cities there was insufficient popular support to warrant such actions (he sent any leaders related to Herod [!] to Rome for Augustus's judgment). At least Simon and the Peraeans, and perhaps Judas, were social bandits; the other incidents involving military confrontations in Judaea are less clearly banditry.

Josephus: Prefects up to Pilate

Josephus knows almost nothing from Archelaus's exile in 6 C.E. until Pilate, so little can be said about social protest during this period. The major point of discussion has been whether Judas was the founder of the "Zealot" movement (of no concern here), with a continuous pattern of revolt through the first six decades of the first century C.E., as Josephus thought. The prevailing view now rejects this claim (Donaldson 1990) because it is so obviously part of Josephus's apologetic concerns. Unlike his earlier picture of individuals and families who resorted to banditry, he emphasizes widespread disturbances, though he has details of important incidents under Pilate, especially the "standards" and "aqueduct" incidents.

Josephus: Procurators after Pilate

His focus on "zealots" is unmistakably apologetic, yet he can keep groups separate, as he does with Eleazar, "who for twenty years had ravaged the country with many of his associates" (Josephus, *B.J.* 2.253), until he was captured and executed by Felix (procurator 52–60 C.E.). When Samaritans murdered a Galilean going up to

Jerusalem and Cumanus (procurator 48–52 C.E.) did nothing, Jews allied themselves with Eleazar and sacked and burned several Samaritan villages (*B.J.* 2.228–31; *Ant.* 20.113–17), which illustrates neatly the officials' presumption of popular support for social protest movements in Palestine, as elsewhere in the Roman world.

Illustrating the other side of conditions first observed under Herod, Florus (procurator 64–66 C.E.) protected brigands, according to Josephus, so that they "were at liberty to practice brigandage, on the condition that he received a share of the spoils" (*B.J.* 2.278–79; *Ant.* 20.255–56). As conditions deteriorated following Eleazar's actions, "the whole of Judea was infested with bands of brigands [*lêstêriôn*]" (*Ant.* 20.124; also 20.121, 185–86; *B.J.* 2.271), so that eventually there was a coalition of brigands, whom Josephus calls "zealots" (*B.J.* 4.134, 160–62, 193, 196, 197, etc.). He believes conditions in the earlier period with individual bandits (sometimes with popular support) were continuous with conditions in the later period when various bands coalesced into a revolutionary movement. And that movement, according to Josephus, was continuous with the extreme zealot movement, which broke out in 66 C.E. on the eve of the revolt. Among several scholarly views we note two: for Horsley and Hanson the zealots coalesced only as a result of rural bandits moving to Jerusalem; for Donaldson, city mobs were the equivalent of rural bandits and were already present in Jerusalem (Donaldson 1990). These conditions—volatile, politicized, and religiously informed—were similar to those of the Hasmonean Revolt.

Historical Reconstruction: Galilee, the Golan, Samaria, Judaea, and Social Protest

Hellenism, Greeks, and Romans

Social conditions in the Holy Land changed frequently between the Persian and middle Roman periods, destabilizing society's institutions and structures and creating the backdrop for social protest. Israel's loss of identity was partially alleviated in the return from exile under the Persians, but those gains were eroded by Alexander the Great's conquest and the deliberate introduction of Greek cities (*poleis*), institutions, and ideals. After more lenient rule by the Diadochoi, the Seleucids wrenched away control of the land in 200 B.C.E.. Under Antiochus IV Epiphanes they attacked Judaism as a religion. The restrictions imposed were an essential background to the Hasmonean Revolt; as Strabo suggests, though he views it negatively, this was a form of social banditry (*lêsteia*) that assumed revolutionary features (1 Mc 1).

As the Hasmoneans acquired the trappings of other late Hellenistic dynasties, destructive internal tensions (75–38 B.C.E.) followed, creating fresh conditions for banditry. Two consequences followed: the Hasmonean struggles (like similar struggles in Syria) led to Pompey's direct involvement (64/63 B.C.E.); the Roman conquest, though limited, altered social and religious institutions, so that *lêsteia* was indirectly encouraged. Herod's early reputation for ridding the Galilee of brigandage resulted in Rome's choosing him to rule. His dynasty then repeated a common pattern: accumulation of wealth, land, and power, with deprivation of small landowners and small businessmen. The localized uprisings on his death reflect the resulting underlying tensions (Fenn 1992; Goodman 1987: 38–42, 139–40). Following the division of the kingdom, Archelaus was unable to rule effectively, though neither Antipas nor Philip experienced similar difficulties; either both were abler, or their regions had been more pacified. The shift in 6 C.E. to direct Roman rule in Judaea under prefects (6–41 C.E.) and proconsuls (44–66 C.E.) created new conditions. After the short interlude under Agrippa I (41–44 C.E.), those difficulties worsened. Roman ineptness together with an ineffectual Jewish elite, respected by neither side; heavy debt load; and religious tensions—all of which are too frequently downplayed—led almost inevitably to full revolt in 66 C.E.

Jesus' Movement as an Instance of Social Protest: The Gospels

The difficulties in discerning what are and are not core traditions related to the Jesus movement are notorious and cannot be considered here. We acknowledge that Q, like the Gospels themselves, contains important information about the early movement. We will draw on material that fits the periods we have outlined above, recognizing that theological and literary interests may well govern the presence and presentation of some material. But theological agendas need not a priori negate the possibility of material reflecting early traditions. While the speeches and specific encounters may be later, the framework or environment, if it fits what we know of the period, may legitimately be used to reconstruct the situation. We will look at selected features of the traditions about Jesus to assess the Jesus movement against the forms of social protest discussed above.

Early Christian literature reflects conditions similar to those Josephus and the Roman literature describe. The difficulties with brigandage of the first century B.C.E. continued in places, especially in the east, into the first century C.E.. While the Gospels refer frequently to the *lêstês* group of words, they quickly disappear from other Christian literature. Paul uses *lêstês* once in 2 Corinthians 11.26 (cf. a quotation from the Septuagint in *2 Clem.* 14.1), but generally speaking brigandage is missing from this literature, as it is also from some secular literature of the same period (e.g., Pliny the Younger).

Jesus was executed between two *lēstai*, despite the implicit embarrassment to the narrative in this admission (Mk 15.27, 32//Mt 27.38, 44; cf. Lk 23.33, 39–43). There is palpable irony in Pilate's including on the *titulus* (the phrase) "King of the Jews" (whether historically accurate or not matters little); literarily it ameliorates the offense of the historical fact. Was Jesus, however, seen as a bandit? On the one hand, three Gospels make it seem that the decision to execute Jesus had little basis in the facts of the case: Mark and Matthew hint at spurious charges against Jesus, while John has Pilate prefer Jesus to be tried according to Jewish law (Jn 18.31). Only Luke, more satisfactorily, permits the notion that Jesus was a popular leader who was "perverting our nation, and forbidding us to give tribute to Caesar, and saying that he is himself Christ a King" (Lk 23.2). This is close to the language of social protest; in general, Luke makes the most historical sense of the trial accounts (Catchpole 1971), even though in the end Pilate concludes, "I find no crime in this man" (Lk 23.4).

At Jesus' arrest the Synoptics have Jesus say, "Have you come out as against a robber with swords and clubs?" (Mk 14.48 pars), consistent with Luke's emphasis. Did the authorities really believe Jesus was a brigand, because they arrested him as a *lēstēs*? The evidence for urban brigands (above) may imply that the authorities had ways to deal with them; certainly his arrest, the charges (according to Luke), and his execution between *lēstai* cohere to give the narrative plausibility. The Jewish authorities—and in the first instance the authorities are Jewish—dealt with Jesus as *lēstēs*. Perhaps Jesus really was seen as leader of a social protest movement who needed to be eliminated.

The Synoptics report Jesus quoting Jeremiah 7.11 about a "robbers' cave" in the "Temple tantrum" incident, contrasting that with Isaiah 56.7 about the Temple as a "house of prayer for all nations" (Mk 11.17 pars). The irony occurs at two levels. On the one hand, all the authors know their stories will end with Jesus crucified between two *lēstai*, so a "robber-look-alike" who proclaims the sacred place of Judaism a place for "robbers" has a wry ring to it. On the other hand, the coin exchanges and the sale of sacrificial animals were services provided for pious pilgrims who came up to Jerusalem from distant places (Sanders 1992; Richardson 1992), not opportunities for profit; as John puts it, the Temple should not be a "house of trade" (Jn 2.16). In John, it is Jesus' "zeal" that "consumes" him, right in the place where he is viewed by the authorities as a "brigand."

Jesus' story in these scenes from the last week of his life intersects with social–political–religious circumstances in Palestine. Jesus was arrested like a robber, tried on charges similar to those that might be used against such a person, executed between two *lēstai*, and another *lēstēs*—Barabbas— is set free (Jn 18.40), at a time when there were public concerns over *lēsteia*. Despite the report that Jesus accused Temple authorities of being "robbers," he himself was dealt with as a "robber."

According to the Gospels, of course, Jesus was not really a *lêstês*. John presents Jesus as the good shepherd (Jn 10.1–18) who watches at the door of the sheepfold for the *lêstês* who climbs over the wall to steal sheep. The parable is heavily christologized—"all who came before me are thieves and robbers"—but its core imagery contrasts Jesus' program to the program of social bandits. The same impression is conveyed by the parable of the Good Samaritan (Lk 10.29–37; L material), whose setting is rooted in the social conditions surveyed in the first half of this chapter. Brigands terrorize the road between Jericho and Jerusalem along the Wadi Qelt; a traveler is set upon by *lêstai*, robbed, and left for dead. Contrary to Seneca's advice, he had money, identifying him as a "have" rather than a "have-not." Yet Jesus' sympathies are with the critically wounded person, not with the social bandits.

In both parables—and parables usually aim for verisimilitude—the vocabulary of social banditry is used, but there is no implied approval. As in the passion narratives, Jesus does not follow a program of "social protest" in the classic model. This is not to say, of course, that Jesus does not have strong peasant sympathies. Obviously he does. His attitudes toward debt and moneylenders, tenant farmers and laborers, dispossessed and weak, show this sympathetic attitude very clearly.

The sayings and parables of Jesus refer to debt, indebtedness, moneylending, financial jeopardy, and debt forgiveness, as, for example, in the unforgiving servant in Matthew 18.23–35 (M); the unjust steward in Luke 16.1–9 (L); the two debtors of Luke 7.40–42 (Lukan redaction); the Lord's Prayer in Q 11.4; love of one's enemies in Q 6.34; the parable of the talents in Q 19.11–27; the saying to lend without return in *Gospel of Thomas* 95; and, of course, the Lord's Prayer (Mt 6.12). These accounts presuppose rural agrarian folk in small villages who are in danger of losing everything because of aggressive loan, interest, and repayment policies. The persons most directly criticized are middlemen, the "steward" or "servant" who is carrying out his master's real or perceived intentions. In turn, these sayings presume estates, accumulation of land, tenant farming, and leases (Kloppenborg 2000), as in the parables of the tenant farmers (Mk 12.1–9 pars; *Gos. Thom.* 65), laborers in the vineyard (Mt 20.1–16 [M]), and make friends with your accuser (Q 12.57–59).

Jesus fits easily into a world of exploited peasants, absentee owners, and middle management, the ones threatened with losses and debts and imprisonment, the others putting additional burdens onto the agrarian poor. The above evidence shows that it was exactly these conditions that led to social banditry among some who had to flee their land to and subsequently eke out a living preying on those who had exploited them. This is a case worth making, even if one holds back from full endorsement. It was only seldom that Jesus protested these conditions directly.

The evidence pulls in different directions, and raises three relevant questions. Did those outside his movement view Jesus as a part of such radical forms of social protest? To what extent was Jesus sympathetic to the more radical social protest that swirled through Palestine during his period? Did his immediate followers hold varying views of Jesus' attitudes toward social protesters? On the last question, it seems likely that various persons among his followers held different views on society and social protest: Simon the Cananean or Zealot?; James and John, the sons of "thunder"; Judas Iscariot (= Sicarius or "dagger man"?). On the first question, it seems almost indisputable that some outside his movement thought of Jesus as just another leader of a minor group of *lêstai*, so that he could be arrested, tried, and executed on these grounds. On the question of Jesus' own views, we suggest that sympathetic as he was to the plight of the exploited peasants, there is little indication that he was sympathetic to the means of those who adopted the life of *lêsteia*.

Notes

1. Quotations are from the Horace White translation.

2. There are actually three minor exceptions to this: in *Ant.* 14.142 Josephus uses *lêsteia* when speaking of Aristobulus and Alexander; in *Ant.* 8.204 he uses *lêsteuô* and *lêstrikos* of Rezon, at the time of Solomon; and in *Ant.* 9.183 he uses *lêstês* of robbers at the time of Elisha. These are minor in comparison to the regularity of use of the terms from Herod onward, as he indicates in the introduction in *War* I.11, using *lêstrikos*.

Civilizational Encounters in the Development of Early Christianity

12

DONALD A. NIELSEN

Introduction: Problems and Perspectives

THE INVESTIGATION OF CIVILIZATIONAL ENCOUNTERS in early Christianity faces some preliminary questions of perspective. What is the temporal framework constituted by the term "early"? Does it refer exclusively to the New Testament era, roughly the first century C.E.? If not, what later centuries should be added? How far back do we need to go in the history of ancient Judaism and other Mediterranean cultures in order to set the stage properly for a study of "early" Christianity?

These questions are related to a second group that focuses on the notions of cultural contacts and encounters. Our conception of these latter concepts in turn influences our view of the temporal limits of "early" Christianity. Must "encounters" refer primarily to open competition and conflict among mutually exclusive religions, or should we also include borrowings and syncretisms? Also, should we focus only on encounters among differing civilizational traditions, or do intracivilizational conflicts within communities over their basic frames of reference also require examination? If these are included, how does this affect our sense of "early" Christianity?

A third dimension of the problem emerges in our effort to delineate the spatial framework for early Christianity. While the movement developed primarily within a Mediterranean setting, it also quickly spread elsewhere—south into upper Egypt and Ethiopia, northwest into the British Isles, and east into further Asia. Should these outlying regions provide a major focus for our study? In what ways should the basic differences that emerged early on between Latin and Greek Christianity be supplemented by other finer discriminations among communities, for example, the distinctive character of Alexandrian Christianity, the special tenor of North African communities or those of Gaul, and so forth?

A final set of questions helps resolve some of these issues. They concern the analytical horizons from the social sciences employed in the investigation. The social scientific study of religious conflicts and encounters implicates a wide range of possible problems. These include the conflicts over ideas and worldviews as well as types of religious organization, the characteristics of the social strata involved, the role of competing political and ethnic communities as well as gendered groups, the varying social psychologies of the participants, the relationships among leaders and followers in movements, the differences between urban and rural regions, and many other related topics. It is necessary to remain sensitive to the implications of these topics for the analysis of civilizational encounters.

These questions are resolved in several ways. My temporal focus is decidedly "long term," and the geographical orbit is "the Mediterranean world" in its ancient configuration (Braudel 1996), especially (with a few exceptions) the major urban centers. From a temporal standpoint, the present study of cultural encounters surrounding "early" Christianity refers to the period from about 200 B.C.E. into the fourth century C.E.

The notion of cultural conflict will also be conceived broadly to include direct cultural competition, encounters between civilizations, syncretisms and borrowings resulting from such competition and encounters, and intracivilizational struggles within Christianity itself over its central doctrines and organization. The analytical focus will be on the fundamental civilizational frames of reference at stake in these encounters. These include the highest level definitions of reality of a cultural community, including its central rationales and cultural logics concerning such topics as time, space, causality, moral and juridical order, the beginning and end of things, the nature of extraterrestrial powers, and others (Nelson 1981: 84). While it will be necessary to touch on the social structural, political, and social psychological features of these struggles, these will be examined only incidentally. In this respect, the present chapter emphasizes the general framework for the study of civilizations and civilizational encounters sketched by Nelson (1981; see Eisenstadt 1992) and subsequently developed by Nielsen (1990a, 1991, 1996a, 1999b), but it also selects from varied perspectives in the sociology of religion, especially neo-Durkheimian theories (Nielsen 1999a; Halbwachs 1992; Harrison 1962; Erikson 1966; Febvre 1973) but also others (Maine 1861; O'Dea 1966; Geertz 1973; Stark 1996; Turner 1975; Weber 1946).

The following topical areas will provide the particular substantive focus for our investigation: aspects of the encounter of Judaism and Hellenism, especially in the work of Philo of Alexandria, and continuities and discontinuities between Jewish and early Christian conflicts with Greco-Roman paganism, especially Greek philosophy, as they appear in the work of the Christian theologian Origen and in the competition between the mainstream of the Christian church and its competitors.

Civilizational Encounters I: Judaism, Hellenism, and the Second Axial Age of Antiquity

Perhaps the most decisive civilizational encounter in the ancient world was that between ancient Judaism and Hellenistic culture, especially Jewish monotheism and Greek philosophy. This encounter marks a second "axial age" in the development of world civilizations that may be as significant as the first axial age (Eisenstadt 1986). In this encounter, the axial age cultural creations of Greek metaphysics and Judaic monotheism were hammered into a new amalgam that not only set the stage for the subsequent development of Christian theology but also for many of the questions at the heart of later Western worldviews in the sciences, metaphysics, and religion.

This encounter emerges out of two highly differentiated cultures, the Hellenistic world and that of late Judaism. Hellenistic culture had since the time of Alexander become the common civilization of the distinct cultural communities of the Mediterranean, penetrating deeply into their fabrics and modifying them. Hellenism's defining role as the ecumenical culture of antiquity was enhanced by the Roman conquests and the solidification of the Pax Romana, which allowed a more thorough dissemination of Greek (and now Greco-Roman) culture—indeed, of many other cultures besides—along the communication routes perfected and secured by Roman power (Peters 1970). Greek thought became differentiated into a variety of individualistic philosophies and cults defined by the distinctive beliefs and practices drawn by each out of the inherited philosophies of Plato, Aristotle, Pythagoras, Epicurus, and the Stoics.

That Hellenistic culture deeply influenced Jewish communities, including Jerusalem itself, is no longer a subject of debate among historians (Hengel 1974). The questions have shifted toward a more precise specification of the dimensions of what is agreed upon as a thoroughgoing trend. This penetration occurred at many levels, not all of them equally central to the present discussion. It affected the language of Jewish religion, synagogue worship, artistic expression, political ideas, and the broader reaches of philosophical and religious thought (Levine 1998). It was also the subject of intense conflict within Jewish circles, which were increasingly divided in the period of the Second Temple not only over the question of "Hellenization" and its implications for Jewish identity but also by the rise within of many parties and sects. These included Pharisees, Sadducees, and politically oriented Zealots; new monastic impulses, including the Essenes; efforts to further extend and also consolidate the oral commentary on the Torah into new written forms, ultimately leading to the codification of the Mishnah (and later the Talmuds); and, of course, the Jesus movement (Baron 1952; Horsley and Hanson 1985; *Faith and Piety in Early Judaism*; Sandmel 1969; Schiffman 1991; Schurer

1973; *Dead Sea Scrolls in English*, Vermes). Indeed, the striking feature of Judaism in the centuries before and after Jesus is the enormous diversity in religious expression, resulting in part from the challenges to Jewish political and cultural identity that emerged during the era of the late Hellenistic and early Roman domination and culminated in the disastrous Jewish wars of 66–67 C.E. and 132–35 C.E. Equally striking amidst this diversity is a persistent core of monotheist belief.

Here I focus on aspects of the civilizational encounter between Judaism and Hellenism and on some continuities and discontinuities between it and the related encounter of early Christianity and Greek culture (Hatch 1957). In particular, I want to discuss the outcomes of this encounter as they appear in the work of Philo of Alexandria and Origen. One of the central themes in this encounter is the divine creation. The image of creation, central to Jewish monotheism, was linked by these writers to the Greek philosophical inheritance in ways that strengthened the basic monotheistic impulse but also resulted in many ambiguities concerning the forces at work in the process of creation. Without this fuller rationalization of the creation image, it is unlikely that the exclusivistic claims of Jewish and especially later Christian monotheism could have been effectively legitimated within the Greco-Roman environment, where convincing religious proofs were advanced primarily through the medium of Greek philosophical ideas. Indeed, early Christian doctrine depended heavily on the foundation of Jewish monotheism, a fact made clear by Eusebius, who repeatedly documents how this one idea served as the lynchpin for everything else (Eusebius, *Hist. eccl.*). Without it, Christianity lacked anchorage, was threatened with doctrinal disintegration, and risked losing the continuity with Judaism that was so central to its further development. Let us turn first to Philo.

Philo was a biblical exegete who is well known for his method of allegorical interpretation (Hanson 1959; Chadwick 1970). However, this was only one aspect of his work. His writings also contain a complex religious philosophy of creation. A central facet of this philosophy is the creation by weight, measure, and number.[1] Philo is hardly alone in his particular way of treating the problem of creation. Indeed, the central image of creation by weight, measure, and number is as clearly enunciated in the Wisdom of Solomon (11: 20). This should not surprise, since that work shares a similar spatiotemporal and cultural location with Philo's. It was written in Greek between the first century B.C.E. and the first C.E. by a Jewish author under Hellenistic influence, probably like Philo in Alexandria. Moreover, both authors work against a tradition of Jewish writings that repeatedly inserted the varied images of creation by weight, measure, and number into their treatments of monotheism, cosmic processes, and moral order. The list of such sources from Ancient Judaism, with which Wisdom and Philo were certainly familiar, include Job (28.23–25; 31.4, 5; 36.26; 37.14; 38.10, 33, 37, 47), Proverbs

(8.27–30, 11.1, 16.2, 24.11–12), Psalms (62.9, 74.12–17, 104.2–3), and the second Isaiah (40.12, 15). Later Jewish works with similar themes include the late prophetic and apocalyptic writings, in particular Ezekiel (40.3; 42.15), Zechariah (2.1–2), Daniel (5.25–28), and 4 Ezra (3.34; 4.6–37) (J. Smith 1975). The list can be expanded by reference to relevant passages from other Jewish Apocrypha and Pseudepigrapha (*Old Testament Pseudepigripha*), some Dead Sea texts (*Dead Sea Scrolls in English*, Vermes, 271–73), rabbinic writings (*Gen. Rab.*; Altman 1956; Sanders 1977), and some New Testament and Nag Hammadi texts (e.g., Rv 21.1, 5, 15; *NHL* 360). The historically earlier texts reveal this complex of images to clearly antedate Wisdom and Philo, within the Jewish religious tradition, although it is not found there in a systematic or rationalized form. This fact is critical to our understanding of the encounter of Judaism and Hellenism. However, the presence of these themes in so many texts from so many different Jewish cultural communities points to a cluster of unifying elements in Jewish monotheistic creation images in what is an otherwise diverse ancient Jewish life. Some of these images almost certainly derive from yet earlier Egyptian ideas (Breasted 1939: 180, 258–61; Rad 1968; Di Lella 1966).

Philo (20 B.C.E.–50 C.E.) is a complex thinker. It is not always easy to sort out the mixture of Jewish religiosity and Greek thought in his work. Louis Ginzberg (1968, V: viii) asked about Philo, "Was he a Jewish thinker with a Greek education, or a Greek philosopher with Jewish learning?" Ginzberg and several others (Wolfson 1962; Belkin 1940; Reale 1990) favored a variant of the former view. Others have come to favor some version of the latter (Dillon 1977; Winston 1981; Berchman 1984). As Nikiprowetsky (1977), Brehier (1908), and Tobin (1983) have noted, Philo's writings are a commentary on scripture rather than a systematic philosophical treatise. Everything about his work needs to be understood from that standpoint. Indeed, Philo repeatedly warns us, in allegorical fashion, that philosophy and the cultural disciplines have the same relation to scripture as Haggar does to Sarah. They are preparatory studies, but the latter represents wisdom and virtue, which is the goal (Winston 1981: 212–13).

Philo's work is closely linked to Middle Platonism, with its amalgam of ideas from Platonic, Stoic, Peripatetic, and neo-Pythagorean sources (Dillon 1977; Berchman 1984), yet his Middle Platonism is grounded in ideas drawn from Jewish Scriptures and traditions. The Hellenistic philosophy is grafted onto a Jewish core, placed in the service of scriptural exegesis, and used in the elaboration of prior Jewish images. In his treatment of creation, especially in his emphasis on creation by precise measure, Philo sounds several central themes. These include (1) the root image, shared with Wisdom, of creation by measure, weight, and number; (2) the role of law and rule in creation and the creator's action; (3) the related neo-Pythagorean number symbolism; (4) the similarly congruent role of the *logos* in the creative process; and (5) and the relationship of these ideas to those about universal moral order, including retribution, judgment, and punishment. If we examine each of these issues in turn, we will understand more precisely aspects of the encounter of Judaism and Hellenism.

(1) The following sentences from Philo's work help us cut into his thinking about creation.

> But Moses held that God, and not the human mind, is the measure and weighing scale and numbering of all things . . . the true and just measure is to hold that God Who alone is just measures and weighs all things and marks out the confines of universal nature with numbers and limits and boundaries, while the false and unjust measure is to think that these things come to pass as the human mind directs. (*Somn.* 2, 193–94; see also *Sacr.* 59–60; *Post.* 35–36; *QG4.* 8; *Prov.* 626)

Here Philo expresses many of his key images. Philo's reference to God as the measure of all things is explicitly meant as a critique of the Protagorean dictum that man is the measure of all things, indeed, as a criticism of any purely human-centered philosophy. It is taken directly from Plato (*Leg.*, Pangle, 103). To the emphasis on the creator working in accordance with measure, number, and weight is added the emphases on equality, divine craftsmanship, and justice. These latter ideas require brief comment. Philo almost always connects the idea of just punishment with the image of divine creation by precise quantitative measure. He also regularly employs the notion that God is a perfect craftsman and much less frequently uses the idea of emanation, or generation, that is, a reproductive metaphor, in describing God's creative work. The key craftsman image derives from Plato (*Tim.*, Cornford, 21–33; see Runia 1986). Finally, Philo's reference to "equality" in the creation is to be understood in the sense of equally balanced or proportioned, that is, as an adjunct to the notions of weight or measures. God takes care for equality in the scheme of things insofar as he balances aspects of the creation against one another, sets opposing forces in balance, and creates a harmonious whole. Indeed, Philo uses musical analogies in this same way to convey the sense of harmony in the whole of creation (*Opif.* 78). All of these modes of argument also allow him to introduce an arithmological, largely neo-Pythagorean, analysis of creation in terms of numbers. His use of number symbolism is also probably indebted to prior Jewish speculations based on the numerological possibilities in the Pentateuch (one God, seven-day creation, Ten Commandments, and many others).

(2) The background in Philo for these creation motifs is his sense that Moses, the author for Philo of the Pentateuch, was a unique kind of lawgiver since he prefaced his law with an account of creation, thus "implying that the world is in harmony with the Law, and the Law with the world" (*Opif.* 3). Anyone who ob-

serves the law becomes a loyal citizen of the world who follows the "the purpose and will of Nature, in accordance with which the entire world itself also is administered" (*Opif.* 3). Despite the use here of Stoic philosophical motifs (cosmopolis and world citizenship), his primary concern is to merge his Jewish monotheism and his idea that God is the source of law (through Moses) with Hellenistic ideas about nature. In the process, he becomes one of the first authors to articulate the idea of laws of nature (Koester 1968). Philo adds to this complex of ideas the further notion that God is one, yet his chief powers are two, goodness and sovereignty. Through goodness he creates, and through his sovereignty he rules his creation (*Cher.* 27–28).[2] As we shall see later, he retains a strong sense of God's sovereign power in the realms of justice, reward, and judgment and, perhaps more important for our purposes, repeatedly links the activities of creation and judgment together in much the same fashion as Wisdom. However, before pursuing this connection, we must return to the examination of several other aspects of Philo's view of creation to gain a fuller sense of how much his work employs images of creation by precise measure.

(3) Philo employs a complex numerological and arithmological symbolism in his account of creation and in his scriptural exegesis generally (Moehring 1978; Robbins 1931; Goodenough 1932). It is a perplexing task to bring his interpretations of the Monad, Dyad, three, four, seven, ten, and other numbers into a systematic and coherent relationship with his other speculations. However, some of these arithmological exegeses have an integral relationship to his central themes. Indeed, he thought this part of his "method" sufficiently important to have written an entire treatise (now lost) on numbers (see *Mos.* 115–16). His speculations on one, six, and seven, in particular, help to link his Middle Platonic neo-Pythagoreanism with his scriptural monotheism and his sense of God as a particular kind of lawgiver and creator, one who operates in accordance with measure, weight, and number. Indeed, it is one of Philo's central intuitions that "Order involves number" (*Opif.* 13, 27–30; *QG1.* 64). The consistent intensity of God's acts of creation result in the perfection of each created thing. In this process of creative perfection, the creator uses to the fullest every number and form (*Her.* 156). Philo's evident devotion to Platonic philosophy, found throughout his work in his repeated reference to the role of "forms" in creation (Winden 1983), should not obscure the fact that he also wishes to identify order (and therefore creation) with number. The perfection of the universe is found in its very mathematical composition. Indeed, the congruence of his arithmological speculations—quite apart from the details of these formulations—with his central image of creation in accordance with weight and measure must be strongly emphasized. Without their grounding in his root image of creation, his arithmological exegeses would be a merely idiosyncratic result of contact with Middle

Platonic and neo-Pythagorean sources. With this grounding established, they can be seen as an integral part not only of his entire exegetical strategy, but as yielding proofs supportive of his religious faith. They also allow him to work more innovatively with his scriptural materials. But it is precisely his root images and exegetical strategy that allow him to make full use of all the neo-Pythagorean methods at his disposal. Another facet of Philo's work involves his use of the *logos* idea in his theory of creation.

(4) *Logos* was a widely utilized category in ancient thought and plays a complex role in Philo as well as early Christianity (Winston 1985; Borgen 1987; Hatch 1957). The following passages provide key images. "Thus God sharpened the edge of his all-cutting word, and divided universal being, which before was without form or quality, and the four elements of the world which were formed by segregation" from animal and plant life (*Her.* 140). In his exegesis of the cherubim, Philo refers to the *logos* as a "fiery sword" and calls it the symbol of divine reason (*Cher.* 28).[3] God alone has the ability to exactly divide in the middle things that are immaterial as well as material (*Her.* 143). His ability to divide things equally, in accordance with precise weight. measure, and number, is one of his central skills as Divine Artificer (*Her.* 144, also 133–34). Philo sees the universe as caused by God and his goodness and created with the material of the four elements, but the instrument through which it was created was the word of God (*Cher.* 127). Elsewhere, in a remarkable visual image, Philo interprets the biblical name of Bezalel, as chief craftsman of the Tabernacle, to mean "shadow" (Ex 31.2ff.) and suggests that God's Word is his shadow, which he uses like an instrument in crafting the world (*Leg.* 96). These and other related usages of *logos* (*Plant.* 8–10, 117; *QG3.* 23; *QE2.* 68) provide a rich set of images. Of central importance is *logos* as a cutter or instrument that divides matter into precise quantities or proportions. Several writers have noted this usage (Goodenough 1932; Moehring 1978; Robbins 1931; Runia 1986), but it has been seen as little more than a Greek embellishment of Philo's main themes. However, the image of a "*logos* cutter" is congruent with his central motif of creation by weight, measure, and number. This theme itself is not entirely Hellenistic in inspiration but has deep reverberations in Philo's Jewish inheritance. In my view, it is precisely the fit of the *logos tomeus* (logos as cutter) concept with Philo's religiously rooted sense of divine creation by precise measure and divine rule by law that appeals to him and allows for its effective use in his overall portrait of the creation process. It is also interesting to see Philo think of *logos* as an instrument or tool. In doing so, he anticipates Emile Durkheim's notion that categories are, in fact, tools of collective thought (Nielsen 1999a).

(5) Philo merges his views of retribution and creative judgment. Other Jewish texts of this period adopt a parallel view. In the Wisdom of Solomon, the idea that God has "arranged all things by measure and number and weight" (Wisdom 11.20)

is closely related to the idea of mirroring punishment or the *lex talionis*. According to Wisdom, during the Exodus, Egypt was punished by a multitude of irrational creatures so they might learn that "one is punished by the very things by which he sins" (Wisdom 11.15–16, also 12.27). In the case of Israel, "through the very things by which their enemies were punished they themselves received benefit in their need" (Wisdom 11.5). God in his power could have punished or even destroyed Egypt more directly in a multitude of other possible ways (Wisdom 11.17–18), but it is precisely because he "arranged all things by measure and number and weight" (Wisdom 11.20) that He achieved his goal only in the manner he did. Finally, in the same spirit, Wisdom affirms that the created world itself serves the God who made it by punishing the unrighteous and benefiting those who trust in God (Wisdom 16.24–27). In order to save Israel in the flight from Egypt, "the whole creation in its nature was fashioned anew" (Wisdom 19.6) and "the elements changed places with one another" (Wisdom 19.18, 24–27). These passages from Wisdom convey the connection between the primary images—creation by measure, weight, number, scales, and balances—and such factors as retribution, punishment, reward, divine power and mercy, and the means employed by God to effect these various outcomes (Winston 1979: 230–35). Philo proceeds similarly. In his exegesis of the Exodus from Egypt and the plagues visited on the Egyptians, he makes an argument remarkably similar to that found in Wisdom (Winston 1979: 232) when he writes, "The punishments inflicted on the land were ten—a perfect number for the chastisement of those who brought sin to perfection. The chastisement was carried out by the four elements (earth, fire, air, water), since God judged that the materials which had gone into creating the world should also be used to destroy the impious" (*Mos. 1.* 96). There are parallel passages in Wisdom and Philo about punishing by means of wild beasts and other creatures (compare Wisdom 11.17ff. and *Mos. 1.* 109). God could have sent greater calamities directly from heaven, but instead used the smallest creatures found in his creation (*Mos. 1.* 110–12). For Philo, as for Wisdom, during the Exodus, the constituent elements of the universe joined in the attack on the Egyptians, and, moreover, "the same elements in the same place and at the same time brought destruction to one people [Egypt] and safety to the other [the Hebrews]" (*Mos. 1.* 143). While in these passages Philo is less explicit about the relationship between the methods of punishment and those of creation, he elsewhere envisions divine punishment in terms of the usual metaphor of weighing and scales. For instance, in his discussion of the punishment of Sodom, he argues that Sodom's evil was so great that "no good could balance the vast sum of evil that weighed down the scale" (*Sacr.* 122). He immediately adds a series of arithmological speculations to demonstrate that a proper number of wisely educated men would have swayed the scales in the other direction. Such passages are frequent in Philo, as are the links between moral judgment and the images of measure and number (see, e.g., *Deus.*

82–85). Philo even repeats the image found in Proverbs and earlier in the ancient Egyptian texts concerning the weighing of the heart in judgment (Prv 24.12; Morenz 1973: 63, 126–31). God's role as creator by precise measure is related to his role as a judge according to law, who weighs mankind upon the scales, but then punishes by means of the creation itself and always "measure for measure" (Winston 1975: 230). The latter idea of *talionic* punishment was important to early Jewish law and generally in the ancient Near East (Diamond 1971: 97–103). It is interesting that it should be so closely connected by Wisdom, Philo, and even later writers (e.g., Origen) to the notion of natural order and retribution by weight, measure, and number. In this form, it seems to be a distinctive product of the encounter between Jewish creation motifs and Greek philosophy.

The varied responses by Jewish thinkers to Greek ideas in the Hellenistic era reflected the conflict over Jewish identity at the time (Hengel 1983; Momigliano 1988; Di Lella 1966). Wisdom defends Jewish cultural autonomy against the threat of total Hellenization and is implicitly critical of Jewish apostates to Hellenism (see also 3 and 4 Mc). This defense takes place through the selective adaptation of Greek ideas and methods of thought to the older, inherited Jewish themes of creation and retribution. The aim is to strengthen the community's moral solidarity by adapting elements of the "other" culture and thereby refining one's own cultural ideals. In the process, its author places added emphasis on the role of creation by measure in its relationship to punishment. The promise to the righteous and the threat to the apostate (as well as the alien) are manifest and linked to a refined Greek conception of just ordering by weight, measure, and number.

It should be recalled that Philo was a prominent member of the Alexandrian Jewish community who participated in the famous embassy to Gaius, wrote about (and was possibly a member of) the religious sect of Therapeutae, and was well connected to the heart of Alexandrian Jewish culture (Winston 1981). Nothing could be further from the truth than the image of him "popping up out of nowhere onto a major position" in Jewish history (Collins 1998: 891). He also goes much further than Wisdom in his use of Greek ideas. The result is a more comprehensive merger of Judaic and Hellenic motifs and also a more universalizing cultural breakthrough (Nielsen 1990: esp. 88–89). There is the question of the relative mix of ideas and images from Hellenism and Judaism.

Genzmer (1952) suggests that the "weight, number, measure" complex was a common "formula" during the Hellenistic and Roman era and, despite its special elaboration by Roman jurists, is ultimately derived from earlier Greek sources. Reese (1970) concurs that the Hellenistic formula is the source of the image of creation in Wisdom, and other authors have documented the debt of Wisdom (as well as Philo) to such Greek ideas (Winston 1979, 1981; Runia 1986; Hatch 1957). The "formula" (weight, measure, number) is, indeed, Greek. It goes back at least to the fifth century B.C.E. and already appears in varying contexts in Euripides, Plato, and Xenophon, although seldom in the context of creation or cosmology and usually in discussions of justice (see Nielsen 1996b: 399–400). This cultural complex was passed down from the earlier period and, as Genzmer notes, is reduced to formulaic status by Hellenistic-Roman times.

However, we must distinguish between this exact "formula" and the wider image of creation in accordance with precise quantity. While creation came ultimately to be expressed in this borrowed formula, it is already conceived of in similar form, although with more varied images and phraseology, in other Jewish writings. For example, Wisdom's use of this image is more complex than a simple formulaic borrowing. Wisdom also uses the formula as an ultimate rationale in a discussion of reward and punishment, "measure for measure," and the recasting of the creation for Israel's benefit. As noted, Philo repeats these proofs. In my view, we are faced with Hellenistic Jewish authors who are thoroughly at home in the later Greek learning, but adopt the "formula" precisely because it is congruent with the current "ideal interests" (Weber 1946: 280) of their communities as well as an antecedent Jewish standpoint descended from earlier biblical traditions. Judaism did not lack creation stories before this time, but the formula lends greater systematic coherence to the images and a fuller "rationalization" of the creation idea (Weber 1976: 399–634). The ancient Near East was generally well stocked with creation myths, although they more often involved the different (if related) idea of a battle between the forces of order and chaos for the control of the universe (Anderson 1984). The newly emerging emphasis on unity, law, and mathematical form in the very constitution of the cosmos is congruent with existing elements of numerology in the Bible, but is now placed at the center of that cosmology.

Koester (1968) has noted Philo's role in the development of the idea of "laws of nature." Here we emphasize the quantitative and mathematical images in his view of natural order. While Philo probably had little contact with the actual scientific work of Alexandrian and other Greek mathematicians (Fraser 1972: I), the spirit of his creation theory already places us in a universe ordered, morally as well as naturally, by precise measure. From the present standpoint, the focus shifts from the question of the Greek sources of the "formula" to the new cultural forms and social functions of the images. Earlier sources of these images in Proverbs, Job, Isaiah, and so forth and, in particular, their relationship to the international wisdom traditions are also important. There are almost certainly Egyptian, possibly also Babylonian and Persian, cultural influences at work, a fact that points to another, yet wider set of intercivilizational encounters in the ancient world (Lambert 1960: 133; Albright 1957: 363).

Durkheim and Mauss noted that changes in key cultural categories are best understood in relationship to the moral histories of their respective societies

(Nielsen 1999a). Communities struggle to establish their cultural boundaries and enhance their solidarity in the face of threats by identifying "deviant" internal groups as negative reference points (Erikson 1966). But when the threat is from an alien culture, the relationship becomes more complex and ambivalent. When a community's identity is defined by reference to its God (or gods), as was largely the case in the ancient world, the God's power and supremacy needs to be enhanced if the community is to ward off the threatening culture. To do this, elements of the alien culture itself are adapted to strengthen the arguments. In the case of ancient Judaism, this was accomplished through the universalization and rationalization of the inherited image of God as creator and judge. The result is a God who claims more universal authority to create and recreate, rule and judge, by precise measure, number, and weight. The categories of Greek philosophy were useful in achieving this goal, but more as a tool or instrument, rather than its central inspiration (Nielsen 1999a: 30). Wisdom and Philo are two of the first if not the first two Jewish thinkers to respond in a systematically creative way to the "modernizing" challenges of their era (Hengel 1974).

Civilizational Encounters II: Christianity and Paganism in Origen's Creation Theology

There are continuities and discontinuities in the transition from the Jewish–Hellenistic encounter to that between early Christianity and Hellenistic thought. The theology of Origen provides a particularly good site for investigating the latter.[4] Origen (c. 185–c. 254 C.E.) was the first Christian thinker to merge Greek ideas with biblical exegesis successfully and create a systematic theology (Hatch 1957; Bigg 1913; Chadwick 1966). While his work owes a large debt to his predecessor, Clement of Alexandria, and to Philo's methods of biblical exegesis, Origen's approach is distinctive (Chadwick 1970). I want to examine his ideas about creation, punishment, and the role of number in them. The similarities and differences between Origen and his predecessor Philo emerge clearly from a focus on this particular subject and allow for a more precise estimate of the similarities and differences between the two civilizational encounters under consideration. The role played in the cosmologies of Origen and Philo by their respective Christian and Jewish commitments also allows us to see the influence of changing religious sentiments on the treatment of a central theme in ancient religious thought. In addition, several remarks will be inserted about Plotinus, whose Neoplatonic system was an influential competitor to Christianity and calls for comparison with Origen, especially concerning the problem of number and creation (Rist 1977; Koch 1932; Berchman 1984).

The emergence of Christianity involved a shift in the locus of religious sentiment. As I have noted above, Philo is emotionally and intellectually committed to the Jewish community of Alexandria, and this commitment leads him to defend Jewish traditions with Greek methods, but work against their being engulfed by Hellenistic culture and eroded by Roman political power and prestige. He maintains the Jewish God's cosmic primacy. Origen's emotional commitment was to Christianity, yet like Philo and Clement before him, his mentality was thoroughly steeped in Greek learning. Indeed, he and Plotinus seem to have shared the same teacher, Ammonius Sacchus. While the urbane Clement moved comfortably in both Greek and Christian worlds and his work reflected little sense of tension between them (Hoek 1988), Origen's religious sentiments drove him instead to seek a more thoroughgoing synthesis between the two and also combat emerging pagan criticism of Christianity (Origen, *Cels.*). As a Christian, he had to reconcile his faith in the cross with its claim to represent the true realization of Jewish biblical prophecies. Finally, he faced an exegetical task complicated by the fact that no authoritative canon existed for Christians, like the Torah had for Jews. At this time, early Christians had no agreed upon reference point against which to measure their theological labors. While this fostered diversity within emerging Christianity, it also threatened disunity. Origen responded to the emerging demand for a Christian canon. His attempt at a synoptic treatment of existing biblical texts, the so-called Hexapla, reflects this effort. Similarly, he struggled, often with controversial results, to define the line between orthodoxy and heterodoxy against other religious currents of his time, for example, Gnosticism (De Faye 1923–28; Hanson 1959). Finally, within the educated Greco-Roman world, which expected that any new religion would be legitimated through a sophisticated philosophical dialectic, Origen needed to make the case for Christianity in precisely this form. Since he was steeped in Greek philosophy, he used it in his proofs, just as Tertullian was later to employ his legal training to develop a parallel dialectic of proof within Latin Christianity.

Origen's interpretations of creation and punishment, and the role of number in these processes, reflect his commitments, his need to create a rational theology through the adaptation of Greek ideas to Christian values, and his perplexities over the relative authority of inherited writings. As we will see, all of these factors figure into the making of his Christian cosmology. This same complex of emotional commitments and intellectual needs also defines the line that separates him, despite their many similarities, from his Jewish predecessor, Philo, on the one hand, and from his pagan contemporary, Plotinus, on the other. Despite their shared attachment to Greek learning, and Platonism in particular, the three thinkers gestated their ideas about cosmic unity out of very different "emotional climates" (Febvre 1973).

Origen opposed Marcion and some Gnostics and argued against the idea that God worked with some body of preexistent matter (Origen, *Princ.*; Butterworth

30). He wrote, "we believe that everything whatever except the Father and God of the universe is created" (Origen, *Princ.*; Butterworth 31). He also upheld the idea that God was always creator, benefactor, and providence and that there was never a time when he was not all these things. At the same time, his Christian allegiances make him identify Christ, the Son, with the wisdom that was always with God from the beginning and through which the creation was prefigured (Origen, *Princ.*; Butterworth 42–43).

More important, for my purposes, is Origen's identification of this creation with precise measure and number. He writes,

> We must suppose . . . that God made as large a number of rational and intelligent beings . . . as he foresaw would be sufficient. It is certain that he made them according to some definite number fore-ordained by himself; for we must not suppose, as some would, that there is no end of created beings, since where there is no end there can neither be any comprehension or limitation. (Origen, *Princ.*; Butterworth 129)

Here, Origen draws on Plato's similar identification of limit with reason (see Plato, *Tim.*). He continues:

> Moreover when the scripture says that God created all things "by number and measure," we shall be right in applying the term "number" to rational creatures or minds for this very reason, that they are so many as can be provided for and ruled and controlled by the providence of God; whereas "measure" will correspondingly apply to bodily matter, which we must believe to have been created by God in such quantity as he knew would be sufficient for the ordering of the world. (Origen, *Princ.*; Butterworth 129–30)

Here, Origen is evidently referring directly to the apocryphal Wisdom of Solomon (11.20). However, he adds to this text a fascinating elaboration and distinction within the overall metaphor. Before commenting further, I would like to first cite two other remarks by Origen, where he reiterates these themes: "Every created thing, therefore, is distinguished in God's sight by its being confined within a certain number and measure, that is, either number in the case of rational beings and measure in the case of bodily matter" (Origen, *Princ.*; Butterworth 324). Finally, there is a lengthy passage in which Origen argues that all things that exist were made by God, except the nature of the Father, Son, and Holy Spirit, and that God created "sons" as beings (presumably the "rational beings" noted above) appropriate to receive the benefits of his creation. This paragraph closes with the familiar statement, paraphrased closely from Wisdom 11.20: "But he made all things by number and measure; for to God there is nothing without either end or without measure" (Origen, *Princ.*; Butterworth 323).

The above passages are generally congruent with Wisdom and Philo. Yet, it is also evident that Origen is developing some new distinctions and employing an overall perspective in part alien to the previous writers. First, Origen's Christian commitments color the entire discussion. He is concerned to determine the canonical standing of previous writings. The apocryphal Wisdom occupies an uncertain place in his thinking. While he expresses reservations about it, since it is "certainly not regarded as authoritative by all" (Origen, *Princ.*; Butterworth 321), he elsewhere views it as an inspired work (*Cels.* 3, 72). As noted above, he adapts it freely to support an important part of his argument. Second, his Christian allegiance requires that he locate Christ in relationship to the inherited stock of ideas. This includes placing the Father as creator in relation to the Son and Holy Spirit (the Trinity problem), identifying *logos* with Christ, and reinterpreting the inherited notion of Wisdom, now also assimilated to Christ as a figure emanating from God. These and other issues are all central to Origen's work; they need to be seen in the light of his innovations in the area of the central metaphor, creation by measure and number.

As noted above, he makes a distinction between number, which applies to the creation of rational creatures, and measure, which has to do with the constitution of bodily matter. The independent role of weight in the Wisdom "formula" has dropped entirely out of Origen's formulation. Many of the older Jewish images of scales and balances in the work of creation and retribution (still found in Philo) are also absent. He focuses on number and measure, with the precise meanings noted. Origen relates them both to the work of God in creation. They are both important, yet subordinate elements of his activity. Indeed, although Origen does not spell out these distinctions very systematically, number and measure also appear to be subordinate to God's Wisdom and to Christ in his role as *logos*. Origen's Platonic perspective leads him to argue that God creates two worlds, an invisible world of ideas or forms and a visible material one (Origen, *Princ.*; Butterworth 253). In Origen's work, the Platonic tendencies have pushed aside some of the Jewish images and been fused directly with his new Christian commitments. These various strands of cosmology are difficult to bring into systematic order and mutual consistency. This is not surprising, given Origen's place as an innovator interested in forging the first Christian theology on Neoplatonic foundations. Some commentators have found greater system in Origen and wanted to see him as a Middle rather than a Neo-Platonist (Berchman 1984). However, I would note that Origen, like Philo, works a good deal of his "philosophy" out of—perhaps into—his scriptural exegesis and uses it to buttress his faith. Origen uses "philosophy" as a means to his end. Its methods and categories serve as a set of interpretive tools, but his emotional commitments lie with Christianity. His sensibility is formed by those commitments as well as the continuity with Jewish writings that they suggest. Second, Origen's particular distinction between number and measure, when set within the context of his work, places him rather closer to the full Neoplatonism of Plotinus than to the latter's Middle Platonic predecessors. A few comparisons between Plotinus and Origen will help clarify this problem.

In his treatise on numbers, Plotinus (*Enn.* 6.6.34) makes a distinction between three senses of number: (1) the One as a "number" quite beyond ordinary number and measure, indeed, itself the source of all subsequent number and measure; (2) ideal numbers, as a sort of system of mathematical formulae, or set of forms from which the visible world emerges; and (3) quantitative number or, more accurately, measure, in the more commonsense meaning of the term, that is, in relation to magnitudes in the physical world (see Plotinus, *Enn.*; Dillon 1991: xcv). The similarities and differences between Origen and Plotinus are worth noting, having a direct bearing on our discussion. I will examine them in reverse order, starting with measure and working upward, so to speak, to the higher principles.

Both Origen and Plotinus confine "measure" to the visible physical world and its creation. This is wholly congruent with their Platonic mode of thought, which locates the physical world in the lowest position of prestige in an ontological hierarchy. They both also connect "number" with rational form, a kind of halfway point between the material world and the ultimate principle of things, although Origen connects number with God's creation of a particular number of rational beings and Plotinus with the entire intermediary world of mathematical forms. Here there emerges a difference between the two authors. Origen thinks in terms of a particular concrete number of created, rational beings, some definite number foreordained by God, since only a definite number can give limit to the universe and be comprehended and only a specific number can be ruled over and provided for by God's providence (Origen, *Princ.*; Butterworth 129–30). Plotinus thinks of his second level of number as a realm of ideal numbers, one corresponding to the visible world and, presumably, a pattern used in its genesis out of the One. He is not concerned with a specific number of rational beings or with their relationship to the work of creation or even less to the problem of divine rulership. Indeed, "creation," in Origen's (and also Philo's) heavily anthropomorphic sense, does not figure at all in Plotinus's account. While I cannot now examine the complex problem of "emanation" in Plotinus (Rist 1967), Origen operates with a fundamentally different set of root images than Plotinus (but see Berchman 1984). This comes out most clearly in an examination of the third sense of number in Plotinus and its relationship to both thinkers' highest principles. These principles differ dramatically from one another. It is at this point that one sees the parting of the ways between Christianity, however much it is influenced by Platonism, and Neoplatonism itself. Origen's first principles are the biblical creator and Christ, however much both may be clothed in Platonic dress, while Plotinus's One is entirely Greek in origin and conception, abstract and remote from the anthropomorphic and human elements attached to Origen's now triune God. Plotinus's One is even more abstract and impersonal than Plato's creative demiurge (Plato, *Tim.*; Dodds 1928).

Origen's conceptualization of creation reveals several things. Not only has Origen truncated the earlier Wisdom "formula," but his Christian concerns have also made him ambivalent about Wisdom's very canonicity and, in general, shifted the overall center of gravity in the discussion of the problem. The comparison with Philo is illuminating. Philo is still free to see number, measure, weight, role of scales, and the balance in creation and existence as manifestations, at one or another level, of God's goodness, rulership, and law. His work manifests what I would call a "pan-arithmism." Origen's focus on Christ's redemptive mission moves a new set of concerns to the forefront: the Trinity, Christ as *logos*, heaven and hell, the Beginning and the End, and so forth. Indeed, in combating his pagan opponents, he is more disposed to argue for the general idea of creation, as such, than about its precise details. It is of particular interest that Philo's image of the *logos tomeus* (*logos* as cutter or instrument) is entirely displaced by the image of Christ as *logos*. Origen's interest in creation has become focused especially on the creation of humanity (i.e., "rational creatures") rather than nature. A more "humanistic" or "personalist" note has been sounded. Of course, Philo is also deeply concerned with the creation of humanity and the human soul (Tobin 1983), but that does not move him to displace his "arithmology" from center stage. On the contrary, he uses it to good advantage in the discussion of these very problems. As we have seen, Origen modifies the number symbolism to correspond to his now clearly diminished sense of the importance of the material world, while Philo can still see this world as an emblem of God and read its meanings from its numerological hieroglyphic. As Hoek (1988: 56, 66, 217, 225–26) has noted, in his comparison of Philo and Clement of Alexandria, the former is more theocentric and cosmological, and focuses on God in his work of creation and rulership, while Clement is more anthropological and salvationist and focuses on the knowledge of God. I would add to this summary characterization that Origen is even more salvationist than Clement, whose personal and intellectual style still retains many of the elements of a this-worldly, urbane Greco-Roman paganism. Origen's quest for certainty in the search for salvation and for authority in the identification of the biblical canon, and his strongly ascetic streak, lead him to a theological synthesis that is simultaneously systematic and personal. It leaves behind Clement's looser, if often startling interpretations and his accommodations between Hellenism and Christianity. It also departs in notable ways from Philo's Jewish perspective, if not entirely from his methods of interpretation. It would seem that the more deeply Christian commitments penetrate the emotional life of the early Christian authors, the less the physical world is seen as having divinely ordained value and the more humanity, especially the individual, and human redemption move to the forefront of religious concern. In the process, as we have seen, many of the images of a precisely quantitative creation drop out of the picture or are greatly modified. This oddly parallels Plotinus's Neoplatonism more than it does Philo's work.

As did Philo, Origen formulated a role for retribution and punishment in history, especially his *Homilies on Genesis and Exodus*. In some respects, numerological considerations actually play a bigger role in Origen's homilies than they do in his analysis of first principles. His scriptural exegeses expound the role played by opposites in the creation in demonstrating its harmonious conjunction (Origen, *Hom. Gen.*; Heine 59, 67). He also provides a fascinating account of the numbers or dimensions involved in the creation of Noah's ark, indeed, where he argues that these numbers and dimensions involve a great mystery (Origen, *Hom. Gen.*; Heine 81–82). Included here are an interpretation of the number 100 that is "shown to be full and perfect in everything and to contain the whole mystery of the rational creation" (Origen, *Hom. Gen.*; Heine 82). Interpretations of the numbers fifty ("the number of forgiveness" and remission of sins), thirty, and the One are also featured. The latter two numbers are significant in connection respectively with the Trinity and with the entire order of the world. Thirty is three times ten, itself a symbolically critical number, as we will soon see, while the One provides a synopsis of almost everything of significance to Origen: one God, one faith of the church, one baptism, one body, one spirit, and one goal of the perfection of God, which goal mankind must try to achieve as it moves from being created in the image of God to becoming perfect in his likeness (Origen, *Hom. Gen.*; Heine 83; *Princ.*; Butterworth 245). Origen's summary in the number one of all the value attributes of his worldview is not at all like Plotinus's use of the One. The latter is a center of power, from which the cosmos is gestated, while the number one for Origen is merely a symbolically convenient vehicle for the summary expression of all that he holds dear. It serves as a starting point for the derivation of the three, or the Trinity, through a process of differentiating the attributes of the one into three separate forces. As noted above, it does not have the same ontological significance as Plotinus's One, nor is Origen's God as unitary or as abstract a conception as that of Plotinus. Finally, Origen provides interesting remarks on the "mysteries of the seventh number" in an interpretation of the design of the Tabernacle, where he also comments on its ten courts and their relationship to the Decalogue (Origen, *Hom. Exod.*; Heine 339–40). The importance of ten reappears in Origen's exegesis of the Exodus account of the plagues visited on Egypt, a scriptural text already central to our analysis.

Origen associates the ten plagues and the Ten Commandments. Moses went to Egypt with a punishing rod that struck Egypt with ten plagues, and it is the law of God that was given to the world "that it might reprove and correct it with the ten plagues, that is the ten commandments which are contained in the Decalogue" (Origen, *Hom. Exod.*; Heine 267). This account is interesting not only numerologically, but also because Origen ties this punishment to the image of the *talion*, or mirroring punishment. For Origen, the world learns "the nature of its errors from the natures of the penalties" (Origen, *Hom. Exod.*; Heine 269). Egypt worshiped beasts and idols and saw the death and suffering of these same things. Origen concludes with the general comment: "To such an extent are the sufferings in the world governed by the forms of their own errors" (Origen, *Hom. Exod.*; Heine 269). While Origen also employs numerological analysis in his account of the Exodus through a brief discourse on the twelve paths created in the Red Sea for the twelve tribes (Origen, *Hom. Exod.*; Heine 283), he also shifts his ground to argue the case for God's goodness in a remarkable but also familiar way. The goodness of the creator also requires obedience to his will. For those who will follow his law, "he compels the elements themselves to serve you even against their own nature" (Origen, *Hom. Exod.*; Heine 282). This entire discussion of the plagues and the "unnatural" action of the elements in the Hebrews' rescue echoes the similar accounts in Wisdom 11.5–6, 19.6. It seems likely, given Origen's familiarity with this text, that he drew liberally on it. However, some major differences of emphasis remain. Foremost is the absence of any direct reference in Origen to the weight–number–measure "formula." Wisdom uses this formula as a pivotal rationale for the understanding of God's work in history. Although, as we have seen, Origen cites it in a truncated form in his account of creation, he does not use it directly in his discussion of divine retribution.

Origen also makes less direct reference than Wisdom to God's recreation of the world to save the Hebrews. For Origen, God "compels the elements" to serve the righteous "against their own nature," while for Wisdom's account of Exodus, "the while creation in its nature was fashioned anew" and "the elements changed places with one another" (Wisdom 19.6, 18). In Origen's account, the elements seem to retain their natures, thus compelling God to struggle against them, so to speak, to achieve his ends. In other words, "natural law" and divine rulership seem to conflict with one another (Grant 1952). This distinction reflects an emerging Christian sensibility about the world, which exists in a fallen and deformed state and is at odds with the divine power. By contrast, for Wisdom God's powers are unparalleled. "For thy all-powerful hand, which created the world out of formless matter," it is a simple task to recreate the universe and recast the elements (Wisdom 11.17). While Origen retains the sense of *talionic* punishment, he does so in a muted form. The Egyptians are punished by means of their own errors, yet the Hebrews do not gain advantage by the same means, as in Wisdom or Philo. In general, Origen accents punishment of the guilty, rather than reward for the righteous.

The salvation of a chosen people directly by its God is replaced by references to Christ and, in a rather tortured exegesis, Aaron's rod becomes a prefigured symbol of the cross (Origen, *Hom. Exod.*; Heine 267–68). In sum, the entire tradition of interpretation of these problems inherited from Wisdom and Philo is subtly transformed by Origen in a Christian direction. In the process, some of the older images slip out of focus and new ones come into view.

Several general conclusions concerning civilizational encounters can be drawn from the above discussion. First, a process of cultural differentiation and excision has taken place in Origen's theory of creation. He has differentiated the notions of number and measure from one another by identifying the former with rational beings and the latter with brute matter. He has also excised the notion of weight from the inherited formula. Also gone are the images of scales, balances, weighing, and so forth, which were important to Wisdom and Philo and were even more central in the older Jewish literature (e.g., Proverbs, Job, the Second Isaiah). Origen has thereby provided a more systematic theological notion of creation.

Second, a process of individuation and "humanization" has taken place in his entire interpretive schema. A common faith in the cross as the central event in a now personally relevant historical narrative has taken precedent over the work of creation and retribution by a unified divine ruler. Moreover, the story of salvation and retribution connected with the history of a people has been supplanted in part by a new emphasis on the universal work of the cross, prefigured in a hidden fashion in this earlier history of Israel, but now superceding it. In the process, there appear new Christian numerological associations that supplement the older arithmological traditions, without entirely dismantling them. The elasticity of this method of thought, the fact that the new speculations need not entirely displace the older ones, points to the instrumental quality of this part of Origen's thinking. Although arithmology was also a tool for Philo, its spirit had a deeper inner connection with the older Jewish images undergoing interpretation. While these tools remain a convenient part of Origen's intellectual equipment, they have a less integral connection with the understanding of creation, or even retribution, than they had in Philo's cosmology.

Third, the search for certainty and authoritative texts permeates Origen's work. Origen's uncertainty about the canonical status of Wisdom allows him to adapt that work more freely to his purposes and, in the process, modify and even ignore parts of the inherited "formula" used by Wisdom. His wide interpretive latitude contributes to the innovative character of his work.

Finally, the merger of theoretical rationality with the new emotional climate provided by Origen's highly ascetic form of Christianity influenced his modification of the inherited creation images. His new emphases—the creation of a specific number of rational beings as a precondition for effective divine rule; the entire omission of the weight idea, so central to the earlier images of God's work by scales and balances; the limitation of measure to the physical world; and the emphasis on the need to struggle against the elements in divine retribution—all imply a creator somewhat diminished in stature, by comparison with the robust monotheistic God of Wisdom and Philo (not to mention Job and Isaiah). They also seem to imply a greater devaluation of the created world itself. The emphasis on Christ's redemptive role has gained a purchase on Origen at the expense of the power of Judaism's One God. While there are certainly strong elements of mysticism, asceticism, and otherworldliness manifest in Philo's life, there is also an emphasis on the intrinsic value of the physical world, precisely because of its divinely created nature. While mathematical and numerological motifs continued to play a role in Christian as well pagan thought in late antiquity (Chadwick 1981; O'Meara 1989), Origen's use of them moves him toward a theological view indifferent, if not hostile to the world, a tendency that began to be substantially reversed only in the high Medieval period, and then only through the recapture of the spirit of those prior syntheses that had combined Platonism with the central creation themes of biblical wisdom literature (see Nelson 1981).

Civilizational Encounters III: Christianity amidst Religious and Philosophic Cults

Christianity's rise to prominence took place in a rich spiritual environment. A variety of religious and philosophical movements and cults competed for followers. This has led some recent commentators to speak of a "religious economy" in which individuals were free to engage in a choice among competing lines of religious goods with varied inducements appealing to differing social and spiritual needs (Stark 1996: 193–96). In such circumstances, one religious cult would attempt to trump another, not only through its intrinsic appeal based on its central differentiating characteristics, but also by borrowing to a greater or lesser extent its competitor's ideas and images, adapting and integrating them into its own system of beliefs and practices. The resulting religious phenomena occupied a spectrum from barely coherent syncretisms to doctrines that, if not entirely unambiguous, effectively integrated a diversity of elements around a coherent core of ideas. To adapt a phrase of Thomas O'Dea (1966), the dilemma of mixed motivation was resolved to allow a broadening of the group's potential membership, but through the specific mechanism of strengthening its basis of symbolic appeal. This involved a double strategy for Christian thinkers: the abandonment of an excessive number of fixed positions and a willingness to adapt to changing circumstances, including those constituted by alien symbols, coupled with an equally strong opposing effort to define Christianity's minimal core symbolic reference points with increasing clarity. The result was that Christianity showed an early flexibility that it would not lose until the fifth century (Troeltsch 1911; Frend 1984). No other religious cult or movement of the era had this quality, to this extent. They tended to move in the opposite direction, either by fixing their religious boundaries through the adherence to prime texts as their major reference point (e.g., in the rabbinical schools, leading to the Mishnah and Talmuds); by insisting on central, unalterable doctrines that made it difficult to adapt to changing circumstances or absorb emerging experiences (the Isis and Osiris cults); or by orchestrating their teachings in a narrow fashion that intrinsically limited their potential followers (e.g., the Mithras cult) (Bell 1975). To adapt Maine's helpful distinction, Christianity was the most "progressive" and least "stationary" of the many ancient religious cults (Maine 1861), in the specific sense of being able to adapt itself to new settings, absorb and transfigure competing ideas, and avoid the risk of premature fixation. Perhaps only Manichaeism had a comparably broad appeal.

As Halbwachs (1992) noted, early Christianity was also faced with the problem of fixing the times and places of its most sacred events (e.g., the sites of the birth of Jesus, the Last Supper, the Crucifixion, Jesus' burial, etc.), locating them as popular pilgrimage sites (Turner 1975) while simultaneously "clothing them with an aura of factuality," to use Geertz's congenial phrase (Geertz 1973: 90), and thus enhancing their doctrinal credibility. This ongoing exercise in the creation and specification of Christian collective memory was itself part of the competition with other religions (e.g., Judaism), which might also have a strong interest in alternative definitions of these times and places. Similar remarks might be made about such Christian holidays as Christmas, which seems to have emerged in the fourth century and resulted, in part, from the adaptation of Mithraic calendrical ideas to Christian needs (Ulansey 1989). In general, through its adaptations of Greco-Roman ideas, especially Stoic natural law philosophy, Christianity increasingly came to provide the basis of a complete "philosophy" of life and social doctrine (Troeltsch 1911), including ideas about family life, the formation of communities, economic practices, and so forth. This gave it an advantage over cults with a more focused appeal (e.g., Mithaism, which was adopted by men, primarily Roman soldiers, and was found everywhere they were garrisoned).

Christianity had been subject to sporadic persecution from the beginning, depending on the shifting policies, motives, and temperament of various emperors. The imperial cult was particularly dangerous to Christianity, as it had already been for Judaism, for it challenged its core ideas and also represented a clever strategy in the pagan battle against the new movement. Under threat of punishment or even death, Christians often lapsed, the incentives of a certificate indicating that they had sacrificed and accompanying freedom making such lapses even more inviting. However, through the reassertion of the authority of the bishops over their communities, the church recovered rapidly after this episode.

A greater danger to Christianity was posed by alternative philosophies such as Manichaeism, which provided a synthetic worldview that found a place for all previous religious prophets, including Christ. Mani himself was born into a Christian sect, the Elkesaites of the Roman and Persian border areas, but underwent a conversion and rejected his religion of birth in favor of preaching his own religious ideas. Augustine's long attraction to the teachings of Mani was typical of members of higher status families (Brown 1967). At the core of Manichaeism was the eternal dualism and opposition between light and darkness. This idea was combined with an historical eschatology that traced the original state of separation of light from darkness, the invasion of light by darkness and their subsequent mingling, and their ultimate and final separation again in the future through the purification light from any admixture with darkness. This goal of world salvation was to be accomplished through a complex set of ascetic practices that included no work, elaborate dietary restrictions, and a prohibition against killing animals. The Manichaens also developed a religious organization that tended to separate the true Elect from the mass of followers, the Hearers, who attended to the bodily needs of the Elect and themselves lived in the world free from such ascetic discipline (Widengren 1965).

Manichaeism was appealing and represented a major challenge to Christianity. It threatened Christianity's central monotheistic worldview, inherited from Judaism, which could find room for evil, but never give it a constitutive role in the universe. The long battles fought among Christian theologians over the precise relationships involved in the Trinity might, at times, risk dissolving Christian monotheism into ditheism or even tritheism, but a principled dualism like Mani's was inadmissible if Christianity were to retain its distinctive theological character and its links to Judaism. Although many Christian groups and movements since the early centuries have lapsed into a dualistic theology, in doing so they have departed from the lodestone of Christian ideas—the notion of one God. In this respect, Manichaeian dualism was (and continues to be) the single greatest threat to Christianity. Also, Manichaeism's stratification of the religious grouping into an ascetic core of the Elect distinct from the mass of followers was incompatible with the universalism of the church structure developing within Christianity, one that could find room for organizational distinctions of rank and office, including ultimately even monasticism, but not for a principled separation of the church into two spiritual grades, one superior to and served by the other. In this respect, Christian opposition to Manichaeism ran parallel to its conflict with other movements, such as Gnosticism and Marcionism, which favored even more a specially qualified elite over the mass (Pagels 1989; Nielsen 1990a: 97).

Conclusion

The above discussion represents only a selective treatment of some episodes of civilizational encounters of particular significance in the development of later Judaism and early Christian civilization, chosen from a much wider array of controversies and problems. The discussion of inter- as well as intracivilizational encounters could easily be expanded and the number of issues multiplied (for fuller surveys see Harnack 1908 and Frend 1984). I have emphasized several shifts in religious and cultural ideals connected with selected figures such as Philo and Origen, especially their treatment of monotheism and creation. I have also focused on struggles within Christianity as well as challenges from without that raised decisive questions at the highest level of definition of a Christian civilization, especially those connected with shaping the unity of doctrine and organizational authority of the church. As we have seen, the problem of refining the church's monotheism was implicated in a large number of other questions (e.g., the number of informing principles of reality, whether monist or dualist, the nature of the Trinity, the problem of original sin and free will, the nature of church authority, continuity with Judaism and the unity of the inherited canon, and so forth). Indeed, as Eusebius (*Hist. eccl.*) repeatedly tells us, monotheism with all its varied implications, operating now, however, within a Christian environment, was perhaps the key doctrinal issue that required elaboration and clarification during the early Christian centuries. It was in turn directly linked to the problem of forging a single, unified church structure. It was what men and women died—and lived—for in the early Christian centuries as it had been earlier in Judaism. As such, it forms a central and necessary thread in the above treatment of civilizational encounters in early Christianity.

Notes

1. This section on Philo draws on Nielsen (1996a).

2. Philo reiterates elsewhere (e.g., *Leg.* 78; *Plant.* 2–4) that God creates everything out of his goodness, an idea that links him closely to Plato (*Tim.*, Cornford 1936: 33–39; Lovejoy 1936) yet is also evidently derived from his scriptural interpretation.

3. I cannot pause to discuss the uses by Jewish and Christian writers of this remarkable symbolism (i.e., word as a sword that cuts matter in a process of creation or destruction), but must focus on Philo's ideas. However, similar images emerge in Revelation 19.12–16 and John I (Dodd 1963), texts probably written under similar intellectual influences.

4, This section on Origen draws on Nielsen (1995), previously unpublished.

Early Christian Culture as Interaction   13

ANTHONY J. BLASI

ULTURE IS ONE OF the most important concepts in the social sciences. It
is also one of the most abused. The early sociologist Pitirim A. Sorokin
generally spoke of "sociocultural phenomena" rather than "culture" because culture does not exist apart from society and because human society is at
best a random and meaningless occurrence without culture. For him, culture was
the meaningful aspect of a sociocultural phenomenon and society was the interactive[1] aspect.

> The most generic model of any sociocultural phenomenon is the meaningful in-
> teraction of two or more human individuals. By "interaction" is meant any event
> by which one partly tangibly influences the overt actions or the state of mind of
> the other. In the absence of such an influence (unilateral or mutual) no sociocul-
> tural phenomenon is possible. . . . A meaningful interaction is any interaction
> where the influence exerted by one party over another has a meaning or value su-
> perimposed upon the purely physical and biological properties of the respective
> actions. (Sorokin 1969: 40)

The expression "culture" has sometimes served as a shorthand reference to sociocultural complexes such as civilizations, so that a material artifact such as an oil
lamp may be taken to be an indicator of a particular "culture." Similarly a mental
abstraction, such as the ideal of charity or the ambition to dominate, may be said
to be an indicator of a particular "culture." Such shorthand statements should not
be equated with social scientific theory. An oil lamp does not indicate anything.
Rather, human individuals indicate to one another and to themselves what one
does with an oil lamp, how one makes an oil lamp, what the value of an oil lamp
is as an object of trade in an agora, and what precautions one should take in the
use of oil lamps. The culture occurs among the people who make such indications.

Similarly, charity and the ambition to dominate do not indicate anything; human individuals set lines of action into motion that benefit one another or coerce one another; those enactments carry out indicated outcomes for which the terms "charity" and "ambition to dominate" come to be used. The people involved do the indicating; the terms that they use are mere labels.

What is at issue is more than terminological precision. When culture becomes separated from interaction in a scholarly approach, it becomes denatured. Particularly troublesome is the practice of taking a "culture" to be a freestanding body of prescriptions, proscriptions, values, attitudes, beliefs, practices, preferences, and propensities to which individuals conform. Not only does "culture" thereby become disembodied and hence removed from the realm of what can be explained through scientific procedures, but humans come to be cast as mere "cultural dopes," "over-conformists," media through which mysterious "social forces" work (Blumer 1969: 83; Garfinkel 1967: 68; Wrong 1961). Theissen (1999: 6) argues well that the term "cultural," if employed, should mean that something is produced by human beings, and that above all it is social action. The argument of the present chapter is not that approaching culture in this way is untenable, since that argument has already been well made, particularly by Herbert Blumer (1969), but that approaching culture as interaction helps make a more convincing account of early Christian sociocultural phenomena.

Background

The school of social scientific thought that has most consistently approached culture as interaction is symbolic interactionism. The expression came originally from Herbert Blumer's essay "Social Psychology" (1937) and subsequently caught on as the name of a professional association and a journal.[2] The intellectual roots of symbolic interactionism go back most immediately to the German scholarly world of the late nineteenth century, in which Wilhelm Dilthey argued that the sciences that studied human life (cultural sciences) were hermeneutic in nature and required adequate depictions of particular sociocultural contexts. In his phraseology, the *Geisteswissenschaften* were unlike the *Naturwissenschaften* in that they were ideographic, portraying the particular, rather than nomothetic, discovering what the philosophers of science call "covering laws." Two famous German sociologists of the day met Dilthey halfway, as it were. Georg Simmel (1971) granted the particularity of interaction situations, but he proposed that similar forms of interaction (e.g., the two-person interaction versus the three-person, interaction for its own sake rather than interaction focused on some "matter," superordination–subordination) would have similar dynamics. Max Weber granted that actual cases of "social action" varied greatly but that pure types of possible social action could be used as yardsticks that the real cases more or less resembled, and that scientific laws would apply to imagined pure types ("ideal types") (1978: 4, 18–22). Similar to Weber's comparative sociology, the famous psychologist Wilhelm Wundt conceived of a folk psychology, albeit limited to a rather distant study of "primitive peoples."[3]

A small number of American scholars studied in Germany in the late nineteenth and early twentieth centuries, appropriated the social scientific perspective they found there, and changed it for their own purposes. The pragmatist philosopher and psychologist George H. Mead, who had studied under Josiah Royce at Harvard and worked in the household of William James as a tutor, studied under Wundt in Leipzig and then attended Dilthey's courses, and possibly Simmel's, in Berlin. Before completing a formal doctorate, he accepted a position from John Dewey at the University of Michigan; Dewey found him so valuable a thinker that he accepted his position at the University of Chicago only under the condition that he could bring Mead with him.[4] William I. Thomas studied folk psychology under Wundt. Robert E. Park, acting on advice from Mead, went to Berlin; his work reveals a great deal of influence from Simmel's sociology. Thomas, who conducted a massive study with Florian Znaniecki of Polish life in rural Europe and in Chicago, made the most he could of "human documents" in order to gain entry into the subjective aspects of collective life (Thomas and Znaniecki 1918–20).[5] Park directed a number of ethnographic or "participant observation" dissertation studies in the sociology department at the University of Chicago; he is known to have encouraged a number of his students to enroll in the "Advanced Social Psychology" course offered by Mead. Mead synthesized the intellectual perspectives of William James, the Germans, John Dewey, and the social activist Jane Addams, and created an original social scientific perspective that gained worldwide attention in the last decades of the twentieth century; his most influential ideas are to be found in the posthumous edition of his Advanced Social Psychology course (1934).[6] Herbert Blumer, who studied under Mead, became the principal social scientific advocate of Mead's perspective.

Culture and Text

In a statement that was in many ways parallel to those by Blumer, anthropologists Leslie White and Beth Dillingham (1973: 9) insisted that culture consists of the activity of "symboling." Symbols per se would be a facet of sociocultural reality, not sociocultural reality itself. White thought that for the scientist to observe a pattern within sociocultural reality and then to take such a pattern to possess a reality of its own would be a fundamental error (White 1954). It would be like looking at constellations of stars and taking the constellations to be real things.

Texts such as those of the New Testament and other early Christian literature are symbols, not human interaction or "symboling." Simply finding patterns in texts will not reflect faithfully the to-and-fro in early Christian contexts from which the texts emerged. Of course, it is not possible to visit the early Christians and watch them in their daily lives. So it is necessary to make do with texts and find in them clues to their originary interactions.

Clues lead us to hypotheses, not facts. They suggest reconstructions that we might make. The relevant reconstructed culture would be that which emerged between an early Christian author and the first intended hearers.[7] Focusing on that interchange to the exclusion of other readings requires no little discipline. For example, consider this controversial text:

ὡς ἐν πάσαις ταῖς ἐκκλησίαις τῶν ἁγίων, αἱ γυναῖκες ἐν ταῖς ἐκκλησίαις σιγάτωσαν, οὐ γὰρ ἐπιτρέπεται αὐταῖς λαλεῖν· ἀλλὰ ὑποτασσέσθωσαν, καθὼς καὶ ὁ νόμος λέγει.

As in all the churches of the saints, the women should keep silence in the churches. For they are not permitted to speak, but should be subordinate, as even the law says. (I Cor 14.33b–34 RSV)

The RSV translators took this passage to be a command ("they are not permitted to speak") about church order, similar to many previous passages in I Corinthians. Modern feminists might change the translation in light of verse 36, where Paul reacts against what the preceding verses present:

ἢ ἀφ ὑμῶν ὁ λόγος τοῦ θεοῦ ἐξῆλθεν, ἢ εἰς ὑμᾶς μόνους κατήντεσεν;

What! Did the word of God originate with you, or are you the only ones it has reached? (I Cor 14.36 RSV)

Thus a modern feminist translation may put quotation marks around verses 33b–35, noting that Paul responds in I Corinthians to a series of issues raised by a letter that some of the Corinthians had sent to him. While that would be an improvement upon the RSV reading and is fine so far as it goes, an interactionist approach would lead one to focus on what is going on between Paul and his intended readers. Paul no doubt thought he was writing only to the people who had sent him a letter, half a dozen or so recently converted Christians. He was chiding them privately: "What! Has the word of God come forth from you? Was it dwelling only in you?" What was the object of his comment? They presumed to speak for God. How? They were interpreting the Law. We can infer from this that the intended hearers had no credentials as Torah interpreters. So the immediate occasion for Paul's response was the clause "as even the law says." What was the legal interpretation the Corinthian correspondents were making? That the law that says women should be subordinate has a bearing on whether they can discuss religious matters in public. That was such a stretch of the legal provision that Paul does not bother to correct it; he only ridicules the pretense of legal interpretation.

For purposes of reconstructing the situation that gave rise to a text, it would appear best to use as many "first meanings" of words as possible, even if that leaves one beginning with a "wooden" or problematic reading.

> As in all the churches of the saints, women should be quiet in the assembly, for it is not entrusted to them to chatter. But "They should be subject," as even the law says. If they wish to learn something, they should inquire of their own husbands at home; for it is unseemly for women to chatter in an assembly. What! Has the word of God come forth from you? Was it dwelling only in you?

The Corinthian correspondents were speaking disparagingly of the women's contributions, calling it "chatter." The law, according to the correspondents, would have the women defer to their own husbands' opinions, not to some other men's. Paul's response is to the suggestion that according to the law women were to be dependent exclusively on their husbands for religious insight. What he was opposing in this particular passage was an attempt to legally support a limiting of women religiously on the basis of a household order.

Note that it is the action in the text that is most relevant culturally. Analogously, in tradition texts such as the Gospels, wherein received texts are reformulated for purposes of being given over to a new audience, tendentious redactive activity is of cultural relevance. It is key to any reconstruction of what was happening between the redactor and the intended audience. What the author or redactor hopes to accomplish in the intended reader is a central feature of the actual interaction among selected early Christians. There may be a set of expected patterns of behavior in the environment of the author or the readers or both, but such expectations are a lesser facet of culture. They are relevant at all only to the extent that the individuals in question make them relevant. Generally expectations of that kind represent ideal culture, a set of statements to which people assent verbally but which they ignore when there is good reason to ignore them. "I don't mean to . . . but. . . ." That which people appear to be accomplishing with their texts should be considered primary data, while evidence of environmental expectations are relevant only and as precisely as conventional verbalizations. Thus it should come as no surprise that early Christian texts frequently reflect the setting aside of "laws."

Historical information needs to be treated with caution. The haphazard circumstances through which literary and archaeological sources preserve information make it unlikely that we have the full story about anything from twenty centuries ago. Moreover, how specific facts were regarded may have gone unspoken, just as many facts are simply cited today, leaving the full meaning of a statement unverbalized. "I was born in Brooklyn, no mean city." "I dropped out of Harvard." "I had a job at the White House in the Nixon administration." "I was in the squad that fired on the protesters at Kent State." Is the Brooklynite speaking humorously on the basis of the hapless borough's reputation, or making a contrast to a small town? Is the Harvard dropout speaking apologetically of an opportunity lost or verbally polishing a badge? Does the erstwhile White House staffer speak of sticking to a task dutifully through trying times or confess to having kept bad company? Is the National Guardsman menacingly threatening to repeat history or is he expressing regrets? The more history we know the more such questions we know to ask, but history does not give us the answers. However, we cannot claim to have much of a grasp of late twentieth-century American life without knowing the place of Brooklyn in humor, the eminence of Harvard among educational institutions, the stigma of the Nixon White House, and the sore spot in the psyche related to the Kent State shootings. But what is the meaning of such symbolic references in given statements?

The fact that a statement denotes and even connotes much less than it brings to mind when used is called "indexicality." The term suggests a parallel with the relationship of an index of a book to the contents of the book's pages or with the relationship of a library catalog to the books on the library shelves. The index and catalog consist of single terms that are but fragments of all that is to be found in the actual indexed locations. Similarly, texts such as those in early Christian literature present but fragments of all that went on in early Christian life. They are incomplete and inadequate.

The Presentness of Culture

Culture is an activity; it is processual in nature. It occurs in the present, specifically the actor's present. Even if one recollects a past activity of "symboling," the act of recollecting occurs in the actor's present, not in a past. The present has an openendedness about it that allows for spontaneity. Consequently one cannot predict accurately how any given session of "symboling" will go. One may have a scenario worked out in elaborate detail—what one is going to tell someone, for instance—but on the spot looking into another person's eyes one says or does something quite different. That is why people find conversations refreshing; they are not simply two-part recitals but creative processes that take unexpected twists and turns. That is why meetings are called in which it is hoped that there will be some back-and-forth among the participants; new ideas and new solutions to problems emerge that the participants would never have come up with individually.

The presentness of cultural activity can make many moments unique and un-recoverable. Many teachers despair at the suggestion that a student be absent from a class and simply "get the notes" from somebody. The attention of the students who were present had been engaged in a certain way, the intellectual scene set up to create a particular perspective for an insight, and a point formulated in terms to fit that particular teaching moment. Notes simply do not recover all of that. In an analogous way, one can hear a passage of music for the first time only once. It will never again strike one in precisely the same way. The second time will be a repeat. The thirtieth time may be several times too often. The appeal of a live perform-ance over a recording comes in the to-and-fro of the performers working in con-cert, eliciting performances from one another that will never again be repeated in precisely the same way. Again, one may read a book in early adulthood and appre-ciate it with a certain level of sophistication; decades later one may read the same book again and appreciate it in a different way with a different sophistication.

"Symboling" occurs not only among people in interaction but also in the imagination. We import (to use Mead's term) the form of society into our imag-ination and carry on implicit conversations. Thus we think in a language. Think-ing, as we generally refer to this process, also occurs in a live present. A thought will strike us differently at different points in time. In the course of thinking about something, we can come up with new ideas that were not thought of before because the presentness of the implicit conversation allows for spontaneity, just as conversations that we enact with others allow for spontaneity.

Mead called cultural phenomena "mind." The process through which mind emerges early in human life, as we will see below, is important in the cultural un-derstanding of religious texts. Mead proposed the situation in which mental phe-nomena do not yet appear—say in the life of a worm. It may be that even before birth humans have a higher psychology than does the worm, but for purposes of discussion it is useful to consider a psychology absolutely devoid of mind. Such a primitive psychology is entirely behavioral—its owner can be conditioned to avoid pain-inducing actions and repeat pleasure-inducing actions. Thus by the use of electric shocks one can train a worm to always bend left and never again bend right. That is not mind, but it is a psychology. To set out toward the emergence of mind, Mead found it necessary to leave the confines of stimulus-response condi-tioning behind, and indeed to break it up so that a stimulus is given by one or-ganism and responded to by a second organism. Using an expression from Wundt, he called the stimulus a "gesture"; he called the response of a second organism to the gesture "meaning."

A typical nonhuman animal does not understand a meaning. A lion, ac-cording to Mead, is not appreciably frightened by its own roar, though fright may be occasioned in another creature by such a roar. For a human to use a symbol that occasions the same meaning in another human that it occasions in the first human, there needs to be a mutual participation in both the gesture and the response to it. Mead analyzed first the mutual participation in gestures by considering the imitative birds. A bird that imitates another bird does so primarily in sound because it can hear itself. The other bird sounds first, and then the imitator makes a sound that it can recall and compare with the sound of the first bird. In order to identify a sound as its own before comparing it and conforming it to the sound of the other, the bird must have some primitive awareness of itself. This kind of "reflexive" awareness seems to be most advanced among humans. Unlike birds, which imitate seemingly to fit into an environment on the basis of a sound-camouflage instinct, human infants imitate sounds in the course of attracting attention to themselves.

The step beyond imitation is imagining how the other will respond to one's own gesture. Having an advanced awareness of oneself, one can imagine oneself in the place of a particular other—usually a parent—and look back at oneself. What will Mother or Father do if one cries? The child experiments with such a gesture and stops midcry to see. Through imitation, the responses that can be anticipated to come from different performances and enactments constitute a repertory or vocabulary after a time. And once "taking" the role of the other (i.e., looking back at oneself from the standpoint of the other), one becomes aware of oneself in a more elaborate way as a "Me." One develops a self-concept. It is not that the self-concept is fashioned by the others whose standpoint one may take, because one still responds to the image that appears from the standpoint of the other. One can be happy or upset by it, accept it or reject it. One responds to such a "Me" as an "I." Thus Mead incorporated the "I–Me" dialectic of William James into his analysis of imitation and symbol. The importance of this for culture is that familial images such as Mother and Father are implicit in the background of all symbolic activity. One may abstract from Mother and Father and other personages from one's childhood toward a general and anonymous standpoint of the other, but one arrives at that anonymous other through particular others from childhood. The anthropomorphic materials for imagining God as an Other are thereby in place.

Cultures, of course, do not exist as particulate symbols that stand in isolation from one another. In fact, the "symboling" activity that we call culture becomes particularly interesting when groups of people associate different lines of "symboling" activity with each other. In the case of early Christian phenomena, for example, we want to know not only what "God," "savior," "messiah," "charity," "baptism," "Eucharist," "resurrection," and "apostle" mean, but how they came to be elements in a common religious subculture. The procedure would involve observing what the early Christians were doing at various points in time, what lines of activity they were fitting together that would involve such symbols with one another. When we understand why they bundled certain symbolic materials together we would have an idea of the early Christians' culture.

Tradition

Early Christianity began within Jewish tradition and then departed from it. Jewish tradition then developed further in its own trajectory, responding in part to Christian cultural activity. Consequently early Christianity was both a break with tradition and a development of tradition. Tradition, of course, consists of those sociocultural phenomena that the people who are engaged in "symboling" activity take to have a past and a future.[8] The individuals are aware of themselves in a present line of "symboling" that began in and is continuing from a past. That kind of awareness is retrospective in quality; it bridges past symbolic presence and present self-awareness. The individual appropriates past symbolic texts in a present state of mind, but that appropriation is not a replication of the experience of people in the past who created the text or who first witnessed it. Just as a note in a musical text is apprehended in different ways, depending on whether it helps comprise one or more chords or comes before and after other notes as part of a melody line, a text of symbols from the past takes on different significances, depending on the sociocultural context in which it is presented. What was revolutionary in the first century may be tradition today; what was sectarian yesterday may be more ecumenical today. In any event, the originator of the text did not create it as tradition; there was no past to it at the time of origination. Rather, the text as originally created stood against a background of other texts that comprised the tradition of the time. Consequently, while there are continuities between a present appropriation of a text and its origination, there are also inherent differences between the two experiences.[9]

A self-awareness is also inherent in retrospection because the individuals perceive the tradition as coming before themselves and extending into a future beyond themselves. The trajectory from past to future necessarily passes through the present collective "self." This is not only the case with people today, organized as they are in modern ethnic, nationality, class, political, and denominational groupings, but also with the people of the first century. There is a world of difference between an isolated rural community breaking with but also extending a tradition and urbanites living in a pluralistic world doing so. What the ruralite may take to be a mere change may become bound up with the dynamics of asserting identity in a pluralistic setting. The heightened sensitivity concerning collective identity may become doubly heightened when the ruralite is exposed to pluralist urban experiences. It is useful to see schism and religious conflict in such a light.

In the situation of religious innovation, such as that of the early Christians, there is something of a tradition deficit. No received text was exclusively Christian; other movements coming out of the Jewish context such as the movement of John the Baptizer and groupings remaining within the Jewish context had as good or better a claim on the Hebrew Scriptures as did the early Christians. What tended to differentiate a Christian tradition from the other trajectories had to be grounded in what was going on in the Christians' collective life of the present and in particular what was giving them a collective identity. They would be looking back upon the received text of the Hebrew Scriptures (often in Greek translation) from the perspective of selves in a pluralist setting wherein there were other collective selves. The figure of the Christ becomes the "fulfillment of the scriptures," functioning as an interpretive key as well as a theological principle under which the legends of Jesus of Nazareth enter into the traditional reading of the Hebrew Scriptures.

The pluralism of identities implicated in the standpoint from which the early Christians received tradition does not stop at the separation of a Christian identity from other identities. There were multiple situations in which early Christians lived, and hence early on there were multiple Christianities. However, no text legitimated a multiplicity of Christianities; that is why Paul could ask whether Christ had been divided (I Cor 1.13). Eberts (1997) identifies four Christian groups that emerged early on in the history of early Christian movements— Disciples, Brethren, Apostles, and Hellenists, led respectively by Peter, James, Barnabas and then Paul, and Stephen.

An antidote to a tradition deficit is institutionalization, which can be defined as the setting up of regularized or routinized patterns of reciprocal activity. Each pattern would consist of a division of labor into roles, a set of expectations or, more strongly, norms and customs, and an articulation of legitimating the emergent institutional order (Linton 1936: 114; Mead 1934: 261; Weber 1978: 31).[10] The tradition deficit in the early Christian movement can explain the rapidity with which Christian leadership structures came to be regularized, even when that regularization entailed departures from the ways associated with the charisma of Jesus or even that of an early figure such as Paul. Soon after the time of Paul, the Deutero-Pauline literature advocates a much more institutionalized church structure than Paul himself knew of.

> Now a bishop must be above reproach, the husband of one wife, temperate, sensible, dignified, hospitable, an apt teacher, no drunkard, not violent but gentle, not quarrelsome, and no lover of money. He must manage his own household well, keeping his children submissive and respectful in every way; for if a man does not know how to manage his own household, how can he care for God's church? He must not be a recent convert. (I Tm 3.2–6a RSV)

Paul himself was reproached often, does not seem to have been married, did not appear to others to be dignified, seemed to have a quarrelsome side, and did not have a household. Thus the author of I Timothy, writing under Paul's name, introduces a number of rules designed to create a particular order in an organized life for early Christianity. The letters of Ignatius of Antioch, dating from the early second century, presuppose an already well-institutionalized local hierarchy of bishop and presbyters, with a deacon serving as something of a manager.[11] The Letter of the Romans to the Corinthians, commonly known as *1 Clement* and probably dating from the late first century, provides evidence of a translocal effort to reinforce the authority of bishops. It provides a historical interpretation of the early Christian movement itself that leads up to a stable structure of church officials (*1 Clem.* 42–44). Similarly the institutionalization of worship patterns (see I Cor 11.23–26; *Did.* 7 and 9–10) can be seen as a response to a tradition deficit, as can the process of establishing a list or κανον of accepted Christian Scriptures.

Much of the literary material that provides evidence of sociocultural processes is produced with the legitimation of the emergent institutional order in mind. Thus lessons such as those of the parables of Jesus could well point to something that distinguishes the Christian subculture of the author from some other subculture, be the latter outside or within the wider Christian movement. Cited traditions handed down within the Christian communities, such as the resurrection narratives mentioned by Paul, often legitimate the structure of the Christian movement itself, in the case of Paul's citation its pluralist character.

> For I delivered to you as of first importance what I also received, that Christ died for our sins in accordance with the scriptures, that he was buried, that he was raised on the third day in accordance with the scriptures, and that he appeared to Cephas, then to the twelve. Then he appeared to more than five hundred brethren at one time, most of whom are still alive, though some have fallen asleep. Then he appeared to James, then to all the apostles. Last of all, as to one untimely born, he appeared also to me. (I Cor 15.3–8 RSV)

At the stage of the history of the early Christian movement in which Paul wrote, oral history and the conformance of that oral history to the Hebrew Scriptures were used in the legitimation of the process by which distinct Christian groups and their leadership structures were institutionalized. The charismatic legitimation from the direct personal influence of Jesus of Nazareth himself was no longer in effect.

Culture and the Affective Life

We have noted that culture as an empirical phenomenon amenable to scientific inquiry consists of "symboling." To reiterate: the activity of "symboling" in turn begins for each person early in life. The individual becomes cognizant of people in the immediate environs, usually parents or parent figures. In order to begin symbolic activity, the individual must first acquire the material aspect of symbols through imitation. Imitation requires a primitive self-consciousness insofar as one must sense oneself in order to compare one's own performance with that of the person whom one would imitate. Unlike the case of imitative birds, however, the imitating human child is not instinctively attempting to blend into the environment so as not to be noticed, but on the contrary tries to call attention to itself. If there is any instinct involved, it is a sociability instinct. In order to "symbol," the child needs to consider its own performance from the standpoint of the others whom it knows, usually its parents, in order to anticipate how those others will respond to its own performance. Accurately anticipating the response of those others is to know the "meaning" of the performance for them. Thus knowledge of such symbols as language is first found in the other and then imported into the individual's mental life. It does not develop independently in isolation and then jump out into a public setting as "genius." When the individual imports the standpoint of the other into its imagination, it not only has a language in which to think but incorporates an objective standpoint into its mental activity, giving it a cognitive capacity that is qualitatively superior to anything the most efficient of central nervous systems could have in social isolation. This is George H. Mead's account of culture, or as he termed it, "mind."

Despite its cognitive focus, Mead's account leads to an important affective development. The self-awareness that is made possible by and arises from social interaction leaves the individual partly in society and partly out, partly identifying with the other and partly distinguishing itself from the other. One abstracts an image of oneself given off by the responses to oneself by others, and one is pleased or displeased with that image, ready to embrace it or reject it. Beginning with one's first others, usually parents, one experiences the social world and the self as bonded together. This sense of bondedness comes to extend toward further others in the social world over time. There are two fundamental emotions that emerge in this experience of social bondedness—pride and shame. Pride signals an intact social bond, and shame signals a threatened one (Scheff 1990: 71). The shame/pride continuum represents a primary social emotion that is generated by the virtually constant monitoring of the self in relation to others. It is implicit in both social interaction and, by virtue of the importation of the perspective of the other into one's own consciousness, even in solitary thought (Scheff 1990: 79). The shame/pride in question is not an abnormal fixation such as that which leads to rigidity in thought and action, but "normal shame," a basically social interest in how one is or would be perceived from the perspective of the other.

Culture, as a "symboling" process that implicates the perspective of the other, has this emotional dimension of normal shame thereby implicit within it. Culture is taken up with bondedness, analogous to the bond between parent and child that is at the origin of the individual's emotional life.

> For our boast is this, the testimony of our conscience that we have behaved in the world, and still more toward you, with holiness and godly sincerity, not by earthly wisdom but by the grace of God. For we write you nothing but what you can read and understand; I hope you will understand fully, as you have understood in part, that you can be proud of us as we can be of you, on the day of the Lord Jesus. (1 Cor 1.12–14 RSV)

"Boast," "proud"—such words reflect an association between writers and audience. "Testimony," "we write," "you can read"—these expressions refer to the authors' very symbolic activity. "Conscience that we have behaved"—here is a reference to the continuous self-monitoring activity. "Understand" and "understand fully"—the cognitive element is never far away. The basic categories represented here all inhere in the very nature of culture and should not be understood to be peculiar to the life and times of an author such as Paul. What are differentiating rather than universal are the contrasts between "earthly wisdom" and the "grace of God" on the one hand and "understand fully" and "understood in part." A cultural social science is one that links such constant universals as pride/shame, symbolic interaction, and cognition, with such historical conjunctures as a group constructing a knowledge system distinct from that of the "world," and the process of upgrading group members from partial to full understanding of that knowledge system.

In the individual's development of the mental life, there is a movement from imitating particular others in "play" to enacting roles that are standardized from a general perspective. Children work at the latter activity in "games" that have rules. Since the time of Mead social psychologists have spoken of a "play stage" and a "game stage," the latter extending well into adolescence. Mead suggested a parallel development of personal morality, and the "moral development" school of thought has sought to elaborate that insight into a general approach (see Kohlberg 1981). A distinction is made between the child's morality of pleasing a parent, an adolescent's morality of obeying rules, and a mature morality of realizing values. Cultural systems have been known to place any one of these foremost. Is one to please Caesar, or must even Caesar conform to the law? Is one to be submissive to the law, or is the "spirit" behind the law such that in the conduct of the individual the law itself becomes superfluous? Just establishing the rule of law over the whims of the ruler of the day is a major civilizational achievement. Establishing occasions for the cultivation of value sensitivity is a rare accomplishment not yet known to be achieved with a civilization-wide scope. At what level of moral development was the early Christian church to aim? This was a cultural issue of great salience in the early Christian movement.

It has already been observed that familial imagery is often used in referring to God. The foundational ability to engage in symbolic activity develops in the process of a child identifying with a parent (or surrogate) and assuming the standpoint of the parent in looking reflexively on itself so as to anticipate accurately what the parent will take a performance by the child to mean. The otherness of the parent with which one needs identify thereby has a primordial presence in all subsequent "symboling" in which the individual may engage. This pervasive and covert presence of the parent in the fully developed consciousness of the human constitutes a cultural resource for giving an image to an omniscient deity who is thought to be immanent in a creative force that maintains the existence of all knowable objects. A faith in such a deity, in contradistinction to a nontranscendent or "low" deity, is not a matter of empirical observation and recognition or of logic because it experientially precedes the objective standpoint that makes observation, recognition, and logic possible. Such a faith is no less mental, but just as a child's awareness of a parent image is as affective as intellectual the believer's affirmations are united with rather than abstracted from the individual's affective development. For that reason religious culture pervades the religious person rather than providing a mere thesis to which the person assents or from which the person dissents.[12] For the same reason, an individual can dissent from a particular cultural symbol as an indicator of a divine reality (i.e., not believe in "God") but nevertheless approach life-in-general religiously. Such a religious non-theism may involve an inconsistency in the sense of negating the very process that gives rise to the religious sentiment, but it involves no logical contradiction in the experienced region of consciousness in which ratiocination takes place.

The question of a religiosity lacking intellectual assent to a given symbolization of the divine is pertinent to the subculture of the early Christian movement. From the perspective of most religions of antiquity, Christianity was a form of atheism. The Christians rejected the cult of the Pantheon of personalities as a pursuit that carried anthropomorphism too far (see Rom 1.23). Thus while the Christians were willing to refer to God as "Father" and to an emanation from the Father as "Word" or "Son" and to a continuing presence of the Son as "Holy Spirit," they took such terms as indicators rather than depictions. Even the narratives of Jesus of Nazareth did not constitute a full account of the Christ Jesus,

> Who, though he was in the form of God, did not count equality with God a thing to be grasped, but emptied himself, taking the form of a servant, being born in

the likeness of men. And being found in human form he humbled himself and became obedient unto death, even death on a cross. (Phil 2.6–8 RSV)

> There was a speech in genesis, and the speech was to God, and the speech was di-vinity. In genesis this was to God. All things came to be through this one, and apart from him nothing came to be that had come to be. In him was life, and the life was the light of humans. And the light shines in the darkness, and the dark-ness has not caught it. The true light that enlightens every human was coming into the world. (Jn 1.1–6, 9, trans. in Blasi 1996: 309)

The early Christian subculture was not atheist by modern standards, but by ancient standards it was as much a system of unbelief as belief since it involved a skepti-cism about the depictability of God. In this respect it resembled Jewish religion.

Fusion

The consciousness that is symbolically endowed, that has an "I" assuming the standpoint of an other and thereby both identifying with and distinguishing itself from the other, has the potential of fusing two dialectically related perspectives. The "I" can cease being concerned primarily with the interests of the "I," and the other can be perceived to have interests that are regarded as if they were one's own. This fusing of perspectives is what underlies the Golden Rule of conducting one-self toward others as one would have them behave toward oneself. In the affective experiences of the individual, fusion brings the person back to the very origin of the objective attitude, challenges its adequacy, and thereby elicits the stance of care first observed in parents (or surrogates for parents).

> In the conception of universal neighborliness, there is a certain group of attitudes of kindliness and helpfulness in which the response of one calls out in the other and in himself the same attitude. Hence the fusion of the "I" and the "me" which leads to intense emotional experiences. The wider the social process in which this is involved, the greater is the exultation, the emotional response, which results. (Mead 1934: 274)

A situation of sympathy is achieved, where the individual's interest comes to be identical to the interests of others (see Scheler 1954: 98–102). Because an expe-rienced fusion of "I" with other undermines the primacy one would otherwise ac-cord the interests of one's self, the individual can act as an ego-less or selfless agent. The motivation for action under a condition of selflessness is to be found in the will of the transcending parent figure, the will of the transcendent deity (Sorokin 1948: 203). William James spoke of a "feeling of being in a wider life than that of this worldly selfish little interests." He noted that this sensation is personified in Christian tradition as God (James 1958: 216). If one is not inclined to greatly anthropomorphize God, that will comes to be understood as the most natural grounds for action, arising from the creative impulse of the deity. Thus an altruistic action is most natural and a selfish one a contrivance. The fully aware human can make such an experience of sympathy itself an object of cognition and discourse and refer to it with such terms as "charity," "philanthropy," and "altruism." In an account of charity, William James speaks of the "shifting of the emotional centre" bringing about a "tenderness for fellow-creatures" (1958: 217). Thus it is possible not only to conceive of charity or a "love ethic" going beyond one's immediate family, circle of associates, community, tribe, or nation, but of extending to all humans and even to all creatures.

As long as culture cannot be empirically dissociated from the interaction that generates it, an adequate account of a love ethic in early Christianity cannot stop at such texts as the Sermon on the Mount (Mt 5.2–7.27) or Paul's discourse on charity (1 Cor 13.1–13). Indeed, it is perfectly possible, as Sorokin notes (1948: 41ff.), for people's verbal affirmations to be contrasted by their courses of action. In the best of all possible research circumstances, one would see evidence of the fusion process occurring. One might look, for example, for the origin of such convictions as "where two or three are gathered in my name, there am I in the midst of them" (Mt 18.20 RSV) and "as you did it to one of the least of these my brethren, you did it to me" (Mt 25:40 RSV).

One aspect of fusion is a tendency toward anomianism. The rule of law is based on a separability of self and other and a "taking" or imaginative assumption of the role of the other so that one can control one's own actions by conformance to the normative expectations of others. In the course of undermining at the affective level the distinction between self and other altruism replaces any legalistic self-control. Simple legal righteousness is thought to be a minimal human achievement, while altruism, experienced as divine, is experienced as something that exists on a higher plane. A genuine altruism is thought to begin only when the minimal legal requirement is transcended. Paul's anomianism might be seen in this light. Moreover, in altruistic actions the individual freely sacrifices rightful interests in favor of the well-being of another. "In contrast to obligatory legal conduct, altruistic conduct is always free from any external compulsion" (Sorokin 1948: 59). Because of this lack of compulsion altruistic actions occasion a sense of freedom.

Feelings of freedom and the "peculiar sense of exultation" (Mead's term, 1934: 273) are experienced as good, as what we moderns would call in our own psychological culture "advanced stages of self-realization." The altruistic individual wants others to experience this as well. Thus this kind of sociocultural development is often accompanied by a missionary zeal to occasion the same experience in others. In the terminology of early Christianity, there is a wish for others to be "converted" and to enter upon the road to "salvation." The legalistic bonds of "this world" can be broken for others as well. From a social scientific perspective, the aim is to account for the emergence of sensations of fusion that in turn generate the missionary impetus.

Closing

The aim of the present exposition has been to suggest problems for inquiry rather than provide a definitive portrayal of early Christian subculture. In part, such a stratagem is predicated on dissatisfaction with much that has been done to date by way of cultural analyses of early Christian phenomena. In part it has been a question of honoring the general purpose of a handbook—giving the reader guidelines that can be used in creative scholarly inquiry. But it also the case that one of the most widely recognized paradigms in the social scientific community—interactionist constructivism—has in general been ignored in social scientific inquiry into early Christianity. This latter situation is truly unfortunate since it is interactionism that has provided theoretical justification for the cultural turn in the social sciences, a turn away from the failed approaches of racial and other biologically reductionist explanations. Most of the advances in social scientific theory in the twentieth century have come within the trajectory of symbolic interactionism or at its margins. What the next century will bring remains to be seen, but it is hard to imagine any progress occurring absent a cognizance of human interaction within the core of "symboling" activity.

Notes

1. Perhaps the earliest formal recognition of the centrality of interaction in human life was Simmel's reference to *Vergesellschaftung* (1971: 9), commonly translated as "sociation." Marx, interested in macro structures, simply presupposed the importance of interaction, to which he referred with the expression *Verkehr* (1978b: 150). In their influential text/anthology, Park and Burgess devoted an entire chapter to social interaction (1924: 339–434).

2. Society for the Study of Symbolic Interaction; *Symbolic Interaction*.

3. Prus (1996: 34–46) provides an excellent history of these intellectual roots.

4. Assessments of the importance of Mead's thought for social science are given, among other places, in Blumer's 1966 essay in Blumer (1969: 61–77); Coser (1971: 333–55); Gurvitch (1958a: 62); and Martindale (1960: 353–59).

5. For insight into the significance of this work, see Blumer (1979).

6. On Mead, see Blumer (1969: 61–77), Joas (1985), and Blasi (1998). Most commentaries on Mead need to be read with caution because they miss the dialectical, constitutive, and processual core of his model of human mind. The introduction by the editor of *Mind, Self, and Society* (Mead 1934) is not recommended.

308   ANTHONY J. BLASI

7. "Hearers" rather than "readers" because of the practice in antiquity of reading texts aloud. Below the two terms are taken to be interchangeable.

8. Berger and Luckmann speak of "intersubjective sedimentation" in a section that bears the heading "Sedimentation and Tradition."

> Intersubjective sedimentation also takes place when several individuals share a common biography, experiences of which become incorporated in a common stock of knowledge. Intersubjective sedimentation can be called truly social only when it has been objectivated in a sign system of one kind or another, that is, when the possibility of reiterated objectification of the shared experiences arises. (1966: 67)

9. This is the hermeneutic problem that Gadamer (1975) in general addresses, but see especially pp. 304–5.

10. Here I differ from Berger and Luckmann (1966: 93), who maintain that legitimation is not necessary in the first phase of institutionalization. Concerning roles, Natanson sees them as "possibilities of social reality through which pure types are actualized in concrete performances" (1974: 213). The "pure types" refer to idealized expectations; there is no suggestion that all role performances are identical. While it is useful for purposes of exposition to speak of interaction as the exchange between two or more co-present individuals, in fact such exchanges are mixtures of spontaneous initiatives and responses and scripted role performances that set limitations on spontaneity; see Stoetzel (1960: 345). Gurvitch cautions that Mead's discussion of interaction absent social structures manifest in concrete roles can be misleading (1958a: 62).

11. See, e.g., the Letter of Ignatius to the Ephesians 2, 4, and 5.

12. Simmel: The "person simply believes, so to speak. Belief in its purest form is active in his soul, but the specific object or content of this faith is not definable in any way" (1997: 45). And: "This point is illustrated by the fact that many deeply religious individuals are indifferent to any kind of dogma, and that the various dogmas are products of the infinite fortuities of history—whereas the religiousness of these individuals is unquestionably the same in essence, even though the content of what they believe in is so diverse" (1997: 46–47).

"Becoming Christian": Solidifying Christian Identity and Content

14

DAVID G. HORRELL

Introduction

HOW DID AN ORIGINALLY Jewish messianic movement come to be a separate religion with its own particular identity and beliefs? How did the identity and content of this new religious movement come to be specifically "Christian," a new and distinct category? Like the other key question about Christian origins—How and why did Christianity come to be the dominant religion in the Roman Empire?—the question of Christianity's separation from Judaism concerns a situation that was in place only after the New Testament period. Although the New Testament writings bear witness to varied degrees of tension between Christ-followers[1] and Jews, and to a developing sense of distinct identity, the schism was certainly not yet definite or complete for some time to come. Some scholars see the period between 70 and 135 C.E. as the key time for the "parting of the ways" and regard some of the later New Testament books (e.g., Matthew, John) as witnesses to the heightened polemic and sense of separation; others argue that the parting is only established some time after this, with the emergence of an authoritative rabbinic Judaism and a powerful "orthodox" Christianity (see Dunn 1991, 1992). We know from Justin Martyr (c. 100–c. 165 C.E.) of Jewish Christians in the second century who continued to follow the Jewish law (*Dial.* 47), and from later writers of the continued involvement of some Christians in the synagogues and of the various Jewish Christian groups that survived into the fourth or fifth century, eventually being marginalized and excluded from both the Christian and the Jewish sides (see Horrell 2000a). So the process of "becoming Christian," becoming something with a distinct and defined identity and content vis-à-vis Judaism, was hardly a swift singular process, and it can only be said to be completed after the period of earliest Christianity, reaching a culmination in the fourth and fifth centuries, with the classic formulations of Christian doctrine at the councils of Nicea (325 C.E.) and Chalcedon (451 C.E.). However, it is in the New Testament period that the foundations of this distinctively Christian identity and content are laid down; in this period of earliest Christianity one can trace the changes and developments that are crucial to the process of "becoming Christian." So here the focus is on the first century C.E. and primarily on the New Testament documents and the evidence they provide for the developing sense of Christian identity and of Christian doctrine and belief.[2]

Resources from the Social Sciences

So how can the social sciences help us to understand this crucial period of earliest Christian history, and specifically the development of Christian identity and content therein? Obviously there is an enormous range of studies, both theoretical and empirical, which could potentially be used to shed light on the subject. What follows is just one approach, using some mainly theoretical studies to construct a framework for understanding.

Structuration Theory

My first and most fundamental theoretical orientation concerns the essentially diachronic, or processual, nature of social life and social structure. In opposition to those traditions of social theory, notably functionalism, that take a synchronic view of social structure and institutions, theorists like Philip Abrams (1982) and Anthony Giddens (1979, 1982, 1984) insist that all sociohistorical analysis must be "an analysis of structuring situated in process in time" (Abrams 1982: xviii); "large-scale systems of social relations do not exist (and persist) independently of their reproduction by human subjects in the course of their daily lives" (Condor 1996: 291). Structure exists only as it is produced and reproduced in and through human action. It exists only in the "process of becoming"; "even apparently stable systems of social relations rely upon continuous social reproduction over time" (Condor 1996: 290). Social psychologist Henri Tajfel, to whose work we shall turn below, insisted that "social groups are not 'things'; they are processes" (1982: 485). Incidentally, this break with the synchrony/diachrony division implies the end of any meaningful distinction between history and sociology.[3]

Perhaps the fullest articulation of this approach to social theory is in Giddens's structuration theory (see Giddens 1979, 1982, 1984).[4] In this theoretical approach, Giddens seeks to transcend the division between action and structure and thus to resolve one of the fundamental problems of social theory. He does so with the conception of the "duality of structure." Giddens explains, "By the 'duality of structure' I refer to the essentially recursive character of social life: the structural properties of social systems are both medium and outcome of the practices that constitute those systems" (1982: 37). Social structure is thus analogous to the structure of language: the rules and resources of a language are simultaneously drawn upon *and* reproduced in the process of speaking or writing. Thus Giddens brings production, reproduction, and transformation to the heart of social theory (Ira Cohen 1987: 306). The central term "structuration" refers to a process, to "the structuring of social relations across time and space" (Giddens 1984: 376).

This theoretical focus on social life as process in time, and on the production, reproduction, and transformation that occur over time, is essential for the understanding of all social relations and structures, even those that are apparently stable. Yet it is especially crucial for the study of a group undergoing rapid change and development, as in the earliest period of Christian origins. Giddens's structuration theory encourages us to appreciate the extent to which the content of Christianity, and the Christian sense of identity, rooted in long-established Jewish traditions, are in *the process of becoming* and are formed and reformed as human agents draw upon the existing rules and resources available to them, simultaneously reproducing and transforming them.

Social Identity Theory

Identity has become something of a buzzword in recent social science and in studies of early Christianity. Yet the apparently simple notion proves to be somewhat slippery to define and use. This is largely because a person's identity comprises a multiplicity of factors, or even a multiplicity of identities, not all of which are relevant, or salient, in every situation (Blasi 1972). One cannot therefore speak simply of someone's "identity" but must rather consider what aspects of identity are being considered and why these are relevant in a particular context. Moreover, one must consider how any particular identity affects or defines other aspects of a person's identity and social conduct. Again this is not self-evident. A particular religious identity, for example, might have little apparent impact on certain other aspects of someone's sense of self, such as their ethnic, familial, or professional identities. Yet in certain circumstances a religious identity can affect, challenge, or redefine other aspects of identity that might in different circumstances be unaffected by that religious commitment. There may come a point at which, say, professional and religious commitments clash, such that a decision has to be made as to which identity will prove determinative; or there may arise a situation in which religious and national identities coalesce, such that religious difference comes to be seen as aligned with national or ethnic difference.

In dealing with the development of Christian identity, we are dealing with *social* as opposed to personal identity; that is to say, with identity based on belonging to a particular and defined *group*.[5] Henri Tajfel's definition of social identity makes this clear:

> social identity [is] . . . that *part* of an individual's self-concept which derives from his knowledge of his membership of a social group (or groups) together with the value and emotional significance attached to that membership . . . however rich and complex may be the individuals' view of themselves in relation to the surrounding world, social and physical, *some* aspects of that view are contributed by the membership of certain social groups or categories. Some of these memberships are more salient than others; and some may vary in salience in time and as a function of a variety of social situations. (1981: 255)

The work of Tajfel and his followers in developing social identity theory may therefore be helpful for understanding the development of Christian identity, as Philip Esler has already shown, in the most detailed application of Tajfel's ideas in New Testament studies to date (Esler 1998b, also 1996, 2000b).

Tajfel's interest in social identity and intergroup dynamics was born from his own life experiences as a European Jew who survived the horrors of World War II (see Tajfel 1981: 1ff.; Turner 1996: 2–4; Billig 1996). The fundamental issue driving his work was that of "the relations between social groups and their conflicts" (Tajfel 1982: xiii) and the question as to how and why, in certain circumstances, a person's attitudes and actions came to be defined on the basis of group membership and of distinctions between ingroup and outgroups.

Experiments carried out by Muzafer Sherif in the 1950s showed that simply categorizing people (boys in summer camps, in the early experiments) as members of one group or another led to an increase of friendships and bonds within the "ingroup" and, in certain situations, hostility toward "outgroup" members (Sherif 1956; Turner 1996: 14–16; Esler 1998b: 42). In other words, merely the sense of belonging to a particular group by itself may engender certain attitudes to those who, in relation to the group boundary, are categorized as insiders or outsiders. In this categorization process, two major principles emerged from Tajfel's research. These are "accentuation and assimilation: people tend to exaggerate the differences between categories and simultaneously minimize the differences within categories" (Brown 1996: 170). Members of the group are seen and described in ways that accentuate their similarities, the features that bind them together, while they are sharply distinguished from outsiders. This process may be referred to as a form of categorization, a process that leads to stereotyping, whether positive stereotyping (of group members) or negative stereotyping (of nonmembers) (see Hogg and Abrams 1988: 68–78).

Tajfel's social identity theory proposed that it was "a psychological requirement that groups provide their members with a positive social identity and that positive aspects of social identity were inherently comparative in nature, deriving from evaluative comparisons between social groups" (Turner 1996: 16; cf. Brown 1996: 179). Various strategies are available to groups and group members to enhance their own positive identity, ranging from leaving the group and joining another (where this is possible) to redefining or shifting the grounds of comparison between groups, so as to give the ingroup a positive identity vis-à-vis the outgroup(s) (see Esler 1998b: 49–55). Clearly, acting as a group or engaging in intergroup comparisons is most likely in a situation where there is "a widely shared belief that 'passing' to another group is undesirable, impossible or very difficult" (Tajfel 1982: 491).

In attempting to refine our understanding as to why intergroup comparisons develop in some situations and not in others, Hinkle and Brown have suggested that there are particular circumstances in which such comparisons are likely to become important for identity: one arises when the cultural setting is one in which collective, group-based achievements and ties are more prominent than individually based competition and achievement; another arises when a comparative ideology pervades the group or its wider context (Hinkle and Brown 1990: 65–68; see also Esler 1998b: 45–49). However, while these sets of circumstances clearly establish the kinds of general context in which intergroup comparisons may arise, there remains the interesting, and more specific, question as to why a *particular* group identity becomes prominent at a particular point in time: out of a range of possible categories and groups to which a person belongs, why is it *this* aspect of their multifaceted identity that becomes the basis for stereotyping and comparison? According to Brown, one from a number of categorical dimensions—race, gender, religion, etc.—tends to dominate in real-life situations, though "which category dimension will assume pre-eminence in any situation is very dependent on particular local circumstances" (Brown 1996: 172–73). Investigating and understanding these "local circumstances" is therefore crucial. What may be especially interesting to consider in the case of early Christianity is the issue as to the conditions under which the sense of a particular group identity develops and assumes predominance for its members. Situations of perceived threat, or of unclear boundaries, or of experienced hostility may all provide such conditions. In particular, it may be interesting to consider the role of conflict.

Conflict

Conflict is generally seen as something negative, something to be avoided, and indeed conflict can involve or lead to the most violent and destructive types of human interaction. It was the lasting contribution of Georg Simmel, in a classic 1908 work, to outline the ways in which conflict contributed to the formation and maintenance of forms of human sociation.[6] Simmel wrote of "the positive and integrating role of antagonism" (Simmel 1955: 18), "the collectivizing effect of conflict" (101), and "the socializing power of competition" (63). Groups, for example, often derive unity and strength from facing external (or internal) opposition: "Conflict may not only heighten the concentration of an existing unit, radically eliminating all elements which might blur the distinctness of its boundaries against the enemy; it may also bring persons and groups together which have otherwise nothing to do with each other" (98–99).

Simmel's groundbreaking work was taken up by Lewis Coser in *The Functions of Social Conflict* (1956), where Coser sets out a series of propositions concerning the characteristics and functions of conflict as outlined by Simmel. These include, for example, its group-binding and group-preserving functions, and the propositions holding that conflict with outgroups increases internal cohesion and creates associations and coalitions (cf. Deutsch 1973: 8–10).

> Far from being only a "negative" factor which "tears apart," social conflict may fulfil a number of determinate functions in groups and other interpersonal relations; it may, for example, contribute to the maintenance of group boundaries and prevent the withdrawal of members from a group. Commitment to the view that social conflict is necessarily destructive of the relationship within which it occurs leads . . . to highly deficient interpretations. (Coser 1956: 8)

Coser's work is formulated within a now largely discredited functionalist framework (cf. Giddens 1977: 96–134 and Horrell 1996a: 33–38) and so needs to be given a rather different theoretical context. As Jonathan Turner has pointed out, functionalism often implies an "illegitimate teleology," the notion that some aspect of social life (in this case conflict) comes about because of its consequences, described as its social function (Turner 1974: 21–27, 52, 72–73). Giddens's structuration theory, briefly outlined above, is explicitly and self-consciously a "non-functionalist manifesto" (Giddens 1979: 7) while at the same time incorporating what Giddens sees as the strength of functionalist approaches, namely their focus on the impact, the unintended consequences, of social activities. Where functionalism speaks of functions, structuration theory, with its insistence on reproduction and transformation through time, refers to the (often unintended) *consequences* of social activity that in turn become the (often unacknowledged) *conditions* of further activity (see Horrell 1996a: 49–50). Within a context of more adequate theoretical framework some of Coser's propositions, derived from Simmel, can help us consider the *impact* of conflict in the history of earliest Christianity. Both internal and external conflicts may arise for particular reasons based in "local circumstances" (and thus are *not* to be "explained" in terms of their social function) and may have an impact—a range of both intended and unintended consequences—on the development of Christian identity and content.[7]

With these various perspectives and questions in mind, I shall consider evidence concerning earliest Christianity in a diachronic manner to see how the process of "becoming Christian" took place. The evidence is, unfortunately, often fragmentary and incomplete, since our primary sources are the theologically committed writings of the early Christians, intended not for the purposes of historical reconstruction but to set down the stories of Jesus and to encourage and exhort the members of the early Christian communities.

From Jesus to the Earliest Church

A vast literature testifies to the difficulties in reconstructing from the gospel records a convincing picture of the historical Jesus.[8] Nevertheless, certain things may be said with confidence. Recent scholarship has, for example, taken on board something that should always have been clear: Jesus was a Jew (cf. Vermes 1983). Thinking, acting, and speaking within a thoroughly Jewish framework, Jesus announced the nearness of the reign of God. Whether this was meant in the sense of an imminent eschatology (the kingdom would soon be ushered in, in a dramatic intervention by God) or whether Jesus thought rather in terms of people taking on the yoke of the kingdom, following the ethics and practices of the kingdom in their lives, is much more open to debate. Whether Jesus saw himself as Messiah (Christ, the anointed one) or not is also highly disputed, but it is clear that he saw himself as having been called to some key role in proclaiming the reign of God and demonstrating that reign in acts of restoration and mercy to those marginalized by poverty, disease, and impurity. Jesus gathered a group of disciples around him and spoke specifically of a close circle of "twelve," probably symbolizing the twelve tribes of Israel (Sanders 1985: 98–106). They are referred to as disciples (*mathêtai*), called, quite literally, to follow Jesus (Mt 9.9; Mk 1.17; etc.) and sent out to announce the message of the kingdom (Mt 10.7; Lk 10.11).

Most prophetic and messianic movements at the time—and there were a number—died out once the central leader had been executed. The Jesus movement did not, however, disappear after the death of its leader. On the contrary, convinced and inspired by their belief in Jesus' resurrection, Jesus' disciples continued to meet in his name and to announce the message that God had made him Lord and Messiah (Acts 2.36).[9] Whatever their beliefs about Jesus during his lifetime, after his death and resurrection his followers were united by the conviction that he was Messiah/Christ and that God had called people to repentance and faith in him.

In terms of social identity, these earliest Christ-followers were Jews, members of Israel: they followed the customs and practices of their ancestral religion, going up to the Temple to pray at the set time (Acts 3.1), following Jewish food regulations (Acts 10.13–14), and so on. Yet they also had a distinct group identity within Judaism, which was itself a diverse and plural phenomenon in the years before 70 C.E., as followers of "the way" (Acts 9.2; 19.9, 23; 24.14, 22), members of the sect of the Nazarenes (Acts 24.5, cf. 24.14). These were probably among the earliest terms applied to the first Christ-followers. They met together as members of this messianic group, sharing fellowship in homes. Entry and membership in their group were marked by rituals that were rooted in the practices of the earthly Jesus: baptism (as Jesus himself was baptized by John: Mk 1.9) and what Luke calls the "breaking of bread" (Acts 2.42), a meal that imitated the Last Supper Jesus shared with his disciples. The content of the movement therefore had both doctrinal and practical aspects. The group was united in the conviction that Jesus is risen, is God's anointed Messiah, and this conviction marked them out from their fellow Jews. A distinctive group identity was also developed through the practical acts of initiation and solidarity: baptism and the Lord's Supper. These acts in themselves embodied central aspects of the group's faith. Baptism symbolized repentance, a turning from sin to obedience to God, and specifically a following in the way of Christ. The Lord's Supper reenacted the meal in which Jesus is recorded as giving meaning to his death, to the shedding of his blood and the giving of his body (Mk 14.22–24 and parallels; 1 Cor 11.23–25) and thus placed the self-giving death of Christ at the center of Christian belief.

According to the accounts, the conflict and opposition that brought about the death of Jesus led at first to the scattering of many of his followers (Mk 14.50). Yet not all dispersed. Some, we are told, met together despite their feelings of fear and uncertainty, thus retaining and even strengthening their sense of solidarity and group belonging (Lk 24.33–43; Jn 20.19). Resurrection appearances, to specific leading figures and to groups of believers (Mt 28.9; 1 Cor 15.4–8) convinced the group that Jesus was alive and led to the enthusiastic proclamation of this conviction despite opposition and external conflict.

Paul and the Beginnings of the Gentile Mission

A decisive moment in the history of earliest Christianity was brought about, at least in part, by conflict, both internal and external. After the rosy picture of Christian beginnings presented by Luke in Acts 1–4 (see Acts 2.41–47, 4.32–35), the ideal community suffered both from deceit (Acts 5.1–12) and internal division (Acts 6.1). The brief record of disagreement between the "Hebrews" and the "Hellenists" (Acts 6.1–6) has long been thought to be of considerable significance for understanding the spread and development of Christianity. It is widely agreed that the two groups or categories referred to here both comprise Jews who were members of the earliest Christian communities. The "Hebrews" were those Christian Jews who originated in Palestine, for whom Aramaic was their first language and who used the Scriptures in Hebrew. The "Hellenists," on the other hand, were Christian Jews of diaspora origin, whose first or main language was Greek, who used the Septuagint (the Greek translation of the Hebrew Scriptures), and who may have been unable to understand the readings and prayers in Aramaic-speaking synagogues (see Hengel 1983: 4–11; Hill 1992: 22–24). Martin Hengel suggests that the seven who are appointed to serve at tables in Acts 6.3 were in fact the leaders of the Hellenist grouping: Stephen, for example, causes controversy in a synagogue of diaspora Jews (Acts 6.8–15) and is recorded as giving a speech critical of his fellow Jews (Hengel 1983: 12–24).

Stephen's subsequent martyrdom marks the beginning, according to Luke, of a persecution against the church in Jerusalem, a case of external conflict (Acts 8.1). From the pieces of evidence available in Acts, it seems plausible that it was the Hellenists in particular who were targeted and scattered from Jerusalem (Hengel 1983: 13, though note the critique of Hill 1992). Whatever was the case, some of these early believers dispersed from Jerusalem and took the Christian message with them where they went. The particular sociohistorical significance of this move was probably twofold: first, the message about Christ came to be formulated in Greek, the *lingua franca* of the eastern Roman Empire (cf. Hengel 1983: x, 24); second, the message began to be shared with non-Jews, a step of enormous significance for the development of Christianity (Acts 11.19–20).

The conversion of non-Jews raised in a practical and forceful way the question of identity: What *are* these new converts? Of what group have they now become members? The message about Christ is presented as a thoroughly Jewish narrative, as a fulfillment of the Jewish Scriptures (cf. Acts 2.14–36; 7.2–53, etc.) and of the promises made by God to the people of Israel. Yet its central focus is Christ and the convictions about who he is; the message centers on the belief that "Christ died for us/for our sins" and that "God raised him from death" (1 Cor 15.3–4). These two convictions stand at the core of early Christian content. So when Gentiles accepted the message about Christ, what did they need to do? More specifically, what new identity, and what marks of that identity, did they need to take on? Clearly the content and marks of Christ-following identity are essential: faith in the risen Christ and initiation into the group of Christ-followers by baptism. Also essential, however, are central Jewish beliefs about the one God, the God of the Jewish Scriptures, who is believed to have acted in Christ, raised him from the dead, and exalted him as Lord. Hence the obvious question: Do these gentile converts need to become Jews? Is the implication of believing in Christ, joining the Messiah's people, that one must adopt the marks of Jewish identity?

This question was to cause division and argument in early Christianity for some time to come; different individuals, and different groups, argued for different answers. What was crucial at this early point in time, less than a decade after the crucifixion of Jesus, was that some early Christian missionaries, maybe some from among the so-called Hellenists, began to welcome gentile converts into the Christian movement *without their having to become full proselytes to Judaism.*[10] Luke records this significant innovation as having first happened in Antioch (Acts 11.20), where, interestingly, he also states that "the disciples were first called Christians" (11.26). This particular identity designation, discussed in more detail below, probably did not develop as early as Luke's account suggests.[11] But Antioch was clearly an important place for the development of a distinctively Christian identity, specifically in terms of the mixed community of Jews and Gentiles that met there, united by their commitment to Christ.

At this point it is time to introduce the figure of Paul, a character with enormous influence on the subsequent development of Christianity, and specifically on the development of Christian identity and content (see Horrell 2000b). We know that Paul, as a zealous Pharisee, persecuted the Christ-followers, until the point when he himself "saw" the risen Christ (1 Cor 9.1; 15.8) and became convinced of his calling by God to take the message of Christ to the Gentiles (Gal 1.15–16). Exactly what Paul did in the first years after his "conversion" is impossible to say for sure. It is often thought that he spent a period in relative isolation and inactivity ("for solitude to rethink his life"—Longenecker 1990: 34). Yet his testimony that he was threatened with arrest in Damascus (2 Cor 11.32–33) may suggest that Paul was doing something more controversial than solitary contemplation: perhaps announcing the news of Jesus' lordship (a potential cause of political controversy) and making gentile converts.

What is more certain is that Paul was attached for some years to the church at Antioch, operating along with Barnabas as a missionary sent out by the church (Acts 11.25–30, 13.1–3, 15.35). This link is significant since Antioch, as we have already seen, was one place where the Christian movement soon began to incorporate Gentiles as well as Jews. Paul saw himself called specifically to be an "apostle to the Gentiles" (Rom 11.13; cf. Gal 2.7), called to the task of spreading the Christian message among non-Jews throughout the Roman Empire.

Early on in his Christian career—though how early is debated, whether from his conversion or somewhat later—Paul came to the conviction that what the Christian message called for from Jewish and gentile converts was faith in Christ and, crucially, that the implication of this was that gentile converts should not adopt the marks of Jewish legal obedience and Jewish identity, specifically circumcision, food laws, and Sabbath observance (Gal 5.1–12; Rom 14.1–14; cf. Dunn 1990: 183–241). Moreover, this new commitment to Christ and its embodiment in communities of believers could for Paul require Jewish Christians to abandon aspects of their previous Jewish identity-defining conduct: by mixing freely with Gentiles in intimate table-fellowship and by abandoning Jewish food regulations they were now deemed to be living in a non-Jewish way (Gal 2.12–16; Holmberg 1998). Certainly Paul considered himself to have "died" to the law that once defined his identity and his conduct (Gal 2.19–20) and was now convinced that "in the Lord Jesus" all foods were clean (Rom 14.14).[12]

Once again conflict seems to have played a significant role in the formulation of these fundamental convictions. In his letter to the Galatians, a hot-tempered and pugnacious letter urging the Galatians not to be persuaded by those Jewish Christians who wanted all converts to be circumcised, Paul refers to a previous incident of conflict and disagreement within the Christian group at Antioch (Gal 2.11–14). The established practice of mixed table-fellowship between Jewish and gentile Christians had been challenged by Jewish Christians coming from James in Jerusalem. The Jewish believers, Peter included, had then withdrawn from this mixed fellowship. This action drew from Paul a public condemnation of Peter and, at least according to his account of the incident in Galatians, a clear presentation of the view that since both Jew and Gentile now based their belonging to God's people, their group identity, in Christ and not on the Jewish law, it was hypocritical and senseless for the Jewish Christians to separate themselves from their gentile brothers and sisters and thus effectively to compel those Gentiles to become Jewish. Indeed, to do so would be to empty the Christian message of its validity. This specific incident of inner-Christian conflict, James Dunn suggests, may have been a crucial moment for the formulation of this Pauline view (1990: 160–63), a view of such central importance for Paul's missionary message and for the development of Christian identity.

This Pauline view is crucial for the development of Christian identity precisely because it creates a group identity that is something new. By insisting that both Jewish and gentile believers find their basis for belonging in Christ and not the Jewish law, and by insisting that gentile believers must not adopt the marks of Jewish identity and legal observance (circumcision, etc.), Paul and other like-minded Christ-followers began the process of clearly demarcating this (Christian) group as something different, distinct from Judaism, a "third race," as some later writers would express it (see Horrell 2000c: 341 with note 65). Gentile converts do not become Jewish, and even Jewish believers may on occasion abandon aspects of their former practice. *Their common group identity is fundamentally defined by Christ and their faith in him.* Indeed, the group may be defined in Pauline terms as those "in

Christ" (*en Christô*). This phrase, and near equivalents like "in the Lord," appears very frequently in the Pauline letters, and is virtually unique to them in the New Testament.[13] To describe an individual (e.g., 2 Cor 12.2), or a group (e.g., Rom 12.5; 1 Cor 3.1) as "in Christ" is to articulate the core identity designation of the group, the boundary that defines insider and outsider (see further Horrell 2000c).

The new identity designation "in Christ" cuts across previous group designations and creates a new and wider group identity. Indeed, without of course using modern sociological language, this is more or less explicitly what the early Christians saw themselves doing. Several times in the Pauline letters we find a baptismal tradition, one which may well have been formulated at Antioch and learned there by Paul, which expresses precisely the sense in which a new unity and identity in Christ cuts across previous major group distinctions, those of race/religion, class, and gender:

> As many of you as were baptized into Christ have clothed yourselves with Christ. There is no longer Jew or Greek, there is no longer slave or free, there is no longer male and female; for all of you are one in Christ Jesus. (Gal 3.27–28; cf. 1 Cor 12.13; Col 3.11)

Just as baptism marks a person's initiation into this new social group, so the Lord's Supper demonstrates and affirms their membership in a group that regards itself as "one body": "we many are one body, for we all partake of the one bread" (1 Cor 10.17). The "body" is an image of the Christian community that Paul develops at length, specifying that this communal "body" is the body of Christ (1 Cor 12.27).

What is happening here is similar to one of the possibilities social identity theorists mention for the reduction of intergroup conflict: that through "recategorization" a new and broader identity transcends and encompasses identities that previously defined and divided separate groups (Brown 1996: 173–75; see further Esler 2000b). However, despite the scholarly tradition of contrasting Christian universalism with Jewish particularism (for a critique see Barclay 1997a), it should be clear that this new identity in Christ constructs a *new* boundary between insider and outsider, rather than transcending any such boundary altogether. The new community in Christ includes Jews and Gentiles, slaves and free persons, men and women, and unites them all; with a common identity in Christ they are brothers and sisters.[14] But the traditional Jewish distinctions between the righteous and sinners, between Jews and "the Gentiles" (*ta ethnê*), the latter being often seen as the repository of idolatry, sexual immorality, and general depravity (see, e.g., Ps 9.15–20, 14.1–7; 4 Ezr 3.28–36; Wis 12.19ff.), are retained but transferred to the distinction between those in Christ and those outside (see 1 Cor 6.9–11; 1 Thes 4.3–5).[15] There is a strong sense of "them" and "us," sometimes expressed in typically sectarian contrasts, as in I Thessalonians 5.5: "you are all children of light and children of the day; we are not of the night or of darkness." However, what *is* universal about the Christian message is its vision that all humanity might ultimately be incorporated within "in Christ" (Rom 5.12–21, 11.32; I Cor 15.22).[16]

So Paul plays a key role in developing a distinctive Christian identity. He never uses the term "Christian"—this probably developed somewhat later (see below)—but his label "in Christ," applied both to individuals and to the group, is functionally equivalent. However, while this group is thus new and distinct in identity from Judaism, Paul clearly claims the positive identity designations of the Jewish people for all who are in Christ. In other words, one of the ways in which Paul builds a positive social identity for members of his "in Christ" groups is by transferring to them the positive labels of Israel, the people of God: the identity designations of the parent community are claimed for the new grouping that is in the process of splitting off (see further Esler 1998b). Thus, for example, all in Christ are equally and without distinction descendants of Abraham (Gal 3.6–4.6, 21–31; cf. Rom 9.8; 2 Cor 11.22), inheritors of God's promise (Gal 3.29, 4.28) and children of the Jerusalem above (Gal 4.26). They are the "people of God" (cf. Rom 9.24–25; 2 Cor 6.16); the Scriptures were written for their instruction (Rom 15.4; I Cor 10.11); the Jewish patriarchs are their fathers (I Cor 10.1; cf. Rom 4.1). They are the ones who possess God's Spirit and who truly fulfill God's law, without living "under" it (Rom 6.14–15; 7.6; 8.1–4; Gal 5.13–26). And despite Paul's polemic against physical circumcision, he describes Christians as "the circumcision" (Phil 3.3; cf. Rom 2.28–29). Indeed, while the interpretation of the verse is disputed, it seems likely that in Galatians 6.16 Paul refers to the church as "the Israel of God" (cf. Gal 4.29; Rom 9.6–8),[17] an Israel whose identity and practice are redefined, reconfigured around Christ and not Torah (cf. Donaldson 1997).

This left Paul feeling acute anguish over what had become of the ethnic people of Israel, his own kinsfolk, to whom the gifts and promises of God irrevocably belonged (see Rom 9–11). His somewhat convoluted sense of the workings of God's purposes enabled him to hold the conviction that "all Israel" would indeed come to be saved (Rom 11.26) and that Israel's "hardening" served a purpose for a time. He would not take the later Christian route of simply declaring that the church had replaced Israel, but rather he held in tension his belief that those in Christ now constituted the people of God with his conviction that Israel was irrevocably the covenant people of God and would thus somehow be saved in the end.

Paul's position on the incorporation of both Jews and Gentiles into a people defined by their being in Christ, establishing a distinctive "Christian" identity, came to be adopted in the following centuries as the orthodox Christian view. However, at the time it was controversial and in conflict with other perspectives. It is clear from Paul's own writings that he came into conflict with Christians from Jerusalem, associates of Peter and James, who took a rather different line on the question of what gentile converts needed to do in order to be accepted into the people of God (Acts 15.1ff.; 2 Cor 11.12–23; Gal 2.1–3.6, 5.2–12). Some advocated full prose-lytism to Judaism, marked by circumcision, while others, James included (according to Acts 15.13–21), urged a minimum of regulations concerning foods and sexual morality, along with full Torah-observance for Jewish Christians (Acts 15.20, 29). The letter attributed to James may or may not come from this early period and from the hand of James himself; a majority of scholars judge it to have been written somewhat later, in the name of James but after his death (see Chester 1994: 12–15). But whatever its date, the letter clearly represents a form of Christianity different in key respects from Paul's. In James there is none of Paul's corporate Christology, the "in Christ" language. There is the Christian affirmation of Jesus as Lord and Christ (Jas 1.1, 2.1), but obedience to the whole Jewish law is also urged (Jas 1.25, 2.8–26, 4.11–12). Polemic against a position like that of Paul's may be implied in James 2.14–26, where, quoting some of the same texts crucial for Paul's case (Gn 15.6; see Rom 4.3), James stresses the need for works as an expression of faith. In short, the letter of James represents a form of early Jewish Christianity rather than the form of Gentile-including Christianity promulgated by Paul (see further Horrell 2000a). With the benefit of hindsight, it is clear to see that the Pauline position was—for better or worse—crucial to establishing Christianity's distinct identity, separate from that of Judaism.

The Passing of the First-Generation Leaders (c. 65–80 C.E.)

In terms used by the famous German sociologist Max Weber, Jesus himself was obviously the central charismatic leader of the Christian movement. But, while Jesus has no successor (Weber 1978: 1123, 1124), some of the key leaders of the first generation of Christian origins, "apostles" (e.g., James, Peter, and Paul), may also be said to be charismatic figures, exercising charismatic authority in the earliest churches (see Holmberg 1978: 150–55). The removal of these figures likely caused trauma and difficulty within the movement, or at least would have been a significant point of transition and development. This is especially so given that a number of these leaders were killed during a short period of time, a time, moreover, that was immediately followed by an external event of considerable significance. We know from Josephus of the killing of James, the brother of Jesus and leader of the Jerusalem church, in 62 C.E. (*Ant.* 20.200). Early Christian sources point to the execution of both Peter and Paul in Rome under Nero, shortly after the great fire of Rome in 64 C.E. (*1 Clem.* 5.2–7; Eusebius, *Hist. eccl.* 2.25.5). Then in 66 C.E. the Jewish revolt against Rome broke out in Palestine, a revolt that was to last for some eight years or so until the fall of Masada to the Romans in 73/74 C.E. A key event during this war was the fall of Jerusalem and the destruction of the Temple in 70 C.E. This event was naturally both profoundly traumatic and significant for Judaism and its subsequent evolution, and also of considerable influence on the development of Christianity. It no doubt fueled and legitimated Christian ideas about God's judgment on Israel for her failure to believe in Christ (cf. Mk 12.1–9; I Thes 2.14–16) and about the church as the new inheritor of Israel's status and identity (cf. Gal 3.29, 4.21–31; Heb 8.1–13; I Pt 2.9–10; *Ep. Barn.* 8.1ff., 14.1ff.).

So what developments took place during Christianity in this period, and what were their implications for the evolution of Christian identity and content? One significant development is that written Gospels began to appear. Certainly traditions about Jesus' life and teaching circulated and were preserved earlier, though when they first began to be recorded in written form is hard to say with confidence. But it is only in this period after the death of the key leaders of the first generation that the written Gospels as we now have them were put together. Mark's Gospel, widely regarded as the earliest of the written Gospels, is dated by many scholars some time in the period 65–75 C.E. (see, e.g., Hooker 1991: 8). The Christian tradition that Mark was "Peter's interpreter and wrote accurately all that he remembered, not, indeed, in order, of the things said or done by the Lord" (Eusebius, *Hist. eccl.* 3.39.15), whether or not it is historically accurate, indicates the impetus behind the writing of the Gospels as being, at least in part, to set down the knowledge of the apostolic generation. Naturally, this desire to record in written form the content of the key traditions of Christianity—the stories of Jesus—was likely to have been stimulated by the deaths of some of those key leaders and original disciples, notably Peter and James.

The significance of the first written gospel is not only that it sets down in written form the narratives about Jesus—though that is significant enough—but also that it does so in a narrative thoroughly infused with post-Easter Christian theology. Mark's Jesus is the Christ, the Son of God, who knows he must go to the cross to give his life for others and knows that he will rise again from the dead (see Mk 8.31; 9.9, 31; 10.32–34, 45). Moreover, the theology expressed by Mark in narrative form seems at least to some degree Pauline (see, e.g., Martin 1972: 161–62; Marcus 2000). Thus Mark's Gospel is significant for the development of Christian content in setting down a written record of the life of Jesus seen through the lens of Christian, specifically Pauline, theology.

The Pauline tradition also receives expression in Colossians and Ephesians, which probably date from this period. Many scholars regard these letters as post-Pauline compositions written in Paul's name some years after his death. The two letters clearly share some kind of relationship, since the content and structure of each is similar, with some material shared in common. One letter was probably based in part on the other, Ephesians most likely using Colossians. The letters share similarities in their theological and ethical teaching: they contain a high Christology, exalting Christ as the head of the church and the one in whom all the fullness of God dwells (Eph 1.22–23, 5.23; Col 1.18–19, 2.9–10, etc.); both contain a similar code of teaching addressed to the various members of the household (Col 3.18–4.1; Eph 5.21–6.9). Colossians addresses a specific situation and confronts the dangerous attractions of a rival philosophy, possibly a syncretistic blend of Jewish and pagan religious elements to which some readers were attracted (for the range of possibilities see Barclay 1997b: 37–55). Ephesians, on the other hand, is not apparently directed to any particular context or problem, and may have been originally intended as a circular letter. While both Colossians and Ephesians reveal developments and changes that occurred after Paul's time, they also represent a clear encapsulation of essentially Pauline theology. In both letters Christ is central as the one in whom God has wrought reconciliation and in whom Christians now live. In Colossians it is emphasized that through Christ God has reconciled to himself "all things, whether on earth or in heaven" (Col 1.20). Believers have "put on" a new nature in Christ, "where there is no longer Greek and Jew, circumcised and uncircumcised, barbarian, Scythian, slave, free, but Christ is all and in all" (Col 3.11). Ephesians emphasizes the reconciliation that has been brought about in Christ between Jew and Gentile. In a quintessential expression of Pauline theology the writer asserts that through the cross of Christ, God has broken down the dividing wall of hostility between Jew and Gentile, creating one new person, one body of people in Christ (Eph 2.14–16). These letters therefore strengthen and consolidate the Pauline contribution to the development of Christian identity and content, affirming the centrality of Christ, the rootedness of Christian identity in him, and the creation of one people from diverse social identities, which is the body of Christ.

It would be misleading to suggest that in this period Christianity develops in anything like a single direction or as a united group: there is, as we shall see in the following section, continuing diversity, disagreement, and division. Christian identity and content are correspondingly diverse. Nevertheless, significant developments do take place, not least within the stream of Christianity that would come to be central to the defined orthodoxy of later times. The deaths of key apostolic leaders and the events of the Jewish war were no doubt catalysts for some of these developments. With the passing of the first-generation leaders, especially those who had been disciples of Jesus, it is understandable that the "gospel" narrative was set down in written form, thus marking a significant step in the establishment of Christian content and tradition in textual form. Moreover, this form of biography of Jesus is also an expression of early Christian theology, which comes to be encapsulated within the historical records of the movement's origins. The key contribution of Paul to the formation of Christian identity is also strengthened in the two letters written in his name, probably during this period. In these letters the status and centrality of Christ are further emphasized and heightened, thus focusing "Christian" identity firmly upon him; and the constitution of the Christian group as a new unity encompassing formerly distinct groups, especially Jews and Gentiles, is further confirmed.

Defining Orthodoxy and Guarding Tradition (c. 80–100 C.E.)

A considerable number of the writings of the New Testament probably belong to this late first-century period of early Christianity, including the Gospels of Matthew, Luke, and John; Acts (Luke's second volume); the pastoral Epistles (1–2 Timothy and Titus); Hebrews; 1 and 2 Peter; Jude; and Revelation. These documents are diverse in both genre and theology and testify to the considerable diversity within the Christian movement at this time. Some of these writings, for example, seem to represent some form of Jewish Christianity, that is, a form of Christianity that recognized Jesus as Lord and Christ but that also practiced full adherence to the laws and customs of Judaism (see further Horrell 2000a). Matthew's Gospel apparently falls into this category: it is only in Matthew that Jesus is said to have come "not to destroy [the law and the prophets] but to fulfill them. . . . So whoever sets aside one of the least of these commandments and teaches others to do so will be called least in the kingdom of heaven. But whoever does them and teaches them will be called great in the kingdom of heaven" (Mt 5.17, 19). Other documents present a thoroughly Jewish picture of Christianity and Christian identity, but, like Paul, claim this Jewish heritage for a Gentile-including Christianity in which full observance of the Jewish law does not seem to be required. Into this category comes the letter to the Hebrews, which presents Christianity as the reality of which Judaism was merely the shadow, now obsolete and passing away (see Heb 8.13, 10.1–10, etc.), and the first letter attributed to Peter, which describes a largely gentile group of believers in terms drawn directly from the Jewish Scriptures: "you are a chosen people, a royal priesthood, a holy nation, a people for God's special possession" (1 Pt 2.9). Although their dating and authenticity are open to debate, there are a number of letters associated with the leading early apostles that may well date from this period: the pastoral Epistles attributed to Paul, the letters of Peter and of James, and the Johannine letters

(1-2-3 John). The Book of Revelation uses the distinctive style and symbolism of the apocalyptic genre.

Given this considerable diversity it is hard to generalize about the developing Christian movement, and generalizations that are offered can easily be misleading. Nevertheless, we can pick out some themes and developments relevant to the topic of Christian identity and content, to the process of "becoming Christian."

Developing Christian Identity

During this period, even in Jewish Christian writings like the Gospel of Matthew, we find an increasing sense of distance from and polemic against Judaism along with a high Christology. In Matthew, for example, there is an extended section of fierce polemic directed at the Pharisees (Mt 23). The historical scenario for this conflict is probably that of the post-70 situation, where the "survivors" of the Jewish war—the Christian sect of Judaism and the pharisaic-cum-rabbinic groups who would rebuild Judaism as rabbinic Judaism—battle to present themselves as the true heirs and interpreters of Judaism's traditions (see further Alexander 1992). For Matthew, it is Jesus, and not the Pharisees, who is the authentic interpreter of the law. Moreover, Matthew presents Jesus as far more than an interpreter of the law: he is Emmanuel, God with us (Mt 1.23), God's beloved Son, Messiah, and Lord (Mt 3.17, 7.21, 16.16, etc.). Commitment to Christ is clearly at the center of Matthew's faith and is expected to be a cause of hostility directed against Christ's followers. And, as Simmel's work on conflict suggests, this hostility seems to result in a greater sense of group identity, of being bound to, and identified by, the very name that is the cause of hostility and persecution: there are a number of references in the Gospels to suffering for "my name" (Mt 10.22, 24.9; Mk 13.13; Lk 21.12, 17; Jn 15.21), specified as "the name of Christ" in Mark 9.41.

In the Gospel of John the sense of hostility and separation from Judaism is even greater. Here Christian claims about Christ have reached the point of being regarded as blasphemous by Jews (cf. Jn 8.57–59) and have apparently resulted in the expulsion of Christians from the synagogues (see Jn 9.22, 34; 12.42; 16.2). We know of a curse upon heretics and Nazarenes (i.e., Christians, or at least Jewish Christians) as the twelfth of the eighteen benedictions used in synagogue liturgy. Scholars disagree as to how early this curse was likely to have been introduced, and in precisely what form (see van der Horst 1994), but something like it may well form something of the background to the situation John describes. An origin for the curse toward the end of the first century seems likely, while Justin Martyr, writing around 160 C.E., provides the strongest second-century evidence for such a custom (*Dial.* 47; Horbury 1998: 67–110).

The first letter of Peter is also addressed to Christians suffering hostility and antagonism, though in this case not apparently from Jews but from the Gentiles among whom they live. The letter is addressed to believers scattered throughout the Roman provinces of northern Asia Minor. These people are currently enduring a "fiery ordeal" because of "the name of Christ" that they bear, a similar phrase to that in Mark 9.41 (see I Pt 4.12–14). It is "the name of Christ" that most clearly defines the social identity of this group, and the hostility directed at them because of that name increases the salience of that aspect of their identity.

According to Larry Miller, the detachment of these Christians from their wider socioreligious context and their formation of a "voluntary utopian group" defined by their commitment to Christ constitutes a form of social protest that meets with reaction from the wider society, both its general populus and its ruling authorities (1999). The instruction contained in I Peter represents a response to this wider societal reaction, calling the letter's recipients both to a nonresistant reaction to their accusers (I Pt 2.1, 2.11–3.9) and yet also to a resistance to the attempt to impose conformity to what society demands: they are to remain committed to fearing God, to doing God's will (1.13–17; 3.13–17; 4.12-19).

Especially notable in I Peter is a single occurrence of the word *Christianos*, the Greek word—a Latinism—transliterated "Christian" (I Pt 4.16). This is one of only three appearances of this word in the New Testament, the other two coming in the Book of Acts (11.26; 26.28). It is important to stress, therefore, that this most well-known identity label was possibly unknown to, and certainly unused by, most of the New Testament writers, appearing only infrequently in two of the later writings of the New Testament.[18] The term *Christianos* most probably originated as a label used by hostile outsiders to denote members of the group of Christ-followers; indeed this seems to be implied in each of the New Testament occurrences. It identifies people as "partisans" or "supporters" of Christ, like the term "Herodians"—meaning partisans or supporters of Herod and his family (see Mt 22.16; Mk 3.6; 12.13)—and appears in Roman writers of the late first to early second century (Pliny, *Ep.* 10.96–97; Tacitus, *Ann.* 15.44; Suetonius, *Nero* 16; see Lüdemann 1989: 138; von Harnack 1905, 15–19). Yet this outsiders' label came to be adopted by the Christians themselves as the primary label designating their social identity, from the end of the first century onward, notably in the letters of Ignatius (very early second century: Ign., *Eph.* 11.2; Ign., *Magn.* 4.1; Ign. *Rom.* 3.2; note also *Did.* 12.4). Ignatius's writings clearly reveal this process of claiming an outsiders' label as a true and valued self-designation: "pray for me . . . that I may not only be called a Christian, but may also be found to be one" (Ign., *Rom.* 3.2); "it is right, then, not only to be called Christians, but also to be Christians" (Ign., *Magn.* 4.1). I Peter, most likely written sometime between 75 and 95 C.E. (Horrell 1998: 8–10), probably marks an important point in the history of this development. The suffering addressees of the letter are urged to avoid any behavior that might lead to them being accused of being a murderer, a thief, or other kind of criminal; but if they are accused of being a Christian, if this is the cause of their suffering, then they should "not be ashamed, but glorify God under that name" (I Pt 4.16). A label applied as an accusation, a cause for punishment, is to be worn with pride, even if suffering is the result. Thus what originates as a negative outsiders' label comes to be adopted as the proud self-designation of the members of the Christian movement.

All of this seems to bear out Simmel's notion, formalized as a proposition by Coser, that "conflict with out-groups increases internal cohesion" (Coser 1956: 87, cf. 38; Still 1999: 121). Because hostility and accusation from outsiders, whether Jews or Gentiles, focuses on the name of Christ, this increases the salience of this aspect of the insiders' shared social identity, increases the extent to which this aspect of their identity defines their commonality and sense of belonging together. The label "Christian" well illuminates this point: applied initially as a term of disdain by outsiders it comes to be the term that insiders proudly bear, the term that expresses what bound them together, the basic badge of group membership.

Fixing Content

Assuming Mark's to be the earliest gospel, it seems that other Christians were not content to leave Mark as the only written record of the Jesus traditions. Since Matthew and Luke evidently knew the Gospel of Mark, and John probably did too (or knew at least some material from the synoptic tradition), it is clear that these subsequent gospel writers sought to supplement, improve, correct, or reinterpret Mark's account. In part this may have been because they had access to material unknown to Mark—the source or sources known as Q—but it is also surely because they wished to present a different portrait of Jesus, to convey different theological emphases. Hence the gospel tradition finds greater diversity of expression in this period, though later writers would seek to reduce this diversity to a single harmonized account (Tatian's second-century *Diatessaron*, a harmony of the four Gospels, was widely used). These gospel accounts also bear some witness to the developing expressions of Christian faith, used in liturgical and ritual contexts. Matthew and Luke, for example, both include a version of the Lord's Prayer, which soon became established as a key Christian prayer (Mt 6.9–13; Lk 11.2–4). All the Gospels give some indications of the importance of the rites of baptism and Lord's Supper: the synoptics record Jesus' baptism (Mk 1.9 and parallels) and preserve the words and actions of Jesus at the Last Supper (Mk 14.22–25 and parallels; cf. I Cor 11.23–25). These narratives thus provide the content and meaning for the ongoing practice of the major Christian rituals. John's Gospel famously does not directly record Jesus' baptism (compare Jn 1.29–34 and Mk 1.9–11), nor does it include a narrative of the Last Supper. Nevertheless, the baptismal and eucharistic imagery in the gospel seem to indicate that for this evangelist too these rituals were an established part of early Christian practice (cf. Jn 3.5, 6.32–58, 13.6–11). A most striking example of a concise liturgical formula is found at the close of Matthew's Gospel, where the risen Jesus commands his disciples to "make disciples of all the nations, baptizing them in the name of the Father and of the Son and of the Holy Spirit" (Mt 28.19). This specific trinitarian formula is found nowhere else in the New Testament and like the term "Christian" represents a late development in the New Testament period. But it is a formula that became central to the content of Christianity, expressing the trinitarian understanding of God that developed out of, but was hardly found as such within, the earliest Christian writings.

The pastoral Epistles, written in Paul's name but reflecting the situation of second- or third-generation Christianity around the end of the first century, exhibit a clear desire to preserve sound teaching, to "guard the deposit" (I Tm 6.20; 2 Tm 1.14) of apostolic doctrine. This concern arises from both the passing of the apostolic generation and the variety of interpretations of the apostolic heritage, which call for the "orthodox" to be distinguished from the "heretical." These letters focus a good deal on the need for "right" conduct among members of the Christian congregations, essentially meaning behavior that is decent and socially respectable according to the standards of the time. Slaves are to be obedient and submissive; women are to be silent and subject to their husbands; church leaders are to govern their own households well, keeping their children in order (see I Tm 2.8–3.12, 6.1–2; Ti 1.6–9, 2.2–10). The pastoral Epistles therefore share with other letters in the later Pauline tradition a broadly conservative social ethic that may in part be a reaction to hostility and conflict with outsiders and to the realization that the "End," the final day of the Lord, was not going to come as quickly as earlier expected (cf. Col 3.18–4.1; Eph 5.21–6.9; 1 Pt 2.18–3.7; 2 Pt 3.8–10). Conflict with outsiders could perhaps be lessened if Christians ensured that they conformed as far as possible to standards of "decent" behavior. At least if they were then the objects of hostility, it would be for the name of Christ alone and not for any other reason (cf. I Pt 4.12–16).

The pastoral Epistles contain a number of passages that encapsulate Christian faith in concise creedal statements. These probably represent traditional, preformed material, included in the letter by the author and known from the context of Christian worship. Some such creedal formulae, christological hymns, etc., are found in the early Pauline letters too (see, e.g., 1 Cor 8.6, 15.3–5; Phil 2.5–11; Col 1.15–20) but there appears to be a greater concentration of such preformed and creedal material in these later letters (cf. Ellis 2000: 310). These formulaic sections are an important aspect of the establishment of solid Christian content: they express in concise and memorable ways the basic core of "the faith" and can be repeated in church meetings as shared declarations of the heart of the Christian message. Probably the best example is in I Timothy 3.16, where a few short and rhythmic lines encapsulate the story of Christ: "Without any doubt, the mystery of our religion is great: He was revealed in flesh, vindicated in spirit, seen by angels, proclaimed among Gentiles, believed in throughout the world, taken up in glory." Other examples may be found in I Timothy 1.17, 2.4–6, 6.15–16; 2 Timothy 1.9–10, 2.11–13; and Titus 3.4–8.

Also highly significant for the establishment of defined Christian content are the few indications in the later New Testament letters concerning the emerging status of earlier Christian writings. For the early Christians "the Scriptures" means the Jewish Scriptures: the Hebrew Bible and its Greek translation, the Septuagint, though the boundaries of the Jewish Scriptures were not firmly fixed until probably late in the first century. But toward the end of the New Testament period we find some evidence to suggest that the process of elevating early Christian writings to the status of scripture had begun. In I Timothy 5.18, in a passage explaining why Christian leaders ("elders") are worthy of support from the church, we find the following scriptural justifications: "for the scripture says, 'You shall not muzzle an ox while it is treading out the grain', and, 'The laborer deserves to be paid.'" The first of these "scriptural" quotations comes from the Book of Deuteronomy (25.4). The second, however, comes from the gospel tradition (Lk 10.7; cf. Mt 10.10). Yet it seems to be quoted as Scripture alongside the citation from Deuteronomy. And in 2 Peter (where, incidentally, the gospel tradition is again quoted: 2 Pt 1.17–18), the letters of Paul are apparently ranked with "the rest of the scriptures" (2 Pt 3.16). What these two references show is that a crucial process in the fixing of Christian content had begun, namely the process whereby certain early Christian writings were regarded as authoritative and canonical, to be reckoned as part of "the Scriptures." This process would ultimately lead, of course, to the formation of "the New Testament," with the Jewish Scriptures taking their place within the Christian Bible as "the Old Testament." Deciding *which* early Christian writings should be accorded this authoritative status took some considerable time, and for the first few centuries of Christian origins a number of writings were disputed as to their status and authority (see Gamble 1985 and Metzger 1987). Some of these disputed writings eventually made it into the canon (e.g., 2 Pt); others did not (e.g., *1 Clement*).[19]

These steps toward the fixing of Christian content, both in concise creedal statements and in treating certain early Christian writings as Scripture, should not be taken to indicate that the movement was anything like united around this solidifying core material. In fact, the impetus for "guarding the deposit," establishing orthodox and authoritative statements and documents, probably came in some considerable part from the sheer diversity within early Christianity. Those who regarded themselves as guardians of the apostolic tradition saw other strands and versions of the faith as dangerous and heretical and thus sought to establish the content of the faith so as to make clear what was sound and what was not (see, e.g., I Tm 4.1–16, 6.2–21, etc.). The succeeding centuries would witness continuing diversity within the Christian movement, with a wide variety of Jewish Christian groups, Gnostic groups, etc., and energetic "anti-heretical" activity on the part of Christians who regarded themselves as representatives of orthodoxy (e.g., Irenaeus, Epiphanius). The eventual triumph of what came to be defined as orthodoxy may have as much to do with social and political power as with the niceties of theological argument: "the Roman government finally came to recognise that the Christianity ecclesiastically organised from Rome was flesh of its flesh, came to unite with it, and thereby enabled it to achieve ultimate victory over unbelievers and heretics" (Bauer 1972: 232).

Conclusions

This sketch of developments in early Christian identity and content has assumed that these phenomena can only adequately be studied and understood as part of an ongoing process. Like all social institutions and structures they are continually in the process of production, reproduction, and transformation, in the process of becoming, and never "arrive" or reach a point where one can say that development "stops." The structuring of the Christian movement is a process situated in time.

Identity

This early period of Christian origins is clearly the crucial period for the development of a distinctively "Christian" identity. Initially there is a group of disciples, followers of the earthly Jesus, who become a group of messianic Jews, convinced that the risen Jesus is God's anointed one, the Messiah. They are known as members of the sect of the Nazarene (after Jesus of Nazareth), followers of "the way." Before long the movement expands to include Gentiles as well as Jews, and key steps in the formation of a new identity are taken. Particularly under Paul's influence, these groups of Jews and Gentiles find their common social identity not in the marks of Jewish belonging—which gentile converts do not adopt—but by being "in Christ," a faith-commitment enacted and embodied in baptism. Yet even this new social identity is rooted in the past, not only because the very notion of the "Christ" is a Jewish one but also because the positive social identity of the "in-Christ" group is based on the claim that it now possesses the special status of Israel: sons of Abraham, inheritors of God's promises, God's special people, etc.

This attempt to develop a positive social identity is comparative in nature, as Tajfel suggests such positive identities are, since the claim to be the *true* people of God, the *real* circumcision, those who fulfill the law in the Spirit's power, and so on, is a claim that contains within it the implication that the other group that claims to hold this status is misguided and has failed.[20] (The question of the extent to which "Christian" identity is rooted in a claim to possess Israel's inheritance in a way that implicitly denies that inheritance to the Jews raises profound problems, much discussed in recent years.)[21]

This new group identity "in Christ" provides a social identity that cuts across and encompasses previous social identity distinctions (Gal 3.28). Yet at the same time it establishes a new boundary between insider and outsider, a boundary that in ideological terms owes much to its Jewish roots, built upon the contrast between the idolatry and depravity outside the group and the holiness and righteousness within. This boundary rhetoric may certainly be seen in terms of Tajfel's two principles of accentuation and assimilation, heightening the sense of distinction between ingroup and outgroup members while minimizing the distinctions among group members. Those inside are holy, righteous, brothers and sisters, children of light, while those outside are unrighteous, unbelievers, destined for destruction—stark examples of forms of stereotyping.

Hostility from outsiders, both Jews and Gentiles, focused on the Christian confession of Christ, though Jews and Gentiles would clearly have had different reasons for finding the confession offensive. This had the presumably unintended consequence of heightening the salience of this aspect of a Christian's complex social identity, increasing the extent to which this factor bound the group together and distinguished them from outsiders. Indeed, the distinctive name "Christian" emerges from the context of hostility, initially voiced as an accusation by outsiders, then proudly claimed by ingroup members and eventually coming to serve as the fundamental group-designator.

Content

The content of Christianity is thoroughly Jewish, though also innovative and distinctive. A basic Christian claim, from the start, is that what God has done in Jesus is a fulfillment of the message of the law and the prophets, the fulfillment of God's promises to his people. As well as essentially claiming for itself the identity of Israel, Christianity therefore claims as its own the content of Judaism, specifically the Jewish Scriptures, although this of course involves considerable reinterpretation (cf. Gal 3.16), for example, spiritualizing the idea of circumcision (Rom 2.28–29; Phil 3.2–4) and portraying the Jewish sacrificial system as but a foreshadowing of the once-for-all sacrifice offered by Christ (Heb 10.1–25). But specifically Christian content develops, based on the conviction that Jesus of Nazareth is God's Messiah, the Christ. The core of Christian content concerns his death and resurrection, expressed in phrases like "he died for us" and "God raised him from the dead." Over time, hymns and creedal confessions develop that encapsulate concisely Christian beliefs about Christ and his redeeming work. Paul's letters are the earliest Christian writings that we possess, the written Gospels emerging after the deaths of the apostles of the first generation. Toward the end of the New Testament period we see the beginnings of the process in which these early Christian writings came to be regarded as Scripture, ranked alongside the Jewish Scriptures, which the Christians already possessed and used as their "bible." Thus it comes to be, after much subsequent disagreement and deliberation, that a body of Christian writings, along with the Jewish Scriptures, are together regarded as containing the authoritative content of Christianity.

Yet along with these written texts and oral confessions of faith, it is important to remember the role of ritual in confirming Christian identity and communicating Christian content. Baptism and Lord's Supper, the two central Christian rituals, celebrated from the earliest days, their varied interpretations notwithstanding, both dramatize and embody key dimensions of Christian faith (see further Meeks 1983: 150–62). Baptism marks the transition from outsider to ingroup member, the transfer from the sinful world to the holy group, the moment when the convert is clothed with Christ and incorporated into him. The Lord's Supper recalls the central narrative about "the Lord Jesus, on the night he was betrayed" and places the self-giving death of Christ at the center of Christian worship. It also serves to affirm the oneness of the members of the group, their common belonging to the body of Christ (1 Cor 10.16–17).

Conflict

At many points in the story of the evolution of Christian identity and content, conflict, both internal and external, appears to play a crucial role in stimulating important developments. Internal conflicts seem on a number of occasions to have been a catalyst for the development of new views, or at least for the forceful articulation of views that prove to be of considerable significance (Gal 2.11–21, etc.). The sense of threat from "heretics" within is part of the motivation for making sure that sound teaching is preserved and set down.

External conflict in the form of hostility, accusation, and ostracism has the (presumably unintended) consequence of developing the group's sense of shared identity by focusing attention on the aspect of identity that unites this group in distinction from outsiders: the name of Christ. In other words, external conflict seems to play a significant role in making the "Christian" part of a person's identity especially prominent, or salient. Without such external opposition to those who confessed the name of Christ, it might have been possible for this aspect of a person's identity to assume a somewhat lower profile. Indeed, at some times and in some places, "Christian" believers were probably rather less sharply distinguished from others, especially Jews, the identity group within which Christianity arose. It seems to have been precisely the times of conflict and hostility that were key moments for the development of distinctive Christian identity.

While conflict does of course have its negative aspects, not least for those facing its pressures, it does seem then that the story of early Christianity bears out Simmel's thesis that conflict plays a significant role in the formation of groups and in the cultivation of group identity. It is through a process riven with conflict and opposition—both internal and external to the Christian movement—that the process of "becoming Christian" occurs.

Notes

1. The term "Christian" appears only rarely in the New Testament and does not emerge as a self-designation until around the end of the first century (see below). The term can anachronistically imply the end of the process of identity-formation that is precisely what we need to study in its emergence; it is therefore perhaps best to avoid using this term as a label for the earliest adherents of the movement. See further Esler (1998b: 3, 44), from whom the term "Christ-follower" is taken—though this label too is a neologism rather than an ancient description.

2. I shall adopt broadly standard views of the dating and authorship of the New Testament writings, though these views are, of course, by no means undisputed. For discussions of the introductory issues of date, authorship, etc., see Schnelle (1998), Johnson (1999), and Brown (1997).

3. So Giddens (1979: 230; 1984: 355ff.), Abrams (1982: x–xi, xviii, 17, 200–201). On this issue see further Horrell (1996a: 26–31).

4. For further detail on structuration theory and its application to New Testament studies see Horrell (1995, 1996a).

5. Tajfel and Turner define a group as follows: "a collection of individuals who perceive themselves to be members of the same social category, share some emotional involvement in this common definition of themselves, and achieve some degree of social consensus about the evaluation of their group and of their membership in it" (quoted in Turner and Bourhis 1996: 30).

6. Subsequent work in the field of social psychology has, without denying the positive consequences of conflict, tended to focus, inter alia, on the differences between destructive and constructive conflict, and on strategies of conflict management and resolution (see Deutsch 1973 and Rubin and Levinger 1995).

7. See also Still (1999: 107–24), for an overview of the social scientific study of intergroup conflict and a valuable list of the range of "potential outcomes of social conflict on groups thus engaged" (120).

8. For accessible overviews of recent debate see Witherington (1995b) and Powell (1998).

9. I Corinthians 16.22 shows that the acclamation of Jesus as Lord goes back to the early Aramaic-speaking believers.

10. Hengel and Schwemer date the beginning of the mission of the "Hellenists" in Antioch to c. 36/37 C.E. (1997: xi). They stress the importance of the Hellenists to the early Christian mission, but also emphasize both that this gentile mission is not strictly pre-Pauline (1997: 31–34, 208, 281, etc.), since Paul was converted in c. 33 C.E., and that Paul was crucial in establishing and justifying theologically the gentile mission (309).

11. Though for a recent argument that the term *Christianos* was coined in Antioch (by the Roman authorities) as early as 39–40 C.E., see Taylor (1994).

12. On all this, see further Horrell (2000c).

13. Deissmann (1926: 140) famously drew attention to the importance of this phrase, and similar equivalents, for Paul; he counted some 164 occurrences. The other occurrences in the NT are in I Peter (3.16; 5.10; 5.14), and may well be due to the influence of Pauline language upon that letter.

14. On the frequency and usage of this sibling-language in the Pauline letters, see Horrell (2001a).

15. Note also Romans 1.19–32 and 3.9–20, where Paul draws on Wisdom 13–15 and on other scriptural texts (mostly from the Psalms) to depict the sinfulness of all humanity, Jew and Gentile alike.

16. On this universal vision and its positive and negative contemporary implications see the stimulating discussion by Boyarin (1994).

17. For arguments in favor of this interpretation, see, e.g., Dahl (1950), Barclay (1988: 98), and Longenecker (1990: 298–99).

18. Taylor (1994) argues for an early date of origin for the term (39–40 C.E. in Antioch), seeing it as a label attached by Roman authorities to the followers of the Messiah who had stimulated Jewish protests in the city. However, the evidence to support the argument is not strong, and the absence of the label from so much of the New Testament is harder to explain if it was coined so early (and the *Didache* is unlikely to have been written as early as Taylor suggests [50–70 C.E.; 1994: 77]. A date in the late first or early second century is more widely accepted).

19. See Ehrman (1998) for an accessible collection of all the Christian writings, canonical and non-canonical, from the first century of Christian origins.

20. Passages from various New Testament texts that express this comparative idea include John 8.31–59; Acts 13.16–52; 2 Corinthians 3.4–18; Galatians 4.21–31; Philippians 3.2–3; and Hebrews 8.1–13.

21. Among many works that could be mentioned, see Gager (1983) and Boyarin (1994).

Sociological Insights into the Development of Christian Leadership Roles and Community Formation

15

HOWARD CLARK KEE

ENTRAL FOR HISTORICAL UNDERSTANDING of the development of leadership roles and community organization in early Christianity, as well as for analysis of early Christian religious beliefs, ethics, and ritual, are the insights that have come from sociology. The mistaken notion that Judaism was the religion of the community, while Christianity was the religion of the individual,[1] has been effectively discredited by those who have noted the importance within the New Testament of redefining the covenant community, and hence have brought sociological insights to bear on the available evidence concerning the origins and early development of Christianity. Some of those who view Christianity in terms of primarily individual experience have turned to psychology as an aid in understanding this religion. But responsible scholarship has shown instead that from the outset Jesus and his followers were promoting a new understanding of the ground of participating in the covenant people that combined features that in some ways matched but in important ways differed from perceptions of the community of faith fostered in Judaism at the turn of the eras. There resulted therefore within early Christianity new, multiple social definitions for the covenant community, involving different criteria for membership, leadership, stance toward both Jewish and Greco-Roman cultural modes, and perceiving the destiny of humanity and of the world. Discernment of these new insights by contemporary historians has been much aided by features of sociological theory and analysis.[2]

Shared Convictions and Modes of Community Identity

Concurrent with recognition and historical analysis of the development of social structure and leadership roles in early Christianity has been the contribution to perceiving these features from perspectives provided by sociology of knowledge,

338 HOWARD CLARK KEE

which has shown how—in all of history and the diversity of human cultures—the shared assumptions of a community are determinative of its values, historical understanding, and sense of destiny.[3] There were, however, not only certain common features shared by the early Christian communities as a whole, but also significant differences among them with regard to specific beliefs, leadership, and group practices. The mix of common and divergent features is sketched below, drawing on insights from sociology.

Focusing on the theme of the group mode of existence of the early Christians, one must note the centrality of their belief that they were not simply divinely redeemed individuals but that they now constituted a community of God's people—the people of the new covenant. This is attested in both the gospel traditions and in the letters of Paul, and found basic expression, for example, in their eucharistic rite. Thus at the Last Supper with his disciples Jesus explained to them that the bread and wine that they shared were to be perceived as "the blood of the covenant" (Mk 14.22–24; Mt 26.28) or as constituting "the new covenant in my blood" (Lk 22.20; I Cor 11.25). The significance of such participation is not merely a personal, individual experience of access to the divine but a symbol of their sharing in the life of the new covenant people. This is seen by them as the fulfillment of the promise of God through the prophet Jeremiah: "I will make a new covenant with the house of Israel and the house Judah" (Jer 31.31). Unlike the earlier covenant with those whom God brought out of Egypt and to whom was given the Law at Mount Sinai—which they broke—this covenant will be based on the law that God will "put . . . within them" and "will write on their hearts." Thus according to Jeremiah, they now will know God in a personal way, will be his people, will experience the forgiveness of sins, and will have personal knowledge of his will (Jer 31.22–34). It is precisely these social factors that are to be seen as operative within the life of the members of the new covenant people founded by and through Jesus, as developed and articulated by the writers of the New Testament.

This conviction of sharing in the new life is also evident in other ways in the various gospel traditions, where there are frequent portrayals of God's new people as a group, rather than their being addressed simply as individuals. That his followers are to experience a new group identity is clear in the parables of Jesus—for example in the parables of the Sower, the Weeds, the Net, the Lost Sheep, the Marriage Feast, the Laborers in the Vineyard, the Ten Maidens, and the Last Judgement, all of which depict the new people of God through images of groups and group relationships. Also, in the Gospel of John Jesus describes the people of God in a variety of inclusive group images: (I) his friendly encounter with the woman from Samaria, who is a member of a religious group (the Samaritans) that had its own temple and priesthood on Mount Gerizim, and its own version of the

Scriptures, and hence was viewed by Jews as alien from the covenant; (2) his designation of himself as the Bread from Heaven, the Light of the World, the Good Shepherd, the Vine joined with his followers, who are the Branches. All of these reports of Jesus' teaching promise to those who respond in faith participation in a new group of God's people. The images and prophetic predictions concerning the new covenant people build largely on traditions from the Jewish Scriptures. A radical difference between the new community and the Israelite understanding of their role as God's people, however, lies in the fact that in the Old Testament there are instructions to the people that they are to have no dealings with people from the other nations. They are to avoid agreements or intermarriage with non-Israelites and are to seek to destroy the places and instruments for worship of other gods. God's love for Israel is the sole basis for their deliverance from slavery, their preservation, and settlement in their new land (Dt 7.1–9). Central is the maintenance of their special social identity. Thus it is a radical redefining of this tradition of group relationship with God that is a central feature of the New Testament. Such social factors as ethnic identity, mode of occupation or religious tradition, and even moral status in no way preclude sharing in the life of the new covenant people as seen in the New Testament and other early Christian writings.

Insights from the Sociologists

The early twentieth-century insights of Max Weber (1864–1920) have had a wide and enduring impact on the study of religion, and especially on the history of Christianity. The title of a collection of his essays in English translation highlights the major feature of his sociological analysis: *On Charisma and Institution Building* (1970). This insight, which is noted by the editor of that volume, S. N. Eisenstadt, in the introduction, makes the historical point that religious movements begin on the level of personal challenge, insight, and commitment under the spiritual power of what is known in this tradition as *charisma*. But they soon begin to take on a more stable and social form as a group of those convinced by these religious claims join to give structure, leadership, and definition to their movement. The issues Weber dealt with concerned these social processes going on historically within a wide range of societies and cultural contexts, especially with the changing modes of leadership. These insights set the pattern for sociological study of religions, especially Judaism and the origins of Christianity.

A more recent analysis of the engagement of sociology with religion has been offered by Thomas F. O'Dea's *Sociology and the Study of Religion*, in the final sections where he deals with "Sociology of Religion: Sociological Theory" and especially with "Sociology and the Study of Religion" (1970: 201–91). O'Dea defines sociology as "the disciplined and systematic study of . . . social structure and social process both in itself and in relation to individual motivation and the ideas and values of the culture" (201). He describes two theoretical modes of functional sociological analysis: (1) seeing societies as social systems that seek stabilization on the basis of a normative consensus and (2) seeing culture as more or less a systematic body of knowledge, traditions, and beliefs that provide an orientation to the participants in terms of both cognition and evaluation (203–13). He perceives the religious traditions as developing in terms of three features: worship, intellectual expressions of beliefs and rules, and the organization of community and leadership (213–14). He summarizes the agenda of sociology of religion as

> the empirical study of the expression of religious experience, religious conceptions, and religious attitudes in the formation and emergence of social relationships, both in terms of the particular forms of religious groups, and beyond their confines, in more secular social institutions and relations, including the reverse influence of social forms (religious and secular) on religious expression and attitude, and belief. (232)

Hence O'Dea sees as essential "a constant dialogue between these disciplines" of religion and sociology (232). Thus for those who perceive and experience this new shared life there is involvement in features of human life and practice that have been discerned and described by sociologists and sociologically focused historians during the last two centuries.

Insights from Sociology of Knowledge

The sociological specialty that has best illuminated and helped to define the convictions shared by members of a religious community is Sociology of Knowledge. This theoretical method developed through the insights of linguistic scholars, such as Ludwig Wittgenstein's study of aphorisms (1969), and historians of the natural sciences—especially Thomas S. Kuhn (1970). Wittgenstein saw language as a form of life—a "language game" that operated on the basis of assumptions and that shapes rules, description of objects, reporting of events, and communication of everything from jokes to prayers. Thus the language of religious experience and communication "cannot be purely private, but is part of a shared public tradition and gains intelligibility because it is anchored in a public history shared by a community" (in Kee 1989: 17). The implications of this perception for historical writing have been drawn out by David Bloor, who contrasts the simplistic notion that words have timeless meaning with the importance of observing that the linguistic conventions used by historians and other writers embody meanings that are "relative to the social setting [of the author] rather than to timeless conceptual models." When changes in meaning occur or conflicts in interpretation of traditions appear we must locate these rival groups and "track down the causes of rivalry," just as we must "try to explain continuities and alliances" between those engaged in appropriation and promulgation of the tradition (quoted in Kee 1989: 18).

In his sociologically oriented *The Interpretation of Cultures*, anthropologist Clifford Geertz has defined culture as "a historically transmitted pattern of meaning embodied in symbols, a system of inherited conceptions expressed in symbolic forms by means of which humans communicate, perpetuate, and develop their knowledge about and attitudes toward life." What symbols do is "to synthesize a people's ethos—the tone, character and quality of life, its moral and aesthetic style and mode—and their worldview—the picture they have of the way things in sheer actuality are, their most comprehensive ideas of order" (1973: 89, 118, 125). Thus the stories that are transmitted in a culture about its origins, the problems of evil, the evidence of divine purpose and power, as well as the rules by which the community is to live and the aims and purpose to which its members are to be devoted, are constitutive of its ongoing existence and its view of the future. It is precisely these features that are evident in the early Christian writings, beginning with the New Testament and continuing into the early centuries C.E. And it is awareness and analysis of them—aided by insights from sociology—that are essential for the responsible study of religious traditions, including those of Christian origins.

Defining Social Identity

One of the norms that was basic for the survival and continuity of the early Christian communities was a common declaration by the members as to their beliefs and expectations about what God had done, was doing, and was going to do to create the new covenant people that they were persuaded Jesus and his followers had launched. The issue of how the people of God were to be defined was a central feature in Judaism in the Roman period, and was treated in a range of ways by the early Christians as well.

Beginning with the apostle Paul, the early Christians produced writings that incorporated statements or reports of the basic beliefs of the community about what God was doing through Jesus for the renewal of his people. The earliest of the testaments were not creeds but summary forms of what was preached or proclaimed about God's purpose at work through Jesus for the group's renewal. The scholarly designation for these is *kerygma*, "proclamation." A prime example of what Paul "proclaimed" appears in I Corinthians, where he reports what had been transmitted to him:

> I delivered to you as of first importance what I also received: that Christ died for
> our sin according to the scriptures, that he was buried, that he was raised again on
> the third day in accordance with the scriptures, and that he appeared to Cephas

[Peter], then to the twelve [other disciples], then to more than five hundred brethren . . . then to James and all the apostles. . . . Last of all . . . he appeared also to me. (15.3–8)

Similarly, in the opening lines of Romans, Paul summarizes the message that he preaches: "the gospel concerning [God's] Son, who was descended from David according to the flesh and designated Son of God in power according to the Spirit of Holiness by his resurrection from the dead: Jesus Christ our Lord" (1.3–5). Paul sees that this message and its meaning are to be proclaimed by those who have been divinely chosen and commissioned as apostles in order "to bring about the obedience of faith for the sake of his name among all the nations."

These features manifest the basic convictions of the new community, but when they are set forth in the Gospels and other New Testament writings, they are linked with, and demonstrated through detailed accounts of Jesus' life, including the miracles attributed to him; his confrontations with the religious and civil authorities, as well as the content and import of his teachings about God and how God's people are to live and serve God; and his execution by the Roman authorities and his resurrection from the dead, with indications of the significance of these events for the community of faith. The diversity of ways in which these features were perceived and described in the Gospels discloses not merely different theological concepts, but also—and most importantly—a range of social structures and community definitions among the early Christians beginning in the first century C.E.

The features by which these communities diverged socially from their contemporaries are evident in the range of answers they offered to the following basic questions: How was one to become a member of the new community? What was the perception of the role of Jesus in making possible participation in the new community? What were the guidelines by which the members were to live—in relation both to other members but also to the wider world? To what extent was there correspondence between their insights and those in other religious traditions—both Jewish and Greco-Roman? Who was to provide leadership for the new movement, and how were the leaders to be chosen? What was to be the structure of the membership of the new community, and how were the leaders to be chosen and given authority? These sociological issues are addressed or implicit throughout the New Testament and in other early Christian writings.

In order to address these issues in a historically responsible way, one must not offer generalizations. Instead, it is necessary to identify the diverse modes by which these factors were perceived and dealt with in the New Testament writings—including the subsequent move toward unification. This analytical process is essential for study of Christian origins.

The Range of Community Structures and Cultural Orientations in Early Christianity

The differences among the Gospels, Epistles, and other traditions represented in the New Testament are not only conceptual but also sociological. Within the Gospels, the letters written by Paul, and the other New Testament Epistles attributed to him and other apostles—or anonymous, like the Letter to the Hebrews—there is evidence of significantly different modes of defining the covenant community.[4] The diversity is analogous to what one finds in the Jewish writings of the two centuries before and after the turn of the Common Era.[5] In my analysis the designations assigned to the social models evident in the Gospels and other New Testament writings are as follows: (1) the Community of the Wise, (2) the Law-Abiding Community, (3) the Community where God Dwells among His People, (4) the Community of Mystical Participation, and (5) the Ethnically and Culturally Inclusive Community. This is followed by a tracing of the development of these communities in the post-New Testament period (Kee 1995: 208–28). All but one of these diverse models as represented within the New Testament are sketched below.

The Community of the Wise: The Q Source and Mark

Within Judaism in the centuries before and after the turn of the eras there was wide concern to grasp and communicate to the community what was perceived to be the wisdom that God was disclosing to his people. This took three major forms: (1) Proverbial wisdom, which was perceived as embodied in timeless truths from God for his people, is most fully represented by the canonical Book of Proverbs. (2) Intellectual wisdom was seen as capable of achievement through a synthesis of insights from philosophy and from divinely granted wisdom. The Wisdom of Solomon and the writings of Philo of Alexandria, which directly correlate biblical tradition and Greek philosophy (Platonic and Stoic), represent this perception of wisdom in Judaism. (3) Insights into the purpose of God as disclosed in the course of history, culminating in the forthcoming triumph of the divine purpose over the powers of evil, are embodied in apocalyptic literature—especially the Book of Daniel, the apocalyptic sections of the biblical prophets,[6] and the postbiblical writings such as the Books of Enoch.[7]

The Gospels, the letters of Paul, and the Revelation of John provide the major evidence for the early Christian apocalyptic perspective and expectations. Beginning with the message of John the Baptist (Mt 3.1–12) and the ministry of Jesus,[8] but also in the letters of Paul,[9] and reaching a climax in the Revelation of John, the New Testament summons the new community to a characteristic apocalyptic stance toward the future: to be steadfast in facing struggle and persecution on the basis of assurance that is offered of what God has already begun to do in order to combat evil and to liberate his faithful people and the soon-coming triumph of God's purpose for renewal of his people and of the whole creation through Jesus Christ.

There is also evidence in the early Christian writings, however, that the authors drew to a considerable extent upon wisdom derived from or reflecting the impact of Greek philosophy. When Paul describes the moral fruits, which the Holy Spirit produces in the lives of the faithful, he includes the role of conscience and commends virtues that are basic in Stoic thought.[10] Thus the hope for renewal of the moral and social order of the world that was affirmed by the Stoics was analogous to that proclaimed by Jesus and the apostles, even though the latter differed from the Stoics by believing in direct divine action through Christ. Yet as a result of the shared hope of cosmic renewal, the Christian message of a coming moral transformation of the universe had a counterpart in the minds of thoughtful pagans in the early centuries of this era. Divine wisdom for both groups concerned not merely timeless truths, but also assurances of the ultimate triumph of truth and justice.

The Community Obedient to the New Law

The Gospel of Matthew pictures Jesus and reports his teaching his disciples in ways that in part resemble and in part contrast with the ancient Jewish biblical tradition of God's having given the law to his people through Moses. Just as Moses received the law and conveyed it at Mount Sinai, so Jesus' basic, comprehensive instruction of his disciples is portrayed as taking place on a mountain (Mt 5.1). Like Israel of old, Jesus was taken to Egypt and then brought back to the land of promise (Mt 2.13–23).[11] His teaching in Matthew is frequently contrasted directly with the Law of Moses: "You have heard it said of old," which is followed by a reference to the Law, and then by Jesus' declaration, "But I say to you." Hence the long-standing authority of Moses as the agent through whom the Law of God was given to the covenant people is now fundamentally challenged and in important ways replaced. The word of Jesus stands in direct contrast to, or in criticism of, what has been viewed in the Israelite tradition of the Law of Moses as providing the divinely intended basis for the shared life and obedience of the covenant people.

Further evidence of an intended contrast between the Law of Moses and the New Law through Jesus is to be recognized by the fact that the main part of this gospel (Mt 3–25) is divided into five sections, just as is the Mosaic Law.[12] Thus Matthew presents Jesus as the one who calls and instructs the new community on the model of Moses. But Jesus is seen as transcending both the role of Moses and the social basis of the nature of the ancient Israelite community: in the new community there will be not only those born in the Jewish community but also "disciples of all nations," who are to observe "all that I commanded you" (28.19–20). Not only do the defining of the social basis for the covenant community and the inclusiveness of its membership transcend what stands in the Mosaic tradition, but so do the depths of the moral commandments (5.19–20).

The Community of Mystical Participation: John

In both Judaism and the pagan religions of the Roman world there was the belief that God—or the gods—had chosen to disclose divine truth to those who came seeking to know it and to live by the principles that it embodied. Although this was to be grasped by individuals, it also brought access to the presence and transforming power of God for a community that shared these insights and sought to live in conformity to them. In the wider Greco-Roman culture, for example, a prime agent through whom divine disclosure was believed to take place was Isis, who was perceived to be the goddess of fertility, but also as the one through whom humans could gain divine knowledge and immortality. Isis's devotees claimed to have access to these divinely given resources.

Furthermore, the Greek philosophers taught that there was a divine principle—the *logos*—that pervaded the universe and was intended to serve as the instrument through which the divine purpose would ultimately be achieved. This term, which means not only "word" but also rational principle, is the very term that the Gospel of John uses in the prologue to identify Jesus. He is the one who brings knowledge of the divine purpose for renewal of God's people and of the whole creation. And it is he who dwells among his faithful people, revealing the glory of God (Jn 1.14). In a series of vivid images, the Gospel of John portrays Jesus as the one through whom there are at work both knowledge of God and power for accomplishing the renewal of his people and of the creation. Facets of these features are present in the identification of Jesus as the Bread, the Wine, the Shepherd, the Way and the Truth, the Life. Mystical participation in the life of this new people is emotional and personal—characterized by love, as set forth in the new commandment (13.34–35). Further, it is not merely intellectual, inward or private experience and mode of life. Instead it is to be shared by the new covenant people as a whole, and it will result in the transformation and renewal of their lives and their view of the future.

The Ethnically and Culturally Inclusive Community: Luke–Acts

In Luke and Acts the social and cultural inclusiveness of the new community is even more explicitly expressed, and it is of course both depicted and symbolized in the second volume—the Acts of the Apostles—in which the community is launched in Jerusalem and soon extends across the Mediterranean region, becoming established in Rome, the capital of the gentile world. But from the beginning of Luke's Gospel the theme of ethnic and cultural inclusiveness is a major factor. This is indicated in Luke's version of the genealogy of Jesus (Lk 3.23–38), which goes back to the first human, Adam, instead of merely to the father of the people of Israel, Abraham, as in Matthew (1.1–17). Jesus is to be the instrument of revelation of God's purpose "to the Gentiles" and to "all peoples" as well as to Israel (Lk 2.29–32). Prior to Jesus' baptism by John, the prophecy quoted from Isaiah 40 is extended by Luke[13] to affirm that through Jesus "all humanity [flesh] shall see the salvation of God."

Similarly, in Luke's account of Jesus' inaugural sermon in Nazareth (4.16–19) there is not only a quotation from Isaiah (61.1–2) to justify his outreach to the poor and oppressed, but also examples are cited of the outreach to non-Israelites by the prophets Elijah and Elisha (4.25–27). This inclusiveness will characterize the ministry of Jesus in Luke and of the apostles in Acts. In addition to Jesus' commissioning his twelve disciples, as in Mark and Matthew (Lk 6.12–16),[14] he sends out seventy to prepare for his coming and to announce the nearness of the Kingdom of God, as well as the doom impending for the people who reject him and his message (10.1–16). Seventy was the symbolic figure among Jews for the number of the nations of the world—as indicated by the designation of the Greek translation of the Hebrew Bible as the Septuagint—which means "seventy," and was intended to symbolize its function as an instrument of outreach to non-Jews, who were thought to comprise seventy nations. It is to this wider world that Luke pictures Jesus reaching out. The seventy messengers of Luke 10 return to report success in their mission to the wider world, and Jesus utters thanks to God that his purpose is indeed reaching out to outsiders. In the same manner, Luke's version of the Parable of the Great Supper (cf. Mt 22.1–10) depicts wider outreach for the gospel. Unlike Matthew's version of this parable, which includes a prediction of God's destroying the city of Jerusalem because its inhabitants rejected Jesus (Mt 22.1–10), Luke's more original version contrasts (1) those who reject the invitation because they are preoccupied with routine earthly matters with (2) the call by Jesus to serve those in need and peripheral to society who accept the invitation he utters and thus will share in the eschatological banquet (Lk 14.15–24). This is a symbol for the fulfillment of God's redemptive purpose for his people. In Luke 18.8–14 there is a contrast between the proudly pious Pharisee who boasted of his moral superiority and a tax collector, whose role involved direct collaboration with the Romans. It was the latter who penitently confessed his sinfulness and was assured of justification before God.

These features in Luke anticipate the broad social outreach of the apostles to the wider Roman world reported in Acts. Their mission reached out to both intellectual leaders—as in the encounter with the scholars on the Areopagus in Athens (Acts 17.16–34)—and to hearings before the Roman authorities, as in Paul's defense before Agrippa, the puppet ruler in Palestine installed by the Romans (25.23–26.32). Dramatically evident in Acts are both the range of opportunities for the Christian messengers to convey their message about Jesus to civil and religious authorities and the diversity of ways in which the significance of Jesus for faith may be presented.

The Shared Rules and Practices of the Communities

In order to achieve the goals and benefits set forth in the traditions of a religious community and to assure its ongoing existence with the passage of time it must articulate the purposes and values for which it was founded and the rules by which its members are to live as they move toward fulfillment of its hopes and expectations. In the case of historic Israel, instruction was given in the name of Moses to the people as they settled in the land of Canaan, which had been promised to them, and began the yearly cycle of producing crops. How were they to express gratitude to God who had brought then there and was providing for their needs? As they presented in the sanctuary the first fruits from their land they were to declare:

> A wandering Aramaean[15] was my ancestor; he went down into Egypt and lived there as an alien, few in number, and there he became a great nation, mighty and populous. When the Egyptians treated us harshly and afflicted us, by imposing hard labor on us, we cried to Yahweh, the God of our ancestors; the Lord heard our voice and saw our affliction, our toil, and our oppressions. The Lord brought us out of Egypt with a mighty hand and an outstretched arm, with a terrifying display of power, and with signs and wonders; and he brought us into this place and gave us this land, a land flowing with milk and honey. (Dt 26.5–10)

To express their gratitude for what God had done to free and provide for his people they were to join in presenting to the Lord the first of the "fruit of the ground" as a celebration of "all the bounty that the Lord God" had given to them (Dt 26.5–11).

For the early Christians, analogous to this communal expression of gratitude for God's action in behalf of the people of Israel is the Eucharist—a New Testament term that comes from a Greek word for rendering thanks. The gratitude to be expressed by the new covenant community is for God's provision of the Messiah whose coming, life, teachings, sacrificial death, and glorious resurrection bring reconciliation of alienated humanity to God for those who trust in this divine act of human renewal. Thus the Eucharist, recalling the bread and wine shared with Jesus by the disciples on the night before his execution, now serves as a communal celebration of what God has done through Christ for the forgiveness and formation of his new covenant people. It is also a symbolic assurance of the ultimate triumph of God's purpose for his people and for creation. This will result in the establishment of the new social order, the Kingdom of God (Mk 14.22–25).

Paul highlights the importance of sharing in this rite as a symbol of the basic unity of God's new people, in spite of differences in social and cultural status among the members (I Cor 11.17–22). One is to be cautious about participation in the communion if certain features of what is used in it are obtained from pagan or ritually impure sources. Crucial is the avoidance of offending observers of Jewish or Greek background, as well as other members of the new community. Similarly, one must avoid eating any substance that is offensive to other members (I Cor 8.10–13). Proper behavior is by no means a purely private matter: one must take fully into account how one's actions affect other members of the community.

Specifics of the ethical standards for the new community derive from at least three sources, but they are at times altered significantly: the Jewish Scriptures, the Jesus traditions, and dominant features of Greco-Roman ethics—especially the Stoic tradition. Examples of these adaptations are as follows: Jesus' commandment that goes beyond the Mosaic prohibitions of killing anyone to a warning of judgment that will come on those who are angry toward or insult a brother or sister (Mt 5.21–22 vs. Ex 20.13; Dt 5.17; 16.18). The Pauline commandment about avoiding divorce and remarriage when one's companion is not converted (I Cor 7.10–11) is different from the rule set down in the Law of Moses. There the issues are a mix of personal choice and ritual defilement: a man may divorce his wife if she displeases him or he finds something objectionable in her, and he may not remarry her if she is subsequently married to another man and then divorced (Dt 24.1–4).

The essential social factor of marriage and divorce is addressed directly by Paul. He builds his case on the subject by urging that one should maintain his or her marital status in spite of personal difficulties and conflict on the ground that the coming of Christ was expected to occur soon, and then all such problems would be resolved and an unbelieving spouse might be converted (I Cor 7.12–16). This position on divorce is different, however, from the teaching of Jesus in Matthew 5.31–32, which reports the permission of divorce in the case of infidelity. Thus the patterns of social relationships at the personal level vary within the New Testament, and diverge from the rules for the people in the Law of Moses.

The fruit of the Spirit—which is the moral transformation that the Spirit produces in the life of the believer, according to Paul (Gal 5.22–23)—includes not only the traditional biblical virtues—love, joy, peace, kindness, goodness, faithfulness—but also those moral qualities that are defined and called for in the Stoic tradition: "endurance" [*makrothumia*], "uprightness" [*chrestotes*], "goodness" [*agathosune*], and most notably, "self-control" [*engkrateia*]. These qualities are not merely matters of inner personal morality; they shape group life and serve as public testimony to the moral qualities that are to be fostered and followed by the members of the new covenant community.

Such cross-cultural facets of early Christianity are also clearly evident in other New Testament writings, as may be noted in an analysis of the Letter to the Hebrews and Letter of James, where Christian beliefs are set forth in perspectives that feature Greek and Roman philosophy and culture. Thus it is clear that the early Christian movement did not take a stand in sharp opposition to Greco-Roman culture as a whole, but instead drew upon its insights and models in literary, social, and conceptual ways.

The most rigid and demanding rules for ethical and social life set forth in the New Testament are those in the Gospel of Matthew, which presents Jesus as offering a new law that is to be fully obeyed, with no provision for relaxing its demands on the members of the new community (Mt 5.17–19; see below). Subsequent development of moral requirements is evident in such post-New Testament writings as the *Didache*. Matching this movement toward more specific ethical standards is the emergence of structures of community leadership.

The Organization and Leadership of the Community

Major factors for the analysis of the modes of early Christian community are, of course, differences in group definition and group formation, especially with regard to the development of leadership roles. It is useful in seeking the distinctive features in the origins of Christianity to note analogous roles and structures in Judaism at the turn of the eras.

LEADERSHIP IN THE NEW COMMUNITY

APOSTLES. The term "apostle" [*apostolos*] is a transliteration based on the Greek verb, *apostello*, which means to send forth. Its meaning corresponds with the English word "envoy" and carries with it the sense of one who has been commissioned to perform an important role. In the case of Paul, it was his encounter with the risen Christ (1 Cor 15.8–10) that resulted in what he perceived to have been God's commissioning him for his special role: "[God] was pleased to reveal his Son to me so that I might proclaim him among the Gentiles" (Gal 1.16). Paul's grasp of the dominant Greco-Roman culture of his time as evident in his skilled, conceptually cultivated writing, his grasp of the prophetic and legal traditions of Judaism, and his ability to communicate across cultural boundaries demonstrates his remarkable suitability to carry out his pioneering role as the apostle conveying the good news about Jesus Christ across the socioculturally wider Roman world.

Divine call and enabling of the apostles were seen as essential for showing the shared life among them and the continuity between them and Jesus, as well as the appropriation of their tradition through what the church proclaimed about Jesus, the ethical demands it made for its members, and the organizational structures that began to emerge in the new community. This principle of continuity accounts for the attribution of the letters, Gospels, and the Revelation of John to apostles. Writings that probably came from the next generation after the apostles—such as the letters of Peter and John, and the so-called pastoral Epistles that claim to have been written by Paul—reflect a later stage in the development of the leadership structure of the church (see below). Also, the authority of the Gospel of Luke and its second volume, the Acts of the Apostles, manifests the importance for early Christians of understanding the apostolic origins, the links for the reliability and transmission of the Christian tradition, as well as for the framework and functions of the leadership that emerged in this new community. From the outset, however, there were certain lesser roles that were nonetheless essential for the growth, instruction, and guidance of the new community, and for combining tradition with the new factors brought by Christ and the work of the Holy Spirit. These are described below.

THE PROPHETS. The leaders in Judaism from ancient times included not only the rulers—judges, priests, Levites—but also those who were perceived to be special messengers from God to his people: the prophets. The prophets in this tradition include not only those whose messages from God to his people were recorded in what have been called the prophetic books of the Bible, but also men and women who down through the history of Israel were the messengers and agents of God who conveyed his purpose and standards to his people. They include Abraham, Aaron, Miriam, and Deborah (Gn 20.7; Ex 7.1; Jgs 4.4)—but also Moses, who is said to have had no equal as a prophet (Dt 34.10), and who became the normative figure. Moses is to be followed one day by a prophet who will convey to all of God's people the divine purpose. Through him they will all respond in faithful obedience (Dt 18.15–18). Other prophetic messengers of God to his people were Elijah and Elisha. Elijah's return to call the people to repentance and to launch the era of divine judgment is predicted in Malachi 4.5–6, and John the Baptist is identified as Elijah in Matthew 11.14.[16] Thus the new faithful community is promised divine messengers.

In Acts 3.17–26, however, Peter is reported as claiming that the prophet whose coming was promised in Deuteronomy 18.15–18 as God's agent for achieving inclusiveness of his people has already arrived and launched this new community: Jesus. In the Q source of the gospel tradition Jesus predicts that the leaders who honor the prophets by building tombs will sadly follow the example of their ancestors, who killed the prophets (Lk 11.49). In the Gospel of John Jesus is likewise identified as a prophet (4.19) but as one who will "receive no honor in his own country" (4.44).

When Paul is describing the roles that the Holy Spirit enables members of the community to carry out, he mentions prophecy (1 Cor 12.10), a role that he ranks as second in authority to that of the apostles (12.28). In Matthew the disciples are warned that they will suffer persecution like that experienced by "the prophets who were before you" (5.12). In Mathew 10.40–41 there is a promise that some hearers will receive the disciples who are prophets just as they received him and in 7.22–23 a warning about those who falsely claim a prophetic role in Jesus' name. In Acts Christian prophets foretell future events (11.27–30), and the predictive role of those empowered by the Spirit is reported in Acts 21.1–14. Paul is depicted in Acts as a prophet granted visions and insights, beginning with his conversion (9.3–6).[17] Continuing with his confrontation with civil authorities (13.9–12) are his vision of the spread of the gospel across the Mediterranean world (16.6–9), the reassurance he is granted of God's safeguarding him against attack (18.9–10), and the prediction that he will stand trial before Caesar (27.23–24). In the Gospel of John the role of the disciples, empowered by the Paraclete—counselor, aide, who is the Spirit of Truth—assures the continuing presence of Christ with the faithful as teacher, enabler, and foreteller of the future of God's purpose (16.13). These who are thus enabled are now sent into the world to proclaim the truth and to persuade others to trust in Christ (17.6–19). This is their prophetic role.

The predictive aspect of prophecy is highlighted in Revelation, where the author has written prophecy (1.3) through his having been commissioned and empowered by God (22.7) and having been granted visions of the future fulfillment of God's purpose of renewal of his people and of the creation (21.9–10; 22.6–7, 9–10, 18–19). Thus in the New Testament, prophecy embodies divinely granted powers of foresight and insight, but these are not personal disclosures for individuals. Rather, they convey to the community the following: what the future purpose of God is, how it is to be fulfilled, and how God's people are to live in preparation for this.

TEACHER/DISCIPLE. Another major mode of communication to God's people of his purpose for them in the early Christian tradition is that of teacher/disciple. These roles were of course at that time abundantly evident in both the Greco-Roman and the Jewish traditions. Paul highlights the importance of the communication of divine wisdom by God to his people—the ability both to grasp it and to communicate it (1 Cor 12.7–8). One important function in relation to communication is that of the scribe. The vast majority of the people in the ancient Near East, as well as in Greco-Roman society, were illiterate. They needed help from those who could read and write for purposes of communication, as well as for forming and keeping records. This was especially important with regard to religious traditions, such as the Jews' keeping and conveying the insights of the prophets and of the legal norms. Josephus, the Jewish historian, depicts the roles of scribes as ranging from village copyists to members of the regional council.

But the Jewish term for scribes, *sopherim*, means "people of the book" and was used for those who gave instruction in the Jewish Bible. The importance of the role of the teacher is indicated in the later books, such as Proverbs and Ecclesiastes, where there are appeals to the reader to apply one's mind to instruction, while those who are capable are to teach others—such as the call to "make instruction shine forth like the dawn" (Sir 34.9–13). And a major figure in the community that produced the Dead Sea Scrolls was called "the Teacher of Righteousness." This scribal tradition—preserving and giving instruction in the sacred texts—was taken over by the early Christians, as is evident from the writings now known as the New Testament.

The teacher/learner relationship is, of course, dominant in the Gospels. The most common term by which the followers of Jesus are identified is "disciple"—more than 250 times in the four Gospels! Jesus does not merely convey information to his followers: he instructs them according to his perception of his role and theirs in the redemptive purpose of God, and it is this message that they are to obey and transmit.

ELDER. In common Jewish usage, "elders" was reserved for heads of a family or clan who were brought together to serve as representatives of the people of Israel as a whole. They made sacrifices and received and conveyed instruction to the people concerning the "words of the Lord" (Ex 24.2). They were the chief figures present when all Israel was gathered, as in Joshua 23–24, and they transmitted the message of the prophets to the people (Is 3.14; Jer 19.1). It was they who represented the people of the land and comprised the council that was the central locus of authority (1 Kgs 20.7; 21.8; 2 Sm 19.16–18; 1 Kgs 8.1). In the periods of Persian and Greco-Roman domination of the land of Israel the elders comprised the official council that was granted a degree of regional autonomy by the major foreign power. The Greek term for this council, *synedrion*, was later transliterated and used to designate the subsequent Jewish religious council, which called itself the Sanhedrin.[18]

BISHOP. This term in English is a loose transliteration of the Greek word *episkopos*, which has a range of meanings: an overseer or guardian, a supervisor or a protector, or a tutor who guides the development of the mind. In the Septuagint (the Greek translation of the Jewish Bible) it refers to both divine and human roles as overseers, in a temple as well as in the army. In the opening of his letter to the Philippians (I.I) Paul uses *episkopos* as well as *diakonos* [deacon] to refer in a general way to the supervisory and subservient roles carried out by the church leaders. Similarly, in Acts 20.17 Paul is reported to have described the role of the elders as "overseers" of the church of God. And in I Peter 2.25 Christ is designated as the shepherd and guardian [*episkopos*] of souls.

In the pastorals (written in the name of Paul in a later generation), there is a detailed description of bishop as a category of official church leadership (I Tm 3.1–7), but with strict personal requirements: married only once, temperate, sensible, dignified, and hospitable. His responsible role with his own family is to be mirrored in his leadership in the church. The fact that he is not to be "a recent convert" confirms the conclusion that this letter comes from later than the first generation of Christians, since then all the members and leaders would have been recent converts. In the Christian writings now known as the Apostolic Fathers— written in the second century C.E.—we have more details about the appointment and the function of bishops. There they are given authoritative, supervisory roles, and all the members of the community are to be subject to them.[19] Ignatius, in his *Letter to the Ephesians*,[20] urges the members in Ephesus to be "joined together in one subjection," submissive to the bishop and the presbytery. The members are to live in "harmonious concord" to God through Christ, based on obedience to the bishop on the part of the presbytery and the members as a whole (Ign., *Eph.* 4–5). The members are to "yield obedience without hypocrisy" (Ign., *Eph.* 3.1). In his *Letter to the Magnesians* Ignatius enjoins respect for the bishop, who carries out his role "according to the power of God the Father" even though he is young. Ignatius goes on to call for submission to the bishop as the agent of god: "Be zealous to do all things in harmony with God, with the bishop presiding in the place of God and the presbyters [elders] in the place of the Council of the Apostles, and the deacons, who are most dear to me, entrusted with the service [*diakonia*] of Jesus Christ." The members are to take care that "there be nothing which can divide you, but [that they] be united with the bishop and with those who preside over you as an example and lesson of immortality (Ign., *Magn.* 6.1–2).

DEACON. The Greek words from which "deacon" is transliterated are the verb, *diakoneo* (which means to render a service to oneself, to other humans or to a deity) and the noun *diakonos*, which refers to the one who performs such service. This service can include menial work, such as waiting on tables, but it includes personal service, providing and caring for those who are in need, as well as offering gifts on the altar of a deity. In the New Testament, however, *diakoneo* and *diakonos* are used

with reference to providing for the needy, and even to suffering for their benefit—
for which Christ is the model in giving his life "as a ransom for many" (Mk
10.45). Those who perform this role in the New Testament include the disciples
and apostles, who follow the model of the suffering Christ. Paul identifies himself and the apostles as servants of God (2 Cor 3.6, 6.4), as well as Timothy (1
Thes 3.2).

Diakonos as a more formal office is implied in Colossians 1.25, where the writer
describes his role as "a divine office" that enables him to reveal the mystery of
God's purpose to the saints. In 1 Timothy 3.8–13 specific qualifications for the
office are laid down: males and females who take on this task are to follow moderation in their lives and show integrity in their piety and doctrine (4.6–8). Thus
"deacon" is not merely a general term for service in the church but has become a
leadership title within the new community. The pattern of defined emergent roles
of service, responsibility, and leadership is clearly developing by the early second
century C.E.

THE CHRISTIAN ROLE OF PRIEST. "Priest" appears in the letters of Paul and the
later New Testament writings as a recurrent metaphor for Christ's sacrificial death
and its basic significance for the community of faith, rather than as a title for an
official role in the church. Only in Romans 15.16 does Paul approach the designation of himself as a priest when he explicitly uses the image of priestly role and
sacrifice in describing his ministry "of Jesus Christ to the Gentiles" as "priestly service of the gospel of God." Yet the term he uses here for his role as minister, *lei-
tourgos*, is clearly akin to our word "liturgy" and implies a mode of sacramental service. Similarly he uses the verb *hierourgonta* with reference to his ministry as "priestly
service of the gospel of God" and describes his success in converting Gentiles to
faith in Christ as a "sacrificial offering" that he is presenting to God. The terms are
largely metaphorical, but they draw on the Jewish tradition of the priests as the divine agents through whom ritual renewal of God's people is accomplished.

Throughout the Letter to the Hebrews, however, the sacrificial death of Christ
and the renewal of his people achieved by that are depicted in imagery that builds
more directly on the priestly traditions of Israel. Priestly features also appear in 1
Peter and Revelation. Thus in 1 Peter 2.5 the community is called to be "built into
a spiritual house, to be a holy priesthood, and to offer spiritual sacrifices acceptable to God through Jesus Christ." In 2.9 the people of God are described in imagery drawn from the Jewish priestly tradition: "a chosen race, a royal priesthood,
a holy nation, God's own people." In the same way Revelation 1.5–6 tells the community that it has been "freed from our sins by [Christ's] blood and made . . . a
kingdom, priests to God and his Father." In the hymn of praise to the Lamb of
God in Revelation 5.9–10, Christ is praised because "[he was] slaughtered and by

[his] blood [he] ransomed for God saints from every tribe and language and people and nation," and "[he has] made them to be a kingdom and priests [in service] to God, and they will reign on earth." Thus the priestly and royal roles are combined in the work to which God has called his new people and that they are being enabled to fulfill. The picture here is primarily that of the significance of a mission to be fulfilled rather than the defining of a formal priestly office.

These are the roles and offices depicted in the New Testament as developing in keeping with the purpose of God for the renewal of his people, and in the outworking of that purpose through the indwelling power and guidance of the Spirit of God.

The Range of Community Structures and Intellectual Orientations

As is evident from the analyses of the evidence offered above, the impact of the Christian message about Jesus and the divine purpose to be achieved through him for renewal of his people and of the creation took different forms, almost from the outset. It was not until Christianity was adopted by the Roman emperor Constantine in the fourth century, however, and councils were assembled and commissioned to establish uniform structures of faith and order, that uniformity of faith and practice was fostered.[21] Up until that time, those who claimed to be heirs of the Christian tradition diverged in significant ways. This was the case with respect to organizational structures within the churches and to defining the community of faith. Regional tensions and ethnic and cultural differences among those who adopted—and adapted—the Christian tradition resulted in a range of authoritarian churchly structures—Greek, Latin, Syriac, Coptic, etc. The diverse basic conceptual models of community for the early Christians may be characterized as follows.

The Eschatologically Oriented

Those for whom Jesus was primarily seen as the divine agent for punitive termination of the present world order and replacement of it by the new order—the eschatological kingdom of God—were content with a minimum of leadership or institutional structures, and devoted their energies to warning the world of the impending cosmic judgment and inviting all who would listen to their message of the good news to recognize Jesus as messenger and agent for the establishment of God's rule in the world, the triumph over the powers of evil, and the reward for the faithful. This type of Christian group produced apocalyptic documents, some of which are included in the New Testament, and others that have survived to the present day. The former are most notably Mark and the Q source in the gospel tradition, the letters of Paul and those attributed to Peter, but especially the Revelation of John. The non-canonical writings of this type include the following: The Ascension of Isaiah, Christian Sibyllines— imitating the Roman writings attributed to the Sibyls predicting the future—and apocalypses attributed to Peter, Paul, and Thomas.[22]

The Mystically Oriented

Building on the mystical religious tradition of direct experience of the deity, as evident in Judaism of the Roman period and subsequently in early Christianity, there developed a belief that it was possible for the faithful seeker to have a personal encounter with the divine. As noted above, this factor became important in Judaism at the time of the turn of the eras—most notably in the writings of Philo of Alexandria, who interpreted the Jewish Scriptures allegorically, perceiving both the legal and the narrative traditions to be expressions of inner experience of the divine by individuals. The features of the Temple and the sacrificial system were interpreted in ways that served to provide a sense of the immediate access for the faithful to the realm of the divine.

That same motif, as noted above, appeared in the Gospel of John, where the images of Christ and of the new community are perceived to be symbolic descriptions of the ways in which the faithful can come into the presence of God through Christ, and can experience immediately the transforming and renewing divine power of God. Unlike some mystical traditions that portray this access to the divine in mostly solitary terms, where the individual has a private experience of the divine, in John's Gospel God is seen as meeting and renewing his people in a variety of corporate images: flock and shepherd, shared bread and wine, vine and branches. The central theme of this gospel is the experience of a new life by the new community through the newly revealed agent of God—Jesus Christ—and the power of renewal that is thus made available to these people who responded in faith to Christ and his message of renewal.

The Ethnically and Culturally Inclusive Community

A third motif that appears in the New Testament texts is the divine intent to form a new community that is inclusive in ethnic and cultural terms. This is embodied and documented in the twin writings of Luke and Acts. That conviction is directly expressed in Peter's sermon as reported in Acts 2.17, where God's Spirit is to be poured out "upon all flesh" (i.e., on all of humanity) with the consequence that "everyone who calls on the name of the Lord shall be saved" (2.21), regardless of race or ethnic origin. That divine purpose of an inclusive covenant community is anticipated and foreshadowed in the Gospel of Luke, but takes on concrete form and reality in the launching of this worldwide program as described in Acts. In Acts the message is expressed in ways that not only reach across cultural boundaries but also transcend religious traditions as well as social distinctions. This is what Paul declares in Galatians 3.28: for those who have trusted in Christ and received the rite of baptism "there is neither Jew nor Greek, there is neither slave nor free, there is neither male nor female; for you are all one in Christ Jesus." Their public testimony to their trust in Christ as God's agent of human renewal places them in the tradition of the children of Abraham—the archetype of the people of God. The resulting intimacy of this new relationship to God finds expression through the Spirit of God who indwells his new people: "God has sent the Spirit of his Son into our hearts, crying, 'Abba, Father'"—a term that connotes the loving intimacy of relationship between father and offspring (Gal 4.6). Humanly contrived as well as genetically transmitted family identity and relationship, which build on and are defined by differences and distinctions, have been overcome by God through the Son for the benefit of the new people that is being formed in response to Christ.

Order and Structure for the Community

Yet human nature, which finds security in well-defined structures and the articulation—and enforcement—of rules and standards, has reacted negatively to the message and model of inclusiveness and to the notion of personal communication of the divine will and purpose by establishing well-defined structures for authority and behavior. These features are especially evident in some of the early Christian writings, as we have noted above: in the Gospel of Matthew with its portrayal of Jesus giving a new law on the mountain, just as in antiquity God did for Israel through Moses. Modification of the authentic Pauline tradition of the inclusiveness of the community—which depends on the love of Christ and the guidance of the Holy Spirit for individual and group moral actions—takes place with the production in the next generation of the Deutero-Pauline writings (Ephesians and the pastorals) with their explicit guidelines for establishing authority roles to guide the churches in their ongoing life. Both the rank and the specific areas of authority are spelled out in these later writings, which seem to have been written in order to document later ecclesiastical authority by attributing it to the earlier tradition in the name of the apostle.

Dealing with Diversity within the Early Christian Traditions

The early Christian writings that came to be preserved and regarded as authoritative in the church by the second century were sufficiently diverse in perspective and content—and for many they were seen as in competition with other Christian writings—that it was felt that a decision must be made as to which of these writings were to be regarded as authoritative for the church. The diversity within

Judaism at the time of Jesus is evident not only from references to different Jewish groups, such as priests, Pharisees, and Sadducees, but also from the Jewish writings that show the influence of Greek philosophy, such as the writings of Philo of Alexandria, who interpreted the Scriptures allegorically. In order to define what Judaism was it was essential to draw up a list of writings to be considered as Scripture.[23] The term that came to be used for the list of those writings considered to be authoritative was "canon," which is from the Greek for "measuring stick." Subsequently, the Christians claimed to be the true people of God and the real heirs of God's promises through the prophets of Israel recorded in the Scriptures. This is evident from Paul's declaration that the death, burial, and resurrection of Jesus are "in accordance with the scriptures," as well as from the dozens of statements in the Gospels and Acts that what Jesus and the apostles did was in fulfillment of the Scriptures. Thus by claiming to be the covenant people, it was essential for the early Christians, as it was for the Jews, to decide which writings were canonical.

This was very important for the Christians in their claim that they were the people of the new covenant—through whom the New Testament was produced—in contrast to the people of the old covenant, whose sacred writings the Christians designated as the Old Testament. Major functions of these Jewish writings included in the Christian canon were to define the old covenant people and the rules by which they were to live and serve God and to identify the promises made concerning God's plan conveyed through the prophets of Israel for the future renewal of his people and of the whole creation. It was along these lines that the decisions concerning the canon of Christian Scriptures set the modes of definition for the new community, the standards by which its members were to live in relation to both the membership and the wider world. The role of its leaders had also to be defined. As we have noted, this process continued down into the second and succeeding centuries.

There was also a necessity for this new movement to deal with groups that challenged the leaders and the majority points of view, claiming to have been given divine truth. Such a group was the Gnostics, who insisted that God had given them special knowledge and insight that differed sharply from the mainstream of Christianity and fostered the development of groups of its adherents. Thus the mainstream Christian leaders had to exercise authority in denouncing such claims and in dismissing from church membership those who adopted such views. The emergence of these sects, with their claims to possess the real Christian truth, led to the heightening of the authority of the central leadership and the specification through formally developed creeds of what the proper beliefs and practices were to be for the members of the church. The result was an increasingly authoritative sense of the role of the leadership and the dismissal and denunciation of those promoting divergent beliefs and practices in the name of Christianity.

Yet by the designation as canonical of the diverse documents that comprise the New Testament, the potential remained—and is operative down to the present day—for a diversity of concepts of the covenant community, of the role of Christ in the purpose of God, of the future of God's purpose for his people and creation, and for the rules and norms by which those who claim to be the people of the new covenant are to live.

Notes

1. This theory is central to Buber, which distinguishes between one type of faith in which one finds oneself in the relationship of faith and is a member of a community— Judaism—and another type in which one is converted as an isolated individual and finds community as one of a group of converts—Christianity (1951: 9). This distinction dominated late nineteenth- and early twentieth-century popular Christian piety. It is reflected in both gospel songs and spirituals of that period: "I come to the garden alone . . . and he walks with me, and he talks with me, and he tells me I am his own"; and "Just a little talk with Jesus makes it right, all right." This individualistic piety has its counterpart in the existentialist interpretation of Christian origins, represented most notably in the work of German New Testament scholar Rudolf Bultmann, who sought to correlate Christian faith with existentialist philosophy, highlighting only private commitment of faith and ignoring the powerful impact of redefined group identity, which pervades the New Testament.

2. An excellent survey of the relationship between sociology and the historical development of religion is offered by sociologist Thomas F. O'Dea, especially section 4, "Sociology of Religion: Sociological Theory" (1970: 201–93).

3. My own historical methods have been directly influenced by these relevant sociological factors, in both theoretical and historical terms (Kee 1980, 1989).

4. I have indicated in detail the diversities with regard to covenant definition among the New Testament writings, as well as the authors' common concern for community identity, in *Who Are the People of God?* (1995).

5. The major options are sketched in chapter 1 of Kee (1995: 17–54), which offers an analysis of "Models of Community in the Literature of Postexilic Judaism."

6. Apocalyptic sections of the canonical prophets include Isaiah 24–27, 56–57 and Zechariah 9–14.

7. The many writings attributed to Enoch—who is said to have been taken up to God rather than to have died (Gn 5.18–24)—were found among the Dead Sea Scrolls, and appear in *OTP* I.

8. From Jesus' initial announcement of the coming of the kingdom of God (Mk 1.14–15) throughout his career of preaching and healing, culminating in his last instruction to the disciples about the events that will precede the coming of God's rule, and his final meal with his disciples—where he speaks of being reunited with them when the kingdom of God has come (Mk 14.25)—the message of Jesus involves preparation for the coming triumph of God's rule. A vivid affirmation of this is offered in the Sayings Tradition (called by scholars the Q source): "If it is by the finger of God that I expel demons,

then the kingdom of God has come upon you" (Lk 11.20). Thus both Mark and Q provide evidence for the perception of the new community as those to whom God has disclosed the wisdom of his purpose for renewal of the world through Jesus.

9. Paul seeks to prepare the new community for the struggles and ultimate triumph of God's purpose through Jesus, especially in I Corinthians 15.20–57 and I Thessalonians 4.13–18.

10. Paul includes Stoic virtues among the fruits that the Spirit produces in the lives of the faithful (Gal 5.22–23). And features of his expectation of the fulfillment of God's purpose also correspond to the beliefs of Stoics about the divine moral renewal of the creation.

11. This experience of Jesus is seen as the fulfillment of the prophetic promise, "Out of Egypt have I called my son" (Mt 2.15; Hos 11.1).

12. The five sections are composed of narrative and discourse: 3.1–7.29, 8.1–10.42, 11.1, 13.52, 13.53–18.35, 19.1–25.46. Following each of these sections is a statement, "When Jesus had finished."

13. In Mark 1.2–3 and Matthew 3.3 the quotation by John ends with "make his paths straight" (Is 40.3).

14. This story is told in Mark 3.13–19 and Matthew 10.1–4.

15. The reference to the major ancestor of Israel as a "wandering Aramaean" recalls the nomadic life of the early Israelites and their shift to a settled mode of existence in the land that they took over—an event regarded as the result of God's action in their behalf, when they returned from Egypt and settled in the land God had given them and from which they now harvested crops. The Aramaeans were a diverse people whose origins were the Syro-Arabian desert, whose language was Aramaic, who spread across Syria and upper Mesopotamia, but who were never united into a single political entity.

16. Similar identification of John and Elijah is offered in Mark 9.9–13 and Matthew 17.9–13.

17. Described again in 16.6–9; 22.6–21; 26.12–18.

18. The term "rabbi," which came to be used for the Jewish religious leaders, was simply a title of honor, meaning "my lord" or "my master." But it came to serve as a designation for those considered to be interpreters and formulators of the ongoing meaning and relevance of the Law of Moses for the Jewish community.

19. For example, 1 Clement 42–44, and extensively in the Letters of Ignatius.

20. Ignatius was probably martyred during the reign of the Roman emperor Trajan (98–117 C.E.). He was bishop of Antioch in Syria and visited and wrote letters to several churches in Asia Minor.

21. Significantly, the creedal formulation that has continued down through history to be appealed to as normative is the creed attributed to Constantine, under whom Christianity became the official religion.

22. These apocalypses are available with introductions and translations in New Testament Apocrypha.

23. This complicated process within Judaism has been superbly analyzed by James A. Sanders in his article on canon in the Anchor Bible Dictionary (vol. I, 837–52).

Establishing Social Distance between Christians and Both Jews and Pagans

16

JACK T. SANDERS

MANY SOCIOLOGISTS HAVE NOTED that one of the most important aspects of group self-definition is boundary drawing—defining who "we" are as over against "them." One of the most comprehensive analyses of this function was given by Talcott Parsons in his study of the evolution of societies. Parsons proposed that basic to all social systems, even at the most primitive level, is "a system of *constitutive symbolism*, which gives members of the society their own self-definition, or collective identity, so that the conception, 'We, the . . . ' is meaningful. This is a kind of answer to the two questions of who and what *we* are" (Parsons 1966: 33).

As Christianity developed after the time of Jesus, its charismatic leader, it necessarily and inevitably followed this pattern of defining itself by drawing boundaries, first between itself and Judaism (as a religion) and then between itself and pagan religion, a complex that comprised both polytheism and civic religion. In the beginning of the new movement, of course, Christianity was a part of Judaism and shared the Jewish concept of boundary between itself and paganism. What, then, led to the boundary drawing between Christianity and Judaism? This is the question that we must investigate first.[1] In pursuing that investigation, we shall need to look at how the situation developed in Judah and Galilee—the Jewish homeland—prior to the first Jewish revolt against Rome (concluded in 70 C.E.) and then between that time and the second revolt (concluded in 135). We shall see that the first revolt precipitated altered relations between Jewish Christians and non-Christian Jews and that the second revolt cemented the cleavage. We shall also see that those altered relations are readily explicable on sociological principles.

When we then turn to the wider world of early gentile Christianity, we shall see that non-Christian Judaism had little interest in that aspect of the new religion, but that there was much competition among different groups of Christians and that the group that was successful was the one that drew the right boundaries between a too-Jewish Christianity, on the one hand, and a too-pagan Christianity, on the other. Here it will be obvious that Christianity followed a normal development as an emerging new religious movement (NRM). To begin, we must assemble the evidence—first for Judah and Galilee before 70.

The most obvious approach would be to turn to the Book of Acts in the New Testament, which provides the only narrative of the first decades of Christianity. Unfortunately, however, there are severe problems with that narrative. Not only is the narrative too much the product of the author's literary skill (Cadbury 1920; Dibelius 1956), but the narrative of conflict between Jewish authorities and the fledgling Jerusalem church is confusing. Chapters 2–4 tell of Jewish persecutions of some of the apostles but not of rank-and-file Christians, but when a general persecution occurs in chapter 8 it is the rank and file who are driven out of Jerusalem while the apostles remain, apparently unhindered. Then there are many statements in the early chapters about the goodwill that the Christians enjoyed among the populace, and there are narratives about thousands of converts; yet when Stephen, a leader of the church, is lynched, it is "the people and the elders and the scribes" (Acts 6:12) who carry out the lynching—thus apparently the general populace. Finally, except for the case of Stephen, Acts never offers a consistent or sufficient rationale for Jewish persecution. Thus we need to look elsewhere for information about the conflict between Christian Jews and others, and for the causes of that conflict. We turn first to the letters of Paul, the former Pharisee (Phil 3:5) and apostle to Gentiles (e.g., Gal 2:1–9), who was active approximately 45–55 C.E.

In several places (1 Cor 15:9; Gal 1:13, 23; Phil 3:6) Paul writes that he formerly, before becoming a Christian, "persecuted" the church. He never, however, gives any content to that persecution. Nevertheless, he sometimes refers to his *being* persecuted as a Christian missionary, and here we do get some content. In 2 Corinthians 11:24 he writes that he "five times received from Jews forty save one," a known synagogue punishment of thirty-nine lashes (Lietzmann 1949: 151); and in Galatians 5:11 he asks, "If I yet preach circumcision, why do I yet suffer persecution?" Since that question comes in the midst of his trying to persuade the gentile Christians in Galatia not to accept circumcision (symbolizing a conversion to Judaism), as some Christians sent from Jerusalem had been trying to persuade them to do, we may assume that the persecution that Paul received had to do with his converting Gentiles to Christianity *as a new religion* rather than as a Jewish movement.

Such persecution likely occurred on Paul's visits to Jerusalem, not in synagogues in the Diaspora. In 1 Thessalonians 2:14–16 Paul advises the Thessalonian Christians that they "have become imitators . . . of the churches . . . in Judaea, for [the Thessalonians] have suffered the same things . . . from [their] own people as they [sc., the Judaean churches] from the Jews." In other words, whatever persecution was occurring in Thessalonica, it was not being carried out by Jews. Back in Judaea, however, some Jewish authorities did persecute Jewish Christians—perhaps those who, like Paul, were severing Christian salvation from its Jewish matrix.

In the early Jewish–Christian layer or source of the present Gospel of Matthew we find further evidence corroborating our conclusions drawn from Paul's letters.[2] In Matthew 23.34 Jesus prophesies that he "will send prophets and sages and scribes to you [sc., the scribes and Pharisees]. You will kill and crucify some of them, and some of them you will flog in your synagogues and harry from city to city." This sequence—kill, crucify, flog, harry—smacks strongly of a temporal sequence, and one may suspect that the Matthean source has been led to this statement because of the traditions of Jewish *killing* of the prophets and *crucifying* of Jesus, and because of what the author knows of *flogging* and *harrying* of Christians. (The parallel in Luke 11.49 has only "kill" and "persecute.") While that suspicion may be debatable, nevertheless, such an understanding of the passage agrees with the evidence from Paul's letters; and the fact that Matthew, like Paul, refers to flogging in synagogues leads us in the direction of seeing the same kind of punishment/persecution involved here as in Paul's statements. Nowhere does Matthew provide clues about the causes of this persecution, and the question of cause is the more puzzling because, in the Jewish-Christian source of Matthew, the Christian mission is clearly restricted to "Israel" (Mt 10.23). Therefore the synagogue flogging known to this Jewish–Christian source cannot have been for the "crime" of admitting Gentiles to Christianity without converting them at the same time to Judaism.

We may also enter into evidence a brief notice in Josephus's *Jewish Antiquities* 20.9.1 (written not long before 100). Josephus writes (in part) that in about the year 62 the high priest Ananus "convened the council of judges and led into it the brother of Jesus called Christ, James by name, and certain others; and making accusation of them as transgressors, he delivered them to be stoned." Here we do have a Jewish killing of Jewish Christians (thus perhaps explaining the "killing" of Mt 23.34), but again without any clarification of motive.

Literature from the period between the wars is a bit more instructive. A major source for this period is the Gospel of John, written apparently sometime before 90. In this gospel we see the earliest stages of the separation of Christianity from Judaism in a particular locale, apparently either in Galilee or somewhere near, and the animosities that accompanied that separation, for a number of the conflict settings in which Jesus appears in this gospel seem clearly to refer to conflicts between Christians and non-Christian Jews at a time when, or shortly after, the Christians were still attending synagogue and considered themselves to be good Jews. That such is the setting of the oldest traditions in the Gospel of John has been demonstrated by a number of studies and is now widely accepted by New Testament scholars (Meeks 1975, 1985: 94–104; Martyn 1978, 1979; Brown 1979; Ashton 1991, esp. 167–75; see also Blasi 1997: 101–70).

In the first place, the Gospel of John several times mentions divisions, schisms, in the Jewish crowd attendant on Jesus, some in the crowd responding favorably to Jesus and some with hostility. These scenes doubtless reflect arguments that took place after Jesus' time. For example, John 7:12 reports that some in the crowd "said, 'He is good'; but others said, 'Nay, but he misleads the crowd.'" Shortly after this division another occurs that is even more complicated, for in 7.40–43 some are convinced that Jesus is "the Prophet," some that he is "the Messiah," and some that he cannot be the Messiah because he comes from Galilee and not from Bethlehem. Consequently, "A schism occurred in the crowd . . . because of him." These arguments about Jesus' identity belong not in his lifetime, but in the early Jewish church where it was necessary to clarify which divine or heroic figure of Jewish belief Jesus was. The Prophet–Messiah debate, we note, appears also in Mark 8.27–29 || Matthew 16.13–14; Luke 9.18–20, and as well in John 1.20–21. People may have discussed Jesus' significance during his lifetime; but the structured argument "Prophet, Messiah, or neither" surely belongs to the early church, as we see from its varied attestation in the gospel tradition.

There is also the Jewish charge that Jesus is a "leader astray" or that he "leads astray" (Jn 7.12, 47). Inasmuch as this charge also appears in Matthew 27.63 and materially in Luke 23.2, 5, and 14—where other words are used to mean that Jesus leads people astray—we seem to have here the earliest identifiable Jewish anti-Christian polemic (see Stanton 1985).

By the end of John 8 the arguments over Jesus' true identity degenerate into the two sides—those for and those against Jesus—hurling insults at each other. Jesus charges that his opponents are children of the devil (8.44), and they counter that he is a Samaritan and has a *daimonion* (v. 48). The tone of the entire section 8:39–59 is quite shrill, and the passage ends with Jesus' opponents throwing rocks at him, at which point he conveniently disappears. John 10:19, finally, reports that "a schism occurred again among the Jews because of these sayings," that Jesus is able to lay down his life and to take it up again (v. 18), etc. When we view these differences of opinion and hostilities as belonging not to the career of Jesus, but to the emerging church in the process of separation from the synagogue, then we can better understand the stages of persecution and separation that followed. The evidence here surely concerns only one congregation—either in Galilee or somewhere a bit to the north or east of there—but it is possible and even likely that similar developments occurred elsewhere.

This gospel also gives evidence of what Martyn (1979: 116–18) called "secret believers" and Brown (1979: 169) "crypto-Christians," people who believed that Jesus was the Messiah but kept their belief secret in order not to fall into conflict with the enforcers of Jewish "orthodoxy." Such people are to be seen in the parents of the blind man whom Jesus heals in John 9. According to this account, after Jesus has restored the sight of the blind man (Jn 9.1–7), certain persons— it is not clear who—conduct him to the Pharisees for reasons not explained. The Pharisees seem to want to discover whether a Jewish legal impropriety has taken place and question both the healed man and his parents (vv. 13–23). The man who has received sight by the hand of Jesus is rather indefinite about who has healed him, and his parents profess ignorance: "Who opened his eyes we do not know. Ask him; he is of age" (v. 21). This reply of course leads the reader to think that the parents of the healed man wanted to protect themselves in some way, and the author of the gospel explains that desire when he then adds, "His parents said this because they feared the Jews; for the Jews had already agreed that, if anyone confessed him as Christ, he would be *aposynagogos*"—that is, would be excommunicated from the synagogue, the congregation (v. 22). The situation that is envisioned here is, therefore, one in which an open confession of Jesus as Messiah (or Christ, to use the Greek term) would lead to exclusion from synagogue participation, and one in which some persons might seek to hide their Christianity in order not to be so excluded.

The conclusion of this story further confirms the impression that the persecution experienced by the early Johannine Christians was expulsion from the synagogue, for we read here that the synagogue authorities "reviled" the man who had received his sight (v. 28) and finally "expelled him." The term *aposynagogos* also occurs in John 12:42 and 16:2, thus providing abundant evidence that expulsion from the synagogue was indeed a punishment that was known in the Johannine tradition. (The term appears nowhere else in all of ancient Greek literature.) In 12.42 we read that "many of the rulers believed in [Christ], but because of the Pharisees they did not confess him so that they would not become *aposynagogoi*" (plural); and in 16:2 we have a prophecy of Jesus that "they will make you *aposynagogoi*." Regarding the authority of the Pharisees to expel persons from synagogues, we may note that such a situation almost certainly implies a setting after the time of the constituting of rabbinic Judaism that followed the destruction of Jerusalem in 70. That would place the setting of John 9.22 and 12.42, at least, toward the end of the first Christian century. John 16.2 places into the mouth of Jesus a prophecy of these coming events.

Not only in the examples that we have considered here, but throughout the gospel, the flash point of hostility between the Christians and other Jews is the claim that Jesus is Messiah.[3] In itself such a belief is hardly a sufficient reason for the kind of hostility that John describes, inasmuch as many Jews, both before and after Jesus, thought that some person or another was Messiah without thereby bringing about such a schism, and one could have raised most of the objections to those other messianic pretenders that John explains were raised to Jesus. In some of the designations of Jesus' messiahship, however, we have a very "high" Christology—that is, Jesus' messiahship makes him equal to God himself. When, for example, Jesus claims that he ("the Son") can raise the dead (John 5.21), or when (10.30) he declares that "I and the Father are one," the concept of what it means to be Messiah has passed into the realm that many Jews would have called the heretical. Jesus is, on this understanding, hardly a messiah in any traditional sense; rather, as Messiah he is God on earth. When this high Christology appears, the expulsion of Christians from the synagogue has apparently occurred *already* (Wahlde 1989: 34–43, 162–64; Blasi 1997: 135–70, esp. 146, 167–68), yet the conflict continues, but around a transformed issue! From this time it is true that "in John the issue between Jesus and the Jews is precisely that Jesus seeks to make himself equal with God" (Segal 1986: 156).

Apparently, therefore, in the traditions lying behind and taken up into the Gospel of John, expulsion from the synagogue was the primary punishment for Christians—that is, for those Jews who confessed Jesus as Messiah—a reaction that has yet to be explained and to which we must return below. The belief that Jesus was (equal to) God will thus have *followed* that persecution and was, doubtless at least in part, prompted by it—a point that also requires fuller explanation below.

In addition to expulsion, John also once mentions the killing of Christians (Jn 16:2), but the future orientation and the subjunctive mood of that sentence should evoke skepticism about whether John actually knows of killings that have occurred: "The hour is coming when everyone who kills you may think to render service to God." Our skepticism is further increased by John 7.19–20, where Jesus suddenly blurts out to his Jewish audience, "Why do you seek to kill me?" and they reply, "You have a *daimonion*; who is seeking to kill you?" If Christian missionaries were occasionally killed by their Jewish audiences (see the discussion of stoning below), John nevertheless reports the Jewish attitude to the theme of killing: Jews are not trying to kill Christians.

Let us turn now to other evidence in the Gospel of John for the stage in Jewish–Christian relations after the period of expulsion, and that is the one in which Jews and Christians understand themselves as different from each other, although the Christians are still—at least predominantly—Jewish. Here we should note especially the metaphor of the shepherd and the sheep in John 10.1–6, where the Johannine Jesus speaks of leading his sheep out of the sheepfold, even of casting them out (*ekballo*, which means literally "throw out," although it is also an idiom for "lead out"), of going before them, and of their following him. This lovely extended figure of speech, in which Jesus appears as the good shepherd, is at variance with the thrice-repeated *aposynagogos*. By speaking, however, of Jesus' leading them out the Christians justify the separation as their own doing, and they escape—in their own eyes, in any case—the opprobrium of being outcasts.

The Gospel of John contains a number of other examples of justifying the Christian position over against the Jewish, of which we may mention only 8.17–18: "In your Law it is written that the witness of two persons is true. I am the one who witnesses about myself, and the Father who sent me witnesses about me." While that saying may have given comfort to the Johannine Christians, nevertheless, the person who maintains that he is himself one of his witnesses and who calls God for his second witness is quite alone; we therefore see the beleaguered state of the Johannine Christians.

Jewish stoning of Christians is mentioned a number of times in the New Testament. Such narratives or prophecies occur in John, Matthew, and Luke–Acts; and Paul refers to his having been stoned. In all these instances save one "to stone" seems to mean "to (attempt to) kill." The incident narrated in John 10, however, presents a rather different caste and merits careful examination. When Jesus says in 10.30, "I and the Father are one," John records the following scene:

> The Jews again picked up stones in order that they might stone him. Jesus answered them, "Many fine works I have shown you from the Father; because of which of those works do you stone me?" The Jews answered him, "For a good work we don't stone you, but for blasphemy, and because you, a human being, make yourself God."

We note two things about this passage. The first is that the cause of persecution is here the same that we were able to identify above as the Christology in contention *after* the expulsion of the Johannine Christians from the synagogue, namely the claim that Jesus was God. The other thing that we note is that the scene clearly describes a mob reaction. It is not an official stoning—a standard method of execution—that nearly occurs; rather, the crowd is so enraged by Jesus' words that it reaches for stones to hurl in its anger. Does this scene not then tell us what kind of stoning early Jewish-Christian missionaries experienced from the hands of their more "orthodox" audiences? Such stonings are inherently more likely than are numerous official executions by stoning, which is the situation implied by Matthew and Luke–Acts. That impromptu stonings, like the contemplated one described in John 10, were more widespread than merely the Christian communities of the Johannine tradition is demonstrated by Paul's statement in 2 Corinthians 11.25 that he "had one time been stoned." Had Paul once been officially executed he would not then have been able to write about it; but if he once so angered a Jewish audience with his preaching that they ran him out of the city by throwing rocks at him, then he might very well write, in the context of listing his many apostolic tribulations, that he had once been stoned. The reason for this stoning will probably have been, as we saw above, Paul's affirming that Jesus' messiahship implied that Gentiles could receive the salvation of God without becoming Jews.

The Jewish persecution of Jewish Christians between the wars therefore seems to have consisted, in at least one location, of expulsion from the synagogue and later rock throwing. It is possible that the rock throwing sometimes resulted in death. The rock throwing was apparently a spontaneous crowd response, and other Christians elsewhere also suffered it, perhaps for a variety of reasons, among which will surely have been that they allowed Gentiles to become full members of the Christian movement without becoming converts to Judaism.

While Justin Martyr wrote, most likely in Rome, several years after the conclusion of the second Jewish revolt, he also provides evidence for Jewish–Christian relations in the Jewish homeland in the period between the wars. In one place Justin refers to the treatment of Christians by the leader of the second revolt. In his *First Apology* 31 he writes, "In the Jewish war that went on recently, Bar Kokhba, the leader of the Jewish revolt, ordered that Christians alone be led to terrible punishments if they did not deny Jesus the Christ and blaspheme." This statement is generally taken to be accurate, and there appears to be no reason to be skeptical about its historical validity, for such action by Bar Kokhba seems understandable. Inasmuch as Bar Kokhba was considered by some to be the Messiah, for others to profess another Messiah would be tantamount to treason against his cause: hence, punishment.

That persecution is too event-specific to provide general information about Jewish–Christian relations, but Justin's *Dialogue with Trypho the Jew* is more informative. It is patterned after a Platonic dialogue and is apparently fictional. It may very well, however, reveal some patterns of Jewish–Christian relations. For one thing, the many objections that Trypho raises to Christianity are so learned that they could hardly be imagined, and he offers interpretations of some scriptural passages that Christians would not have invented, e.g., that Isaiah 7:14, "A virgin is with child and will bear a son" (in the Christian reading of the verse), should read, "A young woman . . ."; and he interprets the child as the son of the ancient Judahite King Hezekiah! Thus some kind of contact with learned Jews and some kind of discussion with them over the meaning of Scripture is given for Justin's environment, and presumably also before his time. (Justin, by the way, had been reared in Sebaste, the older Samaria.) Furthermore, in addition to what Justin knows of Jewish objections to Christian interpretations of Scripture, he also reports that Jews curse Christians and that the Jewish leadership has legislated against any contact with Christians.

When Trypho says (*Dial.* 38) that Jewish "teachers have made a rule not to associate with any of" the Christians, and when Justin accuses Jews (*Dial.* 16) of "cursing in [their] synagogues those who believe on Christ," we may have a reference to a curse inserted surely before Justin's time by rabbis in Galilee into a standard synagogue prayer for the purpose of keeping heretics, perhaps especially Christians, from participating in synagogue prayers. We shall return to this curse presently. Whether it was intended as a curse on gentile Christians is doubtful, but individual Jews may not have made the distinction between Jewish Christians and gentile Christians; and certainly Christians are not likely to have drawn such a line if Jews did not. The most probable way, further, for gentile Christians like Justin to have learned about the curse is from Jewish Christians, not from non-Christian Jews, and such Jewish Christians are unlikely to have drawn the inference for their gentile-Christian companions that the curse concerned only themselves. Whether the Christians so excluded, in any case, were Gentile or Jewish is an issue of little moment for Palestine, where most Christians were Jews.

From the Jewish side there are two literary sources that shed light on early Jewish–Christian relations in Palestine. The first of these is the curse just mentioned, which has come to be known as the *birkat ha-minim*, the blessing (or curse) on heretics (*minim*) inserted into the prayer known variously as the Amida or the Eighteen Benedictions—a prayer that is still regularly recited in synagogues around the world, although the curse no longer appears in the Ashkenazic liturgy but only in the Sephardic. There is some uncertainty about exactly what was in the benediction originally, since the Talmudic and early rabbinic references to it do not give the text. We have noted that Justin was of the opinion that the prayer cursed "us"; and the earliest extant example, from a Talmudic-period (200–500 C.E.) manuscript discovered in Cairo in 1898, reads, "For the apostates may there not be hope if they do not return to Your laws. May the *notsrim* [Nazarenes, i.e., Christians] and the *minim* perish in a moment." There is a fairly general scholarly consensus, however, that the term *notsrim* was added after 150 (e.g., Schiffman 1985: 60). Thus *minim* probably was a catch-all term aimed at other types of heretics as well as at Christians (Kimelman 1981: 232; Simon 1986: 183, 200; Visotzky 1989: 65), although (Jewish) Christians may well have been the main targets. The curse probably was not included in the prayer before c. 80 or 90, since the author of Acts does not mention it (see Rowland 1985: 300), and he certainly would have done so had he known of it. Thus around the end of the first century the move began to exclude Christians from participation in synagogue prayers. Since gentile Christians were not attending such services, they were not—in the first instance, in any case—intended by the curse.

One might think that the curse explains something about the expulsion of Christians from synagogues in the Gospel of John; but John mentions nothing about such a curse, and there seems to be no connection. It appears rather to be the case that the Christian community behind the Gospel of John experienced expulsion, and that later an exclusionary device aimed at Christians (and others) generally was put into place.

The contrast with the period before the first revolt is striking. Then we had evidence of sporadic persecution, even murder; but Christians were still attending synagogue and Temple (so the first chapters of Acts). Now persecution is not a factor (although there may have been rock throwing), and the Christians are, in effect, ousted. Several sources pointed to the earlier persecution. John speaks of exclusion, and the general promulgation of the *birkat ha-minim* implies the universality of that exclusion. Synagogue exclusion, however, is not quite the same thing as social separation, as the next body of evidence will reveal.

Two narratives in tractate *Chullin* of the Tosefta, an early rabbinic document closely parallel to the Mishnah but apparently somewhat later and probably dependent on it (Strack and Stemberger 1992: 169–77), bear on Jewish–Christian relations in Galilee in the early second century. The first:

> The case of R. El'azar ben Damah, whom a serpent bit. There came in Jacob, a man of Chephar Sama, to cure him in the name of Jeshua' ben Pandira, but R. Ishmael did not allow it. He said, "Thou art not permitted, Ben Damah." He said, "I will bring thee a proof that he may heal me." But he had not finished bringing a proof when he died. (*Chullin* 2.22, 23; quoted from Herford 1903: 103)

The event here narrated appears to have taken place not long before Bar Kokhba's revolt began and concerns one of the most famous of the early rabbis, R. Ishmael, and his nephew Ben Damah. That the Jacob (or James) who proposes to cure Ben Damah is a Christian is plainly stated when the narrator tells us that Jacob was a follower of Yeshua' ben Pandera, one of the rabbinic names for Jesus. The learned uncle is of the opinion that to accept such a cure would be a transgression of the Torah, and his unfortunate nephew is unable to controvert that opinion by the use of Scripture before he dies.

From this narrative, therefore, we learn that Jewish Christians in Palestine lived among and had at least occasional contact with other Jews. The corollary of that, however, is that mainstream Jews considered the Christians pariahs, not suitable for regular contact. We also see that the name of Jesus is subject to scorn among the rabbis, yet they do not doubt that one of his followers might effect a cure.

Just following this narrative occurs another concerning the arrest of a rabbi by the Roman authorities on suspicion of being a Christian.

> The case of R. Eliezer, who was arrested for Minuth [heresy], and they brought him to the tribunal for judgment. The governor said to him, "Doth an old man like thee occupy himself with such things?" He said to him, "Faithful is the judge concerning me." The governor supposed that he only said this of him, but he was not thinking of any but his Father who is in Heaven. He [the governor] said to him, "Since I am trusted concerning thyself, thus also I will be. I said, perhaps these societies err concerning these things. *Dimissus*, Behold thou art released."

And when he had been released from the tribunal, he was troubled because he had been arrested for Minuth. His disciples came in to console him, but he would not take comfort. R. Aqiba came in and said to him, "Rabbi, shall I say to thee why thou art perhaps grieving?" He said to him, "Say on." He said to him, "Perhaps one of the Minim has said to thee a word of Minuth and it has pleased thee." He said, "By Heaven, thou hast reminded me! Once I was walking along the street of Sepphoris, and I met Jacob of Chephar Sichnin, and he said to me a word of Minuth in the name of Jeshu ben Pantiri, and it pleased me. And I was arrested for words of Minuth because I transgressed the words of Torah [Prv 5:8], 'Keep thy way far from her, and come not nigh the door of her house, [7:26] for she hath cast down many wounded.'" (*Chullin* 2.24; quoted from Herford 1903: 137–38)

The story is set, apparently, during the time of a general Roman sweep for Christians during the reign of the emperor Trajan, c. 110 C.E. (Herford 1903: 140–41). That the nature of R. Eliezer's presumed heresy was Christianity is clear from R. Akiva's proposed solution to the mystery, and that the trial was before a Roman official is clear from the terms "tribunal," "governor," and *Dimissus*. Acquitted, but still at a loss as to how to understand how he could have been thought a Christian, our rabbi's memory is prodded by Akiva, and he remembers that a Christian named Jacob (or James) had once said something to him, perhaps an interpretation of Scripture (so it is when the story is retold in the Babylonian Talmud, *Avodah Zarah* 16b, 17a), of which he had approved. We also note, incidentally, that R. Eliezer's concluding quotation of Scripture implies that he knew that he should have had no contact with a Christian.

The similarity in outline of these two stories, of course, casts doubt on their historicity. A rabbi who is somewhat lax in his relationships either allows or is willing to allow profitable contact with, in each case, a Christian named Jacob. (Jacob will have been a common enough name in any case, and its popularity among Christians is likely, due to the prominence of two Jameses [i.e., Jacobs] in the early days of Christianity. It may be that rabbis often made Jacob the protagonist of Christian stories, just as English-speaking people make Paddy the protagonist of Irish stories.) A stricter and more eminent rabbi then clarifies the situation. This common pattern, however, need not belie the essential validity of the stories, for they must represent a situation that the narrators could assume to have existed. That is to say that these stories could not have become part of the tradition if they did not reflect a realistic situation, if they were not *typical*. Thus we have evidence, in the period between the wars, that—while Christianity and rabbinic Judaism officially opposed each other—nevertheless social contact probably existed on a day-to-day basis.[4]

To sum up: there were Christians in Jerusalem from the earliest days of Christianity until the Bar Kokhba revolt who considered themselves true and proper

Jews. Of the presence of these Jewish Christians we have sufficient literary evidence. Before the first revolt at least some of these Jewish Christians were a regular presence at the Temple, and there they came into at least sporadic conflict with the temple authorities. This temple leadership, as long as it operated (until 70), sought periodically to destroy Christianity, resorting at times to murder. In and near Jerusalem is also the likely place where Paul first carried out and later received synagogue punishment directed against Christian missionaries. The only apparent cause for this hostility toward the Jewish Christians was that some renegades among them, like Paul, admitted Gentiles into full religious fellowship without requiring those Gentiles to become proselytes to Judaism.

After 70 there were no more temple cults in Jerusalem, but the Jewish Christian community in Judah continued until 135. What the relations of that community were with other Jews we cannot say. We do know of the harsh treatment of some by Bar Kokhba, but that does not reveal a general situation of conflict. For the period between the wars, then, our evidence shifts to Galilee, where we find Jewish Christians being excluded from synagogues and declared heretics. Like their predecessors in Jerusalem a generation before, these Jewish Christians still maintain that they are true Jews; but developing rabbinic Judaism finds them guilty of the heresy of making Jesus equal with God and of causing "enmity and strife" between God and his people. We also cannot know, both for Jerusalem before 70 and for Galilee between the wars, what the full range of social relationships was between Christians and other Jews, for the Christians' conflict in Jerusalem earlier and that in Galilee later was primarily with, respectively, the priestly and the rabbinic leadership. From Galilee, in any case, there is evidence that Jewish Christians received more sympathy from "regular Josephs" and even from some rabbis than from the rabbinic leadership.

Now that we have the evidence, in brief, before us, let us seek the sociological principle(s) at work. We have seen that the separation between Christians and other Jews in the Jewish homeland was more the response of officialdom to the Christians than it was a Christian attempt to be different. If we say, however, that first the priests in Jerusalem and later the rabbinic leadership in Galilee persecuted Christians for their theology and their behavior, we have presented the Christian viewpoint. The viewpoint of the authorities will have been that they were punishing criminals—that is, deviants.

The sociological theory of deviance is derived from the important analysis of society provided by Durkheim (1984), where he explained social stratification as an essential part of a society; or, as a modern follower of Durkheim's ideas puts it, "It seems . . . clear that a social system's specific roles—that is, the specialized roles that distinguish it from other kinds of social systems—tend to develop in response to its specific needs, which in turn are derived from its specific goals" (Eisenstadt 1971: 15). The theory was considerably advanced by Becker (1963), who examined not the causes and functions (or dysfunctions) of deviance, but what it was about society that led to *labeling* certain persons and groups deviants and what it was that led to the punishment of these deviants. For Becker, "the central fact about deviance" was that it was "created by society." Thus he proposed the following axiom: "Social groups create deviance by making the rules whose infraction constitutes deviance, and by applying those rules to particular people and labeling them as outsiders." In short, "Deviant behavior is behavior that people so label" (Becker 1963: 8–9).

Becker then turned to an analysis of kinds of deviance. First recognizing that there were, on the one hand, persons who were perceived as being deviant but who in fact were not (falsely accused persons) and, on the other hand, persons who did in fact break certain rules but were not perceived as having done so (secret deviants), as well as the pure deviants (who both broke rules and were perceived to have done so) (1963: 20), Becker sought to define a "sequential model of deviance" (22–24). This model he called that of "deviant careers" (25–39). Such a career of course begins with a deviant act; yet for Becker the attempt to define a motive for that deviant behavior is mistaken, inasmuch as many more persons contemplate deviant behavior than actually engage in it. Thus "we might better ask why conventional people do not follow through on the deviant impulses they have" (25–27). Since a deviant career cannot be undertaken by one for whom the normal restraints of society are effective, we must rather ask how the constraints are "neutralized." Among a number of possibilities that Becker mentions, we may note especially that the person labeled as deviant may return the charge. "His condemners, he may claim, are hypocrites, deviants in disguise, or impelled by personal spite" (29). On the other hand, there may be cases of conflicting values that lead a normally law-abiding person to violate a law for the sake of a higher principle. (We may think of the "civil disobedience" of various social action groups in our time.)

Against that background, then, we can understand the "career" deviant. Becker proposes the following steps (1963: 30–39): First one will develop "deviant motives and interests" that lead to or provide some kind of pleasure or reward. Next, "one of the most crucial steps . . . is likely to be the experience of being caught and publicly labeled as a deviant." As a result of that labeling, "the deviant identification becomes the controlling one" because such labeling results in isolating the offender from conventional society. Finally, the deviant moves "into an organized deviant group" where his career as deviant is solidified. Becker's characterization of such deviant groups is so appropriate to the subject at hand that it is worth quoting at length.

374 JACK T. SANDERS

Members of organized deviant groups . . . have one thing in common: their deviance. It gives them a sense of common fate, of being in the same boat. From a
sense of common fate, from having to face the same problems, grows a deviant
subculture: a set of perspectives and understandings about what the world is like
and how to deal with it, and a set of routine activities based on those perspectives.
Membership in such a group solidifies a deviant identity. (38)

Later Becker turns to the other side of the issue, "rules and their enforcement"
(1963: 120–34). Here he addresses the fact that rules are selectively enforced. Enforcement requires, he observes, four premises (122). There must be someone to
take the initiative in punishment, and also someone to call public attention to the
infraction; there must be some advantage to the person who calls attention to the
infraction; and this advantage must be seen as varying in kind from situation to
situation. It is not values that determine either deviant action or enforcement
(130–33). Rather, "people shape values into specific rules in problematic situations. They perceive some area of their existence as troublesome or difficult, requiring action" (131). Thus values, ambiguous in themselves, give way to specific
rules.

> If we are to achieve a full understanding of deviant behavior, we must get these
> two possible foci of inquiry into balance. We must see deviance, and the outsiders
> who personify the abstract conception, as a consequence of a process of interac-
> tion between people, some of whom in the service of their own interests make and
> enforce rules which catch others who, in the service of their own interests, have
> committed acts which are labeled deviant. (163)

Erikson (1966) next showed that deviance is constant in society, whereas control of deviance is a form of boundary maintenance brought on by external or internal changes that cause an identity crisis leading to boundary adjustment. Erikson demonstrated this principle by an analysis of Puritan suppression of deviance
at three different times in the seventeenth century.

First there was "the Antinomian controversy of 1636–1638" (Erikson 1966:
71). These "antinomians," led by Anne Hutchinson, "threatened the political outlines of the New England Way by denying that the ministers of the Bay were competent to deal with the mysterious workings of grace" just at a time when there
was some political uncertainty related to John Winthrop's decline from political
favor in Massachusetts (108). (He was defeated in his attempt to be reelected governor in 1634.) Anne Hutchinson was banned in Boston.

Then there were the Quakers. The Quakers had the misfortune to arrive in
Massachusetts in mid-century, just at the time when the rebellion under Cromwell
was coming to its conclusion in England (Erikson 1966: 109–10). This situation

provided a boundary crisis for the New England Puritans, for the New Englanders had thought, when the rebellion broke out in England, that they would participate in the new divine governance. Some had actually been invited back to England earlier by some of the Puritans there "for consultation and advice" (111). Yet the Roundheads preferred, after victory, to endorse toleration, which the New Englanders opposed. This disappointing of New England hopes for being able to chart the course for the new order, now that it had appeared, meant that

> the colony had lost its main reason for existing. The saints had come to the new world to provide an object lesson for the rest of mankind, and when the English Puritans lost interest in the model which Massachusetts had offered for their instruction, the whole project seemed a little pointless. (112)

This identity crisis led to an effort to define the boundaries of the community more precisely; the Quakers were there, and so Massachusetts defined its Puritan boundary by persecuting Quakers.

Finally, there were the witch trials of 1692. While these followed the Quaker persecutions of 1665 by over a quarter century, that period had been marked by identity-threatening crises. Arguments among different groups of the Puritans in 1670 broke the former unity into factionalism; then there was an Indian war in 1675. In 1676 the royalty was back in power in England and King Charles II began to question the Massachusetts charter, and in 1679 he ordered that an Anglican church be established in Boston. In 1686, then, he did revoke the charter and sent an Anglican royal governor to the colony (Erikson 1966: 136–38). Following these severe challenges to the Puritan order, then, the witch trials were held in 1692.

Erikson seems to have made his point, at least for Massachusetts in the seventeenth century.[5] Punishment of deviants occurs when a society experiences difficulties leading to an identity crisis. The society then reaffirms its identity by strengthening its boundaries, and this means the identification and punishment of deviants. Here, then, we have a more complete explanation of an aspect of deviance that Becker had identified but had been unable to explain adequately, namely that equal crimes are not always punished equally. The reason for this phenomenon now seems to lie not in any self-satisfying motivation on the part of the enforcers, but rather in the nature of events. When there is a social-identity crisis, boundary maintenance will follow. Others have made the same point, for example, Berger: "When a challenge [to the social world] appears . . . the facticity can no longer be taken for granted. The validity of the social order must then be explicated. . . . The wrongdoers must be convincingly condemned, but this condemnation must also serve to justify their judges" (1967: 31).[6]

376 JACK T. SANDERS

Only one factor remains to be added to this complex, namely escalation. Given that deviance relationships are interactive—response→response→response, etc.—there will be a spiral of the vigorousness of response. In other words, "an interactionist view of deviance situations seems to imply the likelihood of cycles of increasingly intense hostility and activism among competing groups" (Schur 1980: 199).

Does deviance theory help to explain emerging Jewish–Christian relations in Palestine? Here is the tasting that is the proof of the pudding; for it would have been a miracle had mainstream Judaism not sought to maintain its boundaries during the period that we have been examining by identifying and punishing deviants. Tension existed from the time of the Roman general Pompey's ending of the Second Commonwealth in 63 B.C.E., and relations with Rome deteriorated steadily after Herod's son Archelaus was removed in 6 C.E. and replaced by what became a string of prefects in Jerusalem. During the principate of Gaius (Caligula), in the year 39/40 Jews destroyed an altar of the imperial cult at Yavneh (Jamnia), and the next year the emperor ordered his statue placed in the temple at Jerusalem. Only the skillful maneuverings of the Syrian governor and the murder of Gaius prevented that action. A brief rule, under Roman authority, of Herod's grandson Agrippa (41–44), who put James the brother of John to death, was followed by more prefects, and political tension increased. Furthermore, the social and economic situation deteriorated during these years throughout Palestine. Banditry increased, as did open hostilities. It was thus during the very unsettled years of the later 40s and the 50s that Paul would have been on the receiving end of the punishment that he had formerly meted out. In 59–60 there was a Jewish uprising in Caesarea against the gentile majority there, leading to a considerable loss of Jewish life and property, and a few months later the High Priest Ananus executed James the brother of Jesus along with other Christians. Four to five years after James's death Judah was in open revolt against Rome. The Christians, it would appear, had become the Jewish priesthood's witches (to go back to Erikson's example).

Moreover, we must remember, the Christians were precisely those groups of deviants within Jewish society that were seeking gentile adherents when it was Gentiles who were attacking Jewish boundaries! Of course mainstream Judaism punished those deviant groups. How could it have done otherwise? If we remember that not all non-Christian Jews participated in the punishment or even agreed with it, then we must come back to Becker's observations about enforcers. It is the enforcers of boundaries who punish the deviants, and those enforcers in Jerusalem were the priests—and away from Jerusalem doubtless the synagogue leaders—before 70. As soon as order returned to Galilee following the destruction of 70, the synagogue expulsions that we know from the Gospel of John began, and the curse on the heretics came a decade or two later. Justin, as we noted, knew of Jewish opposition to Christianity that followed the Roman defeat of the second Jewish revolt. Had the boundaries of Jewish society in the Jewish homeland not been under such constant threat during the early decades of Christian development, mainstream Judaism might have tolerated Christianity, Jesus might not have been executed, and Christianity might have remained a Jewish messianic movement that came to include some Gentiles. But perhaps we should not speculate about what might have been.

When we turn to the development of Christianity outside the Jewish homeland we find a spectrum that runs all the way from a consistent Jewish Christianity— one that insists that the only true Christians are Jewish, whether by birth or by conversion, and that advocates Jewish practice (circumcision, dietary laws, Sabbath)— to a pronouncedly gentile Christianity that does not see why it should give up normal aspects of pagan life, especially participation in the public sacrifices (i.e., to pagan gods) and traditional sexual morality, which considered male homosexuality normal and was by no means monogamous (again for men). Such idolatry and sexual practice, we may note, were traditionally those aspects of gentile society most abhorrent to Jews. We need to turn once again to the evidence.

From Paul's letter to the Galatians we learn that the Galatian churches were at first gentile, but that other Christian missionaries had brought to Galatia a Judaizing "correction" to Paul's brand of Christianity. These later missionaries had apparently already persuaded the gentile Christians to take up some Jewish observances, since Paul scolds the Galatian Christians for their "observing days and months and seasons and years" (Gal 4.10). Having been persuaded to observe some Jewish holidays—from Paul's language we should infer Sabbath, New Moon, and New Year at the least, although New Year will probably also imply Day of Atonement and Tabernacles (Sukkot)—the Galatian Christians are considering accepting circumcision. That step has clearly not been taken and is the object of Paul's most strenuous rhetoric in Galatians: "Look, I Paul tell you that if you are circumcised Christ will be worth nothing to you" (Gal 5.2). Thus the Galatian churches are the victims of the argument between Paul, who wants to distinguish Christianity from Judaism (while not giving up its Jewish roots), and the traditionally Jewish Christian missionaries, who think that Gentiles cannot be saved as Christians if they do not convert to Judaism.

If Paul represents a point on our spectrum that is somewhere between the Jewish and the gentile extremes, and if his opponents to whom he refers in Galatians represent the Jewish end of the spectrum, the other end of the spectrum comes into view in the opening chapters of Revelation. To be sure, the author represents a version of Christianity that is apparently more toward the Jewish end of the spectrum than is Paul. In Revelation, in the letters to the seven churches (ch. 2, 3), we find the author arguing, on the one hand, against non-Christian Jews, calling them the "synagogue of Satan" and writing that they "say that they are Jews and are not" (Rv 2.9; 3.9). Apparently, therefore, the view of the author is that the only true Jews are Christian Jews. While the author's Jewishness is everywhere in evidence in this intriguing book—for example, in his vision of a new Jerusalem (Rv 21.2)—he never lets us see how much of Jewish practice he thinks gentile converts to Christianity should take up. Since Paul rejected Sabbath, dietary laws, and circumcision, we should specifically like to know whether the author of Revelation agrees with Paul on that point or whether he endorses the view of the Jewish Christian missionaries who opposed Paul in Galatia; but he is silent on that point.

What the author of Revelation does let us see, however, on the other hand is that he strongly opposes gentile Christian groups that do not reject what are in his opinion idolatry and sexual immorality (Borgen 1995: 37). These groups represent the gentile end of our spectrum. Thus the author scolds the church at Pergamum for countenancing "those who hold the teaching of 'Balaam,' eating food offered to idols and engaging in sexual immorality" (Rv 2.15). Some scholars—like A. Y. Collins (1986: 317; 1979: 20)—point out that "sexual immorality" or "adultery" was a common Jewish metaphorical reference to idol worship and question whether the author of Revelation actually meant to accuse the Pergamene Christians of the former. Yet the author uses similar language in scolding the church at Thyatira for countenancing a self-styled prophetess, "Jezebel," who was also promoting "sexual immorality and eating food offered to idols" (Rv 2.20). We could not prove that he does not employ a standard metaphor for idol worship by referring to sexual immorality, but even if such is the case, still we see that there were Christians in Pergamum and Thyatira who did not distinguish their Christianity sufficiently from pagan life style, in the mind of the author of Revelation.

Paul also attests the existence of such gentile Christians who did not sufficiently follow Jewish custom (in his opinion) in their lifestyles.[7] Revising an earlier communication to the Christian congregation at Corinth, Paul sought in I Corinthians 5.9–13 to clarify his earlier advice on associating with immoral persons. What he had meant, he explained, was "to have no contact with someone called a brother who should be a fornicator or greedy or an idolator or a reviler or a drunk or a robber" (v. 11). In 6.9–10, then, he expanded the list by saying that "neither fornicators nor idolators nor adulterers nor effeminate males [i.e., the objects of pederasts] nor homosexuals nor thieves nor greedy persons nor drunks nor revilers nor robbers will inherit the Kingdom of God." We see that the original list has been expanded to include thieves as well as robbers and to include more explicit types of sexual immorality than the rather vague fornication. Since it is his discussion of a case of notable *porneia* (sexual immorality) that prompts Paul first to give this list, and since he then goes on to discuss various aspects of male–female behavior and then issues related to idol-food, and since he does not further take up a discussion of thieves and robbers, of drunks, or of greedy persons or revilers, we may perhaps infer that these latter forms of undesirable behavior were not at issue in Corinth.

In I Corinthians 8 and 10 Paul also advised the Corinthians on the degree to which they might participate in pagan religious practice. The issue is focused on the eating of *eidolothyta*, sacrifices to idols (I Cor 8.1)—that is, the eating of those portions of sacrifices to the gods that were not either consumed in the sacrificial fire or distributed to the priests. Such portions were on many occasions distributed to the populace, on other occasions sold. Paul first agrees with those gentile Christians in Corinth who saw no reason why they should not eat such food by writing that there is only one God and that these other idols have no real existence (v. 4), yet he went on to point out that the "conscience" or "awareness" (*syneidesis*) of some Christians could be damaged by this practice (v. 7), for they might think that the Christian partakers of idol-food were in fact worshipping the other gods. Therefore it was best not to eat (v. 13).

In chapter 10 Paul pursues a different approach, but to the same end. Here he cites the example of the hungering and thirsting Hebrews in the wilderness after leaving Egypt and the excesses to which their desires led them (v. 7), and then he brings in his theology of the body of Christ, first developed in chapter 6, to conclude, "You cannot drink the cup of the Lord and the cup of false gods, you cannot participate in the table of the Lord and in the table of false gods" (v. 21).[8] The "bottom line" in both chapters is therefore the same: Don't eat. Paul's strong opposition to idolatry and to all sex outside marriage is a Jewish opposition (Segal 1995; Borgen 1995), inasmuch as those are the very aspects of gentile society that Jewish literature of the Hellenistic age most often and routinely condemned (J. J. Collins 1983: 142–43). Yet this is the same Paul who also thought that gentile Christians should not follow the Jewish ritual practices of circumcision, Sabbath (and other festival days), and dietary laws. Very clearly, what Paul (and the author of Revelation) were doing was setting boundaries for the Christian movement. A number of years ago Wayne Meeks labeled this function for what it was:

> The Pauline school abolished circumcision of proselytes and other rules that distinguished Jew from gentile within the new community. . . . Would the abolition of the symbolic boundaries between Jew and gentile *within* the Christian groups mean also lowering the boundaries between the Christian sect and the world? . . . Interaction between sect members and non-Christians is directly at issue in the question posed by the Corinthian Christians, whether one is allowed to eat "meat offered to idols" (I Cor 8.1). (Meeks 1983: 97)

Meeks continued by noting that different Christians in Corinth perceived the boundaries of Christianity "quite differently," and that Paul was attempting to bring clarity into this situation, a task at which he was only partially successful (98, 100).

At this point we could rehearse the sociological discussion of boundary setting at some length, as the function pertains to social movements,[9] new social movements, and new religious movements (NRMs) in particular; but in order not to overextend our discussion we need to be selective. We recall Parsons's analysis cited at the beginning of this chapter.

Many sociologists of religion have seen the function of boundary setting operative in the growth of NRMs, but Rodney Stark's analysis of how NRMs succeed (Stark 1987) seems especially appropriate for our evidence. Stark proposed a set of eight factors important to the success of any NRM, and he considered these factors to be "continuous variables"—that is to say that the more nearly an NRM exemplified all the factors completely, the more likely it would be to succeed. Stark's list has been widely discussed, and several sociologists, Bryan Wilson (1987) among them, have pointed out that Stark has a narrow and inadequate definition of success. Nevertheless, Stark has surely fingered several factors that are important in the *growth and continuation* (which is what he meant by success) of NRMs. Stark's first two factors in the success of new religious movements seem particularly appropriate here. They are "retain[ing] *cultural continuity* with the conventional faiths of the societies in which they appear or originate" and "maintain[ing] a *medium* level of *tension* with their surrounding environment; [they] are deviant, but not too deviant" (Stark 1987: 13).

These points seem to strike Paul's position squarely on the head; for his version of Christianity obviously "retained cultural continuity" with Judaism, understanding Christ and salvation completely within the context of Judaism and the Jewish Scripture. And in the case of I Corinthians especially Paul also seems to try to retain cultural continuity—or to allow the Corinthian Christians to retain it—with Greco-Roman culture as much as possible (but not with the *faith* of Greco-Roman culture). One could almost imagine, further, that Paul was using Stark's second criterion as a guideline when he wrote I Corinthians 5.9–10, "I wrote to you in the [previous] letter not to have dealings with *pornoi*; not, to be sure, with the *pornoi* of this world or with the greedy and robbers or idolaters, since then you would have to exit the world." Thus Paul, in his opposition to normal behavior in the matters of idolatry and sex, deliberately proposes "a medium level of tension with [the] surrounding environment"—that is, that the Corinthian Christians should be "deviant but not too deviant." Another way of making this point might be to say that, for an NRM to grow and prosper, it must not set up impervious boundaries.

By the time Paul's and James's careers had been brought to an end—roughly in the year 60—there was vigorous discussion about where the boundaries were. James and his faction of Jerusalem Christians, in any case, seem basically to have held to the point that Christians *were* Jews but were *not* Pharisees and were perhaps also *not* other varieties of Jews, whereas Paul had a different definition of who Christians were not. As he wrote in Galatians 3.28, Christians were "neither Jew nor Greek" (i.e., Gentile). That is the definition that lies at the heart of formative Pauline Christianity. To state it in Parsons's language, Paul's statement would appear as, "We, the Jews and the Greeks." If in Galatians Paul elaborated one side of that definition (not Jews), in I Corinthians he elaborated the other: not Gentiles.

Let us imagine that one of the other wings of early Christianity had won out over Paul. What if the Jerusalem apostles, in spite of the destruction of Jerusalem, had succeeded in keeping Christianity within Judaism? Or what if the Anatolian gentilizing Christians whom the author of Revelation opposed with the labels of Balaam and Jezebel had succeeded in making Christianity compatible with polytheism? If either one of those ends of the spectrum had triumphed, Christianity might well have perished with the Roman Empire. But those wings did not triumph, and they did not do so because Paul and others like him found the winning formula, which we can now express in Stark's terms, *mutatis mutandis*: cultural continuity with the conventional faith of Judaism, an attempt to accommodate as much as possible to Greco-Roman culture, and a medium level of tension with the gentile environment. Paul found the broad middle. He forged a Christianity that was Jewish to the degree that it forbade idolatry and extramarital sex and was gentile to the degree that it forbade circumcision, Sabbath, and dietary laws. It was thus both and neither. The "third race" had come into existence.

A century after Paul, Justin provides evidence that gentile Christianity, in any case, still defined itself in Paul's way. On the one hand, the entirety of Justin's *Dialogue with Trypho the Jew* shows that Christians argued, in one way or another, with Jews. In this work the gentile Christian Justin and the Jew Trypho argue, albeit cordially, over Christian doctrine and the interpretation of Scripture. Always Justin shows, or thinks that he shows, the Jewish interpretation to be incorrect. Justin also mentions the existence of Jewish Christians, and he says that he approves of them as long as they do not seek to persuade gentile Christians to follow Jewish religious observance (*Dial.* 47). That is exactly Paul's position regarding the relation of Christianity to Judaism. On the other hand, in his *First Apology* Justin takes up the Roman charge that Christians are atheists, and he affirms that Christians pledge not to do any wickedness and that the charges are the result of the influence of demons, thought to be gods, who have also "defiled women and corrupted boys" (*1 Apol.* 5); he adds in chapter 6, "We indeed confess to being atheists regarding these beings considered gods, but not regarding the truest [God] and father of righteousness and of temperance and of the other virtues"—again Paul's position exactly as regards the boundary between Christianity and Greco-Roman culture.

The version of Christianity that survived and continues to survive down to this day formed boundaries between itself and Jewish culture and between itself and Greco-Roman culture. These boundaries were not, however, absolute, inasmuch as important aspects of both cultures became part of mainstream (or, as they would have said, catholic) Christianity. It was the right formula for success.

Notes

Except as noted, all translations of foreign texts in this chapter are the author's own.

1. A more extensive treatment of this issue may be found in Sanders (1993).

2. The early Jewish–Christian layer of Matthew comprises at least chapters 5–7 and parts of chapters 10 and 23; see esp. Betz (1985). See further, Meeks (1985: 110); Betz (1975, 1990); Schille (1970).

3. See esp. Wengst (1990).

4. See Simon, who describes just such a situation for Palestine after 135 (1986: xiii–xiv, 95).

5. For a supporting analysis in a more recent setting, see Richardson (1975).

6. Deviance theory, or, as it is often called, labeling theory, has not been without criticism; see, e.g., Goldthorpe (1991) and Davis (1975). For further support of the theory, however, see Ben-Yehuda (1985) and Liska (1992).

7. For a more detailed discussion of this issue see Sanders (1997).

8. The word is *daimonia*, which originally in Greek merely meant spirit forces of an indeterminate kind but has now obviously taken on the meaning of false gods, i.e., idols.

9. One sociologist of religion who has taken early Christianity seriously as a social movement is Blasi (1988), although he does not deal specifically with the phenomenon of boundary setting.

POWER, INEQUALITY, AND DIFFERENCE

IV

Connections with Elites in the World of the Early Christians

17

PHILIP A. HARLAND

Introduction

SOCIAL SCIENTISTS have long recognized the significance of social networks—intricate webs of connection that exist within a social structure—for understanding and explaining the workings of society. But only in recent decades have scholars begun to appreciate their importance in the ancient context and among early Christians in particular. Such study promises to provide new insights into a long-standing problem with respect to where and how Christianity fit within the social structures and strata of cities in the Roman Empire. Approaching the subject this way helps detail the social avenues whereby Christianity made advances within various strata of society, including the pre-Constantinian elites, and the nature and significance of the interactions between social-religious groups ("associations") and those elites within social networks of benefaction.

Conceptual Preliminaries

Before turning to social structures and networks in the ancient context, it is important to say a few words about four concepts. First, sociologists attempting to understand the social structures of society use the term "stratification" to refer to the hierarchical distinctions or social categories (strata) that develop within virtually all societies as a result of differential access to goods and resources of various kinds, and to power and prestige (cf. Berquist 1995). Second, the concept of "social status" refers to one's position or standing in relation to others within the stratification of a particular society or within a given social structure or group (Harper 1995: 1360). A variety of factors play a role in defining one's status within a social structure, including family background, sex, age, ethnic origins, education, occupation, wealth, and ability. Third, "social mobility" refers to movement from one status category to another (a changing of position in relation to others in the hierarchy of a social structure or group), usually upward, through the acquisition of desired qualities or characteristics, such as education, or through links with others with higher status within social networks (e.g., patronage) (cf. Breiger 1990). The potential for social mobility can vary from one society to another, with some societies (such as modern North American society) being far more open to such movement than others (such as ancient Roman society, where mobility was relatively closed).

The fourth important concept to be outlined here is the "social network," which refers to the webs of ties among actors (individuals, groups, communities) within a social structure. Since the mid-1950s social scientists have come to use the term "social network" as an analytical tool for studying specific phenomena within society in relational terms (cf. Mitchell 1969, 1974; Boissevain 1974; Wellman 1983; Wasserman and Faust 1994); several sociologists have employed this tool in the study of modern religious groups (Kecskes and Wolf 1996; Lofland and Stark 1965; Stark and Bainbridge 1985: 307–24; Welch 1981, 1983). J. Clyde Mitchell defines the social network "as a specific set of linkages among a defined set of persons [or groups], with the additional property that the characteristics of these linkages as a whole may be used to interpret the social behaviour of the persons [or groups] involved" (1969: 2). Relational ties among actors serve as channels for the exchange or flow of resources (tangible or intangible, such as honor) while also providing opportunities and imposing constraints upon those involved in the social relations. We shall find that several insights of the social sciences regarding the patterns of ties that make up a social network serve as helpful exploratory tools for finding what might otherwise remain unnoticed in ancient society, despite the fact that our evidence for social relations in this context is meager and partial. Recent studies by scholars such as L. Michael White (1991), John K. Chow (1992), and Harold Remus (1996) suggest the value in employing such tools in the study of antiquity and early Christianity.

Social Stratification in Greco-Roman Society

A brief discussion of social stratification in the society of the Roman Empire is in order before proceeding to social-religious groups within that context. It is worthwhile distinguishing between the official and the less formal factors that affected one's access to resources, influence, and power within society. The official or *formal* social structure can be illustrated in terms of a steep pyramid of hierarchy, with an extremely small portion of the population at the top and the rest at the bottom (cf. MacMullen 1974b; Alföldy 1985; Garnsey and Saller 1987).

There were four main orders of society: senatorial, equestrian (knights), decurion, and plebeian.

At the very top of the hierarchy were those belonging to the senatorial and equestrian orders, which I refer to as the *imperial elites* (probably about 1 percent of the total population).[1] The emperor and his direct family members were at the peak of power and influence. The senatorial aristocracy consisted of a few families (there was a total of about 600 members, all men, in the Roman senate), who were expected to possess property worth about one million sesterces,[2] from which senators were chosen by the senate or the emperor, the supreme patron. There was a typical career path (*cursus honorum*) through which a senator could pass, culminating (sometimes) in the position of consul and then proconsul of one of the more prestigious provinces (such as Asia).

Membership in the equestrian order required a minimum of 400,000 sesterces, and these knights filled the important offices within the army and sometimes moved into the more prestigious administrative positions in Rome and the provinces. Equestrian standing was also hereditary. Patronage connections within networks, especially with the emperor himself, were an essential factor in advancement through the ranks appropriate to one's official order. And there were occasions when these connections together with success within a family from one generation to the next could mean movement from the equestrian to the senatorial order.

This group of imperial elites had its counterparts, though usually on a more modest scale, in the decurions or *civic elites* (probably about 10 percent or less of a city's population). These were the wealthy families of the provincial communities who assumed the more important positions in the cities, including membership on the council, places on the board of archons, or other important civic positions (e.g., director of contests); they, like the imperial elites, also played the social role of benefactors within the cities, to which I return in a later section. From the mid- to late first century, a very small number of these provincial families with imperial connections began to attain equestrian and, eventually, senatorial standing over generations.

Below the elite lay the vast majority of the population (about 90 percent), the plebeians or masses, including both rural and urban dwellers. City dwellers of this stratum, who are our central focus here,[3] could be quite diverse socially and economically. Mention of this diversity within this nonelite segment of the population brings us to the more *informal* features of social stratification that played an important role both in conjunction with and independently of the official orders and hierarchies. Social mobility from one official order to another was extremely limited, and largely dependent on one's patronage connections with the imperial elites, especially the emperor. However, a variety of factors that affected one's social status and mobility went beyond the legally defined categories; some of these factors, or status indicators, included family, ethnic background, legal standing (free, freed, or slave), occupation (artisans, traders, physicians, etc.), citizenship (civic or imperial), wealth, education, skill, and achievement (cf. Hopkins 1965: 14; Meeks 1983: 54–55). There were, therefore, occasional inconsistencies between a person's official position or order and one's actual status in relation to others within society (see Hopkins 1965). The case of imperial slaves and freedmen within the emperor's household, discussed more fully below, is one of the clearest areas of status inconsistency and vertical social mobility in the empire. Yet there was also a range of possibilities in social status among the (formally) nonelite segments of the city populations, and at least some potential for mobility. Shippers or traders, for instance, could hope to attain greater wealth and prestige within the civic community than, say, local tanners whose work involved undesirable odors and fullers (clothing-cleaners) whose work involved the burning of sulfur and urine. There were some cases where those with origins in the nonelite segment of society acquired some of the status indicators mentioned above, especially wealth, and could then take on the role of benefactor within the city, thereby increasing her or his prestige within the civic context. Social mobility in this sense could result in increased influence and power; we even have some exceptional examples of those formally low on the social ladder, including traders and artisans, actually attaining positions on important civic boards or in significant offices.[4]

Social Networks as Avenues of Group Formation and Dissemination

Group Formation and Recruitment

Sociologists studying the formation and growth of religious groups in the modern context have increasingly recognized the importance of preexisting social ties within networks for the dissemination or expansion of sects, cults, and churches. In studies of the Korean-based Unification Church of the Reverend Sun Myung Moon (Lofland and Stark 1965) and of recruitment to Pentecostal churches (Gerlach and Hine 1970) it was found that, more often than not, prior social contacts or interpersonal connections (through friendship or family) between members of a religious group and a nonmember preceded entrance of new recruits into the group.[5] Subsequent sociological studies confirm the vital importance of social networks not only as a precondition of conversion or membership, but also as a continuing factor in explaining the social workings of a given religious group, be it a cult, sect, or more traditional church (cf. Stark and Bainbridge 1985: 307–24; Welch 1981; Cavendish, Welch, and Leege 1998). Given this stress on social networks and group membership, it is important to consider what types of social connections were at work in the ancient context; this may provide important clues about the social avenues for expansion available to associations of various kinds, including Christian groups.

Associations and Their Social Makeup

Several webs of social network connections, at times intersecting, framed social relations in the Greco-Roman world and could also play a role in the formation and growth in membership of associations, including Christian groups.[6] These overlapping webs include connections associated with family/household, common ethnic or geographic origins, occupational activities, and cultic interests. The social connections that predominate as the basis of a particular group may provide clues regarding the social makeup of a group and avenues for expansion within particular social strata of society. We shall see that similar sets of social connections were at work in the case of both associations and Christian groups, and that both reflect a similar spectrum of possibilities in social composition.

First, the ties of the family and household could play a fundamental role in affiliations and in the membership of associations. Family networks encompassed a far greater set of relations in the ancient context than in the modern West. Household relationships seem to account entirely for the membership and existence of groups like the Dionysiac initiates headed by Pompeia Agrippinilla in Torre Nova, Italy (*IGUR* 160, c. 160 C.E.; cf. *LSAM* 20 = Barton and Horsley 1981 [Philadelphia, Asia][7]), where the whole range of social strata found in the ancient household or *familia* belonged to the group, in this case including free, freed, and servile dependents alongside members of the imperial elites such as Agrippinilla herself, who was married to the influential M. Gavius Squilla Gallicanus (a senator and consul who became proconsul of Roman Asia in 165 C.E.; see Vogliano 1933; Scheid 1986).

Second, one's occupation and the networks of relations it entailed were in many ways a determining factor in social-religious affiliations; daily social contacts in the workshops and marketplaces could often develop into a guild of the more permanent type. A wide range of these occupationally based associations existed in the cities of Asia Minor: producers and dealers of foods (bakers, fishers), clothing manufacturers (leather-cutters, linen-workers, purple-dyers), builders (carpenters, masons), other artisans (potters; copper, silver, or gold smiths), and merchants or shippers. Soldiers fit the bill as well; the dissemination of Mithraism throughout certain segments of the army illustrates the importance of occupational social networks for the formation and growth of associations (Gordon 1972: 103–4). There were also elite associations, such as the Arval Brethren at Rome, formed from the social connections among those whose "occupation" included senatorial imperial offices. On the whole, membership in occupational associations was predominantly male, and in many cases the social makeup of a guild was rather homogeneous in socioeconomic terms; most bakers, for instance, came from a similar background and stratum of society. Nevertheless, there are clear examples of guilds reflecting a spectrum of socioeconomic levels. The fishers and fishmongers at Ephesos (*IEph* 20 = *NewDocs* V, 50s C.E.), for instance, together with their families, contributed toward the building and dedication of the fishery toll office; the one hundred (or so) contributors included Roman citizens (approximately forty-four members) and a mixture of persons of free or freed (between thirty-six and forty-one) and servile status (between two and ten), who are listed in order of the size of their donation, ranging from the Roman citizen who could afford to provide four marble columns to those who could afford to give five denaria or less.

A third important set of social network links, which could often overlap with others, were those formed within the neighborhood where one lived and worked. There are numerous examples of ongoing social-religious groups in Asia Minor that drew primarily on these connections and whose identity was expressed in neighborhood terms (cf. *IEph* 454, 3080; *IGR* IV 788–91 [Apameia, Phrygia]; *IPergamon* 393, 424, 434; *ISmyrna* 714). Apart from elite households, which included dependents, persons living or working in a particular area were more likely to reflect similar social brackets of society, yet such neighborhood associations could include a mixture in terms of occupation (cf. *IPergamon* 393) or gender.

Fourth, social contacts associated with regular attendance at a particular cultic site or common religious interests (i.e., honoring a particular deity), for example, could become the basis for an ongoing association. Remus's (1996) study of social networks at the Asklepios sanctuary of Pergamon demonstrates well the complicated webs of connection that formed in a cultic setting; these connections could also be translated into an association. In the case of the sanctuary at Pergamon, there were groups who called themselves *therapeutai*.[8] Once again, though, there was a range of possibilities in the social levels reflected in these groups; while many associations would have been formed by those of a similar socioeconomic background, others would have more accurately reflected the range of those devoted to honoring a particular deity at a particular site on a regular basis, including both men and women.[9] In the case of socially mixed groups, quite often those with greater wealth and higher social status would act as benefactor and, thereby, acquire leadership positions in the group as a result (cf. *IEph* 4337 [worshippers of Demeter]; White 1997).

A fifth important set of social contacts were those established on the basis of common ethnic background or geographical origin, which could constitute another source of membership for an ongoing group (often devoted to honoring a deity of the homeland). There were various associations of Romans and Alexandrians in the cities of Asia Minor and other provinces (cf. *IGR* I 392, 446, 800), for instance, and groups of Sardians and other Asians in the cities of Italy (*IGUR* 85–87; *IGR* I 147, 458) and Macedonia (*IG* X.2 309, 480; Edson 1948: 154–58). The social makeup of these groups could, of course, vary, with some reflecting a greater spectrum of socioeconomic levels than others. Some associations of Romans in Asia Minor, for instance, drew members from various levels of trade and varying socioeconomic status; a few members could assume local citizenship, attain considerable wealth, and act as benefactors within the city (cf. Hatzfeld 1919: 101–31, 148–74, 297–309).

Not to be forgotten within this category, of course, are the diaspora groups of Jews or Judaeans who could be found in cities throughout the empire. Within the broader context of ethnically or geographically based Jewish networks, several other subsets of social connections, corresponding to the networks outlined above, could be operative in the formation and membership of particular synagogues. The case of the synagogues in Rome, of which there were at least eleven in the first two centuries (some existing simultaneously), is instructive in this regard (see Leon 1995 [1960]: 135–66; Richardson 1998). Three derive their names from the neighborhood where they lived: the Calcaresians from the Limeburner's district, the Campesians from the Campus Martius, and the Siburesians from the Subura district. Two others may very well have been founded by Jews initially from cities elsewhere: the Tripolitans from the city of their namesake either in Phoenicia or North Africa, and the "synagogue of Elaia," perhaps consisting of some former residents (or citizens?) of Elaia in Asia. Both neighborhood and occupational factors played a role in the organization of the Jewish population at Alexandria as well (cf. Philo, *Flaccus* 55; *CPJ* III 454, 468; Kasher 1985: 352–53). Recent studies of the social makeup of Jewish diaspora groups also point to diversity in social levels, occupations, and degree of wealth and influence from one group to the next in various cities (cf. Trebilco 1991; van der Horst 1991: 99–101); the presence of wealthy benefactors among some groups is clear, as at Smyrna, where Rufina, the head of the synagogue, also had a contingent of clients, both freedpersons and slaves (*ISmyrna* 295 = *CII* 741).

Christian Groups and Their Social Makeup

Evidence shows that many of the kinds of social networks outlined above played a role in the growth of Christian groups. Consequently there was diversity in the social composition of various Christian groups, with variations from one group to the next, as was the case with the associations discussed above. First, family-based networks played a key role in the case of some early Christian groups. A pattern of "conversion" and communal gathering portrayed in Acts, but also substantiated elsewhere, is suggestive: again and again an entire family of dependents was baptized along with the head of the household, and then the home was used as a meeting place (Acts 11.14, 16.15, 18.8, cf. I Cor 16.19; Phlm 2; Rom 6.10–16; Col 4.15).

Second, social connections related to ethnicity and geography served as an avenue for the spread of Christianity. Networks among diaspora Jews provided an important matrix within which Christianity could make an entrance into certain cities.[10] Furthermore, it is not hard to imagine regional movements within Christianity, such as Montanism (called the "Phrygian heresy" by opponents), making advances within other areas of the empire by way of emigrants from regions such as the Phrygian region of Asia Minor.

Neighborhood connections were also important. A third-century grave-inscription from Akmoneia is suggestive: a Christian named Aurelius Aristeas promises "the neighborhood of those by the gateway" provisions for regular banquets if they fulfill their obligation by putting roses on his wife's grave once a year (Ramsay 1895–97: 562–63, numbers 455–57).[11] The neighborhood association in question may or may not be devoted to the Christian god as well, but this evidence of social links within networks is significant either way.

Occupational networks were also important for early Christianity, as Hock's work (1980) shows. The Christian group at Thessalonica addressed by Paul seems to provide a good example of a guild of hand-workers, perhaps mainly men (cf. I Thes 2.9, 4.9–12; Ascough 2000). Although we should not take at face value Celsus's characterization of the whole Christian movement as predominantly lower class, there is truth in his observation, about a century after Paul, that attachments through workshops of wool-workers, shoemakers, and clothing-cleaners continued as a key resource for newcomers to some Christian groups (Origen, *Cels.* 3.55). Humphries's (1998) recent case study also suggests the importance of social contacts through trade networks in the dissemination of Christianity and other religious groups in trade centers of northern Italy (third and fourth centuries C.E.). If the purge of Christians from the army in the time of Diocletian is indicative of their considerable presence there by that time (c. 303 C.E.), then it seems that social connections within this arena played some role in the spread of Christianity in the years following our earliest clear evidence of some Christians within a legion in the time of Marcus Aurelius (c. 173 C.E.; Eusebius, *Hist. eccl.* 8.4; cf. Helgeland 1974). In cases where a Christian group drew its membership primarily from occupational or trade networks, the makeup of the group could be more homogeneous, both in socioeconomic level and gender, than was the case with some other Christian groups; but as noted in connection with the fishers at Ephesos, there were cases of socially heterogenous membership in guilds as well.

It is worth placing the present discussion of social networks and the composition of Christian groups, which suggests variety from one group to the next and a range of possibilities from heterogenous to homogeneous membership, within the broader context of debates concerning the social level of early Christianity. Until recent decades, it was quite common for scholars to speak of early Christianity as, in the words of Adolf Deissmann, "a movement of the lower classes" (1910/1927: 8–9). The notion that most, if not all, early Christian groups drew their membership primarily from the most dispossessed and deprived segments of Greco-Roman society is also reflected in some recent studies (cf. Elliott 1990[1981]: 59–100, esp. 70–72). Yet recent years have seen a shift away from this sort of characterization toward an acknowledgment that Christian groups were "more nearly a cross section of society than we have sometimes thought," as Filson observed (1939: 111). Paul's comment to the Corinthians that "not many [of you] were powerful, not many were of noble birth" (1 Cor 1.26), for instance, suggests that *some* were, and recent studies of the Corinthian correspondence show that the presence of both wealthier patrons and those of low social standing within this community accounts for several of the problems that Paul perceives, including the issues of court cases (ch. 6), eating food that had been offered to idols (ch. 8–10), and social divisions at the Lord's Supper (ch. 11; cf. Theissen 1980; Chow 1992; Clarke 1993). Studies by Malherbe (1983[1977]: 29–59), Meeks (1983: 51–73), and others emphasize that although we lack sufficient information to provide detailed profiles of the social level of Christians, the indications we do get suggest that many groups reflect a mixture of socioeconomic levels representing a "fair cross-section of urban society" (Meeks 1983: 73; cf. Judge 1960; Theissen 1982; Holmberg 1990: 21–76). Within this mixture Meeks suggests that the "typical" Christian (in Pauline groups) was the "free artisan or trader" (1983: 73), though, as I have shown, there was certainly a range of possibilities of wealth, prestige, and status within such segments of society. Grant's (1980–81) survey of literary evidence for Christianity in the second century likewise finds a range of possibilities in the wealth, education, and overall status of Christians. It is worth mentioning Pliny the Younger's general observation as Roman governor of Bithynia-Pontus (c. 110 C.E.) that the Christians brought before him represented "individuals of every age and class, both men and women," among them some Roman citizens and two female deaconesses (*Ep.* 10.96.4, 8–9).

Although this emerging scholarly consensus is insightful in most respects, the discussion of social networks and associations above should caution us in generalizing too much concerning the overall social composition of Christianity (or other associations). Meeks (1983: 79), for example, contrasts the (supposed) typically heterogeneous Christian groups to the (supposed) homogeneous character of other associations, which does not do justice to the range of evidence discussed above. Viewing the issue of social composition from the perspective of ancient social networks complicates broad generalizations and points to some of the shared avenues of expansion into certain social strata open to groups of various kinds. Moreover, we need to remain attentive to the differences from one group (Christian or otherwise) to the next, with some groups being more homogeneous, others more heterogeneous, in both social level and gender makeup.

Christians within Elite Strata and Networks: Paths of Vertical Mobility

In the case of the *civic* elites, the wealthier segment of the population who could attain civic office and exert local influence within the cities, we do not have much Christian evidence to work with until the third century; but there are some indicators. There are clear signs that Christianity had to some degree penetrated the ranks of the wealthier stratum in some cities in the first and second centuries; concern for the proper management of wealth within Christian literature confirms the fact that some Christians in Asia Minor and elsewhere were wealthy enough to act as benefactors (and leaders) within the group (cf. pastoral Epistles; *Shepherd of Hermas*). However, we are short on clear evidence of Christians drawn from the segments of society that filled civic offices, with some important exceptions.

Although those of "noble birth" and "power" (I Cor 1.26) among the Corinthian Christians (mid-first century) *could* be among those who assumed important civic positions, it is only in the case of Erastus at Corinth that we have more solid confirmation of this possibility. Paul mentions that Erastus is a civic functionary of some type, an *"oikonomos* of the city" (Rom 16.23). That Erastus was a civic functionary is significant in itself, but it is not clear precisely what position Erastus filled and its level of importance (Paul is speaking in Greek, and the positions in the Roman colony of Corinth would usually be expressed in Latin). The fact that Paul singles out Erastus in mentioning an occupation suggests that the position is one of relatively high status (cf. Theissen 1980: 75–76). Mason's study of Greek equivalents of Latin terms shows that the term *oikonomos* (1974: 71) could be used to describe a number of positions, including treasurer (*dispensator*), overseer (*vilicus*), or even aedile. Any of these positions are candidates in this case, but the position of aedile would be the most influential. The two civic aediles, elected annually, were responsible for management of public streets, buildings, and revenue in a Roman colony, and their position was second only to the chief magistrates, the *duoviri*. If Erastus was an aedile (which we cannot say for sure), it is possible that he can be identified with his namesake in an inscription from first-century Corinth: "Erastus in return for his aedileship laid (the pavement) at his own expense" (see Clarke 1993: 46–57 for full discussion). Perhaps there were other Christians, like Erastus, among the civic elites in the first century, who continued to offer their services to their home city, but we can only speculate.

It is only in the late second and early third centuries (beginning c. 180 C.E.) that we begin to find surviving artifactual evidence for Christians that is distinguishable from the more general archeological record (cf. Snyder 1985). So it is significant that some of the extant monuments or inscriptions, many of which come from Asia Minor, provide glimpses of Christians among the civic elites, playing a significant role in the life of the city. Besides those inscriptions that clearly indicate pride in at least civic citizenship (e.g., Snyder 1985: 138–41, note 5), there are several examples of Christians as members of civic councils in Asia Minor in the mid- to late third century. At Sebaste there was a Christian physician on the council, and at Eumeneia there were several Christians on the council.[12] Membership on the civic council (boule) was reserved for those with considerable wealth who could contribute, as benefactors, to the well-being of the city; only those with high social status within the community would attain the position.

Even more telling is an earlier inscription from Claudiopolis in Bithynia (late second to mid-third century C.E.), which involves a Christian as an important civic magistrate and benefactor of the city:

> For the two purest ones who also had faith in God: Marcus Demetrianos, who served as foremost archon, civic administrator, and director of contests with honor, and the dearest mother, Aurelia Pannychas. Aurelia Demetriane, their daughter, and Domitios Heliodoros, their son-in-law, together with her brother Demetrianos and her uncle Chrysippos erected this tomb as a memorial. (Early-Christian Epitaphs from Anatolia: 80–81, note 3.1 [tr., with adaptations] = IBithDörner II 159)[13]

The board of archons was the most influential civic body in this region, and the post of head of this board would be reserved only for the most wealthy benefactors of the city. Demetrianos's benefactions had evidently included sponsorship of the contests that were so much a characteristic of social life in the city. Here we have a Christian couple of high social status and great influence within the civic context being honored on an epitaph by a family that is proud of both their civic achievements and their "faith in God."

Due to the nature of our evidence, it is difficult to know how representative the cases at Sebaste, Eumeneia, and Claudiopolis are, but they certainly show the potential (and perhaps increasing) presence of some Christians among the civic elites, especially by the third century. It remains most likely, however, that elite members among Christian groups were in the minority, probably reflecting the ratio of elites to general population in civic society more generally. Though evidence is lacking, it is quite possible that the Christian groups at these localities might have used their connections with the city councilors or an archon to further their own interests; gaining permission from the civic authorities to build a meeting place, for instance, would be a plausible benefit of these social network connections.

The presence of Christians among *imperial* elite families or networks is also a difficult area to assess due to the vagaries of our evidence (cf. Harnack 1961[1908]: 33–52; Cadoux 1925 [throughout]; Eck 1971). There is, however, clear and early evidence of Christians belonging to the imperial household or *familia Caesaris*. A few words are in order concerning the imperial household and social mobility before outlining some of the Christian evidence. The *familia Caesaris*, which encompassed all those slaves (*servi*) and freedpersons (*liberti*) in the direct service of the emperor, was divided into two branches: domestic and public (Weaver 1967, 1972). The former, which involved the upkeep of imperial establishments and gardens in Rome and on imperial estates elsewhere, would indeed involve direct social contacts with the emperor and hence access to the most powerful and influential patron in the Roman Empire; yet it was in the public imperial administrative service that there was a wide range of posts, some of which could involve considerable power and influence. In fact, recent scholarship stresses the fact that the civil service of the imperial household was the most important avenue of social mobility in the Roman Empire (cf. Weaver 1967: 4).

Individuals in the administrative service who demonstrated ability and exploited their patronage connections with the emperor usually followed a typical career path leading them to acquire characteristics conducive to social advancement and access to networks of influence, as Weaver's studies (1967, 1972) show. Imperial slaves aged twenty to thirty began in the junior post of assistant (*adjutor*) and would often achieve manumission (transition from the legal status of slave to free) during this period. Next (between the ages of thirty and forty) would come the intermediate posts, including record officer (*a commentariis*), correspondant (*ab epistulis*), accountant (*tabularius*), or paymaster (*dispensator*), positions that entailed some level of education, acquisition of considerable wealth, and exercise of power. Finally, at about the age of forty the imperial freedman would be eligible for the senior posts, including chief accountant, chief correspondent, or supervisor (*procurator*); some procurators would serve alongside their equestrian counterparts in provinces such as Roman Asia. As Finn points out, by retirement (if not earlier) the imperial freedman "had acquired a considerable measure of the criteria which signaled upward change in status" and "his descendants started life fairly well up on the status ladder and could go much further" (1982: 32). The line between imperial freedmen and the official equestrian order was seldom crossed, however (see Weaver 1972: 282–94); yet, as noted earlier, social status and access to networks of influence involved factors beyond the officially or legally defined orders of society.

It is significant that this area of society in which social mobility was most prominent is precisely where we find the clearest evidence (limited though it is) of Christian presence. Moreover, this points to one of the more important processes of vertical mobility whereby Christianity moved up socially in the pre-Constantinian
empire, gradually gaining influence in some of the more important social networks
(cf. Finn 1982). As early as Paul's letter to the Christians at the Roman colony of
Philippi (Phil 4.22, c. 60 C.E.), we hear of Christians as members of "Caesar's
household," probably at Rome. Toward the end of the century there is mention of
Claudius Ephebus and Valerius Vito in the church at Rome (*1 Clem.* 65.1), and their
names suggest strongly that they are freedmen of the Claudian and Valerian households (cf. Jeffers 1991: 29–31).

There are further literary references to Christians among these segments of the
imperial household, especially beginning in the late second century. We hear of an
imperial slave named Euelpistos in connection with the martyrdom of Justin, the
apologist (*Mart. Justin,* c. 165 C.E.). Callistus, Hippolytus's archrival who became
bishop of Rome, was the slave of a Christian imperial freedman named Car-
pophoros, probably a paymaster in Commodus's household (Hippolytus, *Haer.*
9.12, c. 172–92 C.E.; cf. Finn 1982: 34). In Eusebius's *Ecclesiastical History* we encounter several Christians who were imperial slaves or freedmen (mid- to late third
or early fourth centuries), some apparently in important positions of the imperial
administration. These include Dorotheus, who was appointed by the emperor to
take charge of the purple-dye works at Tyre (7.32); Dorotheus, who was honored
as though he were a "ruler or governor" (8.1, 6) before being purged from Diocletian's household along with two other Christians, Peter and Gorgonius; Philoro-
mus, who was entrusted with judicial functions in the imperial administration at
Alexandria (8.9); and Audactus, who "had advanced through every grade of honor
under the emperors, so as to pass blamelessly through the general administration
of what they call the magistracy and ministry of finance" (*Hist. eccl.,* Lake 8.11).[14]

Epigraphical evidence happens to confirm the picture we get from the literature (at least for the third century). An inscription from about 240–50 C.E. sheds
much needed light on this issue and provides us with information about two such
Christians as members of the imperial household (*CIL* VI 8987 = *ICUR* X
27126 = Clarke 1971).[15] Alexander, an imperial slave, erected a memorial for his
deceased son, Marcus, who had been the keeper of the wardrobe in the domestic
service of the emperor. Most importantly for our purposes is the fact that Marcus had acquired an education—a key factor in social advancement—at the
paedogogium ad Caput Africae, a senior administrative training center for the young of
the imperial family (see Mohler 1940: 270–80). As G. W. Clarke points out, the
better graduates of this school "would be well read, well spoken; they would expect to marry non-servile wives (though not yet manumitted themselves), to own

considerable property and other slaves, to receive entree into (though not equal status with) the major social and governmental circles, and thus to wield themselves considerable *de facto* power" (1971: 122–23). Here, then, is a clear example wherein a Christian family was making advancements socially in the service of the emperor, and it is likely that there were others like them.

It is worth mentioning another monument—less securely, though likely, identified as Christian—from the vicinity of Rome (dated 217 C.E.) that provides a similar picture of social mobility. The grave of Marcus Aurelius Prosenes—set up by several of his own freedpersons (*liberti*)—reveals that this imperial freedman had moved his way through the hierarchy of imperial service, even holding several procuratorships (senior positions of considerable influence) under Commodus. Though nothing in the original inscription suggests Christian identity, one freedman named Ampelius later inscribed on the stone the fact that Prosenes was "welcomed before God" (*receptus ad deum*) on March 3, 217, an expression that may best be explained in terms of Christianity (*ICUR* VI 17246; cf. Mazzoleni 1999: 153). Finally, there is evidence in an inscription from Ostia (which is probably Christian), the grave of Basilides, who was an imperial slave serving as assistant to Sabinus, the imperial paymaster for the port, probably around 250 C.E. (*CIL* XIV 1876).[16]

Emperor Valerian's edict of 258 C.E. (soon reversed by Gallienus) not only confirms the presence of Christians within the imperial household, but also suggests that by this time Christianity had begun to make at least some limited headway through elite family networks into the equestrian and senatorial orders. According to a letter of the Christian bishop Cyprian (*Ep.* 80), the edict took measures to eliminate the practice of Christianity among the upper echelons of the imperial elites.

> Senators, prominent men and Roman equestrians are to lose their position, and moreover be stripped of their property; if they still persist in being Christians after their goods have been taken from them, they are to be beheaded. Matrons are to be deprived of their property and banished into exile. But members of Caesar's household (*Caesariani*) are to have their goods confiscated and be sent in chains by appointment to the estates of Caesar. (Trans. Harnack 1961[1908]: 38–39; see Keresztes 1989: 67–81, 258–59)

Specific examples of Christians among the equestrian and senatorial orders in the period before Valerian, however, are few and far between (which may simply be due to the fragmentary nature of surviving evidence). As to Christians of equestrian status, the "brothers" of many ranks that were sifted from the army under Diocletian and his co-emperors (c. 303–305 C.E.) may have included such officers, as Harnack (1981 [1905]: 93) imagined; but we are left with very little information concerning the rank of any Christians who were in the army before this time (since about 173 C.E.; see Helgeland 1974).

We are also short on evidence regarding the senatorial order. Several scholars have argued that the senator and consul (95 C.E.) T. Flavius Clemens and his wife Domitilla, executed for "atheism" by Domitian, were Christians (based primarily on Eusebius's claim [*Hist. eccl.*18.4] that Domitilla was a convert); but the evidence for this is extremely tenuous. It seems more likely that the "atheism" in question is actually Judaism (see Keresztes 1989: 87–93, against Sordi 1986: 43–54). Beginning in the late second century, we hear mention of women from these circles of influence who maintained positive contacts with Christians and were likely converts, such as the wife of a governor of Cappadocia (L. Claudius Hieronymianus) and the wife of a governor of Syria (Tertullian, *Scap.* 3.5; Hippolytus, *Comm. Dan.* 4.18.1–3 [c. 202–4 C.E.]). One could well imagine Christianity making its way through social connections within the households of these influential women. Eusebius mentions Astyrius as "a member of the Roman senate" immediately following Valerian's time (under Gallienus), and all of the other certain pre-Constantinian examples date to the early fourth century (see Eck 1971: 388–91).

It is only beginning with Constantine that Christian senators and equestrians are more commonly attested. Even then, Ramsay MacMullen (1984: 47) can estimate that at least two-thirds of Constantine's government at the upper echelons remained non-Christian (cf. Markus 1974: 90–91). Studies by MacMullen (1984), Markus (1974), Brown (1961), von Haehling (1978), and others are beginning to discern some of the processes through which families of the Roman aristocracy were gradually Christianized in the fourth and fifth centuries. Moreover, although there were few Christians among the imperial elites in the first centuries, there was another important area of potential contacts between Christian groups and both the civic and imperial elites within society: social networks of benefaction or patronage.

Contacts between Associations and the Elites within Networks of Benefaction

Networks of Benefaction and Insights from the Social Sciences

Social networks are not static entities working on the same principles throughout history, but rather systems guided by particular cultural conditions. So it is important to discuss some of the key cultural and social norms, expectations, and roles characteristic of networks of benefaction in the cities of the Roman Empire (especially the Greek East). Virtually all social-religious groups in the world of the Christians, including both Jewish and Christian groups we shall see, were in some way involved in these networks and dependent upon benefaction or patronage for their continued existence.

The late Hellenistic and Roman eras witnessed the emergence of a systematic pattern of benefaction ("euergetism") that worked through social networks and was accompanied by a particular developing cultural worldview, especially in the Greek East (cf. Veyne 1990 [1976]; Gauthier 1985; Wallace-Hadrill 1990: 150–54; Sartre 1991: 147–66). This system is perhaps best explained in terms of webs of reciprocal relations within social networks marked by a clearly differentiated hierarchy, though the potential for relations was quite fluid at all levels. The ultimate patron or benefactor, alongside the gods, was the emperor himself, with the imperial elites coming in second; but perhaps more important for the everyday life of the average city were the civic elites and other inhabitants who had attained considerable wealth (as well as the more successful of those involved in trade or other occupations). The most prominent characteristic of relations within these networks was the exchange of benefits or gifts of numerous kinds (protection, financial contributions for various purposes, legal or other assistance) in return for appropriate honors (monumental inscriptions or statues, leadership positions within the group, yearly proclamation of honors). A clearly defined set of social roles or expectations corresponded to one's position or status within the social structure. Failure of the wealthy to appropriately provide such benefactions was a threat to the position and status they strove to maintain within society. In this sense benefaction became a duty or obligation, not simply a voluntary action. Failure of a beneficiary (individual or group) to fittingly honor a benefactor resulted in shame (cf. Dio Chrysostom, *Rhod., Nest., 3 Fort., Lib.*) and jeopardized the potential for future benefactions, whether this be protection of the community by a god or financial support from a local notable.

Associations were, as we shall see, among the groups and individuals competing within this social system to maintain links with the elites. Several sociological insights are of help in approaching the study of social networks of benefaction and the place of associations within them. Wellman (1983) summarizes several of the most important principles evident in the work of many network analysts, some of which are relevant here. First, ties in a social network are often asymmetrically reciprocal, involving the exchange of resources that may be either material or intangible (e.g., honor, popularity). Thus although the members of a local association or guild differ greatly in status from the wealthy civic or imperial official, relations between the two involve an exchange of resources: money and the prestige of links with a member of the elites for the association, and both honor and nonfinancial forms of support, bringing advantage in competition with other members of the elites, for the official.

Second, ties link network members indirectly as well as directly; that is, links within a network should be understood within the context of larger network structures. Connections between an association and a Roman proconsul or imperial cult high priest, for example, involve a link between the local social networks (in which the association is a clear participant) and larger networks that link the city to province and empire. Third, links connect clusters of relations as well as individuals. The link of an individual association member to someone outside the group links all of the association members to that person. That outside person may be linked to other associations in the same way. Thus clusters of relations lead out to broad networks that often involve influential personages. Finally, networks structure collaboration and competition to secure scarce resources (whether material or otherwise). This principle is particularly apt for our present discussion. We have seen that associations themselves are groups based, in part, on preexisting sets of social network connections, allowing collaboration among members to secure resources, such as benefaction from the elites. On the other hand, associations may compete with one another for access to the limited resource of benefactors within broader social networks.

Mitchell (1969) analyzes social networks in terms of two kinds of dimension. First, there are the morphological dimensions that pertain to the overall shape of the web of ties within a particular social network, something that is difficult to assess owing to the fragmentary nature of ancient evidence. Second, there are interactional dimensions that pertain to the nature of the links themselves; these are "crucial in understanding the social behaviour" (1969: 20). Among the interactional dimensions are *content*, pertaining to the purpose for which a particular link has come into being, be it economic assistance, kinship, religious, or occupational purposes; *directedness*, regarding the direction of the flow of interaction, be it reciprocal or otherwise; *durability*, relating to whether the ties are temporary or ongoing; and, *intensity*, regarding the "degree to which individuals are prepared to honor obligations, or feel free to exercise the rights implied in their link to some other person" (27). All of these dimensions play a role in shaping the social behaviors and interactions of the actors.

Associations and Connections with the Elites

Associations could be among the beneficiaries of family traditions of beneficence, maintaining important links with the provincial imperial elites. The case of a certain Julian family of Asia Minor is illustrative; they were descendents of Galatian and Attalid royalty who entered into imperial service as equestrians and then senators as early as the late first century.[17] Members of this family habitually included associations (though no known Christian ones) as recipients of their benefactions, illustrating the sorts of links that could exist between the elites and local social-religious groups. C. Antius Aulus Julius Quadratus was a prominent Pergamene and senator who assumed the consulate in 94 and 105 C.E. He held numerous provincial offices in the Greek East, including legate in Asia, Bithynia-Pontus, Lycia-Pamphylia, and Syria, and proconsul of Asia in 109–10 C.E. Numerous cities, including his hometown of Pergamon, honored him for his services and benefactions (*IEph* 614, 1538; *ISide* 57; *IPergamon* 436–51). But he was also the benefactor of local associations at home including the synod of young men (*neoi*) and, on more than one occasion, an association devoted to Dionysos, which called itself the "dancing cowherds" (*IPergamon* 440; Conze and Schuchhardt 1899: 179–80, notes 31–32). The cowherds, whose meeting place has been recently excavated (see Radt 1988: 224–28), came into contact with him directly when he was priest of Dionysos Kathegemon. Another relative, Julius Amyntianus, probably Quadratus's cousin, was a member in the Panhellenion institution of Athens, but also the priest of Isis and Sarapis at Tralles for a time, for which the initiates of these Greco-Egyptian deities honored him with a monument (*ITral* 86; post-131 C.E.).

A few sociological observations would be fitting at this point before turning to one final member of this family that had connections with local associations. Considering some of the interactional dimensions of these links in social networks between members of this family and associations of various kinds can help us better to understand the nature of such connections. First, the content or purposes of these instances of interaction—"the meanings which the persons in the network attribute to their relationships" (Mitchell 1969: 20)—are similar, though not necessarily identical. In these cases of asymmetrically reciprocal contacts between the elites and local associations, the participants would clearly understand the links in terms of a benefactor–beneficiary relationship: the exchange of tangible financial aid in return for the far less tangible, though extremely valuable, return of honors. There is more to it than that, though. At one point both men were priests of the deities to whom the associations were devoted, and this would have been a key factor in ensuring benefaction in the first place. The service of these men as priests would on its own warrant reciprocation from the associations, so the content of the link is not limited to a financial component. It should be stressed, however, that the role of benefactor did not necessarily require common religious practice or concerns, which the case of Julia Severa will illustrate.

Owing to the partial nature of inscriptional evidence, it is difficult to assess the durability of links between a certain person and a given association. However, if Quadratus's relations with the Dionysiac cowherds is any indication, there was potential for ongoing links over time. In such cases, the social pressures on both the elites to make further benefactions and the association to respond with appropriate honors (i.e., the intensity of the link) would be considerable. Failure of an association to respond to a benefaction with clearly visible honors in return would be disastrous in its hopes of maintaining links for financial or other reasons with this or any other wealthy person. From this elite family's perspective, such links with local associations were part of a larger set of connections within city, province, and empire that helped to secure family members' high social position and degree of honor within society. These sociological observations concerning the nature of social relations within these networks would also apply to some Jewish and Christian groups.

Some Jewish groups were clearly participants within these same social networks, even maintaining connections with the civic and imperial elites (irrespective of the religious affiliation of a benefactor). Julia Severa, a relative of Quadratus and the others, was a prominent figure in Akmoneia in the mid-first century, acting as director of contests and high priestess in the local temple of the imperial family ("the *Sebastoi* gods"). She was not a Jew, as some have assumed (e.g., Ramsay 1895–97: 639, 650–51, 673; see also Trebilco 1991: 57–60). This prominent and wealthy benefactor maintained links with some local associations, including the elders' organization (*gerousia*), which honored her with a monument (*MAMA* VI 263). Yet an inscription from the late first or early second century (our earliest epigraphical attestation to a synagogue in Asia Minor) reveals that the Jews of the city also had ties with this influential woman:

> The meeting-place, which was built by Julia Severa, was renovated by P. Tyrronius Klados, head-of-the-synagogue (*archisynagogos*) for life, Lucius son of Lucius, also head-of-the-synagogue, and Publius Zotikos, archon, from their own resources and from the common deposit. They decorated the walls and ceiling, made the windows secure and took care of all the rest of the decoration. The synagogue honored them with a golden shield because of their virtuous disposition, goodwill and diligence in relation to the synagogue. (*MAMA* VI 264 = *CII* 766 [tr. mine])

Severa had apparently shown her beneficence by contributing the building in which the Jewish group met sometime around the period 60–80 C.E. (cf. Lk 7.1–5). Along with others who later renovated the building, Severa was honored by the Jewish group with a golden shield and this monumental inscription. The links between these Jews and the civic elites at Akmoneia seem to go beyond this connection with an imperial cult high priestess; P. Tyrronius Klados, the head of the synagogue, was evidently connected with the influential Tyrronius family, either as a relative, freedman, or client (cf. *MAMA* VI = *IGR* IV 654).

This instance of connections between a Jewish group and the elites might be passed off as an interesting exception if not for considerable evidence that further confirms other Jewish groups' links with and honors for (non-Jewish) members of the imperial elites (cf. Harland 2000). Philo mentions that it was customary among Jewish groups in Egypt to set up honorary monuments for the supreme patrons of the empire, the emperors, including "shields, golden crowns, plaques and inscriptions" (*Leg.* 133; cf. *Flaccus* 97–104). We also hear of specific officials of the equestrian or senatorial orders that had links with Jewish groups within networks of benefaction. Jewish groups of Asia passed an honorary decree (c. 12 B.C.E.) for both Emperor Augustus and Gaius Marcius Censorinus, an imperial official of senatorial (consular) rank; a copy was set up (by order of the emperor) in the provincial imperial cult temple (Josephus, *Ant.* 16.165; cf. Bowersock 1964). A Jewish group at Berenike in Cyrenaica set up an honorary monument for Marcus Tittius (c. 24 C.E.), an imperial official of either the equestrian or (more likely) senatorial order; he had acted in a beneficent way toward the city as a whole as well as the Jewish group within it (Reynolds 1977: 244–45, note 17 = Roux and Roux 1949 = *IGR* I 1024; cf. *NewDocs* IV 111). Several inscriptions from the city of Rome show that one synagogue called itself the "Augustesians" and another the "Agrippesians," in honor of their patrons, Augustus and Agrippa (*CII* 365, 425, 503; *CII* 284, 301, 338, 368, 416, 496; cf. Richardson 1998; Leon 1995 [1960]: 140–42). Like other associations, Jewish groups could be among the competitors for connections with influential figures within civic and imperial contexts.

Christian Groups and Connections with the Elites

There is neglected evidence that some Christian groups, like some Jewish groups, participated in these networks of benefaction, sometimes including links with the civic and imperial elites. We know for sure that Christian groups, like their non-Christian counterparts, relied on the benefactions of wealthier members of the group for, among other things, a place to meet, often within the patron's own house (cf. White 1997). Yet the discussion of Jewish groups illustrates well the fact that observance of a common religious practice or cult was *not* a precondition of links with influential figures. Despite the lack of surviving material remains or inscriptions for Christianity in the first two centuries,[18] there is literary evidence that suggests that Christian participation in networks of benefaction could extend beyond the membership of a Christian group, including honors for the elites within society.

There were clearly some Christian leaders, such as the author of Revelation, who condemned honoring influential outsiders (e.g., the emperor, Roman officials) in any way. But others in the first and second centuries were more open to at least some positive contacts with outsiders and some even encouraged Christian groups to engage in typical honorary activities (cf. Harland 2000). The case of I Peter is illustrative of at least one trajectory of Christianity. One of the most important sections in this diaspora letter, which addresses Christian groups throughout Asia Minor (using the metaphor of "exiles"), relates how these Christians were to "conduct yourselves honorably among the Gentiles, so that, though they malign you as evil-doers, they may see your honorable deeds (*tôn kalôn ergôn*) and glorify God when he comes to judge" (I Pt 2.12 [NRSV]). Immediately following this comes a passage filled with the conventional vocabulary of benefaction ("good works," "praise," "honor") that advocates subjection to and honors for influential persons, including the emperor, as one of the means by which tensions with outsiders could be ameliorated.

> For the Lord's sake accept the authority of every human institution, whether of the emperor as supreme, or of governors, as sent by him to punish those who do wrong and to praise those who do right (*epainon de agathopoiôn*). For it is God's will that by doing right you should silence the ignorance of the foolish. . . . Honor everyone. Love the family of believers. Fear God. Honor (*timate*) the emperor. (2.13–17)

The context of this passage suggests that these are not just empty words or merely "a stock phrase taken over from some current formula of instruction in civic duty" (Beare 1958: 117), but rather practical exhortations with direct implications regarding the concrete behaviors of Christian groups and their members that would be observed or even "praised" by influential persons (cf. van Unnik 1980 [1954]; Winter 1994: 11–40; Harland 2000). Together with other evidence from the pastoral Epistles, Polycarp and other Christian leaders in Asia Minor and elsewhere,[19] this evidence suggests it is conceivable that Christians would follow the suggestion of their leaders by actively honoring those in positions of authority, engaging to some degree in social networks of benefaction in Roman society.

A similar mentality concerning the establishment or maintenance of positive connections with the elites seems to be advocated by the author of Luke–Acts (c. 90 C.E.), for instance (cf. Walaskay 1983). The author often portrays Roman officials in a neutral or positive light, such as the Roman centurion at Capernaum (Lk 7.1–10; cf. Acts 10), who had (like Julia Severa) built a synagogue for the local Jews. The proconsul of Cyprus, Sergius Paulus, summons Paul and Barnabas "to hear the word of God," and he ultimately believes the message, according to the author (Acts 13.7–12). It is evidence such as this that leads Vernon K. Robbins to argue that Luke–Acts reflects "a narrative map grounded in an ideology that supported Christians who were building alliances with local leaders throughout the eastern Roman empire" (1991: 202). It seems that the author of Luke–Acts was not alone in his approach.

Some evidence suggests that these alliances and connections between some Christian groups and the elites within social networks would continue in the centuries leading up to Constantine's official adoption of Christianity. Authors of the third and early fourth centuries mention in passing what seems to have been a common practice within some areas. Writing in the mid-third century, Origen of

Alexandria complains that the practice of Christian groups accepting benefactions from the (non-Christian) elites was an increasing problem:

> I admit that at the present time perhaps, when on account of the multitude of people coming into the faith even rich men and persons of position and honor and ladies of refinement and high birth, favourably regard the adherents of the faith, one might venture to say that some become leaders of the Christian teachers for the sake of a little prestige. (*Cels.* 3.9, Chadwick)

Although certainly exaggerating the point, Eusebius's comment that "the rulers in every church were honored by all procurators and governors" (*Hist. eccl.* 8.1) suggests at least some cases of connections between Christian groups and the imperial elites in the years before Constantine. Christian groups, like other associations and Jewish groups, were participants within the networks that dominated social relations in Greco-Roman society.

Notes

I would like to thank Michel Desjardins (Wilfrid Laurier University) and Teresa Harland who provided helpful suggestions for revision.

1. On the following discussion of the senatorial and equestrian orders and civic elites, including numerical information and estimates, see Suetonius, *Aug.* 41.1 and Dio 54.17.3 (1,000,000–1,200,000 sesterces requirement for senators beginning under Augustus); Hopkins (1965: 12); Garnsey and Saller (1987); Alföldy (1985) (on the social structure of the Roman Empire); MacMullen (1974b: 88–120, 183 note 1); and Millar (1977: 275–361, esp. 297–300).

2. To give some sense of the magnitude of this wealth, it is worth noting that an average laborer made about 1,000 sesterces *per year*, and would, therefore, have to work a total of 1,000 years without spending a penny in order to approach senatorial wealth. Due to the nature of inflation and differences in the standards of living from ancient Rome to the modern world, it is very difficult to give equivalents of value in modern currencies (Shelton 1988: 459).

3. Since the Roman economy was primarily agricultural, peasant farmers in the countryside made up the majority of this segment of the population (on the peasantry see Garnsey and Saller 1987).

4. At Thyatira, for instance, there was both a slave merchant (*somatemporos*) and a dyer who at one point assumed the relatively important office of market overseer (*agoranomos*; *TAM* V 932, 991 [second–third centuries C.E.]). There were those who rose to membership in the civic council such as shippers at both Ephesos and Nikomedia, a purple-dyer at Hierapolis, goldsmiths at Sardis (including Jews or god-fearers), and even a baker at Korykos in Cilicia (*IEph* 1487–88; *SEG* 27 828; *IHierapJ* 156; *DFSI* 22–23; *MAMA* III 756 [1–3 C.E.]).

5. The focus on networks revises in part an earlier theoretical framework that emphasized relative deprivation and corresponding ideological appeals of a given group (cult or

sect) as the primary factor in growth of membership. See Gurney and Tierney (1982) on problems with the relative deprivation perspective.

6. Both outsiders and insiders in Roman times described Christian (and Jewish) groups using terminology common to associations generally (cf. Pliny, *Ep.* 10.97; Lucian, *Pereg.* 11; Tertullian, *Apol.* 38–39; and Josephus, *Ant.* 14.215–16, 235). For recent studies of associations, which often argue for the value in comparing associations to Christian or Jewish groups, see Kloppenborg (1993); Schmeller (1995); Kloppenborg and Wilson (1996); Harland (1996, 1999, 2000); and Ascough (1997). Classic studies include Waltzing (1895–1900) and Poland (1909).

7. Abbreviations for inscriptional collections follow the standard outlined in Horsley and Lee (1994).

8. Quite often it is hard to know for sure whether an association is based primarily on such temple connections or on a combination of the networks outlined above, since religion was embedded within the life of virtually all associations and guilds.

9. Remus (1996: 155–64) notes that the orator Aristides did indeed maintain links with those of differing socioeconomic standing at the Asklepios sanctuary, but the most dominant links were those that Aristides maintained with others of similar social, educational, and economic backgrounds.

10. Though Acts may exaggerate the extent to which synagogues were the context for the activity of Paul and other early missionaries, we should not err in the reverse direction by dismissing the importance of Jewish networks for a movement that began as a sect within Judaism and clearly included Jews among its adherents in some cities.

11. The inscription is categorized as Christian based on the warning against violation, which says that if anyone violates the grave, "they will have to reckon with the righteousness of God." This is a variation on the so-called "Eumeneian formula" (see note below).

12. Sebaste: Johnson (1995: 92–93, no. 3.6) = Ramsay (1895–97: 560, no. 451). Eumeneia: Johnson (1995: 82–83, no. 3.2) = Ramsay (1895–97: 519–20, no. 359); Johnson (1995: 84–85, no. 3.3) = Ramsay (1895–97: 525, no. 368); Johnson (1995: 86–87, no. 3.4) = Ramsay (1895–97: 522, no. 364); Ramsay (1895–97: 520–21, no. 361). These are categorized as Christian primarily based on the so-called "Eumeneian formula," which warns that if anyone should disturb the grave, "he will reckon with (the living) God." At Eumeneia and the surrounding Phrygian region, at least, the phrase indicates Christian identity, but not necessarily in the case of inscriptions from other regions (see Calder 1939; Robert 1960: 405–13; Early-Christian Epitaphs from Anatolia: 41–43).

13. Both F. K. Dörner (1952: 59–60) and L. Robert (1978: 414) categorize the inscription as certainly Christian based on the phrase "To the most holy ones who also had faith in God"; the use of "faith" (*pistis*) in conjunction with monotheism is characteristically Christian in inscriptions (cf. *IBithDörner* II 160).

14. Eusebius is prone to exaggerate the positive role of Christians in relation to the empire in the pre-Constantinian era (cf. 5.21, 7.10, 8.1ff.), but the examples provided here seem quite plausible, especially considering our other evidence for Christians within the imperial household.

15. The inscription was identified quite securely as Christian in connection with the phrase "I beg of you, kind brothers, by the one God" (*fratres boni, per unum deum*) by Clarke (1971: 121–22) and has been accepted as such by other experts in Christian epigraphy (cf. Mazzoleni 1999: 153–54).

16. The inscription is categorized as Christian based on the phrase "he sleeps" (*hic dormit*), which seems to have been a Christian usage at Ostia (cf. *CIL* XIV 1877–78), sometimes adding "in peace" (*in pace*) (cf. *CIL* XIV 1887, 1888, 1889). See Cadoux (1925: 560, note 6), who mentions this and two other Ostian Christian inscriptions (*CIL* XIV 1878–79), the latter involving slaves or freedmen of the imperial family in the early fourth century.

17. For the family connections see especially *IGR* III 373–75; PIR² I 147, 507, 701; Halfmann (1979: nos. 5a, 17); and White (1998: 366–71). C. Julius Severus at Ankyra is known to be an *anepsios* (often meaning cousin) of C. A. A. Julius Quadratus of Pergamon, and C. Julius Severus's brother was definitely a man named Julius Amyntianus (*IGR* III 373). Follet (1976: 133) convincingly argues for the probability that this is the same Julius Amyntianus whom we find at Tralles (below), if not a relative in some other way. Scholars are in general agreement that Julia Severa is most likely a relative of C. Julius Severus of Ankyra, and therefore of the others, though we lack an inscription that states it explicitly. The Attalid and Galatian royal ancestry includes Attalos II, Deiotaros, and Amyntas (*IGR* III 373).

18. The lack of surviving *realia* concerning Christian participation in social networks of benefaction is relatively unsurprising in light of the generally partial nature of survival and discovery and the fact that Christians were such a numerically insignificant portion of the population in the first two centuries. The case of Jews at Alexandria in the first century is illustrative: although we know that Jewish groups in Alexandria (a central locus of diaspora Jews) did conventionally erect honorary monuments for imperial or other figures, none have in fact survived.

19. I Timothy 2.1–2; Titus 3.1–2; *Mart. Pol.* 10.2; and Polycarp, *Phil.* 12.3. Compare Romans 13.1–7; *1 Clem.* 60.4–61.3; Tertullian, *Apol.* 21.1; and Melito in Eusebius, *Hist. eccl.* 4.26.7–9.

Government and Public Law in Galilee, Judaea, Hellenistic Cities, and the Roman Empire

18

JOHN W. MARSHALL AND RUSSELL MARTIN

Introduction

IN VARYING DEGREES OF ARTICULATION, the Roman Empire promulgated a body of public law and governmental practice that conditioned social life throughout the regions that Rome ruled. These evolved substantially over time and were applied in different manners among the variety of peoples and regions in the empire. Understanding government and public law is essential for understanding the emergence and development of early Christianity for two reasons: (1) Key players in the prehistory and early development of the movement interacted with the Roman government and were prosecuted for infractions; Jesus, Paul, and Peter are only the most prominent figures to run afoul of Roman government officials. (2) Government and public law significantly conditioned the urban contexts within which nascent Christian organizations formed. The second reason is no less important than the first.

The chronological scope of this study is, in Roman terms, the period from Augustus to Hadrian (31 B.C.E.–138 C.E.), or in Jewish terms, the period from Herod the Great to Bar Kokhba (37 B.C.E.–135 C.E.). The geographical arena is comprised of those areas in which Christianity made its most substantial growth before the end of the period: Judaea and Galilee, Asia Minor and Greece, Egypt, and Rome. Within the context of early Christianity and the social sciences, we examine "government and public law" in order to understand the place of these explicit institutions in the social life of subjects of the Roman Empire. Thus we attend not primarily to the ideal of these institutions but to their actuality—the manner in which they functioned and the manner in which they were received, manipulated, complied with, appropriated, and resisted.

The question "What was law and what was government within the Roman Empire?" is much simpler than its answer. Governance was on one hand an amateur endeavor and could be quite distant from the day-to-day lives of many of the empire's inhabitants, yet on the other hand the power of the emperor himself, channeled through the provincial government, might nail a preacher or bandit onto a cross. The empire could be quite close at hand. Law too was not as clearly bounded as in the modern world. While in the Republic and the earliest days of the Principate laws were passed by the citizen assembly of Rome, through most of our period several other expressions of opinion or principle could hold the force of law. The word of the emperor himself, especially issued in the form of an edict, eventually became a substantial source of law. Letters and replies to inquiries often created what amounted to law in specific situations and sometimes with general application.[1] Beneath the emperor, praetors usually issued an edict at the beginning of their tenure that outlined the principle by which they would apply the law. The edicts issued by various magistrates over their appropriate jurisdictions also constituted law within those spheres—consuls over the business of the Senate, praetors over courts, aediles over public spaces, governors over provinces (Crook 1984: 18–30).

The Structure of Empire

Status

Any discussion of government and public law in the Roman Empire must necessarily begin with the notion of status in the Roman Empire. Neither law nor government functioned, or was meant to function, equally for all inhabitants of the empire. Equality before the law, or equality before the government, was not an ideal in Roman society. Justinian's *Digest* sets forth how status related to treatment under the law and participation in public structures: Is a person free or unfree (slave)? If free, is the person free by birth or by grant, that is to say free or freed? Is the person a Roman citizen, a Latin, or a foreigner? Is the person male or female? Is the person under their own power or that of another, such as children, those unable to care for or represent themselves due to age, illness, etc. (*Digest* 1.5)? Individuals held different rights and duties according to these status differences. Some boundaries were permeable—slaves could be freed, the free or freed could be lawfully or unlawfully enslaved, children grew to adults, women entered into or exited from marriages, foreigners became citizens—but other boundaries were absolute or nearly so. The freedom of a manumitted slave was never really equal to that of a person born free. The differences across these boundaries were often stark: slaves could contract no legal marriage and could be bought and sold (*Digest* 38.2.3).

Imperium

In the aftermath of the battle of Actium (31 B.C.E.), Caius Julius Caesar Octavianus, later titled *Augustus* by the Senate, ruled solely over the possessions of

Rome. The republican system of governance had been severely tried by the civil wars of the preceding decades; though some of its structures remained in place throughout the empire, Augustus's concentration of executive powers transformed the senatorial republic into a monarchial empire. Monarchy exercised baldly was anathema to Latin sensibilities, and Augustus and his successors in this period (Nero excepted) diligently avoided the title *rex* though they were titled βασιλεύς (basileus, king) in the East. Augustus claimed to have restored the republic (Ste. Croix 1981: 350, 621 note 1).

"Imperium" denotes most basically the sovereign power that was held by the emperor and distributed from the sovereign through the hierarchy of governmental, social, and military channels. It also came to refer to the realm within which such control was exercised: the empire. The role of emperor encompassed several types of social relations or roles: the emperor was commander of the military, high priest of the official religions, fount of legislation, and patron of the empire itself.

Provincia

The empire was organized into provinces and client kingdoms. Provincial governors were Roman men of senatorial or equestrian rank sent out for a limited term to govern the province in the interests of Rome. Provinces closer to the heart of the empire and more thoroughly imbued by Greco-Roman culture (notably Greece and Asia) were governed by a proconsul (a former consul). The governance of such provinces did not require a standing army stationed in the province. Provinces of a more volatile disposition and on the borders of the empire were governed by a legate or prefect of equestrian rank supported by one or more legions permanently stationed in the province.

The role of the governor was not to govern for the welfare of the inhabitants of the province but to govern in the interests of Rome. Governors were usually not natives of the provinces they governed and in many cases had little if any sympathy for, or interest in the welfare of, the native inhabitants of the province. Governing in the interests of Rome meant maintaining security and sustaining the stream of tax revenue from the province to Rome. In addition to career advantage through governing effectively in Rome's interest, governors were also concerned with personal enrichment. Though governors were prohibited from direct expropriation of subjects' property, Verres's comment that as governor he needed to make three fortunes—his own, one to pay the debts involved in buying the office, and one to bribe the juror's judging the case against him after his term—illustrates the character of the enterprise (Cicero, *Verr.* 41). This entrepreneurial regime of practice centered on the governor but encompassed a body of retainers, friends, and clients brought by a governor during his term of office and an oligarchy of provincial elites (native, Roman, and Greek) who assisted the Roman governing project. Governors periodically made circuits of their provinces in order to judge the relatively small portion of cases—usually involving threats to or infringements of public order—that merited their direct attention. This is the circumstance that Acts depicts in Paul's trial before Felix and Festus.[2] On coming to his term of office a governor invariably had an effect on the social fabric of the province he governed, both by means of the retinue of assistants, retainers, and functionaries he brought with him as patron, and by means of his cultivation and co-optation of existing native and/or colonial elites to assist in the work and share in the spoils of governance.

The Military

Empire without conquest is inconceivable, and the military was at the center of Rome's power in the ancient world (Webster 1985). Once an army of free citizen volunteers in republican times, the military of the early empire had become a professional army composed of career soldiers and officers, administered by bureaucrats serving in the army within the *cursus honorum*,[3] and supported by foreign auxiliaries.

The Roman army was controlled by generals appointed from the ranks of the Senate. In many cases governors also held the position of general of the units stationed in their province. Assisting the general were military tribunes and a chief captain. These officers were recruited from among the upper classes. The ranks of the army were composed of free citizens functioning as infantrymen and led by centurions. Each centurion led one "century" composed of a hundred legionaries. Six centuries, that is six hundred men, formed a cohort, which was led by a military tribune, usually drawn from the equestrian rank. A legion, led by a general, encompassed ten cohorts and thus six thousand men. These figures are ideal and in actual practice numbers could vary through all the happenstance of war that might reduce numbers and through the practice of forming particular cohorts at double strength.

The military functioned not as a force guarding a border but as a force that could be moved to combat an incursion or put down a rebellion. Such processes were often slow, as the glacial pace at which the Roman army dealt with the rebellion in Judaea in 66–70 C.E. demonstrates,[4] but the result was predictable: revolts rarely had lasting success. Thus deterrence was as important as direct action. Rome's work in opposing its neighbors was not without a mixture of success and failure. On the eastern edge of the empire, conflict with Parthia left a substantial region where Roman sovereignty was only intermittent. In the north also, the regions to the east of the Rhine and the north of the Danube were unstable.

The military did not maintain borders so much as respond to disruptions of sovereignty. In addition to fighting wars on behalf the empire and putting down rebellions within it, the military also functioned within civil conflicts, supporting factions within the government. This was most prominent in the civil wars that led to the Principate itself and again in the year of four emperors, 69 C.E. (see Wellesley 1975). The emperor's command of the military was eventually reciprocated in the military's command of the succession to the imperial office.

The military was a factor in social life under the empire not merely because it facilitated the particular mixture of continuity and repression that characterized the Roman Empire, but also because its potential to mix populations, provide social mobility, and condition the material conditions of life through the characteristics of its members and veterans. The army was also a crucial bearer of Roman culture in its extensive building and engineering projects.[5] The army was a citizen army, but citizenship itself was a broadening category in the first century. Long service in the noncitizen auxiliaries brought citizenship to the retiree and to his children. Upon completion of twenty-five years of service, veterans were entitled to several privileges with social implications: land grants within colonies, the legitimation of "camp marriages," the extension of citizenship to subsequent children born within such marriages. The colonies themselves were outposts of Roman rule and custom, in many cases having special status with regard to taxation and self-governance that enabled them to become important centers of influence. In other cases, veteran-based colonies served as security guarantors of transprovincial road systems. Veteran colonies were a potent social force in the empire.

The counterpart of this accrual of advantage to veteran colonies spread out through the empire was a movement of people to their great disadvantage: the slave economy. The foreign wars fought by the army were a significant source of slave labor for the empire. Revolts within the empire, once quashed, were another means of moving people from freedom to slavery. The combatants not executed—as well as substantial numbers of elders, women, and children—were taken captive and brought as slaves into an economy that assumed and depended on a substantial component of unfree labor.[6] The Roman army was both ladder (for soldiers and veterans) and snake (for its opponents within and without the empire).

Governance, Legislation, and Social Control in Hellenistic Cities

Asia Minor and Greece

Long before the rise of Rome, cities constituted the dominant form of political organization in Greece. Long before the rise of Rome, cities of Greek emigrants

414 JOHN W. MARSHALL AND RUSSELL MARTIN

and eventually Greek-speaking native inhabitants were established in western Asia Minor. This entailed a tradition of municipally focused governance that simultaneously lay in tension with Roman hegemony on an imperial scale and also provided a structure of governance that facilitated the efficient administration of empire.[7]

Status

As with individuals, *status* is the first issue in understanding the governing structure of cities in the Roman Empire in general. The cities of Greece and Asia Minor might be established cities of Greek-style constitution. These were numerous, prosperous, and powerful. Athens, Corinth, Ephesus, Pergamum, Sardis, and Smyrna are only some of the most prominent cities having such status. Other cities were "colonies" in a technical sense, cities created *de novo* or alongside existing cities as a context in which to settle and reward veterans. Such cities had Roman-style constitutions and were, in theory, part of Rome itself. They were governed by the *ius Italicum* rather than the provincial apparatus and were immune to direct taxation (Macro 1980: 675). Philippi, Sinope, and Parum were prominent colonies. "Free" cities were another category. Given their status through a specific grant by an emperor, free cities enjoyed greater freedom from provincial oversight in raising taxes and creating legislation, and often freedom from tributary obligations. Some cities passed in and out of this status, but during much of our period Aphrodisias, Chalcedon, and Ilium, as well as the islands of Chios, Rhodes, and Samos, were free cities (Macro 1980: 676). The combination of personal status, civic status, and municipal and imperial bodies of legislation that were not designed to avoid overlap created a complex legal situation for anything but the most basic offense.

Jurisdiction

Hellenistic cities were usually governed by a constitution created at their founding or refounding. Geographically, cities held jurisdiction over the surrounding countryside (which may have included other urban areas that functioned as de facto cities [Jones 1971: 64–93]). These rural areas were, together with trade, the sources of wealth and surplus that made civic culture possible. With obligations to the empire, the cities' jurisdiction covered tribute and productivity; the point of civic administration was to meet the economic potential and obligations of the city. Often this included direct tribute, but even cities exempt from obligatory tribute raised by the civic government often made donatives and were obliged to be productive economically and in many instances to administer specific levies on trade or other activities. With regard to the populace of the city, the governance focused on the maintenance of the social order. This included policing and judging criminal activity, but mostly providing a field in which the various status groups could play their part and perpetuate themselves. Maintenance of order, maintenance of hierarchy, and fulfillment of obligations to the empire were closely aligned purposes and activities.

Governance itself was an oligarchic endeavor. Rome quite deliberately sought alliances and aligned interests with existing elites among subject peoples. "Democratic" institutions such as citizen assemblies (which never implied a universal adult franchise) were made more oligarchic through the introduction or intensification of property qualifications. Magistracies and liturgies demanded substantial personal resources in order to carry them out and were the preserve, and occasionally the burden, of civic elites. Since many cities retained versions of their ancestral constitutions, the exact structure and nomenclature of civic government varied substantially.

The chief magistrate—by whose name and term of office an individual year of government was designated—might be known as πρύτανις (prutanis), ἵππαρχος (hipparchos), στεφανηφόρος (stephanephoros), ἀρχιπρυτάνις (archiprutanis), or δημιουργός (demiourgos). This officer led a board of magistrates known often as the πρυτανεία (prutaneia), or the ἄρχοντες (archontes). Such boards oversaw finances, legislation, and litigation, as well as representing the city to other cities and to the emperor and his delegates. A γραμματεύς (grammateus), or clerk, did much more than clerical work, running the proceedings of the βουλή (boule, council) and often managing key tasks such as drafting resolutions. An ἀγορανόμος (agoranomos) supervised the markets in terms of both social and economic order, intervening with force or resources to stabilize disturbances—whether scuffles and arguments or inflationary pressures. An εἰρηναρχός (eirenarchos) sought to maintain public order and to bring criminals to justice—small offenses within the city as well as the activities of bandits without were within his purview. Διωγμεῖται (diogmeitai) or ταχεῶται (taxeotai) assisted the eirenarchos. The eirenarchos was also responsible for interrogation—frequently under torture—and the implementation of punishments—frequently corporal and scarcely distinct from interrogation. Though the most serious crimes rose above the civic structure to be judged in a provincial or imperial context, many petty crimes did not draw the attention of civic apparatus and were dealt with apart from a formal legal and judicial system. This is the world of hired guards, vendettas, vengeance and honor, self-defense shading into offense, and the complex tentacles of influence that the powerful wield against the less powerful.

The proceedings of the justice system were manifold, ranging from on the spot censure or beatings by lictors for minor offenses[8] through massive trials with forty or more jurists.[9]

Egypt

More than any other province, Egypt is a special case. Naturally insulated by forbidding desert on three sides and a marshy delta on the Mediterranean coast, Egypt—essentially the Nile valley and delta—achieved political unity long before Roman or Greek administration. Under Roman rule it was an "Imperial Province," the private preserve of the emperor, ruled by a prefect of equestrian rank rather than by a member of the Senate. Members of the senatorial class were forbidden to enter Egypt without the emperor's permission (Tacitus, *Ann.* 2.59). The geography and history of Egypt also facilitated a more intensely centralized administration than was possible in most other provinces (Jones 1971: 296).

ALEXANDRIA. Founded as a Greek city by Alexander the Great on the site of the native Egyptian village of Rhacotis, Alexandria was the administrative capital and chief city of Egypt throughout the Hellenistic and Roman periods. No other city in Egypt rivaled it in any sense. Second in the empire only to Rome, Alexandria had a population of perhaps a million people in the first century (Huzar 1988: 631). Alexandria was from its beginning a multiethnic city consisting obviously of Greek colonists settled by Alexander, native Egyptians, and a substantial population of Jews, as well as "barbarians of every race" (Jones 1971: 303). After Pompey's conquests in the East encompassed Alexandria, Romans became a powerful element of the mixture.

During the first century, though founded as a Greek city, Alexandria was not ruled by an autonomous oligarchic council, but by a board appointed under the auspices of the prefect governing on the emperor's behalf.[10] This board included a number of individuals serving also as imperial officials. The boards oversaw cultural matters and some municipal economics but did not have as much power as the governing bodies of formerly independent city-states or even Roman foundations elsewhere in the empire. A. H. M. Jones sums up the situation concisely:

> Public security was controlled by the commandant of the city and of the nightwatch. In fact, the whole administration of Alexandria was controlled by the Roman government, with the exception of the cultural and religious side, the gymnasium and the temples, the ephebic training and the festivals and games. (1971: 303)

The most famous example of this "religious side" is the well-known Jewish community of Alexandria. Recognized as a πολίτευμα (*politeuma*–distinct community) since the Ptolemaic period (*Let. Aris.* 310), the Jewish community was well established in Alexandria and Egypt as a whole with the advent of Roman rule. Throughout the first century, the Jewish community struggled to assert its rights within Alexandria and to avoid any diminishment of those rights as a result of

Jewish revolts against Rome in Judaea and North Africa. In the aftermath of the latter revolt in 115, the Jewish community in Alexandria was decimated (Eusebius, *Hist. eccl.* 4.2).

EGYPT. Beyond Alexandria was Egypt (so distinct was the capital that often the term "Egypt" did not encompass it). Within Egypt, cities such as Ptolemais and Naucratis, based on Greek constitutions, maintained their civic institutions even if their functions were attenuated relative to those in Greece and Asia Minor. Native cities like Memphis, Thebes, and others that were capitals of nomes developed a rich mix of native and Greco-Roman culture. Egyptian temples continued to function, and temple wardens had substantial powers over order and governance within temple precincts. Administrators from Alexandria, backed up by military forces, oversaw the efficient extraction of surplus from Egypt's agricultural lands. Peasants worked as laborers on imperial lands or temple estates, and most justice was probably meted out by means of the authorities running such estates. Within the villages of Egypt, "Greeks" (i.e., Greek-speaking non-native Egyptians) had recourse to imperial officials, and ultimately to the prefect in Alexandria.

The City of Rome

Like Alexandria, Rome itself sustained a peculiar coincidence of imperial and municipal governance. Many of the affairs of the city—building, infrastructure, economics—were the responsibility of the emperor and the Senate. Other traditional arenas of civic activity—collecting tribute, relating to the imperial governing structure—were not relevant in the capital. The empire belonged to the city.[11] On the matter of civic order, Rome faced challenges equal to or exceeding those of other cities.[12] With a population of perhaps one million and no industrial base to employ the population and distribute wealth, crime was a persistent problem. In the aftermath of the civil wars, Augustus undertook to design more effective means of maintaining order in the city. In addition to a massive building boom that provided much needed employment, Augustus created several military and civic bodies that served the city (and the emperor): the Praetorian guard, the urban cohorts, and the night watchmen. The Praetorian guards, the only military units permanently stationed in the capital, were first and foremost the emperor's personal force securing the palace and the imperial family. Organized into nine cohorts of approximately five hundred men, members of the guard might appear in uniform around the emperor or at official functions, or they might be dressed in plain clothes and concealing weapons among the people of Rome. Though it did not involve itself in crimes committed by one resident against another, the Praetorian guard was a potent force in Rome.

The urban cohorts, only three units of five hundred men commanded by the prefect of the city, were more oriented to crime among the residents of the city whether it affected the security of the emperor or not. Nevertheless, 1,500 men in a city of a million could not respond to most criminal activity. In 7 B.C.E, Augustus divided the city into fourteen wards and each ward into several precincts. The night watchmen (*vigiles*) were assigned to specific precincts of the city. Their primary function was fire control, though they also performed minor policing functions (Reynolds 1926). In addition to the night watchmen, each precinct had minor officials with administrative and religious duties. Trials by jury were reserved for the civil litigation of the upper classes and for the most serious offenses.[13] Judgment by magistrate was more common and could result in exceedingly heavy schedules for those sitting in judgment (Carcopino and Rowell 1991: 205–14).

Governance, Legislation, and Social Control in Galilee, Samaria, and Judaea

With only brief interludes, Jewish experience in their homeland was the experience of foreign rule, ranging from micro-management to client kingship. After Pompey's conquest in 63 B.C.E., a series of administrative arrangements were intended to maintain control of Judaea and Palestine during the Roman civil wars. Herod, who was made "king" of Judaea in 40 B.C.E., was in control from 37 B.C.E.

Governance of Judaea and Galilee

Jews occupied much of Judaea, but many of the cities were predominantly Greek, especially those along the Mediterranean and those that constituted the Decapolis. Galilee and Judaea, accordingly, were uniquely governed in the first century C.E. by a combination of Jewish and Greek institutions that were shaped to meet Roman expectations. Jewish customs and traditions continued both in the countryside and in most villages, towns, and cities (Kasher 1990: 313), but the influence of Greek practices and organizations was particularly evident in the Galilean cities of Sepphoris and Tiberias (Horsley 1995: 171), as well as the Judaean cities of Caesarea and Jerusalem (Tcherikover 1961/1970: 114). Consequently, government and public law in Galilee and Judaea evolved under the impact of changes that reflected the determination of both the rulers and the governed.

Greek culture stressed the worth of every mature individual's contribution to society. Although exceptions to participation were usually made according to age, birth, sex, and ownership of property, those who met the qualifications were recognized as having equal status in determining the way in which public decisions were to be determined and implemented (Jones 1940: 159ff.). An assembly of all eligible citizens selected the magistrates and executive council for specific governing functions, but all elected officials acted on behalf of the citizens who elected them (Radin 1915: 105). Through the institutions of the *ephebate* and gymnasium, every citizen was prepared to assist in the military, political, and religious activities of the community (Hadas 1959: 65). The democratic institutions of Greek cities promoted the active involvement of all citizens in the social and cultural life of society.

The openness and economic prosperity that was characteristic of many of the Greek cities in the eastern Mediterranean was attractive to many faithful Jews in Galilee and Judaea. The residents of these regions were probably aware that Sidon, Tyre, Ptolemais, and the cities of the Decapolis were independent and autonomous, having their own constitutions and capable of establishing their own policies (cf. Mk 3.8, 7.31). The successes of the Maccabees, however, were understood by faithful Jews to mean that God supported only Jewish customs and traditions (1 Mc 13.41; 2 Mc 15.21). The Jews of both Galilee and Judaea, accordingly, were reluctant to give up their divinely revealed laws in order to replace them with arbitrarily chosen constitutions that met only the needs of the citizens. Instead, they were determined to adhere firmly to Jewish law and reject the attractiveness of both independence and autonomy that were the defining characteristics of Greek cities.

Herod and his descendants were able to introduce some of the significant trappings of Greek culture into Sepphoris and Tiberias in Galilee (Josephus, *Ant.* 18.27, 36), as well as Caesarea and Jerusalem in Judaea (*Ant.* 15.268, 331). The Herods knew the limit of Jewish tolerance of Greek culture, however, and did not attempt to introduce an *ephebate* or gymnasium in any of these cities, since these institutions had already been rejected by Jews at the time of the Maccabaean revolt (1 Mc 1.14; 2 Mc 4.9–14). The determination of the Jewish people to maintain Jewish customs and traditions thus restricted the extent to which the Herodian descendants could introduce various aspects of Hellenistic culture.

Although Judaea was governed by Roman prefects and procurators in the periods 6–41 and 44–66 C.E., respectively, the Roman governors knew that there were limits to the extent to which they could introduce foreign practices. Pilate thought that he could succeed in bringing the standards of his cohorts into Jerusalem (*Ant.* 18.55) and tried to coerce the Jews into the acceptance of shields bearing inscriptions denoting dedication to specific individuals (Philo, *Legat.* 299), but the Jews rebuffed his attempts. Gaius's attempt to install a statue of himself in the Temple at Jerusalem resulted in a massive protest that would probably have involved extensive bloodshed had Gaius not been persuaded to abandon the project (*Ant.* 18.261; *Legat.* 203). Only his premature death at the hands of Roman assassins ensured that his ambition would not be revived. The determination of the Jews to preserve their customs and traditions in the first century C.E. is stressed in many of the incidents described by the Gospels, Josephus, and Philo.

The Roman governor of Judaea controlled a small staff and some armed forces. Roman objectives, however, were limited to the maintenance of law and order and the collection of revenue (Garnsey and Saller 1982: 15). The governor's staff, accordingly, included only sufficient personnel to control the armed forces and exact the tribute. The soldiers consisted of approximately 3,000 men, divided into one squadron of cavalry and five cohorts of infantry (*Ant.* 17.266, 19.365, 20.122). They were normally billeted in Caesarea or Sebaste (*Ant.* 19.366), although one cohort was always stationed at the Antonia fortress adjacent to the Temple in Jerusalem (*Ant.* 20.110). The remaining soldiers were occasionally used to patrol Judaea to ferret out any rebel activity (*Ant.* 20.98), but served primarily to make Rome's presence visible in the province. In case of serious border violations or organized rebel activity, assistance could be obtained from the legate of Syria who commanded legions (*Ant.* 18.120). Since the soldiers in Judaea were non-Jewish and held Jewish customs and traditions in contempt, their activities frequently created hostile reactions by the Jewish people (*Ant.* 20.108, 115).

Revenue collection was performed by Jewish officials under the direction of Rome's appointed tax collector (Josephus, *B.J.* 2.405). A Roman official was responsible for the accumulation of revenue (Philo, *Leg.* 199), but could only supervise the transfer of revenue to Rome. The amount of revenue to be obtained was determined by the *princeps* and could not be altered by Roman officials in Judaea (Dio, 52.28.4). The actual collection was performed by local Jewish officials, probably according to the results of a regularly maintained census. Except in 6 C.E., when Judas the Galilaean unsuccessfully tried to incite the Jews to rebel against Rome (*Ant.* 18.4), there was no organized tax revolt, although Tacitus claimed that the Jews pressed for a diminution in tribute c. 17 C.E. (Tacitus, *Ann.* 2.42). The presence of soldiers in Judaea, accompanied by the threat of retaliation by the legions stationed in Syria, was adequate to ensure compliance with Rome's demands.

The Roman administration of Judaea was only supervisory (Sherwin-White 1969: 141). Rome was determined to control the populations of all regions that had access to the Mediterranean in order to ensure her own supremacy (Sartre 1991: 55). The Senate and people of Rome, however, had insufficient resources to maintain both a secure perimeter and a dominating presence in all of the subject territories (Millar 1987: 145). Instead, Rome relied on local leaders to provide leadership in almost every province under her control. In some cases, leadership devolved on the local aristocracies of villages, towns, and cities (Garnsey and Saller 1982: 11). In other cases, Rome assigned responsibility to client princes or priests, who administered the province to meet Roman objectives. Rome allowed Herod's descendants to continue to rule Galilee in the period 4 B.C.E.–44 C.E., whereas high priests were held responsible for the administration of Judaea, 6–66

C.E., although under the control of a Roman governor. The adherence of the Jews in both Galilee and Judaea to Jewish customs and traditions, however, meant that local government in villages, towns, and cities would continue to function much as it had done for centuries.

Civic Governance

A council in a village, town, or city in Galilee or Judaea was frequently identified in the first century C.E. as a συνέδριον (*synhedrion*), συμβούλιον (*symboulion*), or βουλή (*boule*). The use of such Greek terms does not imply, however, that the assembly of persons was organized according to Greek traditions or practices. Rather, the use of Greek terms implies only that the authors of our literary sources wanted to be understood by a Greek-speaking audience, and thus avoided the use of indigenous terms. The councils that governed villages, towns, and cities throughout Galilee and Judaea continued to function according to time-honored traditions. Local officials consisted primarily of those who were wealthy, powerful, or distinguished. The aristocratic structure of local government was maintained in spite of the use of terms that were usually used to depict Greek democratic traditions.

Local officials throughout Galilee and Judaea appointed judges, established magistrates, allocated resources, and made decisions affecting the people within their jurisdiction (Mt 5.22, 25; Jn 7.51). The system was informal but functional, and depended only on the experience, wealth, and power of the participants. The "elders" who constituted a local council could always seek the advice of experts in Jewish law, since Levites, priests, and scribes lived throughout the country and were readily available for consultation (Mk 3.22; Mt 9.3; Lk 11.45). If there was a question regarding Jewish law that could not be decided locally, a decision could be referred to a higher level. A regional council in Galilee or Judaea could be called upon to decide any issues that could not be resolved at lower levels (Josephus, *Vita*, 79; Acts 4.5). The system was conciliatory and recognized the value of both expertise and experience.

The implementation of decisions at the local level depended on the resources available. As heads of families, elders were able to provide both material and human resources, while Levites, priests, and scribes were able to offer both advice and support in the implementation of any decisions. Punishments could thus be carried out according to Jewish law through the use of available local personnel, whether involving corporal punishment (Mt 10.17), excommunication (Lk 6.22), or restitution (Mt 18.23). Every local council was probably able to detain offenders, either with its own resources or those at a higher level (Mt 5.25; *Ant.* 20.215). Capital punishment, however, was probably reserved to the highest council, and, when carried out within an area under Roman jurisdiction, required the approval of the Roman governor (Jn 18.31), but all other forms of punishment could be enacted at the local level without involving higher officials.

Local councils normally fulfilled all the functions of local government without outside assistance. They maintained census records of all persons within their jurisdiction, collected taxes from residents, and made decisions on the allocation of resources for local needs. The most important institution was the local market (Mt 20.3; Lk 20.46), which enabled the residents to exchange the products and services provided by members of the community (Mk 6.36). In addition, local officials considered it their responsibility to provide an adequate water supply (Jn 4.6), passable streets and roads (Lk 10:1), and, where possible, gates and walls for mutual protection (Lk 7.12; Acts 12.10). Local synagogues within each community were organized for regular worship (Lk 13.14), teaching the law (Mk 7.7), and arranging local support to meet the needs of those who were poor, ill, weak, or disabled (Mt 6.1; Lk 21.1). Every community was usually independent and self-sufficient, but exchanged goods and services with members of other communities when its own resources were inadequate to meet its own needs.

The residents of a local community pursued a variety of occupations. Among those specifically mentioned in the Gospels are teacher, fisherman, toll collector, physician, carpenter, soldier, scribe, farmer, tenant, laborer, fuller, merchant, steward, lawyer, banker, guard, builder, judge, hireling, innkeeper, and prostitute. In addition, products that are mentioned imply the presence of a woodsman, smith, miller, baker, and potter. Farmers cultivated various kinds of grain, spices, figs, or olives, and raised sheep, goats, donkeys, cattle, horses, or camels. Most of the occupations mentioned in the Gospels were labor-intensive and involved slaves, employees, or hired persons who did not own property (Mt 20.1, 21.33, 25.14). The people of Galilee and Judaea were thus divided into two distinct classes: a majority who were poor, weak, and victimized, and a minority consisting chiefly of landowners who were rich, powerful, and exploitative (Horsley and Hanson 1985/1988: 48). Whatever limitations may have existed on land ownership did not prevent its consolidation among those who were already wealthy. Poverty had become the norm for the greater part of the population. This is reflected in the Gospels by numerous references to "the poor," including Jesus' statement to his disciples that they would always have the poor with them (Mk 14.7; Jn 12.8). The poverty of the masses was primarily a consequence of exploitation by the wealthy, who were able to control economic affairs through participation in local government.

Most people in Galilee and Judaea lived in unwalled villages that were vulnerable to attack by outsiders. Josephus claimed that Galilee consisted of 204 cities and villages (*Vita* 235), of which the smallest village consisted of more than

15,000 inhabitants (*B.J.* 3.43), but his assertion is almost certainly exaggerated. Caesarea, Jerusalem, and Jericho in Judaea, as well as Sepphoris, Tiberias, and Capernaum in Galilee, were certainly walled cities. On the other hand, Emmaus, Bethany, and Bethlehem in Judaea, and Nazareth, Cana, and Nain in Galilee were probably typical unwalled, rural villages. Some villages, of course, could be fortified in time of war, as was the case with Jotapata and Tarichaeae in 66 C.E. (*Vita* 188). The regular maintenance of walls and gates, however, depended on the importance of the city, and could be carried out only by those who had both the means and resources. This was usually the case only with large population centers that functioned as either territorial capitals or entry points on major highways that were used by caravans. The maintenance of walls, however, could also be interpreted as an offensive activity after the Romans conquered the eastern Mediterranean. Agrippa I organized an effort to improve the walls of Jerusalem, but was prevented by the Romans from completing the project (Josephus, *Ant.* 19.326). The maintenance of defensible cities in Galilee and Judaea could be understood to conflict with the objectives of the *pax Romana*.

Religion and Governance

Religious officials consisted of high priests, priests, Levites, and scribes. The high priests were members of those families from whom high priests were traditionally selected by Herod, the Roman governors, or some of Herod's descendants. High priestly activities were limited almost exclusively to Jerusalem (Mk 11.27; Acts 4.5), where the active high priest performed specific rituals in the Temple (Heb 5.1; Josephus, *Ant.* 18.91). The other high priests were concerned primarily with the peaceful administration of the region to meet Roman expectations. They considered it their responsibility to maintain control of the Jewish people, especially the crowds that regularly assembled in Jerusalem for the major feasts (Mk 14.1; Jn 11.47). They were particularly involved in the resolution of disputes at the highest level, and probably participated in major decisions concerning Jewish law (Acts 5.17, 22.30). Only occasionally did they venture outside Jerusalem to become involved in settling differences that threatened the stability of the country (Josephus, *B.J.* 2.240; Acts 24.1). Their status as representatives of the province of Judaea to the Romans made them appear as collaborators to many fellow Jews, but they were primarily concerned with the preservation of Jewish traditions and realized that this could be achieved only with the cooperation of the Romans.

The priests were privileged to carry out the sacrifices in the Temple at Jerusalem on behalf of the Jewish people (Lk 1.9, 2.24). They were divided into twenty-four courses (1 Chr 24.4, *Ant.* 7.365), however, and spent only a few weeks in Jerusalem throughout the year (Lk 1.8). They lived throughout the country and were occupied with carrying out specific rituals among the people, including an examination of individuals for specific diseases to determine whether they could return to normal life (Mk 1.44). Since many of the priests were also experts in the law, they could assist local officials with legal decisions and could be involved in teaching in synagogues. Josephus considered it the priests' responsibility to "safeguard the laws, adjudicate in cases of dispute, and punish those convicted of crime" (Josephus, C. Ap. 2.187, 193). The frequent references to lawyers and teachers of the law in the Gospels/Acts (e.g., Lk 14.3) probably reflects this distribution of priests throughout the country. Priests were supported primarily by tithes, and since tithes included flocks, herds, grain, wine, and oil (Lk 18.12; Josephus, Ant. 20.181), the priests were also responsible for the collection, storage, distribution, and consumption of the goods that were presented to them.

The Levites, like the priests, were also divided into twenty-four courses and spent only a few weeks at the Temple in Jerusalem each year. They were responsible for maintaining both the security of the Temple and supporting the activities of the priests. The Levites guarded the gates of the Temple and ensured that the Temple boundaries were not violated (1 Chr 23.5; Acts 21.30). Some Levites were skilled in the use of musical instruments and provided liturgical support to the priests, while others sang hymns to accompany the sacrificial ritual (Josephus, Ant. 20.216). When they were not on active duty in Jerusalem, they supported the activities of local officials in the villages, towns, and cities where they lived. Their expertise in maintaining the security of the Temple could be utilized in implementing the decisions of local officials for punishment (Josephus, Ant. 4.214, 9.4; Mt 5.25). They thus probably were involved in the detention of prisoners and enforcing legal decisions, including corporal punishment. Like the priests, the Levites were supported mainly by tithes, and many of their activities involved the receipt and disposition of the various kinds of offerings according to Jewish law.

Scribes did not inherit their traditional responsibilities, like priests and Levites, but fulfilled their functions because they were experts in the law. Many scribes were probably employed by the wealthy as stewards (Lk 16.1), financial officers (Lk 8.3), or secretaries (Josephus, Ant. 20.208) because they were able to carry out the fundamental task of keeping records. Their ability to read and write, moreover, could also be used to teach the law and participate in making legal decisions. A large number of scribes, accordingly, probably supported local officials in activities in local synagogues and councils (Mk 2.6, 14.1). Some scribes may also have been priests and Levites, but most probably became experts in the law because Jewish law was invoked whenever disputes needed to be settled (Mk 7.1; Lk 6.7). The availability of scribes throughout the country was thus a significant factor in both the economic and religious life of the people, and ensured that Jewish customs and traditions would prevail in spite of the strong influence of Greek culture in many centers within the surrounding area.

Religious authorities had only a moral claim on the people of Judaea and Galilee. They could demand that people be obedient to the law and hand over to them the tithes and offerings that the law required. They had no physical means, however, of enforcing their demands. The large crowds who regularly attended the feasts at the Temple in Jerusalem (Acts 2.5; Josephus, *Ant.* 20.106), however, were probably an indication that most of the Jewish residents of both Judaea and Galilee usually fulfilled their financial obligations to the religious authorities (cf. *Vita* 63, 80). Every year, all faithful Jews were required to give to the Levites a tithe of all crops, flocks, and herds (Nm 18.21; Josephus, *Ant.* 4.68). In addition, they were expected to convert a second tithe into cash and spend the proceeds in Jerusalem (Dt 14.22; Josephus, *Ant.* 4.205). A third tithe for poor widows and orphans was demanded in the third and sixth years of every sabbatical cycle (Dt 14.28; Josephus, *Ant.* 4.240). First fruits (Dt 18.4; Josephus, *Ant.* 4.241) and an annual half-shekel tax on every Jew throughout the world (Ex 30.13; Mt 17.24) were also regularly sent to Jerusalem. Most of these obligations were probably met by Jews in Galilee and Judaea in spite of the fact that the religious authorities could not compel compliance.

Most priests and Levites lived among the people and were thus a perpetual reminder of Jewish legal obligations. Since their responsibilities in the Temple required only one week in every twenty-four, the priests and Levites were available to assist local elders in the promulgation and implementation of the law throughout most of the year. In addition, scribes found employment as teachers, secretaries, bookkeepers, and financial administrators throughout Galilee and Judaea. The relation between local and religious officials was complementary and mutually beneficial. Priests and scribes could provide legal expertise in teaching the law and making decisions, while elders and Levites could use their resources and experience to enforce compliance with the law in the implementation of all decisions. The close association of religious and local officials evidenced in the Gospels (e.g., Lk 20.1; Acts 4.5) implies that no serious conflicts in jurisdiction between them arose. Elders supported the religious officials with their tithes, offerings, and material resources, while religious officials supported the elders with their expertise in law and experience in administration. It was a mutually beneficial and satisfactory arrangement that left the implementation of most decisions in the hands of local leaders, while recognizing the legitimacy of the central religious authorities.

With the support of religious officials, local leaders were able to carry out all the prescribed requirements of Jewish law within their villages, towns, or cities. Local officials could use the expertise of priests and scribes in making legal decisions, and the special skills of the Levites in carrying them out. Punishments usually involved restitution, fines, detention, flogging, or excommunication from the community. With the exception of the death penalty, there was no provision of traditional Jewish law that could not be carried out. In Galilee, even capital punishment was probably left in the hands of local officials, who could refer particularly difficult cases to the religious authorities in Jerusalem. In Judaea, on the other hand, the Roman governor probably insisted on reviewing all cases involving the death penalty before they were carried out (Jn 18.31; Josephus, *Ant.* 20.202). Nevertheless, since capital punishment was probably decreed as a punishment only infrequently by Jews in the first century (cf. Jn 8.11), the Jewish people were normally accustomed to living according to the precepts and obligations of Jewish law without interference on the part of Rome's appointed rulers.

Galilee was governed by Herodian princes in the period 4 B.C.E.–44 C.E., and by Roman procurators 44–66 C.E. There is little evidence, however, of the way in which Herod's descendants administered his territory. The Roman *princeps* limited the amount of revenue that a client prince could obtain from his region so that his activities were economically constrained. His armed forces, accordingly, were probably of sufficiently moderate strength to be able to contain any minor threat to the stability of his regime, while not posing a threat to Rome's determination to keep the region subdued. The soldiers were probably billeted in a few of the major cities and were used to monitor activities that were potentially subversive (Mk 6.17; Lk 9.7), and to prevent the armed forces of adjacent territories from violating the boundaries of his tetrarchy (*Ant.* 18.113). The appointment of Agrippa I in 41 C.E. and his replacement by Roman governors in 44 C.E., however, proceeded without any significant interruption, so that the transfer of power must not have required any major structural change in the official administration of the province. All of the evidence indicates that the nominal rulers of Galilee from 4 B.C.E. until 66 C.E. limited themselves to the receipt of revenue, and the maintenance of stability within the boundaries of the territory.

Judaea was governed by Herodian princes in the period 4 B.C.E.–6 C.E. and 41–44 C.E., but Roman prefects ruled from 6 C.E. until 41 C.E. and Roman procurators from 44 until 66 C.E. The official ruler of the province usually resided in Herod's palaces in either Jerusalem or Caesarea while his soldiers were billeted in Caesarea or Sebaste. A permanent garrison was maintained in the Antonia fortress that overlooked the Temple in Jerusalem, but the remaining forces of the ruler were used to periodically patrol the territory to intimidate, disperse, or eliminate potential rebels. The ruler usually reinforced the garrison in Jerusalem at the time of the major feasts in order to forestall any possibility of insurrection. Whether Herodian or Roman, however, the official administrator of the province limited his activities to the receipt of revenue and the maintenance of stability within the region. The smooth transition in power in both 41 and 44 C.E. indicates that no major changes in administration took place. Instead, the nominal ruler who lived in Herod's palaces was replaced while most of the people who were involved in the official administration continued to perform their functions with minimal change.

The Roman appointees who ruled Galilee and Judaea in the period 6 B.C.E.–66 C.E. allowed Jewish law to prevail and made no attempt to impose foreign regulations. Since Rome's official representatives were concerned exclusively with the maintenance of the status quo, they did not become involved in the day-to-day details of administration that continued to be carried out by local and religious officials. The Herodian princes and Roman governors ensured that the country remained peaceful by using their armed forces to remind the people that Rome had the ability to enforce compliance with its objectives, but they usually did not interfere with the way in which Jewish law was either interpreted or implemented. The official administration of the territory thus did not actually "administer" the territory by making decisions on how it should be managed, and the governor did not really "govern" by controlling the actions of the people. Rather, the official ruler ensured only that the region participated in the Roman hegemony of the areas that surrounded the Mediterranean by keeping the territory pacified and economically viable. Roman rule was only an imposition of order that restricted the internal and external activities of those who lived within its reach to be consistent with its perception of its destiny to rule the Mediterranean region.

The presence of armed soldiers in Galilee and Judaea did not mean that streets and roads were secure. Military personnel were utilized to provide territorial security in the region, and frequently acted as bodyguards for Rome's appointed ruler (e.g., Josephus, *Ant.* 18.55), but generally did not provide protection to persons or property. Travel continued to be hazardous, and those who did travel were expected to provide their own security. When journeying to Jerusalem for the regular feasts, participants normally traveled in sufficiently large numbers for their own protection (Lk 2.44; Josephus, *Ant.* 20.118). On the other hand, small numbers of travelers were advised to carry a staff, limited provisions, and no significant amount of money with them (Mk 6.8; Josephus, *B.J.* 2.125). Even under these conditions, travelers were frequently robbed of their meager possessions (Josephus, *Ant.* 20.113; Lk 10.30). Similarly, householders were expected to defend their premises and possessions against thieves (Mt 24.43; Jn 10.1). Police protection did not exist, and individuals needed to be constantly wary of those who thrived by robbing the unprepared. The Gospels contain numerous references to thieves and robbers, and emphasize "watchfulness" as the appropriate precaution.

The autonomy enjoyed by the Jewish people in the first century would have continued if Rome had responded appropriately to the hopes and expectations of the Jewish people. The unacceptable behavior of the Roman *princeps*, the governors he appointed, and the armed forces he controlled, however, incited the residents of Galilee and Judaea to rise in protest. The bizarre behavior of both Gaius and Nero constrained the Jewish people to conclude that they had to be ready to lay down their lives for their principles. The insensitive decisions of Pilate, Cumanus, Felix, and Festus, however, as well as the outrageous actions of the auxiliary soldiers, created a contentious environment in which the people were determined to struggle in order to be able to continue living according to their customs and traditions. Their patience with the Roman governors was exceeded when Albinus and Florus abused their positions by trying to accumulate as much plunder as possible during their brief terms in office. Law and order broke down completely with the result that a great number of people joined the rebellion, expecting a miracle comparable to that of David and the Philistines, Hezekiah and the Assyrians, or the Maccabees and the Syrians.

The fidelity of the Jews in Galilee and Judaea to their traditions continued until the destruction of the Temple in 70 C.E. Their adherence to the law, however, continued unabated in spite of the absence of a national shrine and a hereditary priesthood. The transition was facilitated by the continuity of both local officials and the importance of the activities of the synagogue. The demands of the sacrificial cult were thus reinterpreted symbolically, and the requirements for priestly service were taken up by elders. The observance of Jewish traditions in Galilee and Judaea became comparable to that which had previously been practiced for centuries in the Diaspora. The study of the law and its applicability to daily life could thus continue in spite of circumstances that were radically different from that which prevailed in the first and second Temple periods. The subjugation of the province of Judaea by Rome ensured that Roman government and law would prevail in the land insofar as it was a part of the empire, but Jewish law continued to be effective in the daily lives of most of the Jewish people.

Conclusion

The Roman Empire imposed a measure of control over its territories that was not matched by a measure of uniformity. This applies to the status of people; to the status of civic communities; and to nations, provinces, and kingdoms. Across all this variation law was applied differently as well as were bodies of law and tradition from different sources. The preeminent examples of this for our purposes are, of course, the local power of Jewish law in Galilee and Judaea, the particulars of Paul's entanglement in the legal system as depicted in Acts, and

Jesus' fate as a noncitizen executed in a manner associated with crimes undermining the empire.

Notes

1. Pliny's surviving correspondence with Trajan makes this phenomenon clear.

2. Sherwin-White (1963: 48–70) provides the standard treatment of these trials and what we know of Roman law and judicial process through other sources.

3. Specifically, the ideal progress of a successful male elite career through various offices and magistracies (Jeffers 1999: 182–86).

4. See Dyson (1975) for comparable revolts by other subject peoples. Aberbach (1966) provides and extensive treatment of the Jewish revolt.

5. MacMullen (2000) details the extensive role of the Roman army as an exporter of specifically Roman material culture.

6. Callahan, Horsley, Smith (1998) and Gibson (1999) provide recent overviews of the vast literature on slavery in the ancient world.

7. For tension, note the meaninglessness ascribed to municipal politics in the imperial context. For co-optability, note the cities' efficiency in administering territory and in forming an arena of competition in devotion to Rome such as the desire of cities to host temples of the imperial cult.

8. Apuleius, *Metam.*, Book I provides a hilarious example.

9. See Augustus's Edicts on the composition of juries in Cyrene (Braund 1985: 178–83).

10. Huzar (1988: 661). Huzar provides a reliable overview of the administration of Alexandria focusing on the Julio-Claudian age.

11. See Robinson (1992) on the details of civic administration

12. See Nippel (1995: 85–112) on strategies of maintaining public order.

13. See Robinson (1995) for statutes relating to specific offenses.

Persecution   19

HAROLD REMUS

Early Christians and Persecution: Overview

THAT PERSECUTION WAS PART of the self-consciousness and self-identity of early Christians is evident from the earliest Christian sources. References to "persecute" (διώκειν/*diokein*) and "persecution" (διωγμος/*diogmos*) and to suffering for the sake of Christ appear throughout the New Testament. The apostle Paul in the mid-50s C.E. confesses to having persecuted (διώκειν/*diokein* I Cor 15.9; Gal 1.13; Phil 3.6) "the church of God," and reports that he himself was in turn being persecuted by his fellow Jews (διώκομαι/*diokomai* Gal 5.11). Paul perceived himself to be Jewish (2 Cor 11.22; Rm 11.1; Phil 3.5), though with important ambiguities (Gal 1.13–14; Phil 3.7–8; Barclay 1995b: 113–14). What he perceives to be persecution might therefore be seen by his fellow Jews as legitimate disciplining of a wayward Jew (2 Cor 11.24, 26; cf. Dt 25.3; Josephus, *Ant.* 4.238, 248), presumably for not requiring Jewish observance of gentile converts (Gal 5.11; 4.29, 6.12). For his part, he sees his own actions as intended to "destroy" (ἐπόρθουν/*eporthoun*; Gal 1.13) an undesirable faction within Judaism, that is, as persecution.

The Book of Acts portrays Paul (Saul) prior to his call to apostleship and many other Jews in a similar light: as harassers or persecutors of followers of "The Way" (8.1, 9.1–2, 6.8–7.60, 12.1–2, 21.27–36, 23.12–15, 24.1–9, 25.1–7) or as inciting government authorities against them (13.50; 14.2, 4–5, 19; 17.5–6, 13; 18.12–17; 20.3). These events are reported as taking place in the two decades or so after Jesus' death in 30 or 33 C.E., but they are set down c. 80–85 C.E. or even later (Wilson 1995: 69–71) when this small Jewish sect was becoming distinct from its parent, a religious entity in its own right—"Christian" (Acts 11.26; cf. 26.28, I Pt 4.16)—with its followers subject to expulsion from synagogues

(Jn 9.22, 12.42) and their status in the empire increasingly in question. Nero's torture and execution of a number of Christians in Rome in 64 C.E. on the grounds that they were responsible for a fire that devastated much of Rome (Tacitus, *Ann.* 15.44; Suetonius, *Nero* 16) indicates that also at the upper levels of society Christians were coming to be regarded as distinct from Jews. Whatever their historical value (see Lüdemann 1989), the accounts in Acts properly belong to the later decades of the first century where they constitute "a community-forming story" (Gaston 1986: 128) that depicts a Christian self-identity that is increasingly gentile (1.8; 28.28), distinct from and yet seen as fulfilling the parent Judaism (Gaston 1986: 128–40), with overtones of anti-Jewishness (28.25–27), demarcating it further from Judaism in the eyes both of Jews and the general (gentile) populace (Sanders 1999: 278–79; on third-party roles in conflicts cf. Kriesberg 1973: 277 and Remus 1986).

Although Jews figure on occasion in harassment or persecution of Christians (see Wilson's judicious assessment, 1995: 172–76; for the later period see Fox 1987: 474–87), it is the local gentile populaces who in the period prior to 250 C.E. play the predominant role in initiating actions against Christians, whether apart from government or in the role of *delatores* (plaintiffs; Sherwin-White 1952: 204) hailing Christians before the authorities, who thereupon put the accused on trial. That is, the government, with rare exceptions (*Mart. Pol.* 7.1; Eusebius, *Hist. eccl.* 5.1.8, 14), is not reported as persecuting Christians, if by that one means seeking them out for punishment. Rather, it responds to local accusations (Trajan to Pliny, *Ep.* 10.97). While Nero's torturing and killing of Christians was a case of scapegoating Christians, rather than executing them because they are "Christian" (Barnes 1968b: 34), subsequent accounts—Christian and otherwise—of trials and martyrdoms assume that simply being "Christian" is considered to be a crime sufficient to bring one to trial, whereas denial of the charge, verified by an offering to the deities, brings freedom. "Christian" as a crime is thus distinctive in that one is charged not for what one has done, but for what one is, a situation loudly protested by Christian apologists (Justin, *1 Apol.* 4, *2 Apol.* 2; Athenagoras, *Leg.* 1–2; Tertullian, *Apol.* 1–3).

In much of this period Christians were, in imperial eyes, an insignificant though sometimes irritating minority protected, like the population generally, from anonymous allegations (Trajan to Pliny, *Ep.* 10.97) or frivolous accusations, which, if proved unsubstantiated, redounded on the accuser (Hadrian in Eusebius, *Hist. eccl.* 4.9.3). Martyrdoms would seem to be numbered in the hundreds (Frend 1965: 413; Barnes 1971: 161–62; cf. Origen, *Cels.* 3.8) rather than the thousands at a time when the Christian population has been estimated as increasing from approximately 7,400 in 100 C.E. to 210,000 in 200 C.E. to 1,100,000 in 250 C.E. in a population of 60 million (Stark 1996: 7; Hopkins 1998: 193). That accounts of martyrdoms nonetheless figure so prominently in early Christian sources indicates that the possibility of martyrdom haunted early Christians. It also strongly suggests how important to Christian self-identity, group loyalty, social cohesion and control, maintenance of boundaries, and evangelism—and thus ultimately to survival itself (Riddle 1931; Stark 1997: 163–89; Hopkins 1998: 196–97)—was the professing of Christianity exemplified in the person of the martyr, the "witness" (μάρτυς/martus) unto death who follows in the steps of the archetypal witness, Jesus himself (Rv 1.9, 3.14, cf. 2.13; Eusebius, *Hist. eccl.* 5.2.3; Bowersock 1995).

Beginning with Emperor Decius's edict in 250 C.E. requiring sacrifice to the deities, and continuing off and on until Galerius's edict of toleration in 311, the imperial government undertook initiatives against Christians. The charge again is "Christian," and the litmus test is sacrifice, which Decius required of all persons, not only of Christians. In effect, he was espousing a "religion of empire" in contrast to the customary local religions (Rives 1999). During the time Decius's edict was in effect (250–51 C.E.) some Christians, including leaders, went into hiding, others were killed, and others performed the sacrifices or purchased certificates (*libelli*) attesting that they had done so (examples in English translation in *New Eusebius: Documents*, 228–19; Greek texts and English translations in Knipfing 1923), provoking controversy among Christians about the ecclesiastical status of these *lapsi* (Bryant 1993: 324–28). Beginning in 257 C.E. Valerian, the next emperor, required church leaders and later others as well to sacrifice; confiscated church property; and prohibited Christians from assembling on church property and from using their cemeteries (Potter 1993: 59). A long period of peace that ensued with Gallienus (260–68 C.E.) lasted until the "Great Persecution" (303–11) commenced with edicts that included the requirement of sacrifice, destruction of church property, and confiscation of church books (Eusebius, *Hist. eccl.* 9.10.8; 8.2.4; Gamble 1995: ch. 4). In addition to those Christians tortured and imprisoned, those who died numbered perhaps in the several thousands (Frend 1965: 536–57) in a Christian population estimated at some six million in 300 C.E. (Stark 1997: 7; Hopkins 1998: 193).

On his deathbed and wearied with the attempt to bring Christians back to "the religion of their fathers" (Lactantius, *De Mort. Persec.* 34), Galerius promulgated an edict of toleration in 311 co-signed by his imperial colleagues Constantine and Licinius but rejected by his other colleague Maximin Daza. The Edict of Milan issued by Constantine and Licinius in 313 reinforced the edict of 311, promising free practice of religion to all, including Christians (*Documents of the Christian Church* 21–23). What followed was an increasing imperial favoring and fostering of Christianity, resulting in "a religion of empire," albeit with much fluctuating back and forth during the fourth century as Christians and their opponents confronted one another in various situations and venues.

These government-initiated persecutions, in which Christian rigorists were pitted against Christians accommodationists in battles over conceptions of identity and boundaries, figured significantly in the transformation of Christianity from a sect or cult into a church (Bryant 1993; cf. Weber 1958: 144–54, 254 n. 173) and "a religion of empire."

"Otherness"

Various terms have been used, with numerous variations (Dawson 1998: 29–40), to characterize minority groups. The new Christian social configurations have been called *small groups* or simply *groups* (Meeks 1983: 74), or they have been seen as *voluntary associations* (McCready 1996). Early Christianity is commonly termed a *sect*, specifically a Jewish sect (Cohen 1987: 116; Elliott 1995a; Bryant 1993; Stark 1996: 25). Alternatively, or more specifically, in the early years it is a Jewish *coalition* or *faction* centered on a person, Jesus; subsequently it is a *sect*, "a group-centered faction" within and then increasingly distinct from Judaism (Elliott 1995a: 79–80, 89). Or this Jewish *sect movement* becomes a *cult movement* sufficiently distinct from its parent to constitute in effect a new religion (Stark 1996: 33, 44–45; Stark and Bainbridge 1987), "a universal form of Judaism" (Spivey and Smith 1995: 34; cf. Stark 1996: 49–71).

Common to all of these terms, whether applied to minority groups in early Judaism, in early Christianity, or in the modern period, is a self-conscious deviance from a parent group and/or from society in general that sets the insiders apart from outsiders who, in turn, tend to view these deviants with suspicion or hostility. The deviance may be expressed in a number of ways, many of them found in early Christianity: exclusivity; a distinctive morality and set of beliefs; commitment to the group and to winning others to it; tests of commitment and ways of maintaining and strengthening commitment and boundaries, including expulsion from the group; a promise of salvation in some form in compensation for present or feared deprivation or distress or unattainable goals (Wilson 1970, 1990; Stark and Bainbridge 1987; see the detailed list of early Christian sectarian attributes in Elliott 1995a). Conversionist sects, such as early Christianity was in many aspects, will likely stand in greater tension with the wider society as a result of their recruitment efforts than will introversionist groups that purposely isolate themselves from the outside world. However, sequestration and aloofness (common complaints about early Christians) may in themselves suggest "sinister purposes" and "evil practices" (Wilson 1990: 49), charges also leveled at early Christians. Even the simple fact "that the sect stands apart from the majority may be taken as an implicit rebuke to others. And often, sectarians go further and become explicit critics of contemporary society, its ethos, organization, and its dominant preoc-

cupations" (Wilson 1990: 26–27)—for example, what Galerius's edict of toleration summed up as "the religion of the fathers" from which he said Christians had
departed.

In Galerius's day the "religion of the fathers" was the traditional polytheist wor-
ships of the empire. But earlier, it was the religion of the Jewish ancestors of Christianity from which most Christians had distanced themselves. While Christians were
practicing Jewish observance into the second century and beyond (Justin, *Dial.*
47.2–4; Irenaeus, *Haer.* 1.26.2; Hippolytus, *Haer.* 7.22; Jerome, *Ep.* 112.13, 16; Klijn
and Reinink 1973; Wilson 1995: 158–59), it is the nonobservance of the gentile
entrants into Christianity that became the pattern, provoking from Jews varying degrees of hostility, as noted above (see further Wilson 1995: 6–11, 69–70, ch. 6, esp.
172–94), as well as controversies between Christians and Jews over what constituted
faithfulness to Judaism (e.g., Justin, *Dial.*; Remus 1986; Wilson 1995: ch. 9) and
among Christians sometimes heated debates over who belonged in the Christian fold
and who did not (2 Cor; Gal; Acts 10–12, 15, etc.).

Paul's "attempt to redefine a 'Judaism' without ethnicity and without preserving the national way of life enshrined in the 'ancestral customs' was hugely influential for later Christianity, but was clearly, and understandably, judged a contradiction in terms by his Jewish contemporaries" (Barclay 1995b: 118; cf. Becker
1993: 199). Christians' claims of a Jewish heritage, even while omitting—and
even rejecting and attacking—Jewish observance, aroused Jewish resentment and
hostility, especially if it seemed that Christians were threatening the privileges that
Rome and various cities had granted them (Josephus, *Ant.* 14.190–264,
16.162–73; Sanders 1999: 278–79).

While many in the general polytheist (gentile) populace might regard Jews
with suspicion or hostility because of their "otherness," Jews were nonetheless a
known quantity who enjoyed a long history and imperial recognition (Tacitus,
Hist. 5.5; Origen, *Cels.* 5.25, 41). These polytheist traditionalists were suspicious,
however, of a nouveau movement that seemed to be associated with Judaism but
yet did not observe Jewish practice, and in various ways held itself apart from the
Greco-Roman social world. Traditionalists and Christians alike signaled their
alienation from one another with distinguishing labels and accusations that served
to foster group consciousness and establish and maintain group boundaries, thus
justifying hostile actions against Christians, on the one hand, and Christian resistance to them, on the other.

The various labels applied to Christians by traditionalists presuppose an all-
encompassing social world characterized by certain key concepts that epitomize
the ethos of that world, deviance from which placed one on the outside, in the
category of "other." Chief among these was *pietas* or *eusebeia* (εὐσέβεια), the whole
complex of obligations and duties owed to "family, friends, fellow citizens,

country, and gods" (Shelton 1988/1998: 2; Lewis and Short 1879, s.v. *pietas*; Wilken 1984: ch. 3) and crucial to preservation of the *pax deorum* (harmony with the deities) and thus of the social order. In the terminology of sociology of knowledge, *pietas* was internalized as an "objective reality" in the primary and subsequent secondary socialization (Berger and Luckmann 1967: 60–61, 138–47) that made one a "Roman" or a Carthaginian Roman or an Alexandrian. *Pietas* was essential to the *securitas*, *stabilitas*, and *Romanitas* that various writers celebrated but also perceived as threatened from both within and without (MacMullen 1966; Lee 1971).

Christianity was one such threat, demarcated as "bad religion" through the label *superstitio* (Rives 1995a: 77–78), to which choice adjectives were added: "deadly" (Tacitus, *Ann.* 15.44: *exitiabilis superstitio*), "novel and vicious" (Suetonius, *Nero* 16.2: *superstitionis novae ac maleficae*), "degenerate" and "extravagant" (Pliny, *Ep.* 10.96.8: *superstitionem pravam et immodicam*). By accusing Christians of "hatred of humankind" (*odio humani generis, Ann.* 15.44) Tacitus marks Christians off from Romans representing true humanity. This alien element, he says, invaded Rome where all things frightful and shameful (*atrocia aut pudenda*) converge from every quarter.

Even more telling in marginalizing Christians was the charge that they were *atheists* (Justin, *1 Apol.* 5–6; *Mart. Pol.* 3.2, 9.2–3; Athenagoras, *Leg.* 3.1; Tertullian, *Apol.* 6.10; Clement of Alexandria, *Strom.* 7.1; Arnobius, *Adv. Nationes* 1.29, 3.28, 5.30; Ste. Croix 1963: 24), literally *god-less*, more specifically, image-less, i.e., *aniconic* since, true to their Jewish heritage, they had (in Paul's words) "turned to God from idols, to serve a living and true God" (I Thes 1.9).[1] A Roman official's question to Bishop Dionysius of Alexandria in 257 C.E. expresses common traditionalist attitudes to deity and puzzlement at the exclusivistic nature of Christian piety: What prevents Dionysius from worshiping his god alongside the traditional deities (Eusebius, *Hist. eccl.* 7.11.9)?

While Jews might be, as it were, "licensed atheists" (Ste. Croix 1963: 25) and philosophers might question traditional conceptions of deity, these latter nonetheless took part in the public ceremonies for the deities that were seen as maintaining the *pax deorum* and preserving the social order. At the trials of Christians, their refusal to sacrifice to the deities served as a proof of their Christianity and their atheism as well as a vindication of government action against them and of the common belief that such dereliction of duty provoked divine anger and brought disaster (Fox 1987). This charge—epitomized in Tertullian's famous complaint in 197 C.E. that any disaster evokes the cry "Christians to the lion!" (*Apol.* 40.2)—was systematically disputed by Arnobius (*Adv. Nationes*) during the Great Persecution. It was still being leveled late in the fourth century by Symmachus, the distinguished traditionalist orator, senator, and prefect of Rome (*Relatio.* 3.15–17).

The aniconism that accompanied Christian "atheism" brought Christians further into conflict with polytheists when it resulted in economic loss for makers of images (Acts 19.24–29) and for purveyors of sacrificial victims and their fodder (Pliny, *Ep.* 10.96.10).

Further setting Christians apart from the social order in traditionalists' eyes was the suspicion, as early as the beginning of the second century, that shameful acts (*flagitia*) were associated with the name "Christian" (Pliny, *Ep.* 10.96.2; Tacitus, *Ann.* 15.44). Pliny's examination of lapsed Christians in 112 C.E. reveals that cannibalism is one of the suspected *flagitia* (*Ep.* 10.96.7), a charge that dogged Christians (Justin, *1 Apol.* 26.7; *2 Apol.* 12.2, 5; *Dial.* 10.1; Tertullian, *Apol.* 7.1, 8.3; Athenagoras, *Leg.* 3.1; Minucius Felix, *Oct.* 9.5, 30.1; Eusebius, *Hist. eccl.* 5.1.26, 52) along with that of incest (Justin, *1 Apol.* 26.7; Athenagoras, *Leg.* 3.1, 31.1, 32.1; Minucius Felix, *Oct.* 28, 31.1; Eusebius, *Hist. eccl.* 4.7.11), the two sometimes linked in the phrase "Thyestean banquets and Oedipoean intercourse" (*Hist. eccl.* 5.1.14; cf. Athenagoras, *Leg.* 3.1, 31.1). In Greek lore Oedipus unknowingly married his mother while Thyestes unwittingly ate the flesh of his own children served up to him at a banquet by his brother Atreus as an act of revenge. Whether it was human sacrifice (Rives 1995a: 67–74, 83–84) or cannibalism or incest, such charges were a way of stigmatizing a people or an individual as beyond the pale of civilized society. In 177 C.E., when Christians in Lyons are accused of cannibalism and incest, even persons formerly friendly to them become incensed (Eusebius, *Hist. eccl.* 5.1.14).

Christian dislocation of loyalties from household—the basic unit of society—to church was also perceived as a serious threat to the social fabric (Coyle 1981), exemplified in the Alexandrian mother in 250 C.E. who, loving her Lord more than her many children, refused to deny him under torture (Eusebius, *Hist. eccl.* 6.41.18). The behavior of Christian women was crucial in view of "the symbolic significance of women's behaviour" (MacDonald 1996: 12) in the honor-shame system of the Greco-Roman world (Malina 1981/1993: ch. 2). Conformity to social norms would bring honor on a household, nonconformity shame. The very fact that, contrary to expectations, a Christian woman married to a polytheist partner did not conform to her husband's religion and that of the rest of the household (cf. 1 Cor 1.16; Acts 10.2, 47–48; 11.14; 16.15, 31–33; 18.8; 1 Pt 3.1–6; Meeks 1983: 30–31), or might even divorce or separate from him (1 Cor 7.15; Herm., *Man.* 4.1.6–8; Justin, *2 Apol.* 2), was itself a significant crossing of social boundaries (Justin, *2 Apol.* 2; Grant 1988: 69–73). A Christian wife or fiancée who chose celibacy would produce a frustrated husband or future husband and the possibility of martyrdom for her (*Act. Paul. Thec.*) or for the evangelist who persuaded her to take this unconventional step (*Act. Thom.*). A daughter might disobey her father by persisting in Christianity to the point even of death (*Mart. Perpet.*; Salisbury 1997: 5–14). Women occupying leadership roles in

Christian communities (I Cor 1.11, 11.2–16, 16.19; Rom 16; Phil 4.2; Schüssler Fiorenza 1983; MacDonald 1983; Richardson 1986; Torjesen 1993) might be perceived as a threat to the family system (cf. Sedgwick 1981). Such boundary crossings reflected badly on the households to which these women belonged, generating surmises and rumors of various *flagitia*: sorcery, immorality, and generally shameless behavior (MacDonald 1996).

Outsiders might be forgiven for misinterpreting the "body" and "blood" of the Christian Eucharist, reports or rumors of kissing (I Thes 5.26; I Cor 16.20; 2 Cor 13.12; Rom 16.16; I Pt 5.14; Justin, *1 Apol.* 65.2; Klassen 1992), gatherings of both genders (I Cor 11, 14; Minucius Felix, *Oct.* 9.6) even before dawn (Pliny, *Ep.* 10.96.7; cf. Tertullian, *Cor.* 3.3), or for taking at face value intra-Christian polemic about "overturning the lamp" at such gatherings, i.e., darkening the room so as to conceal sexual promiscuity (Justin, *1 Apol.* 26.7; Tertullian, *Apol.* 7.1; Clement of Alexandria, *Strom.* 3.2.10; Minucius Felix, *Oct.* 9.6; Epiphanius, *Pan.* 26.4–5; Wilken 1984: 17–21).

Celsus (c. 180 C.E.) would seem to have such gatherings in mind when he complains of Christians' secretiveness (Origen, *Cels.* 1.1, 3, 7). However, not much in that world was secretive or private. People lived cheek by jowl and spent much of their time out of doors (Martial, *Epig.* 1.86, 12.57; Tertullian, *Apol.* 42.2; MacMullen 1974b: chs. 2–3; MacMullen 1984: 39-40; Stambaugh 1988: 174–78; Osiek and Balch 1997: 31–32). "Thus, whatever one was or did, everybody knew at once" (MacMullen 1974b: 62), as is evident in I Peter, where the surprise of "Gentiles" at the Christians' dissociation from the common life (cf. MacMullen 1974b: 19-20, 77–78; Clement of Alexandria, *Paed.* 2.2) turns into maligning of Christians (I Pt 4.3–4), part of the general picture of suffering that the author of I Peter envisages for his readers because of their status as "exiles" (1.1) and "aliens" (2.11), or, in modern terms, sectarians (Elliott 1981/1990: 75).

Christians' dissociation from the "everyday," as well as the other distinctive Christian behaviors noted earlier, constitute "markers" setting them off as individuals or as a group in the very public society of their day. In linguistics a marker is that portion of an inflected word that sets it apart from the unmarked form (e.g., the "s" of "visits" or the "-ed" of "visited"); in social settings, clothes, hairstyles, cosmetics, behavior, language, and titles mark differences in gender, status, and belonging (Tannen 1994: ch. 4). The author of I Peter is not alone in taking pains to deflect outside criticism of Christians marked by their behavior (2.11–12, 15, 18–20; 3.9, 14, 16). As is often the case with modern minority groups, New Testament and other early Christian writers are concerned about outsiders' opinion and urge their readers not to offend the general mores (I Cor 10.32, 14.23; Col 4:5; I Thes 4.12; I Tm 3.7, 6.1; Ti 2.5, 10; I Pt 1.11–12, 15; *1 Clem.* 1.1, 47.7; Ign. *Trall.* 8.2), abundantly documented in philosophical writings of the time (Malherbe 1986). The general concern in these passages is that outsiders will have "nothing evil to say of us" (Titus 2.8) and "that the word of God may not be discredited" (2.5). Put positively, the goal is that outsiders will see Christians living good lives, perhaps ask them for "an accounting of the hope that is in you" (1 Pt 3.15)—and be won over.

Many were won over and became Christians, as the exponential growth in Christian numbers cited above indicates. For others, however, "Christian," a label evidently first applied to Christians by gentile outsiders (Acts 11.26; Wilkins 1992) and meaning something like "Christ-devotee" or "Christ-lackey" (Elliott 1981/1990: 79, 2000: 791; cf. "Jesus freak" today), came to epitomize the suspicion and contempt that many felt toward these people who flouted *pietas* and despite their small numbers constituted a "noisy presence" (MacMullen 1984: 13) flaunting their differences and their own supposed superiority. For some, that identity took precedence over the name by which they were known in "the world" (*Mart. Pol.* 3; Eusebius, *Hist. eccl.* 5.1.20), even as in present-day sects one's sectarian identity may overshadow other identities such as one's occupation, memberships in clubs, devotion to hobbies, or other social roles (Wilson 1990: 178–79).

Celsus, the voluble second-century critic of Christians, sums up much traditionalist and, in his case, elitist resentment of what he sees as Christians' disdain of the social order and his disdain of them (Origen, *Cels.* 1.1, 3, 5a, 7, 9, 28, 37, 41; 2.55; 3.22, 44, 55; 4.23; 5.14; 6.34; 7.36, 62; 8.2, 38, 41, 55, 75). Such a group deserves to die out (8.55), and indeed its members are being sought out and executed, their god powerless to deliver them (8.39, 41, 69).

Boundaries

Celsus's polemic is but one of a series of exchanges between Christians and traditionalists on a number of issues (Chadwick 1966; Grant 1952, 1988; Remus 1983). Christian writers point out the how and the why of their divergences from the general mores and through retorsion arguments portray traditionalists as doing the very things of which they accuse Christians (Justin, *2 Apol.* 12.5; Tertullian, *Apol.* 4, 9; Minucius Felix, *Oct.* 29.1, 30.1; Rives 1995a: 74–77).

At the same time Christian writers are at pains to stress Christians' general conformity to everyday values and practices. Far from being practitioners of exotic beliefs that would separate them from everyday life, Christians assert they are present in all the activities of the daily round (Tertullian, *Apol.* 42; *Diogn.* 5). However, from the earliest days those same opinion makers also worry about boundary maintenance. Conversion to Christianity (Nock 1933) meant a resocialization into a social world that included the polytheism described above—stigmatized by Christians as "the/this world" (see below)—but focused on the special bounded community where a heavenly father (Mt 23.9), or a father (1 Thes 1.6; 1 Cor 4.15–16, 11.1) or brother or sister in Christ (Mk 3.31–35; Mt 25.40; 1 Thes 1.4, 2.1, etc.; Meeks 1983: 87), supplanted biological kin after one was "regenerated" through a ritual washing (1 Cor 6.11; Ti 3.5) and sat at table with other members of the household of faith (Gal 6:10; Eph 2:19). These "core social rituals," embodying "significant collective experience" (Bryant 1993: 307), fixed and reinforced boundaries. For example, baptism gave entry to the fold and was requisite for participation in the sacred meal fenced off and presided over by authority figures (Ign. Smyrn. 8.1–2; Did. 7; 9–10; 14; Justin, 1 Apol. 65–67; Tertullian, Cor. 3.3). Such role specializations—apostle, prophet, teacher, bishop, deacon, elder, widows, etc. (Mk 3.14–18 par.; Rom 16; 1 Cor 12.28; Phil 1.2; Acts 6.1–6; 1 Tm 5.3–22; Meeks 1983: 111–39; Richardson 1986; MacDonald 1988)—also functioned to preserve and enhance social cohesion, especially in conflict situations (cf. Kriesberg 1973: 14–15).

One of the chief motivations for joining and continuing in such a community is the promise of salvation in some form. Celsus, as we have seen, taunted Christians with the charge that their god was unable to deliver either their savior or themselves from death. Christians, however, were convinced that the very godforsakenness of Jesus on the cross (Mk 15.34//Mt 27.46) meant their salvation. Death was the portal to a glorious afterlife, a hope and an expectation that marked them off from their polytheist neighbors, as numerous Christian sources (e.g., 1 Thes 1.10; 1 Cor 15; Mt 25; Rv 7.13–17) and a comparison of Christian and polytheist epitaphs across class lines attests (Lattimore 1962). Unquenchable fire awaited those outside the Christian fold, while those within "will laugh unhesitatingly in everlasting joy" (Mart. Pionii 7).

A glorious afterlife is only one of the rewards that attract people to a deviant group and then hold them there. Since such a reward is unattainable in this world, people may settle for "compensators"; in place of the promised immortality, one embraces instead a life prescribed by the group for attaining what is promised (Stark and Bainbridge 1987; Stark 1996). Another compensator in early Christianity was the posthumous fame that martyrs could expect to reap through their death as celebrated in stories written down and circulated among their brothers and sisters in the faith who would (if the authorities permitted) also gather up their remains (Mart. Pol. 18.1–2; Mart. Carp. 47) or treasure even the dust on which the remains had rested (Act. Thom. 170; Brown 1981; Salisbury 1997: 166–72).

For believers who were not prepared or not called upon to witness unto death, the stories and relics made the promise of life after death all the more credible and thus served to strengthen their ties to the community. It was "an agency of salvation" where members sought to live according to the modes of being of the ultimate state of perfected being and, alongside other "saints," experienced the joy(s) of salvation (Wilson 1990: 47–48) while awaiting the fulfillment of the ultimate promise. Among the rewards of belonging was the help available within these Christian communities, which functioned in effect as social agencies at a time when there were none, as was noted by outsiders including notably the emperor Julian (361–63 C.E.), who in his efforts to restore traditional polytheism called for the worshipers of the traditional deities to imitate Christians in caring both for their own and for outsiders (Julian, *Ep.* 22; cf. *Vit. Pachom.* 4).

While these various factors functioned to maintain early Christian groups as strongly bounded communities, Christian leaders were haunted by the question "How complete was conversion?" (MacMullen 1984: ch. 9). That is, how much did converts' original polytheist socialization persist during their resocialization into the Christian social world and threaten community boundaries and cohesion? As early as twenty years after Jesus' death, when Christian sectarian consciousness ran high, one sees Paul wrestling with the lingerings of the socializations his converts brought into the Christian fold from the world of that day. Later, in the second, third, and fourth centuries C.E. when large numbers of nameless persons— "just ordinary folk"—began to enter the Christian fold, many did so without conspicuous changes in their lifestyles and with "the least possible tear in the fabric of already held beliefs" (MacMullen 1984: 1, 21; Markus 1990: ch. 1). This is evident in the warnings voiced by Christian thinkers regarding certain occupations (Lietzmann 1961: 151–52; Remus 1987: 142, n. 47), participation in the shows in the amphitheaters (Tertullian, *Spec.*) or in the schools of the day (Tertullian, *Idol.* 10; cf. later, Basil of Caesarea, *Ad Adolesc.*), or distinctive behavior in even minute matters (Remus 1987: 142–43).

Early Christians might proclaim or be told of the line dividing the "before" from the "after" of their entry into the Christian fold (1 Thes 5.4–5; 1 Cor 6.9–11; 1 Pt 4.3–4; Justin, *1 Apol.* 53.5; *2 Apol.* 2.1–7; *Dial.* 63.5, 119.5, 123.5; Tertullian, *Spec.* 4, 24; *Act. Thom.* 12–15). Every day, however, they were involved in decisions at the borderline that marked them one way or the other: whether to accept an invitation to dinner (1 Cor 10.14–30), or how to live as a woman slave in a polytheist household (Glancy 1998) or as a childless wife (Remus 1999).

It is clear that early Christians inhabited two social worlds. "One is the world they shared with other people who lived in the Roman Empire; the other, the world they constructed" (Meeks 1983: 8). Daily life being so complex, boundaries between the two worlds tended to be permeable and faint. Like traditionalists, Christians employed labels to demarcate boundaries, setting themselves off from outsiders, on the one hand, and encapsulating their self-identity, on the other. Various early Christian sources speak of *the world/this world* (ὀκόσμος/ὀκόσμος οὗτος; *ho kosmos/ho kosmos houtos*: Jn 7.7, 15.18–19; 1 Cor 11.32; Eph 2.2; Col 2.20; Jas 1.27, 4.4; 1 Jn 2.15–17, 4.4–5) or *this age* (ὁ αἰών οὗτος/*ho aion houtos*: Mt 13.22;

Lk 16.8; Rom 12.2; I Cor 1.20, 2.6; cf. 2 Tm 4.10), ruled over by the adversary, Satan, *the god/prince of this age* (2 Cor 4.4; Ign., *Eph.* 17:1, 19:1, etc.; cf. Eph 2.2), *the prince of this world* (Jn 12.31, 14.30, 16:11; cf. I Jn 5.19).

Even though early Christians were of either Jewish or gentile origin, those terms early on came to exemplify conditions and behaviors that demarcated Jews and Gentiles outside the Christian fold from those on the inside: *Jews* or *the Jews* (Jn; I Cor 1.22–23; Rv 2.9, 3.9); *Gentiles* (τὰ ἔθνη/*ta ethnē*; οἱ ἐθνικοὶ/*hoi ethnikoi*: Mt 5.47; Mt 6.7, 32; Mt 18.17; Eph 4.17; I Pt 4.3; cf. Gal 2.15; Latin, *gentiles*: Ambrose, *Ep.* 18.2; *Cod. Theod.* 16.5.46 [409 C.E.]; Latin, *nationes*: Tertullian, *Idol.* 22.1; Arnobius, *Adv. Nationes*). Later, alongside *ethne/ethnikoi* or *gentiles/nationes* the term "pagan" (*paganus*) came into currency (Latte 1960: 371; Athanassiadi and Frede 1999: 4–5) and continues as a common pejorative label to the present day. Thus it is used by Tertullian (*Cor.* 11) at the beginning of the third century and, beginning at the end of the fourth century, in official documents: *Cod. Theod.* 16.7.2 (383 C.E.), 16.10.20 (415 C.E.), 16.10.21 (416 C.E.); *pagani* is cited, from common usage, as an explanatory synonym of *gentiles* in 16.5.46 (409 C.E.).

Christians' consciousness of their own distinctiveness is expressed in terms such as *The Way* (Acts 9.2, 19.9, 19.23, 22.4, 24.14, 24.22); *the church* [ἐκκλησία/*ekklesia*] *of God* (I Cor 1.2; I Tm 3.5) or simply *church* (Mt 16.18, 18.17, etc.); *body of Christ* (I Cor 12); *saints* (I Cor 1.2, 6.1–2, etc.); the chosen and destined ones (Jn 15.16, 19; Rom 8.29–30; I Thes 1.4; Col 3.12; I Pt 1.2, 2.4; Rv 17.14); "a chosen race, a royal priesthood, a holy nation, God's own peo-ple . . . called out of darkness into his marvellous light" (I Pt 2.9). More than any of these, the term "Christian," likely bestowed on them by outsiders (see above), is made their own. Outsiders might use it intending to shame Christians, but those thus reproached are to consider themselves honored (I Pt 4.14). At trials of Christians the simple confession "I am a Christian" is both a badge of honor and the word that can condemn them to death.

The compensators and rewards outlined above that served to maintain bound-aries came with a price, summarized for early Christians in one of the Jesus say-ings. Those who, for the sake of Jesus and of "the good news," leave house or brothers or sisters or mother or children or fields (or, added Eusebius, were de-spoiled of their property or position by covetous traditionalists who accused them to the authorities) are promised all of those in return—"*with persecutions*"—and, in the age to come, eternal life (Mk 10.29–30; Eusebius, *Hist. eccl.*, 4.26.5, 7.15.1–2).

"Persecution" and "Martyrs"

"Persecution" is how Christians were apt to view actions against them, with their identity as individuals and as groups at stake. In their accounts of these events and in whatever traditionalist sources there are on the subject, the competing social worlds outlined above become evident. Latent or implicit conflict becomes overt, permeable boundaries stiffen, faint ones become distinct. Internal Christian conflicts also emerge, with rigorists pitted against accommodationists, Christian "athletes" in the faith at odds with wavering and "everyday" Christians.

The historical value of the Christian accounts of trials, imprisonments, tortures, and executions has been much debated. While it is clear that their rhetoric clouds the historicity of what they report, there is some consensus that some of these accounts, or various recensions of them, also represent firsthand reports; reflect actual procedures before magistrates and proceedings in the arena; offer authentic documents, including diaries of martyrs (*Mart. Perpet.*; *Mart. Pionii*); and are occasionally verifiable from external sources (Lucian of Samosata, *Peregr.* 12–13; Barnes 1968a; *Acts of the Christian Martyrs*; Fox 1987: 433, 435, 460–92; Potter 1993: 56–58; Bowersock 1995: ch. 2; MacDonald 1996: 73–82). Papyri finds of interrogation procedures (Bowersock 1995: 37–38) or the *libelli* of the Decian persecution (Knipfing 1923) enrich Christian descriptions of events, while the papyri fragments that constitute the so-called *Acts of the Pagan Martyrs* provide perspective on the genre of martyr acts.

Moreover, rhetoric is also reality. Christian accounts of interrogations, while shaped for a Christian audience, nonetheless had to meet the criterion of plausibility (Fox 1987: 421). The writers' literary shaping of these critical events also reveals how both they and their audience perceived themselves as a minority in tension with the larger society. In both Christian as well as traditionalist sources one also sees how place, time, actions, actors, and the actors' roles are socially informed and interpreted (Potter 1993; Bowersock 1995).

Traditionalists

Some *delatores* (see above) who accused Christians to authorities may have been concerned about loss of income or livelihood (Acts 19.24–29; Pliny, *Ep.* 10.96.10), but all might have echoed Pliny's expression of satisfaction that, after interrogation and execution of Christians, traditional worship would begin to be restored (*Ep.* 10.96.10). The spectators at interrogations, tortures, and deaths of Christians who cry out "Atheists" (*Mart. Pol.* 3.2, 9.2; cf. Eusebius, *Hist. eccl.* 5.1.9) are expressing concern about the underpinnings of society, fear of angering the deities, and not a little frustration with persons who so willfully refused to participate in the public rites honoring those deities and, indeed, urged others not to do so (*Mart. Pol.* 12.2).

Roman governors were expected to examine Christians who had been brought to their attention by a *delator* or, after 249 C.E., had failed to conform to one of the imperial edicts. Given the depth of feeling sometimes expressed by the populace regarding Christians, these officials might fear a public outcry or riot, a charge of treason, or dereliction of duty if they did not proceed against Christians (*Mart. Pol.* 3.2, 12.2; Eusebius, *Hist. eccl.* 5.1.7–8, 10, 15, 30, 50; *Mart. Pionii* 18; cf. Jn 19.12–15; Barnes 1971: 158–60). More than that, however, over against these disturbers of the Roman order these same authorities felt obligated to uphold that same Roman order, which had nurtured them, situated them in the upper social strata, and, thanks in great part to the Roman emperor, placed them in office.

In examining Christians the procedure the governors followed—*cognitio extra ordinem*, which dealt with matters not covered in the regular criminal code—allowed them wide discretion (Sherwin-White 1952: 205; Ste. Croix 1963: 11–13). Their choices of time and place indicate how they used it to demonstrate Roman authority by making an example of Christians. Polycarp dies on a "Great Sabbath" in 156 C.E. (*Mart. Pol.* 21), martyrs at Lyons during a widely attended local festival in 177 C.E. (Eusebius, *Hist. eccl.* 5.1.47), Pionios on another Great Sabbath in 250 C.E. (*Mart. Pionii* 2, 3), days when the populace did not have to work (*Mart. Pionii*, 3; on the Great Sabbath, Fox 1987: 486–87). Perpetua in 203 C.E. likewise dies on a holiday, the birthday of the future co-emperor Publius Septimius Geta (*Mart. Perpet.* 7.9; 16.3). As to venue, the trials and executions take place in conspicuous urban settings—agoras and arenas—in prominent urban centers: Alexandria, Smyrna, Pergamum, Thessalonica, Carthage, Rome, Lyons. These dramatic public events also offered entertainment—the tortures, immolations, and contests with gladiators and beasts that the populace held dear, much as public hangings, lynchings, and floggings used to be (and in some places still are) community events serving as spectacles affirming the spectators' communal values. For Christians, the trials and executions were "martyrdoms" (see below), public demonstrations of the faith.

In the trials, officials and Christians wage a war of words that reveals representatives of differing groups "talking past one another." Officials threaten, cajole, and plead with Christians in an effort to persuade them to honor the gods of traditional society. Alongside straightforward confessions of Christianity and refusals to deny Christ one finds responses that are oblique and enigmatic—snippets of "insider," "in-group" talk that are part of the superior knowledge that those on trial believe they possess (Eusebius, *Hist. eccl.* 5.1.29–31, 52; *Mart. Pionii* 19). Sometimes Christians offer to teach the interrogator (*Mart. Pol.* 10.1–2).

Celsus (Origen, *Cels.* 1.9; 3.44, 55; 4.23; 5.14) finds such behavior pretentious and presumptuous. The interrogators are also not amused, interpreting anything but capitulation as a flouting of their authority, albeit often reluctantly exercised. Typically, they offer release to those who sacrifice, reportedly even coaching Christians in how to answer to secure their freedom, or dismissing the charges, or once in frustration executing a few of a throng of eager martyrs and contemptuously directing the rest to find death by jumping off cliffs or hanging themselves (Tertullian, *Scap.* 4.3–4; 5.1). Those Christians who offer sacrifice in effect acknowledge the power if not necessarily the authority of the empire. Refusal to do so acknowledges neither, constituting "stubbornness and obdurate obstinacy," a "madness" (*pertinaciam . . . et inflexibilem obstinationem . . . amentiae*) that Pliny was sure deserved to be punished (*Ep.*10.96.3–4; similarly *Mart. Pionii* 20).

The punishments, like most things in that highly stratified world, were likely to follow class and gender lines. Women not outright condemned to death might be sent to a brothel (Tertullian, *Apol.* 50.12; *Mart. Agape* 5; *Mart. Pionii* 7). In Valerian's edict of 258 C.E. Christians of high rank were to have their property confiscated but to be executed only if they persisted in their madness; even then some of special standing might be imprisoned instead (Cyprian, *Ep.* 80.1). Christians who were Roman citizens and/or of standing might be sent to Rome or decapitated rather than sent to the arena, and with little fanfare—at least some officials were not anxious to see those of their own status reduced in the arena to the status of slave, thus blurring social boundaries (Pliny, *Ep.* 10.96.4; *Act. Cypriani* 4–5; Potter 1993: 59–62, 70–71).

Perpetua's diary records that her jailers acceded to her request for better treatment because they believed she and her companions possessed great power but also because of her social status (*Mart. Perpet.* 9; 16). It is her betrayal of her class, epitomized in her unflinching rejection of her father's frantic pleas to her to sacrifice (*Mart. Perpet.* 5–6), that likely most incenses the governor, himself evidently a man of strong religious convictions (Rives 1996) like the governor examining the Scillitan Christians in 180 C.E. who declares to them, "We are religious too" (*Acts Scill.* 3). By that is meant the traditional religion, "the religion of the fathers" from which Galerius said Christians had departed (see above). Galerius, on contemporary evidence, was a religious man, as was Diocletian (Lactantius, *De Mort. Persec.* 10–11; Eusebius, *Vit. Const.* 2.51; Ste. Croix 1963: 27–28; Rives 1995b: 256–58). For both of these noted persecutors of Christians, as well as for the governors who were obliged to examine Christians or for a philosopher like Celsus, refusal of Christians to offer the barest acknowledgment of the gods constituted an unacceptable subversion of the established order and was deserving of imprisonment, torture, or death.

Christians

The mutual incomprehension evident in the exchanges between Christians and the authorities is rooted in the opposing social worlds indicated earlier and anchored in axiomatic underpinnings (Remus 1986). What the authorities perceive as due punishments and executions Christians see as persecution and martyrdom. For at least one fourth-century Christian, Galerius's stubborn determination to persecute Christians quite prepared to die is "madness" (Lactantius, *De Mort. Persec.* 11.3, 4:

furor, insania). For traditionalists, on the other hand, Christians' assertions of the heavenly bliss that awaited them in contrast with the blisters they predicted for their interrogators (*Mart. Pol.* 2; *Act. Scill.* 15; *Mart. Pionii* 7) was puzzling and irritating, and their stubborn persistence in their confession under interrogation or torture was irrational, a madness (as Pliny observed, above; cf. *Mart. Agape.* 3.6), as was their offering of themselves as victims, sometimes in throngs, whether infected with a seeming contagion of martyrdom or in protest of what they perceived as unjust condemnations of Christians (Fox 1987: 442–43).

Christians themselves condemned such "voluntary" martyrdoms (Justin, *2 Apol.* 4; *Mart. Pol.* 4; Clement of Alexandria, *Strom.* 4.10). They were also aware, however, that their beliefs and behavior might be considered madness by outsiders— inevitably, perhaps, considering that they traced their origins to a savior accused of madness (Mk 3.21; Jn 10.20) and proclaimed a message about this crucified savior that was considered foolishness (1 Cor 1.18), madness (Justin, *1 Apol.* 13.4), and shameful (Justin, *Dial.* 131.2) and rendered one mad (Acts 26.24). Moderns have understandably labeled as "a pathological yearning for martyrdom" (Ste. Croix 1963: 23) with "a fanatical ring" (Schoedel 1985: 10) Ignatius's characterizations of himself as "lusting to die" (*Rom.* 7.2)—as "God's wheat" that will become "pure bread of Christ" after it has been ground by the teeth of beasts who are to be coaxed to be his grave (4.1–2). For second-century cultural bellwethers such as Celsus (see above) and Galen (in Walzer 1949: 14–15) Christians had a reputation for ignorance and irrationality, a charge repeated in the late fourth century by the emperor Julian (in Gregory of Nazianzus, *Or. Bas.* 4.102).

Within the Christian social world, however, martyrdom was quite rational, in its very intransigence and drama and its evident power to persuade others. In Tertullian's memorable aphorism, "The blood of Christians is seed" (*Apol.* 50.14: *semen est sanguis Christianorum*). It was precisely martyrdoms that jarred Justin's thinking about Christians before he became one himself: Why did they so willingly embrace death when it would deprive them of the wickedness, pleasure, and cannibalism of which they were said to be so fond (*2 Apol.* 12.2)?

Partly it was (as we have seen) because martyrdom offered, not only fulfillment of the promise of life hereafter and escape from eternal punishment, but also earthly fame after death. Even before the ultimate sacrifice, however, Christian confessors while in prison became minor celebrities attended by other believers who bribed guards for better treatment, brought food and books, received pardons for lapsing, and awaited accounts of visions from these pilgrims en route to paradise (Lucian, *Peregr.* 12–13; Tertullian, *Mart.* 2, *Pud.* 22; *Mart. Perpet.*; Eusebius, *Hist. eccl.* 5.1.45, 5.2.5; Cyprian, *Ep.* 21.2, 27.3, 36.2; on the role of women see MacDonald 1996: 73–82). Ignatius's journey from his bishop's seat in Antioch to martyrdom in Rome—a triumphal procession attended by Christians along the way requiring considerable planning and expense—doubles as public demonstration of the faith for the benefit of outsiders and a vindication of Ignatius's episcopal authority back in Antioch (Schoedel 1985: 10–12).

Lucian of Samosata, drawing on a familiar social category, refers to Jesus as a sophist (*Peregr.* 13), albeit with a prefix—"crucified"—not apt to be associated with those influential social and cultural figures of the second century C.E. (Bowersock 1969; Anderson 1993). Certain gifted Christians also achieved a prominence—or (for many outsiders) notoriety—as, in effect, Christian sophists, whether through their writings (Tertullian; Barnes 1971: ch. 14), engaging in dialogue with their interrogators or the onlookers, or addressing traditionalists and Christians (and sometimes Jews) in the agora (*Mart. Pionii* 4, 12–14), in the tradition of the sophists holding up a mirror to their hearers' society (Bowersock 1995: 44–48). Polycarp is seen by the crowd at his trial as "teacher" and "father" (διδάσκαλος/*didaskalos*; πατήρ/*pater*; *Mart. Pol.* 12), standard epithets of sophists. In prison, we are told, traditionalists come to persuade Pionios and leave amazed at his answers (*Mart. Pionii* 12.1).

In the arena, Christian confessors, the officials, and the spectators participate in another public rite, the spectacle or contest. Even as Paul had portrayed the Christian life as a race, to be run to win the crown of victory (1 Cor 9.24–27), and the Deutero-Paulines as an athletic "contest" or "competition" (ἀγών/*agon*: 1 Tm 6.12; 2 Tm 4.7), so later Christians see the trials and tortures some of them undergo as "contests" (πόλεμος/*polemos*, Eusebius, *Hist. eccl.* 5.2.6), and those contending—men but frequently also women—as "athletes" (ἀθληταί/*athletai*; 1 *Clem.* 5:1; Eusbeius, *Hist. eccl.* 5.1.19; *Mart. Pionii* 22.2) or "competitors" (Eusebius, *Hist. eccl.* 5.1.17: ἀγωνισταί/*agonistai*). Whatever the modern or ancient explanations of the athletes' endurance of immolation, impaling, and dismemberment by wild animals (Salisbury 1997: 167–68), it made a deep impression—both negative and positive—on polytheists and Christians alike, with the Christians recording (and embellishing) the events for the strengthening of their communities (Bowersock 1995: ch. 2; Salisbury 1997).

The martyrs' achievement is heightened when an account points, by contrast, to those Christians who are not athletes and who waver, perhaps not denying Christ at first but ultimately offering the sacrifice that will gain their freedom. Such persons might be stigmatized by other Christians as not really part of the community anyway (Eusebius, *Hist. eccl.* 5.1.48); or they are threatened with dreadful tales of what happened to sacrificers; or offered the chance to redeem a lapse by confession, leading them perhaps to "volunteer" for martyrdom (Fox 1987: 444), which expunges all sins (Tertullian, *Apol.* 50.16).

Was martyrdom madness? As Carl Hempel points out, "to judge the rationality of a decision, we have to consider, not what empirical facts . . . are actually relevant to the success or failure of the action decided upon, but what information concerning such facts is available to the decision-maker. Indeed, a decision may qualify as rational even though it is based on [what others regard as] incomplete or false empirical assumptions" (1965: 464). For the traditionalists who interrogate Christians or cry out against them, Christians' assumptions made little sense. Within the social world of Christians, however, they did (cf. Blasi 1997: 70–72). Martyrdoms were "a group phenomenon" (Stark 1996: 183), events that formed the Christian community. The minority who became martyrs escaped eternal punishment while gaining an eternal reward as well as lasting fame among their brothers and sisters; perhaps some had even resorted to martyrdom as a way to escape debts (Ste. Croix 1954: 83). For the majority—if they had not denied Christ outright (Pliny, *Ep.* 10.96.6)—martyrdoms served to affirm core Christian assumptions and values, demonstrating especially the promise of salvation, even though for themselves it made sense to keep a low profile, or to choose flight (Mt 10:23; Tertullian, *Fug.*), at least temporarily (Cyprian, *Ep.* 16.4), or to be ransomed if imprisoned (Ign. *Rom.* 1, 4), or, during the Decian persecution, secure the *libelli* in one way or another and run the risk of being labeled *lapsi*.

The importance of martyrdoms in the social world of early Christianity has been suggested above. Rodney Stark has argued that early Christians, like new deviant groups generally, faced tough going (1996: 172–89); martyrdoms made Christian claims and promises more credible. Testimonials, so essential to religion, which is commonly social by nature, validate a religion. In a deviant religious group, the most effective testimonials are those by members who voluntarily assume the stigmas that mark the group off from society and are willing to pay the price for doing so. Those prepared to pay the ultimate price of death are the most effective witnesses for the claim that the compensators cherished by the group are indeed credible. Christians who readily went to death proclaiming their certainty that bliss awaited them affirmed for the rest that the same promise held true for them as well and that Christian claims generally were valid.

Various groups and individuals prior and subsequent to Christianity died as a result of their faith or their principles. The terms "martyr" and "martyrdom," however, are Christian coinage of the second century C.E. that came then to be applied retrospectively to the deaths of courageous pre-Christian Jews and notables such as Socrates and, later, to Muslims, Christians, and others who die for their faith, their principles, or a cause (Bowersock 1995: ch. 1).

Conflict and Sociation: The Conversion of the Empire and of Christianity

Kriesberg's "stages" and modes of conflict (1973) are suggestive of important aspects of the conflicts outlined in the preceding sections. Also suggestive is Simmel's contention, followed by Coser (1956), Kriesberg (1973), and others, that conflict is endemic in social relations and is in fact a form of "sociation" (Simmel 1955: 13: *Vergesellschaftung*), i.e., interaction between adversaries. As such, conflict performs a variety of social functions.

The latent conflict inherent in social relations becomes manifest in the case of early Christianity's "otherness" as a result of the public nature of life in that world in general and of religion in particular, with sacrifice to the deities functioning as a litmus test. Other ways in which Christian "otherness" becomes publicly marked have been pointed out above. These markers are discerned, by some on both sides, as incompatible with traditionalist mores. The conflicts that ensue sometimes escalate, sometimes deescalate, over the course of two centuries. Along the way, Roman officials try to persuade Christians to at least a token recognition of the prevailing mores, which they and portions of the populace see as threatened by these deviants. The officials offer accused Christians freedom as a reward for sacrificing, but as the superior power they are also in a position to apply coercion. Some Christians choose that freedom, as early as the turn of the first century. Others flee before being apprehended or simply try to escape notice.

For those brought to trial the only modes of sociation available are what one might call passive resistance (or aggression)—a determined, sometimes defiant, confession of Christianity—and persuasion. Most persuasive is the willingness of some Christians to stake their lives on the principles by which they have been living, embodied in the group to which they have committed themselves and within which they enjoy rewards in the here and now and the promise of life in a hereafter. Their affirmation of this hope for themselves, and the threat of quite the opposite for the officials interrogating them, make clear the dissensual nature of these conflicts. The officials and the traditionalist populace are concerned about a stable society that preserves and is preserved by the *pax deorum*; the Christians are looking to a life that is a perfected continuation of the life experienced within their bounded community. Opinion makers in each group denigrate the goals of the other group, in various ways and in varying degrees.

At the same time there is (as was noted above) commonality. Christians point out their participation in society, that they are not simply "other." "Any specific conflict is not purely conflicting . . . the relations between any two groups have conflicting, cooperative, accommodative, and many other qualities" (Kriesberg 1973: 276). Until 250 C.E. Roman officials, with few exceptions, bother with Christians only in response to accusations by *delatores*. And when it comes to interrogating Christians, alongside threats they also cajole, or suggest ways to comply with the letter of the law. Prison guards accede to requests, accept bribes to provide better treatment, or are even won over to Christianity. Some in the populace are friendly to Christians; others come to hear out imprisoned Christians. Some, like Justin, reflecting on the dissonance between what they have heard about Christians and what they perceive of them firsthand, incline to Christianity. The exponential growth of Christianity indicates something more than just adversarial relations between Jews, polytheistic traditionalists, and Christians; all had to live alongside one another in crowded conditions and of "getting along" despite differences.

Among those forsaking polytheism for Christianity are apologists like Justin, his pupil Tatian, and Tertullian, whose treatises along with those of the learned Christian scholar Origen all speak with some authority in the language of the cultural elite and receive a hearing from some of them (Chadwick 1966; Remus 1983: ch. 9). Persons of the upper class who become Christians in increasing numbers (Cyprian, *Ep.* 80.1) could not be expected to shun positions in civic or imperial administration; in such cases the authorities, for their part, might offer exemption from sacrificing (Eusebius, *Hist. eccl.* 8.1.2).

Boundary maintenance, always a concern for bounded groups and evident already in the earliest Christian sources, becomes increasingly difficult as a group grows in numbers and commitments decline in fervor. Conflicts and rivalries within and between early Christian groups from their inception complicated the issue. One response by Christian leaders was stigmatization, as with Paul's scolding of his opponents (2 Cor 11–12) or Hegesippus's assertion in the second century (followed by Eusebius, *Hist. eccl.* 3.32.7–8; 4.22.4, 7, and many others since) that the church was an unsullied virgin until deviants corrupted it. Another, not unrelated, response was institutionalization (MacDonald 1988), beginning with early leadership role specializations as noted above and then decision-making bodies to rule on disputed issues and groups. "It has seemed good to the Holy Spirit and to us" (Acts 15:28) becomes the leitmotif of these synods and councils, which begin to appear in Asia Minor in opposition to the Montanist prophetic movement in the second half of the second century (Eusebius, *Hist. eccl.* 5.16.9–10) and then developed in other Christian centers as well (Kretschmar 1966). Clergy, especially bishops, carried to the councils the institutional authority they exercised in their regular venues.

Beginning with the Decian persecution of 250 C.E. the tensions between "otherness" and accommodation, evident throughout the conflicts outlined above, become acute as Christians divide over how to deal with the many *lapsi* (Lietzmann 1961: 225–38; Bryant 1993; Rives 1995b: 285–307). Should they be excluded from the Christian fold for violating group norms, as early traditions indicated (1 Cor 5.1–6; Mt 18.15–20), perhaps for all time, as other early traditions insisted (Heb 6.4–6, 10.26–31; Hermas, *Man.* 4; cf. later, Cyprian, *Test.* 3.27, 28; Cyprian, *Lapsi*)? Or should they be offered forgiveness and reconciliation, as other early traditions attested (Mt 6.12//Lk 11.4; Jas 5.15–16; *Did.* 14.1; Justin, *Dial.* 141.2–3), or be readmitted after appropriate acts of penance (2 *Clem.* 16) or a protracted communal process of penance (Tertullian, *Paen.* 9)?

Confronted with multitudes of *lapsi*, Cyprian, the influential bishop of Carthage, articulates the argument—endorsed by other bishops—that readmittance of the *lapsi* is necessary for the sake of "the salvation of the many" (Cyprian, *Ep.* 55.7) in a catholic, that is, inclusive, church. Rigorists like the Novatianists in the Decian persecution and the Donatists in the Great Persecution, who insisted on an earlier, more sectarian ethos with its stricter norms of behavior and more clearly defined boundaries with rebaptism required of persons who switch allegiances, are rendered "outside" of the one, true church that alone has the power to baptize (Cyprian, *Ep.* 69.3).

In these government-initiated persecutions it is thus Christians who increasingly see other Christians as "other" and are labeled—or label themselves—as catholic, orthodox, lax, schismatic, heterodox, heretical. It is the (male) clergy and especially the bishops, whether in the more inclusive or the more exclusivist camps, who define these boundaries, acting, sometimes in concert in synods and councils, as the custodians of the instruments of salvation: the scriptures, the sacraments, and membership in the church. While there were various ecclesiastical means to enforce such norms, circa 268 C.E. these intra-Christian conflicts enter a new stage when a synod of bishops appeals to the emperor to compel Paul of Samosata, bishop of Antioch, whom they had excommunicated, to surrender the church building (Eusebius, *Hist. eccl.* 7.27–30; Fox 1987: 512–14). Both the appeal and Aurelian's ruling—leaving the decision to the bishops of Rome and Italy, which he then enforced—demonstrate how, thanks to centuries of interaction between government and Christians, conflict was developing into cooperation.

In the decades leading up to the Edict of Milan that process was facilitated by shifts in the power relations. Cyprian, for example, was wealthy and well educated and was treated accordingly when apprehended by authorities. His descriptions of his episcopacy echo those of traditionalist authority figures; in relation to laity and the charismatic authority of imprisoned confessors he insists on the bishop's institutionally sanctioned primacy (Rives 1995b: 285–307). Paul of Samosata's retinue and style as bishop reflect his previous tenure in high public office (Eusebus, *Hist. eccl.* 7.30.4–15). Origen, and later Eusebius and Augustine, mount claims that Christianity was the culmination of Greek and Roman culture and its preserver over against, now, the "barbarian" "others" at the boundaries of the empire. The bishops were public figures who embodied those claims, capable of schooling rustic emperors in their truth, and eventually ended up in the imperial governing class with its privileges and perils (Brown 1971: 82–89). They presided over the empire-wide organization that had developed out of the early consciousness of an *ekklesia* linked to other local *ekklesiai* through beliefs, scriptures, rites, letters, personal contacts, common endeavors, and various authority figures both male and female (Meeks 1983: 107–10). While the Catholic bishops could set norms and had various sanctions to enforce them, ultimately, as in the case of Paul of Samosata or the Donatists, they lacked the power to make them stick if there was resistance or division. The empire had that power, and after centuries of trying to preserve the *pax deorum* by hostile measures against Christians, it chose—in the persons of Constantine and his successors—to achieve social stability and cohesion through the Christian deity and his followers.

Christians, once stigmatized, harassed, and oppressed by polytheist traditionalists as "other," were now in a position to do the same to them. At the end of the third century, Ambrose, the powerful bishop of the imperial city of Milan, prevails in a struggle with Symmachus, one of the most powerful Romans of the day, whose *pietas* Ambrose marginalizes as *gentilis* (*Ep.*17.9, 18.1), that is, "pagan," characterizing it as *superstitio* (*Ep.* 17.16)—a term once applied to Christians—and relegating its adherents to minority status (*sectam gentilium*, *Ep.* 18.2). Imperial laws also label that *pietas* as *superstitio*: 16.10.2 (341 C.E.), 16.10.3 (342 C.E.), 16.10.16 (399 C.E.), or as a "pagan" (16.10.20 [415 C.E.]) or an "alien superstition" (16.2.5 [323 C.E.])—that is, as the "other." Whereas being "Christian" was once a crime, it is now *paganus* that is criminalized: see the *Theodosian Code* (*Cod. Theod.* 16.10.21 [416 C.E.], 16.10.25 [435 C.E.]).

Jews, the "third party" in some of the Christian–traditionalist conflicts, became a perennial object of hostility and persecution by Christians, who accuse Jews, as they had once been accused, of cannibalism (Hsia 1992; Malamud 1968), sometimes targeting Jews as scapegoats (Ziegler 1982) as they themselves had once been scapegoated, at other times expelling or forcibly "converting" Jews (Cohen 1982), and in the modern period exterminating them. It was left to prophets—ascetics, monks, reformers, everyday Christians—to recall Christianity, repeatedly, to its origins in a vision of an *ecclesia pura*.

Notes

The author gratefully acknowledges that financial support for this research was received from a grant partly funded by Wilfrid Laurier University Operating funds.

1. Among gentile traditionalists there were also monotheists, but their monotheism accommodated the deities of popular piety as well (Wilken 1984: 148–49; Athanassiadi and Frede 1999); that is, it was not an exclusivistic monotheism. Christians' as well as Jews' monotheism is also more complex than is commonly supposed (Segal 1977; Hurtado 1988; Barker 1992; Athanassiadi and Frede 1999), but both shared a rejection of the polytheism of the Greco-Roman world.

Vulnerable Power: The Roman Empire Challenged by the Early Christians

20

WARREN CARTER

ROME CONTROLLED THE PEOPLES, territories, and materials of the world of the early Christian movement. The empire consisted of organized circuits of power that mobilized relations of meaning and membership, production and discipline (Clegg 1989: 218–19; Mann 1986: 1–33). These power relations ranged from institutionalized organizational forms—position or office, laws, the army, the imperial cult—to personal spheres of operation such as patron–client relationships, ritualized friendship, and kinship (Shaw 1993: 176–78). Together the power networks and relationships provided opportunities for effecting control and compliance. All this worked to control resources and agendas and conceal vested interests, but such power had limits and met with resistance.

That mighty Rome was vulnerable to the first-century Christians has seemed improbable.[1] Superficially, the early Christian movement could appear incapable of challenging the empire. It was a small religious group numbering about 7,000–7,500 in the year 100, a tiny fraction (0.0017 percent) of the empire's population (Stark 1996: 7; Hopkins 1998). Its membership seemed to have been a cross-section of society with no concentration among the ruling elite (Meeks 1983). Even if it had a social program, it did not have access to decision makers who could exert societal influence. In the movement's writings, Jesus urges his followers to "render to Caesar the things that are Caesar's" (Mk 12.13–17 par.), warns them that one who takes the sword will die by it (Mt 26.52b), and does not resist his own arrest and execution. Several passages (Rom 13.1–7; I Pt 2.13–17; I Tm 2.1–2) advocate an "ethic of subordination" (Pilgrim 1999: 7–36). And in case there should be any doubt about who was vulnerable to whom, narratives tell of Jesus' death at the hands of Rome. If this is resistance, it surely appears futile.

However, the issue is worth pursuing. Within a matter of centuries, the world would look very different. The empire, not Christianity, ended. The first-century

453

Christian texts do not simply present Jesus as a submissive, nonthreatening figure but identify him as "king of the Jews," an unashamedly political title (Fredriksen 1999).[2] Josephus calls the emperor Titus "king" (*B.J.* 5.410). Other kings were not welcome in an imperial world, especially when King Jesus announced a kingdom or empire (βασιλεία, *basileia*) that belonged to God (Mk 1.15; Jn 18.36).

The empire struck back; Jesus died by crucifixion at the hands of Roman power and the Jerusalem religious elite. Crucifixion was a form of execution Rome reserved for those who posed some threat, whether violent criminals and robbers (Martial, *Spect.* 9), foreign rebels (Josephus, *B.J.* 2.306, 308; 5.449–53), or slaves (Tacitus, *Ann.* 13.32; Juvenal, *Sat.* 6.219–24; Hengel 1972; O'Collins 1992). It was an extremely painful form of torture for its victim and a very public and intimidating warning about the folly of opposition. The texts have the authorities identify Jesus as a bandit, terrorist, or insurrectionist (Mk 14.48 par.) who meets the fate of crucifixion with other rebels (Mk 15.27; Mt 27.38, 44). It is hard to imagine an imperial power executing him in this manner and in such company if he presented no threat.

When Jesus called upon his followers to "take up the cross and follow" (Mk 8.34 par.), he was not urging compliance and subordination to political powers. Given the significance of crucifixion, his call was nothing short of an invitation to martyrdom in resistance to imperial structures and interests. It invited followers to identify with and join those marginal figures who opposed the empire's order, challenged its commitments, and denied to it the power to intimidate. It also invited followers to join in exposing the limits of the empire's power since Jesus' crucifixion was not the end of the story. Rather, the story asserts that God raised Jesus from the dead. The worst that the empire could do was to put him to death. But that act is shown not to be final.

Despite texts that advocate a subordination ethic, some early Christian traditions viewed the movement's origins in terms of resistance to Rome. Several studies of the historical Jesus develop such a thesis (Beck 1997: 19–49). Paula Fredriksen (1999: 235–59) argues that Pilate crucified Jesus out of fear of the crowds' expectations that God would intervene through this Messiah and "king of the Jews" to defeat Rome and restore the Davidic empire. Herzog (2000: 71, 217–46) proposes that Jesus, "a prophet of the justice of the reign of God," must be understood in his "world of advanced agrarian societies, aristocratic empires, and colonial occupation" as one who challenged fundamental aspects of political, kinship, economic, and social structures. Jesus was crucified for threatening to destroy the Temple—thereby irreparably alienating the priestly aristocracy who controlled it—resisting the tribute, and claiming to be a messiah king, thereby antagonizing Rome.

Parts of the early Christian movement (and texts) did challenge the empire and expose its vulnerability, but not by using military force, economic tactics such as withholding taxes and tribute, or political maneuvers such as assassination and in-

tra-aristocratic conflict. Rather, the Christians presented an alternative social organization and persuasive theological worldview. Existing within the Roman Empire, they contested its social structure and meaningfulness. They could do this because the empire had failed to "penetrate the everyday life of the mass of the
people, urban or rural. It had failed to mobilize their commitment or praxis, or to
give meaning and dignity to their lives" (Mann 1986: 327–28). The Christian
movement profited from the alienation that the elite's system elicited. The empire
was a hierarchical, exclusive, centralized structure that deprived many of its subjects of meaningful community and failed to create a "plausible" ideology (Mann
1986: 23). Using opportunities featured by the empire itself (education, literacy,
travel, trade networks), some early Christians created an alternative, inclusive, and
egalitarian social organization and meaning system that redefined the relationship
of ruler to ruled. By offering a vision and organization for an alternative form of
social interaction, the movement challenged the perception that Rome was the desirable, rightful, invincible ruling power. It rejected the empire's totalizing claims
and version of societal reality that brought benefits to a few and hardships to
many. By contextualizing the empire in God's greater purposes, the Christians de-
mystified it, relativized its power, exposed its shortcomings, burst its illusions
(Brunt 1990: 288–323, 433–80), revealed its lies, and numbered its days. The
texts harbored no illusion that *they* would bring about the collapse or the reform
of the empire. They did not doubt, however, that God would establish the heavenly empire, and that, for the present, faithful embodiment of God's empire in appropriate practices and communities was a necessary alternative. They exposed the
empire's vulnerability by displaying the limits of its claims to human allegiance.

The Roman Empire's Organized Networks of Power

The Roman imperial system has been described as an agrarian society (Lenski
1966; Alston 1998: 227–45) and aristocratic empire (Kautsky 1982; Eisenstadt
1963; Mann 1986: 250–300). Vast disparities of power and wealth are fundamental to such structures (Lenski 1966: 210). Diverse relationships between ruler
and ruled are created and defined by political, military, economic, and ideological
"organized power networks" (Mann 1986). Plutarch (c. 40–120 C.E.) recognized
that societal dominance involved power from political office, participation in political debate, and control of land and peasants; considerable wealth from land
ownership and production; and status or public repute in which others recognize
one's dominant position (*Mor.* 58D).

The emperor and a very small percentage of the population effected control
and submission. Emperor Nero (ruled 54–68 C.E.) described himself standing between the gods and the nations (Seneca, *Clem.* I.2–3; Fears 1975). The emperor

shared the benefits and rewards of this relationship with only a small group. The governing stratum consisted of officials appointed by the emperor (governors and their staffs); bureaucrats; those with inherited wealth, land, and social status; military leaders; and religious officials. It included local elites, governing aristocracies and landowners in the provinces whom Rome turned into allies as common beneficiaries (Nutton 1978; Garnsey 1978; Goodman 1987; Brunt 1990: 282–87). These comprised about 2 percent of the population (Lenski 1966: 219). The wealthy and powerful aristocratic elite exercised power partly at the emperor's pleasure, though also in competition with him.

Ownership of land provided significant power over the lives of others (Lenski 1966: 58). Landowners secured wealth and status and lived well from various rents and taxes on peasant production (Lenski 1966: 220). This small group of less than 5 percent of the population used political and military institutions, especially the powers to tax and to carry out war (Kautsky 1982: 6, 144–55), to legitimate this status quo and enhance their own status within it. Political institutions and offices were a primary source of and protection for political, economic and social inequality and privilege (Lenski 1966: 210). Provincial governors and their staffs, for example, exercised control through tours and assizes, administering justice, collecting taxes, and deploying troops (Burton 1975; Brunt 1990: 53–95, 163–87, 215–54; Austin and Rankov 1995: 123–25, 142–84). There is also evidence for "an internal security agency throughout the empire," the *frumentarii*, charged with the emperor's security and engaged in spying and gathering intelligence on any potential rebellion (Austin and Rankov 1995: 136–37). Control of the state's organization was "the supreme prize" in ensuring "fabulous wealth and immense power . . . privilege, and prestige" (Lenski 1966: 210, 212).

Agrarian empires are, typically, conquest states whereby a group or area of land is forcibly subjugated (Lenski 1966: 195; Said 1993/1994: xii–xiii, 78). The term *imperium Romanum* ("Roman Empire") designates territory gained by Rome's military power (Tacitus, *Germ.* 29.1; Richardson 1991). For Rome, "force is the foundation of political sovereignty" (Lenski 1966: 51). Josephus among many writers attests to the key role of Rome's army in coercing and maintaining submission (*B.J.* 3.107; Rich and Shipley 1993). Luttwak notes the role of "coercive diplomacy" whereby the *possibility* of Roman military action compels and maintains submission. He offers as an example the three-year siege of Masada, by no means the only or best military option. This siege "must have made an ominous impression on all those in the East who might otherwise have been tempted to contemplate revolt: the lesson of Masada was that the Romans would pursue rebellion even to mountain tops in remote deserts to destroy its last vestiges, regardless of cost" (Luttwak 1976: 4). Jewish soldiers had captured Masada in 66 C.E. and killed its Roman guards (Josephus, *B.J.* 2.408). The Romans had to be seen to retaliate.[3] Josephus illustrates the impact of Roman "deterrent power deriving from success" in explaining that because the Gauls are "overawed at once by the power of Rome and by her fortune . . . they submit to the orders of twelve hundred soldiers, they who have cities enough almost to outmatch that number" (*B.J.* 2.372–73; Rajak 1991: 131; Clegg 1989: 222). Also reinforcing the message that military action against Rome was pointless were the "Capta" coins. Vespasian issued "Judaea Capta" coins after the defeat of Judaea in 70 and Domitian issued "Germania Capta" coins after military operations in the 80s (Kreitzer 1996: 136–40). Josephus justifies his lengthy description of Roman military power by making the same point: "If I have dwelt at some length on this topic, my intention was . . . to deter others who may be tempted to revolt" (*B.J.* 3.108, cf. 3.70–107).

In addition to military might, "to rule in aristocratic empires is, above all, to tax" (Kautsky 1982: 150). Control over the land, those who work it, and its product is effected not only through conquest, booty, seizure, and confiscation but also through local and imperial taxes, tributes, rents, and services (Lenski 1966: 217–19). The ruling elite acquired vast wealth by a "proprietary theory of the state" that saw the state as something to be used not for the maximal common good but for personal benefit and, in turn, for the good of one's heirs (Lenski 1966: 214). The threat of military punishment and further loss of land and production by increased tribute and taxes coerced compliance; laws and political offices sought to normalize the exactions. "Taxes provided income for the elite, both local and Roman, that enabled them to maintain their way of life. Nero was led to an awareness of this by his advisors" (Tacitus, *Ann.* 13.50). To ensure the elite's way of life, Roman conquest meant setting in place an infrastructure, often through a general or under the administration of a provincial governor, that would accomplish this exploitation of the provinces. By draining swamps, terracing mountains, irrigating waste lands, and clearing forests (see Aristides, *Roman Oration* 101),[4] Roman soldiers or local landowners, often using forced or slave labor, enhanced the productivity and profitability of their land (Kautsky 1982: 187). Roads and bridges served obvious military purposes (Tacitus, *Ann.* 1.56; 61). They also raised revenue. A saying attributed to Rabbi Simon (*b.Shabb.* 33b) noted the self-serving agenda of such developments: "All that they have made, they made for themselves, they built market places, to set harlots in them; baths, to rejuvenate themselves, bridges, to levy tolls for them." Calgacus, the British chief, agrees. Romans are

> Robbers of the world . . . to plunder, butcher, steal, these things they misname empire; they make a desolation and they call it peace . . . our goods and chattels go for tribute; our lands and harvests in requisitions of grain; life and limb themselves are worn out in making roads through marsh and forest to the accompaniment of gibes and blows. (Tacitus, *Agr.* 31.1–2; Mosley 1991)

Building bridges and roads also provided the means whereby goods were moved from the provinces to Rome, the center of the empire. Aristides, oblivious to the human cost, notes that the provinces supply Rome's aristocracy

> abundantly with whatever is in them. Produce is brought from every land and every sea, depending on what the season brings forth, and what is produced by all lands, rivers and lakes. . . . For what grows and is produced among individual peoples is necessarily always here, and here in abundance. (*Roman Oration* 11; see Pliny, *Pan.* 29; Tacitus, *Ann.* 3.53–54)

All roads, and cargo ships, truly do lead to Rome (Bauckham 1993; Carney 1975: 285–304).

The payment of taxes and tribute also expressed submission to Rome's military power. It paid for maintaining Roman sovereignty, euphemistically termed "peace," "security," and "freedom" (Wengst 1987: 19–26; Zampaglione 1973).[5] Tacitus has the Roman general Cerialis inform the Treviri and Longones in Trier after suppressing their revolt:

> Although often provoked by you, the only use we have made of our rights as victors has been to impose on you the necessary costs of maintaining peace; you cannot secure tranquillity among nations without armies, nor maintain armies without pay, nor provide pay without taxes. (*Hist.* 4.73–74)

According to the speech Josephus attributes to King Agrippa, the Gauls provide Jews with an example of a people who "are yet content to be treated as a source of revenue to the Romans" (*B.J.* 2.372; Rajak 1991).

Not paying tax and tribute was to rebel against Rome's sovereignty (Dyson 1971). Discontent with tributes was a factor in several revolts. Gaul's rebellion against "continuous tributes, the grinding rates of interest, the cruelty and pride of the governors" was put down with military force (Tacitus, *Ann.* 3.40–41). The Frisians refused a tribute of ox-hides and then defeated the troops sent to punish and subdue them (Tacitus, *Ann.* 4.72–73). Vitellius sent troops from Syria to compel the Cietae's payment of tribute (Tacitus, *Ann.* 6.41). Josephus has Agrippa declare to the Jewish people in revolt against Florus in 66 C.E. that their nonpayment of tribute is an "act of war." Paying the tribute would clear them of the "charge of insurrection" (*B.J.* 2.403–4).

"Laws and Roman jurisdiction" were also imposed on the conquered (Tacitus, *Ann.* 15.6), which amounted to payments (bribes) for beneficent action, favorable legal decisions, or appointments to desirable positions (Lenski 1966: 222–24 on Verres; Wengst 1987: 37–40). The ruling class, then, typically created and exercised its power through several interrelated roles—warrior, ruler, administrator, judge, and priest (Kautsky 1982: 161). Certain values or ideologies created, sustained, and interpreted these roles. Kautsky identifies service and duty, maintaining one's honor, and acquiring glory as fundamental (1982: 169–229). Warfare provided an obvious arena (Brunt 1990: 291–300, 440–46, 468–77), but so also did the exercise of rule through taxation and public acts of generosity by "patrons" to religious and civic organizations (Saller 1982; Hanson and Oakman 1998: 70–86). Members of the elite competed with the emperor and with one another for a maximum share of the taxes and services rendered by peasants and artisans (Kautsky 1982: 235–38). Carney discusses Claudius's attempts to ensure a regular grain supply for Rome, an action that involved conflict with aristocratic groups (1975: 285–304).[6]

Contempt for productive or manual labor was another elite value. The absence of such work separated the elite from peasants, and to a lesser degree from more prosperous merchants (Lenski 1966: 250–56). This contempt was expressed in and reinforced by collecting taxes as a primary source of wealth, which was also valued. Wealth was not for investing or accumulating since there was always a continual supply through the elite's exploitation of peasants. Wealth was for conspicuous consumption and display through buildings, clothing, jewelry, military acts, food, celebrations, entertainment, clients and servants, and beneficent civic gestures (a statue, a fountain, a food handout, games, or contests). Such display maintained the distance between the aristocracy and peasantry and reminded the peasants who they were and were not.

This ability to subject and exploit supported another aspect of the aristocratic ideology—a sense of superiority. This superiority was asserted with claims of superior character and race (MacMullen 1974b: 57–65, 138–41). Titus appealed to Roman superiority as a race when prior to the attack on Jerusalem he essentially employed Cicero's century-old argument that "Jews and Syrians were born for servitude" (*Prov. cons.* 10) to urge his troops to victory over "inferior" Jews who have "learned to be slaves" (*B.J.* 6.37–42).

The ruling stratum created retainers to assist it in governing (Lenski 1966: 243–48). These retainers, some 5 percent of the population (Lenski 1966: 245), included "officials, professional soldiers, household servants, and personal retainers, all of whom served . . . in a variety of more or less specialized capacities" (Lenski 1966: 243). Upper-level priests and religious leaders were also retainers (Lenski 1966: 256–66; Saldarini 1988), personalizing and representing aristocratic power among the lower orders, performing its wished-for actions, enacting its decisions, and maintaining its hold over land and people. Their association with and deference to the aristocracy elevated them above most of the common folk and enabled them to share in the benefits of its rule, notably significant power, status, and wealth. Slaves in the imperial household, for example, could exercise great power in controlling access to the emperor (so Helicon, the slave of

Gaius Caligula; Philo, *Legat.*, 166–78). Saldarini correctly locates the Jewish chief priests, Sadducees, leading Pharisees, and scribes among the retainers (1988: 35–49). Josephus presents the chief priests, often allied with "the most notable Pharisees," as consistently pro-Roman in the events leading up to the 66 C.E. war (*B.J.* 2.320, 411).

The verticality and inequality of the empire appeared in the large gap between the ruling class on the one hand and the peasants and urban artisans on the other, with this group occupying something of a middle ground. The masses produced, rather than benefited from, the elite's wealth. Some merchants, those who gained enough commerce to elevate them above most of the population but not enough to join the aristocracy, held a position similar to that of the retainers (Lenski 1966: 250–56; MacMullen 1974b: 88–120). Merchants competed with the land-based aristocracy for control of the economic production, though taxation on commerce ensured further wealth for the elite and limited that gained by merchants (Carney 1975: 98–101).

Peasants and artisans comprised most of the population. Given their illiteracy, they left few records (Mann 1986: 313–17). They do not loom large in the materials left by the elite with their perspective "from above" and profound inattention to the quite different realities experienced by most "from below" (Wengst 1987: 7–11). Peasant and artisan labor produced the goods and services, rendered in taxes and rents (often paid in kind), that sustained the wealth and lifestyle of the ruling elite. Various scholars estimate that between 30 and 70 percent of production was claimed through various taxes (Lenski 1966: 267; Oakman 1986: 72). Forced labor or *corvée*, along with slavery, provided the elite with a ready supply of cheap labor for major building projects or schemes to improve the productivity and profitability of land. The "great majority of peasants who lived in the various agrarian societies of the past apparently lived at, or close to, the subsistence level" (Lenski 1966: 271). Akin to peasants, the smaller class of artisans in the cities, often comprising dispossessed peasants linked to merchants, employed varying degrees of skill to produce goods and services largely for the elite (Lenski 1966: 278–80). Slaves, some of whom exerted authority within households, worked at numerous household and manual tasks (Wiedemann 1981).

Did peasants and artisans take steps to change these power relationships? Lenski argues that peasants were ambivalent. They were aware of the gap separating them from their social superiors, yet they sought to protect and maximize their benefits. Conflicts were inevitable as peasants tried to protect their livelihood by evading the various demands of taxes and services. Mostly these evasionary tactics were nonviolent: hiding produce or lying about production levels to tax collectors, working slowly, pilfering, sabotage (Scott 1985). But at times, led by significant figures, violence occurred in the form of riots or attacks by Robin Hood–like bandit groups on aristocratic property and personnel (Lenski 1966: 273–78; Shaw 1984; Horsley and Hanson 1985/1988).

However, Kautsky attributes a very limited role to conflict. While he recognizes some nonviolent actions on the part of peasants to defend their benefits (Kautsky 1982: 275, 298), he is not convinced that there was interclass struggle (1982: 49–75, 230–46). He argues that it was simply impossible for peasants who lacked access to power to exert any influence on the exploitative relationships created by the elite. To stop working was to starve (Kautsky 1982: 273–78). He describes the peasants as peaceable by disposition, in contrast with the elite, who loved violence and aggressive risk taking expressed in war. The peasants, he says, recognized the aristocracy's superiority in violent conflict. Tied to the land and their work of cultivating it, they were physically isolated from any networks beyond their local context and lacked organization and leadership (Kautsky 1982: 296–306). Lacking organization, fearful of reprisal, and bound to the daily routine and activity, they were organizationally outflanked, and so controlled and exploited by the elite (Mann 1986: 7; Clegg 1989: 218–23).

Kautsky emphasizes the role of imagination or perception in accounting for peasant passivity and resignation: "The peasants cannot imagine a large-scale rebellion and they sense that a local one is utterly hopeless and hence do not normally even contemplate one" (1982: 299). Apart from protecting their own immediate situation against, for example, a tax increase, peasants simply could not conceive of a significant transformation of the social structure or of themselves as agents of that change with a strategy to bring it about. While they knew aristocrats lived a very different and luxurious life free of manual labor, they did not conceive of it for themselves. This fatalism derived from having little control over their natural and social environments. A lack of change was normative (Kautsky 1982: 307–19).

By contrast others warn against misinterpreting this passivity as a failure of imagination or construing it as compliance. The lack of conflict does not mean lack of resistance (Barbalet 1985). The apparent calm may derive from effective repression and may mask a "venerable popular culture of resistance." Nor should one trivialize the "weapons of the weak" that may not have made the imperial system collapse but could be significant as means of limiting power, protecting interests, and expressing dissent from the dominant aristocratic agenda. Such weapons could qualify the power relationships by signaling noncomplicity and indicating that the current demands were not just. They could assert dignity, imagine an alternative, and ensure survival. At times, they could be surprisingly effective in making changes (Scott 1985: 28–47).

As we will see, there may not have been quite the shortage of imagination and abundance of complicity that Kautsky posits. Tacitus narrates a scene in which

Nero is aware that people were complaining about indirect taxes (*Ann.*13.50). Even if fictive, the scene shows the emperor's awareness of and responsiveness to public opposition to taxes. Given that 90 percent of the population paying taxes were peasants or artisans, and given the enormous distance between emperor and people, one can only conclude that protests were widespread, vociferous, and effective enough to make the emperor aware that some people were exercising imagination about fewer and lower taxes. Likewise the attacks on debt-record buildings in Jerusalem and Antioch around 70 indicate others were imagining a world without debt (Josephus, *B.J.* 2.426–27; 7.55, 61). Agrippa acknowledged that numerous Jews, very aware of "injustice" and "servitude," were fanning hopes of "independence" and "liberty" (*B.J.* 2.345–49). With the help of their leaders, Gallic "assemblies and conventicles" imagined a world without Rome's control (Tacitus, *Ann.* 3.40). If an analogy with masters and slaves is appropriate, aristocratic literature is permeated with an awareness that slaves often protested their master's demands in small but significant ways (Carter 1994: 181–83). And Seneca, for one, knew that compliant behavior, however it is coerced, does not imply control over a slave's mind (*Ben.* 3.20.1–2). Acts of imagination seemed possible, and small gestures of protest were important and effective as indications of limits to the imperial system's hold on people's lives.[7]

Religious claims and rituals were deeply woven into this imperial world. Given that words and ritual have performative qualities (Mann 1986: 22–23; Carter 1995), propaganda from elite writers and rituals carried out in the imperial cult gave form to the relationship of power between subject and ruler. They evoked "a picture of the relationship between the emperor and the gods" and "imposed a definition of the world" (Price 1984: 247–48). In evoking and defining, constructing and explaining, religious claims and rituals gave meaning to the political-military and socioeconomic relationships of the empire and solicited compliance with them (Lenski 1966: 209). The challenge for the elite was to gain compliance by convincing the population that imperial control benefited them, even though the system in actuality benefited the elite at the expense of most of the population. Hence one task of the theological claims and ritual was to conceal this coercive power, self-interest, and injustice behind a worldview that claimed divine sanction for the whole imperial enterprise. Another task was to show that well-being for all subjects resulted from the elite's engagement in warfare and taxation at the peasants' expense.

Fears describes an "aura of supernatural legitimation" for the empire that "came to be enshrined in and expressed through the figure of the monarch . . . an image of the ruler as the divine embodiment of cosmic order, divinely ordained to ensure the prosperity of the human race" (1981a: 7–9). A long tradition of propaganda expressed in written, material, and ritual forms, created and sustained the view that the gods had chosen Rome and its emperor to rule the world (Scott 1936; Taisne 1973; Fears 1977, 1981a, 1981b, 1981c). The emperor represented and enacted the rule of the gods on earth. As their agent, he brought about their presence and blessings. His welfare ensured the welfare of the empire (Carter 1998). "The emperor . . . [is] . . . above human criticism because his power is rooted not in human institutions but in his election by the supreme god of the state" (Fears 1981a: 81).

A few examples will illustrate these claims. Virgil narrates Jupiter appointing Romulus founder of Rome and its empire, for which "I set no bounds nor periods of empire; dominion without end have I bestowed." Romans will be "lords of the world" (*Aen.* 1.254, 278–79, 281). Anchises tells Aeneas in the underworld, "Remember, O Roman, to rule the nations with your power—there shall be your arts—to crown peace with law, to spare the humbled, and to tame in war the proud" (*Aen.* 6.851–53). A Roman governor announces to the leader of a German tribe that "all men had to bow to the commands of their betters; it had been decreed by those gods whom they implored that with the Roman people should rest the decisions what to give and what to take away" (Tacitus, *Ann.* 13.51). Aristides surveys in wonder an empire in which "an individual rules over so many people and his officials and emissaries stand so far below him, yet far higher than those over whom they have control" and declares "all is well within the reign of Olympian Zeus." In praising Rome, he declares that "the gods beholding, seem to lend a friendly hand to your empire in its achievement and to confirm to you its possession." He invokes the gods' blessing that "this empire and this city flourish forever and never cease" (*Roman Oration* 89, 104–5, 109). In praising the emperor Trajan, Pliny calls the gods "the guardians and defenders of our empire" and prays to Jupiter for "the safety of our prince" since human "security and happiness depends on your safety" (*Pan.* 94). In writing of the imminent Jewish war, Josephus has Agrippa declare "that Fortune has transferred her favors" to Rome (*B.J.* 2.360, 4.622), and that "without God's aid so vast an empire could never have been built up" (*B.J.* 2.390–91). Josephus expresses similar attitudes in urging Jerusalem to surrender, arguing "that God was on the Roman side" (*B.J.* 5.368) and that "you are warring not against the Romans only but also against God" (*B.J.* 5.378, cf. 396, 412). In Josephus's view, God was responsible for Nero sending Vespasian to command the armies of Syria thereby "shaping the destinies of empire" (*B.J.* 3.6–7). Josephus attributes to Vespasian thoughts that "divine providence had assisted him to grasp the empire and some just destiny had placed all sovereignty of the world within his hands" (*B.J.* 4.622). There is no separation of the political and the religious. The latter serves the former; the former enacts the latter.

The Flavian emperors (Vespasian, 69–79; Titus, 79–81; and Domitian, 81–96) particularly invoked Jupiter's approval (Fears 1981a; Scott 1936). Suetonius signals Jupiter's selection of Vespasian as Nero's rightful successor by describing Nero's dream in which Nero takes the sacred chariot of Jupiter Optimus Maximus to Vespasian's home (*Vesp.* 5.6; cf. Dio 65.1.3). Tacitus (*Hist.* 3.74) and Suetonius (*Dom.* 1.2) note that Domitian found safety during the civil war in the temple of Jupiter Capitolinus. Martial recognizes that Jupiter keeps Domitian safe (*Epig.* V.1.7–8, VII.60.1–2). Silius Italicus (c. 26–101 C.E.) has Jupiter predict:

> The burning of the Tarpeian temple cannot alarm thee;
> But in the midst of the impious flames thou shalt be
> Saved, for the sake of [hu]mankind. (*Punica* 3.609–610)

As a result of Jupiter's favorable intervention and election Domitian rules "the blessed earth with paternal sway" (3.625–6). Statius salutes Domitian:

> A god is he, at Jupiter's command he rules for him the blessed world. . . . Hail ruler of men [*sic*] and parent of gods, foreseen by me and foreordained was thy godhead. (*Silvae* IV.3.128–29, 139–40)

As the gods' elected agents, the emperors manifest the gods' rule on the earth. They do so through military victories. Silius Italicus has Jupiter assure a worried Venus that long into the future Rome will be powerful and successful (*Punica* 3.570–629). Jupiter previews for her the "future events" (3.630) that he has ordained, notably the military successes of the Flavians, first Vespasian, then Titus, and Domitian (3.593–629). Martial and Statius identify Domitian also as the agent of Minerva, goddess of war and the arts. She appears on Domitian's Greek and Syrian coins often in military pose and bearing Jupiter's thunderbolt (Sutherland 1959). Coins issued by various emperors regularly recognize the role of Mars, Victoria, Nike, and Pax in ensuring military success (Scott 1936; Fears 1977, 1981a, 1981b). Vespasian's coins celebrate that through him at the close of the civil war the gods have gifted the world with peace, victory, agricultural prosperity, security, well-being, harmonious relations, and liberty, among many other gifts. Titus and Domitian proclaim similar blessings. Domitian is, for Martial, "the world's sure salvation" (*Epig.* 2.91.1), its "blest protector and savior" (*Epig.* 5.1.7), its "chief and only welfare" (*Epig.* 8.66.6). Statius declares Domitian "Lord of the earth" (*Silvae* 3.4.20), "ruler of the nations and mighty sire of the conquered world, hope of men and beloved of the gods" (4.2.14–15).

Beyond literary propaganda, which could only reach a fraction of the population, other media and rituals promoted these theological claims, created and sustained the relationship of ruler and ruled, and solicited the submission of the empire's subjects to such an exalted and divinely legitimated emperor. Decorated gates, arches, columns, statues, and buildings became bully pulpits. Temples and altars;

various liturgical practices such as prayers, vows, and sacrifices; and festivals such as
the emperor's birthday and accession date, were celebrated with different intensity
and levels of significance in different parts of the empire, utilizing social pressure
to participate (Price 1984; Zanker 1988). Aristides attests the practice of governors who cannot "remain immobile if he but hears the name of the ruler, but he
rises, praises, and reveres him and says two prayers, one for the ruler to the gods
and one to the ruler himself for his own well being" (*Roman Oration* 32). Pliny prays
concerning Trajan, "May you, then, and the world through your means, enjoy every
prosperity . . . [and] that your health and spirits may be preserved firm and unbro-
ken (*Ep.* 10.1). As governor of Bithynia and Pontus, Pliny informs Trajan of a ceremony for taking "our annual vows for your safety in which that of the State is included." In his response Trajan expresses gratitude that "you and the provincials
have both paid and renewed your vows to the immortal Gods, for my health and
safety" (*Ep.* 10.35, 36). Pliny describes that on the day marking the emperor's accession, "we have sincerely implored the Gods to preserve you in health and prosperity as it is upon your welfare that the security and repose of humankind depend.
I have administered the oath of allegiance to my fellow soldiers" (*Ep.* 10.52).

On a larger scale, Josephus's account of Vespasian's and Titus's triumph as a
witness to the "majesty of the Roman empire" (*B.J.* 7.133) clearly displays the in-
termingling of the political, military, and religious relationships. Explicitly religious components contribute to this celebration of Roman power: Vespasian and
Titus stay in the temple of Isis. They offer prayers; sacrifice to the gods; include
images of their gods in the procession, as well as booty from the Jerusalem Temple; offer sacrifices and prayers in the temple of Jupiter Capitolinus; and construct
a temple of peace (*B.J.* 7.123–62).

Such religious propaganda in the service of the empire came into contact with
groups of quite diverse religious understandings and practices. Kautsky emphasizes that this imperial theology was not the religion of peasants (1982: 163–66,
277–78). Generally Rome was tolerant of local traditions. "Roman polytheism
could adapt itself to, and indeed merge with, what we may call the provincial traditions." But tolerance was not that simple.

> The ordinary activities of the Roman authorities both in Italy and in the provinces
> implied continuous attention to the approval of the gods and continuous partic-
> ipation of the gods in the public life of the Romans. The question of believing
> was seldom made explicit, but the question of performing correctly was ever pres-
> ent and committed the ruling class to the preservation of the religious tradition.
> (Momigliano 1986: 107)

Evidence is scarce about the problems that arose from the clash of imperial religious claims with local religious observances. That religion played a role in some

opposition is clear in the Batavian revolt of 69–70 C.E. under Civilis (Dyson 1971: 265–66). Though accommodation dominated, "we can never be certain that these provincial cults could not . . . turn into centres of dissatisfaction and protest against Rome" (Momigliano 1986: 111). A potential conflict lay in the collision of Roman traditions with monotheistic traditions such as Judaism that did not allow merging. Generally, with the exception of Gaius Caligula's attempt to install his statue in the Jerusalem Temple, Jewish observance and worship were not restricted. Roman concerns were appeased by prayers or sacrifices for the emperor's welfare. Another potential conflict lay in the encounter between Roman religious claims and a group with comparable claims about a deity's sovereignty and will. I will discuss Christian groups below, but it can be noted here that Pliny was alarmed enough by reported Christian nonattention to the gods, by such "stubbornness and unshakeable obstinacy," that he executed those Christians who would not invoke the gods and make offerings of wine and incense to the image of the emperor (Pliny, *Ep.* 10.96).

Resistance

Power and resistance stand in relation to each other. One rarely appears without the other. Resistance does not necessarily mean overt conflict; attempts to limit power can take various forms such as indifference or intentional hindrance (Clegg 1989: 208; Barbalet 1985; Lenski 1966: 63–68). Clegg identifies two kinds of resistance: "organizational outflanking" (forming a new power base and alternative system of influence), and a second form that "resists the exercise [of power], not the premises that make the exercise [of power] possible" (1989: 207). Both forms are evident in the first-century Roman Empire, with the early Christian movement exemplifying the first.

MacMullen's analysis of "enemies of the Roman order" includes a spectrum of opponents from aristocrats to members of the lower orders (1966). Aristocratic opposition, often involving a struggle between the senate and the emperor, took primarily literary and philosophical shape. While not advocating republican (or democratic) positions, the opposition rejected a ruler who operated above the law. They sought "security to speak their minds . . . freedom, especially of speech, guaranteed under monarchy" (1966: 33). "Facing the overwhelming power of the Roman state, its opponents had little choice of weapons. They were obliged to strike only through ideas and words, that is, through the philosopher . . . whose formidable figure embodied anger and reproach" (1966: 93). Philosophers were persecuted "because they supplied dangerous ideas and stories to dangerous men" (MacMullen 1966: 70, 82–83; Moles 1983; Sidebottom 1993). Philosophers were expelled from Rome in 66, 71, 89, and 93 (MacMullen 1966: 61–62); others were also exiled, or murdered.

Magicians, astrologers, diviners, seers, and prophets also posed a threat to public order and political security with disruptive or provocative words about the present and future from stars, entrails, or direct revelation (Cramer 1951; Mac-Mullen 1966: 95–162; Potter 1994). So the prophetess Veleda predicted the success of the German forces and destruction of the Roman legions in the Batavian revolt of 69–70 C.E. (Tacitus, *Hist.* 4.61). And Tacitus refers to a Druid prophecy that interpreted the burning of the Capitol in Rome in 69 C.E. as "a proof from heaven of the divine wrath" and predicted Rome's imminent demise and a "passage of the sovereignty of the world to the peoples beyond the Alps" (*Hist.* 4.54). Along with some other factors, Tacitus claims that this prophecy provided incentive for armed revolt.

Ideas, fears, and beliefs were not the only weapons for constructing new power relationships. Urban unrest employed "riots, shouts, blows and bloodshed" (Mac-Mullen 1966: 163). This violence could be motivated by numerous factors from self-protective acts to outright attacks on elite privilege. A crowd rioted in Aspendus in Pamphylia where the elite withheld corn from the locals in order to profit greatly from its export (Philostratus, *Life of Apollonius of Tyana* 1.15; Garnsey 1988). Philo attests the use that Isidore, "a foe to peace and tranquility," made of *collegia* or voluntary associations in Alexandria to cause urban unrest (*Flaccus* 135–37). *Collegia* were often suspected by elites of fomenting conspiracies and factions, of fostering foreign religions, and of promoting undesirable, more egalitarian social structures. They were regular targets of political restriction under Augustus (Suetonius, *Aug.* 93), Tiberius (Suetonius, *Tib.* 36), Claudius (Dio 60.6.6), Nero (Tacitus, *Ann.* 14.17), and Trajan (Pliny, *Ep.* 10.33–34, 92–93, 96–97; Cotter 1996).

Violent opposition also took other forms. Pirates at sea and bandits on land were active, despite Epictetus's boast (*Discourses* 3.13.9) that Rome had curtailed both (Braund 1993). Ubiquitous bandits and their bands of supporters, a category distinct from criminals, violently attacked travelers, stole property, and plundered the rich (MacMullen 1966: 255–68; Shaw 1984, 1993). Shaw argues that while their actions are often presented as a rejection of oppression, more significant is that they exploited a lack of effective imperial control in some areas, notably the lack of civic police or military presence. Bandits secede or withdraw from imperial constraint to establish their own "state-like power that mimics in every way the existing structure of state power" (1984: 50). Josephus, on being appointed governor of Galilee, exerted his authority over brigands he could not disarm, by turning them into mercenaries under his command (*Vita* 77–78, cf. 104–11). He records what seems to be an economics-driven violent protest in Antioch in 70 C.E. when some men burned "the market-square, the magistrate's quarters, the record-office and the law courts-exchange." Its perpetrators, "under the pressure of debts, imagined that if they burnt . . . the public records they would be rid of all demands" (*B.J.* 7.55, 61). Similar attacks occurred in Jerusalem in 66 (Josephus, *B.J.* 2.426–27). One of Jesus' parables narrates the violent and murderous actions of vineyard tenants against the absentee landlord's attempts to gather the rent (Mt 21.34–39).

There were also much larger revolts. Within a year of Nero's death, a Nero pretender terrified Achaia and Asia with an army of criminals, slaves, army deserters in the east, and others "prompted by their desire for a change and their hatred of the present situation." His plan, perhaps to set up a kingdom in Syria or Egypt, ended with his death (Tacitus, *Hist.* 2.8–9). Twenty years later, another Nero pretender joined with Parthia to pose a military threat from the east (Tacitus, *Hist.* 1.2; Suetonius, *Nero* 57). In Gaul, Mariccus raised an army of 8,000 to "challenge the Roman arms" and plunder the wealthy. Tacitus describes him as "pretending the authority of heaven" and as a "liberator of the Gallic provinces, this god—for he had given himself that honor" (*Hist.* 2.61). Dyson discusses five native revolts that occurred just after defeat by Rome's military and as administrative and financial control was being exerted. These new and usually culturally insensitive controls—"taxes in Britain and Dalmatia-Pannonia and possibly in Germany. In the Batavian territory, it was increased recruiting"—made the implications of defeat very concrete, challenged the "whole value system and cultural patterns" of the native society, increased social pressures, and with strong leadership and warrior traditions sparked an armed revolt against Roman control (Dyson 1971: 269–70). Tacitus attributes the Jewish revolt of 66 to the provocative actions of the governor Florus (*Hist.* 5.10).

Bowersock (1986), studying the mechanics of subversion in the provinces, lists three kinds of opposition: local sedition, troublemaking launched by an external power such as Parthia, and regional support for uprisings among Roman soldiers mobilized by an ambitious commander. Only the first of these would appear to really challenge the imperial system, but the other two could provide precedent for any challenge. Local temples often stood at the center of provincial subversion (Bowersock 1986: 315). For example, miracles and prophecies, probably engineered by priests of a particular cult center, were used to destabilize, alienate, or garner support for a person (1986: 297–304). A statue of Julius Caesar supposedly turned from west to east to signal support for Vespasian's candidacy as emperor (Tacitus, *Hist.* 1.86). Vespasian's healing miracles with the aid of Serapis and subsequent vision in the Serapeum functioned similarly (Tacitus, *Hist.* 4.81–82). Galba's candidacy received favorable prophecies (Suetonius, *Galb.* 9), but Germanicus's fortunes suffered with negative oracles (Tacitus, *Ann.* 2.54; cf. 43, 69). Local sanctuaries provided not only miracles and prophecies, but also "lifelong opponents of the Roman government . . . ideological misfits . . . thieves, pirates, kidnappers, and every criminal and sacrilegious person" claiming the right of asylum and ready to engage in any destabilizing activity (Bowersock 1986: 305–6). This range of expressed opposition is evident in responses to Roman rule from Jews both in the Diaspora and in Palestine (de Lange 1978; Goodman 1991). As noted above, Jewish religious leaders generally allied themselves with Rome, actively opposing, for example, the war of revolt in 66 (Josephus, *B.J.* 2.197, 320, 410–14). Gentile members of the elite, such as the wealthier, more powerful, and perhaps more "realistic" citizens of Tiberias and Gamala in Galilee (Josephus, *Vita* 33) or Agrippa in Jerusalem (*B.J.* 2.345–404), remained loyal to Rome (though at some cost, see Rajak 1991: 130–34).

Numerous violent and nonviolent acts of resistance, however, did occur in Palestine. Josephus attests a continual stream of social bandit groups who, inspired by a leader, royal pretender, or prophetic figure and moved by deteriorating socioeconomic circumstances and increased demands from Rome, resorted ineffectively to violent attacks on urban and landowning elites and attempted to redistribute wealth among peasants (Josephus, *B.J.* 2.264–65; Horsley and Hanson 1985/1988; Hanson and Oakman 1998: 86–91). Judas of Galilee found paying tribute to Rome and recognizing Rome's control incompatible with "having God for their Lord" (Josephus, *B.J.* 2.118). An Egyptian prophet gathered a crowd and planned to take Jerusalem from the Romans and become its ruler (*B.J.* 2.261–63). Simon bar Giora echoed Sabbath and Jubilee year traditions (Dt 15.1–18; Lv 25.39–43; Ringe 1985) by promising "liberty for slaves and reward for the free" as he marched on Jerusalem (Josephus, *B.J.* 4.508). Full-scale war broke out in 66, for which Josephus blamed the Zealots (*B.J.* 4.377–88, 5.562–66, 7.259–74) while Tacitus blamed the provocative excesses of the Roman procurators (*Hist.* 5.10–13; Bilde 1979). Agrippa cited misguided enthusiasm, hopes for independence and liberty, and the insolence of the governors (Josephus, *B.J.* 2.345–57).

Nonviolent acts of civil disobedience also expressed resistance. Both urban and rural Jews protested Pilate's introduction of busts of Caesar into Jerusalem; they staged a sit-in, falling "prostrate around his house" for five days. Pilate's subsequent order for his soldiers to kill them met with necks bared for the sword. Pilate withdrew the images (Josephus, *B.J.* 169–74). A vast crowd of Jews gathered on the plain at Ptolemais to beg Petronius not to install the statue of Gaius Caligula in the Jerusalem Temple. After protracted protest and repeated expressions of their willingness to die, Petronius, worried that the land would remain unsown and the tribute unpaid, decided to appeal to Caligula (Josephus, *B.J.* 2.192–203; cf. Tacitus's claim of an armed revolt, *Hist.* 5.9). Philo participated in a delegation to Caligula in Rome to protest mistreatment of Jews in Alexandria (*Legat.*). Andrea Berlin points to the absence of "red-slipped table vessels and mold-made lamps" from sites in Galilee. She suggests the absence of this tableware from houses in

Galilee is a boycott, an anti-Roman statement that rejected Roman control and expressed solidarity and affiliation with a traditional Jewish lifestyle (1999). Rome required a sacrifice offered twice daily on behalf of the emperor (Philo, *Legat.* 157, 317; Josephus, *B.J.* 2.197), but lower priests stopped the sacrifice in 66, an act that Josephus regards as laying the foundation of the war with Rome (*B.J.* 2.409–10). Tribute was withheld from Florus in 66 C.E. (*B.J.* 2.403–4).

Writing provided further visions of transformed power relationships whereby Rome is set in the context of God's purposes and its demise proclaimed. When Pompey took control of Jerusalem in 63 B.C.E., the writers of the *Psalms of Solomon* (2, 8) understood it as divine punishment but also anticipated the day when God's chosen would defeat Roman arrogance and restore God's reign (*Pss. Sol.* 17). The Qumran pesherim employed typical biblical motifs to present a similar vision (4QpNah frgs. 1–2, 2.3–5a; 1QpHab 3–5; Brooke 1991). The Egyptian Sibylline Oracles, especially the third and fifth, offer certainty that Rome will fall and God's people and reign will be restored (3.1–96, 162–294, 350–80, 657–808; Barclay 1996: 216–28). Apocalyptic texts such as *4 Ezra*, written like the fifth Sibylline Oracle after the fall of the Jerusalem Temple in 70 C.E., identify Daniel's fourth kingdom with Rome (*4 Ezra* 12.11) and predict Rome's demise (*4 Ezra* 11.40–45). For life in the meantime, such texts as 4 Maccabees (5.4, 8.15), perhaps originating in Antioch, upheld martyrdom as a likely and noble fate for "philosophers" who refuse allegiance to a tyrant (MacMullen 1966: 82–84). If taking life is "the most effective form of power" (Lenski 1966: 50), martyrdom denies the elite that power by refusing to be intimidated into compliance. Such visionary words, like the sacred texts read at Temple festivals and in synagogues, reminded Jews of a tradition and identity that affirmed a different sovereignty and loyalties—and appropriate actions.

Christian Texts and Communities as Resistance

This resistance to the empire exhibits Rome's diminished ability, despite all its practices and claims, to create and sustain among those under its reign attachments and loyalties to the empire's institutions, officials, and values. Resistance employed numerous means, sometimes but not necessarily involving open conflict, to limit the effects of imperial power. It shows that there was uneasiness with the imperial world. Mann (1986: 306–9) associates this uneasiness with the success of an empire that created unresolved difficulties or "contradictions." He identifies five contradictions: between universalism and particularity, equality and hierarchy, decentralization and centralization, cosmopolitanism and uniformity, and civilization and militarism. At the heart of these is a struggle for community, for social inclusion for the vast majority excluded from official power. However, he disassoci-

ates the contradictions from any deep economic or political foundation, not seeing them connected to issues of exploitation (Mann 1986: 16–17, 309).

In dismissing harsh political and economic factors, Mann appears to overesti-
mate the extent of economic cheer, give too much credence to imperial propaganda, and ignore the factors of political control and economic struggle evident
in the examples outlined above. Stark (1996: 73–94, 147–62) has shown the importance of early Christian attempts to ameliorate, both socially and materially,
the dreadful conditions of many people in urban centers. Yet Mann's emphasis on
issues of community seems well placed. The political and economic grievances he
dismisses are better seen as indicators of the same struggle for social identity to
which he points. The grievances question the sort of world Rome created and
maintained, the sorts of relationship its networks of power shaped, the people it
included and excluded, benefited and deprived. In Mann's terms, they resisted
Rome's hierarchical, centralized, particularistic, and militaristic society and expressed a preference for different communal structures and systems of meaning.

Mann argues that some in the early Christian movement addressed questions
of identity and community. Its social organization and theological claims rendered
the empire vulnerable by supplying the experience of community and a plausible
worldview that the empire had been unable to offer. Making ironical use of aspects of the Roman world—literacy, trade networks, etc. (1986: 310–20)—they
claimed theologically and demonstrated socially that the world did not have to be
organized in Rome's way. They undermined the empire's self-presentation as the
ultimate power that should control and define daily reality. They created and confirmed another relationship between ruler and ruled by appealing to Jewish religious traditions and symbols, to Jesus' life, and by creating alternative communities. Their texts constructed a different vision of reality and divine purposes for
the world and human existence. They contested and relativized imperial claims by
anticipating Rome's demise, and reenvisioned societal relationships, loyalties, and
ethical norms of behavior. Their communities enacted that vision through distinctive practices and structures that were merciful (Stark 1996), inclusive, "universalistic, egalitarian, decentralized, [and] civilizing" (Mann 1986: 307). I will
demonstrate this hypothesis in brief readings of Paul (the seven "genuine" letters),
Matthew, and Revelation.

Paul

Paul was, at least in part, an apocalyptic thinker looking to an end time (Beker
1980/1982). Influenced by Jewish apocalypticism and strong covenant conviction, his universalistic and inclusive gospel announced the vindication of God, the
demonstration of God's faithfulness in setting all creation—Jew and Gentile, male

and female, free and slave, human and nonhuman—in right relationship with God (Rom 3.1–8). God's action was already under way in the death and resurrection of Jesus. Not yet finished, its completion was imminent. Paul's Gospel, cosmic in its extent and apocalyptic in its framework, offered an answer to the crisis with which apocalyptic traditions constantly wrestled. To whom does sovereignty over the world belong (Käsemann 1969: 135)? Paul asserted that creation belonged not to Rome but to God (Rom 1.18–32, 11.33–36; 1 Cor 8.6, 10.26, "the earth is the Lord's" quoting Ps 24.1). The question of sovereignty had a social corollary: to which community did people belong (Mann 1986: 16–17, 309)? God's universal and inclusive sovereignty created inclusive, ethnically mixed communities that provided communal experience and practices alternative to the empire's hierarchical and exclusionary structure.

But the term "apocalyptic" has a further dimension. As much as it announces God's cosmic sovereignty, the word literally means "disclosing" or "revealing." Paul's Gospel discloses or reveals God's sovereignty because its presence is not obvious or self-evident in the world, not discoverable through usual means of observing and knowing. The gospel is the "gospel of God" (Rom 1.1), the Gospel from God and about God.

This double-edged apocalyptic quality of Paul's Gospel presents an immense theological challenge to the Roman imperial system. Fundamental is the claim that there is one God (Rom 3.27), the creator (Rom 1.18–32), whose sovereignty is being established now and will be soon established in full. There is "one Lord" (1 Cor 8.6). Paul of course does not mean the emperor even though the terminology κύριος (kyrios) usually denoted the emperor as the imperial Lord (Deissmann 1910: 355–63; Bureth 1964: 37–45; Beck 1997: 65–68; White 1999: 173–206). While there may be "so-called gods in heaven and earth, indeed as there are many gods and many lords, yet for us there is one God, the Father" (1 Cor 8.6). Paul does not refer to Jupiter/Zeus, "father of men and gods (Virgil, Aen. 1.254; White 1999: 110–72). These "so-called" gods are "beings that by nature are no gods" (Gal 4.8). There are other heavenly powers, but they are powerless in relation to God's love or saving actions (Rom 8.38–39). Not only is this traditional Jewish monotheism dismissive of polytheism as commentators usually note, but it is also a direct attack on the imperial theology and religious propaganda. If there are no such gods, if there is but one divine father and it is not Jupiter/Zeus, Rome's claims to rule at the will of the gods and to present the gods' will, presence, and blessings in the emperor's actions are empty lies. The social corollary, the nonparticipation of Christians in worship ceremonies directed to such gods, whether in houses, guild meetings, meals, civic or imperial celebrations, challenged the divinely sanctioned imperial structure and further loosen loyalties to that system (Mann 1986: 321).

Further, Paul's Gospel reveals that the world under Rome's power was not or-dered according to God's purposes and did not acknowledge God's sovereignty. So Paul sees human existence as marked by misplaced allegiances. Humans do not ac-knowledge the creator but worship creatures (Rom 1.18–32). Images and idols, said to be the dwelling place of demons (1 Cor 10.20–21), express this failure to acknowledge God's sovereignty, as do destructive social relationships (Rom 1.29–31). Images of emperors, such as the one that Gaius Caligula had recently tried to install in the Jerusalem Temple or that could be seen in any city in the em-pire, are included in such a condemnation. The whole imperial system was one of sinfully misplaced allegiance. The powers of sin and death "rule" and "exercise lordship" (Rom 6.9, 14). "Flesh" controls an existence that is hostile to God's purposes (Rom 8.7). This "present age" was evil (Gal 1.4), its wisdom folly com-pared to God's wisdom (1 Cor 2.6). It was marked by "ungodliness and injustice" (ἀδικίαν, Rom 1.18), a scathing condemnation of Rome's hierarchical and ex-ploitative system based on military might. God's wrath or judgment against it was already manifest.

But for Paul God will not allow this situation to continue. Contrary to claims that Rome and the Flavians would rule forever, God will end this unjust and idol-atrous imperial structure. This defeat will occur at the "coming" of Christ. The term "coming" or "arrival" (παρουσία, parousia) is imperial language that an-nounces the arrival of an imperial official, including Titus (Josephus, B.J. 5.410; Deismann 1910: 372–78). At Jesus' arrival, "every rule and every authority and power" are destroyed; "all his enemies are put under his feet" and subjected to God's reign (1 Cor 15.23–28; Phil 2.5–11). God will "triumph." Paul uses the triumph image (2 Cor 2.14) to attest God's sovereignty and contest Roman im-perial displays of victory, as well as to present his own ministry as an obedient slave of this Lord (Kreitzer 1996: 126–44; Versnel 1970).

This triumphant "day of the Lord" will break into the midst of Rome's world, a world of night and darkness in which people mistakenly say, "There is peace and security" (εἰρήνη καὶ ἀσφάλεια, eirēnē kai asphaleia, 1 Thes 5.1–11). Paul unashamedly invokes the common imperial boast of Rome's worldwide gifts, the "peace and security" that result from submitting to Roman military control (Wengst 1987: 19–21; Woolf 1993; Koester 1997: 158–66; Josephus, B.J. 2.572, 584; 3.33, 314; 6.345–46 on Titus; 7.65 on Vespasian; 7.94). But "peace and se-curity" based on submission to Roman military power and expressed in treaties are not the divine will. The claims are false. God will effect salvation from such a world (1 Thes 5.9–10). "The coming of the day of the Lord as an event . . . will shatter the false peace and security of the Roman establishment" (Koester 1997: 162). The savior was not the emperor, though he was often called that (σωτήρ, sōtēr, Josephus, B.J. 3.459, 7.71; Deissmann 1910: 368–69); the savior is Jesus exalted in heaven, returning at any time (Phil 3.20). Horsley (1997: 140) comments that Paul's frequent use of language "closely associated with the imperial religion" indicates "he was presenting his gospel as a direct competitor of the gospel of Caesar."

This final salvation, the completion of God's purposes and establishment of God's reign, was already under way (Rom 1.16–17). While "bad news" for the Roman elite and their allies, God's action was "good news" (εὐαγγέλιον, *euangelion*) for everyone else. Again the term "good news" is a polemical choice since it often denotes the empire's benefits. In the oft-quoted Priene inscription, it celebrates Augustus's birthday and accomplishments of "peace" (Deissmann 1910: 370–72). Josephus calls Vespasian's accession as emperor "good news" (*B.J.* 4.618, 656). But to these imperial claims Paul juxtaposes a very different good news, "the power of God into (εἰς, *eis*) salvation" (Rom 1.16). Again Paul shares vocabulary with the imperial world but redefines its meaning. God's "salvation" is not the same as that of the imperial world: profit for the few and military power that brings destruction and enforced submission under the guise of "peace and security" (Horsley 1997: 140–41; Josephus, *B.J.* 3.136, 4.397, 5.415, 6.365, 7.203). Instead God's saving power frees from imperial powers (Is 40.5, 45.17, 46.13) and creates wholeness or well-being in all the earth (Is 49.6, 52.10; Ps 12.5). God overcomes idolatry and the powers of sin and death and begins to transform the unjust status quo.

This salvation is elaborated in the next clause: the "justice of God is being revealed" (Rom 1.17). "Justice" or "righteousness," another claimed imperial benefit (Georgi 1997: 148–50), involves faithfulness and right relationships (Dunn 1998: 340–46). The revelation of God's justice is necessary precisely because Paul's Gospel reveals the world of Roman imperialism to be a world of "injustice" (Rom 1.18), of faithlessness and wrong relationship. Now God is establishing a different sort of justice or right relatedness, one that includes not a select few but is impartial and extended to all, "the Jew first and also to the Greek," in God's loving, gracious, and merciful purposes (Rom 3.24, 5.5, 8.31–39, 11.28–30).

Central to this act of reasserting God's sovereignty is Jesus' death on the cross. "Christ crucified" is Paul's summary of his gospel (1 Cor 1.23, 2.2). Elliott (1994: 93–139) argues it is Paul's interpreters, not Paul himself, who are guilty of depoliticizing this event. Rome used crucifixion as a prime means of violent torture not only to remove people who threatened the imperial system but also to intimidate anyone else from even contemplating the notion of revolt. Paul does not dwell on the specifics of Jesus' death, but he does draw attention to "faithfulness shown by Jesus"[8] in the face of imperial violence (Rom 3.22, 26; Johnson 1997: 58–61). Paul does identify those responsible for violence—"the rulers of this age" (1 Cor 2.8). The identity of these rulers (ἀρχόντων, *archontōn*) has been much debated: Are they human rulers or heavenly powers? Elliott (1994: 113) argues persuasively that they designate both, "procurators, kings, emperors, as well as the supernatural 'powers' who stand behind them" (see Beck 1997: 51–54). Jesus' death reveals the violence directed against those who oppose the empire. It also reveals Jesus' solidarity with all who endure such tyranny. He too is a victim of imperial violence, a slave (Phil 2.7) who undergoes the fate of many enslaved by the empire.

But the cross also reveals the limits of imperial power. These rulers do the ultimate to Jesus; they kill him (Lenski 1966: 50), but they cannot keep him dead. God overcomes the powers by giving "life to the dead" (Rom 4.17). The powers are not yet defeated, but God liberates Jesus from them as a sign of their imminent defeat (Elliott 1994: 123–24; I Cor 15.23–28). They "are doomed to pass away" (I Cor 2.6). His resurrection also guarantees that with their defeat all who suffer under their coercive power will be set free. Jesus is the first fruit of those who will be raised from death (I Cor 15.20). Hence Paul speaks of Jesus' death as a "redemption (ἀπολυτρώσεως, apolutrōseōs) which is in Christ Jesus" (Rom 3.24). He employs an image that derives from Israel's Scriptures to designate God's liberation of the people from imperial power, the exodus from slavery in Egypt and from Babylonian exile in the sixth century (Dunn 1998: 227–28). Likewise he claims that through Jesus' death God is at work to "treat people as righteous" (δικαιούμενος, dikaioumenos, Rom 3.24), to set them in right relation with God in anticipation of and in solidarity with all of God's creation that will be released from its exploitative use (Rom 8.18–25). This right relationship is for Paul "peace" (Rom 5.1). It is not Rome's accomplishment based on military power, marked by economic injustice, designed to benefit only the elite, and willed by the gods (Georgi 1997: 148–50). It comes "from God our Father" (Rom 1.7) as an expression of God's empire (βασιλεία, basileia) and justice (δικαιοσύνη, dikaiosynē, Rom 14.17). It is the very goal of God's work yet to be completed (Rom 15.13; 16.20).

This understanding of God's power at work in the imperial world, and the encounter of believers with God's action, creates collegia-like communities that acknowledge, experience, and embody God's work (Kloppenborg and Wilson 1996; Ascough 1998: 71–94). Paul uses a political term, that of a "state" or "commonwealth" (πολίτευμα, politeuma) in heaven, to refer not only to the future destiny of these communities but also to identify the basis on which they live their present lives (Phil 3.20). "Heaven," the abode of God, is to determine their present existence (Lincoln 1981: 193) in the midst of Rome's empire.

These communities are marked by "believing," or "faithfulness." Paul placed "faithfulness" at the heart of God's saving work. Salvation or righteousness is "from God's faith(fulness) to human (response of) faith" (Rom 1.17; Dunn 1998: 374). Georgi (1997: 149) draws attention to the deep roots of the "faith" and "believing" (πίστις, *pistis*, πιστεύω, *pisteuō*) terminology not only in the Scriptures but also in imperial claims such as those made in the *Acts of Augustus* 31–33. "The Caesar represented the *fides* of Rome in the sense of loyalty, faithfulness to treaty obligations, uprightness, truthfulness, honesty, confidence, and conviction—all, as it were, a Roman monopoly." Of course such "loyalty" was to be reciprocated by subjects submissive to the emperor's will. Paul's communities of believers commit to an alternative loyalty, to God. In Thessalonica, not to practice idolatry (1 Thes 1.9) was a religious and political matter. Their absence from cultic participation not only removed a means of securing a relationship of loyalty to the emperor but brought affliction and suffering (1.6, 2.14, 3.3–4) from suspicious and antagonistic neighbors and city officials (Donfried 1997). For defense they had "the breastplate of faith and love" and "for a helmet the hope of salvation" (1 Thes 5.8).

The alternative nature of these communities is highlighted by another name. Horsley argues that the common term for church (ἐκκλησία, *ekklēsia*) significantly draws on both its Septuagint usage to denote Israel as the "assembly of the Lord," and its common usage in the Greek-speaking eastern Roman Empire as the citizen assembly of the Greek *polis*. "Paul evidently understood the *ekklesia* of a Thessalonica or Corinth . . . as a political assembly of the people 'in Christ' in pointed juxtaposition and 'competition' with the official city assembly" (Horsley 1997: 208–9).

Other factors indicate the alternative nature of these communities. The use of household language denotes a community related to God the Father, an alternative to imperial society over which the emperor is *pater patriae*, "father of the fatherland." So amidst all the relational imagery of Romans 12 are numerous familial terms including "brothers and sisters" (12.1) and "familial affection" in 12.10 to indicate the love of siblings for each other (φιλαδελφία, *philadelphia*) and of any family relationships (φιλόστοργοι, *philostorgoi*). These communities are not based on kinship but open to all. The redefined familial relationships that embody God's saving love (Rom 5.5, 8.31–39) are part of a rejection of the conventional relationships of patriarchal households. Schüssler Fiorenza points to the baptismal declaration of Galatians 3.28 as a key text determining the "social interrelationships and structure" of the alternative societies of "children of God" (1997: 224–41). "In Christ Jesus" the fundamental distinctions of ethnicity, gender, and social status that define relationships of domination in the imperial world were no longer relevant in the Christian communities. The prominent place of women as coworkers with Paul in preaching and founding and growing churches attests to the same realities. In Romans 16, Paul honors and describes the roles of numerous women with language (διάκονος, *diakonos*, service; κοπιάω, *kopiaō*, work hard, toil) that he uses to describe his own ministry (Rom 16.1–2, 5, 12).

Likewise several acts contest the empire's economic order and offer an alternative. In I Corinthians 11.17–34 Paul is profoundly disturbed by the celebration of the Lord's Supper. Meals provided an important context for displaying socioeconomic status and political power through the range of invited guests (superior patrons, equals, and dependent clients) and through seating order, different qualities of the food served to guests, different sizes of portions, differing qualities of service, and tableware (Corley 1993: 17–79; Smith 1992). That is, meals expressed and reinforced the very vertical structure of imperial society. These inequalities seem to be determining the celebration in Corinth in which some have plenty while others are hungry (11.21). Paul's verdict is that this practice "despise[s] the church of God and humiliate[s] those who have nothing . . . it is not the Lord's supper that you eat" (11.20–22). He orders them to "discern the body" in relation to the significance of Jesus' death (I Cor 2.1–8) and transformed social relationships and practices (I Cor 12.13). His communities are to subvert imperial structures, not reinforce them.

Also to be noted is Paul's uneasiness with the imperial patronage and tribute systems in which he would receive support from those in the churches, either from the "poverty-stricken" or the more wealthy who were looking to enhance their prestige. With some exceptions (Phoebe in Rom 16.1–2), Paul prefers not to imitate the imperial system by either burdening the poor or providing opportunity for the wealthy. He engages in despised manual labor instead (I Cor 9; Horsley 1997: 249–50). Likewise as an alternative to the tributary and centripetal economy of the empire in which the poor support the rich, Paul organized a collection from one subject people to benefit another, the poor in Jerusalem (I Cor 16.1–4; 2 Cor 8–9; Rom 15.25–33). Horsley sees this act as signifying the economic dimension of the international political-religious movement Paul was building with structures and practices alternative to those of the empire (1997: 251–52).

In his attempt to build these alternative communities, there is no doubt about two things. Paul experienced opposition, suffering in what Beker has called a "cruciform" existence (2 Cor 4.7–12, 6.1–10; Beker 1982: 55–59). Second, Paul was not always consistent in enacting his gospel. Various inconsistencies—his use of his own authority, patronage, slavery, the call to respect governmental authority in Romans 13 (Elliott 1997), his use of imperial concepts to depict the triumph (!) of God's empire—indicate that the imprint of the imperial society ran deep even among those who sought an alternative. But whatever the verdict on Paul's efforts, his gospel pronounced God's judgment on the empire's power relationships and called people to discern the times and to live in alternative communities of resistance and of solidarity with those oppressed by its power, in anticipation of God's coming triumph (Elliott 1994: 189–230).

Matthew

Most twentieth-century Matthean scholars have read Matthew in relation to a dispute with a local synagogue. Without denying this, it must also be recognized that this gospel, perhaps written in Antioch in the 80s, originates from and addresses a world shaped by imperial structures and claims. My contention is that the gospel's theology, Christology, soteriology, eschatology, and ethics contested claims that Rome's empire manifested the gods' sovereignty and presence, that the empire was the agent that mediated societal well-being (Carter 1998, 2000b, 2000c). The gospel constructs an alternative understanding of the world and life in it that subverts imperial theology and forms inclusive, more egalitarian communities with an alternative worldview and set of practices.

Concerning sovereignty over human history, the gospel challenges imperial claims that the gods, especially Jupiter, shape history in their choice of Rome and the Flavians as vice-regents to rule over human affairs. The opening genealogical review of God's dealings with Israel attests that God's purposes run through Israel and Jesus, not Rome (Mt 1.1–17; Carter 2000b). The gospel's concern with the enactment of the Scriptures, its scenes of eschatological judgment, Jesus' proclamations about and demonstrations of "the empire of the heavens," about his "Father in Heaven" who is "Father, Lord of heaven and earth" (11.25), about the creator's will from the beginning (19.4), about God's provision of sun and rain for all (5.45), about Jesus' sharing in "all authority in heaven and on earth" (28.19) establish the claim that the world is God's. Far from recognizing that Rome enacts the gods' rule or will, the gospel reveals that Satan controls "all the empires of the world" (Mt 4.8). As the world's leading empire, Rome is the agent of Satan's empire (12.28). "Kings of the earth" (cf. 17.25) like Herod and Pilate, the emperor's representative, always resist God's sovereignty, but the phrase also recalls God's dismissive response (Ps 2.4).

Twice the gospel addresses the issue of paying taxes, a conventional form of recognizing Rome's sovereignty. In both cases, Rome's authority is relativized. In 22.15–22, the religious elite, members of the ruling class allied with Rome, pose the question of the legality of paying taxes to Rome. Jesus uses a coin, a handheld billboard of Roman propaganda bearing the image of the emperor and some words of identification, to frame his answer. "Render to Caesar the things that are Caesar's and to God the things that are God's." In the gospel's point of view, this saying does not mean that God and Caesar are equal, or that God is subordinate to Caesar. What is God's, is other than what pertains to the emperor. Caesar exists but he does not have the absolute power he imagines (Pilgrim 1999: 64–72).

Matthew 17.24–27 depicts Jesus answering questions about paying the post-70 tax levied on Jews by Vespasian (Carter 1999). Vespasian imposed this half-shekel or *didrachma* tax (Josephus, *B.J.* 7.218; Dio 65.7.2) for punitive and propaganda purposes. It reminded Jews of their status as a defeated race; of Rome's superiority; and, in using it to provide for the temple of Jupiter Capitolinus, of Jupiter's sovereignty over history and human affairs. Jesus instructs that they must pay the tax, since kings of the earth, a pejorative phrase that refers in the Psalms to kings opposed to God (Ps 2.7), tax everybody except their own children (Mt 17.26). But paying the tax does not recognize Rome's sovereignty. Rather Jesus instructs Peter to catch a fish and find in its mouth a coin to pay the tax! In their three previous appearances in the gospel, fish have given witness to God's sovereignty (Mt 7.10, 14.13–21, 15.32–39). God supplies the fish and the tax coin. The tax is paid subversively in recognition of God's sovereignty soon to be manifested.

Divine presence offers a second thread. Imperial theology claims that the Flavian emperors reveal the presence of the gods among their subjects. Matthean scholars have long noted the gospel's focus on divine presence. Naming Jesus "Emmanuel" (Mt 1.23) sets the theme. Jesus is God's anointed one, commissioned to manifest God's presence in words and actions (cf. 12.28) and among the gathered and missional community of disciples (18.20, 28.20). The claim of God's presence among people has abundant scriptural warrant, but the manifestation of the gods' presence by rulers is a prominent theme in imperial theology. In citing Isaiah 7.14 (Mt 1.23) the narrative utilizes a text that locates God's presence in resistance to imperialist actions by invoking the Syro-Ephraimite War (Carter 2000a). In a narrative replete with references to the Moses story in which God liberates the people from another tyrant, Jesus enters the world of Herod (Mt 2.1, 3), vassal king of Rome, to expose his limited power. The magi identify Jesus, not Herod, as "the one born king of the Jews" (2.2). Citing Micah 5 and 2 Samuel 5 (Mt 2.6) points to Jesus, not Herod, as ruler. The imperial term "do obeisance" (προσκυνέω) is used in relation to Jesus (2.2, 8, 11), not Herod. Herod's efforts to kill Jesus (Mt 2.4, 7, 8) are thwarted by angel and dream (2.13, 19–20). The narrative refers three times to Herod's death (2.15, 19, 20), God's ultimate frustration of his plans. Two systems clash, the imperial and God's. The imperial system actively opposes God's presence. The narrative exposes the empire as ruthless and murderous, but deconstructs it. It is not ultimate, even though it continues in the person of Archelaus (2.22) and, later, Pilate. By sharing vocabulary with the passion narrative ("King of the Jews," "assemble," "the people," "Messiah," "destroy," "deceived/mocked"), chapter 2 foreshadows Jesus' crucifixion by Pilate as the empire's agent. The empire's ultimate effort to destroy Emmanuel is to crucify him. Resurrection indicates that while the imperial system resists God's presence and has the power to inflict death, God's power and presence overcome death. "All authority in heaven and on earth has been given to me" (Mt 28.18).

A third aspect, that of agency, is implicit. Whereas imperial theology claims the emperor manifests the divine will, presence, and blessing among humans, the gospel claims Jesus as the agent of God's saving presence (1.21–23). Jesus is "Christ," anointed or commissioned to save from sins and to manifest divine presence, blessing, and will in his words and actions (4.17–25, 5.21–48, 12.28).

How does he carry out this commission to save from sins? This commission stands over all of Jesus' life, his words and actions (9.1–8), death and resurrection (20.28, 26.28), and his return. The gospel addresses a post-70 audience, and interprets the fall of Jerusalem in 70 to Vespasian and Titus as God's punishment on the people for their sins (22.7). This kind of perspective had interpreted previous catastrophes: the Babylonian exile (Dt 28–30; 1 Kgs 9.1–9); Antiochus Epiphanes (2 Mc 7.32–36); and Pompey (*Pss. Sol.* 2, 8). Others also use it to interpret the destruction of 70 (Josephus, *4 Ezra, 2 Bar.*). In this post-70 context Matthew proclaims that God's punishment is not final but that God will save the people through Jesus. That salvation is available in part now through Jesus' actions and words manifested through disciples (Mt 10.7–8, 28.18–20), but it will be established in full at Jesus' return or coming (παρουσία). His return, as described dramatically in 24.27–31 with a host of imperial imagery, involves an eschatological battle in which Rome is defeated. "Wherever the corpse is there the eagles (ἀετοί) will gather." Eagles commonly denote imperial powers who punish God's people (Dt 28.47–53; Jer 4.13; Lam 4.19; Ez 17.1–21), but they also denote standards carried into battle by Roman troops displaying the eagle as the symbol of Roman power (Josephus, *B.J.* 3:123; Appian, *Bell. Civ.* 2.61). The eagles gathered with the corpses are fallen Roman troops. Rome, Satan's agent, is defeated by Jesus' return, and God's sovereignty is established over a new heaven and earth (Mt 19.28, 24.35; Carter 2000a, 2000b, 2000c).

The claim that Jesus is God's commissioned agent is made at the expense of the religious leaders, the allies of Rome. Their elite status and commitment to the current social structure are evident in their first appearance as allies of Rome's puppet king Herod (Mt 2.4–6). In their final appearance, they are allies of Rome's governor and soldiers (27.62–66, 28.11–15). As members of the imperial society's elite (Lenski 1966: 256–66; Saldarini 1988: 35–49), they exercise not a restricted "religious" role, but social, economic, and political power, and with detrimental effect. Jesus condemns them because they do not seek "justice, mercy and faith" (23.23). They resist Jesus' claims to be God's agent who offers God's benefits to all of society, especially to those on the margins (9.1–8; 9–13; 12.1–8, 9–14, 22–37; 21.14–16). In defending the status quo, they hinder people from knowing God's empire (23.13) and practice injustice and deceit (27.62–66, 28.11–15). These leaders, along with Rome, are the condemned shepherds in 9.36 (see also Suetonius, *Tib.* 32; Dio Chrysostom, *4 Regn.* 4.43–44; Dio

56.16.3). The image recalls the false shepherds of Ezekiel 34 who maintain a strictly differentiated society to ensure that the elite have plenty at the expense of the rest. They feed themselves but exploit the sheep/people by depriving them of food and clothing, by not strengthening the weak, healing the sick, binding up the injured, or looking for the lost and scattered (Ez 34.3–6). They do not protect the people from nations but let them be enslaved, plundered, frightened, starved, and insulted (Ez 34.27–29). The leaders are condemned because of their imperial style: "With force and harshness you have ruled them" (Ez 34.4). God promises a reversal of these woes with a Davidic prince and God's saving presence (Ez 34.23–24, 30–31). Citing Jeremiah 7 (Mt 21.13) also invokes a chapter that condemns false priestly leadership.

Those who rejected Jesus' teaching and authority rejected also his prophetic attempts to form a different social order (a "domination-free" society) and defend their own privileged location in an iniquitous society sanctioned by Rome ("the domination system"; Wink 1992: 13–137). Their conflict with Jesus reflects a collision of two different visions of society and a struggle over who has the authority to shape society. By describing them as evil like Satan (Mt 6.13, 12.23, 16.4) and tempting Jesus like Satan (4.1, 3; 16.1; 19.3; 22.18), the narrative reveals them to be Satan's agents committed to resisting God's will (cf. 4.8). Jesus announces that they are not God's agents (15.13–14), declares that the privileged societal structure with its inequities of power that they support does not belong to God's empire (20.24–28; 23.5–7, 8–12), and removes their role in God's purposes (21.43). He attacks and condemns their Temple (21.12–17). In response, they ally with Rome to crucify him (Brown 1983: 371–74). Such opposition and martyrdom are inevitable for those, Jesus and disciples, who resist imperial power (16.13–28). Martyrdom denies the empire the power to intimidate. Pilate's power could prevent the execution, but instead he makes it happen. The resurrection reframes Jesus' death as a means of liberation (Mt 20.28), not as an event of shame and defeat.

Imperial theology asserts a fourth claim that the well-being of the world depends on the emperor and submission to him. The gods through the emperor have granted peace, corn, harmony, well-being, and safety. It would seem, though, to be Matthew's view that it is precisely this imperial well-being from which the world needs to be saved! The chapter 2 narrative of Herod's murderous actions follows the 1.21 commission to Jesus to save people from their sins. Chapter 2 demonstrates the sin of the political-religious resistance to God's presence. Summary passages such as 4.23–25 and 9.35–38 present a world in which well-being is absent as many lack the basics necessary for life. The well-being promised by the gospel is, finally, eschatological with a new creation (19.28) and the end of the iniquitous allocation of land and its produce in the exploitative imperial structures (5.5).

But, in the meantime, Jesus and his disciples manifest God's blessings among people, particularly the common people, with the offer of transformation and participation in an inclusive community. Various interconnected terms, often mirroring and contesting imperial claims as with Paul, denote aspects of it—saving (1.21), the empire of the heavens (4.17; 5.3, 10; 6.10), good news (4.23), blessing (5.3–12; 6.9–13), and righteousness or justice (5.10, 20; 6.33)—while numerous gospel stories demonstrate its impact.

Among the first to encounter God's reign manifested by Jesus (4.17; 12.28) were the marginal, "the sick, those afflicted with various diseases and pains, demoniacs, epileptics, and paralytics" (4.23–24; ch. 8–9; 10.8; 11.4–6). These were of no account to imperial power; they were the poor in spirit, not the privileged and powerful (Powell 1996: 463–65; Carter 1997: 23–25; Carter 2000b). Their illnesses—demon possession, paralysis, muteness—arose in contexts of imperial violence, economic exploitation, and social divisions (Theissen 1983: 231–64; Hollenbach 1981; Brown 1983: 366–68; Carter 2000b). They also resulted from hunger and malnutrition among those whose resources have been removed by taxation. Imperial rule was hazardous to one's health. But by healing them and by feeding hungry crowds, Jesus offers God's blessing (5.3), the possibility of a new way of life, of social belonging and economic support, in anticipation of the completion of God's saving purposes when all sickness and lack are healed. This manifestation of God's presence and blessing challenges the imperial and elitist system's discarding of such people. Instead of goods being extracted from below and sent upward, they come freely from above to those below. Disciples are commissioned to continue these transformative practices in cities like Antioch as they announce and realize God's empire (10.7–8; Stark 1996: 147–62).

Another dimension of the alternative way of life of Jesus' community of disciples appears in chapters 19–20 (Carter 1994; Barton 1994). Jesus challenges the four standard aspects of conventional patriarchal households that were basic to imperial society: the rule of husband over wife (Mt 19.3–12), of father over children (19.13–15), of householder over wealth (19.16–30), and of master over slave (20.17–28). A parable of a householder (20.1–16) encapsulates the issue. Jesus subverts this conventional pattern by advocating more egalitarian patterns of human interaction (20.12). In 20.25 Jesus contrasts disciples with "the rulers of the Gentiles [who] lord it over them, and their great men [who] exercise authority over them." He rejects the imperial system in which the exercise of power benefits a few at the oppressive expense of most (Pilgrim 1999: 58–64). Significantly both verbs—lord it over (κατακυριεύω) and exercise authority over (κατεξουσιάζω)—are cognates of words used for God and Jesus. The imperial system's use of power is condemned in part because it claims and misuses what rightly belongs to God/Jesus. The imperial system cannot do what Jesus can do (8.5–13). Jesus' authority means healing and life

(8.8), revealing God's will (7.29), forgiveness and healing (9.6, 8; 10.1), and an extension of God's authority over all things (21.23, 24, 27; 28.18). As Lord (κύριος) he exercises God's salvific will and authority over heaven and earth and over human existence (1.20, 22, 24; 2.13, 15, 19; 3.3; 4.7, 10; 5.33; 11.25, etc.), judgment (7.21–22), disease (8.2, 6, 8; 9.28; 15.22, 25), death (8.21), creation (8.25; 14.28, 30), and the believing community (10.24–25).

Imperial domination is not to be evident among disciples (20.26a). Disciples are to live an alternative social structure as a community of slaves and servants imitating Jesus who gives his life for others. In this inclusive community, well-being is practiced in mercy, love, and life-giving service (5.43–48, 9.13, 12.7). Economic practices provide for, not exploit, the other (5.42, 6.16–18, 25.31–46). As a community of slaves (20.26–27), it is marginal in the dominant culture but does not imitate its hierarchy, domination, and exploitation; it lacks a role for masters (Carter 1994: 161–92). So at the beginning of chapter 21 Jesus enters Jerusalem in a parody of Roman triumphs by riding on a donkey (Tatum 1998; Carter 2000b).

These alternative practices and the worldview that they embody indicate the basic posture of discipleship, a life of resistance to the imperial structure. But this resistance is not violent (5.39). The Roman reconquest of Palestine and destruction of Jerusalem in 70 have shown the futility of that option. Instead of fight or flight, disciples employ active nonviolent resistance (5.38–42) to break the cycle of imperial violence. Jesus offers four examples of how those without power might resist. Instead of the expected submission or violent backlash, actions are chosen that refuse intimidation, seize the initiative, challenge what is supposed to demean, and assert humanness. Turning the cheek, stripping off all one's clothing and offering it to the superior, carrying the soldier's pack a second mile, and using economic resources for the good rather than the exploitation of the other curtail the impact of the imperial system, preserve dignity, seize initiative, and redefine relationships within it (Wink 1992: 175–93).

In addition to the gospel stories, the liturgy of the Matthean community also constructs and maintains its alternative communal identity and worldview. The community's prayer expresses fundamental discomfort with the status quo by praying not only for renewed community in forgiveness and the adequate supply of bread, but also for the coming of God's empire, the establishment of God's will, and deliverance from temptation and evil (Mt 6.9–13; Carter 1995, 2000b: 163–70; Beck 1997: 111–14). The Eucharist strengthens the same eschatological hope (26.29). But liturgy is to be accompanied by merciful actions of feeding the hungry and including the unlovely in communities of disciples (25.31–46). The community is called an assembly (ἐκκλησία, Mt 16.18, 18.17), a term used for potentially dangerous voluntary associations (Kloppenborg and Wilson 1996; Carter 2000b).

The gospel story, then, fashions very different relationships with the imperial world. It contests these four elements of imperial theology: sovereignty, presence, agency, and well-being. It exposes the evil of the present imperial structure as being fundamentally opposed to God's will and condemned to defeat. Jesus' words and actions provide and sustain an alternative worldview and practices for an alternative community.

Revelation

In contrast to the rarely discussed protests of Paul and Matthew, that of Revelation has often been studied. The text combines apocalyptic (1.1), prophetic (1.3), and epistolary forms (1.4) to pronounce judgment on the current oppressive reality, set it in a cosmic context, reassure its audience of God's sovereignty over the difficult present and triumphant future, and exhort faithfulness and resistance, even to the point of death.

Though the specifics are debated, a situation of crisis faces the document's audience, seven churches in cities in Asia Minor. False leaders and teaching, conflicts among religious groups, fading spiritual commitment, disputes with some synagogues, the threat of imprisonment and martyrdom, and social and economic pressure threaten their existence. While some scholars locate this crisis in empire-wide persecution and martyrdom of Christians by the emperor Domitian, a lack of evidence requires a more nuanced understanding of this multifaceted situation (Harrington 1993: 9–11; Boring 1989: 8–23). More convincing is to locate the crisis, at least in part, in the sociopolitical pressure placed on Christians by the imperial cult, especially popular in Asia Minor as a means of uniting people and emperor (Price 1984). All but one of the cities named (Thyatira) had temples for offering vows, prayers, and incense to acknowledge Rome's role as chosen by the gods, and to seek the well-being of the city and the emperor. While participation was not legally mandated, "everyone did it" at meals, trade group gatherings, entertainment, etc. Not to participate was to attract attention, suspicion, and accusations of disloyalty and "atheism" that could lead to legal or political action (Pliny, *Ep.* 10.96–97). Christians, members of a tradition that renounced idolatry and polytheism, were vulnerable. While at least one person in Pergamum, Antipas, was martyred (Rv 2.13), others, perhaps, did not faithfully resist.

Having named this sociopolitical pressure (ch. 1–3), Revelation discerns its much larger context in a cosmic struggle between God and Satan. Three images portray the Roman Empire as being under Satan's control (Pilgrim 1999: 151–61). A beast, combining features of the four beasts representing four world empires in Daniel 7, emerges from the sea (ch. 13). To this beast, the dragon, Satan, "gave its power and throne and great authority." Rome is Satan's designated agent; it blasphemes against God (13.6), wars against God's people (13.7), and demands worship (13.8). A second beast emerges in 13.11, the agent of the first in promoting worship (13.12–16; Scherrer 1984) and in controlling economic activity (13.17). It images the imperial cult along with imperial personnel and structures as the empire's instruments.

Chapter 17 uses a second image, a prostitute who depicts an unfaithful nation. Her great wealth (17.4), identification as an imperial power Babylon (17.5), role as a murderer (17.6), power over all the nations (17.1, 15), and description as "the great city that has an empire over the kings of the earth" (17.18) points to Rome. Judgment on it is announced with a third image, "Fallen is Babylon" (ch. 18). The image invokes another great empire that was used and deposed by God. Chapter 18 also declares judgment on "the merchants of the earth" who bring to Rome the great wealth of the provinces taken in tribute and taxes for the benefit of the elite (18.11–20; Bauckham 1993: 338–83). The book concludes with seven parallel visions that evoke, with numerous colliding images, God's judgment against and victory over her (Rv 19–22).

The violent but terminal nature of the empire appears in another image, that of a lamb wounded or slain but standing. This lamb is first introduced in 5.6 as slain (also 5.12) and in 5.9 with reference to its blood. It represents the crucified Jesus who has suffered the empire's violence and given his life, the inevitable outcome for any "faithful witness" (1.5). But the lamb stands (5.6), attesting the limits of imperial power. God has raised him and installed him in the throne room of heaven where he is worthy to receive praise and to open the seals of the scroll that outlines God's purposes for history (5.6–14). His resurrection means that the empire's violence and deadly power does not give it final say, irrespective of its claims. It cannot thwart God's purposes. The lamb also attests the empire's certain demise. While the nations make war on him, "the Lamb will conquer them for he is Lord of lords and King of kings" (17.14). The document ends with various visions of God's triumph in which the lamb figures prominently (19.7–9; 21.9, 22–27; 22.1–3). The outcome is certain though not yet. The lamb's death and resurrection liberate people from the clutches and claims of the false imperial system to share God's reign and life (5.9–10). Those who have washed in his blood (7.14) share his triumph over the dragon, Satan (12.10–11). They are "called and chosen and faithful" and victorious (17.14).

The presentation of God's judgment on Rome and final victory over it is continuous throughout the book and functions to reassure the audience of God's sovereignty even over such a beastly and Satanic power as Rome. Chapters 2 and 3, in which the various dimensions of the present crisis are named, give way to a sudden revelation of the heavenly throne and worship (ch. 4–5). Every detail asserts God's sovereignty. Aune (1983) argues that the description resembles and parodies the ceremonial of the imperial court with its emphases on dispensing justice, the role of the twenty-four elders, the use of hymns, and the honorific titles. The effect of the move is to put the vicissitudes outlined in the seven letters (Rv 2–3) in the perspective of God's reign and to strengthen the audience in their loyalty to the God who holds supreme sovereignty. Chapters 6–18 focus on the intensifying eschatological distress. Three series of seven visions (seven seals, 6.1–8:1; seven trumpets, 8.7–11:19; seven plagues or bowls 15.1–16.21), organized as a spiral rather than in a chronological sequence, emphasize the enactment of God's judgment. The repetition is telling as God's judgment and the limited power of Rome are repeated repeatedly. But also to be noted are the contrasting scenes of salvation that interrupt the judgment focus. Chapter 7 (7.1–8, 9–17) separates the sixth and seventh seals with visions of the church enjoying God's reign. In 8.1–3 the church is at prayer. Worship is a political protest. In 15.1 the seven plagues are introduced, but detailed description is delayed until the scene of the martyrs praising (Rv 16). The scenes provide encouragement by attesting that even now in the midst of the assertion of Roman power God's saving purposes are under way and experienced by the faithful who also anticipate their completion (Boring 1989: 30–33).

How, then, are followers of the Lamb to live in the meantime? What are they to do about the pressure to honor the emperor in worship? Apocalyptic thinking does not offer an escape from the present but creates faithful engagement with it. Boring outlines six possible options (1989: 21–23). One is to quit following the Lamb while maintaining their jobs, social links, honor, and life. But those who are faithless, "the cowardly, the faithless . . . idolaters," are condemned to the lake of fire (21.8). A second option is to lie, to undergo the formalities of expressing loyalty to Rome, but with reservations and recognition of God as Lord. But "all liars" also belong in the lake of fire (21.8). A third (theoretical) option would be to fight, but the slain lamb invokes Jesus' nonviolent response. Chapter 13.10 echoes Jesus' saying that to live by the sword is to die by it. A fourth possibility would be to lobby to change the law. But given that the imperial system is organized by the ruling elite for its own benefit, this is not an option. A fifth option is to create a synthesis between Christianity and the emperor cult. The abandonment of exclusive loyalty and monotheistic thinking would be necessary. Perhaps this cultural accommodation was somewhat pervasive (is this the "lukewarm" image of 3.16?), that some did not see themselves in any situation of crisis. Such a scenario might account for the book's attempt to create clear boundaries by employing a very strict cosmic and societal dualism. A sixth option was martyrdom. Christians could go about their business and not participate in imperial ritual, but they must know that if some exerted social pressure on them and made legal charges against them, they would face the consequences. "If any one is to be taken captive, to captivity they go. . . . here is a call for the endurance and faith of the saints" (13.10). Pilgrim sees the last option, martyrdom, as the document's exhortation (1999: 161–80). There must be no compromise and no participation in emperor worship (13.8). Followers of the Lamb have different relationships with the emperor. Instead they are to be faithful witnesses like Jesus (1.5), patient and enduring in "counter-communities of Christian resistance in the midst of the enemy's domain" (Richard 1995: 58), and in anticipation of God's final victory and Rome's demise.

Conclusion

I have argued that the mighty Roman Empire, with its power relationships structured to benefit the ruling elite at the expense of most of the population, while simultaneously trying to persuade that population that Rome sought their best welfare and offered them maximum benefit, was vulnerable to parts of the first-century Christian movement. Expressions of protest and resistance indicate, at least in part, that some did not find the social experience and imperial theology plausible and that the empire struggled to command loyalty. The empire's vulnerability lay not in a direct military attack, the threat of assassination or coup, the risk of economic boycott or strike, but in its inability to secure and maintain attachment and loyalty. The very existence of the early Christian communities and texts points to people who did not find the imperial system politically, economically, militarily, or ideologically (theologically) compelling. They created new relationships between ruler and ruled by constructing alternative, inclusive, more egalitarian communities with a more plausible worldview that asserted God's sovereignty and the agency of Jesus, disclosed the limitations of imperial claims, envisioned the certain defeat of Rome, and required appropriate social practices and behaviors. These communities, their practices, and their alternative worldview denied the empire not only the power to control the perceptions, practices, norms, loyalties, and attachments of the present and future, but also (irony of ironies) its very future with visions that it will succumb to the empire of God. Accordingly their threat lay in a combination of theological sabotage, social outflanking, and eschatological extermination.

> There is nothing more dangerous to an ideology than the presence of those who no longer take it for granted. Even without extensive argument, the mere presence of those who do not believe it, sows the seeds of doubt and prepares for that destructive question—But must things after all be as they are? . . . Christianity was at a profound level a deeply subversive force within the empire, because it denied and then undermined the religious legitimation of the ideology upon which the whole system was erected. (A. Kee 1985: 126)

But this does not go far enough. It is not only a matter of "thinking makes it so." In addition to the textual presentations of this alternative worldview, the early

Christian movement organized (Mann 1986: 301–40) in groups, religio-political assemblies (ἐκκλησίαι, *ekklesiai*) that constituted an inclusive, egalitarian, international movement with alternative social structures, rituals, and practices to embody these understandings. In the very midst of the empire, these "new relational fields" lived their vision of different power relationships and so expressed the conviction that the imperial world was not structured according to the divine will and that "things need not be as they are." In so thinking *and* living, they created an alternative empire that exposed Rome's lack of hold on people's loyalties and tapped into an uneasiness that sought different social structures and a compelling understanding of the world.

Notes

1. Momigliano (1987) does not even refer to Christian texts or actions in his discussion of religious opposition to Rome, nor does Bowersock, except to suggest that the "render to Caesar" saying accounts for a lack of Christian opposition (1987: 320). MacMullen includes only a passing reference to Revelation (1966: 145). Kautsky (1982) outlines the elements of aristocratically dominated empires, but all these seem untouched by the early Christians in the first century C.E. (Hanson and Oakman 1998: 69): control of the land and peasants, use of military force, an unchanging social structure, passivity, a popular preference for peace, the lack of any class struggle.

2. Herod, who acknowledges Rome as "masters of the world" (Josephus, *Ant.* 15.387), bore the same title (Josephus, *Ant.* 16.311). Unless indicated otherwise, all citations of ancient writers come from or refer to the Loeb Classical Library editions.

3. Something of the commitment to be seen to be invincible appears in the speech that Josephus has Titus, the emperor Vespasian's son and himself a future emperor (79–81 C.E.), give in addressing his cavalry before attacking the city of Tarichaea in Galilee (*B.J.* 3.472–73, 480; see Mattern 1999).

4. For Aristides, *Roman Oration*, see J. H. Oliver, "The Ruling Power: A Study of the Roman Empire in the Second Century after Christ through the Roman Oration of Aelius Aristides," *Transactions of the American Philosophical Society* 43 (1959): 871–1003.

5. Roman occupation meant a census, an accounting of the resources that would be taxed (Josephus, *Ant* 18.1–3).

6. Stakes in the power game were high. In the first century, at least four emperors were murdered, Gaius Caligula in 41, Claudius in 54, Vitellius in 69, and Domitian in 96. A fifth, Nero, committed suicide in 68 after being declared a public enemy.

7. There was also the very bottom layer of the social structure, comprised of the degraded and expendables. These were people with no skills but only their bodies for labor, and those who performed little labor such as criminals, beggars, the physically deformed, and the sick. Estimates number this group between 5 and 10 percent (Lenski 1966: 280–84).

8. Adopting a subjective genitive reading of πίστις Χριστοῦ.

The Limits of Ethnic Categories 21

NICOLA DENZEY

Contemporary Ethnic Theory

WHAT DO MODERN ANTHROPOLOGISTS AND SOCIOLOGISTS mean by "ethnicity"? Ethnic identity is one way to delimit and define group identity. Determining or uncovering ethnicity involves examining how people articulate difference, the processes by which they draw boundaries between their own group and other groups. Ethnicity denotes an identity constructed, defined, maintained, and changed by and for a group. Within this group, members are bound together by a sense of kinship based on a set of cultural categories such as a shared history, nationhood, language, costume, ancestry, and law.

Some scholars maintain that ethnic identity provides the cultural equivalent to racial identity, where groups are associated through a perceived or posited biological lineage or kinship. The Swedish cultural anthropologist Uffe Østergård, for instance, suggests that *"ethnos* seems to be more suited to cultural than [to] biological or kinship differences" (1992: 32). Often, however, it is difficult to distinguish between the two categories, since both ethnic and racial groups perceive their ties of commonality as deriving from a shared ancestry or kinship. Similarly difficult can be the task of distinguishing ethnicity from religion. Religion, too, can tie members of a group together through common history, practices, and heritage. Religion and ethnicity both respond to changing social circumstance; both are shaped by humans who create and maintain these categories to define identity (MacKay 2000: 107). Certain expressions or manifestations of religion, such as scripture—the Torah within Jewish communities offers an instructive example here—may act as a strong force that ties an ethnic group to its past, building a sense of shared identity or mandate (Romanucci-Ross and de Vos 1995: 21). Alternatively, there are individuals who have fallen away from a religiously defined ethnic group but maintain membership on a secular basis—for example, secular Jews. At the same time, religion and ethnicity may work at cross-purposes. As psychologist and anthropologist George de Vos notes, religious conversion can provoke individuals to deemphasize their ethnic identity and to emphasize in its place participation in a new, transcendent, or universalist community (1995: 21).

In the past thirty years, many scholars of ethnic theory have aligned themselves according to two positions: primordialist and circumstantialist. The second position (which later developed a third, the constructivist movement) grew in response to the perceived limitations of the earlier primordialist school. Proponents of this first position define ethnic identity from "objective" features including language, dress, territory, religion, kinship, and customs. American anthropologist Manning Nash, for instance, defines as a "single recursive metaphor" three cultural markers: kinship, commensality, and religious cult (1989: 11). Ethnic group members feel loyalty, trust, and a sense of commonality with one another because they perceive each other as kin, even if they share no biological ties (Scott 1990: 151; Dubetsky 1976: 435). In the primordialist position, ethnicity and religion alike are perceived as a priori, irreducible social categories.

One of the troubling implications of the primordialist position, when we apply it to the problem of ethnicity in the ancient world, is that it suggests that the content or essential characteristics of distinct ethnicities can be universally known and defined. If we determine the language, location, religion, kinship, and customs of a group, we succeed in determining its true or authentic identity. This position presupposes that there is such an entity as an ethnic group, or such a quality as ethnicity, based on a fixed, predetermined, and often assumed set of cultural markers or categories. This considerably oversimplifies the reality of social groups in the ancient world, concerning which we often have only incomplete and biased data. To give an example, let us imagine that we are Christians living in first-century Antioch. We speak Greek, as do our pagan and Jewish neighbors. Our family is divided (as were many in the ancient world) between those who espouse Christianity and those who have chosen not to convert from the collection of pagan religious options open to them. Like Jews, our family observes the Sabbath and abstains from foods the Hebrew Scriptures have designated as "unclean." We consider ourselves heirs to the true Israel, but through spiritual rather than biological kinship. Are we, then, part of an ethnic group? Which group? Are we Jewish, Christian, Barbarian, Greek, Roman, or Antiochene? What defines one group as identifiably ethnic and another not? Now let us imagine that our neighbors across the street are also Christian, but as gentile converts to Christianity and members of a different community, they do not observe the food prohibitions, but they too speak Greek and believe that Jesus is the Messiah. Are they part of

the same ethnic group as we are, or a different one? Are all these cultural categories—Jewish, Christian, Antiochene, Greek—truly ethnicities?

Primordialist definitions of ethnicity, then, can be too inchoate or generalizing to adequately accommodate the minutiae of difference we find in the range of
Christianities and Judaisms during the first few centuries of the Common Era.
Any definition will soon disintegrate under the force of dozens of commonsense
exceptions. These definitions also oversimplify the boundary-drawing process integral to human social existence. The same individual in first-century Antioch is
likely to identify herself differently in different situations as Jewish, Christian, Roman, or Antiochene, either in solidarity with or in reaction to other groups that
she encounters. If we assert that all these categories are indeed ethnicities, then
"ethnic identity" becomes vague enough to lose its meaning as a marker of difference. If we say that being Jewish constitutes an ethnicity but being Christian
does not, we have to be able to justify our choice of cultural categories and markers that comprise the content of our particular definition of Jewish ethnicity. Primordialist definitions of ethnicity may work if we are considering the ancient
world in generalizing terms, but it will likely not help us to understand individuals or groups unless we examine very carefully our own standards by which we
measure their own constructions of identity—otherwise, any attempts at reconstructing ancient ethnicities are more likely to obscure than to illuminate.

A second implication of the primordialist position, no less troubling than the
first, is that it may quickly degrade into a type of ethnic essentialism, such as the position that Jews were by nature belligerent, or hairsplitting with regard to the interpretation of their Law. Ethnic stereotypes often are reinforced in ideological literature composed by those outside the group. Modern scholars, too, may be influenced
by this ideological or polemical material, particularly if it expresses views already
consonant with their own prejudices. Early Christianity scholar John Meagher, for
instance, once famously remarked that "Antiquity, on the whole, disliked Jews"
(1979: 21), although our extant sources scarcely bear out such a conclusion. Similarly, an earlier generation of scholars often alluded to the attitude of superiority expressed by the Jewish community toward other groups (e.g., Borgen 1992: 125).
New Testament scholar Carl Holladay writes of the "rhetoric of moral superiority"
in Judaism that "derives from a well-developed sense of ethnic identity" (1992:
157). Yet extant Jewish sources rarely express such moral superiority, although this
attitude is abundantly evident in polemical constructions of Jewish identity from the
canonical Gospels. In fact, as early as the first century C.E. Philo (*Virt.* 141) vigorously defended his fellow Jews from the polemical charge of misanthropy.

The methodological pitfalls of the primordialist position, then, make it a dangerous (or at least, inadequate) tool to apply to the problem of early Christian ethnicity. But social theorists have posited a second, revisionist model for ethnic theory

that may prove to be more useful. Norwegian functionalist anthropologist Fredrik Barth proposes a model of ethnicity that is not founded upon a fixed character or essence for the group (Barth 1969; see also Østergård 1992: 36). Developed in reaction to the essentializing inherent in the primordialist perspective (see Eller and Coughlan 1993: 187–92), Barth's circumstantialist position examines groups not by a priori categories such as nationhood or language, but through a group's construction, manipulation, and transgression of boundaries that separate it from others. In other words, circumstantialists focus on contests over boundaries that demarcate and define the group, not the "cultural stuff that it encloses" (Barth 1969: 15). These boundaries are flexible; they are constructed in particular contexts and in response to particular issues. Historian Walter Pohl, for example, employs a circumstantialist model in his investigation of late Roman ethnic identity when he notes that ethnic communities in the Roman Empire were not "immutable biological or ontological essences, but the *results of historical processes*" (1998: 9; emphasis mine).

From a circumstantialist perspective, survival of an ethnic group is not the result of biological reproduction but the outcome of "a continued interest on the part of its members in maintaining the boundaries" (Goudriaan 1992: 76). As soon as the maintenance of ethnic identity is considered irrelevant, Goudriaan notes, the ethnic group disappears. We see this happen in the case of early Christianity, as Christians grow to become the dominant group within the empire. By the time of Constantine's "conversion" in 312 C.E., Christians had successfully redefined the limits of ethnicity and reached great enough numbers that they constituted a clear majority. With imperial patronage of Christianity now secure and the number of pagans clearly in decline, the rhetoric of ethnicity was no longer necessary, along with the concomitant linguistic and conceptual division of Christians as "we" and pagans (or Jews) as "they."

With the circumstantialist discourse of ethnicity, we are better served as we explore the problem of ethnic groups in antiquity. There was a broad range of social classifications that a group could negotiate in its process of self-definition, and which markers out of several they selected varied in response to their own requirements and perceptions of otherness. To return to our Jewish Christian Antiochene family, if the members chose to identify themselves as Christian and to identify their gentile Christian neighbors across the street as non-Christians, we are bound by the limits of their own self-definitions; we cannot impose upon them markers or limitations that they themselves did not emphasize. We cannot call them "ethnically Jewish" if they are emphasizing their status as Christians, even if they circumcise their sons and derive from a Jewish lineage. We are compelled to investigate, too, what historical and sociological factors led to those choices and definitions.

Because ethnicity still constitutes a relatively new conceptual category, much work remains to be done on its general applicability to the ancient world. This chapter offers only the broadest outlines of significant issues and problems that have yet to be fully explored. By drawing on elements from both primordialism and circumstantialism, one of the tasks of this chapter will be to explore the usefulness of the category of ethnicity for understanding Christianity's emergence from its mother religion Judaism. First, we must spend some time defining the term *ethnos* as it was employed in the ancient world. We can then approach the question of whether or not Judaism of the Roman world constituted an *ethnos* at all. Since the Jewish people of the Roman Empire fit many of the criteria modern ethnic theorists set out as defining an ethnic group—yet ancient Christians do not—we may question at which point both primordialists and circumstantialists would claim that Christianity ceases to become an "ethnicity" in the ancient world. The rhetoric and polemics of identity in the New Testament offer fine sources to mine here. Finally, we can investigate some of the ways in which early Christians usurped and altered the concept of *ethnos* to define themselves against other identifiable ethnic groups in the empire. However, a caveat is in order: if we understand ethnicity as an essentialized social reality in the ancient world—in other words, that Jews, Christians, and Romans objectively constituted actual, distinct ethnicities—we face difficulties. If we understand ethnicity as the process of boundary drawing by which one group distinguishes itself from a broader whole, we are better served. The remainder of this chapter, then, will focus on the problems and discourse of "otherness" between Jews, Christians, and Romans in antiquity and the different ways in which we might understand these problems and discourses as constructed in response to social context.

Ethnos as a Category in the Ancient World

Our first task when defining and discussing ethnicity in the ancient world is to establish the semantic nuances of the words *ethnos* and *ethne* in Greek. The instances of the word in Greek literature prior to the Christian era reveal that *ethnos* carried with it none of the resonances or associations that modern sociology assigns it. In the Liddell and Scott Greek-English lexicon (ninth ed., 1997: 480), the word *ethnos* designates distinct, discrete groups of people or animals living together, or a company or body of men. Greek writers employ the term to describe large amorphous groups of animals, synonymous with "swarms" or "flocks." For instance, Sophocles (c. 496–406 B.C.E.) labels groups of wild animals as an *ethnos* (Sophocles, *Phil.* 1147; *Ant.* 344) and Homer (eighth century B.C.E.) uses the terms *ethnea melissôn* and *ethnea ornithôn* to refer to swarms of bees and flocks of birds. The term can also point to a gender; Xenophon (c. 431–352 B.C.E.) writes of *to thêly ethnos*, "the feminine race" and Pindar (c. 522–438) of both the *ethnos gynaikôn* and the *ethnos anerôn*, the female and male "races" respectively. Homer wrote of *ethnos etarôn*, "a band of comrades" or *ethnos laôn*, a "band of men" in the *Iliad*, as well as the *klyta ethnea nekrôn*, the "glorious host of the dead" in the *Odyssey* (Østergård 1992: 31). Three observations are salient here. First, the word *ethnos* originally signified only "group" (or more precisely, "grouping"), not the particular identity of that group in contrast to another one. Second, it suggested that all members of that group were of the same type or category. Third, in the most archaic usage, the term *ethnos* carried neither positive nor negative connotations.

Beyond designating a group that lives and acts in common, the term *ethnos* comes into conventional use during the Hellenistic period as a term employed by one group to identify and classify a perceived other. For Hellenistic Greeks, those identifiable others included Egyptians, Persians, and Babylonians. The playwright Aeschylus (c. 525–456 B.C.E.), for instance, uses it of the Persians (Aeschylus, *Pers.* 43, 56). Aristotle (c. 384–322; *Pol.* 1324.b.10) applies the term to inhabitants of northwestern Greece whose social organization he considered "primitive" in comparison with the Hellenes of the *polis*. In other words, the word *ethnos* developed negative connotations as early as the third century B.C.E., designating a category of social behavior marked by difference, otherness, and implicit inferiority.

We find this new, particularist meaning of the term *ethnos* entering into the discourse of the Roman Empire. In its feminine form *ta ethne*, for instance, later Roman authors such as Appian (second century C.E.) use it to refer to foreigners or inhabitants of the provinces (*Bell. Civ.* 2.13, 26; cf. Herodianus 1.2.1). Arguably, any hegemonic society committed to expansion and domination would develop a discourse of otherness, in which boundaries are carefully demarcated between those who belong to a nation, race, or ethnicity and those who stand outside it. The discourse of ethnicity speaks to the need to define and preserve intact the limits of culture, to impose order on the confusing jumble of identities within and outside the *oikumene*.

Accordingly, we find during the Hellenistic and Roman periods the rise of ethnography as a distinct historiographical genre, a type of literary corollary to the ideology of political expansion. Ethnographic literature is marked by various strategies of distinction, by the drawing of clear conceptual boundaries. This new ethnography—first evident among Greek scientists as early as the fifth century B.C.E.—comes to be manifested in various historiographical genres, including history (e.g., Herodotus, Tacitus), chorography (e.g., Pomponius Mela), and geography (e.g., Strabo). Roman writers categorized "Barbarian" communities by origin (*origo*; *gens*), language (*sermo*, *lingua*), religion (*mores*; *cultus*; *instituta ritusque*), and outward appearance (*habitus corporum*) as well as by more culturally specific categories such as geography and climate, which the Romans understood as crucial to determining character and behavior. There are clear negative implications to this type of taxonomization inherent in the process of defining ethnicity. As Uffe Østergård notes, "when the Greeks called other peoples Barbarians, when the Christians classified non-Christians as Gentiles . . . they did this in order to make them recognize their inferior status. A basically asymmetrical relation was at stake" (1992: 35). This essentially conservative agenda fit Greek and then Roman goals of expansion, conquest, and assimilation. It also provided convenient foils against which to balance Greek, then Roman, notions of virtue.

The term *ethnos* within Hellenistic Jewish and early Christian literature preserves a rather different set of connotations than that which we find in the historiographical or philosophical literature of the classical world. The Arndt et al. *Greek-English Lexicon of the New Testament* (1979: 218) develops an emic–etic distinction between the masculine noun *ethnos*, "nation, people" and the feminine *ethne*, "foreigners."[1] *Ethnos* can refer to outsiders—it is used to refer, for instance, to the Samaritan people (Josephus, *Ant.* 18:85; Acts 8.9)—but more frequently it designates the Jewish people (Philo, *Decal.* 96).

Ethne, however, we often find employed etically. In the Septuagint, for instance, *ethne* translates the Hebrew term *goyim*—all those who stand outside Judaism. This etic use continues in the New Testament, where the word is rendered repeatedly in the Vulgate as *gentilis* and hence into English as "Gentiles," as in Romans 16.4, "all the churches of the *ethne*" (see also Gal 2.12; Eph 3.1). The term *ethne* designates those peoples who are not Christian; it is, in short, a term of exclusion. As an exclusionary term, the word also has the connotation of religious and moral superiority. We see this clearly in constructions such as the *anoma ethne* or "lawless heathen" of the first century *Martyrdom of Polycarp* 9:2. For the most part, however, the term *ethnos* has a range of discernable meanings in the seventy-one instances of the word preserved in the New Testament, and we cannot categorize them as neatly as Arndt et al. (1979) suggest—the term is employed both emically and etically.

To conclude, both the terms *ethnos* and *ethne*, as found in the New Testament, reveal little about what we now term "ethnicity" or "ethnic identity." The word reveals only that those who composed the various writings that comprise the New Testament followed the traditional language of the Septuagint when speaking of other groups of people who were not organized similarly. It is also important to note that the term *ethnos* is construed by modern cultural anthropologists in a manner more nuanced and sophisticated than in ancient parlance. One could argue that to speak of "Jewish ethnicity" or "Christian ethnicity" in antiquity is dangerously anachronistic, since both context and content of the term *ethnos* in the first century before the Common Era and the three centuries that followed remained rather different than what modern social theorists mean by ethnicity in the contemporary context.

The Function of Ethnicity in Roman Definitions of Judaism

Because Christianity emerged out of Judaism, it is worthwhile addressing whether or not primordialists could viably assert that Judaism formed a distinctive, identifiable ethnic group in antiquity, and what set of criteria they invoke to define it as such. The ancient Greeks first encountered the Jews as far back as the sixth century B.C.E., when Jewish refugees from the Babylonian Conquest settled in Sardis in Asia Minor, then called Lydia. Much later, Hellenistic ethnographers such as Hecataeus of Abdera (c. 300 B.C.E.) took a great and generally positive interest in Jewish culture. Overall, the Greeks depicted the Jews as a race of philosophers (Gager 1983: 39). Strabo (c. 63 B.C.E.–24 C.E.) identified the Jews as one of four *ethne* in Palestine, along with Idumeans, Gazeans, and Azoteans (Strabo, *Geogr.* 16.2, 2). The concept of Judaism as an *ethnos*, then, was first and foremost a Greek ethnographical construction. Under Greek rule, Jews themselves came to adopt the term, using it to articulate their own conceptions of nationhood; thus Josephus (c. 37–95 C.E.) in his *Antiquities of the Jews* borrows extensively from Strabo's detailed work on Jewish identity and culture. Philo (c. 20 B.C.E.–50 C.E.), too, employs the term *to ethnos* as a synonym for *oi Ioudaioi* (Philo, *Fug.* 185; *Mutat.* 191; *Abr.* 276). Often, Philo appears to use the term to describe the Jews as a "nation" or "people" set apart from "the whole human race" (Philo, *Spec.* 1.190, 2.263), or from "Greeks and barbarians" (Philo, *Opif.* 28; *Mos.* 2.12; *Mutat.* 35; *Legat.* 83, 102, 141, 145).

If Jews were to the Greeks and Romans a recognized, distinct *ethnos*, they were hardly an invisible minority. They were numerically stronger in the first two centuries of the Common Era than Christians, even after the destruction of the Jerusalem Temple in 70 C.E. Estimates place them at approximately six million out of a total population of sixty million, or between 6 and 10 percent of the population (Wilson 1995: 21). In certain regions, including Palestine, Syria, Egypt, and Asia Minor, their numbers were substantially higher (Wilson 1995: 21). The epigraphic and archaeological data suggest to Stephen Wilson that "Jews retained their identity" in the Roman Empire (Wilson 1995: 21) although they were well integrated into civic life, as the large synagogues at Sardis, Aphrodisias, and Ostia have revealed. Jewish communities also attracted a large number of proselytes, which certainly threatened any attempts by both Jews and Romans to keep Judaism distinct from *Romanitas*. The Roman patrician Seneca, in the first century, thus decried "the customs of this accursed race" that have "gained such influence that [the Jews] are now received throughout the whole world" (Seneca, in Augustine, *Civ. Dei* 6.11).

What measured "Jewish identity" in antiquity? Since the Jews had first caught the interest of Greek ethnographers, they had been identified according to a fairly narrow but consistent set of peculiarities we might understand as marks of ethnicity: they worshipped at the Jerusalem Temple; they circumcised their sons; they observed dietary laws (both Romans and Greeks found the Jewish refusal to eat pork, in particular, as highly peculiar); and they paid the Temple tax. From the second century B.C.E., the Jewish people constituted a protected minority with a distinctive and separate legal status. The emperor Augustus upheld the Jews' right—already established less formally for two centuries—to live according to their ancestral traditions (Philo, *Flaccus* 50; *Legat.* 152–58). Observation of the Sabbath was theirs by legal right, as was the right to recuse themselves from military duty and to pay obeisance to the emperor through prayers rather than through participation in the imperial cult. No other subject peoples held such privileges.

Consistently over time, delineations of Jewish ethnicity shifted—often markedly—during the Roman period, particularly in the wake of the Jewish revolts and the destruction of the Jerusalem Temple in 70 C.E. With the destruction of the Temple, Temple worship could no longer define Jewish identity. The obligation to pay the Temple tax remained after the Temple's destruction, but only because the Roman governments continued to exact it from those Jews who identified themselves as such. With the disbanding of the Sanhedrin and the expulsion of the Jews from Palestine by Hadrian's imperial decree (135 C.E.), the Jewish-run "nation" of Judaea ceased to be a political entity, leaving Jewish identity determined only by its religious or ethnical features. Even these features were fluid, however, as Jews strove to redefine the limits of religious behavior away from Temple observance and toward participation in community-oriented synagogues. For their part, many Romans during this period also actively embraced elements of Jewish identity. As John Gager observes, "not even the war of 66–73 proved that Judaism was incompatible with *Romanitas*" (1983: 66). Menachem Stern also describes the first century as one "marked by the unprecedented diffusion of Jewish ideas and customs among various classes of society. Jewish identity, as its customs and religion entered the Roman mainstream, quickly became divorced from any notion of biological kinship, or even from any concept of "nationhood" (in *Greek and Latin Authors on Jews and Jerusalem* 3, 362).

That the category of Judaism as an *ethnos* becomes inchoate in the first and second centuries is hardly surprising within the ideological parameters of the empire. As a strategy of distinction, ethnicity emphasizes differences rather than similarities. However, a strategy that delimits otherness can only exist within a particular political climate. Within Rome's totalizing regime, Roman ideologies of empire (unlike those of the Late Republic) were concerned with erasing distinctions, not reifying them. Thus in the darkest years for the Jews following the Bar Kokhba revolt (135–38 C.E.), rabbinic literature preserves evidence of severe imperial persecution: cultural markers such as circumcision, Sabbath observance, study of

Torah, and the ordination of rabbis were outlawed (*m.Sabb.* 4.11; *b.B.Bat.* 60b; *b.Ber.* 61b). As Stephen Wilson observes, "Jews were being compelled to live in a manner indistinguishable from Gentiles" (1995: 8).

If, then, Jews of the second century were no longer exempted by laws that disallowed groups from maintaining visible markers of ethnicity in the Roman Empire and had lost their major religious focus in the Jerusalem Temple, did they still constitute an ethnic group? One social theorist, Koen Goudriaan, asserts that they did: "the Jews were and remained a distinct ethnic group just because they themselves as well as the non-Jews focused on Jewish loyalty, in whatever form, to the Law" (1992: 94). Goudriaan argues that Hellenization—and by extension, Romanization—did not automatically entail changes in Jewish ethnic identity, since that identity was based upon a single, irreducible marker: Jews remained "loyal" to Torah.

Yet there are two problems with Goudriaan's conclusion: first, it presupposes that observation of Torah constituted for Jews—and by extension, for us as modern social theorists—an objective measure of ethnicity. But one could argue that the Jews' adherence to Torah was entirely a feature of Jewish religion, not Jewish ethnicity. Second, following Goudriaan's logic, any non-Jews who observed Torah—and there were many gentile converts in the first two centuries of the Roman Empire—would automatically be ethnic Jews. Since Christians likewise observed the Law—although in certain circumstances they did so differently from many Jews—Goudriaan would also have to concede that these Christians were ethnically Jews. To solve this conundrum, a more circumstantialist position might get us closer to the truth. Jews of the first century—particularly Jews of the Diaspora—were deeply engaged with drawing, redrawing, and transgressing ethnic boundaries in a variety of ways (see Holladay 1992: 153). Victor Tcherikover (1970) has emphasized the importance of cultural assimilation for the Jews living in the empire beginning with Hadrian's reign in 117 C.E. Hellenization and Romanization evinced not a loss of Jewish ethnic identity, but new understandings of the contours of that identity.

In summary, it is difficult to access notions of Jewish ethnic separateness in the first three centuries of the empire and the two centuries that preceded it. Accordingly, modern scholars read sources and evidence very differently. Our understanding of the degree to which the Jews maintained a distinct society or actively participated in the broader cultural life of the empire is a matter of interpretation, not fact. The range of interpretations on this matter can be revealed in the professional disagreements of seminal scholars of Judaism such as Elias Bickerman, Martin Hengel (1974/1998), Victor Tcherikover (1970), and E. R. Goodenough (1988), who perceived very different levels of Jewish engagement with Hellenism and Romanization. None of these scholars misrepresents the status of Jewish identity; each simply reads the evidence differently. The difference of perspectives between them serves to highlight the complexity of assigning identities to a group of people in the ancient world based on insufficient and often biased ideological material.

Ethnicity and Ethnic Constructions in the New Testament

Jesus was a Jew living within Judaea. There can be little ambiguity as to his religious affiliation. Yet the Gospels' accounts of his life, composed two generations after his death, reflect the crisis of self-identification that the earliest Christians faced. Neither fully Jewish nor fully Roman, early Christians sought to forge for themselves a new identity. On the one hand, early Christians found themselves beyond the limits of Jewish ethnicity as represented by the Jewish legal status as a distinct nationhood and society. At the same time, as mixed communities of dissident Jews and Gentiles with a utopian and messianic orientation, Christians were more inclined to define themselves as the "true Israel" than as Romans.

Just as we face ambiguity when we seek to determine whether a category of practice such as dietary regulations define ethnicity or religion, the earliest Christians faced similar confusion on where to draw the lines demarcating Jewish religion from Jewish custom. If Jews could be defined ethnically by their monotheism, their unique observances of Torah such as food restrictions, purity laws, and so on, these were the very markers that also defined them religiously. But these same features also defined earliest Christianity. If, on the other hand, Jews could be defined ethnically by their claim to nationhood or their structures of kinship, so could Christians, who also used such categories in a similar way to define themselves. According to categories of modern ethnic theory, it becomes very difficult to distinguish these groups from one another. Instead, we may be less confounded if we search for moments in Christian texts when these ethnic categories become disputed and contested between Christians and Jews, as they strove to formulate new self-definitions. For the purposes of this chapter, we will confine our investigation to two "case studies" in ethnical self-determination: the Gospels of Mark and Matthew.

Our earliest of the canonical Gospels, the Gospel of Mark, reflects the growing chasm between communities of more traditionally oriented Jews and those Jews and proselytes to Judaism who believed that Jesus was the awaited Messiah. Written in the shadow of the Jewish war and the destruction of the Jerusalem Temple in 70 C.E., the gospel reflects some of the earliest attempts of Jesus' followers to define themselves against Judaism. This conflict is articulated most clearly in Jesus' vigorous debates against the Jewish religious authorities. The Pharisees argue with Jesus about fasting (2.18–22), the Sabbath (2.23–3.6), pollution (7.1–8.23, 2.22), divorce (10.2–12), and paying taxes (12.13–17). Significantly, these were all customs that Jews retained in the empire through legal right, yet they were also marks of difference from Roman custom. In a concrete sense, they defined the contents of Jewish identity in the context of the empire.

Mark calls into question the centrality of the Jewish law, particularly rulings on purity and Sabbath observance. In a lengthy discussion of Jewish purity laws (7.1–23) Jesus debates with the Pharisees about the necessity of hand washing before dining (7.2–5) and dietary laws (*kashrut*) (7.14–23). Jesus clearly—and remarkably—abrogates the food laws, declaring that "whatever goes into a person from outside cannot defile . . . for it is what comes out of a person that defiles" (7.18b). To emphasize this point, Mark erases any ambiguity of interpretation with his declaration, "Thus he declared all food clean" (7.19). We learn from this passage at least two things. First, Mark's audience needs to have the contours of Jewish observance mapped out for them; he has to tell them explicitly at 7.3–4 that all Jews follow purity laws. Second, it is equally clear that Mark's community no longer follows these laws; they define themselves against them rather than by them, and thus by extension they define themselves against one feature of Jewish ethnicity.

We find a similar perspective governing Mark's interpretation of the scope of the Sabbath. Twice, Mark recounts controversies over Sabbath observation (2.23–28, 3.1–6). As generations of scholars have noted, in neither case does Jesus reject the necessity of keeping the Sabbath, but suggests mitigating circumstances: it is subject to humane demands (3.4). Still more remarkably, Jesus insinuates that it can be displaced by messianic authority: the Son of Man is Lord even of the Sabbath (2.28).

Scholars have been divided on whether the author of Mark's Gospel was Jewish or Gentile, but recent scholarship has provided persuasive evidence that he was a Gentile, living in a community of Christians in Syria, possibly between Tyre and Galilee (Theissen 1991: 236–49). Because of their largely gentile background, and in contrast to other Jewish Christian groups, this community did not see themselves as continuing Israel. They apparently did not follow purity laws or laws of *kashrut*; Jesus as Messiah also came, in a concrete and immediate way, to replace the Temple as the focus of religious identity. In a real sense, then, the Christians of Mark's community rejected the very heart of Jewish religion, and they drew nothing we might call "ethnic identity" from Judaism. Strikingly, in the two instances when we find the word *ethnos* in the gospel, it reflects Mark's universalism. In Mark 11.17 Jesus notes that the Jerusalem Temple is not exclusively for Jews but is a "house of prayer for all nations"; in Mark 13.10, Jesus notes that the gospel must be preached "to all nations."

Unlike the Gospel of Mark, the Gospel of Matthew apparently emerged from a Jewish-Christian context. Yet the ambiguities of identity politics are never resolved but merely take a different form than they had in Mark. Matthew's Gospel intensifies the field of debate: it excoriates the Jewish authorities with Jesus' harsh antitheses against the Scribes and Pharisees, while simultaneously emphasizing Jesus as the most authoritative interpreter of Torah. The Jewishness of this gospel—and by extension Matthew's community—is clear in Matthew's refusal to translate Aramaic terms, his liberal use of citations from the Old Testament, and above all, his tendency to offer the "nations" or *ethne* as negative examples (see 5.47, 6.7, 18.17).

Matthew's treatment of Jewish law stands in sharp contrast to Mark's. In his version of the narrative in which Jesus and his disciples pluck grain on the Sabbath (Mt 12.1–8), Matthew (as Luke) excises the incendiary messianism of Jesus' claim that the Son of Man rules the Sabbath as its Lord. Similarly, Matthew excludes Mark's claim that all foods are now clean (Mk 7:19) as well as the claim that things from the outside cannot defile (Mk 7.18–19). Matthew's Jesus never abandons Jewish law; by contrast, Jesus comes not to abolish but to fulfill (Mt 5.17). At the same time, Jesus' pronouncement of woes against the Scribes and Pharisees suggests that there was a high degree of rancor between Matthew's community and other Jewish communities. Most likely Matthew's community faced significant opposition from the wider body of Jews, who (judging from the emphasis on Jesus as the new Moses) accused them of ignoring or transgressing the Law.

This rejection of the Law, however, Matthew's Gospel vigorously disputes. Jesus' altercations with the Jewish authorities center around not merely Law but also custom: eating with Gentiles and sinners (9.11), fasting (9.14), the Sabbath (12.2, 14), hand washing (15.1, 12), divorce (19.3), and civic disobedience (22.15–16; see Wilson 1991: 51). Although his community may have loosened some of the restrictions of postbiblical Jewish customs, they likely observed the Sabbath, kept kosher, and (although the gospel is silent on this issue) circumcised their male children. In terms of ethnicity, while Jews and Jewish Christians defined themselves as distinct from one another by virtue of their religious views—particularly their understanding of Jesus as Messiah—outsiders coexisting with them in the same city may have had a difficult time distinguishing them as ethnically distinct.

From the Gospels of Mark and Matthew, then, we are unable to detect a discourse of ethnicity that corresponds to a "primordialist" position. In short, we are unable to find any notion of Christian ethnicity distinct from Jewish ethnicity. Yet Christians of the first century no longer necessarily identified themselves as Jews, although they shared with their mother religion its monotheism, emphasis on Torah, and other postbiblical customs. Here, circumstantialist constructions of ethnicity offer us a more useful model for understanding the dilemma faced by the earliest Christians. The variety of positions early Christians assumed vis-à-vis Judaism reflects an elaborate, extended process of self-definition. They were in the process of drawing and redrawing boundaries, thereby exploring and extending their interpretation of community.

In this summary so far, I have intentionally neglected the case of Paul and his communities. Since the canonical Gospels represent relatively late traditions and exercises in first-century Christian self-definition, Paul remains our best witness for earlier material; his active ministry likely spanned the years 50–70 C.E. I have saved Paul until the end of this discussion because he developed a distinctive notion of "nationhood" that had lasting, measurable influence on the manner in which Christian communities defined themselves for hundreds of years to follow.

Paul himself rarely uses the word *ethnos* in his undisputed letters, employing it only when he refers to the Abrahamic covenant in which God extends his promise to all the *ethne* (Gn 17.4). The biblical doctrine of covenantal election generally circumscribes Jewish ethnic identity. Beyond ratifying nationhood by divine favor, it also suggests both biological and spiritual kinship. Yet Paul invokes the category of "nation" as part of his message that Gentiles are now invited into salvation in Christ (e.g., Rom 4.17, 10.19; Gal 3.8). In Paul's understanding, God's promise to Abraham that Abraham would be the father of the "nations" meant that the ethnical identity of God's Chosen People ought not to be understood as founded solely upon Jewish biological kinship. Whether or not Paul intended to abrogate Judaism in some absolute sense has been a matter of vigorous academic debate (see Reuther 1974; Gager 1983); what is abundantly clear, however, is that Paul considered God's promise of salvation as extending beyond the circumscribed Septuagintal boundaries of Jews as a "chosen people" to include gentile converts.

Paul retains the idea of divine favor defining ethnic identity; yet he deemphasizes biological kinship and emphasizes in its place spiritual community. Paul addresses his communities as "my brethren" no fewer than sixty-five times. In his instructions to them, Paul employs a distinct discourse of otherness. He refers to those outside the community simply as "the outsiders" (*hoi exô*) (1 Cor 5.12 and 13; 1 Thes 4.12; Col 4.5), or the "unrighteous" (*adikoi*; 1 Cor 6.1, 9). We find a corresponding emphasis on "language of belonging" (on Pauline as the "elect," see 1 Thes 1.4; Rom 8.33; Col 3.12; 1 Cor 1.27; Eph 1.4). Accordingly, early Pauline communities policed their boundaries using a rhetoric of difference that circumstantialists might easily construe as a "discourse of ethnicity," even if the "cultural stuff" that Paulinism enclosed may have differed in no significant way from that of other Jewish Christian groups in the first century, in terms of language, dress, and customs.

The Function of Ethnicity in Early Christianity 100–325 C.E.

The past twenty years has witnessed a plethora of studies that explore the sociological factors at work in the formation and development the Jesus movement and early Palestinian Christianity. Here, the work of Gerd Theissen, Richard Horsley,

Sean Freyne, and John Dominic Crossan has greatly illuminated our understanding of Christianity's struggles for self-definition within the matrix of Palestinian Judaism. Yet their work only underscores the fact that before the second century, any divisions between Christians and Jews is likely to be artificial, the product of our own desire to categorize. Indeed, there is some evidence that pagans had difficulty distinguishing between the two. Stephen Wilson notes, "During the early decades of the Christian movement they were, to outside eyes, largely indistinguishable from Jews and therefore treated as such" (1995: 16).

If we attempt to construct an ethnicity for Christians from the end of the first century until the Edict of Milan (313 C.E.) and Constantine's conversion (325 C.E.), we soon run into significant difficulties. The earliest Christians were Jews, and yet, as we have seen from the Gospels, their belief that Jesus was the awaited Messiah quickly put them in conflict with Judaism. If we attempt to classify early Christians initially as of Jewish ethnicity by kinship and biological ancestry, we are confounded when, as early as twenty years after Jesus' death, Paul opens up his communities to Gentiles. The problem of constructing ethnicity becomes clear: No longer Jews by blood, the Christians of Pauline communities also did not share any group identity beyond a religious conviction; they were of different social classes, citizens and noncitizens, either Jews or Gentiles by birth. The Pauline Christians also comprised, by the second century, the bulk of Christians in the empire. For these Christians, their only kinship revolved around a symbolic participation in an eschatologically oriented "body of Christ."

By the middle of the second century, Christians had separated from Judaism, but had also lost many of the cultural markers that defined them in Roman eyes as members of a distinct society. There was no distinctively Christian dress, no food or purity rules, no one quarter of the Roman city where Christians alone lived. Archaeologist Graydon Snyder points out the absence of material evidence for Christianity prior to 180 C.E.; it is impossible to distinguish Christian from non-Christian culture in funerary art, symbols, inscriptions, and even buildings. Snyder notes that it took over a century for Christians to develop a distinctive mode of self-expression (1985: 2). With no identifiable markers of dress, speech, or custom, any Christian community before the Edict of Milan in 313 C.E. was more likely to have been what anthropologist Benedict Anderson terms an "imagined community" (1991), constructed in the hearts and minds of a scattered and otherwise culturally diverse population of Christians. Living under at least the threat of persecution, Christian individuals might have been well known to one another. But they might not have, considering their numbers were so low. For 200 C.E., their numbers ranged from 1 to 1.5 million, or 1.4 percent to 2.5 percent of the population of the empire, which was, at the time, around 60 million (MacMullen 1984: 109–10, 135 n. 26). Robert Grant (1977/1978: 6) estimates that

7,000 Christians lived in Rome at the end of the second century, that is, about 1 percent of the total population of 700,000, or 0.36 percent of the total population of the empire.

Paradoxically, this absence of clear ethnicity whether perceived, constructed, or claimed—combined with their miniscule numbers—actually posed a challenge to Christians in the Roman world. Jews were a recognized and often privileged ethnic minority in the empire. Christians were not. Jews had the weight of antiquity behind their privilege; Christianity, as it separated from Judaism, lost that claim to antiquity. Christianity, as a newcomer on the religious horizon, faced all the problems of a *nouveau riche*. It was a religion without a history, without a clearly defined *ethnos*.

Yet often Christians did find themselves defined as (or defined against) an *ethnos* in the eyes of their pagan contemporaries, primarily through their association with the earlier-defined, perceived *ethnos* of Judaism. Within Roman conceptual horizons, Christianity constituted yet another category of otherness. Christians struggled to defend themselves against such categorization, without successfully finding a home in the broader discourses of membership in the Roman world. They were neither Jews nor pagans, but something entirely other. That otherness marked them as dangerously liminal in Roman society. British historian Robert Markus emphasizes the manner in which outsiders to the Christian cause were more than happy to reinforce this identity of essential otherness by suspicion, calumny, and pogrom: "the whole world conspired together to define the Christians as a visibly identifiable group, or rather groups, sharply marked out in society" (1980–81: 3).

If during the second and third centuries Christians sought to struggle against pagan definitions, it was often in response to implicit comparisons with Judaism. A Jewish critic cited by Origen reveals a deep antipathy between the two groups as Christians sought to develop a new self-identity: "Why do you take your origin from our religion, and then, as if you are progressing in knowledge, despise these things, although you cannot name any other origin for your doctrine than our law?" (Origen, *Cels.* 2.4). Christian ambivalence toward their own spiritual origins reflected a struggle during which time, as John Gager puts it, "Christianity had to deal with Judaism from beneath, that is, from a position of cultural and social inferiority" (1983: 114).

The great apologists of the second century adopt no single strategy to explain Christians' relation to the Jews. Some, like Athenagoras (flourished 176–80 C.E.), ignore the Jews altogether. Others confront the matter more directly and polemically: the *Letter to Diognetus* (c. 130 C.E.) advocates abstention from "the silliness, deceit, fussiness and pride of the Jews" (*Diogn.* 3–4; Loeb trans.). As Stephen Wilson (1995: 31) observes, when the author of the epistle notes that Christians lack an ancestral homeland, language, or distinctive customs, he implicitly contrasts his community with the Jews. The *Letter to Diognetus* also defines Judaism here according to ethnic—as opposed to religious—categories; we are left again with the implication that while Jews constituted some sort of a recognizable ethnic group, Christians did not.

Ultimately, second-century Christians redrew their own limits of ethnicity so as to recircumscribe their conceptual world, placing themselves back securely in the center of that world. They constructed their own definitions of *ethnos* to suit their unique circumstances vis-à-vis the empire. The process of Christian boundary drawing often required that first, new cultural categories of difference had to be constructed, and then, asserted as significant. In a revealing passage, second-century apologist Aelius Aristides marks out Christians as a new people or *ethnos*: Christians are the ones who,

> beyond all the [other] nations (*ethne*) of earth, have found the truth. For they know the God who is creator and maker of everything, and they worship no other God but him. . . . They do not commit adultery, they do not engage in illicit sex, they do not give false testimony, they do not covet other people's goods, they honor father and mother and love their neighbors, they give just decisions. (*Apol.* 15)

As social historian Wayne Meeks has noted, Aristides in his tractate defines Christians first against Babylonians, then Greeks, Egyptians, and finally Jews. These groups, as we have seen, clearly constituted *ethne* in Roman ethnography. Aristides next proceeds to evaluate the religious and social contours of each *ethne*. The Jews Aristides lauds for their monotheism, but also for their compassion in caring for the needy (*Apol.* 14). Meeks observes, "the traits upon which he focuses to distinguish among these different peoples are theological and moral. . . . Thus Aristides has written an apology in the form of comparative ethnography" (1993: 8). Meeks also notes that the Christians are not a natural *ethnos* like the Babylonians, Egyptians or Jews, yet Aristides assumes people will regard them as such (1993: 8).

In a famous passage of his study *The Mission and Expansion of Christianity in the First Three Centuries*, famed church historian Adolf von Harnack characterized Christians of the second and third centuries as a "third race" (*tertium genus*), caught between the conflicting identities of Jews and Romans. The entire sixth chapter of Harnack's book explores Christian self-definition—an ambitious endeavor that set the stage for scores of books on the same topic . All these studies focus on the manner in which Christians crafted a new identity for themselves as a group *extranei a turbis*, "set out from the mass of people," as the North African bishop Tertullian described the Christian community (Tertullian, *Apol.* 31). The fledgling Christian movement came to be considered by some a "third race"—neither Roman nor Jewish but something that confounded the customary strategies of distinction (*Kerygmata Petrou* in Clement of Alexandria, *Strom.* 6.5.41; see also Harnack 1908: 240–78). Ethics, not ethnicity, shaped this new Christian rhetoric of nationhood. Accordingly, Romans often noted Christians as a distinct "people" for positive traits: their aversion to infant exposure and abortion; their care for the ill, indigent, and widowed; and their refusal to attend *munera* or gladiatorial displays (Athenagoras, *Leg.* 31–36; Justin, *1 Apol.* 26, 65–67; Theophilus, *Auto.* 3.9–15). In the Christian discourse of the second and third centuries, morality defined ethnicity, producing what Meeks has termed an "ethnography of morals" (1993: 8).

The Limits of Ethnicity

Finally, let us return to the manner in which Romans engaged in or repudiated the process of ethnicity production. Roman literature and sciences—best reflected in ethnographic writings—constructed a discourse of ethnicity; Roman law ratified ethnic categories by setting parameters for identity, primarily through granting or withholding citizenship. Yet in the expanding, assimilating atmosphere of the empire, strategies of distinction often worked at cross-purposes with cultural hegemony. Accordingly, citizenship could no longer function to police the boundaries of ethnic culture. The *Constitutio Augustiniana* in 212 under the emperor Caracalla granted citizenship to nearly everyone in the empire. Cities lost their status as "significant granters of identity" (Mauss 2000: 435).

By the time of Constantine's conversion in 312 C.E., Christianity became the standard against which foreign people were judged and categorized. We find emerging at that time what historian Michael Mauss has termed a "teleological ethnography of empire" (2000: 436). As Mauss astutely notes, ethnography becomes, in a Christian empire, heresiology. By the fourth century, the categories of "orthodox" and "heresy" had displaced many earlier strategies of distinction. Augustine speaks of the "wide world, which has always been inhabited by many differing peoples." He reflects that these peoples had, in their time, a multiplicity of different customs, religions, languages, forms of military organization, and clothing. Yet Augustine acknowledges only two ontological categories in place of ethnic identities: there existed citizens of the earthly world (*civitas terrena*) and citizens of the City of God (*civitas dei*) (Augustine, *Civ. Dei* 14.1).

From the very earliest identifiable Christian ideological discourse, we find a marked tendency to erase, not to emphasize, ethnicity and other strategies of distinction. Christian communities, then, were often marked internally not so much by otherness, but by the erasure of difference, whether that difference were marked by gender, class, or ethnicity. When Paul claimed in Galatians 3.28 that the Christian community is "all one in Christ Jesus"—that is, in the idealized community that Paul strove to actualize—no room existed for ethnic categories such as "Jew" or "Greek," nor for distinctions of class and gender. Paul's claim that Christians formed a class-

less, genderless, ethnically homogeneous alternate society only became more ideologically freighted as Christianity grew to develop a distinctive rhetoric of empire. As
Walter Pohl notes, ethnic diversity could become a metaphor for disunity (1998: 58);
as such, it could not serve the interests of empire, either pagan or Christian.

In the final analysis, however, we scholars must pay attention to our own constructivist and anachronistic tendencies as we read ancient ideological texts. Ethnicity as a conceptual category, like the discourse of race, is thoroughly modern, having first arrived in the *Oxford English Dictionary* (1953 ed.). It is highly unlikely that
Christians of the first few centuries thought of themselves as an ethnic minority in
the same manner as, let us say, Mexican Americans might in contemporary America.
To assert that they did would be to construct a self-identity for ancient Christians
that does possible violence to the manner in which they thought of themselves. A
second danger is one of essentializing ethnicity. As we do find a discourse of ethnicity—in, for instance, the language of the Christians as a "third nation"—we
should be aware that it derived from a particular group of Christians living in a specific context. We cannot imagine that all Christians of the first three centuries defined themselves against either Judaism or paganism. The discourse of ethnicity,
when we find it, served the ideological agenda of a nascent Christian orthodoxy.
Other Christians apparently had no difficulty keeping the boundaries between themselves and others inchoate or fluid. Christians were buried with their pagan family
members; often read and quoted Homer and Plato; and shared dress, language, a
moral code, and deep, time-honored conceptual understandings of physics, geography, and cosmology, with pagans and often enough, with Jews as well.

Ethnic theory is a relatively new field, and we need to approach thoughtfully its
viability for elucidating the ancient world. Careful work would examine the manner
in which diverse groups in antiquity employed ethnographic material into their discourses of otherness, and under what circumstances they were compelled to do so.
Walter Pohl (1998: 19–20) offers a series of critical questions to guide future work:
When and where did ethnic distinctions matter? What were the cognitive and the political strategies that made use of and created distinct ethnic identities? How diffused
were clear notions of ethnic identity inside and outside the communities in question?
Which criteria were most commonly used to distinguish between ethnic groups, and
what forms of social cohesion did they put into the foreground? These questions
could guide many an inquiry into the limits of ethnicity in the ancient world.

Notes

1. Anthropologists speak of understandings people hold within a culture as *emic* and
understandings developed from an outside perspective as *etic*.

ECONOMIC QUESTIONS V

The Economy of First-Century Palestine: State of the Scholarly Discussion

22

PHILIP A. HARLAND

Introduction

STUDENTS OF JUDAISM AND CHRISTIANITY in the first centuries have become increasingly aware of the need to position their subjects in relation to concrete realities of life, including economic realities. The economic realities of Palestine (encompassing Judaea, Samaria, and Galilee) had drawn the attention of scholars in several fields in the interwar years, but there has been a resurgence in attention since the 1960s. The purpose of this chapter is to sketch in broad strokes the state of the question regarding our knowledge of Palestine's economy, outlining some key issues of debate among scholars and pointing toward some directions for future research. Though in several respects our knowledge of economic realities in first-century Palestine has increased, especially in connection with issues of land, agriculture, trade, and taxation, several ongoing areas of debate, unsolved problems, and methodological difficulties remain. In general Palestine's economy, much like that of other regions in the Roman Empire, was agrarian, based on peasants producing food, but there is room for considerable debate over other features, including the level and importance of trade.

Conceptual Preliminaries

The ancients did not discuss the economy and economic issues in the way that moderns do. From their viewpoint the modern compartmentalization of life into political, social, economic, and religious sectors would be difficult to comprehend; these aspects of life in general comprised a unified whole for those living in first-century Palestine. Thus, as Douglas E. Oakman suggests, "it is necessary to acquire a special set of conceptual lenses when reading ancient literature, including the Bible, in order to perceive appropriately the nature and character of ancient economics" (1991: 34). The definition of economy that is used here would not have occurred to a person in the ancient context. Scholars of antiquity must define the economy in their own terms, while being very aware that they do so, so that the overall workings of ancient societies can be made comprehensible in the present.

For purposes of surveying recent developments in the study of ancient economies and the social sciences, Carney defines an *economy* as "that complex of activities and institutions through which a society manages the production and allocating of goods and services, and organizes and maintains its workers. . . . 'The economy' is not just an aggregate of individuals' actions. Groups, and overall societal interests, are involved" (1975: 140). Politics, power, and social structures are closely related to the nature of the economy since specific groups in a society may attempt to maximize society's utilities, production, and distribution to their own advantage over other groups. In connection with this, the economic situation of specific groups in society, whether groups of peasants or aristocrats, tenants or landowners, hired laborers or craftsmen, will be important.

Since the late 1950s the social sciences have paid greater attention to the nature of peasant societies and have organized a new subdiscipline within anthropology, economic anthropology (cf. Carney 1975; Herskovitz 1952; Wolf 1966; Oakman 1991). Economic anthropology and social scientific studies of peasant societies have provided important insights into the nature of economies in preindustrial societies, some of which are relevant here.

With respect to the social scientific study of ancient economies, Max Weber, as early as 1896, addressed such issues in *The Agrarian Sociology of Ancient Civilizations* (1976; cf. Weber 1952). Works on comparative economics, particularly the studies included in *Trade and Market in the Early Empires* (Polanyi, Arensberg, and Pearson 1957), have been very influential, as has the work of Polanyi (1968). As Carney notes, Polanyi's work basically caused the concept of "economy" in preindustrial society to be redefined along the lines of Carney's definition given above (1975: 139–42). Overall, Polanyi helped to provide a framework for conceptualizing various types of ancient economies or economic exchange systems, including reciprocity, redistribution, and market economies.

There are other social scientific studies of peasant or agrarian societies that are notable for their subsequent influence on students of Judaism and Christianity in antiquity. These include Robert Redfield's *Peasant Society and Culture* (1956), which presents the subsequently influential concepts of "great" and "little" traditions, reflecting elites and peasantry perspectives respectively; Richard A. Horsley and John S. Hanson (1985/1989/1999) and David Fiensy (1991), for instance, are indebted to Redfield in their analyses of economic relations in first-century Palestine. Eric R. Wolf's anthropological study *Peasants* (1966) explains from a Marxian perspective several economic aspects of peasant societies, especially the mechanisms of subsistence-level farming; Oakman's (1986: 49–54) study of the economic context of Jesus draws on this in constructing helpful economic models of the peasant freeholder, tenant, and wage-laborer. Also influential is Gerhard Lenski's *Power and Privilege* (1966), which presents a macro-sociological conceptual framework for discussing social stratification in peasant economies; ancient historian G. Älfoldy (1985) adapted Lenski's model for use in studying the bifurcated social stratification of the Roman Empire, and Fiensy (1991: 155–76) develops the model for analysis of Palestine in the Herodian period.

Overview of the Secondary Literature

A brief overview of the more important secondary literature is also in order. Studies dealing with the economy of Palestine can be roughly divided between the pre– and post–World War II eras; economic questions regarding this region were addressed by scholars of both early Christianity and Judaism, as well as some classicists. F. C. Grant's *The Economic Background of the Gospels* (1926) was among the earliest works to deal with such issues; it remained the standard work on the subject for scholars of the New Testament for nearly fifty years. J. Klausner's essay on "The Economy of Judea in the Period of the Second Temple" held a similar position of influence within the realm of Jewish studies; his survey of the economy, which made extensive use of rabbinic sources for economic realities in earlier centuries, argued that there was "enormous progress both in agriculture and in commerce" (1975 [1930]: 205).[1] Around the same time, J. Jeremias (1969 [1933]) produced his work on Jerusalem in Jesus' time, giving considerable attention to economic conditions and the social stratification of Jerusalem. F. M. Heichelheim (1938), a classicist, dealt with Palestine in his paper on the economy of Roman Syria, arguing that the various districts in the province were economically interdependent. Roughly concurrent with these works on Palestine were those dealing with the economic situation in the empire as a whole, including studies by M. Rostovtzeff (1941, 1957 [1926]), T. Frank (1927, 1936–38), Heichelheim (1958 [1938]), and A. H. M. Jones (1948).

In the postwar years, and especially since the 1970s, there was a burgeoning of interest in social and economic history. Within Jewish studies, Arye Ben-David's *Talmudische Ökonomie* (1974) dealt with the economy reflected in later, rabbinic material; Daniel Sperber (1978, 1991 [1974]) covered issues concerning money, pricing, and land from 200 to 400 C.E. Martin Goodman addressed economic issues in his *State and Society in Roman Galilee, A.D. 132–212* (1983). More relevant for the first century are the essays by Shimon Applebaum (1976, 1977, 1989), discussed more fully below. Most recently, Jacob Neusner (1990) and Ze'ev Safrai

(1994) have researched economic issues as reflected in the Mishnah and Talmuds with very different approaches and results, as we shall see.

Scholars of early Christianity and of the Jewish war (66–70 C.E.) have especially contributed to our knowledge of the economic situation in first-century Palestine. A series of studies by Richard A. Horsley (1979, 1981, 1987, Horsley and Hanson 1985/1989/1999) gives considerable attention to economics in explaining the context of the Jesus movement and other developments in the first century, including banditry and the Jewish war. Still others have concentrated on evaluating the connections between the economic situation in Judaea and the revolt, including Heinz Kreissig (1968, 1970, 1989), who focuses on economic causes from a Marxian perspective, and Martin Goodman, who focuses on the failure of the Judaean aristocracy (alongside other economic and social factors) as the main cause of the war. Several other works approach economics as a means of shedding light more specifically on the context of Jesus and the early Christians, including Sean Freyne's book on Galilee (1980), G. Hamel's *Poverty and Charity in Roman Palestine* (1990 [1983]), and Douglas E. Oakman's *Jesus and the Economic Questions of His Day* (1986). David A. Fiensy's study of the *Social History of Palestine in the Herodian Period* (1991) focuses on shifting patterns in land tenure and how these changes affected the living conditions of the peasantry in the first century.

Once again, research on Palestine since the 1970s coincided with, and was influenced by, studies dealing with economics in the Roman Empire generally. Among the more influential, general works were those by A. H. M. Jones (1974, gathering earlier papers), Ramsay MacMullen (1974a, 1974b), R. Duncan-Jones (1974), and G. E. M. de Ste. Croix (1981/1983). Perhaps most influential from a theoretical perspective was M. I. Finley's *Ancient Economy* (1984 [1973]), which outlines the general characteristics of ancient economic arrangements in terms of a primitivist model, reflecting insights from economic anthropology (covering a period ranging from c. 1000 B.C.E. to 500 C.E.). We will discuss a few other more specialized studies of recent years as we proceed.[2]

The State of Our Knowledge on Palestine's Economy

In surveying the secondary literature on the economy of Palestine, several ongoing issues of concern and debate stand out. These include (1) the agrarian nature of the economy, (2) the relative significance of trade, (3) the distribution or ownership of land, and (4) the social-economic conditions of the peasantry, including the impact of taxation. Through a discussion of agreements and disagreements among scholars in these areas, we will gain a better picture of the state of our knowledge of the economics of Palestine around the beginning of the Common Era. The economy of Palestine should not be understood in isolation; despite regional peculiarities that may be identified, this region was part of the larger economic world of the Roman Empire, and social-economic conditions in the region have their counterparts elsewhere in many respects.

First, the ancient economy of Palestine was an underdeveloped, *agrarian economy* based primarily on the production of food through subsistence-level farming by the peasantry. The peasantry, through taxation and rents, supported the continuance of a social-economic structure characterized by asymmetrical distribution of wealth in favor of the elite, a small fraction of the population. Peasants made up the vast majority of the population (over 90 percent; see Kreissig 1970: 17–87; Fiensy 1990: 155–76). The peasantry included *small landowners* who worked their own land for the subsistence of their families, *tenants* who worked the land of wealthy landowners and paid rent, and a variety of landless peasants who either worked as *wage laborers* on large or medium-sized estates or resorted to other activities such as banditry. The elites, consisting of the royal family, aristocrats, religious leaders, and some priests, drew their primary source of income from medium-sized and large estates. Absentee landlords, living in the cities and benefiting from production in the countryside, were common in this social-economic structure.

Production in Palestine centered on the labor of the peasant household to produce essential foods. The principal products included grain (wheat, barley, millet, and rice), vegetables (onions, garlic, leeks, squashes, cabbages, radishes, and beets), fruits (olives, grapes, figs, and dates), legumes (lentils and beans), spices (salt, pepper, and ginger), and meat (fish, cows, oxen, lambs, goats; cf. Klausner 1975 [1930]: 180–86; Hamel 1990 [1983]: 8–56). The peasant's diet consisted mainly of bread and salt, along with olives, oil, onions, and perhaps some grapes (Hamel 1990 [1983]: 34–35). Distribution of produce and wealth was unequal. And, as emphasized by Oakman (1986) and Halvor Moxnes (1988), the type of exchange or distribution within the economy of Palestine seems best characterized in terms of Polanyi's model of redistribution through a central institution. That is, wealth in the form of rents, taxes, and tithes flowed toward urban centers, especially Jerusalem (and the Temple), and was redistributed for ends other than meeting the needs of the peasantry, the main producers. The city's relation to the countryside in such an economy, then, would be parasitic, according to this view.

This overall agrarian quality of the Palestinian economy coincides with the general character of economies in other parts of the Roman Empire as portrayed by ancient historians. According to Rostovtzeff one of the most striking features of the economic and social life of the empire

is the capital importance of the part played by agriculture. It is no exaggeration to say that most of the provinces were almost exclusively agricultural countries. . . .

[We] may safely affirm that the largest part of the population of the Empire was engaged in agriculture, either actually tilling the soil or living on an income drawn from the land. (1957 [1926]: 343)

Yet despite the general recognition that agriculture was of prime importance, there are several theoretical debates directly pertaining to the agrarian nature of the Roman economy. In particular, considerable scholarly discussion centers on the degree to which ancient economies were qualitatively and/or quantitatively similar to or different from later medieval, early modern, and modern economic arrangements. Closely linked with this issue is the relative importance of trade or commercial activity alongside agriculture. This "modernist" vs. "primitivist" debate provides a context for our discussion of scholarly work on Palestine's economy.

On the one hand is the "modernizing" model or approach of Rostovtzeff. "The ancient world experienced, on a smaller scale, the same process of development which we are experiencing now. . . . The modern development [including capitalism] . . . differs from the ancient only in quantity and not in quality" (cited by Reinhold 1946: 363–64). Hence the free use of terminology drawn from modern capitalistic economies (e.g., "capitalism," "bourgeoisie," "proletariat," "mass production") to speak of the ancient Roman economy, as well as an emphasis on trade or commercial enterprise as a principle source of wealth (cf. Reinhold 1946: 362–68; D'Arms 1981: 11–13).

The "primitivist" model of economy was developed, in part, as a reaction to this "modernizing" approach, but it also draws heavily on insights from economic anthropology. For Finley (1984 [1973]), who is quite representative and influential here, the ancient economy was fundamentally different from subsequent economies (e.g., medieval) not only in quantity but also in quality; it was primitive in line with what we know of other peasant economies—so much so that we are at a loss to make sense of the ancient situation in modern terms. According to this model, as Donald Engels explains,

> the classical world was innocent of many market values and institutions. Classical peasants lived at the margin of human existence and had little or nothing left over after they paid their taxes, rents, and maintenance. Therefore, classical cities could not have been supported by the voluntary exchange of peasant surplus for urban goods and services, since the peasant had little or no surplus at his disposal and no knowledge of a market. (1990: 1)

In such a primitive economy, the city's relationship with the countryside was, primarily, a negative, parasitic one; this is the model of the "consumer city" drawing on resources of the countryside through taxation and rents. The primitivist model has become the dominant view within scholarship in recent years, largely due to Finley's influence (cf. Garnsey and Saller 1987).

Naturally there is a range of scholarly opinion regarding the merits of these two models. Several recent studies propose a more nuanced approach to the question, challenging the primitivist model of the ancient economy as proposed by Finley while also rejecting the modernizing approach of Rostovtzeff (cf. D'Arms 1981). H. W. Pleket and his students, for instance, point out shortcomings in Finley's stark differentiation between ancient and other economies, suggesting that we "may have made the ancient economy too primitive and pre-industrial Europe too modern" (Pleket 1984: 35; cf. Pleket 1983 and Nijf 1997: 11–18). Engels's (1990) recent case study of the economy of Corinth criticizes the widespread acceptance of Finley's primitivist model, particularly regarding the dominant notion of the "consumer city." Instead he proposes further case studies testing alternate models, such as the notion of the "service city," which was "supported by the voluntary exchange of peasant surpluses for urban goods and services" (1990: 1–2). In light of such debates, scholars of Palestine's economy should keep in mind John H. D'Arms caution: "Granted that the Roman Empire was a preindustrial economy—it nonetheless exhibits signs of complexity, order, and system in its institutions, to an extent which makes labels like 'primitive' inappropriate unless they are carefully qualified" (1981: 13). This theoretical debate concerning the nature of ancient economies brings us to the next key issue raised in studies of Palestine's economy.

Although the Palestinian economy centered on agriculture, *trade* was also important. Part of the difficulty in assessing the role of trade in Palestine, as with other aspects of the economy, is that our sources lack the qualitative and quantitative information necessary to evaluate the extent and level of trade on a local or "international" scale. Some scholars such as Grant (1926: 72–75) and S. W. Baron (1952: 250–55) tend to downplay involvement in external or foreign trade based partially on isolated references or prohibitions in the literature (cf. Hamel 1990 [1983]: 97–99 for critique). Josephus, for instance, states the following:

> As for ourselves . . . we neither inhabit a maritime country, nor do we delight in merchandise, nor in such a mixture with other men as arises from it; but the cities we dwell in are remote from the sea, and having a fruitful country for our habitation, we take pains in cultivating that only. (*C. Ap.* 1.60)

We need to remain attentive to the difficulties in moving from rhetoric to reality. Josephus's statement regarding Palestine's lack of trade and later rabbinic restrictions on foreign trade may not be fully reflective of reality. Josephus is writing with an apologetic purpose in mind, and the rabbinic prohibitions should be understood as representing the ideals of the rabbis rather than the real situation with respect to trade, which, evidently, was common enough to warrant the prohibitions. Those who take Josephus's reference at face value fail to recognize the apologetic motive in describing Palestine exclusively in terms of agricultural activities. There is a common inclination among ancient authors who discuss agricultural activities, including Cato (*Agr.* 1.2–4), Cicero (*Off.* 1.150–51), Varro (*Rust.* 2.10.1–3), and Columella (*Rust.* 1.1–17); "treatises on agriculture and morality . . . manifest hostility in differing degrees to trade as a source of income" (Garnsey and Saller 1987: 45). D'Arms's study, *Commerce and Social Standing in Ancient Rome* (1981), for instance, shows how attitudes among, or statements by, elite authors (concerning the need for aristocrats to remain aloof from trade) are quite distanced from the social realities of actual conduct (contra Finley); there is considerable evidence that equestrians and even senators were participants in trade to various degrees (cf. Pleket 1983, 1984 on elite businessmen in the Greek East). So actual trade in Palestine would likely be more significant than Josephus's rhetoric would lead us to believe, as we shall see further below.

In contrast to those who consider trade negligible, scholars such as Klausner (1975 [1930]: 199–200), Kreissig (1970: 57–74), and Applebaum (1976) give more attention to evidence that foreign trade was a significant, though not predominant, aspect of economic activity in Palestine. A distinction should be made between evidence of trade *within* Palestine and trade on a more international scale; it is the degree of international trade that is most debated.

Applebaum's survey of archaeological and literary evidence for imports and exports, for foreign or international trade, is illustrative of the situation, though his conclusion that "[e]conomic activity was predominantly internal" is debatable (1976: 669–80, largely followed here). Regarding imports, Egyptian grain was occasionally imported in times of shortage or famine (Josephus, *Ant.* 15.299–316 [25 B.C.E.], 20.51–52 [46–47 C.E.]), but Palestine was largely self-sufficient for such food staples. The Temple cult required considerable imports, as I discuss below. With respect to clothing, later references in rabbinic literature to sandals from Tyre and Laodicea, goat-hair from Cilicia, and fine linens from Pelusium and India are suggestive of possibilities in the first century. Among the most common items in daily use in antiquity was pottery, so it is significant that archaeological excavations at Samaria, Schechem, Ptolemais, and Ashdod uncovered red glaze both from the east (in the Hellenistic and Roman eras) and from Italy and Gaul (in the Roman era); a stamped jar from Colonia Hadrumetum in North Africa found at Joppa (second century or earlier) is also suggestive of such imports. As Applebaum notes, Palestine was lacking in metals (except copper) and we can assume the import of all necessary ones. The principal exports from Palestine were olive oil (cf. Josephus, *B.J.* 2.591, *Vita* 74–76), dates, opobalsam, and spices. The

Jericho region was renowned for its dates and date-wines, which were in high demand in Rome (cf. Strabo, *Geogr.* 16.763.41; Pliny the Elder, *Nat.* 13.44–49). Products from the opobalsam bush, grown in the Dead Sea area, were exported, including the sap, twigs, and bark, which were used as medical remedies for headaches and problems with eyesight (cf. Pliny the Elder, *Nat.* 12.111; Strabo, *Geogr.* 16.763). By the fourth century, Gaza and Ascalon became well known for their wines. Long-distance luxury items from East Africa, Arabia, India, and the Far East would also pass through Palestine following the usual trade routes.

After surveying this evidence for imports and exports, Applebaum concludes that, although there are indications of limited trade, economic activity in Palestine was "predominantly internal." We need to be more cautious, however, in generalizing from partial and fragmentary evidence; it is often difficult to know whether a particular item among the limited evidence we have should be viewed as representative or exceptional. I would suggest that we need to leave open the possibility that future archaeological work and regionally focused studies may show that trade, including international trade, was more significant than scholars have often thought.

There are other indications of the significance of trade that are worthy of mention here. In many respects, Jerusalem and the Temple were the hub of commercial activity and trade in Judaea. Heavy demands for sacrificial victims for the Temple cult meant that cattle and sheep would have to be imported from elsewhere when local supplies of livestock were short, and incense, consisting of ingredients from various localities (including Ethiopia and India; cf. Applebaum 1976: 674), would also need to be imported. Peter Richardson notes the demands for goods, both domestic and international, associated with the Temple:

> There was heavy traffic from pilgrims to Jerusalem at the major festivals, probably in increasing numbers through the first century B.C.E. and C.E. as the *pax Romana* brought easier travel, more disposable income, and fewer border problems. This meant that Judeans had very large demands made upon them for good roads, lodgings, food, water, and sacrificial victims such as pigeons (doves), sheep, and cattle. Jerusalem was . . . the economic center for taxation, trade, and international links. (1996: 135)

The influx of large numbers of Jews from cities throughout the Mediterranean Diaspora would likely bring with it important social and business network connections to other regions of the empire.

Furthermore, some of Herod's large-scale constructions were designed to foster an increase in trade of a more international character. Richardson notes several potential areas where Herod's attention was drawn to commerce and trade, including the area north of the Winter Palace at Jericho; but most significant was the artificially constructed harbor at Caesarea Maritima, with its harbor installations, warehouses, and stores (1996: 188–91). This was Herod's "showpiece city;

it was a major outlet to the Mediterranean, home for the Judaean navy, the largest harbor in the Mediterranean. Produce, trade, and people flowed in both directions" (1996: 178). Projects and activities of this sort would set the stage for an increase in international trade to, from, and through Palestine in the first century. Trade was likely more significant than often recognized.

But why was international trade not even more predominant in such an economy? The answer appears to lie in the subsistence orientation of much agricultural production in Palestine as in other areas of the empire. According to a qualified primitivist model of economy, the majority of the population lived from the produce of the land with little surplus to sell. As well, the economic situation of the peasantry was not conducive to the regular purchase of imported goods, which would be purchased mainly by the wealthy. Much of the produce extracted by large landowners would be sold to the nonagricultural populations of the city on a local basis if possible rather than exported. Once again, this characteristic seems reflective of other provinces in the Roman Empire, as Garnsey and Saller note, where "agricultural areas inevitably aimed at subsistence rather than the production of an exportable surplus. . . . In general, the backwardness and expense of transport and the relatively low level of demand limited opportunities for profitable investment in commerce" (1987: 44). This statement should be qualified somewhat in connection with our earlier discussion of the primitivist model. Still, in light of this picture of the empire generally, the suggestion that Palestine is a special case in regard to limited trade due to religious factors or prohibitions, as Grant and Baron suggested, is unnecessary.

Returning to the characteristics of the agrarian economy, a third issue addressed by scholars relates to trends in *land ownership*. Many scholars argue that there was a tendency toward the concentration of more land in Palestine into the hands of fewer large landowners at the expense of peasants.[3] Grant identifies lack of land as a cause of economic distress in the years preceding and during the first century (1926: 66), and Klausner identifies forfeiture of land due to indebtedness as a main cause of peasants losing their land and of larger landowners increasing the size of their estates (1975[1930]: 188–89). Kreissig, too, points to the trend toward large estates and an increasing gap between small and large landowners, though he is hesitant to identify any of the large estates as official "royal lands" (i.e., lands in the possession of the current monarch or emperor, often inherited from the preceding dynasty; 1970: 26–27, 31). Applebaum (1976: 633–38, 660–61), Freyne (1980: 165), and, above all, Fiensy (1991: 21–73) convincingly argue that large estates were prominent and on the increase in the years preceding the first century and that they included both royal lands, some of which were given to loyal aristocrats as gifts, and aristocrats' large estates. Fiensy does a good job of plotting out the locations and extent of royal estates known from archaeological and literary information. He identifies royal estates in the Jericho region; the Plains of Esdraelon; western Samaria; Batanea, Gaulanitis, and Trachonitis; the coastal regions; and Idumea and Perea. According to many scholars, the main consequences of this direction in land tenure included an increase in landless peasants and hence of tenancy, day labor, and banditry (cf. Horsley and Hanson 1985/1989/1999: 48–87; Hamel 1990 [1983]: 151–63; Oakman 1986: 72–77; Fiensy 1990; on banditry in Palestine and the empire see Richardson and Edwards, ch. 11, in this volume; Isaac 1984; Shaw 1984).

Once again, this concentration of land ownership within Palestine was part of the larger picture of the Roman Empire as identified by several ancient historians, including Rostovtzeff, MacMullen, and Finley. Rostovtzeff, for instance, notes that there was a

> general tendency throughout the Empire towards the concentration of land in the hands of a few proprietors who lived in the cities. . . . The land was owned by men who were not themselves experts in agriculture but were townsmen for whom land was a form of investment. (1957 [1926]: 344)

The issue of peasant landlessness brings us to a fourth main point regarding the economy: namely, the *social-economic conditions of the peasantry* in Palestine. It is generally acknowledged by most scholars that the economic situation of the peasantry was a precarious one due to subsistence-level farming and various expenses including taxes, rents, and seed, as well as the threat of natural disasters and famine.

The fragmentary nature of the evidence when it comes to quantifiable estimations of taxation, rents, and other expenses helps to explain the difficulty in assessing the economic situation of the peasantry and the varying results of scholars on the extent of the tax burden. In general, Grant, Klausner, Horsley, Applebaum, and Freyne tend to emphasize the extremely burdensome economic situation of the peasantry. New Testament scholars following the lead of Grant, including Horsley and Hanson (1985/1989/1999: 52–63), are inclined to provide, without explanation, a high estimate of as much as 40 percent or more of produce going for taxation and religious dues. On the other hand, scholars such as E. P. Sanders, Hamel, and Oakman are more explicit in stating the calculations behind their estimates. In Sanders's calculation, which seems reasonable, the estimated total burden on the average peasant (assuming a 12.5 percent yearly land tax including taxes and tithes) was no more than 28 percent in most years and, in the worst-case scenario, a total of about 33 percent (1992: 146–69), considerably less than Horsley's calculation of well over 40 percent for the average peasant each year.

Oakman's calculation of taxation is similar to Sanders's, ranging from 20 to 35 percent (1986: 68–72). Oakman suggests that the average amount of produce remaining for subsistence may have ranged from one-fifth to as low as one-thirteenth of the produce based on a yield of 1:5. Oakman provides some useful estimates regarding the peasant family's various expenses, including rents and seed, and regarding the land that would be necessary to fulfill a peasant family's expenditures and food needs (1986: 61). By his estimate, a minimum subsistence plot would have been 1.5 acres per adult, *not* including land that would lie fallow (an additional 1.5 acres per adult) and not including land for the added expenditures of seed, taxes, and rents (1986: 61–66).[4] Oakman suggests that the average seed-to-yield ratio for the Palestinian peasant would have been about 1:5 (cf. Heichelheim 1938: 128; Hamel 1990 [1983]: 127–29). One-fifth of unit production (of each year's yield), therefore, would go toward the seed replacement fund of the next year. Oakman checks his original estimate of 11 bushels of wheat necessary for subsistence per person per year against these hypothetical yield ratios and finds that the calculation is about the same: 1.8 bushels of seed per acre (amount of seed known to have been used in planting) x 1.5 acres (subsistence plot per person) x 5 (fivefold yield) = 13.5 bushels − 1.8 bushels (seed replacement fund) = 11.7 bushels available per year. However, further expenses would be drawn from this amount, including fodder for the peasant's livestock, a reserve for bartering and purchasing various goods and services, and the Temple tithe of one-tenth. These expenses, together with seed replacement, would equal *approximately three-tenths of the harvest* not including rents and taxes, which would range from 20 to 35 percent of total produce by Oakman's estimate. Having outlined these conditions for peasants, it is important to point out that Palestine was not exceptional in its subsistence-level farming and in the various expenses including taxation and rents, which were also faced by peasants in other provinces of the empire.

Methodological Difficulties and Cautions

The works surveyed here raise several methodological issues. First, one of the main difficulties faced by any historian of the ancient world pertains to the nature of our sources, which are fragmentary, partial, and reflective of particular perspectives. The literary sources we do have represent only a haphazard selection from particular places at specific times. For Palestine in the first centuries, there are the Gospels, which were not necessarily written in Palestine and may, therefore, reflect conditions elsewhere; Josephus's writings, which represent the viewpoint of an ancient historian writing (in Rome) from an elite perspective; and various other Christian and Jewish writings that are of unknown date and provenance. For later centuries there are rabbinic writings, the Mishnah and Talmuds, which are problematic for writing the history of the first century; although some of the material preserved within them represents earlier periods, they also represent the viewpoint and sociohistorical setting of the authors or redactors of the material in the third century and beyond. Generally lacking are literary sources representing the perspectives of the peasantry; most sources available for Palestine, perhaps with the exception of some strata of the synoptic Gospels, represent elite perspectives on economic and other conditions, perspectives that were sometimes characterized by a negative view of the peasantry or "people of the land" (*am-ha-aretz*).

Archaeological evidence should play a key role in writing social and economic history. Hamel and Fiensy, for example, illustrate the value of archaeological material in shedding light on ancient economics and the daily living conditions of peasants in Palestine. Fiensy draws extensively on archaeological findings for his survey of large estates (1991: 21–74). Nevertheless, the *realia* available regarding life in the peasant village are also fragmentary. Moreover, the picture of the economy and economic conditions that is drawn from the literary and archaeological evidence we do have is still a partial one.

A second main difficulty in reconstructing a picture of the ancient economy or economic conditions is the lack of (reliable) economic information in the sources we do have. Unlike the modern historian, ancient authors were not interested in presenting an economic history or in providing a collection of economic data, because the modern concepts of economy and economics did not exist in antiquity. Finley notes the care the historian must take in using apparently quantifiable evidence due to the "indifference of most ancient writers to economic matters as well as . . . their casualness and carelessness in giving numbers" (1984 [1973]: 30). Although Finley may overstate the point, he is correct in emphasizing that references to economic conditions and quantifiable economic information are only incidental and can be misleading. Most of the evidence for the ancient economy, then, is indirect.

This leads us to a third main methodological issue in regard to the use of ancient sources for economic and social history. It is essential to ask why the ancient author provided particular information that the historian then considers as evidence for social or economic history. Finley's comments on the nature of the primary sources and the historian's use of them are insightful:

> The first question to be asked about any document is about the reason or motive for its having been written. That question is not asked often enough, because it is unconsciously assumed that motives and purposes are self-evident, that is to say, that they are more or less the same as our own. On the contrary, I would argue that in antiquity the purpose of all documents was either to communicate some information (or misinformation) or to memorialize something, but not to provide data for policy-making or for analysis, past, present or future. (1985: 32)

Finley's comments are applicable to some of the works discussed in this chapter. For example, the debate about the extent of trade based on a passage in

Josephus, discussed earlier, is an illustration of the failure of some scholars to ask the reason or motives underlying the presentation of material by an ancient author.

The use of rabbinic literature in writing social and economic history illustrates the importance of recognizing both the ancient author's motive or purpose in writing and the related issue of the possible gap between the author's ideal presentation and the real social and economic situation, between rhetoric and reality. Its use in historical reconstruction has been a continuing issue, from Klausner's and Heichelheim's seemingly uncritical use of this literature to reconstruct the economy of the Second Temple period to Hamel's more critical use to shed light on village life in Palestine of the first three centuries. A comparison of source-method in the recent works of two scholars of rabbinic Judaism, Jacob Neusner and Ze'ev Safrai, will provide a fitting conclusion to this section on methodology and the use of sources.

Safrai's monograph, *The Economy of Roman Palestine* (1994), approaches the issue of the economy on the assumption that the talmudic sources can be used extensively as representative of the *real* situation when studied critically. Safrai points out that he is following in the methodological path of other Jewish historians including A. Büchler (1912) and G. Alon (1980). Safrai focuses primarily on talmudic literature, alongside archaeological information, to reconstruct various aspects of the economy of Palestine in the period from 70 C.E. to about 350 C.E., with a focus on the latter part of this period. So, for example, Safrai believes that the Jerusalem Talmud, written sometime in the fourth century, contains historically accurate information (which can be separated from other less useful material) regarding the actual economy in an earlier period.

Jacob Neusner's methodological views are quite different. He applies historical-critical methods in the study of Judaism in late antiquity, something that is not often the case, he feels, in the field of Jewish studies. In contemporary Judaic studies, "we routinely deal with premises last found plausible in biblical studies more than 150 years ago" (1991: 70). The application of source, redaction, tradition, and historical criticism, along the lines of the application of these methods in New Testament studies, is essential to the study of rabbinic literature and Jewish history in his view.

Neusner's approach to the economics of the Mishnah greatly contrasts Safrai's. In *The Economics of the Mishnah*, Neusner approaches his subject based on his assessment that the Mishnah represents the *ideal*, not the real: "the authors of the Mishnah tell us how people saw and imagined things, not how things actually were" (1990: 33). Hence to study economic issues in such literature is to study not the actual situation but the authors'/redactors' own ideal perceptions of how economic and other activities should be done. According to Neusner, the rabbis who produced the Mishnah and Talmuds were an elite group removed from the actual situation of the villages in Palestine and, in connection with this, were also unable to ensure the implementation of their suggestions in any nonelite community far removed from them.

Although Neusner's opinions on the genre of the Mishnah and on the specific worldviews he perceives in it are not accepted by all other scholars (see Sanders [1990] on precisely these points), some of Neusner's critical perspectives regarding the use of the rabbinic material for social or economic history are shared by others. Goodman, for example, also makes a similar observation with respect to the use of rabbinic material by historians: "It is an undue credulity about rabbinic effectiveness in social matters that has led to most of the faults in earlier studies and, in particular, to frequent reliance on selected single quotations and laws taken out of context to support theories of social, economic, and religious history" (1983: 8).

How, then, can the rabbinic material (or other literary sources such as the New Testament and Josephus, for that matter) be used in writing social and economic history? The usefulness of the rabbinic materials appears to lie somewhere between the views of Safrai and Neusner. Neusner is correct in suggesting that a social history regarding the economic ideals of the authors or redactors of the rabbinic material can be written, and Safrai is correct in suggesting that references to the actual situation can be found in the literature when analyzed carefully. That is, this literature, like any other, can be useful for social and economic history when used critically with an awareness of the motive of the author or influence of the author's worldview on the material being used. However, the later rabbinic material cannot be uncritically used to reconstruct social and economic realities of earlier centuries. It is essential that the scholar apply historical-critical methods, including source, redaction, tradition, and historical criticism, to the material that is being used in order to differentiate the date of particular material from the date of composition or redaction. Comparison with other literary and, especially, archaeological evidence should play a key role in the evaluation of specific evidence, both for identifying the worldviews that may shape the material and in identifying material that reflects the social or economic realities of particular times and places.

Future Directions for Research

Although a considerable amount of study has been done on economics in Palestine (particularly in the first century but also in rabbinic times), there are several areas that deserve more attention. First, archaeological findings need to be more fully integrated into our understanding of the economy (cf. Applebaum 1976:

631). Some scholars tend to focus on literary evidence to the neglect of artifactual evidence, and when archaeology is used there is a tendency to interpret it in light of literature (e.g., Finley 1984 [1973]; see the critique by Frederiksen [1975: 170]). Artifactual evidence should be considered on its own terms and may, instead, provide alternate perspectives on social and economic life to those we encounter in the literature. Archaeological finds may, for instance, provide important clues regarding the degree to which international trade was important in particular localities of Roman Palestine. Regionally focused case studies of particular cities, villages, and regions may provide a more nuanced picture of local and international trade and commerce.

Second, further research of economic issues in Palestine should be done on macro- and micro-levels and on relating the results to historical developments. On the macro-level, further steps can be taken, along the lines of the research of scholars such as Oakman and Fiensy, to conceptualize the overall structures of the economy and social-economic arrangements in Palestine, particularly with help from the social sciences. Developing explicit models of the ancient economy in Palestine in light of research on the nature of economic arrangements in other ancient Mediterranean societies and in view of the specific economic aspects of Palestine may assist in making sense of disparate economic "facts"; this may be helpful in drawing attention to some of the otherwise less visible dynamics of the economy and of social-economic activities.

On the micro-level, further research into economic aspects of daily village life or the "economy" of the average peasant, along the lines of Hamel's research on food and clothing, will shed further light on the activities and situation of the vast majority of the population. A deeper knowledge of the economic situation of the peasantry will also assist in understanding various phenomena such as banditry, which was also quite common in other areas of the empire.

A third main area requiring further research is *comparison* of the economy and social-economic situation of Palestine with other regions of the Roman Empire. The economic situation of the peasantry deserves comparative attention since some scholars, such as Kreissig and Horsley, appear to place considerable importance on the social-economic plight of the peasantry in explaining social and religious movements particular to Palestine, as well as the Jewish war itself. Such comparative study would help to place the economy of Palestine as we understand it into the overall economic arrangements of the empire, shedding light on both the unique and the typical in regard to economic issues in Palestine.

Finally, the majority of studies on the economy of Palestine concentrate primarily on the situation in the first century and take a synchronic approach to their study. Several scholars utilize their synchronic analysis of economic conditions in explaining key events of the time, especially the Jewish war. Still needed, however, is a more broadly based diachronic analysis of the economy of Palestine, making note of the key points in the history of that region that shaped social-economic arrangements. Such an attempt, though admittedly difficult due to the fragmentary nature of our evidence, may help to show how changes in economic aspects influenced other sociohistorical developments over time, again in relation to trends in the empire as a whole.

Notes

I would like to thank Peter Richardson (University of Toronto) who directed my attention to the economy of Palestine in the first place and who provided numerous and insightful suggestions for an earlier version of this chapter. Anthony J. Blasi was helpful in reworking the earlier work into the present form.

1. Earlier, Emil Schürer (1885 [1983]) had dealt with economic issues in his monumental work. Büchler (1912) had focused his attention on economic issues pertaining to land ownership and demography in the years following the destruction of the Temple in 70 C.E.

2. For more complete bibliographies on the Roman economy, see Garnsey, Hopkins, and Whittaker (1983), Garnsey and Saller (1987), and Parkins and Smith (1998).

3. Scholars are not always clear on the meaning of their terminology for the size of plots of land. H. Dohr's definition of plots is useful (see Fiensy 1991: 24): small = 6–50 acres; medium = 50–315 acres; large = over 315 acres.

4. This figure can be compared with Ben-David's estimate of 16.8 acres for a family of six to nine people (1974: 44), which, unlike Oakman's figure, includes half the land as fallow as well as produce from the land necessary to pay taxes and rent while subsisting comfortably (cf. Hamel 1990 [1983]: 134–36). Fiensy, on the other hand, is more inclined toward the more modest estimate of S. Dar who, based partially on archaeological findings, suggests that peasant (freeholder) families sometimes owned just 6 acres of land (1991: 94–95). Fiensy suggests that many peasant families would be required to seek supplementary income from other sources in order to subsist.

Modes and Relations of Production 23

DIMITRIS J. KYRTATAS

"Working quietly and eating their own food" (2 Thes 3.12): Production and Consumption in the Early Christian Communities

"In the days of Herod king of Judaea" (Lk 1.5): The Historical Character of Christianity[1]

EXAMINING CHRISTIANITY in its historical context is not the only way to investigate its nature, but it is certainly one of the most profitable. Like other religions, Christianity is a historical product: it was founded at a particular time and developed within the limits of existing social conditions. More significantly, its historicity goes part and parcel with its character in a way that has no exact parallel in any other religion of Asia, Greece, or Rome. The most important New Testament documents (the Gospels and Acts) have a clearly historical framework, while the remaining ones constantly remind their audience and readers that their religious teaching, despite its general applicability, was introduced as a response to the moral needs of the period. By proclaiming the imminent coming of the Kingdom of God, the early Christians expressed themselves with an urgency that revealed much of the concrete conditions under which they were living. These concrete conditions were embedded into what became the essence of Christianity.

Stories about King Herod the Great of Judaea, and of Pontius Pilate, governor (*praefectus*) of Judaea, are inseparable from the narratives relating the birth and execution of Jesus. It was an early Christian belief that the time and place of Jesus' appearance upon earth had been premeditated by Divine Providence. For it was only at the beginning of the Roman Empire and within its boundaries that humans were deemed sufficiently prepared to receive his teaching. Augustus, it was argued, had reduced numerous kingdoms to uniformity by bringing them all under his sole rule. In like manner, humanity was being taught to abandon established beliefs in many gods and to accept one God as the Lord of heaven.[2] Such considerations shaped Christianity, while rendering it both a yardstick for history and an object of historical inquiry.

> It was then the forty-second year of the reign of Augustus, and the twenty-eighth year after the submission of Egypt and the death of Antony and Kleopatra (and with her the Egyptian dynasty of the Ptolemies came to an end), when our Saviour and Lord Jesus Christ, in accordance with the prophecies concerning him, was born in Bethlehem of Judaea at the time of the census which then first took place, while Quirinius was Governor of Syria. (Eusebius, *Hist. eccl.* I.5.2, Lake)

Thus began Eusebius, the father of church history, his early fourth-century account of the origins of Christianity. The evangelist Luke, from whom much of this information derives, had added significant historical details to the accounts given by the evangelists Mark and Matthew. Luke thought that it was more appropriate to produce a gospel narrative in the way of Greek historians, like Thucydides. Eusebius was mainly following Luke, but included further detail to make it perfectly clear that the emergence of Christianity should be considered as a historical fact within a historical context. Since the exact timing had been determined by Divine Providence, the historical setting should be proclaimed along with the message of Jesus.[3]

As Christianity continued to grow and expand, church historians kept bringing its history up-to-date. Nevertheless, Christians of all times have been conscious of the significance of the formative years. They have, therefore, regularly looked back to the origins of their religion for inspiration and guidance. Almost all the most important changes in organization, dogma, and morality have been presented as a return to the teaching of the New Testament. The study of early Christianity contributes to the understanding of the Christian religion at large.[4]

"Whatever you eat or drink, do it for the glory of God" (1 Cor 10.31): Consumption in the Early Christian Communities

"One does not live by bread alone," replied Jesus to the temptation of the Devil. Human beings, he claimed, should also be nourished by "every word that comes forth from the mouth of God" (Mt 4.4). Indeed, throughout his mission, Jesus was far more concerned with spiritual instruction than with the material needs of his followers. "Do not worry about your life, what you will eat or drink, or about your body, what you will wear," he told the crowds who had gathered to hear his teaching. "Is not life more than food and the body more than clothing?" (Mt 6.25). Nevertheless, as Jesus was well aware, sustenance and clothing were problems that could not be totally dispensed with.

The New Testament has much to say about the consumption of material goods. Several types or modes of consumption are discussed. For example, while the rich man dressed in purple garments and fine linen and dined sumptuously each day, poor Lazarus, covered with sores, would gladly have eaten his fill of the scraps that fell from the rich man's table (Lk 16.19–31). Jesus even gave instructions concerning etiquette at a wedding banquet, taking account of the formalities related to the social stratification of his society (Lk 14.7–14). For even as consumers, Christians should exhibit their moral character. As Paul clearly expressed, in consuming material goods, believers should always have God in their minds (1 Cor 10.31).

If admonitions regarding consumption are to be properly understood, they must be viewed from within their historical and social context. Fortunately, this is often quite easy. The earliest Christian documents do not have much to say about political and military events. But they are very rich in information regarding the social environment in which Christianity was founded. In the New Testament, the religious duties of men and women toward God are normally presented as duties toward their brethren. "Whatever you did for one of these least brothers of mine, you did for me," said the Lord (Mt 25.40). Thus, relations between humans and the divinity are often discussed in terms of social relations. Topics such as rebellion and obedience, war and peace, riches and poverty, hunger and satisfaction are essential to the moral teaching of the New Testament. Much is also said about attitudes toward all kinds of authorities (political, religious, and domestic) as well as attitudes toward poverty and wealth. Upon examination, even some of the most spiritual instructions reveal their social context and character.

It is sometimes the case, however, that the historical and social context remains veiled, leaving important spiritual issues almost incomprehensible. For example, the practice of consuming meat that had either been "sacrificed to idols" or procured from "strangled animals" caused great disturbances in the early Christian communities. As is evident from Acts, the letters of Paul, and Revelation, Christian views regarding dietary customs were far from unanimous. Yet despite its extreme importance in the New Testament, the topic was almost forgotten in the next generation. The modern reader finds it difficult to understand why a religious problem of such magnitude in primitive Christianity dropped out so abruptly and unexpectedly without being solved at a theological level.

In such cases we must have access to information that was common knowledge in the Roman world. The poor, for example, had almost no other opportunity to consume meat outside pagan religious celebrations; it was only the rich who could afford meat that had not been offered first to a pagan deity. Thus, the theological problem over meat ceremoniously slaughtered was superseded because the underlying social problem proved to be weightier.[5]

"The plowman should plow, and the thresher thresh in hope of receiving a share" (1 Cor 9.10): From Consumption to Production

As a rule, people consume what they possess. It is, therefore, almost impossible to enter into a proper discussion of modes of consumption without considering the origin of wealth and its allocation among the members of a given society. A proper historical and sociological investigation should therefore start from production, move on to exchange and distribution, and finally come to consumption. Just how important production was to the life of the early Christians may be deduced from the frequency with which the problem of securing provisions was addressed.

"Do not worry about tomorrow, tomorrow will take care of itself," Jesus urged his disciples (Mt 6.34). Yet it was because of his own hunger in the desert that the Devil tempted him to turn stones into loaves of bread. The disciples were often anxious over food and drink. They were concerned about their own nutrition as well as the meals of the crowds that gathered to hear Jesus preach. Since the primitive community depended, to a large extent, upon the charity of sympathizers, we may understand why its members felt so insecure. On several occasions, finding food became an acute problem—as it often was in most traditional societies. One of the earliest miracles of Jesus (perhaps the first) was turning water into wine (Jn 2.1–11). Feeding the hungry crowds was not the least admired among his deeds (Mt 14.15–21, 15.32–38). Having asked Jesus to teach them how to pray, the disciples were instructed to ask, among other things, for their daily bread (Mt 6.11; Lk 11.3).

Particular types of production and investment are taken for granted by Jesus in his parables. Men are usually presented as cultivating the land and tending their flocks. Some are also shown to trade, such as the servants who were entrusted with their master's possessions before he left on a journey (Mt 25.14–30). In real life, most of the people surrounding Jesus were free, owning their land and investing their capital in their own interest. The parables make more frequent mention of slaves cultivating their master's land and investing his capital. But in almost all cases the setting is clearly agricultural, with few references to urban life.

In the early church the situation changed considerably. After a very brief period of alleged communal life, most Christians returned to their regular occupations and productive activities. The new communities were soon well organized and had a fixed leadership. They were city-based rather than village-based and included more members engaged in trade and the crafts. One of the main problems faced by the new urban communities was that of supporting their leaders, who were engaged in missionary activities on a full-time basis. Given the low level of productivity in all traditional societies, several brothers and sisters had to make contributions for each member who did not work for a living. As congregations grew and had to support increasing numbers of church officials, widows, and orphans, the Christian churches, as institutions, gradually became heavily involved in productive and distributive activities.[6]

Significant as such matters might have been, very little is said in early Christian documents regarding community assets. We are told next to nothing about the productive and financial activities of churches or how they invested their capital. If we were to rely exclusively upon the few explicit statements made, we would get the impression that the only sources of the early churches were donations and firstfruits offered by the faithful. Yet, there is little doubt that from a very early period the Christian churches owned land as well as urban property. It would have been very strange if they had not made profitable use of their possessions, like all other property owners of the period. Furthermore, since many Christian leaders were involved in usury, it is reasonable to assume that at least part of their profits went to the church treasury.

Why so little is said about production and investment is not difficult to surmise. In the ancient world it was believed that men and women could improve their moral standing by regulating their consuming manners. This was not argued with regard to producing manners. Most people had no opportunity to choose their occupations; they were born into them. More significantly, no one thought at the time that it was possible or even desirable to change the existing modes of production.

In common with everyone else in the period, early Christians took production for granted. They neither passed judgment upon the way it was organized, nor proposed workable alternatives. Religion, they thought, should recommend ways of utilizing wealth, not ways of earning it. In this chapter we attempt to discuss what everybody in the world of the early Christians took for granted. More emphasis is thus lain upon the ways wealth was earned. The most common modes of production in the Roman Empire are considered first, followed by an examination of the effects these modes of production had upon both the structure of the early Christian communities and the early Christian attitudes toward property and wealth.

Modes of Production and Exploitation

Production and Social Stratification

"If anyone was unwilling to work," an early Christian preacher instructed his disciples, "neither should that one eat" (2 Thes 3.10). But in fact, as everybody knew, a lot of people in the Roman world (as in most historical societies) did not depend for their living upon what they produced by their own hands. Part of the wealth available for consumption circulates through some kind of equal exchange system. A producer is almost never able to produce all kinds of goods necessary for his living: he barters part of his surplus with others. Furthermore, a producer has to pay for services rendered and to support the unproductive members of his family (children and the elderly), so as to secure the reproduction of mankind and human labor.

More significantly, part of the wealth produced in a society is extracted from its immediate producers by various means and for various purposes, through what we may call unequal exchange or economic exploitation. In some cases, a surplus of wealth or a surplus of labor is extracted by force, as booty or forced labor; in other cases it is extracted by legitimated means (i.e., means that are accepted by society at large as legitimate), in the form of rent, taxes, customs, or tribute. The most legitimated mode of extracting surplus from the immediate producers is through wages. The laborer sells his labor force in exchange for a wage accepted by convention as reasonable to secure his subsistence. Different types of laborers need of course different wages to reproduce themselves in socially acceptable ways. In return for the wages that he pays, the employer retains the product of the laborer's toil.

Extraction of surplus value or surplus labor (in whatever form) involving unequal exchange or economic exploitation is mainly the result of what is called division of labor, that is, distinct social positions in the process of production. Economic exploitation, in its turn, reproduces division of labor and unequal distribution of the wealth produced. The conquered are exploited by the conquerors; slaves by slave-owners; serfs by landlords; day laborers by the owners of the means of production, whether these means are land, tools, crops, or capital of some other kind. These various types of relations between exploited classes and classes of exploiters, also called the ruling or dominant classes, correspond to as many different modes of production.

By mode of production we should understand the combination of the various elements, structures as well as practices, that contribute to the transformation of nature, through human labor, into wealth—products with social value. In the process of this transformation, both human and nonhuman forces (e.g., machines) are employed. In a more inclusive sense, a mode of production designates also the distribution of the wealth produced among the social agents and social classes in a given society, according to the established division of labor.[7]

The concept mode of production is no more than a theoretical abstraction meant to facilitate a certain type of inquiry. In historical societies, many different modes of production actually coexist. They are articulated between them and support each other, but are more or less clearly distinguishable either by the differences in the forces employed or, more clearly, by the differences in the prevailing social relations. In theoretical parlance, the articulated complex structure of diverse modes of production is sometimes called a social formation, meaning a given society, seen through its producing and distributive capacity.

In most social formations, one particular mode of production proves to be more important than others and becomes dominant. A dominant mode of production is usually the one that secures the reproduction of existing social order, mainly the reproduction of the dominant class divisions. When this reproduction is secured, the whole social edifice appears to function properly. When it becomes unstable, the social edifice starts disintegrating or even crumbling, until a new dominant mode of production is gradually established.

Legitimation of Exploitation

The dominant classes may exercise regular force upon the exploited classes, but no social relations depending upon force alone can remain stable over long periods of time. Booty, extracted for the benefit of conquerors by plunder or looting, is sooner or later transformed into tribute; captives and prisoners are transformed into slaves. The percentage of the surplus extracted is normally smaller, although it may remain the same or even increase. But its extraction in legitimated ways— ways accepted by society as just—makes a great difference to the longevity of the established social order. For whereas payment of tribute or taxes may be sometimes secured by force, it is more often secured by some kind of consent or agreement. The same is more or less true with the employment of slaves. However regularly exercised, force alone may not keep slaves in their permanent posts. In organized societies, even slaves have to accept their position as inevitable, if not, somehow, as acceptable—or even beneficial to them (Kyrtatas 1995).

Legitimation of exploitation normally takes two distinct complementary forms: clearly defined rules (legislation) and more vaguely formulated notions (ideologies). The basic and most fundamental function of law and ideology in most societies is to protect private property (including property of the means of production) and social order. When private ownership is established as a social value, then extraction of surpluses from the immediate producers is accepted as reasonable and just. The legal system and the dominant ideologies combine to provide societies with forms of consciousness. It is through such forms of consciousness that the members of different groups and classes view their place in society.

Modes of Production in the Roman Empire

Basic Characteristics of the Roman World

The Roman world depended, by and large, upon its agricultural production. Manufacture, construction, commerce, services of all kinds (including administration) and the army were of great importance to the economic and social life of the empire. But the vast amount of its energy went into farming and stockbreeding. From its total population, which was at the time of Jesus between fifty and sixty million (at periods, perhaps even more), the percentage of people employed in these two sectors may have been as high as 90 percent.[8] Land was, accordingly, the main source of income for the bulk of the poor and the rich alike. It was also the main source of revenue for the administration, the burden of taxation falling upon agriculture. As has been calculated, the empire derived as much as twenty times more from agricultural tax than from trade and industry taxes.[9]

The uppermost section of the Roman world consisted of three more or less clearly defined groups: the senators, the equestrians, and the decurions. All together, they constituted the dominant classes of the Roman Empire. They were mainly owners of land and slaves, but were often involved in other kinds of profitable activities, such as industry, trade, banking (especially usury), and renting real estate. Being the owners of the principle means of production (land and slaves) they are also called the propertied classes.[10]

The number of senators was very small; including the members of their families they were no more than a few thousand people. Most of them were politically active, especially in Rome, which was their permanent place of residence until a new senate was also established by Constantine in Constantinople. Senators normally had to engage themselves in income-creating activities other than agricultural production indirectly, through their agents. They were also paid extremely large salaries for some of the posts they occupied and directly received part of the taxes collected in the provinces they governed, as well as part of the booty amassed by the armies they led. Like all members of the propertied classes, however, they normally secured their profits by buying more land (empire-wide) and more slaves.

The equestrians were more numerous. They may have been a few tens of thousands, including the members of their families. Only a small proportion of them were politically active, and most of them were less wealthy than most senators. Furthermore, equestrians could be found in almost all the major cities of the empire, although, at the time of Jesus, most of them lived in Rome. The dividing line between them and the senators was never really great; some were regularly promoted to the senatorial order, with which they always shared the same values and social interests.

By far the largest group of the propertied classes were the decurions. They were members of the local councils in the towns of the Roman provinces and filled posts in the most important magistracies. In each town there were normally about 100 decurions. They may have totaled approximately 150,000, including those who were also qualified for office and the members of their families. They were involved in all kinds of profit-making activities, some of them being no more than wealthy peasants. Most of them certainly owned land and slaves. There were great differences in wealth and political power between them and the members of the higher orders. However, because of their significant property and their position vis-à-vis the exploited classes, they also belonged to the ruling classes of the empire. They were mainly responsible for maintaining order in their towns and collecting the appropriate taxes. The ruling classes comprised altogether no more than 1 or 2 percent of the total population.

It is through their eyes, the consciousness of members of the ruling classes, that we get to know the history and culture of the Roman world. With very few exceptions, the most important historians and philosophers of the Roman Empire, such as Tacitus, Suetonius, Cassius Dio, Arrian, Seneca, and Musonius Rufus, were either senators or equestrians. Some, like Plutarch, belonged to the uppermost sections of the local elite. A few, like Herodian and Epictetus were imperial freedmen—an altogether *sui generis* group, sharing the viewpoint of the imperial circles.

A clear dividing line separated the bulk of the Roman population into free and slave. This dividing line was legal (it had mostly to do with political rights) but also determined the mode in which each category was being exploited. The free were often forced to offer their services to state officials or to members of the propertied classes. But they were mainly exploited economically through taxes and rent. Most of them lived near subsistence level. Occasionally, they had to make great sacrifices, face starvation, or abandon their farms and join gangs of robbers (as happened more often in Egypt). But for the most part they were able to produce as much as was needed to maintain their livelihood, support their families, and pay what was asked of them.

The common folk were further divided according to the place of their residence into an urban and a rural section. Those who lived in the cities were often farmers, attending daily to their farms in the hinterland. The rest performed all kinds of manual labor. A few worked for wages, while others were traders or craftsmen. A significant section consisted of people involved in various services.

With few exceptions (the Gospels and the lives of the desert fathers being among the most conspicuous), the whole of the extant literature deals with urban life. It is not difficult to realize how restricted this picture is, given that most inhabitants of the Roman Empire were village-dwelling peasants. From what is known, it is clear that the villages were socially stratified and should therefore be treated as complex rather than simple communities. Rural slaves apart, there were prosperous farmers, poor freeholders, leasehold tenants (who became serf-like *coloni* in the Later Empire), as well as wage earners, living in great uncertainty and anxiety. Villagers had their own culture and their own way of understanding what was going on in the empire. We are sometimes able to get glimpses of their religious sentiments in rural Egypt and a few other provinces (Lewis 1983).

Throughout the imperial period, slaves were quite numerous and of extreme importance to the economy of the empire. In Italy, where their concentration was greatest, they may have accounted for 40 percent of the population (Brunt 1971). In other parts of the empire, the number of slaves was very substantial, in some areas amounting to a third of the total population. All members of the propertied classes owned large numbers of slaves, but so too did many free persons of moderate means—sometimes poor farmers or craftsmen, who needed an extra hand to help them in their work (Hopkins 1978; Bradley 1987). Jesus practically took it for granted that all his listeners had at least one slave plowing or tending sheep in the field (Lk 17.7).

Slaves were found in almost all sectors of Roman society. It is reasonable to assume that most of them were employed in productive activities, especially in the fields where they sometimes worked in chain gangs, as well as in the crafts. But the number of slaves employed in nonproductive services was also considerable. As members of the imperial *familia*, the household of the emperor, they filled many and significant posts in the administration. Occasionally, the slaves and freedmen of the emperor exercised more power than equestrians or even senators.

We know precious little about the feelings of slaves. Some of them were certainly literate and may have expressed their feelings in writing. But everything they ever wrote has perished, almost without a trace. This much, however, is clear: even slaves had learned to accept their position in society. By the time of Jesus, the great slave revolts of south Italy and Sicily all belonged to the past. The ruling classes had learned their lesson and had taken good care to ensure that their slaves would never again be liable to revolt.

Several factors contributed to the docility of slaves. The prospect of emancipation certainly made their fate more bearable. Owners manumitted their slaves frequently. This was sometimes done at a slave's deathbed, but it was also common with slaves who were just thirty years old. The prospect of emancipation served as an incentive; those wishing to gain their freedom were more submissive and more industrious. Normally, they had to buy their freedom, by paying in their lifetime savings. This practice was benevolent to them and also beneficial to masters. It increased the productivity of slaves and enabled masters to recapitalize their property, replacing old slaves with younger ones. When the master was a Roman citizen, the manumitted slave became a Roman citizen himself. Within the imperial *familia*, there was a regular system of promotion, following the principle of seniority (Weaver 1972).

Slavery as an institution did not die out quickly. It retained its significance in production until well into the Middle Ages and was never formally abolished until the modern age. But from the third and fourth centuries onward, many slaves were gradually transformed into serfs. As serfs, they remained under the control of their masters, rendering services to them, and they were also bound to the soil they cultivated, either by law or by custom. They were mainly exploited as unpaid laborers by their landlord and as renters of the land they cultivated on a hereditary basis. Nevertheless, they possessed means of production in a way slaves did not, organizing their labor according to their needs and capacities and reproducing themselves by raising their own families (Ste. Croix 1981: ch. 4.3).

A Mode of Production Based upon Slavery

As a complex and ordered society, the Roman Empire was in constant need of resources. It had to spend great amounts for various purposes, such as public construction projects, the maintenance of an administration and a standing army, and the feeding of the poor in the city of Rome. These resources were amassed both within the borders and from beyond them. Yet there is little doubt that the bulk of imperial revenues derived from taxes paid in by farmers, who also had to contribute to the Roman economy by forced labor.

Part of the taxes exacted may be regarded as corresponding to services rendered by the empire. Most of the public facilities, the administration of justice, and the maintenance of a standing army to guard the borders from external threats, for example, were meant to serve society as a whole. But almost all services were organized in ways corresponding to the class nature of Roman society. Through them, members of the ruling classes (mostly senators and equestrians) secured their social position as governors, generals, etc. We may therefore look on the exploitation of farmers through taxation and forced labor as the mode through which the empire reproduced its socially stratified nature.

Roman society may be also seen in a different and more fundamental way. For however much some senators and equestrians benefited from the distribution of taxes, it was mainly through the exploitation of their land and slaves that the propertied classes, as a whole, secured their privileged position. Slaves never outnumbered free laborers, let alone the free inhabitants of the Roman world at large. There is little doubt that, despite their large numbers and their significance in agriculture, production in the Roman world was basically the work of free peasants and craftsmen. In grain-producing Egypt, for example, agricultural slavery was almost unknown. But it is also clear that the propertied classes extracted most, or at least a very substantial portion, of their surplus by exploiting unfree laborers, most of whom would have been slaves in the strict sense of Roman law. We may thus regard the slave mode of production as dominant because through it the propertied classes secured their position in society (Ste. Croix 1981: ch. 2.3).

In the Roman world, especially during the late Republic and under the Principate, the exploitation of slaves was very profitable to their owners. Due to continuous fighting, millions of people were constantly led into captivity. Captives may be dealt with in many ways: they can be freed when the war is over, slain, or ransomed. But they can also become slaves, treated as permanent property of their captors. This last option is neither always possible nor always desirable. Whatever the case may be, there are certain prerequisites for the conversion of captives into slaves. The society into which they are introduced must be able to keep them under control, circulate them as commodities, and employ them at a profit. Roman society was able to fulfill all these requirements. Once a slave-owning society has been established, slaves may also be reproduced through breeding or other secondary methods, such as piracy and debt-bondage.

The profitability of slaves rested upon their cheapness and extreme exploitation. Being owned by their masters, they were made to work hard, handing in the total of their produce. In return, a master had only to feed, clothe, and shelter them. At their masters' discretion, slaves could also be allowed to keep part of their earnings, either to raise families and thus help create new slaves or to engage in more profitable activities.

Exploitation and Domination

Economic exploitation as an explanatory theoretical category came to the foreground in the nineteenth century. In the modern world, a worker normally offers his laboring capacity in return for wages. The transaction appears to depend upon consent and mutual agreement. As a rule, no law or extra economic coercion forces the laborer to enter upon such a relationship. Having paid the wages agreed, the employer makes use of this capacity for an agreed length of time. In making use of the labor power for which he has paid, the employer reasonably expects to earn more than the agreed wages; otherwise no more is received than spent. The concept of economic exploitation was introduced to explain the extraction of surplus, that is, unpaid labor from the wage earner.[11]

In traditional societies no need for such a concept was ever felt. In the Roman world, which is the topic at hand, the propertied classes derived most of their income through the labor of slaves. From an economic perspective, relations between masters and slaves were thought to be simple. Slaves belonged to a master; their whole body was the property of a master. Hence, everything that was produced through their labor and services, and everything they possessed, just like their bodies and their lives, belonged to their master as well. Thus the ancients had every reason to stress the fact that slaves were, above all, dominated. Domination could explain why the product of their labor went to the master.

From a modern perspective, master and slave relations may be seen in a more sophisticated way. It can be argued that neither a slave nor his laboring capacity belonged to a master as totally as was believed. To begin with, a slave had to be bought or raised at his master's expense. Before being able to make any kind of profit, a master had first to earn as much as he had spent to obtain or raise the slave. Furthermore, a slave had to be fed, clothed, housed, and taken care of, at least to the level of subsistence. Upon manumission, a freedman occasionally could find himself worse off than before. Epictetus the philosopher, an ex-slave himself, had such freedmen argue that while in slavery "someone else kept me in clothes, and shoes, and supplied me with food, and nursed me when I was sick; I served him in only a few matters" (Epictetus, *Discourses* 41.37, Oldfather). Often, to be able to perform his duties properly, a slave was allowed to live above subsistence level—sometimes on his own. This meant that part of what a slave produced did not go to his master at all. It went to the slave himself for his breeding and maintenance—occasionally even for his well-being.

Masters certainly knew that buying and sustaining a slave cost money, but they do not seem to have realized that this money actually "belonged" to their slave. To phrase it differently, the mode in which masters exploited their slaves, by possessing their whole body, concealed the fact that they did not possess all the products of their labor. By stressing domination and ownership, a political and a legal category, ancient authors overlooked exploitation, an economic category.

There is no evidence that masters ever calculated the net profit they made through the employment of their slaves. Production was normally performed at the level of households as economic units, and thus all expenses of whatever kind were added to the same entry. Ancient household organization did not require the evaluation of the productivity of individuals, let alone of "instruments" such as slaves. Of course, masters knew what they earned when they hired their slaves out by the day to a third party; and they knew what slaves working on their own paid in. But as a rule they did not subtract the expenses they made on slaves' behalf.

This concealment of exploitation did not simply affect the logistics of masters. It may have been at least partly responsible for the way in which ancient thinkers tended to regard or rather disregard aspects of the economy at large. Hence, social relations that we would be inclined to consider chiefly in terms of economic implications were in the main viewed with regard to political or moral concerns. This way of reasoning was extended to almost all types of profit-making activities.

Laborers working for wages were not an important element in the Roman economy. But peasants were extremely important, whether they were tenants or freeholders. Most peasants normally remained bound to their productive activities through economic necessity and custom; if these motives did not suffice, coercion was also employed. In the time of Jesus there were laws forbidding peasants to move into cities, but it was mainly through the tax system (the *census*) that they were kept or made to return to their villages. In the Later Empire, from the reigns of Diocletian and Constantine onward, starting with leasehold tenants (*coloni* in the Latin-speaking West and *paroikoi* in the Greek-speaking East), peasants were bound by law, either to the fields they cultivated or to their villages. Thus, hitherto free persons gradually became hereditary serfs (Jones 1958). In the minds of the propertied classes, peasants and other laborers were thus likened, in significant respects, to slaves. No sophisticated theoretical analysis was needed to explain how the products of their labor passed to the propertied classes. Peasants, it was thought, paid in their taxes and their rents because, like slaves, they were dominated. The Roman administration with its tax collectors and, if necessary, with its army saw that no one could escape (Kyrtatas 2002).

"The last will be first, and the first last" (Mt 20.16): Social Stratification and Social Hierarchy in Early Christianity

"The kingdom of Heaven may be likened to a king who decided to settle accounts with his slaves" (Mt 18.23): The Social Structure of the Early Christian Communities

Little is said in the New Testament concerning the ways in which Jesus and his followers obtained their provisions. The impression given is that the first disciples had abandoned their occupations as well as their property for the sake of the gospel (Mk 10.28–9). As far as can be established, before their conversion they had belonged to various sections of the population, although few if any were men of means. A wealthy sympathizer who approached Jesus quickly realized that joining the movement was not for him ("for he had many possessions": Mk 10.17–22), although others may have been less reserved (Jn 3.21). But the majority of them were clearly simple men and women, which does not mean that they were paupers. It may safely be assumed that several of them were farmers (Lk 17.7).[12] A few had been tax collectors; among them, a wealthy chief tax collector (Mk 2.14; Lk 5.27–29, 19.1–10). Beggars were also ready to follow Jesus (Mk 10.46–52). Even the leading disciples were uneducated laymen (Acts 4.13). Four among them were said to have been fishermen (Mt 4.18–22).[13] When Jesus was crucified, some thought of resuming their former tasks (Jn 21.3). Soon they became fully occupied with their religious duties. Most of the leaders became itinerant charismatics and community organizers (Theissen 1978).

After the Pentecost, the first believers in Jerusalem are presented in Acts as living together and having everything in common. Several among them, perhaps most, were property owners. The Levite Joseph Barnabas, who became a missionary, owned plots of land, as did Ananias with his wife Sapphira and others (Acts 4.36–5.1). As is recorded, they would sell their property and possessions and distribute the proceeds among all, according to each one's need (Acts 2.44–45, 4.32). Such wealth was obviously not expected to last forever, but no plans regarding its replacement were made. As new converts joined the community, they would also sell their land or houses, if they possessed any, and hand over to the apostles the proceeds for distribution among those in need (Acts 4.34–35). Those who dared to retain some of the purchase price for themselves were cursed; two of them died (Acts 5.1–11).

This is a somewhat idealized presentation of the earliest Christian community. It is unlikely that a complete common ownership of wealth was ever practiced, let alone organized along clearly defined principles. Even if some kind of property sharing was ever established as a way of living, it died out very quickly. Similar practices were only repeated once or twice in early Christian history. They give the impression of being spontaneous responses to the awe and fear caused by the expectation of the imminent realization of the Parousia. It was never really argued that such was the way all Christians should live. In the later chapters of his work, the author of Acts forgets all about this practice. He takes it for granted that most early Christians pursued their normal business and occupations.

Even if the story in Acts preserves historical information one thing must be underlined. This was not a "communism" of production. Common ownership of the means of production is never as much as implied in the early Christian literature. In this sense, the story of property sharing is quite consistent with Christian reasoning. An urge was often felt to introduce innovations in the prevailing modes of consumption. Believers were thus expected to adjust their table manners in a way pleasing to God. "So whether you eat or drink," says Paul, "or whatever you do, do everything for the glory of God" (1 Cor 10.31). We may therefore call this practice a "communism" of consumption, which was neither meant, nor able to introduce, lasting changes in the basis of the economy.[14]

Our ignorance regarding the occupations of the first disciples is somewhat compensated for by indirect information. Since there is so much talk in the Gospels about fish as foodstuff, it is reasonable to assume that there were several fishermen in the company of Jesus. The parables refer mostly to sowers and sowing, less often to shepherds and merchants (Mt 13, 25.32). On several occasions, the farmers mentioned in the parables are presumed to be owners of the land they cultivate. They till the soil according to their needs and abilities. Buying more land is a constant, if unattainable, dream (Mt 13.44).

The kingdom of heaven was often likened by Jesus to wealthy masters (kings or "businessmen") possessing numerous slaves. Most such slaves normally worked under the direction of their owner or a steward. But an alternative way of administering the master's property is also recorded. The slaves could be left to make the most of what had been allocated to them, working on their own. At intervals or upon arrival (in the case of absentee masters) the lord would settle accounts with them, rewarding those who had increased his property and punishing those who had not (Mt 18.23–34, 25.14–30). Jesus' listeners were clearly expected to identify themselves with the slaves of the parables, not with the masters.

Informative as these parables are regarding the social milieu in which Jesus preached, they have their limits. We may accept their information only when it is corroborated by other evidence. Thus, it is reasonable to assume that the bulk of Jesus' followers were farmers themselves, like some of the heroes in the parables. On a normal working day, the listeners of Jesus were expected to be out in the fields if they were men, or grinding at the mill if they were women (Mt 24.40–41). Some, perhaps most, owned at least one servant of servile status, assisting them in their agricultural labors. Plowing and tending sheep were clearly thought to be a typical servant's task (Lk 17.7). But there is no reason to believe that there were many slaves among the first disciples. In actual fact, not a single real slave is ever mentioned in the Gospels or Acts as being interested in the teaching of Jesus. The master and slave relation was commonly used as a metaphor for subjection and obedience (Martin 1990).

As soon as the movement of Jesus began to spread beyond Palestine it underwent a fundamental change. Whereas the Gospels insist that Jesus preached almost exclusively in rural areas, avoiding even those towns that were in his way, from Acts onward, after the Pentecost, Christian missionaries are only found in the important towns of the empire (Frend 1980; Ste. Croix 1981: ch. 7.4). The originally rural movement of Jesus was transformed into a city-based religion. The countryside was approached again from the late second century onward. But by that time, Christianity had obtained a clearly urban profile.

After the transformation of Christianity into an urban religion we hear little if anything about villagers, shepherds, or fishermen. Farms (*agroi* and *ktemata*), often mentioned in the Gospels, are almost completely forgotten in the rest of the New Testament. The new converts were now drawn from all social strata of the urban population.

Some Christians in the new urban communities were artisans—like Paul of Tarsus; Aquila of Pontus and his wife Priscilla, who were tentmakers (Acts 18.1–3); or Lydia of Thyatira, who was a dealer in purple cloth (Acts 16.14; Theissen 1978; Meeks 1983). In early Christian literature frequent mention is made of craftsmen (cf. *Did.* 12.3), but most Christians were probably farmers who lived in towns and attended daily to their fields. It was taken for granted that a typical community could offer its leaders the "firstfruit of the produce of the winepress and of the threshing floor and of oxen and sheep" (*Did.* 13.3).

From the late second century onward, a section of the Christian communities consisted of members of the local upper classes as well.[15] A few converts could be also found among the Roman elite. There is much evidence to substantiate this estimate (Kyrtatas 1987: ch. 6), but we may safely rely upon the opinion of Eusebius, who argued that from the time of Commodus (180–192 C.E.) "the word of salvation began to lead every soul of every race of men to pious worship of the God of the universe, so that many of those who at Rome were famous for wealth and family turned to their own salvation with all their house and with all their kin" (*Hist. eccl.* 5.21.1, Lake).

Slaves as a social category were not attracted by the teaching of Jesus. Throughout his mission, they constantly make their appearance as servants, and they are also often mentioned in the parables. But the Gospels give us no hint that any of them had joined the group of disciples or even the crowds of sympathetic listeners. To begin with, slaves did not have the freedom to travel as they pleased. Since Jesus was constantly on the move, only runaway slaves could have joined him. Such behavior, however, would have required special encouragement, which was not forthcoming. The company of Jesus was not and did not wish to become a company of outlaws. Only the slaves of disciples could be expected to follow Jesus. If there were any of them in his company, they certainly did not make their presence felt.

After the transformation of the Jesus movement into an urban religion, slaves gradually began to join Christian communities. Very little can be said about their sentiments and expectations, but it is more or less clear that almost all of them belonged to two special and privileged groups. In the Roman world, great importance was attributed to households as social and productive units, especially among the upper sections of society. When the leader of a household expressed interest in new religious rights, his whole *familia* was expected to express interest as well. The early Christian missionaries often addressed themselves to such leaders, in the reasonable expectation that through their conversion the whole household would be baptized, including women, children, and slaves (Acts 11.14, 16.31). It is very difficult to determine the extent to which slaves were actually converted to Christianity along with their masters. But there is little doubt that most of the slaves of whom some concrete information is given in the sources belonged to Christian masters. Indeed, they often appear to be the favorite slaves of their masters, sharing their masters' interests and sentiments.

The second privileged group of slaves represented in the early communities were members of the imperial *familia.* When Paul wrote his letter to the Christians of Rome in the mid-60s, there were already imperial servants among their number (cf. Phil 4.22). Such Christians continued to play a prominent role in the Church of Rome throughout the next centuries, until the time of Constantine. It is very difficult to say whether these people were slaves or freedmen, but the difference was

546 DIMITRIS J. KYRTATAS

not great. All of them were members of a privileged group and to a greater or lesser extent had access to positions of power. The authority exercised by the Church of Rome over much of the Christian movement may to a certain degree have depended upon the influence of the Christian members of the *familia Caesaris*.

The presence of such slaves in the early Christian communities does not alter the fact that the vast majority of their class remained uninterested in the new religious movement. Early Christian literature is devoid of references to rural slaves and slave miners who lived under extremely harsh conditions.

It has been estimated that many early Christians were freedmen. As former slaves, freedmen had certain obligations to their patrons, their former masters. But they were free persons. They had almost all the rights of the freeborn; they could move around as they pleased, become rich, and rise to positions of power. Being a freedman was a one-generation status. A freedman's son could become emperor.[16]

After the conversion of Constantine, the Christianization of the empire progressed steadily with imperial aid, but there was still much to be done (MacMullen 1984). Most slaves employed in production, the bulk of the free peasantry, and the Roman aristocracy were still substantially pagan.[17] It appears that rural slaves converted to Christianity in the process of their transformation into serfs. This transformation gave them some basic freedoms and a family life.

"Everyone should remain in the state in which he was called" *(1 Cor 7.20): Social Mobility and Status Inconsistency*

Social mobility was very limited in the Roman world, as is normally the case in agricultural societies. Peasants, the vast majority of the population, almost constantly hard-pressed, were occasionally given the opportunity to ameliorate their position, but it was hardly ever possible for them to move upward into a different social class. The same applies to most of the exploited masses in the towns of the empire. Social change was almost always restricted to movement within one's own class. But there were two notable exceptions to this rule, which drew the attention of Christian moralists.

In the uppermost section of Roman society, there seems to have been considerable upward mobility from the ranks of town councillors to equestrians and on up to senators. This was mainly due to three factors. First, with imperial aid the senatorial and equestrian orders gradually expanded over the years; second, vacancies were constantly created by the low fertility of the Roman aristocracy;[18] and third, people moving down the social ladder from the nobility into the lower classes had to be replaced by others (Hopkins 1965). Thus, within the dominant classes there was constant competition. Even the wealthiest of the Roman aristocrats felt the urge to increase their wealth.

The second notable exception was the upward mobility of some freedmen. In order to keep them submissive and productive, slaves were not uncommonly given their freedom. As freedmen they found themselves in a new environment, able to pursue their careers and exploit their skills for their own benefit. The Roman world was full of freedmen seeking to improve their position and move into the upper classes. Most opportunities were given to manumitted members of the imperial *familia*. Some of them even succeeded in rising to the highest ranks in a remarkably short time.

Christian teachers reacted to social mobility in a very negative way. In the New Testament, the desire of some Christians to improve their social standing was already being discouraged. Paul was explicit on this issue. "Everyone," he urged his fellow Christians, "should remain in the state in which he was called. Were you a slave when you were called?" he asked. "Do not be concerned but, rather, even if you can gain your freedom, make the most of it [i.e., your slavery]. . . . Brothers, everyone should continue before God in the state in which he was called" (1 Cor 7.20–24). In generations to come this negative attitude became even harsher. Ignatius, bishop of Antioch in the early second century, advised his colleagues not to let slaves be "puffed up," but to make them endure their fate to the glory of God. He argued that such people should not desire to be set free at the church's expense, because they would thus become "slaves of lust" (Ign., *Pol.* 4, Lake; see Harrill 1993).

Christian moralists also reacted negatively to the pursuit of wealth. Wealth, as they saw it, did not constitute a problem in itself. The rich had many opportunities to improve their moral character by spending part of their property for the benefit of the churches and those in need. But the pursuit of wealth, they argued, was an obstacle to moral amelioration. It preoccupied the minds of believers who should be concentrating upon spiritual matters. In addition to that, it required business relations (mostly with pagans) inimical to a pious way of life.[19]

Despite the negative attitude taken by most Christian moralists, there is evidence that some Christians were upwardly mobile. The case of freedmen is of special significance in this context; they were not only given opportunities to become wealthy through hard work, but also belonged to a group with very weak bonds of social solidarity. Upon manumission, they entered a world that accepted them as free but rejected them as peers. To outsiders, they had the stigma of servile origin. Because of their strong status inconsistency they often felt emotional ambivalence and insecurity (Meeks 1983). Most probably sought new relations that would provide a sense of group identity. Hence the importance of religion. While other social groups were closed to newcomers, numerous cults welcomed them and encouraged them to join in. By participating in religious cults, freedmen found themselves inside groups with strong cohesion. The Christian communities seem to have been particularly attractive to upwardly mobile freedmen for this very reason.

Another very important category of upwardly mobile Christians were the church leaders. From an early stage, the missionaries were often supported by the religious communities. "Do you not know," Paul asks the Corinthian Christians, "that those who perform the temple services eat what belongs to the temple . . . ? In the same way, the Lord ordered that those who preach the Gospel should live by the Gospel." Paul himself preached the gospel "free of charge," but this was only because he wanted to avoid obstacles that could make his task less effective (I Cor 9.13–14, 18). Most of the early missionaries were itinerants, finding it difficult to support themselves by their own labor. They had to move around and spend most of their time preaching and organizing the churches (I Cor 9.6–7; 2 Thes 3.8–12).

Most urban churches were soon well organized, under the direction of deacons, presbyters, and bishops. The new clergymen were also supported by the religious communities, receiving firstfruits and other contributions. From the middle of the second century at the latest, some were being paid fixed salaries—a custom that gradually became very common. What is more important, the new leaders took full control of the church funds. The bishop of each city had almost absolute power to make any financial decisions he felt appropriate. Apart from utilizing the community assets, he could also invest them. Although very little is recorded regarding the financial activities of the early church leaders, it seems very likely the most common type of investment was usury. Usury was unpopular with the masses and, hence, bishops were often condemned for practicing it. But it was a very profitable form of banking. All it required was capital and a good name. Christian bishops had both. They could easily find clients both inside and outside their religious communities. Through such activities they helped increase the wealth of their churches, while raising their own financial and social status. Over the following centuries, some of the most important bishops belonged by birth to the upper classes.[20]

Paul's commandment that everybody should remain in the social position in which he received his calling to Christianity sounds very conservative, even reactionary. But it was not necessarily meant to be so. In the early days, all Christians were expecting the end of the world very soon—probably within their lifetime. Concentrating upon the world to come was a matter of priority.

Christian indifference to social status had at least one additional cause. According to the teaching of Jesus, all those who suffer in the present world, including those who are poor and hungry, will receive a high wage (*misthos*) in the world to come (Mt 5.3–11; Lk 6.20–26). The Kingdom of God was not expected to be a world of total equality; in the imagination of the early Christians it had inherited the stratified structure of the Roman world. Hence, indifference to social status was restricted to the temporary period of expectation. Those who fulfilled their religious duties most conscientiously were hoping to find themselves at the top of the heavenly order. The Christian apocalyptic documents that began to emerge from the second century onward gave many details of just how the last would become first and the first last, according to their deeds.[21]

"Hear the parable of the sower" (Mt 13.18): Early Christian Reactions to Modes and Relations of Production

"Should anyone press you into service for one mile, go with him for two miles" (Mt 5.41): Early Christian Attitudes toward Exploitation and Oppression

Like all their contemporaries who did not belong to the dominant classes, the early Christians were clearly unhappy with the exploitation they experienced. This much is clear from the frequency with which the issue comes up in documents. The most ugly forms of what we could call legitimated forms of exploitation were forced labor and taxation. In the Gospels, the technical Greek term for forced labor is used in its verbal form (*aggareuein*). On his arrival in Jerusalem from the country, Simon the Cyrenian was pressed into carrying the cross—a task that he performed without complaint (Mk 15.21; Mt 27.32). Common as they might have been, such duties caused considerable aggravation. Evidently replying to inquiring disciples, Jesus gave a provocative commandment: "Should anyone press you into service for one mile, go with him for two miles" (Mt 5.41).

A similar stance was also taken by some philosophers of the period. Thus Epictetus advised his listeners to treat their whole body like a poor loaded donkey. If it was commandeered (here we have again the technical term *aggareia*) and a soldier lay hold of it, one should let it go, neither resisting nor grumbling. Otherwise one would get a beating and even risk losing the donkey into the bargain (Epictetus, *Discourses* 4.1.79). Such practical wisdom was probably meant to comfort people who were constantly pressed into service. Since they were bound to comply, they should either turn their minds to the future bliss, as taught by Jesus, or to their inner freedom, as taught by the Stoics.

Taxation was another frequent topic of discussion in the company of Jesus. In the Gospels, tax collectors are presented as sinners par excellence (Mt 9.10, 11.19). They are grouped alongside pagans (Mt 18.17) and prostitutes (Mt 21.31). Yet, in spite of their extremely bad reputation, several among them expressed interest in the teaching of Jesus and were accepted into his company. Like those who had approached John the Baptist, they were probably asked to cease collecting more than what was prescribed (Lk 3.12). Feeling guilty for his deeds, the chief tax collector

Zacchaeus proceeded to distribute half of his possessions to the poor and repay any amount he had illegally extorted four times over (Lk 19.2–8).

Since the issue was both hotly debated and caused disturbance in the Jewish world, Jesus was directly asked by some Pharisees and Herodians whether it was "lawful to pay the census tax to Caesar or not." The technical word used in Mark is *kensos*, which basically meant taxes due to Rome as tribute.[22] Jesus and his disciples were clearly aware that tolls (*tele*) and census taxes were normally paid to conquerors not national leaders (Mt 17.25–26). The reply to the direct question was, "Repay to Caesar what belongs to Caesar and to God what belongs to God" (Mk 12.13–17). The wording of the answer reveals just how delicate and controversial the matter was. But there is little doubt that Jesus did not object to the payment. In Matthew's account he objects even less to the payment of the Temple tax (Mt 17.24–27).

The Christian attitude to taxes was standardized by Paul. According to him, all higher authorities were instituted by God. Obedience was therefore due to them not merely out of fear but also because of conscience. Accordingly, all obligations should be paid: "taxes to whom taxes are due, toll to whom toll is due" (Rom 13.1–7). In the next generations, Christian apologists often tried to remind authorities just how loyal they were since they paid their taxes without complaint (Grant 1977/1978: ch. 3).

Regarding wage labor and other forms of legitimated extraction of surplus, Jesus and the early Christians expressed no reservation. When the righteous were promised a great reward in heaven, the word used was *misthos*, wages (Mt 5.12). In general it was argued that laborers deserved their wages (Lk 10.7). In the parables, hired laborers sometimes grumble because they receive less wages than expected (Mt 20.1–16). Elsewhere they complain when they have to deal with demanding masters who harvest where they have not planted and gather where they have not scattered (Mt 25.24). Wages were clearly thought to be the best and most just way of payment; even prophets were said to be rewarded with them (Mt 10.41).

If the disciples of Jesus and the early Christians were admonished to endure oppression, oppressors themselves were regarded as sinners. Oppression was most emphatically condemned when it led to excessive extraction of any kind of surplus. Nevertheless, it was never argued that wealth possessed legitimately was the product of institutionalized oppression or exploitation of slaves, serfs, peasants, or wage earners. Consequently, there was nothing wrong with wealth per se. The only real problem was that the rich were constantly tempted to amass their fortune by whatever means. Wealth was not seen as the product of exploitation but was very often thought to be the cause of oppression.

"What must I do to inherit eternal life?" (Mk 10.17):
Early Christian Attitudes toward Property (Including Slaves)

Regarding wealth, Jesus is recorded as having made some very harsh statements. According to one of them reported by all three synoptic Gospels, he claimed that "It is easier for a camel to pass through the eye of a needle than for one who is rich to enter the kingdom of God" (Mk 10.25; Mt 19.24; Lk 18.25). Jesus had just advised a wealthy sympathizer to sell his possessions and distribute them to the poor (Mk 10.21; Lk 18.22). The version given by Matthew, however, added a qualification: The rich man was only advised to sell his possessions if he wished to become perfect (Mt 19.21). This qualification implied that wealth was not an obstacle to salvation, it was only an obstacle to perfection.

It appears that the most radical stance toward property and wealth corresponds to the itinerant and rural character of the Jesus movement. No sooner did the early Christians become city-based and organized on a permanent basis than the original radicalism was substantially modified. In its new form, after a very brief period of alleged common ownership of wealth, early Christianity focused upon almsgiving. According to an understanding that became dominant and remained unchallenged (except perhaps by some later heretics), Christians wishing to become perfect did not have to distribute their entire property in alms (Lk 12.33). It was up to them to decide just how much was necessary for them to keep.

In the early Christian communities it was thought that almsgiving could create a harmony between rich and poor. "The rich man has much wealth," it was argued by an influential Christian teacher, "but he is poor as touching the Lord, being busied about his riches. . . . But when the rich man rests upon the poor, and gives him what he needs, he believes that what he does to the poor can find reward with God, because the poor is rich in intercession and confession, and his intercession has great power with God" (Herm., *Sim.* 2, Lake; see Hengel 1974/1998 and Osiek 1983). Almsgiving quickly became essential to Christian morals. By being instituted, it gave the churches one of their main missions. At the same time it sanctioned property and canceled all the reservations of the primitive movement regarding possessions and wealth. Since slaves were commonly regarded as property, possession of slaves was also sanctified (Garnsey 1996).

As some Christians gradually moved up the social ladder, and especially when more wealthy people began to join the religious communities in the late second century, a new problem began to trouble Christian moralists. In the Roman world, the rich were in the habit of displaying their wealth and were often prone to extravagance. The luxurious life of many Christians in big cities such as Alexandria was felt by the poorer brethren to be offensive and contrary to a Christian way of life. Asking the rich to abandon their possessions was clearly out of the question.

It seemed reasonable, however, to demand from them restraint. Clement of Alexandria was the most renowned exponent of the theology of moderation (*Paed.*).

By teaching compassion and brotherly love, Christianity ameliorated the treatment of some slaves who were close to their Christian masters. But it had nothing to say about slavery as an institution. Jesus took it for granted. In his parables, production most commonly depends upon the work of slaves. Slaves are often admonished in the parables to work hard and conscientiously; masters are never admonished to treat their slaves with consideration. Consequently, it never occurred to Christian missionaries and teachers to challenge production based upon slavery. The decline of slavery came so late in Western history that it can be in no way attributed to the influence of Christianity (Westermann 1955; Finley 1980).

In the early Christian literature almost nothing is recorded regarding the manumission of individual slaves—a very common practice in the Roman world. In the very few instances that the issue was raised, all the leading Christians were of the same opinion as Paul: "Everyone should remain in the state in which he was called." Slaves were urged not to be concerned with their servile status. Even if they were given the opportunity to gain their freedom, they should rather remain in slavery, making the best use of their condition as slaves, serving their masters in fear and with all due reverence. In their turn, masters were asked to stop bullying their slaves. They both had a common master in heaven (I Cor 7.20–24; Eph 6.5–9). One New Testament author went as far as admonishing slaves to obey their masers with all reverence, not only those "who are good and equitable but also to those who are perverse" (I Pt 2.18; Ste. Croix 1975).

"Neither sowing nor reaping" (Mt 6.26): Early Christian Attitudes toward Production

The sanctification of property and the acceptance of slavery determined Christian attitudes toward production. The principal means of production in the Roman world, land and slaves, as well as its dominant slave mode of production went unchallenged. Ever since, all social relations and all modes of wealth appropriation that were considered by a given society as legitimate were accepted by Christian ethics.

Insofar as early Christianity intervened in matters pertaining to the economy, it was only concerned with modes of consumption. It advocated almsgiving and discouraged exhibition and extravagance. Consequently, no changes in production were recommended or expected to occur. It did not seem possible at that time any more than it does today to transform production by modifying dietary customs and table manners. Yet, before ancient Christianity came to an end, suddenly and unexpectedly, some Christians came very close to introducing a new and hitherto unknown mode of production. It all began just after the middle of the third century, when the Gospel saying "if you wish to be perfect, go, sell what you have and give to the poor" (Mt 19.21) was again read literally and taken seriously. Antony the Egyptian paved the way for numerous others by distributing all his property and seeking salvation in the desert.[23] The ideal was neither to sow nor to reap, but rather to spend a lifetime in contemplation and prayer. But as no human being can live by prayer alone, it soon became evident that some kind of arrangement should be made for provisions.

To secure their livelihood, the desert fathers who began to appear in large numbers in the countryside of the eastern Roman provinces did not reproduce the dominant modes of production. They neither possessed their own land nor exploited the work of slaves. When they did not depend upon charity alone, they worked by their own hands and only kept for themselves the absolute minimum essential for their survival. They established what we could call a desert mode of production, based upon independent and isolated producers, that does not involve economic exploitation of one another. The organized coenobitic monasticism of Pachomius modified this productive system but retained its basic characteristics. Since it had no use for luxury items, the ideal monastery was self-sufficient in a way that almost no village of the period ever aspired to.

By remaining marginal, this minimalist economy of mere subsistence did not alter society; by the fifth century the boundaries that separated the desert hermits from the urban churches were being blurred (Markus 1990: ch. 12). However, it demonstrated that, under certain circumstances, a very radical modification in consumption could revolutionize production. In the Middle Ages numerous Christian groups, by no means all fringe sects, were inspired by this paradigm. The modern socialist movement came also very close to some early Christian precepts. But there was a difference. The communist utopia envisaged a world with free and independent producers. The Christian heavenly utopia envisaged a world with free and independent consumers. In paradise, no one is expected to sow or reap. As visualized in the Revelation of John (Rv 22.2), the tree of life will offer its fruit in such abundance that it will suffice for all.

Notes

1. In this chapter the New Testament is quoted from the *New American Bible*.

2. The earliest known exponent of this theory is Melito of Sardis, who flourished in the second century; the relevant passage is quoted by Eusebius, *Hist. eccl.* 4.26.7, trans. Lake. This topic is examined by Grant (1977/1978: ch. 2).

3. This is not to say that the modern historian accepts as accurate all the information provided by the early Christian authors.

4. For introductions to most historical topics related to the formative years of Christianity see Benko and O'Rourke (1971).

5. This topic is raised and discussed in Theissen (1982).

6. The financial activities of the early churches are not well documented. For a later period see Jones (1960).

7. Mode of production is a central concept of Marxist theory. It is variously understood and explained. Karl Marx gives some important information in his *Critique of Political Economy* and various chapters of *Capital*.

8. All numbers and percentages given in this chapter are no more than estimates of limited value. Nevertheless, they do provide an order of magnitude. On the social structure of the Roman world, with numerical estimates, see Alföldy (1985). On the economy of the Roman world see Garnsey and Saller (1987).

9. This is yet another estimate of limited value, made by Jones (1964: 465).

10. This term is mostly used by Ste. Croix (1981). Much of what I say in this chapter depends upon the information and arguments of this work.

11. One of the most basic and widely read essays by Karl Marx dealing with the concept of exploitation in the modern world is "Wage Labour and Capital," first published in 1849; it is now best known in its 1891 edition, corrected by Frederick Engels (Marx and Engels 1978a).

12. An early witness attests that the grandsons of Jesus' brother Judas were poor farmers; the relevant passage is quoted by Eusebius, *Hist. eccl.* 3.20.1–6.

13. This information has been sometimes challenged on the grounds that it originated from the metaphorical expression "fishers of men" in Matthew 4.19 and Mark 1.17.

14. Interesting comments on this issue were made by Kautsky (1910/1925) and Troeltsch (1931/1932).

15. A well-documented case is Phileas, bishop of Thmuis, who had served as a magistrate in Alexandria and died as a martyr very early in the fourth century.

16. For the probable presence of influential freedmen in the early Christian community of Rome see Osiek (1983) and Jeffers (1991).

17. On the conversion of the aristocracy see Jones (1963) and Brown (1961).

18. To keep property concentrated, very few children were born and raised in most aristocratic families. Due to the high infantile mortality of the period, many of these families did not sufficiently reproduce themselves.

19. This reasoning is made explicit in many Christian treatises. Admonition on these lines was given to the Christians of Rome in *Shepherd of Hermas* and to the Christians of Alexandria by Clement (*Quis div.*). For an analysis of Revelation along such lines see Thompson (1990); this study also locates socially the early Christians of the province of Asia.

20. On upwardly mobile freedmen and church leaders see Kyrtatas (1987: ch. 3 and 6).

21. Most popular were the *Apoc. Pet.* and the *Apoc. Paul.*

22. Luke (20.22) uses the word *phoros* (tribute, tax) in the same context.

23. Athanasius, *The Life of Antony* became the model for the massive hermit movement of late antiquity.

What Would You Do for a Living?   24

DAVID A. FIENSY

HISTORIANS HAVE LONG CONCERNED THEMSELVES with the questions of the theology of the early church. What was the Christology, ecclesiology, or pneumatology of these pioneers of Christianity? These questions, as important as they are, often give the impression that all Christians in the ancient world were theologians or clergymen. This chapter seeks to understand the common church member by reflecting on the kinds of job they held. We soon understand that these were folk not only involved with understanding their faith but also with the mundane task of making a living in a largely non-Christian pagan society.

First, we must define some terms. By early Christianity we mean pre-Constantinian (or from 30 C.E. to 324 C.E.). Some reference might be made to the era of Constantine or a little after, but only to give perspective to the pre-Constantinian time. Second, we will not distinguish between orthodox Christianity and the other types such as Gnostic Christianity, Montanism, the Ebionites, etc. People who considered themselves Christian believers were classed together. We will first examine the occupations that Christians considered unworthy of their new faith. Next we will discuss the occupations actually engaged in by the members of the early church as these occupations are witnessed to by the writings of the New Testament, church fathers, martyrologies, apocryphal literature, non-Christian pagan literature, papyri, and inscriptions.

What Christians Would Not Do for a Living

Occupation and confession were interlinked in early Christianity. We are accustomed in modern Western society to compartmentalizing our jobs, political views, and family relationships from our religious beliefs. The ancients did not do that. One's religion permeated one's political, economic, and kinship values even as one's kinship, politics, and economics permeated one's religious commitments (see Hanson and Oakman 1998). For the early Christians, some occupations were compatible with the new faith and some were not. Even those that were compatible in theory might not be compatible if engaged in improperly.

The Christian prohibition of certain occupations was based on three principles: (1) Occupations that infringed on the moral teachings of the faith were condemned. These included prostitution and all connected with it. (2) Occupations that devalued human life were forbidden. These included the military, gladiatorial contests, and even competitions such as chariot racing where the participants might have to kill or injure someone (though Christians seemed to be in the stands when their fellow Christians were being martyred). In addition, civil magistrates in the church were usually disapproved of because they might have to sentence someone to death. (3) Occupations that participated in idolatry in any way were forbidden. Obviously then one could not be a pagan priest, but some Christians even warned against incense selling, sculpting, masonry, painting, and the like in the service of a pagan temple.

Already in the New Testament there is reference to the occupations based on vice. Paul found it necessary to instruct the Corinthian church members that certain occupations/lifestyles had become unacceptable for the new believers: "Neither sexually immoral persons, idolaters, adulterers, male prostitutes, pederasts, thieves, greedy people, drunken people, verbally abusive people, nor robbers will inherit the kingdom of God and some of you were doing these things" (1 Cor 6.9–10). Thus, the recent converts had to be instructed regarding the relationship of confession to occupation.

Over a century later we again find a listing of unapproved occupations. The two most detailed lists—those of Tertullian of Carthage and Hippolytus of Rome, both around 200 C.E. (see table 24.1)—explicitly refer to prostitutes and all those connected to prostitution. Tertullian says no prostitutes, pimps (*lenones*), panders (*perductores*), attendants of prostitutes (*aquarioli*), or brothel keepers can be accepted because they are connected with immorality (*Idol.* 11; *Apol.* 43; see *Apol.*, Glover 192). Hippolytus's *Apostolic Traditions* lists prostitutes, panders (πορνο–βοσκός), and sodomites (so *Trad. ap.*, Dix 27) or licentious men (so *Trad. ap.*, Easton, 42).[1]

The *Apostolic Traditions* also prohibit Christians from being actors or those who make shows in the theater. We know from other writers that the theater was sternly condemned in the early church. Theophilus of Antioch (C.E. 160) wrote that Christians were forbidden to go to the theater (*Auto.* 3.15). Tertullian maintained that the theater was connected with idolatry (*Spect.*10). Minucius Felix (Rome, 210 C.E.) condemned all shows, mimes, actors, and the theater in general (*Oct.* 37). Cyprian of Carthage (250 C.E.) condemned mimes because they encouraged adultery and

Table 24.1.   Forbidden and Restricted Occupations According to Tertullian (*Idol.* 11, *Apol.* 43) and Hippolytus (*Trad. ap.*)

Tertullian	Hippolytus
Forbidden Occupations	**Forbidden Occupations**
Prostitute	Prostitute
Pimp	Pimp
Pander	Sodomite
Brothel keeper	Actor
Attendant of prostitutes	
	Charioteer
Soldier (but if one at conversion may continue)	Soldier (but if one at conversion may continue; must be taught not to execute people or to take the military oath)
Gladiator	Gladiator
Trainer of gladiators	Trainer of gladiators
	Huntsman in the arena
	One doing wild animal shows
	Public official concerned with gladiatorial shows
Frankincense seller (probably; must not sell to pagan temples)	Priest of idols
	Keeper of idols
	Magistrate of a city
	Military governor
	Teacher of children (but if no other way to make a living may continue)
Magician	Magician
Sorcerer	Charmer
Astrologer	Astrologer
Soothsayer	Interpreter of dreams
	Maker of amulets
	Seller of quack medicines
Occupations with Restrictions	**Occupations with Restrictions**
Plasterer (must not work on pagan temples)	Painter (must not make idols)
Painter (must not work on pagan temples)	Sculptor (must not make idols)
Stonecutter (must not work on pagan temples)	
Bronze worker (must not work on pagan temples)	
Engraver (must not work on pagan temples)	

produced effeminate men (*Ep.* 1.8). A Christian may not, according to Cyprian, remain an actor nor may a Christian teach the art of acting to anyone. If the Christian is a new convert and has no other way to make a living than teaching acting, he must rely on Christian charity (*Ep.* 60.1–2). Novatian (Rome, 250 C.E.) condemned all public shows and Greek contests in poetry, music, and athletics (he specifically mentioned the shot put contest). Although idolatry was the mother of all public amusements and they should be avoided because of that connection, he was also offended that the Greek athletic competitions were in the nude (*Spect.* 1–8). Thus, the Christian opposition to sexual immorality led to prohibiting not only occupations that explicitly depended on that vice (prostitution) but also to prohibiting occupations that could encourage adultery (thus acting/miming and even athletic contests).

The Christian attitude toward military service was usually negative, though at times it could be ambivalent. Condemnations of making war are numerous and found over a wide geographical area. Both Justin Martyr (155 C.E., Rome; *1 Apol.* 39; *Dial.* 110) and Irenaeus (180 C.E., Gaul; *Haer.* 4.34.4) applied the prophecy of turning swords into ploughshares (Is 2:3–4) to the Christian movement and affirmed that Christians were not to make war. Tatian (160 C.E., Rome and Syria; *Oratio ad Graecos* 11) announced that he declined any interest in military command, and Clement of Alexandria (200 C.E., *Paed.* I.12) wrote that Christians are not trained for war but for peace. Cyprian of Carthage challenged his congregation by affirming that the hand that holds the Eucharist must not be corrupted by sword and blood (*De Bono Patientiae*). Origen (230 C.E.; Alexandria and Caesarea) responded to the pagan Celsus's observation (late second century) that Christians were not fulfilling their duty to the emperor by refraining from the military service. Origen argued that Christians did more good for the emperor and his armies by praying for them than others did by fighting under them (*Cels.* 8.68–69, 73). Arnobius (300 C.E., North Africa; *Adv. Nationes* 1.6) maintained that Christians were completely pacifist, preferring to have their own blood shed than to shed the blood of another. Lactantius (300 C.E.; Asia Minor; *Inst.* 6.20) wrote that Christians cannot kill at all, neither in war nor even by accusing someone of a capital crime in a court of law.

Tertullian addressed this issue at length twice. He maintained that to take the military oath of allegiance to the emperor was completely unacceptable for Christians, and that violence contradicted the Christian way of life. When Jesus disarmed Peter in the Garden of Gethsemane, he disarmed every soldier. Since Jesus declared that anyone who lives by the sword will die by the sword, how can any Christian carry one? When Jesus would not even take someone to court to sue him, how can a Christian take part in battle (*Idol.* 19; *Cor.* 11)? Yet, surprisingly, having written these things, Tertullian conceded that if one were already a soldier and converted to Christianity, he might continue, though he must be aware that it would cause great difficulty. The best course of action, according to Tertullian, would be to quit the military (*Cor.* 11).

Clement of Alexandria too seems to have allowed one to remain a soldier if he converted while serving in the military. In the *Protrepticus* 10 he advised that if a person was a farmer when he became a Christian he should continue being a farmer but now one that meditated on God while tilling the fields. If one had been a sailor at his acceptance of the new faith, he could continue sailing the seas but now he should rely on the heavenly captain. And if one had been a soldier when knowledge had taken hold of him, he should listen to the just commander. Thus, it appears that in all three cases, the farmer, sailor, and soldier, the new convert is allowed to continue his occupation but now with a Christian emphasis. The *Apostolic Tradition* of Hippolytus, however, agreed with Tertullian and Clement. A military leader who converts must resign his commission. An ordinary soldier who does so may remain a soldier but must be taught not to execute people and must not take an oath. One already a Christian who wishes to become a soldier must be cast out of the church.

The arrangement given in Hippolytus may record accurately the Christian relationship to the military: Christians converted while in the military could remain if they did not fight in a war. Bainton suggests that Christian soldiers would serve in a police function (1960: 79): guarding the emperor, keeping the peace, aiding governors in provinces, guarding prisoners, caring for the mail, doing secretarial duties, and aiding in fire protection. In these functions Christian soldiers would not be called upon to kill anyone, but if a war began they would have to refuse to fight.

After the accession of Constantine in 324 C.E. the Christian attitude toward war began to change (Hornus 1980: 168; Bainton 1960: 66). Now Christians began to see military service more in terms of just war. If the war is just, so the argument goes, it is possible for a Christian to participate. This idea was developed fully by Augustine in the fifth century, especially in response to the barbarian invasions (*Civ. Dei* 1.21, 26).

In spite of the condemnations of military service, we know of several examples of Christian soldiers. Whether they were all serving in the capacity described by Bainton is unknown and questionable. In the New Testament there are four notable cases of encounters with believing soldiers. John the Baptist encounters some soldiers who ask his ethical advice. John replies that soldiers should not extort or falsely accuse people and that they should be content with their wages (Lk 3.14). Thus there is no instruction to either quit the army or to refrain from battle. Second, Jesus encountered a centurion whose son/servant he healed (Mt 8.5–13; Lk 7.1–10; Jn 4.46–54) and was impressed with the centurion's faith. Third, Acts 10 narrates the conversion of the first Gentile to the faith, Cornelius, a centurion in Caesarea. Upon his conversion, there is nothing indicated about instructions to refrain from warfare. Finally, there is a narrative of a jailer, presumably a soldier, in Philippi who was baptized in the night by Paul and Silas (Acts 16.25–34), again with no information about pacifist teaching.

Cadoux maintains that there is no reliable example of a Christian soldier after the stories of the Acts of the Apostles (late first century C.E.) until the time of Emperor

Marcus Aurelius (160–180 C.E.; Cadoux 1925: 276; cf. Bainton 1960: 67ff.; Hornus 1980: 122). The oft-reported incident of the Legio XII Fulminata or Thundering Legion, which took place around 173 C.E., is the first literary reference to Christian soldiers after the New Testament period. This legion, which contained many Christians recruited in Armenia, was campaigning in Germany when the heat and lack of water threatened their safety. The Christians in the legion prayed for rain and were answered immediately (Dio 72; Eusebius, *Hist. eccl.* 5.5; Tertullian, *Apol.* 5). Thus, this narrative, which may have legendary elements, indicates a large number of Christians in the military in the later half of the second century.

Tertullian himself noted the presence of Christians in the military, even though he opposed their service. He wrote that Christians had by his time filled every place among the pagans, even the military camp (*Apol.* 37). His treatise on a Christian soldier's refusal to wear a laurel wreath refers to many other Christian soldiers who condemned this behavior (*Cor.* 1). The references to soldiers in the *Apostolic Traditions* of Hippolytus also demonstrate that there were numerous Christian soldiers, since Hippolytus found it necessary to handle this problem in some detail. Thus, one gets the impression that by the close of the second century in North Africa and in Rome many Christians served in the military to the displeasure of the Christian leaders.

Eusebius gives us the same impression a century later. He notes that by the end of the third century there were numerous Christians in the imperial palaces, governing provinces, and serving in the military (*Hist. eccl.* 8.1). But in the year 303 C.E. Galerius sought to rid the armies of Christians by forcing them to either renounce their faith or be stripped of their rank (*Hist. eccl.* 8.4). Eusebius reports that many of them (one would think not all, however) left the army at that time. Thus there were enough Christians in the armies to get the attention of Diocletian's lieutenant, Galerius. Also of importance among the literary sources are the martyr narratives. The earliest recorded execution of a Christian soldier was Basileides in 205 C.E., who was executed for refusing to take an oath. Marinus was likewise beheaded in 260 C.E., and Marcellus of North Africa was executed in 298 C.E. On the other hand, Maximilian (295 C.E.), who was being forced into military service, refused to serve; the proconsul tried in vain to convince him to serve by noting that there were already many Christians in the armies. After Maximilian's continued refusal, he was executed by the sword. Three other soldier martyrdoms take place in the early fourth century, before the reign of Constantine: the forty martyrs of Sebaste in Armenia (308 C.E.), Julius the Veteran (Moesia Inferior; 304 C.E.), and Dasius (Moesia Inferior; 304 C.E.). The last account is important because it too refers to "many foolish men who call themselves Christians," in other words who did not behave as uprightly as Dasius (see *Acts of the Christian Martyrs*, xxvii–xlix, 133–279).

In addition to the literary references to Christian soldiers there are several tomb inscriptions. Hornus has identified seven inscriptions that are certainly Christian and four that are probably so (1980: 119–21). He lists among the seven three from Rome, one undated, and two from the third century; three from Phrygia in Asia Minor, two from the third century and one from the early fourth; and one from Thrace. In the four other cases soldiers in grave inscriptions tell of deceased Christian family members. Were the soldiers also Christians or only their family members? Hornus allows that they probably were Christians as well. These are from Dalmatia (late third century), Asia Minor, and Rome. To these inscriptions we should add the papyrus letters described by Judge and Pickering from 297 C.E. in Egypt, which refer to a soldier of "at least moderate means" who was probably a Christian (Judge and Pickering 1977: 52).

Thus there is evidence for Christian soldiers spread throughout the empire. Bainton surmised, however, that the strongest opposition to Christian military service was in the churches in the East. He believes that North Africa was divided on the issue and that Rome was less opposed to Christians in the military (because of the three military epitaphs in Christian cemeteries). The eastern frontier, however, had the most extensive Christian participation in the army (Bainton 1960: 71–72).

Could Christians serve in the army? Probably most Christians frowned on it before the time of Constantine. Nevertheless, the church had the problem of what to do with soldiers who converted. Must they leave the service or could they continue? The church for the most part seems to have settled on the arrangement noted above: stay in the army but do not kill anyone. But even that decision would probably not have been acceptable to every Christian. There were undoubtedly some who fought and killed.

Christians were also concerned about other violent occupations. The gladiatorial contests and even the chariot races concerned them. Theophilus of Antioch (*Auto.* 3.15), Athenagoras (177 C.E., Athens; *Leg.* 35), Minucius Felix of Rome (*Oct.* 37), Tertullian of Carthage (*Spect.* 11, 19) and Cyprian of Carthage (*Ep.* I.7) wrote that Christians were forbidden to witness gladiatorial contests. Tatian condemned both gladiators and boxers (*Oratio ad Graecos* 23); while Clement of Alexandria classed gladiators with parasites, flies, and weasels (*Paed.* 2.1). The *Apostolic Traditions* of Hippolytus forbid receiving anyone into the church who is a gladiator (μονομάχος), a trainer of gladiators, a huntsman in the arena (κυνηγός), or a public official concerned with the gladiatorial shows. Thus no one connected in any way with the gladiatorial contests could, according to Hippolytus, be accepted as a Christian.

There were probably two reasons for this strong denunciation of the gladiatorial contests. First of all the contests involved the taking of human life and feeding the crowd's hunger for watching dying people (Auguet 1972: 46–53). Second, the amphitheater was used to reinforce loyalty to the emperor cult and other local pagan deities (Futrell 1997: 93). Thus the gladiatorial contests were permeated with religious significance. The same reasons lay behind the disgust for chariot races on the part of Christians. Again the *Apostolic Traditions* refuse to admit into the church anyone who is a charioteer (ἡνίοχος). This prohibition is consistent with the condemnation of the chariot games in general found in Tertullian (*Spect.* 9), Minucius Felix (*Oct.* 37), Athenagoras (*Leg.* 35), and Novatian (*Spect.* 5). According to Roland Auguet, the chariot games even more than the gladiatorial contests had the imprint of pagan religion on them. Further, chariot racing often became violent when opponents tried to overturn others' chariots, to the delight of the crowd (1972: 124, 131).

Finally, in this second category of occupations prohibited because of the devaluing of human life is that of civil magistrate (despite the case of Erastus, which will be discussed below). Hippolytus, *Apostolic Traditions*, declares that no magistrate (ἄρχων) of a city who wears the purple may be received for baptism. Tatian had declared that he did not wish to rule (*Oration ad Graecos* 11) while in the *Letter to Diognetus* 10:5 (second century) the desire to dominate others or rule others is condemned. Celsus, the critic of Christianity in the second century, complained that Christians declined public office, neglecting their duty (Origen, *Cels.* 8.75). Minucius Felix wrote, "Nor do we consist of the lowest plebeians even if we do refuse your honors and your purple" (*Oct.* 31). Canon 56 of the Council of Elvira (Spain in 306 C.E.) forbade a Christian to hold the office of the *duovir* or city magistrate (Kyrtatas 1987: 101).

Cadoux suggests five reasons why Christians refrained from seeking or perhaps even accepting public office in the city (1925: 225–26). (1) Such positions were associated with idolatry, and their holders would be expected to participate in pagan rituals. (2) The social standing of most Christians made them unable to seek public office. (3) Christians did not value the worldly glory, and thus the glory of their society. (4) Christianity taught forgiveness and nonresistance, and punishing wrongdoers would contradict this teaching. (5) Christian repudiation of retaliation was so great that they would not endure even watching someone being put to death. Tertullian gives most of these reasons in his treatment of Christians and idols. He declared that Christians could hold public office only if they would have nothing to do with sacrifices, giving public shows, taking oaths, passing judgments on people, or giving penalties (*Idol.* 17). Tertullian's point was that it is not possible to hold a public office and avoid these things.

Yet, we again detect that there were Christian public officials, for Tertullian refers to a dispute in the churches over this matter. Those who argued in favor of Christians holding public office pointed to Joseph and Daniel in the Hebrew Bible, men who were loyal to God but still held important posts in pagan governments

(*Idol.* 17). Thus Tertullian's view was evidently not the only one in the ancient church. Furthermore, Tertullian himself seems to witness the Christian involvement in both the army and the magistracy in a passage admittedly full of rhetorical exaggeration: "We have filled every place: cities, insulae, fortresses, towns, markets, even army camps, tribes, town councils,[2] the palace, the senate, the forum" (*Apol.* 32). Harnack was perhaps overreaching, but not by much, when he suggested that by the end of the third century "the court, the civil service, and the army were full of Christians" (1961: 311). City magistrates who were converted to Christianity, like soldiers, had a difficult decision to make. Undoubtedly, some did give up their positions, but one should not imagine that this was the inevitable choice.

The third and final category of prohibited occupations in the early church was that with a connection to idolatry. Tertullian and Hippolytus condemned any kind of work that had direct association with idolatry and were critical of any that had indirect connection with it. Hippolytus (*Trad. ap.*) excludes from consideration for church membership any priest of idols or keeper of idols. Further, he counsels that Christian sculptors and painters must be taught not to make idols. Thus the occupation was acceptable if it was not used for idolatry. Tertullian verbally thrashed Christian artisans who made idols and attempted to justify their lucrative business by appealing to the apostle Paul's admonition to work with one's hands (*Idol.* 4–5, 7). To his horror, Tertullian could even point to idol makers who had been chosen for ecclesiastical office (*Idol.* 7). He will allow no associations with paganism at all. Thus stucco workers, painters, stonemasons, bronze workers, and engravers must not work on pagan temples (*Idol.* 8). He even has serious doubts about incense sellers since one never knows how the incense will be used (possibly in a pagan ritual, *Idol.* 11). Once again, however, the necessity of condemning such practices indicates that many Christian artisans did work for pagan temples and even fashioned idols for a living.

Also included under this category would be the occupations associated with the magical arts. Hippolytus forbids the occupations of magician (μάγος), charmer, astrologer (αστρολόγος), interpreter of dreams, seller of quack remedies, and amulet maker. Tertullian also condemns Christians who practice astrology for a living and even mentions one in particular who challenged him on this issue (*Idol.* 9). Thus, some Christians were trying to continue telling people's fortunes by the stars. Elsewhere Tertullian maintains that there were among Christians no magicians (*magi*), soothsayers (*aruspices*), diviners (*arioli*), and astrologers (*mathematici*). Allowing for the rhetoric, we would conclude that these occupations would have been rare among Christians since the idolatrous connections would have repulsed most.

Finally, both Hippolytus and Tertullian have reservations about a Christian working as a teacher. Hippolytus urges that if someone teaches children worldly knowledge, it would be better for him to quit teaching altogether. If, however, that person has no other skill (τέχνη) by which to make a living, let him have forgiveness. Tertullian is much less generous about this occupation. He maintained that a Christian should not be a schoolmaster because he would have to teach children pagan literature as well as perform certain customary pagan rites (*Idol.* 10).

The profession of faith on the part of the members of the new religion often resulted in difficult decisions regarding their occupations. Some Christians evidently continued their old lifestyles in about the same way as before conversion, incurring the harsh critique of the ecclesiastical writers (see Harnack 1961: 311). Others must have made sweeping changes such as quitting a military or magisterial post, abandoning a trade or craft, or renouncing any contact with magical practices and the like. Perhaps we should imagine that most Christians, however, stood in the middle of these two extremes, ambivalent and even conflicted over the practical application of their newly found faith.

What Christians Did for a Living

Historians point out that Christian thought brought dignity to manual labor (Agrell 1976: 150–51; Richardson 1952: 43; Latourette 1953: 246; Munier 1992: 469). The classical authors often referred to craftsmen as inferior beings whose bodies were deformed by hard work and whose minds were like those of slaves (Cicero, *Off.* 1.42; Aristotle, *Pol.* 1.5.10; Dio Chrysostom, *Ven.* 7.110; Lucian of Samosata, *Fug.* 12ff.; Burford 1972: 29; MacMullen 1974b: 115ff.). But Pauline references (1 Thes 4.9–12, 1 Cor 9.1–27, Eph 4.28, and 2 Thes 3.6–15) indicate that work was thought of in the Pauline communities as "divinely commissioned for man" (Agrell 1976: 151). Thus Christianity, like Judaism, did not share the disdain for working with the hands that we find so frequently in the Greco-Roman literature. Further, early Christianity was primarily an urban movement. Not many peasants or country folk were involved in the movement until the late third or early fourth century (Meeks 1983: 9–50; Frend 1984: 132, 421–22, 572). The occupations that we would expect to be most often mentioned in the literary sources, therefore, should be urban occupations: skilled crafts and unskilled manual labor. Paul instructed the Thessalonian believers "to work with your own hands" in quietness (1 Thes 4:11). From this and similar texts Best and Meeks conclude that most of the Thessalonian Christians were "manual workers, whether skilled or unskilled" (Best 1972: 176; cf. Meeks 1983: 64). Meeks argues further that this instruction was what Paul in all likelihood typically gave to new converts and that we should therefore conclude that most early Christians throughout the empire were handworkers. This is confirmed by Ephesians 4:28, writes Meeks, where the Deutero-Pauline author again urges the reader to labor with his hands (1983: 65).

Such information as we have for first-century Christianity would seem to agree with Meeks's thesis. We read in the New Testament of a metalworker (2 Tm 4:14), tentmakers (Acts 18:3), a general handworker (I Cor 9.6), Tertius a scribe (Rom 16.22), a purple dealer (Acts 16.14–15, evidently financially well off), and day laborers (Jas 5.4). But the New Testament also gives witness to other occupations: lawyer (Ti 3.13), city manager (Rom 16.23, see below on Erastus), physician (Col 4.14), merchants (Jas 4.13), and soldiers (Lk 3.14, 7.1–10 and Acts 10.1–49, well-to-do centurions, Acts 16.25–34, a jailer). There are also several slaves listed in the New Testament, which we will discuss later.

The literary sources for the second century also indicate that most Christians were handworkers. The *Didache* (100 to 140 C.E. in Syria) admonishes its readers to put guests of the congregation to work: If the guest is a craftsman (τεχνίτης), let him work and then let him eat, but if he is not a craftsman, use your own judgment about whether to feed him (12.3–4). Athenagoras of Athens affirms that among Christians one could find uneducated persons, craftsmen, and old women (*Leg.* 11). Celsus, the pagan detractor of Christianity, charged that the Christian movement consisted of leather cutters, fullers, and woolworkers (Origen, *Cels.* 3.55–56, 58). Eusebius refers to Theodotus the shoemaker, a second-century Christian heretic (*Hist. eccl.* 5.28). Thus, the impression one forms is that most second-century Christians were hand laborers.

Yet there are also references to occupations above mere manual labor. A Christian physician in Gaul was martyred in 180 C.E. (*Acts of the Christian Martyrs*: 77). Callistus, bishop of Rome, was originally a banker and an imperial slave (Hippolytus, *Haer.* 9.7). A second Theodotus, also considered a heretic and a disciple of Theodotus the shoemaker, was a banker (Eusebius, *Hist. eccl.* 5.28). Christians may have been heavily involved in the banking business at some point (Kyrtatas 1987: 124; *NewDocs* 5, 139) since Pliny (*Ep.* 10) mentions in his second-century letter to Trajan that Christians took an oath not to deny a deposit to anyone who asked for it back.

The sources for the third century mention similar Christian occupations. Tertullian referred to sculptors, painters, stucco workers, stonecutters, soldiers, and artisans in general (*Idol.* 4–5, 8, *Cor.* 1). Hippolytus (*Trad. Ap.*) listed painters, sculptors, and soldiers. Tertullian complained that at least one Christian persisted in practicing astrology for a living (*Idol.* 9). Three of the celebrated soldier martyrdoms happened in the third century: the forty martyrs of Armenia (Sozomen, *H.E.* 9.2), Marcellus of Tingis in Mauretania (*Acts of the Christian Martyrs*, xxxvii, 251–59), and Basileides (*Acts of the Christian Martyrs*, xxvii, 133–35). For the brief period of the fourth century before the accession of Constantine we have only reference to two soldiers: both Julius the Veteran and Dasius were martyred in Moesia Inferior (*Acts of the Christian Martyrs*, xxxix, 261; xli, 273–79).

We have postponed until now any discussion of Christian slaves and freed-men. First, we will survey the evidence for Christian slaves/freedmen in general. Next, we will discuss specifically imperial slaves/freedmen.

The New Testament gives evidence to the presence of large numbers of slaves in the early congregations. Paul's long list of greetings to Roman Christians (Rom 16) surely included several slaves and former slaves. Lampe concluded that of the twenty-six persons listed in that text we can identify the origins of four-teen of them. Of these, ten were probably of servile origin. Thus over two-thirds of the names on this list (whose origins can be identified) were slaves or freed persons (Lampe 1991: 228). We have good reason to conclude that the Corinthian church also had a large percentage of slaves and former slaves. Paul's references to the "household of Stephanus" (1 Cor 1.16) and Chloe's people (1 Cor 1.11) indicate large houses with significant numbers of slaves, evidently many of them believers. The much discussed Erastus, the οἰκονόμος or city man-ager/treasurer of Corinth, was probably a freedman (Bartchy 1973: 59–60). Paul even devoted a small letter to the issue of slavery (Philemon). Admonitions to Christian slaves to obey their masters as an act of Christian service also testifies to the importance of slaves in the early Christian community (Eph 6.5–9; Col 3.22–25; 1 Tm 6.1–2; 1 Pt 2.18–21). Finally, the Acts of the Apostles refers to two slaves who were believers in the Way (Rhoda, 12.13 and the Ethiopian Eu-nuch, 8.26-40).

Pliny the Younger, in a letter to Emperor Trajan (*Ep.* 10) written from Asia Mi-nor in 110 C.E., described two female slaves among the sect of Christians. Ignatius, also in 110 C.E., greeted fellow believers in the "house of Tavia" in his *Letter to the Smyrnaeans* 13.2 (in Asia Minor). Evidently this house was a large household with several Christian slaves. In addition, Ignatius admonished slaves of Philippi (Macedonia) to endure their slavery to the glory of God (Ign., *Pol.* 4). Also in the second century was the martyrdom of Blandina, a slave of Gaul, who was tortured to death (Eusebius, *Hist. eccl.* 5.1). Third-century sources also mention slaves. The martyrdoms of Revocatus and Felicitas, Christian slaves, took place in 203 C.E. in Carthage (*Acts of the Christian Martyrs*, xxvii, 108–9). Tertullian wrote that Chris-tians collected charitable donations on a regular basis, part of which went toward caring for aging slaves (*Apol.* 39).

Of special interest are the imperial slaves and freedmen. The career of a slave in the imperial service could be one of upward mobility and increasing wealth. Of-ten sons of slaves would be sent to special schools and then as young men would begin to work their way up through the bureaucratic system (Finn 1982: 31–37). Thus a Christian of lowly origin could in the course of a lifetime of imperial ser-vice acquire great wealth and power. Already in the New Testament we find refer-ence to imperial slaves/freedmen. Paul refers in Philippians to Caesar's household and to the *praetorium* (πραιτώριον; 4.22 and 1.13) where he is imprisoned, probably meaning the slaves in the imperial service (Finn 1982: 33; Kyrtatas 1987: 79).

Toward the end of the first century Clement of Rome wrote his letter to the Corinthian church and sent it by three men named Claudius, Valerius, and Fortunatus. The first two persons bear names suggestive of imperial freedmen, affirms Dimitris Kyrtatas (1987: 79). Lightfoot, followed by others, postulated that Clement of Rome himself was an imperial freedman of the household of the emperor's (Domitian, reigned 81–96 C.E.)[3] cousin, Titus Flavius Clemens (*Clement of Rome*, Lightfoot I.I.25–61; Finn 1982: 33; Kyrtatas 1987: 80, see note 7).

In the second century, the companion of Justin, who was martyred in 165 C.E., was one Euelpistus, one of the emperor Marcus Aurelius's slaves (*Acts of the Christian Martyrs*, 51). Irenaeus indicated that there were believers in the royal court of Caesar (*Haer.* 4.30.1; Kyrtatas 1987: 80–81). Hippolytus named two Christian imperial freedmen, Carpophorus and Callistus, and a Christian imperial concubine, Marcia, in the reign of Commodus (176–192 C.E.; *Haer.* 9.7).

The third century witnessed an increased presence of Christians in the imperial service. Eusebius narrated that the royal house of Emperor Alexander Severus (reigned 222–235 C.E.) consisted mostly of believers (*Hist. eccl.* 6.28). Likewise Emperor Valerian (253–260 C.E.) was said to have filled his place with godly people and have had a veritable church of God in his house until he became alarmed at the growing numbers of Christian bureaucrats and sought to strip them of their power and possessions (Eusebius, *Hist. eccl.* 7.10; Cyprian, *Ep.* 81). By the time of Diocletian (284–305 C.E.) Eusebius could write that in the imperial palaces emperors had been for some time allowing their wives, children, and slaves to adopt Christianity (*Hist. eccl.* 8.1). Under Diocletian, however, many Christian soldiers and imperial slaves were either stripped of their honors or put to death (*Hist. eccl.* 8.1, 8.6). Eusebius narrates especially the martyrdom of Dorotheus and Gorgonius, who along with many other imperial slaves were martyred under Diocletian. Thus by the end of the third century, there seems to have been a growing body of Christian bureaucrats in the imperial system (Kyrtatas 1987: 81–82). Many of these must have acquired great wealth.

The grave inscriptions in Christian cemeteries and catacombs also refer to slaves, although the references are relatively rare (Marucchi 1974: 223; Kajanto 1963: 8). Marucchi lists seven such inscriptions from Italy (1974: 224–27 for slaves and 243 for an imperial freedman). Cadoux cites two inscriptions from the second century that name imperial freedmen (1925: 392). Kaufmann (*Handbuch der altchristlichen epigraphik*, 102) gives the inscriptions from the tombs of three Christian freedmen. Of special interest are quotations of epitaphs of Christian imperial slaves. There are Publius Aelius Rufinus, probably a freedman of Emperor Hadrian (117–138 C.E.) and Marcus Aurelius Januarius, freedman of Marcus Aurelius

(161–180 C.E.). One inscription, from the catacomb of Domitilla, may even connect us with the above mentioned list of names in the epistle to the Romans 16: "Julia, (freedwomen or slave of) Augusta Agrippina. Narcissus (slave of) Augustus Trajan. Agrippinianus put (this here)" (tr. from *Handbuch der altchristlichen apigraphik*, 98); Kaufmann suggested that Narcissus and Julia (both mentioned in Romans 16.11, 15) were husband and wife and former slaves of Nero's mother who were still serving the imperial household in the time of Emperor Trajan (98–117 C.E.). Thus the two listed by Paul were imperial slaves who continued to serve the palace into the second century. Kaufmann affirmed, probably too uncautiously, "The identification of this Narcissus with the one named by the apostle seems to me as good as certain" (99).

One is therefore struck by the frequent mention of Christian slaves both generally and especially with reference to imperial slaves. It is tempting to conclude that a large percentage of the Christian population in the first three centuries was of servile origin. Kyrtatas has argued strongly against this conclusion maintaining that there was only a "small number" of slaves in the early church (1987: 45). He correctly notes that relatively few Christian sepulchral inscriptions indicate servile origins (1987: 48; cf. Kajanto 1963: 8 and Marucchi 1974: 223). But his own evidence would seem to contradict his conclusions. We have as much literary evidence for Christian slaves as any occupation. The relative lack of sepulchral references to servile origin may have been because of the Christian disregard for social ranking (Kajanto 1963: 15; Marucchi 1974: 223; Gal 3.28; Lactantius, *Inst.* 5.14–15). Rather, the literary sources would suggest strongly that from the beginning up through the third centuries there were undoubtedly many slaves and freed persons in the church. Table 24.2 summarizes our results so far.

The inscriptions are also very helpful in discovering what occupations early Christians pursued. We will discuss below the occupations noted on Christian epitaphs or in the few papyri that are clearly Christian. Those inscriptions and papyri identified as Christian (see Keppie 1991: 121–24) may paint for us a landscape of the types of occupations Christians pursued. After we have surveyed the evidence, table 24.3 will summarize our results.

By far the most controversial of the inscriptions comes from first-century Corinth. It reads in Latin: *Erastus pro aed sp stravit.* The epigrapher of the Corinthian materials, John Harvey Kent, understood the inscription as follows: *[praenomen nomen]Erastus pro aedili[ta]te s(ua) p(ecunia) stravit*—"Erastus in return for his aedileship laid (the pavement) at his own expense" (*ICor*, 99). In other words, the Erastus of the inscription paid for a pavement to be laid in return for his being appointed to the office of aedile (commissioner of public buildings). Kent identified this Erastus with the Erastus of Romans 16.23 (see also 2 Tm 4.20; Acts 19.21–22) based on the following three reasons: (1) This inscription dates around the middle of the first century, about the same time as the Epistle to the Romans.

Table 24.2. Christian Occupations in the First Four Centuries Based on Literary Evidence

First Century	Second Century
*Lawyer; #City Manager; *Physician; ^Metal worker; #Tentmaker; #Scribe; *Merchants; *Bankers; ~Day laborers; #Craftsman; +Craftsmen; +Purple dealer; ~Soldier (3); *Imperial slaves; *^#Slaves; Scribe	Physician (Gaul); *Imperial slaves; #~Artisans; ^+Slaves (Gaul); ~Woolworkers; ~Leatherworkers; ~Fullers

Third Century	Fourth Century
*Imperial slaves; @Astrologer; @Sculptors; @Painters; @Stonecutters; @Stucco workers; @Artisans; *@^~Soldiers (also in Mauretania)	Soldiers (Moesia Inferior; Armenia)

*Rome/Italy   #Achaia   @Carthage   +Macedonia   ^Asia Minor   &Egypt   =Dalmatia   ~Syria

(2) The name Erastus was not a common name.[4] Thus one would suspect that any other reference to an Erastus might be the same person. (3) Paul's description of Erastus in Romans 16.23 (the οἰκονόμος or manager of the city) is near enough to an *aedilis* to be the same function. Kent concluded that the Erastus of Romans and the Erastus of the inscription were the same person, that he was probably a freedman, and that he had acquired considerable wealth (*ICor*, 99–100).

Meggitt (following Cadbury 1931: 42–58) recently challenged all three of Kent's arguments. The inscription's date is not clearly the mid-first century, maintains Meggitt; it could be the latter part of the century. The two titles (οἰκονόμος and *aedilis*) could mean the same thing but they are not a perfect fit. Finally, Erastus was not such an uncommon name. Meggitt has found fifty-five examples of the name in Latin and twenty-three in Greek (1996: 218–23).

We would suggest that the date of the inscription is not as crucial as it might seem. Why should we suppose that the date of the inscription has to be the same as the date of the Epistle to the Romans? One can easily imagine that a person such as Erastus would have continued to serve the city of Corinth for many years in the first century. Second, Mason has established without question that the Greek term οἰκονόμος can be used for the Latin *aedilis* (1974: 71). His investigation into the Greek translations of Latin institutions has made it more historically sound to accept that the terms could be referring to the same office (Clarke 1993: 50; Winter 1994: 185–92). Finally, that the name Erastus is found frequently in antiquity is significant but not conclusive. We must ask what are the chances of there being two Erasti in Corinth from approximately the same period of time who held important city offices? A host of historians and commentators have accepted Kent's identification of the two persons (Theissen 1982: 75–79; Meeks

1983: 58–59; Harrison 1964: 100–105; Clarke 1993: 50–56; Winter 1994: 185–92; Fitzmyer 1993: 750). Although one cannot be certain, on the whole it seems better to conclude that these two Erasti were the same person. Thus, one of the earliest inscriptions refers to a wealthy Christian who held a high-ranking office in the city of Corinth.

From the second century in Italy we have the grave of the daughter of a Christian freedman who was an archivist: "Aurelius Primus, freedman of the emperor, record keeper." As noted above, several other second-century grave epitaphs in Rome in Christian catacombs refer to imperial slaves/freed persons (*Handbuch der altchristlichen epigraphik*, 97–99, 106).

The third-century inscriptions and papyrus texts attest to the following occupations: From Italy are a shorthand writer or amanuensis (*notarius*), a woolworker (*ILCV* I, 134, 124), a wagon driver (*Handbuch der altchristlichen epigraphik*, 111), a record keeper, and (surprisingly) the treasurer of the gladiatorial games and of the wine (*Iscrizioni cristiane di Roma*, 30–32). From Nicomedia in Asia Minor is an inscription of a Christian wood-carver (*NewDocs* 5, 127). The sources from Egypt attest to two bankers (*NewDocs* 5, 139), a well-to-do gymnasiarch or director of the gymnasium, three wealthy merchants, and a worker in the central tax administration (Judge and Pickering 1977: 50–51, 69, 70).

From fourth-century Rome and Italy we have inscriptional evidence for Christians as wagon drivers (*Handbuch der altchristlichen epigraphik*, 112), dealers in huts or cottages, a female chamber servant, physicians, a stonecutter or mason, an artisan (*artefex*), and a lawyer (*ILCV* I, 117, 118, 120, 127, 140). From Achaia in the fourth century have come epitaphs of a Christian clothing merchant, innkeeper, teamster, and a pickler who also trapped lobsters and fish (*ICor*, 173–79). The inscriptions from Asia Minor indicate that there were butchers and a (female) physician among the Christians (*NewDocs* 1, 136–37; *NewDocs* 2:16). In Egypt a papyrus text was found from the fourth century that refers to a Christian sailor who was reprimanded for being drunk (*NewDocs* 2, 173). Two inscriptions, one from Carthage and one from Macedonia, name the Christians in the tombs as procurators or managers of large landed estates. Fortunatus of Carthage was the *procurator* of the estate (*fundus*) of Benbenesis (*Inscriptions funéraires chrétiennes de Carthage*, 336). Flavius Callistus was the ἐπίτροπος (steward) of imperial lands (χωρίων δεσποτικῶν) near Thessalonica (*Recueil des chrétiennes de Macédoine*, 118). These were two very important managerial positions, perhaps carried out by wealthy freedmen, sometime in the early to mid-fourth century.[5] Even more surprising is the identification of Ovinius Gallicanus as a Christian consul, reported by T. D. Barnes (1995: 142). Gallicanus, one of the consuls of Rome in 317 C.E., a position only open to those of senatorial rank, made a large donation to a Christian church in Ostia. Thus he appears to have been a Christian and would be the earliest known Christian of such a high rank.

We now summarize the results of our survey of the inscriptions and papyri. To get a sense of both the sweep of the history of Christian occupations and the ancient world in general table 24.3 includes inscriptions/papyri up to the sixth century. It does not list government occupations or military positions after the time of Constantine since the holders of those offices may not have been typical for Christians in the pre-Constantinian age. It does, however, give the inscriptional evidence for soldiers prior to Constantine discussed above under prohibited occupations. The occupations are listed by century with those inscriptions undated placed last. Most of these undated inscriptions would be presumably from somewhere between the fourth and sixth centuries. The vast majority of the Christian inscriptions, however, do not indicate any occupation for the deceased.[6]

Table 24.3.   Christian Occupations in the First Six Centuries Based on Inscriptions and Papyri

First Century	Second Century
#Aedile (Erastus)	*Imperial slaves; *Record keeper

Third Century	Fourth Century
*Woolworker; *Shorthand taker; *Record keeper; *Treasurer of the gladiatorial games; *Wagon driver; ^Wood-carver; &Banker (2); & Gymnasiarch; &Merchant (3); & Tax office administrator (2); *Soldier (3); ^Soldier (3); =Soldier (2); & Soldier; Soldier; @Imperial slave	*Dealer in huts; *Female chamber servant; *Stonecutter; *Artisan; *Physician (2); *Banker; *Lawyer; *Wagon driver; @Chief physician; @Manager of a large landed estate; #Merchant; #Innkeeper; #Teamster; #Pickler; +Manager of an imperial estate; & Sailor; ^Butcher; ^Soldier; *Consul

Fifth Century	Sixth Century
*Chamber servant; *Bread baker; *Stonecutter; *Merchant; *Banker; *Minter; *Lawyer (3); #Poultryman; ^Banker; =Lawyer	*Chief physician; *Goldsmith; *Merchant; *Linen merchant: *Hay seller; *Goat seller; *Pig seller; *Banker (4); *Secretary; *Teacher

Undated

*Dealer in huts; *Shepherd; *Weeder; *Butler; *Slave who carried the child's satchel; *Barber (3); *Miller (2); *Cook; *Pickler; *Tanner; *Pastry maker (2); *Physician (7); *Bread baker; *Butcher; *Carpenter; *Goldsmith; *Ironsmith (2); *Linen maker; *Cobbler (4); *Stonecutter; *Sculptor (2); *Artisan (2); *Builder; *Dice maker; *Mirror maker; *Painter (4); *Merchant (4); Papyrus seller; *Elephant handler (?); *Linen seller (2); *Fruit dealer; *Bottle maker; *Oil seller; *Pig seller; *Fish seller (2); *Banker (2); *Minter (2); *Shorthand writer (3); *Teacher (3); *Lawyer (5); #Captain of the guard; #Bath attendant; #Guardsman; #Grainman; #Pheasant breeder; #Goatherd; #Banker (2) ; ^Architect; &Chief physician; &Scribe; @Merchant; =Sculptor; =Cobbler; Fishseller (Sardinia); Physician (Gaul); ~Purple worker

*Rome/Italy   #Achaia   @Carthage   +Macedonia   ^Asia Minor   &Egypt   =Dalmatia   ~Syria

What did the early church look like? There are certainly references to poor people among the early believers. Paul wrote that there were not many wise, powerful, or noble Christians at Corinth (I Cor 1:26–28). Minucius Felix in the second century admitted that many Christians were poor (*Oct.* 36). Celsus wrote in his attack on Christianity:

> The following are the rules laid down by (Christians). Let no one come to us who has been instructed, or who is wise or prudent . . . but if there be any ignorant, or unintelligent, or uninstructed, or foolish persons, let them come with confidence . . . they desire and are able to gain over only the silly, and the mean, and the stupid, with women and children. (Origen, *Cels.* 3.44, tr. Crombie *ANF* 4, 481–82)

Based on such texts some historians concluded that most early Christians were poor people and slaves.[7] Our survey above, however, does not offer support for this thesis. The overwhelming majority of Christians were not poor, if by poor we mean destitute, starving, and anxious about finances. We found evidence of skilled craftsmen and bureaucrats who would have made at least an acceptable living. I therefore maintain (with Meeks 1983: 64–65) that most Christians were laborers, either skilled craftsmen or unskilled workers. Tables 24.2 and 24.3 support such a conclusion. Further, we have maintained (*pace* Kyrtatas 1987: 45) that a significant minority of Christians were slaves/freed persons as again the evidence in the tables suggests.

Scholars are even beginning to notice clues that indicate that quite a number (a significant minority) of the early Christians were well off. The evidence would require a separate article adequately to cover this issue. In summary, however, the New Testament (Judge 1960: 52–58; Malherbe 1977: 41–57; Winter 1988: 87–103), the second- and third-century Christian authors (Cadoux 1925: 393; Kyrtatas 1987: 101–6; Frend 1984: 132), and the papyri and inscriptions from the second and third centuries (Judge and Pickering 1977: 47–71; *Handbuch der altchristlichen epigraphik*, 101–2; Marucchi 1974: 244–47) refer to Christians of wealth and even a few of significant social standing. Stark too argues that the Christian faith attracted more interest among the wealthy than had been supposed (1996: 29–47). Our survey found references to several wealthy Christians as well.

We should, to be sure, distinguish between wealth and social standing. That there were few Christians of senatorial or equestrian rank before Constantine is a safe conclusion.[8] But that there were many successful, wealthy, and upwardly mobile persons in the Christian movement seems also undeniable. Christianity was a religion of "fairly well-off artisans and tradespeople" (Meeks 1983: 65).

Conclusion

As the Christian movement spread in the first three centuries, it had to decide on the appropriate ethical conduct of its members. New people were coming from every occupation imaginable to seek teaching and baptism. Could converts be allowed to continue in the same line of work as before they came to faith? Increasingly the church leaders said no. Certain principles—sexual immorality, the devaluing of human life, and idolatry—eliminated some occupations and curtailed others. Religious confession had to have an effect on occupation.

Of course, not every church member was compliant to these rules, and it is even probable that not every congregation or locality accepted and enforced the rules of Tertullian and Hippolytus. No group is able to achieve total conformity with its rules. The nonconformists are even hinted at in the very sources that construct the ethical structure concerning Christian labor. We can imagine some Christians quite shameless in their refusal to listen to the church leaders on such ethical questions. On the other end of the spectrum were probably ethical rigorists who would not practice any trade except those narrowly defined as acceptable to the new faith. But common sense would dictate to us that most Christians struggled between conscience and pocketbook to earn a living and remain Christian in an overwhelmingly pagan society.

What would a typical Christian congregation have looked like in the first three hundred years? If you had attended a worship service what sort of people would you have seen?

A representative survey of tables 24.2 and 24.3 present the following results:

Artisans: tentmakers, metalworkers, woolworkers, leather workers, sculptors, painters, stonecutters
Educated artisans: lawyers, physicians, record keepers/shorthand takers, scribes
Merchants: purple sellers, bankers
Bureaucrats: city manager, tax office administrator, imperial slaves/freedmen, managers of large estates, treasurer of gladiatorial games
Soldiers
Slaves

You could have seen people from just about every walk of life. There would have been a few abysmally poor, a significant minority of slaves (in the Roman church several imperial slaves/freedmen), a few soldiers and bureaucrats, almost no people of senatorial or equestrian rank, and a large number of artisans and merchants. We can find no evidence that Christianity appealed to only one social level. If most Christians were artisans and merchants, most urban people in general were from these groups. If very few people of senatorial rank were Christians before Constantine, there were also relatively very few senators in the empire. But virtually every social level is represented in the early church at some point.

The artisans and merchants ranged from the financially secure to the well-to-do. They had little status, but they nonetheless had their craft or business to make a living and contribute to the needs of the church. The majority of Christians were in the large urban group between the miserably poor and the upper classes of senators, equestrians, and decurions (Gager 1975: 96–106).

Notes

1. The *Apostolic Traditions* are extant mostly in the Coptic versions (Sahidic and Boharic). *Trad. Ap.*, Dix gives the Greek words that were transliterated into the Coptic.

2. Town council: *decuriae*; see Glover edition of Tertullian's *Apology* (1953: 168).

3. The dates for Roman emperors are taken from Keppie (1991: 136–37).

4. Kent had also affirmed that this was the only occurrence of the name Erastus among the inscriptions of Corinth. This has proven incorrect. Another Erastus has been found from the second century (Clarke 1993: 55).

5. Ign., *Pol.* 8:2 referred to another ἐπίτροπος around the year 110 C.E. He greeted the wife of the ἐπίτροπος and her household in Smyrna in Asia Minor. That he did not greet the procurator himself probably means that the latter was not a Christian.

6. The largest collection of inscriptions having to do with Christian occupations is found in *ILCV* I, 116–45, with over 170 Latin inscriptions from tombs in Italy, North Africa, Gaul, Sardinia, and Dalmatia, but sometimes lacking dates. Those occupations from Asia Minor, Syria, and Egypt in the fifth and sixth centuries and the undated ones from those regions were given in *NewDocs* 1 and 2. Those occupations cited from Achaia during his time period were given in *ICor*.

7. For a survey of views on the social standing of early Christians see Malherbe (1977: 29–32).

8. Barnes identifies only ten Christians of senatorial rank between 180 and 312 C.E. (1995: 136). For references to Christian senators see Acts of Peter 4; Eusebius, *Hist. eccl.* 6.21 (?), 7.16. Cf. Tertullian, *Apol.* 37 and Cyprian, *Ep.* 81. Were Titus Flavius Clemens, cousin of emperor Domitian, his wife Domitilla, and Anicius Glabrio Christians in 95 C.E.? See Dio Cassius 67.14, Suetonius, *Dom.* 15, and Eusebius, *Hist. eccl.* 3.18. Frend (1965: 214–16) and Cross (1997: 499, 679) doubt it.

PSYCHO-SOCIAL APPROACHES AND PHENOMENA VI

Conflicting Bases of Identity in Early Christianity: The Example of Paul

25

NICHOLAS H. TAYLOR

THE EARLY CHURCH consisted of communities of converts. This may be self-evident in the case of the first generation of Christians, but it nonetheless raises important questions for our understanding of early Christian identity. We need to understand how identity was conceived and perceived and how it changed in the world of early Christianity. The phenomenon labeled conversion in modern parlance is complex, diverse, and variable (Cohen 1989; Taylor 1995; cf. Travisano 1970; Gaventa 1986a). The complex nature of human identity in the ancient world, in particular the cities associated with the Pauline missionary movement, is also salient for this study. Identities transformed through religious conversion become more complex. We need therefore to understand the impact of joining a church on the already complex social identities of the first Christians and how that changed their lives.

A range of diverse social institutions from which people simultaneously derive their social identities is of course not unique to the cities of the eastern Roman Empire where Paul conducted his missions. We do, however, need to recognize the unique features of this society and the characteristics of social identity that it generated for those individuals and groups who derived their identity from the complex web of social structures and relationships that formed the Hellenistic cities. We also need to recognize the cultural forces that gave the individual a very limited role in defining his or her identity (Malina 1981).

The household was the fundamental social unit of Greco-Roman urban society, as is generally recognized (Meeks 1983). For the majority of the population, particularly those with least freedom of association, the household to which they belonged through birth or through a social transaction was the primary source of their identity. Closely related to household membership as a basis of identity were role and status within the household. Whereas the head of a household could

577

exercise considerable autonomy in the wider society and derive further aspects of his, or less commonly her, identity thereby, a subordinate member of the household could function in the wider society largely as a representative and functionary of the household and its owner.

Broader social units were also sources of identity. These would have included the city in which people resided and their ethnic origins, particularly if they belonged to an expatriate enclave such as was common in the cosmopolitan Greek cities. The Jewish synagogues that feature prominently in Acts are an important example of these. Not only were the Jewish communities throughout the eastern Roman Empire an initial point of contact for Christian missionaries, particularly in the various trading centers, but they attracted a variety of adherents from the surrounding gentile society (Cohen 1989; McKnight 1991; Feldman 1993; Goodman 1994; cf. Kraabel 1981, 1982). Both these diaspora Jewish communities (Stark 1996) and the Gentiles who associated themselves with them (Goodman 1994; Taylor 1995) were an important source of converts for Paul and other early Christian missionaries. It is important to recognize here that we are dealing with people whose identity was already complex before their conversion to Christianity and that there would already have been some tension between the identity derived from their various ethnic origins and cultural heritage on the one hand and their place of domicile in the Greco-Roman cities on the other. Meeks has drawn attention to status inconsistency in this situation of complex social identity as a factor in attracting converts to Christianity (1983: 73).

In addition to the principal demarcations of identity and status in terms of ethnic identity and gender, we need to recognize the complexity and often ambiguity and relativity of social rank and status in defining identity. We have already noted that it was the heads of households who could potentially exercise an autonomous role in the wider society, and those of a particular rank and economic means were required to participate in the structures and governance of the city itself. This entailed not merely holding civic office, often at considerable expense to the incumbent, but also participating in the corporate life of the city, including civic cults and festivals of the various deities whose shrines formed a prominent part of the civic landscape, both literally and figuratively. Civic functions, therefore, were also a basis of identity, and for Jewish (and Samaritan) monotheists these posed an obstacle to their identification with their place of residence that many found insuperable.

The issues that have been identified are very broad, and beyond the scope of a study such as this. Rather than surveying them all, this chapter will consider the figure of Paul himself, and then his manipulation of identity motifs to address issues of conflicting identity in the church, with specific reference to identity founded on the heritage of Israel and its relationship to the Christian universalism that Paul espoused. A social scientific theory that has been widely used in the study of early Christianity (Gager 1975; Jackson 1975; Meeks 1983; Hays 1985; Taylor 1996), and that is directly relevant to these issues, is that of cognitive dissonance. In view of the controversy surrounding this theory, some attention must first be paid to its use in the study of early Christianity.

The Theory of Cognitive Dissonance[1]

Leon Festinger and his colleagues developed the theory of cognitive dissonance in a study of a marginal North American religious phenomenon and subsequently applied it to more varied decision making and related activities and processes (Festinger, Riecken, and Schachter 1956; Festinger 1957; Festinger et al. 1964). It has been used in studies of non-Western societies by Douglas (1966) and of Greco-Roman society and religion by Versnel (1990). It was one of the first social scientific paradigms to be applied in biblical scholarship, initially in the study of disconfirmation of eschatological and prophetic expectations (Gager 1975; Carroll 1979). It has subsequently been employed in the study of conflicting beliefs and allegiances in the theology of Paul (Taylor 1996, 1997b; cf. Sanders 1983; Räisänen 1986; Hays 1985), the subject of this study. The use of cognitive dissonance theory in biblical studies has been controversial (Rodd 1981; Stowers 1985; Malina 1986b; Elliott 1993). While the continued use of the theory despite this criticism has been defended recently (Taylor 1998; Horrell 1999), it would nonetheless be prudent to identify and assess the critical issues.

Festinger defines cognitive dissonance as "the existence of unfitting relations among cognitions" (1957: 3), a cognition being any belief, attitude, cultural norm, commitment, or other information. Cognitions may be either consonant, irrelevant to each other, or dissonant. "[T]wo elements are in a dissonant relation if, considering these two alone, the obverse from one element would follow from the other" (1957: 13). Cognitive dissonance, whether generated by logical inconsistency, experience, cultural factors, knowledge, or opinions, or a combination of these, contains within it a pressure to bring about resolution, or at least to reduce dissonance to a tolerable level (1957: 18). This pressure is proportionate to the magnitude of the incompatibility between the cognitions and their significance, *as perceived by the subject*. Dissonance reduction can be brought about through changing beliefs, behavior, or environment, or by introducing new cognitions to the belief system so as either to create consonance or to reinforce a preferred cognition relative to another with which it is dissonant (1957: 19–24).

Festinger's further researches (1964) led to a wider range of applications of cognitive dissonance theory to account for situations where conflicting beliefs are held within a single belief system, as had been provided for though not developed in the original formulation of the theory (1957). Rather than disconfirmation of expectations, the defining criterion became the coexistence of two or more conflicting cognitions within a single belief system, with human decision-making processes and retrospective attitudes to decisions the object of study (cf. Freedman, Sears, and Carlsmith 1978).

Cognitive dissonance theory has been criticized within the social sciences. Rather than a formal theory, it is regarded as "a collection of loosely related ideas" (Brown 1965: 550), lacking clarity in its definition and precision in its predictions (cf. Brehm and Cohen 1962: 311; Fishbein and Ajzeen 1975: 44). Nevertheless, "while remaining frustratingly sparse and informal regarding its specific statement, dissonance theory has been exceedingly productive in terms of the amount of experimentation it has inspired" (McGuire 1966: 3). There has also been criticism of the experimental methods and conditions employed in the formulation and development of the theory (Brown 1965: 603–4), particularly in later laboratory experiments into the postdecision situation (Festinger 1964). However, the endurance of the theory within the social sciences, with publications as recent as 1996 (Mahaffy), is testimony to its value. The issue of immediate concern is its usefulness in the study of early Christianity.

C. S. Rodd (1981) was an early critic of the use of cognitive dissonance theory in biblical studies. His work is directed rather specifically at the early studies of Carroll (1979) and Gager (1975). Stowers (1985) draws heavily on Brown's criticisms (1965) in his critique of the use of the theory by Meeks (1983). More sweeping opposition to use of the theory has come from Malina (1986) and John Elliott (1993). Of Festinger's works, Malina cites only *When Prophecy Fails*, a collaborative study of a particular movement whose expectations were disconfirmed (1956). He makes no reference either to the fuller development of the theory in *A Theory of Cognitive Dissonance* (1957) or to later developments of the theory by Festinger (1964, 1968), his collaborators, and independent scholars (Brehm and Cohen 1962). While Stowers (1985) cites both Festinger's earlier works (1956; 1957), his critique is dependent entirely on Brown (1965). His judgment, in his critique of Meeks's use of the theory in connection with status inconsistency (Meeks 1983: 55, 173–74), is that it "obscures all of the critical questions about beliefs, motives, and intentions" (Stowers 1985: 170). Stowers is well aware that the social sciences do not treat religious beliefs in the same way as disciplines more concerned with ideas, and cognitive dissonance is merely an example of this. The need for scholarship to take due account of ideas and their influence on human behavior is of course incontrovertible, but this does not exclude the tools of the social sciences from contributing usefully to the study of early Christianity. Many of Stowers's concerns are dealt with in greater detail by Malina, but from a perspective of commitment to a more general social scientific interpretation of the New Testament.

Whereas Stowers questions the usefulness of social scientific analysis of the New Testament documents, Malina rejects one theory, cognitive dissonance, in favor of another, Merton's theory of sociological ambivalence (1976), and Mills's theory of normative inconsistency (1983), which derives from it. He argues that Merton and Mills account more adequately for the presence of conflicting ideas within a single cognitive system, and human responses thereto, than does Festinger. Sociological ambivalence applies to situations in which only a limited degree of inconsistency in human perceptions of reality is experienced, as Malina acknowledges (1986: 49). Malina is therefore creating a false dichotomy between the theories of Festinger and of Merton, which, correctly understood, apply to rather different situations.

John Elliott argues that cognitive dissonance "derive[s] from modern social experience with no ancient counterpart" (1993: 97; cf. Stowers 1985). Malina similarly argues that cognitive dissonance theory is not cross-culturally sensitive and is therefore not applicable to the "Mediterranean" world of the first century where "life was riddled with recognized and acknowledged inconsistency" (1986: 38). This ignores the findings of Douglas that the purity systems developed in non-Western societies, with their definition of boundaries and categorization of pure and impure, sacred and profane, serve precisely to resolve the dissonances encountered in everyday life (1966: 49–53). Versnel's study of "henotheism" in the Greco-Roman world (1990), moreover, demonstrates that dissonance and measures to resolve or suppress it were integral to ancient society and its social psychology.

Malina's argument that no stress attached to dissonance in the world of early Christianity (1986: 39) would therefore seem an unjustified generalization (cf. Douglas 1966: 39–53; Versnel 1990). While dissonance has been observed most particularly in modern societies and often been attributed to social change and the complexities in roles and relations that have resulted (Merton 1976; Weigert 1994), the assertion that dissonance or ambivalence accompanies or increases with modernization has not been demonstrated. The relative accessibility of modern societies to analysis does not imply that phenomena, in particular the processes of the human mind, observed there occur more frequently than was the case in extinct societies.

It is of course true that "since dissonance derives from premises about oneself and the world, it must vary with self-concept and world view" (Brown 1965: 598). Malina points to the tolerance of logically inconsistent cognitions as a widespread, cross-cultural, phenomenon and asserts that "in the social setting of earliest Christianity, normative inconsistency was the rule" (1986: 39), with normative values not realizable in daily life (1986: 38). This is equally true of the United States (Malina 1986b: 37), the society in which cognitive dissonance was first documented (Festinger, Riecken, and Schachter 1956). While dissonance may be variously perceived, and the responses thereto are culturally conditioned, cognitive dissonance may be experienced in any society. We need to distinguish between dissonance accepted as normative and tolerated on the one hand, and dissonance that is stressful and generates pressure toward resolution on the other. A continuum in intensity of dissonance needs to be recognized, from levels that can be accommodated without stress to levels that generate pressure toward resolution. Cognitive dissonance theory applies especially to situations where dissonance is experienced at higher levels of intensity, while Merton's theory of ambivalence (1976) is more appropriate to lower levels of dissonance.

Malina asserts that the dyadic nature of human personality in the world of early Christianity militated against introspection, and therefore precluded cognitive dissonance (1986: 38). His corollary is that no inconsistency would be perceived so intensely as to require resolution. Malina would seem more dogmatic than the evidence warrants in excluding any capacity for introspective thought from the ancient mindset, at least among the more literate strata of society. Furthermore, he does not discuss the possibility that dissonance could be a corporate as well as an individual experience, not necessarily the consequence of introspection in the modern individualist sense (cf. Gamson 1992). Festinger formulated the theory of cognitive dissonance precisely in a study of a corporate experience and response thereto, not an individual one. The possibility of a collective and intense experience of dissonance, particularly in a society in which an individual would be so conscious of and sensitive to his or her collective identity, would therefore seem to merit some consideration.

Malina draws upon the work of Snow and Machalek, who argue that cognitive dissonance theory "rests on the . . . assumption that the viability of unconventional beliefs and their organizational carriers is contingent on the existence of elaborate plausibility structures and strategies" (Snow and Machalek 1982: 16; cf. Versnel 1990: 7–8). "[U]nconventional beliefs" can acquire a self-validating nature that protects them from what might be regarded as the logical consequences of disconfirmation (1982: 18–22). Snow and Machalek do not dispute the occurrence of cognitive dissonance, but they observe that "beliefs may withstand the pressure of disconfirmed events not because of the effectiveness of dissonance-reducing strategies, but because disconfirming evidence may simply go unacknowledged" (1982: 23; cf. Versnel 1990: 4). Cognitive dissonance can occur only when the inconsistency is discernible in terms of the plausibility structure within which the individual or group is operating (cf. Weigert 1994: 126, citing Berger 1967). Inconsistencies that are not acknowledged will not generate cognitive dissonance. Nevertheless, when inconsistencies are perceived, cognitive dissonance may result and may generate the drive to resolve the resulting tension.

The perception of inconsistency between values and experience, however normative this may be, does not imply unquestioning acceptance of prevailing circumstances. Human responses to experience and circumstances can vary and are in many ways less predictable than social scientists often suppose (cf. Zygmunt 1972). As well as factors unique to the individual mind that shape perception and interpretation of experience, social context and interaction with others can influence responses to dissonance (cf. Festinger 1957: 41–255). A hostile environment, for example, has been found to aggravate dissonance, and therefore to stimulate the process of resolution (cf. Hardyck and Braden 1962; Carroll 1979: 107).

The dyadic nature attributed to human identity in the world of early Christianity should not be taken to imply uniformity of personality types or of character. Those with social position, education, and wealth would potentially have been able to exercise more independence of mind and of action than others. That some individuals did stand apart and exercise considerable freedom of mind rather than conform to expectations imposed by their environment is surely beyond doubt. Even if such individuals were a small minority in ancient society, their impact on the traditions of early Christianity and other social movements was considerable. That some were sensitive to discrepancies within their belief systems or between their beliefs and the reality they perceived, and that their experience can be illuminated by means of cognitive dissonance theory, is a possibility that cannot be excluded on the basis of the prevalence of dyadic personality in ancient culture. Paul is surely a case in point (cf. Hurtado 1995; Taylor 1996, 1997b). That this is relevant to understanding his manipulation and resolution of conflicting bases of identity, this study will seek to demonstrate.

That cognitive dissonance theory is potentially illuminating when applied to the world of early Christianity has been eloquently if indirectly demonstrated in Versnel's study of henotheism in Greco-Roman religion (1990) and in Carroll's work on the Hebrew prophets (1979). Carroll focuses on the reworking of unfulfilled prophetic traditions as a means to resolving dissonance evoked by their nonfulfillment, but there are other possible applications. Prophets like Amos spoke out against the prevailing order when the Israelite and Judaean kingdoms did not conform either with divine justice or the terms of the Covenant, or indeed with their belief in Yahweh's sole lordship. Cognitive dissonance provides at the very least a heuristic paradigm in terms of which the perceived discrepancy between covenantal faith and quotidian reality could have been experienced and resolution of the resultant tension sought, if not always achieved, through invocation of divine judgement upon the prevailing order. Similarly, prophetic figures who rose in reaction to Roman rule in Judaea, including Judas the Galilean, may have been motivated, as Josephus suggests (*B.J.* 2.118), by the conflict between their perception of divine prerogatives and the reality of Roman rule, and their militancy can perhaps be understood in terms of cognitive dissonance.

There remain situations and phenomena to which cognitive dissonance theory can usefully and appropriately be applied in the study of early Christianity. While Snow and Machalek rightly caution that religious systems have built-in protections against disconfirmation of their beliefs and expectations (1982: 18), it is equally arguable that this built-in protection functions precisely as a plausibility structure, and thereby serves to contain and resolve dissonance (cf. Douglas 1966: 39–53; Weigert 1994: 126, citing Berger 1967). The logic and mechanism of the plausibility system may well not be that of the external analyst, and Stone has rightly asserted that the thinking of the authors of ancient writings, in his specific case apocalypses, must be assumed to be coherent within their own frame of reference (1983: 242). What may appear to the scholar as incoherence or unfalsifiability in belief systems (cf. Snow and Machalek 1982: 19–20) will not necessarily appear so to the believer (cf. Carroll 1979: 104). "Cognitive dissonance is subjectively experienced, it is culturally influenced and socially negotiable" (Prus 1976: 133). If we are accurately to detect and analyze occurrences of cognitive dissonance, therefore, we need to recognize the inner logic of the belief system under investigation. Apparent inconsistencies discerned through the biblical texts can often be accounted for by such factors as presuppositions common to the author and the original readers and hearers but unknown to the modern scholar, in terms of which the document would acquire consistency and coherence.

While it must be conceded to Malina that some degree of inconsistency is normative in any belief system (1986: 38), the distinction needs to be recognized between anomalies that can be tolerated or overlooked and contradictions that create pressure toward some kind of resolution (cf. Carroll 1979: 104; Versnel 1990: 4–8). The value attached to the discrepancy is crucial to determining whether or not cognitive dissonance will result (Prus 1976: 127). We need to recognize that not every occasion of logical incompatibility between beliefs or other cognitions necessarily results in cognitive dissonance, and that the hermeneutical processes of the community and its belief system can in some situations preempt dissonance (Carroll 1979: 106). This would happen, inter alia, when expectations are reinterpreted before they are disconfirmed rather than in the aftermath of disconfirmation, or when paradox and mystery are employed to rationalize and even to sanctify the dissonance.

While less intense levels of ambivalence or dissonance are more adequately and appropriately treated using theories such as that of Merton (1976), there remain within the world of early Christianity situations to which the theory of cognitive dissonance, with its accompanying drive toward resolution, is more appropriate.

The Multifaceted Identity of Paul

That Paul was an ethnic Jew and an adherent of Pharisaism before his conversion to Christianity is of course well known. Recent scholarship has, in various ways, given considerable attention to relating Paul the Apostle of gentile Christianity to his Jewish roots (Stendahl 1976; Sanders 1977, 1983; Boyarin 1994; Räisänen 1985, 1987; Longenecker 1998; Segal 1990a, 1990b; Hurtado 1995; Taylor 1996; Holmberg 1998). The issue of Paul's identity, however, is more complex than the issue of how it changed with his conversion and how his retrospective statements on the subject are to be understood. It is of course important that we recognize the issue of how Paul's identity as a member of Israel was transformed on his becoming a Christian, not least because many, if not the majority, of the first generations of Christians would have undergone a similar process (cf. Stark 1986, 1996). While Hurtado has argued that the conversions of future religious leaders should be understood as categorically different to those of ordinary converts (1995), it must also be recognized that Paul's conversion did not inevitably lead to his becoming a prominent and influential Christian missionary and thinker (cf. Taylor 1992, 1993).

Paul's extant statements about his pre-Christian identity are of course all retrospective. Nevertheless, these, together with allusions found in Acts, are the only information available to us. There are three passages where Paul speaks in his letters of his life before conversion to Christianity, the first of which is sometimes referred to as his autobiographical narrative (Gaventa 1986b; Taylor 1993):

> For you have heard of my former life in Judaism (ἐν τῷ Ἰουδαϊσμῷ), that I persecuted the church of God (τὴν ἐκκλησίαν τοῦ Θεοῦ) violently and tried to destroy it; and I advanced in Judaism (ἐν τῷ Ἰουδαϊσμῷ) beyond many of my own age among my people (ἐν τῷ γένει μου), so extremely zealous was I for the traditions of my forebears. (Gal 1.13–14)

> If anyone else thinks he has reason for confidence in the flesh, I have more: circumcised on the eighth day, of the people of Israel (ἐκ γένους Ἰσραήλ), of the tribe of Benjamin (φυλῆς Βενιαμίν), a Hebrew [born] of Hebrews (Ἑβραῖος ἐξ Ἑβραίων); according to the law a Pharisee (κατὰ νόμον Φαρισαῖος), as to zeal a persecutor of the church (τὴν ἐκκλησίαν), as to righteousness under the law blameless. (Phil 3.4–6)

> Are they [Paul's opponents] Hebrews (Ἑβραῖοί)? So am I. Are they Israelites (Ἰσραηλῖται)? So am I. Are they seed of Abraham (σπέρμα Ἀβραάμ)? So am I. (2 Cor 11.22)

From these passages we can deduce that Paul was an ethnic Jew who traced his ancestry through the tribe of Benjamin. He had lived his life as a pious Jew, and was an adherent of the Pharisaic tradition of interpreting the Law of Moses. It was precisely his devotion to his ancestral traditions that led him to persecute the church.

Paul appears in Acts for the first time at 7.58, supervising the stoning of Stephen. Here he is referred to by his Hebrew name, Saul (Σαῦλος), as opposed to his Greek name by which he is more generally known, and by which he identifies himself in his letters, Paul (Παῦλος). The following verses speak of Paul spearheading a persecution of the church in Jerusalem (Acts 8.1–3). Allusions to his background and earlier life are found in the speeches in which Paul gives after his arrest.

> I am a Jewish man (ἀνὴρ Ἰουδαῖος), born at Tarsus in Cilicia, but brought up in this city at the feet of Gamaliel, educated according to the strict manner of the law of our forebears, being zealous for God as you all are this day. I persecuted this Way (ταύτην τὴν ὁδὸν) to the death, binding and delivering to prison both men and women, as the high priest and the whole council of elders bear me witness. (Acts 22.3–5)

> My manner of life from my youth, spent from the beginning among my own nation and at Jerusalem, is known by all the Jews. They have known for a long time . . . that according to the strictest party of our religion I have lived as a Pharisee (ἔζησα Φαρισαῖος). . . . I myself was convinced that I ought to do many things in opposing the name of Jesus of Nazareth. And I did so in Jerusalem; I not only shut up many of the saints in prison, by authority from the chief priests, but when they were put to death I cast my vote against them. And I punished them often in all the synagogues and tried to make them blaspheme; and in raging fury against them, I persecuted them even to foreign cities. (Acts 26.4–5, 9–11)

Further allusions are made in dialogue and in the narrative. In Acts 18.3 it is mentioned that Paul was a σκηνποιός, conventionally rendered "tentmaker" (cf. Hock 1980), by profession. He mentions frequently that during the course of his missions he supported himself by his own labor rather than depending on the churches for subsistence (I Cor 9.1–23; I Thes 2.7–12; cf. 2 Cor 7.2; 2 Cor 11.7–11, 20). While he does not identify the trade he practiced, it would seem apparent that Paul worked as an artisan.

The more contentious claim that Paul was a Roman citizen by birth (Acts 16.37–39, 22.25–29), though widely disputed in scholarship, forms the rationale of the narrative in the closing chapters of Acts, and is therefore for Luke an essential aspect not only of Paul's identity but also of the story of his journey to Rome (Acts 25.10–12, 21; 26.32). For this reason several recent scholars have affirmed Paul's Roman citizenship (Hengel and Schwaemer 1997; Riesner 1998).

To these various identities, or aspects of his identity, derived from his Jewish heritage and Greco-Roman environment, whether through birth and descent or through acquired social role, Paul added that of a follower of Jesus, or a Christian, on his conversion. We should of course be aware that some scholars argue that conversion is not an appropriate description of Paul's experience, as his Jewish identity was not altered through his vocation to apostleship (e.g., Stendahl 1976: 7–23; Betz 1979: 64–69). This, however, is inadequate in its understanding both of Paul (Gaventa 1986a: 9–42; Segal 1990a: 117–25, 285–300; Taylor 1992: 62–67) and of the complex and varied social and cognitive transformative process that constitutes religious conversion (cf. Straus 1979: 158–65; Snow and Machalek 1983; Rambo 1993). While Paul's conversion did not involve the abandonment and repudiation of all aspects of his previous identity, some at least came to be reevaluated and reinterpreted. This is most apparent in Philippians 3.7–8:

> But whatever gain I had, on account of Christ (διὰ τὸν Χριστὸν) I have counted as loss. Indeed I count everything as loss because of the surpassing worth of knowing Christ Jesus my Lord.

This text reflects a typical convert's appraisal of his previous way of life (cf. Beckford 1978; Snow and Machalek 1983, 1984). Paul's disparagement of his accomplishments and values as a Pharisee, recounted in the previous verses, reflects a reassessment of the commitments and convictions that had characterized his past way of life in the light of the new commitments, convictions, and values he had adopted on conversion to Christ, a process described as "biographical reconstruction" by Snow and Machalek (1983, 1984; cf. Segal 1990a; Taylor 1992, 1993, 1995).

Paul as Convert[2]

Modern studies of conversion have shown that it does not consist simply in the abandonment of one set of beliefs and practices in favor of another (Travisano 1970; Beckford 1978; Straus 1979; Rambo 1993). A more complex process is involved, during which time beliefs and practices associated both with the movement or group that the convert has joined and with that to which he or she had previously been affiliated coexist in the consciousness. It is such situations that may potentially generate cognitive dissonance and the consequent pressure to resolve it. This can be accomplished through changing cognition through adding or eliminating one or more cognitive elements; revising the relationship between and relative importance of existing elements; changing environment to effect removal from exposure to unwanted dissonant information, and increasing exposure to consonant information; changing behavior so as to conform with the dominant and preferred cognitive elements; or attempting to convince others, as a means of reinforcing the preferred convictions (Festinger 1957: 19–24). It is entirely appropriate that scholars such as Segal (1990a) and Gager (1981) have sought to understand Paul's thought in terms of postdecision dissonance (cf. Festinger 1964; Gerhardsson 1961: 289). However, Gager in particular overlooks the temporal distance between Paul's conversion and Galatians, and the developments of the intervening years that shape Paul's portrayal of his conversion and other episodes in his earlier life (cf. Räisänen 1987: 404–7). Galatians reflects a specific historical situation and is neither objective history or autobiography, nor an abstract reflection of Paul's thought; it does not reflect directly the dissonance Paul experienced in the aftermath of his conversion (see Taylor 1992: 123–81 and 1993).

Paul as a Pharisee who had been converted to Christianity would have experienced dissonance between the beliefs and values that belonged to his ancestral religion, Pharisaic Judaism, and those that he acquired in his conversion to Christian Judaism. The new convictions overlapped with, but were nevertheless dissonant to, those Paul had hitherto professed. Conversion brought one set of Jewish loyalties, beliefs, and obligations into conflict with another. Given the ethnic and cultural as well as religious aspects of Judaism, Paul could not have ceased to be a Jew. It was precisely because Paul's Jewish, and specifically Pharisaic, heritage continued to claim his loyalty that cognitive dissonance was generated (*pace*, Collange 1979: 128–30). Research into cognitive dissonance in the postdecision situation has shown that an element of regret enters the cognitive processes after an important decision has been made (Festinger 1964: 83–96, 112–28). Any beliefs that Paul explicitly repudiated would therefore have continued to claim his allegiance and even to cast doubt on his acquired Christian convictions. Still more would those aspects of his Jewish heritage that were fully in harmony with his Christian beliefs have retained his loyalty.

The dissonant convictions that Paul held immediately after his conversion cannot be precisely established (see Fredriksen 1991: 548–58; Räisänen 1987: 415; Sanders 1977: 550–52). It would be anachronistic to project the form of Judaism Paul opposes in his letters, including the autobiographical sections, into his pre-Christian life, or likewise to identify too closely the form of Christianity given expression in his letters with that to which he gave his allegiance in his conversion. We can, however, be certain that, prior to his conversion, Paul had found the Christianity that he encountered so repugnant to his Judaism that he felt constrained to persecute its adherents (Gal 1.13; Phil 3.6; see Fredriksen 1991: 548–58; Hengel 1991: 63–86; Räisänen 1987; Taylor 1992: 87–95). His perception of the Christian faith was fundamentally altered in his conversion, so that he himself became an adherent.

Christian Identity and Cognitive Dissonance in Galatians

Galatians was written in the aftermath of Paul's confrontation with Peter at Antioch (Gal 2.11–14) and in response to the situation this episode occasioned in Paul's life and in the Galatian churches. Paul had been an apostle of the Antiochene church (Acts 13–14; see Haenchen 1971: 364–66; Räisänen 1987: 405; Taylor 1992: 87–95) and had not merely propagated its interpretation of the Christian gospel but had defended it at the Jerusalem conference (Gal 2.1–10; Acts 15.5–21). The Antiochene church included Jewish and gentile members in a single community (Gal 2.12). Issues of Torah observance were not obstacles to this coexistence, which suggests that gentile Christians willingly observed the Law to the degree required by the Jewish Christians, which fell well short of full proselytization and circumcision (see Cohen 1989 and Taylor 1995 for patterns of gentile adherence to Jewish and Christian communities).

Paul clashed with Peter and Barnabas at Antioch over interpretation of the agreement reached at the Jerusalem conference, and in particular the authority of the Jerusalem church to regulate the life of the Antiochene church (see Dunn 1990: 129–82; Holmberg 1978: 32–34; Taylor 1992: 123–39). Paul's failure to rally support isolated him in the church, resulting in his exclusion and consequent loss of status and authority. Galatians is Paul's response to this crisis, an assertion of apostolic status and authority as well as a rationalization of the stand he had taken against Peter and the Antiochene church.

Not only should Galatians not be interpreted as simply reflecting the beliefs Paul had assumed on his conversion, but a complex process of social and cognitive reorientation separates the letter even from the Antioch incident. The crisis in Antioch forced Paul to clarify his position, and, in defending it, radicalize it. Galatians reflects his consequent reinterpretation of what had hitherto been common ground with the church. It is moreover an assertion of personal authority where Paul had previously exercised jurisdiction on behalf of the Antiochene church. Paul's disparagement of his opponents' principles and motives and polarization of their respective positions serves to conceal the dilemmas that had confronted both parties and thereby served to reduce his own postdecision dissonance. His attempt to convince the Galatian Christians serves also to reinforce his own conviction as to the rightness of his position (see Walster 1964). The Christianity defended in Galatians should therefore be understood as a radicalized form of the Christianity hitherto practiced in Antioch. This includes statements regarding the Law and the Covenant.

The issue at Antioch and the preceding conference at Jerusalem was the degree to which gentile Christians were subject to the Mosaic Law. The underlying question was the extent to which ethnic Israel remained the definitive covenant community, to

590 NICHOLAS H. TAYLOR

which gentile Christians needed to belong in order to share fully in the promises to the patriarchs. As a missionary to the Gentiles Paul may have seen the question as whether Jewish ethnic and cultural presuppositions should be allowed to compromise the accessibility of the gospel to the Gentiles. It was the Antioch episode, not his conversion, that brought into conflict Paul's Pharisaic conviction of the election and salvation of Israel and his Christian belief in the universality of the gospel and salvation through Christ (see Räisänen 1986: 187–88 and 1987: 407). Tension between universalism and particularism is widespread in the Hebrew tradition from the time of the Exile (Sanders 1977: 206–11; Fredriksen 1991: 533–48). Paul radicalized this universalism so that salvation through Christ redefined the boundaries of the covenant community, and he identified it with the struggle he had lost at Antioch and thereby with his whole being and apostolic identity. The inextricable bond between the person of Paul, his sense of apostolic vocation to the Gentiles, and the distinctive gospel he proclaimed evolved in the aftermath of the Antioch incident and is given expression in his letters (Taylor 1992: 110–39).

Paul is faced with cognitive dissonance between his convictions as a Christian believing in salvation through Christ and as a Pharisaic Jew believing in the election of Israel. At the same time he is confronting a situation where precisely this issue is impacting on the identity and conduct of gentile converts to Christianity in Galatia. Whereas Paul resolves the problem through asserting the supremacy of Christ, and therefore of identity defined in terms of the gospel, other Christians are interpreting Christ essentially within the Mosaic Covenant, and therefore requiring gentile converts to Christianity to enter the Mosaic Covenant through circumcision and Torah observance.

Paul's radicalized Christian convictions resulted in a sharp dichotomy between Christian faith and Torah observance. This is reflected in his assertion that Jews enjoy no privileged status but relate to God on the same basis as Gentiles, through Christ. Gentile Christians participate, not in the salvation of Israel, but rather in the salvation promised to Abraham, procured through Christ apart from ethnic Israel. The analogy of Hagar and Sarah in Galatians 4.21–31 contrasts the paths of Pharisaic Judaism and Christianity, so that (gentile) Christians, and not Jews, are identified with Sarah and the Covenant. The ethnocentric Mosaic Law, if not repudiated altogether, is relativized both temporally and conceptually and subordinated to the more inclusive Abrahamic Covenant (Burton 1921: 508; Hübner 1984b: 17; Wright 1991: 163). The temporal priority of the latter (Gal 3.17) to some extent at least separates God from the Law (Räisänen 1986: 129). This distance is emphasized further in Galatians 3.19 where the Law is described as having been given through the mediation of angels, implying that the Torah is a less than ultimate revelation of the divine will and purpose. This relativization of the Law, however selective in practice, functions to reduce dissonance by relegating the

Mosaic Law to an inferior level of revelation, thereby curtailing its provisions within parameters implied by the Abrahamic Covenant and the Christian gospel. The Abrahamic Covenant in its turn is subordinated to and interpreted in terms of the Christian gospel. The preferred dissonant alternative, Christianity, is elevated to unique prominence, and the rejected, Pharisaic Judaism, is reinterpreted in terms of and in contrast to the preferred, to which it is unequivocally subordinated. In reducing the Mosaic Law in importance, Paul is able to reduce the dissonance between it and the Christian gospel.

Paul's repudiation of privilege is notably expressed in Galatians 3.26–29, a passage that illustrates most graphically and most idealistically the transformation of Christian identity (cf. Christiansen 1995: 311–20). Before employing this text to illuminate the transformation of identity in early Christianity, it is necessary to consider its proper context. The section "no Jew or Greek, no slave or free, no male and female" (οὐκ ἔνι ἰουδαῖος οὐδὲ ἕλλην οὐκ ἔνι δοῦλος οὐδὲ ἐλεύθερος οὐκ ἔνι ἄρσεν καὶ θῆλυ—Gal 3.28) is widely understood to be an early Christian credal formulary that Paul is quoting, with or without emendation (Schlier 1982: 174–75; Betz 1979: 184–85; Schüssler Fiorenza 1983: 208–12; Longenecker 1990: 156–57; Scroggs 1972). The corollary is that Paul is quoting a formulary already known to the Galatian Christians, presumably arising from his mission preaching there some time previously. The origins of the passage therefore depend on the occasion of Paul's mission to Galatia, and accordingly the much-rehearsed north–south Galatia question. These issues cannot be debated in detail, and I rely here on my previous arguments in favor of the "south" Galatia hypothesis (Taylor 1992; cf. Dunn 1993; Longenecker 1998). In my reconstruction Paul's mission to Galatia was undertaken in association with Barnabas and under the auspices of the church of Antioch during the second decade of Christianity (Taylor 1992). The origins of the credal formulary are therefore to be located in the church of Antioch at a very early date. Such a hypothesis would account for the ethnic contrast between "Jew" (ἰουδαῖος) and "Greek" (ἕλλην—3.28), reflecting a Jewish perception of the composition of the population of a Greek city. This perception would seem to have had little grounding in the Galatian churches, which appear to have been overwhelmingly gentile in composition. An Antiochene origin of the credal formulary could account also for Paul's citation of what was an authoritative statement despite his lack of immediate interest in the issues of slavery and gender (cf. Taylor 1997b).

Paul does not apply the principles expressed in Galatians 3.28 with equal rigor, either in this letter or elsewhere, however much scholars may appeal to interpolation theories to account for passages, particularly in the Corinthian correspondence, that would seem in terms of modern Western canons of consistency and interpretation to conflict with this text (Elliott 1994; Munro 1975; cf. Taylor

1997b). While the formulary itself would seem to presuppose that Christian identity supersedes and eradicates all other bases of social identity, at least within the fellowship of the church if not in the wider society, it is clear that it functions more as an ideological assertion than as a description or reflection of social reality. Still less does it serve any programmatic function in defining life and relationships within the Galatian churches. Paul is concerned primarily with the issue of ethnic and cultural identity within the church and is asserting the right to define the identity of the Galatian Christians. Against those who would define Christian identity in terms of the nation of Israel and the Law of Moses, Paul reinterprets the notion of Israel (6.16) in terms of his redefinition of descent from Abraham (3.29, 4.21–31) and of divine sonship (4.5–7), so that the gentile Torah-nonobservant Christians become in effect the definitive covenant community (cf. Longenecker 1998: 88). In this way the gospel of Christ supersedes the Law of Moses, if not entirely as a rule of life for the Galatian Christians then at least as defining their relationship with Israel and apart from Torah-observant Christianity. The issue of servitude and freedom is raised elsewhere in Galatians only metaphorically and relative to the Mosaic Law (4.1–11, 24–25; 5.1), for which purpose the formulary in 3.28 could be construed as less than helpful. Gender relations and issues are not mentioned elsewhere in Galatians at all. Furthermore, the use of family terminology in verse 26—"sons of God" (υἱοὶ θεοῦ)— and the reference to "seed of Abraham" (τοῦ ἀβραὰμ σπέρμα) in verse 29 emphasizes that it is the issue of identity defined by descent with which Paul is concerned, even if only to refute or to redefine. The Abrahamic Covenant is reinterpreted so as to be defined by faith in Christ rather than biological descent (Christiansen 1995: 312; cf. Longenecker 1998: 83–88, 128–33). Christiansen has perceptively argued that it is the identification of Christ with Abraham's seed that governs the redefinition of identity in Paul's use of the formulary (1996: 312). Christocentric identity is defined "through faith in Christ Jesus" (διὰ τῆς πίστεως ἐν Χριστῷ Ἰησοῦ——Gal. 3.26) and adoption into God's family, with status as children of God and of Abraham superseding previous criteria of identity (Christiansen 1995: 312–13; Meeks 1983: 87–88).

Becoming "in Christ" (ἐν Χριστῷ) defines the change of identity of the Galatian Christians. What Paul is concerned with in this passage, however, is not so much the Galatians' becoming Christian as the nature of Christian identity and conduct of those who have become Christian. No longer at issue is the conflict or contrast between Christianity and paganism or Judaism, but between two alternative notions of Christian identity and two corresponding ways of life. Paul's objective is to assert his definition of Christian identity against that of those influencing the Galatian churches toward an identity more closely bound up with the nation of Israel and the Law of Moses.

The phenomenon described by Snow and Machalek as biographical reconstruction (1983, 1984) is quite apparent in Paul's argument in Galatians, and particularly in this text. Kinship for the Christian is traced no longer through biological descent but through membership in the fictive Christian family descended from Abraham. This is developed further in Galatians 4.21–31, where the Genesis patriarchal epic is reinterpreted so as to define a gentile Christian identity within the Covenant between God and Abraham. Paul's inversion of the relationship between Isaac and Ishmael, Sarah and Hagar, is unlikely to have convinced any reader or hearer familiar with Genesis and not predisposed to such a redefinition of the Covenant as is here expounded, unless already convinced of Paul's authority in the interpretation of the tradition (cf. Longenecker 1998: 88, 128). Paul is opposing the view that gentile Christians need to be incorporated into the covenant people of Israel (Barrett 1985: 44; Longenecker 1998:15–17) through constructing an identity for gentile Christians as the covenant people apart from the physical descendants of Abraham. The identification of gentile Christianity with the promises made to Abraham and inherited in the biblical narrative by Isaac creates both for individual gentile Christians and for gentile Christian communities an identity within the Covenant, one more ancient than that of Law-observant Israel whose identity and Covenant relationship are associated with the later period of Moses. Fictive kinship with Abraham becomes the basis for collective identity in the gentile Christian community. The association of the Jewish people and the Law of Moses with Hagar and Ishmael, with connotations of illegitimacy, servitude, and exclusion from the Covenant, provides the basis for defining this Christian identity apart from the Mosaic Law, as well as reinforcing Paul's repudiation of those proclaiming Torah-observant Christianity in Galatia. At the same time, the pagan past of the gentile Christians, no less than the Jewish past of Jewish Christians and the prevailing state of the Jewish people, is depicted as a time of bondage (4.1–11; cf. Longenecker 1998: 47). Christian identity, as defined by Paul, is acquired through faith (3.7) and adoption as children of God (4.1–7), symbolized through baptism (3.27). In defining Christian identity apart from Israel, and substituting distinctive Christian symbols of incorporation into a distinctive covenant community, Paul is able to control as well as to construct the identity and the lives of the Christian communities that acknowledge his authority.

Christian Identity and Cognitive Dissonance in Romans

Romans was written approximately five or six years after Galatians (Taylor 1992: 51–59). During the intervening period Paul had visited Antioch for the first time since his altercation there with Peter (Acts 18.22). His undertaking the collection project for the Jerusalem church, a prominent theme in the Corinthian correspondence and in Romans, indicates a degree of reconciliation with his former antagonists (Hübner 1984b: 60–65; Taylor 1992: 182–205). Paul's statements relating to Law-observance and the fate of non-Christian Jews are significantly more temperate than in Galatians, which reinforces the impression that Romans and the Corinthian letters were written in a rather different ecclesiastical atmosphere.

Scholars are divided as to precisely what situation Romans addresses (see Donfried 1991; Wedderburn 1988). Paul was conscious of perils facing him in Jerusalem (15.31), and his sense of apostleship to the Gentiles (11.13) may have impelled him to address the church at the center of the empire in case his plans to visit them (1.12–13; 15.23, 28, 32) were frustrated. This does not warrant the description of Romans as Paul's last will and testament (*pace* Bornkamm 1963), as he had definite future plans (1.15, 15.24). Paul was clearly preoccupied with his planned visit to Jerusalem and undoubtedly conscious of its significance for both his Jewish heritage and his Christian convictions, and his thoughts were undoubtedly influenced by these considerations (cf. Jervell 1971; Sanders 1977: 488–89). The recent crisis in Corinth, occasioned partly by antinomian influences (Chow 1992; Marshall 1987; Theissen 1979: 201–317), may have contributed to Paul's more affirmative attitude to the Law. More generally, the *parousia* of Christ had not happened as soon as expected, and in the meanwhile Christianity had spread among the Gentiles to an unanticipated extent while very few of the Jewish people had embraced Christianity (Fredriksen 1991: 562). However, Paul would not have written to the Roman Christians simply to clarify his own thinking on such matters, but on account of their significance for his future plans (1.8–15, 15.22–24). He wished to ensure that there was in Rome a community receptive to his teaching and sufficiently affirmative thereof to support his planned subsequent work (Beker 1980: 59–93; Watson 1986: 97).

However the background to Romans may be reconstructed, the dilemma of the continuing value of the Jewish heritage in the light of the Christian gospel is nonetheless experienced and articulated by Paul in ways rather more subtle and ambiguous than in Galatians. Suppression of the former in favor of the latter is no longer an adequate or satisfactory response to Paul's dissonance, and his allegiance to Israel must be accommodated within his commitment to the Christian gospel for all humanity (cf. Festinger 1957: 264–65; 1964: 21–32, 45–60, 131–44).

Most scholars regard Romans 9–11 as integral to the letter (Dunn 1988: 518–20; Longenecker 1991: 251–65; Moxnes 1980: 33). In these chapters Paul addresses the problem of how the Covenant between God and Israel could be regarded as meaningful in the light of the universality of God's grace that had been demonstrated in his own work as apostle to the Gentiles and in the situation where most of Israel have not accepted their promised Messiah (9.1–5; cf. Dunn 1988: 530; Fredriksen 1991: 562; Segal 1990a: 262; Walter 1984: 132; Watson 1986: 161). His treatment of the issue includes three distinct lines of argument (9.6–29, 9.30–10.21, 11.1–36) in which he "desperately sought a formula which would keep God's promises to Israel intact, while insisting on faith in Jesus Christ" (Sanders 1983: 199). The complexity of Paul's problem can be appreciated if the three arguments of Romans 9–11 are considered.

The first argument (9.6–29) is based on two premises, the remnant theme and the notion of divine sovereignty and predestination, both of which derive from the Torah and Prophets. In the same way as Isaac was Abraham's sole heir, so in successive generations some but not all of Abraham's descendants inherit the Covenant, until the present when only a remnant of Israel receives the gospel (9.6–13). The argument fails in that it does not explain the presence of Gentiles in the remnant of Israel: the archetypal Gentiles Ishmael and Esau are the first to be excluded. Any distinction between lines of natural descent and of Covenant promise (Dunn 1988: 547) cannot be sustained, as the latter is always a remnant within Israel until artificially extended to include gentile Christians. Paul is more concerned with the problem of theodicy that the rejection of Israel poses (cf. Cranfield 1975: 471–73). In Romans 9.14–18 divine justice is equated with divine sovereignty, to the point that might becomes right, and in 9.19–23 divine arbitrariness comes close to fatalism. Paul's only defense against these corollaries of his argument is that humans should not question divine action (*pace* Dunn 1988: 550). The inclusion of Gentiles is supported from the prophetic tradition, but not integrated with the remnant theme. Paul's argument ends somewhat inconclusively, simultaneously defending fatalism and divine mercy (cf. Moxnes 1980: 48; Räisänen 1988: 183–84; *pace*, Munck 1967: 75–79). The Abrahamic Covenant is devalued by the liability to disinheritance of its heirs and the availability of its benefits to others. This applies notwithstanding the liability to judgment recognized by the Hebrew Prophets (cf. Dunn 1988: 561): nowhere do the Prophets threaten sincerely Torah-observant Israelites with exclusion from the Covenant, or promise salvation to Gentiles ahead of Jews.

The second argument (9.30–10.21) is significantly closer to that of Galatians. Christ is the "end of the Law" (τέλος νόμου—10.4); an expression that, however interpreted (cf. Badenas 1985; Cranfield 1979: 519; Dunn 1988: 519), implies the subordination of the Law to an ultimate purpose represented by and culminating in Christ. Discarding that which has served its purpose implies no disparagement (Barrett 1982: 146), but the supersession of the Law is nevertheless unequivocal (*pace*, Thielman 1989: 115). The distinction between Jew and Greek, the latter paradigmatic for all Gentiles, is abolished in Christ (10.12), and there is no continuing Covenant between God and Israel on the basis of racial identity

(Räisänen 1988: 185; Wright 1991: 246). Dunn argues that this reflects one side of a dialectic (1988: 617), the other being the eternal election of Israel (ch. 11). The degree of tension between the two arguments cannot be ignored, and due weight must be given to Paul's rejection of any ethnocentric covenant (cf. Watson 1986: 165). Israel has failed in its pursuit of righteousness through the Law, while the Gentiles have attained salvation through faith in Christ (Dunn 1988: 596; Räisänen 1988: 185–86; Sanders 1983: 40–42; Wright 1991: 240). The logic of salvation by faith is unable to admit the salvation of Israel on any other basis (cf. Longenecker 1989: 102), and the Abrahamic Covenant is effectively supplanted. There is no place for the Covenant Paul had cherished as a Pharisee; he blames Israel for its own rejection and contemplates the irony of the salvation of gentile Christians.

The third argument (11.1–36) reasserts the eternal validity of the Abrahamic Covenant that Paul had cherished as a Pharisee but had been unable to reconcile with his Christian convictions either in Galatians or in his two previous lines of argument in Romans. Resuming his interpretation of the remnant motif, the exclusion of many inheritors of the Abrahamic Covenant becomes a temporary stage in salvation history (11.11). The rejection of Israel, their "hardening" (11.7, 25) and "stumbling" (11.11–12), enables the inclusion of the gentile Christians, in fulfillment of God's ultimate purpose. Gentile Christians are dependent for their salvation on the temporary rejection of Israel (11.19–20, 25), and Paul's own office of apostle to the Gentiles is subordinated to God's overall scheme for the salvation of Israel (11.13). The unbelieving Jew and the believing gentile Christian are in a relationship of mutual dependence (11.17–24), and "gentile believers need to understand their place within the divine purpose, how their blessing not only contributes to but also depends upon the blessing of Israel now in the eschatological present" (Dunn 1988: 669; cf. Moxnes 1980: 50). The Abrahamic Covenant is shown, despite indications to the contrary, to be inviolable, and the salvation of all Israel is assured, but not apart from Christ (Sanders 1983: 194–95; Segal 1990a: 56, 281). Scholars debate the meaning of "all Israel" (πᾶς Ἰσραὴλ—Rom 11.26). Getty (1988: 459) and Wright (1991: 249–50) argue that the term applies to both Jews and Gentiles. Dunn (1988: 520) argues that the church is a subset of Israel. Beker (1980: 334), Refoulé (1991), and Ziesler (1989: 285) argue that the expression refers to ethnic Israel, as do those scholars who maintain separate covenants for Jews and Gentiles (Gager 1983: 193–264; Gaston 1987).

Räisänen has observed that the discrepancies between Paul's three distinct lines of argument in Romans 9–11 give "witness to a process of thought that has not come to an end" (1986: 201–2; cf. Davies 1977: 33; Dunn 1988: 617). Paul's most carefully preconceived and structured letter includes three contradictory attempts to resolve what had for him become a fundamental problem. "Paul the Jew and Paul the apostle of Christ, convinced that God's will is that he be both at once, and therefore never questioning their compatibility," has "more than a little difficulty reconciling his native convictions with those he had received by revelation" (Sanders 1983: 199). The inclusion of all three arguments in Romans indicates that Paul did not reject any of them entirely, but held them in a state of unresolved cognitive dissonance, even if, at the time of writing, the last to some extent supersedes the previous two (cf. Dunn 1988: 668; Räisänen 1986: xvii). Whereas the first two arguments relativize the promises of the Abrahamic Covenant and subordinate them to the Christian gospel, in the third the extension through Christ of salvation to the Gentiles is a subordinate scheme in the salvation of Israel and the fulfillment of the Abrahamic promises.

Conclusions

We have noted that Paul operated in a world in which human beings derived their identity from several sources, and that identity as a member of the Christian body could and frequently did conflict with identities inherited through birth. We have observed ways in which Paul sought to reconcile one specific aspect of conflicting identities, both in his own life and self-understanding and in his dealings with his churches. This was the conflict between membership of Israel and of Christ, particularly as this problem was manifested in the experience of gentile converts to Christianity and those who sought to regulate their association with what was still a predominantly Jewish movement. Cognitive dissonance theory has proved a useful tool in our analysis of the problem and of Paul's response to it.

Notes

1. This issue is dealt with more extensively in Taylor (1998). In the history of psychology, the cognitive dissonance approach is a special case of cognitive balance theory (Heider 1958), which developed in the field theory framework in the mid-twentieth century.

2. This and the following sections are based on work previously published in Taylor (1996 and 1997a).

Dread of the Community: A Psychoanalytical Study of Fratricidal Conflict in the Context of First-Century Palestine

26

RICHARD K. FENN

IF HYAM MACCOBY IS RIGHT, in his excellent treatment of *Judas Iscariot and the Myth of Jewish Evil* (1992), the murder of Jesus was in fact a fratricide: Judas being initially the brother of Jesus himself. Yet, no concern with fratricide can be found in the passage from the Acts of the Apostles in which Peter addressed "the assembled brotherhood, about one hundred and twenty in all" (1.15) about the necessity to replace Judas, "who acted as guide to those who arrested Jesus" (1.16). Note the absence of remorse and guilt in this passage, despite the clear reference to the betrayal of Jesus by Judas. There is only an appeal to internal sources of legitimacy rather than to any charisma that might have been transferred from father to son; he insists that Judas's replacement come from among those "who bore us company all the while we had the lord Jesus with us, coming and going, from John's ministry of baptism until the day he was taken from us" (Acts 1.21–22a).

Whether or not Judas was Jesus' blood brother, as Maccoby (1992: 56ff.) argues, in the synoptics and in Acts Judas's betrayal of Jesus is assumed simply to have been necessitated either by fate, the will of the devil, or his own vicious nature. The sources of violent animosity are thus external to the Christian brotherhood. The murder of Jesus is therefore not compared with the animosity of Jacob for Esau or of Cain for Abel. To be sure, Judas's death was a result of his own guilt or a divine punishment, but there is no attempt in this passage to refer to a besetting, fratricidal conflict that has troubled Israel since its earliest days. This omission of internal sources of fratricidal conflict allows the new Christian brotherhood to be concerned solely with evil as emanating from the old Israel or from Satan, the principalities and powers, or Rome itself. As Maccoby goes on to argue, Judas has become a figure who unwittingly plays his role in a drama of sacrifice and redemption. Even his death assists the sacrificial victory over death itself, as does his part in the execution of the victim, Jesus. However, these are developments, Maccoby argues, that can be traced to Gnostic sources and the mystery cults of the Eastern Mediterranean or of Rome itself, not to biblical sources concerned with fratricide.

The ideology of brotherhood itself does not need to turn Judas into a mythic, even satanic figure; his crime is all too familiar from the history of brotherhoods themselves and from the patriarchal narratives, and from sources like the *Testaments of the Twelve Patriarchs* or from *Jubilees*, all of which would have been more than familiar to the initial brotherhood that Peter has been addressing. Thus, Maccoby may be in error in describing the notion of a drama of sacrifice and redemption to Gnostic sources. For instance, the notion that Judas may have meant his betrayal of Jesus for evil, although God meant it for good, can be traced back to the story of Joseph and his brothers: an epic of fratricidal rivalry. As I will argue below, such an implicit reference to the Joseph story is typical for brotherhoods, like the Galilean, that are peripheral to the priestly brotherhoods centered in Jerusalem itself. It is all the more interesting, therefore, that when it comes time to replace Judas in the brotherhood of Jesus, no reference is made to patriarchal narratives of fratricidal rivalry, especially to the Joseph story, or for that matter to the story of Cain and Abel.

I would argue that in this story, as elsewhere in the account of Judas, we are in the presence of a "comedy of innocence," in which fratricidal hatred and violence within the Jesus brotherhood are ignored or projected outward and thus blamed on external influences, those stemming from Judaeans, scribes and Pharisees, Romans, or other representatives of the forces of evil. Such an assumption of innocence would be particularly necessary at a moment in which the succession is being managed: the succession from the authority of Jesus in person to that embodied in the surviving members of his brotherhood. It is in such moments that old rivalries among members of the brotherhood are most likely to come out, and the threat of violence is therefore greatest. In the case of the brotherhood of Jesus, furthermore, there was no patriarchal authority, no brother designated to represent the father, who could enjoin compliance with his choice of a successor on the remaining brothers. The situation described by Freud in *Totem and Taboo* (1950), in which the brothers revive the memory of the slain father, partly out of guilt for his death and partly out of a need to control their own rivalries, would be most likely under these conditions. That is why Judas is replaced by lot, so that the will of God can be exercised directly, without the need for continuity of succession from one generation to the next. The brotherhood has immediate and direct access to divine authority and thus needs no mediators and no brother to take on himself the role of the father's representative. That role had been taken by Jesus, who suffered the usual fate of the brother who claimed to represent the father.

The relative "innocence" of this account of the succession that replaced Judas among the brotherhood, its lack of reference to fratricide, is all the more remarkable in view of Israel's recent history and of the available literature on its internal conflicts. In the two centuries before the onset of the Christian era, and in the first century C.E. Israel had been plagued by civil war and had developed a literature of mortified reflection on its proclivities to fratricidal conflict. For instance, we will have occasion to examine various passages from the *Testaments of the Twelve Patriarchs* in which remorse over fratricidal rivalry, and injunctions to brotherly love, predominate. In some of these *Testaments* we can discern antipatriarchal elements, whereas others envisage patriarchs as designating their successors in an honored brother, a favored son, in the expectation that the other brothers will accept their lesser lots. It is the designated son, of course, who is the primary target of fratricidal hostility.

A document like *1 Enoch*, which was apparently well known in the brotherhood of Qumran and may well have originated in Judaea, appears to have various elements of the ideology of brotherhoods: warnings against fratricide; a sense of generations as being temporal periods rather than a result of linear succession from father to son; an emphasis on the righteous as opposed to sinners; strong antipathy to potentates and kings; and a notion of a time-before-time, as opposed to the historical course of time, which favors reflection of the succession from fathers to their favored sons. Moreover, some of the more anguished expressions of remorse over fratricide include expressions of longing for the patriarchal presence and blessing, as in some of the *Testaments of the Twelve Patriarchs*. There may well have been a traditional form of fraternal ideology that stressed the dependence of the brotherhood on the blessing and authority of the father, and that allowed one brother to be honored above others as a father to the brotherhood itself. However, this very elevation was the source of considerable rivalry among some brotherhoods, and as Josephus has shown, the brother who assumed extraordinary authority, especially without the consent of all the others, was a prime target for fratricidal anger. It is not surprising, therefore, that the story in Acts finds the brotherhood turning to charismatic sources of selection, the lot, whereby the direct will of God could be expressed, since fratricidal rivalry so often was the result of the father's designation of one son to be his representative among the other brothers. That is why there is a slight contradiction in this passage: a minimal deference to the authority of tradition, if not of patriarchal authority itself. At one point Peter cites two passages from the Psalms of David: one of which refers to letting a place, a homestead, remain uninhabited; the other of which refers to the replacement of one person by another. As Maccoby would no doubt agree, these are merely proof-texts. I mention them here, however, to suggest that, despite the brotherhood's attempt to derive its authority from its own experience and from channels that are neither traditional or hereditary, there is, in the appeal to Scripture, an implicit recognition that the brotherhood is dependent on customary sources of legitimation.

Some brotherhoods were loath to derive their legitimacy from patriarchal sources. These are brotherhoods, I will argue, that are hostile to the political and cultural center. In the first century they were opposed to the ruling priestly brotherhoods in Jerusalem, and to the priestly brotherhoods that monopolized religious and political legitimacy. In this chapter I will explain briefly how this antagonism to the center arose in the events following the return of exiles from Babylon and their establishment of a colonial regime under the auspices of Cyrus, and I will trace later developments of this same antagonism between the center and the Judaean periphery under a variety of Judaean warlords who converted their neighbors by force and who engaged in various forms of ethnic cleansing. Here the point is simply that there were levels upon levels of fratricidal hostility in first-century Palestine: hatred not only heightened by long-standing ethnic tensions among the Israelite brotherhoods but also endemic to the social structure in which fathers designated one son to rule in his name over the others.

Toward the turn of the Common Era there were in Israel a number of groups who in their own eyes at least were what we would call brotherhoods. Some of these, like the Zealots, sought to purify Israel of any internal sources of contradiction. They were against social distinctions that were both invidious and destructive, and thus in the civil war of 66–73 C.E. the Zealots, among others, attacked the priesthood and the nobility. They were also notably hostile to any of their own members who assumed, literally or figuratively, the mantle of leadership; one parading in the vestments of the high priest was killed on the spot for his presumption to authority. Anyone claiming messianic authority would not only arouse the suspicion of Roman authorities but also excite the jealousy of the brotherhood itself. Despite—and because of—the tendency of brotherhoods to eliminate the father, they were badly in need of an ideology that would assign authoritative roles to some brothers without exciting the envy or enmity of the others.

It is no exaggeration to suggest that guilt over these fratricidal struggles was in fact somewhat paralyzing. Not only was there a sense of dread over a future day of retribution, but there was some sophistication about the relation of physical paralysis to guilt over fratricidal motives and impulses. Take, for example, the following passage from the *Testament of Simeon, the Second Son of Jacob and Leah*:

> In the time of my youth I was jealous of Joseph, because my father loved him more than all the rest of us. I determined inwardly to destroy him, because the Prince of Error blinded my mind so that I did not consider him as a brother nor did I spare Jacob, my father. But his God and the God of our Fathers sent his mes-

senger and delivered him from my hands . . . my brother Judah sold him to the Ishmaelites. When Reuben heard this he was sorrowful, for he wanted to restore him to his father. But when I heard it, I was furious with Judah because he had let him go away alive. For five months I was angry with him. The Lord bound my hands and feet, however, and thus prevented my hands from performing their deeds, because for seven days my right hand became partly withered. I knew, children, that this had happened to me because of Joseph, so I repented and wept. Then I prayed to the Lord God that my hand might be restored and that I might refrain from every defilement and grudge and from all folly, for I knew that I had contemplated an evil deed in the sight of the Lord and of Jacob, my father, on account of Joseph, my brother, because of my envying him. . . . Now my father was inquiring about me because he saw that I was sullen. And I said to him, I am inwardly in pain, for I was more sorrowful than all of them because it was I who was responsible for what had been done to Joseph. And when we went down into Egypt and he placed me in fetters as a spy, I knew that I was suffering justly, and I did not lament. (2.6–13, 4.1–3)

This testament is remarkably contemporary for its understanding that the brother who harbors fratricidal desires will suffer from paralyzing anguish and guilt. The crime, for which Simeon pays so dearly, is only imaginary. Simeon himself had not been one of the brothers who had actually harmed Joseph; nonetheless he had desired to do so, regrets that Joseph has been allowed to escape him alive, and feels "responsible for what had been done to Joseph." Simeon's fratricidal wishes, even plans, were tantamount in his own mind to a murderous deed. Not only had Simeon planned to kill Joseph; he also wanted to kill Judah for letting Joseph escape into exile. Thus when Simeon finds himself in fetters because Joseph takes him to be a spy, he finds that his punishment is deserved.

The *Testament of Simeon* represents the sense that Simeon is relegating fratricidal hatred to his youth. It is in their immaturity that brotherhoods tear themselves apart over fratricidal conflict. A similar claim to having made a break with the past can be found in the letters of Paul, who frequently contrasts the new era of the Christian with the childhood of the people of Israel. Thus the psychological insights in the *Testament of Simeon* demonstrate the authenticity of the claim to have made a radical departure from previous fratricidal rivalry. For instance, later in the *Testament*, Simeon acknowledges that fratricidal envy "makes the soul savage and corrupts the body" by causing severe physical and mental disturbances (4.8).

To be sure, there is an ideological element in this text; Simeon attributes the paralysis of his right hand to the Lord who thus inhibits him from acting on his anger against Judah for letting Joseph escape. However, it is not primarily the Lord or Jacob, his father, whose scrutiny causes Simeon's self-awareness. Simeon himself knows that his paralysis is the result of his own murderous passions toward Joseph

and Judah. The *Testament of Simeon* thus indicates that there was a widespread awareness of fratricidal urges as a possible cause of guilt and illness in the soul and body.

Clearly some communities in Israel, in the centuries just before and after the
beginning of the Christian era, sensed the origins of psychosomatic ills in unresolved, highly ambivalent, and intense emotions. To consign these unresolved hatreds to the past thus required an intense form of self-purification and a radical
form of forgiveness. Readers of the canonical Gospels will also recall the frequent
occasions in which the followers of Jesus were reminded that it is inner and spiritual forces that are primarily destructive and that to enter into a new era requires
not only a readiness to give unlimited forgiveness but also a profound cleansing of
the soul.

The future looms larger when a break has been made with the past; thus there
is a confrontation with the end of time that makes such a renunciation of fratricidal passions seem to be eschatological. Anticipations of the future thus dominate the imagination, especially when the past has retreated into a vague source of
unwanted precedent. To enter into a new era is thus to inaugurate the future, but
this inauguration also brings with it a mixed blessing. Not only is the past laid
aside, one has to begin to pay in advance, as it were, for the right to enter into a
new era. Thus it is possible that the paralysis of Simeon's hand was a way of dis-
charging a debt to the past and thus of forestalling a worse punishment on a later
day of judgment and retribution.

To make a break with the past is of course easier said than done. Rituals that
initiate the future call for sacrifice, as if it were necessary to discharge an ancient
debt or to forestall future punishment by paying, as it were, in advance. Furthermore, those who would lift a hand against a brother would understandably find
that hand paralyzed and withered, as though such a punishment for a fratricidal
wish could atone for it or prevent the murderous deed itself. Similarly, the anticipation of such a punishment is a way of forestalling the final day of retribution.
Certainly there is a great amount of passion in Simeon's account: a great deal of
anger, and no small amount of affection between the antagonistic brothers. The
implicit sadistic and masochistic urges are embedded, so to speak, in the text. No
wonder, then, that guilt for murderous wishes toward one's brothers could make
the future an object of dread.

Brotherhoods are themselves attempts to live in the present without deference
to a past dominated by patriarchal authority. On the other hand, such a departure
from the past is seldom complete. The past is invoked even in the attempt to transcend it. We should therefore not be surprised to find that there is an element of
patriarchal ideology in this text. Simeon's patriarchal commands to cultivate
brotherly love and the fear of God were addressed to his sons, and the brothers
whom they are to love are indeed their kin. "And you, my children, each of you

love his brothers with a good heart, and the spirit of envy will depart from you" (*T. Sim.* 4.7). That and the fear of God will drive the evil spirit of fratricide from the heart (*T. Sim.* 3.5). Only then can a future begin that is neither a form of punishment for the fratricidal sins of the past nor a repetition of them in later conflicts. Only a brotherhood fortified from within and thus defended against fratricidal conflict can face the enemies of the clan, who are clearly communal.[1]

It is clear that the *Testament of Simeon* was in circulation and well known during the first century C.E., and that there have been a number of Christian additions to the text. We can therefore speculate with some confidence that a first-century audience existed that was familiar with the social and psychological costs of fratricidal passions; understood, as we might put it, hysterical or psychosomatic symptoms; and wished the present not only to be a radical point of departure form the past but to inaugurate the future.

For a beneficial future to begin, however, required a certain amount of purification from the sins of a fratricidal past. The self-diagnosis of Simeon makes it clear that even a physical paralysis could be understood as the punishment for crimes of the heart and mind. Simeon "repented and wept": sure signs of contrition that could prompt divine forgiveness; and he prayed that his paralysis might be lifted and his hand "restored." Such a purification from a fratricidal history would therefore take the form of prayers for forgiveness. It is in this light that we should understand the implications of Jesus' cure of a paralytic by forgiving his sins: forgiveness being the means of declaring the present free from the past and of letting the future begin. Thus the way would be open to fulfilling the promise of Simeon:

> Make your hearts virtuous in the Lord's sight,
> make your paths straight before men,
> and you shall continually find grace with the Lord and with men. . . .
> If you divest yourself of envy and every hardness of heart,
> my bones will flourish as a rose in Israel
> and my flesh as a lily in Jacob.
> My odor shall be like the odor of Lebanon.
> Holy ones shall be multiplied from me forever and ever,
> and their branches shall extend to a great distance. (T. Sim. 5.2, 6.2)

Note that the image here is of lateral growth: the vine (not explicitly mentioned) and the branches. Indeed it was just such an image that could be found on the walls of the Temple in Jerusalem, and it was a metaphor for the equality and growth of brotherhood. Brotherhoods extend themselves not by the succession from father to son but laterally through growth and proliferation as the "holy ones" multiply and extend themselves through space rather than from one generation to the next.

The Testament of Simeon might therefore reflect an ideology of the victimized and yet preferred son, such as Joseph. Precisely such an ideology characterized the northern Israelites, who compared their national fate with the story of Joseph: "Given the royal connections of the tribe of Joseph in the north, the story of Joseph may originally have played a similar role, perhaps at the expense of the House of Judah, from which the Davidites hailed: the true monarchy is Josephite, not Judean" (Levenson 1993: 205). As Levenson points out, in fact, the parallels between the Gospels and the story of Joseph are quite striking (1993: 203). In fact, the gospel writers appear to have modeled the story of Jesus on that of Joseph. Not only have they adopted the midrashic tendencies of northern Israel, the gospel writers also appear to have used the story of Joseph as a model from which to narrate the history of Jesus and his movement. Jesus is sold into captivity by his brother Judas: Joseph having been sold by his brothers at the instigation of Judah. "*The names are the same*" (Levenson 1993: 203, emphasis added). As Levenson goes on to point out, twenty shekels was the price stipulated for a young male in Leviticus 27.5, whereas the thirty silver pieces referred to in the synoptics may well be a reference to another passage (Zec 11.12–14) in which a shepherd symbolically breaks the fraternal tie between Israel and Judaea. The story of Judas therefore adds a caption, as it were, for those who might otherwise miss the point of the Gospels: that the Passion is a narrative of fratricidal crime. The fraternal bond is broken once again, this time for the price of thirty pieces of silver.

Consider the argument of Hyam Maccoby (1992), who points out that the Judas in the Gospels (Judas Iscariot) can be traced to Judah, the brother of Jesus. His role as a betrayer is the result of secondary elaboration in later texts, but it points to fratricidal conflict among Jesus' "brothers" within the movement. That would explain, of course, why the future remains problematical for all those who do not seize upon the presence of Jesus as an opportunity to be purified of fratricidal impulses and past crimes. Clearly the return of Jesus after the resurrection, in symbolic triumph to reign over his brothers and to reunify the nation, would be an object of dread for all those who had contributed to his rejection and death or who remained paralyzed by their guilt for having broken the fraternal bond in various ways in the past.

Of course, it is difficult to estimate the extent to which a pervasive sense of guilt for a fratricidal history was in fact paralyzing certain quarters in Israel during the first century C.E. Similarly, it is difficult, at this late date, to estimate the extent to which particular ethnic groups who had been victimized by their Judaean brothers felt that "the Jews" deserved a severe punishment for their fratricidal sins. The differences between the *Testament of Simeon* and the *Testament of Reuben* nonetheless suggest that there were strong antipathies between brotherhoods in certain of the provinces, like Galilee, and the brotherhoods that claimed a monopoly on the management of the Temple and the collection of revenues. The hostility between the brotherhood at Qumran and the Hasmoneans would only be another such case in a much larger point.

It is therefore essential to listen closely to a text in order to sound out the voice that is within it. Take, for example, another *Testament*: the words of Reuben to his sons "that you show love, each to his brother" (*T. Reu.* 6.9). Here, however, the injunctions are not only to brotherly love but to sexual restraint and obedience to the tribes of Levi and Judah, appointed respectively to rule as priests and kings. It was these two tribes, Levi and Judah, who had been the primary beneficiaries of Persian authority after the Babylonian exile and had enjoyed the position of surrogate overlords. Exempt from taxation by the Persians, they were entrusted with the administration of the client state of Jerusalem and Judaea, from which they were to extract the usual taxes for their Persian masters. This placed them in a position of patriarchal authority as officials of the Persian regime and as heads of the Temple cult. At the very least, then, the *Testament of Reuben* invokes the authority of priestly brotherhoods with a vested interest in representing what Weber called patrimonial authority: patriarchy with the added support of retinues of servants and administrators, militias, and the power of taxation. No wonder that the *Testament of Reuben* displays an interest in keeping the peace among the various clans and brotherhoods of Israel. Among brotherhoods, some were more equal than others, and those with more access to the political center may well have relied on the borrowed authority of alien patriarchates.

We would therefore not expect to find the same anguished sense of guilt over fratricidal impulses in the *Testament of Reuben* that we do in the *Testament of Simeon*. On the contrary, the brotherhood that claimed the authority to administer the cult and collect taxes would have relied strongly on the force of law and custom and would have claimed to be able to pass their authority from one generation to the next through the succession from father to son. Here simply note the difference between the use of patriarchal ideology in the *Testament of Reuben* and the clear concern of the *Testament of Simeon* with making a break with the past. In this latter text (*Simeon*) we can detect an intense interest with making the present distinct and different from the past and a strong orientation toward the future: a sense of being sickened by fratricidal impulses; feelings of guilt for a fratricidal history; dread of the future as bringing a day of retribution for Israel's past crimes against its brothers.

Of course, *Testaments* that warn against guilt for fratricide could well reflect not only the politics of northern communities but the attempt of Judaeans to co-opt the Joseph theme for their own benefit. Take, for example, another of the patriarchal testaments, the *Testament of Zebulon, the Sixth Son of Jacob and Leah*. Zebulon describes himself as having been moved with compassion by Joseph's appeal to his brothers for mercy: "I was moved to pity and began to weep; my courage grew weak and all the substance of my inner being became faint within my soul. Joseph wept, and I wept with him; my heart pounded, the joints of my body shook and I could not stand" (2.4–5). Zebulon clearly exempts himself from further guilt for fratricide, but he is nonetheless profoundly affected by the fate of Joseph and is moved to sorrow and compassion. Because his other brothers remained hard of heart and angry toward Joseph, however, they eventually were sickened. However, Zebulon reports that he alone remained healthy. Redemption can come only when there is repentance; otherwise the fratricidal sins of the fathers will be repeated among their sons, and the community itself will remain subject to a fatal illness.

There is clearly an element of warning as well as of diagnosis in these texts. The warning is that for those who fail to make a break with past sins, the future will bring sickness and death as a punishment for fratricidal crimes. Indeed, Zebulon reports that "the sons of my brothers were sickly and died on account of Joseph, because they did not act in mercy out of their inner compassion. But you, my sons, were preserved from illness, as you know" (5.4–5). Thus the followers of Jesus were not the only brotherhood to claim for itself release from the past. Christians were not alone in claiming immunity to the ills of the body politic that stemmed from fratricidal passions. It was other brotherhoods, especially the Judaeans and Levites, who would face a future itself of inevitable suffering and death for the fratricidal crimes of the past.

If fratricidal passions are at the root of Israel's inability to escape the past and to enter a future that would be one marked by harmony and justice, what is required is an emotional antidote of greater strength. The one prescribed in the *Testament of Zebulon* will sound familiar to readers of the New Testament: compassion. Remember that Zebulon describes himself as having become deeply moved with compassion by his love for Joseph and fear for Joseph's life; indeed, as Joseph wept, so did Zebulon. In later passages (*T. Zeb.* 7.4) Zebulon describes himself as weeping with all those who are oppressed: the gift of tears and of the heart substituting for more material benefactions to those in need. The model for this compassion is Joseph himself, who did not take revenge on his brothers when they were in need but who also was in his turn compassionate toward those who had wronged him: "Whomever you see, do not harbor resentment, my children; love one another, and do not calculate the wrong done by each to his brothers. This shatters unity, and scatters all kinship, and stirs up the soul. He who recalls evil receives neither compassion nor mercy" (*T. Zeb.* 8.5–6). These injunctions toward brotherly love and compassion were broadened to include "every person" (*T. Zeb.* 7.3, 8.1). They were directed not only at the victimizers but also against the victims who might otherwise mortgage the future to the past in a desire to have a final accounting. Fratricidal motives were to be dreaded not only because they sicken and eventually kill those who harbor them but because they divide the nation and subject it to alien rule and demonic power (*T. Zeb.* 9).

We need to consider what forces kept alive this fear of the paralyzing, indeed fatal effects of fratricide both on the human soul and on the nation as a whole. Certainly fratricide had become endemic in the nation: entire communities being pitched against each other in battles that broke the fraternal bonds uniting Jews. However, there were also structural tendencies that were conducive to fratricidal conflict. On the small scale, within families and within priestly or warrior brotherhoods, there was a profound and intense hatred of any brother who elevated himself at the expense of the others and took on the role of the father. This antipatriarchal motif also shows up in the hatred of brothers toward the son designated by the father as his primary heir, his favored son.

In addition to these dynamics within brotherhoods and among actual brothers, however, was the added tension between certain warrior brotherhoods on the periphery and the concentrations of priestly and patrimonial power at the political and cultural center of Israel. Under the Herodians in particular, the center had become an overwhelming source of power and authority that aroused the enmity of warrior brotherhoods on the northern periphery, in Galilee, Gaulanitis, and Gerasa. This was due not only to the concentration of political, administrative, economic, and social power at the center, which was a magnet for brotherhoods seeking a larger share of the patrimonial power. The enmity of warrior brotherhoods to the center was also a result of the tendency of high priestly families to seek allies in foreign capitals. Thus there were structural factors that kept alive and intensified fratricidal struggles.

Certainly the system kept producing its own effects in each generation: effects that we have seen intensified fratricidal conflict both within and between brotherhoods. For Josephus himself, it appears that each new conflict is reminiscent of an old one. Each new murder recalls a previous fratricide, and ancient fratricides seem to prefigure later conflicts. It is, as Freud pointed out, as if there were a tendency for repressed elements, especially the fratricidal, to repeat themselves.

It is in the light of these structural and endemic tendencies toward fratricide that we are to understand the longing for patriarchal authority. Josephus himself is convinced that the besetting sin of Israel is fratricidal, and that Jews simply loathe any one of their number who seems to exalt himself above the others. To cure a brotherhood of such an endemic tendency would therefore require either a spiritual revolution marked, according to the *Testament of Simeon* and the *Testament of Zebulon*, by contrition, forgiveness, and compassion, or a return to patriarchal rule. It was indeed this longing for the father that Freud found in the memory of a Moses or, earlier, of an Ikhnaton.

However, the power of patrimonial authority, especially of sultans like Herod the Great, met with resistance, however, from certain brotherhoods, which not only sought to undermine that power but to gain it for themselves. Furthermore, any brotherhood that seemed to gain a position of advantage by aligning itself with a patrimonial authority center was itself suspect and a fair target for lesser brotherhoods with more limited access to the patronage of the center. It is understandable, then, if claims to modernity seemed to be more convincing among brotherhoods, lesser especially those that were more removed from struggles for patronage.

In addition to these structural sources of perennial tension, however, we must ask what it was like to live within such a system of chronic fratricidal hatred. That is why I began this introduction with the excerpts from the *Testaments* of Joseph's various brothers, each of whom expressed a sense of guilt and remorse, or of longing and compassion, for fratricidal conflict. To make sense of this undercurrent of foreboding, I would suggest that we return to Freud's notion of social dread: dread, as he put it, of the community.

To understand dread of the community we round up the usual suspects of the social imagination, fantasies, identifications, stereotypes, by which a community fills in the gaps in its social knowledge about itself. Those gaps, I would add, are wider to the extent that the community is engaging in a "comedy of innocence" of the type that we discussed earlier. To the extent that a society is unwilling or unable, therefore, to understand and imagine itself as fratricidal, to such an extent will it imagine that it is strangers, alien brotherhoods, and neighboring communities that harbor such a destructive passion. Within the imagination, of course, it is possible to harbor all sorts of passions, to attribute them to others, especially to those whom one has wronged and would therefore would like to injure or impugn. Every community must then suffer the consequences of those projections.

The consequences of such a quite literally dreadful social imagination can be fatal, as Josephus himself reminds his readers in his stories of individuals who suffered remorse for real or imagined crimes, then felt haunted by their victims, and eventually died. Of course, we do not have direct access to the state of mind of Israelites. Nonetheless, we do have a number of references to the possible return of peoples who had been dispossessed of their lands. As Bickerman points out, certain popular martial stories were more explicit than Scripture in imagining the return of a vengeful brother: "The Bible simply says that Esau planned to revenge himself on Jacob after the death of Isaac, their father, but the Hellenistic storyteller has Esau strike just when Jacob is mourning Leah" (1988: 188). The Jewish warrior communities indeed believed that the Edomites, as well as other neighboring peoples, desired to take revenge for past losses. Like the Edomites, these communities were imagined to be joint heirs who had been killed by their rival brothers, the Israelites, who had forcefully dispossessed these peoples from their own homes and territory. Certainly Esau is the prototype of the wronged brother whose vengeful return must therefore be feared.

In defending themselves against these neighboring, rival brotherhoods, however, Israelites faced the possibility of further intensifying the cycle of fratricidal conflict from one generation to the next. It is no wonder, then, that in some brotherhoods, at least, there was a desire to settle old scores and to rid Israel of its old rivals once and for all. Thus in the *Testament of Judah, the Fourth Son of Jacob and Leah*, it is recorded that, after eighteen years of peace between Jacob and Esau,

> Esau, my father's brother, came up against us with a force powerful and strong. Jacob struck Esau with an arrow, and in death he was carried up to Mount Seir. We pursued Esau's sons, who had possession of a fortified city, which we were unable to enter. Encamping around it, we besieged it. When they had not opened to us after twenty days, I set up a ladder and, holding a shield in position over my head, climbed up in spite of being hit by stones. I killed four of their powerful men while Reuben and Gad killed six others. Then they asked us for peace terms, and following consultation with our father we took them as subjects under tribute. They regularly gave us 200 cors of wheat and 500 baths of oil and 500 measures of wine, until the famine, when we went down into Egypt.

Note that this testament goes well beyond the biblical account of the relation between Jacob and Esau (Gn 27 and 36), to the point of having Jacob actually murder the brother who had once harbored fratricidal designs toward him. Clearly fratricidal warfare had weighed heavily on the communities that wrote or studied this text; a protective barrier between brothers had been breached, and fratricidal warfare had been accomplished.

Note the "comedy of innocence" that accompanies this account of Esau's murder. It was Esau, not Jacob, who launched the first attack. Furthermore, it is only after twenty days of siege had elapsed with an appeal for peace terms, and then only after Judah himself had risked mortal danger in scaling the walls, that the city of Esau's sons is actually attacked. Even after Judah and his allies invaded the fortified city, moreover, there was no wholesale slaughter, but only the death in battle of ten of "their powerful men." Peace terms were then sought, and a relationship established, based on tribute, *until the time of the famine*. Thus the past is only partially laid to rest, and only for the time being.

No doubt these careful qualifications of the damage inflicted by Jacob on Esau were the sign of an uneasy conscience. Bickerman is quite clear that Israel had long sought to deny its history of displacing other peoples (1988: 186). However, a naive ideology of military virtue fortified by divine assistance could no longer serve to provide adequate reassurance and legitimacy once Israel had been severely defeated. The original tendency to attribute Israel's conquests to divine favor ran afoul of later losses, for instance, to the Assyrians. Indeed, contact with racial enemies had long provided Israel with unwelcome reminders that "even according to their own tradition they were intruders in Palestine" (Bickerman 1988: 186).

Furthermore, Bickerman points out that the Edomites, believed to descend from Esau, were blamed for burning the Temple of Jerusalem and were expected to join other neighbors in "a war to recover Isaac's heritage" (1988: 185, 187). Perhaps the rise of the Idumaeans to power under Antipater and his sons may have seemed like a nightmarish fulfillment of this prophecy. The appearance of Idumaeans at the gates of Jerusalem in the civil war of 66–73 C.E. may also have seemed to be the realization of the worst fears of Israel: the return of Esau.

There is other evidence that Israel lived in dread of reprisal for previous crimes, real or imagined, and that to relieve such apprehension the Israelites may very well have resorted to legal fictions or to historical revisionism. Thus the book of Jubilees distorted the facts regarding the Canaanites (Bickerman 1988: 186). According to Jubilees, it was Canaan, not Israel, that had violated an oath to preserve territorial boundaries between peoples. This had been a fictional oath "not to seize other people's possessions," and it was imaginatively attributed to the sons of Noah. The oath had been further reinforced by a curse (Bickerman 1988: 186). Such a curse would have provided ample reason for living in dread of retaliation should the oath itself ever have been broken. To avoid the dread of retaliation and the fulfillment, therefore, of the curse, Israel portrayed another people, the Canaanites, as the guilty party.

This sort of subterfuge conceals a guilty conscience without satisfying it. The underlying truth was that Israel rather than Esau was the one who had stolen the other's heritage, and this truth would return even in disguise. For instance, in biblical terms Esau, the Edomites' ancestor, was imagined to have been a *twin* of Jacob (Bickerman 1988: 184). The twin, of course, is a double of the self, one's mirror image, as it were. Thus in fearing possible reprisals from the Edomites, Israel may have been covertly recognizing an aspect of itself in alien form. More certainly, it would appear that Israel was imagining that its brothers, in this case the Edomites, would displace them from the land that Israel had taken from them by subterfuge or aggression.[2] The curse on the sons of Noah would thus have been fulfilled when the Edomites returned to claim their heritage.

I would also argue that the sons of Esau served as a screen on which to project Israel's internal sources of fratricidal rivalry. Esau, of course, had been Isaac's favorite son, and there was always something precarious about that position. He was the target of all the brothers whose legacies were relatively minor and who had not been selected to represent their father's presence or authority. If to this insult had been added the injury that Jacob inflicted on Esau, however, the wronged brothers would have represented an even more serious threat to the favored son. He would have had an additional reason for their grievance and a more serious score to settle. It is not surprising, therefore, that dread of the fratricidal conflict took on apocalyptic proportions.

Of course, we do not have direct access to any of the hearts or minds of that period. Neither did Josephus, of course, have direct access to what was in the hearts of Herod and his brothers. Nonetheless, in Josephus's interpretation of the fratricidal conflict of the Herodian household we can at least find a witness to the experience of social dread. In describing the death of Herod's brother, Pheroras, Josephus recounts Pheroras's guilt at his own desire to kill Herod: a crime he only contemplated but never actually committed. According to this account, Pheroras had obtained a poison to use on Herod and had entrusted it to his wife. However, in remorse because he knew that Herod had loved rather than hated him, Pheroras urged his wife to destroy that drug "for fear I go to Hades with a devil on my back," (Josephus, *B.J.* I.5). Thus we can safely assume that for some educated Jews of the first century C.E. Hell was a place in which the individual continued to explore and suffer from the past; it was a place from which there could be no release from misgivings, self-punishment, and guilt for real or imagined crimes. Hell was indeed a fitting punishment for fratricidal fantasy as well as a metaphor for the experience of dreading the imagined community.

It will be remembered that the fratricidal hatred between Herod's sons resulted in the execution of two of them, Aristobulus and Alexander, who were accused by another half-brother, Antipater, of plotting to kill their father, Herod. Their spirits, it would appear from Josephus's account, continued to plague the living long after their death. Even if Josephus's account represents a fad among Hellenistic writers to speak of ghosts as though they were real, still it is reasonable to assume that some were indeed capable of being haunted. Indeed, describing the inquisition by Herod into the plot against him, Josephus goes on to say that the "ghosts of Alexander and Aristobulus were prowling around the whole Palace, ferreting out hidden things and bringing them to light, and dragging those remote from suspicion before the inquisitor" (Josephus, *B.J.* I.5). It is worth noting that the appearance of such ghosts could indeed prove not only sickening but fatal. Later, Josephus recounts the death of Alexander's wife as being due to the appearance of her dead husband. Alexander's ghost, it appears, was enraged by his wife's (Glaphyra's) subsequent marriage to the ethnarch Archelaus, his brother, and he threatened her in this way: "'I shall not overlook the insult; I will fetch you back to me whether you like it or not.' She related this dream, and in less than two days she was dead" (Josephus, *B.J.* II.6). Thus the experience of social dread can take on apocalyptic proportions. Consider, for example, another apocalyptic text, *1 Enoch*.

614 RICHARD K. FENN

In one of his visions Enoch is lifted to a high mountain in which he can see the souls of those awaiting final judgment; it is the meantime, in which the spirit of Abel continues to demand satisfaction: "This is the spirit which had left Abel, whom Cain, his brother, had killed; it (continues to) sue him until all of Cain's seed is exterminated from the face of the earth, and his seed has disintegrated from among the seed of the people" (*1 En.* 22.7). This passage suggests that, for some, the present continued to be imbued with the seriousness of the last judgment: an inaugurated and continuing apocalypse. Thus any people who, like Cain, have deprived others of their birthright are subject to being sued by the spirit of Abel. Indeed *1 Enoch* (22.11) sees that the souls of sinners awaiting judgment are being subject to enduring pain.

No comedy of innocence is wholly successful, however, in obliterating the memory of past sins and grievances. The repressed knowledge of violence internal to the community itself is then projected onto a day of future retribution. It is thus understandable that some would seek relief in the coming of someone who, like Abel or the Son of Man, or Jesus on his return, would put an end once and for all to fratricidal conflict. Such relief is found in Enoch's vision of "the One to whom belongs the time before time," who is "the prototype of the Before-Time," (*1 En.* 46.1–2). This is indeed the Son of Man (*1 En.* 46.3), the "Antecedent of Time" so named by the "Lord of the Spirits" who is the "Before-time" (*1 En.* 47.3, 48.2). Enoch speaks of the "Antecedent of Time" as one who was "Before-Time" and in whose hands are all the times of the present and of the future as well as of the past. It is the Antecedent of Time, after all, that views the destruction that he has caused through the flood and promises that there will never be another such disaster (*1 En.* 55.1–2). It is a guarantee to Enoch that the amazing son of Lamech, Noah, will be the last to witness such devastation; after him the future will truly begin.

As dread of the community is translated into apprehension of a future day of judgment, the awareness of fratricidal conflict thus returns in a demand that the community purify itself. The brotherhood, purified of the very passions that are endemic to brotherhoods, must then await a day in which its members will be scrutinized for their fratricidal or patricidal passions. It is as if the community was buying time in order to postpone the immediate and unqualified acknowledgment of its own underlying hatreds. Moral persuasion and exhortations to spiritual purification, accompanied by confessions, take the place of explicit acknowledgments of underlying fratricidal or patricidal motives. Only when the vicious circle of resentment, ambition, and revenge is interrupted, and trust intervenes, will the "enemy's kingdom" be broken (cf. *T. Dan*). All who would emulate the good brother, Joseph, may look forward to a life not only of suffering but of eventual triumph. Thus the *Testament of Benjamin, the Twelfth Son of Jacob and Rachel*, states that "if anyone betrays a righteous man, the righteous man prays. Even though for a brief time he may be humbled, later he will appear far more illustrious, as happened with Joseph, my brother" (5.4). Note how the dream of glory, the fantasy that the mistreated brother will triumph after being humbled, persists despite the apparent repudiation of fratricidal conflict. In the New Testament as well similar promises that the last will be first, and the humbled will reign triumphant, allow the fantasies of retribution and revenge on the last day to persist. Postponing the day of judgment allows fratricidal fantasies to go underground, as it were, covered by the verbiage of spiritual repudiation. As Otto Rank once observed, this commitment to a long period of humiliation, justified by fantasies of eventual triumph, makes for a masochistic social character. I would simply add that it allows social dread to continue, however it may be projected on the screen of a final day of judgment when the secrets of all hearts, as Jesus is reported to have put it, will be revealed. Note also how the continuation of fratricidal motives leads to a longing for a higher authority to intervene: "Whatever it does, or speaks, or perceives, it knows that the Lord is watching over its life, for he cleanses his mind in order that he will not be suspected of wrongdoing either by men or by God" (*T. Benj.* 6.6–7). Only under a fatherly eye will it be possible to replace suspicion with trust and to break the vicious cycle of fratricide and revenge. To overcome dread of the community, it is necessary not only to pray and to engage in self-purification but to accept supervision, both human and divine. One enters into a continuous encounter with a divine tribunal in order to avoid suffering at the last judgment.

The longing for a patriarch who could insist on fraternal harmony thus gave rise to injunctions to the brotherhoods to discipline themselves. In the *Testament of Judah*, the patriarch gives instructions to his sons; he claims that "at no time did I bring grief to Jacob, my father, because everything he said, I did" (*T. Jud.* 17.4). Furthermore, it is clear that the testament invokes a situation in which Judaeans are enjoined to avoid close alliances, sexual or political, with alien peoples. There are strong prohibitions against sexual ties with Canaanites, and a confession of sin by Judah for having had intercourse with a Canaanite woman (*T. Jud.* 14.6, 17.2). Slowly, however, brotherhoods and brothers were enjoined to reach the level of spiritual purification necessary for peace, whether they counted themselves among the victimized or among the victimizers. In the meantime, it would be God alone who maintained close surveillance over the heart and mind of the individual and could discern there any fratricidal tendencies.

It is not enough, however, that sons and brothers, like Joseph, emulate the ideal of the obedient and sacrificial son, who experiences the fratricidal rage of others but does not permit himself to perpetuate it. Not only must the injured brother somehow avoid retaliation or even plans for eventual revenge, a providential order is required, one that will ensure that those who violate the solidarity of brotherhood will suffer and perish in the end, whatever may be their temporary triumph. Thus the *Testament of Benjamin* promises that "Until eternity those who are like Cain in their moral corruption and hatred of brother shall be punished with a similar judgment" (7.5). The guarantees for those who must emulate Joseph are thus rooted in a providential order that not only transcends but triumphs over fratricide. The future must await the day when the "enemy's kingdom" is broken and trust is substituted for revenge.

The *Testament of Benjamin* thus imagined a final judgment that included the Gentiles, but only after Israel itself first had been judged. Only then would the Gentiles be incorporated into the judgment, when the Lord "shall judge Israel by the chosen gentiles as he tested Esau by the Midianites who loved their brothers" (*T. Benj.* 10.10). Clearly fratricidal anger has taken a new turn here and come back to haunt Israel by threatening them with being judged by Gentiles "who loved their brothers." As if to add insult to injury, it is Gentiles who will be Israel's judges: a real turning of the tables on the last day. Dread of the alien has taken on a new source of anxiety; the vision of a community purified of fratricidal hatred has now become a source of accusation from a quarter usually regarded as primitive and hostile to the very existence of Israel itself. In the meantime, therefore, any individual who might resent his brother's advantages and wealth must purify his mind of hatred, and the individual who has been hurt by his brothers must also pursue the path of internal purification. The soul must gain sufficient purity so as to be no longer subject to the weight of others' opinions, because it lives in the knowledge that it is being supervised by God and has been threatened with adverse judgment by an idealized but alien brotherhood.

Why would Israelite brotherhood torment itself with the vision of an idealized gentile community coming to sit in judgment on Israel itself for its own fratricidal tendencies? Remember that Israel must bear the weight of historical guilt for its aggressions against the other peoples of the land. Israel was surrounded by peoples who might indeed long for revenge and the recovery of their lands. In the *Testament of Judah*, for instance, there is a recounting of the successful conquest of Canaanite forces, the demolition of their cities, and the capture and plundering of their populations (*T. Jud.* 3–7). There may well be echoes of the Maccabean period in this narrative of triumphs, as well as cautions against the use of unmitigated force against those who are ethnic "brothers" of the Judaeans. These warnings might also have had a particular currency in the Hasmonean period during the ethnic cleansing instigated by Alexander Jannaeus. No doubt similar echoes were heard during the fratricidal struggles of the first century C.E., particularly during the civil war of 66–73 C.E. The triumphs of Israel were enough to give it an exceedingly guilty conscience and to make it perennially afraid of reprisals by neighboring peoples. The Edomites or their equivalents were always coming back bent on the satisfaction of old grievances.

As I have argued, however, more than a historical memory is at work here. There were structural tendencies as well, which kept alive fratricidal sentiments.

Without this reinforcement from the social order, historical memories of Israel's wars with neighboring peoples might have been allowed slowly to lose their intensity and relevance. Israel was also weighed down by its own internal rivalries, with some brotherhoods chronically resentful over their lesser status and over the privileges enjoyed by wealthier brotherhoods. There would of necessity come a day when such old scores could be finally settled and the vicious cycle of fratricide and the yearning for patriarchal authority broken once and for all.

Not only does dread of the fratricidal aspects of the community perpetuate and intensify longing for a providential order or a patriarchal divinity who will intervene to protect, justify, and avenge the brother who is wronged; patriarchal love is also to be won by becoming the son who is victimized by his brothers. Following Levenson on this point, I would argue that there are two Christologies at work in the New Testament: one focusing on the beloved son sacrificed by the father, for whom Isaac is the main prototype, the other focusing on the son whose preferred status with the father is not only the cause but the consequence of his being victimized by his brother(s). Regarding this latter prototype, Levenson speaks of "a Joseph Christology—that is, a pattern in which the emphasis lies on the malignancy of the slayers rather than on the pious intentions of the father who gave up his beloved son" (1993: 226). That malignancy, Levenson argues, is simply "the homicidal rage" of brothers who wish the lion's share—or even all—of the legacy for themselves and wish to preempt the succession from father to son in their favor (1993: 225). The desire to kill the heir and to monopolize the legacy underlies a variety of texts in both testaments, he argues, as he traces the antecedents of the Parable of the Wicked Husbandmen (Mk 12.1–12) to various passages in the Old Testament and to the midrashic literature. Even the tale of Cain and Abel is to be understood in terms of a contest over inheritance: "It may be pertinent that some rabbinic midrashim attribute the quarrel of the primal brothers to debates over inheritance, such as how the two will divide up the world and which of them should assume Eve after Adam had divorced her" (Levenson 1993: 228; quoting *Gen. Rab.* 22.7).

Certainly the conflict between Jesus and Judas is "a midrashic play on the sale of Joseph by Judah, with Judas, as his name suggests, perhaps typifying the Jews as the homicidal opponents of the beloved son of God. The father's gift has been recast as the brothers' crime" (Levenson 1993: 228, 230).

Following the destruction of Jerusalem in the civil war of 66–73 C.E., it was increasingly difficult to maintain the plausibility either of a patriarchal ideology requiring radical obedience or of a warrior ethic that required radical solidarity. It was clear that to be the favored son of a divine father was no guarantee of protection or rescue. As the author of *4 Ezra* put it, it was necessary to know

> why Israel has been given over to the gentiles as a reproach; why the people whom you loved has been given to godless tribes, and the Law of our fathers has been

made of no effect and the written covenants no longer exist; and why we pass from the world like locusts, and our life is like a mist, and we are not worthy to obtain mercy. But what will he do for his name, by which we are called? (4.23–24)

When "the humiliation of Zion is complete" it is no longer possible to imagine that the patriarch of the universe will protect and defend his favored son (*4 Ezra* 6.20). Even the very institution of patriarchal favor, by which the succession of Israel has been guaranteed, is in radical doubt: "And now, O Lord, behold, these nations, which are reputed as nothing, domineer over us and devour us. But we your people, whom you have called your first-born, only begotten, zealous for you, and most dear, have been given into their hands. If the world has indeed been created for us, why do we not possess our world as an inheritance?" (*4 Ezra* 6.57–59).

When an order, an entire social system, in fact, fails to renew itself, time begins to run out for the people in earnest. Passage after passage in *4 Ezra* speaks of the shortness of time, as is typical of the apocalypse. Time is running out for the wicked, the nation of Israel, and the latter's enemies. The world itself is facing the end of its time, as "salt waters shall be found in the sweet, and all friends shall conquer one another" (*4 Ezra* 5.9). Time is of the essence even for souls in the next life, and the prophet asks God, who has given him a vision of final things, whether time will "therefore be given to the souls after they have been separated from the bodies, to see what you have described to me?" (*4 Ezra* 7.100) The era of fraternal solidarity, as envisaged in the various testaments of Joseph and his brothers, turns out to be an apocalyptic vision rather than an ethic whose time has come. For the author of *4 Ezra*, in fact, the present era is that of Esau, and the age to come will belong to Jacob (5.7–10). It is in this climate of despair over the prospect of a community without fratricidal passions, whether internal or external, that the first Gospels were written. That they should have had a heavy investment in exempting the Christian brotherhoods from the stigma of fratricide is understandable, but they have paid—and others also have paid—a high price for their "innocence."

Notes

1. That is, not only the usual antagonists, such as the sons of Amalek and Ham and the "seed of Canaan," but now also the Cappadocians (*T. Sim.* 6.3).

2. Of course, as Bickerman points out, fictitious and mythological kinship between Israel and other peoples was also used to cement ties with Greeks and to explain enmity with the Romans (1988: 184ff.). In these cases, however, there were clear strategic reasons for the ties, for example, the relationship of Jewish to Spartan colonies.

Conversion in Early Christianity 27

JACK T. SANDERS

OUR CONCERN IN THIS CHAPTER is to understand the conversion of Gentiles (non-Jews) to Christianity in the early decades of the new religion as it left its Jewish matrix and became a universal religion.[1] What was it about early Christianity that was attractive to Gentiles? And what was it about the situation of those Gentiles that disposed—or predisposed—them to conversion? (In order not to extend this chapter unnecessarily we shall have to ignore a discussion of the character of conversion.) Before turning to an examination of the early Christian evidence of conversion, however, it will be helpful to review modern scholarship briefly on the subject and also to acquaint ourselves with a few of the modern studies, that exist in considerable abundance, of conversion to new religious movements (NRMs). This review is necessary in order for us to have the most adequate conceptual framework possible for evaluating the evidence. When we then turn to the evidence itself, our interest will be on conversion to Christianity in the Greco-Roman context, not on Jewish conversion. There is little actual evidence for Jewish conversion (although we know that it certainly existed) in the early church after the time of Jesus, and the phenomenon of following Jesus is better understood under the category of discipleship than under that of conversion.

Of course, the early chapters of the Book of Acts record mass conversions of thousands of Jews in Jerusalem; but these narratives are clearly fanciful and idealized, as can be seen most readily by contrasting the cumulative effect of the conversion narratives through Acts 6.7 with the persecution narrative in Acts 8. The conversion narratives would lead us to believe that a large proportion—if not nearly all—of the population of Jerusalem became Christians within the space of a few days, whereas when the persecution breaks out it empties Jerusalem of all

Christians save the apostles; yet the population of Jerusalem seems hardly diminished. This contrast remains when in the concluding narratives we learn both that there were tens of thousands of Jewish Christians (Acts 21.20) and that "all the multitude of the Jews" (Acts 25.24) opposed Paul before the Roman governor—statements that appear to contradict each other. Consequently, few modern scholars think that there were mass conversions to Christianity in Jerusalem in the days of the apostles.[2] We proceed, therefore, to our review and analysis.

Nock's landmark work, *Conversion*, has focused the modern discussion. Nock distinguished between *conversion* to Judaism and to Christianity and *adhesion* (adherence) to other religious movements, like the religions of Isis and of Mithras. The difference was that conversion meant "the reorientation of the soul of an individual, his deliberate turning from indifference or from an earlier form of piety to another, a turning which implies a consciousness that a great change is involved, that the old was wrong and the new is right" (Nock 1933: 7), whereas in the case of the other religions "a man used Mithraism [for example], but he did not belong to it body and soul; if he did, that was a matter of special attachment and not an inevitable concomitant prescribed by authority" (1933: 14). As Nock's discussion developed, however, he had some difficulty holding firmly to the distinction, as when he wrote that Christianity, like Mithraism, might gain adherents in similar ways (1933: 77), and when he observed regarding some ancient non-Christian texts that "we have . . . a feeling of otherness from the world and a concept of conversion" (1933: 117–18).

Nock also sought to analyze the *mechanics* of conversion in considerable detail. For him the other religions, like those of Isis and Mithras—"cults" in his terminology—won converts or adherents by a variety of means. One individual might bring another to a meeting or service (1933: 77); in the case of Judaism the exclusive and absolute teaching may have been influential (1933: 78); there was the "direct appeal to the eye" of public processions and ceremonies (1933: 80); there were "supposed miracles . . . and the literary propaganda which made them known and enhanced their value" (1933: 83); and beyond this were the public expressions of "hymns and votive offerings and works of art" (1933: 92). But Nock also sought to explain the receptiveness of the general Greco-Roman population for these stimuli, which receptiveness he attributed to "(1) the picture of the universe which arose, above all from astrology, (2) the interest in immortality, [and] (3) an inquisitiveness about the supernatural resulting in a general increase in the tendency to believe" (1933: 99). Then, anticipating modern sociological theory, he observed that "demand creates supply, and this demand was met by the rise of private mysteries" (1933: 116). This point—that the soil, so to speak, was ready for the Christian seeds—is one to which we shall want to return. Yet early Christianity, according to Nock's analysis, lacked most of the appeals to which gentile receptiveness responded. There were no outdoor sermons or other displays, and only the authorities, like those responsible for arresting Ignatius, could finger Christians. What was visible to the public was the martyrs, and martyrdom was effective. Thus Nock laid down an axiom (taken from Tertullian), "The blood of martyrs is the seed of the Church" (1933: 192–94).

MacMullen (1984), among others, has sought to improve on Nock's analysis. He opens his study by showing that conversion to Christianity is not always, and perhaps not generally, a "body and soul" distinction, since even into the early modern period there were people who were Christians but followed practices that were clearly "pagan" in origin. MacMullen thus emphasizes that instead of a black–white distinction between Christian and non-Christian (as in Nock's model), Christianity could blend "into the secular and even the non-Christian without clear demarcation." Indeed, MacMullen seems to have seen the reality of Christian existence here, in contrast to Nock's more idealized view of conversion, and he offers this definition of conversion: "that change of belief by which a person accepted the reality and supreme power of God and determined to obey Him" (1984: 5). We note that this definition leaves practice entirely out of the picture.

As motivation for conversion to Christianity, MacMullen proposes miracles and (like Nock) martyrdoms (1984: 26–30). Also like Nock, he lays emphasis on the fact that after the Pauline mission "the church had no mission . . . ; rather, it left everything to the individual" (1984: 34), and he proposes that people like Justin and Tatian became individual converts as the result of their quests (1984: 30–31). There are thus for MacMullen two classes of early Christian conversions, the lower-class type that responded to miracles and the like and the upper-class type that found Christianity at the end of an intellectual quest (1984: 37–39). Finally, he notes that many persons, albeit a minority within the Christian whole, will have progressed in their understanding of and commitment to Christianity sufficiently to have reached Nock's conversion point (1984: 41).

Throughout his discussion MacMullen notes the importance of individual, often chance encounters—in the marketplace, "in quite obscure settings of everyday," perhaps in homes (1984: 36–37, 41). Without using the term, he has thus seen that conversions take place most often in the context of preexisting *networks*. Yet he also thinks that mass conversions must have been necessary in order to account for the growth of Christianity (1984: 29).[3]

Finally, MacMullen proposes a different "soil" from Nock's in which Christianity could take root. The interest in immortality, according to him, was more apparent than real (1984: 11), and Greco-Roman beliefs appear in general to have been "a very spongy, shapeless, easily penetrated structure" that "positively [invited] a sharply focused and intransigent creed" (1984: 16). Thus where Nock found positive aspects of Greco-Roman belief to which Christianity appealed, MacMullen finds only negativity that was bested by Christianity.

Passing over several more recent studies of conversion to early Christianity, we turn to a still more recent handbook on Roman religions by Beard, North, and Price that brings important new perspectives to the discussion. These authors see quite clearly that conversion to early Christianity must be viewed alongside conversion to the other NRMs (which they call "new cults"), and they have given a lengthy discussion of the phenomenon of conversion to these NRMs in the early empire. The authors first discuss the appeal of the NRMs and propose that the appeal can best be explained "under the term 'transformation': for all these new cults claimed to make much more of an impact than traditional religions on the everyday world and on the after-life of their adherents" (Beard, North, and Price 1998: 287). This transformation the authors see first of all in "a new sense of community" that the NRMs offered that was "stronger" than that offered by traditional religious groups. Membership in such groups was "marked by special initiatory rituals." Thus, membership in the NRMs "affected, in different ways, the everyday life of their members" (1998: 288). "[W]hat was distinctive about the new cults was their drive toward a strong religious identity through strictly controlled rules of behaviour." Furthermore, the NRMs "created new statuses and new ways of life that may have started within the walls of the sanctuary, but extended outside those walls too" (1998: 289).

In the second place, transformation in *some* (albeit not all) of the NRMs had to do with "the fate of the initiate after death." Those NRMs that possessed this trait emphasized it by "construct[ing] death much more sharply as a 'problem'— and, at the same time, offer[ing] a 'solution'"(1998: 289). These authors thus implicitly reject Nock's distinction between conversion and adhesion and posit transformation as the explanatory principle for adhesion or conversion, which they do not distinguish.

Beard, North, and Price then turn to a discussion of the members of the subject NRMs. First pointing out that "male members of the senatorial order appear conspicuously absent from" the NRMs in Rome (1998: 291), they further observe that, "outside Rome, members of local élites (. . . holding the rank of 'town councillor') were involved in these cults much more widely and fully." Mithraism was equally respectable, although in another way, since its adherents were mostly "soldiers, up to the rank of centurion, [and] imperial slaves and ex-slaves" (1998: 294). Furthermore, "by A.D. 200 Christians were found in Rome at every level of society," and they cite the scolding of *Hermas Mandates* 10.1.3 that "many second-century Roman Christians were 'absorbed in business affairs, wealth, friendship with pagans, and many other occupations of this world'" (1998: 295–96). The authors here take note of the Christian ideal of poverty and cite Celsus (further below) on the lower-class membership of the church; but they also astutely note that poverty was, in Christianity, "clearly vested with symbolic, religious significance," thus making it "difficult . . . to trace accurately the presence of the poor (in strictly economic terms) in early Christian communities" (1998: 296). In the opinion of Beard, North, and Price, then, the main NRMs in the early empire attracted a broad spectrum of class and status groups, although Christianity was apparently slower in doing so than were some of its competitors. Again, they refuse to assume that there were conversions of different orders among the various NRMs, although they are aware of individual differences in some cases. The individual differences, however, do not lead them to propose that conversion to one or another of the NRMs was qualitatively different from conversion to the others.

The authors next take up the role of women in the NRMs, and they observe that the possibilities for women's participation varied. Mithraism, of course, admitted no women; but most of the other NRMs did make a place for women that they would normally not have had in the traditional religions of the day. This is true for the worship of the Great Mother, of Isis, and in both Judaism and Christianity. Nevertheless, men retained the primary positions of leadership in all the NRMs (1998: 298–99). The authors conclude their discussion of membership by attacking the notion (without referring directly to Nock or to MacMullen) that "significant sections of the population of Rome had long been searching for some kind of spiritual satisfaction which was eventually offered by the new cults." Rather, they propose, the NRMs on the one hand created "the very needs which they satisfied" and on the other hand offered a transformation that "was rooted and legitimated in the social and political lives of [the] adherents." In other words, the "everyday experience [of the converts] . . . found an echo in the promise of the cults to transform lives." Unfortunately for this last proposal, Beard, North, and Price offer only the example of Mithraism, which allowed soldiers and freedmen the opportunity for advancement, something that the broader culture considered "both desirable and possible" (1998: 300–301). Nevertheless, something that we shall want to consider further below is whether Christianity stood in tension to the culture or not. Did people become Christians in part because Christianity offered a transformation rooted and legitimated in the social and political lives of its converts?

Turning next to the issue of "homogeneity and exclusivity," Beard, North, and Price observe the relative continuity of each of the NRMs across the geographical spectrum, although they are aware that "Isis in Gaul *must* have been a significantly different phenomenon from Isis in Egypt." They speculate that the use of more-or-less standard books in the Isis religion, Judaism, and Christianity may have abetted this uniformity, but they think that "the crucial point must be that these cults defined themselves as international" (1998: 303).

The authors finally, again without specifically rehearsing Nock's adhesion–conversion antithesis, confront the theory head on by proposing that all the successful NRMs under study were *to some degree* exclusive, and in this they are surely correct. They ask first, "Would it be possible at any level to accept the tenets of both the cult of Isis and of Mithras?" and they answer in the affirmative; but the "at any level" must be emphasized (1998: 307). Their examples of exclusiveness are the castrated priests, *galli*, in the service of the Great Mother and certain devotees of Isis, for example, Apuleius's Lucius, whose "newly shaven head [at the end of the *Metamorphoses*] . . . emphasizes that Lucius had no time for any other deity but Isis" (1998: 308–9).

It is clear that Beard, North, and Price have moved the discussion of gentile conversion to early Christianity to a new level by insisting that all conversions to NRMs in the period with which we are concerned must be analyzed together as part of a general phenomenon. Scholars who want to understand early Christian conversion can no longer give prior preference to the notion that Christianity was somehow unique in winning converts in Greco-Roman society. The correctness of this new approach will be more obvious after we take into account sociological (and related) studies of conversion to NRMs in recent times.

Since the 1960s the study of NRMs has occupied many social scientists, so much so that we need a guide. We may conveniently begin with a textbook, Robbins's *Cults, Converts and Charisma* (1988). Summarizing a wide range of sociological studies, Robbins first notes the necessity to distinguish between recruitment and conversion (1988: 64), thus agreeing with MacMullen's opening observation. Commitment or "true" conversion may follow recruitment; or, alternatively, increased understanding may lead the new recruit to drop out of the movement—an aspect of the dynamic of early Christianity that is probably too often neglected in modern studies.

Turning now to the issue of why people join an NRM, Robbins notes a proposal made by Lofland and Stark in 1965 of a way of understanding conversion that has become "the most influential sociological model of conversion-commitment processes in religious movements" (Robbins 1988: 79), namely a "value-added process model" that entails seven stages of conversion. According to this model conversion is accomplished when a person (1) experiences *acute and persistent tensions*, (2) within a *religious problem-solving perspective*, which leads the individual (3) to define himself as a *religious seeker*, after which (4) he encounters the movement at a crucial *turning point* in his life and (5) forms an *affective bond* with one or more converts, after which (6) *extra-cult attachments become attenuated*, and (7) the convert is exposed to *intensive interaction* within the group and ultimately becomes the group's "deployable agent" (Robbins 1988: 79–80).[4] What makes this model especially engaging for our interest here is that, as further sociological studies have shown, the model works only for groups that are "highly stigmatized." Other groups that "do not drastically transform the social roles of converts" or involve the attenuation of extra-cult attachments do not follow this pattern (Robbins 1988: 83).

Were we to stay with Nock's analysis we should be inclined to endorse this model, but MacMullen's analysis would incline us to the opposite view; and the analysis of Beard, North, and Price would seem to tend in the same direction (in their emphasizing the affinity between social status and what the NRMs offered). Was early Christianity at some times and places highly stigmatized and at others not? As MacMullen realized, the actual situation is likely to have been more complex than we may have been wont to recognize.

We need to note two other aspects of Robbins's summary discussion, namely social networks, and defection and deconversion. A great deal of evidence suggests that conversion follows lines of social networks, and Robbins quotes a widely noted summary maxim: "The probability of being recruited into a particular movement is largely a function of two conditions: 1) links to one or more movement members through a pre-existing or emergent interpersonal tie; and 2) the absence of countervailing networks" (1988: 85). The latter condition means that the potential convert is "structurally available." Yet structural availability is subject to other conditions, especially the religious movement's "goals and beliefs about the world" (1988: 86); or, more broadly, there must be a real appeal of the movement to the structurally available person. As Robbins puts it, "A married man with a family might be 'available' for a romantic liaison with Brooke Shields but not with Margaret Thatcher" (1988: 87).[5]

The matter of networks is worth pausing over. If our image of conversion to early Christianity is informed by the accounts of mass conversions in the early chapters of Acts and by the existence of large evangelistic rallies conducted by modern American preachers, we shall surely miss what is probably the most important ingredient in conversion, namely that the convert has or develops an affective tie to someone in the movement before joining. It is in fact known, of course, that modern evangelistic rallies win most of their converts not at the rallies themselves, but through prior evangelistic contact—and such contact readily follows affective lines. Protestant evangelism aside, however, it is also the case that many recent studies of NRMs have shown that most converts are won through networks.

Twenty years ago Stark and Bainbridge published a study that is now almost a classic on this subject (1980). They showed that the "Moonies," for example—the followers of the Rev. Sun Myung Moon—were initially stymied in their attempt at further growth when they first moved from Eugene, Oregon, to San Francisco. "Only when the cult found ways to connect with other newcomers to San Francisco and develop serious relationships with them did recruitment resume" (1980: 1379). Stark and Bainbridge's best example, however, was the Mormon Church (Church of Jesus Christ of Latter-day Saints). Young Mormon men and women are encouraged by the church to go in pairs to places away from their homes seeking converts. Such random visits, however, turn out to be a waste of time for the church. After examining statistics "for all [Mormon] missionaries in the state of Washington during the year 1976–77," Stark and Bainbridge found that only 0.1 percent (!) of all conversions during the year were the result of "door-to-door canvas," whereas 34 percent of conversions came from meetings with potential converts arranged by other Mormons, and fully 50 percent of all conversions occurred when "contact with missionaries took place in the home of [a] Mormon friend or relative" of the potential convert. (Other conversions followed from referrals; Stark and Bainbridge 1980: 1386.) Stark and Bainbridge also sought to discover whether any kinds of conversions occurred in significant proportion *apart from* such networks, and they found that only adoption of such occult beliefs as astrology and the validity of tarot cards fell outside the pattern (1980: 1390–91, 1376).

Nichiren Shoshu America (formerly Soka Gakkai), while not as large as the Mormon Church, maintains a similar growth rate, and the experience of conversions via networks is similar to that for the Mormons and for the Moonies. Out of a total of 345 conversions counted by Snow, Zurcher, and Ekland-Olson in their and in others' studies, 82 percent were the result of social networks, 17 percent of recruitment activity in public places, and 1 percent of information in the mass media (1980: 790–91).

The evidence from NRMs in modern Western societies is clear: conversions come primarily through personal contact within social networks. Can we assume the same for antiquity? Not, to be sure, in the absence of evidence or in the face of evidence to the contrary; but the studies of modern NRMs make it reasonable to think that many ancient conversions to Christianity, and to the other NRMs of that day as well, likely came about as a result of contacts and affective relationships within networks.

We need not linger on the matter of defection, only note it, although it is worth pointing out that the attrition rates of modern American NRMs are "extremely high" (James T. Richardson 1992: 79). We need to remember that in the early days people might have left Christianity as readily as they entered.

A few paragraphs ago we noted the possibility of greater complexity in the matter of conversion to early Christianity than scholars who have studied the issue may have seen. It is now time to complicate that theoretical complexity further by looking at Rambo's inclusive model of conversion (1993). In order not to make this chapter overly long we limit our review of Rambo's model to those parts of it that bear directly on our sources.

Rambo calls his a "holistic model of conversion" (1993: 7). He first emphasizes three aspects: (1) It is "a process over time, not a single event"; (2) it "is contextual and thereby influences and is influenced by a matrix of relationships, expectations, and situations"; and (3) "factors in the conversion process are multiple, interactive, and cumulative. There is no one cause of conversion, no one process, and no one simple consequence of that process" (1993: 5).[6] The bulk of Rambo's book analyzes seven interlocking aspects that may go into any conversion: context, crisis, quest, encounter, interaction, commitment, and consequences.

A part of any *context* might be resistance and rejection; yet a new religious option may appeal to identifiable enclaves within the population. Conversions may also proceed along established paths—that is, following existing "lines of social cleavages"; and conversions are also dependent on congruence—that is, on "the degree to which elements of a new religion mesh with existing macro- and micro-contextual factors" (1993: 36–37).

Noting that Lofland and Stark were "among the first . . . to note the importance of *crisis* in the conversion process," Rambo points out that crises differ. They may be mild or severe, brief or prolonged, etc.; but he sees "two basic types": "crises that call into question one's fundamental orientation to life" and those "that in and of themselves are rather mild but are the proverbial straw that breaks the camel's back" (1993: 46–47).

Here we may note that one of the most discussed issues in the modern sociological study of conversion to NRMs is that of deprivation. In his summary Robbins notes that "many of the theories" that scholars have put forward to explain such conversion are "crisis theories and/or modernization theories" that "tend to pinpoint some acute and distinctively modern dislocation which is said to be producing some mode of alienation, anomie or deprivation to which Americans are responding by searching for new structures of meaning and community" (1988: 60). And Stark reports that before he and Lofland observed conversion to the Unification Church (Moonies), sociologists normally "examined the ideology of a group to see what kinds of deprivation it addressed and then concluded . . . that converts suffered from those deprivations" (1996: 15). On more adequate analysis deprivation seems not to be a factor—or at least not a significant factor—leading to conversion, and so some sociologists refer at times to *relative* deprivation.[7] In light of this ambiguity in the current scholarly analysis of deprivation as a motive for conversion, Robbins appeals for "a cautionary viewpoint" that "would also highlight the constancy and continuity of movements of 'religious outsiders' throughout American history"(Robbins 1988: 60). The implication of that caution would have to be that we must not assume that people who join NRMs always do so because of some deprivation or crisis in their lives, although we should certainly be alert to evidence for such motivation.

We first saw the importance of the *quest* in our review of MacMullen's views; but whereas MacMullen thought of only a few intellectuals as pursuing such a quest, Rambo thinks that "many, if not most, conversions" are "active" rather than "passive," that is, they come about as the result of seeking, at least in some form and at some level (1993: 58). A seeker is thus available to the missionary enterprise of the religious movement, but this availability has to coincide with the nature of the movement if conversion is to work. Thus availability must be structural (we recall Robbins's adultery joke), emotional, intellectual, and religious. Regarding intellectual availability Rambo explains that "it is rare for someone to be converted to an option that embraces an intellectual framework radically different from the person's previous viewpoint"; and religious availability is similar, meaning that "a person's religious beliefs, practices, and life-style are to some degree compatible with the new option" (1993: 60–62). The seeker, finally, must be motivated by one or more psychological needs (enhancing self-esteem, or the like; 1993: 63).

Rambo next discusses *encounter*, where he first defines the role of the "advocate," employing a term that fits a broader field of activity than does "missionary." After first noting that advocate strategy in different groups can run from the "extensive" to the "minimal" and that advocate style can be "diffuse" (seeking to convert whole groups) or "concentrated" (targeting individuals), he observes that advocates' "modes of contact" are extremely diverse (1993: 78–81). Finally, he emphasizes that, to be successful, the advocate must represent desirable benefits, namely "a system of meaning," "emotional gratifications," "techniques for living," "convincing leadership," and possibly "power,"—feeling "filled with power," having "access to power," or the like (1993: 81–86).

Following this discussion Rambo deals with the nature of missionary encounter itself, pointing out that, at first, a new movement normally has only a few converts but that, "as increasing numbers of people adopt the novelty, there is a bandwagon effect, characterized by more and more interest in and less and less resistance to the innovation" (1993: 95). Then he points to missionary and convert adaptations that are part of the encounter process. An advocate may be tolerant toward the potential convert's life and belief, may translate, that is, "communicate the new religious message in a manner that is understandable"; may assimilate—that is, may "utilize the traditions and rituals of an indigenous culture"; may Christianize—that is, cleanse rites and practices of "un-Christian" elements; may acculturate ("go native"); or may incorporate by introducing indigenous concepts into the advocate's Christianity (1993: 97–99). Potential converts, on the other hand, may oscillate between old and new beliefs, may then eliminate "more and more elements of their tradition that were considered incompatible with Christianity" ("scrutinization"), may combine—work out compromises with advocates over new and old beliefs and practices, may indigenize, by which Rambo means taking over equivalent practices to replace ones given up, and, finally, may retrovert (1993: 99–101).

The next stage in Rambo's conversion model is *interaction*, and here he discusses the ways in which the NRM "encapsulates" the convert. The modes of encapsulation are relationships, rituals, rhetoric, and roles. Rambo is persuaded that while some conversions may not involve relationships, most do (1993: 108; likewise Stark and Bainbridge, above); and he means, of course, that the potential convert must establish some kind of meaningful relationship within the NRM before conversion can succeed. Ritual is crucial because, by offering "a form of knowledge that is distinctive from, but as important as, cognitive knowledge," it "helps people to learn to act differently." And of course rituals like baptism that strongly mark the transition from the old ways and the old group(s) into the new are important (1993: 114–16). The importance of rhetoric is that it helps the convert to conceptualize and interpret the changes involved in conversion; and roles, finally, of course integrate the convert into the movement (1993: 118–23).

The importance of *commitment* and *consequences* for early Christianity will be so obvious to most readers that Rambo's observations on these aspects of conversion require little discussion. One point worth noting is his emphasis on the importance of "sustaining surrender." Some groups, in his observation, are better at this (usually through ritual) than are others; thus the less successful groups will also be less successful at holding converts in an active relationship with the movement. Furthermore, the convert's testimony is important to commitment; it helps to cement the conversion. But such testimony also involves "biographical reconstruction," viewing one's past life through the lens of the new self-understanding (1993: 136–37). Consequences are likely to be affective, intellectual, ethical, religious, or social/political (1993: 169); the convert, indeed, *is* not the same person as before.

Rambo's analysis has not met with widespread acclaim among sociologists, primarily because it is so all encompassing and multifaceted. Thus Lofland writes in his review of Rambo's book that it is, on the one hand, "likely the single most comprehensive compendium of the literature on conversion." On the other hand, however, it is an "everything-is-sometimes-true view" that fails to specify "when forms and aspects of conversion occur and when they do not" (1994: 100). This does not mean, however, that Rambo has failed in his attempt to place between two covers *all* facets of conversion, and he seems to have done so. He has provided the broad, theoretical model that allows us to evaluate *all aspects* of individual conversions; and his analysis has subsumed many of the primary aspects of conversion to which Nock, MacMullen, and Beard, North, and Price have called attention.

Finally, before turning to the evidence, let us note a comment by Dawson. He writes,

From a social-scientific perspective, there is still a crucial and easily overlooked element of mystery about why people choose to be religious. . . . So a full explanation of why people choose to convert still eludes our grasp. In these circumstances we must duly appreciate that people may well convert for precisely the reasons the religions themselves say they do: because they have achieved some form of enlightenment or insight into their salvation. (1993: 93)

With that awareness firmly in the backs of our minds, and keeping before us the sociological principles that we have just reviewed, let us turn to the ancient evidence to see what, if anything, we can learn about societal or sociological aspects of early gentile conversion to Christianity.

When we turn to Acts for evidence for the conversion of Gentiles to Christianity, we find that the author is primarily interested in—to use Rambo's terms— encounter, interaction, and commitment, while demonstrating almost no interest in consequences and very little in context, crisis, and quest. People respond to the apostles either following wonders (as in the case of Sergius Paulus in Acts 13.12 or that of the Philippian jailer in 16.30) or as a result of the preaching of the word, as in the keynote conversion of Cornelius in Acts 10 or in the conversion of many citizens of Antioch in Acts 13. While miracles leading to conversion may be performed in view of a crowd, as is the case with the early work of Philip in Samaria (8.6), or before only one observer (the Philippian jailer), normally Acts represents the proclamation of the gospel as a public event in the presence of sometimes large numbers of people. In a few cases, however, the preaching takes place in an individual or small-group setting (Philip with the Ethiopian eunuch in Acts 8, Peter with Cornelius, Paul and his companions with Lydia and a few others in Philippi; cf. esp. 16.13: "We sat down and spoke with the women who had gathered [there]").

Most gentile converts in Acts seem to come from among the group of the "God-fearers," those Gentiles who have some attraction to Judaism and who may be found at synagogue prayer services; but some do not come to Christianity by this route. When we make this division, however, then we immediately note that the only gentile converts who are attracted to Christianity by wonders are those who do not belong among the God-fearers. Thus Samaritans (if we should call them Gentiles) respond to Philip's ministry in Acts 8:6–7 because of "hearing him and seeing the signs that he did; for many of those who had unclean spirits that cried with a loud voice came out [sic], and many paralytics and lame were healed." Sergius Paulus, further, a proconsul (13.7–12), "saw what happened and believed," where "what happened" was Paul's blinding Elymas/bar Jesus, a "Jewish magician and false prophet" (v. 6). To be sure, Acts calls what Paul did "the teaching of the Lord" (v. 12), but it is not the kind of teaching that, for example, Peter gave to Cornelius. The Philippian jailer, whom we have already mentioned, asked about salvation after the prison doors were miraculously opened and Paul and Silas did not leave. No other gentile conversions in Acts come about as the result of wonders, not even that of Cornelius, whose vision prompted him to send for Peter but who believed only after hearing Peter's preaching. All other conversions of Gentiles to Christianity in Acts, most of which are conversions of God-fearers, happen in response to apostolic preaching, whether on a large or on a small scale. The most common strategy for reaching Gentiles in Acts is that of preaching in a synagogue (Paul), but other contacts are varied: The Ethiopian eunuch and the Philippian jailer are chance encounters; Philip in Samaria probably attracted attention first by his healing miracles.

The author of Acts provides very little information about the backgrounds of the converts other than to locate them in their social worlds. Cornelius is a God-fearer and Roman centurion, Sergius Paulus is a proconsul, others are simply Samaritans or a jailer, many are God-fearers. Only the Ethiopian eunuch may be defined as a seeker, for he was attempting to understand Isaiah when Philip encountered him. Acts also presents almost no information about the aftermath of conversion, although the author apparently wants to give the impression of ever-increasing success in the mission. Such a cumulative effect is explicit, however, only in the case of Jewish conversions in Judah (as we noted at the beginning of the chapter). In any case, we learn almost nothing of the consequences of gentile conversions beyond the further "advice" that the missionaries give to the new Christians in Lystra, Iconium, and Antioch that they should "abide in faith" in the face of "many afflictions" (14:22). Probably quite significant here, however, is the note that Paul and Barnabas "commissioned elders" (v. 23). Although the author mentions this commissioning only here, he elsewhere mentions elders in the church(es) with some frequency, so that we can see that he reckons with a continuing structure of leadership in local congregations after the time of first conversions.

Of course, we need to confront the question of whether the author of Acts has given us an accurate picture with regard to early Christian conversion. We know that the picture is inaccurate in at least one respect, the representation of Paul as normally seeking converts first in a synagogue. It has long been recognized that this characterization is so in conflict with Paul's own statements that it cannot be true and must be a schema that the author retrojects onto the earlier period about which he writes. How Paul sought out potential converts will likely remain forever an unanswered question, although we shall see below that Paul himself provides some clues.

Not only does Paul not corroborate the Acts account in the matter of finding converts as the result of synagogue preaching, he also does not corroborate the descriptions in Acts of preaching to large crowds. To be sure, Paul mentions preaching as a main part of his missionary endeavor; in Galatians 1.23 and 2.2 he refers to his preaching "the faith" in the one case and "among the gentiles" in the other,

632 JACK T. SANDERS

and especially in I Corinthians 15 he rehearses the content of his preaching (v. 1–11; Gal 3.1 seems to refer briefly to this same content); but he gives no indication of how large an audience he may have had on any occasion, and what we now know about the spread of NRMs via networks might incline us to think of very small groups or of individuals. Likewise, his remarks in I Thessalonians 2— where he says for example in verse 9 that he was "working night and day not to burden some [of the Thessalonians] and preached the gospel of God to [them]"—provide no information at all about the size of any groups. The fact that he had a full-time job, as we should say, and preached at the same time makes the possibility of his networking and talking to small groups more credible, but there is no proof.

What is clearer, however, is that some persons were attracted to Christianity by Paul's miracles. This he says fairly plainly in I Corinthians 2.4 when he asserts that his "argument" and his "preaching" were "by demonstration of Spirit and power," not in "persuasive reasonings of wisdom." In I Thessalonians 15 he says the same: "Our gospel did not come to you by word only but also by power and by the Holy Spirit and in much certainty." Should we think that, in a culture in which healing miracles took place, Paul meant by this contrast only that he was bombastic? No; surely he meant that he provided visible proof of the power of his Gospel. He may well allude to this same aspect of his missionary activity when he reports in Galatians 2.9 that the Jerusalem Christian leaders "recognized the grace (or: gift) given" to him. With regard to such miracles also we may well think of small audiences, such as households, rather than of the civic demonstrations that Acts describes, but again the evidence is insufficient to allow us to draw a firm conclusion. Yet Paul seems to have relied on miracles, probably healings, as well as on preaching in order to win new Christians. Whether any of the miracles to which he alludes in I Corinthians 2.4 are the same as those that appear in Acts would be impossible to say.[8]

There are two other things that we learn about gentile conversion to Christianity from Paul, namely the insignificant status of converts and that conversion was a process, not an event. The latter is most ably demonstrated by I Corinthians 3.1–2: "I was not able to speak to you as to spiritual persons but as to fleshly persons, as to babes in Christ. Milk I gave you to drink, not solid food; for you were not yet able." Indeed, most of what Paul writes in all his letters involves the assumption that Christians are in process—that they have become Christians, but that they still need to learn what it means to be Christian, both as regards belief (as in the discussion of the resurrection in I Cor 15) and as regards practice, as is the case in chapter 3 ("jealousy and strife," v. 3). As Gaventa writes, "Despite the fact that Paul understands this transformation [of becoming a Christian] to be real and significant, it is never a finished or completed event but is ongoing"

(1992: 49). Such an understanding of conversion as process supports Mac-Mullen's point that converts grow into the faith, and it confirms the sociological distinction between recruitment (joining a movement) and conversion (coming to share the ideology and goals of the movement), and we should thus now think of most conversions, not merely conversions to Christianity, as happening in this way.

The insignificant status is a bit of a problem. Paul says in I Corinthians 1.26–28 that among the Corinthian Christians

> not many are wise in human terms, not many are powerful, not many are well-born; but God chose the foolish of the world in order to shame the wise, and God chose the weak of the world in order to shame the strong, and God chose the low-born of the world and the despised, the nothings, in order to render the some-things of no effect.

One of the problems with this statement is the gender of the nouns. Paul begins with (gender-inclusive) masculine nouns for "wise," "powerful," and "well-born"; but then he brings in a neuter for "foolish," shifts back to masculine for "wise," but then uses neuters for the remaining groups. It seems impossible, however, to see any deliberate theological motive for these shifts, especially in view of the contrast between "foolish" (neuter) and "wise" (masculine). And Paul does, after all, begin this statement by advising, "Look at your calling, brothers." All the "things," then, that God has chosen appear to be the Corinthians whom God called. What Paul says here about the insignificance of Christians in society finds later corroboration in Celsus's criticism of Christians (as a number of authors note). "Their injunctions are like this," Celsus wrote about 180, "'Let no one educated, no one wise, no one sensible draw near'" (Origen, Cels. 3.44).

A problem here, however, is whether what Paul says comports with reality. Is Paul, in other words, skewing the facts here for the sake of effect, in the context of his broader polemic against the wise in Corinth who have a wrong theology? Meeks has shown that such is the case. Relying largely on prosopographical evidence, Meeks reached the "ventured" conclusion "that the most active and prominent members of Paul's circle (including Paul himself) are people of *high status inconsistency* (low status crystallization). . . . Their *achieved* status is higher than their *attributed* status." These people were "independent women with moderate wealth, Jews with wealth in a pagan society, freedmen with skill and money but stigmatized by origin, and so on," who "brought with them not only anxiety but also loneliness, in a society in which social position was important and usually rigid" (1983: 51–72, 73). We thus could say that such people suffered relative deprivation and were therefore prime candidates for conversion to an NRM (cf. Bainbridge 1992: 179–81).

If Paul's labeling Christians the nothings of the world is, then, not an entirely accurate social description, what Meeks has shown is how the label might nevertheless resonate with them, which is of course what has to be explained. (Otherwise they would have exclaimed, "Surely he doesn't mean us!") Especially *after they had become Christians* and had gained a status and security that they had not experienced before (so, in general, Meeks), they might very well have been able to agree that formerly they had been nothings. This agrees with the appeal that Beard, North, and Price proposed for the NRMs in the Roman Empire.

Ephesians 4.11 amends Paul's list of charismatic offices in 1 Corinthians 12 by adding evangelists. Presumably these persons have taken the role of the earlier apostles; but we receive no clarity about exactly what that role was, that is, whether the evangelists spoke to large crowds or contacted people through networks. In the absence of contrary evidence, we shall probably do best to assume networks, as also in the case if 2 Timothy 1.8, which advises the recipient not to be "ashamed of the witness of our Lord," a witness apparently intended for potential converts.

The author of Hebrews expresses the developmental aspect of conversion when, in his discussion of apostasy in 6.1, he refers to the "discussion of the beginning in Christ" that Christians returning after leaving the faith would have to "leave" again in order to proceed again to "completion."

1 Peter brings a new element into view, namely that Christians by their *examples* may bring Gentiles to conversion. In 1 Peter 2.11–12 the author admonishes staying away from a pagan lifestyle but then advises that Christians should turn a good face toward non-Christians, even when the latter abuse Christians, so that "by good works they may gain enlightenment and glorify God on the day of visitation"; and then in 3.1 he proposes that women may be especially effective simply by "being obedient to their own husbands, so that if some are not convinced by reason, they will be won by the women's behavior apart from reason." The author of 1 Peter thus seems to assume the attempt to talk to non-Christians but to encourage a more encompassing attitude toward evangelization, winning converts by good example.

In the New Testament, then, a fairly uniform picture of some aspects of conversion emerges. The early Christian advocates proclaimed the gospel of Christ's death and resurrection, probably to small groups reached through networks, to persons of low status but nevertheless often of some means. Paul also attracted attention by miracles, but others who followed him seem not to have performed them. New Christians were expected to sever their ties with Greco-Roman culture and to grow in their understanding of Christian theology. Where Acts disagrees with this picture (preaching in synagogues and, both there and otherwise, to large crowds), the author has probably misconstrued early Christian history. If there were areas within Christianity during the first century where conversion appeared otherwise, we do not learn of them.

As we round into the second century, we find that the works known as the Apostolic Fathers present us, to the degree that we can learn anything about conversion from them, with a picture similar to the one that we found in the epistles in the New Testament. *1 Clement* 7:5–7 is particularly straightforward, explaining that even in former days God provided preachers of repentance (Noah, Jonah) in response to whom people were saved. Obviously the author considers this pattern paradigmatic. Much of his letter, further, offers advice on Christian living and resembles Paul's letters in revealing the assumption that Christians need advice— that is, that their belief and practice need to improve.

Beyond this, there is little in this collection about conversion, except that Ignatius mentions the influence of example, using language very similar to what we noted in I Peter. "Pray unceasingly," he advises (Ign., *Eph.* 10.1), "on behalf of other people, that they may encounter God. Leave it to them perhaps to be made disciples to you by works." Since Ignatius never mentions the "by reason" of I Peter as the alternative or even normal approach to gaining converts, we might conclude that evangelism as such has ceased by about 110 C.E.; and that impression is strengthened by the observation that neither Ignatius nor Polycarp, for all that they discuss the responsibilities of Christian leaders, ever mentions evangelizing as a responsibility.[9]

The Apocryphal Acts of the Apostles contain numerous conversion narratives, but these narratives are so fanciful that we may ignore them here. Of the several second-century writers classified as Christian apologists, only four present us with material relevant for our discussion of conversion. They are Aristo, Justin, Tatian, and the anonymous author of *Diognetus*.

The *Letter to Diognetus* is a direct evangelistic appeal that hopes to lead the reader(s) to conversion. The author begins (*Diog.* 1) by addressing Diognetus as a seeker. "Since I see you, most excellent Diognetus, applying yourself zealously to learn about the religion of the Christians," he begs to be allowed to lay out the case for Christianity, which he then proceeds to do. He first shows why pagan religion is folly (it is idolatry; 2), and then he argues that Judaism is equally foolish, since it requires sacrifice (3) and furthermore imposes purity regulations (4). Next he presents a positive explanation of Christianity: Christians obey the laws (5:10), they love everyone (5:11), etc., and, "to say it simply, what the soul is in the body, that Christians are in the world" (6:1). Furthermore, Christians accept martyrdom unflinchingly (7:7). Then the author gives a brief exposition of Christ's revelation of God (8) and of Christian soteriology (9), at the conclusion of which he offers the appeal that God "demonstrated in the former time the powerlessness of our nature to attain life, but now he has shown his salvation powerful to save even the powerless" (9:6). Finally, he appeals to his reader(s) to accept Christianity (10:3). "When you have come to know this," he asks, "will you not think [your] joy to be fulfilled? Or how will you not love the one who first so loved you?" And he concludes, "Let your heart be knowledge and your life the true Logos finding room in you" (12:7). Conversion of "Diognetus" is the logical outcome.

If this little gem is not quite, as Quasten (1986: 251) judged it, deserving of "rank among the most brilliant and beautiful works of Christian Greek literature," nevertheless we shall have to agree that it is a well-thought-out and winsome appeal to a seeker (or seekers). This is the kind of presentation that would likely have been effective with seekers and with others already interested in Christianity or for some reason favorably disposed to Christianity because of, for example, network or family contacts with Christians. In a network or family context, such an approach as *Diognetus* could equally well have been oral.

Justin, however, shows us the effectiveness of chance encounter. According to the autobiographical opening of his *Dialogue with Trypho the Jew*, Justin had first followed a Stoic, then a Pythagorean, then a Platonist, under the tutelage of the last of whom he "stupidly hoped to perceive God forthwith" (*Dial.* 2). Then off by himself with his thoughts (3) he was accosted by a stranger who engaged him in philosophical dialogue. After some Socratic-type discussion, the stranger concluded that "those philosophers . . . cannot even say what the soul is," with which conclusion Justin agreed (5). After further showing that traditional philosophers were lacking in true knowledge, the stranger declared that "there were some a long time ago who were much more ancient than all those considered philosophers, blessed and just and devoted to God. . . . They call them prophets. . . . And they glorified God the maker of all and father, and they announced the Christ from him, his son" (7). After the stranger said "many other things" (8), Justin felt "a fire lit in [his] soul, and desire seized [him] for the prophets and for those men who are Christ's friends." Justin the seeker had become a Christian as a result of a form of Christian preaching during a chance encounter. In his *Second Apology* 12 Justin also explains that he had come to admire the Christians, while still in his Platonic phase, because they were "fearless" in the face of death and of other ill treatment.

With Tatian, finally, we have yet another insight into early Christian approaches to conversion, for he, rather than writing to convince others to become Christians, composes an apology showing Christianity's superiority to Greek religion and in the process describes his own path to Christianity as a seeker. Originally an Assyrian, Tatian became a disciple of Justin in Rome but later left the Catholic Church to found the Encratite sect (Eusebius, *Hist. eccl.* 4.29.1). In his *Discourse to the Greeks* 29 he briefly describes his path to Christianity. He first says that he had "taken part in mysteries" and further had "tested the rites organized everywhere by effeminates and hermaphrodites"—doubtless referring to rites similar to those described by Lucian in his *Syrian Goddess*, especially 51–53, and so beautifully satirized by Apuleius (*Metam.* 8:25–28). After, then, further charging that various gods seemed primarily interested in bloody violence, he says that when he "was by [him]self [he] sought in what manner [he] would be able to learn the truth." In the process of his research he "happened upon certain barbarian writings, older as regards the doctrines of the Greeks, but also more divine as regards their error" (29:1). He then mentions the creation of the world and foreknowledge (29:2), implying that it was the Jewish Scriptures that he had read. This narrative leads Tatian to go on at length, with some digressions, to prove that Moses preceded famous Greeks, and that Moses is "older than heroes, cities, spirit beings" (40:1). Here Tatian reaches the end of his *Discourse*. Obviously, therefore, we must assume that he encountered these scriptures within a Christian context, since the truth that he found there led him to become not a Jew, but a Christian.

Tatian's spiritual odyssey to and through Christianity, as well as his mentioning that he discovered the Jewish Scriptures "by [him]self," show him to fit the type of the seeker exactly. Since both he and Justin followed this path, probably we should assume that it was not uncommon, at least in the second century, for intellectuals to come into Christianity in this way, as MacMullen proposed. We note that while Justin's path of seeking that led him eventually to Christianity lay through philosophy, Tatian's lay through the mystery religions, and that both, nevertheless, found the truth that they were seeking in the (Christian interpretation of) the Jewish Scriptures. Only Justin mentions that those scriptures prophesied Christ, but we are forced to assume some such understanding also in the case of Tatian, although he does not express it explicitly.

When we now run up the sum of our evidence we find that we know something about gentile conversions to early Christianity, but that there is much more that we might wish to know. We know that miracles, most likely healings, and martyrdoms played some role in attracting interest in the new religion; but we also have learned that miracles and martyrdoms alone did not lead to conversions, that preaching of the gospel was normally also required.[10] In other cases the preaching alone seems to have sufficed, although we are woefully uninformed about the contexts of that preaching—assuming that we are correct in discounting as idealized historiography the Acts accounts of large crowds. From Paul we learn that the main content of the preaching concerned Jesus' crucifixion and resurrection, and the speeches in Acts confirm that impression. Somewhat later (Justin, Tatian), the pattern seems to have begun with an exposition of the Jewish Scriptures, proving that God had foretold Christ and salvation in ancient times. We also learn that, around the turn of the first–second centuries, the evangelical impetus seems to have declined and that Christian leaders stressed the importance of example. Justin's conversion, some decades later, was the result of a one-on-one chance encounter.

Reading the Jewish Scriptures also convinced some persons to become Christians, something that could have occurred only within a Christian context. The successful line of reasoning seems to have been that these great scriptures are older than anything that the Greeks have, and they have given accurate prophecies, especially about Christ. An outside observer cannot come to those conclusions without Christian interpretation. About those Gentiles who became Christians we know even less than we know about the process. Many were, as Meeks put it, persons of high-status inconsistency (lonely, anxious), but there were also a few who had real status, as well as people of genuinely low status, like slaves. Some intellectuals were clearly seekers.

Finally, an aspect of conversion that has surfaced in several places is the need for continuing instruction after baptism. Without that aspect of gentile conversion, becoming a Christian would have meant a thousand things to a thousand people and would have been, in the last analysis, merely an ephemeral experience.

Let us now bring the two threads of this chapter, the social scientific and the historical, together. If we recall Rambo's model, then we see how well, in general, it fits the evidence that we have of early gentile conversions to Christianity— or perhaps we should say that we see how well our evidence fits into the model.

The *context* for gentile conversion to Christianity was, of course, opportune. We do not have to understand this opportunity theologically, emphasizing with Paul and with many older historians of Christianity that God had "at the right time" (Rom 5.6) inaugurated Christianity,[11] in order to agree with the point; for the opportunity is a historical given, as well. The Greco-Roman world was awash with NRMs from Egypt, Anatolia, and Syria. However numerous the adherents to these religions may or may not have been—and there is no way to know, although we do know that they had many sites—we see that the first decades of Christianity occurred during a time when it was not unusual for people to take up the worship of new, international gods. (Although to speak of the gods as "new" is not quite correct, for, while they may have been new in the sense of being recently imported from elsewhere, they all laid claim to great antiquity.) Nor do we need to decide one way or the other on the much-debated issue of whether there was a widespread "failure of nerve" that opened the way for these new religions. Whatever reasons people had for turning to NRMs, the more important fact is that doing so was a recognized option when Christianity came on the scene.

To be sure, some type of *crisis* must lie behind conversion, and we most likely see such in Meeks's status inconsistency (a variety of relative deprivation). Persons entirely comfortable with their stations in life are unlikely to turn to NRMs, and in the first decades of Christianity (and before) most persons of high status did not—although there are a few notable exceptions. We have also seen good evidence of the role of the *quest* in early Christian conversions. Here Rambo probably steers us toward the right understanding better than MacMullen when he points out that many, if not most, converts are seekers. Why should we think that only intellectuals came into Christianity in this way, merely because we have the autobiographical descriptions of Justin and Tatian and nothing similar from *hoi polloi?* Do we not see, in this matter, how modern sociological analysis can help us to "fill in the blanks" in our often meager historical information? If we cannot demonstrate seeking on the part of others than a few intellectuals, it is at least probable for the majority, especially in view of the fact that so many people were also joining the other NRMs.

Under the subject of the quest we need also to consider the *availability* of potential converts. We have no evidence on the basis of which to judge emotional availability, but the discussion of structural, intellectual, and religious availability brings us back to the point of contention between Nock and MacMullen that we noted at the beginning of this chapter. For Nock there were religious aspects in the culture to which Christianity appealed, whereas Greco-Roman religion for MacMullen was a spongy mass for which Christianity provided some backbone. The argument, as we have seen, can be made both ways, even if we might be inclined to think that MacMullen's position is an example of special pleading. In light of our evidence we may rather recall Rambo's criteria for intellectual and religious availability.

Regarding intellectual availability Rambo observed, as we noted above, that "it is rare for someone to be converted to an option that embraces an intellectual framework radically different from the person's previous viewpoint"; and one is religiously available when one has "religious beliefs, practices, and life-style [that] are to some degree compatible with the new option"(Rambo 1993: 61). Regarding the former condition, we recall that the Christian who led Justin to conversion spoke to him in terms of philosophy, and Justin in turn sought to promote Christianity as the right philosophy. With regard to religious availability, Tatian's example is instructive, since he, having been initiated into several mysteries before he encountered Christianity, probably saw Christianity as the true mystery offering a blessed existence after this life. The examples of Justin and Tatian remind us again that there were other philosophical and mystery-religion alternatives competing with Christianity in Greco-Roman society. Thus for a Gentile to become a Christian in the early decades of the movement was not the radical religious and intellectual break with the past that modern Christians often think it was. Of course Christianity was different from other religious and intellectual alternatives, but it was not totally different.

Since Rambo realizes that *advocate* styles can be quite diverse, we can only readily confirm that we have seen good evidence of such diversity in early Christianity; but his list of *benefits* certainly rings true for all of early Christianity. Christian theology, including its scriptural underpinning, provided a thoroughgoing system of meaning, and evidence of emotional gratification turns up everywhere; we may think of the fire in Justin's breast or of the frequent occurrences of "rejoice" and "joy" in the New Testament. Christianity excelled at offering techniques for living; and first the apostles and later the bishops provided convincing leadership. Everywhere, finally, we see evidence of some manifestation of power, even when it is not a matter of miracles.

Rambo's pointing to missionary and convert *adaptations* opens our eyes to aspects of the growth of early Christianity that we often overlook when we take a strictly historical approach. One of the best examples of an advocate's attempting to engineer convert adaptation, while himself adapting, occurs in I Corinthians in Paul's discussion of "idol food" and of sexual morality.[12] (See the discussion in ch. 16 of Paul's finding the right middle ground for Christianity between Judaism and paganism.)

Another clear example of advocate adaptation is the use of the Socratic dialogue form as a missionary technique. While Aristo's and Justin's written dialogues may have been intended for Christian readers, Justin's account of his own conversion shows that he, himself, was led to Christianity by such an approach; and it is, further, likely that he intended his dialogue as a sort of model for evangelistic style.

Finally we also have abundant evidence that Christianity, in all its forms, made good use of *encapsulation*. Christians met together regularly on Sunday (Rv 1.10) for meals (I Cor 11.20) and for prayers and hymns (Col 3.16)—here we see three of Rambo's 4 Rs, ritual, rhetoric, and roles; and that Christians promoted relationships within the movement is clear from the terms "brother" and "sister." The official offices that Christianity developed—apostle, evangelist, bishop, elder, deacon—also created encapsulating roles, as did the unofficial offices, for example, the charismatic competencies of I Corinthians 12.[13] Of *commitment* and *consequences* it seems unnecessary to write further, as we noted above.

Analyses of conversion by modern sociologists have helped us to understand early Christian conversion. The short answer is that all elements of conversion were present. It is not merely that Christianity provided satisfactory answers to questions that Gentiles were asking (so Nock), although that is certainly true. And it is not merely that Christianity offered a solid alternative to the shallowness and indefiniteness of gentile religion (so MacMullen). While there is some truth to MacMullen's position, it is rather prejudicial, especially with regard to the mysteries and the religion of Isis, which both called for commitment and appealed to gentile longings. At this stage we rest content to have gained clarity regarding what it was about early Christianity itself and what it was about the situation of its converts that caused Gentiles to join the movement. We have seen both that there were abundant personal and social factors that provided fertile ground for a new religion like Christianity and that the Christian movement was simply highly successful—sometimes perhaps by chance—in doing all the right things to promote and to solidify conversion.

Notes

All translations of foreign texts in this chapter are the author's own.

1. A more extensive treatment of this issue may be found in Sanders (2000: 72–128).

2. Cf. Haenchen (1971: 188–89); see further the review of the issue of the number of Jewish conversions in Acts in Sanders (1987: 64–65, 69–71).

3. Gallagher has offered an important corrective to MacMullen's analysis, in that he notes that it is not the real historical core of the miracle stories, as MacMullen proposes (1984: 23), that prompts early Christian conversion, but the stories themselves (Gallagher 1991: 28).

4. For similar analyses see Bainbridge (1978: 12) and Wallis (1984: 41–47, 119–22).

5. Wallis (1986: 195–204) has given a thorough description of people who followed Rajneesh as being structurally available.

6. See also Goldman (1999: 216).

7. See further the further discussion of relative deprivation in Schwarz (1987: 527–28).

8. Many moderns, e.g., Barrett (1968: 65–66) and Betz (1979: 99), find it difficult to believe that Paul performed miracles and propose rather that Paul's preaching was powerful or that the "grace" of Galatians 2:9 is the content of Paul's message. Robertson and Plummer observe that "some Greek Fathers suppose that miracle-working power is meant, which is an idea remote from the context" (1914: 33). The terms "spirit" and "power," however, seem to point to something beyond such twentieth-century psychologizing, which is Robertson and Plummer's context. Surely the fathers, much closer to the cultural reality, had it right. Among modern scholars one may note particularly Weder, who includes Paul, along with the Twelve, the Q tradents, the Stephen circle, and Barnabas as wandering charismatics who "carried Jesus' message *and impact* to people" (1992: 209, emphasis mine).

9. On this point see Goodman (1994: 91–108).

10. Harnack argues that martyrdoms occurred primarily among the lower classes and that "people belonging to the middle classes . . . were left unmolested upon the whole" (1961: 490); and he is followed to excess on this point by Stark, who asserts that "for the rank-and-file Christians the threat of persecution was so slight as to have counted for little" (1996: 80). Stark, however, might have profited from reading Grant where the martyrdoms of the second century are summarized in some of their grisly detail (1970: 85–96).

11. Gager gives a good summary of this traditional explanation of Christianity's early success (1975: 116–18).

12. See further the more detailed discussion of Paul's adaptive procedure here in Sanders (1997).

13. For a similar analysis of early Christian conversion, proceeding from a somewhat different sociological perspective, see Taylor (1995).

References

Abel, Theodore. 1948. The Operation Called *Verstehen. American Journal of Sociology* 54: 211–18.

Aberbach, Moses. 1966. *The Roman-Jewish War (66–70 A.D.): Its Origins and Consequence.* London: The Jewish Quarterly in association with R. Golub.

Abrams, Philip. 1982. *Historical Sociology.* Ithaca, N.Y.: Cornell University Press.

Achtemeier, Paul J. 1996. *1 Peter.* Minneapolis, Minn.: Fortress.

Adam, Andrew K. M. 1995. *What Is Postmodern Biblical Criticism?* Minneapolis, Minn.: Fortress.

Agrell, Goeran. 1976. *Work, Toil and Sustenance.* Trans. Stephen Westerholm. Stockholm, Sweden: Verburm.

Albright, William F. 1957. *From the Stone Age to Christianity.* 2nd ed. New York: Doubleday.

Alexander, Loveday, ed. 1991. Images of Empire. *Journal of the Old Testament Supplement Series* 122. Sheffield, England: Sheffield Academic Press.

Alexander, Philip S. 1992. "The Parting of the Ways" from the Perspective of Rabbinic Judaism. In *Jews and Christians: The Parting of the Ways A.D. 70 to 135,* ed. James D. G. Dunn, 25. Tübingen, Germany: Mohr; Grand Rapids, Mich.: Eerdmans.

Alföldy, Géza. 1985. *Social History of Rome.* Totowa, N.J.: Barnes & Noble.

Alon, Gedaliah. 1980. *The Jews in Their Land in the Talmudic Age (70–640 C.E.).* Trans. and ed. Gershon Levi. Jerusalem: Magnes.

Alston, Richard. 1998. *Aspects of Roman History AD 14–117.* London: Routledge.

Alter, Robert, and Frank Kermode. 1987. *The Literary Guide to the Bible.* Cambridge, Mass.: Harvard University Press.

Altman, A. 1956. The Rabbinic Doctrine of Creation. *Journal of Jewish Studies* 7: 195–206.

Anderson, Benedict. 1991. *Imagined Communities: Reflections on the Origin and Spread of Nationalism.* Rev. extended ed. New York: Verso.

Anderson, Bernhard W., ed. 1984. *Creation in the Old Testament.* Philadelphia: Fortress.

Anderson, Graham. 1993. *The Second Sophistic: A Cultural Phenomenon in the Roman Empire.* London: Routledge.

Anderson, Janice C., and Stephen D. Moore. 1992. *Mark and Method: New Approaches in Biblical Studies*. Minneapolis, Minn.: Fortress.

Andresen, Carl. 1955. *Logos und Nomos: Die Polemik des Kelsos wider das Christentum*. Berlin: de Gruyter.

Applebaum, S. 1976. Economic Life in Palestine. In *The Jewish People in the First Century: Historical Geography, Political History, Social, Cultural and Religious Life and Institutions*. 2 vols. (Compendia Rerum Iudaicarum ad Novum Testamentum), ed. Shemuel Safrai and M. Stern, 631–700. Assen, Netherlands: Van Gorcum.

———. 1977. Judaea as a Roman Province: The Countryside as a Political and Economic Factor. *Aufstieg und Niedergang der römischen Welt* 2.8: 355–96.

———. 1989. Josephus and the Economic Causes of the Jewish War. In *Josephus, the Bible, and History*, ed. L. Feldman and G. Hata, 237–263. Detroit, Mich.: Wayne State University Press.

Appleby, Joyce, Lynn Hunt, and Margaret Jacob. 1994. *Telling the Truth about History*. London: Routledge.

Arav, Rami, and Richard A. Freund, eds. 1995. *Bethsaida: A City by the North Shore of the Sea of Galilee*. Vol. I. Kirksville, Mo.: Thomas Jefferson University Press.

Arnal, William E. 2000. The Parable of the Tenants and the Class Consciousness of the Peasantry. In *Text and Artifact in the Religions of Mediterranean Antiquity: Studies in Honour of Peter Richardson*, ed. Stephen G. Wilson and Michel Desjardins, 135–57. Waterloo, Ont.: Wilfrid Laurier University Press.

Arndt, William, F. William Gingrich, W. Danker, and Walter Bauer. 1979. *A Greek–English Lexicon of the New Testament and Other Early Christian Literature*. Chicago: University of Chicago Press.

Ascough, Richard S. 1997. Translocal Relationships among Voluntary Associations and Early Christianity. *Journal of Early Christian Studies* 5: 223–41.

———. 1998. *What Are They Saying about the Formation of Pauline Churches?* New York: Paulist.

———. 2000. The Thessalonian Christian Community as a Professional Voluntary Association. *Journal of Biblical Literature* 119: 311–28.

Ashton, John. 1991. *Understanding the Fourth Gospel*. Oxford: Clarendon.

Athanassiadi, Polymnia, and Michael Frede, eds. 1999. *Pagan Monotheism in Late Antiquity*. Oxford: Clarendon.

Auguet, Roland. 1972. *Cruelty and Civilization: The Roman Games*. London: Routledge

Aune, David E. 1983. The Influence of Roman Imperial Court Ceremonial on the Apocalypse of John. *Papers of the Chicago Society of Biblical Research* 28: 5–26.

———. 1987. *The New Testament in Its Literary Environment*. Philadelphia: Westminster.

Austin, N. J., and N. Rankov. 1995. *Exploration: Military and Political Intelligence in the Roman World from the Second Punic War to the Battle of Adrianople*. London: Routledge.

Aviam, Mordechai. 1993. Galilee. In *New Encyclopedia of Archaeological Excavations in the Holy Land*, vol. 2, 453–58. Jerusalem: Israel Exploration Society.

———. 1997. A Second-First Century B.C.E. Fortress and Siege Complex in Eastern Upper Galilee. In *Archaeology and the Galilee: Texts and Contexts in the Graeco-Roman and Byzantine*

Periods (South Florida Studies in the History of Judaism 143), ed. Douglas R. Edwards and C. Thomas McCollough, 97–105. Atlanta: Scholars Press.

————, and Peter Richardson. 2000. Josephus's Galilee in *Life* and *War* in Archaeological Perspective. Appendix A in *Josephus, Translation and Commentary*, ed. Steve N. Mason, 177–217. Leiden: E. J. Brill.

Avigad, Nahman. 1980. *Discovering Jerusalem*. Nashville, Tenn.: Thomas Nelson.

Babbie, Earl R. 1979. *The Practice of Social Research*. 2nd ed. Belmont, Calif.: Wadsworth.

Badenas, Robert. 1985. *Christ the End of the Law*. Sheffield, England: JSOT Press.

Bailey, James L., and Lyle D. vander Broek. 1992. *Literary Forms in the New Testament: A Handbook*. Louisville, Ky.: Westminster/John Knox.

Bainbridge, William Sims. 1978. *Satan's Power: A Deviant Psychotherapy Cult*. Berkeley: University of California Press.

————. 1992. The Sociology of Conversion. In *Handbook of Religious Conversion*, ed. H. N. Malony and S. Southard, 178–91. Birmingham, Ala.: Religious Education Press.

Bainton, Roland H. 1960. *Christian Attitudes toward War and Peace*. New York: Abingdon.

Baird, J. Arthur, and David Noel Freedman. 1971. *A Critical Concordance to the Gospels*. The Computer Bible. Vol. I. Rev. ed. Wooster, Ohio: Biblical Research Associates.

Barbalet, J. M. 1985. Power and Resistance. *British Journal of Sociology* 36: 521–48.

Barclay, John M. G. 1988, *Obeying the Truth: A Study of Paul's Ethics in Galatians*. Edinburgh: T. & T. Clark.

————. 1992. Thessalonica and Corinth: Social Contrasts in Pauline Christianity. *JSNT* 47: 49–74.

————. 1995a. Deviance and Apostasy: Some Applications of Deviance Theory to First-Century Judaism and Christianity. In *Modelling Early Christianity: Social-Scientific Studies of the New Testament in Its Context*, ed. P. F. Esler, 114–27. London: Routledge.

————. 1995b. Paul among Diaspora Jews: Anomaly or Apostate? *Journal for the Study of the New Testament* 60: 89–120.

————. 1996. *Jews in the Mediterranean Diaspora from Alexander to Trajan (323BCE–117 CE)*. Edinburgh: T. & T. Clark.

————. 1997a. Universalism and Particularism: Twin Components of Both Judaism and Early Christianity. In *A Vision for the Church: Studies in Early Christian Ecclesiology in Honour of J. P. M. Sweet*, ed. Markus Bockmuehl and Michael B. Thompson, 207–24. Edinburgh: T. & T. Clark.

————. 1997b. *Colossians and Philemon*. Sheffield, England: Sheffield Academic Press.

Barker, Margaret. 1992. *The Great Angel: A Study of Israel's Second God*. Louisville, Ky.: Westminster/John Knox.

Barnes, Timothy D. 1968a. Pre-Decian *Acta Martyrium*. *Journal of Theological Studies* N.S. 19: 509–31.

————. 1968b. Legislation against the Christians. *Journal of Roman Studies* 58: 32–50.

————. 1971. *Tertullian: A Historical and Literary Study*. Oxford: Clarendon.

————. 1995. Statistics and the Conversion of the Roman Aristocracy. *Journal of Roman Studies* 85: 135–47.

Barnett, P. W. 1980/1981. The Jewish Sign Prophets—A.D. 40–70: Their Intentions and Origin. *New Testament Studies* 27: 679–97.

Barnstone, Willis, ed. 1984. *The Other Bible*. San Francisco: Harper.

Baron, Salo W. 1952. *A Social and Religious History of the Jews*. New York: Columbia University Press.

Barrett, Charles Kingsley. 1968. *A Commentary on the First Epistle to the Corinthians*. New York: Harper & Row.

———. 1982. *Essays on Paul*. London: SPCK.

———. 1985. *Freedom and Obligation*. London: SPCK.

Bartchy, S. Scott. 1973. *First-Century Slavery and the Interpretation of 1 Corinthians 7:21*. Atlanta: Scholars Press.

Barth, Fredrik. 1969. *Ethnic Groups and Boundaries: The Social Organization of Cultural Difference*. London: Allen & Unwin.

Barth, Karl. 1918. *Der Römerbrief; The Epistle to the Romans* [English trans. of the 6th ed.]. London: Oxford University Press, 1933.

Bartlett, David L. 1978. J. G. Gager's "Kingdom and Community": A Summary and Response. *Zygon Journal of Religion and Science* 13: 109–22.

Barton, John, ed. 1998. *The Cambridge Companion to Biblical Interpretation* (Cambridge Companions to Religion). Cambridge: Cambridge University.

Barton, Stephen C. 1992. The Communal Dimension of Earliest Christianity: A Critical Survey of the Field. *Journal of Theological Studies* 43: 399–427.

———. 1993. Early Christianity and the Sociology of the Sect. In *The Open Text: New Directions for Biblical Studies?* ed. Francis Watson, 140–62. London: SCM.

———. 1994. *Discipleship and Family Ties in Mark and Matthew: Society of New Testament Studies 80*. Cambridge: Cambridge University Press.

———. 1995. Historical Criticism and Social-Scientific Perspectives in New Testament Study. In *Hearing the New Testament: Strategies for Interpretation*, ed. J. B. Green, 61–89. Grand Rapids, Mich.: Eerdmans.

———. 1997. Social-Scientific Criticism. In *Handbook to Exegesis of the New Testament* (New Testament Tools and Studies 25), ed. S. E. Porter, 277–89. Leiden: E. J. Brill.

———, and G. H. R. Horsley. 1981. A Hellenistic Cult Group and the New Testament Churches. *Jahrbuch für Antike und Christentum* 24: 7–41.

Bastide, Roger. 1971. Mémoire collective et sociologie du bricolage. *L'Année sociologique 1970* (troisième série): 65–108.

Bauckham, Richard. 1993. *The Climax of Prophecy*. Edinburgh: T. & T. Clark.

Bauer, Walter. 1972. *Orthodoxy and Heresy in Earliest Christianity*. London: SCM.

Beard, Mary, John North, and Simon Price, eds. 1998. *Religions of Rome. Vol. 1: A History*. Cambridge: Cambridge University Press.

Beardslee, William A. 1971. *Literary Criticism of the New Testament*. Philadelphia: Fortress.

Beare, Francis Wright. 1958. *The First Epistle of Peter: The Greek Text with Introduction and Notes*. Oxford: Basil Blackwell.

Beasley-Murray, George R. 1987. *John: Word Biblical Commentary*. Vol. 36. Waco, Tex.: Word.

Beck, Norman A. 1997. *Anti-Roman Cryptograms in the New Testament*. New York: Peter Lang.

Becker, Howard S. 1963. *Outsiders: Studies in the Sociology of Deviance.* New York: Free Press.

Becker, Jürgen. 1993. *Paul: Apostle to the Gentiles.* Trans. O. C. Dean, Jr. Louisville, Ky.: Westminster/John Knox.

Beckford, James A. 1978. Accounting for Conversion. *British Journal of Sociology* 29: 259–62

Beker, J. Christiaan. 1980/1982. *Paul the Apostle: The Coming Triumph of God.* Edinburgh: T. & T. Clark; Philadelphia: Fortress.

Belkin, Samuel. 1940. *Philo and the Oral Law.* Cambridge, Mass.: Harvard University Press.

Bell, H. Idris. 1975. *Cults and Creeds in Graeco-Roman Egypt.* Chicago: Ares.

Bélo, Fernando. 1974. *Lecture matérialiste de l'évangile de Marc. Récit—pratique—Idéologie.* Paris: Cerf.; *A Materialist Reading of the Gospel of Mark.* Trans. M. O'Connell. Maryknoll, N.Y.: Orbis, 1981.

Ben-David, Arye. 1974. *Talmudische Ökonomie.* Hildesheim, Germany: Georg Olms.

Ben-Yehuda, Nachman. 1985. *Deviance and Moral Boundaries: Witchcraft, the Occult, Science Fiction, Deviant Sciences and Scientists.* Chicago: University of Chicago Press.

Bendix, Reinhard. 1977. *Max Weber: An Intellectual Portrait.* Berkeley: University of California Press.

Benko, S., and J. J. O'Rourke, eds. 1971. *The Catacombs and the Colosseum: The Roman Empire as the Setting of Primitive Christianity.* Valley Forge, Penn.: Judson.

Berchman, Robert M. 1984. *From Philo to Origen: Middle Platonism in Transition.* Chico, Calif.: Scholars Press.

Berger, Peter L. 1967. *The Sacred Canopy: Elements of a Sociological Theory of Religion.* Garden City, N.Y.: Doubleday; *The Social Reality of Religion.* London: Faber & Faber, 1969.

———. 1969. *A Rumour of Angels: Modern Society and the Rediscovery of the Supernatural.* Harmondsworth, England: Penguin.

———, and Luckmann, Thomas. 1966. *The Social Construction of Reality: A Treatise in the Sociology of Knowledge.* Garden City, N.Y.: Doubleday; Harmondsworth, England: Penguin.

Berlin, Andrea M. 1999. Romanization in Pre-Revolt Galilee. Paper at the conference, The First Jewish Revolt: Archaeology, History and Ideology, sponsored by University of Minnesota and Macalester College, April 1999.

Bernstein, Basil. 1971. *Class, Codes, and Control.* Vol. I. Suffolk, England: Routlege & Kegan Paul.

Berquist, Jon L. 1995. Social Stratification: Modern Theories. In *International Encyclopedia of Sociology.* Vol. 2, ed. Frank N. Magill, 1277–81. London: Fitzroy & Dearborn.

Bertier, J., et al., trans. and eds. 1980 *Plotin: Traité sur les Nombres (Ennead VI.6 [34]).* Paris: Librairie Philosophique: J. Vrin.

Best, Ernest. 1972. *A Commentary on the First and Second Epistles to the Thessalonians.* London: Adam & Charles Black.

Best, Thomas F. 1983. The Sociological Study of the New Testament: Promise and Peril of a Discipline. *SJT* 36: 181–94.

Betz, Hans Dieter. 1975. Eine judenchristliche Kult-Didache in Matthäus 6, 1–18. In *Jesus Christus in Historie und Theologie, Festschrift H. Conzelmann,* ed. G. Strecker, 445–57. Tübingen, Germany: Mohr (Siebeck).

———. 1979. *Galatians: A Commentary on Paul's Letter to the Churches in Galatia.* Philadelphia: Fortress.

———. 1985. *Essays on the Sermon on the Mount*. Philadelphia: Fortress.

———. 1990. The Sermon on the Mount and Q: Aspects of the Problem. In *Gospel Origins and Christian Beginnings, Festschrift J. M. Robinson*, ed. J. E. Goehring, C. W. Hedrick, and J. T. Sanders, 19–34. Sonoma, Calif.: Polebridge.

Bible and Culture Collective. 1995. *The Postmodern Bible*. New Haven, Conn.: Yale University Press.

Bickerman, Elias J. 1962. *From Ezra to the Last of the Maccabees: Foundations of Postbiblical Judaism*. New York: Schocken.

———. 1988. *The Jews in the Greek Age*. Cambridge, Mass.: Harvard University Press.

Bigg, Charles. 1913. *The Christian Platonists of Alexandria*. Ed. F. E. Brightman. Oxford: Clarendon.

Bilde, Per. 1979. The Causes of the Jewish War According to Josephus. *Journal for the Study of Judaism* 10: 179–202.

———, ed. 1992. *Ethnicity in Hellenistic Egypt*. Aarhus, Denmark: Aarhus University Press.

Billig, Michael. 1996. Remembering the Particular Background of Social Identity Theory. In *Social Groups and Identities: Developing the Legacy of Henri Tajfel*, ed. W. Peter Robinson, 337–57. Oxford: Butterworth Heinemann.

Bird, Frederick B. 1982. A Comparative Study of the Works of Charity in Christianity and Judaism. *Journal of Religious Ethics* 9, 2: 157–85.

Bitzer, Lloyd F. 1968. The Rhetorical Situation. *Philosophy and Rhetoric* 1: 1–14.

Black, C. Clifton. 1995. Rhetorical Criticism. In *Hearing the New Testament: Strategies for Interpretation*, ed. Joel B. Green, 256–77. Grand Rapids, Mich.: Eerdmans.

Blasi, Anthony J. 1972. Symbolic Interactionism as Theory. *Sociology and Social Research* 56, 4: 453–65.

———. 1988. *Early Christianity as a Social Movement*. New York: P. Lang.

———. 1993. The More Basic Method in the Sociology of Early Christianity. *Forum* 9: 7–8.

———. 1996. *A Sociology of Johannine Christianity* (Texts and Studies in Religion 69). Lewiston, N.Y.: Mellen.

———. 1997. Marginalization and Martyrdom: Social Context of Ignatius of Antioch. *Listening* 32: 68–74.

———. 1998. George Herbert Mead's Transformation of his Intellectual Context. In *The Tradition of the Chicago School of Sociology*, ed. Luigi Tomasi, 149–78. Aldershot, England: Ashgate.

Blumer, Herbert. 1937. Social Psychology. In *Man and Society*, ed. Emerson P. Schmidt, 144–98. New York: Prentice Hall.

———. 1969. *Symbolic Interactionism: Perspective and Method*. Englewood Cliffs, N.J.: Prentice Hall.

———. 1979. *Critiques of Research in the Social Sciences: An Appraisal of Thomas and Znaniecki's The Polish Peasant in Europe and America*. New Brunswick, N.J.: Transaction Books; New York: Social Science Research Council, 1939.

Bobertz, Charles A. 1993. The Role of Patron in the *Cena Dominica* of Hippolytus' *Apostolic Tradition*. *Journal of Theological Studies* N.S. 44, 1: 170–84.

Bohrnstedt, George W., and David Knoke. 1994. *Statistics for Social Data Analysis*. 3rd ed. Itasca, Ill.: F. E. Peacock.

Boissevain, Jeremy. 1974. *Friends of Friends: Networks, Manipulators and Coalitions*. Oxford: Basil Blackwell.

Borg, Marcus J. 1999a. Seeing Jesus: Sources, Lenses, and Method. In *The Meaning of Jesus: Two Visions*, ed. M. J. Borg and N. T. Wright, 3–9. San Francisco: Harper.

———. 1999b. The Meaning of the Birth Stories. In *The Meaning of Jesus: Two Visions*, ed. M. J. Borg and N. T. Wright, 179–86. San Francisco: Harper.

———, and N. T. Wright, eds. *The Meaning of Jesus: Two Visions*. San Francisco: Harper.

Borgen, Peder. 1987. *Philo, John, Paul: New Perspectives on Judaism and Early Christianity*. Atlanta: Scholars Press.

———. 1992. Philo and the Jews in Alexandria. In *Ethnicity in Hellenistic Egypt*, ed. Per Bilde, 122–38. Aarhus, Denmark: Aarhus University Press.

———. 1995. "Yes," "No," "How Far?" The Participation of Jews and Christians in Pagan Cults. In *Paul in his Hellenistic Context*, ed. Troels Engberg-Pedersen, 30–59. Minneapolis, Minn.: Fortress Press.

Boring, M. Eugene. 1989. *Revelation*. Louisville, Ky.: John Knox.

Bornkamm, Günther. 1963. The Letter to the Romans as Paul's Last Will and Testament. *Australian Biblical Review* 11: 2–14.

Bow, Beverly Ann. 1995. *The Story of Jesus' Birth: A Pagan and Jewish Affair*. Ph.D. thesis, University of Iowa.

Bowersock, Glen W. 1964. C. Marcius Censorinus, Legatus Caesaris. *Harvard Studies in Classical Philology* 68: 207–10.

———. 1969. *Greek Sophists in the Roman Empire*. Oxford: Clarendon.

———. 1986. The Mechanics of Subversion in the Roman Provinces. In *Opposition et Résistances à l'Empire d'Auguste à Trajan*, 23, ed. Adalberto Giovannini, 291–320. Geneva: Entretiens sur L'Antiquité Classique.

———. 1995. *Martyrdom and Rome*. Cambridge: Cambridge University Press.

Boyarin, Daniel. 1994. *A Radical Jew: Paul and the Politics of Identity*. Berkeley: University of California Press.

Bradley, K. R. 1987. *Slaves and Masters in the Roman Empire*. Oxford: Oxford University Press.

Braudel, Fernand. 1996. *The Mediterranean and the Mediterranean World in the Age of Philip II*. 2 vols. Berkeley: University of California Press.

Braund, David. 1985. *Augustus to Nero: A Sourcebook on Roman History 31 BC–AD 68*. London: Croom Helm.

———. 1993. Piracy under the Principate and the Ideology of Imperial Eradication. In *War and Society in the Roman World*, ed. John Rich and Graham Shipley, 195–212. London: Routledge.

Breasted, James H. 1939. *The Dawn of Conscience*. New York: Scribner's.

Brehier, Émile. 1908. *Les Idées Religieuses et Philosophiques de Philo d'Alexandrie*. Paris: Librairie Alphones Picard.

Brehm, Jack W., and Arthur R. Cohen. 1962. *Explorations in Cognitive Dissonance*. New York: Wiley.

Breiger, Ronald L., ed. 1990. *Social Mobility and Social Structure*. Cambridge: Cambridge University Press.

Bridge, Steven L. 1997. To Give or Not to Give? Deciphering the Saying of *Didache* 1.6. *Journal of Early Christian Studies* 5: 555–68.

Bromley, David G., and Phillip E. Hammond, eds. *The Future of New Religious Movements*. Macon, Ga.: Mercer University Press.

Brooke, George J. 1991. The Kittim in the Qumran Pesharim. In Images of Empire. *Journal of the Old Testament Supplement Series 122*, ed. Alexander, Loveday, 135–59. Sheffield, England: Sheffield Academic Press.

Brown, John P. 1983. Techniques of Imperial Control: The Background of the Gospel Event. In *The Bible and Liberation: Political and Social Hermeneutics*, ed. N. K. Gottwald and Richard Horsley, 357–77. Maryknoll, N.Y.: Orbis.

Brown, Peter. 1961. Aspects of the Christianization of the Roman Aristocracy. *Journal of Roman Studies* 51: 1–11.

———. 1967. *Augustine of Hippo: A Biography*. Berkeley: University of California Press.

———. 1971. *The World of Late Antiquity*. New York: Harcourt Brace Jovanovich.

———. 1972. *Religion and Society in the Age of Saint Augustine*. New York: Harper & Row.

———. 1981. *The Cult of the Saints: Its Rise and Function in Early Christianity*. Chicago: University of Chicago Press.

Brown, Raymond E. 1966–70. *The Gospel According to John*. 2 vols. Garden City, N.Y.: Doubleday.

———. 1977/1993. *The Birth of the Messiah: A Commentary on the Infancy Narratives in Matthew and Luke, updated ed.* (Anchor Bible Reference Library). Garden City, N.Y.: Doubleday.

———. 1979. *The Community of the Beloved Disciple*. New York: Paulist.

———. 1997. *An Introduction to the New Testament* (Anchor Bible Reference Library). New York: Doubleday.

———, Joseph A. Fitzmyer, and Roland E. Murphy, eds. 1990. *The New Jerome Biblical Commentary*. Englewood Cliffs, N.J.: Prentice Hall.

Brown, Roger. 1965. *Social Psychology*. New York: Free Press.

Brown, Rupert. 1996. Tajfel's Contribution to the Reduction of Intergroup Conflict. In *Social Groups and Identities: Developing the Legacy of Henri Tajfel*, ed. W. Peter Robinson, 169–89. Oxford: Butterworth Heinemann.

Bruce, F. F. 1954. *Commentary on the Book of the Acts* (New International Commentary on the New Testament). Grand Rapids, Mich.: Eerdmans.

Brunt, Peter A. 1971. *Italian Manpower 225 B.C.–A.D. 14*. Oxford: Oxford University Press.

———. 1990. *Roman Imperial Themes*. Oxford: Clarendon.

Bryant, Joseph M. 1993. The Sect–Church Dynamic and Christian Expansion in the Roman Empire: Persecution, Penitential Discipline, and Schism in Sociological Perspective. *British Journal of Sociology* 44: 303–32.

Buber, Martin. 1951. *Two Types of Faith: A Study of the Interpenetration of Judaism and Christianity*. Trans. N. F. Goldhawk. New York: Harper.

Büchler, Adolf. 1912. *The Economic Conditions of Judea after the Destruction of the Second Temple*. London: Oxford University Press.

Bulmer, Martin. 1984. *The Chicago School of Sociology: Institutionalization, Diversity, and the Rise of Sociological Research*. Chicago: University of Chicago Press.

Bultmann, Rudolf. 1960. *Jesus Christ and Mythology*. London: SCM.

———. 1963. *History of the Synoptic Tradition*. Trans. John Marsh. New York: Harper & Row.

———. 1971. *The Gospel of John: A Commentary*. Trans. G. R. Beasley-Murray, R. W. N. Hoare, and J. K. Riches. Philadelphia: Westminster.

———. 1985. *New Testament and Mythology and Other Basic Writings*. Trans. and ed. Schubert M. Ogden. London: SCM.

Bureth, Paul. 1964. *Les Titulatures impériales dans les papyrus, les ostraca et les inscriptions d'Égypte*. Bruxelles: Fondation Égyptologique Reine Élisabeth.

Burford, Alison. 1972. *Craftsmen in Greek and Roman Society*. Ithaca, N.Y.: Cornell University Press.

Burridge, Kenelm O. L. 1969. *New Heaven: New Earth*. Oxford: Blackwell.

Burton, Ernest de Witt. 1921. *The Epistle to the Galatians*. Edinburgh: T. & T. Clark.

Burton, G. P. 1975. Proconsuls, Assizes and the Administration of Justice under the Empire. *Journal of Religious Studies* 65: 92–106.

Cadbury, Henry J. 1920. *The Style and Literary Method of Luke*. Cambridge, Mass.: Harvard University Press.

———. 1931. Erastus of Corinth. *Journal of Biblical Literature* 50: 42–58.

Cadoux, Cecil John. 1925. *The Early Church and the World: A History of the Christian Attitudes to Pagan Society and the State Down to the Time of Constantinus*. Edinburgh: T. & T. Clark.

Calder, W. M. 1939. The Eumeneian Formula. In *Anatolian Studies Presented to William Hepburn Buckler*, ed. W. M. Calder and Josef Keil, 15–26. Manchester: Manchester University Press.

Callahan, Allen Dwight, Richard A. Horsley, and Abraham Smith, eds. 1998. *Slavery in Text and Interpretation*. Semeia 83/84. Atlanta: Scholars Press.

Cameron, Ron, ed. 1982. *The Other Gospels*. Philadelphia: Westminster.

Carcopino, Jérôme, and Henry T. Rowell. 1991. *Daily Life in Ancient Rome: The People and the City at the Height of the Empire*. London: Penguin.

Carney, Thomas F. 1975. *The Shape of the Past: Models and Antiquity*. Lawrence, Kans.: Coronado.

Carroll, Robert P. 1979. *When Prophecy Failed*. London: SCM.

Carter, Warren. 1994. *Households and Discipleship: A Study of Matthew 19–20*. Journal for the Study of the New Testament Supplement Series 103. Sheffield, England: JSOT Press.

———. 1995. Recalling the Lord's Prayer: The Authorial Audience and Matthew's Prayer as Familiar Liturgical Experience. *Catholic Biblical Quarterly* 57: 514–30.

———. 1997. Narrative/Literary Approaches to Matthean Theology: The "Reign of the Heavens" as an Example (Mt 4:17–5:12). *Journal for the Study of the New Testament* 67: 3–27.

———. 1998. Toward an Imperial-Critical Reading of Matthew's Gospel. *Society of Biblical Literature 1998 Seminar Papers: Part One*. Society of Biblical Literature Seminar Papers 37. Atlanta, Ga.: Scholars Press, 296–324.

———. 1999. Paying the Tax to Rome as a Subversive Praxis: Matthew 17. 24–27. *JSNT* 76: 3–31.

———. 2000a. Evoking Isaiah and Matthean Soteriology: An Intertextual Anti-Imperial Reading of Isaiah 7–9 in Matthew 1:23 and 4:15–16. *Journal of Biblical Literature* 119: 505–22.

———. 2000b. *Matthew and The Margins: A Sociopolitical and Religious Reading* (The Bible and Liberation Series). Maryknoll, N. Y.: Orbis.

———. 2000c. "To Save His People from Their Sins" (Matt 1:21): Rome's Empire and Matthew's Salvation as Sovereignty. *Society of Biblical Literature 2000 Seminar Papers, Society of Biblical Literature Seminar Papers 39.* Atlanta, Ga.: Scholars Press.

Cartledge, Paul. 1994. The Greeks and Anthropology. *Anthropology Today* 10/3: 3–6.

Case, Shirley Jackson. 1923. *The Social Origins of Christianity.* Chicago: University of Chicago Press.

Castelli, Elizabeth A. 1998. Gender, Theory, and The Rise of Christianity: A Response to Rodney Stark. *JECS* 6: 227–57.

Catchpole, David. 1971. *The Trial of Jesus: A Study in the Gospels and Jewish Historiography from 1770 to the Present Day* (Studia Post-Biblica XVIII). Leiden: E. J. Brill.

Cavendish, James C., Michael R. Welch, and David C. Leege. 1998. Social Network Theory and Predictors of Religiosity for Black and White Catholics: Evidence of a "Black Sacred Cosmos"? *Journal for the Scientific Study of Religion* 37: 397–410.

Chadwick, Henry. 1966. *Early Christian Thought and the Classical Tradition: Studies in Justin, Clement, and Origen.* Oxford: Clarendon.

———. 1970. Philo and the Beginnings of Christian Thought. In *The Cambridge History of Late Greek and Early Medieval Philosophy*, ed. A. H. Armstrong, 137–90. Cambridge: Cambridge University Press.

———. 1981. *Boethius: The Consolations of Music, Logic, Theology and Philosophy.* Oxford: Clarendon.

Chalcraft, David J., ed. 1997 *Social-Scientific Old Testament Criticism: A Sheffield Reader.* Sheffield, England: Sheffield Academic Press.

Chance, John K. 1994. The Anthropology of Honor and Shame: Culture, Values and Practice. *Semeia* 68: 139–51.

Chandler, Tertius, and Gerald Fox. 1974. *Three Thousand Years of Urban Growth.* New York: Academic Press.

Charlesworth, James H. 1988. *Jesus within Judaism: New Light from Exciting Archaeological Discoveries.* Garden City, N.Y.: Doubleday.

Chester, Andrew. 1994. The Theology of James. In *The Theology of the Letters of James, Peter, and Jude.* Andrew Chester and Ralph P. Martin, 1–62. Cambridge: Cambridge University Press.

Chilton, Bruce. 2000. *Rabbi Jesus.* Garden City, N.Y.: Doubleday.

Chow, John K. 1992. *Patronage and Power: A Study of Social Networks in Corinth.* JSNTSup 75. Sheffield, England: JSOT Press.

Christiansen, Ellen Juhl. 1995. *The Covenant in Judaism and Paul.* Leiden: E. J. Brill.

Clarke, Andrew D. 1993. *Secular and Christian Leadership in Corinth: A Socio-Historical and Exegetical Study of 1 Corinthians 1–6* (Arbeiten zur Geschichte des antiken Judentums und des Urchristentums, 18). Leiden: E. J. Brill.

Clarke, G. W. 1971. Two Christians in the *Familia Caesaris. Harvard Theological Review* 64: 121–24.

Clarke, John. 1991. *The Houses of Roman Italy 100 B.C.–A.D. 250.* Berkeley: University of California Press.

Clegg, Stewart. 1989. *Frameworks of Power*. London: Sage.

Clifford, Richard J. 1972. *The Cosmic Mountain in Canaan and the Old Testament*. Cambridge, Mass.: Harvard University Press.

Cody, Ronald P., and Jeffrey K. Smith. 1997. *Applied Statistics and the SAS Programming Language*. 4th ed. Upper Saddle River, N.J.: Prentice Hall.

Coenen-Huther, Jacques. 1984. *Le fonctionnalisme en sociologie: Et après?* Bruxelles, Belgium: Ed. De l'Université de Bruxelles.

Cohen, Ira J. 1987. Structuration Theory and Social Praxis. In *Social Theory Today*, ed. Anthony Giddens and Jonathan H. Turner, 273–308. Cambridge: Polity.

Cohen, Jeremy. 1982. *The Friars and the Jews: The Evolution of Medieval Anti-Judaism*. Ithaca, N.Y.: Cornell University Press.

Cohen, Shaye J. D. 1987. *From the Maccabees to the Mishnah*. Philadelphia: Westminster.

———. 1989. Crossing the Boundary and Becoming a Jew. *Harvard Theological Review* 82: 13–34.

Collange, Jean-François. 1979. *The Epistle of St. Paul to the Philippians*. London: Epworth.

Collins, Adela Yarbro. 1979. *The Apocalypse*. Wilmington, Del.: Michael Glazier.

———. 1986. Vilification and Self-Definition in the Book of Revelation. In *Christians among Jews and Gentiles: Festschrift K. Stendahl*, ed. G. W. E. Nickelsburg with G. W. MacRae, 308–20. Philadelphia: Fortress.

Collins, John J. 1983. *Between Athens and Jerusalem: Jewish Identity in the Hellenistic Diaspora*. New York: Crossroad.

Collins, Randall. 1998. *The Sociology of Philosophies: A Global Theory of Intellectual Change*. Cambridge, Mass.: Harvard University Press.

Compier, Don H. 1999. *What Is Rhetorical Theology? Textual Practice and Public Discourse*. Harrisburg, Penn.: Trinity Press International.

Condor, Susan. 1996. Social Identity and Time. In *Social Groups and Identities: Developing the Legacy of Henri Tajfel*, ed. W. Peter Robinson, 285–315. Oxford: Butterworth Heinemann.

Conze, A., and C. Schuchhardt. 1899. "Die Arbeiten zu Pergamon." *Mitteilungun des Deutschen archäologischen Instituts* (A) 24: 164–240.

Conzelmann, Hans, and Andreas Lindemann. 1988. *Interpreting the New Testament: An Introduction to the Principles and Methods of N.T. Exegesis*. Peabody, Mass.: Hendrickson.

Corbier, Mireille. 1991. City, Territory and Taxation. In *City and Country in the Ancient World*, ed. John Rich and Andrew Wallace-Hadrill, 211–39. London: Routledge.

Corley, Kathleen. 1993. *Private Women, Public Meals, Social Conflict in the Synoptic Tradition*. Peabody, Mass.: Hendrickson.

Coser, Lewis A. 1956. *The Functions of Social Conflict*. New York: Free Press; London: Routledge & Kegan Paul.

———. 1967. *Continuities in the Study of Social Conflict*. London: Collier-Macmillan.

———. 1971. *Masters of Sociological Thought: Ideas in Historical and Social Context*. New York: Harcourt Brace Jovanovich.

Cotter, Wendy J. 1996. The Collegia and Roman Law: State Restrictions on Voluntary Associations 64 BCE–200 CE. In *Voluntary Associations in the Graeco-Roman World*, ed. John S. Kloppenborg and Stephen G. Wilson, 79–89. London: Routledge.

Countryman, L. William. 1989 *Dirt, Greed and Sex: Sexual Ethics in the New Testament and Their Implications for Today*. London: SCM.

Coyle, J. Kevin. 1981. Empire and Eschaton: The Early Church and the Question of Domestic Relationships. *Église et Théologie* 12: 35–94.

Cramer, Frederick H. 1951. Expulsion of Astrologers from Ancient Rome. *Classica et Mediaevalia* 12: 9–50.

Cranfield, Charles E. B. 1975/79. *The Epistle to the Romans*. Edinburgh: T. & T. Clark.

Crenshaw, James L., ed. 1976. *Studies in Ancient Israelite Wisdom*. New York: KTAV.

Crook, John A. 1984. *Law and Life of Rome: 90 B.C.–A.D. 212*. Ithaca, N.Y.: Cornell University Press.

Cross, Frank Leslie, ed. 1997. *The Oxford Dictionary of the Christian Church*. Oxford: Oxford University Press.

Crossan, John Dominic. 1973. *In Parables: The Challenge of the Historical Jesus*. New York: Harper & Row.

———. 1991. *The Historical Jesus: The Life of Mediterranean Jewish Peasant*. San Francisco: Harper & Row.

———. 1995. *Jesus: A Revolutionary Biography*. San Francisco: Harper.

———. 1998. *The Birth of Christianity: Discovering What Happened in the Year Immediately after the Execution of Jesus*. San Francisco: HarperCollins.

———. 1999. Historical Jesus as Risen Lord. In *The Jesus Controversy: Perspectives in Conflict*, John Dominic Crossan, Luke Timothy Johnson, and Werner H. Kelber, 1–47. Harrisburg, Penn.: Trinity Press International.

———. 2000. The Relationship between Galilean Archaeology and Historical Jesus Research. Unpublished paper, Society of Biblical Literature Annual Meeting, Nashville, Tenn.

Crouch, James E. 1991. How Early Christians Viewed the Birth of Jesus. *Bible Review* 34: 34–38.

Cullmann, Oscar. 1925. Les récentes études sur la formation de la tradition évangélique. *Revue d'histoire et de philosophie religieuses* 5: 564–79.

———. 1963. Infancy Gospels. In *New Testament Apocrypha, Vol. 1*, ed. Edgar Hennecke and Wilhelm Schneemelcher, trans. R. McL. Wilson, 363–417. Philadelphia: Westminster.

———. 1991. Infancy Gospels. In *New Testament Apocrypha, Vol. 1*, ed. Edgar Hennecke and Wilhelm Schneemelcher, trans. R. McL. Wilson, 414–25. Philadelphia: Westminster.

Czarnowski, S. 1919. *Le culte des héros et ses conditions sociales: Saint Patrick, héros national de l'Irlande*. Paris: Alcan.

D'Arms, John H. 1981. *Commerce and Social Standing in Ancient Rome*. Cambridge, Mass.: Harvard University Press.

Dahl, Nils Alstrup. 1950. Der Name Israel: Zur Auslegung von Gal 6,16. *Judaica* 6: 161–70.

Daly, Mary. 1986. *Beyond God the Father: Towards a Philosophy of Women's Liberation*. London: Women's Press.

Dar, Shimon. 1993. Samaria: Region, The Survey of Western Samaria. *New Encyclopedia of Archaeological Excavations in the Holy Land*. Jerusalem: Israel Exploration Society 4, 1314–16.

Davies, J. K. 1998. Ancient Economies: Models and Muddles. In *Trade, Traders and the Ancient City*, ed. Helen Parkins and Christopher Smith, 225–56. London: Routledge.

Davies, Stevan L. 1995. *Jesus the Healer: Possession, Trance and the Origins of Christianity*. New York: Continuum.

Davies, William D. 1977. Paul and the People of Israel. *New Testament Studies* 24: 4–39.

————, and D. C. Allison. 1988–97. *A Critical and Exegetical Commentary on the Gospel according to Saint Matthew*. 3 vols. Edinburgh: T. & T. Clark.

Davis, J. 1977. *People of the Mediterranean*. London: Routledge.

Davis, Nanette J. 1975. *Sociological Constructions of Deviance: Perspectives and Issues in the Field*. Dubuque, Iowa: Wm. C. Brown.

Dawson, Lorne L. 1998. *Comprehending Cults: The Sociology of New Religious Movements*. Oxford: Oxford University Press.

De Faye, Eugène. 1923–28. *Origène, sa vie, son oeuvre, sa pensée*. 3 vols. Paris: E. Leroux.

Deissmann, G. Adolf. 1910/1927. *Light from the Ancient East: The New Testament Illustrated by Recently Discovered Texts of the Graeco-Roman World*. Trans. Lionel R. M. Strachan. London: Hodder & Stoughton; Peabody, Mass.: Hendrickson.

————. 1911. *Paulus: Eine kultur- und religions- geschichtliche Skizze*. Tübingen, Germany: Mohr; *Paul: A Study in Social and Religious History*, 2nd ed. London: Hodder & Stoughton, 1926; New York: Harper & Row, 1957.

de Lange, N. R. M. 1978. Jewish Attitudes to the Roman Empire. In *Imperialism in the Ancient World*, Peter D. A. Garnsey and C. R. Whittaker, 255–81. Cambridge: Cambridge University Press.

de Silva, David A. 2000. *Perseverance in Gratitude: A Socio-Rhetorical Commentary on the Epistle to the Hebrews*. Grand Rapids, Mich.: Eerdmans.

Desroche, Henri. 1962. *Marxisme et religion*. Paris: Presses Universitaires de France.

Deutsch, Morton. 1973. *The Resolution of Conflict: Constructive and Destructive Processes*. New Haven, Conn.: Yale University Press.

De Vos, George. 1995. Ethnic Pluralism. In *Ethnic Identity: Creation, Conflict, and Accommodation*. 3rd ed. Walnut Creek, Calif.: AltaMira Press.

de Waard, Jan, and Eugene A. Nida. 1986. *From One Language to Another: Functional Equivalence in Bible Translating*. Nashville, Tenn.: Thomas Nelson.

Dewey, Joanna. 1980. *Markan Public Debate: Literary Technique, Concentric Structure, and Theology in Mark 2:1–3:6*. Chico, Calif.: Scholars Press.

Diamond, Arhtur Sigismond. 1971. *Primitive Law, Past and Present*. London: Methuen.

Dibelius, Martin. 1956. *Studies in the Acts of the Apostles*. London: SCM.

Di Lella, Alexander A. 1966. Conservative and Progressive Theology. *Catholic Biblical Quarterly* 38: 139–157. Reprinted in James L. Crenshaw, ed. 1976. *Studies in Ancient Israelite Wisdom*. New York: KTAV, 401–16.

Dill, Samuel. 1958 (1899). *Roman Society in the Last Century of the Western Empire*. New York: Meridian.

Dillon, John. 1977. *The Middle Platonists*. Ithaca, N.Y.: Cornell University Press.

Dilthey, Wilhelm. 1990. *Der Aufbau der geschichtlichen Welt in den geister Wissenschaften*. 3rd ed. Franfurt am Main, Germany: Suhrkamp.

Dodd, Charles Harold. 1963. *The Interpretation of the Fourth Gospel*. Cambridge: Cambridge University Press.

Dodds, Eric Robertson. 1928. The Parmenides of Plato and the Origin of the Neo-Platonic One. *Classical Quarterly* 28: 129–43.

Donaldson, Terence L. 1990. Rural Bandits, City Mobs and the Zealots. *Journal for the Study of Judaism* 21: 19–40.

———. 1997. *Paul and the Gentiles: Remapping the Apostle's Convictional World.* Minneapolis, Minn.: Fortress.

Donfried, Karl Peter, ed. 1991. *The Romans Debate.* Edinburgh: T. & T. Clark.

———. 1997. The Imperial Cults of Thessalonica and Political Conflict in I Thessalonians. In *Paul and Empire: Religion and Power in Roman Imperial Society*, ed. Richard A. Horsley, 215–23. Harrisburg, Penn.: Trinity Press International.

Dörner, Friedrich Karl. 1952. *Bericht über eine Reise in Bithynien.* Denkschriften der österreichische Akademie der Wissenschaften, philosophisch-historische Klasse, 75. Wien, Austria: Rudolf M. Rohrer.

Douglas, Mary. 1966. *Purity and Danger.* London: Routledge & and Kegan Paul.

Drescher, Hans-Georg. 1991. *Ernst Troeltsch. Leben und Werk.* Göttingen, Germany: Vandenhoeck & Ruprecht.

Drosnin, Michael. 1997. *The Bible Code.* New York: Simon & Schuster.

Dubetsky, Alan. 1976. Kinship, Primordial Ties, and Factory Organization in Turkey: An Anthropological View. *International Journal of Middle Eastern Studies* 7: 433–51.

Dumais, Alfred. 1995. *Historicité et foi chrétienne: Une lecture du théologien Ernst Troeltsch.* Québec: Les Presses de l'Université Laval.

Dumont, Fernand. 1980. Les sciences de la religion dans la culture. In *Sciences Sociales et Eglises*, ed. Jean Paul Rouleau and Paul Stryckman, 341–63. Montréal: Bellarmin.

Dunbabin, Katherine. 1991. Triclinium and Stibadium. In *Dining in a Classical Context*, ed. William J. Slater. Ann Arbor: University of Michigan Press.

Duncan-Jones, Richard. 1974. *The Economy of the Roman Empire.* London: Cambridge University Press.

Dunn, James Douglas Grant. 1988. *Romans.* Waco, Tex.: Word.

———. 1990. *Jesus, Paul, and the Law.* Louisville, Ky.: Westminster; London: SPCK.

———. 1991. *The Partings of the Ways: Between Christianity and Judaism and Their Significance for the Character of Christianity.* London: SCM; Philadelphia: Trinity Press International.

———. 1993. *The Epistle to the Galatians.* Peabody, Mass.: Hendrickson.

———. 1998. *The Theology of Paul the Apostle.* Grand Rapids, Mich.: Eerdmans.

———, ed. 1992/1999. *Jews and Christians: The Parting of the Ways A.D. 70 to 135.* Tübingen, Germany: Mohr; Grand Rapids, Mich.: Eerdmans.

Durkheim, Émile. 1963. *Sociologie et philosophie.* 4th ed. Paris: Presses Universitaires de France; *Sociology and Philosophy.* Trans. D. F. Pocock. New York: Free Press, 1974.

———. 1968. *Les formes élémentaires de la vie religieuse.* 5th ed. Paris: Presses Universitaires de France; *The Elementary Forms of the Religious Life.* Trans. Joseph Ward Swain. London: George Allen & Unwin, 1915.

———. 1979. *Le suicide: Étude de sociologie.* 6th ed. Paris: Presses Universitaires de France; *Suicide: A Study in Sociology.* Trans. John A. Spaulding and George Simpson. New York: Free Press, 1951.

———. 1982. *The Rules of Sociological Method*. Ed. Steven Lukes and trans. W. D. Halls. New York: Free Press; *Les règles de la méthode sociologique*. (Quadrige) Paris: Presses Universitaires de France, 1937 (1987).

———. 1984. *The Division of Labour in Society*. London: Macmillan. [Originally *De la division du travail social*, 1893.]

Dyson, Stephen L. 1971. Native revolts in the Roman Empire. *Historia* 20: 239–74.

———. 1975. Native Revolt Patterns in the Roman Empire. *Aufstieg und Niedergang der römischen Welt* II.3: 138–75.

Eastby, John. 1985. *Functionalism and Interdependence*. Lanham, Md.: University Press of America.

Eberts, Harry W., Jr. 1997. Plurality and Ethnicity in. . . . Bibliography #795.

Eck, Werner. 1971. Das Eindringen des Christentums in den Senatorenstand bis zu Konstanin d. Gr. *Chiron* I: 381–406.

Edson, Charles. 1948. Cults of Thessalonica (Macedonia III). *Harvard Theological Review* 41: 153–204.

Edwards, Douglas R. 1992. Religion, Power, and Politics: Jewish Defeats by the Romans in Iconography and Josephus. In *Diaspora Jews and Judaism: Essays in honor of, and in dialogue with, A. Thomas Kraabel*, ed. Andrew Overman and Robert S. MacLennan, 293–310. Tampa: University of South Florida Press.

———. 1994. The Social, Religious, and Political Aspects of Costume in Josephus. In *The World of Roman Costume*, Judith Sebesta and Larissa Bonfante, 153–59. Madison: University of Wisconsin Press.

———. 1996. *Religion and Power: Pagans, Jews, and Christians in the Greek East*. New York: Oxford University Press.

Edwards, O. C., Jr. 1983. Sociology as a Tool for Interpreting the New Testament. *ATR* 65: 431–48.

Ehrman, Bart D. 1998. *The New Testament and Other Early Christian Writings*. Oxford: Oxford University Press.

———. 2000. *The New Testament: A Historical Introduction to the Early Christian Writings*. 2nd ed. New York: Oxford University Press.

Eisenstadt, Shmuel N. 1963. *The Political Systems of Empires*. New York: Macmillan/Free Press.

———. 1971. *Social Differentiation and Stratification*. Glenview, Ill.: Scott, Foresman.

———. 1992. *Jewish Civilization*. Albany: State University of New York Press.

———, ed. 1986. *The Origins and Diversity of Axial Age Civilizations*. Albany: State University of New York Press.

Elias, Norbert. 1970. *Was ist Soziologie?* München, Germany: Juventa Verlag.

Eller, Jack, and Reed Coughlan. 1993. The Poverty of Primordialism. *Ethnic and Racial Studies* 16, 2: 187–92, 199–201.

Elliott, John H. 1981/1990. *A Home for the Homeless: A Social-Scientific Criticism of 1 Peter, Its Situation and Strategy*. Minneapolis, Minn.: Fortress. [1st ed. 1981.]

———. 1985. Review of W. A. Meeks, *The First Urban Christians*. *Religious Studies Review* 11: 329–35.

———. 1986. Social-Scientific Criticism of the New Testament: More on Methods and Models. *Semeia* 35: 1–33.

———. 1993. *What is Social-Scientific Criticism?* (Guides to Biblical Scholarship, New Testament Series). Minneapolis, Minn.: Fortress.

———. 1995a. The Jewish Messianic Movement: From Faction to Sect. In *Modelling Early Christianity: Social-Scientific Studies of the New Testament in its Context*, ed. Philip F. Esler, 75–95. London: Routledge.

———. 1995b. Disgraced Yet Graced: The Gospel According to I Peter in the Key of Honor and Shame. *Biblical Theology Bulletin* 25: 166–78.

———. 2000. *1 Peter: A New Translation with Introduction and Commentary* (Anchor Bible 37B). New York: Doubleday.

Elliott, Neil. 1994. *Liberating Paul: The Justice of God and the Politics of the Apostle.* Maryknoll, N.Y.: Orbis; Sheffield, England: Sheffield Academic Press.

———. 1997. Romans 13:1–7 in the Context of Imperial Propaganda. In *Paul and Empire: Religion and Power in Roman Imperial Society*, ed. Richard Horsley, 184–204. Harrisburg, Penn.: Trinity Press International.

Ellis, E. Earle. 2000. Preformed Traditions and Their Implications for Pauline Christology. In Horrell and Tuckett (eds.) 2000, 303–20.

Emmet, Dorothy. 1972. *Function, Purpose and Powers.* London: Macmillan.

Engels, Donald. 1990. *Roman Corinth: An Alternative Model for the Classical City.* Chicago: University of Chicago Press.

Erdemgil, S., et al. N.d. *The Terrace Houses in Ephesus.* Istanbul: Hitit Color.

Erikson, Kai T. 1966. *Wayward Puritans: A Study in the Sociology of Deviance.* New York: John Wiley.

Esler, Philip F. 1987. *Community and Gospel in Luke–Acts: The Social and Political Motivations of Lukan Theology* (SNTSMS 57). Cambridge: Cambridge University.

———. 1994. *The First Christians in their Social Worlds: Social-Scientific Approaches to New Testament Interpretation.* London: Routledge.

———. 1995. Introduction: Models, Context and Kerygma in New Testament Interpretation. In Esler (ed.) 1995, 1–20.

———. 1996. Group Boundaries and Intergroup Conflict in Galatians: A New Reading of Galatians 5:13–6:10. In *Ethnicity and the Bible*, Mark G. Brett, 215–40. Leiden: E. J. Brill.

———. 1998a. Review of D. G. Horrell, *The Social Ethos of the Corinthian Correspondence. Journal of Theological Studies* 49: 253–60.

———. 1998b. *Galatians.* London: Routledge.

———. 2000a. Models in New Testament Interpretation: A Reply to David Horrell. *Journal for the Study of the New Testament* 78: 107–13.

———. 2000b. Jesus and the Reduction of Intergroup Conflict: The Parable of the Good Samaritan in the Light of Social Identity Theory. *Biblical Interpretation* 8: 325–57.

———, ed. 1995. *Modelling Early Christianity: Social-Scientific Studies of the New Testament in its Context.* London: Routledge.

Farmer, William R. 1964. *The Synoptic Problem: A Critical Analysis.* New York: Macmillan. Macon, Ga.: Mercer University Press, 1976.

Farrer, A. M. 1985. On Dispensing with Q. In *The Two-Source Hypothesis: A Critical Appraisal*, ed. A. J. Bellinzoni, 321–56. Macon, Ga.: Mercer University Press.

Fears, J. Rufus. 1975. Nero as Vicegerent of the Gods in Seneca's *De Clementia*. *Hermes* 103: 486–96.

———. 1977. *Princeps A Diis Electus: The Divine Election of the Emperor as a Political Concept at Rome. Papers and Monographs of the American Academy in Rome* 26. Rome: American Academy in Rome.

———. 1981a. The Cult of Jupiter and Roman Imperial Ideology. *Aufstieg und Niedergang der römischen Welt*, 2.17.1: 3–141. Berlin: Walter de Gruyter.

———. 1981b. The Cult of Virtues and Roman Imperial Ideology. *Aufstieg und Niedergang der römischen Welt*. 2.17.2: 827–948. Berlin: Walter de Gruyter.

———. 1981c. The Theology of Victory at Rome: Approaches and Problems. *Aufstieg und Niedergang der römischen Welt* 2.17.2: 736–825. Berlin: Walter de Gruyter.

Febvre, Lucien. 1973. *A New Kind of History*. Ed. P. Burke and trans. K. Folca. New York: Harper Torchbooks.

Feldman, Louis H. 1993. *Jew and Gentile in the Ancient World*. Princeton, N.J.: Princeton University Press.

———, and G. Hata, eds. 1989. *Josephus, the Bible, and History*. Detroit: Wayne State University Press.

Fenn, Richard. 1992. *The Death of Herod: An Essay in the Sociology of Religion*. Cambridge: Cambridge University.

Festinger, Leon. 1957. *A Theory of Cognitive Dissonance*. Stanford, Calif.: Stanford University Press.

———, and E. Aronson. 1968. Arousal and Reduction of Dissonance in Social Contexts. In *Group Dynamics: Research and Theory*. 3rd ed., ed. Dorwin P. Cartwright and Alvin F. Zander, 125–36. New York: Harper & Row; London: Tavistock.

Festinger, Leon, Henry W. Riecken, and Stanley Schachter. 1956. *When Prophecy Fails*. New York: Harper & Row.

Festinger, Leon, et al. 1964. *Conflict, Decision, and Dissonance*. London: Tavistock.

Fiensy, David A. 1991. *The Social History of Palestine in the Herodian Period: The Land Is Mine* (Studies in the Bible and Early Christianity 20). Lewiston, N.Y.: Mellen.

Filson, Floyd V. 1939. The Significance of the Early House Churches. *Journal of Biblical Literature* 58: 109–12.

Finley, Moses I. 1984 [1973]. *The Ancient Economy*. Berkeley: University of California Press.

———. 1980. *Ancient Slavery and Modern Ideology*. London: Chatto and Windus.

———. 1985. *Ancient History: Evidence and Models*. London: Chatto and Windus.

Finn, T. M. 1982. Social Mobility, Imperial Civil Service and the Spread of Early Christianity. In *Studia Patristica* 17, ed. Elizabeth A. Livingstone, 31–37. Oxford: Pergamon.

Fischer, Claude S. 1975. Toward a Subcultural Theory of Urbanism. *American Journal of Sociology* 80: 1319–41.

Fishbein, M., and I. Ajzeen. 1975. *Belief, Attitude, Intention and Behavior*. Reading, Mass.: Addison-Wesley.

Fitzmyer, Joseph A. 1981. *The Gospel According to Luke I–IX*. Garden City, N.Y.: Doubleday.
———. 1993. *Romans*. Garden City, N.Y.: Doubleday.
———. 1998. *The Acts of the Apostles*. Garden City, N.Y.: Doubleday.
Follet, Simone. 1976. *Athènes au IIe et au IIIe siècle: Études chronologiques et prosopographiques* (Collection d'études anciennes). Paris: Société d'Édition les Belles Lettres.
Foucault, Michel. 1986. Disciplinary Power and Subjection. In *Power*, ed. Steven Lukes, 229–42. Oxford: Basil Blackwell.
Fowler, Roger. 1974. *Understanding Language: An Introduction to Linguistics*. London: Routledge & Kegan Paul.
Fox, Robin Lane. 1987. *Pagans and Christians in the Mediterranean World from the Second Century A.D. to the Conversion of Constantine*. San Francisco: Harper & Row.
Frank, Tenney. 1927. *Economic History of Rome*. 2nd ed. Baltimore, Md.: Johns Hopkins University Press.
———, ed. 1936–1938. *Economic Survey of Ancient Rome*. Baltimore, Md.: Johns Hopkins University Press.
Fraser, Peter Marshall. 1972. *Ptolemaic Alexandria*. 3 vols. Oxford: Clarendon.
Frederiksen, M. W. 1975. Theory, Evidence and the Ancient Economy. *Journal of Roman Studies* 65: 164–71.
Fredriksen, Paula. 1991. Judaism, the Circumcision of Gentiles, and Apocalyptic Hope: Another Look at Galatians 1 and 2. *Journal of Theological Studies* 42: 532–64.
———. 1999. *Jesus of Nazareth, King of the Jews: A Jewish Life and the Emergence of Christianity*. New York: Knopf.
Freedman, David Noel, ed. 1992. *Anchor Bible Dictionary*. Garden City, N.Y.: Doubleday.
Freedman, J. L., D. O. Sears, and J. M. Carlsmith. 1978. *Social Psychology*. Englewood Cliffs, N.J.: Prentice Hall.
Frend, W. H. C. 1952. *The Donatist Church*. Oxford: Clarendon.
———. 1965. *Martyrdom and Persecution in the Early Church: A Study of Conflict from the Maccabees to Donatus*. Oxford: Blackwell; New York: New York University Press.
———. 1980. *Town and Country in the Early Christian Centuries*. London: Variorum Reprints.
———. 1984. *The Rise of Christianity*. Philadelphia: Fortress; London: Darton, Longman & Todd.
Freud, Sigmund. 1950. *Totem and Taboo: Some Points of Agreement between the Mental Lives of Savages and Neurotics*. New York: Norton.
Freund, Julien. 1983. *Sociologie du conflit*. Paris: Presses Universitaires de France.
Freyne, Sean. 1980. *Galilee from Alexander the Great to Hadrian, 323 B.C.E.–C.E. 135: A Study of Second Temple Judaism*. Notre Dame, Ind.: University of Notre Dame.
———. 1995. Herodian Economics in Galilee. Searching for a Suitable Model. In *Modelling Early Christianity: Social-Scientific Studies of the New Testament in its Context*, ed. Philip Esler, 23–46. London: Routledge.
Fruchtel, Ursula. 1968. *Die Kosmologischen Vorstellungen bei Philon von Alexandrie*. Leiden: E. J. Brill.
Funk, Robert W. 1976. The Watershed of the American Biblical Tradition: The Chicago School, First Phase, 1892–1920. *Journal of Biblical Literature* 95: 4–22.

Funk, Robert W., Roy W. Hoover, and the Jesus Seminar. 1993. *The Five Gospels: The Search for the Authentic Words of Jesus.* New York: Macmillan.

———, and the Jesus Seminar. 1998. *The Acts of Jesus: The Search for the Authentic Deeds of Jesus.* San Francisco: Harper.

Furay, Conal, and Michael Salevouris. 1988. *The Methods and Skills of History: A Practical Guide.* Arlington Heights, Ill.: Harlan Davidson.

Futrell, Alison. 1997. *Blood in the Arena.* Austin: University of Texas Press.

Gadamer, Hans-Georg. 1975. *Truth and Method.* New York: Seabury. [Originally *Wahrheit und Methode*, 1960.]

Gager, John G. 1975. *Kingdom and Community: The Social World of Early Christianity.* Englewood Cliffs, N.J.: Prentice Hall.

———. 1981. Some Notes on Paul's Conversion. *NTS* 27: 697–704.

———. 1983. Review of B. J. Malina, *The New Testament World. Interpretation* 37: 194–97.

———. 1983. *The Origins of Anti-Semitism.* Oxford: Oxford University Press.

Gallagher, Eugene V. 1991. Conversion and Salvation in the Apocryphal Acts of the Apostles. *Second Century* 8: 13–29.

———. 1993. Conversion and Community in Late Antiquity. *Journal of Religion* 73:1–15.

Gamble, Harry Y. 1985. *The New Testament Canon: Its Making and Meaning.* Philadelphia: Fortress.

———. 1995. *Books and Readers in the Early Church: A History of Early Christian Texts.* New Haven, Conn.: Yale University Press.

Gammie, J. G. 1990. Paraenetic Literature: Toward the Morphology of a Secondary Genre. *Semeia* 50: 41–77.

Gamson, W. A. 1992. The Social Psychology of Collective Action. In *Frontiers in Social Movement Theory*, ed. A. D. Morris and C. M. Mueller, 53–76. New Haven, Conn.: Yale University Press.

Garfinkel, Harold. 1967. *Studies in Ethnomethodology.* Englewood Cliffs, N.J.: Prentice Hall.

Garnsey, Peter D. A. 1976. Peasants in Ancient Roman Society. *Journal of Peasant Studies* 3: 221–35.

———. 1978. Rome's African Empire under the Principate. In Garnsey and Whittaker, eds., 223–54.

———. 1988. *Famine and Feed Supply in the Graeco-Roman World.* Cambridge: Cambridge University Press.

———. 1996. *Ideas of Slavery from Aristotle to Augustine.* Cambridge: Cambridge University Press.

———. 1998. *Cities, Peasants and Food in Classical Antiquity: Essays in Social and Economic History*, ed. Walter Scheidel. Cambridge: Cambridge University Press.

———, Keith Hopkins, and C. R. Whittaker, eds. 1983. *Trade in the Ancient Economy.* Berkeley: University of California Press.

Garnsey, Peter D. A., and Richard P. Saller. 1982. *The Early Principate: Augustus to Trajan* (New Surveys in the Classics 15). Oxford: Clarendon.

———. 1987. *The Roman Empire: Economy, Society and Culture.* London: Duckworth.

Garnsey, Peter D. A., and C. R. Whittaker, eds. 1978. *Imperialism in the Ancient World.* Cambridge: Cambridge University Press.

Garrett, Susan. 1988. Review of B. J. Malina, *Christian Origins and Cultural Anthropology*. *Journal of Biblical Literature* 107: 532–34.

———. 1992. Sociology of Early Christianity. In *Anchor Bible Dictionary*, ed. David Noel Freedman, vol. 6, 89–99. Garden City, N.Y.: Doubleday.

Gaston, Lloyd. 1986. Anti-Judaism and the Passion Narrative in Luke and Acts. In *Anti-Judaism in Early Christianity. Vol. 1, Paul and the Gospels*, ed. Peter Richardson (with David Granskou), 127–53. Waterloo, Ont.: Wilfrid Laurier University Press.

———. 1987. *Paul and the Torah*. Vancouver: University of British Columbia Press.

Gauthier, Philippe. 1985. *Les cités grecques et leurs bienfaiteurs. Bulletin de correspondance hellénique*. Supplement 12. Paris: De Boccard.

Gaventa, Beverley Roberts. 1986a. *From Darkness to Light: Aspects of Conversion in the New Testament*. Philadelphia: Fortress.

———. 1986b. Galatians 1 and 2: Autobiography as Paradigm. *Novum Testamentum* 28: 307–26.

———. 1992. Conversion in the Bible. In *Handbook of Religious Conversion*, ed. H. Newton Malony and Samuel Southard, 41–54. Birmingham, Ala.: Religious Education Press.

Geertz, Clifford. 1973. *The Interpretation of Cultures: Selected Essays*. New York: Basic Books.

Genzmer, Erich. 1952. Pondere, Numero, Mensura. *Archives d'Histoire du Droit Oriental et Revue International des Droits d'Antiquité* 1: 468–94.

George, Darren, and Paul Mallery. 2000. *SPSS for Windows Step by Step*. 2nd ed. Boston: Allyn & Bacon.

Georgi, Dieter. 1997. God Turned Upside Down. In *Paul and Empire: Religion and Power in Roman Imperial Society*, ed. Richard A. Horsley, 148–57. Harrisburg, Penn.: Trinity Press International.

Gerhardsson, Birger. 1961. *Memory and Manuscript*. Lund: ASNU.

Gerlach, Luther, and Virginia Hine. 1970. *People, Power, Change: Movements of Social Transformation*. Indianapolis, Ind.: Bobbs-Merrill.

Getty, Mary Ann. 1988. Paul and the Salvation of Israel: A Perspective on Romans 9–11. *Catholic Biblical Quarterly* 50: 456–69.

Gibson, E. Leigh. 1999. *The Jewish Manumission Inscriptions of the Bosporan Kingdom* (Texte und Studien zum antiken Judentum 75). Tübingen, Germany: Mohr Siebeck.

Giddens, Anthony. 1977. *Studies in Social and Political Theory*. London: Hutchinson.

———. 1979. *Central Problems in Social Theory*. London: Macmillan.

———. 1982. *Profiles and Critiques in Social Theory*. London: Macmillan.

———. 1984. *The Constitution of Society: Outline of the Theory of Structuration*. Berkeley: University of California Press; Cambridge: Polity.

Gilbert, Margaret. 1989. *On Social Facts*. Princeton, N.J.: Princeton University Press.

Gill, Robin, ed. 1996. *Theology and Sociology: A Reader*. Enlarged ed. London: Cassell.

Gilmore, David, ed. 1987. *Honor and Shame and the Unity of the Mediterranean* (Special Publication of the American Anthropological Association, no. 22). Washington, D.C.: American Anthropological Association.

Ginzberg, Louis 1968. *The Legends of the Jews*. Trans. H. Szolz. Philadelphia: Jewish Publication Society.

Giovannini, Adalberto, ed. 1986. *Opposition et Résistances à l'Empire d'Auguste à Trajan*, 23. Geneva: Entretiens sur L'Antiquité Classique.

Glancy, Jennifer A. 1998. Obstacles to Slaves' Participation in the Corinthian Church. *Journal of Biblical Literature* 117: 481–501.

Glaser, Barney G., and Anselm L. Strauss. 1967. *The Discovery of Grounded Theory*. New York: Aldine de Gruyter.

Goldman, Marion S. 1999. *Passionate Journeys: Why Successful Women Joined a Cult*. Ann Arbor: University of Michigan Press.

Goldthorpe, John H. 1991. The Uses of History in Sociology: Reflections on Some Recent Tendencies. *British Journal of Sociology* 42: 211–29.

Gooch, Peter D. 1993. *Dangerous Food: 1 Corinthians 8–10 in Its Context*. Waterloo, Ont.: Wilfrid Laurier University.

Goodenough, Erwin R. 1932. A Neo-Pythagorean Source in Philo Judaeus. *Yale Classical Quarterly* 3: 115–64.

———. 1988. *Jewish Symbols in the Greco-Roman Period*. Ed. and abridged Jacob Neusner. Princeton, N.J.: Princeton University Press.

Goodman, Martin. 1983. *State and Society in Roman Galilee, A.D. 132–212*. Totowa, N.J.: Rowman and Allanheld.

———. 1987. *The Ruling Class of Judea: The Origins of the Jewish Revolt against Rome A.D. 66–70*. Cambridge: Cambridge University Press.

———. 1991. Opponents of Rome: Jews and Others. In Images of Empire. *Journal of the Old Testament Supplement Series 122*, Loveday Alexander, 222–38. Sheffield, England: Sheffield Academic Press.

———. 1994. *Mission and Conversion: Proselytizing in the Religious History of the Roman Empire*. Oxford: Clarendon.

Gordon, Cyrus H. 1977. Paternity at Two Levels. *Journal of Biblical Literature* 96: 101.

Gordon, J. Dorcas. 1997. *Sister or Wife? 1 Corinthians 7 and Cultural Anthropology*. Sheffield, England: Sheffield Academic Press.

Gordon, Richard L. 1972. Mithraism and Roman Society: Social Factors in the Explanation of Religious Change in the Roman Empire. *Religion* 2: 92–121.

Gottwald Norman K., and Richard Horsley, eds. 1993. *The Bible and Liberation: Political and Social Hermeneutics*. Rev. ed. Maryknoll, N.Y.: Orbis.

Goudoever, J. van. 1959, 1961. *Biblical Calendars*. Leiden: E. J. Brill.

Goudriaan, Koen. 1992. Ethnical Strategies in Graeco-Roman Egypt. In *Ethnicity in Hellenistic Egypt*, ed. Per Bilde, 74–99. Aarhus, Denmark: Aarhus University Press.

Grant, Frederick C. 1926. *The Economic Background of the Gospels*. London: Oxford University Press.

Grant, Robert M. 1952. *Miracle and Natural Law in Graeco-Roman and Early Christian Thought*. Amsterdam: E. J. Brill.

———. 1970. *Augustus to Constantine: The Rise and Triumph of Christianity in the Roman World*. San Francisco: Harper & Row.

———. 1977/1978. *Early Christianity and Society: Seven Studies*. San Francisco: Harper & Row; London: Collins.

——. 1980–81. The Social Setting of Second-Century Christianity. In *Jewish and Christian Self-Definition*. 2 vols., ed. Ed Parish Sanders, 16–29. Philadelphia: Fortress.

——. 1988. *Greek Apologists of the Second Century*. Philadelphia: Westminster.

Greeley, Andrew. 1989. *Religious Change in America*. Cambridge, Mass.: Harvard University Press.

——. 1990. *The Catholic Myth: The Behavior and Beliefs of American Catholics*. New York: Collier/Macmillan.

Green, J. B., ed. 1995. *Hearing the New Testament: Strategies for Interpretation*. Grand Rapids, Mich.: Eerdmans.

Guijarro, Santiago. 1997. The Family in First-Century Galilee. In *Constructing Early Christian Families*, ed. Halvor Moxnes, 42–65. New York: Routledge.

Gundry, Robert H. 1993. *Mark: A Commentary on His Apology for the Cross*. Grand Rapids, Mich.: Eerdmans.

Gurney, Joan Neff, and Kathleen J. Tierney. 1982. Relative Deprivation and Social Movements: A Critical Look at Twenty Years of Theory and Research. *Sociological Quarterly* 23: 33–47.

Gurvitch, Georges. 1947. *Sociology of Law*. London: Routledge & Kegan Paul.

——. 1958a. Brève Esquisse de l'Histoire de la Sociologie. In Gurvitch (ed.) 1958, 28–64.

——. 1958b. Microsociologie. In Gurvitch (ed.) 1958, 172–84.

——. 1962. *Dialectique et sociologie*. Paris: Flammarion.

——, ed. 1958. *Traité de Sociologie, Tome Premier*. Paris: Presses Universitaires de France.

Guthrie, George H. 1994. *The Structure of Hebrews: A Text-Linguistic Analysis*. Grand Rapids, Mich.: Baker.

Habel, Norman C. 1964. *Yahweh versus Baal: A Conflict of Religious Cultures*. St. Louis, Mo.: Concordia Seminary/Bookman Associates.

Hadas, Moses. 1959. *Hellenistic Culture: Fusion and Diffusion*. New York: Columbia University Press.

Haehling, Raban von. 1978. *Die Religionszugehörigkeit der hohen Amtsträger des römischen Reiches seit Constantins I: Alleinherrschaft bis zum Ende der Theodosianischen Dynastie, 324–450 bzw. 455 n. Chr.* Bonn: R. Habelt.

Haenchen, Ernst. 1971. *The Acts of the Apostles*. Philadelphia: Westminster.

——. 1984. *John 1: A Commentary on the Gospel of John Chapters 1–6*. Trans. Robert W. Funk. Hermeneia. Philadelphia: Fortress.

Halbwachs, Maurice. 1971. *La topographie légendaire des évangiles en Terre Sainte*. 2nd ed. Paris: Presses Universitaires de France.

——. 1992. *On Collective Memory*. Trans. and ed. Lewis Coser. Chicago: University of Chicago Press.

Halfmann, Helmut. 1979. *Die Senatoren aus dem östlichen Teil des Imperium Romanum bis zum Ende des 2.Jh.n.Chr.* (Hypomnemata, 58). Göttingen, Germany: Vandenhoeck & Ruprecht.

Hamel, Gildas. 1990 [1983]. *Poverty and Charity in Roman Palestine, First Three Centuries C.E.* (University of California Publications: Near Eastern Studies, 23). Berkeley: University of California Press.

Hampson, Daphne. 1996. *After Christianity*. London: SCM.

Hansen, G. W. 1989. *Abraham in Galatians—Epistolary and Rhetorical Contexts*. Sheffield, England: Sheffield Academic Press.

———. 1993. Rhetorical Criticism. In *Dictionary of Paul and His Letters*, ed. G. F. Hawthorne and R. P. Martin, 822–26. Downers Grove, Ill.: InterVarsity.

Hanson, Kenneth C., and Douglas E. Oakman. 1998. *Palestine in the Time of Jesus: Social Structures and Social Conflicts*. Minneapolis, Minn.: Fortress.

Hanson, Richard Patrick Crosland. 1959. *Allegory and Event*. London: SPCK.

Hardyck, J. A., and M. Braden. 1962. Prophecy Fails Again: A Report on a Failure to Replicate. *Journal of Abnormal and Social Psychology* 65: 136–41.

Harland, Philip. 1993. Banditry in the Roman Empire and Herod the Great. Unpublished paper, University of Toronto.

———. 1996. Honours and Worship: Emperors, Imperial Cults and Associations at Ephesus (First to Third Centuries C.E.). *Studies in Religion/Sciences religieuses* 25: 319–34.

———. 1999. *Claiming a Place in Polis and Empire: The Significance of Imperial Cults and Connections among Associations, Synagogues, and Christian Groups in Roman Asia (c. 27 BCE–138 CE)*. Unpublished Ph.D. Dissertation, University of Toronto.

———. 2000. Honouring the Emperor or Assailing the Beast: Participation in Civic Life among Associations (Jewish, Christian and Other) in Asia Minor and the Apocalypse of John. *Journal for the Study of the New Testament* 77: 99–121.

Harnack, Adolf von. 1905. *The Expansion of Christianity in the First Three Centuries*. Vol. 2. Trans. and ed. James Moffatt. London: Williams & Norgate; New York: Putnam.

———. 1908/1961. *The Mission and Expansion of Christianity in the First Three Centuries*. 2nd ed., 2 vols. Trans. James Moffatt. London: Williams & Norgate; New York: G. P. Putam's Sons/Harper & Brothers.

Harper, Dean. 1995. Statuses and Roles. In *International Encyclopedia of Sociology*. Vol. 2, ed. Frank N. Magill, 1360–63. London: Fitzroy & Dearborn.

Harré, R., and P. Secord. 1972. *The Explanation of Social Behaviour*. Oxford: Blackwell.

Harrill, Albert. 1993. Ignatius, *Ad Polycarp* 4.3 and the Corporate Manumission of Christian Slaves. *Journal of Early Christian Studies* 1, 2: 107–42.

Harrington, Daniel J. 1980. Sociological Concepts and the Early Church: A Decade of Research. *TS* 41: 181–90.

———. 1988. Second Testament Exegesis and the Social Sciences: A Bibliography. *BTB* 18: 77–85.

Harrington, Wilfrid J. 1993. *Revelation: Sacra Pagina 16*. Collegeville, Minn.: Liturgical Press.

Harrison, Jane Ellen. 1962 (1927). *Themis: A Study of the Social Origins of Greek Religion*. New York: Meridian.

Harrison, P. N. 1964. *Paulines and Pastorals*. London: Villiers.

Hatch, Edwin. 1957 (1889). *The Influence of Greek Ideas on Christianity*. New York: Harper Torchbooks.

Hatim, Basil, and Iam Mason. 1990. *Discourse and the Translator*. London: Longman.

Hatzfeld, Jean. 1919. *Les trafiquants italiens dans l'orient hellénique* (Bibliothèque des écoles françaises d'Athènes et de Rome, 115). Paris: E. de Boccard.

Haviland, William A. 1999. *Cultural Anthropology*. 9th ed. Fort Worth, Tex.: Harcourt Brace Jovanovich.

Hayes, John H., and Carl R. Holladay. 1987. *Biblical Exegesis: A Beginner's Handbook*. Rev. ed. Atlanta: John Knox.

Haynes, Stephen R., and Steven L. McKenzie, eds. 1993. *To Each Its Own Meaning: An Introduction to Biblical Criticism and Their Application*. Louisville, Ky.: Westminster/Knox.

Hays, Richard B. 1985. Review of Heikki Räisänen, *Paul and the Law*. *Journal of the American Academy of Religion* 53: 513–15.

———. 1989. *Echoes of Scripture in the Letters of Paul*. New Haven, Conn.: Yale University Press.

Heichelheim, Fritz M. 1938. Roman Syria. In *Economic Survey of Ancient Rome*, ed. Tenney Frank, vol. 4, 121–57. Baltimore, Md.: Johns Hopkins University Press.

———. 1958 [1938]. *An Ancient Economic History*. Leiden: A. W. Sijthoff.

Heider, Fritz. 1958. *The Psychology of Interpersonal Relations*. New York: Wiley.

Helgeland, John. 1974. Christians and the Roman Army A.D. 173–337. *Church History* 43: 143–63, 200.

Hempel, Carl. 1965. *Aspects of Scientific Explanation and Other Essays in the Philosophy of Science*. New York: Free Press; London: Collier–Macmillan.

Hengel, Martin. 1969. *Judentum und Hellenismus*. 2 vols. Tübingen, Germany: Mohr; *Judaism and Hellenism*. London: SCM, 1974.

———. 1972. *Crucifixion*. Philadelphia: Fortress.

———. 1973. *Eigentum und Reichtum in der frühen Kirche*. Stuttgart, Germany: Calwer Verlag; *Property and Riches in the Early Church: Aspect of a Sociological History of Early Christianity*. Philadelphia: Fortress, 1974.

———. 1974/1998. *Judaism and Hellenism*. 2 vols. Trans. John Bowden. Philadelphia: Fortress.

———. 1983. *Between Jesus and Paul: Studies in the History of Earliest Christianity*. London: SCM.

———. 1991. *The Pre-Christian Paul*. London: SCM.

———, and Anna Maria Schwemer. 1997. *Paul between Damascus and Antioch*. London: SCM.

Herford, R. Travers. 1903. *Christianity in Talmud and Midrash*. London: Williams & Norgate.

Hermisson, Hans-Jurgen. 1978. Observations on the Creation Theology in Wisdom. Trans. B. Howard. In *Israelite Wisdom: Theological and Literary Essays in Honor of Samuel Terrien*, ed. John G. Gammie et al., 43–57. Missoula, Mont.: Scholars Press.

Herskovitz, Melville J. 1952. *Economic Anthropology: The Economic Life of Primitive Peoples*. 2nd ed. New York: Knopf.

Hertz, Robert. 1970. *Sociologie religieuse et folklore*. 2nd ed. Paris: Presses Universitaires de France.

Herzfeld, Michael. 1980. Honour and Shame: Problems in the Comparative Analysis of Moral Systems. *Man* 15: 339–51.

Herzog, William. 2000. *Jesus, Justice and the Reign of God: A Ministry of Liberation*. Louisville, Ky.: Westminster John Knox.

Hill, Craig C. 1992. *Hellenists and Hebrews: Reappraising Division within the Earliest Church*. Minneapolis, Minn.: Fortress.

Hill, John M. 1995. *The Cultural World in* Beowulf (Anthropological Horizons). Toronto: University of Toronto Press.

Hinkle, Steve, and Rupert Brown. 1990. Intergroup Comparisons and Social Identity: Some Links and Lacunae. In *Social Identity Theory: Constructive and Critical Approaches*, ed. D. Abrams and M. A. Hogg, 48–70. New York: Harvester Wheatsheaf.

Hirschfeld, Yizhar. 1995. *The Palestinian Dwelling in the Roman-Byzantine Period*. Jerusalem: Franciscan Printing Press.

Hochschild, Ralph. 1999. *Sozialgeschichtliche Exegese: Entwicklung, Geschichte und Methodik einer neutestamentlichen Forschungrichtung* (Novum Testamentum et Orbis Antiquus 42). Göttingen, Germany: Vanderhoeck & Ruprecht.

Hock, Ronald F. 1980. *The Social Context of Paul's Ministry: Tentmaking and Apostleship*. Philadelphia: Fortress.

———. 1995. *The Infancy Gospels of James and Thomas*. Sonoma, Calif.: Polebridge.

Hoek, Annewies van den. 1988. *Clement of Alexandria and His Use of Philo in the Stromateis: An Early Christian Re-Shaping of a Jewish Model*. Leiden: E. J. Brill.

Hogg, Michael A., and Dominic Abrams. 1988. *Social Identifications: A Social Psychology of Intergroup Relations and Group Processes*. London: Routledge.

Holladay, Carl R. 1992. Jewish Responses to Hellenistic Culture. In *Ethnicity in Hellenistic Egypt*, ed. Per Bilde, 139–63. Aarhus, Denmark: Aarhus University Press.

Hollenbach, Paul. 1981. Jesus, Demoniacs, and Public Authorities: Socio-Historical Study. *JAAR* 49: 567–88.

Holmberg, Bengt. 1978/1980. *Paul and Power: The Structure of Authority in the Primitive Church as Reflected in the Pauline Epistles*. Lund, Sweden: C. W. K. Gleerup; Philadelphia: Fortress.

———. 1990. *Sociology and the New Testament an Appraisal*. Minneapolis, Minn.: Fortress.

———. 1998. Jewish Versus Christian Identity in the Early Church? *RevistB* 105: 397–425.

Honoré, A. M. 1968. A Statistical Study of the Synoptic Problem. *Novum Testamentum* 10: 95–147.

Hooker, Morna D. 1991. *The Gospel According to Saint Mark*. London: A. & C. Black.

Hoover, Kenneth R. 1988. *The Elements of Social Scientific Thinking*. 4th ed. New York: St. Martin's.

Hopkins, Keith. 1965. Élite Mobility in the Roman Empire. *Past & Present* 32: 12–26.

———. 1978. *Conquerors and Slaves*. Cambridge: Cambridge University Press.

———. 1980. Taxes and Trade in the Roman Empire (200 B.C.–A.D. 400). *Journal of Roman Studies* 70: 101–25.

———. 1998. Christian Number and Its Implications. *JECS* 6: 185–226.

Horbury, William. 1998. *Jews and Christians in Contact and Controversy*. Edinburgh: T. & T. Clark.

Hornus, Jean-Michel. 1980. *It Is Not Lawful for Me to Fight*. Kitchener, Ont.: Herald.

Horrell, David G. 1993. "Converging Ideologies": Berger and Luckmann and the Pastoral Epistles. *JSNT* 50: 85–103.

———. 1995. The Development of Theological Ideology in Pauline Christianity: A Structuration Theory Perspective. In *Modeling Early Christianity*, ed. P. F. Esler, 224–36. New York: Routledge.

———. 1996a. *The Social Ethos of the Corinthian Correspondence: Interests and Ideology from 1 Corinthians to 1 Clement.* Edinburgh: T. & T. Clark.

———. 1996b. Review of Dale B. Martin, *The Corinthian Body. Journal of Theological Studies* 47: 624–29.

———. 1997. Review of Neil Elliott, *Liberating Paul. Biblical Interpretation* 5: 285–87.

———. 1998. *The Epistles of Peter and Jude.* Peterborough, Ontario: Epworth.

———. 1999. Leadership Patterns and the Development of Ideology in Early Christianity. In Horrell (ed.) 1999, 309–37.

———. 2000a. Early Jewish Christianity. In *The Early Christian World*, ed. Philip F. Esler, 136–67. London: Routledge.

———. 2000b. *An Introduction to the Study of Paul.* London: Continuum.

———. 2000c. Models and Methods in Social-Scientific Interpretation: A Response to Philip Esler. *JSNT* 78: 83–105. (Reply, P. F. Esler, 107–13.)

———. 2000d. "No Longer Jew or Greek": Paul's Corporate Christology and the Construction of Christian Community. In Horrell and Tuckett (eds.) 2000, 321–44.

———. 2001a. From *adelphoi* to *oikos theou*: Social Transformation in Pauline Christianity. *Journal of Biblical Literature* 120: 293–311.

———. 2001b. Review of Ralph Hochschild, *Sozialgeschichtliche Exegese. Journal of Theological Studies* 52: 849–54.

———, ed. 1999. *Social-Scientific Approaches to New Testament Interpretation.* Edinburgh: T. & T. Clark.

———, and Christopher M. Tuckett, eds. 2000. *Christology, Controversy and Community: New Testament Studies in Honour of David R. Catchpole.* Leiden: E. J. Brill.

Horsley, G. H. R., and John A. L. Lee 1994. A Preliminary Checklist of Abbreviations of Greek Epigraphic Volumes. *Epigraphica* 56:129–69.

Horsley, Richard A. 1979. Josephus and the Bandits. *Journal for the Study of Judaism* 10: 37–63.

———. 1981. Ancient Jewish Banditry and the Revolt Against Rome, A.D. 66–70. *Catholic Biblical Quarterly* 43: 409–32.

———. 1986. The Zealots: Their Origin, Relationships and Importance in the Jewish Revolt. *Novum Testamentum* 28: 159–92.

———. 1987. *Jesus and the Spiral of Violence: Popular Jewish Resistance in Roman Palestine.* San Francisco: Harper & Row.

———. 1989. *Sociology and the Jesus Movement.* 2nd ed. New York: Continuum.

———. 1995. *Galilee: History, Politics, People.* Valley Forge, Penn.: Trinity.

———. 1996. *Archeology, History and Society in Galilee: The Social Context of Jesus and the Rabbis.* Valley Forge, Penn.: Trinity Press International.

———, ed. 1997. *Paul and Empire: Religion and Power in Roman Imperial Society.* Harrisburg, Penn.: Trinity Press International.

———, and John S. Hanson. 1985/1989/1999. *Bandits, Prophets, & Messiahs: Popular Movements in the Time of Jesus.* San Francisco: Harper & Row; Harrisburg, Penn.: Trinity Press.

———, and Neil Silberman. 1997. *The Message and the Kingdom: How Jesus and Paul Ignited a Revolution That Transformed the Ancient World.* New York: Putnam.

Horst, Pieter W. van der. 1991. *Ancient Jewish Epitaphs: An Introductory Survey of a Millennium of Jewish Funerary Epigraphy (300 BCE–700 CE)* (Contributions to Biblical Exegesis and Theology, 2). Kampen, Netherlands: Kok Pharos.

———. 1994. The Birkat Ha-minim in Recent Research. In *Hellenism—Judaism—Christianity: Essays on Their Interaction*, 99–111. Kampen: Kok Pharos.

Horton, Fred L., Jr. 1987. Parenthetical Pregnancy: The Conception and Birth of Jesus in Matthew 1:18–25. *SBL 1987 Seminar Papers*, 175–89. Missoula, Mont.: Scholars Press.

House, Paul R., ed. 1992. *Beyond Form Criticism: Essays in Old Testament Literary Criticism.* Winona Lake, Ind.: Eisenbrauns.

Howell, David B. 1990. *Matthew's Inclusive Story: A Study in the Narrative Rhetoric of the First Gospel.* Sheffield, England: Sheffield Academic Press.

Hsia, R. Po-Chia. 1992. *Trent 1475: Stories of a Ritual Murder Trial.* New Haven, Conn.: Yale University Press, with Yeshiva University Library.

Hubert, J. J. 1980. Linguistic Indicators. *Social Indicators Research* 8: 223–55.

Hübner, Hans. 1984a. *Gottes Ich und Israel.* Göttingen, Germany: Vandenhoeck & Ruprecht.

———. 1984b. *Law in Paul's Thought.* Edinburgh: T. & T. Clark.

Hughes, Frank W. 1989. *Early Christian Rhetoric and 2 Thessalonians.* Sheffield, England: Sheffield Academic Press.

Humphries, Mark. 1998. Trading Gods in Northern Italy. In *Trade, Traders and the Ancient City*, ed. Helen Parkins and Christopher Smith, 203–24. London: Routledge.

Hurtado, Larry W. 1988. *One God, One Lord: Early Christian Devotion and Ancient Jewish Monotheism.* Philadelphia: Fortress.

———. 1995. Convert, Apostate, or Apostle to the Nations: The "Conversion" of Paul in Recent Scholarship. *Studies in Religion* 22: 273–84.

Huzar, Eleanor G. 1988. Alexandria ad Aegyptum in the Julio-Claudian Age. *Aufstieg und Niedergang der römischen Welt* II.10.1: 619–68.

Hyland, Susan E. 1998. *Special Birth Narratives: An Analysis of the Scriptural Narratives as Compared with their Contemporary Literature.* Unpublished Ph.D. thesis, Fuller Theological Seminary.

Ilan, Tal. 1992. "Man Born of Woman. . . ." (Job 14:1): The Phenomenon of Men Bearing Matronyms at the Time of Jesus. *Novum Testamentum* 34: 23–45.

Isaac, Benjamin. 1984. Bandits in Judaea and Arabia. *Harvard Studies in Classical Philology* 88.

———. 1990. *The Limits of Empire: The Roman Army in the East.* Oxford: Clarendon.

———. 1992. Banditry. In *Anchor Bible Dictionary*, ed. David Noel Freedman, vol. 1, 575–80. Garden City, N.Y.: Doubleday.

Isajiw, Waevolod. 1969. *Causation and Functionalism in Sociology.* London: Routledge & Kegan Paul.

Jackson, Bernard S. 1972. *Theft in Early Jewish Law.* Oxford: Clarendon.

Jackson, H. M. 1975. The Resurrection Belief of the Earliest Church: A Response to the Failure of Prophecy? *JR* 55: 415–25.

———. 1986. *The Thessalonian Correspondence.* Philadelphia: Fortress.

James, William. 1958 [1902]. *The Varieties of Religious Experience.* New York: New American Library.

Jarvie, I. C. 1973. *Functionalism.* Minneapolis, Minn.: Burgess.

Jeffers, James S. 1991. *Conflict at Rome: Social Order and Hierarchy in Early Christianity.* Minneapolis, Minn.: Fortress.

———. 1999. *The Greco-Roman World of the New Testament Era: Exploring the Background of Early Christianity.* Downers Grove, Ill.: InterVarsity.

Jenkins, Alan. 1979. *The Social Theory of Claude Lévi-Strauss.* London: Macmillan.

Jenkins, Richard. 1996. *Social Identity.* London: Routledge.

Jeremias, Joachim. 1969 [1933]. *Jerusalem in the Time of Jesus.* London: SCM Press.

Jervell, Jakob. 1971. Der Brief nach Jerusalem: Über Veranlassung und Adresse des Römerbriefs. *Studia Theologica* 25: 61–73.

Jewett, Robert. 1985. The Law and the Coexistence of Jews and Gentiles in Romans. *Interpretation* 39: 341–56.

———. 1986. *The Thessalonian Correspondence: Pauline Rhetoric and Millenarian Piety.* Philadelphia: Fortress.

———. 1993. Tenement Churches and Communal Meals in the Early Church: The Implications of a Form-Critical Analysis of 2 Thessalonians 3:10. *Biblical Research* 38: 23–43.

Joas, Hans. 1985. *G. H. Mead: A Contemporary Re-examination of his Thought.* Trans. Raymond Meyer. Cambridge, Mass.: MIT Press. [Originally *Praktische Intersubjektivität:. Die Entwicklung des Werkes von George Herbert Mead.* Frankfurt: Suhrkamp, 1980.]

Johanson, Bruce C. 1987. *To All the Brethren: A Textlinguistic and Rhetorical Approach to 1 Thessalonians.* Stockholm: Almquist & Wiksell International.

Johnson, E. Elizabeth. 1989. *Apocalyptic and Wisdom in Romans 9–11.* Missoula, Mont.: Scholars Press.

Johnson, Luke Timothy. 1997. *Reading Romans.* New York: Crossroad.

———. 1999. *The Writings of the New Testament,* rev. ed. London: SCM; *The Writings of the New Testament: An Interpretation.* Philadelphia: Fortress, 1986.

Johnson, Paul. 1976. *A History of Christianity.* New York: Athenaeum.

Jones, Arnold H. M. 1940. *The Greek City from Alexander to Justinian.* Oxford: Clarendon.

———. 1948. *Ancient Economic History.* Ed. P. A. Brunt. London: H. K. Lewis.

———. 1958. The Roman Colonate. *Past and Present* 13: 1–13.

———. 1960. Church Finances in the Fifth and Sixth Centuries. *Journal of Theological Studies* NS 11, I: 84–94.

———. 1963. The Social Background of the Struggle between Paganism and Christianity. In *The Conflict between Paganism and Christianity in the Fourth Century,* ed. Arnaldo Momigliano. Oxford: Clarendon.

———. 1964. *The Later Roman Empire 284–602.* Oxford: Basil Blackwell.

———. 1971. *The Cities of the Eastern Roman Provinces.* 2nd ed. Oxford: Clarendon Press.

———. 1974. *The Roman Economy: Studies in Ancient Economic and Administrative History.* Ed. P. A. Brunt. Totowa, N.J.: Rowman & Littlefield.

Judge, Edwin A. 1960. *The Social Patterns of Christian Groups in the First Century.* London: Tyndale.

———. 1980. The Social Identity of the First Christians: A Question of Method in Religious History. *JRH* 11: 201–17.

————, and S. R. Pickering. 1977. Papyrus Documentation of Church and Community in Egypt to the Mid-Fourth Century. *Jahbuch für Antike und Christentum* 20: 47–71.

Kajanto, Iiro. 1963. Onomastic Studies in the Early Christian Inscriptions of Rome and Carthage. *Acta Instituti Romani Finlandiae* 2: 1–141.

Kanter, Rosabeth M. 1992. *Commitment and Community.* Cambridge, Mass.: Harvard University Press.

Kapelrud, Arvid Schou. 1963. *The Ras Shamra Discoveries and the Old Testament.* Norman: University of Oklahoma Press.

Käsemann, Ernst. 1969. On the Subject of Primitive Christian Apocalyptic. In *New Testament Questions of Today*, 108–37. Philadelphia: Fortress.

Kasher, Aryeh. 1985. *The Jews in Hellenistic and Roman Egypt.* Tübingen, Germany: J. C. B. Mohr (Paul Siebeck).

————. 1990. *Jews and Hellenistic Cities in Eretz-Israel: Relations of the Jews in Eretz-Israel with the Hellenistic Cities During the Second Temple Period (332 BCE–70 CE)* (Texte und Studien zum Antiken Judentum 7). Tübingen, Germany: J. C. B. Mohr (Paul Siebeck).

Käsler, Dirk. 1988. *Max Weber: An Introduction to His Life and Work.* Trans. Philippa Hurd. Chicago: University of Chicago Press. [Originally *Einführung in das Studium Max Webers.* München, Germany: C. H. Beck'sche, 1979.]

Kautsky, John H. 1982. *The Politics of Aristocratic Empires.* Chapel Hill: University of North Carolina Press.

Kautsky, Karl. 1910/1925. *Der Ursprung des Christentums: Eine historische Untersuchung.* Stuttgart, Germany: J. H. W. Dietz; *Foundations of Christianity: A Study in Christian Origins.* New York: International.

Keck, Leander E. 1974. On the Ethos of the Early Christians. *JAAR* 42: 435–52.

Kecskes, Robert, and Christof Wolf. 1996. *Konfession, Religion und soziale Netzwerke: Zur Bedeutung christlicher Religiosität in personalen Beziehungen.* Opladen, Germany: Leske & Budrich.

Kee, Alistair. 1985. The Imperial Cult: The Unmasking of an Ideology. *Scottish Journal of Religious Studies* 6: 112–28.

Kee, Howard Clark. 1980. *Christian Origins in Sociological Perspective: Methods and Resources.* Philadelphia: Westminster.

————. 1985. Sociology of the New Testament. *HBD*: 961–68.

————. 1989. *Knowing the Truth: A Sociological Approach to the New Testament Interpretation.* Minneapolis, Minn.: Fortress.

————. 1995. *Who Are the People of God? Early Christian Models of Community.* New Haven, Conn.: Yale University.

Kennedy, George A. 1980. *Classical Rhetoric and Its Christian and Secular Tradition from Ancient to Modern Times.* Chapel Hill: University of North Carolina Press.

————. 1984. *New Testament Interpretation through Rhetorical Criticism.* Chapel Hill: University of North Carolina Press.

————. 1998. *Comparative Rhetoric: An Historical and Cross-Cultural Introduction.* Oxford: Oxford University Press.

Keppie, Lawrence. 1991. *Understanding Roman Inscriptions.* Baltimore, Md.: Johns Hopkins University Press.

Keresztes, Paul. 1989. *Imperial Rome and the Christians: From Herod the Great to about 200 A.D., vol. 1.* Lanham, Md.: University Press of America.

Kessler, Martin. 1982. A Methodological Setting for Rhetorical Criticism. In *Art and Meaning: Rhetoric in Biblical Literature*, ed. D. Clines, D. Gunn, and A. Hauser, 1–19. Sheffield, England: Sheffield Academic Press.

Kimelman, Reuven. 1980–81. *Birkat ha-minim* and the Lack of Evidence for an Anti-Christian Jewish Prayer in Late Antiquity. In *Jewish and Christian Self-Definition*, 2 vols., ed. Ed Parish Sanders, 226–44, 291–403. Philadelphia: Fortress.

Kivisto, Peter. 2000. *Social Theory: Roots and Branches.* Los Angeles: Roxbury Publishing.

Klassen, William. 1992. Kiss (NT). In *Anchor Bible Dictionary*, ed. David Noel Freedman, vol. 4, 89–92. Garden City, N.Y.: Doubleday.

Klausner, J. 1975 [1930]. The Economy of Judea in the Period of the Second Temple. In *The World History of the Jewish People. First Series: Ancient Times. Vol. 7: Herodian Period*, 179–205 London: Allen.

Klijn, A. F. J., and G. J. Reinink. 1973. *Patristic Evidence for Jewish-Christian Sects.* Leiden: E. J. Brill.

Kloppenborg, John S. 1988. *Q Parallels: Synopsis, Critical Notes & Concordance.* Sonoma, Calif.: Polebridge.

———. 1993. Edwin Hatch, Churches and Collegia. In *Origins and Method: Towards a New Understanding of Judaism and Christianity*, ed. B. H. Maclean, 212–38. Sheffield, England: JSOT Press.

———. 2000. Isaiah 5:1–7, the Parable of the Tenants and Vineyard Leases on Papyrus. In *Text and Artifact in the Religions of Mediterranean Antiquity: Studies in Honour of Peter Richardson*, ed. Stephen G. Wilson and Michel Desjardins, 111–34. Waterloo, Ont.: Wilfrid Laurier University Press.

———, Marvin W. Meyer, Stephen J. Patterson, and Michael G. Steinhauser. 1990. *Q Thomas Reader.* Sonoma, Calif.: Polebridge.

Kloppenborg, John S., and Stephen G. Wilson, eds. 1996. *Voluntary Associations in the Graeco-Roman World.* London: Routledge.

Klutz, Todd E. 1998. The Rhetoric of Science in the Rise of Christianity: A Response to Rodney Stark's Sociological Account of Christianisation. *JECS* 6: 162–84.

Knight, Douglas. 1990. Sources, Literary. In *Mercer Dictionary of the Bible*, ed. Watson E. Mills, 852–53. Macon, Ga.: Mercer University Press.

Knipfing, John R. 1923. The Libelli of the Decian Persecution. *Harvard Theological Review* 16: 345–90.

Koch, Hal. 1932. *Pronoia und Paideusis: Studien Über Origenes und sein Verhaltnis zum Platonismus.* Berlin: Walter de Gruyter.

Koch, Klaus. 1983. Is There a Doctrine of Retribution in the Old Testament? In *Theodicy in the Old Testament*, ed. James L. Crenshaw, 57–87. Philadelphia: Fortress.

Koester, Helmut. 1968. Nomoe Physios: The Concept of Natural Law in Greek Thought. In *Religions in Antiquity*, ed. Jacob Neusner, 521–41. Leiden: Reidel.

———. 1971. Gnomai Diaphnoi: The Origins and Nature of Diversification in the History of Early Christianity. In *Trajectories through Early Christianity*, ed. James Robinson and Helmut Koester. Philadelphia: Fortress.

———. 1997. Imperial Ideology and Paul's Eschatology in 1 Thessalonians. In *Paul and Empire: Religion and Power in Roman Imperial Society*, ed. Richard A. Horsley, 158–66. Harrisburg, Penn.: Trinity Press International.

Kohlberg, Lawrence. 1981. *Essays on Moral Development.* 2 vols. San Francisco: Harper & Row.

Kraabel, Alf Thomas. 1981. The Disappearance of the "God-Fearers." *Numen* 28: 113–26.

———. 1982. The Roman Diaspora: Six Questionable Assumptions. *Journal of Jewish Studies* 33: 445–64.

Kramer, Hans J. 1964. *Der Ursprung der Geistmetaphysik.* Amsterdam: J. Schippers.

Kreissig, Heinz. 1968. Die Landwirtschaftliche Situation in Palästina vor dem judäischen Krieg. *Acta Antiqua* 17: 223–54.

———. 1970. *Die sozialen Zusammenhänge des judäischen Krieges* (Schriften zur Geschichte und Kultur der Antike, 1). Berlin: Akademi Verlag.

———. 1989. A Marxist View of Josephus' Account of the Jewish War. In *Josephus, the Bible, and History*, ed. Louis H. Feldman and G. Hata. Detroit, Mich.: Wayne State University Press.

Kreitzer, Larry J. 1996. *Striking New Images: Roman Imperial Coinage and the New Testament World: Journal for the Study of the New Testament Supplement Series 134.* Sheffield, England: Sheffield Academic Press.

Kretschmar, Georg, 1966, The Councils of the Ancient Church. In *The Councils of the Church: History and Analysis*, ed. Hans Jochen Margull and trans. Walter F. Bense, 1–81. Philadelphia: Fortress.

Kriesberg, Louis. 1973. *The Sociology of Social Conflicts.* Englewood Cliffs, N.J.: Prentice Hall.

Kselman, John S., and Ronald D. Witherup. 1990. Modern New Testament Criticism. In *The New Jerome Biblical Commentary*, ed. Raymond E. Brown, Joseph A. Fitzmyer, and Roland E. Murphy, 1130–45. Englewood Cliffs, N.J.: Prentice Hall.

Kuhn, Thomas S. 1970. *The Structure of Scientific Revolutions.* 2nd ed. Chicago: University of Chicago Press.

Kyrtatas, Dimitris J. 1987. *The Social Structure of the Early Christian Communities.* London: Verso.

———. 1995. Slavery as Progress: Pagan and Christian Views of Slavery as Moral Training. *International Sociology* 10: 219–34.

———. 2002. Domination and Exploitation. In *Money, Labour and Land: Approaches to the Economies of Ancient Greece*, ed. Paul Cartledge, Edward E. Cohen, and Lia Foxhall. London: Routledge.

Lambert, W. G. 1960. *Babylonian Wisdom Literature.* Oxford: Clarendon.

Lampe, Peter. 1991. The Roman Christians of Romans 16. In *The Romans Debate*, ed. Karl Peter Donfried, 216–30. Edinburgh: T. & T. Clark.

Lapin, Lawrence L. 1973. *Statistics for Modern Business Decisions.* New York: Harcourt Brace Jovanovich.

Lash, Scott, and Sam Whimster. 1987. *Max Weber, Rationality and Modernity.* London: Allen & Unwin.

674 REFERENCES

Lategan, Bernard C. 1992. The Argumentative Situation of Galatians. *Neotestamentica* 26: 257–77.

Latourette, Kenneth Scott. 1953. *A History of Christianity.* New York: Harper & Row.

Latte, Kurt. 1960. *Römische Religionsgeschichte.* Munich: Beck, 1960.

Lattimore, Richmond. 1962. *Themes in Greek and Latin Epitaphs.* Urbana: University of Illinois Press.

Laurence, Ray. 1994. *Roman Pompeii: Space and Society.* London: Routledge.

Laurentin, R. 1957. *Structure et Théologie de Luc I–II.* Paris: Gabalda.

Lausberg, Heinrich. 1998. *Handbook of Literary Rhetoric: A Foundation for Literary Study.* Leiden: E. J. Brill.

Lee, Clarence. 1971. Social Unrest and Primitive Christianity. In *The Catacombs and the Colosseum: The Roman Empire as the Setting of Primitive Christianity,* ed. Stephen Benko and John J. O'Rourke, 121–38. Valley Forge, Penn.: Judson.

Lenski, Gerhard E. 1966. *Power and Privilege: A Theory of Social Stratification.* New York: McGraw-Hill.

Leon, Harry J. 1995 [1960]. *The Jews of Ancient Rome.* 2nd ed. Peabody, Mass.: Hendrickson.

Levenson, Jon Douglas. 1993. *The Death and Resurrection of the Beloved Son: The Transformation of Child Sacrifice in Judaism and Christianity.* New Haven, Conn.: Yale University Press.

Lévi-Strauss, Claude. 1963. *Structural Anthropology.* New York: Basic Books.

Levin, Jack, and James Fox. 2000. *Elementary Statistics in Social Research.* 8th ed. Boston: Allyn & Bacon.

Levine, Lee I. 1998. *Judaism and Hellenism in Antiquity.* Seattle: University of Washington Press.

Lewis, C. T., and C. Short. 1879. *Harpers' Latin Dictionary: A New Latin Dictionary Founded on the Translation of Freund's Latin-German Lexicon Edited by E. A. Andrews.* New York: American Book.

Lewis, Naphtali. 1983. *Life in Egypt under Roman Rule.* Oxford: Clarendon.

Liddell, Henry George, and Robert Scott. 1977. *A Greek-English Lexicon.* 9th ed. Oxford: Oxford University Press.

Lietzmann, Hans. 1949. *An die Korinther I, II.* Tübingen, Germany: Mohr (Siebeck).

———. 1961. *A History of the Early Church. Vol. 2, The Founding of the Church Universal.* Trans. Bertram Lee Woolf. Cleveland: World.

Lightstone, Jack. 1984. *The Commerce of the Sacred: The Mediation of the Divine among Jews in the Greco-Roman Diaspora.* Chico, Calif.: Scholars Press.

Lincoln, Andrew. 1981. *Paradise Now and Not Yet.* Cambridge: Cambridge University Press.

Linton, Ralph. 1936. *The Study of Man: An Introduction. Student's Edition.* New York: D. Appleton-Century.

Liska, Allen E., ed. 1992. *Social Threat and Social Control.* Albany: State University of New York Press.

Lloyd, Christopher. 1986. *Explanation in Social History.* Oxford: Blackwell.

———. 1993. *The Structures of History.* Oxford: Blackwell.

Lofland, John. 1994. Review of *Understanding Religious Conversion,* by Lewis R. Rambo. *Sociology of Religion* 55: 99–100.

————, and Rodney Stark. 1965. Becoming a World-Saver: A Theory of Conversion to a Deviant Perspective. *American Sociological Review* 30: 862–75.

Longenecker, Bruce Ward. 1989. Different Answers to Different Issues: Israel, the Gentiles, and Salvation History in Romans 9 –11. *Journal for the Study of the New Testament* 36: 95–123.

————. 1991. *Eschatology and the Covenant.* Sheffield, England: JSOT Press.

————. 1998. *The Triumph of Abraham's God.* Edinburgh: T. & T. Clark.

Longenecker, Richard Norman. 1990. *Galatians.* Waco, Tex.: Word.

Lovejoy, Arthur O. 1936. *The Great Chain of Being.* Cambridge, Mass.: Harvard University Press.

Lüdemann, Gerd. 1989. *Early Christianity According to the Traditions in Acts.* Trans. John Bowden. Minneapolis, Minn.: Fortress; London: SCM.

————. 1998. *Virgin Birth? The Real Story of Mary and Her Son Jesus.* Harrisburg, Penn.: Trinity Press International.

Luttwak, Edward N. 1976. *The Grand Strategy of the Roman Empire.* Baltimore, Md.: Johns Hopkins University Press.

Maccoby, Hyam. 1992. *Judas Iscariot and the Myth of Jewish Evil.* New York: Free Press.

MacDonald, Dennis Ronald. 1983. *The Legend and the Apostle: The Battle for Paul in Story and Canon.* Philadelphia: Westminster.

MacDonald, Margaret Y. 1988. *The Pauline Churches: A Socio-Historical Study of Institutionalization in the Pauline and Deutero-Pauline Writings* (SNTSMS 60). Cambridge: Cambridge University Press.

————. 1996. *Early Christian Women and Pagan Opinion: The Power of Hysterical Women.* New York: Cambridge University Press.

Mack, Burton L. 1988. *A Myth of Innocence: Mark and Christian Origins.* Philadelphia: Fortress.

————. 1990. *Rhetoric and the New Testament.* Minneapolis, Minn.: Fortress.

————. 1993. *The Lost Gospel: The Book of Q and Christian Origins.* San Francisco: Harper.

————, and Vernon K. Robbins. 1989. *Patterns of Persuasion in the Gospels.* Sonoma, Calif.: Polebridge.

MacKay, D. Bruce. 2000. Ethnicity. In *Guide to the Study of Religion,* ed. Willi Braun and Russell McCutcheon, 96–109. New York: Cassell.

MacMullen, Ramsay. 1966. *Enemies of the Roman Order: Treason, Unrest, and Alienation in the Empire.* Cambridge, Mass.: Harvard University Press.

————. 1974a. Peasants during the Principate. *Aufstieg und Niedergang der römischen Welt* 2.1: 253–61.

————. 1974b. *Roman Social Relations 50 B.C. to A.D. 284.* New Haven, Conn.: Yale University.

————. 1981. *Paganism in the Roman Empire.* New Haven, Conn.: Yale University Press.

————. 1984. *Christianizing the Roman Empire (A.D. 100–400).* New Haven, Conn.: Yale University Press.

————. 2000. *Romanization in the Time of Augustus.* New Haven, Conn.: Yale University Press.

Macro, A. D. 1980. The Cities of Asia Minor under the Roman Imperium. *Aufstieg und Niedergang der römischen Welt* II.7.2: 658–97.

Magill, Frank N., ed. *International Encyclopedia of Sociology.* Vol. 2. London: Fitzroy & Dearborn.

Mahaffy, Kimberly A. 1996. Cognitive Dissonance and Its Resolution: A Study of Lesbian Christians. *Journal for the Scientific Study of Religion* 35, 4: 392–402.

Maier, Harry O. 1991. *The Social Setting of the Ministry as Reflected in the Writings of Hermas, Clement and Ignatus* (Dissertations SR 1). Waterloo, Ont.: Wilfrid Laurier University.

Maine, Henry Sumner. 1861. *Ancient Law.* Notes by F. Pollock. Glouster, Mass.: Peter Smith.

Malamud, Bernard. 1968. *The Fixer.* New York: Dell.

Malbon, Elizabeth S. 1991. *Narrative Space and Mythic Meaning in Mark.* Sheffield, England: JSOT Press.

Malherbe, Abraham J. 1977. *Social Aspects of Early Christianity.* 2nd ed. Baton Rouge: Louisiana State University. Press. Philadelphia: Fortress.

———. 1986. *Moral Exhortation, A Greco-Roman Sourcebook* (Library of Early Christianity 4). Philadelphia: Westminster.

Malina, Bruce J. 1981/1993. *The New Testament World: Insights from Cultural Anthropology.* Atlanta: John Knox. Rev. ed., Louisville: Westminster John Knox.

———. 1982. The Social Sciences and Biblical Interpretation. *Int* 36: 229–42.

———. 1985. Review of W. Meeks, *The First Urban Christians. Journal of Biblical Literature* 104: 346–49.

———. 1986a. *Christian Origins and Cultural Anthropology: Practical Models for Biblical Interpretation.* Atlanta: John Knox.

———. 1986b. Normative Dissonance and Christian Origins. *Semeia* 35: 35–59.

———. 1991a. Honor and Shame in Luke–Acts: Pivotal Values of the Mediterranean World. In *The Social World of Luke–Acts: Model for Interpretation,* ed. Jerome H. Neyrey, 25–66. Peabody, Mass.: Hendrickson.

———. 1991b. First-Century Personality: Dyadic, Not Individualistic. In *The Social World of Luke–Acts: Model for Interpretation,* ed. Jerome H. Neyrey, 67–96. Peabody, Mass.: Hendrickson.

———. 1996a. *Portraits of Paul: An Archaeology of Ancient Personality,* Louisville, Ky.: Westminster John Knox.

———. 1996b. *The Social World of Jesus and the Gospels.* London: Routledge.

———. 1997. Review of R. Stark, *The Rise of Christianity. Catholic Biblical Quarterly* 59: 593–95.

———. 2000. *The Social Gospel of Jesus: The Kingdom of God in Mediterranean Perspective.* Minneapolis, Minn.: Augsburg Fortress.

———, and Jerome H. Neyrey. 1988. *Calling Jesus Names: The Social Value of Labels in Matthew* (Foundations & Facets. Social Facets), Sonoma, Calif.: Polebridge.

Malina, B. J., and R. L. Rohrbaugh. 1992. *Social Science Commentary on the Synoptic Gospels.* Minneapolis, Minn.: Fortress.

Malinowski, Bronislaw. 1954 [1948]. *Magic, Science and Religion.* Garden City, N.Y.: Doubleday.

Malony, H. Newton, and Samuel Southard, eds. *Handbook of Religious Conversion.* Birmingham, Ala.: Religious Education Press.

Mann, Michael. 1986. *The Sources of Social Power. Vol 1, A History of Power from the Beginning to A.D. 1760*. Cambridge: Cambridge University Press.

Manson, T. W. 1951. The Cleansing of the Temple. *Bulletin of the John Rylands Library* 33: 271–82.

Marcus, Joel. 1999. *Mark 1–8*. Garden City, N.Y.: Doubleday.

———. 2000. Mark—Interpreter of Paul. *New Testament Studies* 46: 473–87.

Marius, Richard. 1999. *A Short Guide to Writing about History*. 3rd ed. New York: Longman.

Markus, Robert A. 1974. *Christianity in the Roman World* (Currents in the History of Culture and Ideas). London: Thames & Hudson.

———. 1980–81. The Problem of self-Definition: From Sect to Church. In *Jewish and Christian Self-Definition*. 2 vols., ed. Ed Parish Sanders, 1–15. Philadelphia: Fortress.

———. 1990. *The End of Ancient Christianity*. Cambridge: Cambridge University Press.

Marshall, Peter. 1987. *Enmity in Corinth: Social Conventions in Paul's Relations with the Corinthians* (WUNT 2, 23). Tübingen, Germany: Mohr.

Martin, Dale B. 1990. *Slavery as Salvation: The Metaphor of Slavery in Pauline Christianity*. New Haven, Conn.: Yale University Press.

———. 1993. Social–Scientific Criticism. In *To Each Its Own Meaning: An Introduction to Biblical Criticism and Their Application*, ed. Stephen R. Haynes and Steven L. McKenzie, 103–19. Louisville, Ky.: Westminster/Knox.

———. 1995. *The Corinthian Body*, New Haven, Conn.: Yale University Press.

Martin, Ralph P. 1972. *Mark: Evangelist and Theologian*. Exeter, U.K.: Paternoster.

Martindale, Don. 1960. *The Nature and Types of Sociological Theory*. Boston: Houghton Mifflin.

Martyn, J. Louis. 1978. *The Gospel of John in Christian History*. New York: Paulist.

———. 1979. *History and Theology in the Fourth Gospel*. 2nd ed. Nashville, Tenn.: Abingdon.

Marucchi, Orazio. 1974. *Christian Epigraphy*. Trans. J. Armine Willis. Chicago: Ares.

Marx, Karl, and Friedrich Engels. 1957/1964. *On Religion*. Moscow: Foreign Languages Publishing House; New York: Schocken.

———. 1978a. *The Marx–Engels Reader*. 2nd ed. Ed. Robert C. Tucker. New York: Norton.

———. 1978b. The German Ideology: Part I. In Marx and Engels (1978a), 146–200.

———. 1978c. Wage, Labour, and Capital. In Marx and Engels (1978a), 203–17.

Mason, Hugh J. 1974. *Greek Terms for Roman Institutions: A Lexicon and Analysis* (American Studies in Papyrology, 13). Toronto: Hakkert.

Mattern, Susan. 1999. *Rome and the Enemy: Imperial Strategy in the Principate*. Berkeley: University of California Press.

Matthews, Fred H. 1977. *Quest for an American Sociology: Robert E. Park and the Chicago School*. Montréal: McGill-Queen's University Press.

Mauss, Michael. 2000. Ethnography. In *The Oxford Guide to Late Antiquity*, ed. Glen Bowersock and Peter Brown, 435–36. Oxford: Oxford University Press.

May, David M. 1991. *Social Scientific Criticism of the New Testament: A Bibliography* (NABPR Bibliography Series 4). Macon, Ga.: Mercer University Press.

Mayer, Anton. 1983. *Der zensierte Jesus: Soziologie des Neuen Testaments*. Olten-Friburg: Walter-Verlag.

Mayes, Andrew D. H. 1989. *The Old Testament in Sociological Perspective*. London: Marshall Pickering.

Mazzoleni, Danilo. 1999. Inscriptions in Roman Catacombs. In *The Christian Catacombs of Rome: History, Decoration, Inscriptions*, ed. Vincenzo Friocchi Nicolai et al. and trans. Cristina Carlo Stella and Lori-Ann Touchette, 146–85. Regensburg, Germany: Schnell & Steiner.

McCready, Wayne O. 1996. *Ekklesia* and Voluntary Associations. In *Voluntary Associations in the Graeco-Roman World*, ed. John S. Kloppenborg and Stephen G. Wilson, 59–73. London: Routledge.

McDonald, Lynn. 1993. *The Early Origins of the Social Sciences*. Kingston, Ont.: McGill-Queens University Press.

McGuire, Meredith B. 1981. *Religion: The Social Context*. Belmont, Calif.: Wadsworth.

McGuire, W. J. 1966. The Current Status of Cognitive Consistency Theories. In *Cognitive Consistency*, ed. S. Feldman, 1–46. New York: Academic Press.

McIver, Robert. 1997. Implications of New Data Pertaining to the Problem of Synoptic Relationships. *Australian Biblical Review* 45: 20–39.

McKay, A. G. 1975. *Houses, Villas, and Palaces of the Roman World*. Ithaca, N.Y.: Cornell University Press.

McKnight, Edgar V. 1969. *What Is Form Criticism?* Philadelphia: Fortress.

McKnight, Scot. 1991. *A Light among the Gentiles*. Minneapolis, Minn.: Fortress.

McVann, Mark Edward. 1991. Rituals of Status Transformation. In *The Social World of Luke–Acts: Model for Interpretation*, ed. Jermone H. Neyrey, 333–60. Peabody, Mass.: Hendrickson.

Mead, George H. 1934. *Mind, Self, and Society*. Chicago: University of Chicago Press.

Meade, David G. 1986. *Pseudonymity & Canon: An Investigation into the Relationship of Authorship and Authority in Jewish and Earliest Christian Tradition*. Grand Rapids, Mich.: Eerdmans.

Meagher, John. 1979. As the Twig Was Bent: Antisemitism in Greco-Roman and Early Christian Times. In *Anti-Semitism and the Foundations of Christianity*, ed. Alan Davies. New York: Paulist.

Meeks, Wayne A. 1972. The Man from Heaven in Johannine Sectarianism. *JBL* 91: 44–72. Reprinted in *The Interpretation of John* (Issues in Religion and Theology 9), ed. J. Ashton. Philadelphia: Fortress, 1986, 141–73.

———. 1975. "Am I a Jew?" Johannine Christianity and Judaism. In *Christianity, Judaism and Other Greco-Roman Cults: Studies for Morton Smith at Sixty*. Vol. I, ed. J. Neusner, 163–86. Leiden: E. J. Brill.

———. 1982. The Social Context of Pauline Theology. *Int* 36: 266–77.

———. 1983. *The First Urban Christians: The Social World of the Apostle Paul*. New Haven, Conn.: Yale University Press.

———. 1985. Breaking Away: Three New Testament Pictures of Christianity's Separation from the Jewish Community. In *To See Ourselves as Others See Us: Christians, Jews, "Others" in Late Antiquity*, ed. J. Neusner and E. Frerichs, 93–115. Chico, Calif.: Scholars Press.

———. 1993. *The Origins of Christian Morality: The First Two Centuries*. New Haven, Conn.: Yale University Press.

———. 1996. The Ethics of the Fourth Evangelist. In *Exploring the Gospel of John*, ed. R. Alan Culpepper and Clifton C. Black, 317–26. Louisville, Ky.: Westminster John Knox.

———, and Robert L. Wilken. 1978. *Jews and Christians in Antioch in the First Four Centuries of the Common Era.* Missoula, Mont.: Scholars Press.

Meggitt, Justin J. 1996. The Social Status of Erastus (Rom. 16:23). *NovT* 38: 218–23.

———. 1998a. Review of B. J. Malina, *The Social World of Jesus and the Gospels. Journal of Theological Studies* 49: 215–19.

———. 1998b. *Paul, Poverty and Survival.* Edinburgh: T. & T. Clark.

Meier, John P. 1991. *A Marginal Jew: Rethinking the Historical Jesus. Vol. I: The Roots of the Problem and the Person.* Garden City, N.Y.: Doubleday.

Mendels, Doron. 1992. *The Rise and Fall of Jewish Nationalism.* Garden City, N.Y.: Doubleday.

Merton, Robert K. 1948. The Self-Fulfilling Prophecy. *Antioch Review* (summer): 193–210.

———. 1968. *Social Theory and Social Structure.* New York: Free Press.

———. 1976. *Sociological Ambivalence and Other Essays.* New York: Free Press.

Metzger, Bruce M. 1968. *The Text of the New Testament: Its Transmission, Corruption, and Restoration.* New York: Oxford University Press.

———. 1971. *A Textual Commentary on the Greek New Testament.* 3d ed. New York: United Bible Societies.

———. 1987. *The Canon of the New Testament.* Oxford: Oxford University Press.

Milavec, Aaron. 1989. The Pastoral Genius of the *Didache*: An Analytical Translation and Commentary. In *Religious Writings and Religious Systems. Systemic Analysis of Holy Books in Christianity, Islam, Buddhism, Greco-Roman Religions, Ancient Israel, and Judaism. Volume Two. Christianity*, ed. Jacob Neusner, Ernest S. Frerichs, and Amy-Jill Levine, 89–125. Atlanta: Scholars Press.

Milbank, John. 1990. *Theology and Social Theory: Beyond Secular Reason.* Oxford: Blackwell.

Millar, Fergus. 1977. *The Emperor in the Roman World.* London: Duckworth.

———. 1987. Empire, Community and Culture in the Roman Near East: Greeks, Syrians, Jews and Arabs. *Journal of Jewish Studies* 38: 143–64.

Miller, Larry. 1999. La protestation sociale dans la première lettre de Pierre. *Social Compass* 46: 521–43.

Miller, Robert. 1992. *The Complete Gospels.* Riverbend, Mont.: Polebridge Press.

Mills, Edgar W. 1983. Sociological Ambivalence and Social Order: The Constructive Use of Normative Dissonance. *Sociology and Social Research* 67: 279–87.

Mitchell, J. Clyde. 1969. The Concept and Use of Social Networks. In *Social Networks in Urban Situations: Analyses of Personal Relationships in Central African Towns.* Manchester, England: Manchester University Press.

———. 1974. Social Networks. *Annual Review of Anthropology* 3: 279–99.

Mitchell, Margaret M. 1992. *Paul and the Rhetoric of Reconciliation: An Exegetical Investigation of the Language and Composition of 1 Corinthians.* Louisville, Ky.: Westminster/John Knox.

———. 1996. Review of Neil Elliott, *Liberating Paul. Catholic Biblical Quarterly* 58: 546–47.

Moehring, H. 1978. Arithmology as an Exegetical Tool in Philo of Alexandria. *Society of Biblical Literature Seminar Papers* (Series 13) I: 191–229.

Mohler, S. L. 1940. Slave Education in the Roman Empire. *Transactions and Proceedings of the American Philological Association* 71: 262–80.

Mol, Hans. 1976. *Identity and the Sacred: A Sketch for a New Social-Scientific Theory of Religion.* Oxford: Blackwell.

Moles, John. 1983. The Date and Purpose of the Fourth Kingship Oration of Dio Chrysostom. *Classical Antiquity* 2: 251–78.

Momigliano, Arnaldo. 1975. *Alien Wisdom: The Limits of Hellenization.* New York: Cambridge University Press.

———. 1986. Some Preliminary Remarks on the "Religious Opposition" to the Roman Empire. In *Opposition et Résistances à l'Empire d'Auguste à Trajan,* 23, ed. Adalberto Giovannini, 103–29. Geneva: Entretiens sur L'Antiquité Classique.

Moore, Stephen D. 1989. *Literary Criticism and the Gospels: The Theoretical Challenge.* New Haven, Conn.: Yale University Press.

Morenz, Siegfried. 1973. *Egyptian Religion.* Trans. Ann Kepp. Ithaca, N.Y.: Cornell University Press.

Morgenstern, Julius. 1966. *Some Significant Antecedents of Christianity.* Leiden: E. J. Brill.

Morrow, Raymond A., and David D. Brown. 1994. *Critical Theory and Methodology.* Thousand Oaks, Calif.: Sage.

Mosley, D. J. 1991. Calgacus: Clash of Roman and Native. In Images of Empire. *Journal of the Old Testament Supplement Series 122,* ed. Loveday Alexander, 107–21. Sheffield, England: Sheffield Academic Press.

Moxnes, Halvor. 1980. *Theology in Conflict.* Leiden: E. J. Brill.

———. 1988. *The Economy of the Kingdom: Social Conflict and Economic Relations in Luke's Gospel.* Philadelphia: Fortress.

Mueller, John H., Karl F. Schuessler, and Herbert L. Costner. 1977. *Statistical Reasoning in Sociology.* 3rd ed. Boston: Houghton Mifflin.

Munck, Johannes. 1967. *Christ and Israel.* Philadelphia: Fortress.

Munier, Charles. 1992. Labour. In *Encyclopedia of the Early Church,* ed. Angelo Di Berardino and trans. Adrian Walford. New York: Oxford University Press.

Munro, Winsome. 1975. *Authority in Paul and Peter.* Cambridge: Cambridge University Press.

Munslow, Alun. 1997. *Deconstructing History.* London: Routledge.

Murphy, Nancey C. 1994. *Reasoning and Rhetoric in Religion.* Valley Forge, Penn.: Trinity Press International.

Murphy, Roland. 1990. *The Tree of Life: Explorations of Biblical Wisdom Literature.* Garden City, N.Y.: Doubleday.

Myers, Ched. 1988. *Binding the Strong Man: A Political Reading of Mark's Story of Jesus.* Maryknoll, N.Y.: Orbis.

Nash, Manning. 1989. The Core Elements of Ethnicity. In *The Cauldron of Ethnicity in the Modern World,* ed. Manning Nash, 10–15. Chicago: University of Chicago Press.

Natanson, Maurice. 1974. Phenomenology and Social Role. In *Phenomenology, Role, and Reason: Essays on the Coherence and Deformation of Social Reality,* 190–214. Springfield, Ill.: Charles C. Thomas. [Originally in *Journal of the British Society for Phenomenology* 3 (1972).]

Neirynk, Frans. 1990. Synoptic Problem. In *The New Jerome Biblical Commentary,* ed. Raymond E. Brown, Joseph A. Fitzmyer, and Roland E. Murphy, 587–95. Englewood Cliffs, N.J.: Prentice Hall.

———. 1993. Literary Criticism, Old and New. In *The Synoptic Gospels: Source Criticism and the New Literary Criticism* (Bibliotheca Ephemeridum Theologicarum Lovaniensium 110), ed. Camille Focant, 11–38. Leuven, Belgium: Leuven University Press.

Nelson, Benjamin. 1981. *On the Roads to Modernity.* Ed. T. Hoff. Totowa, N.J.: Rowman & Littlefield.

Netzer, Ehud. 1993. Jericho. *New Encyclopedia of Archaeological Excavations in the Holy Land.* Vol. 2, 682–91. Jerusalem: IAA.

Neusner, Jacob. 1988. Wrong Ways in Historical Study [2]: "The Sermon on the Mount and the Sermon on the Plain" in Ancient Judaism. The Conception of "The Original Tradition," Dating Stories through their Contents, and Making Up Traditions—History in Contemporary Studies of Formative Judaism. In *Wrong Ways and Right Ways in the Study of Formative Judaism: Critical Method and Literature, History, and the History of Religion,* Jacob Neusner, 121–39. Atlanta: Scholars Press.

———. 1990. *The Economics of the Mishnah.* Chicago: University of Chicago Press.

———. 1991. *Studying Classical Judaism: A Primer.* Louisville, Ky.: Westminster/John Knox.

———, ed. 1975. *Christianity, Judaism and Other Greco-Roman Cults: Studies for Morton Smith at Sixty.* Leiden: E. J. Brill.

Neville, David J. 1994 *Arguments from Order in Synoptic Source Criticism: A History and Critique.* Macon, Ga.: Mercer University Press.

Neyrey, Jerome H. 1990. *Paul in Other Words: A Cultural Reading of his Letters.* Louisville, Ky.: Westminster/John Knox.

———. 1994. "Despising the Shame of the Cross": Honor and Shame in the Johannine Passion Narrative. *Semeia* 68: 113–37.

———. 1998. *Honor and Shame in the Gospel of Matthew.* Louisville, Ky.: Westminster/John Knox.

———, ed. 1991. *The Social World of Luke–Acts: Model for Interpretation.* Peabody, Mass.: Hendrickson.

Nida, Eugene A., J. P. Louw, and J. W. Cronje. 1983. *Style and Discourse: With Special Reference to the Greek New Testament.* Cape Town: Bible Society of South Africa.

Nielsen, Donald A. 1990. Max Weber and the Sociology of Early Christianity. In *Time, Place, and Circumstance: Neo-Weberian Studies in Comparative Religious History,* ed. W. H. Swatos, Jr., 87–102. New York: Greenwood.

———. 1991. Natural Law and Civilizations: Images of "Nature," Intracivilizational Polarities, and the Emergence of Heterodox Ideals. *Sociological Analysis* 52, 1: 55–76.

———. 1995. Number and Creation in Origen. Paper presented to the Workshop on the Sociology of Early Christianity, Canadian Learned Societies, June 3, 1995, Montreal.

———. 1996a. La Misura divine: Creazione e retribuzione nel libro della Sapienza e in Filone. Aspetti dell'incontro fra giudaismo ed ellenismo. *Religioni e Società* 11/24: 9–21.

———. 1996b. Pericles and the Plague: Civil Religion, Anomie and Injustice in Thucydides. *Sociology of Religion* 57, 4: 397–407.

———. 1999a. *Three Faces of God: Society, Religion and the Categories of Totality in the Philosophy of Emile Durkheim.* Albany: State University of New York Press.

———. 1999b. Simmel and Genesis. *Social Compass* 46, 4: 455–69.

Nijf, Onno M. van. 1997. *The Civic World of Professional Associations in the Roman East* (Dutch Monographs on Ancient History and Archaeology, 17). Amsterdam: J. C. Gieben.

Nikiprowetzky, Valentin. 1977. *Le Commentaire de l'Écriture chez Philo d'Alexandrie.* Leiden: E. J. Brill.

Nippel, Wilfried. 1995. *Public Order in Ancient Rome.* Cambridge: Cambridge University Press.

Nock, Arthur Darby. 1933. *Conversion: The Old and New in Religion from Alexander the Great to Augustine of Hippo.* Oxford: Oxford University Press.

Nutton, V. 1978. The Beneficial Ideology. In *Imperialism in the Ancient World,* ed. Peter D. A. Garnsey and C. R. Whittaker, 209–21. Cambridge: Cambridge University Press.

Oakman, Douglas E. 1986. *Jesus and the Economic Questions of His Day.* Lewiston, N.Y.: Mellen.

———. 1991. The Ancient Economy in the Bible. *BTB* 21: 34–39.

O'Collins, Gerald G. 1992. Crucifixion. In *Anchor Bible Dictionary,* ed. David Noel Freedman, vol. I, 1207–10. Garden City, N.Y.: Doubleday.

O'Dea, Thomas F. 1966. *The Sociology of Religion.* Englewood Cliffs, N.J.: Prentice Hall.

———. 1970. *Sociology of Religion and the Study of Religion.* New York: Basic Books.

O'Meara, Dominic J. 1989. *Pythagoras Revived: Mathematics and Philosophy in Late Antiquity.* Oxford: Clarendon.

Osborn, Ronald E. 1999. *Folly of God: The Rise of Christian Preaching.* St. Louis: Chalice.

Osiek, Carolyn. 1983. *Rich and Poor in the Shepherd of Hermas: An Exegetical Social Investigation.* Washington, D.C.: Catholic Biblical Association.

———. 1984. *What Are They Saying about the Social Setting of the New Testament?* New York: Paulist.

———. 1989. The New Handmaid: The Bible and the Social Sciences. *TS* 50: 260–78.

———, and David L. Balch. 1997. *Families in the New Testament World: Households and House Churches* (The Family, Religion, and Culture). Louisville, Ky.: Westminster/John Knox.

Østergård, Uffe. 1992. What Is National and Ethnic Identity? In *Ethnicity in Hellenistic Egypt,* ed. Per Bilde, 16–38. Aarhus, Denmark: Aarhus University Press.

Ouedraogo, Jean-Martin. 1997. Des religiosités de virtuoses aux religiosités masses: Aux origines du compromis selon Max Weber. *Social Compass* 44, 4: 611–25.

———. 1999. Esquisse d'une sociologie de la bible chez Max Weber. *Social Compass* 46, 4: 409–39.

Pagels, Elaine. 1989. *The Gnostic Gospels.* New York: Vintage.

Park, Robert E., and Ernest W. Burgess, eds. 1924. *Introduction to the Science of Sociology.* 2nd ed. Chicago: University of Chicago Press.

Parker, Judson Floyd. 1976. *Forester: A Language for Morphological Analysis of Hierarchical Systems, with Reference to Structural Exegesis of the Synoptic Traditions.* Unpublished Ph.D. dissertation, Vanderbilt University.

Parkins, Helen, and Christopher Smith, eds. 1998. *Trade, Traders and the Ancient City.* London: Routledge.

Parsons, Talcott. 1954. *Essays in Sociological Theory.* New York: Free Press.

———. 1966. *Societies: Evolutionary and Comparative Perspectives.* Englewood Cliffs, N.J.: Prentice Hall.

Patrick, Dale, and Alan Scult. 1990. *Rhetoric and Biblical Interpretation*. Sheffield, England: Sheffield Academic Press.

Patte, Daniel. 1976. *What Is Structural Exegesis?* Philadelphia: Fortress.

——, and Aline Patte. 1978. *Structural Exegesis: From Theory to Practice*. Philadelphia: Fortress.

Pearson, Birger A. 1971. I Thessalonians 2:13–16: Deutero-Pauline Interpretation. *Harvard Theological Review* 64: 79–94.

——, ed. 1975. *Religious Syncretism in Antiquity*. Missoula, Mont.: Scholars Press.

Perelman, C., and L. Olbrechts-Tyteca. 1969. *The New Rhetoric: A Treatise on Argumentation*. Notre Dame, Ind.: University of Notre Dame Press.

Peristiany, John D., ed. 1965. *Honor and Shame: The Values of Mediterranean Society*. London: Weidenfeld & Nicolson.

——, and Julian Pitt-Rivers, eds. 1992. *Honor and Grace in Anthropology*. Cambridge: Cambridge University Press.

Perrin, Norman. 1969. *What Is Redaction Criticism?* Philadelphia: Fortress Press.

Peters, Francis E. 1970. *The Harvest of Hellenism*. New York: Simon & Schuster.

Petersen, Norman R. 1978. *Literary Criticism for New Testament Critics*. Philadelphia: Fortress.

——. 1985. *Rediscovering Paul: Philemon and the Sociology of Paul's Narrative World*. Philadelphia: Fortress.

Piaget, Jean. 1970. *Structuralism*. New York: Basic Books.

Pilch, John J. 2000/2001. *Social Scientific Models for Interpreting the Bible: Essays by the Context Group in Honor of Bruce J. Malina*. Leiderdorp: Deo Publishing; Leiden: E. J. Brill.

Pilgrim, Walter E. 1999. *Uneasy Neighbors: Church and State in the New Testament. Overtures to Biblical Theology*. Minneapolis, Minn.: Fortress.

Pippidi, D. M., ed. 1976. *Assimilation et résistance à la culture gréco-romaine dans le monde ancien*. Bucharest: Editura Academiei.

Pippin, Tina. 1997. Ideological Criticisms, Liberation Criticisms, and Womanist and Feminist Criticisms. In *Handbook to Exegesis of the New Testament* (New Testament Tools and Studies 25), Stanley E. Porter, 267–75. Leiden: E. J. Brill.

Pleket, H. W. 1983. Urban Elites and Business in the Greek Part of the Roman Empire. In *Imperialism in the Ancient World*, ed. Peter D. A. Garnsey and C. R. Whittaker, 131–44, 203–7. Cambridge: Cambridge University Press.

——. 1984. Urban Elites and the Economy in the Greek Cities of the Roman Empire. *Münsterische Beiträge zur antiken Handelgeschichte* 3: 3–36.

Plett, H. F. 1985. Rhetoric. In *Discourse and Literature: New Approaches to the Analysis of Literary Genres*, ed. T. Van Dijk, 59–84. Amsterdam: John Benjamins.

Pohl, Walter. 1998. Introduction: Strategies of Distinction. In *Strategies of Distinction: The Construction of Ethnic Communities, 300–800*, ed. Walter Pohl and Helmut Reimitz, 1–16. Leiden: E. J. Brill.

——. 1998. Telling the Difference: Signs of Ethnic Identity. In *Strategies of Distinction: The Construction of Ethnic Communities, 300–800*, ed. Walter Pohl and Helmut Reimitz, 17–70. Leiden: E. J. Brill.

Poland, Franz. 1909. *Geschichte des griechischen Vereinswesens*. Leipzig, Germany: Teubner.

Polanyi, Karl. 1968. *Primitive, Archaic and Modern Economies: Essays of Karl Polanyi*. Garden City, N.Y.: Anchor.

————, Conrad M. Arensberg, and Harry W. Pearson, eds. 1957. *Trade and Market in the Early Empires*. New York: Free Press.

Porter, Stanley E., ed. 1997a. *Handbook of Classical Rhetoric in the Hellenistic Period*. Leiden: E. J. Brill.

————. 1997b. *Handbook to Exegesis of the New Testament* (New Testament Tools and Studies 25). Leiden: E. J. Brill.

————, and Thomas Olbricht, eds. 1993. *Rhetoric and the New Testament: Essays from the 1992 Heidelberg Conference*. Sheffield, England: Sheffield Academic Press.

Potter, David. 1993. Martyrdom as Spectacle. In *Theater and Society in the Classical World*, ed. Ruth Scodel, 53–88. Ann Arbor: University of Michigan Press.

————. 1994. *Prophets and Emperors: Human and Divine Authority from Augustus to Theodosius*. Cambridge, Mass.: Harvard University Press.

Powell, Mark Allen. 1996. Matthew's Beatitudes: Reversals and Rewards of the Kingdom. *Catholic Biblical Quarterly* 58: 460–79.

————. 1998. *The Jesus Debate: Modern Historians Investigate the Life of Christ*. Oxford: Lion; *Jesus as a Figure in History: How Modern Historians View the Man from Galilee*. Louisville, Ky.: Westminster/John Knox.

Price, Simon R. 1984. *Rituals and Power: The Roman Imperial Cult in Asia Minor*. Cambridge: Cambridge University Press.

Prus, Robert C. 1976. Religious Recruitment and the Management of Dissonance. *Sociological Inquiry* 46: 127–34.

————. 1996. *Symbolic Interaction and Ethnographic Research: Intersubjectivity and the Study of Human Lived Experience*. Albany: State University of New York Press.

Quasten, Johannes. 1986. *Patrology. Vol. 1: The Beginnings of Patristic Literature*. Westminster, Md.: Christian Classics.

Rad, Gerhard von. 1951. *Der Heilige Krieg im alten Israel*. Zürich: Zwingli-Verlag.

————. 1968. *Wisdom in Israel*. Nashville, Tenn.: Abingdon.

Radcliffe-Brown, A. R. 1952. *Structure and Function in Primitive Society*. London: Cohen & West.

Radday, Y. T., and Haim Shore. 1977a. An Inquiry into Homogeneity of the Book of Judges by Means of Discriminant Analysis. *Linguistic Biblica* 41/42: 21–34.

————. 1977b. Book of Judges Examined by Statistical Linguistics. *Biblica* 58: 469–99.

————, eds. 1985. *Genesis: An Authorship Study in Computer Assisted Statistical Linguistics*. Rome: Biblical Institute Press.

Radin, Max. 1915. *The Jews among the Greeks and Romans*. Philadelphia: Jewish Publication Society of America.

Radt, Wolfgang. 1988. *Pergamon: Geschichte und Bauten, Funde und Erforschung einer antiken Metropole*. Köhn: DuMont Buchverlag.

Räisänen, Heikki. 1985. Galatians 2.16 and Paul's Break with Judaism. *New Testament Studies* 31: 543–53.

————. 1986. *Paul and the Law*. Philadelphia: Fortress.

————. 1987. Paul's Conversion and the Development of his View of the Law. *New Testament Studies* 33: 404–19.

————. 1988. Paul, God, and Israel: Romans 9–11 in Recent Research. In *The Social World of Formative Christianity and Judaism*, ed. Jacob Neusner et al., 178–96. Philadelphia: Fortress.

Rajak, Tessa. 1991. Friends, Romans, Subjects: Agrippa II's Speech in *Josephus' Jewish War*. In Images of Empire. *Journal of the Old Testament Supplement Series 122*, ed. Loveday Alexander, 122–34. Sheffield, England: Sheffield Academic Press.

Rambo, Lewis R. 1989. Conversion: Toward a Holistic Model of Religious Change. *Pastoral Psychology* 38: 47–63.

————. 1993. *Understanding Religious Conversion*. New Haven, Conn.: Yale University Press.

Ramsay, William Mitchell. 1895–97. *The Cities and Bishoprics of Phrygia*. Oxford: Clarendon.

Rauschenbusch, Walter. 1991 [1907]. *Christianity and the Social Crisis*. Louisville, Ky.: Westminster/John Knox.

Reale, Giovanni. 1990. *A History of Ancient Philosophy, IV: The Schools of the Imperial Age*. Trans. and ed. John Caton. Albany: State University of New York Press.

Redfield, Robert. 1956. *Peasant Society and Culture*. Chicago: University of Chicago Press.

Reed, Jonathan L. 1999. Galileans, "Israelite Village Communities," and the Sayings Gospel Q. In *Galilee through the Centuries*, ed. Eric M. Meyers, 87–108. Winona Lake, Ind.: Eisenbrauns.

————. 2000. *Archaeology and the Galilean Jesus: A Re-examination of the Evidence*. Harrisburg, Penn.: Trinity Press International.

Reese, James M. 1970. *Hellenistic Influences on the Book of Wisdom and Its Consequences*. Rome: Biblical Institute Press.

Refoulé, F. 1991. Cohérence ou incohérence de Paul en Romains 9–11. *Revue Biblique* 98: 51–79.

Reinhold, Meyer. 1946. Historian of the Classic World: A Critique of Rostovtzeff. *Science & Society* 10: 361–91.

Remus, Harold E. 1982. Sociology of Knowledge and the Study of Early Christianity. *SR* 11: 45–56.

————. 1983. *Pagan–Christian Conflict over Miracle in the Second Century*. Cambridge Mass.: Philadelphia Patristic Foundation.

————. 1986. Justin Martyr's Argument with Judaism. In *Anti-Judaism in Early Christianity. Vol. 2: Separation and Polemic*, ed. Stephen G. Wilson, 59–80. Waterloo, Ont.: Wilfrid Laurier University Press.

————. 1987. Inside/Outside: Celsus on Jewish and Christian *Nomoi*. In *New Perspectives on Ancient Judaism. Vol. 2, Religion, Literature, and Society in Ancient Israel, Formative Christianity, and Judaism*, ed. Jacob Neusner et al., 133–50. Lanham, Md.: University Press of America.

————. 1996. Voluntary Association and Networks: Aelius Aristides at the Asklepieion in Pergamum. In *Voluntary Associations in the Graeco-Roman World*, ed. John S. Kloppenborg and Stephen G. Wilson, 146–75. London: Routledge.

————. 1999. "Unknown and Yet Well-known": The Multiform Formation of Early Christianity. In *A Multiform Heritage: Studies on Early Judaism and Christianity in Honor of Robert A. Kraft*, ed. Benjamin G. Wright, 79–93. Atlanta: Scholars Press.

————. 2000. Apuleius to Symmachus (and Stops in Between): *Pietas*, Realia and the Empire. In *Text and Artifact in the Religions of Mediterranean Antiquity: Studies in Honour of Peter*

Richardson, ed. Stephen Wilson and Michel Desjardins, 527–50. Waterloo, Ont.: Wilfrid Laurier University Press.

Rémy, Jean, and Paul-André Turcotte. 1997. Compromis religieux et transactions sociales dans la sphère catholique. *Social Compass* 44, 4: 627–40.

Reuther, Rosemary. 1974. *Faith and Fratricide: The Theological Roots of Anti-Semitism.* New York: Seabury.

Reynolds, Joyce. 1977. Inscriptions. In *Excavations at Sidi Khrebish Benghazi (Berenice). Vol. I: Buildings, Coins, Inscriptions, Architectural Decoration,* ed. J. A. Lloyd, 233–54. Tripoli: Dept. of Antiquities, People's Socialist Libyan Arab Jamahiriya.

Reynolds, Paul Kenneth Baillie. 1926. *The Vigiles of Imperial Rome.* London: Oxford University Press.

Rich, John, and Graham Shipley, eds. 1993. *War and Society in the Roman World.* London: Routledge.

Richard, Pablo. 1995. *Apocalypse: A People's Commentary on the Book of Revelation. The Bible and Liberation Series.* Maryknoll, N.Y.: Orbis.

Richardson, Alan. 1952. *The Biblical Doctrine of Work.* London: SCM.

Richardson, J. S. 1991. *Imperium Romanum*: Empire and the Language of Power. *Journal of Religious Studies* 81: 1–9.

Richardson, James T. 1975. New Forms of Deviancy in a Fundamentalist Church: A Case Study. *Review of Religious Research* 16: 134–41.

———. 1992. Conversion Process in the New Religions. In *Handbook of Religious Conversion,* ed. H. Newton Malony and Samuel Southard, 78–89. Birmingham, Ala.: Religious Education Press.

Richardson, Lawrence, Jr. 1988. *Pompeii: An Architectural History.* Baltimore, Md.: Johns Hopkins University Press.

Richardson, Peter. 1986. From Apostles to Virgins: Romans 16 and the Roles of Women in the Early Church. *Toronto Journal of Theology* 2: 232–61.

———. 1992. Why Turn the Tables? Jesus' Protest in the Temple Precincts. In *SBL Seminar Papers 1992,* 507–23. Atlanta: Scholars Press.

———. 1996/1998. *Herod, King of the Jews and Friend of the Romans.* Columbia: University of South Carolina Press; Minneapolis: Fortress.

———. 1998. Augustan-Era Synagogues in Rome. In *Judaism and Christianity in First-Century Rome,* ed. Karl P. Donfried and Peter Richardson, 17–29. Grand Rapids, Mich.: Eerdmans.

———. 2000. First-Century Houses and Q's Setting. In *Christology, Controversy and Community: New Testament Studies in Honour of David R. Catchpole,* ed. David G. Horrell and Christopher M. Tuckett, 63–83. Leiden: E. J. Brill.

Richter, Philip J. 1984. Recent Sociological Approaches to the Study of the New Testament. *Religion* 14: 77–90.

Riddle, Donald W. 1931. *The Martyrs: A Study in Social Control.* Chicago: University of Chicago Press.

Riesner, Rainer. 1998. *Paul's Early Period.* Grand Rapids, Mich.: Eerdmans.

Ringe, Sharon. 1985. *Jesus, Liberation, and the Biblical Jubilee: Images for Ethics and Christology. Overtures to Biblical Theology 19.* Philadelphia: Fortress.

Riordan, Cornelius, and Allan Mazur. 1988. *Introductory Sociology Workbook*. New York: Harper & Row.

Rist, John M. 1967. *Plotinus: The Road to Reality*. New York: Cambridge University Press.

Ritzer, George. 1988. *Contemporary Sociological Theory*. 2nd ed. New York: Alfred A. Knopf.

———. 1992. *Classical Sociological Theory*. New York: McGraw–Hill.

———. 1996. *Modern Sociological Theory*. 4th ed. New York: McGraw-Hill.

———, ed. 1990. *Frontiers of Social Theory: The New Synthesis*. New York: Columbia University Press.

Rives, James B. 1995a. Human Sacrifice among Pagans and Christians. *Journal of Roman Studies* 85: 65–85.

———. 1995b. *Religion and Authority in Roman Carthage from Augustus to Constantine*. Oxford: Clarendon.

———. 1996. The Piety of a Persecutor. *Journal of Early Christian Studies* 4: 1–25.

———. 1999. The Decree of Decius and the Religion of the Empire. *Journal of Roman Studies* 89: 135–54.

Robbins, F. E. 1921. The Tradition of Greek Arithmology. *Classical Philology* 16: 97–123.

———. 1931. Arithmology in Philo Judaeus. *Classical Philology* 26: 345–61.

Robbins, Thomas. 1988. *Cults, Converts and Charisma: The Sociology of New Religious Movements*. Newbury Park, Calif.: Sage.

Robbins, Vernon K. 1984/1992. *Jesus the Teacher: A Socio-Rhetorical Interpretation of Mark*. Philadelphia: Fortress.

———. 1991. Luke–Acts: A Mixed Population Seeks a Home in the Roman Empire. In Images of Empire. *Journal of the Old Testament Supplement Series 122*, ed. Loveday Alexander, 201–21. Sheffield, England: Sheffield Academic Press.

———. 1995. Social-Scientific Criticism and Literary Studies. Prospects for Cooperation in Biblical Interpretation. In *Modelling Early Christianity: Social-Scientific Studies of the New Testament in Its Context*, ed. Philip Esler, 274–89. London: Routledge.

———. 1996a. *Exploring the Texture of Texts: A Guide to Socio-Rhetorical Interpretation*. Valley Forge, Penn.: Trinity Press.

———. 1996b. *The Tapestry of Early Christian Discourse: Rhetoric, Society and Ideology*. London: Routledge.

Robert, Louis. 1960. Épitaphes juives d'Éphèse et de Nicomédie. *Hellenica* 11–12: 381–413.

———. 1978. Documents d'Asie Mineure. *Bulletin de correspondance hellénique* 102: 395–543.

Robertson, Archibald, and Alfred Plummer. 1914. *A Critical and Exegetical Commentary on the First Epistle of St Paul to the Corinthians*. 2nd ed. Edinburgh: T. & T. Clark.

Robinson, H. W. 1944. The Nature Miracles of the Old Testament. *Journal of Theological Studies* 45: 1–12.

Robinson, John A. T. 1962. *Twelve New Testament Studies*. London: SCM.

Robinson, O. F. 1992. *Ancient Rome: City Planning and Administration*. London: Routledge.

———. 1995. *The Criminal Law of Ancient Rome*. London: Duckworth.

Robinson, W. Peter, ed. 1996. *Social Groups and Identities: Developing the Legacy of Henri Tajfel*. Oxford: Butterworth Heinemann.

Rodd, Cyril S. 1981. On Applying a Sociological Theory to Biblical Studies. *Journal for the Study of the Old Testament* 19: 95–106.

Rohrbaugh, Richard L., ed. 1996. *The Social Sciences and the New Testament Interpretation.* Peabody, Mass.: Hendrickson.

Romanucci-Ross, Lola, and George A. Ross, eds. 1995. *Ethnic Identity: Creation, Conflict and Accommodation.* 3rd ed. Walnut Creek, Calif.: AltaMira.

Rostovtzeff, Michael I. 1941. *The Social and Economic History of the Hellenistic World.* Oxford: Clarendon.

———. 1957 [1926]. In *The Social and Economic History of the Roman Empire*, Ed. P. M. Fraser. Oxford: Clarendon.

Roux, Jeanne, and Georges Roux. 1949. Un décret du politeuma des juifs de Bérénikè en Cyrénaïque au Musée Lapidaire de Carpentras. *Revue des études grecques* 62: 281–96.

Rowland, Christopher C. 1985. *Christian Origins. From Messianic Movement to Christian Religion.* Minneapolis, Minn.: Augsburg.

———, and Mark Corner. 1990. *Liberating Exegesis: The Challenge of Liberation Theology to Biblical Studies.* London: SPCK.

Rubin, Jeffrey Z., and George Levinger. 1995. Levels of Analysis: In Search of Generalizable Knowledge. In *Conflict, Cooperation, and Justice: Essays Inspired by the Work of Morton Deutsch*, ed. Barbara B. Bunker et al., 13–38. San Francisco: Jossey-Bass.

Runia, David. 1986. *Philo of Alexandria and the Timaeus of Plato.* Leiden: E. J. Brill.

Ryken, Leland. 1984. *The New Testament in Literary Criticism.* New York: Frederick Ungar.

———. 1992. *Words of Delight.* 2nd ed. Grand Rapids, Mich.: Baker.

Safrai, Shemuel. 1976. Home and Family. In S. Safrai and M. Stern (eds.), 728–92.

———, and M. Stern, eds. 1976. *The Jewish People in the First Century: Historical Geography, Political History, Social, Cultural and Religious Life and Institutions.* 2 vols. (Compendia Rerum Iudaicarum ad Novum Testamentum). Assen, Netherlands: Van Gorcum.

Safrai, Ze'ev. 1994. *The Economy of Roman Palestine.* London: Routledge.

Said, Edward. 1993/1994. *Culture and Imperialism.* New York: Knopf; New York: Vintage.

Saldarini, Anthony J. 1988. *Pharisees, Scribes and Sadducees in Palestinian Society: A Sociological Approach.* Wilmington, Del.: Michael Glazier.

Salisbury, Joyce E. 1997. *Perpetua's Passion: The Death and Memory of a Young Roman Woman.* London: Routledge.

Saller, Richard P. 1982. *Personal Patronage under the Empire.* Cambridge: Cambridge University Press.

Sanders, Ed Parish. 1977. *Paul and Palestinian Judaism.* London: SCM.

———. 1983. *Paul, the Law, and the Jewish People.* London: SCM.

———. 1985. *Jesus and Judaism.* London: SCM.

———. 1990. *Jewish Law from Jesus to the Mishnah.* Philadelphia: Trinity Press International.

———. 1992. *Judaism, Practice and Belief 63 BCE–66 CE.* London: SCM.

———. 1993. *The Historical Figure of Jesus.* London: Allen Lane–Penguin.

———. 1999. Reflections on Anti-Judaism in the New Testament and in Christianity. In *Anti-Judaism and the Gospels*, ed. William R. Farmer, 265–86. Harrisburg, Penn.: Trinity Press International.

————, ed. 1980–81. *Jewish and Christian Self-Definition*. 2 vols. Philadelphia: Fortress.

Sanders, Jack T. 1987. *The Jews in Luke–Acts*. Philadelphia: Fortress.

————. 1993. *Schismatics, Sectarians, Dissidents, Deviants: The First One Hundred Years of Jewish–Christian Relations*. Valley Forge, Penn.: Trinity Press International.

————. 1997. Paul between Jews and Gentiles in Corinth. *Journal for the Study of the New Testament* 65: 67–83.

————. 2000. *Charisma, Converts, Competitors: Societal and Sociological Factors in the Success of Early Christianity*. London: SCM.

Sandmel, Samuel. 1969. *The First Christian Century in Judaism and Christianity*. New York: Oxford University Press.

Sartre, Maurice. 1991. *L'Orient romain: Provinces et sociétés provinciales en Méditerranée orientale d'Auguste aux Sévères (31 avant J.-C.– 235 après J.-C.)*. Paris: Éd. du Seuil.

Schaberg, Jane. 1990. *The Illegitimacy of Jesus: A Feminist Theological Interpretation of the Infancy Narratives*. New York: Crossroad.

Schapera, Isaac. 1977. *Kinship Terminology in Jane Austen's Novels*. London: Royal Anthropological Institute of Great Britain and Ireland.

Scheff, Thomas J. 1990. *Microsociology: Discourse, Emotion, and Social Structure*. Chicago: University of Chicago Press.

Scheid, John. 1986. Le thiase du Metropolitan Museum (*IGUR I*, 160). In *L'association dionysiaque dans les sociétés anciennes: Actes de la table ronde organisée par l'École Française de Rome (Rome 24–25 mai 1984)* (Collection de l'École Française de Rome, 89), 275–90. Paris: De Boccard.

Scheler, Max. 1954. *The Nature of Sympathy*. London: Routledge & Kegan Paul. [Originally *Wesen und Formen der Sympathie*, 1923.]

Scherrer, Steven J. 1984. Signs and Wonders in the Imperial Cult: A New Look at a Roman Religious Institution in the Light of Rev 13:13–15. *Journal of Biblical Literature* 103: 599–610.

Schiffman, Lawrence H. 1985. *Who Was a Jew? Rabbinic and Halakhic Perspectives on the Jewish Christian Schism*. Hoboken, N.J.: Ktav.

————. 1991. *From Text to Tradition*. Hoboken, N.J.: Ktav.

Schille, Gottfried. 1970. *Das vorsynoptische Judenchristentum*. Stuttgart, Germany: Calwer.

Schlier, Heinrich. 1982. *An die Galater*. Göttingen, Germany: Vandenhoeck & Ruprecht.

Schmeller, Thomas. 1995. *Hierarchie und Egalität: Eine sozialgeschichtliche Untersuchung paulinischer Gemeinden und griechisch-römischer Vereine* (Stuttgarter Bibelstudient, 162). Stuttgart, Germany: Verlag Katholisches Bibelwerk.

Schnabel, Eckhard J. 1985. *Law and Wisdom: From Ben Sira to Paul*. Tübingen, Germany: J. C. B. Mohr, Paul Siebeck.

Schneider, D. 1916. Ianitor. In *Paulys Real Encyclopädie der classischen altertumswissenschaft, neue bearbeitung*, 9, ed. Georg Wissowa, 692–93. Stuttgart, Germany: J. B. Metzler.

Schnelle, Udo. 1998. *The History and Theology of the New Testament Writings*. London: SCM.

Schoedel, William R. 1985. *Ignatius of Antioch: A Commentary on the Letters of Ignatius of Antioch*, ed. Helmut Koester. Philadelphia: Fortress.

Scholder, Klaus. 1987. *The Churches and the Third Reich. Vol. 1: Preliminary History and the Time of Illusions 1981–1934*. London: SCM.

Schottroff, Luise. 1985/1999. "Nicht viele Mächtige": Annäherungen an eine Soziologie des Urchristentums. In *Befreiungserfahrungen: Studien zur Sozialgeschichte des Neuen Testaments*, 247–56. München, Germany: Chr. Kaiser; "Not Many Powerful": Approaches to a Sociology of Early Christianity. In *Social-Scientific Approaches to New Testament Interpretation*, ed. David G. Horrell, 275–87. Edinburgh: T. & T. Clark, 1999.

———. 1993. *Let the Oppressed Go Free: Feminist Perspectives on the New Testament*. Louisville, Ky.: Westminster/John Knox.

———. 1995. *Lydia's Impatient Sisters: A Feminist Social History of Early Christianity*, London: SCM; *Lydias ungeduldige Schwestern: Feministische Sozialgeschichte des frühen Christentum*. Gütersloh, Germany: Kaiser, 1994.

———, and Wolfgang Stegemann. 1978. *Jesus von Nazareth, Hoffnung der Armen*, Stuttgart, Germany: Kohlhammer; *Jesus and the Hope of the Poor*. Maryknoll, N.Y.: Orbis, 1986.

Schottroff, Willy, and Wolfgang Stegemann, eds. 1984. *God of the Lowly: Socio-historical Interpretation of the Bible*. Maryknoll, N.Y.: Orbis.

Schur, Edwin M. 1980. *The Politics of Deviance: Stigma Contests and the Uses of Power*. Englewood Cliffs, N.J.: Prentice Hall.

Schurer, Emil. 1973. *A History of the Jewish People in the Age of Jesus*. Ed. Geza Vermes et al. Edinburgh: T. & T. Clark.

Schüssler Fiorenza, Elisabeth. 1983/1995. *In Memory of Her: A Feminist Theological Reconstruction of Christian Origins*. New York: Crossroad.

———. 1997. The Praxis of Coequal Discipleship. In *Paul and Empire: Religion and Power in Roman Imperial Society*, ed. Richard E. Horsley, 224–41. Harrisburg, Penn.: Trinity Press International.

Schutt, Russell K. 1996. *Investigating the Social World: The Process and Practice of Research*. Thousand Oaks, Calif.: Pine Forge.

Schutz, Alfred. 1964. Making Music Together. In Alfred Schutz, *Collected Papers, Vol. II*, ed. Arvid Brodersen, 159–78. The Hague: Martinus Nijhoff. [Originally, *Social Research* 18, 1(1951): 76–97.]

———. 1972. *The Phenomenology of the Social World*. Trans. George Walsh and Frederick Lehnert. London: Heinemann. [Originally *Der sinnhafte Aufbau der sozialen Welt*. Vienna: Julius Springer, 1932.]

———. 1973. Phenomenology and the Social Sciences. In Alfred Schutz, *Collected Papers I. The Problem of Social Reality*, ed. Maurice Natanson, 118–39. The Hague: Martinus Nijhoff.

———, and Luckmann, Thomas. 1973. *The Structures of the Life-World*. Trans. (from German manuscript) Richard M. Zaner and H. Tristram Engelhardt, Jr. Evanston, Ill.: Northwestern University Press; *Strukturen der Lebenswelt*, Bd. I und II. Frankfurt am Main: Suhrkamp, 1979.

Schwarz, Hillel. 1987. Millenarianism. In *Encyclopedia of Religion*. Vol. 9, 521–32. New York: Macmillan.

Schweitzer, Albert. 2000. *The Quest of the Historical Jesus*. First Complete Edition. London: SCM; *Geschichte der Leben-Jesu-Forschung*. Tübingen, Germany: Mohr, 1913.

Scott, George M. 1990. A Resynthesis of the Primordial and Circumstantial Approaches to Ethnic Group Solidarity: Towards an Explanatory Model. *Ethnic and Racial Studies* 13: 147–71.

Scott, James C. 1985. *Weapons of the Weak: Everyday Forms of Peasant Resistance*. New Haven, Conn.: Yale University Press.

———. 1990. *Domination and the Arts of Resistance: Hidden Transcripts*. New Haven, Conn.: Yale University Press.

Scott, Kenneth. 1936. *The Imperial Cult under the Flavians*. Stuttgart-Berlin: W. Kohlhammer.

Scroggs, Robert J. 1972. Paul and the Eschatological Woman. *Journal of the American Academy of Religion* 40: 283–303.

Scroggs, Robin. 1975. The Earliest Christian Communities as Sectarian Movements. In *Christianity, Judaism and Other Greco-Roman Cults: Studies for Morton Smith at Sixty*. Part 2, 1–23. Leiden: E. J. Brill.

———. 1980. The Sociological Interpretation of the New Testament. *NTS* 26: 164–79.

Sedgwick, Rae. 1981. *Family Mental Health*. St. Louis: Mosby.

Segal, Alan F. 1977. *Two Powers in Heaven: Early Rabbinic Reports about Christianity and Gnosticism*. Leiden: E. J. Brill.

———. 1986. Judaism, Christianity, and Gnosticism. In *Anti-Judaism in Early Christianity. Vol. 2: Separation and Polemic*, ed. Stephen G. Wilson, Waterloo, Ont.: Wilfrid Laurier University Press, 133–61.

———. 1990a. *Paul the Convert: The Apostolate and Apostasy of Saul the Pharisee*. New Haven, Conn.: Yale University Press.

———. 1990b. Paul's Conversion and his Later View of the Law. *Princeton Seminary Bulletin* (Supplement) 1: 55–70.

———. 1995. Universalism in Judaism and Christianity. In *Paul in His Hellenistic Context*, ed. Troels Engberg-Pedersen, 1–29. Minneapolis, Minn.: Fortress Press.

Segal, Judah B. 1961. The Hebrew Festivals and the Calendar. *Journal of Semitic Studies* 6: 74–94.

———. 1963. *The Hebrew Passover from the Earliest Times to A.D. 70*. Oxford: Oxford University Press.

Séguy, Jean. 1980. *Christianisme et société: Introduction à la sociologie de Ernst Troeltsch*. Paris: Cerf.

———. 1982. Charisme, sacerdoce, fondation: Autour de L.M. Grignion de Montfort. *Social Compass* 29, 1: 5–29.

———. 1998. Intensité—extension. In *Compromis religieux et mutations du croire. Aspects théoriques et points historiques*, ed. Paul-André Turcotte, 26–41. Paris: Faculté de Sciences Sociales et Economiques.

———. 1999. *Conflit et utopie, ou réformer l'Eglise: Parcours wébérien ou douze essais*. Paris: Cerf.

Shaw, Brent D. 1984. Bandits in the Roman Empire. *Past and Present* 102: 3–52.

———. 1993. Tyrants, Bandits and Kings: Personal Power in Josephus. *Journal of Jewish Studies* 44: 176–204.

Shelton, Jo Ann. 1988/1998. *As the Romans Did: A Sourcebook in Roman Social History*. Oxford: Oxford University Press.

Sherif, Muzafer. 1956. *Experiments in Group Conflict*. San Francisco: W. H. Freeman.

Sherman, Grace E., and John C. Tuggy. 1994. *A Semantic and Structural Analysis of the Johannine Epistles*. Dallas, Tex.: Summer Institute of Linguistics.

Sherwin-White, A. Nicholas. 1952. The Early Persecutions and Roman Law Again. *Journal of Theological Studies* N.S. 3: 199–213.

———. 1963. *Roman Society and Roman Law in the New Testament.* Oxford: Clarendon Press.

———. 1969. The Empire of Rome: The Roman Government and the Christian Church. In *The Crucible of Christianity: Judaism, Hellenism and the Historical Background to the Christian Faith,* ed. Arnold Toynbee, 123–46. New York: World Publishing.

Sica, Alan. 1988. *Weber, Irrationality and Social Order.* Berkeley: University of California Press.

Sidebottom, Harry. 1993. Philosophers' Attitudes to Warfare under the Principate. In *War and Society in the Roman World,* ed. John Rich and Graham Shipley, 241–64. London: Routledge.

Simmel, Georg. 1968 [1908]. *Soziologie.* Berlin: Duncker & Humblot.

———. 1955. *Conflict* and *The Web of Group Affiliations.* Trans. Kurt H. Wolff and Reinhard Bendix. Glencoe, Ill.: Free Press.

———. 1971. The Problem of Sociology. In *Georg Simmel on Individuality and Social Forms: Selected Writings,* ed. Donald N. Levine, 23–35. Chicago: University of Chicago Press. [Originally Das Problem der Soziologie, in Simmel 1968/1908.]

———. 1997. The Personality of God. In *Essays on Religion,* Georg Simmel, ed. and trans. Horst Jürgen Helle with Ludwig Nieder, 45–62. New Haven, Conn.: Yale University Press. [Originally Die Persönlichkeit Gottes, 1911.]

Simon, Marcel. 1986. *Verus Israel: A Study of the Relations between Christians and Jews in the Roman Empire (135–425).* Oxford: Oxford University Press.

Smith, Dennis. 1992. Meal Customs. In *Anchor Bible Dictionary,* ed. David Noel Freedman, 650–55. Garden City, N.Y.: Doubleday.

Smith, Jonathan Z. 1975a. Wisdom and Apocalyptic. In *Religious Syncretism in Antiquity,* ed. Birger A. Pearson, 131–56. Missoula, Mont.: Scholars Press.

———. 1975b. Social Description of Early Christianity. *RelSRev* I: 19–25.

———. 1978. Too Much Kingdom, Too Little Community. *Zygon* 13: 123–30.

Snow, David A., and Richard Machalek. 1982. On the Presumed Fragility of Unconventional Beliefs. *Journal for the Scientific Study of Religion* 21, I: 15–26.

———. 1983. The Convert as a Social Type. In *Sociological Theory 1983,* ed. Randall Collins, 261–76. San Francisco: Jossey-Bass.

———. 1984. The Sociology of Conversion. *Annual Review of Sociology* 10: 167–90.

———, Louis A. Zurcher, Jr., and Sheldon Ekland-Olson. 1980. Social Networks and Social Movements: A Microstructural Approach to Differential Recruitment. *American Sociological Review* 45: 787–801.

Snyder, Graydon F. 1985. *Ante Pacem: Archaeological Evidence of Church Life before Constantine.* Macon, Ga.: Mercer University Press.

Sordi, Marta. 1983. *The Christians and the Roman Empire.* Trans. Annabel Bedini. London: Croom Helm.

Sorokin, Pitirim A. 1948. *The Reconstruction of Humanity.* Boston: Beacon Press.

———. 1969. *Society, Culture, and Personality: Their Structure and Dynamics. A System of General Sociology.* New York: Cooper Square. [Originally published 1947.]

Sperber, Daniel. 1965. Costs of Living in Roman Palestine I. *Journal of the Economic and Social History of the Orient* 8: 248–71.

———. 1978. *Roman Palestine 200–400—The Land.* Jerusalem: Bar-Ilan University Press.

———. 1991 [1974]. *Roman Palestine 200–400—Money and Prices*. 2nd ed. Jerusalem: Bar-Ilan University Press.

Spivey, Robert A., and D. Moody Smith. 1995. *Anatomy of the New Testament: A Guide to Its Structure and Meaning*. 5th ed. Englewood Cliffs, N.J.: Prentice Hall.

Spradley, James, and David McCurdy. 1988 [1972]. *The Cultural Experience: Ethnography in Complex Society*. Prospect Heights, Ill.: Waveland.

Stambaugh, John. 1988. *The Ancient Roman City*. Baltimore, Md.: John Hopkins University Press.

Stanton, G. N. 1985. Aspects of Early Christian-Jewish Polemic and Apologetic. *New Testament Studies* 31: 377–92.

Staples, Peter. 1970. *The Greek Maccabean Books in the Early Church*. Unpublished Ph.D thesis, University of Nottingham.

———. 1999. Ritual Combat in the Gospels and Josephus: A New Methodological Approach. *Social Compass* 46, 4: 481–92.

Stark, Rodney. 1985. *The Future of Religion: Secularization, Revival and Cult Formation*. Berkeley: University of California Press.

———. 1986. Jewish Conversion and the Rise of Christianity: Rethinking the Received Wisdom. In *SBLSP 1986*, ed. K. H. Richards, 314–29. Atlanta: Scholars Press.

———. 1987a. *A Theory of Religion* (Toronto Studies in Religion). Bern: Peter Lang.

———. 1987b. How New Religions Succeed: A Theoretical Model. In *The Future of New Religious Movements*, ed. David G. Bromley and Phillip E. Hammond, 11–29. Macon, Ga.: Mercer University Press.

———. 1991. Christianizing the Urban Empire: An Analysis, Based on 22 Greco-Roman Cities. *SocAnal* 52: 77–88.

———. 1996. *The Rise of Christianity: A Sociologist Reconsiders History*. Princeton, N.J.: Princeton University Press.

———. 1998a. E Contrario. *Journal of Early Christian Studies* 6: 259–67.

———. 1998b. *Doing Sociology: A Global Perspective*. 3rd ed. Belmont, Calif.: Wadsworth.

———. 2001. *Sociology*. 8th ed. Belmont, Calif.: Wadsworth.

———, and William Sims Bainbridge. 1980. Networks of Faith: Interpersonal Bonds and Recruitment to Cults and Sects. *American Journal of Sociology* 85: 1376–95.

Ste. Croix, Geoffrey E. M. de. 1954. Aspects of the "Great" Persecution. *Harvard Theological Review* 47: 75–113.

———. 1963. Why Were the Early Christians Persecuted? *Past and Present* 26: 6–38.

———. 1975. Early Christian Attitudes to Property and Slavery. In *Church, Society and Politics: Studies in Church History* 12, ed. D. Baker, 1–38. Oxford: Blackwell.

———. 1981/1983. *The Class Struggle in the Ancient Greek World from the Archaic Age to the Arab Conquests*. Ithaca, N.Y.: Cornell University Press; London: Duckworth.

Stegemann, Ekkehard W., and Wolfgang Stegemann. 1999. *The Jesus Movement: A Social History of Its First Century*. Trans. O. C. Dean, Jr. Minneapolis, Minn.: Fortress. [Germany 1995.]

Stegemann, Wolfgang. 1984. Vagabond Radicalism in Early Christianity?: A Historical and Theological Discussion of a Thesis Proposed by Gerd Theissen. In *God of the Lowly:*

Socio-historical Interpretation of the Bible, ed. Willy Schottroff and Wolfgang Stegemann, 148–68. Maryknoll, N.Y.: Orbis.

Stendahl, Krister O. 1976. *Paul among Jews and Gentiles.* London: SCM.

Still, Todd D. 1999. *Conflict at Thessalonica: A Pauline Church and Its Neighbours.* Sheffield, England: Sheffield Academic Press.

Stoetzel, Jean. 1960. La Psychologie des Relations Interpersonnelles. In *Traité de sociologie, t. 2nd.* Georges Gurvitch, 339–52. Paris: Presses Universitaires de France.

Stoldt, Hans-Herbert. 1980. *History and Criticism of the Marcan Hypothesis.* Trans. and ed. Donald Niewyk. Macon, Ga.: Mercer University Press.

Stoller, Paul. 1995. *Embodying Colonial Memories: Spirit Possession, Power, and the Hauka in West Africa.* London: Routledge.

Stone, Michael E. 1983. Coherence and Inconsistency in the Apocalypses: The Case of "The End" in 4 Ezra. *Journal of Biblical Literature* 102: 229–43.

Stowers, Stanley K. The Social Sciences and the Study of Early Christianity. In *Approaches to Ancient Judaism, vol. 5, Studies in Judaism and its Greco-Roman Context* (Brown Judaic Studies, 32), 149–82. Atlanta: Scholars Press.

———. 1986. *Letter-Writing in Greco-Roman Antiquity.* Philadelphia: Westminster.

Strack, Hermann L., and Günter Stemberger. 1992. *Introduction to the Talmud and Midrash.* Minneapolis, Minn.: Fortress.

Straus, Roger A. 1979. Religious Conversion as a Personal and Collective Accomplishment. *Sociological Analysis* 40, 2: 158–65.

Strecker, Georg. 1979. *Eschaton und Historie.* Göttingen, Germany: Vandenhoeck & Ruprecht.

Streeter, Burnett H. 1925. *The Four Gospels: A Study of Origins.* New York: Macmillan.

Sutherland, C. H. V. 1959. The Intelligibility of Roman Imperial Coin Types. *Journal of Roman Studies* 49: 46–55.

Taisne, A. -M. 1973. Le thème du triomphe dans le poésie et l'art sous les Flaviens. *Latomus* 32: 485–504.

Tajfel, Henri. 1981. *Human Groups and Social Categories.* Cambridge: Cambridge University Press.

———, ed. 1982. *Social Identity and Intergroup Relations.* Cambridge: Cambridge University Press.

Talmon, Yonina. 1962. Pursuit of the Millennium: The Relation between Religious and Social Change. *Archives Européennes de Sociologie* 3: 125–48.

Tannehill, Robert C. 1975 *The Sword of His Mouth.* Missoula, Mont.: Scholars Press.

Tannen, Deborah. 1994. *Talking from Nine to Five: How Women's and Men's Conversational Styles Affect Who Gets Heard, Who Gets Credit, and What Gets Done at Work.* New York: Morrow, 1994.

Tatum, W. Barnes 1998. Jesus' So-Called Triumphal Entry: On Making an Ass of the Romans. *Forum* 1 N.S.: 129–43.

Taylor, Justin. 1994. Why Were the Disciples First Called "Christians" at Antioch? *Revue Biblique* 101: 75–94.

Taylor, Nicholas H. 1991. The Composition and Chronology of 2 Corinthians. *Journal for the Study of the New Testament* 44: 67–87.

———. 1992. *Paul, Antioch and Jerusalem: A Study in Relationships and Authority in Earliest Christianity* (JSNT Supplement Series 66). Sheffield, England: JSOT.

———. 1993. Paul's Apostolic Legitimacy: Autobiographical Reconstruction in Galatians 1:11–2:14. *Journal of Theology for Southern Africa* 83: 65–77.

———. 1995. The Social Nature of Conversion in the Early Christian World. In *Modelling Early Christianity: Social-Scientific Studies of the New Testament in its Context*, ed. Philip F. Esler, 128–36. London: Routledge.

———. 1996. Paolo: Fariseo, cristiano e dissonante. *Religioni e Società* 11/24: 22–39.

———. 1997a. Paul, Pharisee and Christian: The Gentiles, the Law, and the Salvation of Israel in Light of Cognitive Dissonance Theory. *Theologia Viatorum* 24: 45–65. [First published as Taylor 1996.]

———. 1997b. Paul for Today: Race, Class and Gender in the Light of Cognitive Dissonance Theory. *Listening* 32, 1: 22–38.

———. 1998. Cognitive Dissonance and Early Christianity: A Theory and Its Application Reconsidered. *Religion and Theology* 5: 138–53.

———. 1999. The Temple in Early Christian Eschatology. Paper presented at the meeting of the New Testament Society of South Africa in Port Elizabeth.

Tcherikover, Victor. 1961/1970. *Hellenistic Civilization and the Jews*. Trans. Shimon Applebaum. Philadelphia: Jewish Publication Society of America; New York: Athenaeum.

Tenney, M. C. 1960. The Footnotes of John's Gospel. *Bibliotheca Sacra* 117: 350–64.

Theissen, Gerd. 1978. *The First Followers of Jesus: A Sociological Analysis of the Earliest Christianity*. London: SCM [Germany 1977.]; *Sociology of Early Palestinian Christianity*. Philadelphia: Fortress.

———. 1979/1988. *Studien zur Soziologie des Urchristentums* (Wissenschaftliche Untersuchungen zum Neuen Testament 19). 3rd ed. Tübingen, Germany: Mohr-Siebeck.

———. 1982. *The Social Setting of Pauline Christianity: Essays on Corinth*. Philadelphia: Fortress.

———. 1983. *The Miracle Stories of the Early Christian Tradition*. Philadelphia: Fortress.

———. 1985. Review of W. Meeks, The First Urban Christians. *Journal of Religion* 65: 111–13.

———. 1987. *Psychological Aspects of Pauline Theology*. Philadelphia: Fortress.

———. 1991. *The Gospels in Context*. Minneapolis, Minn.: Fortress [Germany 1989].

———. 1992/1993. *Social Reality and the Early Christians: Theology, Ethics and the World of the New Testament*. Minneapolis, Minn.: Fortress.

———. 1999. *The Religion of the Earliest Churches: Creating a Symbolic World*. Trans. John Bowden. Minneapolis, Minn.: Fortress. [*Eine Theorie de urchristlichen Religion*, 1999.]

Thielman, Frank S. 1989. *From Plight to Solution*. Leiden: E. J. Brill.

Thistleton, Anthony C. 1992. *New Horizons in Hermeneutics*. Grand Rapids, Mich.: Zondervan.

———. 1999. Communicative Action and Promise in Interdisciplinary, Biblical, and Theological Hermeneutics. In *The Promise of Hermeneutics*, ed. R. Lundin, C. Walhout, and A. C. Thiselton, 133–239. Grand Rapids, Mich.: Eerdmans.

Thomas, William I., and Dorothy Swain Thomas. 1970 [1928]. Situations Defined as Real are Real in Their Consequences. In *Social Psychology through Symbolic Interactionism*, ed. Gregory P. Stone and Harvey P. Farberman, 154–55. Boston: Ginn-Blaisdell.

Thomas, William I., and Florian Znaniecki. 1918–20/1956. *The Polish Peasant in Europe and America*. 5 vols. Chicago: University of Chicago Press, 1918 (vols. 1–2); Boston: Badger, 1919–20 (vols. 3–5)/New York: Dover.

Thompson, Leonard. 1990. *The Book of Revelation: Apocalypse and Empire.* Oxford: Oxford University Press.

Thuren, Lauri. 1995. *Argument and Theology in 1 Peter: The Originas of Christian Paraenesis.* Sheffield, England: Sheffield Academic Press.

Tidball, Derek J. 1983. *An Introduction to the Sociology of the New Testament.* Exeter, England: Paternoster.

Tobin, James. 1983. *The Creation of Man: Philo and the History of Interpretation.* Washington, D.C.: Catholic Biblical Association of America.

Tomasi, Luigi, ed. 1998, *The Tradition of the Chicago School of Sociology.* Aldershot, England: Ashgate.

Torjesen, Karen Jo. 1993. *When Women Were Priests: Women's Leadership in the Early Church and the Scandal of Their Subordination in the Rise of Christianity.* San Francisco: Harper.

Toulmin, Stephen. 1958. *The Uses of Argument.* Cambridge: Cambridge University Press.

Tracy, David. 1978. A Theological Response to *Kingdom and Community. Zygon* 13: 131–35.

Travisano, Richard V. 1970. Alternation and Conversion as Qualitatively Different Transformations. In *Social Psychology through Symbolic Interaction,* ed. Gregory P. Stone and Harvey A. Farberman, 594–606. Waltham, Mass.: Ginn-Blaisdell.

Trebilco, Paul R. 1991. *Jewish Communities in Asia Minor.* Cambridge: Cambridge University Press.

Trible, Phyllis. 1994. *Rhetorical Criticism: Context, Method, and the Book of Jonah.* Minneapolis, Minn.: Fortress.

Troeltsch, Ernst. 1911,1931/32. *The Social Teaching of the Christian Churches.* 2 vols. Trans. Olive Wyon. New York: Harper; Macmillan; London: George Allen & Unwin.

Tuckett, Christopher M. 1983. *The Revival of the Griesbach Hypothesis: An Analysis and Appraisal.* Cambridge: Cambridge University Press.

Tuma, Elias H. 1971. *Economic History and the Social Sciences: Problems of Methodology.* Berkeley: University of California Press.

Turcotte, Paul-André. 1990. Recherche-action et sociologie historique: Questions de méthode. In *Les études pastorales à l'université: Perspectives, méthodes et pratiques,* ed. Adrian M. Visscher, 222–37. Ottawa: Les Presses de l'Université d'Ottawa.

———. 1999a. A l'intersection de l'Église et de la secte, l'ordre religieux. *Sociologie et sociétés* 22, 2: 65–80.

———. 1999b. Les médiations dans le christianisme: Points théoriques et tracés socio-historiques. *Cahiers de recherche sociologique* 33: 85–117.

Turner, Bryan S. 1996. *The Blackwell Companion to Social Theory.* Oxford: Blackwell.

Turner, John C. 1996. Henri Tajfel: An Introduction. In *Social Groups and Identities: Developing the Legacy of Henri Tajfel,* ed. W. Peter Robinson, 1–23. Oxford: Butterworth Heinemann.

———, and Bourhis, Richard Y. 1996. Social Identity, Interdependence and the Social Group: A Reply to Rabbie et al. In *Social Groups and Identities: Developing the Legacy of Henri Tajfel,* ed. W. Peter Robinson, 25–63. Oxford: Butterworth Heinemann.

Turner, Jonathan H. 1974. *The Structure of Sociological Theory.* Homewood, Ill.: Dorsey.

———. 1987. Analytical Theorizing. In *Social Theory Today,* ed. Anthony Giddens and Jonathan H. Turner, 156–94. Cambridge: Polity.

Turner, Victor. 1975. *Dramas, Fields and Metaphors: Symbolic Action in Human Society*. Ithaca, N.Y.: Cornell University Press.

Ulansey, David. 1989. *The Origins of the Mithraic Mysteries*. New York: Oxford University Press.

Unnik, W. C. van. 1980 [1954]. The Teaching of Good Works in I Peter. In *Sparsa Collecta: The Collected Essays of W. C. Van Unnik*, 83–105. Leiden: E. J. Brill.

Vaage, Leif E. 1994. *Galilean Upstarts: Jesus' First Followers According to Q*. Valley Forge, Penn.: Trinity Press International.

Vanhoozer, Kevin J. 1998. *Is There a Meaning in This Text? The Bible, the Reader, and the Morality of Literary Knowledge*. Grand Rapids, Mich.: Zondervan.

Vermes, Geza. 1983: *Jesus the Jew*. London: SCM.

Versnel, Henk S. 1970. *Triumphus: An Inquiry into the Origin, Development and Meaning of the Roman Triumph*. Leiden: E. J. Brill.

———. 1990. *Ter Unus: Inconsistencies in Greek and Roman Religion I*. Leiden: E. J. Brill.

Veyne, Paul. 1990 [1976]. *Bread and Circuses: Historical Sociology and Political Pluralism*. Trans. Brian Pearce. Alen Lane, England: Penguin.

Via, Don Otto, Jr. 1967. *The Parables: Their Literary and Existential Dimension*. Philadelphia: Fortress.

Visotzky, Burton L. 1989. Prolegomenon to the Study of Jewish-Christianities in Rabbinic Literature. *Journal of the Association for Jewish Studies* 14: 47–70.

Vogliano, Achille. 1933. La grande iscrizione bacchica del Metropolitan Museum. *American Journal of Archeology* 37: 215–31.

Vorster, Johannes N. 1990. Toward and Interactional Model for the Analysis of Letters. *Neotestamentica* 24: 107–30.

———. 1992. Dissociation in the Letter to the Galatians. *Neotestamentica* 26: 297–310.

Wackenheim, Charles. 1992. Trois initiateurs: Engels, Weber, Troeltsch. *Social Compass* 39, 2: 183–205.

Wahlde, Urban C. von. 1989. *The Earliest Version of John's Gospel: Recovering the Gospel of Signs*. Wilmington, Del.: Michael Glazier.

Walaskay, Paul W. 1983. *And So We Came to Rome: The Political Perspective of St Luke*. Cambridge: Cambridge University Press.

Wallace, Walter. 1971. *The Logic of Sociology*. Chicago: Aldine-Atherton.

Wallace-Hadrill, Andrew. 1988. The Social Structure of the Roman House. *Papers of the British School at Rome* 56: 43–97.

———. 1990. Roman Arches and Greek Honours: The Language of Power at Rome. *Proceedings of the Cambridge Philological Society* 216: 143–81.

———. 1994. *Houses and Society in Pompeii and Herculaneum*. Princeton, N.J.: Princeton University Press.

Wallis, Roy. 1984. *The Elementary Forms of the New Religious Life*. London: Routledge & Kegan Paul.

———. 1986. Religion as Fun? The Rajneesh Movement. In *Sociological Theory, Religion and Collective Action*, ed. Roy Wallis and Steve Bruce, 191–224. Belfast: The Queen's University.

Walster, E. 1964. The Temporal Sequence of Post-Decision Processes. In *Conflict, Decision, and Dissonance*, ed. Leon Festinger et al., 112–28. London: Tavistock.

Walter, Nicholaus. 1984. Zur Interpretation von Römer 9–11. *Zeitschrift für Theologie und Kirche* 81: 172–95.

Waltzing, Jean-Pierre. 1895–1900. *Étude historique sur les corporations professionnelles chez les Romains depuis les origines jusqu'à la chute de l'empire d'Occident* (Mémoires couronnés et autres mémoires publiée par l'Académie Royale des Sciences, des Lettres et des Beaux-Arts de Belgique, 50). Brussels: F. Hayez.

Walzer, Richard L. 1949. *Galen on Jews and Christians*. London: Oxford University Press.

Wanamaker, Charles Arthur. 1990. *The Letters to the Thessalonians*. Grand Rapids, Mich.: Eerdmans.

———. 1995. "Like a Father Treats His Own Children": Paul and the Conversion of the Thessalonians. *Journal of Theology for Southern Africa* 92: 46–55.

———, and Nicholas H. Taylor. 1999. Paul and the Construction of Christian Identity (*Studiorum Novi Testamenti Societas* Seminar Paper).

Wasserman, Stanley, and Katherine Faust. 1994. *Social Network Analysis: Methods and Applications*. Cambridge: Cambridge University Press.

Watson, Duane F. 1988. *Invention, Arrangement, and Style: Rhetorical Criticism of Jude and 2 Peter*. Atlanta: Scholars Press.

———. 1992. Chreia/Aphorism. In *Dictionary of Jesus and the Gospels*, ed. Joel B. Green and Scot McKnight, 104–6. Downers Grove, Ill.: InterVarsity.

———, and Alan J. Hauser. 1994 *Rhetorical Criticism of the Bible: A Comprehensive Bibliography with Notes on History and Method*. Leiden: E. J. Brill.

Watson, Francis B. 1986. *Paul, Judaism, and the Gentiles: A Sociological Approach* (SNTSMS 56). Cambridge: Cambridge University Press.

Weaver, P. R. C. 1967. Social Mobility in the Early Roman Empire: The Evidence of the Imperial Freedmen and Slaves. *Past & Present* 37: 3–20.

———. 1972. *Familia Caesaris: A Social Study of the Emperor's Freedmen and Slaves*. Cambridge: Cambridge University Press.

Weber, Max. 1946. *From Max Weber: Essays in Sociology*. Trans. Hans H. Gerth and C. Wright Mills. New York: Oxford University Press.

———. 1946. The Protestant Sects and the Spirit of Capitalism. In Weber 1946, 302–22.

———. 1952. *Ancient Judaism*. Trans. and ed. Hans H. Gerth and Don Martindale. Glencoe, Ill.: Free Press.

———. 1958, 1976 (1919–20). Author's Introduction. In Weber 1958, 13–31.

———. 1958. *The Protestant Ethic and the Spirit of Capitalism*. Trans. Talcott Parsons. New York: Charles Scribner's Sons. [Die protestantische Ethik und der geist des Kapitalismus. *Archiv für Sozialwissenschaft und Sozialpolitik* 20 and 21 (1904–5).]

———. 1970. *On Charisma and Institution Building*. Ed. S. N. Eisenstadt. Chicago: University of Chicago Press.

———. 1976 [1896]. *The Agrarian Sociology of Ancient Civilizations*. Trans. R. I. Frank. London: NLB.

———. 1978. *Economy and Society. An Outline of Interpretive Sociology*. 2 vols. Ed. Guenther Roth and Claus Wittich. Berkeley: University of California Press. [Originally *Wirthschaft und Gesellschaft. Grundriss der verstehenden Soziologie*, 1922; definitive ed. Johannes Winckelmann. Tübingen, Germany: J. C. B. Mohr (Paul Siebeck), 1964.]

Webster, Graham. 1985. *The Roman Imperial Army of the First and Second Centuries A.D.* 3rd ed. Totowa, N.J.: Barnes & Noble Books.

Wedderburn, Alexander John Maclagan. 1988. *The Reasons for Romans.* Edinburgh: T. & T. Clark.

Weder, Hans. 1992. Disciple, Discipleship. In *Anchor Bible Dictionary,* ed. David Noel Freedman, vol. 2, 207–10. Garden City, N.Y.: Doubleday.

Weigert, Andrew J. 1994. *Mixed Emotions.* Albany, N.Y.: State University of New York Press.

Welch, Kevin W. 1981. An Interpersonal Influence Model of Traditional Religious Commitment. *Sociological Quarterly* 22: 81–92.

———. 1983. Community Development and Metropolitan Religious Commitment: A Test of Two Competing Models. *Journal for the Scientific Study of Religion* 22: 167–81.

Wellesley, Kenneth. 1975. *The Long Year A.D. 69.* London: Paul Elek.

Wellman, Barry. 1983. Network Analysis: Some Basic Principles. *Sociological Theory* 1: 155–200.

Wells, Peter S. 1999. *The Barbarians Speak: How the Conquered Peoples Shaped Roman Europe.* Princeton, N.J.: Princeton University Press.

Wendland, Ernst R. 1992. Cohesion in Colossians: A Structural-Thematic Outline. *Notes on Translation* 6/3: 28–62.

———. 1994. A Comparative Study of "Rhetorical Criticism," Ancient and Modern—with Special Reference to the Larger Structure and Function of the Epistle of Jude. *Neotestamentica* 28/1: 193–228.

———. 1996. Finding Some Lost Aspects of Meaning in Christ's Parables of the Lost—and Found. *Trinity Journal* 17 NS/1: 19–65.

———. 1998. Dear Children versus the Antichrists: The Rhetoric of Reassurance in I John. *Journal of Translation and Textlinguistics* 11: 40–84.

———. 2000. *Preaching That Grabs the Heart: A Rhetorical-Stylistic Study of the Chichewa Revival Sermons of Shadrack Wame.* Blantyre, Malawi: CLAIM.

Wengst, Klaus. 1987. *PAX ROMANA and the Peace of Jesus Christ.* Philadelphia: Fortress.

———. 1990. *Bedrängte Gemeinde und verherrlichter Christus: Ein Versuch über das Johannesevangelium.* 3d ed. Munich: Chr. Kaiser.

Westermann, William L. 1955. *The Slave Systems of Greek and Roman Antiquity.* Philadelphia: American Philosophical Society.

White, John L. 1999. *The Apostle of God: Paul and the Promise of Abraham.* Peabody, Mass.: Hendrickson.

White, L. Michael. 1990, 1997. *The Social Origins of Christian Architecture.* 2 vols. Valley Forge, Penn.: Trinity Press International.

———. 1998. Counting the Costs of Nobility: The Social Economy of Roman Pergamon. In *Pergamon: Citadel of the Gods. Archaeological Record, Literary Description, and Religious Development,* ed. Helmut Koester, 331–71. Harrisburg, Penn.: Trinity Press International.

———, ed. 1991. *Social Networks in the Early Christian Environment: Issues and Methods for Social History. Semeia* 56: 1–202.

White, Leslie A. 1954. Review of *Culture: A Critical Review of Concepts and Definitions* by A. L. Kroeber and C. Kluckhohn. *American Anthropologist* 56: 461–68.

———, with Beth Dillingham. 1973. *The Concept of Culture*. Minneapolis, Minn.: Burgess.

Whitehead, Neil L. 1995. The Historical Anthropology of Text: The Interpretation of Ralegh's *Discoverie of Guiana*. *Current Anthropology* 36, 5: 3–74.

Widengren, George. 1965. *Mani and Manichaeism*. New York: AMS Press.

Wiedemann, Thomas. 1981. *Greek and Roman Slavery*. Baltimore, Md.: Johns Hopkins University Press.

Wilckens, Ulrich. 1980. *Die Brief an die Römer*. Neukirchen-Vluyn, Austria: Neukirchener.

Wilken, Robert L. 1984. *The Christians As the Romans Saw Them*. New Haven, Conn.: Yale University Press.

Wilkins, Michael J. 1992. Christian. In *Anchor Bible Dictionary*, ed. David Noel Freedman, vol. 1, 925–26. Garden City, N.Y.: Doubleday.

Wilson, Bryan R. 1961. *Sects and Society*. London: Heinemann.

———. 1970. *Religious Sects: A Sociological Study*. New York: World University Library.

———. 1973. *Magic and the Millennium: A Sociological Study of Religious Movements of Protest among Tribal and Third-World Peoples*. New York: Harper & Row.

———. 1987. Factors in the Failure of the New Religious Movements. In *The Future of New Religious Movements*, ed. David G. Bromley and Phillip E. Hammond, 30–45. Macon, Ga.: Mercer University Press.

———. 1990. *The Social Dimensions of Sectarianism: Sects and New Religious Movements in Contemporary Society*. Oxford: Clarendon.

———. 1998. Church-Sect Theory. In *Encyclopedia of Religion and Society*, ed. William H. Swatos, Jr., 90–93. Walnut Creek, Calif.: AltaMira.

Wilson, Stephen G., ed. 1986. *Anti-Judaism in Early Christianity. Vol. 2: Separation and Polemic*. Waterloo, Ont.: Wilfrid Laurier University Press.

———. 1995. *Related Strangers: Jews and Christians, 70–170 C.E.* Minneapolis, Minn.: Fortress.

———, and Michel Desjardins, eds. 2000. *Text and Artifact in the Religions of Mediterranean Antiquity: Studies in Honour of Peter Richardson*. Waterloo, Ont.: Wilfrid Laurier University Press.

Winden, J. C. M. 1983. The World of Ideas in Philo of Alexandria: An Interpretation of De Opificio Mundi, 24–25. *Vigiliae Christianum* 37: 209–17.

Wink, Walter. 1992. *Engaging the Powers: Discernment and Resistance in a World of Domination*. Minneapolis, Minn.: Fortress.

Winston, David. 1975. Philo's Theory of Cosmogony. In *Religious Syncretism in Antiquity*, ed. Birger A. Pearson, 157–71. Missoula, Mont.: Scholars Press.

———. 1979. *The Wisdom of Solomon*. Garden City, N.Y.: Doubleday.

———. 1985. *Logos and Mystical Theology in Philo of Alexandria*. Cincinnati, Ohio: Hebrew Union College.

———, trans. and ed. 1981. *Philo of Alexandria: The Contemplative Life, the Giants, and Selections*. New York: Paulist.

Winter, Bruce W. 1988. The Public Honouring of Christian Benefactors: Romans 13:3–4 and 1 Peter 2:14–15. *Journal for the Study of the New Testament* 34: 87–103.

———. 1994. *Seek the Welfare of the City: Christians as Benefactors and Citizens. First-Century Christians in the Graeco-Roman World*. Grand Rapids, Mich.: Eerdmans.

Witherington III, Ben. 1994. *Jesus the Sage: The Pilgrimage of Wisdom*. Minneapolis, Minn.: Fortress.

———. 1995a. *Conflict and Community in Corinth: A Socio-Rhetorical Commentary on 1 and 2 Corinthians*. Grand Rapids, Mich.: Eerdmans.

———. 1995b. *The Jesus Quest. The Third Search for the Jew of Nazareth*. Carlisle, U.K.: Paternoster.

———. 1998a. *The Acts of the Apostles: A Socio-Rhetorical Commentary*. Grand Rapids, Mich.: Eerdmans.

———. 1998b. *The Paul Quest: The Renewed Search for the Jew of Tarsus*. Downers Grove, Ill.: InterVarsity.

———. 2001. *The Gospel of Mark: A Socio-Rhetorical Commentary*. Grand Rapids, Mich.: Eerdmans.

Wittgenstein, Ludwig. 1969. *On Certainty*. Oxford: Blackwell.

Witztum, Doren, Eliyahu Rips, and Yoavi Rosenberg. 1994. Equidistant Letter Sequences in the Book of Genesis. *Statistical Sciences* 9: 429–38.

Wolf, Eric R. 1966. *Peasants* (Foundations of Modern Anthropology). Englewood Cliffs, N.J.: Prentice Hall.

Wolfson, Harry A. 1962. *Philo: Foundations of Religious Philosophy in Judaisms, Christianity, and Islam*. 3rd ed. rev. 2 vols. Cambridge, Mass.: Harvard University Press.

Woodward, Kathryn. 1997. Concepts of Identity and Difference. In *Identity and Difference*, ed. Kathryn Woodward. London: Sage.

Woolf, George. 1993. Roman Peace. In *War and Society in the Roman World*, ed. John Rich and Graham Shipley, 171–94. London: Routledge.

Worsley, Peter. 1968. *The Trumpet Shall Sound*. New York: Schocken.

Wortham, Robert A. 1999. *Social-Scientific Approaches in Biblical Literature*. Lewiston, N.Y.: Mellen.

Wrede, William. 1971 [1901]. *The Messianic Secret*. Cambridge: James Clarke.

Wright, Nicholas Thomas. 1991. *The Climax of the Covenant*. Edinburgh: T. & T. Clark.

———. 1999. The Mission and Message of Jesus. In *The Meaning of Jesus: Two Visions*, ed. Marcus J. Borg and N. T. Wright, 31–52. San Francisco: Harper.

Wrong, Dennis H. 1961. The Oversocialized Conception of Man in Modern Sociology. *American Sociological Review* 26:183–93.

———. 1995. *The Problem of Order*. Cambridge, Mass.: Harvard University Press.

Wuellner, Wilhelm. 1987. Where Is Rhetorical Criticism Taking Us? *Catholic Biblical Quarterly* 49: 448–63.

Yasukata, Toshimasa. 1986. *Ernst Troeltsch: Systematic Theologian of Radical Historicality*. Atlanta, Ga.: Scholars Press.

Zampaglione, Geraldo. 1973 *The Idea of Peace in Antiquity*. Notre Dame, Ind.: University of Notre Dame Press.

Zanker, Paul. 1988. *The Power of Images in the Age of Augustus*. Ann Arbor: University of Michigan Press.

———. 1998. *Pompeii: Public and Private Life*. Cambridge, Mass.: Harvard University Press.

Zetterberg, Hans L. 1965. *On Theory and Verification in Sociology*. 3rd enlarged ed. Totowa, N.J.: Bedminster.

Ziegler, Philip. 1982. *The Black Death*. Harmondsworth, England: Penguin.
Ziesler, John A. 1989. *Paul's Letter to the Romans*. London: SCM.
Zygmunt, Joseph F. 1972. Movements and Motives. *Human Relations* 25: 449–67.

Ancient Authors

Works from antiquity are cited in parentheses by author and title; when Latin abbreviations of the work are used, they are taken from the list at the front of the volume. Specific editions or translations cited in chapters are listed in this section.

Appian. *Appian's Roman History*. 4 vols. Trans. Horace White (Loeb Classical Library). Cambridge, Mass.: Harvard University Press, 1938.
Clement of Rome. *The Apostolic Fathers, Part I: S. Clement of Rome*. Trans. Joseph B. Lightfoot (Loeb Classical Collection). London: Macmillan, 1890.
Epictetus. *Discourses*. Trans. W. A. Oldfather. London: Collins, 1925.
Eusebius. *Ecclesiastical History*. Trans. Kirsop Lake. London: Collins, 1978.
Hermas. *The Shepherd*. Trans. Kirsopp Lake. In Clement, *Apostolic Fathers*.
Hippolytus. *The Treatise on the Apostolic Tradition*. Trans. and ed. Gregory Dix. London: SPCK, 1937; *The Apostolic Tradition of Hippolytus*. Trans. and ed. Burton Scott Easton. Cambridge: Cambridge University Press, 1943.
Ignatius. *Letter to Polycarp*. Trans. Kirsopp Lake. In Clement, *The Apostolic Fathers*.
Origen. *Origen: Contra Celsum*. Trans. Henry Chadwick. Cambridge: Cambridge University Press, 1953.
———. *Homilies on Genesis and Exodus* (The Fathers of the Church, Vol. 71). Trans. Ronald E. Heine. Washington, D.C.: Catholic University of America Press, 1982.
———, *On First Principles*. Trans. G. W. Butterworth. New York: Harper Torchbooks, 1966.
Philo of Alexandria. *Questions on Exodus*. Trans. R. Marcus (Loeb Classical Library). Cambridge, Mass.: Harvard University Press, 1953–1962b.
———. *Questions on Genesis*. Trans. R. Marcus (Loeb Classical Library). Cambridge, Mass.: Harvard University Press, 1953–1962.
———. *Philo of Alexandria: The Contemplative Life, the Giants and Selections*. Trans. David Winston. New York: Paulist, 1981.
———. *Works*. 10 vols. Trans. and ed. F. H. Colson and G. H. Witaker (Loeb Classical Library). Cambridge, Mass.: Harvard University Press, 1929–1962.
Plato. *The Laws of Plato*. Trans. Thomas L. Pangle. Chicago: University of Chicago Press, 1988.
———. *Plato's Cosmology: The Timaeus of Plato*. Trans. and ed. Francis M. Cornford. Indianapolis, Ind.: Bobbs-Merrill, 1937.
Pliny the Younger. *Selected Letters of Pliny*. Trans. Gerald B. Allen. Oxford, Clarendon, 1915.
Plotinus. *The Enneads*. Trans. Stephen MacKenna and ed. abridged John Dillon. New York: Penguin, 1991.
Plutarch. *Fall of the Roman Republic: Six Lives by Plutarch*. Trans. Rex Warner. London: Penguin, 1972.

Seneca the Elder. *Controversiae*. 2 vols. London: Heineman, 1924.

Tertullian. *Apology, de Spectaculis with an English Translation*. Trans. Terrot Reaveley Glover. Cambridge, Mass.: Harvard University Press, 1953.

Compilations of Ancient Sources

Acts of the Christian Martyrs. Ed. Herbert A. Musurillo. Oxford: Clarendon, 1972.

Acts of the Pagan Martyrs: Acta Alexandrinorum. Ed. Herbert A. Musurillo. Oxford: Clarendon, 1954.

Apostolic Fathers: Greek Texts and English Translations of Their Writings. Trans. and ed. Joseph B. Lightfoot and J. R. Harmer; ed. Michael W. Holmes. Grand Rapids, Mich.: Baker, 1992.

Critical Edition of Q. Ed. James M. Robinson et al. Minneapolis, Minn.: Fortress, 2000.

Dead Sea Scrolls in English. 3rd ed. Ed. Geza Vermes. New York: Penguin, 1987.

Documents of the Christian Church. 2nd ed. Ed. Henry Bettenson. Oxford: Oxford University Press, 1963.

Early-Christian Epitaphs from Anatolia (SBL Texts and Translations, 35). Ed. Gary J. Johnson. Atlanta: Scholars Press, 1994.

Faith and Piety in Early Judaism: Texts and Documents. Trans. George W. E. Nickelsburg and Michael E. Stone. Philadelphia: Fortress, 1983.

Greek and Latin Authors on Jews and Jerusalem. 3 vols. Ed. Menahem Stern. Jerusalem: Israel Academy of Sciences and Humanities, 1974–1984.

Handbuch der altchristlichen Epigraphik. Ed. Carl Maria Kaufmann. Freiburg: Herder, 1917.

Inscriptions funéraires chrétiennes de Carthage: Carthage Intra et Extra Muros, vol. I. Ed. Liliane Ennabli. Rome: École Française, 1991.

Iscrizioni cristiane di Roma. Ed. Carlo Carletti. Florence: Centro Internazionale del Libro, 1986.

New Eusebius: Documents Illustrative of the History of the Church to A.D. 337, Based upon the Collection Edited by . . . B. J. Kidd. Ed. J. Stevenson. London: SPCK. 1957, 1963.

New Testament Apocrypha. 2 vols. Ed. W. Schneemelcher and trans. R. McL. Wilson. Louisville, Ky.: John Knox/Westminster, 1992.

Novum Testamentum Graece. 27th ed. Trans. and ed. Barbara Aland, et al. Stuttgart, Germany: Deutsche Bibelgesellschaft, 1993.

Prosopographia imperii romani. Ed. Edmund Groag, Arthur Stein, and Leiva Petersen. Berlin: Walter de Gruyter, 1933, 1966.

Recueil des chrétiennes de Macédoine du IIIe au Vie siècle. Ed. Denis Feissel. Athens: École Française d'Athènes, 1983.

Bibliography

COMPILED BY JEAN DUHAIME
(WITH THE COLLABORATION OF MIKE ARCIERI,
AURORE CONKIC, AND PAULE-RENÉE VILLENEUVE)

This bibliography includes selected books and articles published up to the year 2000. They are arranged according to broad divisions currently used in scholarship on the New Testament and Early Christianity.

Abbreviations

ABD	*Anchor Bible Dictionary*
AJT	*Asia Journal of Theology*
ANRW	*Aufstieg und Niedergang der römischen Welt*
ArchEurSoc	*Archives européenes de sociologie*
ATR	*Australasian Theological Review*
AUSS	*Andrews University Seminary Studies*
BBR	*Bulletin for Biblical Research*
BibInt	*Biblical Interpretation*
BJRL	*Bulletin of the John Rylands University Library of Manchester*
BK	*Bibel und Kirche*
BR	*Biblical Research*
BTB	*Biblical Theology Bulletin*
BZ	*Biblische Zeitschrift*
CBQ	*Catholic Biblical Quarterly*
CTR	*Criswell Theological Review*
CurBS	*Currents in Research: Biblical Studies*
CurTM	*Currents in Theology and Mission*
CV	*Communio viatorum*
DBM	*Deltion Biblikon Meleton (Athens)*
EgT	*Église et théologie*
EspVie	*Espirit et Vie (Langres)*
EstBib	*Estudios bíblicos*

ETR	*Études théologiques et religieuses*
EvQ	*Evangelical Quarterly*
EvT	*Evangelische Theologie*
ExpTim	*Expository Times*
FoiVie	*Foi et vie*
Forum	*Foundations & Facets Forum*
HBD	*HarperCollins Bible Dictionary*
HBT	*Horizons in Biblical Theology*
HR	*History of Religions*
HTR	*Harvard Theological Review*
HTS	*Harvard Theological Studies*
IBS	*Irish Biblical Studies*
Int	*Interpretation*
JAAR	*Journal of the American Academy of Religion*
JAC	*Jahrbuch für Antike und Christentum*
JBL	*Journal of Biblical Literature*
JECS	*Journal of Early Christian Studies*
JES	*Journal of Ecumenical Studies*
JETS	*Journal of the Evangelical Theological Society*
JFSR	*Journal of Feminist Studies in Religion*
JR	*Journal of Religion*
JRelS	*Journal of Religious Studies*
JRH	*Journal of Religious History*
JSNT	*Journal for the Study of the New Testament*
JSP	*Journal for the Study of the Pseudepigrapha*
JTS	*Journal of Theological Studies*
JTSA	*Journal of Theology for Southern Africa*
LTP	*Laval théologique et philosophique*
LumVie	*Lumière et vie*
MelT	*Melita theologica*
Mils	*Milltown Studies*
MTSR	*Method and Theory in the Study of Religion*
MTZ	*Münchener theologische Zeitschrift*
Neot	*Neotestamentica*
Notes	*Notes on Translation*
NovT	*Novum Testamentum*
NTS	*New Testament Studies*
NTT	*Norsk Teologisk Tidsskrift*
PRSt	*Perspectives in Religious Studies*
RB	*Revue biblique*
RelSRev	*Religious Studies Review*
ResQ	*Restoration Quarterly*
RevistB	*Revista bíblica*

RivB	*Rivista biblica italiana*
RQ	*Römische Quartalschrift für christliche Altertumskunde und Kirchengeschichte*
RR	*Review of Religion*
RrelRes	*Review of Religious Research*
RSR	*Recherches de science religieuse*
RTP	*Revue de théologie et de philosophie*
SBFLA	*Studii biblici Franciscani liber annus*
SBLSP	*Society of Biblical Literature Seminar Papers*
SEÅ	*Svensk exegetisk årsbok*
SecCent	*Second Century*
SJT	*Scottish Journal of Theology*
SNTSMS	*Society for New Testament Studies Monograph Series*
SNTSU	*Studien zum Neuen Testament und seiner Umwelt*
SocAnal	*Sociological Analysis*
SocRel	*Sociology of Religion*
SR	*Studies in Religion*
ST	*Studia theologica*
SVTQ	*St. Vladimir's Theological Quarterly*
Tbei	*Theologische Beiträge*
TBT	*The Bible Today*
ThTo	*Theology Today*
TLZ	*Theologische Literaturzeitung*
TRev	*Theologische Revue*
Tru	*Theologische Rundschau*
TS	*Theological Studies*
TynBul	*Tyndale Bulletin*
TZ	*Theologische Zeitschrift*
USQR	*Union Seminary Quarterly Review*
VC	*Vigiliae christianae*
VF	*Verkündigung und Forschung*
WD	*Wort und Dienst*
WTJ	*Westminster Theological Journal*
WUNT	*Wissenschaftliche Untersuchungen zum Neuen Testament*
ZNW	*Zeitschrift für die neutestamentliche Wissenschaft und die Kunde der älteren Kirche*
ZRGG	*Zeitschrift für Religions- und Geistesgeschichte*
ZTK	*Zeitschrift für Theologie und Kirche*

General

Bibliographies and Review Articles

Barbaglio, G. 1988. Rassegna di studi di storia sociale e di recherchi di sociologia sulli origine christiani. *RivB* 3: 377–410, 495–520.

Best, T. 1983. The Sociological Study of the New Testament: Promise and Peril of a Discipline. *SJT* 36: 181–94.

Duling, D. C. 1994. BTB Readers Guide: Millennialism. *BTB* 24: 132–42.

Edwards, O. C. 1983. Evans, C. A. 1989. *Life of Jesus Research : An Annotated Bibliography* (New Testament Tools and Studies 13). Leiden : E. J. Brill.

Evans, C. A. 1989. *Life of Jesus Research: An Annotated Bibliography* (New Testament Tools and Studies 13). Leiden: E. J. Brill.

Gager, J. G. 1982a. Shall We Marry Our Enemies? Sociology and the New Testament. *Int* 36: 256–65.

———. 1983. Social Description and Sociological Explanation in the Study of Early Christianity: A Review Essay. In *The Bible and Liberation: Political and Social Hermeneutics*, ed. Norman K. Gottwald and Richard Horsley, 428–40. Maryknoll, N.Y.: Orbis.

Hanson, K. C. 1997. Greco-Roman Studies and the Social-Scientific Study of the Bible : A Classified Periodical Bibliography (1970–1994). *Forum* 9/1–2: 63–119.

Harrington, D. J. 1980. Sociological Concepts and the Early Church: A Decade of Research. *TS* 41: 181–90.

———. 1988. Second Testament Exegesis and the Social Sciences: A Bibliography. *BTB* 18: 77–85.

Kaestli, J. -D. 1996. Milieu du Nouveau Testament–Judaisme–Christianisme ancien. *Bulletin de Bibliographie Biblique* (Lausanne) 18: 1–121.

Kümmel, W. G. 1985. Das Urchristentum. II. Arbeiten zu Spezialproblemen. b. Zur Sozialgeschichte und Soziologie der Urkirche. *Tru* 50: 327–63.

May, D. M. 1991. *Social Scientific Criticism of the New Testament: A Bibliography* (NABPR Bibliography Series 4). Macon, Ga.: Mercer University Press.

Neyrey, J. H., et. al. 1986. Review Articles on Two Social Scientific Studies of the Bible. *BTB* 16: 107–18.

Osiek, C. 1989. The New Handmaid: The Bible and the Social Sciences. *TS* 50: 260–78.

Poucet, J., and J. M. Hannick. 1997. *Aux sources de l'Antiquité gréco-romaine: Guide bibliographique.* Bruxelles: Artel.

Riesner, R. 1986. Soziologie des Urchristentums: Ein Literaturüberblick. *Tbei* 17: 213–22.

Schmeller, T. 1989. Soziologisch orientierte Exegese des Neuen Testaments: Eine Bestandsaufnahme. *BK* 44: 103–10.

Scholer, D. M. 1987. Understanding the New Testament in its Contexts: A Review Article. *Perspective in Religious Studies* 14: 259–70.

Scroggs, R. 1983. The Sociological Interpretation of the New Testament: The Present State of Research. In *The Bible and Liberation: Political and Social Hermeneutics*, ed. Norman K. Gottwald and Richard Horsley, 337–57. Maryknoll, N.Y.: Orbis.

Segalla, G. 1982. Sociologia e Nuovo Testamentico—Una rassegna. *Studia Patavania* 29: 143–50.

Introductions and General Works

Artus O., and Baudoz, J. -F. 1997. L'évolution de la pratique exégétique dans les trente dernières années: Nouveaux champs de recherche et principaux débats actuels. *Transversalités* (Paris) 62: 177–98.

Bartlett, D. L. 1978. J. G. Gager's "Kingdom and Community": A Summary and Response. *Zygon Journal of Religion and Science* 13: 109–22.

Barton, J., ed. 1998. *The Cambridge Companion to Biblical Interpretation* (Cambridge Companions to Religion). Cambridge: Cambridge University.

Becker, J., ed. 1993. *Christian Beginings: World and Community from Jesus to Post-Apostolic Times.* Trans. A. S. Kidder and R. Krauss. Louisville, Ky.: Westminster/Knox. 1993.

Clines D. J. A., S. E. Fowl, and S. E. Porter. 1990. *The Bible in Three Dimensions: Essays on Celebration of Forty Years of Biblical Studies in the University of Sheffield* (JSOT Supplement Series 87). Sheffield, England: JSOT Press.

Elliott, J. H., ed. 1986. Social Scientific Criticism of the New Testament and Its Social World. *Semeia* 35.

Esler, P. F., ed. 1995. *Modelling Early Christianity: Social-Scientific Studies of the New Testament in its Context.* London: Routledge.

Gager, J. G. 1975. *Kingdom and Community: The Social World of Early Christianity.* Englewood Cliffs, N.J.: Prentice Hall.

Gewalt, D. 1971. Neutestamentliche Exegese und Soziologie. *EvT* 31: 87–99.

Göll, H. -P. 1985. Offenbarung in der Geschichte: Theologische Überlegungen zur sozialgeschichtlichen Exegese. *EvT* 45: 532–45.

Green, J. B., ed. 1995. *Hearing the New Testament: Strategies for Interpretation.* Grand Rapids, Mich.: Eerdmans.

Hawthorne, G. F., and O. Betz. 1987. *Tradition and Interpretation in the New Testament: Essays in Honor of E. Earle Ellis for His 60th Birthday.* Grand Rapids, Mich.: Eerdmans.

Johnson, L. T. 1986. *The Writings of the New Testament: An Interpretation.* Philadelphia: Fortress.

Kee, H. C. 1980. *Christian Origins in Sociological Perspective: Methods and Resources.* Philadelphia: Westminster.

———. 1985. Sociology of the New Testament. *HBD*: 961–68.

Mainville, O., ed. 1999. *Écrits et milieu du Nouveau Testament: Une introduction.* Montréal: Médiaspaul.

Moxnes, H. 1988a. Sociology and the New Testament. In *Religion as a Social Phenomenon: Theologians and Sociologists Sharing Research Interest,* ed. E. Karlsaune, 143–59. Trondheim, Norway: Tapir.

Muvar, V. 1975. Towards a Sociological Theory of Religious Movements. *Journal of the Scientific Study of Religion* 14: 229–56.

Nielsen, D. A. 1990. Max Weber and the Sociology of Early Christianity. In *Time, Place, and Circumstance: Neo-Weberian Studies in Comparative Religious History,* ed. W. H. Swatos, Jr., 87–102. New York: Greenwood.

Norelli, E. 1987. Sociologia del Cristianesimo primitivo: Qualche osservazione a partire dall'opera di Gerd Theissen. *Henoch* 9: 97–123.

Paulsen, H. 1997. *Zur Literatur und Geschichte des frühen Christentums: Gesammelte Aufsatze* (Wissenschaftliche Untersuchungen zum Neuen Testament 99). Ed. U. E. Eisen. Tübingen, Germany: Mohr Siebeck.

Porter S. E., and D. Tombs, eds. 1995. *Approaches to New Testament Studies* (JSNT Sup. Ser. 120). Sheffield, England: Sheffield Academic Press.

Porter, S. E., ed. 1997. *Handbook to Exegesis of the New Testament* (New Testament Tools and Studies 25). Leiden: E. J. Brill.

Rowland, C. 1985. Reading the New Testament Sociologically: An Introduction. *Theology* 88: 358–64.

Scroggs, R. 1986. Sociology of the New Testament. *Listening* 21: 138–47.

Smith, J. Z. 1975. Social Description of Early Christianity. *RelSRev* 1: 19–25.

Theissen, G. 1979/1988. *Studien zur Soziologie des Urchristentums* (Wissenschaftliche Untersuchungen zum Neuen Testament 19). 3rd ed. Tübingen, Germany: Mohr-Siebeck.

Tidball, D. 1983. *An Introduction to the Sociology of the New Testament.* Exeter, England: Paternoster.

———. 1985. *The Social Context of the New Testament.* Grand Rapids, Mich.: Zondervan; Carlisle, England: Paternoster.

Turcotte, P. A., et al. 1992. *The Sociology of Christianity's Beginnings: Social Compass* 39: 179–275.

Tolbert, M. A. 1993. Social, Sociological and Anthropological Methods. In *Searching the Scriptures*, vol. 1. Ed. E. Fiorenza. New York: Crossroad.

Methods

GENERAL

Albl, M. C., P. R. Eddy, and R. Mirkes, eds. 1993. *Directions in New Testament Methods* (Marquette Studies in Theology 2). Milwaukee, Wis.: Marquette University.

Bossman, D. M., ed. 1992–93. International Conference on the Social Sciences and the Second Testament Interpretation (Spain, 1991). *BTB* 22: 50–95, 98–142; 23: 4–39.

Brown, S. 1989. New Directions in Biblical Interpretations. *TBT* 27: 197–202.

Bruce, F. F. 1990. Modern Criticism, Social World Studies of Israel and Early Christianity and Questions of Interpretative Method. In *The Bible in Three Dimensions: Essays on Celebration of Forty Years of Biblical Studies in the University of Sheffield* (JSOT Supplement Series 87), ed. D. J. A. Clines, S. E. Fowl, and S. E. Porter. Sheffield, England: JSOT Press.

Craffert, P. F. 1996. Relationships between Social-Scientific, Literary and Rhetorical Interpretation of Texts. *BTB* 26: 45–55.

Domeris, W. R. 1988. Social Scientific Study of the Early Christian Churches: New Paradigms and Old Questions. In *Paradigms and Progress in Theology*, ed. A. G. Van Aarde and W. S. Vorster, 378–93. Pretoria: Human Sciences Research Council.

———. 1995. Sociological Studies and the Interpretation of the Bible. *Scriptura* 54: 203–13.

Douglas-Klotz, N. 1999. Midrash and Postmodern Inquiry: Suggestions Toward a Hermeneutics of Indeterminacy. *CurBS* 7: 181–93.

Duhaime, J. 1994. Approches socio-critiques de la Bible. In *Entendre la voix du Dieu vivant* (Lectures bibliques 41), ed. J. Duhaime and O. Mainville, 201–19. Montréal: Médiaspaul.

Duling, D. C. 1995. Social-Scientific Small Group Research and Second Testament Study. *BTB* 25: 179–93.

Dunnill, J. 1996. Methodological Rivalries: Theology and Social-Science in Girardian Interpretations of the New Testament. *JSNT* 62: 105–19.

Eisenstadt, S. N., and L. Roninger. 1980. Patron–Client Relations as a Model of Structuring Social Exchange. *Comparative Studies in Society and History* 22: 42–77.

————, eds. 1984. *Patrons, Clients and Friends: Interpersonal Relations and the Structure of Trust in Society*. Cambridge: Cambridge University Press.

Elliott, J. H. 1986. Social-Scientific Criticism of the New Testament : More on Methods and Models. *Semeia* 35 : 1–33.

————. 1993a. *What is Social-Scientific Criticism?* (Guides to Biblical Scholarship, New Testament Series). Minneapolis, Minn.: Fortress.

Esler, P. F. 1994. *The First Christians in their Social Worlds: Social-Scientific Approaches to New Testament Interpretation*. London: Routledge.

Fenn, R. K. 1987. Sociology and Social History: A Preface to a Sociology of the New Testament. *JSP* 1: 95–114.

Gottwald, N. K., and R. A. Horsley, eds. 1993. *The Bible and Liberation: Political and Social Hermeneutics*. Rev. ed. Maryknoll, N.Y.: Orbis.

Grawitz, M. 1986. *Méthodes des sciences sociales* (Précis Dalloz). Paris: Dalloz.

Haynes S. R., and S. L. McKenzie, eds. 1993. *To Each Its Own Meaning: An Introduction to Biblical Criticism and Their Application*. Louisville, Ky.: Westminster/Knox.

Hochschild, R. 1999. *Sozialgeschichtliche Exegese: Entwicklung, Geschichte und Methodik einer neutestamentlichen Forschungrichtung* (Novum Testamentum et Orbis Antiquus 42). Göttingen, Germany: Vanderhoeck & Ruprecht.

Horrell, D. G. 2000. Models and Methods in Social-Scientific Interpretation: A Response to Philip Esler. *JSNT* 78: 83–105. (Reply, P. F. Esler, 107–13).

————, ed. 1999. *Social-Scientific Approaches to New Testament Interpretation*. Edinburgh: T. & T. Clark.

Hynes, W. J. 1981. *Shirley Jackson Case and the Chicago School: The Socio-Historial Method*. Chicago: Scholars Press.

Isenberg, S. R. 1980. Some Uses and Limitations of Social Scientific Methodology in the Study of Early Christianity. *SBLSP* 1980: 29–49.

Jobling, D., P. L. Day, and G. T. Sheppard, eds. 1991. *The Bible and the Politics of Exegesis: Essays in Honor of Norman K. Gottwald on His Sixty-Fifth Birthday*. Cleveland, Ohio: Pilgrim.

Kelsey, D. H. 1987. Biblical Narrative and Theological Anthropology. In *Scriptural Authority and Narrative Interpretation*, ed. G. Green, 121–43. Philadelphia: Fortress.

Malina, B. J. 1982. The Social Sciences and Biblical Interpretation. *Int* 36: 229–42.

————. 1983. Why Interpret the Bible with the Social Sciences? *American Baptist Quarterly* 2: 119–33.

————. 1991. Interpretation: Reading, Abduction, Metaphor. In *The Bible and the Politics of Exegesis: Essays in Honor of Norman K. Gottwald on His Sixty-Fifth Birthday*, ed. D. Jobling, P. L. Day, and G. T. Sheppard, 253–66. Cleveland, Ohio: Pilgrim.

Matthews, V. H., and D. C. Benjamin. 1994. Social Sciences and Biblical Studies. *Semeia* 68: 7–21.

Meeks, W. A. 1986. A Hermeneutic of Social Embodiment. *HTR* 79: 176–86.

Morgan, R., and J. Barton. 1988. Theology and the Social Sciences. In *Biblical Interpretation*, 133–66. Oxford: Oxford University.

Mosala, I. J. 1986. Social Scientific Approaches to the Bible: One Step Forward, Two Steps Backward. *JTSA* 55: 15–30.

Neyrey, J. H. 1986. Social Science Modeling and the New Testament. *BTB* 16: 107–10.

Osiek, C. 1992. The Social Sciences and the Second Testament: Problems and Challenges. *BTB* 22: 88–95.

Pagàn, S. 1996. Poor and Poverty: Social Distance and Bible Translation. *Semeia* 76: 69–79.

Pilch, J. J., ed. 2000a/2001. *Social Scientific Models for Interpreting the Bible: Essays by the Context Group in Honor of Bruce J. Malina.* Leiderdorp: Deo Publishing; Leiden: E. J. Brill.

Powell, J. 1989. Social Theory as Exegetical Tool. *Forum* 5/4: 27–40.

Quivy, R., and L. van Campenhoudt. 1988. *Manuel de recherche en sciences sociales.* Paris: Dunod.

Robbins, V. K. 1996a. *Exploring the Texture of Texts: A Guide to Socio-Rhetorical Interpretation.* Valley Forge, Penn.: Trinity Press.

———. 1996b. *The Tapestry of Early Christian Discourse: Rhetoric, Society and Ideology.* London: Routledge.

Rodd, C. S. 1990. Sociology and Social Anthropology. In *A Dictionary of Biblical Interpretation,* ed. R. J. Coggins and J. L. Houden, 26–28. London: SCM Press

Rohrbaugh, R. L. 1987. Models and Muddles: Discussion of the Social Facets Seminar. *Forum* 3: 23–33.

———. 1993. Social Science and Literary Criticism: What Is at Stake? *HTS* 49: 221–33.

———, ed. 1996. *The Social Sciences and the New Testament Interpretation.* Peabody, Mass.: Hendrickson.

Scroggs, R. 1980. The Sociological Interpretation of the New Testament. *NTS* 26: 164–79.

Segal, R. A. 1989. *Religion and the Social Sciences.* Atlanta: Scholars Press.

Slater, T. B. 1993. Sociological Methodology and the New Testament. *Biblebhashyam* 19: 237–48.

Stowers, S. K. 1985. The Social Sciences and the Study of Early Christianity. In *Approaches to Ancient Judaism. Vol. 5, Studies in Judaism and its Greco-Roman Context* (Brown Judaic Studies, 32), 149–82. Atlanta: Scholars Press.

White, L. J. 1986. The Bible, Theology and Cultural Pluralism. *BTB* 16: 111–15.

Wilder, A. N. 1987. Biblical Hermeneutics and American Scholarship. In *Neutestamentliche Studien für Rudolf Bultmann zu seinem siebzigsten Geburtstag,* ed. W. Elteser, 24–32. Berlin: Töpelmann.

ANTHROPOLOGY

Borchgrevink, T., and M. Melhuus. 1989. Text as Reality–Reality as Text. *ST* 43: 35–59.

Craffert, P. F. 1995. The Anthropological Turn in New Testament Interpretation: Dialogue as Negotiation and Cultural Critique. *Neot* 29: 167–82.

Destro, A., and M. Pesce. 1995. *Antropologia delle origini cristiane* (Quadrante 78). Rome-Bari: Laterza.

Douglas, M. 1966. *Purity and Danger.* London: Routledge & Kegan Paul.

Feeley-Harnick, G. 1982. Is Historical Anthropology Possible? The Case of the Runaway Slave. In *Humanizing America's Iconic Book: SBL Centennial Addresses 1980,* 95–126. Chico, Calif.: Scholars Press.

Isenberg, S. R. 1975. Mary Douglas and Hellenistic Religions: The Case of Qumran. *SBLSP* 1975. Missoula, Mont.: Scholars Press, 179–85.

————, and D. E. Owen. 1977. Bodies, Natural and Contrived: The Work of Mary Douglas. *RSR* 3: 1–17.

Laplantine, F. 1995. *L'anthropologie* (Petite Bibliothèque Payot 227). Paris: Payot.

Leach, E. 1982. Anthropological Approaches to the Study of the Bible during the Twentieth Century. In *Humanizing America's Iconic Book: SBL Centennial Addresses 1980*, 73–94. Chico, Calif.: Scholars Press.

Malina, B. J. 1981/1993. *The New Testament World: Insights from Cultural Anthropology.* Atlanta: John Knox. Rev. ed., Louisville: Westminster/John Knox.

————. 1986. *Christian Origins and Cultural Anthropology: Practical Models for Biblical Interpretation.* Atlanta: John Knox.

————. 1989a. Christ and Time: Swiss or Mediterranean? *CBQ* 51: 1–31.

————. 1989b. Dealing with Biblical (Mediterranean) Characters: A Guide for U.S. Consumers. *BTB* 19: 127–41.

————. 1991. Scienze sociali e interpretazione storica: La questione della retrodizione. *RivB* 39: 305–23.

————. 1993. *Windows on the World of Jesus: Time Travel to Ancient Judea.* Louisville, Ky.: Westminster/Knox.

McVann, M., ed. 1994. Transformations, Passages, and Processes: Ritual Approaches to Biblical Texts. *Semeia* 67: 7–232.

Moxnes, H. 1983. Kropp som symbol: Bruk av sosialantropologi i studiet av Det nye Testamente. *NTT* 84: 197–217.

————. 1993. New Testament Ethics: Universal or Particular? Reflexions on the Use of Social Anthropology in New Testament Studies. *ST* 47: 153–68.

Neusner, J. 1980. The Talmud as Anthropology. *Religious Traditions* 3: 12–35.

Pilch, J. J. 1991. *Introducing the Cultural Context of the New Testament* (Hear the Word). Vols. 1–2. New York: Paulist.

————. 1994. Secrecy in the Mediterranean World: An Anthropological Perspective. *BTB* 24: 151–57.

Rogerson, J. W. 1990. Anthropology. In *A Dictionary of Biblical Interpretation*, ed. R. J. Coggins and J. L. Houden London: SCM.

Schnelle, U. 1991. *Neutestamentliche Anthropologie. Jesus–Paulus–Johannes* (Biblisch-Theologische Studien 18). Neukirchen-Vluyn: Neukirchener Verlag.

Segal, R. A. 1984. The Application of Symbolic Anthropology to Religions in the Greco-Roman World. *RSR* 10: 216–23.

Stegemann, W. 1999. Kulturanthropologie des Neuen Testaments. *VF* 44: 28–54.

Taylor, W. F. 1996–97. Cultural Anthropology as a Tool for Studying the New Testament. *Trinity Seminary Review* 18: 13–27, 69–82.

White, L. J., ed. 1993. Mediterranean Socio-Cultural Perspectives on the Bible. *BTB* 23: 91–134.

Worgul, G. S. 1979. Anthropological Consciousness and Biblical Theology. *BTB* 9: 3–12.

PSYCHOLOGY

Bucher, A. A. 1992. *Bibel-Psychologie: Psychologische Zugänge zu biblischen Texten.* Stuttgart, Germany: Kohlammer.

Drewermann, E. 1985. *Tiefenpsychologie und Exegese.* Olten-Freiburg, Switzerland: Walter.

Ellens, J. H. 1997. The Bible and Psychology, an Interdisciplinary Pilgrimage. *Pastoral Psychology* 45: 193–208.

Goldbrunner, J. 1989. Um eine neue Dimension der Schriftauslegung. *TRev* 85: 271–78.

Jodelet, D., et al. 1970. *La psychologie sociale* (Les textes sociologiques 3). Paris: École Pratique des Hautes Études.

Leiner, M. 1995. *Psychologie und Exegese: Grundfragen einer textpsychologischen Exegese des Neuen Testaments.* Gutersloh, Germany: Kaiser–Gutersloher Verlagshaus.

———. 1997. Die drei Hauptprobleme der Verwendung psychologischer Theorien in der Exegese. *TZ* 53: 289–303.

Marchadour, A. 1997. Rencontre entre psychanalyse et Bible. *Chronique* (Toulouse) 4: 25–36.

Pilch, J. J. 1997. Psychological and Psychoanalytical Approaches to Interpreting the Bible in Social-Scientific Context. *BTB* 27: 112–16.

Rollins, W. G. 1983. *Jung and the Bible.* Atlanta: John Knox.

———. 1996. The Bible and Psychology: New Directions in Biblical Scholarship. *Pastoral Psychology* 45: 163–79.

———. 1999. *Soul and Psyche: The Bible in Psychological Perspective.* Minneapolis, Minn.: Fortress Press.

Segal, R. A. 1987. Jung and Gnosticism. *Religion* 17: 301–36.

Slusser, G. H. 1986. *From Jung to Jesus: Myth and Consciousness in the New Testament.* Atlanta: John Knox.

Theissen, G. 1993. Identité et expérience de l'angoisse dans le christianisme primitif: Contribution à la psychologie de la religion des premiers chrétiens. *ETR* 68: 161–83.

SOCIOLOGY

Aguire, R. 1985. El método sociologico en los estudios biblicos. *Estudios Eclesiásticos* 60: 305–31.

Alvarez-Verdes, L. 1989. El método sociológico en la investigación bíblica actual: Incidencia en el estudio de la ética bíblica. *Studia Moralia* 27: 5–41.

Anderson, B. W. 1985. Biblical Theology and Sociological Interpretation. *Theology Today* 42: 292–306.

Ansart, P. 1990. *Les sociologies contemporaines* (Point, Anthropologie–Sciences humaines 211). Paris: Seuil.

Aron, R. 1967. *Les étapes de la pensée sociologique.* (Tel) Paris: Gallimard.

Atkins, R. A. 1988. Three Problems in Using Sociological Methodologies in New Testament Materials and Their Solution Using Grid-Group Analysis. In *Proceedings, 8,* ed. P. Redditt, 35–48. Georgetown, Ky.: Eastern Great Lakes & Midwest Biblical Societies.

Baasland, E. 1984. Urkristendommen i sosiologiens lys. *Tidsskrift for Teologiog Kirke* 54: 45–57.

Blasi, A. J. 1990. On Precision in Studying Ancient Palestine. *SocAnal* 51: 395–99.

———. 1993. The More Basic Method in the Sociology of Early Christianity. *Forum* 9: 7–8.

———. 1997. Sociology of Early Christianity: By Way of Introduction. *SocRel* 58: 299–303.

Cahill, M. 1984. Sociology, the Biblical Text and the Christian Community Today. *African Ecclesiastical Review* 26: 279–86.

Caulley, T. S. 1995. Sociological Methods in the Study of New Testament: A Review and Assessment. *ResQ* 37: 36–44.

Coleman, J. A. 1999. The Bible and Sociology. *SocRel* 60: 125–48.

Cotterell, P. 1986. Sociolinguistics and Biblical Interpretation. *Vox Evangelica* 16: 61–76.

De Villiers, P. G. R. 1984. The Interpretation of a Text in the Light of Its Socio-Cultural Setting. *Neot.* 18: 66–79.

Duling, D. C. 1985. Insight from Sociology for New Testament Christology: A Test Case. In *SBLSP 1985*, ed. K. H. Richard, 351–68. Atlanta: Scholars Press.

Durkheim, E. 1937. *Les règles de la méthode sociologique.* (Quadrige) Paris: Presses Universitaires de France (1987).

Holmberg, B. 1991. *Sociology and the New Testament: An Appraisal.* Minneapolis, Minn.: Fortress.

Kee, H. C. 1989. *Knowing the Truth: A Sociological Approach to the New Testament Interpretation.* Minneapolis, Minn.: Fortress.

———. 1992. A Sociological Approach to New Testament Interpretation. *Drew Gateway* (Madison, N.J.) 61: 3–21.

Laub, F. 1989. Sozialgeschichtliche Exegese : Anmerkungen zu einer nuen Fragestellung in der historischkritischen Arbeit am Neuen Testament. *MTZ* 40: 39–50.

Neusner, J. 1981. Max Weber Revisited: Religion and Society in Ancient Judaism with Special Reference to the Late First and Second Centuries. *SecCent* 1: 61–84.

Olsson, B. 1984. Ett hem för hemlösa: Om sociologisk exeges av NT. *SEÅ* 49: 89–108.

Ouédraogo, J. -M. 1999. Esquisse d'une sociologie de la Bible chez Max Weber. *Social Compass* 46: 409–39.

Richter, P. J. 1984. Recent Sociological Approaches to the Study of the New Testament. *Religion* 14: 77–90.

Schluchter, W., ed. 1985. *Max Weber Sicht des antiken Christentums.* Frankfurt am Main, Germany: Suhrkamp.

Stark, R. 1996. *The Rise of Christianity: A Sociologist Reconsiders History.* Princeton, N.J.: Princeton University Press.

Stevenson, E. 1979. Some Insights from the Sociology of Religion into the Origins and Development of the Early Christian Church. *ExpTim* 90: 300–305.

Taylor, W. F. 1989. Sociological Exegesis: Introduction to a New Way to Study the Bible. Part I: History and Theory. *Trinity Seminary Review* (Columbus, Ohio) 11: 99–110.

Theissen, G. 1974. Theoretische Probleme religionssoziologischer Forschung und die Analyse des Urchristentums. *Neue Zeitschrift für systematische Theologie und Religionsphilosophie* 16: 35–36.

———. 1983. The Sociological Interpretation of Religious Traditions: Its Methodological Problems as Exemplified in Early Christianity. In *The Bible and Liberation: Political and Social Hermeneutics*, ed. Norman K. Gottwald and Richard Horsley, 38–58. Maryknoll, N.Y.: Orbis (Germany 1975).

Tidball, D. 1985. On Wooing a Crocodile: An Historical Survey of the Relationship between Sociology and New Testament Studies. *Vox Evangelica* 15: 95–109.

Touraine. A. 1974. *Pour la sociologie* (Points Sciences humaines 55). Paris: Seuil.

Turcotte, P. -A. 1999. Les médiations dans le christianisme: Points théoriques et tracés socio-historiques. *Cahiers de recherche sociologique* 33: 85–117.

Venetz, H. -J. 1985. Der Beitrag der Soziologie zur Lektüre des Neuen Testaments. In *Methoden des Evangelien-Exegese*, ed. G. Schelbert et al., 87–121. (Theol. Berichte, 13). Zurich: Benziger.

Watier, P. 2000. *Le savoir sociologique* (Sociologie du quotidien). Paris: Desclée de Brouwer.

Weber, M. 1958. *The Protestant Ethic and the Spirit of Capitalism*. Trans. Talcott Parsons. New York: Charles Scribner's Sons. [Die protestantische Ethik und der geist des Kapitalismus. *Archiv für Sozialwissenschaft und sozialpolitik* 20 and 21 (1904–5).]

Yamauchi, E. 1984. Sociology, Scripture and the Supernatural. *JETS* 27: 169–92.

SOCIOLOGY OF KNOWLEDGE

Berger, K. 1977. Wissenssoziologie und Exegese des Neuen Testaments. *Kairos* 19: 124–33.

Gnuse, R. K. 1990. Contemporary Evolutionary Theory as a New Heuristic Model for the Socioscientific Method in Biblical Studies. *Zygon* 25: 405–31.

Hindson, E. E. 1984. The Sociology of Knowledge and Biblical Interpretation. *Theologia Evangelica* 17: 33–38.

Nineham, D. 1975. A Partner for Cinderella? In *What about the New Testament? Essays in Honour of Christopher Evans*, ed. M. Hooker and C. Hickling, 143–54. London: SCM.

———. 1977. *The Use and Abuse of the Bible: A Study of the Bible in an Age of Rapid Cultural Change*. New York: Harper.

Remus, H. E. 1982. Sociology of Knowledge and the Study of Early Christianity. *SR* 11: 45–56.

Rohrbaugh, R. L. 1987. Social Location of Thought as a Heuristic Construct in the New Testament Study. *JSNT* 30: 103–119.

Syreeni, K. 1999. Wonderlands: A Beginner's Guide to Three Worlds. *SEÅ* 64: 33–46.

Background

Jewish

Achtemeier, P. J. 1989. Omne verbum sonat The New Testament and the Oral Environment of Late Western Antiquity. *JBL* 109: 3–27.

Auneau, J. 1981. Le temple de Jérusalem et la société juive au Ier siècle. *Masses Ouvrières* 37: 38–59.

Bonneau, G., and Duhaime, J. 1996. Angélologie et légitimation socio-eligieuse dans le livre des Jubilés. *EgT* 27: 335–49.

Brooten, B. *Women Leaders in the Ancient Synagogue: Inscriptional Evidence and Background Issues*. Chico, Calif.: Scholars Press.

Cate, R. L. 1989. *History of the Bible Lands in the Interbiblical Period*. Nashville, Tenn.: Broadman.

Clements, R. E. 1989. *The World of Ancient Israel: Sociological, Anthropological and Political Perspectives. Essays by Members of the Society for Old Testament Study*. Cambridge: Cambridge University.

Cohen, S. J. D. 1999. *The Beginnings of Jewishness: Boundaries, Varieties, Uncertainties* (Hellenistic Culture and Society 31). Los Angeles: University of California Press.

Collins, J. J. 1989. Judaism and Preparatic Evangelica in the Work of Martin Hengel. *RelSRev* 15: 226–28.

Cousin, H., ed. 1998. *Le monde où vivait Jésus*. Paris: Cerf.

Davies, W. D., and L. Finkelstein. 1989. *The Cambridge History of Judaism. Vol. 2: The Hellenistic Age*. Cambridge: Cambridge University.

Edersheim, A. 1994. *Sketches of Jewish Social Life*. Rev. ed. Peabody, Mass.: Hendrickson.

Eisenstadt, S. N., and R. Lemarchand, eds. 1981 *Political Clientelism and Development*. Beverly Hills, Calif.: Sage.

Fenn, R. K. 1992. *The Death of Herod: An Essay in the Sociology of Religion*. Cambridge: Cambridge University.

Fiensy, D. A. 1991. *The Social History of Palestine in the Herodian Period: The Land Is Mine* (Studies in the Bible and Early Christianity 20). Lewiston, N.Y.: Mellen.

Freyne, S. 1980. *Galilee from Alexander the Great to Hadrian, 323 B.C.E.–C.E. 135: A Study of Second Temple Judaism*. Notre Dame, Ind.: University of Notre Dame.

Goldenberg, R. 1997. *The Nations That Know Thee Not: Ancient Jewish Attitudes towards Other Religions* (Biblical Seminar 52). Sheffield, England: Sheffield Academic Press.

Goodman, M. 1987. *The Ruling Class of Judea: The Origins of the Jewish Revolt against Rome* A.D. *66–70*. Cambridge: Cambridge University Press.

Grabbe, L. L. 1989. The Social Setting of Early Apocalypticism. *JSP* 4: 27–47.

———. 1995. *Priests, Prophets, Diviners, Sages: A Socio-Historical Study of Religious Specialists in Ancient Israel*. Valley Forge, Penn.: Trinity Press International.

Guijarro Oporto, S. 1995. La familia en la Galilea del siglo primero. *EstBib* 53: 461–88.

Hengel, M. 1989. *The Zealots: Investigations into the Jewish Freedom Movement in the Period from Herod I until A.D. 70*. Edinburgh: T. & T. Clark.

Horbury, W., W. D. Davies, and J. Sturdy, eds. 1999. *The Cambridge History of Judaism. Vol. 3: The Early Roman Period*. Cambridge: Cambridge University Press.

Horsley, R. A. 1986. Popular Prophetic Movements at the Time of Jesus. Their Principle Features and Social Origins. *JSNT* 26: 3–27.

———, and J. S. Hanson. 1985/1989/1999. *Bandits, Prophets, & Messiahs: Popular Movements in the Time of Jesus*. San Francisco: Harper & Row; Harrisburg, Penn.: Trinity Press.

Isenberg, S. R. 1974. Millenarism in Greco-Roman Palestine. *Religion* 4: 26–46.

———. 1975. Power through Temple and Torah in Greco-Roman Palestine. In *Christianity, Judaism and other Greco–Roman Cults: Studies for Morton Smith at Sixty*. Pt 2, 29–52. Leiden : Brill.

Kealy, S. P. 1997. Galilee in Jesus' Time. *Proceedings of the Irish Biblical Association* 20: 81–94.

Keith, K. 1992. The Background of the New Testament Diversity in First-Century Judaism and Its Contemporary Implications. *Louvain Studies* 17: 131–51.

Lang, G. 1989. Oppression and Revolt in Ancient Palestine: The Evidence in Jewish Literature from the Prophets to Josephus. *SocAnal* 49: 325–42.

Levine, L. I., ed. 1992. *The Galilee in Late Antiquity*. New York: Jewish Theological Seminary of America.

Mayer, G. 1987. *Die jüdische Frau in der hellenistich-römishen Antike.* Stuttgart, Germany: Kohlhammer.

McLaren, J. S. 1991. *Power and Politics in Palestine: The Jews and the Governing of Their Land, 100 B.C.–A.D. 70* (JSNT Sup. Ser. 63). Sheffield, England: JSOT.

Neusner, J., A. J. Avery–Peck, and W. S. Green, eds. 2000. *The Encyclopaedia of Judaism.* 3 vols. Leiden: E. J. Brill.

Newsom, J. D. 1993. *Greeks, Romans, Jews: Currents of Culture Belief in the New Testament World.* Philadelphia: Trinity Press.

Oakman, D.E. 1991. The Ancient Economy in the Bible. *BTB* 21: 34–39.

Pastor, J. 1997. *Land and Economy in Ancient Palestine.* London: Routledge.

Riches, J. K. 1990. *The World of Jesus: First-Century Judaism in Crisi.* (Understanding Jesus Today). Cambridge: Cambridge University.

Rohrbaugh, R. L. 1991. The City in the Second Testament. *BTB* 21: 67–75.

Safrai, Z. 1994. *The Economy of Roman Palestine.* London: Routledge.

Saldarini, A. J. 1990. *Pharisees, Scribes and Sadducees in Palestinian Society: A Sociological Approach.* Wilmington, Del.: Michael Glazier.

Sanders, E. P. 1992. *Judaism, Practice and Belief 63 BCE–66 CE.* London: SCM.

Schwartz, D. R. 1992. *Studies in the Jewish Background of Christianity* (Wissenschaftliche Undersuchungen zum Neuen Testament 60). Tübingen, Germany: Mohr-Siebeck.

Stemberger, G. 1995. *Jewish Contemporaries of Jesus: Pharisees, Sadducees, Essenes.* Trans. A. W. Mahnke. Minneapolis, Minn.: Fortress.

Testa, E. 1988. Le conseguenze della distruzione di Gerusalemme secondo la litteratura rabbinica e cristiana. *SBFLA* 38: 173–209.

Weiner, E., and A. Weiner. 1990. *The Martyr's Conviction: A Sociological Analysis* (Brown Judaic Studies 203). Atlanta: Scholars Press.

Weinfeld, M. 1995. *Social Justice in Ancient Israel and in the Ancient Near East.* Jerusalem: Magnes Press, Hebrew University.

Greco-Roman

Alfödy, G. 1985. *The Social History of Rome.* Totowa N.J.: Barnes & Noble.

Anderson, G. 1994. *Sage, Saint and Sophists: Holy Men and their Associates in the Early Roman Empire.* London: Routledge.

Badian, E. 1983. *Publicans and Sinners: Private Enterprise in the Service of the Roman Republic.* Ithaca, N.Y.: Cornell.

Balsdon, J. 1979. *Roman and Aliens.* Chapel Hill: University of North Carolina.

Benko, S., and J. J. O'Rourke, eds. 1971. *The Catacombs and the Colosseum: The Roman Empire as the Setting of Primitive Christianity.* Valley Forge, Penn.: Judson.

Bettini, M. 1991. *Anthropology and Roman Culture: Kinship, Time, Images of the Soul.* Trans. J. Van Sickle. Baltimore, Md.: Johns Hopkins University Press.

Botha, P. J. J. 1992. Greco-Roman Literacy as Setting for New Testament Writings. *Neot* 26: 195–215.

Bowman A. K., E. Champlin, and A. Lintoit, eds. 1996. *The Cambridge Ancient History. Vol. 10. The Augustan Empire, 43 B.C.–A.D. 69.* 2nd ed. Cambridge: Cambridge University.

Bradley, K. R. 1987. *Slaves and Masters in the Roman Empire: A Study in Social Control.* Oxford: Oxford University Press.

———. 1991. *Discovering the Roman Family: Studies in Roman Social History.* Oxford: Oxford University Press.

Brown, J. P. 1981. The Role of Women and the Treaty in the Ancient World. *BZ* 25: 1–28.

———. 1983. Techniques of Imperial Control: The Background of the Gospel Event. In *The Bible and Liberation: Political and Social Hermeneutics,* ed. N. K. Gottwald and Richard Horsley, 357–77. Maryknoll, N.Y.: Orbis.

Bush, A. C. 1982. *Studies in Roman Social Structure.* Washington, D.C.: University Press of America.

Cantarella, E. 1987. *Pandora's Daughters: The Role and Status of Women in Greek and Roman Antiquity.* Trans. Maureen B. Fant. Baltimore, Md.: Johns Hopkins University Press.

Carney, T. F. 1975. *The Shape of the Past: Models and Antiquity.* Lawrence, Kans.: Coronado.

Crook, J. A., A. Lintott, and E. Rawson, eds. 1994. *The Cambridge Ancient History. Vol. 9, The Last Age of the Roman Republic, B.C. 146–43.* 2nd ed. Cambridge: Cambridge University Press, 1994.

Evans, C. A., and S. E. Porter, eds. 1997. *New Testament Backgrounds: A Sheffield Reader* (Biblical Seminar 43). Sheffield, England: Sheffield Academic Press.

Ferguson, E. 1993. *Backgrounds of Early Christianity.* 2nd ed. Grand Rapids, Mich.: Eerdmans.

Finegan, J. 1997. *Myth & Mistery: An Introduction to the Pagan Religions Biblical World.* Grand Rapids, Mich.: Baker.

Finley, M. I. 1973. *The Ancient Economy.* Berkeley: University of California Press.

Gardner, J. F. 1986. *Women in Roman Law and Society.* Bloomington: Indiana University Press.

———. 1989. The Adoption of Roman Freedmen. *Phoenix* (Toronto) 43: 236–57.

Garnsey, P. 1999. *Food and Society in Classical Antiquity* (Key Themes in Ancient History). Cambridge: Cambridge University Press.

———, and R. Saller. 1987. *The Roman Empire: Economy, Society and Culture.* London: Duckworth.

Garrison, R. 1997. *The Greco-Roman Context of Early Christian Literature* (JSNT Sup. Ser. 137). Sheffield, England: Sheffield Academic Press.

Goodman, M., and J. Sherwood. 1997. *The Roman World B.C. 44–A.D. 180* (Routledge History of the Ancient World). London: Routledge.

Grant, R. M. 1992. *A Social History of Greece and Rome.* New York: Charles Scribner's Sons.

Hardwick, M. E. 1989. *Josephus as a Historical Source in Patristic Literature through Eusebius* (Brown Judaic Studies 128). Atlanta: Scholars Press.

Harris, W. V. 1989. *Ancient Literacy.* Cambridge, Mass.: Harvard University.

Isaak, B. 1998. *The Near East under Roman Rule: Selected Papers* (Mnemosyne: Bibliotheca Classica Batava, Supplementum 177). Leiden: E. J. Brill.

Jeffers, J. S. 1999. *The Greco-Roman World of the New Testament Era: Exploring the Background of Early Christianity.* Downers Grove, Ill.: InterVarsity.

Kraemer, R. S. 1983. Women in the Religions of the Greco-Roman World. *RelSRev* 9: 127–39.

———. 1992. *Her Share of the Blessings: Women's Religions among Pagans, Jews and Christians in the Greco-Roman World.* New York: Oxford University.

Lendon, J. E. 1997. Social Control at Rome. *Classical Journal* 93: 83–88.

MacMullen, R. 1974. *Roman Social Relations 50 B.C. to A.D. 284.* New Haven, Conn.: Yale University.

Malherbe, A. J. 1986. *Moral Exhortation, A Greco-Roman Sourcebook* (Library of Early Christianity 4). Philadelphia: Westminster.

Martin, L. H. 1990. The Encyclopedia Hellenistica and Christian Origins. *BTB* 20: 123–27.

Miles, R., ed. 1999. *Constructing Identities in Late Antiquity.* London: Routledge.

Phillips, C. R. 1986. The Sociology of Religious Knowledge in the Roman Empire to A.D. 284. *ANRW* 2.16.3: 2711–73.

Price, S. R. F. 1984. *Rituals and Power: The Roman Imperial Cult in Asia Minor.* Cambridge: Cambridge University Press.

Rawson, B., ed. 1986. *The Family in Ancient Rome: New Perspectives.* Ithaca, N.Y.: Cornell University Press.

Stevens, M. 1990. Paternity and Maternity in the Mediterranean: Foundations for Patriarchy. *BTB* 20: 47–53.

Watson, A. 1987. *Roman Slave Law.* Baltimore, Md.: Johns Hopkins University Press.

Gospels–Acts

General

Arens, E. 1990. Los Evangelios en la perspectiva sociológica: Algunas observaciones y reflexiones. *Paginas* (Lima) 104: 71–86.

Braun, W. 1999. Socio-mythic Invention, Graeco-Roman Schools and the Sayings Gospel Q. *MTSR* 11: 210–35.

Engelbrecht, J. 1988. Trends in Miracle Research. *Neot* 22: 139–61.

Hanson, K. C. 1997. The Galilean Fishing Economy and the Jesus Tradition. *BTB* 27: 99–111.

Hollenbach, P. W. 1986. *From Parable to Gospel: The Infancy Narratives in Social Context.* New York: Crossroad.

Jacobs-Malina, D. 1994. Gender, Power and Jesus' Identity in the Gospels. *BTB* 24: 158–66.

Johnson, M. D. 1988. *The Purpose of Biblical Genealogies, with Special Reference to the Setting of the Genealogies of Jesus* (SNTSMS, 8). 2nd ed. Cambridge: Cambridge University Press.

Kingsbury, J. D., ed. 1997. *Gospel Interpretation: Narrative-Critical & Social-Scientific Approaches.* Harrisburg, Penn.: Trinity Press.

Locklin, R. B. 1999. To Teach as the Evangelists Did? An Experiment in New Testament Theology. *Koinonia* 11: 65–102.

Malina, B. J., and R. L. Rohrbaugh. 1992. *Social Science Commentary on the Synoptic Gospels.* Minneapolis, Minn.: Fortress.

Matthews, V. H., and D. C. Benjamin, eds. 1994. Honor and Shame in the World of Bible. *Semeia* 68: 1–161.

Percy, M. 1997. The Gospel Miracles and the Modern Healing Movements. *Theology* 99 793: 8–17.

Robbins, V. K. 1987. The Woman Who Touched Jesus' Garment: Socio-Rhethorical Analysis of the Synoptic Accounts. *NTS* 33: 502–15.

Schmidt, T. E. 1987. *Hostility to Wealth in the Synoptic Gospels* (JSNT Sup. Ser. 15). Sheffield, England: JSOT.

Theissen, G. 1985. Localkoloritforschung in den Evangelien: Plädoyer für die Erneurung einer alten Fragestellung. *EvT* 45: 481–99.

———. 1991. *The Gospel in Context.* Minneapolis, Minn.: Fortress [Germany 1989].

Tilborg, Van S. 1986. *The Sermont on the Mount as an Ideological Intervention: A Reconstruction of Meaning.* Assen, Netherlands: Van Gorcum.

Jesus

JESUS AND JESUS MOVEMENT

Alter, M. G. 1994. *Resurrection Psychology: An Understanding of Human Personality Based on the Life and Teachings of Jesus.* Chicago: Loyola University Press.

Ben-Chorin, S. 1985. Jesus, der Proletarier. *ZRGG* 37: 260–65.

Capps, D. 2000. *Jesus: A Psychological Biography.* St. Louis, Mo.: Chalice.

Carlson J., and R. A. Ludwig, eds. 1994. *Jesus and Faith: A Conversation on the Work of John Dominic Crossan.* Maryknoll, N.Y.: Orbis.

Chilton, B. D., and C. A. Evans, eds. 1995. *Studying the Historical Jesus: Evaluations of the State of Current Research* (New Testament Tools and Studies 19). Leiden: E. J. Brill.

Cothenet, E. 1996. Jésus, 70 ans de recherches. *EspVie* 106: 353–62.

Crossan, J. D. 1991. *The Historical Jesus: The Life of Mediterranian Jewish Peasant.* San Francisco: Harper & Row.

Davies, S. L. 1995. *Jesus the Healer: Possession, Trance and the Origins of Christianity.* New York: Continuum.

Derrett, J. D., and M. Duncan. 1973. *Jesus' Audience: The Social and Psychological Environment in Which He Worked.* New York: Crossroad.

Duling, D. C. 1999. The Jesus Movement and Social Network Analysis (Part I: The Spatial Network). *BTB* 29: 156–75.

———. 2000. The Jesus Movement and Social Network Analysis (Part II: The Social Network). *BTB* 30: 3–14.

Ebertz, M. N. 1987. *Das Charisma des Gekreuzigten: Zur Soziologie der Jesusbewegung* (WUNT, 45). Tübingen, Germany: Mohr-Siebeck.

———. 1992. Le stigmate du mouvement charismatique autour de Jésus de Nazareth. *Social Compass* 39: 255–73.

Fiensy, D. 1999. Leaders of Mass Movements and the Leader of the Jesus Movement. *JSNT* 74: 3–27.

Freyne, S. 1988. *Galilee, Jesus and the Gospels: Literary Approaches and Historical Investigations.* Philadelphia: Fortress.

Funk, R. W. 1986. Jesus Seminar Contributions in 1986. *Forum* 2: 3–80 Mr; 3–78 Je; 3–128 S.

Gnilka, J. 1990 *Jesus von: Botschaft und Geschichte* (Herders Theologischer Kommentar zum Neuen Testament, Supplementband 3). Freiburg, Germany: Herder.

Grant, C. 1999. The Greying of Jesus. *ExpTime* 110: 246–48.

Hollenbach, P. W. 1981. Jesus, Demoniacs, and Public Authorities: Socio-Historical Study. *JAAR* 49: 567–88.

———. 1983. Recent Historical Jesus Studies and the Social Sciences. *SBLSP 1983.* Chico: Scholars Press, 61–78.

———. 1985. Liberating Jesus from Social Involvement. *BTB* 15: 151–57.

Horsley, R. A. 1987. *Jesus and the Spiral of Violence: Popular Jewish Resistance in Roman Palestine.* San Francisco: Harper & Row.

———. 1994. *Sociology and the Jesus Movement.* 2nd ed. New York: Continuum.

———. 1995. Archeology of Galilee and the Historical Context of Jesus. *Neot* 29: 211–29.

———. 1996. What Has Galilee to Do with Jerusalem? Political Aspects of the Jesus Movement. *HTS* 52: 88–104.

Houtart, F. 1980. *Religion et modes de production pré-capitalistes.* Bruxelles, Belgium: Éd. Universitaires. Chap. VII: La religion dans la formation sociale de la Palestine du premier siècle et l'acteur socio-religieux Jésus, 218–60.

Kazmierski, C. 1986. Has the New Testament Censored Jesus? *BTB* 16: 116–18. [Review of A. Mayer *Der zensierte Jesus. Soziologie des Neuen Testaments.*]

Kee, H. C. 1977. *Jesus in History: An Approach to the Study of the Gospels.* 2nd ed. New York: Harcourt Brace Jovanovich.

Kelly, J. L. 1994. *Conscientious Objections: Toward a Reconstruction of the Social and Political Philosophy of Jesus of Nazareth* (Toronto Studies in Theology 68). Lewiston, N.Y.: Mellen.

Lohfink, G. 1984. *Jesus and Community: The Social Dimension of Christian Faith.* Philadelphia: Fortress.

Machovec, M. 1978. *Jésus pour les athées* (Jésus et Jésus-Christ, 5). Paris: Desclée.

Mack, B. L. 1985. The Innocent Trangressor: Jesus in Early Christian Myth and History. *Semeia* 33: 135–65.

Malina, B. J. 1986. Normative Dissonance and Christian Origins. *Semeia* 35: 35–59.

Mayer, A. 1983. *Der zensierte Jesus: Soziologie des Neuen Testaments.* Olten-Friburg, Switzerland: Walter-Verlag.

Meier, J. P. 1999. The Present State of the "Third Quest" for the Historical Jesus: Loss and Gain. *Biblica* 80: 459–87.

Oakman, D.E. 1985. Jesus and Agrarian Palestine: The Factor of Debt. In *SBLSP 1985,* ed. K. H. Richards, 57–73. Atlanta: Scholars Press.

———. 1986. *Jesus and the Economic Questions of His Day.* Lewiston, N.Y.: Mellen.

Parsons, H. L. 1985. The Commitment of Jesus and Marx: Ressources for the Challenge and Necessity of Cooperation. *JES* 22: 454–73.

Pilch, J. J. 1995. Insights and Models from Medical Anthropology for Understanding the Healing Activity of the Historical Jesus. *HTS* 51: 314–37.

Pixley, George V. 1983. God's Kingdom in First-Century Palestine: The Strategy of Jesus. In *The Bible and Liberation: Political and Social Hermeneutics*, ed. N. K. Gottwald and Richard Horsley, 378–93. Maryknoll, N.Y.: Orbis.

Remus, H. 1997. *Jesus as Healer* (Understanding Jesus Today). Cambridge: Cambridge University.

Riches, J. K. 1980. *Jesus and the Transformation of Judaism*. London: Darton, Longmann & Todd.

Sanders, E. P. 1993. *The Historical Figure of Jesus*. London: Allen Lane–Penguin.

Sanders, J. T. 1988. The Criterion of Coherence and the Randomness of Charisma: Poring through Some Aporias in the Jesus Tradition. *NTS* 44: 1–25.

Scheffler, E. H. 1995. Jesus from a Psychological Perspective. *Neot* 29: 299–312.

Smith, D. 1985. Jesus and the Pharisees in Socio-Anthropological Perspective. *Trinity Journal* 6: 151–56.

Stegemann, E. W., and W. Stegemann. 1999. *The Jesus Movement: A Social History of Its First Century*. Trans. O. C. Dean, Jr. Minneapolis, Minn.: Fortress. [Germany 1995.]

Stegemann, W. 1987. Aspekte neurer Jesusforschung. *Der Evangelische Erzieher* 39: 1–27.

Stenger, W. 1986. Sozialgeschichtlicher Wende und historischer Jesus. *Kairos* 28: 11–22.

Theissen, G. 1976. Die Tempelwiessagung Jesu: Prophetic im Spannungsfeld von Soziologie urchristlicher Missionare. *TZ* 32: 144–58.

———. 1978. *The First Followers of Jesus: A Sociological Analysis of the Earliest Christianity*. London: SCM [Germany 1977].

———. 1989. Jesusbewegung als charismatische Wertrevolution. *NTS* 35: 343–60.

———. 1997. Jesus und die symbolpolitischen Konflikte seiner Zeit: Sozialgeschichtliche Aspekte der Jesusforschung. *EvT* 57: 378–400.

Vaage, L. E. 1994. *Galilean Upstarts: Jesus' First Followers According to Q*. Valley Forge, Penn.: Trinity Press International.

Venetz, H. -J. 1983. Der zensierte Jesus. *Orienterung* 47: 250–52.

Verdoodt, A. 1999. Critique de l'approche de J. D. Crossan à partir de la sociologie et de l'histoire. *Social Compass* 46: 471–79.

Yarbro-Collins, A. 1987. The Origins of the Designation of Jesus as the "'Son of Man." *HTR* 80: 391–407.

Zeitlin, I. M. 1988. *Jesus and the Judaism of His Time*. Cambridge: Polity.

———. 1990. Understanding the Man Jesus: A Historical-Sociological Approach. *Ultimate Reality and Meaning* 13: 164–76.

DEATH AND RESURRECTION OF JESUS: SURVIVAL OF HIS MOVEMENT

Craffert, P. F. 1989. The Origins of Resurrection Faith: The Challenge of a Social Scientific Approach. *Neot* 23: 331–48.

Crossan, J. D. 1998. *The Birth of Christianity: Discovering What Happened in the Year Immediately after the Execution of Jesus.* San Francisco: HarperCollins.

Jackson, H. M. 1975. The Resurrection Belief of the Earliest Church: A Response to the Failure of Prophecy? *JR* 55: 415–25.

Kent, J. A. 1996. The Psychological Origins of the Resurrection Myth. *Faith and Freedom* 49: 5–22.

Pickett, R. 1997. *The Cross in Corinth: The Social Significance of the Death of Jesus* (JSNT Sup. Ser. 143). Sheffield, England: Sheffield Academic Press.

Reichardt, M. 1997. Psychologische Erklarung der Ostererscheinungen? *BK* 52: 28–33.

Schottroff, L., and W. Schottroff. 1988. *Die Macht der Auferstehung: Sozialgeschichtliche Bibelauslegungen* (Kaiser Taschenbücher 30). Munich: Kaiser.

Vorster, W. S. 1989. The Religio-Historical Context of the Resurrection of Jesus and Resurrection Faith in the New Testament. *Neot* 23: 159–75.

Wanamaker, C. A. 1999. The Conversion of Jesus' Disciples and the Emergence of Christianity. *JTSA* 104: 16–31.

Matthew

Anderson, J. C. 1995. Life on the Mississippi: New Currents in Matthean Scholarship 1983–1993. *CRBS* 3: 169–218.

Balch, D. L., ed. 1991. *Social History of the Matthew Community: Cross-Disciplinary Approaches.* Minneapolis, Minn.: Fortress.

Capps, D. 1985. The Beatitudes and Erikson's Life-Cycle Theory. *Pastoral Psychology* 33: 226–44.

Carter, W. 1999. Paying the Tax to Rome as a Subversive Praxis: Matthew 17.24–27. *JSNT* 76: 3–31.

Crosby, M. H. 1988. *House of Disciples: Church, Economics, and Justice in Matthew.* Maryknoll, N.Y.: Orbis.

Duling, D. C. 1992. Matthew's Plurisignificant "Son of David" in Social Science Perspective: Kinship, Kingship, Magic, and Miracle. *BTB* 22: 99–116.

Humphries-Brooks, S. 1991. Indicators of Social Organisation and Status in Matthew's Gospel. In *SBLSP 1991*, ed. E Lovering, 31–49. Atlanta: Scholars Press.

Levine, A. -J. 1988. *The Social and Ethnic Dimensions of Matthean Social History.* Lewiston, N.Y.: Mellen.

Love, S. L. 1994. The Place of Women in Public Setting in Mathew's Gospel: A Sociological Inquiry. *BTB* 24: 52–65.

Malina, B. J. 1984. Jesus as a Charismatic Leader? *BTB* 14: 55–62.

———, and J. H. Neyrey. 1988. *Calling Jesus Names: The Social Value of Labels in Matthew* (Foundations & Facets. Social Facets). Sonoma, Calif.: Polebridge.

McVann, M. 1989. The Making of Jesus the Prophet: Matthew 3:13–4:25 (Temptation as Rite of Passage). *Listening* 24: 262–77.

Overman, J. A. 1990. *Matthew's Gospel and Formative Judaism: The Social World of the Matthean Community.* Minneapolis, Minn.: Fortress.

Pamment, M. 1981. Witch-Hunt. *Theology* 84: 98–106.

Pilch, J. J. 1986. The Health Care System in Matthew: A Social Science Analysis. *BTB* 16: 102–6.

———. 1989. Reading Matthew Anthropologically: Healing in Cultural Perspective. *Listening* 24: 278–89.

Riches, J. K. 1983. The Sociology of Matthew: Some Basic Questions Concerning Its Relation to the Theology of the New Testament. In *SBLSP 1983*. Chico, Calif.: Scholars Press, 259–71.

Rohrbaugh, R. L. 1993b. A Peasant Reading of the Parable of the Talent\Pounds: A Text of Terror? *BTB* 23: 32–39.

Saldarini, A. J. 1994. *Matthew's Christian-Jewish Community* (Chicago Studies in the History of Judaism). Chicago: The University of Chicago.

Sim, D. C. 1998. *The Gospel of Matthew and Christian Judaism: The History and Social Setting of the Matthean Community* (Studies of the New Testament and Its World). Edinburgh: T. & T. Clark.

Viviano, B. T. 1990. Social World and Community Leadership: The Case of Matthew 23:1–12, 34. *JSNT* 39: 3–21.

Vledder, E. -J. 1997. *Conflict in the Miracle Stories: A Socio-Exegetical Study of Matthew 8 and 9* (JSNT Sup. Ser. 152). Sheffield, England: Sheffield Academic Press.

———, and A. G. Van Aarde. 1994. The Social Stratification of Matthew Community. *Neot* 28: 511–22.

———. 1995. The Social Location of the Matthew's Gospel. *Vidyajyoti* 59: 437–48.

White, L. J. 1986. Grid and Group in Matthew's Community: The Righteousness/Honor Code in the Sermon of the Mount. *Semeia* 35: 61–90.

Wick, P. 1998. Der historische Ort von Mt 6, 1–18. *RevistB* 105: 332–58.

Mark

Barraclough, R. 1992. Power-sharing in the Kingdom of God: A Political Paradigm in Mark 10:35–45 and Parallels. In *In the Fullness of Ttime*, ed. D. Peterson and J. Pryor, 45–56. Homebush West, NSW, Australia: Lancer.

Beavis, M. A. 1989. *Mark's Audience: The Literary and Social Setting of Mark 4:11–12* (JSNT Sup. Ser. 33). Sheffield, England: JSOT Press.

Bélo, F. 1974. *Lecture matéraliste de l'évangile de Marc*. Paris: Cerf.

Best, E. 1986. *Disciples and Discipleship: Studies in the Gospel According to Mark*. Edinburgh: T. & T. Clark.

Bonneau, G. 1998. *Prophétisme et institution dans le christianisme primitif* (Sciences bibliques 4). Montréal: Médiaspaul.

Delorme, J. 1999. Jésus mésestimé et impuissant dans sa patrie (Marc 6, 1–6). *Nouvelle Revue théologique* 121: 3–22.

Derrett, J. D. M. 1979a. Contributions to the Study of the Garasene Demoniac (Mk 5:1–20). *JSNT* 3: 2–17.

———. 1979b. Spirit Possession and the Gerasene Demoniac. *Man* N.S. 14: 286–93.

Kee, H. C. 1977. *Community of the New Age: Studies in Mark's Gospel*. Philadelphia : Westminster.

Mack, B. L. 1988. *A Myth of Innocence: Mark and Christian Origins*. Philadelphia: Fortress.

Matera, F. J. 1987. *What Are They Saying about Mark?* New York: Paulist.

May, D. M. 1987. Mark 3:20–35 from the Perspective of Shame Honor. *BTB* 17: 83–87.

———. 1990. Leaving and Receiving: A Social Scientific Exegesis of Mark 10:29–31. *PRSt* 17: 141–51, 154.

Myers, C. 1988. *Binding the Strong Man: A Political Reading of Mark's Story of Jesus.* Maryknoll, N.Y.: Orbis.

Neyrey, J. H. 1986b. The Idea of Purity in Mark's Gospel. *Semeia* 35: 91–128.

Nuefeld, D. 2000. Jesus' Eating Transgression and Social Impropriety in the Gospel of Mark: A Social Scientific Approach. *BTB* 30: 15–26.

Pilch, J. J. 1985. Healing in Mark: A Social Science Analysis. *BTB* 15: 142–50.

Robbins, V. K. 1984/1992. *Jesus the Teacher: A Socio-Rhetorical Interpretation of Mark.* Philadelphia: Fortress.

Rohrbaugh, R. L. 1993. The Social Location of the Markan Audience. *BTB* 23: 114–27.

Ruiz Pérez, M. D. 1998. El feminismo secreto de Marcos. *Communio* 31/1: 3–23.

Selvidge, M. J. S. 1983. And Those Who Followed Feared (Mark 10:32). *CBQ* 45: 396–400.

Smit, J. 1994. The Sociological Explication of Conflict in the Gospel According to Mark. In *The Relevance of Theology for the 1990s,* ed. J. Mouton, 585–601. Pretoria: Human Science Research Council.

Staples, P. 1993. The Cultural Management of Space and Time in the Narrative of the Gospel of Mark. *Forum* 9/112: 19–45.

Suh, J. S. 1991. *Discipleship and Community: Mark's Gospel in Sociological Perspective* (Nexus Monograph Series 1). Claremont, Calif.: Center for Asian-American Ministries, School of Theology at Claremont.

Theissen, G. 1977. "Wir haben alles verlassen" (Mc. X 28): Nachfolge und soziale Entwurzelung in der jüdischpalästinischen Gessellschaft des I. Jahrhunderts n. Ch. *NovT* 19: 161–96.

———. 1984. Local- und Sozialkolorit in der Geschichte von der syrophönikischen Frau (Mk 7:24–30). *ZNW* 75: 202–25.

Thompson, W. G. 1987. Mark's Gospel and Faith Development. *Chicago Studies* 26: 139–54.

Vouga, F. 1995. Das Markusevangelium als literarisches Werk: Eine Weiterentwicklung des paulinischen Evangeliums? Überlegungen zur Problematik Schriftlichkeit/Mündlichkeit. *WD* 23: 109–24.

Waetjen, H. C. 1984. *A Reordering of Power: A Socio-Political Reading of Mark's Gospel.* Philadelphia: Fortress.

Wilde, J. A. 1974. *A Social Description of the Community Reflected in the Gospel of Mark.* Ph.D. dissertation, Drew University, Madison, N.J.

Luke–Acts

Abraham, M. V. 1987. Good News to the Poor in Luke's Gospel. *Bangalore Theological Forum* 19: 1–13.

Arens, E. 1999a. El año de gracia del Señor: Observaciones y reflexiones sobre el jubileo. *Páginas* 160: 46–56.

Arlandson, J. M. 1997. *Women, Class, and Society in Early Christianity: Models from Luke–Acts.* Peabody, Mass.: Hendrickson.

Balch, D. L. 1995. *Through Peasant Eyes: More Lukan Parables, Their Culture and Style.* Grand Rapids, Mich.: Eerdmans [1980].

Beydon, F. 1986. Luc et ses dames de la haute société. *ETR* 61: 331–41.

Braun, W. 1995. *Feasting and Social Rhetoric in Luke 14* (SNTSMS 85). Cambridge: Cambridge University.

Buckley, F. J. 1990. Healing and Reconciliation in the Gospel According to Luke. *Emmanuel* 96: 74–80.

Cassidy, R. J. 1978. *Jesus, Politics, and Society: A Study of Luke's Gospel.* Maryknoll, N.Y.: Orbis.

———. 1987. *Society and Politics in the Acts of Apostles.* Maryknoll, N.Y.: Orbis.

Cazeaux, P. 1989. A propos de Luc 18, 9–14: Le pharisien et le publicain. *Masses Ouvrières* 424: 79–87.

Combrink, H. J. B. 1996. A Social-Scientific Perspective on the Parable of the "Unjust Steward." *Neot* 30: 281–306.

Cuvillier, E. 1990. Luc et les christianismes primitifs. *ETR* 65: 93–99.

Czachesz, I. 1995. Socio-rhetorical Exegesis of Acts 9:1–30. *CV* 37: 5–32.

Daube, D. 1982. Shame Culture in Luke. In *Paul and Paulinism: Essays in Honour of C. K. Barret*, ed. M. D. Hooker and S. G. Wilson, 355–72. London: SPCK.

Davies, D. J. 1995. Rebounding Vitality: Resurrection and Spirit in Luke–Acts. In *The Bible in Human Society* (JSOT Sup. Ser. 200), ed. M. R. Carroll, 205–24. Sheffield, England: JSOT Press.

Domeris, W. R. 1993. Cellars, Wages and Gardens: Luke's Accommodation for Middle-class Christians. *HTS* 49: 85–100.

Edwards, D. R. 1991. Surviving the Web of Roman Power: Religion and Politics in the Acts of the Apostles, Josephus, and Chariton's Chaereas and Callirhoe. In *Images of Empire*, ed. L. Alexander, 179–201. Sheffield, England: JSOT Press.

Elliott, J. H. 1991a. Household and Meals vs Temple Purity: Replication Patterns in Luke–Acts. *BTB* 21: 102–08.

———. 1991b. Temple vs Household in Luke–Acts: A Contrast in Social Institutions. In *The Social World of Luke–Acts: Models for Interpretation*, ed. J. Neyrey, 211–40. Peabody, Mass.: Hendrikson.

Esler, P. F. 1987. *Community and Gospel in Luke–Acts: The Social and Political Motivations of Lukan Theology* (SNTSMS 57). Cambridge: Cambridge University.

Fiensy, D. A. 1999. The Importance of New Testament Background Studies in Biblical Research: The "Evil Eye" in Luke 11:34 as a Case Study. *Stone–Campbell Journal* 2: 75–88.

Garrett, S. R. 1989. *The Demise of the Devil: Magic and the Demonic in Luke's Writings.* Minneapolis, Minn.: Fortress.

Gill, D. W. J. 1994. Acts and the Urban Elites. In *The Book of Acts in Its First Century Setting.* Vol. 2, ed. D. Gill, 105–18. Grand Rapids, Mich.: Eerdmans.

Goulder, M. D. 1988. *Luke: A New Paradigm* (JSNT Sup. Ser. 20). Sheffield, England: JSOT Press.

Gowler, D. B. 1991. *Host, Guest, Enemy and Friends: Portrait of Pharisees in Luke Acts* (Emory Studies in Early Christianity 2). New York: Peter Lang.

Kee, H. C. 1990. *The Theology of Acts.* Valley Forge, Penn.: Trinity Press International.

Kilgallen, J. J. 1990. Social Development in Lucan World. *Studia Missionalia* 39: 21–47.

Kirk, A. K. 1999. Peasant Wisdom, the "Our Father" and the Origins of Christianity. *TJT* 15: 31–50.

Klauck, H. -J. 1996. *Magie und Heidentum in der Apostelgeschichte des Lukas* (Stuttgarter Bibelstuden 167). Stuttgart, Germany: Katholisches Bibelwerk.

Kraus, T. J. 1999. "Uneducated," "Ignorant," or even "Illiterate"? Aspects and Background for an Understanding of αγραμματοι and ιδιωται in Acts 4.13. *NTS* 45: 434–49.

Kraybill, D. B., and D. M. Sweetland. 1983. Possessions in Luke–Acts: A Sociological Perspective. *Perspectives in Religious Studies* 10: 215–39.

LaHurd, C. S. 1994. Rediscovering the Lost Women in Luke 15. *BTB* 24: 66–76.

Liu, P. 1992. Did the Lukan Jesus Desire Voluntary Poverty of His Followers? *EvQ* 64: 291–317.

Loubster, J. A. 1994. Wealth, House Churches and Rome: Luke's Ideological Perspective. *JTSA* 89: 59–69.

Maguerat, D. 1997. Magie, guérison et parole dans les Actes des apôtres. *ETR* 72: 197–208.

Mitchell, A. C. 1992. The Social Function of Friendship in Acts 2:44–47 and 4:32–37, *JBL* 111: 255–72.

Moxnes, H. 1986–87. Meals and the New Community in Luke. *SEÅ* 51–52, 158–67.

———. 1987. The Economy of the Gospel of Luke in Light of Social Anthropology. In *Urkristendommen* 2, 1–35. Oslo: University of Oslo.

———. 1988. *The Economy of the Kingdom: Social Conflict and Economic Relations in Luke's Gospel.* Philadelphia: Fortress.

———. 1991. Social Relations and Economic Interaction in Luke's Gospel: A Research Report. In *Luke–Acts: Scandinavian Perspectives*, ed. P. Luomanen, 58–75. Helsinki: Finnish Exegetical Society

———. 1994. The Social Context of Luke's Community. *Int* 48: 379–89.

Neyrey, J. H., ed. 1991. *The Social World of Luke–Acts: Model for Interpretation.* Peabody, Mass.: Hendrickson.

Oakman, D. E. 1992. Was Jesus a Peasant? Implication for Reading the Samaritan Story (Luke 10:30–35). *BTB* 22: 117–25.

Pokorny, P. 1992. Die soziale Strategie in den lukanischen Schriften. *CV* 34: 9–19.

Sanders, J. T. 1987. *The Jews in Luke–Acts.* Philadelphia: Fortress.

Scheffler, E. H. 1988. A Psychological Reading of Luke: 35–48. *Neot* 22: 355–71.

Sloan, I. 1993. The Greatest and the Youngest: Greco-Roman Reciprocity in the Farewell Address, Luke 22:24–30. *SR* 22: 63–73.

Spencer, F. S. 1999. Out of Mind, Out of Voice: Slave-Girls and Prophetic Daughters in Luke–Acts. *BibInt* 7: 133–55.

Stoops, R. F. 1989. Riot and Assembly: The Social Context of Acts 19:23–41. *JBL* 108: 73–91.

Tyson, J. B., ed. 1988. *Luke–Acts and the Jewish People: Eight Critical Perspectives.* Minneapolis, Minn.: Augsburg.

Van Staden, P. 1988. A Sociological Reading of Luke 12: 35–48. *Neot* 22: 337–53.

———. 1991. *Compassion—The Essence of Life: A Social-Scientific Study of Religious Symbolic Universe Reflected in the Ideology/Theology of Luke* (Nervormde Teologiese Studies Supplement 4). Pretoria: University of Pretoria.

West, T. C. 1999. The Mary and Martha Story: Who Learns What Lesson about Women and Ministry. *Quarterly Review* 19: 135–52.

Zylstra, C, 1991. Anthropological Consideration for the Book of Luke. *Notes* 5: 1–13.

John

Bahr, A. M. 1991. God's Family and Flocks: Remarks on Ownership in the Fourth Gospel. In *Covenant for a New Creation*, ed. C. Robb and C. Casebolt, 91–104. Maryknoll, N.Y.: Orbis Books.

Blasi, A. J. 1996. *A Sociology of Johannine Christianity* (Texts and Studies in Religion 69). Lewiston, N.Y.: Mellen.

Braun, W. 1990. Resisting John: Ambivalent Redactor and Defensive Reader of the Fourth Gospel. *SR* 19: 59–73.

Brown, R. E. 1979. *The Community of the Beloved Disciple*. New York : Paulist.

Busse, U. 1995. The Relevance of Social History to the Interpretation of the Gospel According to John. *Skrif en kerk* 16: 28–38.

Carter, W. 1990. The Prologue of John's Gospel: Function, Symbol and the Definitive Word. *JSNT* 39: 35–58.

Cosgrove, C. H. 1989. The Place Where Jesus Is: Allusions to Baptism and the Eucharist in the Fourth Gospel. *NTS* 35: 522–39.

Destro, A., and M. Pesce. 1995b. Kinship, Discipleship and Movement: An Anthropological Study of John's Gospel. *BibInt* 3: 266–84.

Draper, J. A. 1992. The Sociological Function of the Spirit/Paraclete in the Farewell Discourses in the Fourth Gospel. *Neot* 26: 13–29.

Kieffer, R. 1989. *Le monde symbolique de Saint Jean* (LD 137). Paris: Cerf.

Liebert, E. 1984. That You May Believe: The Fourth Gospel and Structural Development Theory. *BTB* 14: 67–73.

Lombard, H. A. 1998. Orthodoxy and Other-Worldliness of the Church: Johannine Perspectives on Christianity on a New South Africa. *Neot* 32: 497–508.

Malina, B. J. 1985. The Gospel of John in Sociolinguistic Perspective. *Center for Hermeneutical Studies Protocol* 48: 1–23.

———, and R. L. Rohrbaugh. 1998. *Social-Science Commentary on the Gospel of John*. Minneapolis, Minn.: Fortress.

Meeks, W. A. 1966. Galilee and Judea in the Fourth Gospel. *JBL* 85: 159–69.

———. 1972. The Man from Heaven in Johannine Sectarianism. *JBL* 91: 44–72. Reprinted in *The Interpretation of John* (Issues in Religion and Theology 9), ed. J. Ashton, 141–73. Philadelphia: Fortress.

———. 1967. *The Prophet-King. Moses Traditions and the Johannine Christology*. Leiden: E. J. Brill. Supplement to *Novum Testamentum*, vol. 14.

———. 1975. "Am I a Jew?" Johannine Christianity and Judaism. In *Christianity, Judaism and Other Greco-Roman Cults: Studies for Morton Smith at Sixty.* Vol. I, ed. J. Neusner, 163–86. Leiden: E. J. Brill

———. 1976. The Divine Agent and His Counterfeit in Philo and in the Fourth Gospel. In *Aspect of Religious Propaganda in Judaism and Early Christianity,* 43–62. Notre Dame, Ind.: University of Notre Dame.

Neyrey, J. H. 1986c. "My Lord and My God": The Divinity of Jesus in the Fourth Gospel. In *SBLSP 1986,* 152–71. Atlanta, Scholars Press.

———. 1988a. *An Ideology of Revolt: John's Christology in Social-Science Perspective.* Philadelphia: Fortress.

———. 1995. The Footwashing in John 13:6–11: Transformation Ritual or Ceremony? In *The Social World of the First Christians,* ed. L.White et al., 198–213. Minneapolis, Minn.: Fortress.

Petersen, N. R. 1993. *The Gospel of John and the Sociology of Light: Language and Characterization of the Fourth Gospel.* Valley Forge, Penn.: Trinity Press International.

Rebell, W. 1987. *Gemeinde als Gegenwelt: Zur soziologischen und didactischen Funktion des Johannese-vangelium* (Beiträge zur biblischen Exegese und Theologie 20). Frankfurt: P. Lang.

Reim, G. 1988. Zur Lokalisierung der Johannischen Gemeinde. *BZ* 32: 72–86.

Rensberger, D. 1988. *Johannine Faith and Liberating Community.* Philadelphia: Westminster/John Knox.

Sandford, J. 1993. *Mystical Christianity: A Psychological Commentary on the Gospel of John.* New York: Crossroad.

Segovia, F. F. 1995. The Significance of Social Location in Reading John's Story. *Int* 49: 370–78.

Von Wahlde, U. C. 1995. Community in Conflict: The History and Social Context of the Johannine Community. *Int* 49: 379–89.

Epistles–Revelation

Paul and Pauline Christianity

Adams, E. 2000. *Constructing the World: A Study in Paul's Cosmological Language.* Edinburgh: T. & T. Clark.

Adeyemi, M. E. 1991. A Sociological Approach to the Background of Pauline Epistles. *DBM* 10: 32–42.

Álvarez Verdes, L. 1999. El carismatismo en Pablo: Aproximación sociológico–teológica. *EstBíb* 57 : 23–38.

Barclay, J. M. G. 1992. Thessalonica and Corinth: Social Contrasts in Pauline Christianity. *JSNT* 47: 49–74.

Bartchy, S. S. 1999. Undermining Ancient Patriarchy: The Apostle Paul's Vision of a Society of Siblings. *BTB* 29: 68–78.

Barton, S. 1982. Paul and the Cross: A Sociological Approach. *Theology* 85: 13–19.

———. 1984. Paul and the Resurrection: A Sociological Approach. *Religion* 14: 67–75.

Blasi, A. J. 1991. *Making Charisma: The Social Construction of Paul's Public Image*. New Brunswick, N.J.: Transaction.

Botha, P. J. J. 1998. Paul and Gossip: A Social Mechanism in Early Christian Communities. *Neot* 32: 267–88.

Brownrigg, R. 1989. *Pauline Places: In the Footsteps of Turkey and Greece*. London: Hodder & Stoughton.

Callan, T. 1986. Competition and Boasting: Toward a Psychological Portrait of Paul. *ST* 40: 137–56. Reprint: *JRelS* 13 [1987]: 27–51.

Castelli, E. A. 1991. *Imitating Paul: A Discourse of Power* (Literary Currents in Biblical Interpretation). Louisville, Ky.: Westminster/Knox.

Clark, G. 1985. The Social Status of Paul. *ExpTim* 96: 110–11.

Corrigan, G. M. 1986. Paul's Shame for the Gospel. *BTB* 16: 23–27.

Craffert, P. F. 1999. The Pauline Household Communities: Their Nature as Social Entities. *Neot* 32: 309–41.

De Vos, C. S. 1999. *Church and Community Conflicts: The Relationships of the Thessalonian, Corinthian and Philippian Churches with Their Wider Civic Communities* (SBL Dissertation Series 168). Atlanta: Scholars Press.

Ellis, E. E. 1989. *Pauline Theology: Ministry and Society*. Grand Rapids, Mich.: Eerdmans.

Fitzpatrick, J. P. 1990. *Paul, Saint of the Inner City*. New York: Paulist.

Fredriksen, P. 1986. Paul and Augustine: Conversion Narratives, Orthodox Traditions, and the Retrospective Self. *JTS* 37: 3–34.

Funk, A. 1981. *Status und Rollen in den Paulusbriefen: Eine inhaltsanalytische Untersuchung zur Religionssoziologie* (Insbrucker Theologische Studien, 7). Innsbruck, Austria: Tyrolia.

Gager, J. G. 1981. Some Notes on Paul's Conversion. *NTS* 27: 697–704.

Gallagher, E. V. 1984. The Social World of Saint Paul. *Religion* 14: 91–99.

Garmus, L., ed. 1990. *Sociologia das Comunidas Paulinas* (Estudos Biblicos 24). Petropolis, Brazil: Vozes.

Gielen, M. 1990. *Tradition und Theologie neutestamentlicher Haustafelethik: Ein Beitrag zur Frage einer christlichen Auseinandersetzung mit gesellschaftlichen Normen*. Frankfurt: Hain.

Hock, R. F. 1978. Paul's Tentmaking and the Problem of His Social Class. *JBL* 97: 555–64.

———. 1979. The Workshop as a Social Setting for Paul's Missionary Preaching. *CBQ* 41: 439–50.

———. 1980. *The Social Context of Paul's Ministry: Tentmaking and Apostleship*. Philadelphia: Fortress.

Holmberg, B. 1978/1980a. *Paul and Power: The Structure of Authority in the Primitive Church as Reflected in the Pauline Epistles*. Lund, Sweden: C. W. K. Gleerup; Philadelphia: Fortress.

———. 1980b. Sociological Versus Theological Analysis of the Question Concerning a Pauline Church Order. In *Die paulisniche Literatur und Theologie*, ed. S. Petersen, 187–200. Göttingen, Germany: Vandenhoeck & Ruprecht.

Jaquette, J. L. 1995. *Discerning What Counts: The Function of the Adiaphora Topos in Paul's Letters*. Atlanta: Scholars Press.

Judge, E. A. 1972. St. Paul and Classical Society. *JAC* 15: 19–36

————. 1984. Cultural Conformity and Innovation in Paul: Some Clues from Contemporary Documents. *TynBul* 35: 3–24.

Laato, T. 1995. *Paul and Judaism: An Anthropological Approach* (South Florida Studies in the History of Judaism 115). Atlanta: Scholars Press.

Lodge, J. G. 1985. All Things to All: Paul's Pastoral Strategy. *Chicago Studies* 24: 291–306.

Louis, A. F. 1990. The Psychological Wisdom of Pauline Theology. *Center for Hermeneutical Studies Protocol* 60: 29–34.

Lüdemann, G. 1989. *Opposition to Paul in Jewish Christianity*. Minneapolis, Minn.: Fortress.

MacDonald, M. Y. 1988. *The Pauline Churches: A Socio-Historical Study of Institutionalization in the Pauline and Deutero-Pauline Writings* (SNTSMS 60). Cambridge: Cambridge University Press.

Malina, B. J. 1981. The Apostle Paul and Law: Prolegomena for a Hermeneutic. *Creighton Law Review* 14: 1305–39.

————. 1986. "Religion" in the World of Paul. *BTB* 16: 92–101.

Meeks, W. A. 1979. "Since Then You Would Need to Go Out of the World": Group Boundaries in Pauline Christianity. In *Critical History and Biblical Faith*, ed. T. J. Ryan, 4–29. Villanova, Penn.: College Theology Society/Horizons.

————. 1982. The Social Context of Pauline Theology. *Int* 36: 266–77.

————. 1983a. *The First Urban Christians: The Social World of the Apostle Paul*. New Haven, Conn.: Yale University.

————. 1983b. Social Functions of Apocalyptic Language in Pauline Christianity. In *Apocalypticism in the Mediterranean World and the Near East*, ed. D. Hellholm, 687–706. Tübingen, Germany: Mohr-Siebeck.

Moxnes, H. 1989. Social Integration and the Problem of Gender in St. Paul's Letters. *ST* 43: 99–113.

Paloma, P. E. 1998. Poverty and Saint Paul. *Quaerens* (Quezon City) 2, 1: 93–144.

Schlosser, J., ed. 1996. *Paul de Tarse: Congrès de l'ACFEB (Strasbourg 1995)* (LD 165). Paris: Cerf.

Schöllgen, G. 1988. Was wissen wir über die Sozialstructur der paulinischen Gemeinden? Kritische Anmerkungen zu einem neuen Buch von W.A. Meeks. *NTS* 34: 71–82.

Schütz, J. H. 1974. Charisma and Social Reality in Primitive Christianity. *JR* 54: 51–70.

————. 1975. *Paul and the Anatomy of Apostolic Authority*. New York: Cambridge University Press.

————. 1980. *Paul and Power: The Structure of Authority in the Primitive Church as Reflected in the Pauline Epistles*. Philadelphia: Fortress.

Stegemann, W. 1987. War der Apostel Paulus ein römischer Bürger? *ZNW* 78: 200–229.

Stoers, S. K. 1984. Social Class, Public Speaking and Private Teaching: The Circumstances of Paul's Preaching Activity. *NovT* 26: 59–82.

Summers, S. 1998. Out of My Mind for God: A Social-Scientific Approach to Pauline Pneumatology. *Journal of Pentecostal Theology* 13: 77–106

Taylor, N. H. 1992. *Paul, Antioch and Jerusalem: A Study in Relationships and Authority in Earliest Christianity* (JSNT Supplement Series 66). Sheffield, England: JSOT.

————. 1996. Paolo: Fariseo, cristiano e dissonante. *Religioni e Società* 11, 24: 22–39.

———. 1997. Paul for Today: Race, Class and Gender in the Light of Cognitive Dissonance Theory. *Listening* 32, 1: 22–38.

Theissen, G. 1987. *Psychological Aspects of Pauline Theology.* Philadelphia: Fortress.

Watson, F. 1986. *Paul, Judaism, and the Gentiles: A Sociological Approach* (SNTSMS 56). Cambridge: Cambridge University Press.

Wedderburn, A. J. M. 1987. *Baptism and Resurrection: Studies in Pauline Theology against Its Graeco-Roman Background* (WUNT 44). Tübingen, Germany: Mohr–Siebeck.

Paulinian Corpus

Agosto, E. 1998. Social Analysis of the New Testament in Hispanic Theology: A Case Study. *Journal of Hispanic/Latino Theology* (Collegeville, Minn.) 5: 6–29.

Anderson, C. 1993. Romans 1:1–15 and the Occasion of the Letter: The Solution to the Two-Congregation Problem in Rome. *Trinity Journal* 14: 25–40.

Arnold, C. E. 1989. *Ephesians: Power and Magic: The Concept of Power in Ephesians in Light of Its Historical Setting* (SNTSMS, 63). Cambridge: Cambridge University Press.

Barton, S. C. 1986. Paul's Sense of Place: An Anthropological Approach to Community Formation in Corinth. *NTS* 32: 225–46.

Bassler, J. M. 1984. The Widow's Tale: A Fresh Look at 1 Tim 5: 3–6. *JBL* 103: 23–41.

BeDuhn, J. D. 1999. "Because of the Angels": Unveiling Paul's Anthropology in Corinthians 11. *JBL* 118: 295–320.

Blasi, A. J. 1995. Office Charisma in Early Christian Ephesus. *SocRel* 56: 245–55.

———. 1999. L'idéologie de l'Église chrétienne primitive dans l'epître de saint Paul aux Romains et la lettre de recommandation de Phébée. *Social Compass* 46: 507–20.

Blue, B. B. 1991. The House Church at Corinth and the Lord's Supper: Famine, Food Supply and Present Distress. *CTR* 5: 221–39.

Botha, J. 1994. *Subject to Whose Authority? Multiple Readings of Romans 13* (Emory Studies in Early Christianity 4). Atlanta: Scholars Press.

Callahan, A. D. 1993. Paul's Epistle to Philemon: Toward an Alternative Argumentum. *HTR* 86: 357–76.

Corry, N. 1999. Questions of Authority, Status and Power. *Scripture* 70: 181–94.

DeMaris, R. E. 1995. Corinthian Religion and Baptism for the Dead (1 Corinthians 15:29): Insights from Archaeology and Anthropology. *JBL* 114: 661–82.

DeSilva, D. A. 1999. Hebrews 6:4–8: A Socio-Rhetorical Investigation (Part 2). *TynBull* 50: 225–35.

Diaz Mateos, M. 1990. "La solidaridad de la fe": Eclesologia de la carta a Filemón. *Páginas* (Lima) 101: 23–39.

Duquoc, C. 1999. Mission d'Israël dans le temps de l'Église. *LumVie* 48 (no. 242): 51–61.

du Toit, A. B. 1998. God's Beloved in Rome (Rm. 1:7). The Genesis and Socio-Economic Situation of the First Generation Christian Community in Rome. *Neot* 32: 367–88.

Engberg-Pedersen, T. 1987. The Gospel and Social Practice According to 1 Corinthians. *NTS* 33: 557–84.

Georgi, D. 1986. *The Opponents of Paul in 2 Corinthians: A Study of Religious Propaganda in Late Antiquity.* Philadelphia: Fortress.

Gill, D. W. J 1993. In Search of the Social Elite in the Corinthian Church. *TynBul* 44: 323–37.

Gooch, P. D. 1993. *Dangerous Food: 1 Corinthians 8–10 in Its Context.* Waterloo, Ont.: Wilfrid Laurier University.

Gundry-Volf, J. M. 1994. Celibate Pneumatics and Social Power: On the Motivation for Sexual Ascetism in Corinth. *USQR* 48: 105–26.

Hammerton-Kelly, R. 1985. A Girardian Interpretation of Paul: Rivalry, Mimesis and Victimage in the Corinthian Correspondence. *Semeia* 33: 65–81.

Heiligenthal, R. 1984. Soziologische Implikationen der paulinischen Rechtfertigungslehere im Galaterbrief am Beispiel der "Werke des Gesetzes." Beobachtungen zur Identitätsfindung einer frühchristlicher Gemeinde. *Kairos* 26: 38–53.

Holland, G. S. 1988. *The Tradition That You Received from Us: 2 Thessalonians in the Pauline Tradition* (HUT 24). Tübingen, Germany: Mohr-Siebeck.

Holmberg, B. 1990. Sociological Perspective on Gal 2, 11–14 (21). *SEÅ* 55: 71–92.

———. 1998. Jewish Versus Christian Identity in the Early Church? *RevistB* 105: 397–425.

Horrell, D. G. 1993. "Converging Ideologies": Berger and Luckmann and the Pastoral Epistles. *JSNT* 50: 85–103.

———. 1995. The Development of Theological Ideology in Pauline Christianity: A Structuration Theory Perspective. In *Modeling Early Christianity*, ed. P. F. Esler, 224–36. New York: Routledge.

———. 1996. *The Social Ethos of the Corinthian Correspondence: Interests and Ideology from 1 Corinthians to 1 Clement.* Edinburgh: T. & T. Clark.

Jewett, R. 1997. Gospel and Commensality: Social and Theological Implications of Galatians 2:14. In *Gospel in Paul* (JSNT Supp. Ser. 108), ed. A. Jervis et al., 240–52. Sheffield, England: Sheffield Academic Press.

Johnson, L. A. 1999. Satan Talk in Corinth: The Rhetoric of Conflict. *BTB* 29: 145–55.

Keck, L. E. 1996. God the Other Who Acts Otherwise: An Exegetical Essay on 1 Cor 1:26–31. *Word and World* 16: 437–43.

Keightley, G. M. 1987. The Church's Memory of Jesus: A Social Science Analysis of 1 Thessalonians. *BTB* 17: 149–56.

Lincoln, A. T. 1999. The Household Code and Wisdom Mode of Colossians. *JSNT* 74: 93–112.

MacDonald, M. Y. 1990. Women Holy in Body and Spirit: The Social Setting of 1 Corinthians 7. *NTS* 36: 161–81.

Malherbe, A. J. 1987. *Paul and the Thessalonians: The Philosophic Tradition of Pastoral Care.* Philadelphia: Fortress.

Marshall, P. 1987. *Enmity in Corinth: Social Conventions in Paul's Relations with the Corinthians* (WUNT 2, 23). Tübingen, Germany: Mohr.

McClane, C. D. 1998. The Hellenistic Background to the Pauline Allegorical Method in Galatians 4:21–31. *ResQ* 40: 125–35.

Meggitt, J. J. 1996. The Social Status of Erastus (Rom. 16:23). *NovT* 38: 218–23.

Meyer, R. 1989. *La vie après la mort: Saint Paul défenseur de la résurrection* (La Pensée Chrétienne). Lausanne, Switzerland: Belle Rivière.

Míguez, N. O. 1989a. La composición social de la Iglesia en Tesalonica. *RevistB* 51: 65–89.

———. 1989b. La ética cristiana: Una opción contra Hegemónica. *Cuadernos de Teologica* 10, 2: 15–25.

———. 1989c. Pablo y la revolución cristiana en el primer siglo. *Cuadernos de Teologica* (Buenos Aires) 10: 67–80.

Mitchell, A. C. 1993. Rich and Poor in the Courts of Corinth: Litigiousness and Status in I Corinthians 6:1–11. *NTS* 39: 562–86.

Moxnes, H. 1985. Paulus og den norske vaeremåten: "Skam" og "aere" i Romerbrevet. *NTT* 86: 126–40.

———. 1988a. Honor and Righteousness in Romans. *JSNT* 32: 61–78.

———. 1988b. Honor, Shame and the Outside World in Paul's Letter to the Romans. In *The Social World of Formative Christianity and Judaism*, ed. J. Neusner, 207–18. Philadelphia: Fortress.

Murphy-O'Connor, J. 1976. Christological Anthropology in Phil 2, 6–11. *RB* 83: 25–50.

———, with introduction by J. H. Elliott. 1983. *St. Paul's Corinth: Texts and Archaeology.* (Good News Studies 6). Wilmington, Del.: Michael Glazier; 2nd ed., Collegeville, Minn.: Liturgical Press 1990.

Nanos, M. D. 1999. The Jewish Context of the Gentile Audience Addressed in Paul's Letter to the Romans. *CBQ* 61: 283–304.

Neyrey, J. H. 1986a. Body Language in I Corinthians: The Use of Anthropological Models for Understanding Paul and His Opponents. *Semeia* 35: 129–70.

———. 1986b. Witchcraft Accusations in 2 Cor 10–13: Paul in Social-Science Perspective. *Listening* 21: 160–70.

———. 1988b. Bewitched in Galatia: Paul and Cultural Anthropology. *CBQ* 50: 72–100.

Peterlin, D. 1995. *Paul's Letter to the Philippians in the Light of Disunity in the Church* (NovTSup 79). Leiden: E. J. Brill.

Petersen, N. R. 1985. *Rediscovering Paul: Philemon and the Sociology of Paul's Narrative World.* Philadelphia: Fortress.

Pietersen, L. 1997. Despicable Deviants: Labeling Theory and the Polemic of the Pastorals. *SocRel* 58: 343–52.

Pretorius, E. 1998. Role Models for a Model Church: Typifying Paul's Letter to the Philippians. *Neot* 32: 547–71.

Rowe, A. 1990. Silence and the Christian Women of Corinth: An Examination of I Corinthians 14: 33b–36. *CV* 33:41–84.

Russel, R. 1988. The Idle in 2 Thes 3: 6–12: An Eschatological or a Social Problem? *NTS* 34: 105–19.

Savage, T. B. 1996. *Power through Weakness: Paul's Understanding of the Christian Ministry in 2 Corinthians* (SNTSMS 86). Cambridge: Cambridge University Press.

Schreiber, A. 1977. *Die Gemeinde in Korinth: Versuch einer gruppendynamischen Betrachtung der Entwicklung der Gemeinde von Korith auf der Basis der ersten Korintherbriefes.* Münster, Germany: Aschendorff.

Taylor, N. H. 1996. Onesimus: A Case Study of a Slave Conversion in Early Christianity. *Religion and Theology* 3: 259–81.

Tellbe, M. 1994. The Sociological Factors behind Philippians 3:1–11 and the Conflict at Philippi. *JSNT* 55: 97–121.

Theissen, G. 1974a. Soziale Integration und sacramentales Handeln: Eine Analyse von I Cor. XI 17–34. *NovT* 16: 179–206.

———. 1974b. Soziale Schichtung in der korinthischen Gemeinde: Ein Beitrag zur Soziologie des hellenistischen Urchristentums. *ZNW* 65: 232–72.

———. 1974/75. Legitimation und Lebensunterhalt: Ein Beitrag zur Soziologie urchristlisher Missionare. *NTS* 21: 191–221.

———. 1975. Dir Starken und Schwachen in Korinth: Soziologische Analyse eines theologischen Streites. *EvT* 35: 155–72.

———. 1979. *The Social Setting of Pauline Christianity: Essays on Corinth*. Philadelphia: Fortress.

Toews, J. E. 1990. Paul's Radical Vision for the Family. *Direction* 19: 29–38.

Vassiliadis, P. 1991. Equality and Justice in Classical Antiquity and in Paul: The Social Implications of the Pauline Collection. *SVTQ* 36: 51–59.

Verner, O. C. 1983. *The Household of God: The Social World of the Pastoral Epistles*. Chico, Calif.: Scholars Press.

Wetherington, B. 1995. *Conflict and Community in Corinth: A Social-Rhetorical Commentary on 1 and 2 Corinthians*. Grand Rapids, Mich.: Eerdmans.

White, L. M. 1987. Social Authority in the House Church Setting and Ephesians 4:1–16. *ResQ* 29: 209–28.

Williams, R. 1997. Lifting the Veil: A Social-Science Interpretation of I Corinthians 11:2–16. *Consensus* (Waterloo, Ont.) 23: 53–60.

Winbush, V. L. 1987. *Paul, the Worldly Ascetic: Response to the World and Self Understanding According to I Corinthians 7*. Macon, Ga.: Mercer University Press.

Wire, A. C. 1990. *The Corinthian Women Prophets: A Reconstruction through Paul's Rhetoric*. Minneapolis, Minn.: Fortress.

Wortham, R. A. 1996. Christology as Community Identity in the Philippians Hymn: The Philippians Hymn as Social Drama (Philippians 2:5–11). *PRSt* 23: 269–87.

Wuellner, W. H. 1973. The Sociological Implications of I Corinthians 1:26–28 Reconsidered. In *Studia Evangelica 6*, ed. E. A. Livingstone, 666–72. Berlin: Akademie-Verlag.

Young, F. M., and D. F. Ford. 1988. *Meaning and Truth in 2 Corinthians*. Grand Rapids, Mich.: Eerdmans.

Catholic Epistles

JAMES
Becquet, G., et al. 1987. *La lettre de Jacques: Une lecture socio-linguistique* (C.E. 61). Paris: Cerf.

Elliott, J. H. 1993. The Epistle of James in Rhetorical and Social Scientific Perspective: Holiness-Wholeness and Patterns of Replication. *BTB* 23: 71–81.

Meynard-Reid, P. U. 1988. *Poverty and Wealth in James*. Maryknoll, N.Y.: Orbis.

Panackel, C. 1989. The Option for the Poor in the Letter of St. James. *Biblebhashyam* 15: 141–53.

Penner, T. C. 1999. The Epistle of James in Current Research. *CurBS* 7: 257–308.

Perdue, L. G. 1981. Paraenesis and the Epistle of James. *ZNW* 72: 241–56.

Wachob, W. H. 2000. *The Voice of Jesus in the Social Rhetoric of James* (Society for New Testament Studies Monograph Series 106). Cambridge: Cambridge University Press.

Wall, R. W. 1990. James as Apocalyptic Paraenesis. *ResQ* 32: 11–22.

PETER

Balch, D. L. 1986. Hellenization–Acculturation in 1 Peter. In *Perspective in First Peter*, ed. C. Talbert. Macon, Ga.: Mercer University Press.

Campbell, B. L. 1998. *Honor, Shame, and Rhetoric of 1 Peter* (SBL Dissertation Series 160). Atlanta: Scholars Press.

Charles, J. D. 1998. The Language and Logic of Virtue in 2 Peter 1:5–7. *BBR* 8: 55–73.

Elliott, J. H. 1979. *1 Peter: Estrangement and Community.* Chicago: Franciscan Herald.

———. 1990. *A Home for the Homeless: A Social-Scientific Criticism of 1 Peter, Its Situation and Strategy.* Minneapolis, Minn.: Fortress. [1st ed. 1981.]

———. 1998. The Church as Counterculture: A Home for the Homeless and a Sanctuary for Refugees. *CurTM* 25: 176–85.

Giesen, H. 1998. Lebenszeugnis in der Fremde: Zum Verhalten der Christen in der paganen Gesellschaft (1 Petr 2:11–17). *SNTSU* 23:113–52.

Lamau, M. L. 1988. *Des chrétiens dans le monde : Communautés pétriniennes au 1er siècle* (LD 134). Paris: Cerf.

Miller, L. 1999. La protestation sociale dans la première lettre de Pierre. *Social Compass* 46: 521–43.

Prostmeier, F. -R. 1990. *Handlungsmodelle em ersten Petrusbrief* (Forschung zur Bibel 63). Würzburg, Germany: Echter.

Puig Tarrech, A. 1980. Le milieu de la première épître de Pierre. *Revista Catalana de Theologia* 5: 95–129, 331–402.

Wire, A. 1984. (Review of) Elliott, *A Home for the Homeless. RelSRev* 10: 209–16.

1–3 JOHN

Aune, D. E. 1981. The Social Matrix of the Apocalypse of John. *BR* 26: 16–32.

Malina, B. J. 1986. The Received View and What It Cannot Do: III John and Hospitality. *Semeia* 35: 171–94.

Mitchell, M. M. 1998. "Diotrephes Does Not Receive Us": The Lexicographical and Social Context of 3 John 9–10. *JBL* 117: 299–320.

Perkins, P. 1983. *Koin-onia* in 1 John 1:3–17: The Social Context of Division in the Johannine Letters. *CBQ* 45: 631–41.

Revelation

Arens, E. 1999b. El cordero y el dragón: El Apocalipsis ¿una teología política? *Páginas* 158: 6–14.

Bauckham, R. J. 1991. The Economic Critique of Rome in Revelation 18. In *Images of Empire* (JSOT Supp. Ser. 122), ed. L. Alexander, 47–90. Sheffield, England: JSOT Press.

Callahan, A. D. 1999. Apocalypse as Critique of Political Economy: Some Notes on Revelation 18. *HBT* 21: 46–65.

DeSilva, D. A. 1992a. The Revelation to John: A Case Study in Apocalyptic Propaganda and the Maintenance of Sectarian Identity. *SocAnal* 53: 375–95.

———. 1992b. The Social Setting of the Revelation to John: Conflicts Within, Fears Without. *WTJ* 54: 273–302.

———. 1997. The Construction and Social Function of a Counter-Cosmos in the Revelation of John. *Forum* 9: 47–61.

De Villiers, P. 1997. Oracles and Prophecies in the Greco-Roman World and the Book of Revelation in the New Testament. *Acta Patristica et Byzantina* (Pretoria) 8: 79–96.

Du Rand, J. A. 1990. A Socio-psychological View of the Effect of the Language (Parole) of the Apocalypse of John. *Neot* 24: 351–65.

Elliott, J. H. 1993. Sorcery and Magic in the Revelation of John. *Listening* 28: 261–76.

Esler, P. F. 1993. Political Oppression in Jewish Apocalyptic Literature: A Social-Scientific Approach. *Listening* 28: 181–99.

Ford, J. M. 1990. Persecution and Martyrdom in the Book of Revelation. *TBT* 28: 141–46.

Lunny, W. J. 1989. *The Sociology of the Resurrection.* Victoria, BC: Heron.

Pilch, J. J. 1992. Lying and Deceit in the Letter to the Seven Churches: Perspectives from Cultural Anthropology. *BTB* 22: 126–35.

———. 1993. Visions in Revelation and Alternate Consciousness: A Perspective from Cultural Anthropology. *Listening* 28: 231–44.

Slater, T. 1999. *Christ and Community: A Socio-Historical Study of the Christology of Revelation* (JSNT Sup. Ser. 178). Sheffield, England: Sheffield Academic Press.

———. 1998. On the Social Setting of the Revelation to John. *NTS* 44: 232–56.

Staples, P. 1996. D. W. Riddle e la funzione sociale di apocalissi e martirologi: Un recupero critico. *Religioni e società* 11/24: 48–62.

Stanley, J. E. 1986. The Apocalypse and Contemporary Sect Analysis. In *SBLSP 1986*, ed. H. R. Kent, 412–21. Atlanta: Scholars Press.

Thompson, L. 1986. A Sociological Analysis of Tribulation in the Apocalypse of John. *Semeia* 36: 147–74.

Worth, R. H. 1999a. *The Seven Cities of the Apocalypse and Greco-Asian Culture.* New York: Paulist.

———. 1999b. *The Seven Cities of the Apocalypse and Roman Culture.* New York: Paulist.

Yarbro Collins, A. 1984. *Crisis and Catharsis: The Power of Apocalypse.* Philadelphia: Westminster.

Early Christianity

Social World and Social History

Barton, S. C. 1997. Early Christianity and the Sociology of the Sect. In *The Open Text: New Directions for Biblical Studies?*, ed. F. Watson, 140–62. London: SCM.

Benko, S. 1985. *Pagan Rome and the Early Christians*. Bloomington: Indiana University Press.

Blasi, A. J. 1997. Marginalization and Martyrdom: Social Context of Ignatius of Antioch. *Listening* 32: 68–74.

Borgen, P., V. K. Robbins, and D. B. Gowler. 1998. *Recruitment, Conquest, and Conflict: Strategies in Judaism, Early Christianity and the Greco-Roman World* (Emory Studies in Early Christianity). Atlanta: Scholars Press.

Bovon, F. 1994. The Church in the New Testament, Servant and Victorious. *Ex Auditu* 10: 45–54.

Brown, R. E., and J. P. Meier. 1983. *Antioch and Rome: New Testament Craddles of Catholic Christianity*. London: G. Chapman.

Bryant, J. M. 1993. The Sect–Church Dynamic and Christian Expansion in the Roman Empire: Persecution, Penitential Discipline, and Schism in Sociological Perspective. *British Journal of Sociology* 44: 303–32.

Carmichael, J. 1989. *The Birth of Christianity, Reality and Myth*. New York: Hyppocrene.

Castelli E. A., and H. Taussig, eds. 1996. *Reimagining Christian Origins: A Colloquium Honoring Burton L. Mack*. Valley Forge, Penn.: Trinity Press

Chamberland, L. 1999. À propos d'un récent ouvrage de Gerd Theissen. *LTP* 55: 309–14.

Culdaut F., et al. 1991. *A la naissance de la parole chrétienne: Tradition et écritures au deuxième siècle* (Suppléments aux Cahiers Évangile). Paris: Cerf.

Cwiekowski, F. J. 1992. Early Churches in the Early Church. *Catholic World* (Mahwah, N.J.) 235, 1406: 58–62.

Donaldson, T. L., ed. 2000. *Religious Rivalries and the Struggle for Success in Caesarea Maritima*. Waterloo, Ont.: Wilfrid Laurier University Press.

Donfried K. P., and P. Richardson, eds. 1998. *Judaism and Christianity in First-Century Rome*. Grand Rapids, Mich.: Eerdmans.

Drexhage, H. -J. 1981. Wirtschaft und Handel in den früchristlichen Gemeinden (1.–3. Jh. n. Chr.). *RQ* 76: 1–72.

Duhaime, J. 1992. L'univers des premiers chrétiens d'après J. G. Gager. *Social Compass* 39: 207–19.

Dumortier, F. 1988. *La patrie des premiers chrétiens*. Paris: Éd. ouvrières.

Ferguson, E., ed. 1993. *Studies in Early Christianity: A Collection of Scholarly Essays*. Vol. 1–18. New York: Garland.

Fernandez Vargas, V. 1979. El púlpito como medio de communicación de masas. Los primeros tiempos: La génesis de la unificación Iglesia Estado. *Revista Internacional de Sociologia* 37, 29: 105–16.

Fox, R. L. 1988. *Pagans and Christians in the Mediterranean World from the Second Century A.D. to the Conversion of Constantine*. San Francisco: Harper & Row.

Gager, J. G. 1979. (Review of R. M. Grant *Early Christianity*, A. J. Malherbe *Social Aspects of Early Christianity*, etc.). *RelSRev* 5: 174–80.

Garrett, S. R. 1992. Sociology of Early Christianity. *ABD* 6: 89–99.

Gottlieb G., and P. Barcelo, eds. 1992. *Christen und Heiden in Staat und Gesellschaft des zweiten bis vierten Jahrhunderts* (Schriften des Philosophischen Fakultär der Universität Ausburg 44). Munich: Vögel.

Gottwald, N. K., ed. 1993. *The Hebrew Bible in its Social World and in Ours* (SBL Semeia Studies). Atlanta: Scholars Press.

Grabbe, L. L. 1995. *Sects and Violence: Judaism in the Time of Hillel and Jesus.* Hull, England: University of Hull Press.

Grant, R. M. 1977/1978. *Early Christianity and Society: Seven Studies.* San Francisco: Harper & Row; London: Collins.

————. 1990. Early Christianity and the Creation of Capital. In *The Capitalist Spirit*, ed. P. Berger. San Francisco: ICS Press.

Grosby, S. 1996. The Category of the Primordial in the Study of Early Christianity and Second-Century Judaism. *HR* 36, 140–63.

Hamel, G. 1990. *Poverty and Charity in Roman Palestine, First Three Centuries C.E.* (University of California Publications: Near Eastern Studies, 23). Berkeley: University of California Press.

Harriss, O. G. 1984. The Social World of Early Christianity. *Lexinton Theological Quaterly* 19: 102–14.

Hartin, P. J. 1993. The Religous Nature of First-Century Galilee as a Setting for Early Christianity. *Neot* 27: 33–50.

Hazlett, I., ed. 1991. *Early Christianity: Origins and Evolution to AD 600. In Honour of W.H.C. Frend.* London: SPCK.

Hellholm D., H. Moxnes, and T. K. Seim, eds. 1995. *Mighty Minorities? Minorities in Early Christianity—Positions and Strategies (Essays in Honour of Jacob Jervell on His 70th birthday, 21 May 1995).* Oslo: Scandinavian University Press.

Hengel, M. 1974. *Property and Riches in the Early Church: Aspect of a Sociological History of Early Christianity.* Philadelphia: Fortress.

Hexter, J. H. 1995. *The Judeo-Christian Tradition.* 2nd ed. New Haven, Conn.: Yale University Press.

Hodgson, R. 1989. Valerius Maximus and the Social World of the New Testament. *CBQ* 51: 683–93.

Johnson, E. A. 1979. Constantine the Great: Imperial Benefactor of the Early Christian Church. *JETS* 22: 161–69.

Kee, H. C. 1988. (Review of J. E. Stambauch, D. L. Balch, *The Social World of the First Christians*). *CBQ* 50: 147–49.

————. 1995. *Who Are the People of God? Early Christian Models of Community.* New Haven, Conn.: Yale University.

Kee, H. C., et al. 1991. *Christianity: A Social and Cultural History.* New York: Macmillan.

Kelly, J. F. 1997. *The World of the Early Christians* (Message of the Fathers of the Church 1). Collegeville, Minn.: Liturgical Press.

Keresztes, P. 1989. *Imperial Rome and the Christians: From Herod the Great to about 200 A.D., vol. 1.* Lanham, Md.: University Press of America.

Kyrtatas, D. J. 1987. *The Social Structure of the Early Christian Communities.* London: Verso.

Lampe, P. 1987. *Die stadtrömische Christen in den ersten beiden Jahrhunderten: Untersuchungen zur Sozialgeschichte.* Tübingen, Germany: Mohr-Siebeck.

B. A. 1997. *The Emergence of the Christian Religion: Essays on Early Christianity*. Harris-
Penn.: Trinity Press.

R. I. 1985. Wisdom and Power: Petronius' Satyricon and the Social World of Early
istianity. *ATR* 67: 307–25.

M. 1989. The Transformation of a Religious Document: From Early Christian
itings to Canon. In *From Ancient Israel to Modern Judaism*, ed. J. Neusner, E. Frerichs, and
Sarna, 133–48. Atlanta: Scholars Press.

o, A., ed. 1991. *Orígenes des cristianismo, Antecedente y primeros pasos*. Córdoba, Argentina:
diciones El Almendro.

t, D. 1992–93. Explaining the Christianization of the Roman Empire: Older Theo-
ies and Recent Developments. *Sacris Erudiri* 33: 5–119.

darini, A. J. 1992. Jews and Christians in the First Two Centuries: The Changing Paradigm. *Shofar* 10/2: 16–34.

nders, J. T. 1993. *Schismatics, Sectarians, Dissidents, Deviants : The First One Hundred Years of Jewish–Christian Relations.* Valley Forge, Penn.: Trinity Press International.

———. 2000. *Charisma, Converts, Competitors: Societal and Sociological Factors in the Success of Early
Christianity*. London: SCM.

Smith, J. Z. 1990. *Drudgery Divine: On the Comparision of Early Christianity and the Religions of Late
Antiquity* (Chicago Studies in the History of Judaism). Chicago: University of Chicago
Press.

Speyer, W. 1989. *Frühes Christentum im antiken Srahlungsfeld: Ausgwählte Aufsatze* (WUNT50).
Tübingen, Germany: Mohr-Siebeck.

Stambaugh, J. E., and D. L. Balch. 1986. *The New Testament in Its Social Environment* (Library
of Early Christianity I). Philadelphia: Westminster.

Stark, R. 1991a. Christianizing the Urban Empire: An Analysis, Based on 22 Greco-Roman Cities. *SocAnal* 52: 77–88.

———. 1991b. Epidemics, Networks and the Rise of Christianity. *Semeia* 56: 159–75.

Stroumsa, G. G. 1999. *Barbarian Philosophy: The Religious Revolution of Early Christaianity* (Wissenschaftliche Untersuchungen zum Neuen Testament 112). Tübingen, Germany:
Mohr-Siebeck.

Theissen, G. 1988. Vers une théorie de l'histoire sociale du christianisme primitif. *ETR* 63:
199–225.

———. 1992. *Social Reality and the Early Christians: Theology, Ethics and the World of the New Testament*. Minneapolis, Minn.: Fortress.

———. 1999. *The Religion of the Earliest Churches: Creating a Symbolic World*. Trans. John Bowden.
Minneapolis, Minn.: Fortress. [*Eine Theorie de urchristlichen Religion*, 1999.]

White, L. M. 1988. Shifting Sectarian Boundaries in Early Christianity. *BJRL* 70: 7–24.

———. 1991. Social Networks: Theoretical Orientation and Historical Applications. *Semeia* 56: 23–36.

———, ed. 1991. Social Networks in the Early Christian Environment: Issues and Methods for Social History. *Semeia* 56: 1–202.

White, L. M., and O. L. Yarbrough, eds. 1995. *The Social World of the First Christians: Essays in
Honor of Wayne A. Meeks*. Minneapolis, Minn.: Fortress.

Leutzsch, M. 1989. *Die Wahrnehmung Wirklichkeit im "Hirten des*
ligion und literatur des Alten und Neuen Testament 15(
denhoeck & Ruprecht.

Lieu J., J. North, and T. Rajak, eds. 1992. *The Jew among Pagans a*
pire. London: Routledge.

Lieu, J. M. 1987. The Social World of the New Testament. *Epw*

Long, W. R. 1989. Martin Hengel on Early Christianity. *RelStudR*

Longstaff, T. R. W. 1990. Nazareth and Sepphoris: Insights into (
suppl. 11: 8–15.

Malherbe, A. J. 1977. *Social Aspects of Early Christianity.* 2nd ed. Baton R(
University Press; Philadelphia: Fortress.

Malina, B. J. 1978. The Social World Implied in the Letters of the Chri
tyr (named Ignatius of Antioch). In *SBLSP 1978*, vol. 2, ed. P. J. Ach
Missoula, Mont.: Scholars Press.

———. 1994a. Establishment Violence in the New Testament World. *Scrip*

———. 1994b. Religion in the Imagined New Testament World: More (
Lenses. *Scriptura* 51: 1–26.

Meeks, W. A. 1979. *Zur Soziologie des Urchristentums: Ausgewählte Beiträge zum frühchrist*
schaftsleben in seiner gesellschaftlichen Umwelt (Theol. Bucherei 62). Müchen, Germ;

Meyer, B. F. 1991. The Church in Earliest Christianity: Identity and Self-Defini
Master Journal of Theology 2/2: 1–19.

Mimouni, S. C. 1998. *Le judéo-christianisme ancien. Essais historiques* (Patrimoines). Par
1998.

Morsey, D. 1991. Economics and the Bible: A Response to Patton. *Journal of Interdisci*
Studies 3: 121–25.

Moxnes, H., ed. 1997. *Constructing Early Christian Families: Family as Social Reality and Meta*
London: Routlege.

Neusner, J., P. Borgen, E. S. Frerichs, and R. Horsley, eds. 1988. *The Social World of Form*
tive Christianity and Judaism: Essays in Tribute to Howard Clark Kee. Philadelphia: Fortress.

Nineham, D. 1982. The Strangeness of the New Testament World. *Theology* 85: 171–77,
247–55.

Nouailhat, R. 1988. *Les premiers christianismes.* Paris: Errance.

Osiek, C. 1984/1992. *What Are They Saying about the Social Setting of the New Testament?* New
York: Paulist.

———. 1990. The Second Century through the Eyes of Hermas: Continuity and
Changes. *BTB* 20: 116–22.

———. 1993. The City: Center of Early Christian Life. *TBT* 31:17–21.

———. 1996. The Family in Early Christianity: "Family Values" Revised. *CBQ* 58: 1–24.

Patten, P., and R. Patten. 1991. *The World of the Early Church: A Companion to the New Testament.*
Lewiston, N.Y.: Mellen.

Patton, J. W. 1991. Is There a Christian Political Economy? *Journal of Interdisciplinary Studies*
3: 11–30.

Wiefel, W. 1972. Erwägungen zur soziologischen Hermeneutic urchristlicher Gottesdien-stformen. *Kairos* 14: 36–51.

Williams, D. H. 1989. The Origins of the Montanist Movement: A Sociological Analy-sis. *Religion* 19: 331–51.

Wilson, S. G. 1995. *Related Strangers: Jews and Christians, 70–170 C.E.* Minneapolis, Minn.: Fortress.

Wimbush, V. L. 1993. Contemptus Mundi: The Social Power of an Ancient Rhetorics and Worldview. *USQR* 47: 1–13.

Winkelmann, F. 1990. Zur Entstehung und Ausbreitung des Christentums. *Das Altertum* (Berlin) 36: 182–89.

Social Organization

CHRISTIANITY AS A SOCIAL MOVEMENT

Atwood, D. J., and R. B. Flowers. 1983. Early Christianity as a Cult Movement. *Encounter* 44: 245–61.

Beaude, P. -M. 1995. Christianisme et modèles d'appartenance au 1er siècle. *Revue de l'In-stitut Catholique de Paris* 56: 67–83.

Bergmann, W. 1985. Das frühe Mönchtum als soziale Bewegung. *Kölner Zeitschrift für Soziologie und Sozialpsychologie* 37: 30–59.

Best, E. 1986. A First-Century Sect. *IBS* 8: 115–21.

Blasi, A. J. 1988. *Christianity as a Social Movement.* New York: P. Lang.

Brox, N. 1994. *History of Early Church.* London: SCM.

Castelli, E. A. 1998. Gender, Theory, and The Rise of Christianity: A Response to Rod-ney Stark. *JECS* 6: 227–57.

Cothenet, E. 1989. La secte de Qumrân et la communauté chrétienne. *EspVie* 99: 488–94.

Desprez, V. 1991. Christian Asceticism between the New Testament and the Beginning of Monasticism: III Egypt and East. *American Benedictine Review* 42: 356–74.

Dumais, M. 1990. La vie de la communauté chrétienne et sa portée missionnaire dans l'Église des temps apostoliques. *Neue Zeitschrift fur Missionsweissenchaft* (Immensee) 46: 49–61.

Eberts, H. W. 1997. Plurality and Ethnicity in Early Christian Mission. *SocRel* 58: 305–21.

Grech, P. 1990. The Daily Life of Second-Century Christians. *MelT* 41: 87–96.

Hengel, M. 1997. Das früheste Christentum als eine jüdische messianische universalistis-che Bewegung. *TBei* 28: 197–210.

Hopkins, K. 1998. Christian Number and Its Implications. *JECS* 6: 185–226.

Horrell, D. 1997. Leadership Patterns and the Development of Ideology in Early Chris-tianity. *SocRel* 58: 323–41.

Johnson, L. T. 1989. The New Testament's Anti-Jewish Slander and the Conventions of Ancient Polemic. *JBL* 108: 419–41.

Judge, E. A. 1960. *The Social Patterns of Christian Groups in the First Century.* London: Tyndale.

Kaye, B. N. 1984. Cultural Interaction in the New Testament. *TZ* 40: 341–58.

Klutz, T. E. 1998. The Rhetoric of Science in the Rise of Christianity: A Response to Rodney Stark's Sociological Account of Christianisation. *JECS* 6: 162–84.

McGowan, A. 1994. Eating People: Accusations of Cannibalism against Christians in the Second Century. *JECS* 2: 413–42.

Meeks, W. A. 1985. Breaking Away: Three New Testament Pictures of Christianity's Separation from the Jewish Community. In *To See Ourselves as Others See Us: Christians, Jews, "Others" in Late Antiquity*, ed. J. Neusner and E. Frerichs, 93–115. Chico, Calif.: Scholars Press.

Myre, A. 1987. Le christianisme était-il une secte à l'origine? *Médium* 28/29: 37–40.

Riches, J. K. 1995. "Neither Jew nor Greek": The Challenge of Building One Multicultural Religious Community. *Concilium* (New York) 1: 36–44.

Rousseau, P. 1990. The Development of Christianity in the Roman World: Elaine Pagels and Peter Brown. *Prudentia* 22: 49–70.

Scroggs, R. 1975. The Earliest Christian Communities as Sectarian Movements. In *Christianity, Judaism and Other Greco-Roman Cults: Studies for Morton Smith at Sixty. Part 2*, 1–23. Leiden: E. J. Brill.

Stegemann, W. 1979. From Palestine to Rome: A Social Process in Early Christianity. *Concilium* (New York) 125: 35–42.

Vouga, F. 1998. L'attrait du christianisme primitif dans le monde antique. *RTP* 130: 257–68.

House Church

Ade Odumuyiwa, E. 1991. A Historical Note on Christianity and Jewish Culture in the Early Century (AD 29–70). *AJT* 5: 286–95.

Collins, R. F. 1990. House Churches in Early Christianity. *Tripod* 55: 3–6 (in Chinese), 38–44 (in English).

Klauck, H. -J. 1981a. Die Hausgemeinde als Lebensform im Urchristentums. *MTZ* 32: 1–15.

———. 1981b. *Hausgemeinde und Hauskirche im frühen Christentum*. Stuttgart, Germany: Katholisches Bibelwerk.

Lampe, P. 1993. Family in Church and Society of the New Testament Times. *Affirmation* 5: 1–20.

Laub, F. 1986. Sozialgeschichlicher Hinter und ekklesiologische Revelanz der neutestamentlichfrüchristlichen Haus- und Gemeinde- Tafelparanese–ein Beitrag zur Soziologie des Frühchristentum. *MTZ* 37: 249–71.

Osiek, C., and D. L. Balch. 1997. *Families in the New Testament World: Households and House Churches* (The Family, Religion, and Culture). Louisville, Ky.: Westminster/John Knox.

Vogler, W. 1982. Die Bedeutung der urchristlichen Hausgemeinden für die Ausbreitung des Evangeliums. *TLZ* 107: 785–94.

Weiser, A. 1990. Evangelisierung im Haus. *BZ* 34: 63–86.

RANK AND STATUS

Alfaric, P. 1947. *Les origines sociales du christianisme*. Paris: Cahiers rationalistes.

Bowman A. K., and G. Woolf, eds. 1994. *Literacy and Power in the Ancient World*. Cambridge: Cambridge University.

Countryman, L. W. 1980. *The Rich Christian in the Church of the Early Empire: Contradictions and Accomodations.* Lewiston, N.Y.: Mellen.

Gottwald, N. K. 1993. Social Class as an Analytic Hermeneutical Category in Biblical Studies. *JBL* 112: 3–22.

Guenther, B., and D. Heideebrecht. 1999. The Elusive Biblical Model of Leadership. *Direction* 28: 153–65.

Hollenbach, P. W. 1987. Defining Rich and Poor Using the Social Sciences. In *SBLSP 1987*, 50–63. Atlanta: Scholars Press.

Judge, E. A. 1980. The Social Identity of the First Christians: A Question of Method in Religious History. *JRH* 11: 201–17.

———. 1982. *Rank and Status in the World of the Caesars and St. Paul.* New Zealand: University of Canterbury.

Junod, E. 1995. L'Eglise des premiers siècles fut-elle une "minorité religieuse"? *Le Supplément* (Paris) 194: 74–93.

Kee, H. C. 1992. Changing Modes of Leadership in the New Testament Period. *Social Compass* 39: 241–54.

Kippenberg, H. G. 1978. *Religion und Klassenbildung im antiken Judäa: Eine religionssoziologische Studie zum Verhaltnis von Tradition und gesellschaftlicher Entwicklung.* Göttingen, Germany: Vandenhoeck & Ruprecht.

Kyrtatas, D. J. 1995. Slavery as Progress: Pagan and Christian Views of Slavery as Moral Training. *International Sociology* 10: 219–34.

Malina, B. J. 1978. Limited Good and the Social World of Early Christianity. *BTB* 8: 162–76.

———. 1986. Interpreting the Bible with Anthropology: The Case of the Poor and the Rich. *Listening* 21: 148–59.

———. 1987. Wealth and Poverty in the New Testament and Its World. *Int* 41: 354–67.

Martin, D. B. 1991. Ancient Slavery, Class, and Early Christianity. *Fides et Historia* 23: 105–13.

Osiek, C. 1983. *Rich and Poor in the Shepherd of Hermas: An Exegetical Social Investigation.* Washington, D.C.: Catholic Biblical Association.

———. 1992. Slavery in the Second Testament World. *BTB* 22: 174–79.

Pilch, J. J. 1981. Biblical Leprosy and Body Symbolism. *BTB* 11: 108–13.

Rohrbaugh, R. L. 1984. Methodological Considerations in the Debate over the Social Class of Early Christians. *JAAR* 52: 519–46.

Schöllgen, G. 1984. *Ecclesia sordida? Zur Frage der sozialen Schichtung frühchristlicher Gemeinden am Beispel Karthagos zur Zeit Tertullians.* Münster, Germany: Aschendorff.

Smith, R. H. 1983. Were the Early Christians Middle-Class? A Social Analysis of the New Testament *CTM* 7: 260–76. Reprinted in N. K. Gottwald and R. A. Horsley, eds. *The Bible and Liberation: Political and Social Hermeneutics.* Maryknoll, N.Y.: Orbis, 441–57.

Soares-Prabhu, G. M. 1985. Class in the Bible: The Biblical Poor as a Social Class? *Vidyajyot* 49: 322–46.

Stark, R. 1986. The Class Basis of Early Christianity: Interferences from a Sociological Model. *SocAnal* 47: 216–25.

Van Zyl, H. C. 1998. The Evolution of Church Leadership in the New Testament—a New Consensus? *Neot* 32: 585–604.

ROLES

Bendix, R. 1985. Umbildungen des persönlichen Charismas: Eine Anweindung von Max Webers Charismabegriff auf das Frühchristentum. In *Max Webers Sicht des antiken Christentum: Interpretation und Kritik*, ed. W. Schluchter, 404–43. Frankfurt am Main, Germany: Suhrkamp.

Blasi, A. J. 1986. Role Structures in the Early Hellenistic Church. *SocAnal* 47: 226–48.

Countryman, L. W. 1981. Christian Equality and the Early Catholic Episcopate. *ATR* 63: 115–38.

Downey, M., ed. 1991. *That They Might Live: Power, Empowerment and Leadership in the Church.* New York: Crossroad.

Giles, K. 1989. *Patterns of Ministry among the First Christians*. Melbourne: Collins Dove.

Green, H. A. 1991. Power and Knowledge: A Study in the Social Development of Early Christianity. *SR* 20: 217–31.

Jeffers, J. S. 1991. *Conflict at Rome: Social Order and Hierarchy in Early Christianity*. Minneapolis, Minn.: Fortress.

Kalluveetil, P.1989. Social Criticism as the Prophetic Role: A Biblical Prolegomenon. *Jeevadhara* 19: 133–60.

Kyrtatas, D. J. 1988. Prophets and Priests in Early Christianity: Production and Transmission of Religious Knowledge from Jesus to John Chrysostom. *International Sociology* 3: 365–84.

Love, S. L. 1994. Gender, Status and Roles in the Church: Some Social Considerations. *ResQ* 36: 251–66.

Maier, H. O. 1989. The Charismatic Authority of Ignatus Antioch: A Sociological Analysis. *SR* 18: 185–99.

———. 1991. *The Social Setting of the Ministry as Reflected in the Writings of Hermas, Clement and Ignatus* (Dissertations SR 1). Waterloo, Ont.: Wilfrid Laurier University.

Sabourin, L. 1989. *Early Catholicism and Ministries: Bibliographical Commentary*. Burlington, Ont.: Trinity.

Schmeller, T. 1989. *Brechungen: Urchristliche Wandercharismatiker im Prisma soziologisch orientierter Exegese* (Stuttgarter Bibel-Studien 136). Stuttgart, Germany: Katholisches Bibelwerk.

Strand, K. A. 1991. Church Organization in First-Century Rome: A New Look at the Basic Data. *AUSS* 29: 139–60.

Theissen, G. 1973. Wanderradikalismus: Litteratursoziologische Aspekte der Überlieferung von Worten Jesu im Urchristentum. *ZTK* 70: 245–71.

WOMEN

Borsch, F. H. 1990. Jesus and Women Exemplars. *ATR* suppl. 11: 29–40.

Bremmer, J. 1989. Why Did Early Christianity Attract Upper-Class Women? In *Fructus centecimus: Mélanges offerts à Gerard J. M. Bartelink*, ed. A. Bastiaensen et al., 37–47 Dordrecht, Netherlands: Kluwer.

Clark, E.A. 1998. Holy Women, Holy Words: Early Christian Women, Social History, and the "Linguistic Turn." *JECS* 6: 413–30.

Clark, S. B. 1980. *Man and Woman in Christ: An Examination of the Role of Men and Women in Light of Scripture and the Social Sciences.* Ann Arbor, Mich.: Servant.

Corley, K. E. 1993. *Private Women, Public Meals, Social Conflict in the Synoptic Tradition.* Peabody, Mass.: Hendrickson.

Corrington, G. P. 1985. Salvation, Celibacy and Power: "Divine Women" in Late Antiquity. In *SBLSP 1985*, ed. K. H. Richard, 321–25. Atlanta: Scholars Press.

———. 1988. The "Divine Women"? Propaganda and the Power of Celibacy in the New Testament Apocrypha: A Reconsideration. *ATR* 70: 207–20.

D'Angelo, M. R. 1990. Women Partners in the New Testament. *JFSR* 6: 65–86.

Davies, S. L. 1980. *The Revolt of Widows: The Social World of the Apocryphal Acts.* Carbondale, Ill.: Southern Illinois University Press.

Dewey, J. 1997. Women in the Synoptic Gospels: Seen but Not Heard? *BTB* 27: 53–60.

Dutcher-Walls, P. 1999. Sociological Directions in Feminist Biblical Studies. *Social Compass* 46: 441–53.

Elliott, J. H. 1984. (Review of) E. S. Fiorenza *In Memory of Her. New Catholic World* 227: 238–39.

Fiorenza, E. S. 1979. Word, Spirit, and Power: Women in Early Christian Communities. In *Women of Spirit*, ed. R. R. Ruether. 29–70. New York: Simon and Schuster.

———. 1983a. *In Memory of Her: A Feminist Theological Reconstruction of Christian Origins.* New York: Crossroad.

———. 1983b. "You Are Not to Be Called Father": Early Christian History in a Feminist Perspective. In *The Bible and Liberation: Political and Social Hermeneutics*, ed. N. K. Gottwald and R. A. Horsley, 473–81. Maryknoll, N.Y.: Orbis.

Gillman, F. M. 1993. The Ministry of Women in the Early Church. *New Theology Review* 6: 89–94.

Guarino, J. 1991. The Role of Women in the First-Century Church. *Catholic World* 235/1406: 74–77.

Ide, A. F. 1998. *Martyrdom of Women: A Study of Death Psychology in the Early Christian Church to 301 CE* (Women in History 13B). 2nd ed. Las Colinas, Tex.: Tangelwüld.

Irizarry, E. T. 1991–92. From Participation to Segregation: Women in the Primitive Church; De la participación a la segregación: La mujer en la iglesia Christiana Primitiva. *Homines* 15–16: 273–282.

Kaestli, J. -D. 1989. Les actes apocryphes et la reconstruction de l'histoire des femmes dans le christianisme ancien. *FoiVie* 88/5: 71–79.

Kee, H. C. 1992. The Changing Role of Women in the Early Christian World. *ThTo* 49: 25–38.

Kopas, J. 1990. Jesus and Women in Matthew. *ThTo* 47: 13–21.

Kraemer, R. S. 1980. The Conversion of Women to Ascetic Forms of Christianity. *Signs* 6: 298–307.

Love, S. L. 1987. Women's Role in Certain Second Testament Passages: A Macrosociological View. *BTB* 17: 50–59.

MacDonald, M. Y. 1990. Early Christian Women Married to Unbelievers. *SR* 19: 221–34.

———. 1996. *Early Christian Women and Pagan Opinion: The Power of Hysterical Women.* Cambridge: Cambridge University Press.

Maloney, L. M. 1991. The Argument for Women's Difference in Classical Philosophy. *Concilium* 6: 41–49.

Meeks, W. A. 1974. The Myth of the Androgyne: Some Uses of a Symbol in Earliest Christianity. *HR* 13: 165–208.

Montgomery, H. 1989. Women and Status in the Greco-Roman World. *ST* 43: 115–24.

Mullins, P. 1999. The Public, Secular Roles of Women in Biblical Times. *Mills* 43: 79–111.

Newsom, C. A., and S. H. Ringe, eds. 1993. *The Women's Bible Commentary.* Louisville, Ky.: Westminster/Knox; London: SPCK, 1992

Osiek, C. 1994. Women in the Church. *TBT* 32: 228–33.

Paul, C. 1989. A Plethora of Phoebes. *Faith and Culture* 15: 75–86.

Portefaix, L. 1989. Women and Mission in the New Testament: Some Remarks on the Perspective of Audience. A Research Rapport. *ST* 43: 141–52.

Robbins, V. K. 1994. Socio-Rhetorical Criticism: Mary, Elizabeth and the Magnificat as a Test Case. In *The New Literary Criticism and the New Testament* (JSNT Sup. Ser. 109), ed. E. S. Malbon, 164–209. Sheffield, England: Sheffield Academic Press.

Rook, J. 1991. Women in Acts: Are They Equal Partners with Men in the Earliest Church? *McMaster Journal of Theology* 2/2: 29–41.

Ruether, R. R. 1979. *Women of Spirit: Female Leadership in the Jewish and Christian Traditions.* New York: Simon and Schuster.

Schottroff, L. 1980. Frauen in der Nachfolge Jesu in neutestamentlicher Zeit. In *Frauen in der Bibel* (Traditionen der Befreiung, Sozialgeschichtliche Bibelauslegugen. Band 2), ed. W. Schottroff and W. Stegemann, 91–133. München, Germany: Kaiser.

———. 1983. Women as Followers of Jesus in the New Testament Times: An Exercise in SocialHistorical Exegesis of the Bible. In *The Bible and Liberation: Political and Social Hermeneutics*, 418–27. Maryknoll, N.Y.: Orbis.

———. 1994. *Lydias ungeduldige Schwestern: Feministische Sozialgeschichte des frühen Christentum.* Gütersloh, Germany: Kaiser.

Seim, T. K. 1989. Ascetic Autonomy? New Perspectives on Single Women in the Early Church. *ST* 43: 125–40.

Stark, R. 1995. Reconstructing the Rise of Christianity: The Role of Women. *SocRel* 56: 229–44.

Stegemann, W. 1997. Women in the Jesus Movement in Social-Scientific Perspective. *Listening* 32: 8–21.

Thurston, B. 1998. *Women in the New Testament: Questions and Commentary* (Companion to the New Testament). New York: Crossroad.

Urban, P. A. 1989. Jesus Speaks to the Sexes. *RR* 48: 922–29.

Beliefs, Practices, Values

GENERAL

Barnard, L. W. 1978. Early Christian Art as Apologetic. *JRH* 10: 20–31.

Barton, T. 1994. *Ancient Astrology, Sciences of Antiquity.* London: Routledge.

Benoît, A., and C. Munier. 1994. *Le Baptême dans l'Église ancienne (Ier–IIIème siècle)* (Traditio Christiana 9). Bern, Switzerland: Lang.

Bossman, D.M. 1987. Authority and Tradition in First-Century Judaism and Christianity. *BTB* 17: 3–9.

Bryant, J. M. 1998. Wavering Saints, Mass-Religiosity, and the Crisis of Post-Baptismal Sin in Early Christianity: A Weberian Reading of "The Shepherd of Hermas." *ArchEur-Soc* 39: 49–77.

Cabaniss, A. 1989. *Pattern in Early Christian Workship.* Macon. Ga.: Mercer University Press.

Feeley-Harnick, G. 1981. *The Lord's Table: Eucharist and Passover in Early Christianity.* Philadelphia: University of Pennsylvania Press.

Gager, J. G. 1982. Body-Symbols and Social Reality: Ressurrection, Incarnation and Acetism in Early Christianity. *Religion* 12: 345–64.

Gamble, H. Y. 1995. *Books and Readers in the Early Church: A History of Early Christian Texts.* New Haven, Conn.: Yale University Press.

Gonzalez, J. L. 1990. *Faith & Wealth: A History of Early Christian Ideas on the Origin, Significance, and Use of Money.* San Francisco: Harper & Row.

Hurtado, L. W. 1988. *One God, One Lord: Early Christian Devotion and Ancient Jewish Monotheism.* Philadelphia: Fortress.

Mantzaridis, G. 1975. La naissance du dogme relatif à l'unité de l'Église. *Social Compass* 22: 19–32.

Marshall, I. H. 1989. Church and Temple in the New Testament. *TynBul* 40: 203–22.

McGowan, A. 1999. *Ascetic Eucharists: Food and Drink in Early Christian Ritual Meals* (Oxford Early Christian Studies). Oxford: Oxford University Press/Clarendon.

Miller, R. J. 1990. Death and Victory. *TBT* 28: 145–52.

Mitchell, N. 1998. The Economics of Eucharist. *Worship* 72: 354–65, 452–63.

Pilch, J. J. 2000. Dreams. *TBT* 38: 174–78.

———, and B. J. Malina, eds. 1993. *Biblical Social Values and Their Meaning: A Handbook.* Peabody, Mass.: Hendrickson.

Sawicki, M. 1994. *Seeing the Lord: Resurrection and Early Christian Practices.* Minneapolis, Minn.: Fortress.

Schoenfeld, E. 1989. Justice: An Illusive Concept in Christianity. *RRelRes* 30: 236–45.

Wermik, U. 1975. Frustrated Beliefs and Early Christianity. A Psychological Enquiry into the Gospels of the New Testament. *Numen* 22: 96–130.

Williams, R. B. 1979. Reflections on the Transmission of Tradition in the Early Church. *Encounter* 40: 273–85.

Young, N. H. 1994. The Sectarian Tradition in Early Christianity. *Prudentia* Supplement: 178–97.

BEHAVIOR

Droge, A. J., and J. D. Tabor, eds. 1992. *A Noble Death: Suicide and Martyrdom among Christians and Jews in Antiquity.* San Francisco: HarperCollins.

Ferguson, E. 1993. Early Christian Martyrdom and Civil Disobedience. *JECS* 1: 73–83.

Hartman, L. 1998. "Do Not Grieve as the Others Do": Reflections on Family Rites in the Early Christian Period, Especially Those Concerning Cases of Death. *SEÅ* 63: 249–60.

Keck, L. E. 1974. On the Ethos of the Early Christians. *JAAR* 42: 435–52.

Meeks, W. A. 1986a. *The Moral World of the First Christians* (Library of Early Christianity 6). Philadephia: Westminster.

———. 1986b. Understanding Early Christian Ethics. *JBL* 105: 3–11.

Modritzer, H. 1994. *Stigma und Charisma im Neuen Testament und seiner Umwelt: Zur Soziologie des Urchristentums* (Novum Testamentum et Orbis Antiquus 28). Fribourg: Universitatsverlag.

Wengst, K. 1988. *Humility: Solidarity of the Humiliated: The Transformation of an Attitude and Its Social Relevance in Greco-Roman, Old Testament, Jewish and Early Christian Tradition.* Philadelphia: Fortress.

Wimbush, V. L., and R. Valantasis, eds. 1995. *Ascetism.* New York: Oxford University Press.

CONVERSION

Draper, J. A. 1993. The Role of Ritual in the Alternation of Social Universe: Jewish-Christian Initiation of Gentiles in the *Didache. Listening* 32: 48–67.

———. 2000. Ritual Process and Ritual Symbol in *Didache* 7–10. *VC* 54: 121–58.

Esler, P. F. 1992. Glossolalia and the Admission of Gentiles into the Early Christian Community. *BTB* 22: 136–42.

Finn, T. M. 1997. *From Death to Rebirth: Ritual and Conversion in Antiquity.* New York: Paulist.

Gaventa, B. R. 1986. *From Darkness to Light: Aspects of Conversion in the New Testament.* Philadelphia: Fortress.

Kee, H. C. 1993. From the Jesus Movement toward Institutional Church. In *Conversion to Christianity,* ed. R. Hefner, 47–63. Berkeley: University of California Press.

Lieu, J. M. 1998. The "Attraction of Women" in/to Early Judaism and Christianity: Gender and Politics of Conversion. *JSNT* 72: 5–22.

MacMullen, R. 1983. Two Types of Conversion to Early Christianity. *VC* 37: 174–92.

———. 1986/87. Conversion: A Historian's View. *SecCent* 5: 67–81.

Nguyen Van Phong, J. 1972. Essai de construction et d'utilisation d'un modèle de conversion religieuse suivant l'exemple constantinien. *Revue Française de Sociologie* 13, 4: 516–49.

Parente, F. 1987. L'idea di conversione da Nock ad oggi. *Augustinianum* 27: 7–25.

Sanders, J. T. 1999. Did Early Christianity Succeed because of Jewish Conversions? *Social Compass* 46: 493–505.

Stark, R. 1986b. Jewish Conversion and the Rise of Christianity: Rethinking the Received Wisdom. In *SBLSP 1986,* ed. K. H. Richards, 314–29. Atlanta: Scholars Press.

HEALING, MAGIC AND MIRACLES

Aune, D. E. 1980. Magic in Early Christianity. In *Principat.* ANRW 2, 23/2. Ed. W. Hasse. New York; Berlin: Walter de Gruyter.

Avalos, H. 1999. *Health Care and the Rise of Christianity.* Peabody, Mass.: Hendrickson.

Barrett-Lennard, R. J. S. 1994. *Christian Healing after the New Testament: Some Approaches to Illness in the Second, Third and Fourth Centuries.* Lanham, Md.: University Press of America.

Borgen, P. 1981. Miracles of Healing in the New Testament: Some Observations. *ST* 35: 91–106.

Bovon, F. 1995. Miracles, magie et guérison dans les Actes apocryphes des apôtres. *JECS* 3: 245–59.

Bremmer, J. N., ed. 1998. *The Apocryphal Acts of Peter: Magic, Miracles and Gnosticism* (Studies on the Apocryphal Acts of the Apostoles 3). Leuven, Belgium: Peeters.

Galipeau, S. A. 1990. *Transforming Body and Soul: Therapeutic Wisdom in the Gospel Healing Stories* (Jung and Spirituality). New York: Paulist.

Gallagher, E. V. 1982. *Divine Man or Magician? Celsus and Origen on Jesus.* Chico, Calif.: Scholars Press.

Graf, F. 1994. *Magic in the Ancient World* (Revealing Antiquity 10). Cambridge, Mass.: Harvard University Press.

Guijarro Oporto, S. 2000. La dimensión política de los exorcismos de Jesús: La controversia de Belcebú desde la perspectiva de las sciencias sociales. *EstBíb* 58: 51–77.

Kee, H. C. 1983. *Miracle in the Early Christian World: A Study in Socio-Historical Method.* New Haven, Conn.: Yale University Press.

Kollmann, B. 1996. *Jesus und die Christen als Wundertäter: Studien zu Magie, Medizin und Schamanismus in Antike und Christentum* (Forschungen zur Religion und Literatur des Alten und Neuen Testaments 170). Göttingen, Germany: Vandenhoeck & Ruprecht.

Lattke, M. 1985. New Testament Miracle Stories and Hellenistic Culture of Late Antiquity. *Listening* 20: 54–64.

Meyer, M., and P. Mirecki, eds. 1995. *Ancient Magic and Ritual Power* (Religions in the Greco-Roman World 129). Leiden: E. J. Brill.

Mills, W. E. 1986. Glossolalia as a Sociopsychological Experience. In *Speaking in Tongues: A Guide to Research on Glossolalia*, ed. W. E. Mills, 425–37. Grand Rapids, Mich.: Eerdmans.

Pilch, J. J. 1995. Sickness and Long Life. *TBT* 33: 94–98.

———. 1997. Understanding Healing in the Social World of Early Christianity. *BTB* 22: 26–33.

———. 2000. *Healing in the New Testament: Insights from Medical and Mediterranean Anthropology.* Minneapolis, Minn.: Fortress.

Remus, H. E. 1982ba. Does Terminology Distinguish Early Christian from Pagan Miracles? *JBL* 101: 531–51.

———. 1982b. "Magic or Miracle"? Some Second Century Instances. *SecCent* 2: 127–56.

———. 1983. *Pagan–Christian Conflict over Miracle in the Second Century.* Cambridge Mass.: Philadelphia Patristic Foundation.

Schoedel, W.R., and B. J. Malina. 1986. Miracle or Magic? *RelSRev* 12: 31–39.

Theissen, G. 1983. *The Miracle Stories of the Early Christian Tradition.* Philadelphia: Fortress.

Yamauchi, E. 1983. Magic in the Biblical World. *TynBul* 34: 169–200.

Author Index

General discussions without specific scriptural references are listed in the subject index.

Biblical References Index

13.34–35	345
14.2	133
14.30	442
14.31	129
15–17	129, 234
15.16	442
15.18–19	441
15.19	442
15.21	326
16.2	238, 366–67
16.11	442
16.13	351
17.6–19	351
18.17–18	367
18.31	264, 422, 426
18.36	454
18.40	264
19.14	135
20.19	316
20.30–31	129
21	129
21.3	542

Acts of the Apostles

1.1	65
1.1–5.16	128
1.1–12	133
1.8	432
1.14	112
1.15–16	599
1.21–22	599
2.5	425
2.5–13	230
2.14–36	131
2.17	356
2.21	356
2.37–42	238
2.41	131
2.41–47	316
2.44–45	131, 543
3.1	316
3.12–26	131
3.17–26	350
4.3	131
4.4	131

4.5	421, 423
4.7	128
4.8–12	131
4.13	542
4.32	543
4.32–35	131, 316
4.32–37	234
4.34–35	543
4.36–5.1	543
5.1–11	543
5.1–12	316
5.17	423
5.18	131
5.29–32	131
6.1	316
6.1–6	235, 317, 440
6.7	619
6.8–7.60	431
6.8–15	317
6.12	362
7.58	586
8.1	317, 431, 619
8.1–3	586
8.2–3	235
8.6–7	630
8.9–13	239
8.14–40	227
8.26–40	566
9.1–2	431
9.2	316, 442
9.3–6	351
9.31–11.18	128
10	630
10.1–49	565
10.2	99
10.13–14	316
10.44–48	99
11.14	392, 545
11.19	230
11.19–20	317
11.19–26	235
11.20	318
11.25–30	318
11.26	318, 327, 431, 439

Subject Index

Page numbers in italics indicate tables. Specific scriptural references are listed in the biblical references index.

Dead Sea Scrolls, 250
Dead Sea Scrolls in English, 270–71
Deborah, 350
Decius, Galerius, 433
deconversion, 625–26
decurions profit-making activities, 536–37
deductive reasoning, 71, 73, 75–77, 149
defection, 625–26
delatores, 443, 449
Delos, 85
democratic institutions, 419
desert hermits, 553
desert-mountain-temple axis, 212–14,
    218–19n22
deviance, 372–76, 434
deviant, but not too deviant, 380
Dewey, John, 54
diakoneo, 353–54
diakonos, 353–54
Dialogue with Trypho the Jew (Justin Martyr),
    368, 381, 636
diaspora Jews, 230, 391
Diatessaron (Tatian), 328
Dibelius, Martin, 5
Didache, 69–70, 137, 140–41, 349, 440,
    450, 544, 564
Didascalia, 101
dietary laws, 250, 319, 377–79, 499–501,
    531–32, 640
difference in means test, 158–61
Digest (Justinian), 410
dining customs, 93–95, 99
dining rooms, 88, 94; seating arrangements,
    90, 99, 477
Diocletian, 445, 567
Dionysiac cowherds, 402
Dionysius, 96
Dionysius of Alexandria, 436
disciples, 300, 315, 483; first called
    Christians, 318; occupations of, 542–43,
    586
Discourse to the Greeks (Eusebius), 636–37
discrepancies. *See* inconsistencies
diversity: within early Christianity, 229–34,
    243–44, 342–55; ethnic, 507

divine conception. *See* virginal conception
divine presence, 479–80; personal
    relationships with, 531
divine sovereignty, 472–73, 475, 478, 480,
    483–85, 595
division of labor, 534
divorce, 348, 437, 499
doctrine, Christian, 310
Documents of the Christian Church, 433
domination, 43, 540–42
Domitian, 463–64
domus, 88, 92
domus ecclesiae, 96, 100–103
Donatists, 451
donkeys, 483
doorkeeper *(ostiarius)*, 91
Dorotheus, 397, 567
Double Festal Octave, 206–9, 212, 218n13
dragons, 484
dramaturgical sociology, 56
dread: of the community, 610, 614; of
    reprisal, 612–16; social, 610–18, 613
dreams, 116, 120
duplications of material, 131–32
Dura Europa, 83, 96
dyadic personality, 26n17
dysfunction, 34–36

Early Christianity as a Social Movement (Blasi), 9
Ecclesiastical History (Eusebius), 392, 397, 406
economic anthropology, 512–13
The Economic Background of the Gospels (Grant),
    513
economic exploitation, 534, 540–42
The Economics of the Mishnah (Neusner),
    524–25
economic status, 145
economy: defined, 512; modernist model of,
    516–17; of Palestine, 511, 514–22,
    525–27; primitivist model of, 516–17,
    520; religious, 287; Roman Empire, 477,
    515; slave economy, 413, 538
Edict of Milan, 433, 451, 503
edicts, 410; confiscating Christian property,
    445; eliminating Christianity, 398; for